The Life of
ANDREW JACKSON

ANDREW JACKSON
A portrait by Samuel Lovett Waldo. From the original in the Metropolitan Museum of Art, New York City.

The Life of
ANDREW JACKSON

COMPLETE IN ONE VOLUME

BY

MARQUIS JAMES

Author of The Raven,
A Biography of Sam Houston

PART ONE: *The Border Captain*
PART TWO: *Portrait of a President*

THE BOBBS-MERRILL COMPANY
Indianapolis PUBLISHERS New York

THE LIFE OF ANDREW JACKSON
COPYRIGHT, 1938
By MARQUIS JAMES

ANDREW JACKSON
The Border Captain
COPYRIGHT, 1933
By MARQUIS JAMES

ANDREW JACKSON
Portrait of a President
COPYRIGHT, 1937
By MARQUIS JAMES

PRINTED IN THE UNITED STATES OF AMERICA
BY THE HADDON CRAFTSMEN, INC., CAMDEN, N. J.

PART ONE
ANDREW JACKSON
The Border Captain

PART ONE
To the Memory of My Mother
RACHEL MARQUIS JAMES

PART TWO
To the Memory of My Father
HOUSTIN JAMES

CONTENTS

Part One

The Border Captain

CHAPTER		PAGE
	Book One: The Orphan	
I	The Garden of the Waxhaws	3
II	An Officer's Boots	17
III	Dice and Bear's Oil	30
	Book Two: The Robe	
IV	The Mero District	45
V	Tidings from Harrodsburgh	62
VI	Robes of Justice	79
VII	"Truxton" against "Ploughboy"	95
VIII	A Long Spoon	115
	Book Three: The Sword	
IX	Old Hickory	141
X	Red Eagle	155
XI	Storm Clouds	174
XII	"Push on the Troops"	189
XIII	The Escape of Gabriel Villeré	200
XIV	The Mud Rampart of Rodriquez Canal	218
XV	The Silvery Carpet	234

CHAPTER		PAGE
XVI	"The United States versus Andrew Jackson"	250
XVII	A Changing World	265
XVIII	The Florida Adventure	285
XIX	General Jackson Calls on Colonel Callava	302
XX	The Border Captain	319

CONTENTS

Part Two

Portrait of a President

Book Four: A Reluctant Candidate

XXI	The Nashville Junto	335
XXII	A Grass Hat	354
XXIII	The Canvass	374
XXIV	The Election	398
XXV	The Bargain	414
XXVI	A Preoccupied Cincinnatus	446
XXVII	End of Flight	473

Book Five: The "Reign"

XXVIII	The Haggard Hero	487
XXIX	Emergence of a Quiet Statesman	508
XXX	Throb of a Distant Drum	529
XXXI	A Greek Temple in Chestnut Street	553
XXXII	Martin Van Buren's Masterpiece	567
XXXIII	Mr. Biddle's Dilemma	583
XXXIV	A Sword Against Disunion	603
XXXV	"A Knightly Personage"	623

CHAPTER		PAGE
XXXVI	Mr. Biddle's Biggest Gamble	647
XXXVII	Doom of the Bank	664
XXXVIII	The Etiquette of Collecting Twenty-five Million Francs	681
XXXIX	The Prairie Rose	699
XL	The Scepter Passes	717

Book Six: Twilight of a Chieftain

XLI	Shadows on the Hermitage	727
XLII	A Taper Burning Low	746
XLIII	Last Leave	762
	Notes	788
	Bibliography	895
	Personal Acknowledgments	909
	Index	923

ILLUSTRATIONS

Part One

The Border Captain

Tennessee, 1788–1804, a map	*Front end paper*
Andrew Jackson, a portrait by Waldo	*Frontispiece*
	FACING PAGE
The War in the Waxhaws	32
"The Brave Boy of the Waxhaws"	33
	BETWEEN PAGES
Where Andrew Jackson Spent His Youth, 1767–1784, a map	48–49
	FACING PAGE
Earliest Known Autograph of Andrew Jackson	64
Where Jackson was Married, 1791	65
Judge Jackson, a portrait about 1804	72
The First Hermitage	73
The Cost of Education, a check payable to Cumberland College drawn by Jackson, 1811	88
Rachel Jackson, a miniature by Anna C. Peale, 1815	89
"Old Hickory," a portrait by Vanderlyn, 1819	96
General Jackson, a portrait by Jarvis, 1815	97
Battle of Tohopeka, a map	128
The Creek Campaign of 1813–1814	129
Invitation to a Victory Dinner to Andrew Jackson, 1814	136
In Formal Dress, a portrait of Jackson by Vanderlyn, 1815	137
The Six Water Routes to New Orleans Defended by Andrew Jackson	152
The Villeré House, Pakenham's Headquarters below New Orleans	153
The Night Battle, a painting by Pape	160
Battle of December 23, 1814, below New Orleans, a map	161
	BETWEEN PAGES
Battle of New Orleans, January 8, 1815, a map	176–177

	FACING PAGE
The Macarté House, Jackson's Headquarters below New Orleans	192
A Presentation Portrait, Jackson at New Orleans, by Vallée, 1815	193

	BETWEEN PAGES
A Participant's Conception of the Battle of New Orleans, a painting by Laclotte	240–241

	FACING PAGE
Jackson in 1817, an engraving	256
The Florida Campaign, 1818, a map	257
Andrew Jackson, a portrait by Earl	288
In the Byronic Manner, a portrait of Jackson by Sully	289
The Second Hermitage	320

ILLUSTRATIONS

Part Two

Portrait of a President

	FACING PAGE
Andrew Jackson, a portrait by Ashel B. Durand	352
Jackson in Florida, a pencil sketch	353
"The Nation's Hero and the People's Friend," a bas-relief by William Henry Rinehart	384
The Gentleman from Tennessee, a portrait by Ralph E. W. Earl	385
Andrew Jackson, a portrait by Thomas Sully	416
Old Hickory Toasts His Friends—Bill for a wine dinner to some of his political supporters	417
Rachel Jackson, a portrait by Earl	448
Andrew Jackson, a drawing by James Barton Longacre	449

	BETWEEN PAGES
The Coffin Handbill, a campaign poster of 1828	464–465

	FACING PAGE
Emily Donelson, mistress of the White House, a portrait by Earl	480
Andrew Jackson ("Jack") Donelson, private secretary to the President, a portrait by Earl	481

	FACING PAGE
Souvenir of an Unpleasant Evening for Mrs. Eaton—card of invitation to the President dinner at which the Secretary of War's wife was snubbed	512
Andrew Jackson, junior, adopted son of the President, a portrait by Earl	513
Andrew Jackson Hutchings, ward of General Jackson, a portrait by Earl	520
Andrew Jackson, a portrait by Thomas Sully	521
The Third Hermitage, Jackson's home as remodeled in 1831	536
Sarah Yorke Jackson, the President's daughter-in-law, a portrait by Earl	537
A White House Bride—Mary Eastin	544
"King Andrew I," a campaign cartoon of 1832	545
"A Fine Old Well-Battered Soldier," a portrait of General Jackson by Earl	576
Two White House Young Ladies—Mary Eastin and Mary Ann Lewis	577
A White House Belle—Mary Coffee, a portrait by Earl	608
One of the White House Babies—Rachel Jackson Donelson, a portrait by Earl	609
Jackson and Biddle Sever Business Relations—Canceled checks showing withdrawal of Jackson's personal balance from Bank of the United States for deposit in a private bank	640
The White House	641
Rachel Jackson, the General's first grandchild, a portrait by Earl	672
"Qui Paye Ses Dettes S'Enrichit," a French cartoon on the spoliation claims	673
The Fourth Hermitage, completed 1835	704
A bust of General Jackson	705
Jackson at New Orleans, 1840, a portrait by Jacques J. Amans	736
Jackson in Retirement, a drawing by William H. Brown	737
In an Invalid's Chair, a daguerreotype by Mathew B. Brady	768
The Dying Chieftain, a portrait by George P. A. Healy	769
	BETWEEN PAGES
Jackson's Last Letter, a facsimile	784–785
The United States of the Jackson Era	*Back end paper*

PART ONE

The Border Captain

BOOK ONE

THE ORPHAN

Make friends by being honest, keep
them by being steadfast.
ELIZABETH JACKSON to her son.

ANDREW JACKSON

CHAPTER I

THE GARDEN OF THE WAXHAWS

1

THE allure of a graceful name had something to do with the fact that nineteen families made up their minds to sail with the Andrew Jacksons from Larne, in Ireland, for the "Garden of the Waxhaws." But these tenant farmers from County Antrim were not adventurers to the manner born, and on second thoughts soberer counsel prevailed. In the end just two households accompanied the Jacksons, and it required only the North Atlantic crossing in April and May of 1765 to modify their impulse to rise in the world.

At what appears to have been the settlements along Conowingo Creek in Lancaster County, Pennsylvania,[1] peopled by Scotch-Irish of earlier transplantings, the little party rested from the sea-leg of the journey. Frankly homesick and discouraged, Mr. Jackson's neighbors said they would remain in Pennsylvania among people who spoke their own burry brogue, rather than lay out for wagons and like costly gear requisite to a farther excursion of nearly five hundred miles to the Waxhaws.

It was not in the power of Mr. Jackson, or of any one, to contend successfully that the route to the Waxhaws bore an especially friendly reputation. True, "The Great Waggon Road" from Philadelphia thrust itself confidently enough as far as York, but once across the Potomac and beyond the comforting shelter of the Blue Ridge, this air of assurance diminished until the Carolina highlands were attained under the less sophisticated title of Catawba Traders' Path. The neighbors lacked the heart to undertake the Path, and, indeed, two years more found them back in Ireland.[2] But Andrew Jackson was for the Waxhaws and would not be dissuaded.

2

There seems to have been more to this young man than met the eye or has descended in tangible form to posterity. Son of a comfortably well-off linen weaver and merchant of Carrickfergus, he had forsaken an apprenticeship in that calling to take a small farm from which he maintained a vicarious contact with the world. His brother Sam was a sailor who rolled on his tongue the names of exotic ports and places. The voyage just completed had been on board a vessel in which Sam served before the mast, an association that probably elevated Andrew Jackson among the passengers to something of a lay authority on navigation.

Another circumstance of import was the knowledge of America that Andrew had derived from a second brother, Hugh Jackson. Late of His Majesty's Forty-Ninth Regiment of Foot, Hugh had accompanied Braddock in Virginia, Wolfe at Quebec and Amherst at the surrender of Montreal. He had fought Cherokees in the Waxhaws and hunted with the docile Catawbas. Indeed, the present expedition was of Hugh's inspiration, and would have tackled the New World under his experienced leadership except for an insuperable domestic obstacle. Home from the wars, Hugh had taken a wife, and, smiling at her remonstrances, extolled America in such large terms that twenty families placed themselves at his disposal for emigration. Belongings were made ready, passage money got in hand; but Mrs. Hugh Jackson simply declined to leave Ireland and nothing could budge her. The crestfallen grenadier hauled down his flag, which all but ended the project, seventeen of the families refusing to embark.[3]

Andrew Jackson's mate was of different goods. In the snapping blue eyes and brisk little body of red-haired Elizabeth Hutchinson burned a zeal for accomplishment that made handicaps seem to resolve themselves in her favor. A five-months-old baby boy at the breast and one of two years by her side only sharpened the desire of this mother for the land of spacious opportunity. Moreover, four of Betty Jackson's sisters already had traversed the Catawba Path and were in the Waxhaws, married, settled and, from all accounts, doing well. Three of these enterprising Hutchinson girls appear to have crossed the ocean unmarried, and, finding North-of-Ireland husbands in Pennsylvania or Virginia, accompanied them into the southwestern wilderness. The fourth and eldest, Margaret, had sailed to join her husband, George McKemey, who had come out alone and established himself in the Waxhaws.[4]

The family of Andrew Jackson followed the trace of these pioneers.

With the breadth of Virginia behind them, they crossed the uplands of North Carolina—not a lonely journey, for the newcomers found themselves a part of a great tide of emigration spilling southwestward over the Catawba Path. Residents of Hillsboro, North Carolina, counted a thousand wagons going through in this same year of 1765. But the tide had thinned by the time the Jacksons forded the stony-bedded Yadkin and rested their blown horses by the impressive log court-house which dominated the cluster of cabins calling itself Salisbury. This was the last town they saw. Salisbury distinguished itself by a greater degree of primitiveness and by the vocabulary of the tavern-talk, which was not so much of Philadelphia and the north as of Charles Town and the Low-Country.

At Salisbury the Catawba Path veered toward the mountains of the West and the true unknown. But the Jacksons changed roads. Salisbury also marked the wilderness end of the trail over which appeared at intervals the post-rider, a weather-stained and cosmopolitan personage, with the royal mail from Charles Town and all the word-of-mouth gossip of the country intervening. The post route saw Mr. Jackson into the Garden of the Waxhaws, which at first sight may have struck him as having been rather enthusiastically named.

3

But after weeks of sleeping under a wagon it was something for a man to have his wife and two young ones out of the weather. In point of fact he was lucky, and must have known it, for a few of the transient acquaintances met on shipboard or during the long overland trek looked forward to the prospect of starting life in the New World under the sponsorship of so large a colony of kinfolk and connections as received the Andrew Jacksons into the Waxhaws.

Mrs. Jackson's sister Jennet,[5] called Jane, was the wife of James Crawford, a well-to-do man by frontier reckoning. Five years before they had come from Cumberland County, Pennsylvania.[6] Now slaves tilled their bottom-land fields on Crawford's Branch of Waxhaw Creek, and their residence had a pleasing situation on a knoll commanding the post road. It was roomy enough to accommodate Mr. Crawford's large family and still offer hospitality to the passing traveler. Margaret Hutchinson and her husband, George McKemey, bought a farm of their own the following year[7] and built a cabin with a stone chimney on the post road two and a half miles from the Crawfords'. Mary and Sarah Hutchinson who were married to John and Samuel Lessley[8] lived—shortly afterward, at any rate—within two or three miles of their sisters.

The streams of immigration from the north by way of the Catawba Path and from the south over the Charles Town-Salisbury Road, merged on this rim of civilized life called by the Indian name of Waxhaw. The more desirable lands had been preempted by 1765, and older residents had acquired a sufficiently colonial point of view to damn the Stamp Tax. The land that Andrew Jackson took seems to have represented choice tempered by expediency. It was on Ligget's Branch near the headwaters of Twelve Mile Creek and the most isolated of any of the lands belonging to husbands of the Hutchinson sisters—being about four miles from the post road, eight miles from McKemey's and ten from the plantation of James Crawford, the most substantial of the in-laws. The red soil was washed and thin. The stand of pine and hickory and oak was drubbed and scrubby-looking. After traveling three and a half thousand miles for a new home had Andrew Jackson gone twenty miles farther he might have found land more inviting to the plow-iron. But he would not have been so near his wife's relations.

Even the Ligget's Branch tract was not vacant. Thomas Ewing was on it, though by what authority no surviving record discloses.[9] He might have filed with the Governor the officially requisite form of "entry," or rested content for the time being with "tomahawk rights," —his blaze on trees roughly bounding his claim,—tranquil in the knowledge that they would be respected by community sentiment regardless of how a remote Royal Governor might feel about it. Probably he had thrown up a shack and cleared a field.

Neither entry paper, tomahawk rights nor clearing invested Mr. Ewing with anything he could legally convey, but frontiersmen were not hair-splitting constructionists in that particular. Therefore, Thomas Ewing and Andrew Jackson made a private dicker by which the latter occupied this portion of the public domain. The following spring a busy provincial surveyor and two chain bearers appeared in the Waxhaws. They ran a line around the Jackson place "Beginning at a White Oak South side of the creek by a small Branch & thence

N 10 E 180 Poles"—a pole being sixteen and a half feet—"to a Red Oak" and so on, enclosing "200 acres being in . . . the county of Mecklenburgh Province of North Carolina."[10]

The rule-bound surveyor entered the homestead in the books as that of Thomas "Yewing."

4

With no sense of insecurity on this account, Andrew Jackson made a late crop and entered into the expanding life of the Waxhaws. New settlers appeared from north and south, falling upon the woods with axes and mauls. New fields were brought to the plow, new cabins dotted the red creeks that snaked westward toward the tumbling Catawba River. Henry Eustace McCulloh gave the land, and other bigwigs, like the Alexanders, the Polks and the Phifers (who had a crest on their silver), combined to promote a court-house for Mecklenburg County which they insisted should be more pretentious than the court-house at Salisbury. The first story was built of brick, the second of logs, and, however roundly they might extirpate her husband's Stamp Tax, these sentimental Irishmen named their work of beauty Charlotte, for George III's yellow-haired girl queen.

Yet for some time Sugar Creek Church was to rival the court-house and taverns of Charlotte as the fixed center about which affairs of the locality revolved. This was due to the importance that Scotch-Irish Presbyterians attached to their faith and to the robust personality of the Sugar Creek pastor, Reverend Alexander Craighead, whose wine-glasses were regarded as the finest in the county. Something for those wine-glasses or, failing in that, simply rye whisky, would have been acceptable to many clergymen and to most schoolmasters in part payment for their services. Salisbury and Camden, in South Carolina, the market towns of the Waxhaws, were each a wagon journey of three or four days, and it paid a farmer to refine his grain into liquor at home, thus reducing the bulk of the produce he carried away to sell. James Crawford owned a still and made whisky of his neighbors' grain for sixpence a gallon in toll.

Although they lived within the orbit of its influence, the Andrew Jacksons did not attend the Sugar Creek Church, but drove some twelve miles southwest to Waxhaw Church to worship with Mrs. Jackson's relations.

Waxhaw Church was on the road to recovery from an unfortunate incident. A pioneer of the region, Robert Miller, had built the meeting-house on his farm and begun to hold services. He proved "a man of popular talents and lively," but these very qualities contributed to his downfall in "little more than a year [when] . . . too much familiarity with a young woman . . . laid [him] under a sentence of excommunication for violating the seventh commandment."[11] The disgraced preacher deeded to the community the church house with four sloping acres for a burial ground and departed. The countryside never saw Mr. Miller again, though it was years before he was forgotten; and a wayfarer was the more welcome to the warmth of a Waxhaw fireside when he brought news of the proscribed wanderer who lived by odd jobs, teaching school or preaching under trees, as he dared not enter a house of God.

The congregation had been on the point of discouragement in its quest for a preacher to succeed Mr. Miller when there descended from the Cherokee country over the mountains a slender, quiet-spoken young man on horseback, distressed by his failure to win the Indians from the creed of their fathers. William Richardson was an English-born patrician and a Master of Arts of the University of Glasgow. The missionary accepted the beclouded pulpit, and, by virtue of his ecclesiastical standing, Waxhaw Church became the only pastorate in the Back-Country enjoying full Gospel ordinances. If anything more were needed to complete the recrudescence of Waxhaw Church, it seemed to be supplied when Doctor Richardson rode to Sugar Creek and brought back a wife from the household of the celebrated Reverend Alexander Craighead.

This particular addition to the luster of the Waxhaws was presently viewed in different lights, however. The vivacity of Virginia-born Nancy Craighead smacked a trifle too much of the liberal ways of the Low-Country aristocracy. Although the new minister continued to be perfection, a sentiment developed that some of Mrs. Richardson's fine qualities were unsuited to her husband's station. But these insinuations failed to impress Betty Jackson. The new parishioner from Twelve Mile Creek liked the high-spirited Nancy and they became friends.

5

Elizabeth Jackson was soon in need of the consolation that friendship could offer. In February of the second year, when she was about to bear her third child, Andrew strained himself lifting a log, it was said, and took to bed in great pain. While a heavy snow fell in the southerly Waxhaws Andrew Jackson died.

Neighbors sat beside the body in Old-Country fashion to guard it from hostile tenants of the invisible world, handing around the whisky gourd to fortify their spirits against the responsibilities of the occasion. The provision of such cheer formed an admissible charge against a deceased's estate, and a few months later when another Mecklenburg County pioneer passed to his reward a record was deposited at the new court-house, along with his will, to show that seven gallons of rye were on hand to enable those left behind to submerge their grief. On the morning after the wake Mr. Jackson's coffin was put on a sled drawn by a mule. Mrs. Jackson and her two boys, Hugh, four, and Robert, two, were bundled into a wagon and the procession started for Waxhaw Church.

It was hard work getting the sled over the broken ice of the creeks and "branches" that intersected the curving road, as James Findley, who assisted, recalled to the end of his days. But Mr. Findley also remembered that they had "liquor along & would stop at the branches . . . & take a drink."[12] At the McKemey cabin the procession received reenforcements and doubtless more refreshment. James Crawford's would have been the next stop and perhaps it was there that an especially appreciated jug of brandy was introduced among the pall-bearers who had made the cold march from Twelve Mile Creek. "The brandy was good and the host was kind and before they knew it night was upon them."[13]

Wagons carrying the mourners splashed over the Waxhaw Creek ford, vague in the winter twilight, while the sled escort left the road to cross the ice. The company was huddled in the dark at the graveside when the pall-bearers arrived with the sled—but not the body.[14] This painful disclosure sent them scurrying back, fortunately to recover the corpse of Mr. Jackson where it had caught in the brush after slipping off of the sled while they were negotiating the steep south bank of the creek. The classical diction of that strangely environed scholar, William Richardson, pronounced its promise of life everlasting, and the dust of the novitiate backwoodsman became one with the red earth of the Waxhaws.[15]

6

Elizabeth and her boys slept that night at the home of one of Mrs. Jackson's sisters, one would think Jane Crawford, whose house was nearest by two miles and the best provided for the reception of guests. Before sunrise a few mornings later "at the plantation whereon James Crawford lived . . . on the 15th of march in the year 1767,"[16] Elizabeth Jackson's third son was born. Such is General Jackson's own statement as to the place of his birth. In the opinion of the present reviewer it is the best evidence available bearing on the issue, though several of his biographers have accepted an elaborate and interesting tradition that he was born at George McKemey's.[17] In any event, Elizabeth named the baby Andrew, carried him to be baptized in Waxhaw Church and took up her permanent abode under the Crawford roof.

7

But not as a poor relation. Elizabeth Jackson maintained her inherited equity in the two hundred acres on Ligget's Ranch, and in 1770 when a clear title could be conveyed, paid "fourteen Pounds Current Money of North Carolina" to Thomas Ewing who deeded the property to "Hugh, Robt and Andrew Jackson,"[18] by which instrument the youngest of the brothers became a landed proprietor at the age of three. Moreover, there was need for an active woman in a household teeming with eight Crawford offspring besides the three little Jacksons, for Mrs. Crawford was an invalid. Elizabeth Jackson's competent hand must have been especially useful at this time when the master of the home was preoccupied by a turmoil that had seized the Waxhaws, turning neighbor against neighbor. The controversy was over the location of the boundary between North and South

Carolina and threatened the validity of every land title in the community.

A band of armed "South Men" roamed the countryside, asserting the claim of the southern province to the greater part of the Waxhaws. They drove off a surveying party running lines for grants under authority of North Carolina, defied a sheriff's posse, and dispersed only after a company of militia stacked arms on the post road. When the militia departed the South Men reassembled, this time with Thomas Polk, one of the personages of the region, on their side.

James Crawford and George McKemey were North Men, their titles bearing the emblems of North Carolina authority. As a matter of fact this authority had not the force of law, their holdings, as well as many other North Carolina land grants in the Waxhaws, being well within the precincts of South Carolina. Thus it is to no purpose to debate, as has been done interminably, in which house Andrew Jackson was born, in expectation of determining thereby in which province he was born. As the boundary was ultimately fixed by a compromise, the McKemey house stood four hundred and seven yards in North Carolina territory, while the Crawford house remained in South Carolina. In 1767, however, when Andrew Jackson was born, both houses were on the soil of South Carolina, over which North Carolina exercised a vigorously contested jurisdiction.

The contest had begun in 1764 when surveying commissioners representing both provinces discovered that, owing to an earlier surveyor's error, a guesswork line then in use was more than eleven miles south of the thirty-fifth parallel of latitude which actually separated the respective provinces. The controversy flared and simmered until 1772 when by a compromise the North Men carried the day in the Waxhaws. North Carolina was awarded most of the eleven-mile strip east of the Catawba River in exchange for a strip about equal in area west of the Catawba.[19] Even this arrangement failed to shift James Crawford's place from South Carolina to North Carolina, but Mr. Crawford was able to obtain at Charles Town a new grant confirming him in possession. The two hundred acres of the Jackson minors, having always been in North Carolina proper, were outside of the zone of contention.

8

The settlement of the boundary issue, when Andrew was five years old, enabled his elders to focus their concern on other topics, such as the deportment of the minister's wife. Nancy Craighead's husband had made a name for himself. He organized an "academy" at Waxhaw Church and imparted instruction in Greek and Latin. He went on long wilderness journeys, building churches and rejuvenating congregations. These enterprises were profitable to Doctor Richardson as well as to the Lord. The clergyman acquired a plantation that prospered under the toil of ten slaves. His two-story "manse" was one of the sights of the Waxhaws, his library its pride. His "literary evenings" were mentioned with awe on a frontier where the social tone was otherwise fixed by cock-fights, log-rolling and funerals. As no children blessed his union with Nancy Craighead, the pastor brought from England a nephew, William Richardson Davie, whom he reared as his son and sent to college at Princeton, New Jersey. Such magnificence captivated the Celtic imagination of Elizabeth Jackson who determined that one of her own sons should wear the cloth. Her "fresh-looking," eager face glowed at the prospect toward which she bent all her bustling energy. "Betty Jackson . . . [was] very conversive," wrote a woman who knew her, "[and] could not be idle. She spun flax beautiful"—being, indeed, a spinner's daughter. "She spun us heddie-yarn for weaving and the best and finest I ever saw."[20]

Alack, neither success nor Elizabeth Jackson's tribute encompassed happiness for Doctor Richardson. His solitary rides became longer, his silences deeper.

On the evening of July 20, 1771, William Boyd rode up from Rocky Creek, on the other side of the Catawba, the emissary of a new settlement from Ireland, to solicit the guidance of Reverend Richardson. At the same time the minister's wife, who had been to a quilting party, arrived at the house. She showed Mr. Boyd to her husband's study where Doctor Richardson was found in an attitude of prayer, but dead with a bridle twisted about his throat.

After a feverish consultation, the Waxhaw Church trustees announced that the minister had died during his devotions, but said nothing of the bridle. Every one attended the funeral and Mrs. Richardson ordered the finest tombstone that was to be seen in the Waxhaws for many years. The coat of arms of her husband's family was on it, with a bust in low relief and seventeen lines of carving to recount his virtues. The widow celebrated the arrival of this monument from Charles Town by marrying George Dunlap, a member of a large and wealthy local family whose sires had done almost as much as the Hutchinson sisters to populate the Waxhaws.

The news about the bridle leaked and the swift consolation Nancy Craighead found in the arms of Mr. Dunlap gave wings to conjecture. In vain the trustees—two of them Dunlaps—insisted that their deletion of the story of the tragedy was designed to shield the good name of the church from the stain of suicide. Among a faction of the congregation, all too ready to believe ill of Nancy, passed the whispered sentiment that other hands than his had buckled the fatal bridle about the neck of William Richardson. Rumors multiplied, passions mounted and a year after the interment the population of the Waxhaws met at the church to determine according to the ancient wisdom of the Scottish clans the innocence or guilt of Elizabeth Jackson's friend.

The grave was opened, the coffin exhumed, the skeleton of the late M.A. of Glasgow bared to view. Nancy Craighead was sternly directed to touch her finger to the forehead of the skull. If the finger bled she had murdered her husband.

Nancy touched but the finger did not bleed.

Then and there she would have stood acquitted, but for her brother-in-law, Archibald Davie. Mr. Davie had practically lived on the bounty of the late Reverend Richardson and regarded the future with concern. He seized Nancy's fingers and thrust them cruelly against the skull. She sobbed hysterically, then raised her hand—triumphant. There was no blood.[21]

9

Mr. William Humphries reopened the school at Waxhaw Church. Andrew Jackson attended this select institution while his brothers made out at a school of fewer pretensions. Andy was the bright one in the matter of letters. He could read when he was five. At eight he wrote "a neat, legible hand" and had a passion for maps.[22] Mrs. Jackson decided that her youngest was to be the preacher of the family, but Andrew, the man, remembered more clearly the winter evenings when his mother's tart rapid speech recounted "the sufferings of their grandfather at the seige of Carrickargus [Carrickfergus] & the oppression by the nobility of Ireland over the labouring poor."[23]

It was a time for splendid plans. The Waxhaws flourished. An active market for indigo, corn and barley transformed cabins into houses. Slave-traders from the Coast paraded their wares up the post road and auctioned them off at Charlotte. They were mostly "new niggers," raw from holds that plied the Middle Passage, South Carolina having abandoned its extensive attempt to enslave the non-warlike Indians[24] who only curled up and died for all the white man's pains. Virginia and Low-Country thoroughbreds began to replace the "grass ponies" of an earlier decade. Pastures were fenced and filled with cattle. "Cow-pens" became a fixture, where beef was fattened for the market. To accompany a "drive" to the seaboard was the zenith to which a Back-Country boy's ambition might aspire. The red dust rising from the heels of the herd twinkled like gold in the sunshine: a foretaste of fabulous Charles Town.

Andrew's uncle, James Crawford, better than kept abreast of these changes. His lands increased eightfold and ran to the Catawba River four miles away where he built a grist mill. There was more room in the large house now since the three eldest Crawford girls were married and had houses of their own. A son, Thomas, also married and his father deeded him a hundred and fifty acres. Then Aunt Jane died and Andrew's mother became the actual head of woman's domain on the busy farm.

But for all his lands and goods Uncle James played second fiddle to his brother, Robert Crawford, who owned the place adjoining on the south and was called "Esquire" because of his participation in public affairs. Squire Robert's residence, which Andy passed every day on his way to school, was the most elaborate of the countryside and the boy was proud of a connection so important.

10

Just now the Squire had his hands full. Following the Tea Party, of which a lengthy account reached the distant Waxhaws, the Crown had closed the port of Boston thinking a slender menu would coax his subjects there into a more amenable frame of mind. But it was not so. Boston appealed to her sister colonists against this indignity and nowhere was the response prompter or more substantial than in South Carolina. The Waxhaws sent corn, barley and cattle to vary the diet of rice that went from the Low-Country. Thus waist-bands in Boston did not shrink, and Charlotte's better-half blundered again. Musketry rattled on Lexington green and at Concord bridge. Its afterclap prompted his Excellency the Governor of South Carolina, a seafaring man by profession, to remove his official seat aboard a vessel in Charles Town harbor, where the Governor of North Carolina presently arrived to bear him company.

Home-made governments popped up in the places of these departing worthies, and express riders ranged the farthest trails with proclamations calling for measures of defense. South Carolina's answer was immediate. "Every man turned himself into a soldier; even the children . . . drilling with sticks."[25] The Waxhaw militia company elected Robert Crawford its captain.

In June of 1776 Captain Crawford's command took the field to help repel the invader. In July it returned, covered, if not with glory, at any rate with mosquito welts, and the Captain out of pocket eleven pounds, five shillings "South Currency," for "English flour" and pork to sustain his troops on the march to Charles Town.[26] But the Waxhaw men had been present during the astonishing defense of that port which confounded British plans for a comprehensive land-and-water subjugation of the southern rebels. They had lain in Lynch's pasture on the Neck ready to salute with their long rifles a British landing force in case the fleet should best the log fort on Sullivan's Island, thus clearing the way for a descent on the city. The fort bested the fleet, however, and, as the landing force mired in the mud, Captain Crawford's company had only to slap gnats and listen to the cannonade six miles down the harbor.

The Philadelphia newspapers which came by post from Charles

Town were more than ever an event. Neighbors came miles to Captain Crawford's house to hear them read aloud, column by column. The post of "public reader," always important, acquired new dignity. Nine-year-old Andy Jackson was, to use his own language, "selected as often as any grown man in the settlement." His voice was "shrill," but he "could read a paper clear through without getting hoarse . . . [or] stopping to spell out the words."[27] This was achievement in an environment where some of the men and nearly all of the women signed their names "X." The Hutchinson sisters could write, but George McKemey could not. James Crawford may have spelled and evidently pronounced his name "Crafford,"[28] as deed drawers and clerks frequently entered it that way in the records.

The papers that came in August after Captain Crawford's return contain momentous news. "Thirty or forty" citizens came to his house to hear it. Andy had prepared for his audience and read "right off," long words and all:

"In Congress, July 4, 1776. The Unanimous Declaration of the Thirteen United States of America. When, in the course of human events . . . ."[29]

CHAPTER II

AN OFFICER'S BOOTS

I

ANDY's precocity in the unorthodox use of biblical names might have disturbed his mother's pious ambition to see her son an ornament of the pulpit had he been less considerate about swearing around the house. Thus Elizabeth Jackson's aspiration remained a bright hope extinguished only by her courageous death. Sixty years after that event an old man looking wistfully toward the sunset embraced the faith. Then, remembering the boy fidgeting through the long sermons at the Waxhaw meeting-house who had noticed on his mother's lap a Bible covered with checked cloth, Andrew Jackson covered his own Bible in the same way.

The repulse of the British at Charles Town in 1776 brought three years of comparative peace to the Carolinas, while the northern Colonies carried on the war. Andy entered his thirteenth year, a tall, lean, remarkably agile, freckle-faced boy with bright blue eyes, a shock of tousled hair that was almost red and a temper in keeping. He would fight at the drop of a hat, by that means mitigating a misfortune that would have ruined the prestige of an ordinary boy. Andy had a habit of "slobbering" which he was unable to control until almost grown, but a jest at this circumstance spelled combat, whatever the odds. George McWhorter, a schoolmate at Mr. Humphries's, tried it often, with the same result, "& . . . said that Jackson never would give up, although he was always beaten, as he, McWhorter, was much the stronger of the two."[1]

Andy was a reckless horseman and few could best him in a foot-race or jumping match, but he was too light to wrestle. "I could throw him three times out of four," another classmate said, "but he would never *stay throwed*. He was dead game and never would give up."[2] Like all frontier boys, Andy had used a musket from the time he could lift one. Some of his friends gave him a gun to fire that had been loaded to the muzzle. The recoil sent Andy sprawling. He sprang to his feet with eyes blazing.

"By God, if one of you laughs, I'll kill him!"³

South Carolina filled wagons with grain and long trains creaked up the slope from Waxhaw Creek where Captain Crawford had built a bridge. They passed Andy's house on their northward trek to General Washington's encampments. In 1778, when he was eleven, Andy himself participated in the great adventure of a cattle drive to Charles Town. There were profits from these undertakings, and in pursuit of the goal she held for her youngest son, Mrs. Jackson sent him to Francis Cummins's "classical" boarding school in the New Acquisition. This was the name given the territory across the Catawba which South Carolina had received from North Carolina to settle the Waxhaw boundary.

Nothing survives to indicate the progress Andrew Jackson made in the classics, but the oldest document to be found among his personal papers bears the date, "March the 22d 79," and lifts a corner of the curtain on the extracurricular activities of the new pupil. "A Memorandum," it is entitled, "How to feed a Cock before you him fight Take and give him some Pickle Beaf Cut fine. . . ."⁴

2

While Andy was experimenting with Latin declensions of which he remembered nothing, and cock-fighting on which he became an authority, Captain Crawford's militia company received its second summons to oppose a British thrust at South Carolina. Savannah had fallen, Georgia was overrun, and a King's army advanced upon Charles Town. Andrew Jackson's brother Hugh, aged sixteen, joined his "uncle's" company. James Crawford sent two of his sons and a valuable wagon, with a hired driver, to haul the troops' provender. A mounted company also marched under Lieutenant William Richardson Davie, godson of the late Waxhaw Church pastor.

They returned victorious but at a price. Several had fallen in the action at Stono Ferry which helped to roll the British back into Georgia. Davie was badly wounded and left behind. James Crawford's wagon was lost. Hugh Jackson, ill and ordered not to fight,

AN OFFICER'S BOOTS

had fought anyhow, and after the battle died of "the excessive heat ... and fatigue of the day."[5]

Another British army sailed for the South, and again the Waxhaws went to the defense of Charles Town, this time unsuccessfully. On the twelfth of May, 1780, South Carolina's capital fell and General Lincoln and his army became prisoners. Robert Crawford—a major now, with a silver-mounted sword—also was captured, but released on parole.[6] Colonel Thomas Sumter with a few bands of unparoled militia escaped toward the Back-Country to reorganize and resist. He was opposed by two of the most energetic officers who served their royal master in America, the Earl of Cornwallis and Lieutenant-Colonel Banastre Tarleton.

Chaos imperiled the Revolutionary cause. Outspoken Tories who had fled the Province after the American victory of '76 returned in the wake of the invaders. Soft-spoken Tories who had stayed showed their true colors, and the weak-kneed everywhere begged the King's protection. Sumter not only had to elude British regulars but also Tory militia that sprang up in his path. Major Crawford took the perilous step of breaking his parole. He reformed his shattered command as mounted militia. Sumter himself appeared in the Waxhaws —a giant over six feet tall and weighing two hundred pounds, cool, unharassed and afraid of nothing. The distracted community rallied about him.

The classical school having disbanded, Andrew Jackson hung about the Major's camp, all boyish usefulness, and, as one born to it, picked up the manual of arms and "some idea of the different evolutions of the field."[7] But Major Crawford left his youthful connection behind when he joined Colonel Buford, whose small regiment, in retreat toward Virginia, was resting in a creek bottom some ten miles to the eastward. A day or so later, on May 29, 1780, came shocking news, confirmed in a few hours by wagons filled with wounded. Marching his cavalry one hundred and fifty-four miles in fifty-four hours, Tarleton had obliterated Buford's force, leaving one hundred and thirteen dead. Waxhaw Church was filled with the wounded, where Andy and Robert Jackson helped their mother minister to the sufferers on the straw-covered floor. From three members of their own household who had been there—Joseph, William and James Crawford, junior—they heard the story of the "massacre" that made the name of Tarleton a byword in the Waxhaws.

A large British force moved up to Crockett's plantation, a few miles south of the Crawfords', and Tory marauders began to drive off horses and other live stock. Nor were the English themselves as considerate as inhabitants thought they might have been. Had he fallen into the hands of the enemy Major Crawford's neck would have been a grave embarrassment to him. But the Major managed to avoid the Redcoats, being more fortunate in that respect than "Mr. Adam Cusack . . . [whom] Major Weymss, of the sixty-second regiment deliberately hung . . . though charged with no other crime than . . . shooting at some British officers across the river."[8] This intensified the resentment of the patriots who felt that some allowance should have been made for Mr. Cusack's poor marksmanship, as he had not hit any of the officers. Yet the British commander meant to be just and promised security to all who would sue for the King's mercy. Elizabeth Jackson, her boys, and such Crawfords as were not already fugitives, declined to sue. Driving their live stock before them, they retired into near-by North Carolina where Sumter stood guard.

3

This exile was of very short duration. The British were obliged to withdraw and the émigrés came back, followed by Sumter at the head of six hundred men of whom Major Davie's "dragoons" were the corps d'élite. Major Crawford, "on a three quarters Blooded gelding 15 hands high,"[9] his two sons and three nephews rode with the dragoons. Andrew Jackson, aged thirteen years and four months, could keep out of it no longer. With his sixteen-year-old brother Robert, he presented himself at the encampment, and, in one of his few allusions to his military service in the Revolution, which were always brief and modest, relates that the dragoon commander made him "a mounted orderly or messenger, for which I was well fitted, being a good rider and knowing all the roads."[10] Major Davie gave his boy adherent a pistol, and remained to the end of Andrew Jackson's life his absolute ideal of an officer and a gentleman.

Three weeks thereafter, on August 6, 1780, the mounted orderly "witnessed," as he said, the notable assault on the fortified British post at Hanging Rock where the dragoons dismounted under fire and with the infantry stormed the works. But for the disorganizing effect of plundering the enemy's camp which contained an excellent store of rum, Sumter would have captured the whole British force. It was a victory, nevertheless, and brought recruits to Sumter who pushed south to cooperate with Horatio Gates, lying near Camden with four thousand men ready to attack Cornwallis and confident of victory. Andy and his brother returned, however, to Waxhaw Church with the wounded, among whom was their cousin, James Crawford, junior.

Ten nights later the Jackson boys may have heard hoofs on the post road in front of their home and seen a cluster of hard-riding men stream by in the moonlight. It was General Gates and staff fleeing in advance of the wreck of their army which Cornwallis had annihilated in the most smashing victory British arms have gained on American soil. But Sumter, having captured one of Cornwallis's supply trains, fell back to defend the Waxhaws, halting at Fishing Creek to rest his command. There Tarleton surprised him completely. Sumter escaped to Charlotte on an unsaddled horse and without a hat, accompanied by a naked drummer boy who was taking a bath in the creek when the British cavalry struck. Major Crawford escaped on foot, leaving behind the fancy gelding and his silver mounted sword.[11] William and Joseph Crawford were captured.[12]

4

The Smart family lived on the post road five miles below Charlotte. Father and sons were in a North Carolina militia regiment that had been with Gates at Camden. The countryside knew of the disaster through the wild tales of fugitives who had strewn the roads, but the Smarts had no word of their men-folk. A vigil was kept upon the highway and every traveler from the south beset for news. Fourteen-year-old Susan perceived the approach of a figure on horseback in a cloud of sultry September dust. She hailed him and a boy reined up, dirty and tired-looking, with a battered broad-brimmed hat that flopped over his face. His long legs almost met under the belly of the worn little grass pony he bestrode. Susan wanted to smile, and perhaps something in her appraising eyes told the rider that he was not regarded precisely in the light of a cavalier.

"Where are you from?" asked Susan Smart.

"From below," the boy replied briefly.

"Where are you going?"

"Above."

"Who are you for?"

The boy answered the delicate question without equivocation: "The Congress."

Susan indicated that they were rebels together and asked for news from "below."

"Oh, we are popping them still," said the boy.

Susan thought the "we" assumed a good deal. "What's your name?" she asked.

"Andrew Jackson."[13]

Susan told her story and Andy related what he knew of the fate of Gates's army, which was far from reassuring. The army was no more. The population of the uplands was in panic-stricken flight before the invasion, and the roving bands of outlaws who cloaked their depredations with whichever standard was ascendant. The British commander-in-chief had moved into the Waxhaws, quartering himself in Robert Crawford's house and penning this proclamation.

"WHEREAS, notwithstanding . . . His Majesty's unparalleled clemency . . . [certain] deluded subjects . . . either in the service of the rebel Congress . . . or by abandoning their plantations . . . [oppose] His Majesty's just and lawful authority . . . I have ordered the estates . . . belonging to traitors above described to be sequestered. . . . GIVEN under my hand . . . in the Wacsaw . . . the sixth day of September one thousand seven hundred and eighty. CORNWALLIS."[14]

Tarleton's cavalry raked the countryside, harrying the fugitives. But the late mounted orderly could have informed Miss Smart that his recent commanding officer, the splendid Davie, and his "uncle," Major Crawford, had rallied a remnant of Sumter's command and kept the field. "Farming utensils were wrought into rude arms . . .

pewter dishes moulded into bullets," Andrew Jackson recalled in later years.[15] Tarleton replied to this impertinence by seizing the plantation of James Wauchope,[16] a captain under Davie. By a swift march and a dashing assault Davie surprised him there. A fierce fight swirled about the homestead, which, catching fire, drove the family out-of-doors—and into the arms of Captain Wauchope. The Captain had only time to embrace his wife and children, when Davie gave the signal to retire, richer by a herd of fine horses and a large stand of captured arms. He left sixty British dead in the Wauchope yard.

Five days later, on the morning of September twenty-sixth, Andrew Jackson, his mother and brother Robert, approached Charlotte from the south. The houses were there but the villagers had taken to the woods. Behind the stone wall of the courthouse square lay Davie with twenty men. Across the road behind a garden fence were two companies of North Carolina militia. Their rifles commanded the southern road. They were expecting Cornwallis and had orders to delay his advance at any hazard. The Jacksons passed through the waiting battle line three hours before Davie took the British columns unaware and made Cornwallis lose a day.

Mother and Robert found refuge with the McCollochs in Guilford County, but Andrew dropped off with the Wilsons, six miles east of Charlotte and closer to the scene of action. Mrs. Wilson was a sister of George McKemey. She had a son named John who was about Andy's age, but of different temperament. John grew up to become a locally distinguished preacher who never forgot Andy's robust language or the way he flourished weapons. Once John found him in an absolute fury mowing weeds on the assumption that they were British soldiers. John was not sorry when his playmate left, and forty-four years later declined to vote for him for President.[17]

5

Some of the victims of the débâcle of 1780 did not stop until they reached the steep green valleys "up west" beyond the mountains, where dwelt a buckskin-clad race of men who had taken little more than an academic interest in the war, but regarded hospitality as a duty. Nolichucky Jack Sevier passed the sign—and a thousand followers, white by blood, half-Indian in appearance and technique of war, carried their Deschert rifles and tomahawks to the Sycamore Shoals. In five days they were across the divide at Roan Knob with eighty miles behind them. At King's Mountain, assisted by Virginians and South Carolinians, they wiped out a formidable British force. Dropping back over the Blue Ridge by a water-gap and through the Big Smokies by a wind-gap they overcame a horde of Cherokees that had hung like a cloud on their rear. Under these circumstances Andrew Jackson, annihilating weeds at the Wilsons', heard for the first time in his life the name of John Sevier.

This neighborly turn broke the precedent of defeat, and Nathanael Greene arrived to help restore the fortunes of the Revolution in the South. The Back-Country word "cow-pens" was glorified by a victory and the hamlet of Guilford Court House gave its name to a battle that revised Cornwallis's plans entirely. Waxhaw refugees began to filter back to their desolated farms.

Major Robert Crawford was on hand to receive them, his house still a military post, but American, with sentinels mounting guard and officers tramping in and out. He bought of William Wrenn, a neighbor, sixty-six bushels of corn "for the Use of the Destressed Inhabitants . . . January ye 16th 1781."[18] The redeemed countryside became an armed camp, every man sleeping within reach of a weapon, and the houses of the principal Revolutionary partizans guarded by Crawford's mounted militia. Andrew and Robert Jackson reentered the ranks and were assigned to the domicile of Captain Land across the Catawba River. One night the picket was asleep, except one of their number, a British deserter, who was dozing when he heard a noise.

"The Tories are on us!" he yelled, seizing Andy by the hair.

Jackson slung a short-barreled musket, loaded with nine buckshot, into the fork of an apple tree. He saw figures crouching in the shadows. He cocked his gun and challenged. When a second hail was ignored Trooper Jackson fired. A volley from the shadows killed the deserter. Jackson dived into the house and with his six companions began to shoot from windows. A second defender dropped, dying by Jackson's side. Andy's uncle, James Crawford, was hit. With only four rifles to answer them the assailants were pressing the fight when, in their rear, a bugle sounded the cavalry charge. The Tories dashed for their horses. The defenders were mystified until a solitary neighbor, Mr. Isbel, appeared with a bugle.[19]

At other times the Tories were more successful. Young Martin McGary had married Betty Crawford and settled on some of the Crawford land where Waxhaw Creek enters the Catawba. Returning on a furlough from Major Robert's command, he found his house ransacked and his wife dead of fright from a Tory raid. His first-born babe survived its mother by only a day. This unhinged the mind of Mr. McGary who became a one-man army in quest of Tories, prowling the roadside thickets with a two-shooting rifle, one barrel loaded with ball for long range, the other with buckshot for close quarters.

A body of British dragoons moved on the Waxhaws to help the Tories, and Major Crawford gathered his squadron to resist. One of the points of assembly was the church. On April 9, 1781, the Jackson brothers and forty others were there when a group of mounted men in country dress was seen approaching by the road. A reenforcement under Captain Nesbit, thought the party at the church. When a few hundred yards away the screen of men without uniform, who were Tories, turned aside and a company of dragoons with sabers drawn charged the meeting-house.

Eleven of the forty men were captured and the church was set on fire. Springing on his horse, Andy dashed away by the side of his cousin, Lieutenant Thomas Crawford, with a dragoon at their heels. They sought to shake pursuit in the swampy "bottom" of Cain Creek. Andrew got across but Crawford's horse mired and the dragoon, after wounding his quarry with a saber, made him a prisoner. Jackson found his brother and the two spent a chilly night in the brush. In the morning they crept to the house of Lieutenant Crawford to convey the news to his family. But a Tory named Johnson had seen them and the boys were surprised at their breakfast by a file of dragoons. While his men wrecked the furnishings of the house, the officer in command "in a very imperious tone," directed Andy to clean his boots.

"This order he very promptly & positively refused, alleging that he expected such treatment as a prisoner of war had a right to look for."[20]

The officer lifted his sword and aimed a violent blow. The boy threw up his left hand. It was cut to the bone, and a gash on his head left a white scar that Andrew Jackson carried through a long life that profited little to England or any Englishman.

The wounded boy was ordered to mount a horse and guide the English party to the house of a noted Whig named Thompson. Threatened with death if he misled them, Andrew started off in the proper direction. He knew that Thompson, if at home, would be on lookout and prepared for flight. By road the party could have approached very near to the house without being seen. But Andrew took a path through a field which brought the British within sight of the house while half a mile away. Thompson saw them, and, leaping on a horse, escaped by swimming a swollen creek.[21]

6

Andy paid for his audacity by marching forty miles to Camden without a morsel of food or a drop to drink. When he tried to slake his aching throat by scooping up a little water from streams they forded, the soldiers would hustle their fourteen-year-old prisoner on.

The British military prison at Camden was the District jail house with a stockade around it. Andrew was confined on the second floor of the house where the only food was a scanty issue of stale bread once a day. His youthful appearance attracted the notice of an English officer, however, who engaged him in conversation. When Jackson complained of the lack of food, the officer made an investigation which disclosed that the rations contractor, a Tory, was taking too short a cut to financial independence. Another Tory had taken Andy's coat and shoes. His wounds had not been dressed and he was ignorant of the fate of his brother and his cousin, for as soon as their relationship was discovered the three had been separated. Robert Jackson also had reached Camden ill as a result of a saber cut from the British subaltern with muddy boots. A few days after the boys' arrival smallpox, the panic-spreading scourge that killed a tenth and marked a fifth of mankind, invaded the crowded prison.

AN OFFICER'S BOOTS

But deliverance seemed near when General Greene encamped just beyond the British works upon Hobkirk's Hill, clearly visible from the north window of the jail. One evening, as he afterward related, Andy saw "an american soldier . . . supposed to be a deserter . . . coming in from the american lines to the [British] redoubt." The activity that followed raised a hope among the prisoners that the British were preparing to retreat. But this ended "about sunset [when] a carpenter . . . came into our room with a plank, and nailed up the windows" while the guard of Tory soldiers "told us Green was on their lines without artillery, and they intended to make a second Gates of him, and hang us all. . . .

"Being anxious to see the Battle . . . [and] having only a razor blade which was allowed us to divide our rations with, I fell to work to cut out a pine Knot, out of the plank . . . obstructing the view of Greens encampment, and with the aid of a fellow prisoner compleated my object before day, making an aperture about an inch and a half in diameter which gave a full view of Genl Greens situation." The morning of April 25, 1781, found Andy with his eye to the peep-hole, describing events to his comrades. "The British army was . . . drawn up in column, under cover of the stockade and Col. Kershaws houses." Silently it moved out, circling under the cover of woods to surprise the American flank. It reached a road at the foot of Hobkirk's Hill when suddenly "it recd. a severe fire from the american piquet, and was seen to halt."

The check was momentary, however. The picket retired, "keeping up a brisk fire of musquetry" while the British deployed and advanced "in order of Battle up the Hill." On the heights Andrew saw the American camp spring to life. "The British supposing Green had no artillery," advanced boldly, "the officers in front . . . [of] their men, when Greens battery opened!" This was a surprise to the prisoners as well as the British, and they cheered as Andy relayed the news: the enemy in confusion; "many wounded;" others "running helter skelter." But the red line steadied and engaged the American infantry, "when the american squadron of horse . . . charge [d] them on their left and rear, and cut off the retreat. . . . Never were hearts more elated than ours at the glitter of americans swords . . . which promised immediate release to us. . . .

"How short was our Joy. . . . The *roar* of our cannon ceased and the sound of our small arms appeared retiring."[22] The Americans' last hope was the cavalry, which the British attacked with such vigor that it barely was able to join the main body, already in retreat. The failure of a single American company had lost a battle half won. A day or so later Andrew was stricken with smallpox.

At this moment Lord Rawdon, the British commander, was receiving a caller, a brisk, blue-eyed little Irishwoman whose country attire showed the stains of travel. Elizabeth Jackson had ridden all the way from the Waxhaws to second the request of an American militia captain for an exchange of prisoners, and to ask that her two wounded boys be among the number. His lordship was a kindly man, and probably he admired the rebel mother's pluck. In any event the Jackson brothers and three neighbors were liberated.

Robert was so weak from smallpox and an infection of his wound that he had to be held on a horse. Mrs. Jackson rode another pony. Andrew walked, barefooted, bareheaded and without a coat. A beating rain drenched the little cavalcade. They put Robert to bed raving. In two days he was dead and Andrew was delirious. For several weeks little more tangible than hope sustained Elizabeth Jackson in her fight to save her remaining son.

7

Though Cornwallis, now fortifying Yorktown, had virtually taken the war out of the Carolinas, the British held Charles Town where two of James Crawford's sons lay with "ship fever" in the floating British prison. As soon as Andrew was out of danger Elizabeth Jackson, Mrs. George Dunlap (Nancy Craighead), and a lady named Boyd set out to nurse the boys from home.

Andy's mother understood the risk of the undertaking. "Kissing at meetings and partings was not so common as now," Jackson said of that leave-taking. Simply "wiping her eyes with her apron," Elizabeth stammered some words of "a mother's advice." She told her son to make friends by being honest and to keep them by being steadfast. "Andy . . . never tell a lie, nor take what is not your own, nor sue . . . for slander. . . . *Settle them cases yourself.*"[23]

They found Joseph Crawford beyond help. William was saved but it cost the life of his nurse. On an unrecorded day in November,

1781, Elizabeth Jackson was hastily buried with other victims of the plague in an unmarked grave on the gloomy flat of Charles Town Neck, a mile from Governor's Gate. With this news Andrew received a small bundle containing his mother's spare clothes.[24] "I felt utterly alone," the orphan said, "and tried to recall her last words to me."[25]

CHAPTER III

Dice and Bear's Oil

I

The war was over, except to sign the papers, but it was not paid for. Accordingly, on December 12, 1782, Major Robert Crawford and Andrew Jackson, "being Duly Sworn . . . appraise[d] for the use of the publick . . . for William Crawford Owner viz one Bay Horse Brands unknown to the appraisers—Value £150."[1] This animal, which young Mr. Crawford had lost at the time of his capture at Sumter's Surprise, formed only a part of his bill against the state. There was a "Waggon, Gears and hand screw taken in Beauforts defeat," "one horse lost at hanging Rock," pay as "centinel," as "adjutant," "as Issuing Commissary" and many other items footing up to sixteen hundred and twenty-five pounds. Mr. Crawford's claim reached the state auditor in rather good order, but this eagle-eyed servant of South Carolina's gaunt Treasury whittled it down to thirteen hundred and thirty pounds, paper currency, for which the petitioner accepted one hundred and ninety pounds[2] in sterling money to restore his farm and contemplate the blessings of liberty. Yet in this liquidation William Crawford had fared better than most.

The blessings of liberty seemed somehow illusory. Major Robert Crawford had served seven years and in six campaigns, the staunch comrade of one whom another generation would mention with the great light-horse leaders of the war. But in 1783 Colonel William R. Davie was simply a pleasant young gentleman of English birth and no occupation who had spent his inheritance in his adopted country's service. He went off to North Carolina to undertake the practise of law, leaving the Major to his muddled accounts.

Major Crawford had neglected until 1783 to file a claim for the money laid out for flour and pork on the march to Charles Town in '76. The seller's receipt for the money? queried the meticulous auditor. Fortunately the Major had kept it. Proving a claim for services and losses in maintaining a "station" on his property and for timber and fences destroyed was a more difficult matter. A piece had become torn from the appraiser's certificate. The Major's copy of the missing part was not accepted without a great deal of quibbling.[3] And auditors had other ways of diminishing their popularity. "James Craford Certifies to Wm Craford's acc^t & the latter the former's by which means the publick are liable to Great Impositions."[4] Impositions, indeed! More than one harassed veteran washed his hands of it and impulsively set his face toward the gray roof of the Big Smokies. "Up West" was liberty from auditors, from debtors' jails and taxes.

Martin McGary left in quest of peace in heart. He had killed twenty Tories but it was no use.

2

Andrew Jackson, aged fifteen and publicly certified as a competent judge of horse-flesh in a region where every one knew something of horses, made his home at George McKemey's for a while and then with Major Crawford, where a Captain Galbraith also was sojourning. Andy mimicked the rich Highland brogue of Captain Galbraith who lost his head, and, seizing a horsewhip, announced his intention of imparting a lesson in deportment. Andy coolly suggested that before lifting his hand the Captain would do well to prepare to meet his Maker.[5] Whereupon the Major stepped in, and shortly afterward apprenticed his youthful connection to a saddler. This lasted for six months, after which Andy turned up at a school, or several schools, if all claims advanced in behalf of casual educational institutions of that frontier are valid. More probable is the essence of tradition involving the juvenile Jackson in an exhilarating cycle of personal encounters, horse racing, cock-fighting and gambling.

This was the state of affairs when Hugh Jackson, a weaver and merchant of Carrickfergus, Ireland, passed to his reward, leaving his American grandson a legacy which Jackson later valued at "three or four hundred pounds sterling."[6] Andy set out to claim his money at Charles Town—or Charleston since the war, unless one would contradict the General Assembly to whom the royal name, standing apart, seemed inconsistent with the triumph of freedom's cause.

Thus it was that the Revolutionary orphan found himself on a March day of 1783[7] leaving the Quarter House Tavern possessed of a fortune sufficient to begin his life auspiciously—which Andrew Jackson, according to his lights, meant to do. Three or four hundred pounds sterling would have worked wonders with the acres on Twelve Mile Creek of which the death of his brothers had put Andrew in sole possession. Half of the sum would have seen him through college. But it was not toward the Garden of the Waxhaws or the classroom that thrifty Hugh Jackson's heir turned his horse's head.

From the Quarter House it was four miles by the Broad Path to Charleston's battered military wall, a native work of masonry contrived of oyster shells and lime. On either side of this road rice-fields alternated with a jungle of moss-curtained live-oak, palmetto, myrtle and fine-leafed little cassina trees with their bright red Christmas berries. Vine-covered gate-posts framed a prospect of white-and-brick plantation seats—Belmont, the ruined home of the Pinckneys; Accabee, the Dart place—a stimulating overture to the richest and gayest of American cities.

The long occupation of Charleston by the British army had made refugees of all the great families who had turned their backs on the King. A few had gone to the Waxhaws[8] where Andy had made acquaintances among the boys of his age. This was natural. Andrew Jackson belonged to all the aristocracy there was in the Back-Country, and think you him not oblivious to this fact. The Low-Country émigrés had pressed courteous invitations to which Andrew could hardly have anticipated an opportunity to comply so soon.

Beyond the fortifications the Broad Path became Meeting Street paved with English cobblestones transported as ballast. The town was a little shabby, though not to Andrew's eyes, but lively with the stir of reclamation. In great houses windows long dark gleamed again, neglected gardens took form and fragrance and gave up silver buried at the roots of magnolia trees. "There is courtesy here, without stiffness or formality," wrote a German traveler. Neither "domestic circumstances" nor "religious principles" stood in the way of "pleasures of every kind." A French dancing master was spon-

The War in the Waxhaws

A steel engraving by John Sartain, executed about 1850. From the private collection of Mrs. Mary French Caldwell of Nashville.

"The Brave Boy of the Waxhaws"

A print by Currier & Ives which appeared in 1876 and has, of course, no authority as an historical document other than that which time and the affections of the American people have bestowed upon the productions of these famous lithographers. From the gallery of the North Carolina Historical Commission, Raleigh.

sored by the "first minister of the town" who knew how to retain the favor of his parishioners. "Milliners and hair dressers . . . grow rich."[9] And of course there were the races, for which "courts of justice" closed, "all the schools were regularly let out," and merchants put up their shutters. "Clergymen and judges" joined the procession to the track, and the stones of Meeting Street rang as "Splendid equippages" rolled by, displaying "liveried outriders—gentlemen in fashionably London made clothes."[10]

Horses, horses. In the talk at McCrady's Tavern and the paddock at New Market, the late fight for freedom loomed merely as a vexatious interruption to the historical progress of affairs on the Charleston turf. "Not only were horses thrown out of training" by the hostilities, "but on the appearance of Lord Cornwallis' army they were . . . hid in the swamps." In no Colony or Province did a larger proportion of the gentry espouse the rebel cause, George III "being neither a sportsman nor a horseman."[11] They bore their parts well, these Low-Country dandies, and now they were back to exchange reminiscences—of their horses.

Twice Captain James, "surest scout of Marion," had made escapes impossible to explain, except by the fact that he rode Roebuck. And imagine Mr. Ravenel's indignation upon finding his Lucy ("out of Rose by imported Friar") ridden by a *servant* of the American Colonel Maham. Mr. Ravenel presented himself to General Marion. He had decided to join the Army. That was good, said Marion. But there was only one horse in the corps that Mr. Ravenel desired to ride. Yes? said General Marion. Yes, replied Mr. Ravenel, Colonel Maham's servant's horse. It was arranged. . . . And Red Doe was at the post again, but a couple of years before she had carried a British officer at the head of a firing squad to execute an American soldier named Hunter. The condemned man asked the officer to dismount as he had something of importance to communicate. Thinking the prisoner meant to reveal military information the officer complied. No sooner did his foot leave the stirrup than a single bound landed Hunter in the saddle, and Red Doe flashed into a thicket before the astonished soldiery could close their mouths.[12]

Andrew Jackson had the qualities his late sovereign lacked. He was both a sportsman and a horseman but, alack, his luck was bad. The legacy dwindled and disappeared. The young adventurer was in debt to his landlord, and, one evening wondering how he could pay it, strolled into a place where dice clicked across a tap-room table in a high-stake game of rattle and snap. A player offered two hundred dollars against Andrew's horse. Andy thought for a while and then requested the dice. He cast and won. The landlord was paid and Andy left for home with "new spirits infused into me."[13]

3

After that Andrew was not long for the Waxhaws, where one occupation seemed as unstable as the next. He went to school at Queen's Museum in Charlotte. He taught a school near home. Girls as well as horses swam within his ken. Susan Smart thought "Ande" a "lank, leaning-forward fellow." She also remembered his eyes, and that there was "something very agreeable about him."[14] Mary Massey is said to have entertained a less favorable opinion,[15] but Mary Crawford received Andrew's ardent addresses with a sense of satisfaction not shared by her father, the Major. On December 4, 1784, Andrew Jackson acted as an appraiser of "a Bay horse of James Crawford Lost in the Service of the State,"[16] and a few days thereafter was gone for ever from the scenes of his boyhood. Some have said it was to be shut of reproaches over his squandered inheritance. Local tradition adds a complication over Mary Crawford and a tender parting "on the bank of the Catawba." In any event, of that farewell Jackson carried away a memory to be recalled at strange hours and places as when, across the débris of fifty years, a silver snuff-box found its way from the hands of a lonely widower in the White House to Mary Crawford Dunlap in the Waxhaws.[17]

Andy spent Christmas of 1784 at the lively Rowan House in Salisbury, North Carolina, where refreshment for man and beast cost four shillings a day. The spirit of Yuletide may have favored the wayfarer for he persuaded Spruce Macay, who already had two young scapegraces in charge, to let him read law in his office.

The new protégé of Mr. Macay—pronounced Macoy—was soon known and long remembered by the inhabitants. "Andrew Jackson was the most roaring, rollicking, game-cocking, horse-racing, card-playing, mischievous fellow, that ever lived in Salisbury . . . the head of the rowdies hereabouts . . . more in the stable than in the office."[18] But there was something instantly attractive about this tall young Celt, not eighteen when he came to Salisbury, with intense blue eyes and a long, fair, pock-marked, apperceptive face interestingly seamed by a scar that lost itself in his ruddy hair. An acute imagination animated that face—an imagination of action, fierce in its loyalties and its hatreds, projecting through dim generations of Scottish rains and Irish mists to strike confusion in the breast of this plunging orphan on a savage hinterland across the ocean.

Not that Salisbury would have fancied being called a part of a savage hinterland. The Waxhaws—yes; but in Salisbury a native of the Waxhaws could feel that he had accomplished a steep social climb. Salisbury was an old town at the beginning of the Revolution. It was not large—some fifty families—but no southern towns were large. Several of those families, including that of Spruce Macay, were wealthy and maintained mansions with a Low-Country flavor. What of it? Andrew Jackson who had been to Charleston declined to be terrified by Salisbury. He dressed as well as, or better than, he could afford. Debts or not, he rode a good horse; and no horse was ridden better. If liquor, cards and mulatto mistresses filled the rôles that legend assigns to them in the history of the student's residence in Salisbury, these diversions were enjoyed in a company that enabled Andrew to attain a position of leadership among the socially eligible bloods of the countryside.

Nor were the young ladies of quality indifferent. Nancy Jarret "often met him at parties, balls and . . . at the house of my relative, Mr. McKay. I knew him as well as I did any other young man when I was a single girl . . . for his ways and manners . . . were most captivating. . . . We all knew that he was wild . . . that he gambled some and was by no means a Christian young man. . . . When he was calm he talked slowly and with good selected language. But . . . animated . . . he would talk fast with a very marked North-Irish brogue. . . . Either calm or animated there was something about him I cannot describe except to say that it was *a presence*. . . . This I and all the other girls in Salisbury . . . talked about among ourselves."[19]

Their mothers also talked. Two hundred Waxhaw acres did not support Andrew Jackson's scale of living. They feared that he gambled not always as a sportsman who can afford to lose, but as an adventurer who has to win. They would have been glad to hear that salutary progress in his legal studies promised a swift removal of the captivating "presence" from Salisbury.

They heard the contrary. Judges rode the circuit, trailed by a curious following of lawyers and sharpsters. Courts came and went, filling the sprawling Rowan House with patrons and the town with news: Ordered, that "Susannah Hartman, Orphan, 13 years old, be bound to Paul Rodsmith to serve till she shall attain the age of 18." . . . Recommended, that James Hughes be "exempt from Taxes being poor, aged & infirm and having a large family." . . . Ordered, that John Fraize "keep the County free from all Costs respecting a Bastard child begot on the Body of Dorotha Goose.". . . Ordered, that tavern proprietors serve, on request, "small Beer or Grog" with dinners at no extra charge.[20]

John McNairy completed his preparation in the office of Mr. Macay and was admitted to the bar, but the conclusion of Andrew Jackson's second year in Salisbury found him engrossed principally by his duties as a manager of the Christmas ball. It was the ambition of the gilded youth of Salisbury that this affair should eclipse all precedent.

It did so. Every one came—never the girls more beautiful, the young men more gallant: no flaw anywhere until a flurry at the door stopped the music, stopped the dancing. There stood Molly and Rachel Wood, mother and daughter, the only white prostitutes in Salisbury. Moreover, their cards of invitation were in order. Speechless chaperons shooed their charges into a buzzing group at the far side of the hall.

Andrew Jackson approached them. He "humbly apologized." He alone had sent the cards to Molly and Rachel Wood, as "a piece of fun," not thinking for an instant they could misunderstand. One story is that Jackson was half-forgiven, another that he had no choice but to follow Molly and Rachel into the night.[21]

4

Not long after the Christmas ball Andrew parted company from Spruce Macay and attached himself to Colonel John Stokes, one of the most brilliant figures in the annals of the North Carolina bar. If Colonel Stokes's convivial habits cost him a conspicuous place in history, they also sponsored a sympathetic view of the contiguous problems of youth and wild oats. Moreover, the Colonel had lost a hand at Buford's Defeat and may have been nursed at Waxhaw Church by Andy and his mother. In place of the missing hand he wore a silver knob, and, whether pleading a cause in court or leading a tap-room chorus, dramatized his points by bringing the knob down on a table so that it rang like a bell.

After six months of John Stokes's guidance, the pupil joined the itinerant court at Wadesborough. On September 26, 1787, Judges Samuel Ashe and John F. Williams, after examination, directed that "Andrew Jackson . . . a person of unblemished moral character, and . . . competent . . . knowledge of the law," be admitted to "practice . . . in the said several courts of pleas and quarter sessions . . . with all and singular the privileges and emoluments which . . . appertain to attorneys."[22]

In November the court arrived at Salisbury. "The girls had a habit," wrote Nancy Jarret, "of going to the court-house when any friend or acquaintance . . . was to be licensed." They saw Andrew in "a new suit, with broad-cloth coat [and] ruffled shirt . . . his abundant suit of dark red hair combed carefully back . . . and, I suspect, made to lay down smooth with bear's oil. He was full six feet tall and very slender, but . . . graceful. . . . His eyes *were* handsome . . . a kind of steel-blue. I have talked with him a great many times and never saw him avert his eyes from me for an instant."[23]

One of the judges advised Jackson to try his fortunes "up West" and he left Salisbury with the court. The end of the short North Carolina winter found Lawyer Jackson a fairly seasoned circuit campaigner for a boy not old enough to vote. But it was all on the side of experience rather than the more negotiable emoluments which appertain to attorneys. At Richmond he is supposed to have defended a thief on a guarantee of acquittal or no fee. The defendant got the whipping post and his counsel left town owing a board bill. At Martinsville he loafed with two friends who kept a store, and visited at the pleasant home of his schoolmate, John McNairy. At Johnsonville Colonel William Moore rode his horse into the courtroom and was fined fifty pounds after a posse had dismounted him.

There, in his first case of record, Barrister Jackson was successful in an action against the Coroner growing out of a family dispute among the county officers.[24]

Brighter prospects spread before him. Andrew had made himself agreeable as a guest of the influential McNairys whose neighbor was Governor Martin, of North Carolina. Indeed, he had organized the first known celebration of the anniversary of the Battle of Guilford Court House, with speeches, horse-races and a cock-fight.[25] North Carolina extended to the Mississippi. The westernmost reach of this domain was hardly explored, but one hundred and eighty miles beyond the regular outposts of civilization, astride a vague stream named Cumberland, a band of settlers had made an island for themselves which they called the Western District of the state. Jackson's eye was on the Western District, and the most plausible explanation of what followed seems to be that, to smooth his own path, he communicated this interest to John McNairy,[26] by no means a timid young man, but also by no means an adventurer, probably because his future was provided for at home, while Jackson had his way in the world to win. In December of 1787 the Legislature dignified the Western District with a Superior Court and elected John McNairy to its bench.[27] No legislative provision was made for an attorney-general, as the public prosecutor was called. This appears to have been a disappointment to Jackson,[28] until it occurred to him and McNairy that this officer could be appointed by court, thus providing the sought-for means of financing a reconnaissance of the West.

5

It was a triumph of enterprise as well as luck, for with all his impetuosity there was a shrewd streak in the composition of this superficially irresponsible young Back-Country dandy. Andrew Jackson had got what he was after, a pioneering trip de luxe with the prospect of comfortable fees to pad the prickly edges of life in the new land of promise, where thousands of unhappy countrymen would have sold their shirts for a chance to swing an ax.

Jackson had watched the western fever mount as the trickle of disillusioned soldiers swelled to a bold stream of restless men from Georgia to New Hampshire, who converged upon the mountain passes as the best escape from the fruits of a revolution that seemed to have soured on the vine. The national government of the Amercan "Confederation," a frail enough reed in war-time, had declined to a simulacrum of bankrupt authority, unable to meet interest on its debts, to command respect abroad or obedience at home. Reflective men who had borne arms in support of the flaming watchwords of independence brooded over the failure of the democratic experiment. Nathaniel Gorham, presiding officer of Congress and weary of the humiliation, caused a brother of Frederick the Great to be approached with a view of establishing a monarchial government to avert retrocession to England, who, believing her moment near, complacently retained troops on our soil. Nor could the states keep peace within their several households. Massachusetts had contended against armed rebellion, while others forestalled it by mixed displays of courage and cowardice.

North Carolina's problems arose chiefly from the isolated character of her ultramontane settlements which had little in common socially, economically or politically with the eastern part of the state. These settlements comprised two geographically distinct groups the most remote of which was the Western District athwart the Cumberland, accessible only by traversing nearly two hundred miles of Indian country. As the keen Jackson probably knew, the Western District was speculating already on the advantages of an independent political future. The other transmountain settlements filling the narrow Holston, Nolichucky and Watauga Valleys just beyond the crest of the Blue Ridge, were past the speculating stage. They had seceded from the parent commonwealth under the title of the State of Franklin. This circumstance gave a lively cast to the proposed journey of Messrs. McNairy and Jackson who must pass through Franklin, where other North Carolina officials riding in on horseback had ridden out on rails, and held themselves fortunate for the privilege.

Franklin stood by republican institutions. Its legislators traveled to their meetings with rifles under their arms which sustained the spirits by a chance shot at an Indian or North Carolina partizan, democratically equal in their eyes; sustained the body by adding to the mound of game outside the log house in Jonesborough where the lawmakers conducted their deliberations. Otter skins were legal tender which might have placed the fiduciary system of Franklin on a sounder basis than some of the paper-stuffed treasuries nearer the seaboard but for the undermining influence of counterfeiters. Bales of what had passed for otter pelts were found to be raccoon with otter tails sewed on. But as the Legislature had also monetized a number of other articles, including "good" whisky, a collapse of the state's credit was averted. The personality of their Executive remained, however, the greatest resource of the over-mountain men.

The Governor of Franklin was John Sevier—pronounced Seveer. Without him it is hard to see how the state could have lasted three months. With him it had lasted three years. The history of Nolichucky Jack was a legend among the people who had known him most of his life. He could shoot the straightest, ride the hardest, and dance the best. He was tall, handsome, a soldier and a cavalier. The belle of the valleys was Catherine Sherrill. An attack on Watauga Fort caught her outside the walls. Under a "hail" of arrows, she tried to climb the stockade, slipped and was snatched to safety by John Sevier. This enabled Bonny Kate to choose among a shoal of suitors. Just before he started for King's Mountain, she married Nolichucky Jack. His military record surpassed Cæsar's—at any rate, in the eyes of the border legion he had led in twenty-six battles against the Indians and one against the British without defeat.

But when Andrew Jackson arrived at Morganton in the foothills to prepare for his journey West he learned, to his great satisfaction, that victory had incredibly deserted the banner of John Sevier. North Carolina had moved against him with the sinister weapon of tact. There was no arrow in the quiver of Nolichucky Jack to contend with such womanish artifices. His right-hand man, John Tipton, had gone over to the foe, and, cocking a rifle, declared himself a court sitting by North Carolina authority ten miles from Sevier's capital at Jonesborough. Sevier raided this tribunal and was ready for civil war. So was Tipton, and the poison of conciliation had had its effect. Nolichucky Jack's force melted at the first encounter. Two of the Governor's sons were captured. Tipton ordered them hanged, but cursing himself for his weakness, signed a reprieve. Sevier, senior, plunged into the wilderness and began an Indian campaign— a stratagem ever calculated to burnish the fortunes of a frontier captain.

The Spanish Minister to the United States continued to address him as Governor and the nebulous rumors of western intrigue with Madrid glowed anew. Louisiana was on every lip. Explanations of this circumstance ranged from a comprehensive frontier conspiracy to open the Mississippi to western commerce by the capture of New Orleans, to the creation of a separate republic beyond the mountains under protection of Spain as a buffer to hostile encroachment by the seaboard Confederation.

Irrespective of this complication, the absence of Sevier gave North Carolina an opportunity she did not neglect. A "loyal" court was established in Jonesborough. In April of 1788, McNairy joined Jackson at Morganton where a red road rolled away toward the high blue mist. No time could be lost if they were to open court on the Cumberland for the session of the second quarter of the year. With two pistols slung from his saddle, a beautiful rifle lashed to the pack of his stout "bat" mare and trailed by a troop of hunting dogs Andrew Jackson departed, adequately prepared to defend the dignity of the Old North State while in transit through the seduced domain of Nolichucky Jack.

In quiet Salisbury Nancy Jarret sighed. Her graceful friend "would get himself killed" the next thing she knew.

BOOK TWO

The Robe

"Do what is *right* between these parties. That is what the law always *means*."

Judge Jackson to a jury.

CHAPTER IV

THE MERO DISTRICT

I

ANDREW JACKSON stated with pride that the stout mare carried "half a dozen books" over the windy summits of the Blue Ridge. Of these Matthew Bacon's *Abridgement of the Law* was the sheet anchor of the journeyman solicitor. Or so it seemed to Waightstill Avery who found himself opposed to young Mr. Jackson in a suit before the Superior Court at Jonesborough, where Jackson and McNairy had decided to tarry, finding it impossible to get through to Nashville in time to open court before the autumn session. Waightstill Avery, of Morganton, was a personage in North Carolina, a wise and scholarly old lawyer mellowed by the experiences of life. He liked Jackson and had gone out of his way to be helpful to him, but this did not deter him, in an address to the court, from twitting his adversary upon the liberal doses of Bacon that spiced his arguments.

Andrew squirmed in his seat, and when Colonel Avery concluded, he blurted out, probably forgetting to suppress his Irish accent:

"I may not know as much law as there is in Bacon but I know enough not to take illegal fees!"

Silence in the log court-room. Colonel Avery arose to ask if Mr. Jackson meant to imply that he had taken illegal fees.

"I do, sir," replied Andrew Jackson.

"It's false as hell!" shouted Waightstill Avery.[1]

Mr. Jackson was writing rapidly on a fly-leaf of his Bacon. He tore out the page and bowing—"Your obedient servant, sir"—presented it to Colonel Avery.

The promptitude with which the unknown stripling had invoked the Code of Honor against one of the most popular men in that part of the country rather captured the fancy of Jonesborough. The yea and nay and tergiversation that forms the half-concealed background of most duels dims their glamour. A word and a challenge was the Code in its purest ray.

Some of the most respectable gentlemen of the place civilly approached Andrew Jackson with the inquiries and offers of mediation that etiquette required. Jackson admitted that he did not impute dishonesty to Colonel Avery, but ignorance of the statute governing fees in a certain instance. Avery's remark, however, had ended the discussion as an explanation now might be construed as an act of cowardice. Avery had no desire at all to fight. He had charged an unwarranted fee, but had returned it, and so declined to take the first step toward an amicable adjustment with Jackson, thinking the armor of his reputation sufficient against the cause of this quick-tempered young man.

Colonel Avery entered the court-room the next morning without taking notice of Mr. Jackson's challenge. Near the end of a tense day, the ignored one took up his quill again.

"August 12th 1788
"Sir

"You rec^d a few lines from me yesterday & undoubtedly you understand me. My charactor you have injured; and further you have Insulted me in the presence of a court and a large audianc I therefore call upon you as a gentleman to give me satisfaction . . . & further . . . an answer immediately without Equivocation and I hope you can do without dinner untill the business is done. . . . y^r obt S^t

"An^{dw} Jackson[2]

"Coll^o Avery"

The Colonel could sustain his attitude of indifference no longer. His second, John Adair, called on the challenger. Details were arranged and the two met on a hill south of town at sunset. But conciliators had accomplished their end. Both parties fired in the air and shook hands.

"Mr. Jackson," said Colonel Avery producing a parcel, "I feared that in event of my wounding you mortally you would be inconsolable in your last moments without your beloved Bacon."

Jackson undid the wrappings and exposed a side of smoked pork. The laugh that went up died on the lips of the company assembled. Jackson was not laughing and two of the gentlemen stepped anxiously to his side. It took Andrew Jackson thirty years to perceive the humor of Colonel Avery's bold little pleasantry.[3]

2

In September of 1788 the Cumberland Road was opened across the Cumberland range and one hundred and eighty miles of Cherokee country, linking the former State of Franklin with the ultima thule on the shores of Cumberland River. Andrew Jackson, accompanied by a negro girl he had bought of Micajah Crews for two hundred dollars,[4] joined the first immigrant train to use the new trail. The state furnished a guard of sixteen men under Martin McGary, late of the Waxhaws, who, deprived of his occupation of eliminating Tories, had found Indians the best substitute available. Aside from the pursuit of his hobby, Mr. McGary was one of the gentlest of men, and could stop a baby from crying as quickly as its mother. But it was Jackson's alertness one night that put the train in so bristling a state of defense that a Cherokee war-party forebore to attack. Four hunters were scalped on the spot, however, a few hours after the caravan had left. On another night Jackson shot a panther and tomahawked its cub when they tried to kill a colt. On Sunday, October twenty-sixth, the wagons climbed to the crest of a bluff overlooking the Cumberland. Inside a shambling fence built to keep the browsing buffalo at a distance, stood, in order of importance, two taverns, two stores, one distillery, one court-house and a fringe of cabins, bark tents and "wagon camps." Andrew Jackson had reached the theater of his labors.

Nashville's court-house was a hewn-log structure eighteen feet square with a porch on the south side. Its interior was filthy. Doors askew and sagging window-shutters leered the community's contempt for authority. The courts of the Western District had sunk in the slough of disrespect that marked the decline of the old Confederation. Horses were hitched to the stocks and whipping-post. Twenty-six-year-old John McNairy took the bench on November third[5] and quickly changed all this, in so far as the jurisdiction of the Superior Court was concerned. If the sheriff could not sustain him, he knew his twenty-one-year-old prosecutor would. Debtors, defying the law's machinery, had banded together to run the town.

Andrew Jackson espoused the cause of the creditors. In thirty days he had enforced seventy writs of execution[6] and changed the attitude of Nashville toward its wheels of justice. This was the kind of lawyer the property owners of Nashville wanted and the prosecutor got all the private business he could handle. Money was scarce but land was illimitable, inasmuch as it belonged to no one except the Indians. Mr. Jackson became a land holder almost before he knew it.

Of Nashville's two taverns, the young prosecutor probably would have preferred "King" Boyd's "notorious" Red Heifer had not his official course placed him in opposition to the interests of so many of Mr. Boyd's patrons. Boyd also owned the distillery whose prosperity was founded on the new and far-reaching discovery that whisky could be manufactured from corn. Therefore, one finds Mr. Jackson gracing the table of the Widow Donelson's blockhouse, which, on first thought, strikes an observer as an out-of-the-way abode for one so actively employed at Nashville. To reach Mrs. Donelson's it was necessary to ferry the river and take the Kentucky Road northward for six or seven miles, then branch off on a poor trail for three or four miles more. A man as eager for advancement as Jackson would not have undertaken this ride twice daily without good reasons, and good reasons Jackson had.

Residence at the Donelsons' established him with a family first in numbers and second or third in influence along the Cumberland. Moreover the landlady's youngest and most beautiful daughter, Rachel, had lately arrived at the blockhouse after an absence of four years.

The return of Rachel Donelson Robards to her mother's house had provided the Cumberland with a mildly stimulating topic of conversation. Her deep dark eyes and full flexible lips had inadvertently spelled trouble for men before, and when, early in 1789, her husband suddenly appeared in Nashville the apprehension grew that this might happen again. For those dark eyes had met the level glance of Andrew Jackson—and found it quite undisturbed by the proximity of jealous Captain Robards.

3

Restless and energetic John Donelson was born in Somerset County, Maryland, April 7, 1725. His father was an importer, his maternal

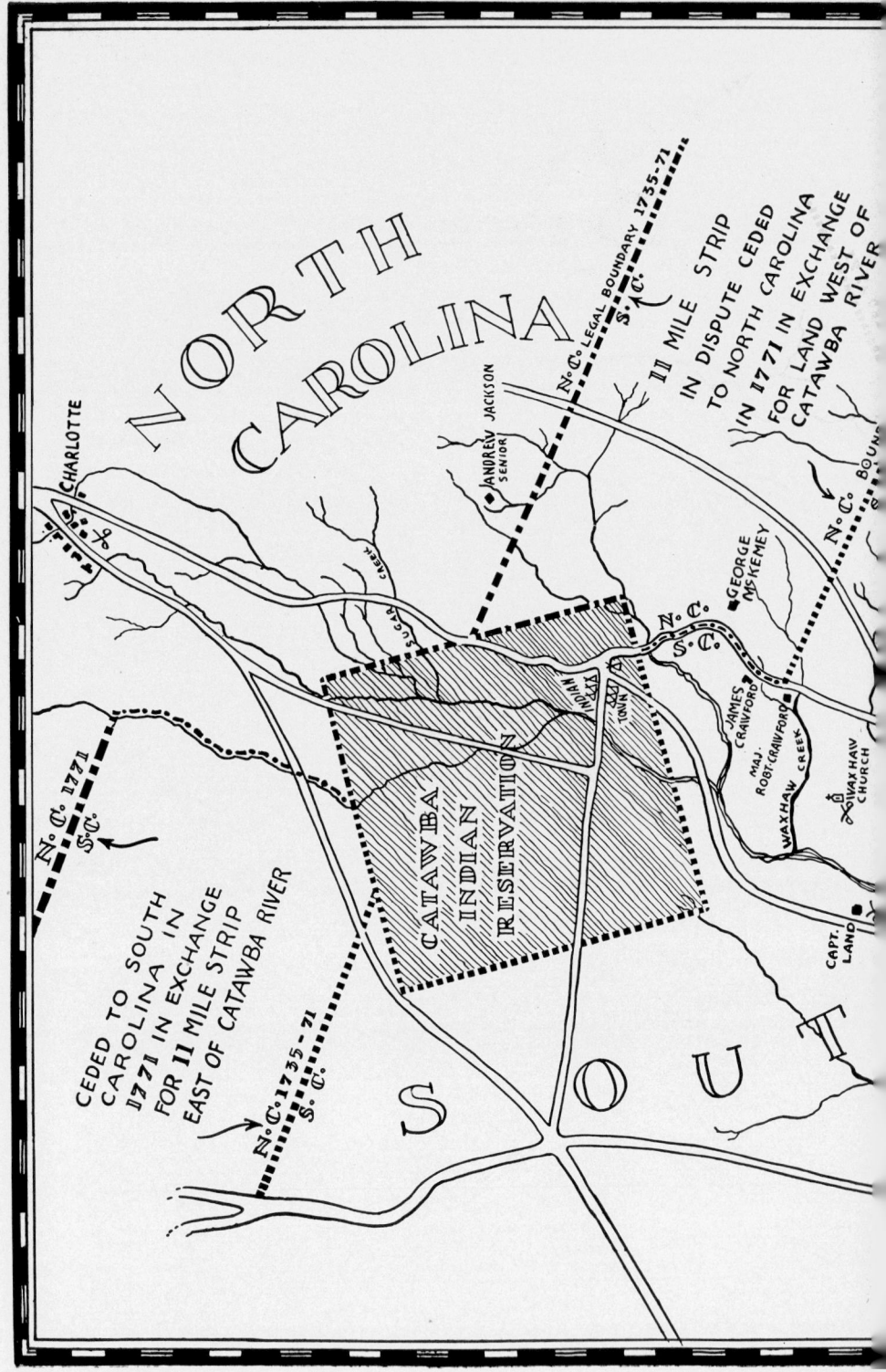

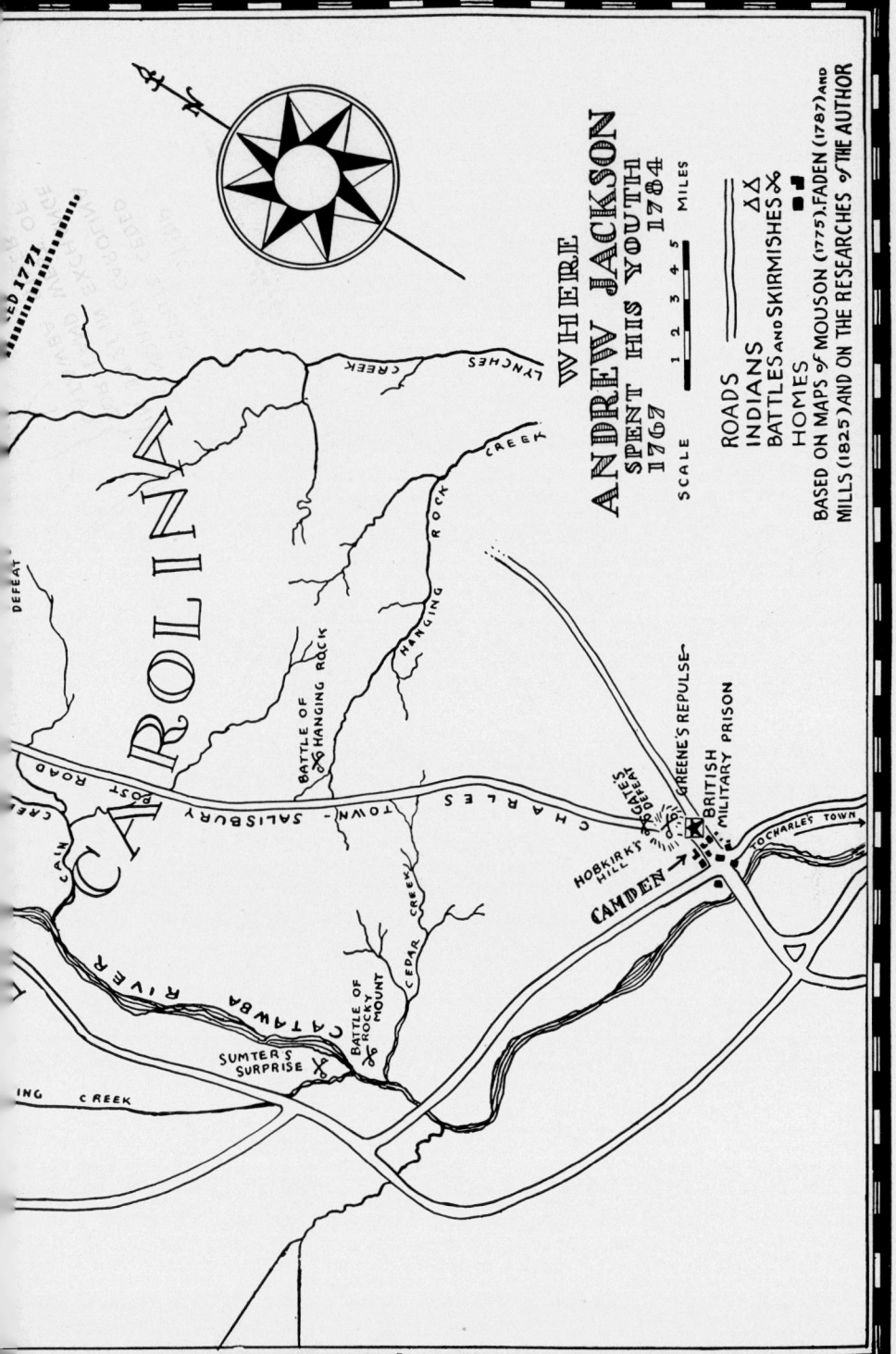

grandfather an Episcopal clergyman, a great-uncle the first president of the college of Princeton, New Jersey. John Donelson removed to Virginia where his star ascended. He was vestryman for two parishes, surveyor for two counties and thrice elected to the House of Burgesses. He was a lieutenant-colonel of militia and a friend of Colonel George Washington. As a Cherokee treaty-maker, his services were extolled to the Home Government. He married Rachel Stockley of Accomac County, Virginia, born in "a mansion, an old Hanoverian hip-roofed house" built by her great-grandfather who had represented that county in the House of Burgesses.[7] Eleven children had been born John and Rachel when, in 1778, a speculation in an iron-works in Pittsylvania County swept away the accumulations of thirty prosperous years.

Under the stress of ill-fortune the close-knit family threatened to disintegrate. The eldest daughter Mary and her husband, John Caffery,[8] succumbed to the lure of Louisiana and made preparations for the immense journey. The second son, John, junior, who was engaged to be married, prepared to accompany the Cafferys as far as the Kentucky District, as western Virginia was called, to locate a new home in the blue-grass. Colonel Donelson's travels had taken him into over-mountain North Carolina where he knew John Sevier, James Robertson and other principals of that semi-independent domain. Colonel Donelson had about decided to go along with his son to Kentucky, when Robertson urged him to enter into partnership to plant a settlement in the valley of the Cumberland, of which the "long hunters" brought such enticing stories. The Colonel consented and the family agreed to begin their several westward journeys together.[9]

Robertson went overland with a party of men to find the best place to settle and to put in a crop of corn. Donelson was to bring the families by water—a project as audacious as any of its kind in our history—down the Holston to the Tennessee, down the Tennessee to the Ohio, up the Ohio to the Cumberland and up the Cumberland until he should meet Robertson. Donelson's sketchy charts could only approximate the distance, which was nine hundred and eighty-five miles. One hundred and twenty women and children, with forty men to handle the boats and fight Indians, presented themselves at the rendezvous, Fort Patrick Henry. Colonel Donelson's flag-ship, the flatboat *Adventure*, carried his wife and eleven children, several slaves and the household silver, engraved "JD^e." John, junior, made a flying trip back to Virginia for his bride and dubbed the trip their wedding journey. This light-hearted view found echo in the ringing laugh of the Colonel's youngest, his little minx of a Rachel, tanned as an Indian and agile as a boy. She was thirteen.

"December 22, 1779.—Took our departure and fell down to the mouth of Reedy Creek," wrote a Colonel Donelson in his "Journal of a Voyage intended by God's Permission, in the good boat Adventure." For the first five weeks all went well except that the coldest weather in years filled the river with ice.

"Sunday, the 27th [of February] Struck the Poor-valley. . . . In much distress.

"Monday, February 28th, 1780—Got off the shoal after landing thirty persons to lighten our boat. . . . Lost sundry articles. . . .

"March 2d—Rain and . . . Mr. Henry's boat being driven on a point of an island . . . was sunk. . . . Reuben Harrison went out a hunting and did not return. . . .

"Tuesday 7th—Very windy. . . . Smaller crafts in danger. . . . Wife of Ephraim Peyton delivered of a child."

Indians in war-paint stalked the boats.

"Wednesday 8th—Must regret the unfortunate death of young Mr. Payne [killed by an Indian] . . . and the more tragical misfortune of poor Stuart, his family and friends to the number of twenty-eight. . . . Being diseased with the small-pox, it was agreed that he should keep [his boat] some distance to the rear; and he was warned each night when the encampment should take place by the sound of a horn. The Indians . . . killed and took prisoners the whole crew: their cries were distinctly heard.

"We are now arrived at the Whirl or Suck. . . . John Cotton['s] . . . canoe was overturned and the little cargo lost. . . . The company concluded to assist him in recovering his property . . . when the Indians . . . firing down . . . occasioned a precipitate retreat to the boats. . . . We have now passed through the Whirl . . . except the family of Jonathan Jennings, whose boat ran on a large rock . . . where we were compelled to leave them, perhaps to be slaughtered."

With the Jennings party was Mrs. Peyton, whose husband had

gone overland with Robertson, and day-old babe. They met the Indian onslaught with rifle-fire. The baby was killed first. A man drowned. Two were captured. The rest saved the boat and joined the fleet. Running the Muscle Shoals was another "dreadful" experience. More Indian ambuscades. Food ran low. On the Ohio famished men struggled at the sweeps to force the boats up-stream. The Cumberland River was picked by lucky guesswork. Food ran out. "Killed a swan, which was very delicious."

"Monday Ap^l 24th 1780 This day we arrived at our journey's end . . . where we have the pleasure of finding Capt. Robertson & his Company . . . [and] a few log Cabbins on a Cedar Bluff."[10]

Such was the odyssey of Rachel Donelson terminating on the day a sandy-haired boy a few months older than she peered through a knot-hole in Camden jail to announce the battle of Hobkirk's Hill.

4

The Cafferys had parted from the family at the Ohio to float on toward Louisiana. John, junior, and his bride had stopped off in Kentucky. On a rich level stretch, later called Clover Bottom, six or seven miles up the Cumberland from the bluff, the Colonel encamped his family and put in crops. But sixty days later the water rose and flooded him out, the family taking refuge at the blockhouse of Casper Mansker, a retired long hunter who had settled his family about ten miles distant the year before. There the Donelsons remained until the end of summer when the river had receded and some corn and cotton was found to have survived. While gathering this in, the Colonel was attacked by Indians and lost a slave or two. The Indians were within their treaty rights in expelling him from this land, and the consequent inability of Donelson to perfect his title led him to abandon the Cumberland and join John, junior, in Kentucky in the autumn of 1780.

Father and sons entered homesteads in Mercer County, the boys buckling down to work, two of them becoming deputy county surveyors, while their impatient sire sought a shorter road to the redemption of his fortunes. He made three hazardous trips to the region of Muscle Shoals upon whose contiguous lands the old speculator had cast an approving eye from the deck of the *Adventure*. For four years the Colonel was gone most of the time. His children were growing up and marrying, and the light of childhood faded from the "lustrous dark eyes" of Rachel, to be succeeded by something that stirred men with desire. "She was irresistible to men," recorded a female relation. "Medium heighth, beautifully moulded form, full red lips," a glowing, olive, oval face "rippling with smiles and dimples."[11] Suitors came from leagues away. In 1785 Rachel married Lewis Robards before she was eighteen.

About the same time the Indians drove Colonel Donelson from Muscle Shoals, ending his hopes in that direction. Whereupon he turned his attention again to the Robertson settlement on the Cumberland, and, such was the hold of this veteran pioneer on his large family, that despite his failures, all followed him thither, excepting Rachel and her husband.[12] But even Robards wavered, going so far as to "enter" six hundred and forty acres which apparently had been recommended by his father-in-law.[13]

Although Rachel was said to be her father's favorite, it is easy to understand why she stayed in Kentucky. She had married extremely well, her husband's family being one of the most prominent in Mercer County. The young couple lived with Robards's mother, a well-connected and proud old Virginia lady, whose stone residence was called the finest in the vicinity of Harrodsburgh. Perhaps Mrs. Robards dipped snuff instead of smoking a pipe as her border-bred daughter-in-law did, but she liked Rachel. Three years went by and Peyton Short, a young attorney, came to board at the house. He liked her, too. Then John Overton, a law student and remote connection by marriage, joined the family circle.[14] He had not been there "many weeks before I understood that Captain Robards and his wife lived very unhappily on account of his being jealous of Mr. Short,"[15] who showed the irresistible Rachel "perhaps a little more than ordinary politeness." The Captain, "surprising them chatting together on his mother's porch,"[16] placed a grave construction on the tête-à-tête. Although the elder Mrs. Robards took the side of her son's wife and Short "swore" to the innocence of their relations, Robards "ordered his wife . . . never to show her face in his house again,"[17] and wrote the Donelsons to send for her.

As the old Colonel had been killed by Indians—or white outlaws, the family insisting that no Indian could kill their father—Samuel Donelson took his sister away. A subdued Rachel reappeared at her mother's blockhouse ten miles from Nashville, "withdrawing herself from all places of pleasure, such as balls, parties, etc."[18] A few weeks thereafter Andrew Jackson became one of the household. The somber light in eyes that were made for laughter did not elude the notice of the border cavalier. "Always polite, [he] was particularly so to the beautiful Mrs. Robards," observed a boy who was doing chores about the place.[19]

John Donelson's widow did not have to keep boarders, but she welcomed a man of Jackson's stamp as a protection against Indians. Besides the boy, George Davidson, the only other white man about the house was John Overton, who had taken up residence at the blockhouse about the same time as Jackson with whom he divided a bed in a cabin apart from the main house. Overton had come to practise law in the new settlement and also as an emissary of Lewis Robards, who, finding himself more unhappy away from his wife, asked forgiveness. As a friend of both parties and a connection of the Robards family, Overton conveyed this overture, and discussed the whole matter freely with Jackson.

Some progress must have been made for, in the early spring of 1789, Robards himself appeared on the Cumberland, began improving his land and pressing his importunities for a reconciliation. Rachel gave in, and there is a local tradition that she lived for a while on her husband's river farm,[20] but both seem to have spent most of their time at the blockhouse. In any event coming upon Rachel and her mother in tears one day, Overton learned that Robards had made a scene over Andrew Jackson.

All, except Robards, seemed to understand the gravity of a careless use of this man's name. Overton promised the women he would do what he could, and pleaded with Robards "that his suspicions were groundless."[21] The husband, however, was determined to see it otherwise, and a suppressed "commotion" clutched the household. Overton felt that he should acquaint Jackson with "the unpleasant situation," but shrank from so delicate a duty.[22]

5

The departure of the court brought a measure of composure to the blockhouse. John McNairy's jurisdiction formed a community fifty miles long and twenty miles wide straddling the winding Cumberland. Judge and prosecutor rode up the river to Gallatin and down it to Ashland holding court. A scene of vibrant activity met their eyes. The Cumberland Road was proving a great thing for the Western District. "Movers" filed in to enlarge the frontiers of this island of elementary civilization. White men stood together against the Indians who saw their hunting-grounds depleted, and against the forces of Nature. "Did a neighbor wish to erect a cabin, or roll his logs, or gather his harvest each man was a willing hand and in return received aid from others. . . . Did a man want a bushel of salt he received it in exchange for a cow and a calf . . . and the force of moral sense sustained by public sentiment was a stronger guarantee than all forms of law."[23]

John McNairy superseded "Judge Lynch" and "Chief Justice Birch." Court and retinue reined their horses at the habitation nearest to where night found them, ate hog and hominy with the family, drank burnt-barley "coffee" and spread their saddle blankets on the floor. At Gallatin Mr. Jackson encountered an echo of the resentment of the Nashville debtors. While he was speaking with a gentleman in the street, a local bully shouldered up and deliberately trod on Jackson's boots. Without a word the slender prosecutor picked up a slab of wood and knocked the man down.[24]

Mr. Jackson returned from the tour with a larger comprehension of the remote forces molding the fortunes of the salubrious valley. Candles burned late in the cabin which he used as an office as well as sleeping quarters; and this preoccupation helped to guard the secret of the blockhouse. On February 13, 1789, the "dull and heavy" weather being an encouragement to correspondence, Mr. Jackson wrote to Brigadier-General Daniel Smith, an officer of the Revolution, now commanding the militia of the Western District.

"I had the pleasure of seeing Capt Fargo yesterday who put me under obligations of seeing you this day but as the weather . . . prevents my coming up . . . I comit to you in this small piece of paper the business he wants with you." This officer was a person of importance, continued Mr. Jackson, "the commission of Capt. under the King of Spain . . . being an honorable title in that country," where military prefixes were bestowed more frugally than on an American frontier. "He is related to his Excellency"—his Excellency being identification enough in Nashville for Don Estéban Miró, the Governor of Louisiana. Moreover the visit of Captain Fargo did not appear to be without the knowledge of this personage. "He [Fargo] expresses a great friendship for the welfare and harmony of this country; . . . he wishes you to write to the governor informing him the desire of a commercial treaty with that country; he then will importune the Governor for a permit to trade to this country which he is sure to obtain; . . . then he will show the propriety of having peace with the Indians for . . . the benefit of the trade . . . and also show the governor the respect this country honors him with." Mr. Jackson begged General Smith to do Captain Fargo the honor of seeing him "before he sets out for Orleans."[25]

Andrew Jackson's solicitations in favor of the Spanish officer formed a part of an interesting arrangement of Western affairs. The Cumberland settlers' compliment to Estéban Miró, to which Jackson alluded, was at the moment a topic of spirited discussion on both sides of the mountains. They had changed the name of their community from Western District to "District of Mero," as it was written in the nonchalant orthography of the frontier. "It seemed strange [to the East]," wrote a local historian who lived through the events he described, "that the name of an officer of a foreign government . . . should be given to a great political section of the country which might perhaps sustain that name for many ages. . . . Why select a Spaniard . . . at the very time when that nation unjustly withheld from us the free navigation of the Mississippi, and when this very officer was the one chosen by the Spanish courts to see that exclusion executed?" Did the people of the Cumberland see "more congeniality between their circumstances and Spanish connections than . . . the prostrated . . . Atlantic confederacy?" Were they concerned with the dark maneuvers of "certain political characters in Kentucky . . . accused of intriguing with Spanish agents to detach the western country from the Union?"[26]

In brief, they were. The winter he left Salisbury, Mr. Jackson had seen the "prostrated Confederacy" throw its dying energies into the convocation of a convention to write a new constitution as a last cast to sustain independence by federal union. This Constitution had now been adopted by enough states to make it binding on the adopters. Electors were being chosen to designate General Washington the head of the new government, and the authority of his name stirred many hearts to hope. But North Carolina had no share in this. The Western delegates voting aggressively for rejection, she had declined the Constitution and was not a part of the Republic. Isolated Mero found more interest in the man at New Orleans whose name it had taken than in the retired soldier of Mount Vernon.

Thanks to the respectably placed gentlemen in Kentucky who had paved the way to a private understanding with Señor Miró, Cumberland tobacco found an enormously profitable market in New Orleans, a port legally closed to American products. Two things the West must have to prosper: peace with the Indians and the New Orleans market. The East could give it neither. Spain, controlling the powerful Creeks, could give it much of one and all of the other.

To this add the feeling in the West that the new experiment at union would fail and the West be left to fend for itself. Should that come to pass, over-mountain men would need an ally to resist the confidently contemplated British attempt at reconquest.

6

Brigadier-General Daniel Smith must have been amused by Mr. Jackson's solicitations in behalf of the man he called Fargo, in the flesh, Captain André Fagot, a Frenchman in His Catholic Majesty's service. They revealed Nashville's new lawyer as a man of enterprise —such enterprise, indeed, as to triumph unconsciously over the formality of fact in the present premises.

Finding Jackson a newcomer, Monsieur Fagot had drawn a long bow. It being a cold wet evening and something to dispel the chill in order, the visitor's estimate of himself seems to have expanded until a veritable kinsman of Estéban Miró evolved. But surely Fagot had not charged Jackson to carry this tale to Smith. That could only have been Jackson's own idea of a way to impart a more enticing cast to the visitor's speculations.

THE MERO DISTRICT

Actually Smith and Fagot were old acquaintances. As far back as 1785, the American militia officer and trader on the Cumberland had transacted official and private business with the Spanish militia officer and trader on the Illinois. Smith knew Fagot to be no relative of Miró. He knew Fagot had never seen Miró. But there is no indication that Smith chided Jackson for his excess of zeal, which, after a talk with Fagot, the Brigadier-General decided had been in a good cause.

On the other hand Smith wrote a letter to Miró introducing "Mr. Fagot" in whom the Cumberland people "have very great confidence . . . and beg leave to refer your excellency to him for a particular intelligence. We have honored our district with your Excellency's name . . . and I should look upon myself as much honored by a Correspondence from you."[27] James Robertson, the first citizen of the Cumberland, also wrote: "Every thinking person in this Country" wished "to be on good terms" with the government "in possession of the mouth of the Mississippi. Nature seems to have designed the whole Western Country to be one people." Robertson's letter was carried to New Orleans by "Cap^{tn} John Bosley my son in law who is desirous of seeing" Louisiana "with a view of settling there."[28] Smith's letter was carried by André Fagot. The "particular intelligence" to which Smith referred, was communicated verbally, however. Miró relayed it to Madrid in these terms:

"The inhabitants of the Cumberland . . . would in September send delegates to North Carolina . . . to solicit from the legislature . . . an act of separation, and . . . other delegates . . . to New Orleans with the object of placing the territory under the dominion of his Majesty."[29]

To this important intelligence, Estéban Miró replied by letter in the polished but restrained idiom of intrigue. "His Excellency Danl Smith Brig.^{r} gral & Commander of Miró District &ca, &ca, &ca. I have had the greatest satisfaction in the honour I received in being acquainted that the Inhabitants of your District have distinguish[ed] my name . . . for the denomination of that country, which impels me" to any number of good wishes for their "prosperity. . . . I anxiously expect the consequences of the operation you are to transact in September."[30]

As a matter of fact the Cumberland already had a representative in New Orleans, and an exceptional spokesman he was. Born in Philadelphia and educated by the Jesuits in France, Dr. James White had been a delegate from North Carolina to the Congress of the defunct Confederacy. At his ease in salon or cabin, and no stranger to the conventions of Latin diplomacy, this sophisticated surgeon had not inspired a feeling of unreserved trust in the breast of Don Estéban. Nevertheless, the Governor asked him to carry to the Cumberland his letter to General Smith and to communicate certain additional reflections which were not committed to paper.

7

Governor Miró's Creek allies lent an effective stimulus to the negotiations. "On the 20th of January [1789] the Indians killed Capt. Hunter and dangerously wounded Hugh F. Bell," wrote a local chronicler. "A party of white men collected and pursued the Indians . . . [who] fired upon the pursuers, killed Maj. Kirkpatrick, and wounded J. Foster and William Brown. . . . In the spring of this year, at Dunham's Station, the Indians killed a man of the name of Mills; in May they killed Dunham, and in the summer Joseph Norrington and another Dunham. They kept up hostilities during the whole summer and killed a number of persons whose names are not remembered. . . . Near the mouth of Sulphur Fork of Red River, the Indians fell upon two moving families by the name of Titsworth and killed their wives and children. Killed Evan Shelby and Abednego Lewellen as they were hunting in the woods. . . . Came to Buchanon's Station and scalped John Blackburn near the spring on the bank of the creek, and left a spear sticking in his body."[31] On an average of once in ten days throughout 1789 some one was killed within a few miles of Nashville.

Andrew Jackson continued his travels. In March he saved the lives of three companions by a perilous crossing of the Emery River on a raft. In June he joined a militia company in the relief of beleaguered Robertson's Station where Nashville's founder had been wounded. The Indians fled. With nineteen others Jackson pursued for ten miles and surprised them at dawn,[32] breaking the dismal sequence of defeats.

In September Don Estéban Miró penned a proclamation offering peace and liberal bounties of land to American emigrants, which had "the obvious tendency" to "draw off the [Cumberland] settlers," and "make them desirous of a Spanish alliance."[33] Jackson was among the first to be drawn off.[34] At Natchez, second in importance only to New Orleans and the focal point of most of the American emigration, he was entertained at the homes of the most influential Americans of the district, including Abner Green and Thomas Marston Green, junior, brothers from Virginia. Abner had prospered sufficiently to purchase the summer home of Manuel Gayoso de Lemos, the Spanish commandant. Thomas had constructed in that far world a white pillared replica of a Virginia plantation manse. There were not two such homes in North Carolina west of the mountains. Mr. Jackson was impressed. Acquiring a tract of excellent land where Bayou Pierre meets the Mississippi thirty miles above Natchez, he ordered one hundred and ninety dollars' worth of supplies, including white wine, from a Natchez merchant,[35] built a log house and projected the construction of a race-track and other improvements. He arranged to sell slaves to the Greens,[36] to be delivered at Bayou Pierre, and posted home in time for the April, 1790, term of court at Nashville where, in one hundred and ninety-two cases on the dockets, Andrew Jackson was employed in forty-two.

The solicitor was getting on—"a restless and enterprising man," as a son-in-law of Abner Green, who was a friendly critic, described him, "embarking in many schemes for the accumulation of fortune, not usually resorted to by professional men."[37] The revenue from his law business regularly went into deals in land and sometimes in slaves. "List of Negroes for A Jackson," reads an accounting, "One fellow Daniel about 28 years old sawyer 250 One Wench Kate [aged] 32 150" and three young ones making the sum of seven hundred and ten pounds.[38] Rachel's brother, Stockley Donelson, needed a loan. Jackson advanced the money taking Donelson's promise to repay with "one likely Country born Negro boy or girl ... on or before the 1st day of December next ensuing."[39]

In May of 1790 Jackson was preparing to return to Natchez when a party of Kentuckians arrived from there with "a Negro Fellow named Tom or Peter" who called himself a freedman, but turned out to be "a Run away slave of M^r. Petit of New Orleans." Here was another chance for the Cumberlanders to show their good will. "I have requested M^r. Andrew Jackson, a Gentleman of Character & Consideration, very much respected in this Country, & generally esteemed, to take Charge of the Negro, & deliver him to your Excellency"—James Robertson to Commandant Gayoso.[40]

8

If Mr. Jackson made this trip,[41] he was back by July. But a great deal happened before he went.

Forty-two cases at the April term, and plans for a three-hundred-mile ride to Natchez had failed to occupy Jackson sufficiently to subjugate the jealous emotions of Lewis Robards. Accordingly, upon John Overton devolved the long-deferred task of telling his friend how matters stood. Mr. Overton did this with suitable tact, suggesting that the sensibilities of all the ladies of the household would be spared if he and Jackson sought other lodgings.

Jackson agreed, but, before he took his departure, accidentally encountered Robards "near the orchard fence." In the circumspect language of Overton, Jackson "began mildly to remonstrate" with Robards "respecting the injustice he had done his wife." Robards offered a fist fight. Jackson said he would fight in the manner of gentlemen. According to Overton,[42] Robards refused the invitation to a duel with a torrent of abuse, though a Donelson family tradition mentions an informal exchange of "harmless shots."[43]

Jackson left the house but not the neighborhood, transferring his belongings to the blockhouse of Casper Mansker, the hospitable pioneer who had once sheltered the entire Donelson clan. Rachel and her husband composed their difficulties and the latter part of May or sometime in June when business called Robards to Kentucky, the two parted affectionately. Jackson was then on his way to Natchez—that is, if he went at all. During the journey to Kentucky Robards astonished a traveling companion, who had witnessed the farewell to his wife, with an "ill-natured" remark that "he would be damned if ever he would be seen on the Cumberland again." "I observed," said Robards's companion, "that the friends of Mrs. Robards . . . perhaps would not consent for her to go back to Kentucky to live. He said he did not care what they liked."[44]

Rachel did go back, but only to quarrel immediately and irretrievably, and to flee. "Rachel Robards," recites the record of the Court of Quarter Sessions, Harrodsburgh, Mercer County, Kentucky, commenting on that flight, "Rachel Robards did, on the [*sic*] day of July, 1790, elope from her husband, said Lewis . . . with another man."[45] The man was Andrew Jackson.

CHAPTER V

TIDINGS FROM HARRODSBURGH

I

MATTERS had not eventuated precisely as Brigadier-General Daniel Smith foretold to Estéban Miró. Mero District and the old State of Franklin petitioned for a separation successfully enough, but meantime North Carolina had ratified the Constitution and rejoined the United States. Consequently the trans-mountain region was not let loose to cast its favor where it listed, but, under the long name of Territory of the United States of America South of the River Ohio, became a subsidiary of the new Federal Government into which George Washington was infusing a likely amount of back-bone.

Thus without soliciting their approval, the United States draped the mantle of its citizenship about the surprised residents of the Cumberland. Yet the Spanish intrigue declined to die. "We cannot but wish for a more interesting connection," James Robertson assured Estéban Miró. "The United States afford us no protection."[1] And more remarkable is the number of Don Estéban's correspondents who were able to recommend themselves to General Washington for posts of preferment in the new territory. William Blount was appointed governor and Daniel Smith secretary. Robertson took Smith's baton as military commander of Mero, and John Sevier, who had miraculously restored himself to power and favor, was made brigadier-general of the Eastern or Washington District. Dr. James White represented the territory in Congress.

Having taken the oath of allegiance to the United States on December 15, 1790,[2] Andrew Jackson was retained "during good behaviour" as public prosecutor of Mero under the title of attorney-general.[3] His behavior was very good. "The thanks of this Court are tendered to Andrew Jackson, Esq., for his efficient conduct," was the entry spread upon the minutes in Sumner County after the prosecutor had preserved the dignity of the bench in a rough and tumble fight.[4]

Indians continued to suggest the blessings of a Spanish alliance. "They killed Alexander Neely at the fort where Anthony Bledsoe had lived; also a young woman of the name of Morris. They killed at Mayfield's Station John Glen who had married the widow Mayfield, and three persons at Brown's Station a few miles from Nashville. They wounded John McRory, and caught and scalped three of Everett's children and killed John Everett."[5] A man did not go for a bucket of water without his gun, and tobacco was hoed under guard within sight of Nashville's court-house on the bluff. When the wild blackberries were ripe, young blades had two good reasons for accompanying the girls on their errands.

2

Jackson's foray into Kentucky had delivered Rachel to the home of her sister Jane, wife of Colonel Robert Hays, one of the substantial citizens of the valley.[6] In this "elopement," to use the dark title it was presently to wear before a jury, Jackson appears to have acted simply as an agent of the Donelson family in the rescue of an unhappy daughter of their house from an intolerable domestic entanglement. Once before the jealous nature of Robards had made it necessary for the family to bring her away. It seems that this time Rachel's brothers consented to let one so eminently qualified by temperament as Jackson go in their stead. Events proved this to be a tragic blunder, but the harsh interpretation eventually put upon it seems an afterthought on the part of Captain Robards, or his legal adviser, United States Senator John Brown, of Kentucky. Otherwise how could he have followed his wife back to the Cumberland as he did in July or early August, 1790, to make a final plea for reconciliation? Had Robards believed then, as he later claimed,[7] that the journey with Jackson was evidence of moral delinquency, he would not have done this.

However useful Robards's punctual reappearance may be now as evidence of his wife's innocence of wrong-doing, at the time it presented a problem. Rachel was definitely finished with her husband. But Robards stayed on, continuing his persuasions. One day he accompanied a berry-picking expedition, and something he said about Andrew Jackson flew to the ears of the prosecutor.

Jackson told Robards that if he should associate his name with Mrs. Robards's again he would cut off the Captain's ears and was "tempted to do it anyhow." To put temptation out of Mr. Jackson's way, Robards procured a peace-warrant, which a constable served. Constable, a guard, the prisoner, Robards and a file of the curious started for a magistrate's. Turning to one of the guard, Jackson asked for his hunting knife which was handed over after the prisoner had whispered that on his honor he would harm no one. Unsheathing the blade Jackson ran his thumb along its edge and directed his most penetrating stare upon Captain Robards. Jackson partizans claimed that Robards fled, and, no complainant appearing, the magistrate dismissed the charge.[8] Less friendly testimony avers that Magistrate Robert Weakley placed Jackson under bond to observe the peace toward Robards who had stood his ground.[9]

He could not have stood it long, however, for shortly he was in Kentucky again, threatening to swoop upon the Cumberland and carry off his wife by force.[10] The Donelson women were "much distressed," Mr. Overton says, and Rachel prepared for flight. A small party of traders under the elderly John Stark, an American-born Spanish subject, were fitting out for Natchez. Rachel asked them to take her away.

The trading route to Natchez was by way of the Cumberland, Ohio and Mississippi—two thousand wilderness miles dark with sagas of Indian ambuscade. One returned overland by the Chickasaw Road, later called the Natchez Trace, which for twenty years sustained the reputation of the most evil thoroughfare in the West. Though an old friend of the family, Colonel Stark shrank from the responsibility of adding a woman to his company. He mentioned his fears to Overton and then to Jackson who paced the compound at Mansker's Station with "symptoms of more than usual concern."[11] But there was no dissuading Rachel. Her determination was formed. From the deck of the *Adventure*, she had heard Indian arrows sing and seen the glint of scalping knives. She did not fear them now.

The visible signs of Jackson's anxiety increased until Overton asked him what was the matter. It was Rachel, Andrew replied, with bitter

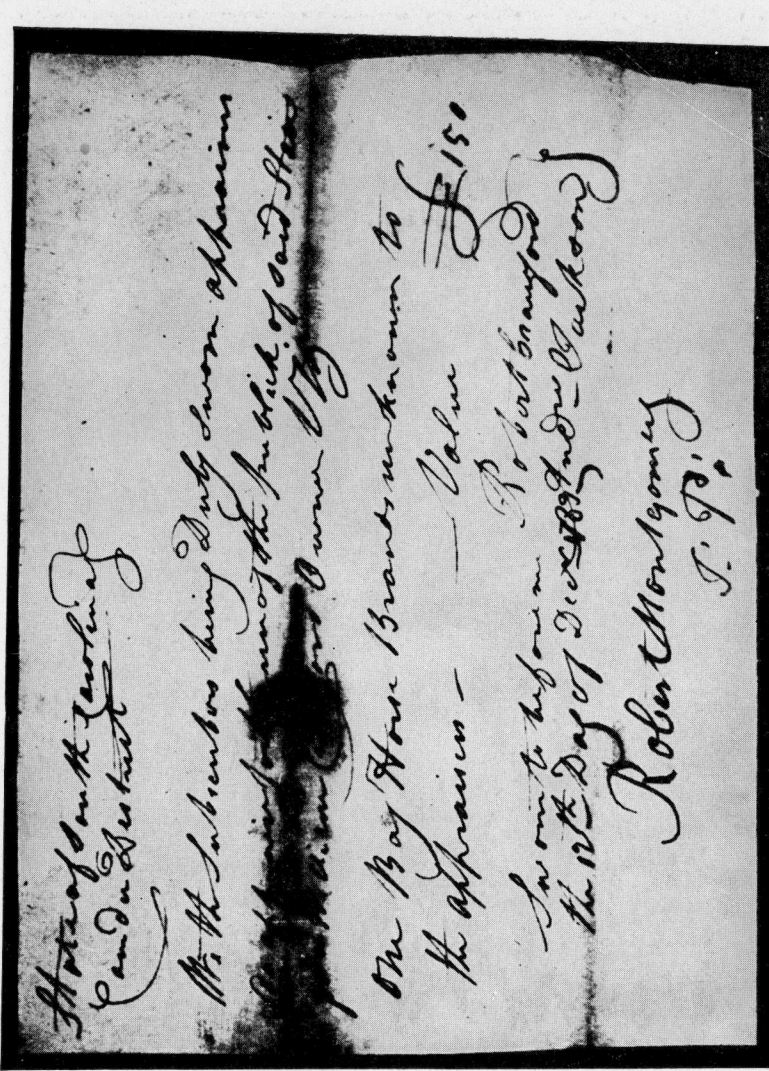

EARLIEST KNOWN AUTOGRAPH OF ANDREW JACKSON

Dated December 12, 1782, though the terminal figure might be mistaken for a "9". Jackson, then fifteen years old, acted as a member and scribe for a board of appraisers which valued a horse which his cousin had lost in the military service during the Revolution. From the archives of the Historical Commission of South Carolina, Columbia.

WHERE JACKSON WAS MARRIED IN 1791

Springfield, the Residence of Thomas Marston Green, junior, near Natchez. From a photograph made in 1922 and now in the private collection of Mrs. Samuel G. Heiskell of Knoxville.

TIDINGS FROM HARRODSBURGH

self-reproach for "having innocently and unintentionally been the cause of . . . [her] loss of peace and happiness."¹²

The peace and happiness of Mrs. Robards meant much to Andrew now, for he loved her.

Stark renewed his "urgent entreaties" that Jackson join the expedition, and, after more torments of indecision, he committed his law business to Overton and departed with the flotilla "in the winter or spring"¹³ of 1791.

3

It was a flight from nothing, for the mercurial Robards had altered his course of action. Instead of dashing upon Nashville with intentions of carrying Rachel away, he closeted himself with John Jouitt, his brother-in-law. Jack Jouitt, to whom Virginia had presented a ceremonial sword for his part in the Revolution, was one of the most popular members of the Legislature. He was familiar with the estrangement over Peyton Short and believed Lewis had acted too hastily in that instance, but now he consented to sponsor Robards's petition to the General Assembly at Richmond for a divorce.

In those days divorces were usually granted by legislative act, but the committee of the Assembly to which Robards's petition was referred rejected it, and reported a bill which merely gave the husband the right to go to court with evidence in support of his allegations. This bill was passed on December 20, 1790, twelve days before Kentucky ceased to be a part of Virginia.¹⁴

"*An Act concerning the Marriage of Lewis Roberts;*

". . . It shall and may be lawful for Lewis Roberts to sue out of . . . the Supreme Court of the District of Kentucky, a writ against Rachel Roberts, which . . . shall be published for eight weeks successively, in the *Kentuckey Gazette*; whereupon the plaintiff may file his declaration . . . and the defendant may appear and plead. . . .

"A jury shall be summoned . . . to inquire into the allegations contained in the declaration; . . . and if the jury . . . shall find in substance that the defendant hath deserted the plaintiff, and that she hath lived in adultery with another man since such desertion . . . THEREUPON the marriage between the said Lewis Roberts and Rachel shall be totally dissolved."¹⁵

Had Lewis Robards been an illiterate backwoodsman it would be easy to believe that he might have misinterpreted this rather unusual procedure of the Assembly, and honestly assumed that the enabling act constituted a divorce. But under the circumstances it is impossible to explain his behavior on grounds of ignorance.

Robards made no move to take his case into court, but countenanced the false report that he had obtained a divorce through the customary legislative channels. He wrote in a friendly vein to Rachel's brother-in-law, Robert Hays: "I shall depend on you and Mr Overton That theire is no advantage taken of me in My absence at Cumberland. You will plase Right by first Opportunity if the Estate is divided as I may no how to get my [due? Manuscript illegible]."[16] I can discover no reason why Robards should have anticipated a partition of his Cumberland holdings except as a consequence of a supposed divorce. This letter apparently reached Nashville not long after the departure of Jackson and Rachel for Natchez. Its tone discloses an absence of hostility toward Jackson's most intimate friends that is difficult to understand except under the assumption that, as far as Robards was concerned, bygones were bygones and Rachel had been given her freedom[17] without scandal.

Three months later, however, the scandalous nature of the Robards allegations were known to the Donelsons. Their anger flamed, and on the heels of this Andrew Jackson returned to report Rachel safely installed with the family of Abner Green, twenty-three miles from Natchez. Jackson's "first impulse was to pursue Robards and at the pistol's point make him retract."[18] That he failed to do so is not the most easily comprehended fact of his impulsive life. Instead, he besought Mrs. Donelson for "permission to offer his hand and heart to her daughter." "Mr. Jackson," said the good lady, "would you sacrifice your life to save my poor child's good name?" "Ten thousand lives, madam, if I had them."[19] And under the spur of this spirited pledge, Andrew was off again over the Chickasaw Road's perilous three hundred miles to Natchez.

Rachel had endeared herself to the rich Abner Greens who lived in a mansion that had once been the country seat of Don Manuel Gayoso de Lemos, the Spanish commandant of Natchez. Her old vivacity had begun to return and she was in demand as a guest at the homes of neighboring planters to whose prosperity, incidentally,

Andrew Jackson had contributed by the introduction of slaves and Yankee goods through his trading post on Bayou Pierre.

When Andrew broke the news of the divorce the life seemed to go out of her. "I expected him to kill me but this is worse."[20] But the enveloping tenderness of Andrew's wooing soothed the bruised spirit of Rachel and her sharp anguish passed.

4

A few miles from the shaded Gayoso mansion stood stately brick Springfield where Thomas Marston Green, junior, lived. In August of 1791, Rachel Donelson Robards and Andrew Jackson exchanged the wedding vows in its tall parlor. Each was twenty-four years old. The tradition in the Green family is that Thomas Marston Green, senior, in his capacity of magistrate, performed the ceremony.[21] Mary Donelson Wilcox said that it was performed by a Catholic clergyman.[22]

In any event the couple retired to Jackson's establishment at Bayou Pierre, where a log house in a clearing on the bluff looked down on the incredible Mississippi and a summer sea of treetops rolling toward the horizon from the low western shore.

The rhythm of the river imparted a pulse to the palpable stillness. At night a trailing image of the moon swam by in the water. Rachel's cares swam with it, and the life she had left seemed as remote as a half-forgotten, evil dream. The newlyweds entertained; and a garrulous and gay old bachelor named George Cockran wrote his hostess a flowery thank-you. "I cannot lose the remembrance of the agreeable hours . . . at Bayou Pierre."[23]

Nor could Rachel—ever.

5

"Amid the joyous congratulations of her relatives and a large circle of mutual friends,"[24] Jackson brought his bride to the Cumberland in October of 1791. There were great doings. Robert Hays, "Lord Chief Joker and General Humbugger of North America West of the Appalachian Mountain," convoked his hilarious "court." A certificate of appointment as "High Marshall," countersigned by

"Andrew Jackson, Attorney General," was issued to Samuel Donelson,[25] putting the three brothers-in-law in close control of this unique society whose secrets were available only to rousing good fellows of approved social standing.

The wild lands Jackson owned in the West were unsuited to home-making for the bride whom he meant to give the best the Cumberland afforded. So he bought out John Donelson,[26] whose Poplar Grove plantation filled Jones's Bend,[27] a hairpin curve formed by the sea-green, inviting Cumberland which moved so leisurely as to suggest the wish to prolong a pleasant journey. The house—its site still marked by "Jackson's Well"—stood about the center of the hairpin on land too level to reveal the river, though one could follow its course by the half-circle of haze-clad hills along the yonder bank.

Yet the honeymoon had ended too soon for Rachel. The demands of romance had kept her husband rather long from his official duties and growing private practise. A surge of activity caught up the solicitor. At the four terms of court at Nashville in 1793, Jackson appeared in two hundred and six of the four hundred and thirty-five litigations of record.[28] In 1795, he completed his twenty-second trip between Nashville and Jonesborough[29] over the Cumberland Road, a distance of four thousand, four hundred miles, representing seven hundred and fifty hours in the saddle.

An urge to riches and social rank seemed to impel this activity. Jackson was little attracted to the type of renown diffused by political office, an attitude not greatly modified during the years to come. He took pride, however, in his election as a trustee of Davidson Academy. Possibly this was because of his own irregular schooling, though more probably because it associated him with Reverend Thomas B. Craighead, master of the little school and a brother of his mother's friend in the Waxhaws. Nor did the quest for wealth obscure a flair for the profession of arms. Mr. Jackson became judge advocate of the county militia, accepting a draft on the public revenues for "Two young Likely second Rate Cows and calves . . . for Services performed,"[30] but, contrary to frontier precedent, declining casual use of the title of captain to which this distinction gave him a technical right.

In larger matters the attorney-generalship suited Mr. Jackson well. It was independent of the whim of an electorate. It brought one into contact with land and Indian problems, which meant association with a class of pioneers who were shedding coonskin caps and hunting shirts for broadcloth. Among this category of frontiersmen—the owners of slaves, the breeders of horses, the holders of local offices and titles—Andrew Jackson was born and had spent his life. This aristocracy of the border might pass supercilious remarks on the Tidewater gentility, but, nevertheless, imitated it in all that environment would allow.

Jackson had only a rough idea of how much land he owned or laid claim to. Much of it he had never seen,[31] but he knew that some day the ceaseless tide of settlers would make it valuable. Then Andrew Jackson could build himself a house with a race-path and a cockpit, such as he remembered on Charleston Neck, and follow the life of a gentleman. The waiting wife at Poplar Grove, desiring only her husband's companionship, prayed that the time might not be long.

Before that should come to pass much remained to be decided. Ultimately would the Cumberland be governed from New Orleans or from Philadelphia? What of security from the Indians? The United States had sent an emissary to the Cherokees—Colonel John McKee, a Virginian, who had spent an attractive youth among the Indians and possessed their confidence. Governor Blount believed McKee the man to persuade the Indians to peace. Mr. Jackson differed. "John McKee Dear Sir: . . . The late proclaimed peace . . . [has been] attended with . . . Depredations and Murders . . . not Less than Twelve Men killed and wounded in this District. Why do we now attempt to hold [another] Treaty with them. have they attended to the Last Treaty. I answer in the Negative then why do we attempt to Treat [again]. . . . With the highest Exteem ANDREW JACKSON."[32]

The sentiments of Colonel McKee are not available, but, if they represented the truth of the situation, Jackson may not have thought them worth preserving. Whites and not Indians had first broken the treaty of 1791, to which Jackson alluded, and several earlier treaties as well. Until 1785 not only every white settler south of the Cumberland but the town of Nashville occupied land in violation of treaty stipulations. This was in accord with the usual white procedure of making a treaty guaranteeing the Indians certain territory, breaking it and writing a new treaty to legalize the violation.

The Cherokees were perhaps the most intelligent of North American Indians, and had a feeling of nationality that was very old. They were British allies during the Revolution. We made a separate peace with them in 1785, recognizing their sovereign character and fixing the limits of their "Nation," where Cherokee law was to be supreme. Settlers punctually overran this boundary. The Cherokees first protested and then used violence as the treaty gave them a right to do. Spanish diplomacy made profitable use of the situation. President Washington was so incensed at the disregard of Western land speculators for the pledged word of the United States that he threatened to send the Regular Army to uphold the rights of the Indians. To avert this the treaty of 1791 was negotiated. Through it the Cherokee chiefs yielded more territory.[33] Land-hungry whites violated this treaty on the day it was signed, and indignant Mr. Jackson, if not then, was shortly afterward a participant in the violation.

The whites paid for this behavior. With Spanish ball and powder the Cherokees carried war into the settlements. They cut off Poplar Grove from Nashville and attacked Robert Hays's blockhouse, killing two of its defenders.[34] But the heaviest blows fell later when Knoxville, the territorial capital, was threatened. Jackson was in the neighborhood at the time. On August 29, 1793, he and Lieutenant Telford attempted a reconnaissance from Henry's Station. Hearing a fusillade in the direction of the fort they retreated only to fall into an ambush. "The Lieutenant was taken and . . . put to death. . . . Mr. Jackson made his escape" and alarmed "the whole frontier."[35]

John Sevier mobilized his militia brigade, and, after waiting in vain for Federal authorization made a dashing invasion of the Cherokee Nation. The fighting power of the Cherokees never recovered from this campaign, which also closed the military career of Nolichucky Jack—thirty-five battles, thirty-three victories.

6

In December of 1793, Sevier's success had made it possible to relax vigilance at home. Andrew Jackson and John Overton journeyed on law business to Jonesborough, where Overton said he accidentally encountered a transcript of certain proceedings before the Court of Quarter Sessions at Harrodsburgh, Kentucky, during the autumn term just closed:

"On the 27th day of September, 1793, this day came the plaintiff by his attorney, and thereupon came also a jury . . . who being duly sworn well and truly to inquire into the allegation in the plaintiff's declaration . . . do say, that the defendant, Rachel Robards, hath deserted the plaintiff, Lewis Robards, and hath, and doth, still live in adultery with another man. It is therefore considered by the court that the marriage between the plaintiff and the defendant be dissolved."[36]

This was overwhelming news. It revealed the false character of the report of a divorce by the Legislature which sent Andrew Jackson impulsively posting to Natchez in 1791. Robards had waited two years before exercising his right to sue under the enabling act.

The tidings from Harrodsburgh stunned Andrew Jackson. When Overton suggested the "propriety" of a second marriage ceremony Jackson refused to consider it. Before God, he declared, and in "the understanding of every person in the country," Rachel had become his wife at Natchez. "Nor was it without difficulty," observed the tactful Overton, "that he could be induced to believe otherwise."[37]

7

Such is the story John Overton gave the public in 1827[38] when Andrew Jackson's marriage became an issue in his second contest for the presidency. Its peculiarities are inescapable. One is asked to believe that on the return from escorting Rachel to Natchez in 1791, Jackson, a lawyer, accepted without professional inquiry the report that Robards had obtained a divorce from the Virginia Assembly, and swept Rachel into an irregular marriage. Then one is asked to believe that a man with as many gossiping rivals as Jackson, lived on the Cumberland trail for two years undisturbed by the slightest suspicion of the illegality of that union, when a simple inquiry at Richmond should have disclosed that no divorce had been granted.

But one must believe these things for they are true. Not even Jackson's political enemies of 1827, always merciless with the truth and often reckless of it, claimed anything else. Evidence of the general belief on the Cumberland that a divorce was granted in 1791 is ample.[39] Evidence to the contrary is absent.

Mr. Overton has emphasized the statement that the discovery of the true state of affairs came as a surprise. In this he is corroborated by eighteen other prominent residents of the Cumberland who in 1827 united in the declaration that "neither Mrs. Jackson or Gen. Jackson . . . [had] any knowledge of" the "judicial proceeding" of 1793 until it was over.[40]

This is quite possible, but in view of the court records, it is unfortunate that none of the nineteen deponents give any evidence to support their assertion.

The discovery was in December. Yet in the April preceding, Robards, through his attorney, Senator Brown, had publicly instituted his suit with a plea that the marriage be dissolved "according to an act of the Assembly . . . made and provided," on the ground that "said Rachel . . . did . . . on the—[sic] day of July . . . 1790, elope from her husband."[41] This was spread upon the records of the court and there is nothing to indicate that these records were not at all times available to public inspection.

Postponement of the case from the April to the September term of court gave more time for the news of Robards's action to circulate. On August sixth Thomas Allen, Clerk of the Court, directed the Sheriff to "summon Hugh McGary and John Cowan to appear . . . at the Court House on the third day of September court next . . . the truth to say in behalf of Lewis Robards in a certain matter of controversy . . . between said Lewis, plaintiff, and Rachel Robards, defendant."[42] Of these witnesses John Cowan bore a name very respectable in that part of Kentucky and Hugh McGary, a frontier soldier and Indian fighter, was famous. Incidentally, he was a brother of Martin McGary, the Waxhaw Tory slayer who married Jackson's cousin.

JUDGE JACKSON

An engraving from a portrait made about 1804. Reproduced by courtesy of the Tennessee State Library, Nashville.

THE FIRST HERMITAGE

Erected as a blockhouse prior to 1795 when Jackson bought it. Remodeled, it was Jackson's residence from 1804 until 1818 or 1819. From a print in the collection of Mrs. Samuel G. Heiskell of Knoxville.

But in one very important respect Robards, or his attorney, had not complied with the terms of the enabling act, which provided that notice of his intention to go into court should be published "for eight weeks consecutively in the *Kentuckey Gazette*." This newspaper was widely read on the Cumberland and a notice therein could not have escaped Jackson, preoccupied as Cumberland settlers were at the time with Indian raids. No publication, however, was made. This omission, which the writer finds difficult to dismiss as an oversight, lends some color to the theory that Robards sought to obtain the divorce clandestinely, avoiding a contest of his allegations.

When the case was called in September, McGary swore to a story that persuaded a jury of the truth of Robards's charge. In 1827 Jackson's defenders asserted that McGary, then dead, "must have" perjured himself. It was said that the first time he saw Jackson and Rachel together was during their return from Natchez after the marriage in 1791, Jackson and McGary quarreling over measures against a meditated Indian attack.[43] Hugh McGary was said to have taken his revenge on the witness stand. This may be true, though the act is not in character with the known annals of his conspicuous life.

8

"Know all men by these presents that we, Andrew Jackson, Robert Hays and John Overton, of the County Davidson and Territory of the United States of America South of the River Ohio, are held and firmly bound . . . in the sum of one thousand pounds to be paid . . . if there shall . . . hereafter appear any lawful cause why Andrew Jackson and Rachel Donelson, alias Rachel Roberts should not be joined together in holy matrimony."[44]

This was the usual marriage bond and was dated January 7, 1794. On January seventeenth a license was issued and the ceremony probably performed on the same day.[45]

Thus ends the charted record, but not the human record of this romance.

The subtle attrition of an inner disquietude that began to wear upon the buoyancy of Rachel stamps the wounding character of the second ceremony. The exactions of the statute had been satisfied to the humiliating letter. Nor was Rachel joined to a mate who looked alone to such conventional forms to defend his wife's good name. Andrew Jackson's pistols were in order, and for thirty-three years they kept slanderers at bay. But a defense may be so energetic as to recoil upon the mind of the defended.

9

A military foray from Nashville in defiance of Federal authority completed the subjugation of the Cherokees and opened the way to riches for Andrew Jackson. The volume of new settlers doubled and trebled. It would be only a question of time until the vast and vacant lands the solicitor had acquired for ten cents an acre in services would be worth five dollars. In March, 1795, he started for Philadelphia to sell at once some thirty thousand acres on his own account, fifty thousand acres held jointly with John Overton and eighteen thousand acres on commission for Joel Rice.

John Overton sent a "Memorandum" in the wake of his partner. "Be canded and unreserved with the purchasers . . . and particularly inform them that" the fifty thousand acres "are situate without the [boundaries of land open to white settlement as fixed by the] Treaty of Holston"—the Cherokee treaty of 1791. In other words this land belonged to the Indians and no white man legally owned or could convey a foot of it. "If you purchase Negroes yourself in any of the northern States, be careful . . . to subject yourself to the penal Laws," added Mr. Overton, but before posting the letter he crossed out the "canded and unreserved" paragraph substituting a marginal note: "This . . . to your discretion. Perhaps it would be best to raise . . . few difficulties."[46]

The trip to Philadelphia was Mr. Jackson's first visit to a center of culture since his descent upon Charleston with his grandfather's inheritance. He found it much less enjoyable. Jackson was an abrupt trader, used to naming his price which the other side could take or leave. This worked well enough in the West where Mr. Jackson was under no compulsion and could abide his time for bargains.

TIDINGS FROM HARRODSBURGH

Not so in Philadelphia where time was an ally of the prospective purchaser. Twenty-two days of chaffering, bickering and delays, with Jackson's temper getting shorter all the time—twenty-two days of "difficulties such as I never experienced before . . . The Dam'st situation ever man was in,"[47] and the bargains were struck. David Allison, a merchant and speculator with apparently unbounded credit, bought twenty-eight thousand eight hundred and ten acres of Jackson and Overton for ten thousand dollars.[48] Payment was by a series of notes, maturing at intervals over a period of about four years.

Of the seller's candor concerning the title to the Indians' acres nothing appears, but Andrew Jackson's meanest enemy never questioned his personal honesty. Anticipating the acquisition of treaty-protected hunting-grounds was a regular part of business foresight on a frontier.

There was now a multitude of things to do and little time for them. Jackson meant to establish a trading post on the Cumberland. He bought five thousand dollars' worth of goods from Meeker, Cochran & Company, giving some of Allison's notes in payment. Allison suggested that the firm of John B. Evans & Company was also worthy of patronage—a natural sentiment, Mr. Allison being a secret partner in the concern. He walked into the store with Jackson and told Mr. Evans to let his friend "have goods to any amount." Jackson's bill came to one thousand four hundred and sixty-six dollars and sixty-six cents for which he tendered a note of Allison's. "Mr. Evans . . . requested me to put my name on the back of it. I did so, but . . . did not conceive I stood security for the payment of the note."[49] A rather odd conception, but Jackson was in a great haste, with the formidable shipping details still to arrange: wagons to Pittsburgh at eight dollars a hundredweight; there a boat to be bought and manned for Kentucky; thence by wagon to Nashville, bringing the total outlay for transportation to six hundred and sixty-four dollars and eighty-six cents cash.[50]

Far behind his schedule the harassed man of business reached Knoxville in June, picked up twenty-five hundred dollars on a quick local transaction and, "fatigued even almost to death," pushed on toward Poplar Grove without a day's delay.[51]

10

Politics bubbled merrily in the Territory South of the River Ohio.⁵² Mr. Jackson did not call himself a politician, but, as a traveler with latest tidings from the nation's capital, he suggested the impeachment of George Washington, "for the Daring infringements on our Constitutional rights"⁵³ by the use of his influence to obtain ratification of John Jay's treaty which acknowledged England's right to search our ships at sea. The President deemed the treaty preferable to war. Young Mr. Jackson would have fought.

The Territorial Legislature ordered a census, and, if the returns should show sixty thousand inhabitants, directed the Governor to call a constitutional convention to prepare the way for admission to the Union as a state. That was how the resolution read, but it attracted some of its support on the supposition that the convention might be a means of devising a separation from the Union. Owing to the extraordinary competence of the enumerators, the census showed seventy thousand inhabitants. The convention was ordered, and, Jackson being elected a delegate from Davidson County, accepted the honor at some inconvenience to himself.

During the recent ascendency of his prospects, Mr. Jackson had undertaken an expansion of his domestic arrangements. A finer plantation called Hunter's Hill was purchased and work begun on a new residence which tradition described as a large one of cut lumber, a specification of magnificence. An estate manager was engaged. "The Barer Mr. David lile is the man I . . . send you for an Overseer. . . . Put your Negroes Under him . . . and keep Out of the field yourself. . . . My Comp.ᵗˢ to Mʳˢ Jackson. MARK MITCHELL."⁵⁴

This stride toward life in the Tidewater manner was imperiled by news from Philadelphia which virtually disorganized Jackson's affairs. Allison had defaulted his obligations, and the firms of Meeker and of Evans warned Jackson to prepare to cover the Allison notes with cash—not land, salt, cow-bells or other circulating media of the frontier. The one bright spot was the mercantile establishment Jackson had opened with the Meeker-Evans goods. Possibly its profits would retire the notes.

TIDINGS FROM HARRODSBURGH

Under these circumstances, in January of 1796, the constitutional convention met at Knoxville and appropriated two dollars and a half to cover the chairman's dais with oil-cloth. Although Delegate Jackson seldom addressed this dignitary, he was one of the silent forces of the convention. He is said to have proposed the new state's name, Tennessee.[55] The proletarian aspect of the constitution alarmed eastern Federalists. Any man could vote upon six months' residence in a county, a freeholder upon one day's residence; the owner of two hundred acres was eligible to the Legislature, of five hundred acres to the governorship. Nor was this all. Tennessee declared free navigation of the Mississippi to be "one of the inherent rights of . . . this state." This the United States had specifically denied, but Tennessee said she would come into the Union on her own terms or secede. On February seventh the convention adjourned, giving the Federal Government forty-nine days in which to make up its mind.

Without awaiting the pleasure of Congress, Tennessee organized an administration under John Sevier who had graced the chief magistracy of one outlawed state. Former Governor Blount (pronounced Blunt) and William Cocke went to Philadelphia as senators, but found no red morocco chairs at their disposal. The forty-ninth day had come and gone, but Federalist members blocked the recognition of Tennessee. Washington had declined a third term, and Federalists anticipated trouble enough for Candidate Adams without raising up another state sure to vote for Jefferson and perhaps for Burr. On June first they gave in. The old Spanish threat had served its last end.

II

The first of the Allison notes was due and the store's profits could not pay it. Jackson acted resolutely. He traded the store to Elijah Robertson for thirty-three thousand acres of land and sold the land for twenty-five cents an acre to James Stuart, of Knoxville, taking in part payment a draft for four thousand five hundred and thirty-nine dollars and ninety-four cents on Senator Blount in Philadelphia who was indebted to Stuart.

Jackson had championed the Union in Tennessee, though his

own county, angered by the lofty attitude of the Federalists, voted five to one against joining.[56] But now that she had joined, Tennessee was entitled to one member in the House of Representatives. Andrew Jackson was elected without opposition. With the Blount draft in his pocket he set out for Philadelphia in November of 1796.

It was a sad leave-taking for Rachel. Since the day she had said her wedding vows a second time some deep interior instinct told this woman that her hope of peace on earth lay in obscurity. Married to an ordinary man this boon would have been hers as a matter of course. But Rachel was married to Andrew Jackson. She shuddered as the world of affairs, the hostile world that had inflicted a terrible brand upon her, reached out to claim her husband.

Rachel Jackson's long flight from fame and the scrutiny that falls on the famous had begun.

CHAPTER VI

ROBES OF JUSTICE

1

On December 5, 1796, Representative Jackson presented his credentials to the Speaker. Two days before a Philadelphia tailor had delivered a "black coat & breeches." Yet the pleasing impression left with Miss Nancy Jarret, of Salisbury, North Carolina, on the occasion of an earlier investiture, was not duplicated in the reflections of fastidious Albert Gallatin who looked on from his seat in the House Chamber. "Tall, lanky uncouth-looking personage . . . queue down his back tied with an eel-skin; . . . dress singular, . . . manners those of a rough backwoodsman."[1]

The backwoodsman himself seems to have carried away no memory of the occasion, however, for once in the seclusion of his lodgings his thoughts were all of Hunter's Hill. A hurried note went to Robert Hays. "I beg you to amuse Mrs Jackson. let her not fret. I am disturbed in mind about her."[2]

On December eighth Mr. Gallatin may have felt the deportment and attire of the gentleman from Tennessee in still greater contrast with their surroundings, for enough red leather chairs had been moved into the paneled hall of the House to accommodate a joint sitting with the Senate. A shining coach drawn by four cream-colored horses halted in Chestnut Street. General Washington made a stately entrance, his tall military form richly clad in black, a symbol of decorum and dignity. A deep rich voice pronounced his farewell to Congress in a lofty and, in its concluding lines, a moving address.

Three days later members of the House found on their desks a draft of the customary reply to the President's speech, prepared by a committee. Not all of the committee were Federalists, but the impending withdrawal of General Washington to private life inspired a tribute to his public services and a rather decorative expression of good wishes "for the decline of your days." The perfunctory motion for its adoption by unanimous consent failed, and for two days the reply was pulled apart line by line, and put together again with the scrupulous substitution of tweedle-de-dum for tweedle-de-dee.

To these important labors the lawgiver from Tennessee contributed nothing, but he wrote Robert Hays somewhat gleefully of the "Considerable degree of warmth" that marked the debate. The President's supporters, he added, "wish to Cultivate a close friendship with Britain at the Expense of a war with the French Republick. . . . The British are daily Capturing our vessels [and] impressing our seamen . . . but from the presidents speech it would seem that . . . all the Depredations on our commerce was done by the French. . . . Attend . . . my Dear little Rachael and sooth her in my absence. If she should want for anything [get] it for her."[3]

In silence Mr. Jackson heard a handful of unterrified patriots explain that Washington's reputation was overrated, that his tours of the country resembled "royal progresses" and hence were unrepublican. Indeed a corrupting consequence of this practise might have been cited in connection with the President's southern journey. He was entertained by Major Robert Crawford, where that sincere republican soldier had outdone himself in imitation of regal splendor, and the guest's touch had made a bed historic.

When a vote could be delayed no longer, a North Carolina statesman demanded a roll-call that posterity might know where the people's legates stood in this crisis. The journal of the House betrays that sixty-seven stood for the felicitous response, twelve opposed. Andrew Jackson was one of the twelve.

2

The points that had most impressed Mr. Jackson in the criticism of General Washington's statesmanship concerned our Indian policy, the Jay treaty and the responsibility that a governing régime always bears for hard times. Two months after Jackson reached Philadelphia, the Bank of England suspended specie payments, the signal for a world-wide depression which in the United States already was severe.

Though a rich man, Senator Blount had been caught by the stringency and was unable to honor the draft which Jackson presented.

Allison did not have a ready dollar. Jackson's situation was critical. To cover his endorsements then due, he had to discount Blount's paper for what he could get. Into the chasm went the price of his store—thirty-three thousand acres of land which twenty years later were worth two hundred thousand dollars.

In the domain of public finance Mr. Jackson was more successful. A member of John Sevier's unauthorized Cherokee campaign of 1793 had asked Congress for compensation for his military services. The plea was rejected with sharp comment on the nature of the expedition by the Secretary of War. Jackson blandly introduced a resolution to reimburse Tennessee for the expenses of the entire expedition, which he supported with a crisp speech. "That war was urged. . . . The knife and the tomahawk were held over the heads of women and children. . . . It was time to make resistance. Some of the assertions of the Secretary of War are not founded in fact."

Administration parliamentarians moved to refer the subject to the Committee on Claims. "I own," countered Jackson, "that I am not very well acquainted with the rules of the House, but . . . [why] this very circuitous mode of doing business?"[4] Nevertheless, the resolution was shunted aside. On the next day Jackson revived it. His concise language held the attention of the House. James Madison came to the unknown Representative's support. The question was referred to a special committee, "Mr. A. Jackson chairman," and the treasury of Tennessee enriched by twenty-two thousand eight hundred and sixteen dollars.

The Member from Tennessee did not address the House again. For one thing he hardly had time to do so. "I am the only representative from the State. Consequently all the business of the State in the house of representatives devolves on me. . . . [I serve] on all [standing] Committees, . . . and also on Many select ones."[5]

He was disappointed when a count of the electoral ballots for a successor to General Washington revealed the triumph of Adams over Jefferson by seventy-one to sixty-eight. But Jackson was able to obtain from the incoming administration the promise of a United States marshalship for his brother-in-law Robert Hays. "Take care of my little rachael until I return," he charged the prospective marshal.[6]

Representative Jackson also voted for a proposal to build three naval frigates; against the purchase of peace by paying tribute to Algiers; against an appropriation of fourteen thousand dollars to buy furniture for the presidential residence in the new capital on the Potomac—and, on the expiration of his term, March 3, 1797, quit Philadelphia distinguished, except in the eyes of his constituents, for little more than his eel-skin.

3

Knoxville gave its Representative a rousing reception, extravagant with predictions. Not a little dismayed, perhaps, that one can not eat his cake and have it too, Mr. Jackson shook himself free of back-slapping admirers and mounted to his tavern chamber.

"My Dearest Heart

"With what pleasing hopes I view the future when I shall be restored to your arms there to spend My days . . . with you the Dear Companion of my life, never to be separated from you again. . . . I mean to retire from . . . publick life. . . .

"I have this moment finished My business here . . . and tho it is now half after ten o'clock, would not think of going to bed without writing you. May it give you pleasure to Receive it. May it add to your Contentment until I return. May you be blessed with health. May the Goddess of Slumber every evening light on your eyebrows . . . and conduct you through . . . pleasant dreams. Could I only know you . . . enjoyed Peace of Mind, it would relieve my anxious breast and shorten the way . . . until . . . I am restored to your sweet embrace which is the Nightly prayer of your affectionate husband."⁷

Declining to seek reelection, Jackson permitted the office to go to William Charles Cole Claiborne, a peripatetic politician late of Richmond, New York and Philadelphia, and in May of 1797 sequestered himself at Hunter's Hill.

Alas for Rachel, her period of happiness was brief. In July Tennessee welcomed another returning hero: Jackson's friend and political mentor, William Blount, whose claim to the laurel rested upon the fact that the Senate had expelled him for "a high misdemeanor." The West ever had been engagingly indifferent as to whether it achieved control of the Mississippi through Spain's friendship or her enmity—which, however, did not deceive Señor Miró. With the expanding prestige of the Federal Government, one heard less talk of a Spanish alliance and more of a Spanish war. Mr. Blount favored an economical war by inciting the Creek and Cherokee Indians to join the British in the conquest of West Florida, which the Senate felt to be an ineligible occupation for one of its members.

But Tennessee approved. It elected Mr. Blount to the State Senate before he got home, whereupon an intricate situation over the succession at Philadelphia enticed the Cincinnatus of Hunter's Hill into the party councils. Jackson owed much to Blount's influence and could not desert his patron in an hour of adversity. After a feverish period of hesitation, the vow of political celibacy was suspended and Rachel's husband, at thirty, accepted the senatorial toga that had been so modishly worn by William Blount.

Responsibilities were confronted punctually. The year before Jackson had been a candidate for major general of militia. After causing his defeat on the ground of inexperience, Governor Sevier had made an allusion to the ambitions of the aspirant which Jackson considered incompatible with the dignity of a United States Senator. Judge John McNairy also was concerned in the affair. Jackson addressed to these gentlemen notes containing the formal inquiries preliminary to a dueling summons. The scene dissolved, however, upon the receipt of dignified but palliative replies satisfying alike the demands of etiquette and of honor.[8]

The Senator-Elect departed for Philadelphia. "Try to amuse Mrs. Jackson," he wrote en route to Robert Hays. "I left her *Bathed in Tears* . . . [which] indeed Sir has given me more pain than any event in my life."[9]

4

Mr. Jackson made his appearance before the Upper House in "florintine Breeches" and a black coat with a velvet collar, fresh from the bench of his Philadelphia tailor. He attended a large and brilliant dinner given by Senator Aaron Burr and remarked on the excellence of the wines. They formed a fragrant memory to be recalled on convivial occasions for many years.

A bag of trifles—a Cherokee boundary, job-seekers letters—filled his routine, but his real interest, like that of the country, lay across the ocean. Newspapers remained the favorite literature of the late public reader of the Waxhaws. He devoured the foreign dispatches, sending long digests of them to Tennessee. "France is now turning her force toward Great Britain. . . . Should Bonaparte make a landing on the English shore, tyranny will be humbled, a throne crushed, and a republic spring from the wreck."[10] This soldier was the Senator's hero. A fortnight later the news of his conduct was not so reassuring, however. Jackson feared he might make peace with England. "Should that Happen, Perhaps France may give america a sweep of her tail."[11]

And if France did not, the chances were that England would. It seemed inevitable that we should be drawn into this war. But the thing was to get on the proper side. The Federalists leaned toward England, a name which to Andrew Jackson delineated the livid face of a dragoon lieutenant with upraised sword. The Tennessee Senator favored the French, but was obliged to confess privately that on the whole their leaders were a tricky lot.

The session dragged. David Allison went to jail for debt and more of his notes for which Jackson was liable fell due. In April of 1798 the Senator obtained a leave of absence to grapple with his personal affairs. Their aspect was so forbidding that he returned home and resigned his seat, but this proved no obstacle to the conclusion of an item of unfinished senatorial business. Although Jackson was actually the successor of Blount, and the representative of his views in the Senate, technically Joseph Anderson had been elected in Blount's place, whereas Jackson, on the same day, had taken the seat vacated rather unwillingly by William Cocke. This had led to some free expressions of opinion by Cocke. To clean the slate Jackson invited his predecessor to a duel, but Cocke wavered and friends smoothed things over.[12]

With equal resolution Jackson tackled his problem of finances. The ledger at Hunter's Hill showed a profit. Very well, increase it. Mr. Jackson verified the report that this new "cotton engine," or "gin" as the negroes called it, did the work of forty hands. He bought one. Whisky was almost the same as cash. A "distilery" was added to the plantation equipment, and its product sold at the new mercantile establishment Jackson had opened on his farm in partnership with Thomas Watson.

In six months the ex-Senator had his head above water, but little more, when he accepted an appointment to the bench of the Superior Court, often called Supreme Court because, when sitting together, its justices comprised the highest tribunal in the state.

5

"New Port, Tennessee, March 22nd 1803
"My Love: . . . Colo Christmas . . . has promised to . . . deliver some garden seeds and this letter. . . .
"On the 15th instant in Jonesborough Mr. Rawlings stable burnt down. . . With the utmost exertion I saved my horse . . . having nothing on but a shirt . . . I wish my cotton planted between the 15th and 25th of April. I hope the apples trees . . . received [no] injury from the frost. . . .
"May health and happiness surround you is the sincere wish of your affectionate Husband."[13]

Mr. Justice Jackson had become a personage, his counsel sought, his favor courted. Four years on the bench saw him the most popular servant of the law that Tennessee ever has had, and perhaps the most useful. Certainly no one did more to inculcate a sentiment of respect for courts which in a border society often matures slowly. The tribunals of Judge Jackson were a synthesis of the man who presided: swift, untechnical, fiercely impartial, fiercely jealous of prerogatives and good name. "Judge Jackson, Dear Sir: The little illnature which you observ'd on yesterday evening in my language I am sorry to bring to recollection . . . and wish . . . in oblivion . . . yr Hmble Servt. GEORGE M. DEADERICK."[14] "A report has been in circulation that I . . . [did] utter and speak the following words (to wit) [']As honest a man as Andrew Jackson was called he had stolen his Bull['] If I did speak the above words they were groundless and unfounded. . . . MICHEL GLEAVE."[15]

But this did not surround Rachel with happiness. She had been married eleven years, and life was still a lonely improvisation, first with Andrew absent in the quest of money, now the quest of power

—which an unshakable intuition warned Rachel must some day recoil against her.

Yet how happy they could be together. The fine house at Hunter's Hill stood high, commanding a view of the beautiful river where Jackson had his store, his private landing and a ferry. Sometimes when Mr. Jackson—never "Judge" to Rachel—came home, the old-time Cumberland clan would be on hand to receive him—Rachel's innumerable connections, with their shoals of children; Overtons, Robertsons, Manskers and miscellaneous belles and beaux of Rachel's girlhood. Old friends were the best friends: a cask of whisky, a dozen pot-pies, the nimblest fiddler in Davidson County, and a rollicking dance tune such as used to make the rafters of John Donelson's blockhouse ring. The years fell away, cares fell away and Rachel was herself again.

Judge Jackson had as good a time as any. He retained his liking for companionship, a glass around, a song and a story. But the gayest night has its end, and Rachel's busy husband might ride away at dawn without touching a pillow. He would return with his friends from the encircling world of affairs. They were studiously attentive to Judge Jackson's lady and one has no reason to suspect them of hypocrisy, though Rachel made her morbid reservations. Andrew fought this shyness. He strove to draw her into the enlarging sphere of his interests. After supper she must join the gentlemen over their brandy by the fire. Jackson would fill a fresh clay pipe and light it for her with a coal, the same as when they were alone. Only for Rachel it was not the same.

As this sensitiveness grew she sought the solace of religion. No road was too bad or weather too inhospitable to keep Rachel Jackson from a household visited by sickness or death. She loaned tools and gave advice to new settlers. She was the idol of the slave quarters and the mainstay of Lile, the manager at Hunter's Hill. But her particular fondness was for children of whom there were usually from one to half a dozen about the house. She borrowed them from overworked wives of neighbors and new settlers. The swarming progeny of her brothers and sisters came in relays to stay with their aunt who was, in fact, "Aunt Rachel" to every youngster of the countryside.

Jackson too was a favorite of the children, indulging their wants and sharing their pastimes. He was tumbling on the floor with one of the Donelson offspring when Aunt Rachel burst into tears.

"Oh, husband! How I wish we had a child!"

Andrew took her in his arms.

"Darling, God knows what to give, what to withhold."[16]

6

It was a modest account that Rachel received from her husband of the Jonesborough fire, wherein Judge Jackson had subdued a midnight panic and saved the town. His principal assistant was Russell Bean, who had rushed into the burning barn, "tore doors from their hinges to release the horses, scaled the roofs of houses, spread wet blankets and," in the estimation of one witness, "did more than any two men except Judge Jackson."[17] The fact that this hero was a jail-breaker and fugitive from justice[18] imparted a certain savor to his conduct.

Russell Bean was also a veteran of King's Mountain, and the first entirely white child born in the territory which was to become Tennessee. This, however, did not satisfy his mind as to the accuracy of Pliny's contention that babies may appear in this world from no other cause than the fertilizing effect of moonbeams. Indeed, Mr. Bean's estrangement from the law had followed his clipping the ears of an unsponsored infant born to Mrs. Bean. When the fire was out he declined to submit to arrest, and, armed to the teeth, undertook to interview his wife's seducer.

On the following morning Bean stood off a posse of ten men and Judge Jackson directed the sheriff to summon as many men as necessary and bring Bean in. The sheriff was obliged to report failure. He had found that his quarry enjoyed a certain sympathy from a public that saw the law in arms against a poor leather-shirt, while a merchant had as yet escaped any serious consequences of his amours. Jackson read the sheriff a stinging lecture and court adjourned for dinner. With two associate justices Jackson was on his way to the hotel when the irritated sheriff, taking his instructions literally, summoned the three of them to help take Bean. Two of the judges put themselves on their dignity. Jackson asked for firearms. Advancing with a leveled pistol, he invited Bean to surrender or be shot down. Bean surrendered.[19]

The rise of Judge Jackson had not been achieved without the mastery of obstacles. Tennessee was predominately Republican, but the ascendant party lay in separate camps—the old Blount group in which Jackson became more and more conspicuous, the other ruled lock and stock by John Sevier. To the Jackson wing belonged most of the land barons and men of wealth, while Nolichucky Jack, whose State of Franklin had cost him a fortune, backed the third estate and made the clearings ring with his criticism of the "nabobs." That was how the dice fell. Actually Sevier was of genteel Huguenot lineage and patrician bearing, tempered by the easy social intercourse of the frontier on which he had spent his life. When he went to Philadelphia he wore a powdered wig, which was something Andrew Jackson would not do. Beneath the noisy democracy of Franklin, Sevier and other wealthy men had scrupulously perpetuated their shadily acquired land titles.

The difficulty between these men was that, temperamentally, they were too much alike. Where either sat was the head of the table.

Their gallery was enlarging. Without counting emigrants at more than one turn of the road, census enumerators in 1800 were able to discover one hundred and five thousand inhabitants of Tennessee. Where Prosecutor Jackson had picked his way over the fallen timbers of an Indian trace, Judge Jackson traversed a "road" rutted by the broad tires of Conestoga wagons. Lines were run. The click-clock of axes beat a ceaseless rhythm of destruction and growth. Sawpits rasped; a new tavern rose at the fork of the road: a new county, a new court-house, a new court. The stimulation of these acts of creation made bodies strong and minds buoyant. To those who fight for it daily, life has a flavor the protected never know. Frontiersmen acquired an unhesitant faith in themselves and their new country, and in dealing with the impediments to their progress, a convenient disregard for the conventions.

The first settlers had come out largely on their own, in flight from the transitory disappointments of the Revolution. Nowadays settlers started in much as their predecessors—sheltered by a wagon camp until the cabin was raised, eating corn-meal and game until a crop was made. But most of them no longer took their land first-hand

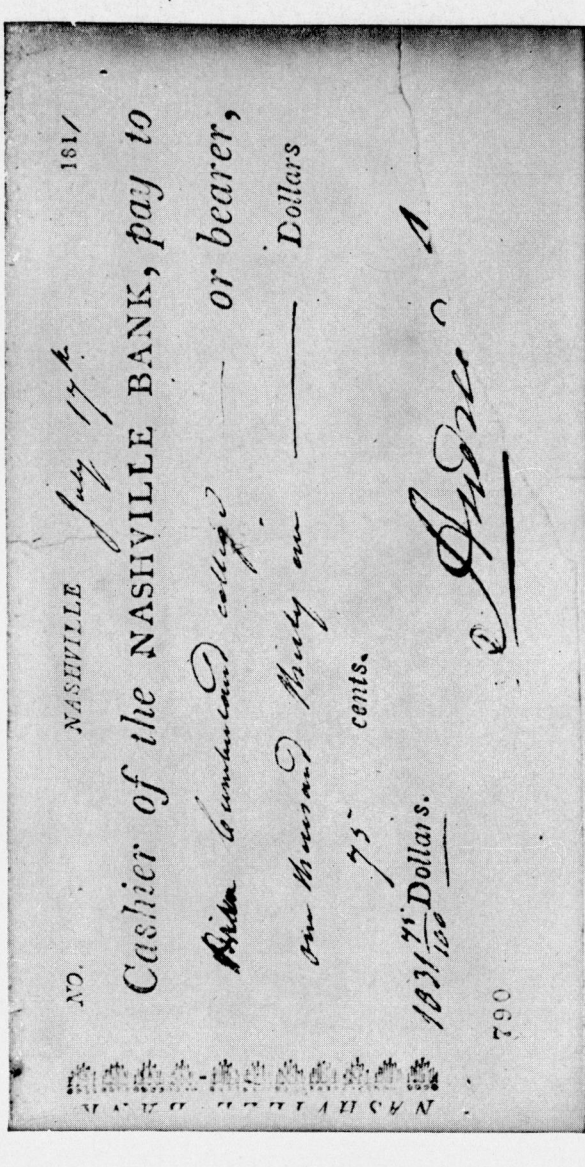

A Believer in Education

General Jackson was an active supporter of Cumberland College at Nashville and an officer of its forerunner, Davidson Academy. This check, made at a time when Jackson was striving to pay the debts of his trading house, was probably in payment of tuition for his various wards. Checks were commonly cancelled in that day by tearing off a part of the signature. From the Jackson Papers, Library of Congress.

RACHEL JACKSON

A miniature on ivory which Jackson wore about his neck for thirty years. Painted by Anna C. Peale in Washington, December, 1815. Reproduced from a copy in the collection of Mrs. Samuel G. Heiskell of Knoxville.

from the state. They took from the big land companies who acquired it by the hundred-thousand-acre swoop. They were somewhat under the ægis of those monopolies, which distributed literature fluently descriptive of the Western paradise, offered counsel on emigrant outfits, owned stores that sold them, sometimes roughed out roads and furnished guards for trains. The companies were deeply and often corruptly concerned with politics. By this nearly invisible system seaboard capital had its hands on the entrails of Western development, and, with all its evils, made that development more rapid, and possibly more secure than, hit or miss, it might have been.

Andrew Jackson was on the side of the capitalists. His first case in Nashville in 1788 had landed him as champion of the creditors against the debtors. Jackson desired wealth. It seems to me that this impulse led him into public life—via the constitutional convention and Congress. But his record is clean. Barring a little finesse in Indian matters, which was customary, no hint of irregularity renders the dim beginnings of his career of a color with those of a few of our other Western immortals. On the bench Jackson was rectitude embodied. His law library was presentable,[20] and his acquaintance with it ample for the time and place. No written decision by him is known, that practise being inaugurated by Jackson's successor, John Overton. But tradition preserves the essence of his frequent charge to juries. "Do what is *right* between these parties. That is what the law always *means*."

The frontier was hailed at the time, and has been generally regarded, as a spontaneous democracy. This quality was apparent. Less easily perceived was the cloaked influence of the land companies, peopling their fiefs with settlers, and silently imparting to the loquacious and active pattern of Western expansion the faint impress of a modified feudalism. When Jackson went on the bench he abandoned his law practise, largely concerned with landowners' interests, for a salary of eight hundred dollars a year. The legal safeguarding that his own extensive private holdings required was entrusted to hired lawyers. But Jackson's habits of thought—or, rather, impulse—had been formed. He belonged with those who wore the beaver hats. Nolichucky Jack had made a virtue of necessity by espousing the cause of those who skinned the beavers.

7

The rift and threatened duel between these natural antagonists in 1797 had their origin in the fact that on his way to Philadelphia as a Member of Congress the autumn before Jackson had picked up a piece of information involving the validity of certain large-scale land deals in East Tennessee. As the transactions had taken place before the separation of the over-mountain region from the mother state, Jackson relayed what he had heard to Governor Ashe, of North Carolina. Ashe called upon Sevier for the records. The Tennessee Governor failed to comply but agents of Ashe obtained the papers anyhow. Whereupon Sevier, Senator Blount and others met at Blount's house in Knoxville and formed a plan for retrieving the documents, and if this could not be done, to burn the building in which they were. Neither of these earnest designs succeeded, however. The land papers were carried over the mountains to North Carolina, and then Sevier began to perceive in Andrew Jackson a man of unsound political ideals.

In North Carolina an investigating committee quietly pursued its study of the land papers. Stockley Donelson was found to be involved, but when Jackson heard that his participation in the scandal was small beside that of John Sevier he probably sensed a deeper satisfaction of virtue rewarded. In March of 1798, when Jackson was on his way home to resign from the Senate, the committee made its report to Governor Ashe. The Napoleonic magnitude of the attempted theft lifted it from the category of sordid or common crimes. By forged warrants and other means Nolichucky Jack and other gentlemen of eminent good name had labored to possess themselves of something like one-fifth of the area of Tennessee. Ashe called upon Sevier for the extradition of some of the guilty, which was refused. The sensational report of the investigators was then filed away without publication and an inexplicable hush fell over the whole affair before the public understood what had happened.[21]

Sevier kept his hold on the governorship for three consecutive terms, the limit permitted by the Constitution. In 1801 Jackson's friend, Archibald Roane, succeeded him, after which, in 1802, the Judge won another victory over his rival. The field officers of the militia were to elect a major general. Jackson and Sevier received seventeen votes each. Roane broke the tie in favor of Jackson, depriving Sevier, thirty years a soldier, of the military rank on which he had set his heart.

The new General forebore the martial airs. He preferred the title of Judge and used it except at musters of the militia. This was a prudent thing to do. General Jackson might have the rank, but the military reputation was Nolichucky Jack's.

As Governor Roane neared the end of his term, the conservatives laid careful plans for his reelection. This was crass effrontery in the eyes of John Sevier who regarded Mr. Roane's incumbency as a courtesy interregnum dictated by the letter, though not the spirit, of the Constitution. The old leader meant to have back his throne and began to stump the state with telling effect.

In this critical situation Jackson decided that the only way his man could win would be to unmask Sevier's connection with the land fraud. It was done in an article contributed by Jackson to the Knoxville *Gazette*.[22] Remarkable gifts of imagination had inspired this imperial attempt at swindling. The same gifts saved John Sevier from the effects of Jackson's disclosure. The history of Tennessee was still the biography of Nolichucky Jack, who had mastered every crisis in its annals and his. He mastered this one. Evading, denying, confusing, he stormed the settlements as the persecuted friend of the poor. Jackson had made Sevier's guilt plain to any thinking person, overlooking only the fact that in the glamourous presence of Nolichucky Jack people did not think. Beating Roane easily, the old warrior resumed office in triumph, his legendary fame glowing with new luster from its brush with the "aristocrats." He pardoned the oppressed leather-shirt, Russell Bean, and, shortly thereafter, Judge Jackson arrived in Knoxville.

On Saturday, October 1, 1803, he adjourned court after hearing two prosy debt suits. There were other exits from the courthouse, but Jackson chose a door that framed the gesticulating form of John Sevier on the steps haranguing a crowd which included most of the members of the Legislature. The Governor spoke of his services to the state, for emphasis shaking, in its scabbard, the old cavalry sabre he always wore. The presence of the Justice was acknowledged with an allusion which moved Jackson to interpolate that he himself had performed public services which, he believed, had not met with the disapproval of his fellow citizens.

"Services?" thundered Sevier before Jackson could get in a word about the land scandal. "I know of no great service you have rendered the country except taking a trip to Natchez with another man's wife!"

An unearthly light invaded the blue eyes of Andrew Jackson. The crowd stood as if transfixed. Sevier drew his sword.

"Great God!" cried Jackson. "Do you mention *her* sacred name?" Clubbing his walking stick, he lunged at John Sevier.[23]

8

The crowd surged forward. Pistols were drawn, shots fired and a bystander grazed by a ball before Jackson and Sevier, surrounded by partizans, were borne away in opposite directions.

Captain Andrew White carried Jackson's challenge to the Executive Residence. When no reply had been received on Monday morning, Jackson sent White to jog the Governor's memory. Not until he had called several times did he receive Sevier's answer. The Governor would be "pleased" to meet Judge Jackson, but the interview could not take place in Tennessee, which had adopted the conventional statute against dueling.[24]

Jackson replied instantly, charging Sevier with "subterfuge," and offering to fight in Georgia, Virginia, North Carolina, or on Indian territory "if it will obviate your squeamish fears. . . . You must meet me tween this and four o'clock this afternoon . . . or I will publish you as a coward."[25] Sevier crisply replied that the seconds could proceed with their duties relating to "time and place of rendezvous."[26] Yet he did not suit action to word, and restrained his second, young Captain Sparks. To others the Governor protested that his age, his proven courage, and the poverty which an untoward issue of events would visit upon his family should exempt him from Jackson's demands.

All very true, but not the Code. It was easy to read the discomfiture of Captain Sparks. But forces were at work. Jackson was encircled by a pressure for peace. He was importuned on the ground of respect for his judicial robes—a high consideration, but Rachel's

ROBES OF JUSTICE

honor was higher. He would resign from the bench, he said, but Sevier must fight, or stand publicly proclaimed a coward. Jackson wrote the proclamation, but friends persuaded him to delay giving it to the *Gazette*.

Two days passed. No word from Sevier whose friends pleaded absorption in state business. But Jackson's stock was rising. Thirty-three prominent citizens of Knoxville signed a petition asking him not to desert the bench "at this momentous crisis." Two days later a similar petition[27] attracted forty-three signers, including some old supporters of Sevier. Captain Sparks forsook the Governor's cause and left town.

Jackson did not desert the bench. On October fifth he presided at the trial of Stephen Duncan, whom a jury found not guilty of murder. On October sixth he presided at the trial of Joseph Duncan who was found "guilty of feloniously slaying . . . Joseph Remenhill." On October seventh John Stuart was acquitted of "house stealing." On October eighth a jury found John Childress guilty of murder.[28]

October ninth was Sunday again, and at the Sign of the Indian King Tavern Jackson found leisure to write Sevier what he said would be his last communication.

"In the publick streets of Knoxville you appeared to pant for combat. You ransacked the vocabulary of vulgarity. . . . You . . . took the sacred name of a lady in your polluted lips, and dared me publickly to challenge. . . . I have spoken for a place in the paper for the following advertisement:

"'To all who shall see these presents Greetings.

"'Know ye that I Andrew Jackson, do pronounce, publish, and declare to the world, that his excellency John Sevier . . . is a base coward and poltroon. He will basely insult, but has not the courage to repair. ANDREW JACKSON.'

"You may prevent the insertion of the above by meeting me in two hours after the receipt of this."[29]

No answer came in two hours. On the following morning Judge Jackson sentenced Joseph Duncan and John Childress to be hanged,[30] and returned to the Sign of the Indian King where a saucy but unsatisfactory note from Sevier was delivered by the Secretary of State.[31]

Jackson improved the rough draft of his proclamation and gave it to the *Gazette*, wherein it appeared on the following day at the customary rates for advertising. Knoxville was in a ferment. With one companion, Dr. Thomas J. Van Dyke of the Regular Army garrison at Kingston, Jackson set out for the Cherokee boundary at Southwest Point, in the belief that the ultimate insult of "publishing" would compel Sevier to follow.

For five days they encamped at the Point and had started to leave when Sevier appeared with several armed men. Andrew Greer rode ahead and addressed Jackson who suddenly left off speaking and drew a pistol, dismounted and drew a second pistol. Turning, Greer perceived Sevier "off his horse with his pistols in his hands advancing" on Jackson. Twenty steps apart they halted and began to abuse each other, "the Governor damn[ing] him to fire away." After a little of this both put away their arms. There were more words and Jackson rushed at Sevier saying he was going to cane him. Sevier drew his sword, "which frightened his horse and he ran away with the Governor's Pistols." Jackson drew a pistol and "the Governor went behind a tree and damned Jackson, did he want to fire on a naked man?" George Washington Sevier, the Governor's seventeen-year-old son, drew on Jackson and Doctor Van Dyke drew on Washington.[32]

Members of the Sevier party dashed up making amicable signs. They got the three men to put away their guns and suggested that the Governor relinquish the field, which he did, swearing at Jackson and receiving the Judge's comments in return as long as either could hear.

At Kingston an alert sentry shouted, "Turn out the guard, Governor of the State!" A sixteen-gun salute in his Excellency's honor[33] restored the poise of Nolichucky Jack.

CHAPTER VII

"Truxton" against "Ploughboy"

I

Andrew Jackson voted for Thomas Jefferson in 1796 and again in 1800 when, by a narrow squeak, some good came of it. Aaron Burr was the Republican vice-presidential nominee although, as the Constitution then read, only a tacit understanding distinguished candidates for president from those for vice-president. As Colonel Burr received the same number of votes in the Electoral College as Mr. Jefferson, the choice passed to the House of Representatives before whom Burr permitted himself to stand for the presidency, and thirty-six ballots were required to dismiss his ambition. Thus the new Administration took charge, embarrassed by a coolness between the two most exalted officers of the land. This failed, however, to retard the spirited fructification of republican principles in an order forbidding army officers to wear their hair in queues—a notable badge of reaction—and in the Louisiana Purchase. These topics Judge Jackson bracketed in a single communication to his President.

"Sir, ... The golden moment ... when all the Western Hemisphere rejoices at the Joyfull news of the cession of Louisiana, ... we hope will not be ... [marred] by the scene of an aged and meritorious officer ... before a court martial for the disobedience of an order to deprive him of the gift of nature ... worn by him both for ornament and convenience."[1] Colonel Thomas Butler had distinguished himself in the Revolution. President Washington sent him to Tennessee to expel settlers from Indian lands. The courtesy and courage with which the old soldier discharged his unpopular duty won the friendship of Jackson, opposed as he was to Federal collaboration in Indian matters. "Sir the removal of such an officer for ... his well known attachment to his locks, ... gray in the service of his country, opens a door for the greatest tyranny."

The morale of the Army seemed important to Jackson, for the

joyful news about Louisiana might entail a fight. Spain saw through the trick of Bonaparte, who had acquired the American colony only to derange a broad scheme of Spanish policy by selling out to the United States while the Spanish flag yet flew over New Orleans. Estéban Miró's successor made gestures that looked like resistance. Andrew Jackson made a gesture. Without instructions from the War Department and without cutting his hair, on the day he wrote the President concerning Colonel Butler, Jackson directed his militia "to be in order at a moment's warning to march."[2]

Spanish officialdom drew in its horns, however, and Brigadier-General James Wilkinson, author of the charges against Butler, floated down the river with a parcel of Regulars. Before a circle of unenthusiastic Creoles he unfurled the Stars and Stripes in front of the Cabildo at New Orleans.

2

A governor of the new acquisition was to be appointed and Jackson desired the post. It was important. A vast domain must be brought under our administration and a keen lookout kept for war with Spain.

Americanization of the illimitable Valley and its port of New Orleans, so profoundly altered the economic destinies of a continent that men stood breathless before the prospect. In a convulsion of speculation no scheme seemed too chimerical, no project too disproportionate to existing resources of capital to be undertaken with an enthusiasm that for the moment swept all before it. Jackson plunged in, dispatching John Coffee to offer twenty-five thousand dollars for certain salt springs "in the Illinoi" and to go as high as thirty-five thousand to get them. This came at a moment when Jackson was so strapped that to pay three hundred and seventy-five dollars "freitage" on five tons of iron he had bought in East Tennessee he pledged his salary certificates. At Hunter's Hill John Hutchings was loading fifty-six thousand and seventy-nine pounds of cotton and a consignment of skins for New Orleans which Jackson confessed must be sold "at any market [price] . . . to save ourselves." Yet plans were for continued expansion, Jackson himself departing for Philadelphia

OLD HICKORY

Painted in 1819 by John Vanderlyn in New York and placed in the City Hall where it still hangs. The head was made from life during Jackson's festive visit after his Florida campaign. John James Audubon, the ornithologist, posed for the body and in 1821 pronounced the whole the only good likeness of Jackson he had seen,

GENERAL JACKSON

From a painting executed at New Orleans in 1815 by John Wesley Jarvis who was in the city at the time of the battle. In 1819 Samuel Swartwout pronounced the likeness "inimitable."

to spend twelve thousand dollars for merchandise. He was concerned only over the thousand or fifteen hundred dollars ready money he must raise to bring it home.³

But the important thing he expected to bring home was the governorship of Louisiana which would end all his pecuniary difficulties. Jackson laid his route therefore by way of the new seat of government on the Potomac.

Mr. Jefferson had received Andrew Jackson's name, very respectably endorsed, but kept his counsel. Hopeful news intercepted the traveler, however, and he wrote Rachel to try to be cheerful until "I . . . return to your arms, dispel those clouds that hover around you and retire to some peaceful grove [in Louisiana] to spend your days in domestic quiet."⁴

In Washington Judge Jackson put up at Conrad's boarding house, the most presentable of six or seven inns at the foot of a grassy hill, wormed by paths leading to the unfinished Capitol. A miry road surmounting a gentler rise of ground a mile away revealed the Executive Mansion which Congressman Andrew Jackson had sought to deprive of fourteen thousand dollars' worth of furniture—a blank-looking edifice with pink plastered walls, striped in front by square white pillars hugging the wall in half relief. The pink house wore an air of abandonment and, indeed, had been forsaken in favor of the President's own thirty-one-room Monticello in which the architect had foreseen almost every human need except the cost of maintenance.

Judge Jackson did not go to Monticello. "A call under present existing circumstances might be construed as the act of a courteor . . . cringing for office."⁵ So the candidate posted to Philadelphia on a sick horse to dicker for queensware and calico, an occupation not made more congenial by receipt of intelligence that the governorship had gone to the peripatetic William Charles Cole Claiborne, who already had deserted Tennessee for the fresher field of Natchez. Yet the least intimation of resentment was precluded under the code by which Andrew Jackson lived and died, for Claiborne was his friend. After an extravagant purchase of parlor chairs "and a settee" for his wife, the empty-handed office-seeker started home to recast his plans.

3

The new furniture never saw the inside of the handsome house at Hunter's Hill. Swathed in "blanketts" it arrived with the rest of Jackson's goods in two keel boats at Johnson's landing, Nashville, in the middle of July, 1804. Jackson was already on the ground and the expense of transportation, one thousand six hundred and sixty-eight dollars and five cents, including twenty gallons of whisky to sustain a crew of fourteen on the sixteen-day pull from the mouth of the Cumberland,[6] had taken his last penny. Hutchings crowned this with a report of the utter failure of his crucial New Orleans expedition to realize the profits needed.

Jackson's fortunes were on the brink. He resigned from the bench[7] on which he had served for six years, relinquishing the office which, of all he ever held, afforded the greatest measure of satisfaction, excepting only his military career. He sold the apple of his eye, Hunter's Hill. "I [have] turned myself out of house and home . . . purely to meet my engagements."[8]

From Johnson's landing a brown road slanted up the rock-faced bluff, past a warehouse and a disused fort at the river's edge. A rabble of cabins escorted this path until it assumed the dignity of Market Street, accommodating ten buildings without crowding, five to a side and no two occupying the same level. Four were two stories high, seven were frame and two brick. De Monbreun's tap-room was stone, and its proprietor a son of the voyageur from Quebec who was the first white man to dwell permanently on the site of Nashville. Wooden awnings converted the fronts into shady lounging places. Horses switched flies and stamped dust at the hitching rails.

Market Street terminated in a square occupied by a stone courthouse, jail, whipping-post and stocks, and a shed where farmers sold their wares from wagons. A few primitive cedars intercepted the sun and the stumps of others were handy to sit on. Facing the square stood Talbot's and Winn's taverns and Parker's new and splendid Nashville Inn at which Jackson usually stayed when in town. Next to the Inn was a cockpit where Jackson would forget his troubles for an hour. He owned a bird named Bernadotte. "Twenty dollars on my Bernadotte! Who'll take me up?"[9]

John Coffee, who luckily had not purchased the salt springs, took charge of the keel boats, and discharging some cargo that Jackson had carried as a favor to Nashville friends, pushed up the looping Cumberland to Hunter's Hill. If the boats were unloaded there, it was only to pack again and abandon the place,[10] already sold, in favor of a six-hundred-and-forty-acre tract, called the Hermitage, two miles nearer Nashville by road, but fifteen miles nearer by the river. This fertile rolling property Jackson had acquired at the height of his land-hunger days in 1795. Adjoining were six hundred and forty acres where Lewis Robards had tried to make a home in Tennessee for Rachel Donelson. In 1796 Jackson had added this to the Hermitage estate, but in his present extremity had been obliged to lump it with Hunter's Hill in the painful sale to Edward Ward.

A thousand young peach and apple trees gave a pleasing aspect to the Hermitage land, but Rachel's Philadelphia settee and her harpsichord from Hunter's Hill had hard work to give the blockhouse that became their new abode a look of residential formality. This did not disturb a frontier woman whose gayest memories recalled many blockhouses not unlike this—one great room downstairs, puncheon floor, hewn joists overhead, blackened by the smoke of the fireplace that would devour a cord of wood on a wintry day, two rooms above and detached kitchen. Twenty-five feet away and connected by a passage Jackson built another log house for guests. The "manse" at Hunter's Hill had harbored years of loneliness, and Rachel left it not unhappier for a change of fortunes that promised to keep her husband at her side.

4

Thomas Watson had been supplanted as Jackson's mercantile partner by young John Hutchings, whose principal qualification appears to have been that he was one of Rachel's nephews. The firm reopened at Clover Bottom where the Lebanon Road crossed Stone's River, three miles from the Hermitage and eight miles from Nashville. Branch stores were retained at Lebanon and Gallatin. Broadcloth, costing five dollars a yard in Philadelphia, brought fifteen in Tennessee. Rifles, skillets, grindstones, salt, coffee, calico and allspice went in trade for cotton, tobacco, pork, pelts and negroes that Jackson & Hutchings expected to turn into cash in New Orleans. "Sales are dull, small quantities of Cotton planted . . . [but] our A. Jackson . . . [having] made sale of his possessions . . . we flatter ourselves [we] will be able to meet all our debts next spring."[11]

They might have done so had the senior partner been content to concentrate his talents upon the conduct of the store. The spring of 1805, however, found our A. Jackson caught up in another train of projects. An intoxicating incense of speculation perfumed the air. From the Upper Louisiana wilderness came a rumpled sheet with four scrawled lines that must have cost its author as much labor as a day in his pits.

"Ste Genevieve 28th Feby 1805
"Sir I have discovered a Lead mine on White river
"Wm Hickman"[12]

But Jackson's new adventure lay nearer the home and as it concerned horses, nearer the heart. William Preston Anderson and his brother Patton[13] had begun the construction of a race course on the beautiful oval meadow a few hundred yards from Jackson & Hutchings's establishment—the land upon which Rachel Jackson's father had encamped his large family at the conclusion of the voyage in the *Adventure*. Apparently the Andersons got beyond their depth for Jackson and Hutchings took over a two-thirds interest in the race course and, as was Jackson's way, enlarged the undertaking. A small army of workmen fell to building a tavern, booths for hucksters and a keel-boat yard.

Thus old debts were unpaid, fresh obligations contracted. Nor was the dull state of sales all that Andrew Jackson found wrong with the cotton trade, on which he placed his principal anticipations for recruited fortunes. The cotton trade was becoming an intricate operation with the planter at one end and the manufacturer in England, or New England, at the other. Between them cropped a facile corps of factors, agents, jobbers, bankers, insurers and shippers, speaking a strange tongue in the performance of mysterious services by which the isolated planter saw his anticipated profits quartered and halved. The run of planters, encompassed by the system, submitted.

But not Jackson, "a cool shrewd man of business . . . rarely wrong; but whether wrong or right hard to be shaken." And harder still to be imposed upon. "He knew his mind. . . . 'I will take or give so much; if you will trade, say.' . . . A man . . . utterly honest, *naturally* honest; would beggar himself to pay a debt and did so."[14]

And just as ardently would he resent a charge he felt unjust.

"I am truly sorry," wrote Planter Jackson, "that any of our cotton has taken its direction to Liverpool. . . . The expense will destroy the profits."[15] This transaction had been made at New Orleans by John Hutchings who had a knack for doing things almost right. The general agents for Jackson & Hutchings were Boggs, Davidson & Company, widely known cotton brokers of Philadelphia who, like most eastern firms, maintained a junior partner at New Orleans. After further inquiry Jackson accused this partner, N. Davidson, of hoodwinking Hutchings into the English shipment of one hundred bales. One hundred and thirty-three bales, however, had gone "in the brigg Maria" to Philadelphia, as Jackson desired. But the invoice showing their disposition upon arrival reached Clover Bottom two bales short and further diminished by deductions for insurance, interest and commissions which Jackson thought excessive.[16] Mr. Davidson sought to lay the blame on Hutchings. Jackson gave him a short answer: "You are regardless of truth . . . and . . . *we shall meet.*"[17]

5

On the west bank of the Hudson an acquaintance of Andrew Jackson had already "met" his man. Indicted for murder, he hid on an island off the Georgia coast to while away the warm days composing whimsical letters to his daughter and revolving audacious courses in his mind. Congress convening in December of 1804, Aaron Burr came out of concealment and with flawless composure resumed his functions as Vice-President of the United States. The Senate never had a better moderator, and at this session the trial of Supreme Court Justice Chase made the post one of conspicuous responsibility. It would have taken an unreasonable enemy to complain of Burr's conduct of this trial, marked, as a spectator said, by the impartiality of an angel and the rigor of a devil.

As March fourth, ending his term of office, approached, the Vice-President took leave of the Senate with words so dignified and, for one of his position, so moving that hearers, not the partizans of Aaron Burr, shed tears. Writing playfully to Theodosia of the legal proceedings that imperiled his safety, he vanished to reappear on the safe ground of the West.

This seemed normal. It would be nearly correct to say that Eastern disapproval constituted an endorsement in Western eyes. Burr's duel with General Hamilton had, if anything, enhanced a reputation already high in the West for the part he had played as a Senator in obtaining the admission to the Union of Tennessee. Moreover, the West prided itself as a land of regeneration for victims of inhospitable fortune.

Aaron Burr chose to exploit these facilities as no man had attempted before. Previous to leaving Washington he had surveyed the field: vast Louisiana, annexed at the displeasure of England, Spain and most of its inhabitants; Kentucky and Tennessee, lately involved in an intrigue of secession. In Washington he had whispered to the British and Spanish ministers a scheme for separating the Mississippi Valley from the Union, had spoken with a visiting junta of angry Creoles and with Brigadier-General James Wilkinson who had raised the Stars and Stripes at New Orleans. To each he had unfolded an enterprise different in detail.

Cincinnati and Louisville acclaimed the traveler. At Frankfort he was the guest of United States Senator Brown. He saw many of the leading Kentuckians, and particularly those concerned with the old Spanish plot. For public purposes Colonel Burr's mission was to recruit colonists for a Ouichata River tract in Louisiana, which all but the very naïve took as a subterfuge for a military invasion of Texas, a stroke entirely compatible with the conscience of the West. In private audiences there was a story for the palate of every hearer: England was supporting him or not; war with Spain inevitable or impossible, as the needs of the instant might require. He would seize Mobile or all West Florida, Texas or all Mexico—anything to be agreeable, or to win promises of men and of money. The certain intent of a scheme so elastic has not been ascertained to date, but the conquest of Mexico with the possible adhesion of the lower Mississippi Valley to form an empire over which Aaron I should preside with Princess Theodosia, is a vision contrived, perhaps only half seriously, for a dazzled coterie of his intimates.

After the brilliant sojourn in Kentucky, Burr could think of but one more preliminary before dropping down the river to sow his seeds in the fertile soil of Louisiana. He made a side trip to Nashville, principally to renew a half-forgotten senatorial acquaintance with Andrew Jackson.

6

Their meeting arranged itself. On May 29, 1805, all the Cumberland turned out to greet the distinguished caller. Mr. Jackson rode to town early, proposed a ringing toast at a public dinner, and carried off the honored visitor to the Hermitage. Until he heard the name in Frankfort, Andrew Jackson probably had not crossed Aaron Burr's mind in all of seven years, but the perfect houseguest was not the one to permit a hint of that. He was glad he had come. His Kentucky friends had not mistaken the latent strength of this rangy, restless Tennessean.

On the other hand Andrew Jackson remembered Aaron Burr very well: his championship of the cause of Tennessee in the tense controversy over admission to the Union, his dextrous leadership of the Republican bloc in the Senate. And perhaps as distinctly as anything else the frontiersman remembered the brilliant dinner of 1797 in Philadelphia, for he had not ceased to speak of it when the subject of table wines came under review. Jackson did his honest best to reciprocate this hospitality. The result deserves mention for Aaron Burr, as competent as any American of his generation to pass on such matters, was captivated.

"I could stay a month with pleasure,"[18] he privately assured his daughter.

Five days were enough. Jackson was his—on the basis of a highly correct colonization proposal to cloak a spring at Texas when (the now "inevitable") war with Spain should become an actuality.[19] As a Westerner with some practical knowledge of land settlement and military expeditions, Jackson did not think everything would go off as simply as Burr had outlined,[20] but the end was so laudable that he could not withhold his patronage. The most promising thing was Burr's assurance of the secret complicity of Henry Dearborn, the Secretary of War.[21]

In New Orleans the late Vice-President spoke French with the natives, charmed every one, and, upon his departure, the Ursuline sisters prayed for him. It was no longer necessary to seek out men or to initiate proposals. Men sought him. In August he was again on the Cumberland. "For a week I have been lounging at the house of General Jackson, once a lawyer, after a judge, now a planter; a man of intelligence, and one of those prompt, frank, ardent souls whom I love to meet. The General has no children, but two lovable nieces [of Rachel] made a visit of some days, greatly to my amusement. If I had time I would describe these girls, for they deserve it."[22] Showered with attentions the conspirator slipped eastward. Diplomatic and financial aid from abroad was his next requirement; and the facile Colonel was prepared, in a pinch, to reshape his program to accommodate Spain should England fail him. In the West, however, the stage had been set, with Andrew Jackson impulsively in the train of Aaron Burr's dark attractive star.

7

The duties of hospitality had distracted General Jackson from his always-heavy correspondence. Edward Ward, one thousand four hundred and fifty-one dollars and eighty and a half cents behind schedule with his payments for Hunter's Hill, sought to discharge a part of the arrears with negroes. "Had negroes been offered," Jackson wrote as soon as his guest had gone, "before Mr. Hutchings descended the river with negroes for sale they would have been recd." But cash had been promised, and now Jackson must have it. "As to your offer of giving property at valuation . . . if my creditors would receive their debts thus I would meet every demand in four hours." Jackson repeated that his "sacrifice . . . of house and home" had been to pay his debts. "Creditors are growing clamorous and I must have money."[23]

Jackson did not exaggerate. "as a Considerable time has Elapsed Sence we have had the pleasure to hear from you & your acc^t. still unsettled . . . Sorry we are to say you have betrayed that Confidence we had placed in you."[24] That from one Philadelphia wholesaler. This from another: "we certainly have expected and ought, according to promise to have our money . . . and we cannot help thinking from the Character and knowledge we have of General Jackson but what . . . [it] must have been sent. If not, we must beg . . ."[25]

8

Moreover there had been other disappointments, equally annoying. In the spring races of 1805 over the Hartsville course, Lazarus Cotton's gelding Greyhound had beaten Jackson's Indian Queen in three heats. This was more than a blow to the flat purse of Jackson. It was a blow to his pride. The meeting had been a thoroughgoing triumph for Greyhound. He had won every race he entered, including one with Truxton, a Virginia horse of splendid repute. The victory had stripped Truxton's owner, Major John Verell, clean and his last asset, this big bay race horse, was about to be seized for debt.

Jackson yearned to avenge his own reverse. He had seen Truxton run. He sized up the stallion which stood fifteen hands and three inches high, was beautifully formed and had white hind feet. He searched his pedigree: got by imported Diomed out of Nancy Coleman, in the stable of Thomas Goode, Chesterfield County, Virginia. He believed Truxton had lost to Greyhound because of ill-condition. Hard up as he was, Jackson made Verell an offer of fifteen hundred dollars for Truxton on these terms: Jackson to assume Verell's debts to the extent of eleven hundred and seventy dollars and give three geldings worth three hundred and thirty dollars, with a bonus of two other geldings should Truxton "win a purse in the fall ensuing."[26]

By this proposal Andrew Jackson staked much on his knowledge of horse-flesh, for he was near, if not within, jail bounds for debt. But as far back as he could remember, he had been accustomed to trust his knowledge of horses and only once—when he had taken his grandfather's legacy to the New Market track in Charleston—had it seriously failed him.

So he bought Truxton and matched him immediately for a return race with Greyhound at Hartsville for a side bet of five thousand dollars. How Andrew Jackson raised five thousand dollars at this critical juncture is a point the present reviewer is unable to clarify. But he raised it and with Verell undertook to put Truxton in shape for the race. Jackson's training methods were severe. He worked a horse to the limit of endurance, but somehow implanted in him a will to win, a circumstance which, as much as anything, epitomizes the character and elucidates the singular attainments of Andrew Jackson.

The race was the last event of an already memorable season and all Middle Tennessee was there. Greyhound went to the post the favorite on the strength of his previous victory and the talk that Jackson had worn out Truxton in training.

Betting had been heavy. "Hundreds of horses," wrote Congressman Balie Peyton who had the story from Jackson himself, and "numerous 640 acre tracts were staked."[27] Jackson accepted fifteen hundred dollars of additional wagers in "wearing apparel." His friend Patton Anderson, "after betting all his money and the horse he rode," put up fifteen horses belonging to others, "many of them having ladies saddles on their backs." "Now, I would not have done that," said Jackson,[28] making a fine distinction on the side of abstract morality. It is likely that the horses of Mrs. Jackson and her favorite niece, Rachel Hays, were among the fifteen. These ladies were ardent patrons of the turf, and once rode home from Clover Bottom without their gloves.

But everything turned out all right this time. Truxton won and Anderson treated "to a whole barrel of cider and a basket full of ginger cakes."[29]

This victory did more than ease the finances and replenish the wardrobe of Andrew Jackson. It established him in the first file of Western turfmen, a position he held for more than twenty years, and which, if Andrew Jackson had achieved no other claims to recognition, would have perpetuated his name in the fragrant memorabilia of stud-book, race path and paddock.

After beating Greyhound, Jackson immediately bought him and added him to his stable at Clover Bottom. Captain Joseph Erwin, of Nashville, offered to run his Tanner at Clover Bottom's fall meeting in 1805 against all comers for five thousand dollars.

Jackson accepted and trained sixteen horses, Truxton and Greyhound among them. On the day of the race Greyhound was led out on the track. He won in three heats.[30]

Since his defeat of Greyhound the stud fees of Truxton had been an appreciable source of revenue to General Jackson, thus cutting the income Captain Erwin derived from his famous stallion Ploughboy. After the defeat of Tanner Erwin desired more than ever to reestablish the reputation of Ploughboy, and matched him against Truxton for the best two of three two-mile heats, two thousand dollars side, eight hundred forfeit. Four persons were interested in the stake on Truxton's side—Jackson, Verell, William Preston Anderson and Captain Samuel Pryor, who was to train Truxton. On Ploughboy's side were Erwin and his son-in-law, Charles Dickinson. Before the day of the race, Ploughboy having gone lame, Erwin withdrew him and paid the forfeit.

9

Captain Patton Anderson of Bachelor Hall was as free with the reputations of his adversaries as with the horses of his friends. Shortly after the payment of the forfeit, he entertained a gathering at Bell Brothers' store in Nashville with an unpleasant story to the effect that Erwin and Dickinson had attempted to discharge their obligation with notes, not due or payable, as had been agreed. When Dickinson heard of this he asked youthful Thomas Swann, who had been present, to repeat what Anderson had said. The notice delighted Mr. Swann. It was a feather in the hat of a cub lawyer, newly come from the College of William and Mary with a lofty Tidewater attitude toward the backwoods, to be drawn into a gentlemen's controversy involving such personages as Charles Dickinson and Andrew Jackson.

As every one knew, relations between these two were strained already. Dickinson was twenty-seven years old, a man of fashion and success. John Marshall had been his preceptor in the law. At Nashville his polished manners had won many friends, but lately there had been a rift when, in convivial company, Mr. Dickinson made an allusion to Rachel Donelson's matrimonial history. Confronted by Jackson he had apologized, saying that he was drunk when he spoke. But Jackson soon heard of a repetition of the offense and begged Captain Erwin, an old acquaintance, to restrain his daughter's husband "in time." "I wish no quarrel with him," said Jackson, adding that Dickinson was being *"used* by my enemies,"[31] the Sevierites. The stimulus to talk afforded by the Sevier affray had shown Jackson that public quarrels were not the best means of casting a blanket of oblivion over the chapter in his marital relations that he wished forgotten.

In this situation Thomas Swann, whose law practise was not a burden, rode to Clover Bottom. A Saturday crowd was loafing, and probably drinking, about the fire at the store. Patton Anderson started to repeat his story of the forfeiture when Jackson interrupted to say that it was incorrect. The General then gave an account of what had happened which differed little from Anderson's, except by the absence of an imputation of trickery. Jackson said Erwin first had proffered eight hundred dollars in notes not due. Jackson protested that he must have at least half in matured notes, as Verell and Pryor needed money for their share. Dickinson then offered notes of this character for four hundred dollars, and Jackson accepted Erwin's notes for the balance[32]—all being easy to understand in a region where banks were unknown, currency scarce and notes of hand a common media in "cash" transactions of more than a few dollars. Jackson's recital was a mild rebuke to Anderson whose brother, Preston, had been present at the payment. Nevertheless, Swann shouldered into the conversation, and ran to Dickinson with an exasperating version of it. When Dickinson applied for an explanation, Jackson told him that some one had been retailing "a damned lye."

This brought from Swann a letter which usage marked as a curtain-raiser for a challenge. Jackson's reply began firmly but moderately, as a man of experience addressing a youthful stranger, to the effect that offense had been taken where none was intended, and that Swann was being used as a catspaw. Then came the thunderclap. *"The base poltroon and cowardly talebearer will always act* in the background. you can apply the latter to Mr. Dickinson. . . . I write it for his eye."[33]

Two missives reached Clover Bottom in answer. The first, from

Dickinson, called Jackson an equivocator and a coward and dared him to challenge. Learning that before dispatching these provocative lines Mr. Dickinson had boarded a boat for New Orleans, Jackson did not reply. The second note was from Young Swann. "Think not I am to be intimidated by your threats. No power terrestrial shall prevent the settled purpose of my soul. . . . My friend the bearer of this is authorized to make complete arrangements in the field of honor."[34]

Jackson sent word that he would not fight Swann, but would come to town and cane him for his impudence, which he did, though the devastating effect desired was modified when the General's spur caught against a chair and tripped him backward almost into the fireplace of Winn's Tavern.[35]

Jackson and his friends hoped that this might end matters, but they were disappointed. Nathaniel A. McNairy, a younger brother of Judge McNairy, immediately presented himself in Swann's interest, demanding "satisfaction" for the caning. Jackson declined. "He would not degrade himself" by accepting a challenge from one "he knew not as a gentleman." But he offered alternatives. He would repair to "any sequestered grove" and shoot it out with Swann, with the understanding that the affair should not be known as a gentleman's duel; or he would meet McNairy in a duel. McNairy repelled these proposals in a scene that furnished slender guarantees of future peace.[36] Moreover, the word had reached Nashville that on his way south Dickinson was entertaining himself with pistol practise.

The most even-tempered and least selfish of Andrew Jackson's lifelong friends was John Coffee, a big awkward man, careless of dress, slow of speech, but kindly, tactful and wise. Coffee had witnessed the assault on Swann. He had heard the conversation with McNairy and the tidings of Dickinson's target exercises. Before the eventful day was over he, John Verell and Jackson sat down together. Coffee produced a paper. "General Jackson and Major John Verell covenant with each other, that the first of them that is known to drink ardent spirits . . . is to pay the other a full and compleat suit of clothes . . . this 24th day of January, 1806."[37] It was a bargain. Coffee folded the paper and put it in his wallet.

10

Thomas Swann transferred the controversy to the columns of the *Impartial Review and Cumberland Repository,* Nashville's only newspaper, taking nearly a column to vindicate his position. General Jackson replied with two columns (the editor was one of Rachel's innumerable relatives), paying his respects to McNairy as a meddler and to Swann as "the puppet and lying valet for a worthless, drunken, blackguard scoundrel, . . . Charles Dickinson."[38] Young McNairy published a lively retort, involving John Coffee who challenged. At the meeting McNairy unintentionally fired before the word, wounding Coffee in the thigh. In reparation he offered to lay down his pistol and give his adversary an extra shot.

Clearly Jackson was reserving himself for the return of Mr. Dickinson, a circumstance which moved venerable General James Robertson, Nashville's founder, to take pen in trembling hand and write a long and painful letter. He begged Jackson not to fight. "Your courage . . . & reputation" did not require that mode of vindication. The old gentleman had the delicacy not to mention Rachel, but any issue of events, he argued, would militate against Jackson. Should he lose, "your Country besides . . . your Famnley" would suffer. Should he win it would be a Pyrrhic triumph. Jackson was besought to reflect on the gravity of taking "the life of your Fellow Mortal. might this not make you miserable so long as you lived, instant Colo Burr. I suppose if dueling Could be Jestifiable it must have bin in his case and it is beleaved he has not had ease in mind since the fatal hour. . . . Once for all let me tell you . . . avoid . . . a duel."[39]

But events were in the full cry, each day adding to the public excitement. The match between Truxton and Ploughboy was rearranged, with feeling between the backers of the rival stallions more tense than ever. "Gentlemen . . . would do well," counseled the *Impartial Review,* "not to put their mares to horses until after the race, as at that time will be seen . . . whether or not *Ploughboy* merits the attention of sportsmen and gentlemen breeders." On the day[40] Coffee met McNairy the *Review* was able to announce the particulars of the event following:

"On Thursday the 3d of April next will be run the greatest and most interesting race ever run in the Western country between *Gen. Jackson's* horse
TRUXTON
6 years old carrying 124 pounds and *Capt. Joseph Erwin's* horse
PLOUGHBOY
8 years old carrying 130 lbs. . . . For the sum of 3,000 dollars."

On the great day all roads led to Clover Bottom where Jackson surveyed "the largest concourse of people I ever saw assembled, unless in an army."

Had they come to witness his triumph or his humiliation? About Truxton's stall a knot of excited men talked and gestured. In the midst of them stood Jackson, his long face very grave. Two days before, in the course of his rigorous training, Truxton had "got a serious hurt to his thigh, which occasioned it to swell verry much."[41] No amount of liniments or rubbing or stable lore had been able to reduce the swelling. Clearly the big stallion was not himself and the positive Anderson, horse-wise Verell, conservative Coffee and Trainer Sam Pryor, in fact all of Jackson's friends, recommended that he pay the forfeit and postpone the race. Jackson went over his horse again, minutely—spoke to him, stroked his nose. When Andrew Jackson spoke to a horse he looked in its eyes, as he looked at men. No, gentlemen, he said, Truxton would run.

The Erwin stable was jubilant. Major William Terrell Lewis rushed out to offer any amount on Ploughboy. Two thousand dollars were covered. Truxton's supporters were slow to wager. They had come on the field ready to back their choice with everything they had. One pen was filled with horses, brought for the purpose, another with negroes, chuckling and nudging one another in expansive enjoyment of their association with an important event; but the injured thigh chilled the ardor of Truxton partizans. Ultimately they risked ten thousand dollars, a large sum, but Jackson said it would have been twice as much had his horse been in condition.

The contenders were led out under a lowering sky. The heats were to be two miles. "All things prepared, the horses started . . . Truxton under every disadvantage." But he slipped into the lead, held it, increased it, and passed the finish line going away.

The victory had been dearly bought. The bay horse limped on his injured hind leg. A front leg had gone lame. Upon one of his good legs "the plate had sprung and lay across the foot." It did not seem that he could last another heat.

A hard-beating rain came as the horses returned to the post. The drum tapped. Through the April downpour the crowd saw the long bony body of the bay glide ahead of Ploughboy with effortless ease. The Erwin phalanx was speechless. Truxton ran away from their horse, winning "without whip or spur [by] sixty yards . . . in 3 m. 59 seconds. by two watches, by another 3 m 59 1-2, by Blufords pendulum 4 m. 1 second, by one other in 3 m. 57 seconds."[42]

The sublimity of this triumph sent the spirit roaring above the dusty vexations of the trading house with its cloud of duns. Something of the inextinguishable will he had imparted to Truxton Andrew Jackson dreamed now of imparting to armies.

II

What more likely moment for a skilful letter from Aaron Burr? "You have doubtless before this time been convinced that we are to have no war"—with Spain, upon which all of Burr's plans, as Jackson understood them, depended. "The object of the administration appears to be to treat for the purchase of the Floridas . . . This . . . is a secret to those only who are best entitled to know it—our citizens."

Yet a timid administration which shrank from an easy war of conquest was backing into a dangerous war of defense. "Notwithstanding the pacific temper of our government there is a great reason to expect hostility, arising out of the expedition under General Miranda." This flaming South American patriot had equipped ships at New York for a descent upon Venezuela. "And it would not surprise me if . . . Paris and Madrid" should retaliate by seizing "our vessels in the ports of these kingdoms" and moving against New Orleans.

Any military force to meet this invasion should "come from your side of the mountains. . . . I am glad to learn that you had your division reviewed; but you ought" to do more. "Your country is full of fine materials for an army, and I have often said a brigade could be raised in West Tennessee that would drive double their number of Frenchmen off the earth. I take the liberty of recommending to you to make out a list of officers from colonel down to ensign for one or two regiments, and with whom you would trust your life and your honor. If you will transmit to me that list, I will"—easily now, Colonel Burr—"I will, in case troops should be called for, recommend it to the Secretary of War."[43]

Burr got his list.

12

At New Orleans John Hutchings awaited a barge flotilla laden with cotton, barrel staves and negroes, upon which the year's profits depended. Jackson penned him a great account of the horse race, receiving in return a story of the barges' delay and a falling market. But New Orleans knew of Truxton's victory! "I am truly sorry that mr. Dickerson . . . left here before this pleasing nues reached me, so I might have had the pleasur of seeing . . . [his] aggoney."[44]

On May twentieth Mr. Dickinson was in Nashville. On the twenty-first he handed a "card" to Editor Eastin of the *Review*, whose next number was due to appear on May twenty-fourth. On the twenty-second General Thomas Overton, a militia brigadier and a brother of Jackson's intimate, John Overton, took the word to Clover Bottom. Jackson bade him read the article and bring back the gist of it.

Overton returned, his face flushed with excitement. "It's a piece that can't be passed over. General, you must challenge."[45]

Jackson rode to the newspaper office and read the piece himself. Though rather long and wordy, the last paragraph came to the point. The "Major General . . . of the Mero district . . . [is] a worthless scoundrel, a poltroon and a coward." After which the writer airily announced his departure "the first of next week for Maryland."[46]

On the day before publication Overton carried Jackson's challenge to Dickinson, whose response is a model of its kind.

"May 23d, 1806
"Gen Andrew Jackson,
    "Sir, Your note of this morning is received, and your request shall be granted. My friend who hands you this will make the necessary arrangements. I am etc.
"CHARLES DICKINSON."[47]

CHAPTER VIII

A Long Spoon

I

On Thursday, May 29, 1806, Andrew Jackson rose at five o'clock, and after breakfast told Rachel that he would be gone for a couple of days and meanwhile he might have some trouble with Mr. Dickinson. Rachel probably knew what the trouble would be and she did not ask. Rachel had had her private channels of information concerning the Sevier affray. At six-thirty Jackson joined Overton at Nashville. Overton had the pistols. With three others they departed for the Kentucky line.[1]

Mr. Dickinson and eight companions were already on the road. "Good-by, darling," he told his young wife. "I shall be sure to be at home to-morrow evening." This confidence was not altogether assumed. He was a snap shot. At the word of command and firing apparently without aim, he could put four balls in a mark twenty-four feet away, each ball touching another. The persistent tradition on the countryside, that to worry Jackson he left several such examples of his marksmanship along the road, is unconfirmed by any member of the Dickinson or Jackson parties. But the story that he had offered on the streets of Nashville to wager he would kill Jackson at the first fire was vouchsafed by John Overton, the brother of Jackson's second, a few days after the duel.

Jackson said he was glad that "the other side" had started so early. It was a guarantee against further delay. Jackson had chafed over the seven days that had elapsed since the acceptance of the challenge. At their first interview, Overton and Dr. Hanson Catlett, Mr. Dickinson's second, had agreed that the meeting should be on Friday, May thirtieth, near Harrison's Mills on Red River just beyond the Kentucky boundary. Jackson protested at once. He did not wish to ride forty miles to preserve the fiction of a delicate regard for Tennessee's unenforceable statute against dueling. He did not wish to wait a week for something that could be done in a few hours. Dickinson's excuse was that he desired to borrow a pair of pistols. Overton offered the choice of Jackson's pistols, pledging Jackson to the use of the other. These were the weapons that had been employed by Coffee and McNairy.

As they rode Jackson talked a great deal, scrupulously avoiding the subject that burdened every mind. Really, however, there was nothing more to be profitably said on that head. General Overton was a Revolutionary soldier of long acquaintance with the Code. With his principal he had canvassed every possible aspect of the issue forthcoming. "Distance . . . twenty-four feet; the parties to stand facing each other, with their pistols down perpendicularly. When they are READY, the single word FIRE! to be given; at which they are to fire as soon as they please. Should either fire before the word is given we [the seconds] pledge ourselves to shoot him down instantly." Jackson was neither a quick shot, nor an especially good one for the western country. He had decided not to compete with Dickinson for the first fire. He expected to be hit, perhaps badly. But he counted on the resources of his will to sustain him until he could aim deliberately and shoot to kill, if it were the last act of his life.

On the first leg of the ride they traversed the old Kentucky Road, the route by which, fifteen years before, Andrew Jackson had carried Rachel Robards from her husband's home, the present journey being a part of the long sequel to the other. Jackson rambled on in a shrill voice. Thomas Jefferson was "the best Republican in theory and the worst in practice" he had ever seen. And he lacked courage. How long were we to support the affronts of England—impressment of seamen, cuffing about of our ocean commerce? Perhaps as long as Mr. Jefferson stayed in office. Well, that would be two years, and certainly his successor should be a stouter man. "We must fight England again. In the last war I was not old enough to be any account." He prayed that the next might come "before I get too old to fight."

General Overton asked how old Jackson reckoned he would have to be for that. In England's case about a hundred, Jackson said.

He spoke of Burr. A year ago, this day, Jackson had borne him from the banquet in Nashville to the Hermitage. He recalled their first meeting in 1797 when both were in Congress. Jackson also met General Hamilton that winter. "Personally, no gentleman could help liking Hamilton. But his political views were all English." At heart a monarchist. "Why, did he not urge Washington to take a crown!"

Burr also had his failings. He had made a mistake, observed Jackson with admirable detachment, a political mistake, when he fought Hamilton. And about his Western projects the General was none too sanguine. Burr relied overmuch on what others told him. Besides, there was Jefferson to be reckoned with. "Burr is as far from a fool as I ever saw, and yet he is as easily fooled as any man I ever knew."

The day was warm, and a little after ten o'clock the party stopped for refreshment. Jackson took a mint julep, ate lightly and rested until mid-afternoon. The party reached Miller's Tavern in Kentucky about eight o'clock. After a supper of fried chicken, waffles, sweet potatoes and coffee, Jackson repaired to the porch to chat with the inn's company. No one guessed his errand. At ten o'clock he knocked the ashes from his pipe and went to bed. Asleep in ten minutes, he had to be roused at five in the morning.

2

The parties met on the bank of the Red River at a break in a poplar woods. Doctor Catlett won the toss for choice of position, but as the sun had not come through the trees this signified nothing. The giving of the word fell to Overton. Jackson's pistols were to be used after all, Dickinson taking his pick. The nine-inch barrels were charged with ounce balls of seventy caliber. The ground was paced off, the principals took their places. Jackson wore a dark-blue frock coat and trousers of the same material; Mr. Dickinson a shorter coat of blue, and gray trousers.

"Gentlemen, are you ready?" called General Overton.

"Ready," said Dickinson quickly.

"Yes, sir," said Jackson.

"*Fere!*" cried Overton in the Old-Country accent.

Dickinson fired almost instantly. A fleck of dust rose from Jackson's coat and his left hand clutched his chest. For an instant he thought himself dying, but, fighting for self-command, slowly he raised his pistol.

Dickinson recoiled a step horror-stricken. "My God! Have I missed him?"

Overton presented his pistol. "Back to the mark, sir!"

Dickinson folded his arms. Jackson's spare form straightened. He aimed. There was a hollow "clock" as the hammer stopped at half-cock. He drew it back, sighted again and fired. Dickinson swayed to the ground.

As they reached the horses Overton noticed that his friend's left boot was filled with blood. "Oh, I believe that he pinked me," said Jackson quickly, "but I don't want those people to know," indicating the group that bent over Dickinson. Jackson's surgeon found that Dickinson's aim had been perfectly true, but he had judged the position of Jackson's heart by the set of his coat, and Jackson wore his coats loosely on account of the excessive slenderness of his figure. "But I should have hit him," he exclaimed, "if he had shot me through the brain."

With a furrow through his bowels Charles Dickinson tossed in agony until evening when friends eased him with a story that Jackson had a bullet in his breast and was dying. At ten o'clock he asked who had put out the light.

Rachel heard the news and fell on her knees weeping. "Oh, God have pity on the poor wife"—Mrs. Dickinson was with child—"pity on the babe in her womb."

3

Andrew Jackson had kept his friend, George W. Campbell, in Congress, but he could make little headway against Sevier, fortified in the governorship and licking his lips in anticipation of the fight for a fifth term against an opposition whose leader had too many irons in the fire. In the national theater Jackson's criticism of the foreign policy of the Administration had been similarly barren of result, though its tone was that of the growing voice of the West. An imperious championship of Colonel Butler, of uncut hair, had been without avail, Mr. Jefferson countenancing a court martial which disclosed a diffidence toward authority extending, alas, further than a mellow attachment to his queue. Now, despite personal misgivings, Jackson espoused the cause of Aaron Burr whose cloudy moves fell more and more under the critical scrutiny of the Government.

Nor did the smoke that curled from the poplar clearing minister to the renown of the militia general. The dead man's friends were numerous and respectable. Some also were friends of Jackson whose obdurate pride disguised the serious nature of his wound. "Oh, he pinked me," was the frivolous concession that left a public, devoured by curiosity, to turn elsewhere for details, and to hear them from Dickinson partizans: Jackson, trivially wounded, taking "illiberal and unjust advantage" of a defenseless man.[2] Jackson misled his closest friend in Tennessee, John Overton, as to the extent of his injury,[3] and neither by word nor sign did he imply that he had killed Charles Dickinson from any motive more presentable before morality than a race-track row.

The funeral had been largely attended. All the Sevierites were there. A mass meeting followed at which a petition, bearing seventy-two names, was presented to the *Impartial Review* asking the editor to dress his paper in mourning "as a tribute of respect for the memory, and regret for the untimely death of Mr. Charles Dickinson." It was proposed, however, to publish the names of only five or six signers as representative of a much larger number. At this Jackson bestirred himself. From his bed he wrote Eastin that a publication "so novel" should be accompanied by the names of all its sponsors, "that the public might judge whether the true motive of the signers were a tribute of respect to the deceased or something else." When the editor sent word that identities would be disclosed, the Sevierites took cover, and twenty-six names were withdrawn. But forty-six signers stood their ground, including such old supporters of Jackson as Alexander Craighead and Dr. Felix Robertson, a son of Nashville's founder.[4]

Summer dragged on. The barge flotilla en route to New Orleans was scattered by a storm, only four out of seven boats reaching a bad market. Jackson's wound healed slowly, with Dickinson's bullet too close to the heart to be removed. September brought cooler weather and signs of activity. "Col. Burr is with me; he arrived last night. . . . Say to Gen. O[verton], that I shall expect to see him here tomorrow with you. . . . Say to Gen. Robertson . . . I know . . . he will be happy in joining in any thing that will show a mark of respect to this worthy visitant."[5]

The mark of respect took the form of a reception at Talbot's Hotel at which Jackson introduced Burr to the company. They entered arm in arm, the host an inch over six feet tall, his guest about four inches over five. Ladies exclaimed at the courtly appearance their General made in the uniform he wore more often now, an appearance nothing over-shadowed by propinquity to one of the most engaging gentlemen of his day. That night Jackson indited a memorandum to his militia officers of so unconfidential a nature that a copy was sent to the *Review*. Spanish troops were "encamped within the limits of our government . . . within the Territory of New Orleans!!! . . . They [have] imprisoned . . . five of the good citizens of the United States" and "cut down and carried off" an American flag. Tennesseans must hold themselves "in complete order and at a moment's warning ready to march."

The General was grateful to his guest for the startling information from which this dispatch was derived. But the elasticity of Burr's narratives, and the persistence of unpleasant rumors, left some of Jackson's friends frankly confused. After the worthy visitant had passed on up to Kentucky doubts began to plague shrewd old General Robertson. "He dined with me and I was several times in his company. He told me he expected to make settlements . . . on the western waters. I endeavored to find out how the Executive of our government was held with, but he was so guarded, I gained little satisfaction."[6]

4

On the score of reticence Colonel Burr had little choice. In justice to himself he hardly could divulge the entire failure of the winter's effort to obtain money, that the Executive was highly suspicious, and that, in fact, he had determined upon a hazardous throw with the help of only one confidential ally of importance. But this confederate was Brigadier-General James Wilkinson whom Burr apparently considered sufficiently deft at intrigue to insure success. Like Burr, James Wilkinson had been a colonel in the Continental line. As a trader in Kentucky after the war, he became the heart and center of the old Spanish cabal, and finally a secret agent of the Spanish crown in receipt of a salary. This machination faded and Wilkinson joined another Kentucky secession flurry in 1796. When the United States acquired Louisiana, he was back in the Army under the personal ægis of Jefferson. Through everything he had maintained his good standing with Spain and his name on its pension roll as spy No. 13.

From Kentucky Burr sent Jackson thirty-five hundred dollars with a commission to build and provision five river boats. The work was begun at Clover Bottom by John Coffee, and Patton Anderson recruited a military company for the expedition.

In the midst of this clattering activity a young man of pleasing address turned from the Lebanon Road into the level lane that led to the Hermitage. His name was "Capt Fort" and he came to Jackson "an entire stranger . . . introduced to me by letter."[7] The Captain professed "to be on his way from N. York to join . . . Burr."[8] He spent the night at the Hermitage and a part of the following day, speaking freely and a trifle importantly, of the Burr project, which at length he "incautiously" characterized as a scheme "to divide the union."[9]

If the young man's object had been to impress his host, he succeeded. "I sternly asked how they would effect it. He replied by seizing New Orleans and the bank, shutting the port, conquering Mexico, and uniting the western part of the union to the conquered country." "With Warmth" Jackson demanded how this was to be done. "He replied by the aid of Federal troops, and the Genl at their head."

The General was Wilkinson, of whom Andrew Jackson was prepared to believe anything evil—Wilkinson the nemesis of Colonel Thomas Butler, who had privately attributed his troubles to a knowledge of the Spanish connections of his superior.

"I asked him if he had this from the Genl. He said he had not. I asked him if Col. Burr was in the scheme and he answered that he did not know . . . that he was, that he hardly knew Col. Burr.

... I asked ... from whence he got his information [and] he said from Col. Swartwout in New York."[10]

Jackson knew Samuel Swartwout, of New York, to be one of Burr's lieutenants. He knew Wilkinson to be concerned with Burr's plans, though not how deeply. Fort saw that he had said too much. With the boring blue gaze of Jackson upon him he hedged, "attempted to take [me in] to explain &., &."[11] Too late. "It rushed into my mind like lightning" that the treasonable project broached by Captain Fort and the project in which Andrew Jackson was leagued with Burr were the same.[12] Like lightning Jackson's quill flew at such a rate that one sheet would be finished before the ink on its predecessor was dry. "In strong tones" Burr was told that until "my suspicions ... were cleared from my mind no further intimacy was to exist between us."[13]

To Daniel Smith, Jackson's successor in the United States Senate, went a long letter. "Whilst ... not in the possession of Testimony that would authorize names to be used ... I have no doubt but there is a plan on foot ... in concert with Spain to seize New-orleans, and Louisiana, and attempt to divide the union. ... permit me to bring to your view how it might be" done. "A difference exists between our government and Spain, their minister at open war with our executive. A designing man forms an intrigue with him to regain the purchased territory. This designing man intrigues with the general of our army. ... The Spanish forces under pretext of defending their frontier marches a formidable force within two hundred miles of New Orleans. Your Governor of New orleans organizes the militia ... but your general orders him home at the verry moment he is advancing to ... the Sabine." At the same time "a descent is made from the ohio and uper Louisiana on New Orleans ... [where] two-thirds of its inhabitants [are] into the plan. The Town falls an easy pray. ... The conquerors ... shut the Port ... and hold out to all the western world to join and have ... profitable commerce." By stopping the mails the conspirators keep Washington in ignorance until the game was in their hands. "I hope I may be mistaken but I as much believe that such a plan is in operation as I believe there is a god. ... You may say to the president . . . that the[y] have no time to lose . . . to watch over their general, . . . and give orders for the defense of Neworleans."[14]

To Jefferson himself Jackson tendered the services of his command "in the event of . . . aggression . . . FROM ANY QUARTER."[15]

He did not wait for the President's warning to reach New Orleans, but wrote Governor Claiborne direct. "I fear Treachery has become the order of the day. Put your Town in a state of defence. . . . Keep a watchful eye on our Genl., and beware of an attack . . . from Spain. . . ." Jackson then subtly recognized Governor Claiborne as a confederate in the "innocent" Burr plot to subjugate Mexico. "I love my country and government. I hate Dons. I would delight to see Mexico reduced, but I will die in the last Ditch before I would . . . see the Union disunited. . . . Your sincere friend ANDREW JACKSON."[16]

5

On November 3, 1806, the day that Jackson received the order to build flatboats, United States District Attorney Joseph Hamilton Daviess petitioned the Federal Court at Frankfort, Kentucky, to arrest Aaron Burr for treason. On the bench was Harry Innes, associate of Wilkinson in the early Spanish plot and himself formerly, if not then, a pensioner of Spain. He denied the motion but granted a request to summon the grand jury to consider evidence against Burr. On Andrew Jackson's day of feverish letter-writing, November twelfth, the little court-room at Frankfort was thronged, the town agog to hear the presentation. Burr appeared with his attorney, young Henry Clay, also the legal representative in Kentucky of Jackson's trading house.

To the astonishment of every one Mr. Daviess asked the dismissal of the jury. His chief witness, he said, had fled to Indiana. Adjournment amid laughter for Daviess, cheers for Aaron Burr.

Accompanying news of this proceeding Andrew Jackson received a letter from Burr containing "the most sacred pledges that he" entertained no "views inimical to the united States."[17] Jackson was puzzled—and Thomas Jefferson no less so. For months the President had had reports of Burr's designs, but little as was the love he bore Aaron Burr, Jefferson was not a hasty man and his apprehensions, like Jackson's, were devoid of anything one could put a finger on.

James Wilkinson now overcame the deficiency. For some time this soldier had been confronted by the necessity of deciding whom he could most profitably betray—the United States, Spain, or Aaron Burr. On the eighth day of October, 1807, at Natchitoches, Louisiana, he received from the hands of Samuel Swartwout a message from Burr which he spent the night decoding. On the following morning he decided to betray Burr, but twelve days elapsed before he dispatched the cunning letter to Jefferson doing so, and another to Mexico City demanding one hundred and ten thousand dollars for the service. On November twenty-sixth the President proclaimed the existence of a military conspiracy by "sundry persons . . . against the dominion of Spain." "Faithful citizens" were warned to shun it, authorities to seize boats and apprehend the unnamed guilty. With this communication on its way Joseph Hamilton Daviess, nephew of John Marshall, made his third appeal for Burr's arrest. Again witnesses failed him; Burr walked from the court-room to a ball in his honor.

A fortnight later, however, confusion struck the Burr camps on the Ohio. Responsive to the President's proclamation the Governor of Ohio seized Burr's boats at Marietta. Adherents dived into their holes, except thirty men under romantic Harman Blennerhasset who fled down the river. Riding ahead of this disastrous news Burr reached Nashville on December seventeenth. The *Impartial Review* chronicled his appearance in two short sentences.[18] General Jackson was absent when he presented himself at the Hermitage. Rachel received him coolly and did not ask him to stay. He put up at the Clover Bottom tavern where Jackson paid a stiff call, taking John Coffee as a witness.

"After much vehement denial Burr [assured] Jackson *upon his honor* that his object . . . [had] the approbation of our govt & . . . pulled from his pocket a blank commission signed by Mr. Jefferson saying, 'Gentlemen, I suppose this will satisfy you.' "[19]

Jackson's suspicions were quelled to the extent that he released two boats (all Burr desired), and permitted seventeen-year-old Stockley Hays, Rachel's nephew, bound for school at New Orleans, to go on one of them. Patton Anderson's military company remained at home, however, and the Hays boy carried confidential letters to Governor Claiborne.[20]

6

Burr and boats departed at dawn on December twenty-second. They had gone too far to be overtaken when Jefferson's proclamation came, and Andrew Jackson learned[21] that it takes a long spoon to sup with the devil. "Last night at the hour of nine," chronicled the *Impartial Review* on January third, "commenced the burning of the Effigy of Col. Aaron Burr." There had been a similar cremation three days before. In threshing exhortations from the foot of the pyre, Thomas Swann and Charles Dickinson's father-in-law joined the names of Jackson and the fugitive. The town boiled with excitement and citizens lately flattered to be seen in Burr's company were loudest in their deprecation of his infamy.

The panic was not confined to Nashville. At Pittsburgh Captain Read reported to the War Department that an army from Tennessee with Jackson at its head was on the march to join Aaron Burr. The responsible Richmond *Enquirer* was "happy to hear that General Wilkinson had been tampered with unsuccessfully," but unhappy that it could not say the same "of a militia general in Tennessee."

While frightened friends and exultant foes proclaimed their loyalty about a fire in the court-house square, the Hermitage presented a scene of torrential activity as Jackson moved to confront the crisis believed to imperil the Union. At eleven o'clock on New Year's night he had received a communication—"I cannot call it an order"—from the Secretary of War: "a milk and water thing . . . the merest old-woman letter you ever saw."[22]

Jackson's characterizations were appropriate.

"War Department Dec 19, 1806
"General Jackson,
"Sir:
". . . It appears that you have some reason for suspecting that some unlawful enterprise is in contemplation on the western waters. There can be no doubt, but that many persons are engaged in some such enterprise; and before this reaches you, it is not improbable, that a general movement will have commenced.—

"It is presumed that the Proclamation of the President . . . will have produced every exertion . . . and . . . that you will have been among the most jealous opposers of any such unlawful expedition, as appears to be initiated, by a set of disappointed, unprincipled, ambitious or misguided individuals, and that you will continue to make every exertion in your power, as a General of the Militia, to counteract and render abhortive, any such expedition. . . . About Pittsburgh it is industriously reported among the adventurers, that they are to be joined, at the mouth of the Cumberland, by two Regiments under the Command of General Jackson—such a story might afford you an opportunity of giving an effectual check to the enterprise if not too late I am etc.

"HENRY DEARBORN"[23]

Contrast this nebulous, hinting thing, from the Government's responsible minister of defense, written in the light of information from a hundred quarters, with the decisive expressions of his frontier servant after one conversation with Captain Fort. The more Jackson conned it, the angrier he became. Did Dearborn really wish Burr molested?

The Secretary's letter was acknowledged: "The first duty of a soldier is to attend to the safety . . . of his country. The next is to attend to his own feelings when they have been . . . wantonly assailed."[24]

Assuming that Dearborn did wish Burr taken, Jackson put two brigades under arms. Volunteer companies were called for. Jack Morrell was dispatched with word to Captain Bissell, commanding the Regular Army post at Fort Massac on the Ohio, to intercept armed boats and to call on Jackson for reenforcements if necessary. The flames died in the court-house square, and men began to understand that a better way to prove their fealty was to put themselves at the disposal of Jackson. Old General Robertson gave this an aspect of completeness by ceremoniously tendering the service of the "Corps of Invincibles," Revolutionary veterans.

7

Major General Jackson's rôle as protector of the Republic might have electrified the country, as it did the Cumberland, had the

Union been in danger. It soon fell out, however, that the military aspect of Burr's "expedition" had been comically exaggerated. Jack Morrell returned with a tart reply from Captain Bissell. The peace of the United States had not been jeopardized within his jurisdiction. Colonel Burr had passed down the river with ten unarmed boats manned by six men each. The Captain had no orders to detain him and implied that he required no instruction in his duties from a militiaman. So Burr floated down the Mississippi in ignorance of furore behind him, or the trap in front where Wilkinson was slapping dupes in jail and thunderously laying waste to the aspirations of his fellow-conspirator. "Wilkinson is entirely devoted to us," wrote the Spanish Minister. "The President confides in his fidelity"—Senator Smith to General Jackson.

When his eyes at length were opened Burr deserted his boats and slipped into the wilderness.

"Burr and his expedition . . . [are] a thread bare topic," wrote a resident of the Cumberland. "The Volunteers pretty well tucked out waiting for nothing."[25] With the imagined peril of the nation out of the way, General Jackson could undertake a soldier's "next" duty. He believed Dearborn as deeply involved with Burr as himself, though wanting courage to acknowledge it—a suspicion from which time has not absolved the Secretary. Sending his army home, the Cumberland commander immersed himself in the toils of composition. Ordinarily Jackson wrote rapidly, just as he spoke. He wrote rapidly now, but nothing seemed to suit. He struck out and recast. This was unusual, for Jackson was a man who knew his own mind at all times and had the habit of expressing himself clearly in the first words that came to him. But this time he was dissatisfied and, taking a fresh sheet of paper, began anew. "Henry Dearborn, Sir. . . . Colo. B. received at my house all that hospitality that a banished patriot . . . was entitled to. . . . But sir when proof shews him to be a treator I would cut his throat with as much pleasure as I would cut yours on equal testimony."[26]

Still dissatisfied Jackson wrote a third draft, which he sent. Though slightly less quotable than the foregoing, it nevertheless holds its own place among communications from a subordinate to a Secretary of War.

"You stand convicted of the most notorious and criminal acts of dishonor, dishonesty, want of candour and justice. . . . You say Sir that it is industriously reported amongst adventurers that they are to be joined at the mouth of cumberland by two regiments under the command of Gnl Jackson. Such a *Story* might afford him an opportunity of giving an effectual check to the enterprise, if not too late. After I have given the most deliber[ate] consideration to your expressions, . . . I cannot draw from them any other conclusion but this: that you believed me concerned in the conspiracy [and] that I was a fit subject to act the traitor of traitors, as others have done, and that the . . . Secretary of war . . . [could] buy me up without honour."

The "others" Jackson identified as "yr. much loved Genl. Wilkinson" and the Secretary himself. "Was anything in . . . [the order of December nineteenth] that would have authorized . . . [Burr's] arrest? . . . There was not. . . . What . . . the Secretary at war . . . has done is unworthy of . . . a . . . man of honor. I care not where, when, or how he shall . . . [undertake to resent this language]. I am equally regardless of . . . [his] defense before the world. I know it cannot be . . . either tenable or true."[27]

Secretary Dearborn offered no defense. He made no move to resent his correspondent's language. The communication was passed over with the complete dignity of silence and Henry Dearborn said nothing more of Andrew Jackson's relations with Aaron Burr.

Jackson also labored manfully to expose James Wilkinson, but vital evidence remained elusive. Deserted by every one, Burr was taken in disguise, a few miles from the frontier of Spanish Florida, and safety. The ardor with which the Administration continued to repel the least whisper against Wilkinson, clinched Jackson's conviction that "Jamy" could hardly be the only official tarred with Burr's brush.

8

Behind the desk of the Speaker, in the graceful hall of the House of Delegates at Richmond, sat a tallish man in his fifties—jet-black hair, jet-black eyes, and the demeanor and homely dignity of a shrewd country lawyer. If his quick glance strayed to the windows it may have been to recall how as a young member of the Virginia As-

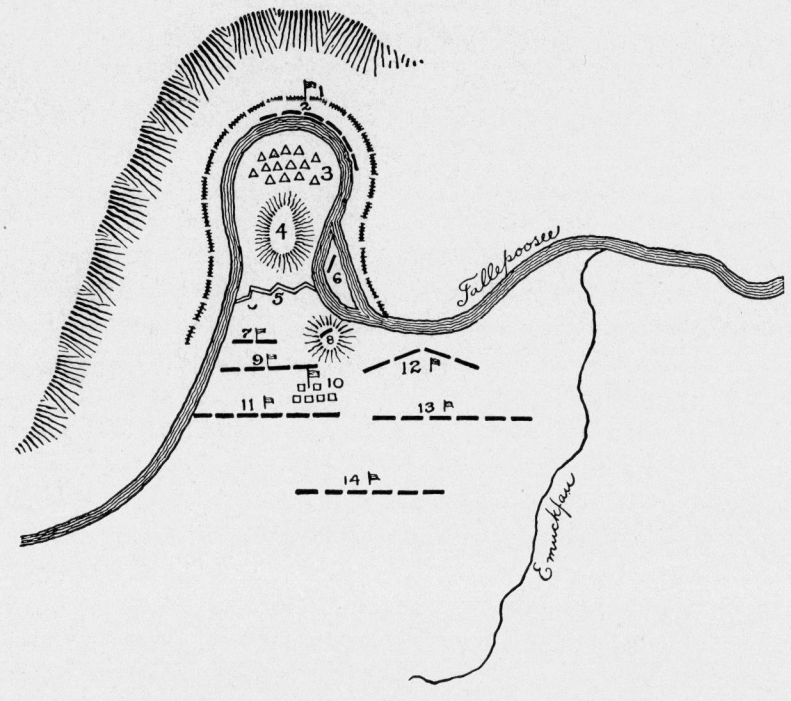

Battle of Tohopeka

From a sketch accompanying Jackson's report of the engagement to Governor Blount of Tennessee, now in the Tennessee Historical Society archives at Nashville. (1) Coffee's cavalry. (2) Friendly Cherokees. (3) Creek village. (4) Broken ground. (5) Creek breastwork. (6) Island. (7) Jackson's advance guard. (8) Artillery on a small hill. (9) Regulars. (10) Wagons, packhorses and wounded. (11 to 14) Militia.

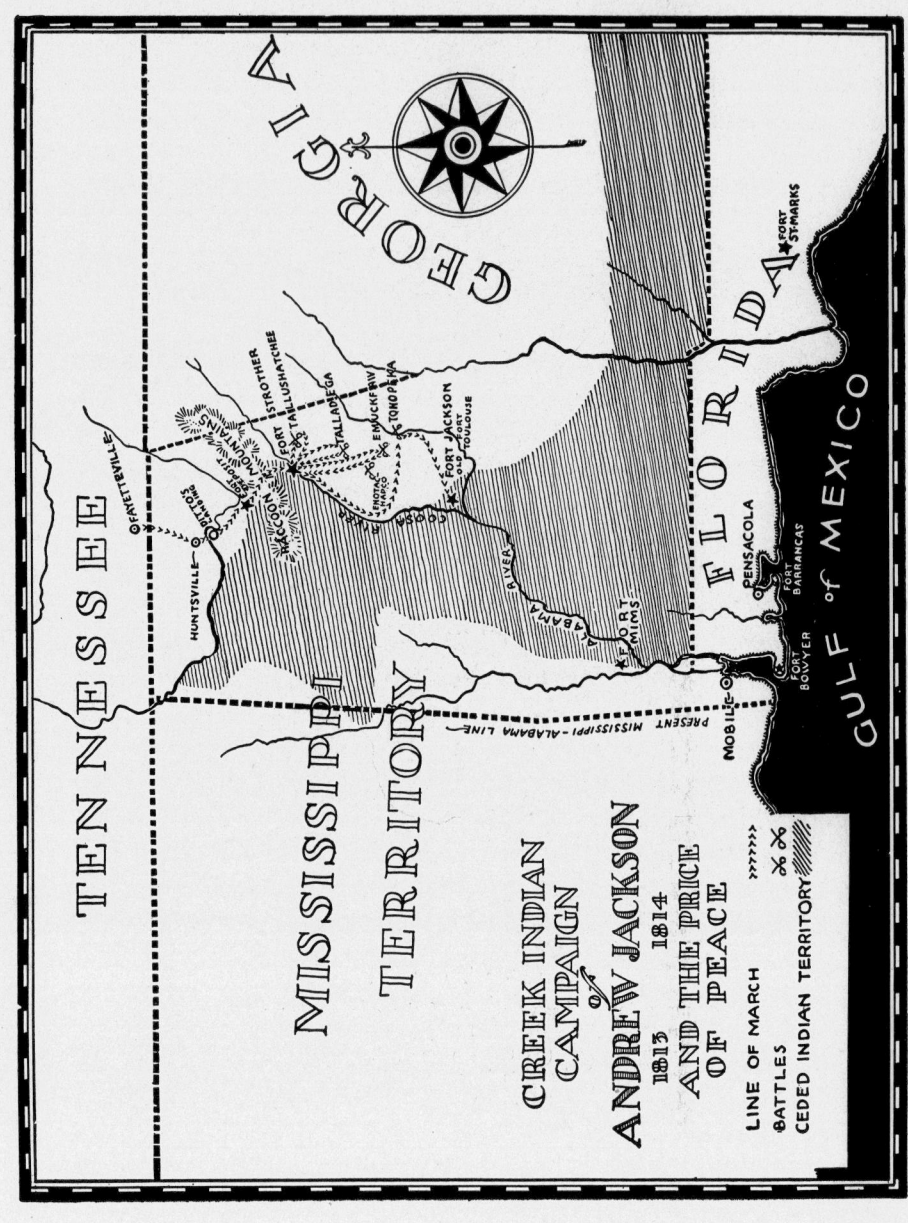

sembly he had pitched horseshoes on the State-House green. Before Chief Justice John Marshall bowed the accused, Aaron Burr, perfection in dress and composure. He had been escorted from a comfortable apartment in the penitentiary by a guard of honor of two hundred gentlemen. Behind him was the eminent counsel of the United States and for the accused; behind them a press of forms and faces, of powdered wigs and ruffled shirts, diffusing an odor of snuff and Madeira. Minds went back to the celebrated trial two years before when Aaron Burr sat in the seat of judgment and a Justice of the Supreme Court in that of the judged.

"May it please the Court," began Colonel Burr, very pale. He said the law for the formation of the grand jury had been evaded, William Branch Giles and Wilson Carey Nicholas being on the panel in violation of the rules of procedure. Giles was a United States senator, Nicholas a former senator, both allies of Thomas Jefferson and enemies of Aaron Burr.

John Marshall ruled for the accused, and the stillness deepened. The grand jury was formed with the lank Murat of the House of Representatives, John Randolph, as foreman—Thomas Jefferson's relative, but not his protégé. District Attorney Hay moved for an adjournment. His key witness had not appeared. On the next day he made the same request for the same reason, and on another day repeated it. The missing witness was Brigadier-General James Wilkinson, by whose testimony the prosecution promised to establish the treason of Aaron Burr. The defense sensationally demanded a subpœna duces tecum directing the appearance of the President of the United States. For four days Marshall listened to argument, and issued the subpœna which Jefferson refused to obey. Still no Wilkinson. Public opinion began to incline toward the prisoner at the bar.

The trend was not hindered by the attitude of another witness under subpœna of the prosecution. Andrew Jackson had responded promptly and had been told to wait. In high company and low, on the thronged sidewalk of Brick Row, in smoke-fogged Eagle Tavern and the jostling crowd that trampled the State-House green, he denounced James Wilkinson; and as delay succeeded delay, asked if Thomas Jefferson held himself above the law.

After twenty days Wilkinson obeyed the summons. People lined the streets to scan the stout form in full panoply of rank, the strong face, big, brandy nose and steady eyes. They saw young Samuel Swartwout, whom Wilkinson had jailed in the South and stolen his watch, shoulder him from a walk. They heard Andrew Jackson call him "a double traitor" and "pity the sword that dangles from his felon's belt, for it is doubtless of honest steel!"[28]

The waiting witness wrote William Preston Anderson. "Tell . . . Mrs. Jackson . . . not to be uneasy. . . . I am more convinced than ever that treason never was intended by Burr; but if ever it was, you know my wishes—that he may be hung."[29]

It required a loud explosion to penetrate the preoccupation at Richmond, but this was provided by the broadside guns of the English warship *Leopard* when they raked our unready *Chesapeake*, killing or wounding twenty-one men to get four presumed British deserters. A savage cry rang through the West. "On my Conscience and Faith and Honour," wrote one friend of Andrew Jackson, "I hope that war will take place."[30] So hoped Tennessee's Major General, and when Mr. Jefferson turned to diplomacy he announced that he "would address the people from the steps of the State-House after the adjournment of court." He spoke for an hour. "Mr. Jefferson has plenty of courage to seize peaceable Americans . . . and persecute them for political purposes. But he is too cowardly to resent foreign outrage on the Republic. An English man-of-war fires on an American ship . . . so near his Capital that he can almost hear the guns, and what does he do? . . . A year or more ago I gave at a dinner to Aaron Burr the toast—'Millions for defence; not a cent for tribute.' They change that tune on this side of the mountains. . . . 'Millions to persecute an American; not a cent to resist England!'"[31]

The prosecutor released General Jackson from his subpœna.

9

In January of 1810 Rachel stepped from her carriage at the Hermitage with a bundle in her plump arms. It was a baby, and the baby was hers—to have for ever, and not for a week or a season, to grow fond of and to lose as she had lost so many others. In 1804 Edward Butler died, making Jackson guardian of his children, Anthony Wayne Butler, Edward George Washington Butler and two girls whose names—did he resist Betsy Ross and Molly Pitcher?—are unknown to your chronicler.[32] In 1805 Edward Butler's brother, Colonel Thomas Butler, his locks still unshorn, had failed to survive his court martial. One of his last letters begged Jackson to extend a father's guidance to his boys. And when Samuel Donelson died, Jackson carried his two sons, John and Andrew Jackson, to the Hermitage, to raise and to school them as his own. Jackson felt a peculiar solicitude for these bright children. He had held the grapevine ladder by which their mother had taken silent leave of her obdurate parents for a midnight wedding.[33] The Donelson boys were at the Hermitage now with little William Smith, a pathetic child, born to a neighboring couple after the normal expectancy of such an event had passed, and grown sons and daughters were disputing over the prospective division of the estate.[34]

The new baby made four. On the third night before Christmas, the wife of Severn Donelson, had borne twins. The mother, barely surviving, could not suckle two infants. Her sister-in-law had carried one away, which Rachel and Andrew legally adopted and christened Andrew Jackson, junior. The mistress of twenty slaves submerged herself in the service of her new love. He grew strong and brightened the hearthside of the blockhouse with a promise of cheerfulness and tranquillity.

This promise was needed. As he had abandoned the law in which he prospered and public life in which he had won a name, General Jackson now relinquished trade in which he had failed. The house of Jackson & Hutchings had never rightly caught the tide that carried many to fortune with the annexation of Louisiana. As that tide ebbed, the firm struck the shoals of slack times and closed its doors. The last statement of its condition showed liabilities of twenty-one thousand four hundred and thirty-six dollars and sixty-one cents against twenty-five thousand, two hundred and eighty-three dollars and fifty-two cents in assets, mostly customers' bills, probably half of which were never collected.[35] John Coffee, a silent partner, gave Jackson notes for his share of the debts, and returned to surveying. When his friend drew upon the inexhaustible supply of Rachel's nieces for a wife, Jackson opened his iron strong-box and presented the notes to the bride.

Store debts were gradually depleted by earnings of the Hermitage plantation and racing stable. For five years General Jackson had not lost an important race without being able to compensate immediately with a victory. Truxton had won more than twenty thousand dollars in prizes and his progeny was becoming famous. During the general simplification of his affairs Jackson had sold his Clover Bottom track to the Nashville Jockey Club. In 1811 he entered Decatur, a Truxton colt, in the fall meeting. Jackson had ambitions for Decatur and was chagrined to see him beaten by three-year-old chestnut mare Maria, owned by Jesse Haynie of Sumner County. In fact, Maria lowered the Jackson colors all along the line, winning six races and losing none.

The turfman's leisure hours were spent in the company of a translation of the French army regulations, and in applying its precepts to his militia division. Again and again this division reached for its arms as the commander could not conceive of an Administration longer enduring the arrogance of England. "My only pride is [that] . . . my soldiers has confidence in me, and on the event of war I will lead them to victory. Should we be blest with peace I will resign my military office and spend my days in the sweet calm of rural retirement."[36]

But Jackson foresaw only war or a perpetuation of the dishonor which he had come to regard as synonymous with the régime of Thomas Jefferson. In 1808 this had led him to support James Monroe for the presidency, perhaps on the theory that any one Jefferson opposed would be preferable to the Administration's altar boy, Madison. Actually, however, in 1808 and for a long time after, Colonel Monroe was more friendly in England than was either Madison or Jefferson. Nevertheless, the election of Madison continued a policy of non-resistance and things drifted along much as before. Each fresh climax that made drums to beat along the Cumberland splintered in futility. Acquitted of treason but reindicted for high misdemeanor, Burr had fled the country. An effort to deprive Wilkinson of his rank failed with Madison's approval. "On the eve of war and a Treator at the head of the army!"[37]

Such were the occupations of Andrew Jackson when in 1811 George Washington Campbell rode to the Hermitage to see his friend alone. Mr. Campbell had resigned from Congress for a place on the State Supreme Court of Errors and Appeals, in consequence of which he had privately discovered an error.

The financial troubles entrammeling Jackson date from David Allison's failure at Philadelphia in 1796. Allison died in a debtor's prison after making a futile effort to free himself by mortgaging to Norton Prior eighty-five thousand acres of land on Duck River in Tennessee. Prior had asked Jackson to join him in a foreclosure against Allison's heirs, but Jackson being on the bench referred the matter to John Overton who successfully prosecuted the action in a Federal Court. In the liquidation Jackson obtained five thousand acres which he sold in parcels to settlers, giving them warranted titles, binding himself, should the titles prove unsound, to buy back the land, not for what he sold it, but for what it should be worth when the titular defect appeared. The wilderness Jackson sold had become orderly fields of grain and bobbing cotton worth a fortune. Judge Campbell said that Jackson was liable for all this. His titles were not good. The Federal Court had been without jurisdiction in the foreclosure suit.

"I became alarmed and . . . went to Mr J Whitesides." United States Senator Whiteside was the most celebrated lawyer in Tennessee. He told Jackson not to worry. What the Allison heirs did not know would never help them, and in any event they were without funds to redeem the mortgage. "I told Mr. Whitesides that I had never sold any land but what I thought the title was good" and that he would perfect his titles for the protection of "those honest men" on Duck River.[38]

Andrew Jackson had been rather showy, the Administration thought, in his proffers of life and fortune to protect the nation's honor. With no show he rejected the advice of a crafty lawyer, and imperiled his fortune beyond hope of extrication to protect his personal honor. That is one aspect of the case as General Jackson's admirers in later years were pleased to point out. Another aspect of it establishes that under the proper sponsorship honesty may be not only the best policy, but the best paying one. Jackson rode to Georgia where the Allison heirs lived in poverty and told them everything. "I have a claim," he said in effect, "against the estate of David Allison for twenty thousand dollars. I will surrender that claim in exchange for your release upon these eighty-five thousand acres." Had the Allisons refused the cat would have been out of the bag and Jackson face to face with ruin. To satisfy his moral compunctions Jackson took that chance. But the heirs did not refuse, and the sagacious bargainer returned to Tennessee armed with legal instruments enabling him to convey proper titles to the purchasers of his own five thousand acres and to demand his own price for the same service to those who had sold the other eighty thousand acres.[39]

Jackson had saved himself by an act that can hardly be stripped of its attributes of courage and of honest impulse, but other acts, equally courageous, equally honest in Jackson's view, did not frame him in so fair a light: a brawl at Clover Bottom wherein Jackson covered the starting post with his pistols to prevent a race he believed had been fixed;[40] a war over the slave trade against Silas Dinsmore, government agent of the Choctaws, which constituted a rather presumptuous disregard of the authority of the United States.[41] Then David Magness concluded a long and hitherto indecisive feud with Patton Anderson by killing him, and Jackson vowed that the slayer of his friend should hang.

The village of Franklin became a smaller Richmond, Jenkin Whiteside, John Haywood, Felix Grundy and other immortals of the border bar contending in the cause célèbre. Jackson roared upon the scene and, none too steady on his feet, delivered a taproom harangue which a stranger would have found impossible to associate with the man who once had sustained with a pistol the prerogatives of courts in Tennessee. Jackson took the stand as a character witness for Anderson. On cross-examination alert Felix Grundy, one time to be Attorney-General of the United States, pecked away at the General's portrait of the peace-loving nature of the deceased. Had not Major Anderson frequently been in "difficulties"? Had he not made numerous enemies?

"Sir," quoth Andrew Jackson, "my friend was the NATURAL ENEMY OF SCOUNDRELS!"[42]

Magness received a light sentence for manslaughter and Jackson shook his fist under the nose of one of the jurors.

10

In a blustery February twilight the truculent Major General gazed into his great fireplace, brooding. Between his knees nestled Andrew, junior, and a lamb the master of the Hermitage flocks had carried out of the storm.[43] "From my persuits for several years past, from many unpleasant occurrences . . . during that time . . . my mind . . . [has taken] a turn of thought that I have laboured to get clear of."[44]

Not money worries this time. The old embarrassments were nearly sponged out,[45] but Jackson had proof that solvency is no guarantee of felicity. George M. Deaderick was rich—president of the Nashville Bank, the only bank in Tennessee, and symbol of the retreat of the frontier. Careful as he was of fresh investments, General Jackson had taken fifty shares in it.[46] Yet Mr. Deaderick was unhappy, his wife's "use of her eyes" bringing reproaches that had caused an estrangement. "By the expressions of the eye as much levity & Viciousness can be expressed as by the tongue,"[47] the harassed husband assured Jackson, asking him to try to patch up matters. A desperate letter from Deaderick indicates the measure of the General's success. "I do solemnly declare to you that I never have conveyed an Idea to Mrs Deaderick or to any other individual that I . . . suspected you had any carnal knowledge of her." This pretty story was the work of a lady who wished to annoy her husband. "You will not I know," pleaded the banker, "Abandon a . . . friend."[48]

And other thorns sprang from seed that should have borne only flowers of contentment. Generously had Jackson fulfilled the dying request of old Colonel Thomas Butler and become, in truth, as a father to his sons. He had seen the oldest boy Robert grow to be a fine man more than six feet tall, and an embodiment of the virtues that warmed the heart of Andrew Jackson.

Of all her nieces Rachel's favorite was Rachel Hays, a lively laughing girl in whom the older woman could see the reflection of herself in the zestful blockhouse days. When Robert and Rachel began to keep company no one looked on with more approving eyes than the couple at the Hermitage. Naturally, it was too much to expect that Robert's suit for a belle such as Rachel Hays should be undisputed. Half a dozen other blades danced attendance on her, and in this connection a foul tale reached her uncle's ears. Jackson ran it down and stood over George Blakemore who with quill and ink acknowledged himself a liar.[49]

So Rachel and Robert were married and nothing seemed wanting to insure their happiness. Robert owned lands and negroes and was looked upon as one of the coming young men of the Valley. Alack, they quarreled, and over the most sordid of matters: money. Robert wished to save, Rachel to spend. "Our friend R.B.," a cousin of the bride wrote to General Jackson, "[is] doom'd to . . . the melancholy effects of imprudence in a wife. Good God! . . . What a reward for Aunt J[ackson]."⁵⁰

But the deepest cuts came from the slinking whispers that touched the "sacred name."

Rachel Jackson was forty-three. Her short figure had grown rather stout, but her movements were quick and agile, her olive countenance unlined, and the round black eyes young and fine. She owned a carriage but preferred the saddle. She wore good clothes, but neglected the styles. Nashville was no longer frontier, but Rachel remained a frontier woman, clinging to the fragile images of a bygone day that had witnessed her last touch with happiness—a day when something less superficial than silks constituted the resources of charm in a Cumberland belle. With these resources Rachel may have been endowed too well. In any event twenty years of piety shining in every act of her life, of boundless generosity, charity and kindness, of ministrations to the troubled, the sick and the orphaned had not erased a record at Harrodsburgh, or stilled tongues wagged by consciences enjoying an ease Rachel could not attain.

At this late time it seemed the work of her own sex. The retribution of Charles Dickinson had established that Jackson could deal with men. But women were another case as, after Mrs. Deaderick, the General had reason to suspect. He sent Lem Hutchings to Sumner County to conduct "a strict inquiry." The mission was a failure. "I cannot learn that Betsy has said anything injurious of Mrs. Jackson."⁵¹ Jackson himself wrote to solicit the help of the wife of a neighbor. She replied in confusion. "I pledge you that Mrs Bell did not either directly or indirectly say anything tending to injure the reputation of Mrs. Jackson."⁵²

A man pursuing a shadow.

11

"Unpleasant occurrences" in sooth, and, one suspects, the hidden source of much of the rancor and rashness that has left its impress on painful episodes: Dickinson, Burr, Silas Dinsmore, Patton Anderson.

A TRIBUTE TO MERIT.

Brig. Gen. J. Coffee is invited to partake of a PUBLIC DINNER, to be given by the citizens of Nashville and its vicinity, to MAJ. GEN. ANDREW JACKSON, at the Nashville Inn, on Thursday, the 19th inst. as a proof of their decided approbation of the gallant and meritorious manner, in which he has conducted and terminated the Creek War.

DINNER on the Table at 3 o'clock.

John Childress,
Geo. M Deaderick,
Jno. Sommerville,
John Bird,
Alexander Richardson,
Roger B. Sappington,
Ephraim Prewett,
Andrew Hynes,
James Jackson.
} Committee.

May 12, 1814.

APPROBATION OF HIS NEIGHBORS

Though showered with honors it was simple tributes of this kind that General Jackson preferred. For more than fifty years the Nashville Inn was the local rendezvous of the famous and the fashionable. From the Jackson Papers, Library of Congress.

IN FORMAL DRESS

Painted by John Vanderlyn, it is believed in 1815, and hung in the Council Chamber of the Charleston City Hall as a tribute to a native South Carolinian. Reproduced from a photograph of the original in the collection of Mrs. Samuel G. Heiskell of Knoxville.

The pass to which such episodes had brought the man who at twenty-one was Attorney-General, at thirty-one United States Senator and Superior Judge, all with eyes could see. Jackson saw this much and more. He saw the pass to which the pursuit of fame had brought his domestic happiness. He strove to blot out the unpleasant image "to divest myself of those habits of . . . gloomy reflections. . . . I find it impossible."[53] The poisoned arrows had struck home.

The man of action behaved with resolution. A confidential letter went to a confidential friend. "In order to try the experiment how new scenes might relieve me from this unpleasant tone of thought," Andrew Jackson was prepared to relinquish the gains of a lifetime in Tennessee and exchange the equivocal coin of public reputation for the tranquil obscurity of another frontier[54] by which he hoped to restore his peace of mind and that of the woman he loved.

One of the Donelson nephews was dispatched on a tour of inspection of Mississippi. A young Army officer at Natchitoches reported on the soil, climate and crops of Louisiana, adding, for completeness, a paragraph about the people. "The creole women . . . surpass the world at intrigue, . . . & I can only admire their taste in Generally preferring an american."[55]

The choice fell on Washington County, Mississippi. The landscape was reminiscent of Bayou Pierre where the unforgettable honeymoon had been spent and the rolling current of the great brown river washing the base of the bluff recalled the felicity of the past. The Hermitage was offered for sale to a horse-trading acquaintance, the splendid Wade Hampton of Charleston.[56] United States Senator Whiteside was petitioned for an insignificant judgeship in Mississippi Territory. "If the salary . . . is $1000 I will accept."[57]

BOOK THREE

THE SWORD

"What, retrograde under these circumstances? I will perish first!"
GENERAL JACKSON to Governor
Blount of Tennessee

CHAPTER IX

OLD HICKORY

1

"I FEAR you cannot read this scroll," Jackson closed a long and depressing business letter. "I write it in the night and with the Rheumatick in my right rist so that I can scarcely wield the pen."[1]

But in seven days he had recovered the use of his writing hand.

"Hermitage, March 7 1812
"VOLUNTEERS TO ARMS!

"*Citizens!* Your government has yielded to the impulse of the nation. . . . War is on the point of breaking out between the United States and . . . great Britain! and the martial hosts . . . are summoned to the Tented Fields! . . .

"A simple invitation is given . . . [for] 50,000 volunteers. . . . Shall we, who have clamoured for war, now skulk into a corner? . . . Are we the titled Slaves of George the third? the military conscripts of Napolon? or the frozen peasants of the Rusian Czar? No— we are the free born sons of . . . the only republick now existing in the world. . . .

"Are we going to fight to satisfy the revenge or ambition of a corrupt ministry? to place another diadem on the head of an apostate republican general? . . . No . . . we are going to fight for the reestablishment of our national charactor, . . . for the protection of our maratime citizens, . . . to vindicate our right to free trade. . . .

"The period of youth is the season for martial exploits; and . . . how pleasing the prospect . . . to . . . *promenade* into a distant country . . . and [witness] the grand evolutions of an army of fifty thousand men. To view the stupendous works of nature, . . . Niagra, . . . Montmorenci, . . . carrying the republican standard to the heights of abraham. . . .

"ANDREW JACKSON
"Major General"[2]

141

2

Perhaps from a feeling of delicacy for Tennessee's pride in its military prowess, the General omitted to mention that the "invitation" to whip England had been extended to the other states as well.

Yet Andrew Jackson was under no apprehension as to the popularity in the East of the inevitable conflict. The fact that the East opposed war was virtually reason enough to insure its acceptance in the West, and, regardless of glib economic theories or ponderous ones, this spite-fence of antagonism more than anything else produced the division of sentiment which was to embarrass our military effort from the first. The Embargo, the Non-Intercourse Acts, the Orders, Decrees, and the rest bore about as heavily on the shipping and commercial interests of New England as on the agricultural West. The personality of Napoleon Bonaparte had more to do with it than these things. Jackson's predilection for him, and his persevering inclination to see good in his acts despite the allusion in the call to arms, was but a reflection of Western opinion. The Corsican was an architect of new frontiers, let the chips fall where they may, and so were our pioneers. He cared little for precedent. Nor did they. He was a careerist. So were they. He created a feeling of nationalism that Frenchmen had not known before. Our borderers did the same in America. All this turned frontiersmen against England whom the conservative East supported as a protagonist of the existing order against the destructive occupations of a marauding opportunist.

The choice cost the East the leadership in affairs it had exercised since the nation's beginning. The swift overthrow came spectacularly with the organization of the Twelfth Congress in December, 1811. From the young West had swarmed young men, schooled in resentment for the humiliation that had degraded us as a neutral in the cross-fires of England's death grapple with the Emperor. The East tried to sneer at the "War Hawks," but soon discovered its inability to match for eloquence, enthusiasm and force such men as Henry Clay and Richard M. Johnson of Kentucky, Felix Grundy of Tennessee, John C. Calhoun and Langdon Cheves of South Carolina. With a scattering of Eastern allies as young as themselves, they captured Congress and swept Clay—"Harry of the West"—into the speakership of the House, an office soon to become almost second in public esteem to the presidency.

Like a bracing breeze from the mountains their ardor aroused a lethargic nation. It aroused the Administration where the War Hawks were able, by degrees, to make an ally of erstwhile pro-English James Monroe, who had become Secretary of State. In Tennessee old John Sevier once more had served the constitutional limit of three consecutive terms to be succeeded by Jackson's friend Willie Blount.[3] A change of air altogether.

The rush of these events had obliterated the plan to leave Tennessee, which one of Rachel's nephews living in Natchez had opposed from the start. "You have been able to read the Characters of men. In their actions; here another Volume will be presented to our view in which human baseness will take up a considerable part. . . . Were I in your situation [I] would not move."[4] For Rachel's sake, one hopes that he was right.

June 18, 1812, the House balloted on the war resolution. Tennessee, Kentucky, Ohio, Georgia and South Carolina did not cast a vote against it. Connecticut, Rhode Island and Delaware did not cast one for it. New York voted two for war, eleven for peace; Massachusetts eight to six for peace. But the resolution prevailed seventy-nine to forty-nine.

Anticipating the result a courier was already in the saddle. Lexington, North Carolina, saw him "tear through" without stopping, "his horse's tail and his own long hair streaming in the wind. . . . 'Here's the Stuff! WAR WITH ENGLAND!! WAR!!'" Billy Phillips had learned horsemanship under the eyes of Andrew Jackson. He had ridden Truxton. At seven in the evening of June twenty-first, he clattered into the dusty Square at Nashville, having covered eight hundred and sixty miles over primitive roads and three mountain ranges in nine days to the hour.[5] Spreading like quicksilver, the news evoked "a unanimous huzau. . . . Had any other sentiment been Express^d. . . . [the author] would have been Tarred & Feathered."[6]

General Jackson offered the President his militia division of twenty-five hundred trained men for instantaneous service and promised to have them before Quebec in ninety days. "He can most certainly do so," exclaimed Blount in an endorsement calculated to melt the antipathy of the Administration toward the Tennessee Commander. "At the present crisis he feels a holy zeal for the welfare of the United States, and"—in case the War Department had not forgotten Aaron Burr—"at no period in his life has been known to feel otherwise. . . . He delights in peace; but . . . has a peculiar pleasure in treating his enemies as such."[7] General Jackson's attitude toward his enemies was a matter the present Secretary of War could establish by reference to the correspondence of his predecessor, Henry Dearborn.

Jackson's proffer was perfunctorily accepted but no orders came to take the field. As for Quebec, the Department had other plans. General Henry Dearborn was told off to lead the dash against the city on the rock, and nine months after receiving his orders took up the line of march. Meantime Hull surrendered Detroit without a shot; Wilkinson assumed command at New Orleans; two of Jackson's regiments and Brigadier-General James Winchester were called to assist Harrison in the North, but there was no call for the Commander.

Aaron Burr landed penniless in New York after four years of wandering in Europe. Martin Van Buren who, as a law student and a rather too carefully dressed young man, had enjoyed the patronage of Burr, was brave enough to perform some courtesies. "I'll tell you why they don't employ Jackson," Burr told him. "It's because he is a friend of mine."[8]

3

The Major General saw his dream of paralyzing Canada by a lightning stroke against trivial opposition—and it was trivial—come to naught. He saw an alternative plan for a descent upon the Floridas come to naught. He saw the Northwest lost and our soil invaded. "The news . . . almost killed me." His offer to march "any minute" with a thousand mounted men and retake Detroit was not accorded the civility of an acknowledgment. He saw the Indians, quick to sense the direction of the wind, swell the ranks of the enemy. As idle weeks became idle months, he beheld a decline of the esprit which for eleven years he had labored to implant in his division.

As a recreation for his mind, General Jackson interested himself in the autumn meeting of the Nashville Jockey Club.[9] Hoping for marching orders he had neglected his horses. The presence of Jesse Haynie's little chestnut mare Maria, however, recalled too vividly the humiliation of the year before. Ed Bradley's Dungannon was to race Maria and Bradley was confident of victory. To share in the triumph Jackson bought an interest in Dungannon. But Maria beat him more easily than she had beaten Jackson's Decatur in 1811.

In the same month, October of 1812, the War Department requested of Governor Blount—not General Jackson—fifteen hundred men to reenforce James Wilkinson at New Orleans. The plain implication of the Department's request was that Jackson's services were not desired.[10] And the galling part was that the troops were to be used in the occupation of West Florida, an enterprise which Jackson had originally outlined to the Department and offered to undertake alone. Dearborn for Quebec, Wilkinson for Florida: Jackson might suggest campaigns, but their execution was entrusted to the Administration's favorites.

Willie Blount turned to his friend. Would Jackson accept a subordinate command under Wilkinson?

The man who already had asked for service on every front and advanced money from his own pocket for the purchase of rifles until promissory notes bearing the autograph of Andrew Jackson were currency in Tennessee, replied: "I cannot disguise my feelings. had the Secretary of War directed you to call me . . . into the field . . . [with the] compensation of sergeant I should have been content, but he has not even daigned to name me," or his treasured division. "But . . . should your Excellency believe that my personal service can promote" the country's welfare, "all I ask is" a chance to fight.[11]

Blount was in a quandary. A difference of opinion had arisen between him and the Major General over the mode of selecting field officers for the militia. Blount favored the old and popular method of election by the men. Jackson insisted that they should be appointed by the Commander. "We want Men Capable of Command—who will fight and reduce their soldiers to strict obedience."[12] This was an advanced position for a militia general in 1812. The Governor's hands fluttered over the seventy blank commissions the War Department had sent already signed in order to get the Tennessee force in the field without delay. He consulted lawyers, and, after agonies of indecision, took up one of the papers and filled in the name of Andrew Jackson, who thus became a Major General of United States volunteers, in the war at last by a small side door.

4

The sea-green Cumberland freezes at Nashville four or five times in a century. It froze from bank to bank on December 10, 1812, the day set for the rendezvous of the fifteen hundred volunteers. Twenty-five hundred responded. From every quarter of Middle Tennessee they came, by companies, by platoons, by ones and twos, ahorse and afoot, in dark-blue and nut-brown homespun and in buckskin hunting shirts. A few of the officers sported white pantaloons and waistcoats. These men had been reared with arms in their hands and they came with rifles. "Smooth-bore muskets," General Jackson had advised, "do not carry straight. They may be good enough for Regular Soldiers, but not the Citizen Volunteers of Tennessee."

Against the zero cold they were not so well armed, however. Jackson's neighbor and the army quartermaster, Major William B. Lewis, had assembled a thousand cords of wood, expected to last the life of the encampment. It was burned that night as Jackson himself made the rounds to keep sleeping men from freezing. At six o'clock he stamped the snow from his boots in front of a tavern fire. A well-known citizen who had spent the night in bed deprecated the lack of preparation for the troops. "You damned, infernal scoundrel," blazed the Major General. "More of that talk and I'll ram that hot andiron down your throat."[13]

The War Department accepted two thousand and seventy men. Jackson borrowed sixteen hundred and fifty dollars[14] to cover his extraordinary personal expenses, and on January seventh Colonel John Coffee's regiment of cavalry filed down the Natchez Trace while the General and two infantry regiments boarded flatboats. With "Four beautifull stand of Colours" waving and minute guns firing, cables were slipped and the great scows glided from the view of an huzzahing populace. "It is a bitter pill to have to serve with . . . Wilkinson . . . but I go in the true spirit of a soldier."[15] Taking his dueling pistols, however.

The Ohio was a grinding field of ice. General Jackson went ashore to reconnoiter and to write a letter.

"My Love:

"I have this evening received your affectionate letter . . . [and] your miniature. I shall wear it near my bosom; but this was useless for my recollection never fails me of your likeness.

"The sensibility of our beloved son has charmed me. . . . He will take care of both of us in our declining years. . . . Kiss him for his papa and give him nuts and ginger cake [I send].

"I thank you for your prayers. I thank you for your determined resolution to bear our separation with fortitude. We part but for . . . a few fleeting weeks when the protecting hand of Providence . . . will restore us to each others arms. . . .

"It is now 1 o'clock in the morning—the candle nearly out. . . . May the angelic hosts that reward and protect virtue and innocence and preserve the good be with you until I return, is the sincere supplication of your affectionate husband."[16]

Despite ice, an earthquake that had terrorized inhabitants and changed the currents of the Mississippi, and the loss of three men and one boat, the Commander's sleepless energy brought the flotilla off Natchez, distant two thousand miles by the route it had come, in thirty-nine days. On shore in the dark Major Carroll gave him a packet of mail.

"Your letter . . . was everything to me. . . . Where'er I go, where'er I turn, my thoughts, my fears, my doubts distress me. Then a little hope revives again and that keeps me alive. . . . Do not my beloved husband let love of country, fame and honor, make you forget [me]. . . . You will say this is not the language of a patriot, but it is the language of a faithful wife. . . .

"Our little Andrew often does he ask me in bed not to cry, papa will come again and I feel my cheeks to know if I am shedding tears. . . .

"Your dearest friend on earth
"RACHEL JACKSON"[17]

Another communication was from "Head Quarters, New Orleans."

"Sir, I have received from his Excellency Governor Blount . . . [information that] you were about to move from Nashville with one thousand four hundred infantry and Riflemen, and six hundred and seventy dragoons, destined to this city. . . .

"I beg leave to refer you to my letter of the 22nd. Inst., and must repeat my desire that you should halt in the vicinity of Natchez. . . .

"With consideration and respect,

"I have the honor to be Your Obedt Servant

"JAMES WILKINSON"[18]

The letter of January twenty-second was couched in terms that exceeded the bounds of ordinary military courtesy. "Several reasons prevent my calling you lower down the river. . . . Vizt. the impracticability of providing for your horses, . . . the health of the troops; . . . the policy of holding your corps on the alert" within equal striking distance of Pensacola, Mobile and New Orleans—wherever needed. General Wilkinson had ordered provisions to Natchez. General Jackson would find Brigade Inspector Hughes on the ground to muster the troops into Federal service, and Paymaster Knight to pay them. "Those officers [will] give every aid and facility . . . and if it is in my power to add to the comfort of the band of patriots under your orders, it is only necessary to point out the mode to me."[19]

5

Jackson perceived the military logic of Wilkinson's polite "requests" and encamped his troops. A week, a fortnight passed—and no orders. At New Orleans the subtle commandant was pondering the next phase of his problem of keeping Jackson at a distance, when news came of Winchester's disastrous defeat in Canada. Jackson asked the War Department to send him to the northern front.[20] Rachel learned of it, though not from her husband. "Oh how hard . . . Love of Country the thirst for Honour . . . is your [ruling] motive."[21]

Fifteen more days of fretful waiting for Jackson and a short letter came from John Armstrong, the Secretary of War:

"The causes for embodying ... the Corps under your command having ceased to exist, you will on receit of this consider it dismissed from public service and ... deliver over to Major General Wilkinson all articles of public property. ... Accept for yourself and the Corps the thanks of the President of the United States. I have the honor to be. ..."[22]

By countermanding the Florida venture the government had enabled the War Office to rescue General Wilkinson from his quandary as to what to do with Jackson.

Instead of recognizing the celerity with which the Tennessean had thrown an army into Natchez as the most creditable military accomplishment of the war to date, the Government had dismissed that army from service eight hundred miles from home, without pay or rations, without transportation or medicine for the sick. Nor was the blow softened by the sugary observations of Wilkinson, regretting that although "the policy of the Government" prevented "the maturation of our association in arms ... you still have it in your power to render a most acceptable service to our Government by encouraging" his abandoned troops to enlist in the Regular Army. After which the lucky schemer wished his brother officer "pleasant weather" on his journey home.[23]

Should Jackson disband his army, he saw Wilkinson getting the bulk of Tennessee's fine soldiers without their commander by a mere promise of something to eat. Passing the word to drum from camp the first Regular recruiting officer to approach his men, Jackson posted a fiery proclamation vowing to march the Tennesseans home intact "on my own means and responsibility"[24]—at best an inglorious finale to the grand adventure his ringing words had promised the youth of Tennessee.

In strong but respectful terms he notified Secretary Armstrong and Wilkinson of his refusal to obey that part of the order calling for demobilization on the spot. His command was mostly boys. He had brought them from home, and would take them back at his own expense if they had to eat their horses on the way. Then he wrote his wife. "Kiss my little Andrew for me and tell him his papa is coming home."[25]

Though seething at "the wicked machinations of Armstrong and W—n,"[26] he repressed his feelings out of hope for service in Canada.

Firmness obtained twenty days' rations from Wilkinson's quartermaster. Eleven wagons for the desperately ill were hired by the Commander, who altogether laid out more than a thousand dollars for the sick. The other ailing rode horses, three of them Jackson's own, while the General marched on foot. Such things could not be without effect on soldiers whose feeling toward their commander had hitherto been one of respect rather than affection, for Jackson was not the hail-fellow type of militia officer. The column moved at the pace of veterans—in a wilderness where streams had to be bridged and the road hacked through swamps. Jackson was everywhere—up and down the toiling line, with the sick, where the rations were distributed—and always on foot, until the men began to offer their horses.

"He's tough," an admiring voice observed in the ranks after the General had passed by. "Tough as hickory," said another naming the toughest thing he knew. The word somehow seemed to suit the tall, striding man in a mussed uniform and muddy boots. "Hickory" he became to that company. The sobriquet took, and before the first settlements were reached was the property of the army with the affectionate prefix "Old" for completeness.[27] In fine array General Jackson led his command into Tennessee to be showered with honors, but none so great or lasting as the name that had sprung from the hearts of his soldiers.

6

While on vacation from his classes at the College of William and Mary, Thomas Hart Benton had once seen Judge Jackson on the bench. The memory of it was never forgotten by this youth with the form of an athlete and a flare for Roman oratory. As a young lawyer in Franklin, Tennessee, Benton joined the local militia company of General Jackson's division and became its captain. He assisted in the prosecution of Patton Anderson's slayer and began to visit at the Hermitage. He had started on the Natchez expedition as one of the General's aides-de-camp and was not afraid to voice opinions differing from those of his chief. He returned the colonel of a regiment aglow with a desire for a military career.

Jackson gave him letters of introduction to take to Washington in furtherance of this ambition as well as Jackson's never-ceasing effort to get into the field. Moreover he was charged with straightening out the General's property accounts held up by the auditors in consequence of disregarding the order to disband at Natchez. Henry Dearborn's tardy invasion of Canada had been defeated and driven out. Another commander for the St. Lawrence was inevitable. The War Department was raising several new regiments of Regulars. Jackson's friends in Washington were quietly working to have two of them recruited from Tennessee with their man in command.

Benton was energetic and effective. Jackson's accounts were passed. While there is little doubt of the President's desire to get along without the services of Andrew Jackson, his unjust treatment at Natchez had been due to the normal bungling of the War Office rather than collusion with Wilkinson to humiliate intentionally. Benton obtained a lieutenant-colonelcy in the Regular establishment. That was the end of success. Tennessee got only one Regular regiment—to be raised in the eastern part of the state outside of Jackson's military jurisdiction. To Major General James Wilkinson, attended by every favor and facility the War Department could confer, went the honor calculated to crown our eagles with victory on the St. Lawrence.

Another young man who returned from Natchez with the esteem of Old Hickory was William Carroll,[28] the brigade inspector. Billy Carroll had come from Pittsburgh a few years back to open a hardware store which had been very successful. He was one of the best-dressed sparks in Nashville. An inspector's rôle is not a sure passport to popularity, and a selfish streak in Carroll made his advancement more than ordinarily grating. As soon as the brigade was mustered out in May, Lieutenant Littleton Johnston challenged him. Carroll declined on the ground that Johnston was not a gentleman. The bearer of Johnston's message, Jesse Benton, a brother of General Jackson's envoy, then challenged.

Carroll asked Jackson to be his second. Jackson said he was too old for such a thing, and moreover that the quarrel should be adjusted amicably. As a matter of fact Jackson was guarding his behavior, still hoping for a crumb of favor from Washington. He rode to Nashville to act as peacemaker. He talked with Benton and everything seemed settled until others put in their oars, among them Joseph Erwin and Thomas Swann.

Jackson was indignant at the way his friend had been crowded, and above all at the rattling of Charles Dickinson's bones. "May the angelic hosts protect virtue and innocence," he had written to Rachel, and stood ever ready to extend to those hosts any mundane aid in the discharge of their duties that circumstances might seem to him to require. However faint the allusion or tenuous the trace to touch the Sacred Name, Andrew Jackson never let it pass.

To maintain his standing Carroll was obliged to accept Benton's challenge. Jackson accompanied him to the field. The affair that followed provided Tennessee with a standing jest for many years. Benton fired, and, in a fit of panic, doubled up at the waist so that the most conspicuous part of his person exposed was that covered by the seat of his trousers. Into this target Lieutenant-Colonel Carroll plumped a bullet which did far more injury to the spirit than to the flesh.[29]

7

Lieutenant-Colonel Benton heard of the duel while on his way from Washington. In Nashville he took his stand by his brother and avoided the Hermitage. Gossips made the most of this and Jackson heard that Benton had threatened to challenge him. In a fatherly letter he asked if this were true. Benton replied straightforwardly that it was not, but added that he thought it "very poor business of a man of your age and standing to be conducting a duel about nothing between young men who had no harm against each other." And there were other observations showing that Benton chose to believe the accounts circulated by Jackson's enemies. This brought a stern reply. The Bentons went home to Franklin, but busybodies kept at Jackson until he exclaimed that he would horsewhip Tom Benton the next time he saw him.

Six weeks passed. On the morning of September 4, 1813, the Benton brothers arrived in Nashville and took their saddle-bags to the City Hotel, to avoid, Colonel Benton said, a possibility of unpleasantness, as Jackson and his friends were accustomed to make their headquarters at the Nashville Inn, diagonally across the Court-

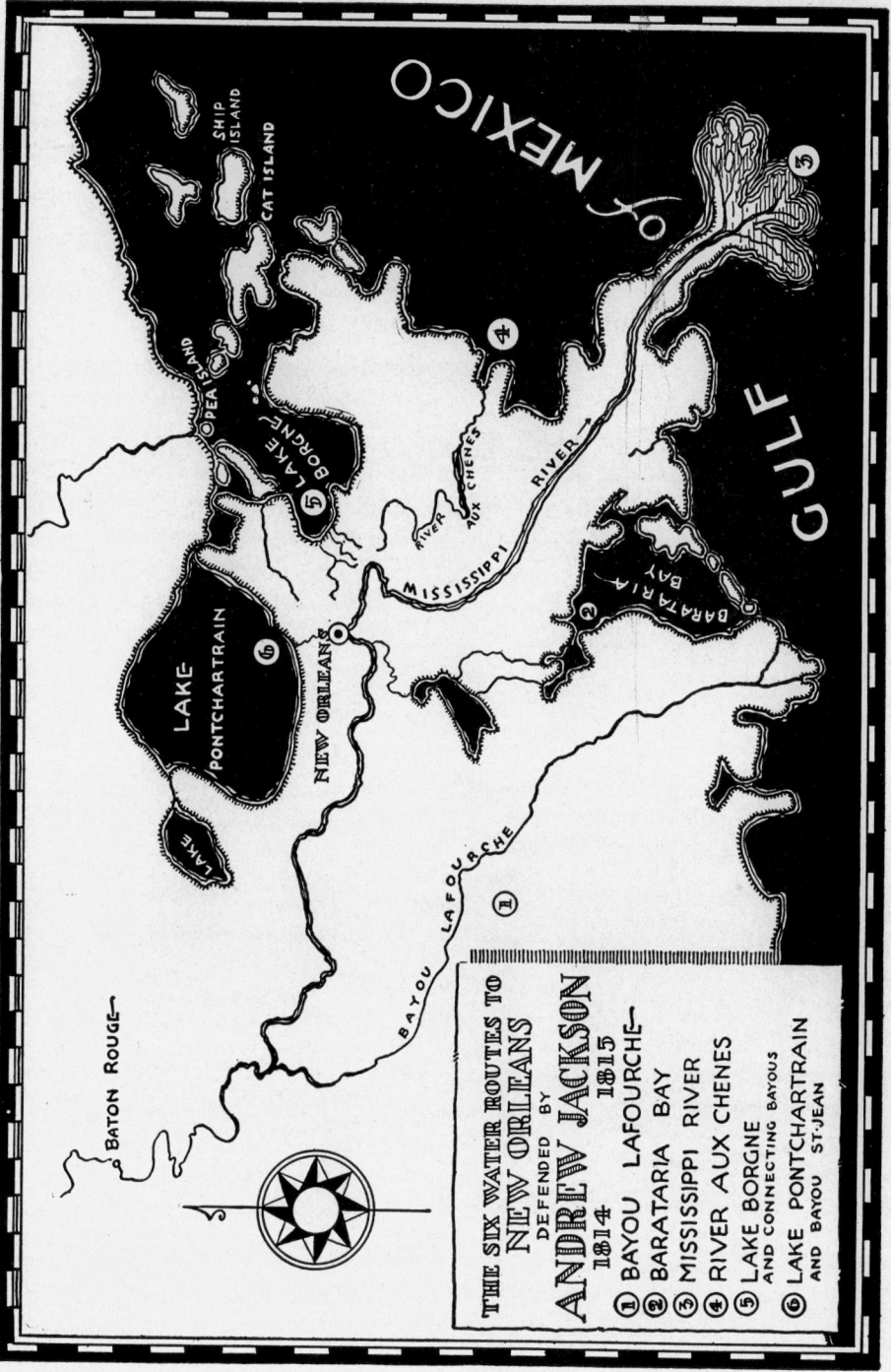

THE VILLERÉ HOUSE

Headquarters of General Pakenham Below New Orleans.

The country residence of Major General Jacques de Villeré of the Louisiana militia. On its gallery his son Major Gabriel Villeré was captured by the British advance guard. The house was demolished in 1920 to make room for an oil refinery. This photograph from the private collection of Stanley Clisby Arthur of New Orleans.

House Square. Each of the Bentons wore two pistols. At about the same time Jackson, Coffee and Stockley Hays arrived at the Inn, all armed and Jackson carrying a riding whip. The news was over town in a moment. Jackson and Coffee went to the post-office, a few doors beyond the City Hotel. They went the short way, crossing the Square and passing some distance in front of the other tavern where the Bentons were standing on the walk.

Returning, Jackson and Coffee followed the walk. As they reached the hotel Jesse Benton stepped into the barroom. Thomas Benton was standing in the doorway of the hall that led to the rear porch overlooking the river. Jackson started toward him brandishing his whip. "Now, defend yourself you damned rascal!" Benton reached for a pistol but before he could draw Jackson's gun was at his breast. He backed slowly through the corridor, Jackson following, step for step. They had reached the porch, when, glancing beyond the muzzle of Jackson's pistol, Benton saw his brother slip through a doorway behind Jackson, raise his pistol and shoot. Jackson pitched forward, firing. His powder burned a sleeve of Tom Benton's coat. Thomas Benton fired twice at the falling form of Jackson and Jesse lunged forward to shoot again, but James Sitler, a bystander, shielded the prostrate man whose left side was gushing blood.

The gigantic form of John Coffee strode through the smoke, firing over the heads of Sitler and Jackson at Thomas Benton. He missed but came on with clubbed pistol. Benton's guns were empty. He fell backward down a flight of stairs. Young Stockley Hays, of Burr expedition memory, sprang at Jesse Benton with a sword cane and would have run him through had the blade not broken on a button. Jesse had a loaded pistol left. As Hays closed in with a dirk knife, Benton thrust the muzzle against his body, but the charge failed to explode.

General Jackson's wounds soaked two mattresses with blood at the Nashville Inn. He was nearly dead—his left shoulder shattered by a slug, and a ball embedded against the upper bone of that arm, both from Jesse Benton's pistol. While every physician in Nashville tried to stanch the flow of blood, Colonel Benton and his partizans gathered before the Inn shouting defiance. Benton broke a small-sword of Jackson's that he had found at the scene of conflict. All the doctors save one declared for the amputation of the arm. Jackson barely understood. "I'll keep my arm," he said.

Friends vowed to even the score. "I'm literally in hell here," Tom Benton wrote and left town.[30]

The feud was blotted out by news of a Creek uprising and the massacre of two hundred and fifty persons at Fort Mims in Mississippi Territory (now Alabama). The horrors of Indian warfare, which Tennesseans knew so well, were at their doors. A committee on public safety hastened to the Hermitage. Jackson was too weak to leave his bed but he was strong enough to make war.

"By the eternal these peple must be saved."[31]

Before the state authorities could act to save them and before the Federal Government knew what had happened, Coffee's cavalry was forming up. "The health of your general is restored," Jackson wrote, propped against a pillow. "He will command in person."[32] The Governor authorized an expedition of twenty-five hundred men and Jackson promised to march with it in nine days.

CHAPTER X

RED EAGLE

I

THE destroyer of Fort Mims was William Weatherford, a personage of unusual family history. His great grandfather, Captain Marchand, had carried the fleur-de-lis from New Orleans to the upper waters of the Alabama, thereby establishing a minute claim to immortality, which was acknowledged by a dot on a map swept by lace cuffs at Versailles where a circle of scented little men fumbled with the iron Frontenac's dream of New France. The Captain found his post of command a lonely one, but this was mitigated in 1722 when a girl of the godlike Creek Clan of the Wind consented to share his exile behind the sodded ramparts of Fort Toulouse on the River Coosa. The wilderness representative of the arms of France was less fortunate, however, in his relations with his soldiers, who mutinied and slew him, by that means removing a father's protecting hand from a small demi-French daughter named Sehoy. But the gods intervened in favor of their own. Sehoy's good looks proved to be protection enough.

A minor chief married her first. Then Fort Toulouse changed hands and Sehoy Marchand changed husbands, returning to her birthplace as consort of the English Captain Tait. The new Commander welcomed to his solitary post Lachlan McGillivray, a presentable young Scottish tourist of wealthy family. The visitor paid his host the compliment of departing with Sehoy. He built her a house on the Coosa, surrounded her with servants and accumulated a fortune in the Indian trade. Sehoy bore him a family, which one day Trader McGillivray forsook to spend life's afternoon beneath the wet clouds of Scotland, telling, one imagines, some wonderful stories.

By this time Alexander McGillivray, the trader's son, was old enough to make a man's decisions concerning life. Of commanding bearing and polished address, this youth showed little trace of his quartering of Indian blood. Lachlan had seen to his education at Charleston and desired him to be a white man. Alexander tried the life of his parent's preference, but, on the whole, it bored him so that he fell back upon the culture of the wigwam and a career in which French urbanity, Spanish deceit, Scotch thrift and Creek savagery saw him far—his boast being that no Yankee blood polluted his veins.

In the American Revolution McGillivray was a British colonel. During a subsequent recrudescence of French influence, one of his sisters became the mistress of General Leclerc Milfort. Under Miró he was a Spanish civil servant, usefully involved in the Cumberland intrigue, and so first came within the sphere of Andrew Jackson. But whatever his relation to the uncertain white counter-theme of Indian affairs, Alexander McGillivray retained the principal chieftainship of the Creeks, controlled the Seminoles, and was faithless to the interest of neither. In 1793 he died, a brigadier-general in the United States Army, worth one hundred thousand dollars, and was buried with Masonic honors in a Spanish gentleman's garden at Pensacola.

For twenty years men and nations had learned that success on the southern borderland required the good-will of McGillivray. Charles Weatherford, another Scotch trader, achieved this boon by marrying a half-sister, *née* Tait. Mr. Weatherford's comfortable house, his blooded horses and his hospitality were known to every traveler of distinction who fared that way. His children also were border-line cases to whom was presented a choice of races. John Weatherford chose the Caucasian and has not been heard of since. William chose the Creek.

As Red Eagle this nephew of the fantastic McGillivray won his place at the council fires, but events were several years in shaping a field suitable to the scope of his talents. In 1810 one of the remarkable personalities of American history, Tecumseh, visited the Creeks to exploit his dream of a Lakes-to-Gulf confederacy to smother the white infiltration. Red Eagle was stirred, but the glow died. There were other tribes with more cause for complaint than the Creeks. Under McGillivray the Creeks had held their own. After him Benjamin Hawkins came as agent for the United States Government—

an anomaly among such officials, being both honest and able. His defense of treaty rights won him a much higher regard among Creeks than among whites.

In October of 1811 Tecumseh returned. Land-seekers had been aggressive and the red genius made the most of it. His magnetism and matchless eloquence swept away most of the young Creeks. Red Eagle, thirty-one years old, emerged from a state of moody contemplation. Then came war with England. Medicine-men said the Great Spirit had contrived this opportunity. Hawkins, the Creek's true friend, pleaded dramatically but in vain. With the crimson war-club, or red stick, dangling in the squares of their encampments, the braves rose under William Weatherford. Settlers fled to stockades. Weatherford moved against the largest of these, the fortified residence of Samuel Mims, a well-to-do Creek half-breed who had cast his lot with the whites. Seventy Louisiana militia under Major Daniel Beasley, a half-breed, guarded the fort. On August 30, 1813, the seven-eighths white leader of the Creeks surprised his half-white adversary. When the butchery was over, Red Eagle shamed his army, but before the world accepted its conduct—a duty inseparable from leadership.

2

On October seventh, Old Hickory took command of his infantry at Fayetteville. Coffee's cavalry was in Red Eagle's country. Jackson broke camp on the eleventh, and, hearing that Coffee was in danger, marched thirty-two miles in nine hours before learning that the rumor was false.[1] The next day he joined the cavalry at Ditto's Landing on the Tennessee River below the outpost settlement of Huntsville (now Alabama).

The haggard man with an arm in a sling had done more than make a new record for the movement of infantry. He had taken the first step in a bold winter campaign, all clear to his rapid mind. The second step was to move twenty-four miles along the Tennessee to its southernmost dip where part of his army began to throw up defenses called Fort Deposit, which was to be the main base of supplies. The rest of the army plunged into the wilderness with axes to hew a road across the Raccoon Mountains to the Ten Islands of the Coosa River fifty miles away where the advance supply base was to be. There Jackson planned to begin fighting.

From his bed at the Hermitage he had spread spies among the enemy. They were white men and mixed-breeds whose homes were the woods. He had sent emissaries to those Creeks who remained friendly; also to the Cherokees and to the Choctaws. In this way enough was learned of Weatherford's numbers and dispositions[2] to form the plan for an offensive, ranging southwestward from the Ten Islands, in which Red Stick towns would be destroyed and armed bands exterminated in battle. This done, Jackson would push on to Mobile, opening from Tennessee to the Gulf a highway of much importance to the United States. Then, although nothing in his orders contemplated it, the crowning stroke: invasion of Florida, seizure of Pensacola,[3] and elimination of the insidious influence of Spain, silent ally of Britain and open supporter of the Creeks.

The project of the impetuous Tennessean was complete in itself, and much more comprehensive than the suppression of an Indian insurrection. Jackson prepared to accomplish it alone. He did not ignore the fact that he was subordinate to old Major General Pinckney of the Regular Army, commanding the Department of the South; or that Georgia, Louisiana and Mississippi Territory also were dispatching militia columns against the Creeks, and that a Regular regiment at Mobile was supposed to cooperate. Neither did he rely on help from those quarters, a wise resolution as matters fell out. He did, however, count on a junction with twenty-five hundred East Tennessee troops under John Cocke.

And first of all he counted on supplies. Fort Deposit was completed, but there was little to put into it. The civilian contractor system, in vogue in our armies, was a weak reed under favorable circumstances. In the wild country where troops moved with the celerity of Jackson's, it failed from the first. In six days the road to the Coosa was cut "over mountains more tremendous than the Alps," as a participant vowed with perfect sincerity. Jackson stormed at the delinquent contractors, discharged one set and engaged another. Coffee was sent to forage Indian corn. An appeal was dispatched to the inhabitants of Mississippi: "There is an enemy I dread much more than I do the hostile Creek, . . . that meagre-monster 'Famine.'"[4]

On the next day Jackson wrote privately, "I am determined to push forward if I have to live upon acorns,"[5] and, publishing battle instructions,—"the charge with the bayonet will be the signal of victory. Your general has pledged his reputation upon it"[6]—began to march with less than two days' rations.[7]

Red Stick scouts slipped through the trees beside the toiling column. Chief Pathkiller of the Cherokees sent word of Weatherford's threat to Indians who failed to espouse his cause. "Brother," wrote Jackson, "the Hostile Creeks will not attack you until they have had a brush with me; & that I think will put them out of the notion."[8] To his aide, John Reid, he said he would die rather than retreat.[9] Arriving on the Coosa in three days, the army began to cut trees for the stockade of the advance base which was named Fort Strother. Here General Jackson renewed for sixty days, and sent back to Tennessee, a personal note for one thousand dollars which he had owed for nearly a year.[10]

Thirteen miles away two hundred Red Sticks were at the village of Tallushatchee. Coffee was sent with one thousand troops to destroy them. The first battle of the campaign was fought the following morning, November 3, 1813. "We shot them like dogs," said Davy Crockett, present and shooting.[11] No warrior escaped and eighty-four women and children captives were taken. Coffee lost five killed, forty-one wounded. "We have retaliated for Fort Mims," Jackson reported in literal truth.[12] Among the prisoners a handsome child attracted the notice of the Commanding Officer. He was three, the age of another boy much in the thoughts of the turbulent General. The Creek women would not take care of him. His parents were dead, they said. "Kill him, too." With his one good hand, Jackson dissolved some brown sugar in water and coaxed the child to drink. Then he sent him to Huntsville to be looked after at his personal expense.[13]

3

Weatherford had his hands full. Jackson's whirlwind invasion had won Indian allies and kept others on the fence. To put his own house in order, the red leader turned from his white adversary to the Creek town of Talladega which had declared for Jackson. On November seventh Jackson was dictating an order to Brigadier-

General James White, commanding the advance of Cocke's East Tennessee division, to hasten to Fort Strother when news of Talladega came from an Indian wearing a deer tail in his hair, the sign of friendship prescribed by Jackson. Talladega was in imminent danger, the Indian said, being surrounded by a thousand of Weatherford's braves. The informant himself had crept through the hostile lines in a hog's hide. Jackson added a postscript for White to march with all speed as he was leaving his sick and wounded in camp insufficiently protected. He told the Indian to creep back and tell his friends that help was coming.

Talladega was across the Coosa and thirty miles to the southward. There was no road. At one o'clock in the morning, Jackson began to move his army over the river. The following sunset the men dropped in their tracks, six miles from the beleaguered town. Jackson was ill of dysentery. While the army slumbered he sat against a tree in agony, questioning scouts who had been sent to ascertain the topography of Talladega, the disposition of the enemy and of the force he was to relieve. At midnight came an express from White saying that "a positive order" from Cocke would prevent his protecting the fort. This left two hundred sick, all the stores of the army and its line of communication at the mercy of an enemy whose intelligence service was nearly perfect, and who could outmarch even Jackson. Yet to retreat without giving battle would be a blow to white prestige that would send every doubting Indian in the region to Weatherford's standard.

Not having slept, Jackson, at four in the morning, gave word to arouse the army. As soon as light began to show through the treetops, the columns were in motion.

The sun was an hour high when they deployed for battle on November 9, 1813. The men were hungry. Half a mile away, they could see friendly Indians gesticulating from their ramparts, but no foe was visible. Jackson ordered a crescent-shaped formation, with the points toward the town, and sent three mounted companies to raise the enemy and court an attack. The men making the half-moon saw them ride warily through the brush and dead autumn grass, saw the exchange of signs with the Indians in the fort, saw two Indians rush from the fort, seize the bridle of Captain Russell's horse and point earnestly to a tree-lined creek.

THE NIGHT BATTLE

Jackson riding to the rescue of the guns, below New Orleans, December 23, 1815. From a painting by W. A. C. Pape, date unknown, which has hung in the St. Charles Hotel in New Orleans for more than fifty years.

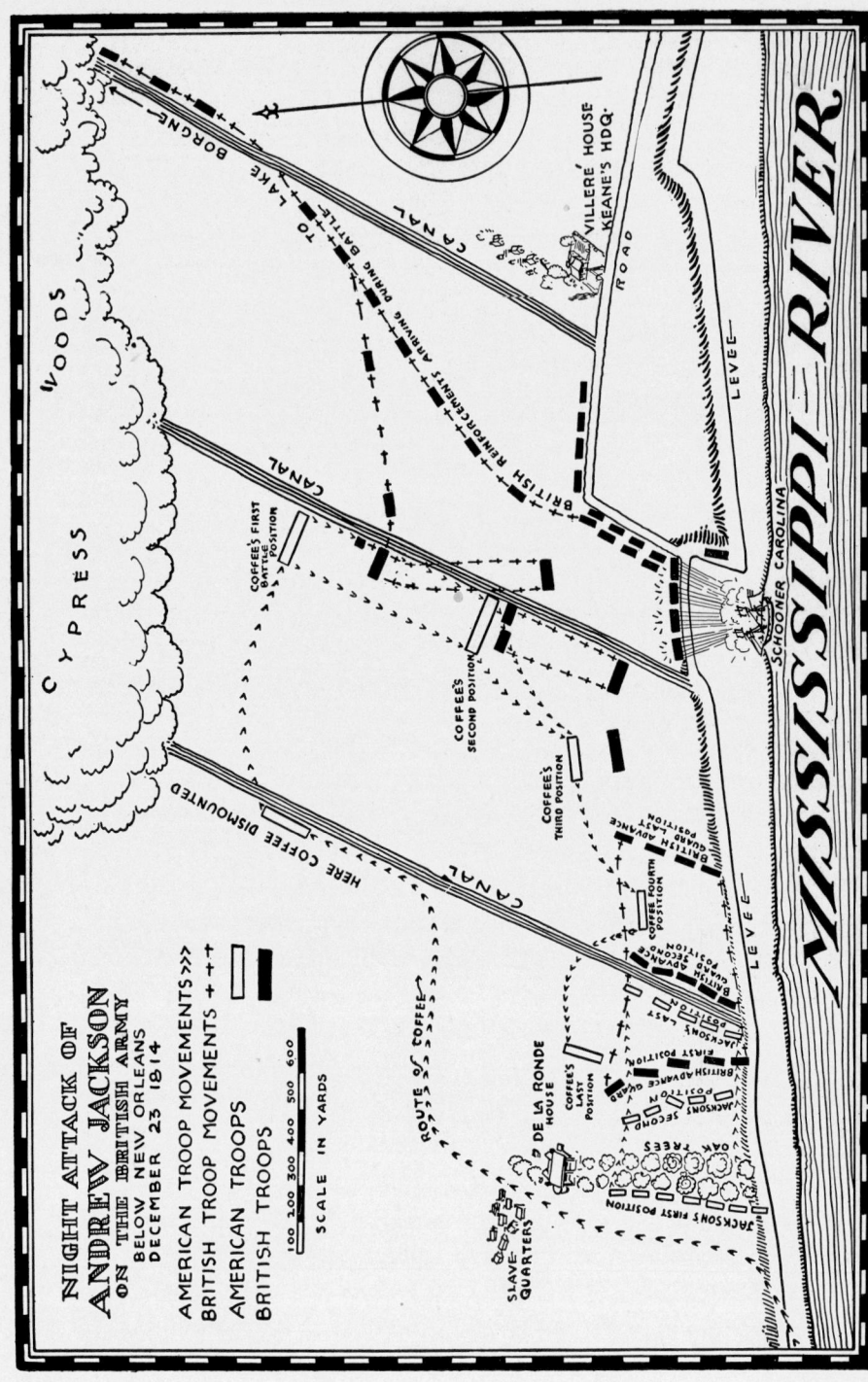

The warning was not a moment too soon. A volley roared from the creek bank, and the hostiles burst from their cover "like a cloud of Egyptian locusts, and screaming like devils."[14] With the painted warriors in pursuit, the cavalrymen galloped back toward the main body. When the heedless Indians had been drawn within range, their quarry wheeled from the line of fire.

A volley from Jackson's curving battle line staggered the charge, but did not stop it. Weatherford's naked men met the whites with guns and arrows and tomahawks. The tips of Jackson's crescent pressed forward and joined. The encircled Creeks were falling in heaps before the superior arms of their adversaries when a detachment of volunteers gave way. Seven hundred Red Sticks poured through in flight.

Cavalry closed the gap and the battle went on until inside the ring of Jackson's line lay three hundred dead Indians, fifteen dead whites.[15]

4

Two stinging defeats within six days were bad for Weatherford, and although entirely without rations, Jackson wished to plunge ahead and take advantage of his victories. Cocke's order, which left Fort Strother defenseless, alone prevented Old Hickory from going on to what might have been a speedy conclusion of the war.

With eighty-seven wounded and nothing to eat, Jackson returned to the fort the second day after the battle, hoping to find supplies and to resume operations. Not a pound of rations had reached the stockade. Before leaving for Talladega, Jackson had directed the surgeons to draw upon his private stores should others not arrive. These had all been consumed except a few pounds of biscuit. Jackson immediately ordered them distributed among the wounded, though no one in camp had greater need than the commanding officer for a special diet. So wracked by dysentery that he could hardly stand, Jackson confronted his trials with a fortitude from which his stomach never recovered. During a paroxysm he would half-suspend himself by dangling his arms over a horizontal sapling pole, and in this position sometimes remain for hours. The only succor of two thousand men was a few cattle. Jackson ordered them butchered, taking for himself and staff only the offal, on which he lived without bread or salt while moving heaven and earth to rouse the ration contractors.

Petitions came from the different commands, urging a return to civilization to replenish stores. The troops were respectful. No thought of abandoning the war was expressed. By one expedient and another Jackson put them off. To remove the wounded, he said, would cause the death of many. The story was told of a soldier who asked the General for something to eat. "I will divide with you what I have," Jackson replied, drawing from his pocket a handful of acorns.[16]

Complaints soon grew bitter. Jackson's force was composed of two brigades of United States volunteers, Natchez expedition "veterans," and one brigade of militia. The militia was the first to try to take matters into their own hands and start home. Jackson threw some volunteers across their path and they returned to quarters. When the volunteers tried to leave, the militia stopped them.[17] Summoning the brigade commanders, Jackson renewed his promise of supplies, and, after a ringing appeal, asked them to ascertain if their commands would stand by the wounded and by the campaign. Coffee's volunteer cavalry voted to stick. Robert's militia would stay for three or four days. Despite all their brigadier could do, Hall's volunteers voted to go. This cut deeply. Hall's brigade was a part of the old division that had sworn to follow Jackson to Quebec. The Commander published an order. "If supplies do not arrive in two days we march back together."[18]

Two days and no supplies. Four days. With men and mounts starving, Jackson yielded on November seventeenth. Twelve miles from the fort they met one hundred and fifty beeves and nine wagons of flour. When they had eaten their fill, Jackson ordered the army to return to Fort Strother, excepting Coffee who was to take his command in search of forage for the horses. The infantry ranks formed, grumbling. At the command to march a single company moved out—toward Tennessee. Others prepared to follow. Officers were powerless.

Jackson put spurs to his horse. A detour brought him in front of the mutineers where Coffee happened to be with a handful of his cavalry. Forming them across the road, Jackson threatened the deserters with a volley unless they faced about. He did not speak twice.

Rejoining the main body Jackson rode among the men. Finding

Hall's entire brigade on the point of desertion, he seized a musket and backed his horse into their path. Jackson's left arm was in a sling. Resting the barrel of the musket on his horse's neck, he swore to shoot the first man to move a step in the wrong direction. John Coffee walked to one side of his General. Major John Reid, the handsomest man in the army, took the other side. A loyal company deployed in their rear. For some grim minutes the army stood thus; then the discontented brigade trudged sullenly toward Fort Strother and Jackson returned the musket, which was found to be too badly out of order to fire.[19]

On November twenty-seventh a note for seven hundred and fifty-four dollars fell due. The General was obliged to renew.[20]

5

On December second he rejoined his troops at Fort Strother with extensive plans to move against Weatherford on December tenth.[21] He discovered, however, that Hall's brigade, comprising the bulk of his force, had made other arrangements for that date. A volunteer's term of service was one year. The brigade had been sworn in on December 10, 1812, for the Natchez expedition, after which they had been released until the recall in September. At the instigation of certain officers, a majority of the men contended that time spent at home counted toward their year of service, which would expire on the day the General had set for a resumption of operations.

Nor was this Jackson's only concern. Impossible instructions came from Major General Pinckney, viewing the situation from his headquarters at Charleston, South Carolina. The Louisiana and Mississippi expedition had accomplished little. After a brush with the Red Sticks Georgia's expedition was in retreat. A strong Creek faction which had sued for peace after Talladega was again on the war-path, and Weatherford had doubled the army opposing his vexed adversary at Fort Strother. The moral value of the two victories had been lost.

Jackson's patience, never abundant, was exhausted. Irritable and ill, he used language that failed to promote an understanding with the volunteers. Without yielding an inch, he prepared, however, to replace them, and dispatched appeals to Tennessee for reenforcements.

Should the volunteers leave before new troops arrived Jackson and his one brigade of steadfast militia would be exposed to annihilation.

On December sixth a note for one thousand dollars was payable. Jackson had renewed it the day he left Nashville. He was obliged to renew again, but omitted to do so until the eighth, a species of delay of which he was not often guilty. Sunday, December ninth, was a day of tension. A backwoods chaplain delivered a sermon which a supporter of Jackson was moved to answer in a speech that did not please the volunteers who had announced their departure from camp on Monday. Among the loyal was a nephew of Nolichucky Jack who asked a small favor. "If you can Spare as much Whiskey as will wearm a half Douzen of Good Heerited fellows you will Oblige Your friend & Hum^b, Svt Charles Sevier."[22] The General himself wrote to John Coffee whose cavalry was still absent refreshing the horses: "What may be attempted tomorrow I cannot tell," but should the volunteers succeed in quitting the fort Coffee was to intercept them. Should they resist arrest "you will immediately open fire."[23]

Jackson did not have to wait until the morrow to learn the determination of the men. At eight that evening, he was informed the brigade planned to slip away during the night. With the loyal militia under arms near by, he paraded the volunteers outside the walls where the astonished brigade found their line covered by the two little brass cannon that comprised the post's artillery. Jackson addressed them. He was tired of argument, he said, and "done with entreaty." If they meant to desert, let them try it now. If they meant to be soldiers, they should return to quarters.[24] The ranks stood motionless.

With "feelings better to be Judged than expressed," Old Hickory gazed at the wayward soldiers "I once loved as a father loves his children."[25] Ordering the gunners to light their matches, he rode within the field of fire. "I demand an explicit answer." The lines stirred. Several officers hastened forward. They promised that the brigade should remain until relieved by reenforcements.

Three days later Cocke from East Tennessee marched in "with 1450 of as fine looking Troops as you ever saw," as Jackson wrote Coffee directing him to rejoin the main body ready for battle.[26] Hall's brigade was read from camp and they were scarcely out of sight when Jackson was informed that the time of most of Cocke's fine-looking troops would expire in ten days, when they, too, expected to go home.

Old Hickory declined to waste rations or breath on such men and wounded their pride by packing them off in twenty-four hours. Everything now depended on the cavalry, ordered to come on by forced marches. Alas for the stout Coffee, who had yet to fail Andrew Jackson as a soldier or as a friend. His men also were volunteers. Meeting Hall's brigade streaming northward, they broke camp while their commander lay ill and joined the deserters. "Can it be true what I hear!" exclaimed Jackson.[27]

Then came the blow that seemed to foretell the end of Andrew Jackson's military career. Governor Blount threw up the sponge, advising the evacuation of Fort Strother and a retreat to Tennessee. It was a literal summons to join the dismal file of funking military chieftains whose crowded march into the limbo had distinguished our management of this war. One ill-calculated step and Andrew Jackson should bear company with the dim shapes of Hull, Dearborn, Hampton, Izard, Chandler, Winder—the list could be lengthened.

When General Jackson received Blount's letter, he had slept only two hours in two nights, for the five hundred effective men remaining of his deciduous military organization had begun to falter. Word of the Governor's loss of heart, coming in response to Jackson's burning petition for conscription in order to maintain an army in the field, would have reduced them to panic. At twelve-thirty o'clock in the morning on December 29, 1813, Jackson began his long reply by observing, in a general way, that Mr. Blount had merely "recommended" a withdrawal. "Still, if you had ordered me peremptorily to retrograde with my troops," Old Hickory declared that he would have refused to obey. With his back to the wall, Jackson cast everything his passionate being possessed into the scale to restore the ebbing courage of the Executive.

The Governor was reminded that he had "bawled aloud for permission to exterminate the Creeks." He was reminded that the Legislature of Tennessee had pledged the Federal Government to keep thirty-five hundred men in the field until this was done. "And are you my Dear friend sitting with yr. arms folded, . . . recommending me to retrograde to please the whims of the populace. . . . Let me tell you it imperiously lies upon both you and me to do our duty regardless of consequences or the opinion these fireside patriots, those fawning sycophants or cowardly poltroons who after their boasted ardor would . . . let thousands fall victims to my retrograde."

To "see how you and myself would appear in the painting," Jackson sketched the desperate consequences of a retreat that would add five thousand wavering Choctaws, Cherokees and hitherto friendly Creeks to Weatherford's cause.

"Arouse from yr. lethargy—despite fawning smiles or snarling frowns—with energy exercise yr. functions—the campaign must rapidly progress or . . . yr. country ruined. Call out the full quota—execute the orders of the Secy of War, arrest the officer who omits his duty, . . . and let popularity perish for the present. . . . Save Mobile—save the Territory—save yr. frontier from becoming drenched in blood. . . . What retrograde under these circumstances? I will perish first."[28]

6

These lines and a supporting thrust from an unexpected quarter—the War Department—made a changed man of Governor Blount. But before new troops could reach the Coosa, Robert's militia, so long faithful, went home; their three months' term was up. Jackson had declared that if two men stayed by him he would hold Fort Strother. For a few hours he held it with one hundred and thirty,[29] including a cavalry company under John Coffee, composed of ex-officers who had refused to join the men in desertion.

As the last of the militia walked off eight hundred recruits arrived from Tennessee. Already they were beginning to sense the irksome side of military life. Jackson gave them no time for reflection, but at once marched southward where the Red Sticks were gathering. On the night of January 18, 1814, the expedition encamped on the site of the Battle of Talladega. The men were undisciplined, the officers not much better. With such material Jackson knew he must fight now or never. He pressed toward Weatherford's stronghold at Tohopeka, or the Horseshoe Bend of the Tallapoosa River. On the night of January twenty-first he bivouacked at Emuckfaw Creek, seventy miles from Fort Strother and three from Tohopeka. Before dawn the Creeks attacked.

They hoped to take the whites by surprise, but Jackson's green men had been ready all night. By firing at the flashes of the Indians' guns, they held off the enemy until it was light enough to see. Then Jackson threw in his reserve of one company and charged. The enemy gave way and Coffee went forward with half of the command to reconnoiter the Creek position at Tohopeka. He found it too strong to attack and hastened back, fearing Jackson might be cut off. Coffee's men had scarcely thrown themselves down to rest when a clatter of musketry came from the pickets on the left of the line. Coffee called for two hundred men to flank the assailants, but only fifty-four, including the ex-officers' company, followed him.

Alarm guns sounded on the right and pickets ran in firing. This was the main attack. Jackson led the reserve, one company, into action, riding up and down the firing line. Gliding from tree to tree, the Red Sticks came on behind a stiff barrage of musketry and arrows. They prepared to charge, but Jackson charged first. The Creek line faded into the woods. Two hundred Indian allies who had joined Jackson on the march had done well in the battle. They closed the events of the day by relieving Coffee's outnumbered band which, with its leader wounded, was hotly pressed.[30]

The indecisive fight was susceptible of some military and enormous popular advantages. A diversion had been created for General Floyd's column. The report of a glorious victory for the new troops would stimulate recruiting in Tennessee. On the other hand Jackson was in a ticklish situation. Seventy miles from an unprotected base he was surrounded by an enemy in superior force. An attack on Weatherford's position at Horseshoe Bend being out of the question, he could only withdraw.

The night after the battle his men slept on their arms. Having buried the dead, who included Major Alexander Donelson, and made litters for the wounded of the skins of dead horses, their cautious retirement began. The country was wild and roadless. Weatherford's men—noiseless, invisible, a part of the leafless landscape of winter—crept alongside the nervous column. That evening Jackson reached Enotachopco Creek. The Red Sticks hovered near and the whites bivouacked in expectation of an attack. None came and on the morning of January twenty-fourth they began to cross the creek.

Enotachopco Creek was broad and cold, its banks steep and sparsely wooded. Jackson had distributed detailed orders in case of an attack on front, flanks or rear. The advance-guard, the wounded and part of the flank columns were on the other side, the artillery company with one brass cannon was in the creek, and the center column was preparing to follow when alarm guns banged in the rear. Jackson heard them "with pleasure." He had laid a trap for an attack from behind. The rear of the three columns were to hold the Red Sticks while the front of the flank columns, recrossing the stream above and below, surrounded them—a repetition of the tactical principle of Talladega.

Jackson was on the bank of the creek. Imagine his "astonishment and mortification," when "I beheld the right and left column of the rear guard precip[i]tately give away . . . in shamefull retreat," their colonels with them.[31] As the fleeing men tumbled down the declivity, the center column also gave way, despite the efforts of its commander, William Carroll. Only this officer and twenty-five men stood between the scalping knife and the panic-stricken mass splashing in the water.

Jackson's shrill oaths clove the din. "When they heard his voice and beheld his manner," many preferred to confront the Red Sticks instead. On the far bank John Coffee staggered from a litter and brought a company to Carroll's support. Lieutenant Armstrong fired the six-pounder using the butt of a musket as a rammer and a musket ramrod to pick the flint. "Save the cannon," he cried as he fell with a ball through his body. Ordering the retreating colonels under arrest, Jackson took hold of the embattled line. "In showers of balls he was seen performing the duties of subordinate officers," wrote one who was there, "rallying the alarmed," and "inspiriting them by his example. . . . Cowards forgot their panic, . . . and the brave would have formed round his body a rampart with their own."[32]

7

Emuckfaw and Enotachopco added to Jackson's other battles afforded news in pleasing contrast to the war's established precedent. The Administration press, famished for anything that looked like a victory, printed columns in which a wealth of patriotic ardor repaired the paucity of accurate detail without, however, exaggerating the difficulties against which the Commander on the Creek front had contended. A "blue light," or anti-war, newspaper in New England might spare only twelve lines for events so remote, but its serves-us-right attitude toward defeat was deranged by a prideful swelling of hearts among common men that here at least was one soldier, named, as it appeared, Andrew Jackson, who could win battles.

But the woman waiting at the Hermitage received the news with other emotions.

"My Dearest Life, I received your Letter by Express. . . . how did it feel. I never Can disscribe it. I Cryed aloud and praised my god For your safety. . . . how long o Lord will I remain so unhappy. no rest no Ease I cannot sleepe. all can come hom but you. . . . I hope the Campaine will soon end the troops that is now on their way will be sufficient you have done now more than aney other man ever did before you have served your County Long Enough. . . . you have been gon six monthes. . . . oh Lord of heaven how Can I beare it. Colo Hayes waites. . . . our Dear Little Son sayes maney things to sweet papa. . . . your faithfull wife untill Death. RACHEL JACKSON."[33]

Colonel Hayes brought troops. Jackson had demanded five thousand men of Governor Blount—more than he needed and doubtless more than he expected to get. But he got them all, hastily raised and poorly equipped. By the time half of them had crowded upon Fort Strother the old troubles recommenced. But when the Thirty-Ninth United States Infantry marched in, Jackson felt himself master of any eventuality. The Regulars "will give strength to my arm and quell mutiny."[34] "With a continuation of the smiles of fortune I shall soon put an end to the Creek war."[35] A professional view of discipline began to emphasize the distinction between Jackson's position and the position of all subordinates. *This* army would not slip through his fingers. When the second senior officer, Major General John Cocke, seemed to doubt that Jackson meant it, he was relieved of his sword and sent home in arrest. A similar fate befell Brigadier-General Isaac Roberts.

Old Hickory was putting the final touches to his plans to end the Creek war when interrupted by a row outside his tent. A seventeen-year-old boy was defying the Officer of the Day with a rifle.

"Shoot him! Shoot him!" cried Jackson.[36]

Private Woods belonged to a company that had caused much trouble. But Jackson did not know that Woods was a new recruit, in service less than a month as a substitute for his conscripted brother, and not involved in the company's previous behavior.[37] He was convicted of mutinous conduct and sentenced to be shot, but the camp refused to believe "that a militiaman would . . . for any offense be put to Death."[38]

After two sleepless nights[39] the Commanding General approved the action of the court. At ten in the morning of the fourteenth of March the army formed in hollow square. In the center, a squad of Regulars leaned on their smooth-bore muskets of seventy caliber. At headquarters Jackson penned a dispatch. "A private (John Wood) having been sentenced to death by a court martial, that ceremony is now in the act of execution. . . . I have ordered the line of march to be taken up at 12 o'clock with seven days bread rations and two of meat, . . . direct for Emuckfa."[40] Having brought up to date a statement of his private indebtedness the General was now ready for battle.[41]

8

Dawn of March 27, 1814, saw Jackson's field army of two thousand men at the Horseshoe Bend of the Tallapoosa where eight hundred warriors awaited the battle upon which they staked everything. The Horseshoe enclosed one hundred acres, furrowed with gullies and covered by small timber and brush. Across the neck of the peninsula was a log breastwork with two rows of portholes. At the point was a fleet of canoes to insure an avenue of retreat.

Jackson surrounded the Horseshoe. Coffee's scouts swam the river and carried off the canoes. A thousand men were drawn upon the land side to storm the works. "Any officer or soldier who flies before the enemy without being compelled to do so by superior force . . . shall suffer death."[42] At half past ten o'clock the six-pounders' flat echo flapped through the naked woods. Their round balls sank harmlessly in the soft pine logs and Creek sharpshooters kept the gun crews close to the ground.

Jackson delayed the infantry attack until the Creek women and children could be carried across the river to safety. This took until twelve-thirty o'clock, when the drums of the Regulars beat the long roll and the infantry charged. Major Lemuel P. Montgomery of the Thirty-Ninth Regiment was the first man on the works. He reeled back dead. Half hidden by smoke, a tall boy in Regulars' blue and brass, Ensign Sam Houston, scaled the logs, and, waving his sword, leaped down on the other side.

There was a hard fight at the rampart, but it was overrun. The Red Sticks retreated in small bands into the rugged terrain where twenty battles raged at once. "Arrows, and spears, and balls were flying," recorded Ensign Houston, "swords and tomahawks gleaming in the sun."[43] The bands fought to the last man. A power more than moral sustained their courage. The Great Spirit had promised victory. Oblivious to the conflict, the priests of their religion moved among the braves, chanting the rituals, and falling as the warriors fell. The tide would yet turn, they said. The sign would be a cloud in the heavens.

In the middle of the afternoon Jackson offered life to all who would surrender. During the lull a small cloud appeared. The Red Sticks fired upon the messenger of peace and resumed the battle with passionate fury. "The *carnage* was *dreadfull*."[44] The sign of deliverance brought only a quiet shower and the "peninsular was strewed with the slain." At dusk one band held out in a little covered fortress at the bottom of a ravine. An invitation to surrender was refused "with scorn," and a volunteer storming party of Regulars driven off. Jackson set fire to the stronghold with flaming arrows; the battle was over.

Five hundred and fifty-seven Indian dead were counted on the ground and the river held two hundred more. Jackson had lost forty-nine killed and one hundred and fifty-seven wounded. From the field the victorious Commander carried "a warrior bow and quiver . . . for my little andrew."[45]

He expressed two regrets. "Two or three women & children were killed by accident,"[46] and a mischance of events had kept Weatherford away from Horseshoe on the day of the battle. Weatherford had commanded at the massacre at Fort Mims. He had been the moving spirit of the insurrection. The white sought his corpse as evidence of the Mosaic law fulfilled.

Jackson moved south where Weatherford was reported to be rallying a few Red Stick remnants on the Hickory Ground at the junction of the Coosa and the Tallapoosa—sacred soil which, in the Creek belief, no enemy could tread and live. But on Jackson's approach, the shaken warriors scattered. The flag was raised over the moldering walls of Fort Toulouse which was rechristened Fort Jackson. One or two of the Creek leaders fled to Florida. Others came in and surrendered. But where was Weatherford? The thought of his quarry safely on Spanish soil exasperated General Jackson.

A tall, light-colored Indian presented himself at the post. His body was bare to the waist, his buckskin breeches and moccasins badly worn. He was unarmed and on foot.

The Commanding General was leaving his quarters.

"General Jackson?" inquired the Indian.

"Yes."

"I am Bill Weatherford."

Reputed eye-witnesses have given two versions of Jackson's response. "I am glad to see you *Mr.* Weatherford."[47] "How dare you show yourself at my tent after having murdered the women and children at Fort Mims!"[48]

They went inside. The General's aide, young John Reid, was present.

"Weatherford," he wrote in a private letter, "was the greatest of the Barbarian world. He possessed all the manliness of sentiment—all the heroism of soul, all the comprehension of intellect calculated to make an able commander. . . . You have seen his speech to Genl Jackson, . . . but you could not see his looks & gestures—the modesty & yet the firmness that were in them.

"'I am come,' he said, 'to give myself up. I can oppose you no longer. I have done you much injury. I should have done you more . . . [but] my warriors are killed. . . . I am in your power. Dispose of me as you please.'

"'You are not,' said the general, 'in my power. . . . I had ordered you . . . brought to me in chains. . . . But you have come of your own accord. . . . You see my camp—you see my army—you know my object. . . . I would gladly save you & your nation, but you do not even ask to be saved. If you think you can contend against me in battle go & head your warriors.'

"'Ah,' said Weatherford, 'well may such language be addressed to me now.[49] . . . There was a time when I . . . could have answered you. . . . I could animate my warriors to battle; but I can not animate the dead. . . . General Jackson, I have nothing to request . . . [for] myself. . . . But I beg you to send for the women and children of the war party, who have been driven to the woods without an ear of corn. . . . They never did any harm. But kill me, if the white people want it done.'"

Jackson poured his guest a cup of brandy. He promised to help the women and children. Weatherford promised to try to persuade the remaining braves to peace. General Jackson extended his hand. Red Eagle took it, and strode from the ruined fort in which his mother had been born—vanishing from the view of the astonished soldiery, and from history, a not entirely graceless figure.

CHAPTER XI

Storm Clouds

I

Rachel and Andrew, junior, joined the victor at Huntsville and the return became a triumphal progress. "I can but imperfectly communicate to you the feeling of the people. Your standing . . . is as high as any man in America," John Overton wrote and he added a "hint." "There are mean people whose greatest gratification is to irritate you, and thus lessen your fame if they can." Judge Overton hoped that his old friend would watch his temper.[1]

A large part of the population of the Cumberland lined the road entering Nashville to receive the first home-coming soldier-hero of the war. On the court-house steps Representative Felix Grundy did the honors, Jackson responding without vanity, in boast, or in mock modesty. A state banquet was followed by the presentation of the first of an eventual arsenal of ceremonial swords. General Jackson then treated the community to an example of what any soldier who had done his duty might expect of his old commanding officer:

"I have the pleasure to inform you that Captain Armstrong and his lady is now with me, . . . united in the holy bonds of matrimony." General Jackson addressed the bride's father, Josiah Nichols, whose brick mansion still looks upon the Lebanon Road a few miles from the Hermitage. The bridegroom was the plucky artillery lieutenant at Enotachopco. "I hear with regreat that this union did not meet with approbation. I have been acquainted with Captain Armstrong since his childhood. so have you! Is there a blemish in his charector? . . . he is honest, he is brave, he is enterprising, . . . and without a cent of property he is worthy of any lady, of any family, of any fortune. . . . Be good enough to present my respects and that of Mrs. Jackson to Mrs. Nichol, and assure her untill her daughter meets with a full forgiveness from her, she will find in Mrs. Jackson the tender care of a mother, and both will find in me the care of a father. on friday . . .

I am to have my friends with me to partake of a dinner, will you and your lady do Mrs. Jackson and myself the pleasure of dinning with us."[2]

2

Speaking of Tennessee, Judge Overton was correct. Enemies had been crushed by the irrefutable logic of victory. The powerful clique of ex-officers of the autumn army that had deserted and all but succeeded in persuading Blount to call the General home, dared not make a sound. Old Sevierites said Jackson should be the next governor.[3] And the man they honored had changed. From the nadir of a tap-room shooting scrape, he had gone forth to return master of himself as well as of the Red Sticks, the sure and resolute Jackson of Mero District days.

Throughout the country Administration newspapers printed long accounts of the Horseshoe, and the opposition found itself unable to duplicate the succinct journalism that had distinguished its earlier references to the campaign. Several Administration personages would have preferred to see editorial encomiums bestowed elsewhere, but the conduct of the favorite generals had rendered this difficult. The only other military commander eligible to felicitation was William Henry Harrison, a non-favorite, who, seeing much of his good work in Canada undone by the ineptitude of James Wilkinson, resigned from the Army in disgust. After some prodding the major-generalcy in the Regular establishment thus vacated was tendered on May 28, 1814, to Andrew Jackson[4] with the command of the Seventh Military District, embracing Tennessee, Louisiana and Mississippi Territory. The War Department did not expect, however, that this should afford General Jackson further opportunities for distinction. The fighting was over on the southern front, Secretary Armstrong said. Rumors of Spanish efforts to stir the Indians to fresh hostility were incredible, and "the report of a B. naval force on our Southern coast . . . of nearly the same character." Jackson was instructed to dismiss all troops, except a thousand men, and rest from his exertions.[5]

The new Commandant had other plans. When he left his bed to lead the expedition against Weatherford, Andrew Jackson's true goal had been Pensacola. It was Pensacola now. But another matter came first. The War Department had announced that General Pinckney, Jackson's nominal superior during the Creek campaign, and Benjamin Hawkins, the veteran United States agent of the Creeks, would make the treaty of peace with the defeated Red Sticks. The choice was not popular in the West. Pinckney was a decent old Charlestonian whose martial force had been usefully spent in the Revolution. Hawkins was an appointee of George Washington and embodied the Father's views of Indian affairs. By a series of blunt moves, Jackson supplanted these gentlemen as peacemaker and the frontier was assured of a representation of its own ideas.

On the day that a tailor in Murfreesborough measured the General for "one suit of full dress uniform, . . . [with] Gold Epaulettes, . . . all of the best quality," an express arrived with Florida news through Jackson's own channels: British marines arming and inciting Indians to a renewal of hostilities. "We ought to be prepared for the worst," Jackson warned the Secretary of War. "*Query*. . . . Will the government say to me, . . . 'proceed to —— [*sic*] and reduce it.' If so I promise the war in the south has a speedy termination and the British influence forever cut off from the Indians in that quarter."[6]

3

Twelve days later he was at Fort Jackson, inviting the chiefs to council. "Destruction will attend a failure to comply."[7]

They came, chieftains and sub-chieftains of the war-party who had surrendered at discretion, and expected a stern peace; leaders of the Creeks who had sided with Jackson, anticipating reward for their loyalty—all attended by the retinues that their rank required. The retinues of the Red Sticks were pitiful. "Could you only see the misery and the wretchedness of those creatures," Jackson wrote to Rachel, "perishing from want of food and Picking up the grains of corn scattered from the mouths of horses."[8] Yet to complain would have been beneath the dignity of an occasion when one must assume a brave appearance at any inconvenience. Their lean faces masks of oriental reserve, they gathered their robes of ceremony over empty stomachs and confronted the man with whom they must barter for their fate.

The mind of the Indian was a deep mind, perhaps at its best in a

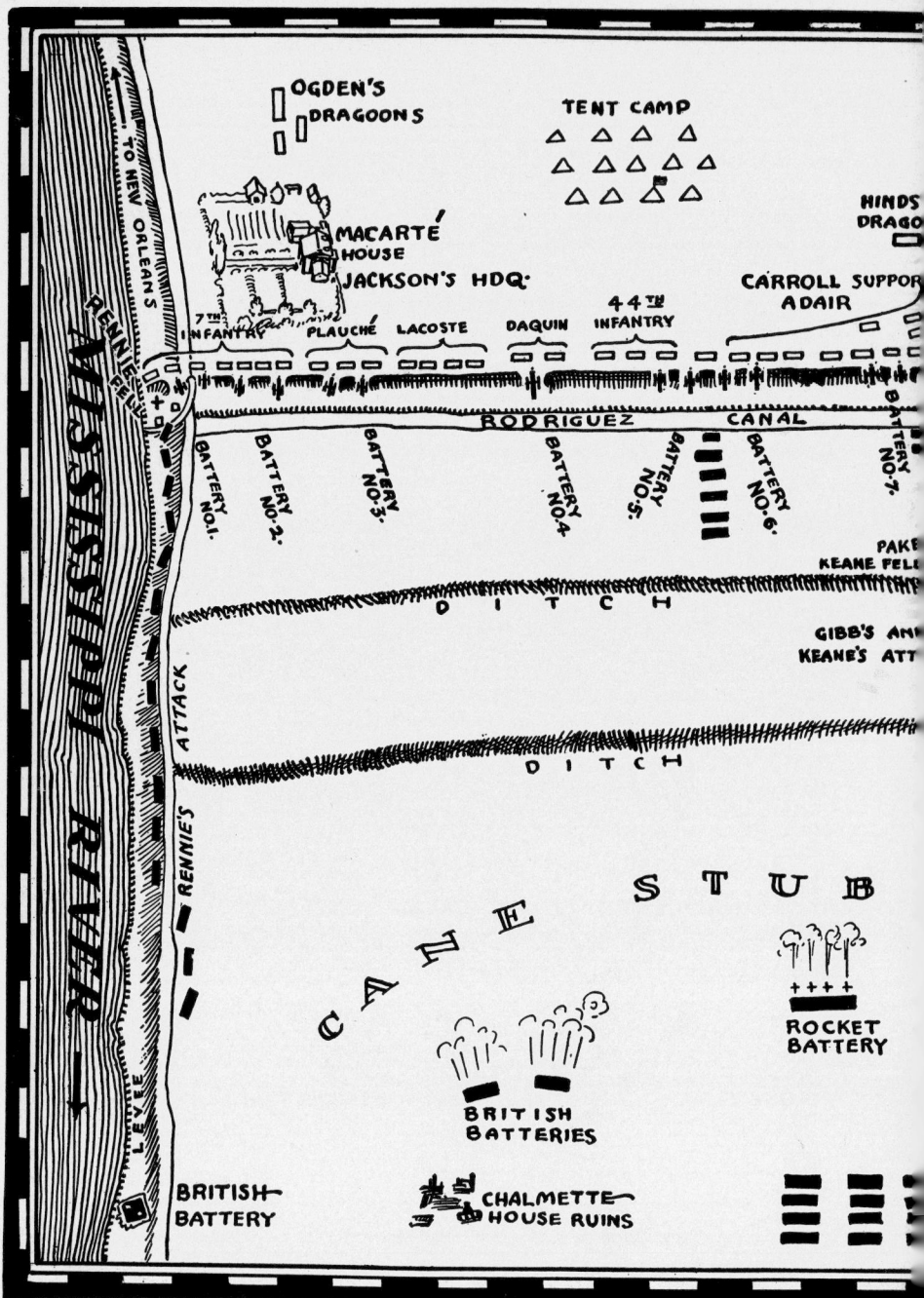

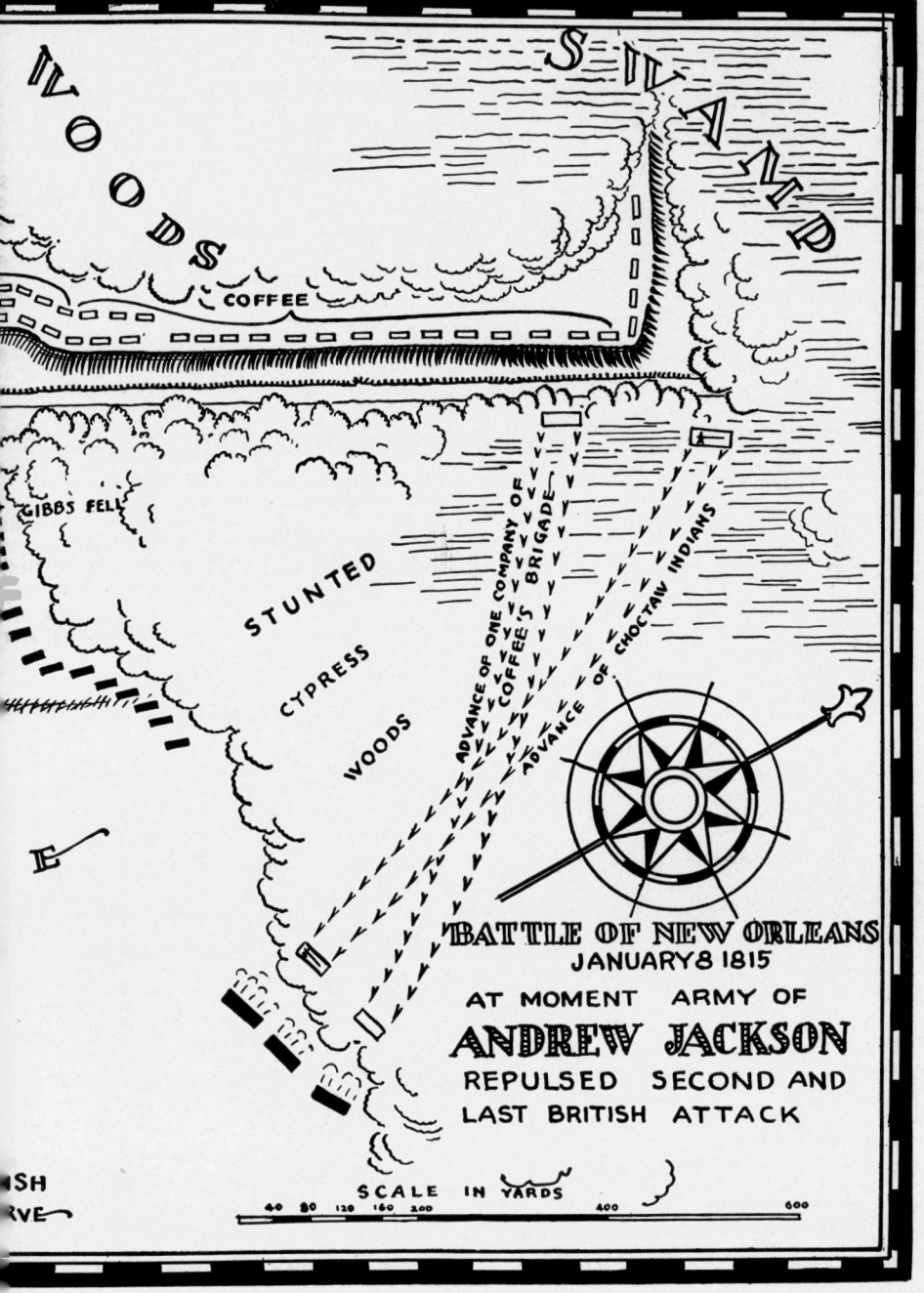

STORM CLOUDS 177

council of this kind. He reasoned subtly and rather well, clothing his thoughts in language which for beauty and color is surpassed by that of no race on earth. He would contend cunningly for an advantage, but an agreement was quite as likely to be respected by him as by the frontiersmen through whom his ideas of civilization were formed. In the present instance the negotiators knew the man with whom they dealt. The Indian name for Jackson was Sharp Knife.[9] He was hard, but, having given his word, he kept it.

The Creeks reposed their hopes in ceremonious delay, a strategy already begun with Pinckney and Hawkins. They had no opportunity to continue it with Jackson who called the delegations before him and addressed them briefly, speaking first to the loyal Creeks. "Friends and brothers, you have fought with the Armies of the United States, many of you . . . by my side." Then to the Red Sticks: "Friends and Brothers, you have followed the counsel of bad men." The war, he said, had been expensive. To pay for it and to avert the possibility of future war the United States must indemnify itself with land from the whole Creek people. "Brothers, the terms of peace I hold in my hand. . . . [They] will be read to you."[10]

The translators performed their task. An Indian was schooled from childhood to control the lines of his face against a betrayal of surprise or dismay, and so without comment, when the reading ended, the Creeks withdrew to their foodless camps. They were thunderstruck. In all the checkered narrative of our dealings with the Indian people, General Jackson's terms are unequaled for exorbitance. They cast a long shadow, giving the authority of distinguished approval to a precedent that was to accomplish the ultimate ruin of the red race more quickly than otherwise might have been. Since the result was inevitable, perhaps it was better thus. The Indian was of flint; one could only break him for he would not bend. But one issue was possible in his struggle against the Caucasian who always has conquered. Because of its directness and swiftness, the method of Andrew Jackson was probably the more humane in the long run. At least, he did not clothe it in the diaphanous disguise of nice excuses.

Jackson demanded the surrender of twenty-three million acres, or half of the ancient Creek domain. This territory now comprises one-fifth of the state of Georgia and three-fifths of Alabama. There was slight distinction between the lands of friend and foe. Nearly half of the territory demanded belonged to tribes whose braves had fought throughout the war under the banners of the whites. To the government Jackson perfunctorily explained his terms on grounds of policy. The frontiers of Georgia and Tennessee were removed from hostile threat. The remaining Creek lands were separated from the deleterious influence of Florida. The coveted highway from the Cumberland to Mobile was assured. To the West explanations were superfluous. The frontier gazed with hungry eyes upon a land speculator's New Jerusalem.

In private council the hearts of the Creeks sank. An attempt to ameliorate the brutal terms was delegated to two chiefs who had fought with Jackson in the late campaign. On the following day the General and his suite received them. The eloquence of Big Warrior and of Shelokta touched every white man who heard it. Jackson answered them at considerable length. The interest of his country, he said, would permit no amendment to his demands. Through the territory the Creeks must relinquish "leads the path that Tecumseh trod. That path must be stopped. Until this is done your nation cannot expect happiness, mine security." Those who signed the treaty would be received as friends, those who refused, as enemies. They must decide that night, but whoever declined to sign would be given safe-conduct to Pensacola.[11]

"Face" was important to an Indian. The negotiators could not return to their people without a concession, however trivial. Of the land they were asked to surrender, they proposed that three square miles be given to General Jackson "as a token of gratitude." Similar gifts were suggested for Benjamin Hawkins and two others. Jackson replied in a friendly speech. With the consent of the President of the United States, he would accept the gift and "appropriate its value to aid in clothing their naked women and children." The chieftains replied that "they did not give to General Jackson land to give back to them in clothing; they want him to live on it, and when he is gone his family may have it; and it may always be known what the nation gave it to him for."[12] There is subtlety in the last words.

On August 9, 1814, thirty-five friendly chiefs and one who had been hostile signed the extraordinary treaty.[13] A "disagreeable business" was done, the General wrote Rachel, and "I know your humanity would feel for them."[14]

4

Not for an instant had Jackson taken his eyes from Florida. His first act on arriving in the Creek country was to dispatch observant and reliable John Gordon, a man of the woods and captain of a scout company, to Pensacola. He bore a letter to the Commandant demanding the surrender of two fugitive chiefs and an explanation of the British proceedings on Spanish soil. "Disagreeable consequences" were intimated in event of an unfavorable answer.[15] Gordon's interview with the Spanish officer was brief. Don Matteo González Manrique observed that Jackson's communication was "Impertinent" and that the hospitality of Spain would not be withdrawn from the chiefs. On his return, Gordon further reported that the British were establishing a military base at the mouth of the Apalachicola, and that a Spanish fleet was expected to join the British men-of-war off the coast.[16]

From other sources the observations of Captain Gordon were confirmed. British marines had landed and a captain of their number was drilling the Indians while regiments of black troops were being mobilized at Jamaica. "I calculate on some warm work with them and the Indians in the course of the fall season,"[17] Jackson informed John Coffee. To Secretary of War Armstrong he wrote: "You will pardon me for suggesting that the months of September and October are those in which we may anticipate a blow."[18]

Jackson had received no reply to his *"Query"* for tacit consent to strike at the root of the trouble in Florida and this puzzled him. The Secretary was equally puzzled. He had written a sleek letter, explicit enough to send the Commander of the Seventh District into Florida, but vague enough to support a disavowal should this become diplomatically desirable. But when General Jackson received this communication the war was over. The delay has the color of intrigue, though in later years Armstrong declared it was Madison who held up the letter.[19] Jackson was left, therefore, to act on his own responsibility, which is probably what he would have done in any case.

The day after the Indian treaty was signed he had made up his mind to act.

"My love

"This is the last letter you will receive from this point . . . as tomorrow at 12 I embark for Mobile." But the separation was nearly at an end. From Mobile Colonel Robert Butler, Rachel Hays's husband and the General's ward, would return to Tennessee "for the purpose of bringing you to me." "I have wrote John Hutchings to have you a good pair of horses procured, and I wish your carrige repaired or exchanged for a new one—you had better vissit Nashville and make this arrangement with the carriage maker yourself— you must recollect that you are now a Major Generals lady in the service of the U. S. and as such you must appear elegant and plain, not extravagant, but in such state as Strangers expect to see you— a good Supply of Eatable such as our country yields will add verry much to our comfort. . . . Let a house be built for your Sister Cafferry." She was Mary, the oldest of the Donelson sisters, who with her young husband had journeyed from Virginia to Louisiana by the rivers in 1780, reared a family and in her widowhood come to Tennessee to enjoy the protection that Jackson extended to so many of the numerous company of his wife's relations. "Say to Genl Overton he knows I would write if I had time. May heaven protect you is the prayer of your affectionate Husband."[20]

General Jackson was aware that he invited his wife to a theater of lively scenes. He had asked Blount to summon troops. "Dark and heavy clouds hang over us."[21]

5

The storm those clouds foretold had already broken, though it was a month before Jackson began to receive the news.

"Wellington's army to America! . . . Bonaparte dethroned. Peace in Europe; English coming to swallow U. S."[22] So recorded a diarist of Dedham, Massachusetts, who refused to speak to his brother, the distinguished Fisher Ames, because of his opposition to the war.

Ten thousand Peninsular veterans disembarked at Quebec to invade the East, while Sir Alexander Cochrane's fleet was to divert attention along the Atlantic littoral. As a finishing blow the most formidable military and naval expedition the New World had seen moved toward its secret rendezvous at Jamaica to subjugate the South. A fringe of this stupendous effort was what Andrew Jackson had detected in Florida.

Cochrane struck first. He seized and annexed most of Maine. He burned Eastport, captured Nantucket, sacked or laid under tribute the Cape Cod towns and made a foray into Long Island Sound. New England shuddered. Banks buried their specie and people fled. A good many Blue-lights renounced their British sympathies and the scurrying of militia companies contributed to the confusion. Other reformed lukewarms, groping for a scheme of resistance, began to prepare the way for the Hartford Convention. A few border-line traitors among them, supported by a wide-spread sentiment in New England, were to give this assembly the hard name of a secession conspiracy. Believing the worst Andrew Jackson declared that had he been in the East, he would "have hung every man of them."[23] Later he graciously modified this opinion, saying he would have hanged only "the three principal leaders."[24]

But with Andrew Jackson on the Alabama and an English fleet off Boston harbor, sufficient of the anti-war party in high places stood its ground to present a bewildering spectacle—Paul Revere's copper-clad dome atop the State-House illuminated in honor of the Allies' victory over Napoleon!

The Quebec army marched and Cochrane entered the Chesapeake for an experimental thrust toward Washington, defended by a force of militia thrice the size of the invaders. The government disappeared by as many exits as the city afforded. The militia proved almost as nimble. A band of Navy seamen sold their lives dearly but Washington was leisurely occupied and the Capitol and President's House burned. Alexandria was plundered, Baltimore shelled and the middle seaboard clutched by panic. Philadelphia frantically fortified, New York fortified. Then came tidings of an American defeat at Plattsburgh by the expedition from Quebec.

It was false. By an astonishing victory on Lake Champlain, Commodore John McDonough had broken up the invasion, and sent ten thousand Wellington veterans limping back to Canada. One could count on the Navy! Bonfires flared and flags flew in great celebrations, as if such din could substitute for self-respect or repair the naked objects of degradation that scarred our coast from Penobscot to Potomac. The menace from Quebec was removed and Cochrane stood to sea—for Jamaica and New Orleans, it transpired. At the time it was enough to know that he had gone. New England dismissed her homeguards, dug up her money and resumed a sophisticated stare upon allusion to what a crude man like Andrew Jackson styled "our nation's Honour."

6

With the Third United States Infantry, five hundred and thirty-one strong, General Jackson reached Mobile on August 22, 1814, two days before the fall of Washington. He sent a runner to overtake Butler, en route to fetch Rachel from Tennessee.

"His B. M. ships Hermes, Carron and Sophy has arrived at Pensacola . . . and taken possession. The Orpheus is expected in a few days with 14 sail of the line and many transports with 10,000 Troops. It is further added that 14 sail of the line and Transports has arrived at Barmuda, with 25,000 of Lord Wellingtons army &c. &c., before one month the British and Spanish forces expect to be in Possession of Mobile and all the surrounding country.

"The[re] will be bloody noses before this happens. I have ordered the different Indian agents to enroll every warrior that will take the field. I have called on all the militia I am authorized under orders of the Government. . . . See Captain Deaderick and Captain Parish and say I expect them in the field with . . . a Betalion and the favorite six pounder. . . . I want about 1000 horse with Genl Goffee." A page of this, calling up men. "Cause the Contractors to . . . [forward] 6 months rations for three thousand men. . . . Say to Mrs. Jackson I have not time to write. . . . Before this reaches you we may have a brush."[25]

Next day he found time to write Rachel. She must defer her visit. "I pray you be calm and Trust to that superintending being who has protected me in the midst of so many dangers and kiss little Andrew for me affectionately adieu."[26] With a British fleet at hand the Commandant of Pensacola sent Jackson an insolent reply to the message delivered by John Gordon. Jackson's rejoinder contained a sentence that captivated his imperiled little army: "An Eye for an Eye, Tooth for Tooth and Scalp for Scalp."[27] But before the Old Testament could be employed as a guide for the regulation of affairs at Pensacola, Jackson surmised he would meet the British at Mobile. Major Lawrence was sent with one hundred and sixty men to repair abandoned Fort

Bowyer on the spit commanding the pass that connected Mobile Bay and the Gulf. To hold the pass was Mobile's only chance of safety.

Lawrence strove day and night at the fort. In the drowsy little waterside town, Jackson's cyclonic energy confirmed the easy-going French-Spanish inhabitants' worst opinions of "Americans." They chattered knowingly in groups and helped when they were paid for it. Soon it became impossible to pay them. "I have not a dollar," Jackson informed the Government, "to purchase an Express horse, nor can the Quarter Master procure one on credit, and the Mail arrives here only once a month."[28]

7

Intelligence of the enemy, however, arrived daily. Spain had shed the pretense of neutrality. At Pensacola, a few hours' sail from Fort Bowyer, an English fleet rode at anchor and in the casemates of Fort Barrancas lounged English marines. Captain George Woodbine distributed scarlet jackets and sought to instruct his astonished Indian allies in the manual of arms! The Cross of St. George was unfurled beside His Catholic Majesty's standard over the residence of Don Matteo Manrique. The Commandant's guest was Lieutenant-Colonel Edward Nicholls, an Irishman whom Wellington thought well of. The Colonel had not been long on the scene when he penned—and composition seems to have presented few difficulties to this soldier—an order of the day:

"You are called upon, . . . to perform long marches through wildernesses, swamps and water-courses; your enemy, . . . inured to the climate, will have great advantages. . . . But remember the . . . glory of your country."[29]

This was followed by a proclamation:

"Natives of Louisiana; on you the first call is made to Assist in Liberating . . . Your paternal soil. . . . American Usurpation . . . must be Abolished. . . . I am at the head of a large body of Indians, well armed, disciplined and commanded by British officers—a good train of artillery, seconded by . . . a numerous British and Spanish squadron. . . . Be not alarmed at our approach. . . . A flag over any door, whether Spanish, French or British, will be certain Protection."[30]

With these engaging documents there came to Jackson's hands the letter of a resident of Pensacola intended for a business friend in Mobile. "Great events are in embrio. . . . I tremble for what you already have at stake in case of resistance. . . . All the Mobile will fall an easy prey and before one month it will be your inevitable fate again to change masters."³¹

The American Commander had been following the moves of Colonel Nicholls since he had appeared in Havana a month before. Fortunately for Jackson, the Colonel loved the sound of his own voice. In Cuba he had talked too much for a military man, and his words had found their way to the alert Commander at Mobile. According to Nicholls the British would occupy Pensacola as a base, then seize the mouth of the Mississippi and Mobile, and, marching on Baton Rouge, cut off New Orleans from above and below. Slaves were counted on to join the black regiments of Jamaica and help was expected from the Louisiana Creoles.³² With the landing at Pensacola the first step in this broad program had been taken.

Fortunately also this opportune disclosure of British intentions was no surprise to Jackson, who, putting himself in the enemy's shoes, had come to virtually the same conclusion as to the most practicable way to move on New Orleans. During the Indian conference Jackson had warned Claiborne to prepare for an attack. But the Governor was not impressed. As a courtesy to a friend, he ordered his militia to be "ready," but nullified the force of his act with an opinion that the idea of an invasion was too "chimerical" for serious attention. By now he had changed his mind, however. While Nicholls was addressing the Louisianians, Claiborne addressed Jackson. "I have a difficult people to manage, . . . Native Americans, Native Louisianians, Frenchmen, Spaniards (with some English). . . . *That ardent Zeal* which the Crisis demands" was lacking. Unless "Louisiana [militia] is supported by a Respectable Body of Regular Troops . . . I fear . . . we shall be enabled to make *but a feeble Resistance*."³³

8

Serious as Jackson knew his situation to be it was not possible to follow every tentacle of the vast British effort that was encompassing him. On the second day after Colonel Nicholls had signed his procla-

STORM CLOUDS

mation, His Majesty's brig *Sophie* sailed under the guns of Barrancas and stood to sea. On September 3, 1814, she approached with care a narrow strait between two low green islands of the Louisiana coast.

A small brick fort materialized against the foliage. It flew no flag. The *Sophie* fired a signal gun and a boat containing four men at the oars and a fifth in the bow left the beach. It was met by a gig carrying two English officers. One of them requested "Monsieur Laffite." He was told, in French, that Laffite might be seen on shore.

On the yellow beach a motley press of barefooted seamen crowded to the water's edge. The King's servants did not like their looks and were glad when a glance from their guide dissolved this gallery. On a breeze-swept porch overlooking Barataria Bay, the guide turned to his visitors.

"Messieurs, I myself am Laffite."

Captain Lockyer of the brig *Sophie* and Captain McWilliams of the Royal Colonial Marines introduced themselves. Perhaps they appraised rather closely the man of whom they had heard so much. He was thirty-four years old, tall and sunburned. His countenance was pleasant, his address polite, and he had a peculiar habit of closing one mild brown eye when he spoke. He wore a green shirt, open at the throat. His wavy brown hair was tossed by the wind.

The time of the Englishmen's visit had been happily chosen, said Jean Laffite. It was the hour of dinner.[34]

9

Possibly Governor Claiborne might have sensed more quickly the peril of a British invasion had it not been for the dust of his lesser war against Jean Laffite. "Emboldened by the impunity of past trespasses," the Barataria pirates "no longer conseal themselves . . . but setting the Government at defiance in broad daylight carry on their infamous traffic."[35] Mr. Claiborne offered five hundred dollars for the capture of Laffite.

Ten years among them had failed to acquaint William Charles Cole Claiborne with his Latin constituents. Five hundred dollars! Monsieur Laffite redeemed the dignity of the scene by offering thirty thousand dollars for the apprehension of Mr. Claiborne, and the Hôtel du Trémoulet chuckled over its coffee and cordials. Laffite's sail continued to comb the Gulf for Spanish ships, his only quarry, and to bring them into Barataria. The cargoes were offered for sale to New Orleans merchants, who sometimes were apprized of their arrival by advertisements in the *Louisiana Gazette,* inviting an inspection of goods before buying. While Jackson, with a weather eye on the Gulf, wrote his Creek treaty, Mr. Claiborne labored with a handpicked Grand Jury. This body terminated its toils with a broad deprecation of piracy and an expression of regret that convictions should be "difficult . . . even where the strongest presumptions of guilt are offered."[36]

From his comfortable quarters at Barataria, Captain Laffite noticed the activities of the Grand Jury in a letter to the *Gazette,* adding: "Please to inform the public that several prizes have latterly been brought to Barataria. . . . Notes of any of the Banks of New Orleans will be received for goods sold."[37] Whereupon Pierre Laffite was arrested. The Laffites' lawyer, Edward Livingston, sought his release on bail. It was refused. This depressed Jean, who was fond of his brother. He himself had spent four years in a Spanish prison, and to his misfortune attributed his present attitude toward society.

Jean Laffite was a native of Bordeaux, the second of five brothers. After short terms in the British and the French navies and in Napoleon's artillery, he turned his hand to piracy in the Caribbean where an English house-cleaning had brought the profession to low estate. Laffite restored it to a plane not enjoyed since the royal patronage of Elizabeth. He had a warehouse in Royal Street, New Orleans, and a blacksmith shop in St. Philip Street, where skilled slaves fashioned grills for French and Spanish houses. Jean was little at sea, the maritime branch of the business being in the charge of Pierre Laffite and Dominique You, a dandified little fellow with a hot temper. For the touch it afforded with gentility, Jean instructed the youth of first families in the use of the sword. He brought his younger brothers from France, intending that their acquaintance with the polished world should penetrate beyond the fencing ground. Marc Laffite promised to fulfill these expectations. He studied law and was elected a local magistrate.

But all the quiet influence, by no means small, that Jean could bring to bear failed to open prison doors for Pierre Laffite. Claiborne was elated. His "difficult" population might not support him against

England. Against Laffite he did not require their support. In New Orleans were a handful of Regulars and a few small gunboats. Governor Claiborne conferred with Master Commandant Patterson of the Navy and with Colonel Ross, Forty-Fourth Infantry. An expedition to destroy the fort at Barataria was arranged.

Jean knew of this plan almost as quickly as it was made, but he lay in his hammock on the cool porch and lifted not a hand to forestall it. His first desire was the release of his brother. Unusual means would be necessary, but there were ways by which such means might be applied. He was turning over expedients in his mind when the *Sophie's* signal gun boomed off Grand Terre.

The English officers long remembered the delicacy of the food and wines and the splendor of the plate that graced the table of Jean Laffite. Over fragrant cigars Captain Lockyer unfolded his papers.

The first was the proclamation of Colonel Nicholls.

The second was a letter to "Monsieur Lafite or the Commandant of Barataria:" "I Call upon you, with your brave followers, to enter into the Service of Great Britain, in which you shall have the rank of Captain. . . . I hope to cut out other work for the americans than oppressing the inhabitants of Louisiana. Your property shall be guaranteed to you, and your persons respected. . . . Be expeditious in your resolves, and rely on the verity of your humble servant, EDWARD NICHOLLS."[38]

Another letter was from Sir William H. Percy, commanding the squadron at Pensacola. Sir William addressed Laffite in a different tone. He must be England's ally or her enemy. "Monsieur Le Feete . . . I hold out [to you] a War instantly destructive . . . but trust that the inhabitants of Barrataria, consulting their own interest, will not make necessary . . . such extremities . . . [but will] assist Great Britain in her just and unprovoked war against the United States." In this event "the security of their property [and] the blessings of the British Constitution" would be their reward. "Given under my hand on Board H. M. Ship Hermes."[39]

So the rumored descent upon New Orleans was to be a fact. Moreover, the British offer seemed a solution to all the difficulties that beset Jean Laffite. He would be protected against the meditated attack by Patterson and Ross. Pierre would be free.

Jean told Captain Lockyer he would reply to his proposals in writing. The officers returned to their ship and a letter followed them.

"If you could grant me fifteen days . . . to put my affairs in order . . . I will be entirely at your disposal."[40]

10

The *Sophie* departed from Barataria on September fourth. With the *Hermes*, *Carron* and *Childers*, she stood off Mobile Point on September twelfth. Colonel Nicholls landed marines, Indians and a howitzer in the rear of Fort Bowyer. On the thirteenth he exchanged shots with the fort at long range. The men of war moved into the pass and began to make soundings. Sir William H. Percy had hoped for Jean Laffite as an ally in the attack impending.[41] His small vessels would be in no danger of grounding. But the British Commander was confident, nevertheless. His guns outnumbered those of the fort seventy-eight to twenty.

Major Lawrence watched these preparations through a glass and when darkness fell dispatched Lieutenant Roy in a small sailing vessel for reenforcements. Mobile was thirty miles away and against the high wind Roy had a difficult passage before him.

But it was a good night to journey in the other direction. Jackson was still at Mobile. Knowing nothing of the presence of the British at the Point, he decided to slip over and inspect Lawrence's preparations for defense. At ten o'clock boarding a schooner with a small guard, he headed for the pass.[42]

CHAPTER XII

"Push on the Troops"

I

AFTER ten thousand miles on the curling currents of Western rivers, this was Andrew Jackson's introduction to salt water. The wind stiffened, and at one o'clock in the morning the schooner hailed the vessel of Lawrence's messenger beating up the bay. From Lieutenant Roy, Jackson learned that Fort Bowyer was beseiged by superior forces on land and on water. Timely news! Sixty minutes more and the wind might have carried into the pass a prize of more consequence to Sir William Henry Percy than Lawrence's awkward little fort on the sand spit.

Jackson's schooner put about for Mobile to hasten reenforcements to Lawrence. For fourteen hours the small vessel tacked against the storm, making land at two in the afternoon, September 14, 1814, at the mouth of Dog River. Jackson leaped into a pirogue and ordered a course to Mobile. A pirogue on a river is one thing, on Mobile Bay in dirty weather another, but Jackson reached the town by nightfall. He called Captain Laval's company to arms. There was not a sea-going craft in the port. Jackson embarked them on a boat he had used to descend the Alabama, with instructions to transfer to the schooner should they meet it, but at all hazards to reach Fort Bowyer.[1]

The next day was one of anxious waiting. If the fort fell Jackson meant to resist at Mobile. "Lose no time," he ordered the Governor of Mississippi, "in facilitating the arrival of five hundred infantry and the *four troops of Cavalry*."[2] The sixteenth dawned without news, and Jackson sent confidential officers by land and by water for intelligence from the front.

A few hours later Captain Laval and his company returned by schooner. Their story threw garrison and town into a state of excitement. On the afternoon of the fifteenth they had run up within four miles of the fort, but were unable to land because the battle was on, the four British vessels letting loose their broadsides against the walls, while the force of marines and Indians waited on the land side to attack when ships' bombardment had done its work. "Great was the exertions & valiantly the action fought."[3] Laval's men cheered when they saw the British flag-ship disabled and abandoned. Then the flag on the fort when down. Had Lawrence struck? The marines and Indians advanced. The flag reappeared on a makeshift staff, the enemy's land forces retired, and the battle was resumed with new fury. Toward midnight the firing slackened, both fleet and fort seeming to have spent themselves. A glowing light revealed the angular contours of the works, followed by a vivid flash and a roar. Something had blown up. Laval declared the magazine of the fort had gone and started for Mobile. But some of the sailors on the schooner thought the explosion was on board the disabled British ship.[4]

The night brought no more explicit news, and General Jackson learned to appreciate something of the trials of Claiborne with his "difficult population to manage." Spies in regular correspondence with the enemy reported Jackson's every move.[5] A visiting merchant from New Orleans, suspected of complicity in this business, was lodged in the guardhouse. The belief that the fort had fallen was received with undisguised satisfaction, and Lieutenant Guillemard, of the Spanish Army, who had brought Manrique's latest to Jackson, became an object of friendly attention.[6] Jackson's answer to this was: "Push on the troops from Tennessee."[7]

A few hours later saw Lieutenant Guillemard at Jackson's headquarters in a nervous sweat for his passport. The word had come, proving Laval mistaken and the sailors right. The British themselves had blown up the *Hermes* to avert its capture. Lawrence's victory was complete,[8] and Jackson was jubilant. "Sir Wm. has lost his ship, and the Col [Nicholls] an eye . . . and have retired to Pensacola to rest. . . . We will be better prepared to receive them on the next visit."[9]

2

Having put the British off for two weeks, Jean Laffite wrote a lengthy letter to Jean Blanque at New Orleans. "I make you the repository of a secret on which perhaps depends the tranquility of our country." Monsieur Blanque was a member of the Legislature and one of the political powers in Louisiana. Laffite enclosed the documents of Captain Lockyer. "Our enemies exerted on my integrity a motive which few men would have resisted. They have represented to me a brother in irons, a brother who is to me very dear! of whom I can become the deliverer! . . . From your enlightenment will you aid me in a circumstance so grave."[10]

With this was also enclosed the following communication for Blanque to deliver:

"A Son Excellence Monsieur
"W^m C, C, Clayborne, Gouverneur
"del' Etat de la Louisiane:

"MonSieur

"In the firm persuasion that the choice which was made of you for . . . Office of first Magistrate . . . has been by the Esteem & accorded by Merit, I address Myself to you with confidence for an object on which can depend the Safety of the State. I offer to Return to this State many Citizens Who perhaps have lost to your eyes that sacred title. I offer . . . Their Efforts for the Defense of the country.

"This point of Louisiana that I occupy is of Great Importance in the present situation. I offer myself to defend it. . . . I am The Lost Sheep who desires to return to the flock . . . for you to see through my faults such as they are. . . .

"In case, Monsieur Le Gouverneur, that your Reply should Not be favorable to my ardent wishes I declare to you that I leave immediately so Not to be held to have Co-operated with an invasion. . . . This can not Fail to take place, and puts me entirely at the judgement of my conscience.

"I have the Honor to be, Monsieur Le gouverneur,

"LAFFITE"[11]

The outlaw had the quality of loyalty to friends and most of his friends in New Orleans, notably his legal adviser, Edward Livingston, were supporters of the United States. Moreover, alliance with the British would involve peace with his implacable enemy Spain.

Claiborne was deeply impressed by Laffite's correspondence, which contained the clearest disclosure of British intentions yet known in America. Hard as it was on his pride, the Governor agreed that this put a new face on the pirate's affairs. "There is in this city a much *greater Spirit of Disaffection* than I had anticipated, and among the faithfull Louisianians There is a *Despondency* which palsies all my preparations. . . . Laffite and his associates might probably be made useful to us."[12] The sailing of the Patterson-Ross expedition to destroy Barataria was therefore delayed and the commanders summoned to a council at the Executive Residence. These officers denounced Laffite's papers as forgeries and a design to outwit justice. They dominated a stormy conference. Claiborne yielded and the expedition sailed. But that very night Pierre Laffite mysteriously escaped from jail, and the impertinent *Gazette* twitted the authorities.

Pierre joined Jean at Barataria with word of the impending attack. Jean made no move to resist, though a British fleet was within call. Pierre was free and the promise implied was kept. With a few personal followers the Laffites slipped away to the Côte Allemand, a stretch of river above New Orleans, to await events. On September sixteenth, the day after Lawrence's victory at Fort Bowyer, Barataria was rifled and burned. Goods worth half a million dollars were carried to New Orleans, the spoil of a bloodless raid, a circumstance which detracted but little, however, from the stirring prose of Colonel Ross's official report to General Jackson.[13]

Though Mr. Claiborne permitted the raid on the assumption that the Laffite papers had been forged, he sent copies of them to Jackson on the assumption that they were genuine and contained military intelligence of first importance. General Jackson was not a man readily to see himself in error and this drew him also into an equivocal position. Jackson had denounced Laffite and seconded the plan for the destruction of Barataria. Now he used the pirate's information and enjoyed a gift of claret from his confiscated cellar[14]—with no thanks to Laffite for either. He roundly rebuked Claiborne because "those wretches, the refugees from Barataria . . . should find an asylum in your city. . . . Cause them to be arrested."[15] And if this were not enough the Laffites were noticed in a proclamation Jackson sent to New Orleans in answer to Colonel Nicholls's literary composition. "Can Louisianians, can Frenchmen, can Americans ever stop to be Slaves or allies of Britain . . . [or] place any confidence in the honor of Men who have courted an alliance with . . . the Pirates of Barrataria? . . . Have they not insulted you by calling on you to associate . . . with . . . this hellish Banditti?"[16]

Governor Claiborne reported the address "well received," despite comment of the *Gazette*, a journal never unfriendly to the interests

JACKSON'S HEADQUARTERS BELOW NEW ORLEANS

The residence of Augustin Macarté which stood behind the rampart of the Rodriguez Canal. It was hit more than a hundred times during the three battles before those defenses. Reproduced from a daguerrotype made before the Civil War and now in the private collection of Stanley Clisby Arthur of New Orleans.

A Presentation Portrait

A miniature on ivory done at New Orleans in 1815 by Jean François Vallée, a Frenchman under the spell of the Napoleonic tradition. Contrast this with the cruder, though better, likeness (facing page 176) made at the same time by Jarvis. Jackson's inscription "Headquarters N. orleans, May 1st 1815" is a sentimental anachronism, the General having left the city in April. This reproduction from an engraving in the private collection of Emil Edward Hurja of New York City.

of Laffite.[17] Claiborne may have been so deficiently informed as to believe what he said, though the fact is General Jackson's allusion to the Baratarians was a blunder.[18] That the consequences were not disagreeable is due to the good management of Edward Livingston. A curious odor of ships attends this distinguished family, Edward's brother having financed Robert Fulton and his grandfather Captain William Kidd. Edward himself had served with Andrew Jackson in the House of Representatives, being one of the twelve immortals to vote, with Jackson, against a congenial reply to Washington's address of farewell. In 1804 a scandal in municipal politics and the ruin of his private finances had driven Mr. Livingston from the mayoralty of New York City to seek a restoration of his fortunes in Louisiana, and to find it in a law practise which, among other things, imparted respectability to the calling of Laffite.

Louisianians who might not listen to Claiborne would listen to Livingston. Elected chairman of a committee of defense created with Gallic éclat in the coffee room of the Hôtel du Trémoulet as a result of Laffite's disclosures, he became Jackson's most effective champion at New Orleans. The committee did little except to vote a sword to Lawrence, but Livingston did much. While Claiborne congratulated himself on the "victory" over Laffite and bombarded Jackson with alarms over the undefended state of the city, the questionable loyalty of its cosmopolitan population, and rumors of a slave insurrection,[19] Livingston strove to repair these conditions. He sent Jackson a useful description of the six water approaches to the town with suggestions for the defense of each, requiring four thousand men. He asked Jackson to pay the city a visit—"Tho' short it would have an happy effect"[20]—solicited a place on the General's staff for himself and sent a bottle of Laffite's claret, without, however, calling the "hellish banditti" by that name.

In Congress the relations of Jackson and Livingston had been close. In 1804 Jackson felt that if he himself could not get the governorship of Louisiana, Livingston should have it.[21] The formal though polite tone of the letters now passing between them gave no indication of their earlier intimacy. Jackson studied the water approaches, but it was to Claiborne he applied for additional enlightenment.[22] He drank the claret as honest booty, but declined Mr. Livingston's proffer of official services[23] and turned to other things.

3

General Jackson did not think the British would use a water route to New Orleans, but would advance on the city by way of Mobile. "A real military man, with full knowledge of the geography of . . . this country, would first possess himself of that point, draw to his standard the Indians, and march direct to the walnut Hills [site of the present city of Vicksburg] . . . and being able to forrage on the country, support himself, cut off all supplies from above and make this country an easy conquest."[24] The activity at Pensacola, the attack on Fort Bowyer, everything the British had done, and all that Jackson or any one[25] had learned of their intentions could be construed as supporting this view. A glance at the broad instructions to the army and naval commanders at Negril Bay, in Jamaica, where the great expedition was taking form, would have left one little wiser. To enable the English Government "to exact its cession as a price of peace," orders were to occupy Louisiana by advancing directly upon New Orleans or through Mobile, at discretion. Nicholls's free talk in Havana had indicated an attempted advance through Mobile.

Jackson moved, therefore, to meet the enemy in that quarter, and moved alone, because for a month during and after the occupation of Washington, he was, in effect, without a Government to report to. On his own responsibility Jackson demanded troops from Mississippi, Tennessee and Kentucky, though Kentucky was outside his military jurisdiction, using all his passionate art to stir in Western hearts the will to battle. Stricken with fever and unable to sign his name,[26] he dictated one of these letters. The response was rather encouraging, except in the matter of arms and supplies. A "patriotic" letter from Rachel was worth a new regiment. "The burning [of] the capitol," her husband replied, "may be a disgrace, . . . but it will give impulse and energy to our cause, the change too, in Secretaries of war will add much. . . . Say to my son . . . he must never cry . . . and learn to be a soldier. I wish the horses kept in good order and my coalts well fed."[27]

Salutary, indeed, had been the change in the War Department. The first officers of the Administration upon the scene of desolation after the retreat of the British from Washington were Madison and Monroe. The President was on the verge of nervous prostration and Monroe took charge. Expelling Armstrong from the Cabinet, he assumed the duties of the War Office without relinquishing those of Secretary of State and planned to wage the war as it had not been waged before. The Treasury was empty, recruiting for the Regular establishment discontinued for want of funds, and the cry of disunion raised in New England.[28] In the blackest hour since Valley Forge, James Monroe pinned his hope for deliverance on emergency measures for raising money, federal conscription for raising men— and on Andrew Jackson. He found one hundred thousand dollars to place at the Southern Commander's disposal and his validated levies for troops, adding Kentucky and Georgia to the territory from which he could draw.[29] "A war of seven years," an attaché of the War Office informed Jackson, "may be expected."[30]

Simultaneously Jackson found time to outline to a friend in Congress his own idea of the government's duty. "The whole force Britain can bring into the field we are now contending against [and] it is daily increasing." To meet this there must be "unanimity of feeling . . . and . . . action in the deliberative councils of the nation." Men must be provided without "calculating the expense." "The spirit of mutiny and desertion that pervade our militia" must be removed, and "their term of service [extended] to one or two years," making them, for all practical purposes, Regular troops.[31] Had the two men conferred, General Jackson's recommendations could not have been more agreeable to the energetic Secretary of War.

Meantime peace negotiations had been opened at Ghent where the British Commissioners displayed an attitude somewhat similar to that of Andrew Jackson toward the Creeks. And despite all that Madison and Monroe could do to pump new life into the war, New England was for ending it on any terms. But the West chose to keep up the fight. Brigades, regiments and isolated companies began to people the wilderness above Mobile—their frontier dress and weapons forming a picture in acute contrast to the British Regulars on board the transports en route to the rendezvous at Jamaica. Jackson's illness passed almost as quickly as it had come upon him.[32] He began to station the gathering units strategically, and to reiterate the old plea for supplies. From a Tennessee regiment came the monotonous militia story of insubordination and mutiny. Jackson ordered two hundred men in arrest and convoked a court martial to sift for the guilty. But on the whole the news was good. "Coffee's near approach gives . . . confidence to me."[33] Coffee led eighteen hundred men, each riding his own horse and carrying his own rifle. "Every one of my boys wants to get within fair buckrange of a red coat!"[34]

On October twenty-fifth the General quit Mobile for Pierce's Stockade on the Alabama, where a large force of the new troops was concentrated. A frontier dream of twenty years was in the execution: Jackson meant to strike at Pensacola. "As I act without the orders of the government, I deem it important to state to you my reasons. . . . The safety of this section of the union depends upon it . . . [and] Pensacola [has] assume[d] the character of British Territory. . . . I feel a confidence that I shall stand Justified to my government. . . . Should I not . . . the consolation of having done the only thing in my own opinion which could give security to the country . . . will be an ample reward for the loss of my commission."[35] This letter to Mr. Monroe had several possible uses. In case of diplomatic consequences it would give an innocent appearance to the record. In any case it would be an excellent nerve tonic for Mr. Madison, and for Monroe too, if he should heed it, though in reality Jackson had private assurances that the Secretary personally would approve of the expedition.[36]

On November second Jackson marched with three thousand men, seven hundred of them Regulars. On the sixth he was before Pensacola. Major Peire of the Forty-Fourth Infantry accompanied a flag of truce "to require that the different forts, Barrancas, St. Rose, and St. Michael, should be immediately surrendered, to be garrisoned . . . by the United States, until Spain . . . could preserve unimpaired her neutral character."[37] The flag was fired upon—by the English, it later came out—and Major Peire retired without delivering his message.

4

Jackson stormed the town in the morning. The principal defenses of Pensacola were constructed to meet an attack from the west along the white beach, the beach on the east side being narrow and difficult of access. Jackson was encamped on the main road entering the town from the west, just out of range of the guns of St. Michael and seven British men-of-war in the bay. An hour before dawn he led the bulk of his army out quietly and began to circle the town, while five hundred of Coffee's men started a noisy demonstration on the west.

When sunrise disclosed the maneuver the dispositions for assault on the east had been made. There was no time for the fleet to change its position, but a battery was posted at the head of a street and garden walls looking eastward were manned by infantry. The Americans advanced in three columns, one on the beach and two above it. Captain Laval of the Third Infantry captured the battery after its third fire. The assailants swarmed up the streets, clearing garden walls and roofs as they went. The General was standing over Captain Laval, who had been seriously wounded, when he was told that Commandant Manrique, old, infirm and trembling, was stumping about with a white flag in distracted quest of Jackson. The two met at the Government House where the surrender of the forts was arranged while a British sally in small boats was beaten back. The Spanish killed time and displayed such bad faith in the surrender of Fort St. Michael that Jackson was obliged to defer until the following morning a projected attack on Barrancas, fourteen miles away and garrisoned by the British. At three A. M. Jackson was ready to march when an explosion rocked the earth beneath his feet. The British had blown up Barrancas. Whereupon they fled to their shipping which put to sea.

The bird Jackson had hoped to bag had flown, and, fearing it was headed for Mobile, he dropped his useless prizes and in three and one-half days was on the Tensas ready to support Fort Bowyer.[38]

The dash upon Pensacola was a daredevil thing, and the General's personal historians have confessed disappointment "in the object he had principally in view."[39] Washington was shocked, not so much over a violation of the nominal neutrality of Spain, as over Jackson's absence from the vital points of Mobile and New Orleans, not even Monroe reckoning upon the celerity with which this man could move an army. But the immediate and local results were wholesome. The expedition exalted Coffee's men, who failed not to note how punctiliously the Red Coats had kept out of "buck range," leaving the honor of defense to the Spaniards. It ruined British prestige among die-hard Creeks and Seminoles. Deserted by allies who had promised so much, they fled destitute into the Florida wilderness. It disgusted Manrique with the same allies and mightily altered the tone of his communications. "Exmo Señor Dⁿ. Andres Jackson. . . . Permit me . . . to sign myself, with additional consideration and respect, your most faithful and grateful servant, who kisses your hands."[40] It thrilled the West, the only part of the country properly supporting the war. It enhanced Jackson's confidence in his troops and theirs in him.[41]

5

New Orleans continued to call. "I renew the entreaty," wrote Livingston, "that you will pay us a visit . . . and overawe disaffection."[42] Claiborne was little more cheerful. "The Legislature has not as yet done anything to damp the public. . . . But I fear, I much fear, they will."[43] These fears wearied Jackson, who adhered to the belief that the enemy would move on the city through Mobile.[44] "The Citizens of New Orleans have addressed me," he informed Monroe. "My whole force would not satisfy the demands they make."[45]

Jackson had not neglected New Orleans. He had requested Claiborne to embody the militia, and the War Department to send arms by way of the Mississippi. He had directed Lieutenant-Colonel McRae of the Regular Army to take command of the city and put the forts in condition for resistance. He had sent his inspector-general, Colonel Arthur P. Hayne, to report on this work. But despite all this Livingston's plea that the situation required the dominating presence of the Commander himself was not without basis.

Returning to Mobile from the Pensacola excursion, Jackson decided to go, though not until he had placed Mobile and surrounding country in a bristling state of defense. Militia and friendly Indians ranged westward to keep hostile Seminoles and Creeks at bay.[46] Fort Bowyer was strengthened "until I feel a conviction . . . that ten thousand troops cannot take it."[47] Other Regulars and militia were stationed at Mobile and posts to the northward from whence they could be thrown where needed in event of attack. Command of the whole was given to Brigadier-General James Winchester, trained in Jackson's Cumberland militia division before the war. "Fort Bowyer . . . [is] the Key of communication between . . . [Mobile] and New Orleans," Jackson instructed him. . . . "[It] must be maintained."⁴⁸

To cover New Orleans proper Jackson sent Coffee toward Baton Rouge to await reenforcement by Carroll's newly mustered militia from Tennessee and Thomas's from Kentucky. With these dispositions in the making, General Jackson glanced at the politico-military situation as a whole. With specie payments suspended by nearly all banks west of the Hudson, with New England Federalists crying for peace at any price, and the Governor of Massachusetts upbraiding the American commissioners at Ghent for rejecting the British demand for the cession of the Northwest, Andrew Jackson felt sufficiently unterrified to forward to Monroe a suggestion for the reduction of Canada. "I leave for N. Orleans on the 22d [of November, 1814], and if my health permits, will reach there in 12 days." The leisurely pace was to afford "a view of the points at which the enemy might effect a landing."⁴⁹

General Jackson was five days on his way when the British armada —ten thousand seamen, fifteen hundred marines, nine thousand six hundred troops—sailed from Negril Bay. The presence of officers' wives gave decks a holiday air. They brought their prettiest frocks, these ladies, prepared for a lengthy sojourn in New Orleans concerning the social tone of which they had made diligent inquiry. The attitude of Major General Keane reflected this expression of confidence. Counting on another Bladensburg victory, he had decided to forego the tactically superior route through Mobile and to embarrass Jackson's calculations by disembarking directly on the Louisiana coast.

This posture of affairs was certain to bring disappointment to some one. For the altered blockhouse at the Hermitage was also astir with preparations of departure. Confident that Mobile would be the scene of the fighting, General Jackson had written his wife to descend the river to New Orleans. In the thirteen months past they had been together fewer than thirty days. Mrs. Jackson asked her vivacious niece Rachel Hays Butler to accompany her, and none could say that Aunt Rachel had not taken to heart her husband's suggestions as to the style of travel suiting "a Major Generals lady in the service of the U. S." She had a thirty-ton keel boat fitted out at an expense of four hundred and fifty dollars.⁵⁰

CHAPTER XIII

THE ESCAPE OF GABRIEL VILLERÉ

I

A CREOLE[1] lady of New Orleans, whose identity seems lost to history, surveyed the dining-room of J. Kilty Smith with an eye of serene approval. Formal silver and Sèvres patterned the white damask. The kitchen steamed with a "rich and savory" breakfast, "prepared in that style of cookery for which the Creoles are renowned."[2] Madame had fulfilled her duties in distinguished style. Monsieur Smith could be proud of the hospitality he was about to tender le grand Général Jackson.

The host was one of the first "American" merchants to come to New Orleans and one of the most successful. His home, a few miles north of the city near the junction of the Carondelet Canal with the Bayou St. Jean, had been the country seat of an affluent Spaniard of an older day. But as a bachelor who surmised that his preparations for welcoming Andrew Jackson to the gates of New Orleans might profit by a feminine touch, Mr. Smith had solicited the collaboration of the wife of a wealthy neighbor.

It was the morning of December 1, 1814.[3] The chill night mist breathed up by the swamps reluctantly dissolved beneath a sullen sky, revealing the old road past the Smith place following the Bayou St. Jean into New Orleans. This stream twisted through the swamp like a dark green serpent and the road was muddy and broken. But General Jackson had traversed worse thoroughfares on his journey from Mobile. He had come slowly, integrating the troublesome topography with the map that Claiborne had sent him. His observations had confirmed him in the opinion that it would be the part of wisdom for the British to attempt their invasion through Mobile, or at nearest make a landing at the mouth of the Pascagoula,[4] thirty miles west thereof, and attack New Orleans from above. At Fort St. Jean on Lake Pontchartrain, a few miles from the

Smith place, Major Hughes of the Seventh Infantry and Major Chotard of the Louisiana militia had joined the party. There were not more than three or four others, including Jackson's adjutant-general, Robert Butler, and his military secretary, handsome John Reid.

At Mr. Smith's reins were thrown to stable-boys and the party welcomed on the merchant's spacious gallery. The young officers chatted gaily, but the appearance and demeanor of the Commanding General was a shock to Mr. Smith and the temporary mistress of the manse who observed him narrowly: "A tall, gaunt man, very erect, . . . with a countenance furrowed by care and anxiety. His dress was simple and nearly threadbare. A small leather cap protected his head, and a short blue Spanish cloak his body, whilst his . . . high dragoon boots [were] long innocent of polish or blacking. . . . His complexion was sallow and unhealthy; his hair iron grey, and his body thin and emaciated like that of one who had just recovered from a lingering sickness. . . . But . . . [a] fierce glare . . . [lighted] his bright and hawk-like eye."[5]

The elaborate breakfast was wasted on the guest of honor whose querulous digestion permitted him to eat only a few spoonfuls of boiled hominy. Moreover, he was eager to be at his work of the day. Glancing at his watch, he "reminded his companions of the necessity of their early entrance into the city."[6]

Mr. Smith's neighbor was piqued, but the General received no hint of it in the smooth alloy of her drawing-room manner. Madame was not sure whether she had been the victim of a jest or her friend the victim of a hoax. She who had seen officers of Napoleon knew a "grand général" by the outward signs—"plumes, epaulettes, long sword and moustache." "Ah! Mr. Smith . . . you asked me to . . . receive a great Général. I make your house comme il faut, and prepare a splendid déjeuner, . . . all for . . . an ugly old Kaintuck flat-boatman."[7]

When a Louisiana lady said Kaintuck flatboatman there was little one could add to the degree of disparagement.

2

At the last moment carriages appeared to convey the shabby General and his staff to the city. He had initiated his own arrangements for quarters in New Orleans, however, a circumstance that had come about in a curious way. The dismay of the Spanish over the nimble retreat of the British from Pensacola had been genuine. During his short stay in that city, Jackson was entertained by the elegant Don Juan Ventura Morales who had been Spanish Intendant at New Orleans before the transfer of Louisiana to the United States, and later was expelled by Claiborne for plotting against the American régime. Surely Jackson knew Don Juan's history. Yet he believed his protestations of friendship which indeed may have been sincere in that Don Juan was prepared to accept the Americans temporarily as the lesser of a choice of evils. Jackson left Pensacola carrying a letter of introduction to Don Juan's son-in-law, Bernard de Marigny de Mandeville, of New Orleans. From Fort St. Jean Jackson had sent this letter into the city, with an intimation that he would appreciate the use of Marigny's residence as his personal headquarters.[8]

But the carriages had not been sent out by Marigny and they did not convey the General to the Marigny house. They conveyed him to the residence of the lately deceased Daniel Clark, an Irish adventurer picturesquely involved in Louisiana politics since the Miró conspiracy. On the gallery of this large house, Jackson was formally received in the presence of a crowd that filled the street despite the unheralded nature of his arrival, the early hour, and the threatening sky. Governor Claiborne was there, tall, immaculate and truly happy to shed his responsibility for the safety of the city. Commandant Patterson was there, "a compact, gallant-bearing man, in the neat undress naval uniform, his manner slightly marked by hauteur,"[9] and none too popular as the "conqueror" of Laffite. Rotund, affable little Mayor Girod bowed and bobbed about. But the personage of the occasion was tall, high-shouldered, ungraceful Edward Livingston. The welcoming committee was of his choosing. Bernard Marigny, the only person in New Orleans whose hospitality Jackson had solicited, was not invited to the gallery, and dark reflections filled his active Latin mind as he hung on the fringe of the crowd.

Claiborne addressed his fellow-citizens with "fluent elocution." Girod addressed them with fluent elocution plus gestures. The rain began to fall and soon "all present," as Monsieur Marigny recorded, "were wet, muddy and uncomfortable; but the Mayor (given to singing madrigals to persons in power) assured the General that 'The sun is never shining more brilliantly than when you are among us!' "[10] The General responded briefly. Edward Livingston advanced to render his remarks into French. When this man spoke one forgot his unprepossessing exterior. His manner was assured, his voice rich, his diction flawless. General Jackson, he translated, pledged himself "to protect the city, . . . drive their enemies into the sea, or perish in the effort."[11]

The effect was "electric. . . . Countenances cleared up. Bright and hopeful were the words and looks of all who . . . caught the heroic glance of the hawk-eyed General."[12]

The hawk-eyed General mounted his horse, and, with Livingston at his side, rode to the Place d'Armes where four gorgeously uniformed companies of New Orleans militia waited in the downpour. The élite of the town comprised this battalion—sons of planters, merchants, bankers—with a sprinkling of soldiers of fortune and refugees from Santo Domingo (now called Haiti), where the slave uprising under L'Ouverture had uprooted French dominion. Jackson passed down the line: the Carabiniers d'Orléans of Captain Plauché; the Dragons à Pied of Captain St. Gême, a salty little French rooster whose five feet of stature was exalted by a twelve-inch plume in his cap; the Francs of Captain Hudry; the Chasseurs of Captain Guibert; the Louisiana Blues of Captain Maunsel White, an Irishman. Seasoned soldiers in the ranks, and there were men who had followed Napoleon, felt a wordless unity with the one that had come to lead them.

At the three-story building at Number 106 Royal Street set aside for his headquarters, Jackson made Livingston an aide-de-camp with the rank of colonel, and began to consider the situation. The total of arms in the city did not exceed twenty-five hundred muskets and seventy-five hundred pistols, the latter captured from the Baratarians.[13] No government rifles had arrived, but a shipment of molasses had come overland from Boston in the same barrels in which it had left New Orleans two years before.[14] This much the War Department had contributed toward the defense of the city whose warehouses bulged with cotton, sugar, and sirup, accumulated in consequence of the British blockade. The Commander also began to sense the quicksand of jealousies and doubtful loyalty that had mired Claiborne.

He was to dine with Colonel Livingston whose wife, a Santo Dominican of exotic beauty, had repelled the idea of bringing "that wild Indian-fighter" in contact with polished society. "He will capture *you* at first sight," said her husband dryly.

Madame Livingston could have spared herself the worry that her dinner would be anything but a success. Andrew Jackson's first appearance in New Orleans society was a triumph which was to repeat itself many times. Colonel Livingston discovered the secret of the General's easy victory at his wife's dinner.

"I ushered General Jackson into the drawing-room . . . in the full-dress uniform of his rank, . . . a blue frock-coat with buff facings, white waistcoat and close fitting breeches. . . .

"'Madame and Mesdemoiselles, I have the honor to present Major-General Jackson of the United States Army.'

"I had to confess to myself that the new . . . uniform made another man of him. He had two sets of manners: One for headquarters . . . the other for the drawing-room. . . .

"Of the twelve or more young ladies present . . . not more than three could speak English. . . . However, . . . we placed the General between Madame Livingston and Mlle. Eliza Chotard, an excellent English scholar. . . . Of our wines he seemed to fancy most a fine old Madeira and remarked that he had not tasted anything like it since Burr's dinner at Philadelphia in 1797. . . ."[15]

But despite the success of General Jackson with Madame Livingston's guests, a tactical error had been committed at the dinner, from the effects of which the General was to suffer innumerable embarrassments. Bernard Marigny had not been invited.

Colonel Livingston was the acknowledged leader of the "American" element, but his influence with the Creoles, though considerable, had been exaggerated. Under his chaperonage Jackson could not hope to complete the conquest of "society" in New Orleans, a not unimportant adjunct to the coordination of all preparations for the defense of the city. True, Madame Livingston was French and therefore could be a great aid, but—and what a difference this made in a social hierarchy almost as rigid as the courts of the Louis—she was a Santo Dominican.

There was no prouder name in Louisiana than de Marigny de Mandeville, about which the lambent traditions of Creole aristocracy cluster in their finest flower. Bernard was twenty-nine, unassailably rich, and a leader of the faction in the State Legislature that had effectively checked attempts at a rampant Americanization of Louisiana. He accepted the snub and abided his time. In the morning, as he understood, General Jackson and staff were to take up their residence in the Marigny town-house by the river—which should alter very materially the sudden ascendency of the parvenu Colonel. Monsieur Marigny, who knew the salons of Paris and of London, would show General Jackson what correct entertainment was, and would acquaint him with the real rulers of Louisiana. For Marigny was impressed with Jackson and wished him well—under the proper auspices, naturally.

On the morning of December second Bernard Marigny paced his spacious drawing-room. The apartments set aside for the General and his official family were in order. Breakfast had been prepared. When Jackson had not arrived at noontime Marigny went abroad for news. "M. Pelletier Delahoussaye . . . told me that the General had changed his mind and would remain at Dr. Kerr's on Esplanade Street. I was astonished."[16] A call at the Kerr residence verified this intelligence. Firm in the clutches of the "Americans," General Jackson was poring over a map. The hospitality of a Marigny had been rejected. Incredible happenings are a part of war.

3

General Jackson was also astonished, but for a different reason: "the total ignorance I have found among all descriptions of persons of . . . [the] topography" of the country[17] surrounding New Orleans. This topography is unique, and knowledge of its peculiar intricacies indispensable to any plan for the defense of the city. Jackson clung to the belief that if New Orleans were attacked it would be from above, a contingency that could arise only after Winchester's defeat at Mobile, which the Commander regarded as improbable. But now that he was on the ground his duty was to fend against the other alternative, a direct assault on the city from the Louisiana coast.

New Orleans lies about one hundred and five miles from the mouths of the Mississippi. For the most part the country intervening is neither land nor water, but a geological laboratory where land is being made. If one would behold the completed product, however, he must wait for another fifty thousand years. At the present moment, the more finished parts of this leisurely labor of Nature comprise dank cypress swamps peopled by alligators and muskrats and lugubrious pelicans. In the less finished parts where the forming soil is too unstable for trees, marsh reeds rear their bright green blades six feet high, tough as hemp and sharp as knives. The whole is schemelessly patterned and webbed by streams and sloughs and lakes, which in 1814 afforded no less than six definable approaches to the environs of the city. This much Jackson had known from his study of an imperfect map and from information supplied by Livingston before his departure from Mobile.

The map I have provided to assist the reader's understanding of these six routes is, I hope, much clearer than the one General Jackson was obliged to use. Glancing from west to east one first encounters the Bayou La Fourche. This narrow deep stream is in reality a mouth of the Mississippi. It breaks away from the parent river about midway between New Orleans and Baton Rouge, entering the Gulf eighty miles west of the delta.

Next is Barataria Bay which lies seventy miles west of the mouths of the Mississippi, and by a series of water courses affords communication with the Mississippi at a point opposite New Orleans. This was the route Laffite used to bring his booty to the city.

Then comes the Mississippi River which was the usual mode of approach.

East of the Mississippi are River aux Chênes and Bayou Terre aux Bœufs. These sluggish streams, navigable to small boats, almost touch the Mississippi in the vicinity of English Turn, a bend in the river fourteen miles below the city.

The next approach is Lake Borgne. This arm of the Gulf scallops the east side of the delta, reaching within six miles of the Mississippi just above English Turn. Its possession would afford an enemy two possible routes to the city: first, by ascending Bayou Chef Menteur to the Plain of Gentilly, a treeless belt of dry land about a mile wide, and second, by crossing the six miles from the lake shore to the Mississippi. Approximately five miles of this was swamp, passable only by a series of finger-like bayous concerning which Jackson could get little precise information. But having passed this swamp an enemy would find himself on a strip of firm ground bordering the river, the seat of some of the richest cane plantations in Louisiana, with a road along the levee leading directly into the town.

The last route General Jackson had to consider is through Lake Pontchartrain, which is reached from Lake Borgne by the narrow strait of the Rigolets. Mastery of the lake would admit an enemy to the city by way of Bayou St. Jean and the road leading along its bank which Jackson had recently traversed. The bayou itself was navigable for vessels of a hundred tons to a point within two miles of the city. The route of the lakes and the Bayou St. Jean ranked next to the Mississippi River as an artery of the city's water-borne commerce.

Not until his arrival in New Orleans did Jackson comprehend the difficulty of defending these six routes. He had spent his life among a frontier race whose security depended upon unsleeping vigilance. At fourteen he had been sufficiently familiar with Waxhaw trails to serve William Richardson Davie as a courier. But this was not the state of affairs in New Orleans, "an opulent and commercial town," as Jackson said, made soft by "the habits . . . of wealth."[18] "The numerous bayous & canals"—the only roads through the swamps—"appear almost as little understood by the inhabitants as by the Citizens of Tennessee. True every man will give you an exact description of the whole & every man will give you an erroneous one."[19] Such is the General's own statement of the case, which is not, however, to be taken altogether literally. Perhaps only by contrast to backwoodsmen could citizens of New Orleans be called ignorant of the unique geography of their country; and in any event, despite the handicaps, within twenty-four hours after his arrival Jackson had gathered a vast fund of reasonably accurate topographical information.

The next move was to send detachments armed with axes to fell trees and obstruct the smaller streams—Bayou La Fourche, the waterways from Barataria Bay, Bayou Terre aux Bœufs, Bayou

Chef Menteur, and the innumerable creeks—called coulées—which, like so many treacherous fingers, stretch from Lakes Pontchartrain and Borgne toward the Mississippi.[20]

There remained the lakes themselves and the Mississippi River, through which progress of an enemy could not be hampered by such elementary means. Five small gunboats cruised Lake Borgne under command of Lieutenant Thomas Ap. Catesby Jones of the Regular Navy. This force was too slender for fighting. Its duty, therefore, was one of reconnaissance—to watch for a sight of British sail at the mouth of the lake, and, should enemy vessels enter the lake, to stand back out of range and keep New Orleans informed of the movements of the invader. It was calculated that the shallow waters of Borgne, necessitating the transfer of a landing force from sea-going transports to vessels of light draft, would afford time for the gunboats to perform their mission. The route of the lakes long had given the military authorities of Louisiana the greatest concern, but Jackson felt that his precautions in this direction were sufficient for the time being at least. Indeed, with the means at his disposal, there was nothing more that the Commander could have done.

This sweeping activity, the spreading of men from Bayou La Fourche on the west to the mouth of Lake Borgne on the east, was the work of forty-eight hours after leaving the breakfast table of J. Kilty Smith. But the task was only fairly begun. Jackson now turned his personal attention to the Mississippi, which he descended on December 3, 1814, the day following the chilly call of Bernard Marigny.

Wisely he determined to attempt no defense of the river below Fort St. Philip, fifty miles from the mouths. There he ordered two auxiliary batteries erected. At English Turn, fourteen miles below the city, he designated additional batteries, which planters turned out their negroes to erect. On his return to New Orleans, after an absence of six days, there was no indication of the designs of the enemy. The General was able to assure Secretary Monroe that the military situation was in hand. The works projected would render the Mississippi impassable for hostile troops. "The Gun Boats on the Lakes will prevent the British from approaching in that quarter. . . . Fort Bowyer will be their point of attack."[21] So confident was Jackson of this that he hoped for word that Rachel had begun her journey.

But on the next day there was news of the enemy to engage his attention. Lieutenant Jones reported their vessels arriving off Cat and Ship Islands, near the mouth of Lake Borgne. The news threw New Orleans into a state of alarm, though Jackson was not surprised or disturbed. "I expect this is a faint," he informed Coffee near Baton Rouge, "to draw my attention to that point when they mean to strike at another—however I will look for them there and provide for their reception else where."

And while waiting to see which way the cat should jump, here was a morsel for General Coffee to chew on. "I see in the Nashville Gazette that *'Packolett has beat the noted horse Doublehead with great Ease.'*"

True, this was not the best turf news that Old Hickory, who owned Pacolet, could have wished, but it took some of the sting from the triumph of Jesse Haynie's little chestnut mare Maria which continued to beat every horse that Andrew Jackson or any one else sent against her.

"I have only to add," concluded General Jackson, "that you will hold your Brigade in compleat readiness to march. . . . We may, or may not have a fandango with Lord Hill in the christmas holidays."[22] Originally the British ministry had intended that Lord Hill should command the expedition against Louisiana.

4

Next morning Jackson departed for the reedy shores of the lakes, Chef Menteur and the Plain of Gentilly, where old fortifications were strengthened, new ones begun and lines of resistance projected. This required four days. Jackson's accomplishments, in the face of his illness from dysentery, had amazed the people and drawn the majority of them to him. "General Jackson, his presence revived spirits . . . and rescusitated Clabo [Claiborne] the very day he entered the town," Pierre Favrot wrote to his wife. Like most Creoles Monsieur Favrot had slight use for the Governor. "He is good for nothing, . . . a third rate lawyer."[23]

Yet the benefits of Jackson's labors were not conceded on all hands.

There still remained the wounded sensibilities of Bernard Marigny who was a power in the Legislature and this body adopted a critical attitude toward the measures of the Commanding General. Waterfront lodging houses abounded with sailors, but Commandant Patterson was unable to recruit crews for the naval schooner *Carolina* and the ship *Louisiana* that lay in the river. It was subtly intimated, no doubt by Livingston, that a word from General Jackson would repair this difficulty. Jackson had steadfastly declined to receive the services of the Laffites or their followers, though some of the latter who were out of jail slipped past complaisant mustering officers. It was argued that infantry might be improvised, but artillerymen and sailors were another matter. Jackson needed both, and the Baratarians were skilled cannoneers and intrepid seamen. The General insisted, however, that he would get along without the "hellish banditti," and asked the Legislature to permit him to impress seamen. The Assembly airily replied by asking Jackson to procure an amnesty for the Baratarians.[24]

Evidences of defection, if not treason, were visible in the city. Consternation followed the circulation of a story that the object of the British expedition was to return Louisiana to Spain, a suggestion not displeasing to a good many Creoles. Jackson thought the situation grave enough to warrant a blunt warning. "Believe not such incredible tales—your government is at peace with Spain—it is the . . . common enemy of mankind . . . that . . . has sent his hirelings among you with this false report. . . . The rules of war annex the punishment of death to any person holding secret correspondence with the enemy."[25]

This was published on the morning of December 15, 1814, after which Jackson repaired to the Plain of Gentilly to resume his survey of the terrain. Should a battle be fought near New Orleans he believed that this would be the place.

A hard-riding courier found him there. The news was bad and wholly unexpected. A swarm of British vessels had overwhelmed Jones's five gunboats. Lake Borgne was in the hands of the enemy.

5

Panic threatened New Orleans.[26] "The enemy was on our coast with a presumed force of between nine and ten thousand men;

whilst all the forces we had yet to oppose him amounted to no more than one thousand regulars and from four to five thousand militia."²⁷ Two thousand militia would be about accurate.²⁸ Jackson galloped to his headquarters in Royal Street, and for thirty-six hours the place shook with his tumultuous energy. Too ill to stand he lay on a sofa, and, whipping up his strength by force of will and an occasional sip of brandy, exhausted a corps of robust aides with the dictation of orders, the enlistment, concentration and dispatch of troops, and the multitudinous details which before another sun had set were to transform frightened New Orleans into an armed camp.

A battalion of free Santo Dominican negroes who had stood with the whites against the legions of L'Ouverture, marched to reenforce the defenses of Chef Menteur. Captain Newman of the Regulars, guarding the pass to Lake Pontchartrain, was ordered "to defend his post to the last extremity."²⁹ Fort St. Philip was told to resist "while a man remained alive to point a gun."³⁰

To Coffee near Baton Rouge: "You must not sleep until you reach me."³¹ To Billy Carroll who had left Tennessee by water two months before with a division of raw levies and had not been heard from since: Hasten! "Our lakes are open to . . . the enemy, and I am prepared to . . . die in the last ditch before he shall reach the city."³² Similar orders to Hinds's Mississippi Dragoons and Thomas's Kentucky militia. Yet the man of action remained a calculating strategist, viewing the campaign as a whole, which, were the British to exercise the same degree of caution, must be a long one. Provisions for six months were ordered. To Winchester at Mobile: "Fort Bowyer . . . must be . . . defended at every hazard. The enemy has given us a large coast to guard; but I trust . . . to . . . defeat him at every point."³³ To the Secretary of War went a reassuring account of the posture of affairs concluding: "We have no arms here. Will the Government order a supply?"³⁴

Crowning these labors of a night and a day, Jackson proclaimed martial law and a levée en masse.

"No persons will be permitted to leave the city. . . . No vessels, boats or other craft will be permitted to leave. . . . Street lamps shall be extinguished at the hour of nine at night, after which time persons of every description found in the streets, or not in their respective homes . . . shall be apprehended as spies."³⁵

The panic subsided. "General Jackson had electrified all hearts," one witness recorded. "New Orleans presented a very affecting picture . . . [of] citizens . . . preparing for battle, . . . each in his vernacular tongue singing songs of victory. The streets resounded with *Yankee Doodle, the Marseillese Hymn, the Chant du Depart,* . . . while . . . at the windows and balconies . . . beauty applauded valour."[36] The Ursuline sisters said special prayers.[37] Editor and staff of the newspaper *Friend of the Laws* repaired to camp, informing subscribers that they could be "more usefully . . . employed in defending the country than satisfying the public appetite for news."[38]

6

Yet one class of recruits, equally eager, Jackson stubbornly declined to accept—the Baratarians.

Livingston exercised his persuasive wiles in vain, although the story was about that Dominique You, the most celebrated of Laffite's sea captains, had offered the solicitor fifteen thousand Spanish dollars to procure his release from jail.[39] Major General Jacques Phillippe de Villeré of the Louisiana militia had no better luck than Livingston.[40] Jackson thought well of the courteous old Creole, however, and well of the soldierly qualities of many of his command, notably cocky little St. Gême, with the foot-high plume in his cap. General Villeré refrained from mentioning that in his non-military character Captain St. Gême was a partner of the proscribed Laffites. A committee of the Legislature, Messieurs Marigny, Rafignac and Louaillier, visited the headquarters in Royal Street. They were accompanied by Auguste Davézac, a brother of the beautiful Madame Livingston. These gentlemen enlarged on the patriotic services already rendered by Captain Laffite, and the unsurpassed qualifications of his followers as swamp guides and artillerymen. To no purpose. "The General was inexorable," reported Marigny. "The committee retired, saddened by . . . his decision."[41]

But the committee did not despair. It sought Judge Dominick Hall of the United States District Court, a magistrate who would have been at home on a Tennessee bench when Andrew Jackson rode the circuit. The offenses of the Baratarians, being in contravention to Federal laws, came within the purview of Judge Hall. "I am general under these circumstances," said Hall. He advised his callers to obtain from the Legislature a resolution suspending proceedings against the buccaneers.[42] This done, the Judge released Dominique You and the others from jail—at a possible saving to Captain You of fifteen thousand Spanish dollars.

Thus Jean Laffite, who had made a pretense at hiding, was provided with a safe conduct to walk the thoroughfares of New Orleans in security until nine o'clock at night. He walked to 106 Royal Street and requested an audience with General Jackson. After all others had failed, the mild-mannered pirate had resolved to state his own case.

It was an audacious resolution, but audacity was a feature of the trade of Jean Laffite.

No narrative of the interview appears outside the pages of fiction, a circumstance for which history is the poorer. Major A. Lacarrière Latour, Jackson's chief of engineers, knew Laffite well and immediately after the campaign collected his military correspondence. The brief and bald sentences of Major Latour tell all that we shall probably ever know of the singular meeting of these singular men. "Mr. Laffite solicited for himself and for all Baratarians, the honour of serving under our banners, that they might have an opportunity of proving that if they had infringed the revenue laws, yet none were more ready than they to defend the country.... Persuaded that the assistance of these men could not fail of being very useful, the general accepted their efforts."[43]

Artillery detachments were formed under Dominique You and Captain Belluché. The defenses of the route from Barataria Bay to the city of New Orleans were strengthened. "Fortify yourself at the ... Temple," Jackson commanded Major Reynolds. The Temple was an Indian mound made by oyster shells. "M^r. Jean Lafite has offered his services to go down and give you every information.... Dismiss him as soon as possible as I shall want him here."[44]

The chief of the hellish banditti was succeeding with his new associate in arms. This was a habit of his.

7

A soft breeze stirred the fronds of the palm-trees, a warm sun brightened the gray towers of St. Louis Cathedral, and the time-stained walls of the solid Cabildo. The streets enclosing the Place d'Armes were thronged with people. It was Sunday, December 18, 1814, and they had been called from their beds, not alone by the Cathedral bells' unfailing invitation to mass. Since dawn the town had echoed the roll of drums, the music of bugles and the tramp of marching men, as General Jackson prepared to review his troops. All routes led to the revered Place which had witnessed the formal authentication of much of the volatile history of Louisiana. Here, fourteen years before, James Wilkinson had raised the Stars and Stripes before an audience that smiled when the halyards fouled and the flag stuck half-way up the staff. But now the flag flew high, and the ring of people parted as the "Battalion of Uniformed Companies"—Major Plauché, Captains St. Gême, Guibert, White, Roche —swung into the Square. They cheered again, though with less abandon, for the "Battalion of Free Men of Color," Santo Dominican negroes under white officers. Their mobilization had been Jackson's own idea, carried out in the face of a considerable body of local opinion as to the propriety of placing arms in the hands of former slaves.

The General appeared, splendidly mounted.

"Vive Jackson!"

His "eye brightened, the careworn expression of his face cleared up"[45] at the enthusiasm of the populace. Colonel Edward Livingston read the General's address. The rhetoric probably was Livingston's but the spirit was Jackson's and both exactly what the people wanted.

Two mornings later, on December twentieth, John Coffee halted his advance-guard of eight hundred men on the Avart plantation four miles above the city. He had marched one hundred and thirty-five miles in three days.

Louisianians had heard much about Coffee. They beheld "a man of noble aspect, tall and herculean in frame, yet not destitute of a certain natural dignity. . . . His appearance . . . on a fine Tennessee thorough-bred was striking." Equally striking to the city-folk who flocked to see them pitch camp was the aspect of Coffee's weary men "in their . . . dingy . . . woollen hunting-shirts, copperas-dyed pantaloons, . . . hats . . . of the skins of raccoons and foxes, . . . belts . . . in which were stuck hunting-knives and tomahawks, . . . [and] unkempt hair and unshorn faces."[46] These veterans had traveled light, carrying "nothing but their pieces, cartouch-boxes and powder-horns—their bullets were usually in their pantaloons pockets. . . . They had no idea of military" drill, but spectators found comfort in the tale that these soldiers were concerned only with "the more important part of their calling which . . . was quietly to pick out their man . . . and 'bring him down.'"[47]

Nor was this all the good news. A few hours behind Coffee, Carroll's long-unreported flotilla, bearing the new Tennessee division three thousand strong, hove in sight.[48] Until thirty hours before, Jackson had been without word of Carroll beyond the bare fact that he had left Nashville on the seventeenth day of November. Carroll had made the trip by water in violation of orders from both Jackson and Governor Blount, "but neither when I arrived or at any subsequent period has the General mentioned the subject to me."[49]

There were reasons. Carroll had embarked with raw recruits. He arrived with fairly disciplined men. While half of a company plied the oars, the other half drilled on the boat decks. Starting virtually unarmed, they had overtaken and brought along a shipment of eleven hundred muskets that a War Department contractor had sent by slow freight to minimize the carrying charges. On a boat fitted with forges, Tennessee blacksmiths had put all guns in order and fabricated "fifty thousand cartridges in the best manner, each containing a musket ball and three buck shot."[50] Jackson's failure to receive word of his subordinate's progress was due to no fault of the latter. Carroll had sent messengers overland, but, on account of storms and high water, had beaten all except the fleetest of them to New Orleans.

The same causes delayed the Eastern mails. Jackson had heard nothing from Washington for sixty days. Perhaps this was just as well. Any news from that distracted quarter would have been dismal news. The efforts of Madison to rally the country continued to meet opposition at every step, the call for the Hartford Convention crowning all. Congress refused to create a national army and refused the means to pay what troops we had. The Conscription Bill which

Jackson had urged so vigorously was on the road to defeat. The Treasury was bare. James Monroe rode from bank to bank in Washington soliciting loans in the banks' own depreciated currency, adding his personal credit to the guaranty of the United States. New England Federalists called for peace at any price. They would accept the humiliating terms by which the British demanded a third of Maine and a large slice of the Northwest. They stormed against the American commissioners at Ghent for rejecting them. By the Eternal! Had Old Hickory heard of that!

Cheered by the presence of Coffee and Carroll, he returned to Royal Street, easier in mind than he had been since the loss of the gunboats. His military position was correct. With every approach to the city, as he imagined, either blocked or guarded, he had only to await an alarm that would betray the direction of the enemy's contemplated advance. Although he believed the British would attempt the route of the Plain of Gentilly, Jackson was not committed to that line of defense. He was committed to nothing except to attack the British when and where they should show themselves. His best troops—those of Coffee, of Carroll, the Regulars, Hinds's Mississippi Dragoons and Plauché's Uniformed Companies—he kept under his hand at New Orleans ready to throw in any direction.

Early on the morning of Friday, December twenty-third, the waiting General wrote Robert Hays a family letter, tranquil in the belief that "since . . . the capture of our gun boats . . . the British had made no movement of importance. . . . *All well*."[51]

But all was far from well, as by mid-forenoon Jackson received an inkling from Colonel Pierre Denis de La Ronde,[52] in command of militia pickets assigned to watching all possible routes through the swamp from Lake Borgne to the Mississippi. The Colonel's courier reported "several sail of vessels" in a position that suggested the possibility of a landing that would threaten the vital point of English Turn. Forthwith Jackson dispatched his chief of engineers, Latour, to reconnoiter.[53]

Latour left at eleven. He had been gone about an hour and a half when Augustin Rousseau flung himself from a lathered horse in front of 106 Royal Street and dashed inside with the most overwhelming news of the campaign. He told Jackson the British were eight miles from town. They had captured Villeré's plantation, five miles above English Turn. Rousseau himself had witnessed the surprise of an American picket belonging to the regiment of Colonel de La Ronde.[54]

The story was incredible. Every approach in that region Jackson had ordered blocked and had received reports that his directions had been executed. Yet Rousseau had the air of a man telling the truth. The General retired to his sofa to turn the matter over in his mind. A sentry rapped at the door and announced "three gentlemen . . . having important intelligence."

Colonel de La Ronde, Major Gabriel Villeré and Dussau de la Croix, a friend of Edward Livingston, rushed into the room. The clothing of the officers was stained with mud and they were nearly breathless. Their appearance prepared Jackson for the worst.

"What news do you bring, gentlemen?" he asked.

"Important! Highly important!" cried de la Croix. "The British have arrived at Villeré's plantation! . . . Major Villeré was captured by them and has escaped!"

Young Villeré was a son of the ranking officer of the Louisiana militia and the son-in-law of Colonel de La Ronde. A cataract of French tumbled from his lips, de la Croix translating. The English had accomplished what Jackson had labored day and night to avert. Unseen they had landed on the shore of Lake Borgne. Undiscovered they had penetrated the five miles of swamp which Jackson believed his vigilance had transformed into an impassable barrier between the lake and the sugar plantations along the Mississippi.

Whose blunder or treachery, or what military skill or luck or magic had got them there was more than the agitated militiamen could explain. Nor was this a moment to probe for explanations. It was enough to know that the enemy stood in force on the river, eight miles by highway from the city. Already Villeré's story had corroboration. Latour had seen the British troops and dispatched Major Howell Tatum to headquarters with the news.

Jackson sprang from his sofa. "With an eye of fire and an emphatic blow upon the table," he cried:

"By the Eternal, they shall not sleep on our soil!"

This flushed mood passed with the abruptness of a summer storm. Jackson's tone grew calm. Inviting his visitors to sip a glass of wine with him, he called his military secretary and his aides.

"Gentlemen, the British are below. We must fight them tonight."[55]

It was then two in the afternoon.

CHAPTER XIV

THE MUD RAMPART OF RODRIQUEZ CANAL

I

BY A bold scheme tenaciously carried through, the British had landed from Lake Borgne with a degree of secrecy that has not favored another modern military expedition.

On December 10, 1814, ten days after Jackson's arrival at New Orleans, the wooden walls of England came to anchor off the white beaches of Ship and Cat Islands at the mouth of the lake: fifty-odd sail of various rigs and sizes, from the huge *Tonnant*, Nelson's prize at Abouquir, to restless gun-brigs pitching in the swell. Ladders went over the sides, and down them streamed lines of red-tunicked men, as Keane crowded his troops on board lighter craft for the invasion of the lake. They were tried troops: four regiments of the Army of the Chesapeake which had fought at Bladensburg, burned Washington and fought again at Baltimore; a brigade of Wellington's veterans, straight from their victories over Napoleon's armies in Spain; the kilted Ninety-Third Highlanders, a "praying regiment" fetched from a detail of Empire building at the Cape of Good Hope; two West India regiments, mainly Jamaican negroes supposed to be adapted to the Louisiana climate; complete trains of artillery, a rocket brigade, sappers, engineers.

The little islands were uninhabited, but from the *Tonnant* Vice-Admiral Sir Alexander Cochrane perceived that his arrival had been observed. Just out of range, the fast gunboats of Lieutenant Thomas Ap. Catesby Jones hovered impudently about the British front, meanwhile informing Jackson of the enemy's arrival. From Maine to Maryland our shores had felt the quick and hard hand of the acrid old admiral. With the same promptitude he moved to efface the obstacles to his mastery of Lake Borgne. A fleet of gun-brigs in battle line sailed forth, making a show calculated to gladden the eye of the Admiral and correspondingly disconcert Mr. Jones with his five gunboats. But Jones was clever and he knew the lake. Dexterously he lured the fleet aground in shallow water and darted out of sight. Admiral Cochrane lost no time in taking another tack. He manned barges and cutters with volunteers under Captain Lockyer. This enterprising mariner had been duped by Jean Laffite and he had been defeated at Fort Bowyer, but now his time had come to be served by better fortune. After rowing thirty-six miles, Lockyer found Jones becalmed and unable to maneuver. With forty-five boats and twelve hundred men, he attacked the American's five boats and hundred and eighty-two men. The fighting was savage, Lockyer was wounded. Jones was wounded and every fourth man on his slippery decks went down.[1] After two hours of battle, British boarders carried the day. The last of the gunboats struck at twelve-forty o'clock, December fourteenth.

Jackson was now without "eyes" on Lake Borgne. Under the prodding of Cochrane, General Keane wasted not a moment in starting his army toward New Orleans. Pea Island in the upper reach of the lake was selected as a rendezvous. For six days and six nights the seamen of the fleet plied from ships to island and island to ships. It was a pull of thirty miles, but Cochrane was relentless, and some of the crews were at the oars four days without relief.

Their passengers had no holiday excursion. "Than this spot," wrote a subaltern, "it is scarcely possible to imagine any place more completely wretched, . . . a swamp containing a small space of firm ground at one end, and almost wholly unadorned by trees of any sort of description, . . . the interior a resort of wild ducks and . . . dormant alligators. . . . The army . . . without tents or huts, or any covering from the . . . heavy rains such as an inhabitant of England cannot dream of, and against which no cloak can furnish protection. . . . As night closed . . . severe frosts . . . [congealed] our wet clothes to our bodies." There was no fire-wood. The only ration was "salt meat and ship biscuit . . . moistened by a small allowance of rum."[2] Many of the Jamaica negroes died from exposure.

"Yet, in spite of all this, . . . from general down to youngest drum-boy, a confidant expectation of success seemed to pervade all ranks." A similar expectation pervaded several citizens of Louisiana who shared with the visitors the discomforts of Pea Island. They "entertained us with accounts of the alarm experienced at New Orleans, . . . the rich booty that would reward its capture," and promises of "a speedy and bloodless conquest."[3] Veterans of the Chesapeake campaign who had seen the Americans fly before Washington could believe the bloodless part. On December twentieth, while Jackson was meeting Coffee and Carroll, General Keane managed a review of his army on the dry end of the island.

The vital question confronting the British commanders was answered. A place to land in secret had been discovered. The route of Chef Menteur and the Plain of Gentilly was too obvious and too closely watched by Jackson. Naval Captain Spencer and Army Captain Peddie had cruised the coast-line in search of a likelier spot. At first their quest was disappointing. Bayou after bayou that might have afforded a route through the swamp had been blocked with fallen trees. But at length they came upon one, the only one apparently, on the whole coast that was open—the Bayou Bienvenue.[4] This almost fatal neglect on the part of Americans remains unelucidated. The existence of Bayou Bienvenue was known to Jackson who had issued "express orders in writing" for its obstruction.[5] Another peculiarity of the case is that one of the sources of this stream was on the plantation of Major General Jacques de Villeré, commandant of the Louisiana militia, to whom the execution of Jackson's orders had been entrusted.[6] General Villeré was the father of Major Gabriel Villeré.

Near the bayou's mouth Spencer and Peddie came upon a collection of palmetto huts raised on piles above the marsh and inhabited by Spanish and Portuguese fishermen. With these fishermen the English scouts quickly reached an understanding. The fishermen made daily journeys to New Orleans with their wares, Villeré and other landowners affording them right-of-way. Disguised in blue smocks obtained from their guides, the British officers and three fishermen ascended Bayou Bienvenue on the night of December eighteenth, branched off on Bayou Mazant and emerged on Villeré's plantation. So enthusiastic was Peddie over his coup that when he took a drink from the Mississippi he pronounced the water cool and sweet. Back at Pea Island he communicated the exhilarating intelligence that New Orleans was defended by less than five thousand men. The estimate was nearly correct.

THE MUD RAMPART OF RODRIQUEZ CANAL

At dusk on the evening of December twenty-second, the British advance-guard of two thousand and eighty men and two guns[7] appeared in small boats off the mouth of Bayou Bienvenue. "The place . . . was as wild as it is possible to imagine. Gaze where we might nothing could be seen except . . . tall reeds. . . . Yet it was such a spot, as above all others, that favored our operations. No eye could watch us, or report our arrival to the American General."[8] Or so the invaders imagined. They learned, however, that since the visit of Spencer and Peddie, an American picket of twelve men had been stationed a short distance up the bayou. The success of the whole British plan hinged upon the suppression of this outpost. The job was expertly done and one of the prisoners was led before Keane and Cochrane for interrogation.

His name was Joseph Rodolphe Ducros and his brief turn beneath history's proscenium had a share in important consequences. Ducros said that Jackson commanded from twelve to fifteen thousand men in New Orleans and had four thousand at English Turn. He stuck to his story, and, for that matter, probably believed it, Jackson being the last general on earth to understate his numbers. Other prisoners corroborated Ducros. Curiously enough this estimate of the American strength tallied almost exactly with the one Cochrane had received from emissaries Jackson had sent to inquire about prisoners taken in the gunboat battle.[9] The repetition of this exaggeration of Jackson's force had its effect. Could the fishermen be mistaken? The white-haired fighter in worn sea-clothes was disturbed, something that did not happen every day.

At daybreak on the twenty-third, when, so far as Jackson knew, the British army was still aboard shipping at Cat Island, the red-coated column began to pick its way through the swamp. Engineers went ahead, clearing an excuse of a road over the narrow rim of soggy ground that hugged the bayou. At length, however, the soil grew firmer and the mud-spattered men moved more rapidly through a cypress woods, from which they emerged on to the Villeré plantation. Before them stretched a field of cane stubble. Beyond this stood the white Villeré house, its low rectangular lines half-concealed by an orange grove.

Colonel William Thornton of the Eighty-Fifth Light Infantry, one of the ablest regimental commanders in the British Army, deployed a few companies under cover of the woods. They swept forward in a semicircle to surround the house.

It was ten-thirty in the morning. Major René Philippe Gabriel de Villeré sat on his father's gallery contemplating the river through the smoke of a Spanish cigar. His brother, Célestin, was cleaning a rifle. The Major commanded the picket at the fishermen's village, and, under his father, was responsible for the security of Bayou Bienvenue. He deemed it secure enough until a file of British infantrymen, traversed his line of vision. A few moments later the crestfallen young Creole surrendered to Colonel Thornton.

This energetic officer begged Keane not to halt. They could reach New Orleans in two hours, probably before Jackson was aware of their presence on the mainland. Thornton believed the fishermen had given a correct idea of the size and scattered state of Jackson's army, with its main body four miles above the city. But Keane was afraid Ducros had told the truth. He was in the enemy's country with only two thousand men, and, moreover, a reenforcement of three thousand was due from Pea Island at midnight. So strong outguards were posted and the troops ordered to bivouac.

A clatter of musketry in the plantation yard brought the General to his feet. Gabriel Villeré had leaped a fence and escaped.

2

Andrew Jackson was not a Keane. In the face of Villeré's tremendous news, he made the most daring and most far-reaching decision of his career, when on the instant, he concluded to attack. "I will smash them, so help me God!"[10]

Couriers flew along the roads and drums beat the assembly. The hawk-eyed Commander remained tranquil. Orders were issued with "no unnecessary words, even of excitement or encouragement."[11] Preparations for the battle completed, he ate a little boiled rice, dropped on his sofa and was asleep in a moment.[12]

At four o'clock he was in the saddle beside the road that surmounted the levee near the old French barracks below the city. A thousand men under Carroll stood in the cane stubble near by. This was the reserve, in readiness to march where needed. Hinds's Mississippi dragoons had already disappeared at a gallop down the levee road to reconnoiter. In their wake had gone the Seventh Infantry with orders to engage the British should they advance, and to hold them at any cost until Jackson could get up with his main body. These troops had not as yet arrived on the field and every moment of waiting was critical. Any instant Jackson expected to hear firing on his front and he was none too sanguine as to his rear, which the enemy could fall upon by way of a branch of the Bayou Bienvenue; but Carroll was supposed to take care of trouble in that locality. Anxiously, too, Jackson gazed across the yellow river at the schooner *Carolina*, moored to the western bank. Seamen clambered among the rigging, the vessel cast off and drifted slowly down with the current in the direction of the enemy.

At five o'clock the December sun had slipped behind the treetops. With half of his main body—five hundred-odd mounted gunmen under Coffee, two six-pound field pieces under escort of a company of marines, and eighteen Choctaw warriors under half-French, half-Indian Pierre Jugeat—Jackson joined the advance-guard at the Rodriquez Canal, two miles from the British position. Hinds sent good news. The enemy was not more than two thousand strong, he said, and was preparing to camp for the night. Plauché's picturesque battalion arrived panting, having run most of the ten miles from Fort St. Jean. The Forty-Fourth Infantry, Daquin's Santo Domingo blacks and Beale's excellent New Orleans militia company made Jackson's force complete.[13] He now had on the field two thousand one hundred and sixty-seven men.

Dusk deepened, faintly outlining a misty moon. The damp air grew chill. Jackson moved forward until Versailles, the plantation château of Colonel Denis de La Ronde came into view. A double row of oaks,[14] planted in 1783 on the Colonel's twenty-first birthday, led from a private boat landing on the levee to his gate. Behind this screen Jackson arranged his army for battle.[15]

The field of cane stubble grew darker. Versailles and the slave village behind it surrendered their identity, and, lingering for a few moments as nebulous dark lumps, dipped into the uniform blackness of the night-conquered plain. Accouterments were muffled, orders passed in whispers. So silently did Jackson's men move out that the pickets of the enemy, five hundred yards away, suspected nothing. Keane's camp fires "burning very bright," recorded Jackson, "gave a good view of his situation."[16] The guns and the marines remained on the levee. The Seventh Infantry, the battalions of Plauché and Daquin, and the Forty-Fourth Infantry formed in that order on the left, reaching as far as the gardens of Versailles. Coffee's men filed noiselessly into the black plain. Guided by Denis de La Ronde and Pierre Laffite,[17] they passed behind the château, and began a wide detour calculated to bring them in position to strike the enemy's flank and rear.

At six-thirty the shadowy bulk of the *Carolina* floated abreast Jackson's position. Livingston went aboard and gave Commandant Patterson orders to open fire on the British main position at seven-thirty. At eight Jackson would attack.[18] "The Caroline," wrote Jackson, "passed in Silence, . . . sliding gently down the current."[19] A cold fog, seeping in from the river swallowed her up and began to dim the moon and the camp-fires of the unwatching enemy. Jackson inspected the line to see that every soldier had "plenty" of ammunition, and then returned to his post behind the guns on the levee. Men drew their coats closer about them and strained their eyes in the wake of the vanished *Carolina*.

At exactly thirty minutes past seven o'clock a great red patch glowed through the fog and faded; a roar and a rolling echo: the *Carolina* had opened fire.

The consternation in the British camp was apparent. Jackson waited his full half-hour. When the British, feeling that they had only the schooner to deal with, had concentrated most of their forces against it, the American infantry advanced. From his post on the levee, Jackson could see nothing more than the shapes of the artillerymen and the rumps of their horses, but he could hear in the dark to his left orders and oaths in French and in English. The infantry had got off badly. They stumbled into a stake-and-rail fence and a wet ditch which the militia battalions were slow getting over. The line opened a ragged fire and the British outposts replied with a stiff volley. From the Seventh Infantry came the cry that the lagging militia "are firing into us." Yet the Regulars pressed on and the British fell back. The six-pounders opened and a quarter of a mile ahead the *Carolina* continued her raking bombardment. Gun flashes far out on the black plain revealed that Coffee was engaged. This much, and this much only, could the Commanding General discern

THE MUD RAMPART OF RODRIQUEZ CANAL 225

of his battle, a lieutenant's fight from the start, every platoon for itself.

Staff officers dressed the infantry line and directed the militia's fire toward the enemy. But the British resistance stiffened. Keane had sent up reenforcements under Thornton, and wherever that soldier appeared an adversary had his work cut out for him. The heaviest fusillade yet sprayed the six-pounders. Our fire slackened. The British line moved up. Our marines gave ground. A wounded horse reared, overturning one of the limbers. The guns were in imminent danger.

Jackson dashed into the fight. The air was stiff with lead.[20]

"Save the guns!"[21]

The marines rallied about their General, a company of the Seventh Infantry rushed to the rescue and the guns were saved.[22]

"Charge! Charge! Push on the bayonet!"[23] The Regulars leaped forward.

"*A la bayonette!*"[24] Plauché and Daquin were in the thick of it. On the left things were going better now.

And Jackson traced Coffee's progress, a thousand yards away, by the twinkle of his rifles.

3

Between twelve and one o'clock Coffee was back on the levee without his horses,[25] but with a parcel of prisoners including Major Mitchell who had applied the torch to the Capitol at Washington. The gunmen had ranged through the British position, roughly describing a circle two miles in extent, and fighting wherever an enemy presented. Friend could not be distinguished from foe much beyond a saber's length. "In the whole course of my military career I remember no scene at all resembling this," a British officer related. "An American officer, whose sword I demanded, instead of giving it up . . . made a cut at my head."[26] Captain John Donelson, junior, substantiates the Englishman's complaint of unprofessional conduct. "I charged on near Lord Pakenham's quarters [meaning Keane's, in the Villeré house], made several prisoners and killed several. . . The enemy having discovered my position immediately fell on my rear. . . . [shouting] that they were General Coffee's men, having by some means learned the General's name. They advanced within about ten steps, ordered us for d—d rebels to lay down our arms. ... I answered them, they be d—d, and ordered my men to open a fire."[27]

While Coffee was making his eventful tour, the battle line on the river bank drove the enemy advance-guard behind a fence and a ditch separating the de La Ronde and Lacoste plantations. Colonel de La Ronde returned to enjoy the personal satisfaction of finding the enemy evicted from his property.

At nine-thirty firing had begun to diminish. At midnight the black field was still. Ominously still, suspected Jackson, who knew that Keane was being reenforced. British prisoners put his strength at six thousand. Above all, Jackson was still uncertain of the enemy's plans. Keane had surprised him on Bayou Bienvenue, and, fearing he might attempt the same feat elsewhere, Jackson declined to draw men from Chef Menteur and other posts to strengthen his present force. A determination to resume the offensive at dawn was therefore abandoned, and Jackson consulted his engineers about a protected position where he might await the enemy's pleasure.[28] At four o'clock in the morning he began to withdraw his army, and daybreak saw it behind the Rodriquez Canal with only a façade of cavalry in front to observe the movements of the British two miles away.

The Americans had lost twenty-four killed, one hundred and fifteen wounded and seventy-four prisoners. Keane's losses were forty-six killed, one hundred and sixty-seven wounded, sixty-four prisoners.[29] Jackson had displayed unusual generalship, first in his instantaneous decision to attack, turning a surprise into a counter-surprise, a phenomenon so rare that it has no name in the glossary of military terms; and second, in his present decision to take the defensive. On the morning of December twenty-fourth, Keane had four thousand seven hundred and three effectives on the field, exclusive of staff, against whom Jackson's nineteen hundred and fifty-four might have fared differently from the night before.

4

General Jackson's next move was to have "the whole city and country ransacked for intrenching tools,"[30] horses, vehicles, muskets

THE MUD RAMPART OF RODRIQUEZ CANAL 227

and men. The provost guards redoubled their vigilance. Every person found abroad without a pass was ordered under arrest, this measure being enforced against the careless as well as the suspect. "Before two days," expostulated Mayor Girod, "the Guard House will be full."[31] The inexorable Jacksonian will was unleashed—an instrument by which he believed he could accomplish anything. Had Charles Dickinson shot him through the brain, Andrew Jackson counted on the power of sheer resolve to sustain him long enough to kill his adversary. This mood possessed him now. His determination was formed to fight below New Orleans; if beaten there, to fight in New Orleans; if beaten there, to fight above New Orleans—to fight until no living thing could withstand his ineradicable impulse to victory.

This was fury—but of the cool, calculating sort. "As the safety of the city," he assured Monroe, "will depend on the fate of this army, it must not be incautiously exposed."[32] Dawn of December twenty-fourth groped through a sullen fog. The conditions were ideal for a hostile attack, but none came. At four in the afternoon Hinds in command of cavalry pickets, reported the British still receiving reenforcements, but making no preparations to advance. "I expect the enemy is pretty sore to day," Jackson informed Governor Claiborne.[33] The army had found the Rodriquez Canal a dry grass-grown ditch twenty feet wide and about four feet deep. It was an abandoned mill-race running from the levee to the woods on the plantation of Augustin Macarté. Thirty yards in the rear of this ditch Jackson made his line which by nightfall on the twenty-fourth bore some resemblance to a field entrenchment stretching from the river to the woods. The work went on in the darkness, one rank sleeping on its arms while another toiled at the rampart. Jackson slept none at all. He was never off the line. He ate his rice in the saddle.

So opened Christmas Day. At a salvo of artillery in the direction of the British camp, spades were dropped and rifles caught up. A messenger from Hinds reported, however, that the red coats merely were saluting the arrival of a new commanding officer, whom rumor quickly identified as Wellington himself.

He was, in fact, the Duke's brother-in-law, Major General Sir Edward Pakenham. Born in a mansion in County Antrim, where Andrew Jackson's parents also first saw the light of day, the hero of Salamanca had justified by valor and ability the exertions that family and friends had made for his advancement. He had fought his way up from subaltern, and something of a subaltern he remained, in appearance and in the simplicity of his manner. A round boyish face belied his thirty-seven years and a mischievous glint in his blue eyes shielded the methodical brain behind them. No unpleasant story of Ned Pakenham survives, and singularly enough Andrew Jackson had heard many stories about him. Dr. Redmond Dillon Barry and Pakenham had gone to college together in Dublin, the latter to leave for fields of glory and the former for the orderly hills of Sumner County, Tennessee, to practise medicine, to race horses, and open his home to Rachel and Andrew Jackson during the meetings at the Gallatin course.[34]

The presence of the popular Commander infused spirit into the British troops whose disturbed state of mind since the night of the battle General Jackson had rightly surmised. They had landed prepared to take over the civil administration of New Orleans, with appointments from tide-waiter to collector of customs already designated. An inspection of the dispatch case of General Pakenham would have disclosed the enlarging scope of English aims. He had brought a commission as governor of Louisiana and the Regent's promise of an earldom to adorn the office.

The methodical soldier moved discreetly toward a realization of these rewards. He perceived the injudicious position of his army and the disagreeable result of its not having advanced on the twenty-third. The report was that he spoke of withdrawing and landing in another quarter, only to be crushed by the scorn of the weather-beaten veteran in a seaman's rough coat. The lower ranks of the British Army shared Admiral Cochrane's opinion of the inferior military qualities of the Americans. Their not entirely misleading name for them was Dirty Shirts, inspired by the homespun raiment of the prisoners they had taken from Coffee in the night battle. The belligerent Admiral declared that if the army shrank from the risk his sailors would carry the Dirty Shirt lines and march into the city. "The soldiers could then bring up the baggage," the old tar added.[35] But he agreed that no advance should be attempted until the *Carolina* and the *Louisiana*, which lay in the river above the British position, were removed. Guns from the fleet were sent for and Pakenham began to dig emplacements for a battery.

THE MUD RAMPART OF RODRIQUEZ CANAL

Along the American line of defense, Jean Laffite cast an appraising eye. The retired pirate had learned the art of entrenching from engineers of Napoleon Bonaparte. The plan of Jackson's works was the conception of Major A. Lacarrière Latour, an able man, and Captain Laffite hesitated to raise an issue of its virtues with the General. He pointed out to Livingston, therefore, that the line which ended at the cypress woods was too short. It should be carried through the woods to the impassable swamp. "Otherwise, [the enemy] might turn our left."[36] Livingston conveyed the suggestion to Jackson at once and the extension was ordered. Hinds's scouts saw the work on the British batteries and reported the enemy to be fortifying. At the same time word came that the enemy was landing troops on the Plain of Gentilly and driving the Americans before them. From the first Jackson had feared the Bayou Bienvenue demonstration might be a feint. Claiborne was in command at Gentilly. Jackson sent two hundred Tennesseans under Latour to reenforce him and spent another night without sleep and without news. "Uncle Jackson . . . looks very badly," observed Captain Donelson, "and has broken very much."[37]

On December twenty-sixth Latour returned to report that the alarm at Gentilly had been a ruse. A few sailors had landed and set fire to the grass. Jackson was now convinced that Pakenham's main attack would be against his present position. A part of Carroll's division was called up to help prolong the rampart through the woods. Other outlying posts were stripped to reenforce the river end of the battle line, and Jackson slept for the first time in three nights.

5

He slept more soundly than did a good many residents of New Orleans, four miles away, where the restrictions of martial law and the strain of suspense were beginning to tell. An underground current of criticism rasped nerves already raw. "While . . . explosions of musketry and artillery reminded them that their sons were facing war-like soldiers, . . . old inhabitants . . . lamented that the protection of the city had been confided to an utter stranger . . . who . . . had hardly ever met any but an Indian enemy."[38] And what of the march of events? Jackson had lost the gunboats. He had been surprised by the landing at Villeré's. He had promised to sweep the enemy into the lake and failed to do so. Curbstone Vaubans viewed the mud bulwark behind the Rodriquez Canal and returned to town with long faces. They spoke with some of General Jackson's young gentlemen volunteers who had flown to the front to risk life and fortune on the field of honor only to have shovels thrust in their hands, and, what is more, required to use them. The connection between military glory and blistered palms remained obscure.

Suppose the mud rampart should not hold. "Jackson . . . openly declared," said Vincent Nolte who was there, "that he would imitate the example of the Russians at Moscow, and consign the whole city to the flames" rather than see its rich stores fall to the enemy."[39] Jackson openly declared nothing of the kind, although the secret of his intentions had been rightly guessed by Mr. Nolte. A great quantity of powder was placed aboard a vessel manned and ready to stand up-stream.[40] Jackson's "conduct in this respect was considered by some as an evidence of his deeming his defeat a probable event."[41] Captain Thomas L. Butler represented the commanding officer in New Orleans, charged, among other things, with the enforcement of martial law. Thomas Butler was a nephew of the Revolutionary colonel of uncut hair, a ward of Andrew Jackson and a close-mouthed young man. Subterranean whispers continued to carry the ominous refrain of Moscow. The wealthy of New Orleans feared for their property. When Fulwar Skipwith, president of the State Senate, demanded the nature of Butler's orders in case of an evacuation of the city, the Captain declined to give them.[42]

On the evening of December twenty-seventh Colonel Declouet, commander of a militia regiment, was in New Orleans on leave from duty. Declouet was a member of a distinguished Creole family and a former state senator. Before the street lights were extinguished, he repaired to the home of his old friend Magloire Guichard, Speaker of the Lower House of the Legislature, and heard from that gentleman's lips some remarkable observations. He understood Guichard to say that certain members of the Legislature were prepared to make terms with the British to preserve New Orleans from the fate of Moscow.[43] Among the names mentioned was that of Bernard Marigny. Declouet was frightened. He was aware of the risk any man took in questioning Andrew Jackson's authority at this desperate juncture. Moreover, the Colonel had come straight from the mud line and was loyal to his indomitable Commander.

6

This conversation took place at the close of a day when the news from Jackson's army had increased the apprehensions of New Orleans.

Early that morning of December twenty-seventh, at his headquarters in the Macarté plantation mansion, Andrew Jackson had awakened from the first repose he had enjoyed since taking the field. This galleried house and its trampled garden stood a hundred yards behind the rampart of the Rodriquez Canal. From an up-stairs window he could survey his line, and, after an old Frenchman lent him a telescope, he had a view of the British encampment. He had hardly risen on December twenty-seventh before a mighty blast of artillery brought him to his post of observations with the telescope. Pakenham's new batteries were letting go at the *Carolina*. In thirty minutes the schooner was in trouble. Her fire had ceased and the crew began piling over the sides. They departed none too soon. With an explosion that rattled windows in New Orleans and threw flaming fragments the width of the river, the *Carolina* blew up.

Then the batteries turned upon the *Louisiana*. Jackson had anticipated this and had sent word that she must be saved at any risk. Already he could see Lieutenant Thompson frantically spreading sail. But against the current the whisper of a breeze did not serve to slacken the ship's cable. Under a rain of red-hot shot the boats were launched and manned and lines passed to them. A shell tore up the *Louisiana's* deck. Boat crews pulled at the oars. The next moment was like an hour. On the tattooed arms of these striving seamen depended, perhaps, the fate of New Orleans, for half of Jackson's remaining artillery was aboard the *Louisiana*. The American line watched breathlessly. Could the sailors do it? . . . Then, vaguely perceptible, the big ship moved. A mighty cheer from the mud line. They towed her out of danger.

The day continued one of industry for the Yankees. A twenty-four pounder and an old brass twelve-pound howitzer, slightly out of repair, were established behind the Rodriquez Canal by seamen from the late *Carolina*. Jackson began a second line of defense along the Canal Dupré, two miles in the rear of the first and only two miles from the city. This precaution provoked fresh alarms in New Orleans.

Preparations in the British camp seemed to foretell an attack in the morning. In the evening strong enemy outposts were pushed forward in an effort to insure a night of rest for the main body. Jackson upset this plan for a comfortable night, sending down small bodies of snipers to harry the English with false alarms. "Scarcely had the troops lain down," wrote a British lieutenant, "when they were aroused by a sharp firing at the outposts." Columns were formed, ready to meet an attack of the entire American army. In the stubble the snipers lay on their bellies as still as deer hunters. "But as soon as . . . [our columns] were dispersed, the same cause for alarm returned and they were again called to ranks. Thus the entire night was spent . . . [without] the main body . . . obtaining any sound or refreshing sleep, . . . than which nothing is more trying to . . . [the] spirits of an army."[44]

The eastern horizon began to glow behind the British position and the black plain to turn to purple. Jackson was at his window. Rice birds in the orange trees set up their morning chatter and a shout turned the Commander's glance to the levee. He saw a band of "red-shirted . . . desperate-looking men, all begrimed with . . . mud, hurrying . . . toward the lines."[45] Baratarians under Dominique You. They knew their business and promptly swabbed and charged a second twenty-four that had been heaved into place during the night. It was hardly day when a messenger from Hinds brought word that the British were advancing. At twenty-five minutes past eight a cloud of singing meteors rimmed arcs of fire across the sky. *Crash!* The meteors pelted about the mud rampart and the Macarté house. Their detonations shook the earth. The enemy had opened with Congreve rockets, a new and terrifying, but seldom fatal, bit of pyrotechnics on which they laid great store.

The rockets were attended by a cannonade from ten guns and this barrage was not without effect on the Americans, half of whom were in battle for the first time in their lives. On rearing horses Jackson's aides patrolled the entrenchment, warning the men to hold their fire. Jackson caught sight of the infantry of the enemy. In two compact columns it advanced, one column next the river, the other bordering

THE MUD RAMPART OF RODRIQUEZ CANAL

the woods. Carroll and Coffee *must* be reenforced. They held the weakest part of the line against which the British right was aiming. Dropping his telescope, the Commander leaped into the saddle and dashed through the shower of rockets toward the swamp.

Abner Duncan, a prominent lawyer of New Orleans and a volunteer aide, halted him.

"I am the bearer of a message from Governor Claiborne," gasped Duncan. "The Assembly are about to give up the country to the enemy!"

"Have you a letter from the Governor?" demanded Jackson.

"No, General."

"Who gave you the intelligence?"

"Colonel Declouet."

"Where is Declouet?" screamed Jackson's high voice. To be heard above the din the men were shouting at the top of their lungs. Soldiers began to gather around. Partly for their benefit, Jackson yelled that he did not believe the news and that Declouet should be arrested.

The Commander glanced over his breastwork. On came the British columns. The red and green and tartan of their regimentals bright against the gray cane stubble, the bayonets agleam in the morning sun presented quite the majestic spectacle that General Pakenham intended it to be. The right column next to the woods, not half a mile away now, spread forward a fan of skirmishers. Carroll's and Coffee's men lay behind that flank of line, where the mud rampart was hardly waist high and the canal a ditch that a man could leap.

"The Governor expects orders what to do!" screamed the aide.

"I don't believe the intelligence, but tell the Governor to make a strict inquiry, . . . and if they persist to blow them up!" Jackson shouted back.[46]

The colorful mass flattened with impersonal precision from column into line, the formation of assault. The sight effaced the yelling Duncan from Jackson's thoughts. He loosened his reins to gallop toward his imperiled left.

CHAPTER XV

THE SILVERY CARPET

I

FROM the deck of the *Louisiana* Master Commandant Daniel T. Patterson trained his glass on the advancing British infantry. The enemy's artillery raised yellow plumes in the water, but the square-built seaman favored them with little notice. His orders were to break up the infantry assault, and this involved a nice piece of timing. He must fire not too soon and not too late. The gunners held their matches ready. Not a fortnight ago this crew had been swept up from the streets of New Orleans—"men of all nations, English excepted"[1]—and much depended on them to-day.

The left column of infantry, nearest the river, continued to advance. It was within five hundred yards of Jackson's line. On the border of the woods, the right column was deploying to attack and Jackson, having just got rid of Duncan, was riding toward Coffee's menaced flank. Patterson's primary business was with the left column. He made a signal and a wall of flame leaped from the starboard guns of the *Louisiana*. Five puffs of smoke rose from the mud rampart behind the Rodriquez Canal: the land guns had joined in.

Pakenham's splendid left column wavered, halted. Mounted officers reassuringly scurried beside it. The column began to melt into line, presenting a less compact target. Patterson's gunners ripped that line with the accuracy of sharpshooters. It fell apart like a broken string of beads and men began to take cover wherever they could find it. The advance on the left was stopped.

But the British right did not waver. Small-arms crackled on the edge of the woods. Less exposed to our artillery, a spirited young colonel was able to lead a thrust at a detachment that Carroll had sent into the woods in front of the rampart. The Tennesseans were falling back on their entrenchments and the flank was in danger. Then, inexplicably to the Americans, the attack ceased and the British halted just out of rifle range. Orders had come from Pakenham for his right to wait until the riddled force by the river could resume its advance. To expedite this Sir Edward pushed forward two field pieces near the levee.

2

The lull at the edge of the woods gave Jackson a chance to strengthen Carroll and Coffee, and when this was done he returned to his headquarters. There he found Bernard Marigny pacing the floor.

The Senator had been waiting some little while for the General. He had arrived with a "heart enraged,"[2] but the wait during the thunder of bombardment had subdued his emotions considerably. However, he greeted Jackson with a demand for his reasons for closing the State Legislature.

Abner Duncan had been gone from the battle-field less than two hours, and, if Jackson was astonished to learn the drastic turn events had taken in New Orleans, he gave no sign. Instead, he listened to Marigny's passionate defense of the Assembly and was rather favorably impressed. This increased Senator Marigny's confidence in his powers of persuasion until presently he asked the forbidden question. What were the General's plans in case the battle should go against him? Jackson closed the interview:

"If I thought the hair on my head knew my thoughts on that subject I would cut it off and burn it. . . . Return to . . . [your] Honorable body and say to them from me, that if I was so unfortunate to be beaten from they [sic] lines . . . and compelled to retreat through Neworleans, they would have a *warm session*."[3]

Senator Marigny did as was told, apparently quite satisfied with the results of his mission. He had faced the fire of British batteries. He had faced Andrew Jackson. And he lingered on the field long enough to bring to the anxious city assurances that the enemy's attack had failed.

Not until after the battle did the Commander learn that Abner Duncan had taken large responsibilities on his shoulders, Andrew Jackson himself seldom displaying greater originality in the interpretation of the orders of a superior. What had happened was this: Early in the morning Colonel Declouet had come to the camp to apprize Jackson privately of his conversation with Magloire Guichard. Failing to find him, he imparted his story to Duncan who relayed it to Jackson as a message direct from Claiborne. Jackson's instructions to have Claiborne look into the matter had been communicated to the Governor by Duncan as an unconditional order to prevent the Legislature from sitting. Claiborne acted immediately and Marigny, confronted by the barred doors of the Assembly chambers, had posted to the battlefield.

The assurances of a victory that he carried back to New Orleans were not exaggerated. The awesome British attack never recovered from the blows of Patterson's artillery on its left, and sputtered out like a display of fireworks. When the field guns, with which Pakenham hoped to restore his fortunes, were within range, the *Louisiana* wrecked them and resumed its vicious sweep of the inactive infantry. The five land guns also combed the plain for troops crouching behind fences and the ruined buildings of Chalmette plantation. Unable to reestablish his left, Pakenham ordered it back, and the men crept to the rear as best they could. The right, however, withdrew in formation, bitter in the belief that had the command been "Forward" it could have turned Jackson's flank.

So ended, on December 28, 1814, the second battle for New Orleans. A discriminating use of the military vocabulary saved General Pakenham from a confession of defeat. He called the engagement a "reconnaissance in force." In later years a subordinate could speak with more candor. "In spite of our sanguine expectations of sleeping that night in New Orleans, evening found us occupying our negro huts at Villeré's, nor was I sorry that the shades of night concealed our mortification from the prisoners and slaves."[4]

3

Three days and three nights of dazzling activity followed the victory. Every house in New Orleans was searched for firearms and entrenching tools. But tension in the city relaxed when the Legislature was permitted to resume its sittings. Three batteries of naval guns were erected across the river. The number of guns in the mud line was increased from five to twelve, affording protection to the left

THE SILVERY CARPET

which Pakenham might have turned on the twenty-eighth had he known how weak it was. The emplacement of these guns was a work of great labor and considerable ingenuity. Cotton bales were sunk into the yielding soil and wooden platforms built upon them. The cheeks of the embrasures in the rampart were faced with cotton bales plastered with mud.[5]

The soul of this preparation was Jackson. "Although . . . ready to sink under the weight of sickness [and] fatigue, . . ." wrote his chief of engineers, "his mind never lost for a moment that energy which [caused] insurmountable obstacles" to melt before him. This "energy . . . spread . . . to the whole army, . . . composed of heterogeneous elements . . . speaking different languages, and brought up in different habits. . . . There was nothing . . . it did not feel capable of doing if he ordered it to be done."[6]

By day a desultory fire from Jackson's cannon made life miserable in the British encampment. By night he kept the enemy's nerves on edge, sending down "hunting parties" to stalk sentries as a frontiersman stalked his game—the first extensive use of the raiding party, now a common feature of minor tactics. The British appeared so cowed and inactive that Jackson arranged a treat for his hard-working troops and a tonic for the citizens of New Orleans. A formal review was announced to take place behind the lines on New Year's morning.

But the British were not cowed or inactive, and they had their own plans for New Year's Day. The air of idleness that overhung their camp had masked the almost incredible toil by which Cochrane's sailors brought naval guns from the fleet seventy miles away—guns with which the short-tempered Admiral expected to silence Jackson's cannon, breach his mud wall and open the way to New Orleans. The British had not counted on a long delay at the threshold of a well-provisioned city, and their ration stores were low. The night of December thirty-first closed in foggy and pitch dark. Under a strong escort of infantry, seventeen pieces of ordnance were painfully dragged forward. Seven hundred yards from the Rodriquez Canal batteries were set up within easy range of the American front. The men worked quietly. Only the dull sound of their sledges reached Jackson's lines where, for some reason, the Dirty Shirt hunters rested from their exertions.

4

The fog's fleecy veil threatened to dim the splendors of Jackson's review. Shortly before eight o'clock the first of the visitors, several ladies among them, arrived from the city. A band was playing. The troops assigned to parade were forming up, their uniforms and accouterments scrubbed clean of the stains of the less engaging aspects of military life. Jackson had completed his morning inspection of the rampart, and, stretching himself on his couch, awaited the beginning of the review. Suddenly the room grew lighter. The fog dissolved as if touched by a hand of magic. Parade weather after all.

A thunderous clap drowned the music of the band. The Macarté house rocked amid a shivering of glass and a rain of plaster. Jackson rushed to a door. The sky was aflame with rockets. The walled-in garden was being plowed by shells. The troops assembled for the parade were dashing toward the safety of the rampart. Spectators went flying in every direction. Shouting to his aides to follow, Jackson started for the garden gate. A ball erupted a geyser of earth that almost buried Robert Butler.

At Battery Number One by the river Captain Humphrey, a veteran Regular, "dressed in his usual plain attire [and] smoking that eternal cigar [was] cooly levelling his guns." The British batteries erected during the night were guarded by low mounds of earth and hogsheads filled with sugar. They presented small targets, and it was some moments before Humphrey was satisfied with the aim of his twelve-pounders.

"Let her off," he said at length.[7]

Jackson passed on. At Battery Number Three fierce little Dominique You examined the enemy works through a glass. A cannon shot grazed his arm.

"I'll make them pay for that!" exclaimed the pirate.[8]

The picked gunners from the English fleet, veterans of Nelson and of Collingwood, were superior to the army artillerists against whom Jackson had contended on the twenty-eighth. One hundred balls struck the Macarté house. In the river a boat laden with supplies was disabled. Along the rampart cotton bales were torn apart and set on fire. The carriage of one of Dominique You's twenty-fours was broken. A thirty-two and a twelve were silenced. A rocket blew up a caisson of ammunition. At this tremendous explosion the British gunners, believing their work was done, suspended their fire. The infantry, behind them waiting to attack, sent up a cheer. It was answered by a broadside from Jackson's guns.

The pungent smoke blotted out everything. The Americans blazed into it by guess. An infantry thrust against the left of the line in the woods was warmly received by Coffee's riflemen. The chance that Pakenham had on the twenty-eighth against that flank was not to be his again. Toward noon the enemy artillery fire began to slacken. At one o'clock their guns in the center and on the right ceased to fire. At three the battery on the levee had quit and Cochrane admitted another failure.[9] The defenders had won the third battle for New Orleans.

General Jackson rummaged the ruins of the Macarté house. He had lost his overcoat,[10] and overcoats were at a premium in his army. The search was futile, and, throwing himself on his couch, Jackson asked John Reid to take an order. "The Major General Tenders to the troops he has the honor to command his good wishes for a happy new year, and especially to those officers & men at the pieces of Artillery. . . . Watch Word Fight on—— The Contractor will issue half a gill of whiskey around."[11]

That night, while the men drank it, the British hauled their guns to the rear.

5

"The enemy occupy their former position," Andrew Jackson wrote to James Monroe two days after the battle, "and are engaged in strengthening it; Our time is spent in the same employment and in exchanging long shot with them. . . . I do not know what may be their further design—Whether to redouble their efforts, or apply them elsewhere. . . . I am preparing for either event."[12]

The pounded first line was repaired, the second line was strengthened, a third line just below the city was begun. Under the relentless pressure of this preparation, the yeasty enthusiasm of some of the militia organizations began to droop. One battalion laid down its shovels. Jackson gave the officers of the recreant organization a talking to that enabled them to persuade their men of the intrinsic nobility of lowly labor in an exalted cause.[13] Nor did he soften his words to the Secretary of War. "The Arms I have been so long expecting have not yet Arrived, All we hear of them is that . . . the man . . . entrusted with their transportation has halted on the way for the purpose of private speculations. . . . This negligence . . . [threatens] the defeat of our armies."[14]

On January fourth the long-delayed Kentucky division under Thomas began to arrive. Livingston reported them unarmed.

"I don't believe it," exclaimed Jackson. "I have never seen a Kentuckian without a gun and a pack of cards and a bottle of whisky in my life!"[15]

Nevertheless, these particular Kentuckians had only seven hundred guns to twenty-three hundred and sixty-eight men.

On the sixth Jackson learned from deserters and from the evidence of his own telescope that the British were preparing another attack. The arrival of a fresh brigade had put new heart into Pakenham's weary troops. Boats were being dragged from Lake Borgne to the Mississippi, which added a new element of uncertainty. Did Pakenham mean to attack on the west side of the river, where Jackson had a rude line defended by only five hundred and fifty Louisiana militia under Brigadier-General David Morgan?

On the seventh the British were detected bundling cane stalks into facines and making ladders. From this Jackson decided the real attack would be against his main line with perhaps a demonstration against Morgan. Accordingly, he reenforced this officer with five hundred Kentuckians, only one hundred and seventy of whom, however, had arms. The main body of the Kentuckians went into bivouac in the rear of Jackson's line as a reserve. Four hundred rusty Spanish *escopetas* were taken from the Veteran Guard, on police duty in New Orleans, so that every second man of the reserve possessed a fowling piece of some kind.

Toward evening Jackson received information from which he concluded that the British intended to attack before dawn. He ordered half of the force at the rampart to remain at their posts while the other half slept. The General himself turned in early. On the floor of the same room lay his aides Butler, Reid, Livingston and

A Participant's Conception of the Battle of New Orleans

An excellent tactical representation painted in water colors in 1815 by Hyacinthe Laclotte, an engineer in General Jackson's army. Rennie is storming the bastion by the river and Keane obliquing across the field

the support of Gibbs by the woods. The whereabouts of the original of this unusual painting is not known. This reproduction is from a contemporary and rare engraving made in France by Philibert-Louis Debucourt, and now in the collection of Albert Lieutaud of New Orleans.

Davézac, with only their sword-belts unbuckled and pistols laid aside.

They had not been asleep long when a figure entered the dark hallway and spoke to the sentry at the door. Jackson was awake before the sentry could call him.

"Who's there?" he demanded.

It was a courier with a note from Commandant Patterson who reported strong enemy detachments preparing to cross the river toward Morgan's position. "I would therefore beg leave most earnestly to recommend an increase of our present force."[16]

"Tell General Morgan," Jackson replied, "that . . . the main attack will be on this side, and I have no men to spare. He must maintain his position at all hazards."[17]

The General glanced at his watch. It was after one in the morning of January 8, 1815. "Gentlemen," he said, addressing his aides, "we have slept enough."[18]

The group passed out into the creeping cold of the clammy night for a last survey of the lines. Lieutenant Billy Phillips, of Phillips's Ride remembrance, led the General's horse. On the extreme right by the river, a bastion protruded some thirty yards to the front, flanking the Rodriquez Canal. It had been built three days before at the earnest suggestion of subordinates, Jackson yielding against his own judgment, as he said, "for the first time in my life."[19] It was held by Beale's City Rifles, a crack militia company from New Orleans, and one company of the Seventh Infantry. Next was Battery Number One, commanded by Captain Humphrey of the "eternal cigar," then the Seventh Infantry, then Battery Number Two, Lieutenant Norris of the late *Carolina*.

The men spoke in low tones and they did not speak much. Their laughter was a little off key. The wait before a battle produces a sensation for which there is no name.

Next were Plauché's Uniformed Companies; then the Baratarians' battery where a circle of men crouched about a mound of red embers dripping coffee in the Creole way.

"That smells like better coffee than we can get," remarked Jackson. He turned to Dominique You. "Smuggle it?"

"Mebbe so, Général," rejoined the little captain, filling a cup for his commander.

"I wish I had five hundred such devils in the butts," said Jackson.[20]

Lacoste's negroes. . . . Daquin's negroes. . . . Battery Number Four, Lieutenant Crawley of the Navy. . . . The Forty-Fourth Infantry. . . . Battery Number Five, Colonel Perry. . . . Battery Number Six, Lieutenant Spotts. Rank had little to do with Jackson's selection of battery commanders. It was ability to handle the guns.

Carroll's division was next. Old Hickory espied a grandson of Nashville's founder. "Joe, how they using you? Wouldn't you rather be with Aunt Lucy than with me?" Aunt Lucy was Joe's mother. "Not by a damned sight, General," retorted Private Robertson. "Stick to 'em, Joe." He clapped the boy on the back and passed on. It was astonishing how many of the Tennesseans Jackson could call by name.[21]

The visit to Battery Number Seven called for a different style of military etiquette. Its commander, General Garriques Flaugeac, had led a division in Egypt under Napoleon. Battery Number Eight, a few yards away, was manned by Tennesseans, in charge of a Regular Army corporal.

Here the line entered the stubby cypress woods and Coffee's sector began. For a few yards the moss-hung trees grew from ground fairly firm and then the swamp began. For two weeks Coffee's men had breathed its odors of decay and, standing to their waists in the viscous slime, had cut trees to prolong the mud line with a breastwork of logs for a distance of six hundred yards. In front of this rampart, trees had been removed to afford a field of fire. Back of the rampart was a log walk for the men to stand on. They crowded about the General, who called out names by the sound of voices and exchanged greetings in the intimate vernacular of the West. If Andrew Jackson had a favorite corps in his army it was Coffee's which had taken the most difficult post in the battle line and borne the hardest labors with the least complaint.

At three o'clock Jackson stopped at Battery Number Eight to dictate an order for Brigadier-General Adair, acting in the place of Thomas who was ill, to bring up the Kentucky reserve and distribute it in two lines at the point behind the works where the commands of Carroll and of Coffee joined. Here, near the margin of the woods, he believed the British would make their real attempt to break through. This gave Jackson a total of five thousand one hundred and seventy-two men on his line, or about all he could crowd in.[22]

At six o'clock a milky light paled the little fires over which men rubbed their hands for warmth. Noting the direction of the wind, Major Latour said the fog would clear in an hour. Pickets reported the enemy formed in column on the plain of Chalmette plantation not half a mile away. Jackson sent Billy Phillips for his telescope and stood on the parapet with Carroll and Adair. From the field in front a rocket rose with a shrill sigh and burst into a bluish silver shower. It was answered by a rocket from the river bank.

"That is their signal for advance, I believe,"[23] said Andrew Jackson, whose life until now had been a preface to this moment.

6

Edward Michael Pakenham was not a man ordinarily to take counsel of his fears, which he had done when he fired that *"fatal ever fatal rocket,"* as a British officer afterward named it.

Sir Edward had been up nearly all night only to witness one miscarriage of arrangements after another. First, Colonel Thornton, commanding the forces that were to assail Morgan across the river, had got off four or five hours late and then, because of a shortage of boats, with less than half of his force of fourteen hundred men. He was to make the first attack, plow through Morgan, seize Patterson's batteries and turn them on Jackson's rear. Pakenham's advance against the mud rampart was to consist principally of two columns. Twelve hundred men under Keane would make a demonstration by the river, while twenty-one hundred under Gibbs breached the line near the margin of the woods. To occupy Coffee further a regiment of West Indian negroes was to attack through the trees. A third column of fourteen hundred under Lambert would remain in the center of the field to go where the fortunes of battle might call. It was a devastating scheme to box in Jackson's position with hostile fire. And the crux of the whole plan was that all attacks should take place in the dark. The British had had enough of Dirty Shirt marksmanship in broad daylight.

Mismanagement trod the heels of delay. At the head of the

main striking force under Gibbs was placed the Forty-Fourth Regiment to carry facines for bridging the canal and ladders for scaling the rampart. The selection of this corps is unaccountable; its lack of discipline was notorious. The column was in position, though late, and awaiting the signal to move when General Gibbs discovered that the Forty-Fourth had neither facines nor ladders. Three hundred men were sent back to get them.

With the thin January dawn breaking about him, Pakenham was almost frantic. There was no sign from across the river that Thornton had begun his attack. The chance to fall on Jackson's line in darkness was slipping away. Yet, in his exasperation, he dared not face old Cochrane with a proposal to postpone the assault.

So his signal flared. Keane answered. Of them all he alone was ready. The Forty-Fourth had not returned with the facines and ladders. For an instant, Gibbs hesitated, then sent his column forward in the blundering but brave British way. Still no sign of Thornton. Could Pakenham have but known—his Colonel was just landing on the opposite shore, having been dragged far from his objective by the unexpectedly strong river current.

A breeze broke ragged patches in the fog—one more tragedy for Pakenham, a God-send to the Americans.

General Jackson was standing on the parapet when a caprice of the wind unmasked the British advance. They were immediately in front, not more than six hundred and fifty yards away, and headed straight for the point behind which Jackson had massed his reserve. Andrew Jackson never forgot the sight that met his eyes. A heavy frost had embossed the cane stubble with silver. Across this shining carpet moved a field of red tunics latticed by white cross-belts, and a pulsing hedge of bayonets that gave an impression of infinity.

The American rifles were ineffective beyond four hundred yards. Jackson called to Carroll and Adair to pass the word for each man on the fire-step to pick out his target and "to aim above the cross plates."[24]

"The men were tense, but very cold," related one of them. "The enemy was now within five hundred yards. . . . Then—boom! went our first guns, . . . the long brass 12-pounder . . . commanded by Old General Fleaujeac.... Then all the guns opened. The British batteries,... concealed from us by the fog replied, directing their fire by the sound of our guns,... their flashes light[ing] up the fog... into all the hues of the rainbow."[25]

Cannon smoke billowed forward and "spoiled" the aim of the riflemen. This was as bad as the fog, shouted Adair. Jackson directed Batteries Seven and Eight to cease firing. When the air cleared the red line was within three hundred yards and coming at a run. Shells from the center batteries furrowed the ranks. They closed up and came on. Jackson could not suppress his admiration of the sight.[26] Carroll's and Coffee's men pressed their cheeks to their rifle stocks, each bringing his "bead" to bear above the beltplate of a British soldier.

"*Fire!*"

A sheet of orange flame flared from the parapet. The rank stepped down to reload. Another took its place.

"*Fire!*"

The second rank gave way to the third.

"*Fire!*"

The solid front of the British column was now a skirmish line. But this came on. The ranks behind it thinned, like teeth snapping from a comb. But they came on. The shining field was red with British coats. Advancing ranks tripped over them, the precise lines began to buckle, to bunch, and open a premature and ragged fire. "Never before," related an English lieutenant, "had British veterans quailed. But it would be silly to deny that they did so now.... That leaden torrent no man on earth could face. I had seen battle-fields in Spain and in the East... but nowhere... such a scene" as this.[27]

A figure on horseback appeared in the van—Gibbs, shouting to the men to push on with the bayonet. But the foreranks had turned toward the rear, throwing the column in confusion. Two more horsemen dashed to the front—Pakenham and his aide, Captain McDougall. Sir Edward's horse went down. A ball shattered the rider's right arm. He threw himself on McDougall's black pony. But the column was in retreat.

Out of range it reformed, the men throwing off their heavy knapsacks. Keane, on the left, perceiving the plight of Gibbs, obliqued across the field with the praying Ninety-Third Highlanders. This regiment, in which every man was six feet tall, was ordered to lead the second assault. Its commander, Colonel Dale, handed his watch and a letter to a surgeon. "Give these to my wife," he said. With swinging kilts the Scots came on across the stubble.

Blasts of grape rutted their line. They came on.

"*Fire!*" A musketry volley mowed them. Those who were left trailed arms and came on.

"*Fire! Load! Aim! Fire!*" There is British corroboration for Jackson's statement written on the field that his riflemen fired "with a briskness of which there have been but few instances, perhaps in any country."[28]

The Scots stumbled among their dead and the dead of the first attack. Colonel Dale was dead. Pakenham and Gibbs were dying. Keane was down, with a ball through his neck. One hundred and fifty yards from the rampart the leaderless Highlanders halted and huddled together. Other corps pressing up from behind bred confusion, then panic. Officers shouted and struck men with the flats of their swords. Major Wilkinson of the Twenty-First North Britain Fusiliers ran forward. Perhaps a hundred men followed and perhaps two-thirds of these gained the Rodriquez Canal, thirty yards from the black line's smoking face.

Twenty clambered up the bank and charged the works. Wilkinson scaled the parapet and fell gasping into the arms of Major Smiley of the Kentucky militia. He lived for two hours and the Kentuckians covered him with their colors.

When Keane went to the relief of Gibbs he left the left column along the river to Rennie, the gallant young colonel who had threatened Coffee's sector on the twenty-eighth. More favored by the fog than Gibbs had been, Rennie stormed the lines almost on the heels of the American pickets. He penetrated the bastion protruding from our line and perished there.

The last order Pakenham gave before he received his third and mortal wound was for Lambert to throw in the reserve. But this officer decided the battle was beyond redemption. As best he could he withdrew the whole British army from the stricken field.

At half past eight the American infantry ceased to fire. The batteries ceased at two. The silvery carpet had changed back to gray cane stubble. "I never had," said General Jackson, "so grand and awful an idea of the resurrection as . . . [when] I saw . . . more than five hundred Britons emerging from the heaps of their dead comrades, all over the plain rising up, and . . . coming forward . . . as prisoners."[29]

Andrew Jackson was not called a religious man, but when he looked upon those British dead and heard the report that his own loss was seven killed, six wounded,[30] his heart was filled with awe and his mind with wonder. "The unerring hand of providence shielded my men."[31]

7

Yet the battle was not ended. Across the river the long-delayed Thornton was moving against Morgan's works. Jackson climbed on top of his scarred parapet and peered anxiously into the mist.

"Take off your hats and give them three cheers!" he shouted, though Morgan's men were a mile and a half away.[32]

The cheers were given too soon. Gun-flashes showed that Morgan was falling back. Jackson's enthusiasm yielded to wrath and then to alarm. In the rear of Morgan's line were Patterson's batteries, still playing across the river on the retreating British. Morgan's withdrawal turned into flight. As Thornton pressed on the batteries ceased to fire. Patterson was spiking his guns. Should Thornton find even one of them undisabled, he could rake Jackson's position from river to swamp, Pakenham's original plan.

Hinds was begging Jackson for permission to pursue and cut up the fugitive army in front of him,[33] but Jackson refused until he could see how matters should eventuate on the western bank. General Jean Humbert, a Napoleonic exile, was sent across the river with four hundred men to drive back Thornton. He returned to say that the troops objected to the leadership of a foreigner.

After his almost incomprehensible victory, the night of January eighth was one of anxiety for Jackson. Thornton still held a position of enormous tactical possibilities. But on the morning of the ninth, Jackson learned, to his relief and astonishment, that Thornton had recrossed the river and joined the main body. General Lambert had called him back, considering the army too low in morale to attempt the exploitation of its success on the western bank.

Over the showing of his own army on the western bank, Jackson was bitter. In anger he dashed off a note to Monroe that Morgan's defeat had averted "the entire destruction of the enemy's army."[34] The entire destruction of a British army had been an accomplishment for which General Jackson had lived since he was thirteen years old. Monroe was further informed that the responsibility lay squarely on "a strong detachment of the Kentucky troops . . . [which] ingloriously fled." To this conclusion Jackson clung, despite protests of Adair and others, including a court of inquiry, presided over by William Carroll, which later was to find the conduct of the Kentuckians "not reprehensible." General Morgan blamed "Major Arnaud of the second brigade of Louis[a] militia . . . [who] abandoned his post in a most shameful manner."[35] The court of inquiry also placed the blame on Major Arnaud.[36]

Nothing is easier than armchair criticism after a battle. Jackson has had enough of it to relieve the monotony of hero-worship, but the fact remains that in matters small and large his generalship was excellent and considerably superior to that of the English. As to fighting qualities there was no comparison. But the responsibility for the failure on the western bank was Jackson's. He placed the incompetent Morgan in command there, permitted him to locate his line badly, and then refused sufficient troops to defend it.

8

With Thornton gone from the other side of the river, Jackson was ready to carry out Hinds's suggestion of the day before and complete the ruin of the British army. Livingston declared it would be a useless exposure of lives. "What do you want more? . . . The city is saved."[37] Even Coffee and Adair hesitated to "hazard an attack with raw militia on the open plain."[38]

As for the British, their only desire apparently was to quit their forlorn camp unmolested. For ten days they made elaborate preparations to protect their narrow avenue of retreat to Lake Borgne. On the night of January eighteenth, leaving fires alight, Lambert piloted his broken command over the five miles of swamp, the

THE SILVERY CARPET

soldiers stumbling and struggling to extricate their feet from an entangling evergreen called Laurel of the Conqueror. At the mouth of Bayou Bienvenue shallow boats awaited them. Already on its way to the fleet was the body of "General Pakenham in a casket of rum to be taken to London. What a sight for his wife who is aboard and who had hoped to be Governess of Louisiana."[39]

The next morning when Jackson rode toward the littered encampment a British surgeon met him with a petition for considerate care of eighty badly wounded who could not be removed. They were carried to New Orleans and given the same attentions as the American sick and wounded.

A few days later Jackson received a communication from General Keane, who was with the British fleet off Cat Island, offering "any price" for the return of the sword he had lost in battle.[40] Jackson marveled at the lapse of pride that could permit a request so exceptional.[41] He sent the General his sword promptly and with it a letter, entirely correct and military, and on the whole perhaps one of the most satisfying epistles Andrew Jackson ever wrote.

"The General Commanding the American forces, having learned that Major General Kean . . . has expressed a wish for . . . his sword, . . . feels great satisfaction in having it ordered returned to him. . . . The undersigned, feeling for the misfortunes of the brave, begs that Genl Kean will be assured of his wishes for his speedy restoration."[42]

CHAPTER XVI

"The United States Versus Andrew Jackson"

I

January of 1815 was one of the bleakest months it has been the lot of a President of the United States to endure. Behind the eight walls of Colonel Tayloe's Octagon House to which the British had driven him when they destroyed the Executive Mansion, James Madison shifted his anxious gaze between two remote points on the map—Hartford, Connecticut, and New Orleans. From either locality might issue news that would be the doom not only of his Administration, but of the Union.

Disaster had followed upon disaster. The war was a failure, the armies unpaid, the Treasury empty. Our coast was blockaded, business disturbed, taxes doubled. From Albany to Savannah banks had suspended specie payments. Then in December, like twin clouds obscuring the last gleam of hope, the great expedition equipped at an expense of one million pounds sterling converged upon Louisiana, and the "New England Convention" sat in the State-House at Hartford. The Administration press branded the latter as a plot to dismember the Union, an allegation the journals of New England did little to repel. "Throwing off all connection with this wasteful war," said one, "[and] making peace with our enemy . . . would be . . . a manly course."[1]

A dearth of news increased the tension. A discreet observer sent to Hartford by Mr. Madison might as well have remained at home for all he learned, so closely did the delegates guard their deliberations. As for Louisiana, after news of the loss of the gunboats three Southern mails in succession failed to arrive. Then a post that had left New Orleans at daylight on December twenty-fourth brought the word which appeared to confirm the worst forebodings. The British had made a surprise landing "with 6,000 men;" a battle was in progress.[2] And after that silence. An army officer employed the

"UNITED STATES VERSUS JACKSON"

time to demonstrate to an Administration congressman that New Orleans was indefensible.

On January fifth the Hartford Convention adjourned and published its report, which was received with mixed emotions. With old George Cabot in the chair, the Convention had been kept in leash by the moderates. The report contained ample sop for the radicals—the iniquities of the Administration set forth, the war denounced, defeat conceded—but considering the temper of New England, the body of recommendations was conservative. A strong argument in favor of union prefaced the opinion that secession should be contemplated only as "the work of peaceable times and deliberate consent." This on one hand. On the other a peremptory demand that Congress empower each state to carry on the war to suit itself, raising and directing armies independently of Federal authority.

Harrison Gray Otis and two other gentlemen departed from Boston on February third to lay the Hartford report before the general Government. They meant to take a firm tone with Mr. Madison. New England had been patient, for two and a half years remaining aloof from the major concerns of the war. No applause for Lundy's Lane, for Plattsburgh or Tohopeka. A motion for a vote of thanks to Captain Lawrence for the capture of the *Peacock* was rejected by the Massachusetts Legislature as "not becoming . . . a moral and religious people to express any approbation of military or naval exploits."

But now reserve had been discarded. New England had spoken and did not intend her breath should be wasted.

What, indeed, could little Mr. Madison do except listen and submit!

Supremely confident, Mr. Otis and his companions proceeded toward the capital. At any hour they expected to meet an express with news from the South which would finish the Administration.

Sunday Blue Laws detained the envoys for a day at New Haven. Ice in the Hudson put them back another twenty-four hours. And still no news. Three black crows preceded their coach into Philadelphia. "These are *ill omened* birds," observed Otis, "and . . . when augury was in fashion would have been considered sad precursors of three Ambassadors."[3]

Augury, it seems, had gone out of style too soon. At Gadsby's Hotel in Baltimore the three ambassadors learned of "The *Miraculous* success of our arms at N Orleans . . . [which] will probably put the Administration on stilts, and augur no favorable issue for our mission."[4]

The gentlemen who had expected to shake Washington with their tread tiptoed through a scene of celebration, ringing with the name of Jackson. The Administration was on stilts a mile high, and Mr. Otis was thankful for the shelter of a respectable Georgetown boarding house where several other bewildered New England statesmen also waited for the fever to pass. It did not pass. On February fourteenth Otis wrote his wife. "At this moment a rumor of peace . . . throws the natives into a great bustle." Mrs. Otis was cautioned to remember, however, that Madison had been taken in by such rumors before. Still, the letter remained unsealed until post-time, in the hope of later advices.

They were not long coming. Cannon boomed, bells rang, men paraded. "Peace! Peace! Victory!" A disciplined New England conscience guided the pen of Harrison Gray Otis. "Gods holy name be praised. . . . I say again, Gods name be praised."[5]

For ten days the august embassy withstood the lampooning its ridiculous position evoked and then left town. Mr. Otis grimly resumed his seat in the Massachusetts Legislature in time to vote for a resolution giving the Lord exclusive credit for the battle of New Orleans. General Jackson was not mentioned.

2

The Almighty was already aware, however, that the General entertained similar views. Riding from the deserted British camp on the morning of January nineteenth, he dictated a note to the Abbé DuBourg, head of the Catholic clergy of Louisiana. "Revd. Sir, The signal interposition of heaven . . . requires . . . some manifestation. . . . Permit me therefore to entreat that you will cause a service of public thanksgiving to be performed in the Cathedral."[6]

Two days later Jackson returned to New Orleans and the city gave him a Latin welcome. Pierre Favrot, seated by a window overlooking the Place d'Armes, undertook to describe it to his wife.

"At this moment there are more than 2500 people in the Place awaiting the arrival of the General . . . at least 1000 women, ladies & young girls." New Orleans gave itself over to fêting the heroes and Monsieur Favrot wrote no more that day. The rigors of the siege were forgotten, Jackson suspended the nine o'clock curfew and the gaiety lasted into the night. In the morning Favrot finished his letter. "8 A.M. Never my dear, have I seen such a crowd. . . . All the troops arriving to the strains of military music & of the cannons, . . . more than 12000 people of whom 8000 were armed. . . . Tomorrow they . . . will crown the General; twelve young girls will strew his path with flowers. . . . They are practicing at Mme. Floriant's."[7]

Madame Floriant fulfilled her duties with imagination. Two of the little girls took their places under a triumphal arch, one holding a wreath of laurel, one a paper inscribed with the words of a song. From the arch to the door of the gray cathedral stood two lines of children, "all dressed in white, . . . and wearing a silver star on their foreheads. Each . . . held in her right hand a flag . . . and in her left a basket . . . of flowers."[8] The sight touched the heart of the child-loving soldier. When the little girl under the arch had sung her song (to the tune of *Yankee Doodle*), General Jackson bent down and requested a copy of it, which he sent with an affectionate note to one of the Hays youngsters in Tennessee. At the door of the church he was received by the Abbé DuBourg in his robes of office and attended by a college of priests. A transcript of his remarks went to the little Hays child's father with this modest comment: "The language is good and the sentiments sublime altho' . . . as it respects myself too flattering."[9]

The choir began to chant the majestic lines of the *Te Deum*. The people in the church took up the hymn. It spread to the lips of the throng that filled the square as all New Orleans poured forth its gratitude for deliverance.

3

On the following day New Orleans awakened somewhat amazed to find itself, to all intents, once more in a state of siege. The tight restrictions of martial law were reimposed. Militia companies which had looked forward to prompt disbandment were marched into camps and set to drilling. Reserve companies not under arms before because there were no arms to give them were called out, the dilatory cargo of War Department rifles having arrived. Andrew Jackson expected his victory to have bearing on the tedious negotiations he assumed to be in progress at Ghent, but he took no chances.[10] He knew the tenacity of the English and their reputation for losing every battle except the last one. Moreover, boarding their boats on Lake Borgne, they had recovered sufficiently to boast a little. "We have missed the victory," a captain was heard to declare, "but we are going to get General Wellington, and . . . come back. . . . We did not count on having to do with Frenchmen. Your . . . Dirty Shirts are not much."[11]

The army in Louisiana was not alone to feel the hand of discipline. When Jackson left Mobile in November, two hundred Tennessee militiamen were under arrest for mutiny. In December they were tried. The court condemned six of the ringleaders to death and the others to penalties less severe. The papers in the case reached Jackson probably about January first. After the victory of the eighth there was time to study them. On the day before he was crowned with laurel at the Cathedral, Jackson dictated a lengthy memorandum which shows that he had considered the findings of the court with scrupulous care. He approved the sentences.[12]

Jackson foresaw a need for discipline on the Alabama. "The last account from the enemy," he wrote, "they were steering towards Mobile," evidently in contemplation of a "stroke." But "Winchester is prepared and must defeat them. . . . If they return [here] I am ready."[13]

This state of readiness was maintained at a sacrifice of much popularity. The Lower House of the Louisiana Legislature voted Jackson a sword, but the proposal was killed in the Senate, no one working harder to that end than Bernard Marigny. A lengthy resolution of thanks, however, was adopted. It was studded with names—captains, majors, colonels, generals—the author must have written with a roster of the army before him. But in this long list of the conspicuous and the obscure nowhere appeared the name of Andrew Jackson. The Legislature had taken its revenge for December twenty-eighth.

Martial law bore cruelly upon the population. "General," the patriotic Abbé DuBourg wrote in unaccustomed English, "a Number of unfortunate half starved women of Terre Aux Bœufs fall at your feet to redemand you their husbands."[14] Civil authorities chafed to resume their functions and picked quarrels with the military. Claiborne urged the discharge of some of the militia. Jackson refused like a shot, reminding him that the enemy was only four days' sail away. The reminder had little effect. The militia began to desert, Private James Harding taking the trouble to state his reasons in writing to the Commanding General. "Dear Sir, My wife was turned into the Street by the land lord . . . and she wrote me to go home."[15] A court martial ordered him to be shot, but Jackson quietly withheld his approval of the sentence.

On February nineteenth word came that Fort Bowyer had fallen to the English, but, before Jackson could give effect to his flaming determination to recapture it, Edward Livingston returned from a mission to the British fleet with a rumor that the war was over.

New Orleans forgot Fort Bowyer as completely as if it were in China. But Jackson did not forget it. He published a proclamation warning that the report of peace might be a "stratagem" on the part of "an artful . . . enemy . . . to put you off your guard. . . . Fort Bowyer . . . must and will be speedily retaken."[16]

New Orleans declined to attach importance to Fort Bowyer. It had ears only for the news of peace. Counting houses, coffee houses, offices and shops seethed with milling throngs. Bids on cotton, bids on sugar, tobacco, pelts. Prices climbed and the truth or falsity of the rumor of peace would spell the difference between riches and ruin to some of the bidders. The wharves and warehouses of New Orleans were piled with the accumulations of two years, cut off from export by the British blockade. On confirmation of the rumor of peace the value of exportable products would jump one hundred per cent. Manchester's looms were starved for American cotton, and New England's little better off. Peace would deflate the prices of imports in the same proportion.

At Washington, at Philadelphia—almost any place one pries into this subject of the peace news, one finds that a favored few by underground means were informed in advance of officials for whom the dispatches were intended. Some such leak seems to have occurred at New Orleans. Livingston arrived on February nineteenth and publicly gave out a report based on a copy of a London newspaper that had just reached the British fleet. But he knew more. Admiral Cochrane, with whom Livingston was personally acquainted, had exhibited a Foreign Office bulletin anouncing a treaty at Ghent "by [which] hostilities will cease as soon as . . . ratified by the President of the united states . . . and the Prince regent."[17] Indeed Cochrane had given Livingston a copy of this bulletin to deliver to Jackson with a hasty note of "sincere congratulations."[18] When Colonel Livingston reached New Orleans he turned his dispatch case inside out before the Commander. The note from Cochrane was not there. It did not arrive until the morning of February twenty-first, by a British launch flying a white flag. Meanwhile had Edward Livingston seen fit to tell his friends privately that the peace rumor rested on a foundation more substantial than a newspaper report, the information would have been priceless. An incident suggests that some such thing occurred.

Jackson hardly had time to acknowledge Cochrane's message when he heard boys crying handbills in the streets: "A truce-boat from Admiral Cochrane . . . has just brought to General Jackson official news of a treaty concluded at Ghent . . . and a request for a cessation of hostilities."[19]

The handbills were issued by the Louisiana *Gazette* whose editor enjoyed the confidence of Colonel Livingston. Jackson sent John Reid scurrying through crowded Royal Street with a bristling order for the *Gazette* to destroy "every copy of so *unauthorized and improper a notice*" and to publish the retraction which General Jackson had dictated.

"The only official news . . . received by no means declares that a truce is to take place until the treaty be . . . ratified. . . . The Commanding General again Calls upon his fellow Citizens and Soldiers to recollect that . . . until . . . [peace] is properly announced" there can be no "relaxation in the army under his command."[20]

These words had no effect. The tide of speculation reduced Louisiana militia commands to skeletons as brokers, planters and merchants in the ranks declined to see themselves outdone by rivals not in service. Cotton rose from six to sixteen cents. The river front whitened with sail as ships long idle were loaded and made ready for sea, but Jackson forbade them to weigh anchor. though it is

JACKSON IN 1817

A steel engraving believed to have been made in France, where Jackson was very popular after beating the English. From the private collection of Emil Edward Hurja of New York City.

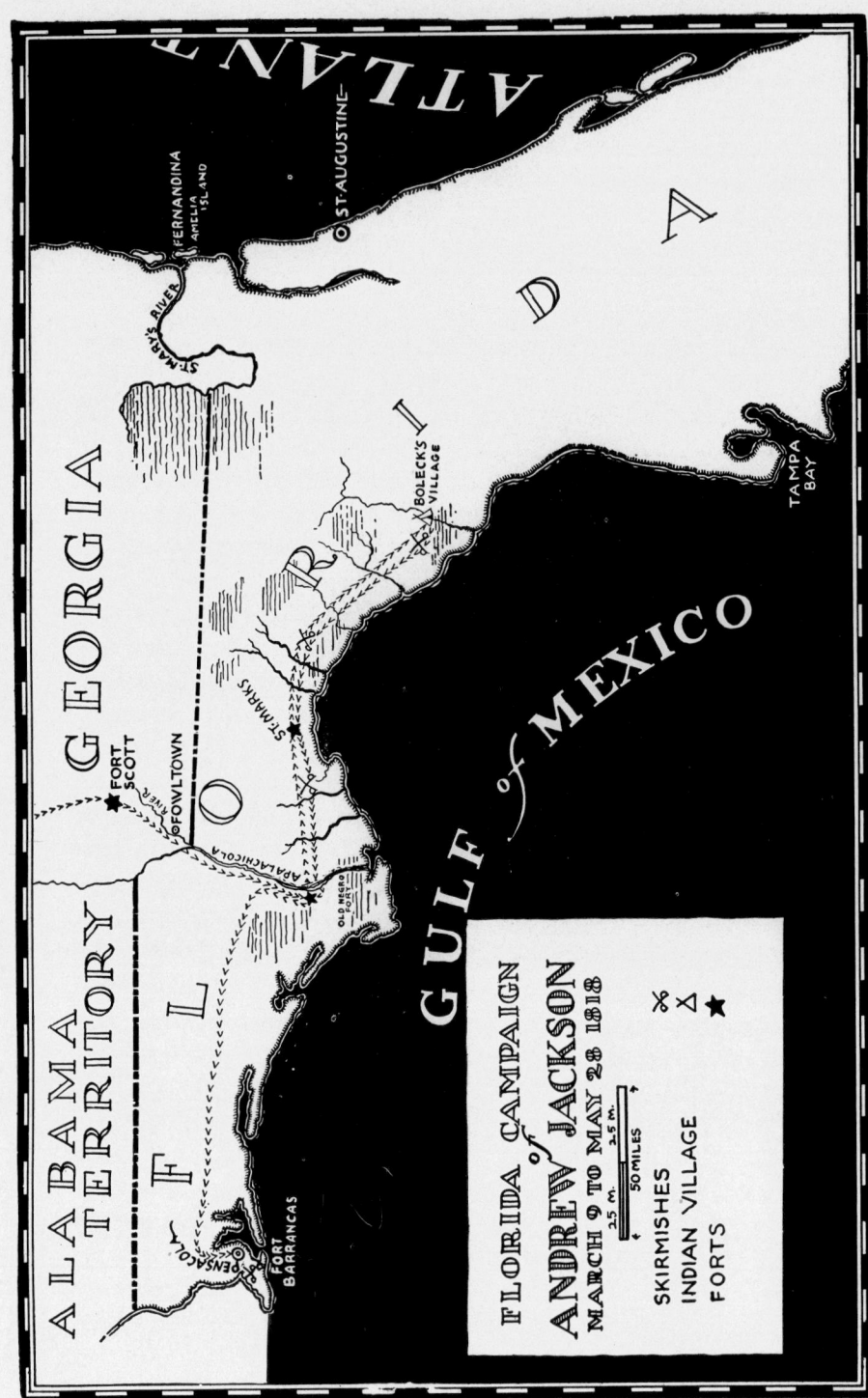

probable that some of his own cotton lay on the wharves. The stronger he was opposed the more tightly he clutched the mace. Each day brought nearer the inevitable eruption that was to display the defects of the qualities that had made Andrew Jackson the savior of Louisiana.

4

On to this taut stage stepped Rachel and Andrew, junior, after "a tollerable pasage in 25 days"[21] on the refurbished Cumberland keel boat. In December their departure had been postponed by news of the British landing, but they had left the day following receipt of the tidings of the eighth of January.[22] Rachel's coming was a signal for a partial suspension of hostilities between the General and the militia and, for the moment, supplanted the treaty rumor as the pièce de resistance of drawing-room small-talk, while the Creole community prepared to entertain a lady who had been preceded by such engaging descriptions of her virtues. Rachel seemed unaware of the especial attention. Joy alone consumed her. At last, she was reunited with the husband who had been gone from her side more than seven months.

Madame Livingston took her in charge. This family had become truly devoted to Andrew Jackson who reciprocated with his confidence and his friendship. Their home was a quiet harbor where he could shed the cares of headquarters, take their little daughter Cora on his knee, and send her to bed with a story. At first Cora's mother was rather alarmed by the responsibility of rendering Aunt Rachel presentable to New Orleans society. Mrs. Jackson was forty-seven. Her short figure had grown so stout that in describing her the natives repeated an old French saying, "She shows how far the skin can be stretched."[23]

It was skin honestly tanned by the wind and sun of Tennessee, for during her husband's absence Rachel had been the active manager of Hermitage plantation. Her black hair was without a strand of gray, her large dark eyes still young, her generous lips ready for a frank warm smile, revealing teeth that would have been the pride of a duchess. But her clothes—*mon Dieu!* Mrs. Jackson's wardrobe ignored the pageant of style even as revealed to remote Nashville.

With invitations to plays and dinners pouring in, not to mention the great celebration of Washington's birthday, Madame Livingston surrounded her guest with folds of goods and a corps of French needlewomen. When General Jackson lifted the censorship from the press, a caricaturist represented Aunt Rachel standing on a table while Madame Livingston tugged at the strings of a pair of stays in an effort to reestablish her waist-line.[24]

It was Mrs. Jackson's first visit to a city larger than Nashville. "I have seen more already than in all my life past it is the finest Country for the Eye of a Strainger but a Little while he tir[e]s of the Disipation. . . . So much amusement balls Concerts Plays theatres &c &c but we Dont attend the half of them. I herd a band of musick a few Evinings since."[25]

The elegant Creole ladies smiled behind their fans, but very soon Rachel's simplicity and her unaffected kindliness won them.

Preparations for the Washington's birthday dinner and ball were bewildering. For days the upper floor of the French Exchange had been in the hands of a Committee on Arrangements whose selection resulted in the usual contest for supremacy between the French and "American" contingents of society. "to give you a disseription [of their handiwork] is beyond the power of my pen," Rachel asserted, but her fresh, frontier eyes caught details that were lost to the sophisticated. "The Splendor, the brilliant assemblage the Magnificenc of the Supper and orniments of the room with all our greate Characters in Large Letters of Gold on a Long Sheet of Glass about four Inches wide with Lamps behind that they might be read as we Sat at Supper I was placed opposit the Motto Jackson and Victory ar one on the table a most Ellegant piremid on the top was Vivi Jackson in Large Letters on the other Sid the Immortal Washington— ther was a gold ham on the table . . . to say nothing . . . [of] the orniments and S[u]pper."[26]

After the supper, to say nothing of the gold ham, had disappeared the merry company formed for dancing. The guests of honor finally consented to treat their hosts to a pas de deux as it was done in blockhouse days in the Mero District. A member of the Committee on Arrangements observed them, perhaps still a little resentful because Jackson had allowed him only the pre-peace-rumor price for his cotton used to mount guns behind the Rodriquez Canal. "To see these two figures, the general a long, haggard man, with limbs like a skeleton, and Madame le Generale, a short, fat dumpling, bobbing opposite each other . . . to the wild melody of *Possum up de Gum Tree* . . . was very remarkable."[27]

5

"I have given you," concluded Rachel, "some of the flowers now the thorns." The nights of vigilance and days of toil in the swamps were taking their toll of the unacclimated troops from Tennessee and Kentucky. Hospital tents were full. "Major Read tells me this morning nearly one thousand have died." Yet, with the Louisiana militia approaching a state of mutiny, these soldiers bore their lot without complaint. Jackson labored incessantly. "of all men in Erth he Does the most Business from Day Light to ten at night."[28]

He had much business to do. French citizens in the militia had found that they could obtain discharge by registering their nationality at the French consulate. Creoles were quick to perceive the advantages of this arrangement and the obliging consul, Louis de Tousard, began a land-office business in French citizenship papers. Jackson matched the trick by deporting the holders of such papers to Baton Rouge.[29] Tousard made a theatric protest and was deported also.

Any number of actual French subjects, having neglected to obtain certificates, remained in the city. They sympathized with their exiled compatriots. Moreover, at the first ebb of Jackson's popularity, Governor Claiborne had made himself accessible to those opposed to the measures of the Commander. Relations between the two had become strained during the campaign. *La Courrière de la Louisiane* strode boldly into the breach on March third, publishing a lengthy communication which gave a formal cast to coffee-house criticism. Did General Jackson forget that Frenchmen and men of French blood had virtually won his battles? "It is high time the laws should resume their empire; . . . that citizens accused of any crime should be rendered to their natural judges; . . . that having done enough for glory the moment for moderation has arrived."

This was defiance and it acted as a match to powder. Louisiana troops at Chef Menteur mutinied, and a company in the city ordered to replace them refused to march.³⁰ Jackson demanded the name of the author of the *Courrière* article and was surprised to hear that it was Louis Louaillier, a member of the Legislature who had distinguished himself by his support of the war. Louaillier was a naturalized Frenchman. Jackson ordered his arrest and on Sunday, March fifth, a file of businesslike Regulars closed about him on the steps of the Exchange Coffee House. The prisoner threw up his hands and shouted that he was being borne away against his will by armed men. A Creole lawyer offered his services on the spot and sped to the residence of Federal Judge Hall with a petition for a writ of habeas corpus. It was granted. The Major General's answer was to arrest Hall for "a[i]ding abbetting and exciting mutiny within my camp," and to lock him in the Barracks with Louis Louaillier.

Rachel wrote on that day that her husband, though "busy," seemed much improved in health and spirits.

6

Morning found the town in an uproar. A crowd filled Royal Street in front of General Jackson's headquarters. It parted to admit the passage of a horseman, a road-stained stranger in the uniform of a Regular captain. The rider was a courier, twenty days from Washington, with a sealed packet for General Jackson and a letter identifying him as the bearer of official news of peace. An hysterical cry went up:

"La paix! La paix!"

In the mind of the populace there could be no doubt of it now. Jackson ripped open the packet. Several official papers tumbled out, but there was not a line in one of them about peace.³¹

Jackson accepted the situation as a clerk's blunder and hurried a note to General Lambert at Fort Bowyer. "I have . . . little doubt in my mind that the treaty . . . has been ratified. . . . I pray you to receive . . . [assurance] of the satisfaction I feel in reflecting that our Correspondence begun as Commander of hostile armies should terminate as officers of nations in amity."³² No assurance, or any word whatever, was addressed to the perplexed citizens of New Orleans until the following day when General Jackson admitted the probability of peace, and, with soldierly words of praise, released the drafted militia of Louisiana. The exiled holders of Tousard's certificates were permitted to return.

But volunteer troops were retained and Louaillier was placed on trial before a court martial on seven fearful-sounding charges, ranging from mutiny to "general misconduct." The president of the court martial was Brigadier-General Edmund P. Gaines of the Regular Army, a competent and conscientious officer. After two days of deliberation the court declared itself without jurisdiction in six of the seven charges, and on the remaining charge, that of being a spy, acquitted the prisoner.

In a black rage Jackson rejected the findings and sent Louaillier back to the Barracks. The Major General appreciated, however, the futility of trying Hall even by a court of his own choosing, and detailed a squad of soldiers to escort the Judge out of town and let him go.

Forty-eight hours later, at daybreak on March 13, 1815, New Orleans awakened to the boom of minute guns. At last General Jackson had received official notice of the ratification of peace. With the same paralyzing promptitude with which he had gathered them into his hands when the crisis came, the Commander laid aside his extraordinary powers. Martial law was revoked and military prisoners released, including Louaillier and Private James Harding. The Mississippi, Kentucky and Tennessee troops were told to make ready for home, and the remainder of the Louisiana militia was dismissed. "Farewell, fellow-soldiers. The expression of your General's thanks is feeble."[33]

The volatile city surrendered to the emotions of jubilee, an about-face in which self-congratulation assumed the sublimer form of hero-worship. Huzzahing crowds enveloped the Royal Street headquarters. Coffee houses that two days before had rumbled with denunciation rang now with toasts to Old Hickory. The Sister Superior of the Ursuline nuns who viewed the carnival from their latticed windows begged that General Jackson would visit them again. The officers of the Battalion of Uniform Companies, representing most of the distinguished Creole families, presented a glowing and significant address, which indicates the unspontaneous nature of much of the recent opposition. "Leaving to others the task of declaiming about . . . *constitutional rights,* we are content with having fought . . . for them."³⁴

In a carefully worded reply in which he admitted with disarming candor infringement on personal rights guaranteed by the Constitution, Andrew Jackson developed his hypothesis on the subject of authority. "The laws must sometimes be silent when necessity speaks. . . . My first wish . . . has been to be useful to my country."³⁵

In the midst of these occupations General Jackson celebrated his forty-eighth birthday on the fifteenth of March. A few old friends came to offer their felicitations. They found the chief in a mellow mood. The years rolled back to the scenes of childhood and he spoke of his mother. "How I wish *she* could have lived to see this day." He told of her heroic resolve to nurse the prisoners of war at Charleston and repeated her farewell: make friends by being honest, keep them by being steadfast; be truthful, be sincere, be brave. . . .

"Gentlemen. . . . [those] words have been the law of my life."³⁶

7

Dominick A. Hall did not subscribe to the imperial doctrine of authority enunciated by the Major General. Hall was born in England, but neither the United States nor the prerogatives of the bench had a stauncher defender. He had braved the frown of Jackson in preparing the way for the participations of the Baratarians in the late campaign. He had welcomed the Louaillier case as an opportunity to contest the Commander's right to supersede habeas corpus proceedings by martial law. Returning to the city during the rejoicing, he quietly resumed his seat on the bench and permitted the hero to enjoy his hour.

But on March twenty-first he issued a summons directing Andrew Jackson to show cause why he should not be held in contempt for his refusal to recognize the writ of habeas corpus in the case of Louis Louaillier. Ten days of legal fencing followed, Jackson's counsel (Edward Livingston, et al.) disputing the jurisdiction of the court over acts of their client during the period of martial law. Popular opinion was as strongly on the side of Jackson as it had been on that of Hall and Louaillier a fortnight before. Nor was Judge Hall any more terrified by threats than General Jackson had been. He ruled against Jackson on every count and directed the defendant to appear and receive the sentence of the court.

Andrew Jackson was not ignorant of the force of the theatrical values in a court-room. Faultlessly attired in civilian dress, he left his carriage and made his way on foot through the throng that packed Royal Street in front of the little red-tiled Spanish building where Judge Hall presided. The room was crowded almost to suffocation. In their red shirts and holiday sashes, the Baratarians were present in force ready for anything. The General had no more zealous partizans than these mariners, many of whom, but for Dominick Hall, would still have been in jail. Jackson reciprocated this loyalty. In his most sprightly contributions to the belles-lettres of the war, the "hellish banditti" had become "my comrades in arms," and the brothers Laffite, "those gentlemen."[37]

The General entered amid perfect decorum, but as Judge Hall emerged from his chambers a storm of jeers broke from the Baratarians. Leaping to his feet, Jackson silenced them with a gesture reminiscent of the public prosecutor of Mero District. Then he turned toward the bench and inclined his head in a slight bow.

Judge Hall lowered the dramatic tone of this spectacle by dryly directing the clerk to proceed.

"The United States versus Andrew Jackson."

The defendant arose. "When called upon to show cause why an attachment for contempt of this court ought not to run against me, I offered to do so. . . . You would not hear my defense. . . . Under these circumstances I appear . . . to receive the sentence of the court. . . . Your Honor will not misunderstand me as meaning any disrespect, . . . but as no opportunity has been furnished me to explain . . . my conduct, so it is expected that censure will form no part of that punishment which your Honor may imagine it your duty to perform."[38]

It was an astute protest, but the urbane Dominick Hall was undisturbed by this representation of a patriot entangled by a manipulation of the law's machinery. Judge Hall had the measure of his man. It was impossible to forget, he said, the important services of the defendant to the country, and for that reason imprisonment would form no part of the sentence. "The only question was whether the

Law should bend to the General or the General to the Law." The defendant had declined to respond to the interrogatories of the District Attorney. This left the Court no alternative but to adjudge him in contempt. A fine of one thousand dollars and costs was imposed.[39]

Jackson walked out of the court-room the idol of the cheering crowd. They unhitched the horses and dragged his carriage to the Exchange Coffee House. The General stood on the seat of the vehicle and signed for quiet.

"I have," he said, "during the invasion exerted every one of my faculties for the defense and preservation of the constitution and the laws. . . . Considering obedience to the laws, even when we think them unjustly applied, as the first duty of a citizen, I did not hesitate to comply with the sentence you have heard, and I entreat you to remember the example."[40]

Dominick Hall not being present, the scene was wholly Jackson's.

CHAPTER XVII

A Changing World

I

WITH the nation as well as New Orleans at his feet the hero bore his honors becomingly. If anything, he grew a little weary of the laurel. The departure from New Orleans was taken in triumph—public farewells, private leave-takings, exchanges of costly gifts. A purse was raised to discharge the fine imposed by Dominick Hall, but Andrew Jackson waved it aside requesting that the money be distributed among the families of soldiers who had fallen in battle. Rachel, too, had her farewells to say and she addressed some lines "To the ladies of Orleans,"[1] which may have come from the pen of John Reid, though, if it were possible, one should suspect Madame de Staël.

On the evening of May 15, 1815, General Jackson, Rachel and little Andrew descended from their coach at Nashville into a changing world. The bounteous blessings of peace and prosperity lay upon a smiling land—trade reviving, crops moving, coin clinking across the counters in Market Street and the Square. From a pit of disillusionment the new order had issued with the celerity and perfection of a miracle. Peace and Victory! It mattered not that the victory was gained fifteen days after the commissioners had put their names to the articles at Ghent, and had had no bearing on the negotiations. It mattered not that the peace secured to us scarcely one specific trophy promised by the enthusiasts whose buoyant rhetoric had swept the republic into War in 1812. Enough to know that Andrew Jackson had met the British and sent them reeling. Through his agency a treaty, "honorable," yes, in that it failed of national humiliation, was touched with the wand of glory and transformed, redeeming the self-respect of a spiritually bankrupt people. Not even Rachel could resist. She dropped her "Mr. Jackson" and began to speak of "the General."

Once more she was looking forward to a quiet life with her husband at her side. This time it seemed as if she were really to have it. The General had declined to show himself about the country and retired to his log residence to resume the management of his plantation. The Army was reorganized into two divisions, Jackson retaining command of the South, where his military duties promised to be nominal since the detail work devolved upon capable Edmund P. Gaines. The Major General's pay of twenty-four hundred dollars a year, with forage and rations allowances of sixteen hundred and fifty-two dollars more, had got him out of debt for the first time since 1796.

Thus the old financial worries were gone. Truly, Rachel and her husband now had nothing to stop the flow of their lives into the normal ways of the contented countryside. They visited back and forth among the neighbors and their old friends, comfortably and without ostentation. The pride of the General's heart was Andrew, junior, now five and a half, and Jackson was pleased to observe that "he behaved like a soldier" in the face of danger. Andrew's horse had run away, but the plucky child "stuck to him for half a mile" and when thrown "never hollowed."[2] The late Samuel Donelson's two sons still lived at the Hermitage, but Junior's especial playmate was Lincoyer, the little Creek Indian boy General Jackson had found half-starved among the dead at Tallushatchee and fed with his own hands.

His indifference to applause stimulated curiosity and the victor of New Orleans remained the most talked-of man in the country, interest undiminished by the fact that the public knew, and apparently could learn, very little about the man it honored. The War Department was obliged to write for a portrait before it could proceed to design the gold medal Congress had voted.[3] A resident of Lexington, Kentucky, wagered a "Considerable" sum that he was born in Ireland,[4] whereas an Eastern newspaper declared him a native of Devonshire.[5] North and South Carolina asserted their divergent claims. As a general response to such inquiries Jackson turned John Reid loose among his papers to write a biography, and addressed himself to preparations for the forthcoming meeting of the Nashville Jockey Club.

2

Much was at stake here. During the war Jackson had made an effort to maintain his stable, with the immediate object of defeating Jesse Haynie's chestnut mare Maria just as soon as he could send the British about their business. When Maria humbled his colors so thoroughly in 1811, the General punctually inaugurated a search for a horse to beat her and with this quest the fighting of three campaigns interfered only slightly. Pacolet had been acquired while Jackson was with the Natchez expedition. From that front the General wrote Colonel William R. Johnson of Kentucky to send to the Hermitage "the best 4-mile horse in Virginia, without regard to price."[6] Johnson had bought the dapple-gray six-year-old Pacolet for one hundred and seventy-nine dollars. He sold him to Jackson for three thousand. At home in the summer of 1813, Jackson did not think he had made a bad bargain. The grueling training began, but the Creek uprising kept Old Hickory from the fall meeting that year. It was just as well, for Pacolet injured an ankle and Jackson paid a forfeit of five hundred dollars rather than risk defeat.

While facing the British at Mobile in the summer of 1814, Jackson purchased Tam O'Shanter in South Carolina and Stump-the-Dealer in Georgia to train with Pacolet. Meantime a Kentucky sportsman named DeWett turned up in Nashville with a mare that observers thought should distance Maria. Jackson ordered the Hermitage stables placed at his disposal. But to no purpose. Stump-the-Dealer was scratched and Pacolet reserved to race Doublehead. Maria easily won from Tam O'Shanter and from the DeWett mare. But there was some balm in the fact that Pacolet beat Doublehead, which news Jackson included in his order to Coffee announcing the arrival of the British off the Louisiana coast.

The battle of January eighth out of the way, the General filled his letters home with expressions of solicitude for his horses and directions for their training. Yet, as the autumn meeting of 1815 approached, he felt that he had nothing fit to contend with Maria, and so gave his support to the DeWett mare and to Edward Ward's Western Light in whom he had a partnership interest. Maria was first matched against the DeWett entry in a half-mile dash for three side bets, five hundred dollars on the first quarter, five hundred on six hundred yards, and five hundred on the finish. She won all wagers, the last by a hundred feet. Then she beat Western Light, taking for her owner a bet of one thousand dollars.

But Jackson was not done. Himself an old rider, he believed that with the right jockey in the saddle the DeWett mare could best Maria over a two-mile course. Accordingly, he hired of Colonel Lynch in Virginia a negro rider named Dick who bore a great reputation. Unquestionably General Jackson was unaware of the secret of Dick's consistent triumphs, for Jackson's most unbending enemy never accused him of shady work on the track. A salient factor in Dick's success was his reputation among fellow jockeys as a conjurer. Most professional riders were negroes, usually slaves, drenched with the superstitions of their race. They were privileged and sometimes pampered characters. A skilful jockey, such as Lynch's Dick or Colonel George Elliott's hunchback Monkey Simon, would command on the block a price equal to that of a first-class race-horse. As in the case of Dick they were frequently hired at fancy figures for a single race or for a season.

The race in which Dick was to ride the DeWett mare attracted more attention than any turf event in Tennessee since Truxton had beaten Ploughboy. The match was for a side bet of one thousand dollars, Maria giving her opponent one hundred and twenty yards distance. Maria's trainer was Berry Williams, who had served in Jackson's Creek campaign and was destined for fifty years to be a figure on Western and Southern tracks. He instructed his rider to give Maria her head at the tap of the drum, take the lead and never relinquish it.

To Williams's amazement Maria started leisurely, and the DeWett mare passed the stands at the end of the first mile a good hundred and twenty yards ahead. Williams yelled to his rider to give her the spur, but Maria kept on at the same speed until she struck the back stretch. Then the spectators saw a sight that taxed the credulity of their senses. The chestnut mare leaped forward like lightning. Such a burst of speed had never been seen on a Tennessee track. The hundred-and-twenty-yard lead diminished, vanished. Maria went ahead and thundered home the winner by one hundred and eighty yards. When Williams demanded an explanation, his rider declared

A CHANGING WORLD

that Dick had put a "spell" on him, saying that should he attempt to pass him before they had gone a mile and a quarter, he would lift him from the saddle by a wave of his whip.

Jesse Haynie offered to match Maria against any horse on earth, one to four mile heats, for five thousand dollars.

"Make it fifty thousand," exclaimed Jackson, "and consider me in with you. She can beat any horse in God's whole creation."[7]

Maria had licked Old Hickory, a circumstance so unusual that he could never forget the little mare. Twenty-two years later an old friend sat with Jackson at the Hermitage enumerating his triumphs, and no other American, before or since, has enjoyed so long or so stormy a reign as a popular idol. Was there anything Jackson ever had seriously undertaken and failed to accomplish? the friend inquired.

"Nothing that I can remember," he said simply, "except Haynie's Maria. I could not beat her."[8]

There was consolation in the fact that neither could any one else. The chestnut mare never lost a race, or a heat.

3

Five months of rest restored General Jackson's health. His fortunes were restored by the rise of tobacco and cotton prices and a timely assertion of his claim to the Duck River land obtained from the Allison heirs in 1811.[9] On October 2, 1815, his cash balance with the Nashville Bank was twenty-two thousand one hundred and seventeen dollars.[10] He yearned for activity, and poor Rachel could see there was no want of opportunities to satisfy this yearning. Meantime he seemed to have overcome, to an extent, his diffidence toward the plaudits of the multitude.

Officers of the New Orleans army, scattered to every quarter of the country, kept interest kindled with expanding sagas of their Commanding Officer, and boomed advance subscriptions for John Reid's book. "You are the favorite . . . in the *New England* States," wrote Arthur Hayne,[11] and there was much truth in the statement. Federalist leaders who had staked the political future of their glory on an inglorious termination of the war found themselves deserted by their followers, with the national elections only a year away.

Returning from a trip in October, William Carroll reported "many of the leading characters of . . . K.y OHio and Penna, . . . are solicitous that you should become a candidate for the next President. . . . I should be glad to know your views."[12]

What views General Jackson imparted are not known, but a few days later when, with his wife and son, he departed for Washington, ostensibly on military business, the pulses of Jackson men quickened. Another friendly observer reported that even General Adair, whose sensibilities had been ruffled by Jackson's reference to the behavior of the Kentucky troops on the west bank, "had little doubt with proper management . . . you might be elevated to the highest office in the American Government. . . . I have friends in Balto . . . of the same sentiments. . . . Will you be good enough to call on those gentlemen?"[13] Anthony Wayne Butler also sent a letter in the wake of his guardian. "On my way through Pennsylvania and Virginia I had numerous conversations with persons of the first consideration . . . and found a strong disposition . . . to run your Name for the Presidency. . . . I . . . [urge] you to stand a candidate."[14]

The reference to congressmen was important in view of the approaching caucuses at which, according to custom, the members of Congress would designate the candidates of their respective parties. The dramatic termination of the war and the crowning misfortune of the Hartford Convention had so disorganized the Federalists that it seemed as if they might let the election go by default. Thus it only remained for the Republicans to agree on their man. James Monroe had emerged from the war with the highest prestige of any member of the Administration, not the least conspicuous feather in his cap being his mettlesome support of Jackson at New Orleans. In this way, he had associated himself with the great event that imparted a rosy cast to what otherwise would have been the unstimulating end of a war, about which the less said the better. This state of affairs placed Colonel Monroe in a position that no aspirant except William H. Crawford of Georgia dared to challenge. Although the abler man, Crawford's post as war-time minister to France had deprived him of opportunities for popular distinction. During the crisis Monroe had been both Secretary of State and of War, but when the rewards in the War Office had been reaped, Crawford was summoned home to take over this portfolio. He made considerable headway against the claims of Monroe, though it appears that many congressmen secretly hoped for a new man with sufficient popular appeal to the imagination of the electorate to justify the desertion of both announced candidates.

A collateral factor in the situation was the increasing distrust of the system of congressional nominations which the people, afflicted with the growing pains of democracy, felt excluded them from the councils that governed the nation.

In New York Aaron Burr, an outcast to whom personal aspirations were impossible, pondered the case with singular clarity and detachment. He had lost his talented Theodosia, whom he had loved even more than he had loved ambition. He desired an occupation for his mind and an activity to arouse his son-in-law, Governor Joseph Alston of South Carolina, from his brooding. And he had not forgotten the conduct of Andrew Jackson at Richmond. He wrote to Alston.

"A Congressional Caucus will, in the course of the ensuing month, nominate James Monroe for Pres^t. . . . I have often heard your opinion of these Congressional Nominations. . . . Independently of the manner of the nomination . . . the Man himself is . . . Naturally dull & stupid, . . . indecisive, . . . hypocritical. . . . Pretends, I am told, to some knowledge of military matters, but never commanded a platoon. . . . In the revolutionary war . . . he acted a short time as aide to L^d. Stirling who was regularly drunk, . . . Monroe's whole duty being to fill his Lordship's Tankard. . . . As a lawyer Monroe . . . never . . . [tried] a cause of the Value of a hundred pounds.

"The Moment is extremely Auspicious for breaking down this degrading system. . . . If then there is a man in the U. S. of firmness and decision & having standing enough to afford even a hope of success it is Your duty to hold him up to public view—— That man is Andrew Jackson—— Nothing is wanting but a respectable Nomination . . . [prior to] the Proclamation of the . . . Caucus, and Jackson's success is inevitable. . . .

"Exhibit yourself then & emerge from this State of Nullity—— You owe it to yourself—— You owe it to me—— You owe it to your Country—— You owe it to the memory of the dead——"

Before posting this letter, Burr learned that Jackson was on the way to Washington. "If you have any confidential friend . . .

[there] charge him to caution J against the perfidious Caresses with which he will be overwhelmed." Then a second postscript: "Our project is wonderfully advanced." Alston was to inform Jackson that "Communications have been had with every State to the Northward," and to solicit the "names of persons in the Western States . . . whom you may address."[15]

4

Joseph Alston replied that he was too encompassed by grief, "too entirely unconnected with the world," to interest himself in "anything." It did not matter, for, in his own way, Andrew Jackson had disposed of the cloud-castle of his aspiring friends.

On the first stages of the journey to the capital, he maintained a silence that was beginning to wear a significant aspect when Lynchburgh, Virginia, was reached. Here a prodigious reception awaited, to which Thomas Jefferson had come, a long day's ride from Charlottesville. This was an event in itself. Mr. Jefferson seldom had need to leave his curious mansion on the mountain. The world had pressed a path to the door, coaxing from his books, his violin and his memories an untidily attired old man richest in honors of living Americans, though master of Monticello only by the indulgence of creditors. Mr. Jefferson and General Jackson had not met since 1798, and, since Jackson's speech on the State-House green at Richmond, few had been willing to sponsor a reunion—a situation that very nearly had kept Andrew Jackson out of the war.

At a banquet attended by three hundred persons, the founder of the Republican Party lifted his glass.

"Honor and gratitude to those who have filled the measure of their country's honor."

General Jackson responded.

"James Monroe, late Secretary of War."[16]

The estrangement was over, and without loss of countenance by either party. Jackson had supported Monroe for president against Jefferson's candidate, Madison, in 1808. But the philosophic Jefferson possessed the seemly faculty of retaining a personal regard for some of the men from whom he differed politically. James Monroe had studied law in his office and the exigencies of politics had failed

A CHANGING WORLD

to disturb their social relations. Now Mr. Jefferson supported his old pupil's aspirations for the presidency, and was delighted to see that General Jackson did so.

A mind less embittered than Aaron Burr's might have discerned a motive beneath the shining surface of the welcome the Administration gave Andrew Jackson in the capital. Young John Reid could hardly find time for a personal letter. "To tell every thing would require a book. . . . This week . . . two *special invitations* to dinner; one . . . from *Jimmy* [Monroe] *himself*, the other . . . from Dolly and her husband." At first the traveling biographer was more than a little apprehensive over the outcome of his subject's call on the Secretary of War. There had been some talk of a polite, though official, request for additional enlightenment on the Hall-Louaillier business at New Orleans. Jackson ascended the steps of the War Office *"fully prepared"* to give it. Mr. Crawford was not in the city and the acting Secretary, Mr. Dallas, received the General who launched impulsively into his exposition. Mr. Dallas interrupted. Explanations were not in order. Anything General Jackson had done at New Orleans was quite all right. "The President as well as the heads of departments" were happy and satisfied. John Reid breathed easier. "I think now I see the horizon *blue before me*."[17]

And so thought Andrew Jackson when his sojourn in the city was ended and his carriage jolted over the frozen January roads toward Tennessee. So thought Rachel from whose spirit a weight of dread had been lifted by that toast at Lynchburgh. But her husband had plowed and sown another field.

Next to New Orleans Andrew Jackson regarded the Creek treaty as his most enduring claim to fame. Speaking from the conviction of experience, he had fired the mind of Monroe with a vision of this wilderness empire transformed into homesteads, a perpetual diadem for the crown of the new Administration. The old frontiersman's blood raced to contemplate the sweat and smoke and hurly-burly of it all. Through the management of Mr. Monroe General Jackson was charged, in broad language, with the pacification of the Southern border, where, under British and Spanish influence and the crushing terms of the treaty, the Indians were becoming restive again. Commissioners had been ordered into the field to survey the conquered lands. Jackson was delegated to protect them. And upon himself he took the additional responsibility of seeing that their lines should embrace the ultimate acre nominated in the bond.

Yet this could not be the end. No open-minded person could devote an hour's consideration to the subject without appreciating the futility of efforts for permanent peace in the South as long as Florida remained in the hands of Spain. Mr. Jefferson had initiated pourparlers for purchase of the province, but the matter lagged. At the head of an army on the border, Jackson might become a providential instrument for bringing these negotiations to a satisfactory conclusion; and certain it seems that he and Monroe had discussed this delicate contingency without reserve.[18]

Thus the scope of the alluring task Andrew Jackson had set to round out his public career.

5

At Nashville a letter awaited from John Coffee, the only one of the three commissioners designated to run the Creek treaty lines who was at his post. The Indians were in bad temper, and, without waiting for his colleagues, Coffee had begun work alone. Warmly complimenting his old friend, Jackson told him to proceed irrespective of the other commissioners. To the Indians he dispatched a succinct warning and himself started south to make a general reconnaissance.[19]

He rode with a heavy heart, having just received news of the death of John Reid. Jackson had grown extremely fond of this gifted young man. They had parted at Reid's home, in Virginia, where John desired to remain at the bedside of a sister hopelessly ill of consumption. The General and Rachel had slipped away leaving a note of farewell. "How can I apologise for not taking leave of your amiable mother & sisters? I have but one [excuse]. I saw their distress I was fear full (if Possible) it would heighten their sorrow—— I could not bear to take leave of the family and not bid adieu to the *amiable* the *dying Maria*."[20] A fortnight after the burial of Maria her brother was stricken with a mysterious fever and died in twenty-four hours. Jackson resolved that the biography should be finished and the proceeds reserved for Reid's widow and little children in Tennessee. He volunteered to advance the cost of printing. Deluged with offers to complete the book, he accepted that of John Henry Eaton, a wealthy lawyer and planter of Franklin, Tennessee, with a frontier reputation for scholarship.

The tour of observation inevitably brought the General to New Orleans. At a private gathering Judge Hall offered his hand. "I received it and . . . my mind . . . tells me I have done right. . . . The hatchet is buried."[21]

Prospects for peace in other quarters, however, were not so reassuring. British agents, operating from the safe refuge of Florida, had spread the report among the Creeks that the treaty of Ghent required the United States to restore the lands Jackson had taken from them. Another source of alarm was Negro Fort on the Apalachicola River in Florida sixty miles below the Georgia line. This stronghold had been built by the British during the war. With three thousand small arms and a thousand barrels of powder, it was now in the hands of fugitive slaves under the determined leadership of one of their number named Garçon. With the horrors of Santo Domingo fresh in Southern minds, Georgia was in a state of excitement. Jackson told Gaines to awe the Indians with a show of force and gave him permission to destroy Negro Fort "regardless of the ground it stands on."[22]

En route home he wrote his old partner in trade, John Hutchings. "A great speck'l [speculation] . . . on the allabama" seemed imminent and was more than the old fortune hunter could resist. "I have been making some conditional contracts for land on the coast, and am . . . [contemplating] the purchase of a sugar estate."[23]

The great speculations and the private plans and public policies of General Jackson were thrown into confusion by the action of Secretary of War Crawford in modifying the celebrated Creek treaty.

With the preoccupations of war past, the drum-head nature of the procedure by which Jackson had "negotiated" this instrument had gradually become apparent. To effect his ends the American peacemaker had snatched at will lands from friendly as well as hostile Creeks. This was well known. Now it transpired that in the twenty-three million ceded acres were four million belonging to neither Creek faction but to the Cherokees and Choctaws who had been Jackson's allies in the war against Weatherford. Indian boundaries were always vague, and the General had recognized a shadowy Creek claim to this territory solely that he might include it in the booty.

Crawford returned the four million acres to the Cherokees and Choctaws. The announcement was made a few days after the Congressional Caucus had given Monroe, by the surprisingly narrow margin of eleven votes, the Republican nomination that was equivalent to election. It probably afforded the Secretary additional satisfaction to endow his act of justice with the color of a rebuke to his successful rival's agent in the Southwest.

The effects of the admonishment were short-lived, however, and gained for Mr. Crawford only the unrelenting enmity of Andrew Jackson. A howl went up from the West, and Madison sent Jackson to get the land back. He succeeded, naturally, though not without having to pay the Cherokees and Choctaws one hundred and eighty thousand dollars. Jackson bargained as closely over this indemnity as if it were to come from his own pocket.[24] Meantime Gaines had blown up Negro Fort, killing two hundred and seventy of its occupants, and a measure of peace settled on the Southern border.[25]

6

But an uncertain peace in more ways than one, and President-Elect Monroe began to choose his Cabinet with care.

He declined to select as Secretary of War the man of Jackson's choice, William H. Drayton of South Carolina, turning to Henry Clay who loftily refused the place as unworthy of his attainments. Clay wished to be Secretary of State, a post also coveted by William H. Crawford, whose presidential hopes, though deferred, had not been abandoned. Mr. Monroe disappointed both of these men, however, and earmarked the Department of State for John Quincy Adams, late minister to England and member, with Mr. Clay, of the peace commission at Ghent. This son of the second President was a singular man—polished, learned and lonely—who after three decades of unselfish and distinguished devotion to the public service remained virtually without one intimate personal or political friend. Yet a youthful aloofness, deepening to austerity, masked a wistful heart and at times an almost romantic turn of mind. Adams was fifty, but years of unremitting labor and intellectual solitude had given a drawn and set cast to once-handsome features, and he looked older than he was. To see him now it seemed incredible that he should have confessed, even in the privacy of his thoughts, to a secret boyhood passion for a Parisian actress.

Mr. Monroe made a restrained gesture of tendering the War Office to Jackson, "tho' I doubted whether I ought . . . to draw you from the command of the army to the South, where in case of any emergency no one could supply your place."[26] Jackson did what seems to have been expected of him and declined. "I have looked forward to that happy period when . . . I would retire from public life" as soon as the frontier should be safe.[27]

The interim of superficial tranquillity continued big with change. In the East, the gilded aura of lush prosperity had begun to pale as our young factories met the strangling competition of European imports. This swelled the torrent of settlers plunging toward the Edens of the frontier—Ohio and Indiana in the North and, with the Administration's especial benediction, General Jackson's Alabama acquisitions in the South. In the face of great rivalry for this choice site, the Cypress Land Company bought at government auction an immense acreage below the Muscle Shoals of the Tennessee River toward which architects of empire had cast longing glances since the days of John Donelson, the elder. John Coffee was a leading spirit of the Cypress Land Company and Jackson owned a few shares of its stock. This concern laid out the town of Florence where speculation reached its climax, town lots selling for thirty-five hundred dollars and near-by cotton land for eighty dollars an acre. Jackson acquired a lot or two and some of the cotton land, paying for the latter two dollars an acre which was the lowest bid the government would entertain.[28] But by common understanding, when the great benefactor who had made this land available came forward with an offer, no one bid against him. John Henry Eaton and Captain John Donelson, junior, likewise expressed their confidence in the ultimate issue of events by making a heavy purchase in Florida.

Money for these ventures gushed from the strong boxes of Western banks. Tennessee's banking policy remained fairly conservative, only two institutions being chartered in addition to the now celebrated Nashville Bank in which Andrew Jackson was a small stockholder. But across the line in Kentucky were fifty-nine banks, or seventeen more than in the State of New York, all of them printing their own currency. This display of fictitious capital made credit easy. Farms uncleared were mortgaged, crops yet unsowed were pledged and the money used to enlarge the ever-expanding rainbow of speculation.

A Tidewater atmosphere began to drift with the blue mists across the Appalachians. The Cumberland Valley was frontier no longer. The début of William Carroll's steamboat, the *Andrew Jackson*, on the sea-green water was a spectacle as certain to draw an audience as the General himself. Sons were building fine houses on the sites of their fathers' cabins. Life slipped into a slower tempo, gaining in grace what it lost in robustness. One generation had tamed the land, another was being tamed by it. The Cotton Kingdom was being planted, its astonishing harvest to bring forth, to subjugate, and one day destroy an era.

Change, change. Within the same month two youthful faces vanished from the Hermitage family circle. John—"Jacky"—Donelson III died in military service on the Alabama and his brother Andrew Jackson Donelson departed for West Point. "On these children," confided General Jackson to their grandfather, old General Daniel Smith, "I had built my hopes for happiness in my declining days. . . . They . . . always appeared as my own."[29]

Jackson looked back upon his own student days at Salisbury with a degree of perspective. "I was but a raw lad then."[30] He hoped Cadet Donelson might be something better. "in your intercourse with the world . . . be courteous to all, but make confidents of few [as] a young man is too apt to form opinions on speecious shows . . . and to bestow confidence . . . [unwisely]. Amonghst the virtuous females you ought to cultivate an acquaintance, and shun . . . the others. . . . I recommend economy . . . [but] shun parsomony. . . . You are authorized to draw on me for money."[31]

Mr. Monroe's difficulties in filling the War Office to his satisfaction continued, and for several months the post remained in the hands of an acting secretary, George Graham, a hold-over from the Madison régime. On the day Monroe assumed the presidency, March 4, 1817, Jackson wrote him a lengthy letter, departing from the theme of ardent congratulation only long enough to pick a bone with the War Department. Graham had ordered a major of engineers from Jackson's jurisdiction to New York without consulting the Southern Commander. To Monroe Jackson remonstrated against this irregularity. Had the President replied by return post Jackson would not have had his letter in less than forty days. He waited forty-nine days and then issued an order forbidding subordinates to obey the commands of the War Department unless they should come through him.[32] This remarkable military paper made the rounds of the press, and in August the New York *Columbian* published an article characterizing it as an effort by Jackson to protect his favorites. An anonymous correspondent forwarded this to Jackson, with the salty observation that it had been written by Winfield Scott who had called the order "an act of mutiny."[33] This drew from Jackson a courteous letter to Scott expressing disbelief in the report, but asking Scott's assurance to that effect.[34]

Winfield Scott was an ambitious major general without command, and he seems to have been very badly informed as to the character of his Southern colleague. Otherwise it is difficult to believe that he would have replied in a vein so condescending and contentious. Though disclaiming authorship of the newspaper article, General Scott admitted having privately pronounced the order in question "mutinous . . . and . . . a reprimand of the . . . President"—a sentiment he was quite at liberty to entertain, but his manner of expressing it was subtly provocative.[35] Jackson's rejoinder was a challenge to a duel in language that does not materially enhance his reputation for moderation. Disdaining the use of "tinsel rhetoric" he undertook to render his meaning clear by calling the Northern general *"a hectoring bully"* and one of an undisclosed number of *"intermeddling pimps and spies of the War Department."*[36] Scott replied that his correspondent had the better of him as a master of epithet and declined an affair of honor on religious grounds, adding that his life would be risked to a better purpose in "the next war."[37]

General Jackson enlivened this period of military inactivity with further proof that his talents for unproductive controversy amounted, at times, to genius. In Kentucky a history of the war had appeared, with some critical observations on Jackson's attitude toward the Kentucky troops on the west bank at New Orleans, which the General noticed in a letter to the *Kentucky Reporter*. "A forgery of the blackest kind," "wicked, willful and corrupt" and "Spanish dish" were some of the gems that dropped from his pen. John Adair came forward with a defense of the Kentuckians. After a spirited exchange of letters, Jackson prepared a third communication which William Carroll apparently was able to persuade his chief to withhold, on the well-reasoned assumption that "You stand on too high an emminence to gratify the Editors of the Kentucky news papers."[38]

Meanwhile another of the General's wards, Edward George Washington Butler, took his departure for West Point, and the prolific correspondent paused in the midst of the Kentucky conflict to indite a word of counsel to Andrew Jackson Donelson. "My son, I wish you . . . and Edward . . . to live in the harmony of brothers . . . and by . . . obedience to your superiors . . . merit . . . the Esteem . . . of all."[39]

7

Over these scenes crept the shadow of Florida, rendered more portentous by the rumble of revolution that rocked Spain's fabulous empire from the Louisiana border to Tierra del Fuego. During his sojourn in Washington, General Jackson and Colonel Monroe had discussed the prospect as practical men, and allusions to the subject continued in their correspondence. Monroe referred to his subordinate's unsponsored seizure of Pensacola in 1814. "I was not very severe on you for giving the blow, nor ought I have been for a thousand considerations, which I need not mention."[40] In point of fact very little need be mentioned between these gentlemen who understood each other perfectly. Monroe expressed his pleasure at the swarming of settlers upon the Jackson treaty lands. "As soon as our population gains a decided preponderance in those regions Florida will hardly be considered by Spain as a part of her dominions."[41] Very well put, Mr. Monroe.

Mexico was in revolt, affording fresh employment in freedom's cause to a number of military characters of vague nationality who had stood behind the mud wall of Rodriquez Canal. Weary of repose and honors, Jean Laffite sailed for Galveston Bay and once more the diversion of Spanish cargoes contributed to the prosperous appearance of Royal Street. From the cluttered desk of Edward Livingston emanated proof of the impeccable legality of everything. He kept Jackson informed, and, carried away by the clarity of his demonstration of the high-minded zeal of his clients, importuned the General to go to Texas and lead them.[42]

This activity served the useful purpose of inserting one more thorn in the flesh of Spain. But with the sure instinct that so often enabled him to pick the essential thing from a jungle of miscellaneous detail, Andrew Jackson kept his eyes on Florida. There was much of interest to follow: fortifications stripped of troops to oppose dominions in revolt; Pensacola with "not enough Gunpowder to fire a salute;"[43] Spanish authority sunk to a charade of shabby grandeur.

Then as now the lazy waters of St. Mary's River formed part of the boundary between Florida and Georgia. In the Atlantic, off the mouth of this international stream within gunshot of shore, lay Amelia Island on whose sands sprawled the village of Fernandina. It was a poor and impermanent-looking place of wood and thatch and sunburnt plaster, but these appearances were deceptive. The current value of chattels stored in the flimsy shacks was something like five hundred thousand dollars. Fernandina was the Barataria and the Galveston of the Atlantic, maintaining about the same cordial relations with merchants in Savannah, Charleston and Baltimore as did the Laffites with New Orleans. A decent regard for some of the freer traditions of smuggling enabled the Fernandians to surpass in volume the commerce of their rivals in the Gulf. Perhaps the high mark of conservatism in the profession was established when Messrs. Laffite and Livingston declined traffic in negroes, who, since the war, had become one of the most profitable items in the American import trade. The result was a scarcity of field-hands in Louisiana. Livingston purchased a plantation, and, hearing that Jackson had forty negroes for sale, he offered twenty-four thousand dollars for the lot, eight thousand down.[44]

In June of 1817, an attractive professional adventurer from South American fields named Gregor MacGregor convinced a coterie of Baltimore business men that, without injury to their interests, they could assist the sacred cause of liberty by financing the deliverance of Fernandina from the "yoke" of Spain. Accordingly, he "captured" the town, wrote some marvelous proclamations and departed in quest of reenforcements. During his absence "Commodore" Louis Aury, late client of Edward Livingston and associate of Jean Laffite, dropped in from Galveston with a stolen ship, the *Mexico Libre*, and declared Amelia Island a part of the Mexican Republic. These incidents so disturbed the settled order of smuggling along the Atlantic coast that persons of influence began to complain. Meantime our perpetual negotiations for the purchase of Florida emerged from a period of hibernation, and President Monroe saw in the Amelia Island situation a chance to apply pressure upon Spain. A naval expedition was ordered to send Aury on his way and to hold Fernandina in trust for His Catholic Majesty.

While this sturdy feat of diplomacy was being realized, Brevet Major General Gaines attacked a party of Seminoles at Fowltown just north of the Florida border. These Indians had declined to vacate lands included in the Creek cession of 1814. The Administration had expected trouble with them, and was prepared for it, entirely aware that the Seminoles, like the buccaneers of Amelia, might serve as convenient pawns in the larger gamble for Florida. The War Department ordered Gaines to continue his offensive against the Indians, pursuing them into Spanish territory if necessary, but to molest no Spanish military post without further instructions.

8

Andrew Jackson had declared he would resign from the Army, rather than withdraw his celebrated order forbidding subordinates to obey commands of the War Department unless transmitted through him. With the Florida crisis looming the President wrote a long and conciliatory letter, begging Jackson not to leave the service at such a moment, but stating frankly that he could not accept "this order [which] involves the naked principle of the power of the Executive over the . . . army."[45] Jackson's friend, Congressman John Rhea, intervened in behalf of the President. Every member of the Administration, he said, including William H. Crawford, now Secretary of Treasury, wished Jackson to retain his command.[46] With the naval force against Aury on the sea, a compromise was arranged in which Monroe went as far as a President could go without abdicating his authority.[47]

In this arrangement the President was skilfully counseled by the man he had finally selected for Secretary of War—John Caldwell Calhoun—and if one may judge by the vigor with which the Secretary attacked his duties, Mr. Monroe must have been glad he had taken his time to fill this post. The new Cabinet officer was a restless man, with darting eyes, and a swift speech in which lingered a trace of something Andrew Jackson would have recognized instantly. For Calhoun was Back-Country Scotch-Irish from South Carolina, his forebears even more obscure than Jackson's. After Yale and a marriage that ended financial anxieties, he had gone to Congress in 1811 as a War Hawk. His career in the House was sufficiently distinguished to cause him, at thirty-five, to think twice before taking the War Office.

On December 26, 1817, Mr. Calhoun ordered General Jackson to Georgia. His instructions were very broad. "Adopt the necessary measures to terminate . . . [the] conflict."[48]

While Mr. Calhoun's communication was on the way to Tennessee, General Jackson received a copy of the Gaines order which the Department had previously forwarded as a matter of information. At a glance he perceived its weakness, and, not for the first time in his life, undertook to stiffen the spine of an executive. "Suppose," he wrote Monroe, "the Indians . . . take refuge in either Pensacola or St. Augustine. . . . General Gaines . . . has to halt before the . . . [town and] communicate with his Government; in the meantime the militia grows restless, and he has to defend himself with regulars. The enemy, with the aid of Spanish friends and Woodbines British Partizens, or, if you please, with Aury's force, attacks him, what may not be the result? defeat and massacre."

General Jackson proposed a simpler plan. "The whole of East Florida [should be] seized and . . . this can be done without implicating the Government." How? "Let it be signified to me through any channel, (say Mr. J. Rhea) that the possession of the Floridas would be desirable . . . and in sixty days it will be accomplished."[49]

Five days after this letter had started north the order for Jackson to supersede Gaines reached Nashville. By the same post came a note from the President. "The mov'ment . . . against the Seminoles . . . will bring you on a theatre where you may possibly have other services to perform. . . . Great interests are at issue. . . . This is not a time for repose . . . untill our cause is carried triumphantly thro'."⁵⁰

"Other services. . . . Great interests. . . . Our cause." Mr. Monroe seemed to be himself again.

CHAPTER XVIII

THE FLORIDA ADVENTURE

I

MR. MONROE's patriotic importunities were scarcely necessary to stir the General from his "repose." A brigade of New Orleans veterans was called to arms. The Governor of Tennessee being absent, Jackson swore them in on his personal responsibility. When funds for their equipment gave out, he advanced four thousand dollars from his private purse. Eleven days after receiving the orders from Washington he was on the road with the advance guard of two mounted companies. "My love, . . . I have left you . . . with greater regret than I have ever done. I hope that God who controls the destinies of nations . . . will permit me to return to you in a short time. . . . With my prayers for your preservation and happiness. . . . adieu."[1]

On the night of February 13, 1818, the advance-guard bivouacked on the bank of Big Creek, four miles from Hartford, Georgia. There Jackson received a packet of mail among which, as he always claimed, was a letter from Representative Rhea transmitting President Monroe's "approval" of Jackson's suggestion to effect an unofficially authorized seizure of Florida and let the diplomats sweep up the débris. In later years, when the incident became the core of a muddy controversy, Monroe denied that he had empowered Rhea to convey any such assurances. In my opinion the evidence favors Monroe's contention on this specific point. On the other hand— and this is far more important—the evidence is clear that the Administration understood General Jackson's intentions toward Florida, and, by the absence of any restraining sign or syllable, gave its consent to them. For instance, after he received word of the occupation of St. Marks, Secretary of War Calhoun wrote Governor Bibbs of Alabama: "General Jackson is vested with full power to conduct the war as he may think best."[2] Mr. Calhoun knew perfectly what

Andrew Jackson thought "best" for Florida, having, indeed, read the General's unambiguous letter to Monroe, the answer to which, Jackson asserted, was received at Big Creek.

Be that as it may, during the night of March ninth, General Jackson reached Fort Scott, near the Florida border, and at dawn took formal command of eight hundred Regulars and nine hundred Georgia militia. The militia was restless and all were hungry, but Andrew Jackson was no stranger to such conditions. With one quart of corn and three rations of meat per man, the army took up the line of march for Florida at noon. Streams were bank high and the trail was a quagmire. In five days the struggling column gained the site of Negro Fort, where a boat-load of army flour ascending the Apalachicola, by permission of the Spanish authorities, provided the first square meal the troops had eaten in three weeks. The next day they were put on half rations and set to repairing the fort while the Commander took stock of his situation.

"It is reported to me that Francis and Peter McQueen," Creek leaders who had fled to Florida after their defeat in 1814, "are now exciting the Seminoles to . . . acts of hostility. . . . With them it is stated . . . [are] Woodbine, Arbuthnot and other foreigners."[3]

2

Francis, Woodbine, Arbuthnot. . . .

When General Jackson traced those names, he struck deeply into the dark pattern of Florida politics where the practised hand of England had not ceased from troubling. After the battle of New Orleans Colonel Edward Nicholls had returned to his old stamping-ground. He negotiated a military alliance with the Florida Indians —Spanish subjects and American fugitives—and sailed in triumph to London with the chief Francis. This was a bit too raw and the Foreign Office felt compelled to repudiate the treaty, but sent Francis home with marks of friendship including the scarlet regalia of a brigadier-general. Then came Captain George Woodbine, whose official connection with Whitehall was more tenuous, though when occasion required he signed himself "on His Britannic Majesty's service in the Floridas." With an eye for his own prospects as well as those of his sovereign, the Captain had acquired a grant of land which would be his to enjoy only in the event that the province remained out of American hands. The transaction brought the interests of Captain Woodbine in collision with those of General Jackson's Tennessee neighbors, Eaton and Donelson, whose Florida investments had been made with other expectations in view.

The last personage on the scene was Alexander Arbuthnot, a Scottish merchant of Nassau who appeared in the province as a trader, and, by charging the Indians honest prices and taking an interest in their welfare, established a profitable commerce. This abuse of the ethics of the Indian trade estranged other mercantile interests in Florida, notably the celebrated Scottish house of Forbes & Company, which, seeing how the wind was blowing, had begun amicable intrigues with the Americans. Arbuthnot went his way. In his seventy years he had acquired a suit of flowing white hair and a gentle though confident air with the world. He had no official connection with his government, and regarded Woodbine as a man of low principles. His only friends were Indians. "They have been ill treated by the English," he wrote in his diary, "and robbed by the Americans," but he regarded the Americans as the worse offenders and made no effort to conceal his opinion. Beside secret council fires he became immersed in Indian statecraft, and, by accepting a power of attorney from the Creek refugees, gave to his utterances a cast that brought upon his person a burden of responsibility. The wildest rumors concerning him reached the United States. The authoritative Niles's *Register* of Baltimore declared Alexander Arbuthnot to be Woodbine in disguise, and, if captured, that he should suffer the fate of "a sheep-killing dog."

Jackson received word that the Indians had demanded arms of the Spanish commandant at St. Marks and were probably now in possession of the town. He marched at once, sending Naval Lieutenant Isaac McKeever with a few small gunboats to blockade the west coast of the peninsula and prevent escape of the fugitives by water. Without resistance, Jackson lowered the Spanish colors from the stone fort at St. Marks. But the Indians had departed and the Americans' only prisoner was an old gentleman with snowy hair, taken in the commandant's quarters while preparing for flight. Mr. Arbuthnot accepted arrest quietly, and General Jackson spared a moment to record the events of the week.

"St. marks, April 8, 1818

"My Love, on the 1st of april I . . . had a small affair with the Indians in which we lost one man killed (Tucker) and four wounded all Tennesseens. . . . Entered the Town of St. marks on yesterday. . . . Capt [Lieutenant] McKeever . . . was fortunate enough to capture on board his flotilla the noted Francis the prophet and Homollimicke [another Creek chief and leader in a recent massacre]. . . . The Capt having the British colours flying they supposed him to be part of Woodbines Fleet. . . . These were hung this morning. I found in St. marks the noted Scotch villain Arbuthnot. . . . I hold him for trial. I leave Tomorrow in hopes . . . with the smiles of heaven to put an end to the war. . . . Kiss my Two sons and accept my prayers for your health and happiness until I return yr affectionate Husband."[4]

"My two sons" were Andrew, junior, and his Creek Indian playmate, Lincoyer.

General Jackson left St. Marks on schedule. Plunging into a jungle that had changed little since De Soto's time, he hoped to surprise the Indians at the village of Chief Boleck (or Bowlegs) on the Suwanee River, one hundred and seven miles away. Two skirmishes barely interrupted the march. Boleck's place was reached in eight days. The reed huts were empty. The Chief and his people had scattered like quail into the swamps. But during the night there blundered into an American picket Lieutenant Robert C. Ambrister of the Royal Colonial Marines, and another Englishman, Peter B. Cook, probably the two most astonished persons in Florida.

On one of their negro servants was found a letter from Arbuthnot to his son. "Tell my friend, Bowleck, that he is throwing his people away to attempt to resist such a powerful force as will be drawn on Sahwahnee."[5] Cook admitted that the letter had been read to the Indians, and General Jackson began to understand why he had advanced two hundred and thirty miles into Florida's wet wilderness without meeting the Indians in a proper battle.

3

The one hundred and seven miles from St. Marks to the Suwanee, over which no white army had passed before, had been covered in

A Much Discussed Portrait by Ralph E. W. Earl

Painted at the Hermitage in 1820. The artist carried it to New Orleans in 1821 with a letter of introduction to Mayor Rafignac from Jackson pronouncing it "a more correct likeness of myself than perhaps you have ever seen." The city purchased the canvas, which still hangs in the City Hall. On April 29, 1821, John James Audubon recorded in his journal: "*Great God* forgive Me if my Jugment is Erroneous— I Never Saw A Worst painted Sign *in the streets of Paris—*" Later portraits by Earl possess real merit, however.

IN THE BYRONIC MANNER

Thomas Sully's portraits of Thomas Jefferson, Stephen Decatur, Queen Victoria and the Marquis de Lafayette are distinguished, which cannot be said of his Jackson. The artist appears to have been laboring, at the time, under the influence of Byron who also had sat for him. Copy from collection of Mrs. Samuel G. Heiskell of Knoxville.

eight days. Returning, Jackson made it in five, and, on the morning of April 26, 1818, issued an order for the trial of Arbuthnot and Ambrister. The court met at noon in the stone fort. Eight of its members were officers of the Regular service, five of the militia or volunteers. The president was General Gaines who had presided over the court martial at New Orleans which disappointed the anticipations of the Commander in the trial of Louis Louaillier.

Arbuthnot was arraigned on charges of exciting the Indians to war, spying and giving aid to the enemy. Two witnesses for the prosecution were agents of Forbes & Company whose hostility to the prisoner impairs faith in their testimony. A third witness was Ambrister's companion, Peter B. Cook, who bore Arbuthnot a grudge. His story that Arbuthnot had warned Boleck of Jackson's advance was corroborated, however, by John Lewis Phoenix, master of the prisoner's schooner. Moreover the documentary evidence found aboard this vessel was clear and uncontroverted. In Arbuthnot's handwriting were appeals from Boleck and other chiefs to the British Governor at Nassau for troops, arms and ammunition with which to fight the Americans; communications in the Indians' behalf to the British Minister at Washington and to the Governor of Havana; statistics on the strength of the hostile Indians and the munitions they needed to wage war.[6] On the twenty-seventh the case against Arbuthnot was completed and he was given until four o'clock the following afternoon to prepare his defense.

The second prisoner to face the court presented an appearance in contrast with that of the aged and anxious merchant. Robert Christy Ambrister was a well-born English adventurer who had lived by the sword in many lands and climes. Wounded on the field of Waterloo he was made a member of Napoleon's guard at St. Helena. Then, in the Orient, he had been suspended from command for a year for dueling. Coming to Nassau to pass this enforced vacation as a guest of his uncle, Governor Cameron, he fell in with George Woodbine. As a soldier Ambrister knew the gravity of his position and the weight of the evidence against him. To a charge of "assuming command of the Indians in . . . war with the United States," he pleaded "guilty, and justification."[7]

At four o'clock on April twenty-eighth Arbuthnot was called in to offer his defense. His language was dignified. He wished to avoid, he said, an appeal to sympathy, "though I am persuaded that sympathy no where more abounds than in a generous American breast." With some justice he argued against the admissibility of certain evidence. He admitted the sale of ten kegs of powder to Boleck, but contended this was no more than the Indians needed for hunting. No explanation of the damaging contents of "sundry letters purporting to be written by myself" was attempted, however, and the manifest evidence that they had been written by Arbuthnot remained unchallenged. "May it please the honorable court I close my reply . . . fully persuaded that should there be cause for censure my judges will . . . lean on the side of mercy."[8]

He was found guilty and sentenced to be hanged. Such was the retribution of "the noted Scotch villain" whose principal villainy had been to treat the Indians decently, without regard for the United States, his own country, General Jackson, or any one. Yet, taking a military view of the evidence, he was guilty as charged.

At five o'clock Ambrister faced the bar. The attractions of this prisoner's personality had won him many well-wishers among the officers of General Jackson's army. Ambrister was an excellent talker. His cell was crowded every evening. Summoned to plead for his life, he detained the court no more than sixty seconds with a word of appreciation of its courtesies and a frank petition for mercy.

The verdict of a court martial is determined by the vote of two-thirds of its members. On a poll of the court Ambrister was sentenced to be shot. After the finding had been recorded, one member asked to reconsider his vote with the result that the sentence was reduced to fifty lashes and confinement for one year.

The following morning, while the army was falling in to march, Andrew Jackson approved the sentence of Arbuthnot "and . . . the finding and first sentence . . . of Robert C. Ambrister, and disapproves the reconsideration."[9] The prisoners received the word of doom stoically. A drum beat assembly for the platoon assigned to conduct the executions.

"There," said Ambrister, "a sound I have heard in every quarter of the globe, and now for the last time."[10]

A girl in London was waiting to marry him.

4

In four days Jackson was back at Fort Gadsden, as the new post on the site of Negro Fort had been named.

On May fifth he notified Calhoun that he would invade West Florida and probably take Pensacola. On the seventh he marched. "The continued wading of water . . . first destroyed our horses, and next our shoes, the men are literanny barefoot."[11] On the twenty-fifth Pensacola was invested. On the twenty-eighth it surrendered. On the twenty-ninth, in the most sweeping exemplification of imperial powers he had exercised in Florida, Jackson seized the royal archives, appointed one of his colonels military and civil governor, and declared in force the "revenue laws of the U. States."[12]

On May thirtieth he departed for Tennessee and the frontier's acclaim of his exploits billowed across the mountains. It was the diplomats' turn now.

5

They had their work cut out. One dispatch after another, like chapters of a swashbuckling serial, apprised Washington of Andrew Jackson's career in Florida. "The storm," wrote John Quincy Adams, "is rapidly thickening."

On the night of July seventh the Secretary was routed from his bed by a message that Don Luis de Oñis, the Spanish Minister, had rushed back to the city. Members of the Administration, Mr. Adams excepted, stood a little in awe of this vigorous official whose commanding presence breathed a semblance of life into the hollow shell of Spanish power. Only a fortnight before James Monroe had begun to rest easier when the smooth assurances of his Secretary of State sent the Minister away to enjoy the cooling breezes of his summer place in Pennsylvania. He returned in the middle of the night with a surging communication on the subject of Florida. "In the name of the King, my master, I demand a prompt restitution of St. Mark's, Pensacola, Barrancas, and all other places wrested by General Jackson from the Crown of Spain. I demand . . . indemnity for all injuries and losses, and the punishment of the general."[13]

For three days the Cabinet met at noon and continued in session until five, the members dispersing exhausted by the heat of the weather and of their discussions. At the outset, as Adams recorded in his diary, "the President and all the members, . . . except myself, are of the opinion that Jackson acted not only without, but against his instructions; that he has committed war upon Spain, . . . which if not disavowed" would ruin the Administration. Calhoun and Crawford took the lead in urging the restoration of the captured forts and a flat disavowal of Jackson's acts, the Secretary of War going so far as to intimate that the General was a party to the Eaton-Donelson land gamble. Their arguments impressed the President. Jackson had not made out a case for himself, declared Mr. Monroe, with an anxious allusion to what the newspapers were saying about the danger to the Administration's prestige. He referred to the Crawford organs in Virginia and Georgia which already had set themselves to advance the political fortunes of their man at the expense of the Florida campaign.

Against them all stood the thin-lipped, perspiring New Englander, who had spent a third of his life abroad and had not the remotest connection with the mottled Western intrigue against Florida from which Monroe now sought to disengage himself. Adams contended that Jackson was guilty of "no real . . . violation of his instructions; that his proceedings were justified by . . . necessity." Did the Administration, he asked, wish to deal with him as Elizabeth had dealt with Walter Raleigh—to have the benefit of his services, and then abandon him? Thus John Quincy Adams championed Andrew Jackson's cause at every turn, until, at the end of the third day, his hands trembled from fatigue so that he was obliged to neglect his famous diary.[14]

On the fourth day, June 18, 1818, the Cabinet made its decisions. Though his opinion had prevailed in part, Adams characterized them as "weakness and confession of weakness." He prepared a note to de Oñis stating that in taking the posts Jackson had acted on his own responsibility for which, however, he could not be censured, and that the forts would be given up. Attorney-General Wirt drafted for the press a paragraph calculated to conciliate all shades of popular opinion. So much for the Administration's endeavor to appease Spain and

THE FLORIDA ADVENTURE 293

the public. Another, and equally delicate, task remained—that of appeasing Andrew Jackson. The President took this upon himself.

6

His long letter opened with the interesting assurance that "nothing" would be withheld. General Jackson had been called into service, wrote Mr. Monroe, under orders previously issued to General Gaines. These instructions sanctioned an invasion of Spanish territory, but precluded the occupation of military posts. "An order to attack a Spanish post would . . . authorize war" which was more than a President could do. "Congress alone possesses the power." Therefore, "in transcending the limits prescribed by those orders you acted on your own responsibility."

But on this point the President sought to put his subordinate at ease. "I am aware that cases may occur when the commanding general, acting on his own responsibility, may safely pass the limit . . . [of his orders] with essential advantage to his country." For instance: "The officers and troops of the neutral power forget . . . their neutral character; they stimulate the enemy to make war; they furnish . . . arms; . . . they take an active part in their favor. . . . The general . . . pursues them to their post, . . . attacks and carries it, and rests on those acts for his justification."

The flaw in this justification was that the General had not thought of it first. His dispatches omitted to aver that Spanish officers had incited the Seminoles to war, furnished arms or participated in the struggle. True Jackson had said something about the occupation of St. Marks and Pensacola being necessary to the pursuit of the enemy, but his words were not explicit. The President dropped the subject for a moment, however, and addressed himself to the more ticklish business of excusing the return of those posts to Spain.

"If the Executive refused to evacuate . . . [them] it is not improbable that war would immediately follow, . . . and we do not foresee that we should have a single power in Europe on our side. Why risk these consequences? . . . There is much reason to presume that this act will furnish a strong inducement to Spain to cede the territory, providing we do not wound her too deeply. . . . The manner in which we propose to act will exculpate you from censure, and promises to obtain all the advantages you contemplate."

Now back to the matter of justification. The President said it would be necessary to establish that the posts had been seized in retaliation for the misconduct of Spanish officers. "You must aid in procuring the documents necessary for this purpose. Those you sent . . . do not, I am satisfied, do justice to the cause. . . . Your letters to the Department were written in haste, under the pressure of fatigue. . . . If you think it proper to authorize the secretary or myself to correct . . . [certain] passages, it will be done with care."[15]

Unlike Napoleon, whom he admired for many things, the Commander of the Southern Division did not regard history as a fable agreed upon. His Florida dispatches remain in the files of the War Department as he wrote them. Nor is this the only evidence of the Jacksonian touch that illuminates the reply to James Monroe. The elaborate war scare was not mentioned. The President's concern over the Spanish officers was dismissed with scant respect, though Jackson promised to get up stronger evidence of their rascality. The body of the letter dealt with the President's disclaimer of responsibility. Accompanying the copy of the order originally issued to Gaines, which forbade the violation of Spanish forts, Calhoun had sent a letter directing Jackson to "adopt the necessary measures to terminate . . . hostilities." This letter did not state that Gaines's order was to be binding on Jackson. Always a latitudinarian in such matters, the General had followed the letter and not the order. For this Old Hickory was ready to accept responsibility. "I never have shrunk from it and never will."[16]

A break with the Administration seemed to impend. Jackson wrote in confidence to a Philadelphia politician. "Being a sincere friend of Mr. Monroe . . . it is not my desire to injure him unless impelled in my own defense. . . . Had the government held the posts until the guarantees were given stipulated in the Articles of Capitulation . . . I would have been more than willing to have taken on myself all responsibilities, but when my country is deprived of all the benefits resulting from my acts I will not consent to bear . . . responsibility that ought to be those of another. My situation is . . . delicate. I must for the present be silent."[17]

Was Jackson holding over the head of the President the celebrated Rhea letter said to have been delivered at Big Creek? In any event Monroe was afraid of the General, and he had reason to be. What an explosion if Old Hickory should learn that during those warm days in July both the President and Mr. Calhoun had proposed to save their skins by throwing Andrew Jackson to the wolves. The Secretary of War also was uneasy, and nimbly he changed his course and deftly he covered his tracks. Within sixty days after he had argued by the hour to break down Adams's stubborn refusal to accede to a disavowal of Jackson a complete somersault had been achieved. Meeting Captain James Gadsden of the Regular service and one of Jackson's confidential officers in Florida, Mr. Calhoun praised the results of the campaign and deplored the fact that certain of his unfeeling Administration colleagues would sacrifice "their best friend" to "screen themselves."[18]

Mr. Monroe's difficulties increased. A timid attempt to induce Jackson to confess that he had "misunderstood" the Secretary's instructions failed to budge the adamant soldier an inch.[19] On top of this came an ultimatum from Madrid. The restoration of the posts was not enough, exclaimed His Majesty's Minister for Foreign Affairs. Jackson's actions must be disavowed and Jackson himself "suitably punished" or negotiations for the purchase of Florida were at an end.

James Monroe turned to his Secretary of State. Mr. Adams had defended General Jackson to his fellow Cabinet officers in July. Let him do it now.

Gladly John Quincy Adams undertook the task and composed a withering dispatch that would fill twenty pages of this volume, all of it excellent—and much of it true. Mr. Adams labored alone, without the connivance of any one. No subterranean request for doctored documents or planted evidence. The Secretary of State interpreted documents to suit his requirements and extemporized testimony by the power of assertion.

"The President," he said, "will neither inflict punishment nor pass censure upon General Jackson for that conduct—the vindication of which is written in every page of the law of nations, . . . self defense." On the contrary, "suitable punishment" of the commandant of St. Marks and the governor of Pensacola was demanded for their "defiance and violation of the engagements of Spain with the United States." If these officers were powerless, "the United States can as little compound with impotence as with perfidy, and Spain must immediately make her election" and properly defend Florida, "or cede to the United States a province of which she retains nothing but the nominal possession."

Jackson's occupation of the forts was contrasted with that of Nicholls in 1814, who had not only seized the defenses of Pensacola but had blown up the largest of them. "Where is his Majesty's profound indignation at that?" The subsequent history of Florida was reviewed —Woodbine, Amelia Island, Arbuthnot, Ambrister—"this narrative of dark and complicated depravity; this creeping and insidious war, this mockery of patriotism, these political philters to fugitive slaves and Indian outlaws. . . ." The paper closed with a threat. Should it become necessary again to take "forts and places in Florida," the unconditional surrender of them must not be expected.[20]

Thus a Jacksonian spirit in the Cabinet to support Jacksonian measures in the field.

7

The General prepared for a quiet winter at the Hermitage. "My eyes are weak and my hand trembles."[21] He needed recreation, and on a Sunday in October, 1818, drove to Nashville where a Methodist Conference was in session.

Peter Cartwright had rounded out twenty of the two score years as a circuit rider that made him the frontier's most celebrated priest of religion. Subtler persuasions failing, he had been known to knock a sinner down and drag him to the throne of grace. Not without misgivings, a local pastor had invited him to fill the pulpit on this Sunday morning. The announcement brought out the town. Reverend Cartwright read his text in a ringing voice.

"What shall it profit a man if he gain the whole world and lose his soul?"

He paused to let the words sink in. General Jackson entered the church and walked slowly down the aisle. Every seat being taken, he stood for a moment leaning against a pillar.

Mr. Cartwright felt a tug at the tail of his coat.

"General Jackson has come in!" the Nashville minister whispered. "General Jackson has come in!"

The whisper was audible to most of the church. Peter Cartwright's hard jaw tightened. He gave the minister a look of scorn and confronted his congregation.

"Who is General Jackson? If he don't get his soul converted, God will damn him as quick as a Guinea nigger!"

After the sermon Reverend Cartwright was advised to leave town. "General Jackson will chastise you for your insolence."

"Two can play at that game," said Cartwright, and accepted an invitation to preach at a country church near the Hermitage. Jackson invited him to dinner.[22]

Certain other critics of the General were not to get off as easily. It was too early to judge of its effect abroad, but the domestic success of Mr. Adams's Florida dispatch had been instantaneous, and of this William H. Crawford and Henry Clay took particular note. With Mr. Adams, these gentlemen aspired to the presidency in 1824. They were pained to see a rival winning so much applause. Nor did they fail to consider that General Jackson's undimmed popularity boded no good to their expectations. When Congress convened the two were soon at work. In the House a resolution was prepared disapproving the execution of Arbuthnot and Ambrister.

His renown as Andrew Jackson's biographer had helped to elevate to the United States Senate John Henry Eaton who advised the General to leave Florida matters in the hands of his friends. But Colonel Robert Butler urged his guardian to come to Washington and direct the fight for his military reputation. Representative Felix Grundy wrote in the same style. "It is natural that you (now near the close of an illustrious life) should feel sensibly for your fame—and . . . I have no doubt but y^r presence would inspire many with correct sentiments."[23]

On the morning of January 23, 1819, a gaunt figure on horseback muffled in a borrowed greatcoat thumped across the Long Bridge that spanned the Potomac. At Strater's Hotel General Jackson dismounted cold and ill, but resolved to "defeat these hellish machinations,"[24] if it were his last accomplishment on earth.

8

Machinations they were. On January twelfth the House Committee on Military Affairs had reported against the executions of Arbuthnot and Ambrister. In a savage onslaught Thomas W. Cobb of Georgia, Crawford's spokesman in the lower chamber, broadened the issue to include disapproval of the occupation of Pensacola, and proposed bills prohibiting the execution of captives taken in an Indian war, or the invasion of foreign territory without authority, except in fresh pursuit of an enemy. Men less consumed by the fires of ambition might have awaited the tranquillization of our foreign relations before attempting the destruction of their country's greatest soldier and of any member of the Administration who should stand with him. The situation does not render more difficult of belief a rumor that came to Jackson's ears that, unwilling to wait until 1824, Crawford and Clay plotted to overthrow Monroe in 1820.[25]

The House dropped all other business. Galleries were crowded, aisles packed and cuspidors overturned. It was feared that the temporary edifice in which Congress met pending the rebuilding of the Capitol might not stand the strain. Not since the trial of Aaron Burr had the country's interest been captured by such a spectacle. Jackson's defenders were on hand and they made their points well. On the twelfth day of the debate Speaker Clay descended from his dais to crush them. The Kentuckian and General Jackson had long been casual friends, viewing Western problems through Western eyes, as during the Burr affair, which, in its most innocuous guise, contemplated a violation of Spanish sovereignty. At Ghent Mr. Clay would sit too late at cards to please John Quincy Adams, though he was invariably on hand in the morning bearing his part to get the better of the third-rate Englishmen at the other side of the table. Returning to Kentucky he was warmly received, but there was no blinking the fact that another Westerner had gained the first place in the admiration of his countrymen. This became more apparent when Mr. Monroe passed over Henry Clay in his quest of a Secretary of State.

The Speaker began by disclaiming any ill-will toward General Jackson. He was actuated, he said, by principle. His first attack was directed against the Creek treaty, which, though it had been a subject of discussion for four years, Mr. Clay read for the first time on the eve of this debate. The Creek treaty is a vulnerable document, but so superficial had been Mr. Clay's perusal that he missed or overshadowed the most assailable points by a rhetorical, and incidentally baseless, outburst that Jackson had sought to deprive these worthy barbarians of the consolations of their native religion. The Florida part of the speech showed more careful preparation, but here again the orator failed to make the most of his opportunity, except in the use of language. He closed with a murky implication which every act of Andrew Jackson's life, good or bad, refutes. "Recall to your recollections the free nations which have gone before us. Where are they now and how have they lost their liberties? If we could transport ourselves back to the ages when Greece and Rome flourished, and, . . . ask a Grecian if he did not fear some daring military chieftain, covered with glory, some Philip or Alexander, would one day overthrow his liberties? No! no! . . . [he] would exclaim, we have nothing to fear for our heroes. . . . Yet Greece had fallen, Caesar passed the Rubicon. . . ."26

Mr. Clay's utterance caused a sensation. Three days after its delivery, General Jackson reached Washington, and, declining public hospitalities, closeted himself with his supporters. From that moment until the end of the twenty-three days of argument, Jackson's lieutenants dominated the declamatory scene. Old Hickory sat in his hotel room, the center of an ever-increasing press of homage-bearers, guiding, inspiring, directing. Mr. Clay was answered in kind by Poindexter of Mississippi, and while the Jackson proponents did not disdain oratory they did not rely on it as the opposition did. Every truth and half-truth that could be regimented in support of their position was used and generally used well.

In granting that personal ambition played a conspicuous part in the Clay-Crawford assault on Jackson's Florida raid, it should not be assumed that, by contrast, loftier motives were the sole spur of the General's defenders. Many vehicles already were hitched to the soaring star of Old Hickory, and individual aspirations played their part in his defense. On the face of the facts it would be nearly as easy to make out a case against Jackson as for him, and the careful student of the record may well be astonished at the inherent weakness of an attack engineered by such resourceful men as Crawford and Clay. At the outset they underestimated their task, which, with Adams brazening and bluffing his way with the diplomats and Jackson himself bringing lieutenants in the House under the hypnotic sway of his will, was not one to be approached as casually as Mr. Clay, for one, approached it.

On February eighth the votes were taken.

"Resolved, That the House of Representatives . . . disapproves the execution of Alexander Arbuthnot and Robert C. Ambrister." Ayes, 50; noes, 90.

"Resolved, That the Committee on Military Affairs . . . prepare . . . a bill . . . prohibiting" the execution of captives in Indian warfare without executive authority. Ayes, 57; noes, 98.

"Resolved, That the late seizure of Pensacola was" unconstitutional. Ayes, 65; noes, 91.

"Resolved, That" a bill be prepared prohibiting the invasion of foreign soil, without authorization of Congress, except in fresh pursuit of an enemy. Ayes, 42; noes, 112.

It was the greatest triumph since New Orleans.

9

The victor left Washington with the ostensible object of visiting his godsons at West Point. Philadelphia waylaid him with an ovation, which, gathering momentum, lasted four days. The modest manners of the guest pleased every one. At a vast public dinner, speakers electrified the air with controversial allusions. Thanking his hosts briefly, General Jackson raised his glass.

"The memory of Benjamin Franklin," he said.

New York had more time to prepare. Beginning with the presentation of the freedom of the city in a gold box, its reception lasted five days. The guest was amenable, but he kept his bearings. A banquet at Tammany Hall, many of whose leading lights were active Crawford men, was thrown into confusion when General Jackson blandly offered a toast to Governor DeWitt Clinton whom he had never seen, but knew as the head of the anti-Crawford wing in New York.

At four o'clock in the morning of February twenty-seventh, residents of Baltimore were roused from their slumbers by salvos of artillery hailing the approach of the hero. Here Jackson received great news. In Europe Adams's aggressive note on Florida had carried all before it. England had dropped her protest over Arbuthnot and Ambrister. Spain had renewed the purchase parley, and on February 22, 1819, Adams and de Oñis had signed a treaty ceding Florida to the United States for five million dollars. At five o'clock on the evening of March first, Jackson took his place beside the Mayor of Baltimore at a banquet. At nine he took leave of the company and boarded a stage which entered Washington before day.

It was not the tidings of the Florida treaty, however, that called the General to the capital in such haste. Unmindful of the verdict of the House, the popular approval of the same, or, indeed, the Adams-de Oñis treaty, the United State Senate had undertaken to pass upon the propriety of General Jackson's late campaign. John Henry Eaton was a member of the committee to whom the task was delegated, but Abner Lacock, of the Crawford camp, was the chairman and ruling figure. This quiet and effective Pennsylvanian had gone about his duties, undeterred, as he later said, by a story that General Jackson meant to establish the purity of his motives in Florida by "cutting off the ears" of critical Senators.[27]

Though calm in tone, the report of the Lacock committee was penetratingly critical of the invasion. The Administration, however, conceived the idea of forestalling action until Congress should die on March fourth. Jackson's precipitous appearance on March second did not promise to facilitate this velvety stratagem, especially when the rumor reached the streets that he had come to town to cane Senator Eppes of Virginia, a member of the Lacock committee and a nephew of Thomas Jefferson. Captain Stephen Decatur, with whom Jackson had struck up an instantaneous friendship, has been pictured dashing across Washington in a cab, and intercepting the General on the steps of the Capitol, where he was able to dissuade him from his intention.[28] In any event no caning occurred, and, when Congress and the report faded from the scene together, the hero graced a levee at the reconstructed Executive Mansion gleaming with its first coat of white paint. "The company pressed about him" until it seemed to observant John Quincy Adams that General Jackson was giving the reception.[29] How it seemed to Mr. Monroe is something Mr. Adams did not attempt to say.

CHAPTER XIX

General Jackson Calls on Colonel Callava

I

The silvering logs of Hermitage blockhouse had begun to confess their years. "Say to my overseer that on my return I will expect my house . . . prepaired in such a way as will prevent the nothern blast from entering."¹ But the tide and tone of the times prescribed that the family seat of the most popular man in America be something more than a shelter against the northern blast. Twenty years before, as an industrious frontier solicitor, Andrew Jackson's Hunter's Hill was the equal for elegance of any residence in the Cumberland Valley. Misfortune had brought him to the Hermitage and the threshold of oblivion, but the years of flailing struggle against debt and disappointment had bred a retrospective tenderness for its logs, and General Jackson was content to spend the remainder of his days in their friendly company. Returning from Florida enfeebled by dysentery, he reflected that these days would not be many, and that Rachel deserved a better home.

As soon as he was able to be about he showed a neighbor, William B. Lewis, the site of the new house, a stretch of pasture land almost perfectly level, a few hundred yards southwest of the blockhouse and screened by a wood from the highroad a quarter of a mile away.

Lewis suggested a more commanding situation which, indeed, had been the General's personal choice.²

"No, Major," he said, "Mrs. Jackson chose this spot, and she shall have her wish. I am going to build this house for *her*. I don't expect to live in it myself."³

Commanding situations formed a small part of Rachel's desires in this world, and the house⁴ was built in the secluded meadow—a plain rectangular structure of brick which was burned and oak timbers for the most part cut and shaped on the plantation. It faced south, with a front of about eighty-five feet, the depth being somewhat greater.

From a small porch, such as were more commonly seen on New England than on Southern houses, one entered a hall which ran the length of the house. On the right and left, in front, were the parlors. Back of the parlor on the left was the dining room, back of the parlor on the right the bed chamber of General and Mrs. Jackson, a northeast room. Upstairs were five or six sleeping rooms. The General's office was a small brick building on the west side of the house; the kitchen and house-servant quarters in the rear.

On his return from the East in April, 1819, General Jackson engaged William Frost, a "regular bred english Gardner,"[5] to lay out the grounds. The result was a beautiful lawn, shaded by gigantic trees, and, on the east side in view of her bedroom window, Rachel's particular sanctuary—an orderly acre of flowers, traced by curving brick-edged walks.

The guest chambers were seldom vacant and Rachel and Andrew rarely sat at their table alone. Judge John Overton—who had known Mrs. Jackson as the bride of Lewis Robards—Senator Eaton, Governor McMinn, youthful Gaston Davézac of New Orleans clicking his heels and conveying his father's respects; Edward Ward talking horses and Alabama land; a cloud of Donelson kin; Sam Houston, a tall handsome young lawyer in whom the General was beginning to take an exceptional interest; Dr. James C. Bronaugh of the Army, flint-and-trigger duelist, beau sabreur and the General's personal physician; officers reporting from distant posts; politicians, speculators, a Sunday-School picnic; the traveling curious with letters of introduction from persons who had shaken the General's hand, say, at the stage station in Perth Amboy the winter preceding; brisk young aides-de-camp on fancy horses, plying to and from Division Headquarters at Nashville: the new Hermitage was not an idle place. And it rang with childish laughter, for Rachel and Andrew had taken another ward to raise, Andrew Jackson Hutchings, the six-year-old orphan of the junior partner of Jackson & Hutchings of Clover Bottom memory. General Jackson had kept the President waiting for an answer to a letter while he journeyed by forced rides to Alabama to comfort the last hours of his dying friend with a promise to care for his boy.[6]

There were other domestic problems. "Dear Uncle I am . . . confined in the Common Jaoll . . . for an assault on John McKinley in which I displayed the patriotism which should be engrafted in the bosom of every free born American. . . . S. D. HUTCHINGS."[7] "D[r]. Uncle Herewith you will find enclosed a letter . . . on the subject of my Brother Anthony's suspension from Yale College. . . . C[AROLINE] S. BELL."[8] But the Hermitage mail pouch was not without its compensations. "I send you a Barrel of what I think good old Whiskey. . . . Respect & friendship. EDWARD WARD."[9]

Ralph E. W. Earl, an itinerant portrait painter, and member of a talented though eccentric family of artists, caught Rachel's fancy. "I can say with truth a more Correct young man I never knew."[10] Jane Caffery, a niece of Rachel, caught the fancy of the artist. He married her and prepared to settle down to confine the practise of his profession to meeting the active demand for likenesses of General Jackson. The bride died a few months after the ceremony. "My Friend," wrote Rachel, "you have not to weep as thos who have no hope. Angels wafted Her on Celestial wings to that blooming garden of roses that has no thorns."[11] Like his father before him Earle had been a wanderer from boyhood who had never known a home. Mrs. Jackson carried him off to the Hermitage where he remained for seventeen years.

In the summer of 1819, General Jackson rode to Georgia to greet another visitor. Earle went to Nashville for a few days, and a letter followed him. "Pleas to Look in the post office for Letters for me. I feel Lonely and unhappy. . . . I have lived a life of hope, I hope to Die in the Faith. . . . I would write you a long letter but perhaps not so as to be all together Exceptable Adieu Dear sur and believe Me your Sincere friend RACHEL JACKSON"[12]

But not to Mrs. Jackson alone did the persisting lamp of fame bare the imperfections inherent in the human plan. The General had gone to Georgia to welcome James Monroe to Tennessee. Two years before the President had undertaken the experiment of showing himself to the country, which no Executive since Washington had done. He had promised to visit Nashville then, but wrote Jackson that the Spanish situation would not permit. This tour was a success. The raw-boned, six-foot President was a shy man, an able lieutenant though a mediocre chieftain, whose timidity had grown with the exactions of independent leadership until one could scarcely recognize in him the draconian Secretary of War of 1814, braced by the shadow of Mr. Madison's responsibility. Applause seemed to renew his failing self-assurance, but, like most men with an interior sense of insecurity, he was jealous. In 1819 a second journey carried the Executive through the Carolinas and into Georgia where Jackson joined the entourage. Immediately the crowds were larger, the plaudits heartier, altogether a salutary thing until the presidential party made the unfortunate discovery that this was because of the presence of Andrew Jackson. Over the War Path to Knoxville, over the Cumberland Road to Nashville, the procession filed amid continuous ovation; and thence by the Kentucky Road to Lexington, where General Jackson turned back, and the homage, if less strident, was at least the President's own.

2

Having put on a brave face for Mr. Monroe (and for General Jackson), Tennessee turned again, amid a clamorous conflict of counsel and convictions, to the infinite perplexities of a life disordered.

Moving westward the creeping paralysis of hard times had reached the frontier. To put currency on a sounder footing, the government-supported Bank of the United States had opened its doors in 1817 with branches from Portsmouth to New Orleans. The Bank of the United States redeemed its paper in coin on demand, and, as fast as the currency of wildcat banks fell into its hands, they were pressed to do the same. The wildcat banks began to call loans and the financial house of cards in the West toppled. A cry of rage went up against the government bank. Tennessee excluded its branches from the state by imposing a tax of fifty thousand dollars a year, and, departing from a policy of moderation, chartered a "litter" of independent banks to accommodate the imagined financial needs of the communities. For a little while every one was flush; then came a reckoning. Throughout the West independent banks fell like nine-pins in the face of the demand that they honor their paper money. The Nashville Bank was obliged to suspend specie payments, though it managed to keep open. The government bank's demand for the redemption of the paper that flooded the West revealed conditions that would have fascinated a finance minister of Louis XVI. One bank had twenty-seven thousand dollars in specie with which to redeem three hundred and ninety-five thousand dollars in notes; another thirty-five thousand dollars to cover five hundred and thirty-four thousand dollars' worth of paper.

The collapse had come at an awkward moment for General Jackson. The new Hermitage had drained his reserve of cash. He had loaned money freely. He was deep in Alabama speculations on his own account and with partners, notably John Coffee and the late John Hutchings. Over the latter's interests he established a protectorate for the benefit of the Hutchings boy. On the eve of the débâcle, he had joined his old friends, John Overton and James Winchester, in the founding of Memphis, "on the American Nile," as the prospectus defined it. The promoters spent a good deal of money clearing the bluff, laying off squares and streets—one named Jackson, naturally—and building a court-house and jail. Russell Bean, hero of the Jonesborough fire, was engaged as marshal to keep the peace. His duties were not arduous. The queen of the American Nile attracted few investors, peaceable or otherwise, though it proved a suitably isolated asylum for General Winchester's son when he married the quadroon mistress of Colonel Thomas Hart Benton. Before the reviving river trade established the fortunes of Memphis, Jackson had disposed of his interest.

Middle Tennessee was prostrate. Between five and six hundred suits for debt clogged the courts in Davidson County. In a single action Andrew Jackson brought the law upon one hundred and twenty-nine persons who owed him.[13] His situation was serious. He must meet obligations maturing in Alabama or sacrifice thousands of dollars he had poured into his ventures there.[14] Debtors cried out for relief from the public funds. Bills went before the Legislature to set up loan offices and to stay the collection of debts. Jackson and Edward Ward were the only men of prominence in the Cumberland Valley to oppose them, Jackson sending the Legislature a protest which it declined to receive on the ground that the language was disrespectful.[15] The bills were passed.

To this turmoiled scene came the news that America had congratulated itself too soon on the acquisition of Florida. Spain hesitated to ratify the treaty. Jackson's impulse was to rush to Washington, but he did not have the money for the journey.[16]

3

He wrote to James Monroe. "I am wearied with public life. . . . I have been accused of acts I never committed, of crimes I never thought of, and secretly . . . charged . . . in the Senate . . . of doing acts in my official capacity to promote my private interest." This was an allusion to the Eaton-Donelson land purchase in Florida, from which the Lacock committee had sought to draw false inferences. Jackson was deeply hurt. "I have laboured through life to establish an honest Charactor. . . .

"I had hoped that our affairs with Spain would have been finally settled by her ratifying the treaty, and nothing would have arisen to prevent me from" leaving the Army. "But Sir you know my services is my countries as long as" the country should need them. Yet he prayed for peace. "I have therefore to request that you . . . say to me . . . at what time it will be proper . . . to tender my resignation. . . . Have the goodness to present Mrs. J. and myself to your amiable lady . . . and believe me to be Yr mo. ob. serv."[17]

The storms that beat about the haughty spirit beat more fitfully now. The intervals of calm were longer. An old slave Peter pined for his children and grandchildren. General Jackson located them in East Tennessee and increased his debts eighteen hundred dollars in order to unite the family at the Hermitage, "object, humanity."[18] At West Point Andrew Jackson Donelson joined other cadets in a protest against "kicks and cuffs" and the use of the ball and chain as aids to the mastery of the military profession. This precipitated a controversy during which young Donelson wrote home for permission to resign rather than embarrass his uncle by a scene. He remained at the Academy, however, and eventually was graduated second in the class of 1820.

Andrew and Rachel followed with pride the progress of this studious, spirited youth and his letters were an event at the busy Hermitage, General Jackson's only complaint being that they did not come oftener. "Your aunt and myself . . . [were] fearfull from your long silence that you were sick. . . . You can attend to nothing more beneficial than writing. It . . . expands the mind, and will give you . . . an easy habit of communicating your thoughts. there is nothing so beautiful in writing as a plain easy stile. . . . Altho Mr. Jeffersons writings has met with the approbation that they merited I have always thought that the chasteness of Mr. Madison excelled any american author I ever read." The man preparing to withdraw from the world could judge impartially, untroubled by the remembrance of how many times the chaste style had been employed to defeat the desires of Andrew Jackson. "It is by habit that this ease and plainness of stile which I call elegance is to be acquired. . . .

"When you know the pleasure it gives me to read your letters why not amuse yourself by writing to me. Choose you own subject—and handle it in any way your judgt may direct. . . . This will give you confidence in yourself, which to become great you must acquire, keeping you mind allways open to reason, . . . but never yielding your opinion until the Judgt. is convinced. Independence of mind and action is the noblest attribute of man. . . . [It] gives a peaceful conscience, and when the public voice, being misled, disapproves the course, innocence smiles . . . at . . . clamour [until] time dispells the mists of error from their eyes . . . truth ultimately prevails. . . .

"If we remain at peace I wish you to study law and live with me. if we have war . . . I will have you with me, but . . . war is a great evil . . . and a curse to any nation. . . . I enclosed you in my last one hundred dollars in a bill of the Branch bank of the U States— I am anxious to know whether it reached you, there are so many roberies of the mail."[19]

Within three weeks the philosopher of the Cumberland came to the assistance of Time to dispel the mists of error from the Florida issue. The bad faith of Spain was apparent, and she had potential allies in Crawford and Clay who seemed willing to go to any lengths to feather their nests at the expense of Adams and the treaty. Adams pressed the President into a position of defiance, and Jackson received confidential instructions to prepare a military movement calculated to awe the Spanish. He replied instantly. "My health is very precarious, but . . . with the smiles of heaven I will endeavour to place once more the american Eagle upon the ramparts of the Barancas Pensacola, St. Marks and reduce Ft St augustine and then beg leave to retire if I survive."[20]

The first person awed by these sentiments was the President of the United States.

But there was no retreat. Mr. Calhoun asked for details of a program involving only Regular troops, and twenty-four hours after his dispatch had reached Nashville the answer, in Jackson's slanting scrawl, was on its way. This compact and able military document embodied a plan for war against the full power of Spain, no less, on a front from New Orleans to Charleston, complete to an "Estimate of the Teams . . . required . . . for the Field Artillery"—the rapid work of a man who knew his resources, those of the enemy, and his own mind exactly. The Commander was under no delusion that Florida would prove the easy prey that she had been in 1818. "Garrisons at Pensacola and Barrancas . . . may be estimated at 500 regulars and 300 militia. . . . St. Augustine is one of the strongest Fortres in the World with the exception of Quebeck and Gibraltar. . . . St Marks is a strong place, . . . and well defended will cost many lives to take by Storm. . . . I might be 75 days employed in the reduction of the . . . posts, . . . but with the Smiles of Heaven I hope not to be half that time." As ever with Jackson to think was to strike. Orders had gone, he said, and, by the time this communication should reach the Secretary, the troops would be in motion.[21]

Then taking a fresh sheet of paper, Old Hickory indited a private letter to the Secretary of War. Would it embarrass the government if he should seize Cuba also? Mr. Calhoun treated the request with elaborate deference to Jackson's views. He, also, favored the acquisition of Cuba, but felt "we ought at present limit our operations to Florida."[22]

Mr. Monroe had had his lesson. He halted the movement of troops against Florida, determined to consult Congress before turning Andrew Jacksoon loose on Spanish soil again. Secretary of Treasury Crawford declared our finances would not bear the strain of war and Congress hesitated. Jackson fumed. "Had Congress acted with the . . . feeling . . . our national charector demanded the Don long since, cap in hand, would have paid his respects to our President, with the treaty ratified."[23]

Something like this eventually happened when, in February, 1821, Francisco Dionisio Vives, the Spanish Minister, delivered the ratified treaty. Before the document was actually in his hands, Mr. Monroe offered Jackson the governorship of the new acquisition. His communication reached the Hermitage on the ninth or tenth of February with a request for a prompt answer, as the President must send his nomination to the Senate on March third. Jackson answered at once declining the office, and the letter went to Nashville to await the departure of the bi-weekly mail.

4

This letter, had he received it, would have dissipated the web of dilemma which increasing vacillation and a nervous fear of Jackson had spun about James Monroe. A President owes something to his public, and Mr. Monroe was not without a feeling that he did not appear at his best in the company of Andrew Jackson. As early as 1818, a solution was suggested that seemed to possess so much intrinsic merit that Monroe took it to his old preceptor, Thomas Jefferson. How about sending General Jackson on a mission to Russia? The patriarch threw up his hands. "Good God, he would breed you a quarrel before he had been there a month!"[24]

Jackson's repeated requests for Monroe to name the day of his retirement had been sincere. Had the compliments with which the President sugared his correspondence during the two years past been equally sincere, there would have been no problem. Congress had reduced the Army which required the demotion of one major general commanding troops. There were only two such, Jacob Brown, head of the Northern Division, and Jackson. Brown had hastened to Washington, and, with Winfield Scott and other friends of William H. Crawford, waged a campaign in his own behalf. Jackson had done nothing, but, by accident or design, the oft-stated plea for retirement dropped from his letters. Now that the skies were serene, Monroe would be more comfortable with the comparatively colorless Brown at the head of the Army, but a high regard for the amour propre of the Southern Commander caused him to hesitate. The governorship was a way out and Mr. Monroe called Senator Eaton to the White House, flattered him, and declared that Jackson could remain in the Army if he wished, but that he hoped he would undertake the more important, the much more important, work of organizing an administration in Florida.[25]

The Florida landowner was easily persuaded. Other political and military satellites of Jackson were quick to perceive the advantage during these lean times of a patron in a position to distribute public appointments. Off to the Hermitage sped a letter from Eaton saying that Jackson's friends in Congress were determined to have him appointed whether he would accept or not, and hinting at a "strong political reason" for the step.[26] On the heels of this missive a delegation from Nashville hurried up the guitar-shaped drive. Over Rachel's remonstrances,[27] Jackson consented to reverse his decision on condition that his letter of refusal had not left the post-office. A horseman was off to Nashville like a bullet. He brought back the letter. Jackson crumpled it and "reluctantly" wrote another, accepting the appointment on condition "that I may resign as soon as the Government is organized."[28] Willing hands sped this to Nashville, the delegation departed, and the weary old soldier fell to reckoning the speed a post rider should make to Washington over the long red road that Andrew Jackson knew so well. At best he would not make it before March first. A forty-eight-hour delay, then, and Mr. Monroe would name another man. "My hopes are that the letters will not reach there [in time]."[29]

5

But they did.

In the remarkable space of eight days, General Jackson and Rachel arrived in New Orleans by steamboat on April 22, 1821. On board was their carriage, newly glassed, curtained with "Broad Lace" and upholstered in "Moroco Skins," at an expenditure of one hundred and sixty-three dollars. A new set of harness had cost another one hundred and sixty dollars, less an allowance of twenty-five dollars for the old.[30]

This equipage was not out of place in New Orleans. "Great Babylon," wrote Rachel, "is come up before me. Oh, the wickedness, the idolatry of this place! unspeakable riches and splendor. The attention and honors paid to the General far excel the recital of my pen. They conducted him to the Grand Theatre . . . [which] rang with loud acclamations, Vive Jackson. Songs of praise were sung by ladies, and . . . they crowned him with . . . laurel. The Lord has promised his humble followers a crown that fadeth not away; the present one is already withered the leaves falling off. . . . Oh, farewell! Pray for your sister in a heathen land."[31]

Mrs. Jackson found their next tarrying place, Montpelier, Alabama, smaller than New Orleans, but as sinful per capita. "The Sabbath entirely neglected and profaned. The regiment [of United States troops] . . . no better than the Spaniards. . . . The General, I believe, wants to get home again as much as I do. . . . [He] wishes he had taken my advice. . . . Amen. RACHEL JACKSON."[32]

She was right about her husband. The General had regretted that letter of acceptance since the instant it left his hand. His impulse was to recall it "but my word is out and I must comply."[33] For another thing, he could not disappoint the President whose "solicitude . . . arose from feelings of friendship, and a desire to give evidence that he fully approved my course in the Seminole campaign, as well as believing that my name would have some weight in establishing the Government over the Floridas."[34] A third reason for taking the office was to help his friends. A list of suggested appointments to subordinate posts had been forwarded to the President. Andrew Jackson knew the advantage steady income gave a man starting out in a strange country. Under such auspices he had come to the Cumberland in 1788. But as soon as Congress could meet and extend a territorial form of government to Florida, friends must fend for themselves. "I retire to my farm and there spend my latter days."[35] Through the efflorescent aura of official compliment, General Jackson had begun to discern that it required a lenient view of the facts to construe his present mission as a promotion in the public service. Twice he had borne the flag into Florida under circumstances that had made the world look on. Now he carried it as a figure in a ceremonial. A gust of pride eddied up in a private line to Coffee. "I never can condescend to become a governor of a Territory after the office I have filled."[36]

Moreover, despite all his protestations, as the day neared for Andrew Jackson to lay aside his sword, a singular depression of spirit weighed upon him. In nine years of active service he had grown accustomed to command. Army life had opened natural avenues of expression for talents always a little robust for ordinary pursuits. He loved the camaraderie of camp and barracks and was loath to leave it. He had formed more and closer ties of friendship than in any other period of his life. Though American soldiers had not known such discipline since the day of Von Steuben, Jackson's men adored him.

The General found it equally hard to part from his superiors, Mr.

Adams's challenging loyalty was apparent to the world, while the mellifluous phrases of Messrs. Monroe and Calhoun obscured a shadowy hour when but for Adams the conquest of Florida would have been repudiated. "I have my D'r Sir read your letter with great pleasure, the principles you have laid down for political guide through life will . . . lead you to compleat triumph over your enemies and your country to safety and happiness." The quick eyes of John C. Calhoun must have glowed at these lines, for he, too, was in the lists for the presidency. "Before this reaches you our military relations will have ceased, but my breast will allways cherish . . . that friendly feeling . . . your honourable conduct towards me ever since you have been placed in the Department of war was well calculated to inspire. this feeling for you will never cease during life."[37]

Andrew Jackson had hoped to enter Pensacola again as a soldier—a soldier seated beside his wife in a carriage, it is true, rather than riding at the head of a barefooted army—but even this was not to be. The day designated for his retirement, June 1, 1821, found him marooned at Montpelier where he penned a moving order of farewell. It had not been distributed, however, when the late Commander of the Southern Division chanced upon an address to the troops elucidating an easy theory of discipline which was susceptible of the interpretation that General Jackson had been too severe on the men. Moreover this order was signed "Jacob Brown, Commander-in-Chief, under the President, of the Armies of the United States." This title Jackson had never achieved, the office having lain vacant until the announcement of Jackson's retirement, which was in reality a compliment to Jackson as Brown was his senior in the service. Although his name had passed from the Army rolls, Jackson recalled his order of farewell and added a stiff "P. S." of a hundred lines to say that, contrary to the opinion of the Commander-in-Chief, the trouble with the military establishment was that discipline was too lax.[38]

6

The vertical rain crushed down like a water-fall compressing the elastic forms of the Pride of China trees and making a pond of the Plaza. Rachel had seen rain like this every day since she had come to Pensacola. But in no time the flood would run off into the bay, or sink into the porous white sand, and the sun reveal the premeditated brilliance of the walled-in gardens. Before her gallery had ceased to drip, people were abroad and bare feet whispered on the damp sand beneath her windows like the sound of a little stream.

"Fine flowers growing spontaneously, for they have neglected their gardens expecting a change of government. . . . All the houses look in ruins, old as time."[39] Mrs. Jackson was somewhat mistaken as to the age of those sun-washed, shuttered houses with plastered walls of faded blue and green and yellow. Their time-stained appearance was the work not so much of years or neglect as of the extraordinary powers of tropical nature to triumph over human endeavor.

"The inhabitants all speak Spanish and French. Some speak four or five languages. Such a mixed multitude you, nor any of us, ever had an idea of. . . . Fewer white people by far than any other. . . . I am living on Main Street which . . . [gives] me an opportunity of seeing a great deal from the upper galleries." There was a great deal to engage the eye. "We have a handsome view of the bay, . . . the most beautiful water prospect I ever saw." Languorous movement, vivid colors—the sea, the foliage, the houses, the garb and the complexions of people. Seamen strolled with knives in their belts and coins burning their pockets; absurd little Spanish soldiers; yellow women with well-turned limbs and insinuating glances; Jamaica blacks bearing prodigious burdens on their heads; a fish peddler filling the street with incomprehensible cries; a Seminole Indian with a set expression of unfriendliness; a grandee in his carriage. "And must I say the worst people here are the cast-off Americans?"[40]

"The Sabbath profanely kept; a great deal of noise and swearing in the streets; shops kept open; trade"—a broad term—"going on, I think, more than on any other day."[41] This disturbing environment so carried away Mrs. Jackson's mulatto maid Betty that Rachel was obliged to report her delinquencies. "She can behave herself," wrote General Jackson, "or Mr. Blair . . . [will] give her fifty lashes and if he does not . . . as soon as I get possession I will order a corporal to give it to her publickly."[42]

The General was not, therefore, in possession.

After five weeks of delay at Montpelier, he had sent Rachel and her household into the city alone, expecting almost every day to follow. But delay succeeded delay, and nothing takes more from the imposing character of a ceremonial than a want of punctuality. The first postponement was occasioned by the tardiness of the United States sloop of war *Hornet*, which was to bring from Havana the authorization for Don José Callava, Governor of West Florida, to make the formal transfer. Jackson was certain that the officials were purposely "amusing" our Colonel Forbes in Havana, in order to detain the *Hornet* while Florida slave-smugglers and miscellaneous importers took advantage of the last benevolent days of Spanish sovereignty. "How Irksome . . . to remain here with my arms Folded not able to prevent those illegal practices."[43] Nor was the tedium relieved by the arrival of a copy of the *National Intelligencer* containing a roster of the President's appointments to subordinate situations in General Jackson's Florida government. Not a name that Jackson had suggested was on it. Not one. Jackson wrote to Doctor Bronaugh, in Pensacola, with Mrs. Jackson, and for whom he had solicited the office of Receiver of Public Money. "I am determined never to be associated with such men. . . . Say to my friend Call [another of the Jackson candidates] not to despond. . . . I am too sick to write more."[44]

Eventually the *Hornet* reached Pensacola, and, in an exchange of flowery letters, the formal negotiations with Callava began. They struck a snag promptly when Callava proposed to remove the cannon from the fortifications. Jackson said that by explicit instructions from the President the cannon must be considered a part of the fortifications, specifically ceded by Article II of the treaty. Callava replied that by explicit instructions from the King under no circumstances could the cannon be considered as a part of the fortifications, ceded by Article II of the treaty. The difference of opinion was given time to expand by failure of the vessels, which were to carry away the Spanish garrisons, to arrive on schedule.

Never a man to pursue a long-range discussion when he could meet the other party face to face, General Jackson entered Florida without invitation, but with the Fourth Infantry, encamped fifteen miles from Pensacola and in courteous terms invited an interview with Don José. The Governor's reply breathed those exquisite compliments before which the oafish bulk of the English language retreats in confusion. Only a violent illness, threatening to extinguish life itself, deprived Señor Callava of the pleasure of visiting General Jackson's camp. "I have the honor to acquaint your Excellency, that in your quality as

Commissioner, you may when it suits your pleasure, and in the manner you deem most expedient, exhibit your credentials to me."[45]

So that was it. If General Jackson wished to see Colonel Callava, he must pay the first call—not omitting to bring his credentials.

General Jackson's idea of the formalities, like his ideas concerning the cannon, differed from those of his Spanish colleague. "Etiquette due me as a stranger and to my rank" required that the first call should come from Callava.[46] For the present, however, he limited himself to a fervent prayer for the restoration of His Excellency's health and the hope of a meeting (at his camp) before long.[47] A letter to Coffee used up less ink. "I would sink the place and him with it before I would visit him."[48]

It is a pity that some one like Coffee was not there in the place of the General's young and ornamental aides-de-camp—some useful friend with the forthrightness to tell his chief that he was on the wrong side of this etiquette issue. By international usage Callava was entitled to receive the first call. On occasions, there could be no greater stickler for punctilio than General Jackson, and this was an occasion when, had he been properly enlightened, certainly no Spaniard would have surpassed him in politeness.

While Callava continued diplomatically indisposed, Jackson fell ill in reality. Doctor Bronaugh recommended his immediate removal to Pensacola. He refused to go. Rachel came out from town. Her persuasions were futile. "He said when he came in it should be under his own standard, and that would be the third time he had planted that flag on that wall."[49]

Jackson moved his camp to a mosquito-ridden flat two miles from the wall and pressed Callava for a settlement of the artillery question. After first making sure that Jackson would accept, the Governor "proposed" an elaborate "compromise" (which Jackson had already suggested), the guns remaining in our possession, Jackson giving receipt for them. Ruffled by Jackson's failure to call, the urbane Callava continued to take his revenge by those subtle tactics of postponement for which the Spanish seem to possess an especial genius. Finally he proposed to deliver the province on July seventeenth at ten in the morning. Jackson replied that unless the delivery was made at ten A. M. July fifteenth certain small money penalties would be invoked. Callava replied with an air of offended innocence. He would pay the fines, but delivery could not take place before the day and hour he had specified. "God preserve Your Excellency many Years."

"My feelings as a soldier," replied General Jackson on his last day with the mosquitoes, "correspond with yours, death before an undue condescension. . . . I will be in Pensacola early tomorrow morning to breakfast with Mrs. Jackson, whom our unfortunate misunderstanding has prevented me from visiting since she has been in Pensacola. . . . Will you . . . breakfast with . . . [us] . . . at half after Six or Seven, when I shall have the pleasure of introducing you to my Officers, who know well how to appreciate a soldiers merits." Yet, these hearty words did not go without a final and rather strained effort to bring the Spaniard to General Jackson's terms in the matter of official precedence. Would Callava visit the camp that evening? Jackson asked in a tone strangely akin to entreaty. "I am without a horse, or I should meet you and conduct you: but I send my nephew Lt. A. J. Donelson . . . to conduct you to the Camp, where you will meet a cordial welcome, . . . but be assured that I have no wish to expose your health. . . . Should we not meet . . . before 10 o'clock tomorrow, . . . I shall then take you by the hand as a soldier and a friend, and am certain that after further acquaintance we will know how to appreciate each other."[50]

7

They did not meet until ten o'clock—on July seventeenth. From her balcony Rachel saw the American and Spanish troops facing each other in front of the Government House with flag staff between them. A silent crowd lined the boundaries of the square. Respectfully, but silently, it made a lane for General Jackson and his suite which moved splendidly accoutered and mounted (the General having found a horse) to the steps of the Government House. "O how solemn was his pale countenance when he dismounted," noted Mrs. Jackson. "Recollections of perils and scenes of war . . . presented themselves to view."[51] Quite possibly, though all that the crowd could see was General Jackson in the act of calling on Colonel Callava.

In a few moments they descended the broad steps together. The sternness of the General's countenance had relaxed a little. Callava was smiling. He made a striking appearance—tall, well-formed, blond, not more than forty, and seemingly recovered from the malevolent illness which had prevented him from breakfasting with General Jackson. The dignitaries passed between the lines of troops who raised their arms to salute. The Fourth Infantry band began *The Star Spangled Banner* and the royal standard of Spain fluttered to half-staff.

The Stars and Stripes were raised to a level with it. Aboard the *Hornet* in the bay boomed the first of twenty-one guns, after which the Spanish flag came down and the American ensign went up. Florida was ours.

On the Sunday following, Colonel Callava and staff gave themselves the pleasure of dining with Governor Jackson. They were enchanting guests.

CHAPTER XX

THE BORDER CAPTAIN

I

THE President had not stinted his Governor of Florida as to the extent of his authority. He was clothed with "all the powers . . . heretofore exercised by the Governor and Captain-General and Intendant of Cuba, and by the Governors of East and West Floridas," with the exception of granting land and laying "new or additional" taxes.[1] No American civil servant, before or since, has held in his hands such regal rights. General Jackson expressed himself as satisfied.

On assuming the duties of his office, the Governor found that, despite the delays of Callava, none of the Monroe appointees to subordinate offices had arrived. General Jackson was not greatly dismayed. The town was filled with place seekers—Army officers left without employment by the reduction of the military establishment, politicians, adventurers and the various driftwood of hard-times, many of them without a dollar in their pockets. "The vessels are daily coming in loaded with people," observed Rachel.[2] Before the General's entrance into the city one poor wretch had thrown himself on Mrs. Jackson's mercy. She promised that her husband would do something for him. Jackson made him Port Warden, and the other posts of the absent appointees were promptly filled with friends.

This relief was transitory. Twenty applicants contended for every position. As the Monroe men began to arrive and appropriate the more desirable spoil, the ranks of unemployed Jackson adherents swelled and the Governor began to perceive his gleaming scepter a thing of paste and brass. The positions he could fill with any degree of permanence were few and their rewards small.

Every aspect of the Florida business was small. The white population of the territory did not greatly exceed in numbers the armies Andrew Jackson had created and commanded in the New Orleans campaign. It was segregated in communities remote from one another

—the most feasible communication between Pensacola and St. Augustine being by water around the tip of the Cape—rendering the tasks of administration largely the work of local functionaries. This left little for an executive of Jackson's caliber to do, as, until Congress should meet, the Spanish machinery of government remained intact, with no extension of the United States laws except those dealing with the customs and with slave smuggling. For Jackson this was the labor of a few days, after which many an official in his situation and state of health would have given thanks for the opportunity to enjoy the sunshine, and the Gulf breezes that cooled the broad galleries of the Government House. Even Rachel, whose enthusiasm for Florida was tempered by many reservations, said their domicile was "as pleasant as any in town," and that Pensacola was the most healthful place she had ever seen.

The Governor was in no mood for relaxation, however, and before a week was out there was something in his activities that vaguely suggests the occupations of the Emperor at Elba. He undertook the duties of a town constable, demolishing gambling houses and closing the shops and bazaars on Sundays. "Fiddling and dancing not heard any more on the Lord's day," wrote Rachel in triumph. "Cursing not heard. What, what has been done in one week!"[3]

2

Other officials were more inclined to yield to the mutation of destiny and accept the restful nature of their responsibilities. Spanish residents of quality abandoned their reserve, finding some of the American Army officers and their families indeed quite presentable. One of these was Lieutenant Andrew Jackson Donelson. Another member of the Governor's household not wanting for polite attentions was Mrs. Jackson's niece and companion, Narcissa Hays. Rachel bought her a pair of silk slippers to wear to parties. Colonel Callava who remained as a Commissioner of the King proved eminently popular with the military set, whose duties were not arduous. The tedium was abated by an affair of honor between two young officers, in which Doctor Bronaugh acted in his professional capacity. He brought the news of the result to the Executive. Lieutenant Randal had shot Lieutenant Hull through the heart, Hull's pistol, of the hair-

THE SECOND HERMITAGE

Built in 1818 on a site selected by Mrs. Jackson. The structure on the left was General Jackson's office. This representation, from an engraving owned by Emil Edward Hurja, of New York City, was made before Jackson's English gardener had transformed the grounds. In earlier editions of this volume a likeness of the Hermitage appeared in this space which the Tennessee Historical Society, from which it was obtained, and the writer erroneously believed to be of the house built in 1818. Actually it represented the edifice above as extensively remodeled in 1831.

trigger type, having stopped at half-cock. "By God," exclaimed the experienced Jackson, "to think that a brave man would risk his life on a hair trigger."[4]

Under the terms of the "compromise" whereby the cannon were left on the fortifications, Jackson had given a receipt for the guns, pending their eventual disposition, and Colonel Callava was to receipt for the provisions which, under the treaty, the United States furnished the Spanish troops while en route to Cuba. When Jackson's aide called on Callava for his signature acknowledging an inventory of the rations, he was put off by a plea of a return of the Colonel's enigmatic illness. Eventually a document from Callava was delivered to the Government House, which, when translated, proved to be no receipt. Whereupon, Jackson declared his own receipt for the ordnance void, warning Callava that his duplicity "can injure no one but Your Excellency and Your Government.... This closes my correspondence on this subject forever."[5]

The incident had its influence on the lively pattern of social life in Pensacola, though without diminishing the popularity of the Colonel who managed to retain in his circle several officers of the Fourth Infantry as well as some of the civil appointees of Mr. Monroe, notably Judge Eligius Fromentin of the Federal District Court. To this company belong John Innerarity, a member of the Cabildo or town council of Pensacola. For ten years this tall, Hispanicized Scot had been resident manager of Forbes & Company. Royal Governors, British soldiers, international adventurers came and departed, but since the reign of Alexander McGillivray Forbes & Company remained the actual rulers of Florida. The Scottish house had dealt with McGillivray by making him a partner.[6] It had covertly assisted Andrew Jackson in removing Alexander Arbuthnot as a troublesome commercial rival. Like a white shadow John Innerarity glided through the weaving labyrinth, never on the losing side.

3

John Quincy Adams used to tell how he dreaded the arrival of the Florida post, never knowing what strange, new problem would spring from the mail bag. When Henry M. Brackenridge, Alcalde of Pensacola, waited on the Governor on the twenty-first day of August,

1821, he brought an interesting story that was destined to sharpen the Secretary's apprehensions. Mr. Brackenridge had received a caller, he told Jackson, in the person of Mercedes Vidal, a free octoroon, the natural daughter of Nicolas Maria Vidal, a Spanish official who had died in 1806 leaving large holdings of land in Louisiana and other property in Pensacola to his half-caste children. The estate had gone into the hands of Forbes & Company for settlement. Some years passed, and, when the beige-complexioned Vidals received nothing, they applied to the courts for an accounting. A number of judicial orders were served on John Innerarity to deliver the records in the case to the courts, but the merchant complied with none of them until peremptory demand was made in 1820. Then he produced a few papers which a court auditor pronounced irregular and presumptive of fraud. Governor Callava signed a decree directing Innerarity to bring forth his accounts as executor under Vidal's will within ten days, and to deposit in the royal treasury certain sums of money within five days. He evaded this decree and presently Governor and trader were on their old terms of intimacy.

Meantime Mercedes Vidal had not been inactive. By the exercise of personal wiles, she had obtained copies of sufficient of the records to substantiate her story. The originals, she said, along with the papers bearing on other estates, had been spirited from the municipal archives, and were now at the residence of Lieutenant Domingo Sousa, a clerk of Callava, in readiness for transportation to Cuba.[7]

Jackson immediately sent Brackenridge to demand the papers of Sousa, who refused to relinquish them without an order from Callava. The Governor slept on the matter and the next morning sent Colonel Robert Butler to bring both Sousa and the papers before him. He brought Sousa, but not the papers, which the terrified Lieutenant admitted he had conveyed to the residence of Colonel Callava.

Jackson had every right to the Vidal and other estate papers. Callava had no right to them. The Governor did not hesitate. He sent Butler, Brackenridge and Doctor Bronaugh to demand the documents of the Commissioner and to say that, if the demand were refused, Sousa would be imprisoned. The four reached the Callava house at four o'clock. They were informed that the Commissioner was dining with Colonel Brooke of the Fourth Infantry. When Callava had not returned at five o'clock, the party proceeded to Colonel Brooke's a few doors away. Mr. Brackenridge entered the house.

The dinner was over. Colonel Callava, John Innerarity, Judge Fromentin and several ladies were on the gallery fronting the bay. The Alcalde stated his errand and Callava jumped up and began to declaim on the inviolability of his person as Royal Commissioner. He declared that he would neither surrender the papers nor return to his house, and Colonel Brooke announced that no civil process should be served on his premises. He followed the Alcalde to the gate complaining about the way his guests had been disturbed.[8]

Later the American emissaries found Callava at his home with John Innerarity and courteously renewed their request. An hour was consumed explaining and trying to bring the slippery Spaniard to accede. At length Callava said that his illness, which had returned coincidentally with the appearance of the Americans, had become so severe that he must refrain from further discussion. Jackson's aides were on the point of leaving when Callava added that if a list of the papers were presented to him in writing he would give them up. Brackenridge procured a list, whereupon Callava with Innerarity beside him, invented pretexts for repudiating his promise. As the Americans withdrew, Innerarity remarked significantly: "The die is cast."[9]

Jackson took these words as a call to battle. "Sir," he directed Callava's late host, Colonel Brooke, "you will furnish an officer, sergeant, corporal, and twenty men, and direct the officer to call on me by half past eight o'clock for orders. They will have their arms and . . . twelve rounds of ammunition."[10]

Butler, Brackenridge and Bronaugh accompanied the soldiers to the residence of Colonel Callava. A small light burned in one room, but no one answered the knocks of the Americans. Butler entered the hall with two or three soldiers and guided their steps toward the lighted room. Callava was in bed, though fully clothed except for his military blouse. He demanded the reason for a visit "at that time of night."[11] The request for the papers was repeated, and refused. Butler said in that case he had no alternative but to ask the Colonel to appear before the Governor. The Spanish officer exclaimed that he might be murdered but that he would not quit his house alive. With as much delicacy as the situation permitted, Robert Butler stated that he had received his orders and would obey them. He motioned a file of soldiers into the room. Deliberately Callava put on his coat, and, taking up his sword, made a formal tender of it to Lieutenant Mountz commanding the guard. The token of surrender was declined and at ten o'clock Don José was escorted before Governor Jackson sitting in his capacity as chief magistrate, or judge, of the Floridas in the audience chamber of the Government House.

4

The Governor had not left his office since early in the morning. The yellow rays of the lamps overhead etched more deeply the lines on his alert but thin and weary face. He politely waved Callava to a seat at the table facing him. Beside the prisoner sat Cruzat, his secretary. Brackenridge took a chair at one end of the table to act as interpreter. Every other seat in the dim chamber was occupied. Tall Innerarity's lean countenance was intent. Andrew Jackson had not abandoned his habit of looking people in the eyes when he addressed them. Without useless preliminaries he began the interrogation of Callava.

"Were or were not the papers mentioned in a schedule handed to you by H. M. Brackenridge, Alcalde of the city of Pensacola, delivered by Domingo Sousa at your house this day?"[12]

Colonel Callava stood up, looked at his watch and at the audience. He asked permission to write his answer. After writing a few words, he complained that his eyes were weak and asked if he could dictate to his secretary. He began to dictate in a low tone, and some one whispered to the Governor that instead of replying to the question Callava was illuminating the record with a protest against his arrest. The sharp voice of the Governor stopped Cruzat's pen in the middle of a word. An answer to the question was demanded, yes or no.

Colonel Callava replied that he was before the Governor in his capacity as Commissioner of Spain and declined to answer except as he saw fit. Jackson interposed that he was before him "as a private individual, charged with refusing to surrender papers" belonging to the archives and with being a party to an attempt to remove them from the territory.[13] The question was repeated. Callava refused to answer and Antoine Fullarat, his butler, was called before the interrogator. He corroborated the story of Sousa on the delivery of the papers to Callava's house and said that they were still there.

Jackson crisply demanded that Callava surrender the documents. The Colonel replied by objecting to the testimony of a servant and began to harangue the spectators on the indignities done the person of a Spanish Commissioner. Jackson cut him short. He did not wish to hear the word commissioner again. Callava was here as an "individual," amenable to the laws of the territory, charged with complicity in the theft of public documents. The exchange became too rapid for Brackenridge's translating. He asked Cruzat, then Innerarity, to help him and as Callava's friends to remove any impression of a mistaken rendering of his words. They refused.

Jackson tried persuasion. He urged Callava to surrender the papers and to avoid the consequences his refusal must entail. He urged Innerarity and others of the Callava retinue to employ their influence. It was futile. Callava began another speech. The chamber was in a babble. The Governor yelled to Callava to stop and to Brackenridge to stop him, but the confusion went on. The yellow lamplight gleamed on the high cheek-bones. The blue eyes were afire. Quivering with wrath Andrew Jackson seized a paper from the pile before him and splashed his angular autograph at the bottom. So be it with those who opposed the strong waters of his will.[14]

General Jackson had convened his court armed against all contingencies. The paper he had signed was a commitment remanding José Callava to the city jail. Had it stipulated the military dungeon of Fort Barrancas, the case would have been grave enough, though at least the dignity of prisoner of state would have been preserved to Colonel Callava. But the dingy little calabozo, reserved for offenders of the meanest kind—Callava's band was speechless. At the moment its sole occupants were Domingo Sousa and a homeless youth from New Jersey charged with shooting snipes on the communal lands, contrary to municipal regulation.

It was after midnight when the Colonel and his servant, Fullerat, escorted by a crowd of Spanish officers and sympathizers, reached the lockup. By degrees their normal faculties returned. The spirit of Callava rose above the tormenting malady his flesh was heir to. Food and champagne were brought. Corks were drawn and the prisoners went on a bender.

5

Next morning General Jackson issued the requisite warrant of search, and the testamentary papers in the cases of Nicolas Maria

Vidal and of three other decedents were taken from the Colonel's files. Jackson had what he wanted and so he signed an order for the release of the prisoners, a kindly instrument, including in the broad sweep of its magnanimity the liberation of the snipe shooter. But stay. Before this act of amnesty could be executed, Judge Fromentin issued and caused to be served on the Officer of the Day a writ of habeas corpus in favor of Callava. Immediately Jackson cited the Judge to appear "and show cause why he has attempted to interfere with my authority." The prisoners were released in obedience to the order of the Governor and not the writ of the Judge.

Fromentin replied that a delicate state of health precluded him from leaving his home, where he remained in expectation of arrest. Jackson failed to gratify this wish, however, and on the following day Eligius Fromentin appeared at the Government House. To this meeting he had traversed a long road. Born in France and ordained as a priest of the Society of Jesus, this gentleman had been left without occupation by the shopping of the clergy during the Revolution. Turning up in Maryland as a college professor, he married into an influential family there, drifted to New Orleans, and in 1812 was elected to the United States Senate. The end of his term found the Bourbons and the Jesuits in clover in France. Fromentin reappeared in Paris with a petition for restoration to his priestly office. The discovery of the American marriage proving an obstacle to the realization of this devout desire, the ex-Senator returned to New Orleans and reembraced his wife. Through the exertions of her family, James Monroe had named him to the Federal bench in Florida in place of the eminent though less widely traveled John Haywood, of Tennessee, who was Jackson's choice.

In the Vidal case Governor Jackson had taken a few short-cuts to justice, as he perceived it.[15] But his procedure had been by no means as irregular as that of Fromentin, not to mention Callava. Fromentin was without jurisdiction except in litigation pertaining to the revenue laws or the importation of slaves. He had issued his writ at the request of John Innerarity and others without asking to see the warrant of commitment, and had it served by a private citizen. Jackson's citation halted him in the act of preparing bail for Callava, the legality of whose confinement he had yet to determine. "The lecture I gave the Judge," wrote Jackson in another contribution to John Quincy

Adams's mail bag, "will, I trust, for the future cause him to obey the spirit of his commission, . . . instead of attempting to oppose me."[16]

In a mauve cloud of indignation Don José soared off to Washington and plumped his protests before the Spanish Minister. A long and fantastic account from the Colonel's pen of his scandalous treatment in Florida was published by the *National Intelligencer*.[17] As in the past John Quincy Adams supported Jackson. The bold declarations of the Secretary of State provoked a curious echo within the white walls on Pennsylvania Avenue. "The *momentary* gov^t. of Florida," James Monroe described it to a friend, "for *temporary* is too strong a term. . . ." This was boldness with a degree of safety, Mr. Monroe being quite aware that Andrew Jackson was moving mountains to be out of Pensacola at the first moment possible. Yet to be altogether secure, the presidential confidant was warned against divulging "[this] sentiment, . . . in consideration of the high temper of the general."[18]

On October 5, 1821, the high-tempered General informed Mr. Monroe that "having organised the Government, . . . and it being in full operation,"[19] he was going home. The President asked him to remain, but, long before his letter reached Florida, the handsome carriage, drawn by four white horses, had emerged from the Government House gate and crossed the flowering Plaza. A sentry presented arms, and the Gargantuan quit the land of Lilliput.

When he was well on his way, Colonel Brooke distributed invitations to a ball. "A great constellation of Spanish beauties," John Innerarity and Judge Fromentin were there, but Jackson partizans heard the cadenced thrum of guitars from afar. "It is impossible," one lamented, "to describe the vacuum in the society of this place occasioned by the departure of yourself."[20]

6

How peaceful the Hermitage. "Our place looks like it had been abandoned for a season, But we have a cheirful fire for our friends, and a prospect of living at it for the . . . ballance of our lives. I have sent on my resignation by Doctor Brunaugh."[21]

It was over, this uncertain adventure into which Andrew Jackson had been drawn by an unreciprocated sense of loyalty to the President and a wish to help his young friends. Rachel again felt a release from the alien and unassimilable world against which she had striven for thirty years. She and Andrew undertook to make their home comfortable for the decline of their days. In the great hall stood seven cases of furniture and table silver purchased at New Orleans. The freight bill was two hundred and seventy-three dollars and seventy-five cents. However Rachel might deplore the wicked luxury of the complaisant Creole town there was no denying the comfort of good French beds. "1 Bedstead, of Mahogony, fluted, $100" was for her own and Andrew's tall south chamber; likewise "1 Matress of fine ticking, $45, 1 moschetto Bar of muslin, $16, 1 Counterpane knotted, Marseilles, $24."[22] There was also a new sideboard and something to fill its decanters: "18 Gallons Best Brandy $45, 1 half pipe Old Madeira, $275; 1 Bll Old Whiskey $29.75. 6 Boxes Claret $72, 2 do $26, 1 Cask Porter $28, 3 bottles Bitters $3, 6 Boxes Cigars $24, 2 Boxes Brandy fruits $16."[23] In all sufficient to impart a mellow cast to conversation beside the cheerful fire for many a winter's evening. And to prove that no human experience is wholly barren, Rachel had brought away from Florida a preference for Spanish cigars.

These domestic preparations promised to afford an answer to a letter of inquiry from an old friend of the General, Seth Lewis, who wrote: "Since we saw each other both of us have passed through a variety of Scenes, and we are now approaching the evening of our lives. Your career has been brilliant but stormy—mine more humble but more peaceful. . . . We have both had time and opportunity to make a full trial of the gifts of fortune, as they are usually called, and to form a correct Judgment of their real value. We have both pursued them with the same object in view— We have pursued them as a means of happiness. Have they yielded us that happiness? For myself I must answer . . . in the negative, . . . and I presume your answer . . . must be the same."[24]

Seth Lewis presumed too much. His friend was content and the measure of his contentment was in proportion to the sincerity of his resolution to exchange a brilliant career for a quiet one. General Jackson was fifty-five and looked ten years older. His hair bristled up like the crest of a hussar's helmet, but it was almost white. His remaining strength he meant to dedicate to the service of his family. Besides the Hermitage he had the affairs of two other plantations to direct—his own place at Florence and the Hutchings boy's legacy at Huntsville.

The cotton yield of 1821 was satisfactory, and, after two years of depression, men looked to spring for signs of the rainbow. The General's crop was ginned by New Year's and he planned to send it to New Orleans on his own account rather than accept the prices of Nashville and Alabama commission merchants. Waiting for the winter rains to fill the rivers that were to float his produce to market, he boxed up his public papers and declined an invitation to tour the North and the East. Other concerns, he said, engaged him. "I have my little sons including Lincoyer, at school, and their education has been greatly neglected in my absence."[25]

He subscribed for twenty newspapers from all parts of the country. They littered the floor of his study whose walls were a reliquary of his military past. With a faculty which, as always, was half discernment and half leaping instinct, he surveyed the nest of new national problems irresistibly centering about slavery—and remained inert before them. "The Missouri [Compromise] question . . . will be the entering wedge to separate the union. . . . I hope I may not live to see the evils that must grow out of this wicked design of demagogues, who talk about humanity, but whose sole object is self agrandisement."[26]

7

Already there was a theater in Nashville, with a brick sidewalk in front, and they were speaking of street lamps to light the steps of the new era. The town claimed thirty-three hundred inhabitants, counting eight hundred slaves. Fifty municipally owned negroes kept the clay thoroughfares tidy in dry weather and passable in wet. Busier shops and stores and statelier homes were not to be seen elsewhere between Lexington and Natchez. The Nashville Inn had adorned its front with a three-story gallery and its barroom with a billiard table. While still well patronized the cockpit on the vacant lot next door was losing its refined social tone. Davidson Academy had become Cumberland College, General Jackson contributing one thousand dollars toward the erection of the new buildings. The two Andrews, as he called his adopted son and the Hutchings boy, attended its elementary classes. Nieces and grandnieces of Rachel pursued the genteel arts at the Nashville Female Academy.

The tradition of the sword was fading from the Hermitage family. Colonel Robert Butler and Lieutenant Andrew Jackson Donelson followed the head of their clan into retirement, Butler to restore his plantation, Donelson to study law at Transylvania University in Kentucky. "Amuse yourself occasionally, with history," counseled his uncle, "amonghst which if to be had, I would recommend to you the history of the scottish chiefs. I have always thought that sir William Wallauce . . . was the best model for a young man. In him we find a stubborn virtue, . . . too pure for corruption, . . . allways ready to brave any danger for the relief of his country or his friend."[27]

Young Mr. Donelson did not have to seek so far afield for a model. Striding the level acres of Hermitage farm was another Celtic chieftain, a man of fire and tenderness, of strong and sincere, if sometimes rash, emotions—a product of the vibrant forces that had swept him, thirty-four springs before, across the gusty Blue Ridge into the Western wilderness. He had helped to beat back that wilderness from the Mountains to the Mississippi and to raise the frontier to an almost equal partner with the seaboard in the management of public affairs. By virility, experience and, since the war, the prestige of victory, pioneers compensated for the disparity of their numbers. They lived close to the machinery of government. They had seen it made: "offices" for the registration of land titles housed in immigrant wagons, courts in log cabins; Indian wars, Indian treaties; every man a soldier and a servant of the law. Thus county governments had taken shape, and over them territorial and state régimes from which it was an easy step for the frontiersman with all the aplomb in the world to shoulder into the councils of the nation.

Yet, in 1816, the greatest of the race had drawn back from the presidency. Nor did five more years on the plinth of popularity alter his resolution. A New York editor took sly cognizance of the lingering ambition of a few of the General's friends. Jackson thrust the sheet from him. "Do they think I am such a damned fool! No sir; I know what I am fit for. I can command a body of men in a rough way; but I am not fit to be President."[28]

So the old border captain: heart-beat of a throbbing era, turning his face toward the shadows enclosing the epoch that had made him, a national hero high above the ignoble rivalries of politics.

He wrote young Captain Richard Call not to despair. Despite all that Jackson could do, this demobilized officer had been left at Pensacola without employment. "Believe me when I first met you in the field . . . my opinion was formed of you. . . . Your soldier like conduct when deserted by your company . . . drew my particular attention to you to see a gallant youth of Eighteen abandoned by his captain and company all retiring from the field of Honour, and you left alone, determined to die rather than tarnish your military fame. I regret our separation but still more I regret that injustice and inattention of the executive in not having provided for you agreeable to his promise and my expectation. But my dear Call I have been Tossed upon the waves of fortune from youthood, I have experienced prosperity and adversity. . . . It was this that forced into action all the energies of my mind. . . . Pe[r]mit me to say to you that long experience has made me well acquainted with human nature. It is well to study it as you progress through life—you will find many . . . who by their openness of conduct . . . obtain your confidence that it may be betrayed. Guard against such impositions."[29]

8

Andrew Jackson deemed that he had guarded against them well. To Mr. Monroe's affectation of regret at Jackson's determination to close his public career, the General responded with smooth civility. Before him lay a letter dated from Augusta, Georgia, and signed "FRIEND." Jackson was not a man ordinarily to lay great store by anonymous communications, but he could not deny that this one was exceptional. Six months later found him still speculating on the identity of the author.[30]

"I have long known the President of the U. States and understood his character, . . . dull and stupid—cold & selfish, . . . under the dominion of a pride so inordinate that nothing short of universal homage can satisfy. . . . Upon this pride you inflicted a wound when you consented to attend him . . . through part of his Southern & western Tour— In that journey Mʳ. President intended to play the great man, but . . . Genl. Jackson . . . attracted all eyes. . . . Hence the intrigue to get you from the Army, hence the submissiveness to a dictation from Genl Brown, Genl Scott & M^r. Crawford— hence all your measures are traversed, your recommendations neglected. . . . When you were appointed Governor of Florida they told your friends it was a compliment to you—amongst themselves they said it was *to get rid of you.* at the head of the army you were still formidable, . . . as a Govr. of a Territory, a mere colonial prefect, soon forgotten." The letter closed by saying that Crawford would be the next President "unless someone other than Adams is taken up." Jackson was urged to "rouse the western Country" to an appreciation of this posture of affairs."[31]

This was a seductive invitation for support for the cause of Calhoun, and not the last of its kind. Faithful Doctor Bronaugh, who carried his chief's resignation to Washington, wrote from the capital. "The course which M^r. Adams has pursued in relation to Callava & Fromentin does him much credit," Don José having been rebuffed and the Judge rebuked. "He is an honest and independent politician. . . . This is also [true of] M^r. Calhoun, . . . but M^r. Monroe in my opinion never acts without a view to his popularity. M^r. Adams & M^r. Calhoun on every occasion speak in the most decided approbation of all your acts in Florida."[32]

The General's withdrawal from public life had caused a vacuum not alone at Pensacola. The Eastern press continued to conjure up implications touching the presidential contest. They remembered the toast to DeWitt Clinton. Was it the mark of a covert alliance? inquired the New York *Advocate*. This was more than the retired soldier could permit to pass unchallenged, and the result was Andrew Jackson's first expression on the looming campaign of 1824. "I have an opinion of my own on all subjects, and when that opinion is formed I persue it *publickly*, regardless of who goes with me. . . . You are at liberty to say in my name to both my friends and enemies, that I will as far as my influence extends support Mr. Adams unless Mr. Calhoun should be brought forward. . . . As to Wm. H. Crawford you know my opinion I would support the Devil first."[33]

Now would they leave him to the contemplation of his fire?

THE END OF PART ONE

PART TWO

Portrait of a President

BOOK FOUR

A Reluctant Candidate

> "If I was to travel to Boston where I have been invited that would insure my election.—But I would feel degraded the balance of my life."
>
> Andrew Jackson to one of his campaign managers.

CHAPTER XXI

THE NASHVILLE JUNTO

I

THE gray weariness of winter was taking leave of the Cumberland Valley in March of 1822. Impertinent little redbud trees and graceful dogwood brightened the small-growth of the copse which screened the Hermitage from the highroad a quarter of a mile away. Northern rains had fallen and northern snows melted to swell the brown bosoms of southern rivers. The warehouses of General Jackson's two plantations were empty. His Hermitage cotton and his Melton's Bluff cotton from Alabama had begun the long journey to the sun-washed wharves of New Orleans[1] to be sold directly to forwarders, thus eliminating the takings of local middlemen which cut so deeply into the profits of planters too poor or too unenterprising to provide their own transportation.

Still, the best price this cotton could hope to command would not exceed eleven cents a pound. The dead weight of a depression in trade, which three springs before had laid in monotonous ruin the bright edifice of a fictitious prosperity, continued to press cruelly upon the West and the South. Dismal columns of sheriffs' sales, marshals' sales and notices of foreclosure and of execution darkened the pages of Nashville's newspapers; of lands and goods and slaves offered at sacrifices. Friends of General Jackson who a few years before had been reckoned as affluent in their circumstances were not exempt. The Nashville Inn was bankrupt, and former Congressman Felix Grundy advertised to sell his plantation on Mill Creek, with "a good orchard, several excellent springs and a distillery."[2] The Nashville Bank, in which General Jackson was a small shareholder, kept open its doors and paid a dividend of four per cent; but none was paid to stockholders in debt to the bank, and sixty thousand dollars in profits were sequestered to meet "probable losses by the late disastrous change in business."[3]

Similarly prudent management characterized Andrew Jackson's administration of his private affairs. Owing to his long absences from home on public business, the retired soldier's expenses had been heavy that winter, yet he was able to meet obligations with agreeable promptitude, to pay his taxes, to take advantage of a hard-times bargain now and then and, while other places were running down, to build and better about both his Tennessee and his Alabama properties. He and Rachel continued their unostentatious charities, and there were even a few luxuries for the Hermitage. His cotton shipped, Jackson placed an order with Thomas Barron & Company, wine merchants and fancy grocers of New Orleans: "4 demij mad.ª wine 64, 1 cask best claret 65, 21 Boxes Johnsons wine 22, 1 Box sp candles 13.28, 1 do Best Raisens 4.50, 1 Keg almonds 7." The General was fond of almonds, though they had no place in the diet of a man trying to rid himself of dysentery.[4]

An important aspect of life at the Hermitage was changed, however. The stalls of the great racing stable were empty. The defeat of Western Light and the DeWett mare by Jesse Haynie's Maria in 1815 had convinced General Jackson that the itinerant nature of official duties made it impossible to attend properly to the minutiae of his racers' training—and Jackson's horses ran best when prepared for their contests under the eye of the master. So gradually the stable had been sold, all excepting Truxton. Who could have sold Truxton? Jackson gave him to one of the Butlers who carried the big stallion away to Mississippi. So it was that, although the Hermitage remained as well provided with horseflesh as any plantation on the Cumberland, the animals were no longer bred or trained for the track.

But other details were much the same. Newspapers remained the General's favorite reading, and the twenty to which he subscribed protected the red carpet on the floor of his study. Despite the repeated and abrupt assertions that his retirement from public life this time was to be permanent, the name of Andrew Jackson figured in these journals almost as prominently as that of any other American. The press had not exhausted the abundant controversial possibilities of the General's tenure of the governorship of Florida; and occasionally there were even more interesting personal mentions. In January the Philadelphia *Aurora* contained an item that went the editorial rounds. This writer "understood" that there were seven candidates for the presidency. "If a choice of Clinton or Jackson could be made, then our country would prosper."[5]

To these insinuations Jackson had said nothing publicly, but his private answer was no and no and no.

Nevertheless, one Nashville and one Knoxville newspaper[6] insisted upon an answer to the question: Why this preponderance of presidential talk centering about Mr. Monroe's three Cabinet officers, Adams, Crawford and Calhoun? "The name of Andrew Jackson to a document would command more respect than the signatures of all the secretaries in the nation." Therefore, an observer might have been more than casually interested to learn that during the second week of March, 1822, Old Hickory had put his signature to the first public communication since his departure from Florida five months before. The notice was addressed to the editor of the Nashville *Whig*:

"YOUNG TRUXTON
"(*One of the best sons of the celebrated running horse Truxton, by Diomed.*)

"SIXTEEN hands and one inch high, a beautiful dark bay, of fine bone and sinew, and great in action, will stand one half of his time at my stable, where I now live, the other half of his time at the stable of Mrs. Donelson, widow of Col. Wm. Donelson, deceased . . . at the moderate price of three hundred pounds of good merchantable seed Cotton . . . or eight dollars cash. . . . His colts are finely formed, large and strong, fit for saddle or geer, or any other use . . ."

"ANDREW JACKSON."[7]

2

Rachel also glanced at the newspapers occasionally, and in her tall east chamber she, too, was engaged with a pen for she owed her niece, Mary Donelson, a letter.

"I do hope they will now leave Mr. Jackson alone." Mister, again, not General. "He is not a well man and never will be unless they allow him to rest. He has done his share for the country. . . . In the thirty years of our wedded life . . . he has not spent one-fourth of his days under his own roof. The rest of the time away, travelling, holding court, or at the capital of his country, or in camp, or fighting its battles, or treating with the Indians; mercy knows what not. . . .

"Through all such trials I have not said aye, yes or no. It was his work to do, he seemed called to it and I watched, waited and prayed most of the time alone. Now I hope this is at an end. They talk of his being President. Major Eaton, General Carroll, Mr. Campbell, the Doctor and even the Parson . . . come here to talk, talk everlastingly about his being President. In this as all else I can say only, the Lord's will be done. But I hope he may not be called again to the strife and empty honors of public place."[8]

3

Visitors continued to come and to breathe life into the topic which above all others threatened the peace of mind of Rachel Jackson. Even now a traveler was turning from the Lebanon Pike into the level lane which traversed the copse of hickory and oak and sycamore and made its way between the brick gateposts to join the driveway that led to the house.

General Jackson's caller was a friend whose fealty had withstood the changing fortunes of a quarter of a century. Moreover George Washington Campbell's name, like his present errand, bore the stamp of patriotic initiative. He was born in Scotland plain George Campbell, and while attending the College of New Jersey at Princeton he had interpolated the "Washington." Then coming to Tennessee to practice law, he presently found himself in Congress largely through the instrumentality of Judge Andrew Jackson. Those were the days when Judge Jackson, of the nabob wing of the Republican Party, was disputing for control of the state with the leathershirt wing captained by John Sevier. Through all that followed, G. W. Campbell had served the cause of his patron, and served it well, rising to become Secretary of the Treasury. Able, conciliatory, persuasive in debate and in negotiation, he yielded one point only to gain two in the end.

After General Jackson's military raid into Florida, President Monroe had looked about for a post that would get his peppery commander out of the way until the storm subsided. The embassy at St. Petersburg fell vacant. Its remoteness particularly appealed to the

THE NASHVILLE JUNTO 339

President. He consulted his venerated preceptor, Thomas Jefferson who, with incidental profanity, assured the Executive that if Andrew Jackson went to St. Petersburg we should have a quarrel with Russia in a month. So General Jackson was wheedled into accepting the governorship of Florida, where there was a quarrel in less than a month, but helpless Spain was not the empire of the Romanovs.

Thus it was that tactful George Washington Campbell, rather than the forthright frontier soldier, had journeyed to the banks of the Neva, there for three winters to endure the cold green fogs and the interminable state dinners, and to see three of his children die in one week of typhus. After this Campbell had fled to Tennessee, arriving in the autumn of 1821 when General Jackson was on his way home from Pensacola.

Before a cheerful fire the two friends lighted their pipes and found a great deal to say. Old Hickory was as firm as ever in his decision to be done with public life. He spoke of his health which was bad when he left Florida and had mended slowly. A distressing cough and inflammation of the lungs had added themselves to the dysentery contracted in the Creek campaign.

"I am no longer a young man. I can't stand the fatigues and privations I used to. George, do you realize we are getting old? I'm fifty-five!"

The returned diplomat ventured that the General was merely tired. The mission to Florida had been too much. But a few months' relaxation would restore him. Adroitly Campbell built up the concept of his friend again in the throbbing prime of his powers with new vistas of glory unfolding before him. A fact. Did not Jackson comprehend that he was "by no means safe from the presidency in 1824—"

With an arresting sweep the fingers of Old Hickory plowed his unruly gray hair. The lines of the long, appreciative face were taut. The intense blue eyes kindled.

"I really hope you don't think, George, that I'm damned fool enough to believe that!"

Then, relaxing his severity a little: "No, sir; I may be pretty well satisfied with myself in some things, but I'm not vain enough for that."[9]

The words had an air of finality, the preparations to enjoy the

Hermitage a look of permanence. Knowing well that Andrew Jackson's self-made rules of life were never so likely to set other regulations at naught as when too abruptly opposed, the listening diplomat permitted the conversation to seek its own level.

4

There was much else to speak of. Captain Alpha Kingsley had taken over the insolvent Nashville Inn, and was making a brave effort to restore the fortunes of the pleasant house of entertainment which was General Jackson's favorite place of resort when in town. . . . Sam Houston, the handsome and rather baroquely attired young lawyer, was getting on despite hard times and convivial habits. A card in the *Whig* announcing a relocation of his office assured the public that he "can be found at all times where he ought to be." Nevertheless, those who knew Sam best would continue to expect him at the sociable bar of the Nashville Inn at any time after three in the afternoon. . . . On Court House Square over J. Decker's confectionery, Rachel's protégé, Ralph E. W. Earl, the artist, had opened a "Museum of Natural and Artificial Curiosities." Among the latter were several portraits of General Jackson. . . . Despite the low state of public finances, work continued on the great bridge across the Cumberland, buoyantly voted in more prosperous times. . . . Thomas Yeatman offered cash for cotton, tobacco and "a few likely *Young Negroes*."[10] . . . But better bargains in negroes were said to be available in Kentucky, and the General had asked Andrew Jackson Donelson, still pursuing his legal studies at Transylvania University, to be on the lookout for a good buy.

In Kentucky bargains of every character awaited the purchaser so fortunate as to possess real money. The collapse in 1819 of the wildcat bank and paper currency craze had intensified the financial depression in the Ohio River Valley and the Southwest. This proved a lesson to most states, but not to Kentucky where debtors had taken charge of the Legislature. A replevin law was enacted, a new state bank erected on the ruins of the old, and its paper styled "legal tender." This money immediately fell to fifty cents on the dollar and, when a justice of the Supreme Court declared the replevin law unconstitutional, he was hauled before the Legislature for removal, which was the beginning of a long course of judge-breaking in Kentucky.

Nearly every instinct and interest of Andrew Jackson's long life set him in opposition to this undisciplined rising of the masses. As a former judge, a sound money man and a creditor rather than a debtor, the shrewd old frontier aristocrat was anxious that his namesake at Transylvania should view matters correctly. To young Mr. Donelson went another of a long series of letters of counsel: "The conduct of Kentucky . . . augurs the destruction of our republican government—for let me tell you that all the rights secured to the citizens under the constitution are worth nothing . . . except guaranteed to them by a virtuous and independent Judiciary. . . . I hope Kentucky will . . . preserve the . . . Judiciary unimpaired by faction or the designing demagogues of the day— ? which side of this does Mr. Clay take."[11]

Perhaps it discomfited the General a little to learn that Mr. Clay had taken the sound-money side.

Though Tennessee escaped some of the tribulations of economic reconstruction that beset her sister commonwealth to the north, the lines were drawn between the Haves and the Have Nots. Jackson stood with the Haves. After the crash of 1819 he had opposed the popular stampede which, taking control of the Assembly, enacted a law "staying" the collection of debts and set up loan bureaus for the relief of private debtors from public funds. The next round of the battle was fought out in the election of 1821, with the governorship as stake. Andrew Jackson's neighbor and one-time racing-stable partner, Edward Ward, bore the conservative standard against William Carroll, who espoused the cause of "the people." Viewing the contest from Florida, Old Hickory was bitter at the defection of the man he had raised from obscurity to be second in command at New Orleans; and, indeed, there was something peculiar in the sudden revelation of elegant Billy Carroll as a crusader for the poor.

Ward was pictured as a slave-holding land baron, and his college education enumerated among the reasons why an awakened electorate should reject him. As champion of the *sans culottes*, Carroll had numbers on his side, yet few anticipated the devastating nature of the triumph that awaited: Ward carried only two counties in the State.

Once Carroll was in office the dire prophecies of the conservatives remained unfulfilled, however. Instead of a revolutionist, William Carroll was proving a sagacious and practical liberal leader, deftly controlling his radical followers and, without alienating their support, averting the destructive extremes which might have swept Tennessee into the sea of troubles that engulfed Kentucky. But the shining testimonial to the Governor's skill was his reappearance at the Hermitage on what seemed to be the old basis of intimacy, and his participation in the persistent conversations that so disturbed the heart of Rachel.

5

Yet there seemed to be little tangible cause for her uneasiness. March stretched into sunny April, April into May and a month of rain. But it was warm and Mr. Decker, the confectioner, advertised "*ICE CREAMS AND ICE PUNCH* every day."[12] A journeyman dentist established himself in a room next to Sam Houston's law office. "Those who desire his services had better avail themselves of the present opportunity," ran his card in the *Whig*, "for unless business will justify him in making a permanent residence in Nashville he will leave the Western country in the ensuing fall."[13]

On one of his frequent visits, Houston brought to the Hermitage a rare tale of a duel between General John Cocke and a Mr. Darden. General Jackson's relations with the Cocke family had been singularly disappointing. Twenty-five years before he had challenged John Cocke's father, but friends intervened and prevented a meeting. Houston's story was that in this latest affair of honor Cocke had worn a bullet-proof "shield," afterwards found in a hollow tree. Sam promised to recover the shield and place "it in Mr. Earl's museum for the inspection of the curious."[14]

"Houston," declared Old Hickory, "is a truly noble-minded fellow" who deserves a seat in Congress "at our next election."[15]

This, however, was no evidence that Jackson's interest in public affairs went deeper than a desire to be of service to his friends; in particular to young men who like Sam Houston had marched in his battle-sore little armies.

To another such soldier, Captain Richard K. Call, he found occa-

THE NASHVILLE JUNTO 343

sion to express his creed of public service. Call, who had settled where Jackson left him in Florida, wrote to ask his former chief's advice about running for Congress. His election would strengthen Jackson's hand in Florida as well as in Congress, a circumstance no current candidate for the presidency could have overlooked.

The General responded that Captain Call should consider carefully before embarking on a public career. He would not thereby establish himself financially, and would lose the law practice he had created. "On the other hand society has claims on every individual who compose it, and if your country calls on you to represent her . . . you are bound to obey that call; the services of every man belongs to his country when that country requires it, and with this principle I have commenced and will end my life."[16]

Jackson's health had much improved when a cold contracted at church in Nashville,[17] brought an alarming relapse. Colonel James Gadsden, another of Jackson's subalterns now farming in Florida, wished to compile a history of the Jackson campaigns, and wrote to remind his old commander that he had promised his military files for that purpose. Old Hickory replied that he would have them collated and sent. "I resign to you my papers with great pleasure; with the request that they be . . . returned to my adopted son. . . . I have been oppressed with a violent cough and have been recently vissited with my old bowell complaint, which has weakened me very much, having . . . in the last twelve hours upwards of Twenty passages. . . . In short Sir I must take a rest or my stay on Erth cannot be long."[18]

The hand of the sick man trembled as he signed his name, but the day's writing was not done. Andrew Jackson Donelson again stood in need of advice. "Whatever may be thought of the pretentions of Mr. Clay to the presidency by the Kentuckians he has not the prospect of being elected. Virginia . . . will not support him— But my young friend keep yourself from the political vortex . . . until your age & experience will justify your country in calling you. . . . Let this be a stimulant to your application to your studies. . . . Prepare yourself for the bar and . . . be able to meet . . . even Mr. Clay in Forensic debate."[19]

Still in school were four other youngsters whom the childless couple at the Hermitage regarded as their own. Andrew, junior, the adopted son aged twelve, and his cousin, Andrew Jackson Hutchings, attended the elementary classes of Cumberland College in Nashville. Their holidays were a source of joy to Rachel and General Jackson. Lincoyer, the Creek Indian refugee, went to a country school near the Hermitage. Daniel Donelson was at West Point and on the honor roll of his class. Andrew, junior, was too immature for one to judge of his capacities, but of all the young ones—eleven or more—whom the General and Mrs. Jackson had reared and educated, "Jack" Donelson, at Transylvania University, showed the greatest promise. Each week from one to four long letters were exchanged by Old Hickory and his nephew.

"My wish is that you complete your education fully. . . . Your talents if life lasts will lead you to fill the highest stations in our Government. . . . That you may fill them with benefit to your Government and honour to yourself I have drew your attention to the Models of patriotism such as Wallace [the Scottish chieftain] and Washington."[20]

And more specifically:

"I look forward . . . to the time when you will be selected to preside over the destinies of america."[21]

6

The homecoming of United States Senator John Henry Eaton with the latest under-cover gossip from Washington gave fresh impetus to the purpose of Andrew Jackson's friends. The little group that shared his confidences was an interesting one. In all the country, boiling as it was with political intrigue in behalf of avowed candidates, it is doubtful whether one could have found the counterpart of the singular company which gathered in remote Nashville to attempt to introduce, against his will, another aspirant into the race.

There was John Overton, Old Hickory's oldest friend in Tennessee, who knew, for instance, the private secrets of Rachel's and Andrew Jackson's courtship as no other man knew them now that Lewis Robards was dead. With scarcely a ripple to mark his progress, the unobtrusive stripling lawyer who once shared a bed in a blockhouse with Prosecutor Jackson had become one of the wealthiest, wisest and quietest men in the West. Deliberately this self-effacing figure has sought to elude the vigilance of History. On his deathbed he all but obliterated the traces of his masterful hand in the campaign of 1824 by directing his son-in-law to burn before his eyes his papers, including Jackson's letters, which pertained to political subjects.[22] There was also Eaton of histrionic air, who might plume himself on having "made" Andrew Jackson Governor of Florida. Although he fell short of genius, the Senator was sufficiently adept at the political arts to keep his local colleagues *au courant* with the complicated and capricious pattern of the national situation. There was William Berkeley Lewis whose plantation lay near the Hermitage. In this drama Lewis was an actor whose motives and true rôle puzzled even his contemporaries. Better than six feet tall, with shoulders as broad as a door, he was an imposing figure. His intellectual attainments were of less heroic mold; yet there is no denying an unaccountably effective quality to the man and his works. For several years Lewis had enjoyed a small reputation as one of Andrew Jackson's confidants. In this he found a satisfaction which observed the limitations of good taste. He held no public offices and was unknown outside Davidson County. In the War of 1812 he had not gained or apparently aspired to a rank above that of commissary major.

Such was the inner circle. On the fringe were Felix Grundy, a scheming man of flexible convictions, G. W. Campbell, Sam Houston, George Wilson, editor of the Nashville *Gazette* and three or four others, not including William Carroll. With this intimate coterie the Governor was still on probation, his visits to the Hermitage and conciliatory overtures notwithstanding.

By April of 1822 the members of this junto had pretty well mapped out General Jackson's destiny. Their plan was apt because so agreeable to the temper of the hour. It was audacious because almost diametrically opposed to the position Andrew Jackson had previously maintained in politics. They meant to sweep aside precedent, ignore party machinery which they knew they could not control, and plant the flag of their man amid the restless masses groping for leadership.

Hitherto national tickets had been selected by congressional caucuses of the different parties. This system and the method of choosing electors in the various states, combined virtually to exclude the people from participation in the selection of a president. It made for party solidarity, and no other method yet devised has brought forward as nominees men of larger calibre. The caucus belonged to a day when the country was governed by leaders who imposed their will, rather than by popular men who must propitiate to preserve their prestige. Thus it was undemocratic and out of step with the times. Moreover, the disappearance of the Federalist Party made a caucus less necessary because of the lack of opposition. Meantime the lean years had made men think, made them eager to grasp the reins of government and contend against abuses by which they saw themselves ground down and their last cow taken. All this reacted against the caucus.

And the junto perceived another salient circumstance. Secretary of the Treasury William H. Crawford was the "regular" Republican candidate because he controlled most of the party machinery. In a caucus he might have more votes than the combined votes of all other aspirants. But Crawford must pay for this advantage. He must confront the mounting popular resentment against the caucus system, meanwhile bearing the responsibility for necessarily painful items of the nation's fiscal policy during a period of diminished revenues and increased taxes. He must contend also against the personal ill-will of Andrew Jackson who abided by his declaration to "support the Devil" before he would support William H. Crawford.[23]

The junto's next problem was to start the ball rolling. After much discussion, the decision was reached amid elaborate secrecy that the Tennessee Legislature would be the best agency to present Jackson's name to the nation. This would afford a sponsorship to suit the most popular palate. The present Assembly was a thoroughgoing creation of the people—so much so that two years before it had rejected as "disrespectful" a communication from General Jackson inveighing against the enactment of the stay law and loan bureau bill.

This being agreed upon, William B. Lewis said he was going to North Carolina to pay his wife's family a social visit. Mrs. Lewis's father was United States Senator Montfort Stokes of Wilkesboro who had known Andrew Jackson as a rollicking law student. Colonel John Stokes, who prepared Andy for his bar examination after another tutor had disclaimed further responsibility for the future of so wild a youth, was the Senator's brother. Major Lewis's conversations with his father-in-law turned to political topics. "I . . . found him a warm, personal friend and admirer of General Jackson," recorded the Major, "but he gave not the slightest intimation that he preferred him for the presidency. This occasioned me some uneasiness."

Lewis believed Montfort Stokes's support essential to the success of the Jackson cause in North Carolina and, when his visit was drawing to a close, nothing remained but to lay the case before the Senator "without reserve." He spoke of the quiet activities of the General's Nashville friends. Stokes was surprised. He asked if the little group really expected to place Jackson in the race.

"Unquestionably," replied Lewis, and to prove it he revealed the covert scheme for nomination by the Legislature.

The old politician was interested, but not swept off his feet by the novel proposal.

"What support," he inquired, "do his friends expect him to get, if nominated?"

"They expect him to be supported by the *whole* country," Lewis replied.

"Then," said the Senator dryly, "he will certainly be elected."

But the son-in-law had made an impression. Assuming a more serious tone, Montfort Stokes spoke of his long acquaintance with Andrew Jackson. He admired "no living man" more, but, in the forthcoming campaign he said his support was already pledged to Secretary of War John C. Calhoun.[24]

"This was very unwelcome news to me," wrote Lewis—doubly so because Lewis knew that Jackson himself, though at present for John Quincy Adams, probably would transfer his allegiance to Calhoun should the South Carolinian's name be formally brought forward.[25] The unwelcome news, however, made it plain that the junto had no time to lose. It must get the name of its man in the lists before he committed himself to Calhoun, as Stokes had done.

"Suppose," ruminated Lewis, "Mr. Calhoun should not be a candidate. Can you support the General as your next choice?"

Senator Stokes replied promptly, "Yes, with great pleasure."[26]

This conversation terminated the sojourn of Major Lewis with his wife's relations. Hurrying across the mountains he arrived in Nashville about June 1, 1822.

7

The returned emissary received pleasing news. General Jackson was in better health, and for Old Hickory health always meant activity. Even now he was absent from home, having ridden to Alabama to inspect his Melton's Bluff Plantation, and incidentally to adjust one of those difficulties which more and more had begun to disturb the tranquillity of a southern planter's days.

"50 DOLLARS REWARD

"RAN AWAY from the plantation of Gen. Andrew Jackson . . . in Franklin County (Ala) . . . Gilbert, a negro man, about 35 or 40 years of age, very black and fleshy, with a full round face, has a scar on one of his cheeks, but not recollected which. . . .

"JOHN COFFEE"[27]

The euphemisms and amenities of the black code were in the making. The word "slave" seldom met the eye or ear. One spoke of "servants," "the hands" or "the force"; and "slavery" was translated as the South's "peculiar domestic institution." Something of the oblique character of dueling correspondence came to feature the announcement of a runaway. A gentleman might lend his own name to a public offer of the services of his stud horse, but in the case of a fugitive negro his overseer or a friend usually undertook that obligation to society.

"Ran away from Col. E. Wards, a negro man named CHARLES. . . .

"CHAMBERLAYNE JONES."[28]

Notices of escaping slaves were eagerly read and discussed. The prospect of a man-hunt arouses a deep-seated instinct. Nor were the cash rewards to be overlooked. But underneath all this lay the consciousness of a threat to the economic order upon which, for better or for worse, the cotton states staked their future. The social position of the owners was sufficient to insure attention to the losses of General Jackson and Edward Ward, but features inherent in the escape itself might elevate to temporary distinction a citizen otherwise obscure.

"$250 REWARD

"A man by the name of George W. Harvy, after loitering in few days about the plantation of Maj. Thos. B. Scott . . . did on Friday last steal a remarkable likely bright mullato woman, named POLLY, about twenty years old, light hair, inclined to curl a little. . . . They will no doubt travel as man and wife as she . . . would . . . pass as a white woman. . . . They will undoubtedly try to reach the free states . . . or some Spanish Territories. . . .

"JOHN SCOTT."[29]

Harvy, a young Georgian, had been Scott's overseer. He had fallen in love with the blonde mulatto who could pass for white and they were to have a child. Scott discharged him and other employment in the neighborhood was hard to find. Harvy bought two horses and a suit of man's clothing for the girl. Waiting until the master was absent in Nashville, they made their perilous bid for happiness, apparently finding it in a new land, under a new name and, for Polly, a new race—for Major Scott's reward was never claimed.

General Jackson was an ideal slave-owner. He called the force at the Hermitage, numbering about a hundred, "the family"; and relations between the bond and the free were marked with instances of genuine and reciprocal attachment. Over the sixty slaves at Melton's Bluff, on the Tennessee River near Florence in northern Alabama, Jackson was endeavoring to establish a similarly patriarchal relationship. This proceeded slowly for the planter must deal with them through an overseer and good overseers were hard to find. Moreover the negroes themselves were suspicious. Jackson had acquired them, along with Melton's Bluff, from a former river pirate who had ruled his hands with a horsewhip.[30]

Upon learning of the flight of Gilbert, Jackson cautioned his Alabama overseer, Egbert Harris: "I have only to say, you know my disposition, and as far as lenity can be extended to these unfortunate creatures, I wish you to do so; subordination must be obtained first, and then good treatment."[31] The overseer lacked his employer's ability to handle men, and when Jackson reached Melton's Bluff three other negroes were missing. Old Hickory took command and all were recaptured; "and although I hate chains, I was compelled to place two of them in irons."[32] Meantime the stand of corn had suffered from inattention, buildings were out of repair and, in all, General Jackson was a fortnight putting matters to rights.

With that friend of friends, John Coffee, who now made his home on a neighboring plantation in Alabama, Old Hickory journeyed northward, arriving at the Hermitage on June 22 to plunge into the newspapers that had accumulated during his absence. He fumed at a political attack on John Quincy Adams, rejoicing at Adams's vigorous answer, which offered a theme for another letter of advice to Jack Donelson. "This exposure by Mr. Adams . . . has increased . . . his popularity in the west and south."[33]

8

General Jackson's absence had afforded the junto a splendid opportunity to further its aims.

The presentation of another ceremonial sword was arranged for July 4, after which Old Hickory contemplated a trial of the curative waters at Harrodsburgh Spring, Kentucky. On June 27 Felix Grundy sent a note saying that his inability to leave home obliged him to deliver in writing a message which, he intimated, he would have preferred to communicate orally. "The subject . . . is this, Your friends wish to know, whether there is any cause; unknown to them, which would render it improper . . . to exercise their own discretion . . . in bringing forward your name . . . for the office of Chief Magistrate of the United States. The General Assembly will meet next month. Then is the time to take a decisive step."[34]

General Jackson had received letters from every quarter of the Union asking the same question in one form or another. He had answered none of them. He did not answer Mr. Grundy's communication and, indeed, apparently laid it aside without a careful reading.[35]

General Jackson received his sword from the hands of Governor Carroll. This was followed by an enormous barbecue at McNairy's Spring on the purlieus of the town. Festivities closed with a ball at the Nashville Inn. Nowhere in the oratory or long round of toasts was breathed an allusion to the topic in every mind—the presidential election.

The departure for Harrodsburgh was delayed. After these ceremonies guests lingered at the Hermitage, obliging Jackson to cancel the trip to Harrodsburgh. Meantime the Legislature convened at Murfreesborough,[36] the capital, and, amid the commotion caused by the burning of the courthouse where the lawmakers held their sessions, the apparently casual arrival of Sam Houston escaped comment. Felix Grundy also was there and in his place as a member of the Lower House which took refuge in the Presbyterian Church.

The Hermitage, too, was the scene of activity. The General started to write Jack Donelson a long letter on the evils of Kentucky's banking policy, but he was unequal to more than a short note. "My cough sticks by me, and the pain in my side and shoulder [from Jesse Benton's bullet] continues." He thought that a rest and change of scene might bring relief. "I have agreed to travel with Genl Coffee next week to the Assembly and spend a few days— perhaps this may be beneficial."[37]

If Andrew Jackson had read Felix Grundy's letter, he was not dealing candidly with Rachel's nephew—a circumstance out of character with Jackson.

On the following day, July 17, the General wrinkled his brows over an item in the Nashville *Whig*.

"GREAT RACING! ! ! . . . The prize to be run for is the *Presidential Chair*. . . . There have already four states sent their nags in. Why not Tennessee put in her stud? and if so, let it be called *Old Hickory*. . . ."

Before another sun had set the Nashville *Clarion* put the case rather less breezily. "A new candidate for the Presidency, being number fifteen," would presently be brought forward by "the friends of the nation." This entrance of Andrew Jackson into the lists would serve the useful purpose of saving the other fourteen candidates from any amount of bootless exertion. For, "having done more than any man now living," continued the *Clarion* in a matter-of-fact way, General Jackson was unquestionably the choice of "the people, in justice to themselves."[38]

After reading the above, Old Hickory concluded a long letter to his former aide and military physician, James C. Bronaugh, in which the presidential question was disposed of briefly. "You will see from the papers that my name has been brought forward. To every application to me, I give the same answer—that I have never been a candidate for any office. I never will. . . . But when the people call, the Citizen is bound to render the service required. I think Crawford is lost sight of. . . . I am told Mr. Adams is at present the strongest in this state."[39]

The proposed visit to the capital was abandoned, the General explaining to Jack Donelson that he had received a "hint" of what was in the wind.[40] It appears that Old Hickory had got around to reading Grundy's letter.

Meanwhile, at Murfreesborough, the junto's plan went forward. On July 20, 1822, Representative Pleasant M. Miller of Knoxville, a son-in-law of William Blount, Andrew Jackson's first political mentor across the mountains, placed the following before the Lower House of the Legislature:

"The members of the general assembly of . . . Tennessee, taking into view the great importance of the selection of a suitable person to fill the presidential chair . . . have turned their eyes to *Andrew Jackson,* late major-general in the armies of the United States. In him they behold the soldier, the statesman, and the honest man; . . . calm in deliberation, cautious in decision, efficient in action. . . . " Therefore, "*Resolved* . . . that the name of major-general Andrew Jackson be submitted to the consideration of the people of the United States . . ."[41]

The ayes were unanimous.

Old Hickory received the news with little show of interest. He made no public acknowledgment, writing privately to Bronaugh: "I have never been an applicant for office. I never will. . . . I have no desire, nor do I expect ever to be called to fill the Presidential chair, but should this be the case . . . it shall be without exertion on my part."[42]

Affairs at Murfreesborough, however, were not unfolding according to the design of the junto. The Lower House had behaved handsomely, but the obstinacy of the Senate presented difficulties to which day after day of silence gave embarrassing emphasis. The pride that Tennesseans, irrespective of caste, had in their first citizen was insufficient to overcome, at once, the resentment of some of these legislators over Jackson's unparliamentary characterization of their hard-times emergency laws.

Not until August 3 did the senators appear well enough in hand

ANDREW JACKSON
President of the United States 1829-1837
From a portrait made at the White House in 1835 by Ashel B. Durand,
now owned by the New York Historical Society.

Jackson in Florida

A pencil sketch, owned and copyrighted by Emil Edward Hurja of Washington, D. C. The artist was William Henry Rinehart.

THE NASHVILLE JUNTO 353

for the manipulators to chance a vote. Then the resolution was adopted unanimously, though rather than vote aye and lacking courage to vote nay, "some one or two gentlemen quit the house."[43] Glowering down from his six-feet-six, the ordinarily urbane and always stylishly waist-coated Sam Houston eyed the recalcitrants darkly. "They will repent this!" he said.[44]

CHAPTER XXII

A Grass Hat

I

THE New York *Evening Post* observed that if the country were under martial law General Jackson by all means would be the best man for President.[1] This not being the case, the *Post* continued its cordial allusions to Secretary of the Navy Smith Thompson, one of a treeful of early birds.

In general, however, editors remained on the fence, waiting for time to diminish their problem by narrowing down the field of aspirants. "Not one in fifty," complained the Knoxville *Register*, "have *come out*."[2] The *Columbian Observer* of Philadelphia presented three-quarters of a column of florid encomium of Jackson's career as a soldier though, alack, no syllable on the topic so dear to the hearts of the Nashville Warwicks.[3]

Nearer home several issues of Salisbury's *Western Carolinian* passed over in silence the action of the Tennessee Legislature, while continuing to criticize Crawford's administration of the Treasury, assail the caucus, and give other indications of an impulse to take up the battle of the common man. Eventually the coup at Murfreesborough was noticed with a commendation of General Jackson's military services. As to the presidency, however, this influential newspaper "could point to several men who are greatly preferable." Old Hickory might be a dependable pilot in a storm, but "in times of tranquility and with brisk and favorable gales we should greatly fear he would carry too much sail."[4] All of which bore the threatening aspect of preparing the way for a declaration in favor of John C. Calhoun, whom Nashville's schemers saw as their most dangerous competitor in North Carolina.

Except in Tennessee, the opening gesture of the junto had not achieved a "good press."

2

The gray-haired soldier seemed sincerely unconcerned. "Believe me my Dr Andrew," he assured Rachel's nephew. General Jackson never addressed his namesake as Jack. "Believe me my Dr Andrew I never had a wish to be elevated . . . to the executive chair. . . . My sole ambition is to pass to my grave in retirement. But as the Legislature of my state has thought proper to bring my name forward without consulting me, I mean to be silent—and let the people do as seemeth good unto them."[5]

Silence, of course, was not refusal. It merely conformed to Jackson's rule of conduct not to seek a public office or to shun a public responsibility. Yet, beneath a calm exterior the quick blood of the old warrior stirred a little. The man who had never, in season or out declined a challenge, took a quiet satisfaction in construing the action of the Legislature as a fling at Crawford and the congressional caucus.[6]

Jack Donelson did not share his uncle's indifference to the Legislature's nomination. Anxious to be in the thick of things, he wrote of abandoning his studies and returning to the Hermitage. Although Jackson needed the services of a secretary, he suggested that young Donelson keep to his books. "The Presidential election will not give me either trouble or pain."[7] The General asked for details of the law course at Transylvania. "It is sheer Legal knowledge, abstracted from Politicks, that I wish you to learn—not the absurd doctrine that the Legislature is the people."[8]

The Legislature not the people! Had the statesmen at Murfreesborough suspected such heresy more than one or two of them would have braved Sam Houston's scowl. For Jackson had expressed the conservative and not the popular thought of the country. What a morsel that would have been for the Messrs. Crawford, Adams, Calhoun and Clay, as each, mindful of the awakening of the masses, strove to clothe himself in the garments of the people's true and original friend.

3

Notwithstanding the timidity of editors, some political entrepreneurs did not fail to perceive that a national hero, the common man's toast on all occasions, might cut a wide swath in a campaign in which the substratum seemed determined to play a leading rôle. Mr. Clay was especially anxious about the western vote, but before he could decide what to do James Monroe had undertaken to maneuver Old Hickory gracefully out of the race. The President availed himself of a method employed once before, when he found the Florida governorship a handy means of relieving himself of Andrew Jackson's overshadowing presence—a stratagem rendered the more innocent in appearance by the collaboration of John Henry Eaton. The first week in January, 1823, the Senator from Tennessee again was summoned to the Executive Residence. This time the President flattered him with an exposition of our relations with Mexico.

The Mexican question was a stepchild of the Florida problem, so expeditiously solved by Jackson's military raid and the hardly less robust diplomacy of John Quincy Adams. To smooth the ruffled feathers of Spain, and to accommodate our own expansionists who wanted Florida in a big hurry, Adams had incorporated in the treaty of annexation a clause recognizing the Sabine River as the boundary between the United States and Mexico, thus relinquishing a shadowy claim to the Rio Grande. At the moment, Jackson had consented to this;[9] only to regret it when the West set up a howl, for the eyes of our pioneers were on the fertile savannas of Texas. Our desire for Texas prompted Mr. Monroe to suggest to Senator Eaton the advisability of the preliminary of sending a minister to Mexico City; and for this post who was better qualified by experience than Andrew Jackson? No one was better qualified, yet the case presented certain perplexing difficulties. "He has been nominated for President," blandly continued the Executive, "and you know he has my good wishes." But, pursued Mr. Monroe, "I'm afraid it may be thought & said if nominated for the Mexican mission that it is done . . . to get him out of the way."

To this entirely true statement, Eaton replied that while "some might say so the genl would impute nothing of the sort."[10] The Senator asked for time in which to consult Jackson's friends, and a few days later returned to give his acquiescence to the appointment. At the same time Eaton gave Jackson his first intimation of what had happened. "If you accept, well and good; if not, no disservice will be produced."[11]

The Senator understated the case. A refusal would be tantamount to an announcement of Jackson's readiness to stand for the presidency. But Eaton was careful to leave with Monroe the impression that the General would accept.

The nomination of Andrew Jackson to be Envoy Extraordinary and Minister Plenipotentiary to Mexico was confirmed by the Senate and the formal commission dispatched to the Hermitage with a personal letter from the President. "I have intended this as a new proof of my confidence in your integrity and patriotism and of your ability to execute a very high and important trust. Should you accept it, you will be put aboard a public vessel with your family." Mr. Monroe explained that Senator Eaton had been consulted "on the propriety of making . . . the nomination in respect to yourself at this interesting moment" and that he favored it "decidedly."[12]

4

These exercises in statecraft coincided with the marketing of the Hermitage cotton crop which, in the early spring of 1823, seemed to absorb General Jackson to the exclusion of all other matters. The quiet life of the Hermitage was restoring the planter's health. He would have avoided the local celebration of the anniversary of the Battle of New Orleans had he been able to do so politely. "You know I am opposed to pomp & parade but," he added honestly, "the sincere approbation of the community must be acknowledged to be gratifying. . . . I see in the last Intellegencer that Mr J. Q. Adams has given Mr Clay a severe dressing. . . . You will see in the quill of Mr Adams a happy nack at satire."[13]

The severe dressing had failed, however, to diminish the energy with which Henry Clay pursued the presidency. The Kentuckian had joined Crawford and Calhoun in rendering obsolescent the code established by General Washington when the office sought the man. With little concealment these aspirants personally directed their campaigns. Mr. Monroe's proposal to send Jackson to Mexico sharpened the efforts of Mr. Clay to obtain the western vote without division. The Kentucky Legislature answered the Assembly of Tennessee with a resolution endorsing its favorite, and missionary work to the same end was begun in Ohio, Missouri, Alabama and Louisiana. Jackson's perfect silence, his failure to give his closest friends a sign which the freemasonry of politics might identify as conveying tacit approval of their labors, strengthened the cause of Mr. Clay and cheered his adherents.

Cautiously Clay scouts infiltrated through Tennessee. When the Legislature of Ohio nominated Mr. Clay, Governor William Carroll of Tennessee sent the Kentuckian a letter of felicitation, expressing regret that the Alabama Legislature should have adjourned without taking similar action. "If General Jackson should cease to be a competitor," continued the Governor, "you may rely with the utmost confidence on the support of Tennessee. . . . In a conversation with Mr. Grundy a few days ago he assured me that if the prospects of General Jackson became hopeless he would be for you and that he would endeavor to have you nominated at the next meeting of our Legislature."[14] Felix Grundy was never the most constant of men, and just now he and General Jackson found themselves on opposite sides of a land controversy.

So far so good, but the eastern post brought from Congressman Henry Shaw of Massachusetts, working in the Clay interest there, a picture of the situation drawn on a larger canvas. This placed the Jackson candidacy in a different light. One hundred and thirty-two electoral votes were necessary for a choice, and at present Crawford appeared to have one hundred and fourteen, Adams was a distant second with forty-eight; next Clay, forty-one—Kentucky, Missouri, Illinois, Indiana and Ohio; next Calhoun, thirty-nine—South Carolina and Pennsylvania; and lastly Jackson, nineteen—Tennessee, Mississippi, Alabama and Louisiana. The question of the withdrawal of either Jackson or Calhoun was a delicate one at present, however. Mr. Shaw quoted Daniel Webster as saying that "at heart" Massachusetts preferred Calhoun to Adams, who would be the only beneficiary of the withdrawal of Calhoun at this time. The withdrawal of Jackson, continued Shaw, would present Crawford with six votes from Tennessee and two or three from Mississippi, bringing the votes of the Secretary of the Treasury to the dangerous aggregate of one hundred and twenty-three or twenty-four.[15] Thus the need for caution in any attempt to disperse the Jackson following or to remove the General from the race.

Old Hickory a stalking horse for Henry Clay: a piquant speculation to say the least. Yet the suggestion of Congressman Shaw contained a good deal of common sense, and in the political arena stranger things have come to pass.

A similarly complacent attitude toward the Jackson movement was imputed to Adams and Calhoun,[16] who preferred to see a body of western votes temporarily in the hands of a man who showed no sign of going through with the canvass than to see them pledged to an aggressive rival like Crawford. The Florida campaign furnished the basis of the hope each of these gentlemen entertained of becoming the ultimate beneficiary of the Jackson activity in the West. Adams's support of Jackson in Florida had been courageous and real. To no other man in the Government was Old Hickory so deeply indebted. Mr. Calhoun's support existed largely in the domain of expedient afterthought. In the secrecy of those warm Cabinet discussions of the summer of 1818, the Secretary of War had been outspoken against Jackson's imperial behavior. But, as the popular tide swung in the soldier's favor, Mr. Calhoun swung with it and began an umbrageous courtship of the commander of the Southern Division. Beguiled into the belief that all along Calhoun had stood with him on the Florida issue, Jackson viewed with favor the progress of Calhoun's prospects in the West.[17] Punctually the Secretary of War had accepted at face value Jackson's coolness to the Murfreesborough resolutions, explicitly writing the General, "It will be manifest in six months that I am the only man from slave holding states that can be elected."[18]

This situation enhanced interest in the proffered mission to Mexico. Should Jackson accept, it would be necessary for Clay, Adams and Calhoun to revise their plans of campaign in the West. And the Nashville junto's exhilarating vision would dissolve entirely.

5

John Henry Eaton continued to cruise about Washington, interviewing Jackson's friends as to the advisability of accepting the Mexican appointment. Mr. Adams unselfishly favored it. So apparently did the others to whom Eaton spoke, excepting only Mr. Calhoun who thought the General could better serve his country by remaining at home.[19] As the Secretary of War imagined, this might better serve his own cause, too.

Old Hickory himself considered the subject with care, soliciting the opinions of Joel R. Poinsett, our soundest authority on Latin-American affairs, and of Mrs. Jackson. Reasoning from different premises, each offered the same advice.

"I have the pleasure," General Jackson scrawled to the President with more than his usual haste, "to acknowledge recpt. of your letter.... I cannot accept.... Under the present revolutionary state of Mexico, caused by the despotic acts of Iturbide [who had overthrown the republic and proclaimed himself emperor] ... the app of a minister from the United States ... might help Tyrant Iturbide in rivitting ... Despotism upon his country.... Added to this Mrs Jackson could not be prevailed on to go."[20]

The Nashville junto took a deep breath, congratulated their chief upon his decision,[21] and sedulously spread the impression that the refusal of the diplomatic appointment made Jackson a receptive candidate. The General himself could not have been blind to this. During the progress of the Mexican negotiations Eaton himself had said as much, writing letters such as no man would address to Old Hickory without knowledge that the General's early aversion to presidential politics was undergoing a change. One of these communications revealed how well the scheming Senator understood the temperamental weaknesses of his patron.

"It is incumbent on you therefore to act with the caution that belongs to you.... Commit not your opinions; nor let the malevolence whatever insinuating shape it may assume, drag you into any *news paper* controversy. Already are Mr. Crawfords folks seeking to convey the idea that you have not consented to be placed before the nation.... The enquiry has several times been made of me

& I have generally replied that ... you would not decline any call of your country. ... Should any man of standing and character address you on the subject I suggest ... a reply ... in sentiment & language like this. 'That you had at no period of your life sought ... after office ... and ... altho ... retired ... from public service ... yet if your country should think it in your power to ... promote her happiness it would be a departure from the uniform course of your life to refuse.'"[22]

6

Governor Billy Carroll had a clear right to support Mr. Clay or anyone else he might prefer, but to make that support effective while still professing friendship for General Jackson called for strict heed to the rules of discretion. Difficult as it was for Andrew Jackson's intent nature to see good in those who opposed him, nevertheless there were occasions when he respected an open adversary. But duplicity he could never condone. Therefore, when Carroll elected to write letters in Henry Clay's behalf, he should have selected his confidants with care. He did not do this, for the substance of his letters was at once relayed to the Hermitage. Old Hickory took fire, exhibiting an interest in the campaign which the overtures of all his friends had been unable to elicit.

"Carroll has been writing ... that Clay will get the unanimous vote of Tennessee. I mean at first oportunity to shew the Governor this letter. ... His friends shall also see it, and I suppose the individuals of Tennessee will inquire by what right he attempted to give lye to the expression of the Legislature of the state."[23]

A kind word for the Murfreesborough resolutions! The quotation is from a letter to John Coffee in Alabama, which continued: "Should the people take up the subject of my nomination in the south, and west, as they have in Pennsylvania they will soon undeceive Mr. Clay's friends. If the people of Alabama, Mississippi, and Louisiana, follow the example of Pennsylvania, they will place Clay and Crawford ... *Dehors the political combat.*"[24]

John Coffee had been in Nashville when the Murfreesborough plan was hatched. If, with the Nashville junto, he had suffered on account of Jackson's want of enthusiasm for that work of art, now he had an oil for his wounds. Clay and Crawford must be defeated. To this end Jackson was ready to go to the extremity of permitting the use of his name as a candidate. Moreover he had made a specific recommendation: "Follow the example of Pennsylvania."

7

Had the foremost political seers of the generation sat at Andrew Jackson's elbow as he wrote they could have imparted no better advice than to follow the example of Pennsylvania. The fact that Old Hickory should have discerned this is tribute to his intuition and evidence of the fact that, from the quiet of his study, he had followed the vagrant currents and source-springs of the campaign with more penetration than his ambitious friends had dared to hope.

Pennsylvania favored a protective tariff, internal improvements at the expense of the Federal Treasury, and sound banking. Calhoun and Clay were both high-tariff, internal-improvements and sound-banking men; and Mr. Clay had dramatized these issues more effectively than any other American in public life. Further to enhance his attractions in the eyes of Pittsburgh especially, Harry Clay was a Westerner, at home in the vernacular of trans-Appalachia and reflecting its social outlook with his fast horses, his game cocks and his devotion to the pleasures of the taproom. These virtues would appear to have given him an advantage over Mr. Calhoun who lacked them, but such had not proved to be the case. One reason was the bringing forward, by Tennessee, of the name of Andrew Jackson, known friend of Calhoun and known foe of Clay.

Unlike Nashville, Pittsburgh supporters of General Jackson were not embarrassed by the propinquity of the General himself, throwing cold water on their efforts. Andrew Jackson was known to Pittsburgh as early as 1795 when he transshipped there, from wagons to flagboats, merchandise destined for the trading post at Hunter's Hill. When the war brought Jackson fame, Pittsburgh recalled and embroidered these half-forgotten visits. James Riddle, Jackson's old bootmaker, whose native wisdom had elevated him to the bench of the court of common pleas, had many a tale to tell. Robert J. Walker, a twenty-one-year-old lawyer, David Lynch, a tobacco forwarder, and Robert Steele, a storekeeper, listened to these stories and formed a "Jackson Committee" in Pittsburgh. Their advertising agent was Edward Patchell, a coal miner and nomadic preacher without parish, who ranged the countrysides expounding the glory of Jehovah and of Andrew Jackson.

The response, as one of Mr. Patchell's associates admitted, was limited to "the lower and middle classes of society"[25]—small farmers, miners, river men and artisans. Jackson committees multiplied and began to call mass meetings. Such a gathering in Pittsburgh formally considered the question of the presidency. "Wm. H. Crawford received one vote, H Clay five, J. Q. Adams two, J. C. Calhoun four and Gen Andw Jackson upward of 1000."[26] A meeting at Harrisburg made the choice of Jackson unanimous, and H. W. Peterson, a barkeeper, wrote to ascertain if the General approved of his name "being used at this time as a candidate."[27]

Andrew Jackson had received similar communications almost without number, many of them from persons well situated in life. He had replied to none. Yet he answered Mr. Peterson, apparently without knowing anything more about him than his name. The nature of this response suggests that the political advice of Senator John Henry Eaton had not fallen on barren soil. Another significant fact is that the copy of the letter found in Jackson's files after his death is in the handwriting of Major William Berkeley Lewis, charter member of the Nashville junto.

The letter bears the date of February 23, 1823, which was four days after the Mexican mission had been declined. The General began by reiterating that he had been "richly repaid" for his services to his country, and longed only to perpetuate his retirement and "be a spectator merely of passing events." Yet—"my undeviating rule of conduct through life . . . has been neither to seek or decline public invitations to office. . . . As the office of Chief Magistrate of the Union . . . should not be sought, . . . so it cannot, with propriety, be declined. . . . It was with these impressions, I presume, . . . that the Members of the Legislature of Tennessee . . . thought it proper to present my name. . . . My political creed prompts me to leave the affair uninfluenced by any expression on my part . . . to the free will of those who have alone the right to decide."

"H. W. Peterson   "Your obedient, &c
                                                ANDREW JACKSON"[28]

When this momentous communication reached Harrisburg John M. Farland, an unemployed newspaperman, got his hands on it long enough to strike out the name of Mr. Peterson and substitute "Dauphin County Committee." In this form the letter reached the Harrisburg *Commonwealth* from whose columns it was quickly reproduced by the press of the whole country.[29]

Hitherto John Farland has been overlooked in the scramble to discover those responsible for General Jackson's political career. He has his place. The democratic genesis of the Jackson movement in Pennsylvania had been established beyond the necessity of addressing the candidate's formal announcement to the proprietor of a river-front grogshop.

8

Though his ardor to crush Crawford and Clay seemed to transcend any expectation of winning himself, Andrew Jackson had lifted his eyes to the hills. His acquiescence in the rôle of candidate gave the campaign the external form it was to exhibit to the country until election time. The contest of 1824 beheld the meeting and parting of two political generations. It witnessed the opening of the schisms that were to wreck the Republican Party and remold it, Andrew Jackson's violent moderation superseding the mild radicalism of Thomas Jefferson as the swelling, dividing, diverging stream of American life swept toward the climactic cataracts of the 'Thirties. Superficially the contest wore the aspect of a clash of personalities rather than of issues. Nevertheless, early in 1823, it was possible to distinguish differences of principle as well as of personality in four of the five aspirants among whom it was now apparent that the country must choose a president.

The first candidate invariably considered was Secretary of the Treasury William H. Crawford who, though the field was united against him as against no other man, entered the spring of 1823 the leading contender.

The greatest strength of Crawford lay in the tactical position into which he had maneuvered his cause. He asserted himself to be the "regular" candidate of the party, the only "true Jeffersonian." The claim to regularity was vindicated by control of the machinery of the party and insistence on the traditional caucus method of nomination which he, alone of the candidates, could dominate. The claim to authenticity as a Jeffersonian was vouched for by the support of the sage of Monticello himself; and the adhesion of venerable James Madison made Crawford veritably the candidate of the fading Virginia Dynasty which, through a working agreement with New York, had controlled the presidency for twenty-four years. The political dictator of New York, Martin Van Buren, respected that ancient understanding, and, setting his face against strong popular pressure, prepared to deliver the State's vote to Crawford by virtue of his whip hand over the Legislature.

So much for Crawford's political strength. His popular strength was not coextensive, being limited in the main to the southern aristocracy which honored the Secretary as a state-rights advocate, opposed to a tariff and internal improvements. Actually his utterances on these issues were evasive so as not to make the burden of his northern supporters, particularly Van Buren, any heavier.

Crawford was a southern man, born in an impoverished but genteel family in Virginia, and reared in Georgia where he won his way back among the people of his own class, the final victory being a marriage into the manor-house nobility. Boyhood had been a struggle: to obtain a classical education; to support a widowed mother and a cluster of sisters and brothers; to restore his family to its place in the social scale. In every case he had triumphed. The battle had left no scars, but on the other hand had imparted understanding and a hearty approach to men in every walk of life. Crawford was a giant in size, in muscular strength and mental vitality. A mellow sense of humor and a booming laugh took the sharpness out of an otherwise too persistent ambition which on occasions did not hesitate at intrigue to promote its ends. Lacking the statesmanlike breadth of John Quincy Adams or of Calhoun, Crawford was as intently self-seeking as the latter, though the easy camaraderie of his manner helped to disguise it.

During a time of trial William H. Crawford had been a satisfactory Secretary of the Treasury, but in hard times that post is ill-calculated to engender popular enthusiasm. Mr. Crawford's commitment to a caucus was a source of weakness as well as strength and placed attractive cards in the hands of his adversaries. The appeal of his principles was limited to the wealthy class of the South. His support in other quarters, though impressive, was in the hands of politicians against whom the tide was rising.[30]

9

The aspirant second to Crawford in 1823 was John Quincy Adams.

With DeWitt Clinton eliminated in his own state by the dexterity of Martin Van Buren, Adams was the only northern candidate in the race. This was a source of much prestige and placed him first among the voters of New England and New York as well, though Mr. Van Buren had no intention of giving New York's voters a voice in the selection of presidential electors. Mr. Adams's friendly attitude toward the tariff and internal improvements helped him in the Middle States and in the West. He despised slavery and all its works but, abiding by the Missouri Compromise, confined his acidulous observations to the privacy of his diary.

No candidate possessed higher proved qualifications or was as generally respected by his adversaries; and in all but the final stages of the contest no candidate adhered more faithfully to the vanishing school of political ethics which precluded a display of personal interest in his fortunes. John Quincy Adams belonged to the generation of the founding fathers, having served every president since Washington. He made admirers but not friends. Looking at himself as objectively as he would look at a problem of government he discerned the reason. "I am a man of reserve," reads the diary, "cold, austere and forbidding manners. My political adversaries say a gloomy misanthrope; and my personal enemies an unsocial savage. With a knowledge of the actual defects in my character, I have not the pliability to reform it."

In this campaign, as always, he stood much alone. "An undercurrent of calumny has been flowing in every direction adapting its movements to the feelings and the prejudices of the different parts of the country. It has a story for Pittsburg and a story for Portland, a misrepresentation for Milledgeville and a lie for Lexington. . . . I have no countermining at work. . . . I make no bargains. I listen to no overtures for coalition. I give no money. I push no appointments of canvassing partisans to office."³¹

Thus did Mr. Adams put the case for himself, and put it rather too well. J. Q. Adams wanted the presidency more than he had wanted anything in his starved and singular life—but he was slow to make up his mind to adopt the most effective means of getting it. Yet, like Crawford and Calhoun he had his newspaper in Washington, the aggressive *National Journal*. Like his rivals, he found loans for his editors and public printing for their columns. And eventually Mr. Adams was to go much farther than that.

10

With Crawford carrying the frayed banner of old-line Republicanism and Adams steering a middle course, Secretary of War John Caldwell Calhoun strode forth a frank champion of the "new" school of Jeffersonians developed by the war. Of late years hard times and the consequent drift back to sectionalism had tended to outmode the "new" school; but the Hamiltonian sweep of Calhoun's nationalism and the challenging vigor of his advocacy served to recapture, for the moment, something of the one-for-all-and-all-for-one spirit of 1811.

Even South Carolina, by logic the property of Crawford, was carried away. The Palmetto State might rebel at the moderate tariff and public improvements views of J. Q. Adams; but sentimental pride in the brilliance of a native son prevailed over the extreme position of Calhoun on those same issues. In North Carolina, too, the Secretary of War promised to give his colleague of the Treasury the battle of his life. In New England Calhoun was the only candidate with a chance against Adams, being particularly strong with former Federalists angered by the "desertion" of the statesman from Braintree on the war question. "He is conceded," declared one enthusiastic supporter, "*almost* a northern man."³²
A newspaper in New York City came out for Calhoun, increasing the concern of Mr. Van Buren. His high tariff and improvement policies had early captured the party organization in Pennsylvania, where the spontaneous Jackson manifestations were looked upon

as helpful backfire against the encroachments of Clay. As to the West, Calhoun had Jackson's word for it that he stood first in the hearts of the frontiersmen.

As 1823 opened Crawford, though leading, had ceased to gain. Adams gained slowly. But Calhoun's fortunes appeared to be distinctly on the rise. An untoward accident to the Adams cause or to that of Mr. Clay and the presidency seemed within the grasp of the eager South Carolinian. He pursued his ambition a little less openly than Clay. He was not yet forty-one, a grave, restless being, of whom a friend said, "I have never heard him utter a jest."

II

Next, Henry Clay, Speaker of the House of Representatives, a "Kentucky gamester in politics"; tall, angular, careless of attire and rather unfavored of countenance yet, withal, the most personable of the condidates.

He was born in Virginia during the Revolution, the son of a hand-to-mouth rural clergyman who also gave dancing lessons. Fatherless at four, orphaned at seventeen, Harry Clay had made his way in a world ever responsive to the charms of an engaging temperament and the sheen of a mind so quick and so apt as to find little need for exercises in depth. As a barrister, an hour's preparation sometimes would suffice to dazzle a jury and rout a less agile adversary who had spent weeks methodically formulating a case. So natural was his behavior that Mr. Clay was said to be the only man who, while arguing before the United States Supreme Court, could walk to the bench and take a pinch of snuff from one of the boxes reserved for the use of the justices.

In 1811 the War Hawks had huzzaed him into the speakership of the House which, under his flashing leadership, plumped a country picturesquely unready into war. He represented that spirit now but only in the West was he able to make headway against Calhoun who stood for the same things. From the first his candidacy was almost purely local, and never able to rise above it. His friends early saw that the best chance for victory lay in throwing the choice into the House where the influence of the Speaker remained paramount. To achieve this he must neatly divide the vote of the West with General Jackson and, in any event, strive to keep a single western vote from his other rivals.

12

These were the four leading contenders when his letter to Harrisburg definitely added the name of General Jackson to the roll.

All his life Andrew Jackson had been something of a law unto himself, stripping of their usual authority the conventions that govern the commonality of mankind. It was so with Jackson the candidate. Other aspirants might be northern men or southern men or western men, but not Jackson. Policies and principles might bait and bedevil *them*, but not Jackson. Where did he stand on the tariff? He did not say and no one else attempted to say. Internal improvements? The same. Caucus? Against it, of course. Currency and banking? Jackson was a sound money man identified with the economic group supporting the Bank of the United States: not a very flattering recommendation for a candidate of the western proletariat. Did it make any difference with Jackson? Not appreciably. Did his silence on tariff or improvements make any difference? None.

As "the nation's hero" he was above such things. In good time no doubt the General would consent to tell the people all they needed to know.

Thus far he had said that he did not wish the office and would do nothing to obtain it, but if elected, he would serve from a sense of duty. He said no more and this Roman reticence became more formidable than all the words of his fretting rivals. What call for words from one whose deeds shaped so large? Did not the world know Andrew Jackson to be infallible in decision and instantaneous in action; that victory was his habit and the republic's glory his diadem? Mr. Adams had drawn the mantle of an aloof dignity about him, but as yet Adams stood almost alone whereas a corps of the ablest politicians of the day was silently surrounding Jackson. They caught the possibilities of their man's unique deportment. While others offered controversial issues, they offered an axiom: Old Hickory, the Nation's Hero and the People's Friend.

13

The pulse of the campaign beat faster. First to feel the changed tempo was Calhoun, still addressing affable letters to the Hermitage while his eyes turned toward Pennsylvania, the keystone of his hopes. A friend penned a cheerful report. "Pennsylvania unquestionably will support Calhoun. . . . The movements for Jackson have been made by the grog shop politicians & the rabble. . . . A republican convention will be called, which will secure a fair expression of the popular voice, & . . . nominate Calhoun."[33]

Supporters of Mr. Clay, too, found the Jackson candidacy exhibiting more life than they had bargained for. In Pennsylvania "Gen. Jackson has so possessed the public mind that your friends have been unable to make much headway. . . . He is supported by exactly that school . . . who would otherwise have been for you."[34] In Alabama a veritable "contagion" for Jackson was "spreading largely through the influence of Gen Coffee. . . . Your friends have at present a difficult part to play. Believing that Gen Jackson will not finally be a candidate we have deemed it bad policy to give the slightest offense."[35]

On the whole, though, Clay remained hopeful of sufficient western votes to enable him to fight the final round of his battle on the familiar floor of the House. Thomas Hart Benton was in Tennessee again. That State had seen little of Benton since 1813 when he changed his residence to Missouri as a consequence of a tavern brawl in which Andrew Jackson's arm was broken by a bullet. In St. Louis he had improved as a marksman, killing his man in a duel and eventually winning a seat in the United States Senate. Mr. Benton now toured the West in the quiet interest of Mr. Clay. "Jackson out of the way . . . Tennessee will go for you,"[36] he wrote.

In Baltimore William H. Crawford also strove to trade upon the popularity of the soldier. A pro-Calhoun observer on the Chesapeake sized up the situation in this way: "I am pretty confident that unholy bargains have been made for votes. . . . Friends of Mr. Crawford here will get up a ticket for Jackson to divide" the opposition.[37] The South Carolinian professed to be undisturbed. "An effort is making for Jackson in the City of Washington," he wrote. "This will do no harm. . . . The interest both of Mr C--d & Mr Clay is greatly distressed. . . . The rise of Genl Jackson will be fatal to the latter."[38]

When he penned these grave lines, Mr. Calhoun was in greater distress than either Crawford or Clay. A serious and unexpected blow had fallen in Pennsylvania where the state convention, held March 4, 1823, and upon which the immediate prospects of the entire Calhoun campaign depended, had declined to endorse the Secretary of War. Up to the moment the delegates took their places, Mr. Calhoun had hoped for a nomination there. His workers in other states had been assured of it. The voice of Pennsylvania was to sweep hesitant North Carolina and New Jersey into the Calhoun fold. It was to inaugurate a drive upon Maryland, New York and New England. George M. Dallas had journeyed from Philadelphia to Harrisburg to transmit to the country the pleasing intelligence that would set this machinery in motion.

He transmitted news of a stunning reverse, for the convention passed over the presidential question in silence, limiting its labors to the selection of a State ticket.[39] Though Calhounites assuaged their disappointment as best they could, it was difficult to conceal the fact that the South Carolinian's keystone had cracked.

14

Aunt Rachel's favorite sister Jane Hays, whose hospitable blockhouse beside the Cumberland once sheltered the unhappy wife of Lewis Robards, had left the valley that was her home for forty years to share the rigors of a new frontier in western Tennessee with her married son Samuel. When the longing for familiar scenes and faces become too acute she would write a letter.

"How does my dear sister Jackson do. I cannot take up my bonnet and meet you at sister Betsys or sister Marys, . . . smoke our pipes, laugh and talk over occurrences of former days, each one taking the words out of the others mouth. . . . It was a pleasant neighborhood. . . . You will regret leaving it sister Jackson and your fine farm and comfortable house, for the city of Washington when the General is elected President, for there is no doubt of his election from the present popular opinion. I hear you are about to build a church in the neighborhood, this will add to its pleasantness, but you will miss our good Mr. Hodge. O, how often I think of him hovering over the sick bed of my dear departed husband. . . . You may get more flowery speakers, but none that will disseminate the truths of the Gospel with more faithfulness.

"I hope you wont give out your intention of visiting us. I have right comfortable cabins, plenty of chickens, flow in milk and butter, the barrens abound with strawberrys— hurtleberrys abundant in the swamps, sloes, service berrys and grapes— do come and see us. You shall be met by the Hickory Guards, styled in honor of your General. . . . The uniform is very handsome, a hickory leaf wrought on the skirts of the coat."[40]

Yes, Rachel would have enjoyed a visit with her Sister Hays—all except the Hickory Guards She envied Jane's seclusion and gratefully would have exchanged the Hermitage for a cabin in the woods, there to enjoy the society of her husband free of the intrusions of a tale-bearing world.

True, the Hermitage neighborhood was to have its church house. Though not a church member, General Jackson had made the largest contribution to the erection of this edifice, where Rachel could kneel in pious supplication that Andrew might never leave her side again to become President or for any other reason. Thus continued the unceasing struggle against the claims of fame in which Rachel had won her little victories, but in the end the world that was in arms against her always had its way. The world fought unfairly and under false colors, like an Indian creeping up inside a deer skin. Always some unsuspected device. Even now, alongside the letter of Sister Hays, a courteous communication from a gentleman of Philadelphia lay on Rachel's table.

"Mrs. General Jackson:

". . . I have been favoured with an opportunity to forward to you an *American Grass Hat or Bonnet* . . . made by Miss Pike and Miss Andrews, both under the age of twelve.

"I am, Madam . . ."[41]

Bless the children! Rachel would wear the hat.

"Colonel Robert Patterson:

". . . I accept the bonnet, sir, as a just emblem of the sphere in which my sex should move, and be useful to our country. . . .

"Your obedient, humble servant . . ."[42]

A GRASS HAT

As innocent a thing as this grass hat made by two little girls served as an instrument for Pennsylvania protectionists to sound out the General on the tariff:

"General A. Jackson;

"Sir: I have this day forwarded a Grass Bonnet or Hat, made by *American* hands, and of *American* materials, which I request your lady to accept . . . as a token of gratitude for . . . your distinguished services . . . especially during our late contest with Great Britain. The offering is small, sir: but it is hoped it will be . . . worn as an encouragement to *domestic manufacturers.*

"I have the honor to be . . .

"Robert Patterson."[43]

Small, indeed, the offering, but mighty the response it drew forth:

"Hermitage, near Nashville, May 17, 1823

"Sir—A few days since, I had the pleasure to receive the Grass Hat. . . . Mrs. Jackson will wear with pride a hat made by American hands, and made of American materials: its workmanship . . . will be regarded as an evidence of the perfection which our domestic manufactures may hereafter acquire, if properly fostered and protected. Upon the success of our manufactures, as the handmaiden of agriculture and commerce, depends in a great measure, the independence of our country. . . .

"Accept, sir . . .

"Andrew Jackson."[44]

The Grass Hat Letters placed Old Hickory in the race, not to confound the ambitions of Crawford or Clay or to assist those of Adams or Calhoun, but to win for himself. Eighteen months of subtle graduations had sufficed to complete the metamorphosis from explosive refusal[45] to open consent to his own candidacy. Like a train of ignited powder these communications, including Rachel's, ran the rounds of the press.

CHAPTER XXIII

THE CANVASS

I

FAIRFIELD, the residential seat of William Berkeley Lewis, lay on the Lebanon Pike some twelve miles west of the Hermitage. The easy financial circumstances of the retired commissary officer had absolved him from anxiety over the low price of cotton during the most pessimistic period of the current depression in trade. With commerce showing signs of revival and cotton quotations plodding upward on the New Orleans exchange, Major Lewis found less distraction than ever from his labors to advance the cause of his neighbor toward the fragrant gardens of political preferment. For a time in the spring of 1823, he had acted as amanuensis to the General, this term of service coinciding with the production of the epochal Dauphin County Committee and Grass Hat Letters. Andrew Jackson Donelson, having completed his legal studies and taken up his abode at the Hermitage, released the Major for employment in other fields.

He found one under his own roof when William Polk of Raleigh paid a visit to Tennessee. General Polk, a Revolutionary soldier and one of North Carolina's famous men, came from the Waxhaws where he had known Andrew Jackson as a child. Formerly a Federalist but now a man without a party, General Polk's personal influence at home remained unimpaired. As the conversation wore around to the campaign, Lewis heard his guest brand Adams as "a *damned Traitor*," and Jackson as an old and valued friend, but nothing was said as to his preference for President.

After bidding his guest good night, Major Lewis retrieved from his store of papers a copy of a letter that General Jackson had written James Monroe, then President-elect, under date of November 12, 1816. At that time Mr. Monroe was wrestling with the problem of Cabinet selections and Jackson had suggested Colonel William Drayton, a South Carolina Federalist, as Secretary of War. "Party feelings ought to be laid out of view," he wrote, "by selecting those the most honest, possessing capacity and firmness."[1]

Next morning finding General Polk taking the air in the garden, Major Lewis handed him Jackson's letter.

The old Federalist was surprised. "Did General Jackson really write this?"

"Certainly," said Lewis.

"Then he is my man," the North Carolinian replied.[2]

2

With the tactics of a determined and skillful fighter, John Caldwell Calhoun met his unexpected rebuff in Pennsylvania with slashing blows. On other fronts he sought to consolidate his positions before the poison from Harrisburg should have a chance to spread or the enemy to exploit his advantage. Skirmishes were won and hopes ascended. In Washington Congressman George McDuffie, of South Carolina, convalescing from a dueling wound inflicted by a Crawford retainer, condensed for wider dissemination buoyant reports streaming in from the scenes of action.

"Mr. Calhoun is rising rapidly in all quarters. . . . New Jersey will give . . . [him] an undivided vote."[3] "Calhoun taking like wild fire in the western part of New York."[4] "The strongest indications are given that New England, believing that Mr. Adams cannot be elected, will . . . support Mr. Calhoun."[5] (The Secretary himself was striving to win over the singularly inert Daniel Webster.)[6] "In the western states Calhoun . . . [is] clearly next to Jackson & Clay in their respective strongholds."[7]

One competent observer, John Pendleton Kennedy of Baltimore, viewed these broad claims with an active distrust. To the director of Calhoun's Maryland campaign, Colonel Virgil Maxcy of Tulip Hill Plantation, near Annapolis, he wrote a long letter. "What do you think of the *people*"—that new and unpredictable element in a presidential contest—"of Baltimore being all alive for Jackson?" They were two to one for him. This reflected merely the vagaries of the populace, of course, and not the wholesome judgment of the politicians. Nevertheless, rather than court defeat or even victory by a small majority, Mr. Kennedy asked if it would not be wiser for Calhoun, who was so young, to withdraw in favor of the New Englander and rest content to be Adams's "*premier . . . for the next 8 years.*"⁸

The embattled minister of war repelled the thought, however, and threw his reserves into the fight for North Carolina where, true to his word, William Polk had come out for Jackson. There had been a time when Mr. Calhoun was glad to see the development of Jackson strength in this State, as once he had looked upon it as an ally in Pennsylvania. Now, unless something were done, the enthusiasm for Old Hickory might prove another case of the tail wagging the dog. "Our cause with the people," a Calhoun lieutenant wrote from Raleigh, "would . . . succeed if"—and it was a big if—"the friends of Jackson, who seem to be *intoxicated with military glory*, do not start a ticket for him."⁹

3

Crawford, too, was losing ground. To the structural defects already discernible in the Georgian's political edifice was added another, as he failed to develop that secondary strength deemed so important in a crowded contest where last-minute horse trades might tell the tale. Granted the Secretary of the Treasury was first in Georgia, North Carolina, Virginia, Delaware and New York. These states could not elect him, and in what states was he the runner-up? While grappling for a solution of this difficulty, Crawford's campaign organization was staggered by the most overwhelming personal calamity which has assailed a pilgrim toiling the steep slope toward the presidency.

In August or early September, 1823, Mr. Crawford left Washington, his jovial mood unruffled by the clouds upon the horizon of his fortunes, his enormous frame apparently bearing with ease the burden of fifty-one years. A fortnight later a form under a sheet was carried into a house in the Virginia hills. The Secretary of the Treasury was paralyzed in every limb, speechless, nearly blind and nearly deaf. Friends, whom it was indispensably necessary to inform of the tragedy, waited anxiously to ascertain whether his mind, too, were gone.

So closely was William H. Crawford guarded during the next year and a half, so many were the tricks to dissemble his true condition, so few, and they so close-mouthed, knew the facts, that even now it seems impossible to reconstruct what had happened. The most probable story is that a paralytic stroke had been induced by an overdose of lobelia prescribed by a country physician treating an attack of erysipelas.[10]

The stricken man rallied and the bedside watchers learned that his mind was unimpaired. Nor was this all. The blow that had prostrated the flesh could not prevail against the spirit of William Harris Crawford and, as soon as his thick tongue could mumble a word, it was for his friends to carry on the fight because he would get well. Then the world received its first news of the affliction that had befallen the candidate. A paragraph in the Crawford press announced that the Georgian was convalescing from the painful illness.

General Jackson was the first to feel the effects of the suffering man's refusal to ask for quarter. Crawford had a strong ally in Tennessee, United States Senator John Williams, who had made trouble for Andrew Jackson before and was prepared to do it now. The Senator was up for re-election by the Legislature and, so carefully had he prepared his lines, victory seemed a foregone conclusion. Colonel Williams had long filled Washington with tales of Jackson's weakness in his home state, and rather late in the day the General's presidential monitors realized that the defeat of Congressman John Rhea, Jackson's preference for Senator, would endow this assumption with an unpleasant amount of credibility.

John Henry Eaton and Major Lewis hastened to Murfreesborough to save the day for Rhea. The Williams managers, already on the ground, had combed Tennessee for men who had felt the hard hand and harsh temper of old Jackson—not an inconsiderable company when a prospect of retaliation seemed sufficiently bright to bring them into the open.

Eaton and Lewis toiled as men possessed, but every effort splintered against the pledged and unbreakable Williams majority. The best combination they could contrive for Rhea lacked three votes of victory.[11] "It became necessary," related Lewis, "now to play a bold game."[12] Unless Jackson were to lose what had developed into an important battle, he himself must enter the lists against Williams.

Eaton and Lewis put his name forward and dispatched a messenger to the Hermitage, imploring the General to come to Murfreesborough and inspire the waverers with his presence. Old Hickory refused, refused even to sanction the use of his name; but an admission was drawn from him that if elected he would serve. A second, a third envoy posted to the Hermitage, the last one on the night of September 30, and the Assembly was to vote on the morrow. Old Hickory held his ground.[13]

When the Legislature convened at seven o'clock in the morning on October 1, 1823, the Jackson forces made a desperate attempt to obtain a postponement for two days. Davy Crockett led a successful fight against delay[14] and preparations for the roll call went forward amid signs of soul-searching anguish among legislators, confronted with the choice of repudiating their pledges to John Williams, a power in eastern Tennessee, or flying in the face of the gray-haired Hero. Seven men switched their allegiance and the vote was Jackson, thirty-five; Williams, twenty-five. Thus was an astonishing triumph clutched from the shadow of defeat when a reverse, as Lewis believed, "might possibly have destroyed . . . his prospects for the presidency."[15]

"I have been elected senator," the victor wrote wearily to John Coffee, "a circumstance which I regret more than any other in my life.[16] . . . To leave . . . Mrs. Jackson . . . fills me, as well as her, with much regret."[17]

4

Want of promptitude was never a failing of Andrew Jackson. Although utterly unprepared to leave home, the Senator-elect departed for Washington during cotton ginning time, a planter's busiest season when expenses were greatest and debts heaviest. To defray the cost of his journey, it was necessary to accept a personal loan from John Overton and, to meet outlays at home, to dispatch Jack Donelson to Alabama for the collection of fifteen hundred dollars owing him there.

Jackson began the eight-hundred-and-sixty-mile journey on horseback attended only by John Henry Eaton and a colored body servant. Except on one day when a mail coach afforded refuge from the rain, he remained in the saddle all the way to Staunton, Virginia. At Fredericksburg the party boarded a steamboat which arrived in Washington a little after daylight on December 3.

Anxious letters sped back to Rachel.

"Staunton Novbr. 28th 1823.
"My Love
"I have been greeted by the people wherever I have halted, to avoid much of which was one reason why I took the stage, & even then in many places . . . were collections who hailed & stopped the stage, This through Virginia [a Crawford stronghold] I did not calculate on. . . . Were you only with me I could be satisfied— But should providence once more permit us to meet, I am solemnly resolved, with the permission of heaven, never to separate, or be separated from you in this world."[18]

"Newburn Virginia Novbr. —
"My Love
"The separation, so unlooked for, from you . . . has oppressed my mind very much, still I hope that your mind is become calm. . . . I hope you will not permit yourself to want for anything."[19]

"City of Washington
"Decbr. 3d. 1823
"My Love
"I have not heard from you . . . [and] am anxious to receive a letter. . . . I have been treated with marked attention. . . . Altho this is gratifying . . . my heart is with you & fixed on Domestic Life. . . . Without you this will be a Tedious and unpleasant winter present me to the Andrews [the adopted son and Andrew Jackson Hutchings], . . . write me often and believe me to be your affectionate husband."[20]

Modestly lodged at Major William O'Neale's boarding house, General Jackson immediately became the most conspicuous personage in Washington. In vain did he seek the seclusion of his rooms where he had expected to dine privately with Eaton and Richard K. Call, the Delegate from Florida Territory. "There is nothing done here but *vissiting* and *carding*," he complained to Rachel. "You know how much I was disgusted with Those scenes when you and I were here [in 1815]."[21] Eaton helped with his patron's mountainous correspondence, even writing to Mrs. Jackson. "The general is in very fine health, and just as good sperits. . . . He is constantly in motion to some Dinner party or other, and tonight stands engaged at a large Dancing party at Genl Browns."[22]

The anticipated tedium of these obligations was not altogether realized. Jackson, who always liked people about, enjoyed himself. For evening wear he ordered a "pr of Sup fine Blk mill'd cassimere Pantaloons," and had his dress coat spruced up with new silk-covered buttons. Nor was he oblivious to the fact that the hospitable attentions coming his way did no harm to the cause of a candidate. As his mind dwelled anew on the demonstrations that had attended his progress through Virginia, the vexatious features of that journey, as recounted to Mrs. Jackson, began to disappear. The General found time to give Jack Donelson a considerable account of a reception at Fredericksburg, to which was added this significant instruction: "Nothing from my pen is to appear in print, whatever may be used under other names—or as coming from a friend in Virginia. . . . Take care of Mrs. Jackson and attend to the little Andrews— Write me often and make known to me the amount of my cotton crop."[23]

As usual, Jackson's cotton brought satisfactory prices, the state of the market considered, twenty-seven bales being selected for export to France at a cent and a quarter a pound in excess of the highest New Orleans quotations.[24] Also, as usual, there were extraordinary demands on this income. From New Haven arrived a letter saying that the General's troublesome ward, Anthony Wayne Butler, a student at Yale, had neglected to honor a draft for one hundred and fifty dollars. Jackson forwarded one hundred dollars, reminding Anthony's creditors that this was all he had authorized them to advance the young man, but promising to see that the balance was paid.[25] From New Orleans came further light on the financial affairs of the widely distributed Butler family which Jackson had so long befriended. A draft of Robert Butler and Dr. William E. Butler for three thousand dollars was protested, and Jackson called upon as endorser to pay. He immediately directed the Nashville Bank to place one thousand and eight dollars to W. E. Butler's account, and advised his New Orleans brokers to advance another one thousand and eight dollars out of the proceeds of the cotton revenue.[26] Apparently the Butlers themselves scraped up the remaining nine hundred and eighty-four dollars.

5

General Jackson's appearance in the capital outmoded one form of electioneering hitherto used with considerable effect by partizans of Old Hickory. No longer could their broadsides proclaim:

"With the exception of this great man
The Hero of Orleans
ANDREW JACKSON
all the candidates have toiled through the winter at Washington seeking . . . to press themselves into favour. Why is not
JACKSON *there*?

"Because he has a soul that towers above intrigue. . . ."[27]

But now that the Hero was, indeed, "there," the only embarrassment fell upon his rivals who had cherished lingering hopes that something might occur to dissuade the Tennessean from making a finish fight of it. Senator Eaton, Sam Houston—a member of Congress—and others of the old Nashville junto were correspondingly elated, though they knew their work to be far from complete.

On the frontier Andrew Jackson had made his fame by methods that were uncompromising and direct. Now Old Hickory found himself on a stage which called for a modification of the border technique.

Major General Winfield Scott was in the city when Jackson arrived. General Scott's refusal to meet his military associate in a duel in 1817 had not ministered to that soldier's prestige in Army circles. When gossips ran to Scott with the tale that Jackson meant to challenge him again, Scott decided to do nothing to avoid a collision. On December 5, when Jackson presented his credentials to the presiding officer of the Senate, General Scott ranged the corridors of the Capitol in the hope that Jackson would see him.

For six days Scott frequented the Senate wing of the Capitol without encountering Jackson—a circumstance that suggests adroit management by friends of both parties. Then General Scott sent the Senator a note of restrained politeness soliciting a meeting on any terms that Jackson might elect. Old Hickory responded the same day suggesting that the meeting be "on friendly terms."[28] And so it was.

Meantime another little tableau had been unfolding in the Senate Chamber. Jackson took a seat on the floor, only to notice that the adjoining chair was occupied by Thomas Hart Benton. This was the nearest these gentlemen had been to each other since 1813, when Tom Benton's brother had fired into Andrew Jackson's body two bullets that nearly cost his life. Perceiving the situation, several senators offered to exchange places with Benton, but he declined. Jackson also refused the proffer of another seat—all this taking place without a sign of recognition passing between the old acquaintances.

A few days thereafter the junior Senator from Tennessee was appointed chairman of the Committee on Military Affairs and Senator Benton made a member of the same body. Without rising Jackson turned to him. "Colonel, we are on the same committee; I will give you notice when it is necessary to attend." "General," replied Benton, "make the time to suit yourself." As a meeting of the committee broke up, Senator Benton exchanged civilities with the chairman and asked about Mrs. Jackson's health. In the old days Tom Benton had been a favorite of Aunt Rachel. One afternoon the two senators found themselves face to face in the drawing room of the Executive Mansion. Benton bowed and Jackson held out his hand.[29]

From these signs Henry Clay concluded that Jackson had "resolved upon a general amnesty"—the benefits of which presently were, indeed, offered to the Speaker himself. A number of Tennessee congressmen, who maintained a "mess" at Mrs. Claxton's boarding house on Capitol Hill, waited on the Kentuckian with an invitation to a dinner at which Jackson had consented to be present. Clay was not a man to harbor personal resentments. He attended the dinner after which Jackson and Eaton took him to his lodgings in their carriage. Later the General gave a rather large dinner at which three competitors for the presidency—Clay, Adams and Calhoun—honored his board.[30]

These events damaged the authority of the widely propagated stories of Old Hickory's implacable hatreds and original ideas of etiquette. "It will afford you great pleasure to know," John Henry Eaton informed Rachel, "that all his old quarrels have been settled. . . . The General . . . is in harmony and good understanding with everybody."[31]

6

Nor was Old Hickory blind to the effects of his reformed deportment. Of the reconciliation with Scott he wrote to a Tennessee friend, "This has destroyed the stronghold . . . of those whose minds were prepared to see me with a Tomahawk in one hand and a scalping knife in the other."[32]

It was somewhat true. Representative Daniel Webster, supporting Adams without enthusiasm because really more attracted to Calhoun, wrote his brother: "General Jackson's manners are more presidential than those of any of the candidates. He is grave, mild and reserved. My wife is decidedly for him."[33] Senator Elijah Hunt Mills of Massachusetts who had violently opposed Jackson on the Florida question, considering "him little advanced in civilization over the Indians with whom he made war," confessed to Mrs. Mills that "these opinions [were] unfounded. . . . He is exactly the man with whom *you* would be delighted."[34]

"I get on pretty well amidst the intrigue for the next presidency," Old Hickory himself admitted, "as I touch not, handle not of that unclean procedure[35] . . . I intermix with . . . [no] president makers . . . and should the choice of the people fall upon another it will give me no pain . . . [unless] the choice fell upon Wm H. C. . . . [which] would be a great curse to the nation."[36] Declining a social invitation from a Virginia friend the Senator wrote: "Your request to vissit Richmond cannot be complied with . . . [because] it . . . would be attributed to any thing than the real cause. . . . My course is to . . . take no step which may have imputed to it a disposition to recommend myself to anyone."[37]

Sam Houston complained that the General kept too close to his lodgings. "He has not yet been to the Rep's Hall,"[38] a chamber much in the eyes of the other aspirants, owing to the ultimate probability that the election would be decided by the Lower House. Nevertheless, for one so explicit in his professions of disinterestedness and so ostensibly withdrawn from the practical affairs of the campaign, General Jackson was able to sprinkle his private letters with some remarkably apt political comments. "Mr. Vanburen can not *manage* New York."[39] "A gentleman of N. Carolina of the first respectability

... says if Pennsylvania declares for me N Carolina is certain."[40] "South Carolina, alab, Mississippi, Louisiana, Tennessee, Kentucky, ohio and Maryland will all come out in my favour."[41]

The effect was not lost on observant James Buchanan, a representative from Pennsylvania. "He is a real & not a nominal candidate."[42]

While the General's cultivation of the elect in Washington was repelling stories of his coarse manners, no effort was made in the country at large to diminish the Hero's appeal to the less exalted strata of society. In North Carolina General Polk was receiving reports from every county. One informant brought to light the advantage accruing to Jackson from the fact that so many voters could not read. "[Therefore] they are illy acquainted with the character and qualifications of the [other] candidates," scholarship not being a requisite to an appreciation of "the glorious exploits which have crowned the military career of Jackson."[43] Wrote another: "Printers may puff, office men may dogmatize, politicians may calculate, . . . but rely on it, the effectual voice of the people, now . . . scarcely recognized amidst the clamor will be uttered in favor of Andrew Jackson."[44]

Meantime the great and near-great of the capital continued their courtship. Calhoun, Clay and Adams returned the Tennessean's hospitality, the Secretary of State pre-empting the most fitting of days—January 8—for a reception which was one of the winter's shining events. For a week Mrs. Adams had been preparing decorations of tissue paper and evergreens. Chalked on the floor were eagles, flags and a motto, "Welcome to the Hero of New Orleans." A thousand guests viewed the sight. "The ladies climbed on chairs and benches to see General Jackson," one who was present informed Dolly Madison. "Mrs. Adams very gracefully took his arm and walked through the apartments."[45]

After this the General assured Rachel that a forthcoming levee at the President's would terminate his social activities for the season.

7

Yet Jackson did not want for pleasurable company to lighten his few leisure hours. "The kind attention of my friend Eaton has been great, and to him I feel truly indebted for the comfortable quarters

"The Nation's Hero and the People's Friend"

A bas-relief by the distinguished American sculptor, William Henry Rinehart. The artist grew up during Old Hickory's heyday and began work shortly before his death. This is one of his early pieces. It is owned by Emil Edward Hurja of Washington.

The Gentleman From Tennessee

This is probably the best of Ralph E. W. Earl's many portraits of General Jackson. The original, painted in 1835, is owned by Charles W. Frear of Troy, New York.

we occupy. . . . Mr Oneale's amiable wife and two daughters take every pains. . . . This family has been wealthy but by misfortune has been reduced to keeping a boarding house. . . . In the evening Mrs. Timberlake the maryed daughter whose husband belongs to our Navy plays the piano delightfully, and every Sunday evening entertains her pious mother with sacred music. . . . Every Sunday we spend at church. on last Sunday I went to the Presbyterians, today a Baptist. . . . Mrs Timberlake has requested me to present you with her respects. . . . Accept of my prayers for your happiness and believe me your affectionate Husband."[46]

John Eaton was in truth a kindly man, to which Major O'Neale as well as General Jackson could testify because it was to Eaton that the Major owed the roof above his head. For more than twenty years William O'Neale had prospered as proprietor of the Franklin House, strategically situated midway between Washington and Georgetown. Sunning himself in the reflected renown of his patrons the host expanded into something of a personage about the capital. In this tavern house the O'Neales' six children were born. Friendly guests obtained West Point nominations for two of the boys, and the three girls were excessively pampered, children being a rarity in Washington in a day when few statesmen subjected their families to the discomforts of the unfinished city.

The eldest of these daughters was Margaret: a small, apple-cheeked brunette, vibrant, clever and strangely alluring. Before she was fifteen the trail of romances in her wake gave Peggy O'Neale a certain distinction. On her account the nephew of an Acting Secretary of the Navy had killed himself; two young army officers had passed a challenge to a duel; an elderly general was in a state of distraction; an elopement with a major had been forestalled only because, in climbing from a window, Peg overturned a flower-pot which awakened her father. This miscarriage of plans had afflicted Margaret with a broken heart from which she did not recover for a week. Next Peg was immured in a boarding school in New York City where a captain in our armed forces attracted the new pupil's favorable notice. A runaway marriage was agreed upon but, when the Captain made an awkward speech in returning a handkerchief his fiancée had dropped, the young lady decided that he was not the man of her choice.

One Sunday afternoon the following summer a tall, blond Adonis from Virginia, named John B. Timberlake, caught sight of Miss O'Neale through a window of the Franklin House and announced to a chum his intention of making her acquaintance by six o'clock in the evening. He allowed himself more time than was necessary and by eleven had received Margaret's promise to marry him.[47] Peggy had frequently declared a brisk elopement to be, in her opinion, the most zestful approach to the delights of matrimony. But so enduring was her ardor for Mr. Timberlake, that she consented to wait for a month. The ceremony was performed in the tavern parlor by a Presbyterian minister of Georgetown, on July 18, 1816. The bride was sixteen. Though none of the bridegroom's family came, Major O'Neale was able to make quite an event of the wedding.

John Timberlake was a purser in the Navy, at the moment on furlough because of a discrepancy in his accounts. O'Neale set his son-in-law up as a merchant, an experience which cost the old gentleman fifteen thousand dollars. About this time Senator John Henry Eaton of Tennessee had appeared at the Franklin House—twenty-eight years old, wealthy and a widower. He opened his pocketbook to the hard-pressed landlord, pulled wires to send Timberlake to sea again, and by his amiable attentions sought to compensate Peggy for the loss of her husband's society. In this he succeeded so well that Mrs. Monroe sent a note desiring her not to attend the presidential receptions to which, as a naval officer's wife, she was eligible. "Mrs. Timberlake," a member of Congress from Virginia recorded, "was considered as a lady who would . . . dispense her favors wherever she took a fancy. . . . Eaton's connection with . . . [her] was notorious."[48]

When O'Neale failed in business Eaton took over the Franklin House, sold it to the Baltimore hotel owner, John Gadsby, and provided the O'Neales with a smaller property in which to begin anew. Meantime Timberlake had returned, again in bad odor with the Navy Department, for his bookkeeping had not improved. With these accounts still unsettled, Eaton posted a bond of ten thousand dollars and obtained a fresh berth for the purser on the frigate *Constitution* which weighed anchor for a cruise that was expected to last four years. The sailor departed on this voyage shortly after

General Jackson, Senator Eaton and Congressman Richard K. Call established their abode at O'Neale's.

The three gentlemen took their meals in a private room and Peggy formed the habit of joining them to pour the coffee. Her talent for table talk charmed the General almost as much as the piety of her demeanor on Sundays. Another admirer was Call who associated more freely with his colleagues on Capitol Hill than did General Jackson and, in the barroom beneath the legislative chambers, heard Mrs. Timberlake's name used without reserve. This appeared to increase the emotional confusion which beset Captain Call, owing to the fact that a girl in Nashville whom he loved was under parental injunction not to correspond with her suitor. In any event one afternoon Call returned home in advance of his messmates and took Peg in his arms. It was necessary to emphasize her remonstrances with a fire-shovel before the puzzled young man left the room.

Tearfully Mrs. Timberlake complained to Jackson that she had been "grossly insulted." She could hardly have come to a more sympathetic person. Eaton's infatuation was too patent for disguise, but had not Jackson himself courted a woman mismated to another? Moreover Old Hickory knew from experience what gossip could make of such a state of affairs. Call admitted to Jackson the truth of Peg's accusation, offering as his excuse that "she was a woman of easy virtue and familiar with others," whom he named. Old Hickory was unconvinced. "I gave him a *severe lecture* for taking up such ideas of *female virtue* unless on some positive evidence of his own."⁴⁹

The incident clouded the pleasant family intercourse Jackson had come to enjoy, for Peg did not again appear at the gentlemen's table.

8

The campaign's increasing complexity offered a diversion. William H. Crawford did not participate in the polite exchanges which marked the relations of the other four candidates. He had been removed from Virginia to his home in Washington where, despite the assurance of partizans, the Secretary of the Treasury remained a very sick man, shut up in a dark room and seen by almost no one. This was not, however, the only reason for Mr. Crawford's isolation.

"Calhoun, Clay, Jackson & Adams have a perfect understanding," noted Congressman McDuffie. "[They are out] to give the Caucus a death blow. The explosion will blow up Mr. Crawford . . . & end his hopes forever."[50]

But should the coalition fail to give the caucus a mortal wound, the effects of the explosion would be more detrimental to the allies than to Mr. Crawford. Although his cause had declined since the middle of 1823, Crawford remained the strongest single candidate, since only the candidacy of Jackson, starting from scratch, had made measurable gains in that time. Moreover, the anti-caucus candidates were bolder in speech than in action. For all their impassioned war-cries—"Shall Congress or the People elect our President?"—the caucus was an old and respected institution. The record fails to confirm the implication that had Jackson, Adams, Clay or Calhoun been able to raise up the support in Congress enjoyed by Mr. Crawford, there would not have been so much high-minded indignation against the caucus.

At length the Jackson people made the first move. Glowing with the victory which had sent the General to the Senate, Jacksonians in the Tennessee Legislature adopted a resolution against the caucus mode of nomination in which they asked the assemblies of the other states to concur.

Georgia, Virginia and New York declined, as was expected of Crawford states. But elsewhere the result was disappointing. Ohio and North Carolina refused to act. South Carolina could not agree on a report. In Pennsylvania consideration was postponed indefinitely. Rhode Island laid the resolution on the table and Maine approved the caucus. Only Maryland and Alabama stood with Tennessee.

The Crawford managers had not been in better mood since their candidate's illness. Their contention—in the words of Eaton—that "he who was strongest before congress would assuredly be strongest before the nation"[51] seemed to possess an uncomfortable amount of logic. Mr. Crawford's competitors redoubled their efforts and their imprecations. The caucus was "undemocratic"; it was "unconstitutional"; it encouraged "bargain" and "intrigue"; it deprived the "sovereign people" of an "unalienable right" to something more than spear-bearing rôles in the selection of a president.

Four-fifths of the politicians and four-fifths of the newspapers of the United States thundering against the caucus made an impression. The practical object was to render that mode of nomination so unpopular that Crawford would drop it and take his chances before the country. But the sick man was not intimidated. He could not afford to be. He knew the caucus to be the best shot in his locker, his strength among congressmen being greater than his strength with the voters. On January 21, 1823, Andrew Jackson wrote: "A *caucus* is the last hope of the friends of Mr Crawford, and I have no doubt it will be attempted—with what success time will determine. But it appears to me that such is the feelings of the nation that . . . a congressional caucus would politically Damn any name put forth by it."[52]

The last sentence expressed a hope rather than a conviction, for Jackson men still toiled to avert the convocation of a caucus. They failed. A caucus was ordered, whereupon the opposition decided to boycott it. On the evening of February 14, 1824, lamps in the colonnaded Hall of Representatives were lighted. Anti-caucus members and their friends crowded the galleries, making a noisy show. The floor was reserved for caucus members who were slow to arrive. "Adjourn, adjourn," came the mocking cry from the gallery. An alarmed caucusite suggested a postponement, only to be opposed by Van Buren who knew it was now or never. When sixty-six gentlemen had put in an appearance, they went through the form of nominating Crawford for president and Albert Gallatin for vice president.[53]

Crawford had polled the votes of more than a fourth of the Republican membership of Congress, a figure no rival could have attained. But the Fabian tactics of the opposition made it a blow struck in the air. "The caucus," dispassionately observed Webster, "has hurt nobody but its friends. . . . Mr. Adams and General Jackson are likely to be the real competitors at last."[54]

9

These words of Webster seemed prophetic when four days after the caucus the battle-flag of John C. Calhoun fell in the dust.

This dénouement came with heart-breaking suddenness. Since

the preliminary reverse in pivotal Pennsylvania, the energy Calhoun threw into the fight to hold his lines had served as an autohypnotic, restoring a measure of confidence to the Secretary and his followers. And not without reason. From Maine to Louisiana Calhoun was, in all but a few states, still second choice at least. No other aspirant could exhibit popularity so widely spread.

Pennsylvania was to hold a state convention on March 4. The state was aboil with town and county mass meetings shouting advice to the delegates. Almost without exception these gatherings favored Jackson. Calhoun pinned his faith on populous Philadelphia and on the management there of his capable friend George Mifflin Dallas.[55] On the evening of February 18 Mr. Dallas addressed a meeting of the ward leaders of the city. His partiality to Mr. Calhoun, he said, was well known, but the hour had come when "predelictions must be sacrificed: the cause of the nation . . . [is] at stake." The speaker introduced a resolution urging "all sound Democrats" to unite in favor of "a single illustrious individual . . . ANDREW JACKSON."[56]

This turned Washington upside down. "The movement at Philadelphia," wrote Mr. Calhoun, "was as unexpected to me as . . . to any of my friends. . . . Had Penª decided favorably the prospect would have been most fair. Taking the U. S. together I never had a fairer prospect than on the day we lost the State." Though bitterly disappointed, the practical South Carolinian wasted no more ink on lamentations. The remainder of a six page letter dealt with proposals for clinching the vice presidency.[57]

Nominating Jackson with one dissenting vote, the Pennsylvania convention changed the complexion of the swiftly paced campaign. In North and South Carolina, in Maryland and New Jersey, the Calhoun organizations went over to Jackson virtually lock and stock, receiving in exchange second place for their man on the ticket. With Old Hickory thus clearly in the van, his lieutenants renewed their threats to Clay in Kentucky, Ohio, Illinois and Missouri, and licked their chops over Van Buren's discomfiture occasioned by a bill to transfer the selection of New York's electors from the Legislature to the people. New England felt the stir for Jackson. "I have no doubt," Old Hickory wrote William Berkeley Lewis, "if I was to travel to Boston where I have been invited that would insure my election— But this I cannot do— I would feel degraded the balance of my life."[58]

10

The persistent anxiety as to how Rachel would react to triumphs which her husband knew she did not desire wore on the conscience of the prospering candidate. His long letters to her contained little of politics. "My love, remember that you have promised me that you would bear up in my absence— recollect that your health much depend upon your keeping your mind calm & at ease." He tried to see that she was never alone. "I am grateful to your nieces for staying with you, present me affectionately to them."[59] While awaiting the decisive word from Pennsylvania, he "rejoiced" to learn from Jack Donelson that she "keeps up" her "spirits." "I have always wished my name had not been brought before the nation. . . . I am tired of this place and will leave it as soon as I can." Before the letter went into the post the news came from Harrisburg. In a post-script the impulses of a candidate superseded those of a solicitous husband. "This will carry the South and West." Would Donelson relay the tidings to the Nashville editors "without giving my name?"[60]

The Pennsylvania victory and consequent demotion of Mr. Calhoun's ambitions assumed the nature of birthday gifts to Andrew Jackson, who on March 15 entered his fifty-eighth year. "I had," he wrote to Rachel, "a few friends to dine"—about twenty, as appears, including Messrs. Adams, Clay and Calhoun.

On the morrow these gentlemen met again, with a great many others, to honor General Jackson on the occasion of the last public ceremonial that was to draw him from O'Neale's during his sojourn in Washington. "This morning at 11 I was requested to attend Mr Monroe to receive the medle voted me by Congress on the 27th Fbry 1815." The delay of this presentation had been occasioned in part by the General's tardiness in furnishing a portrait to guide the artist who fashioned the token. "You are aware how disagreeable to me these shows, and I performed it not without a tremor which always seises me on such occasions."

Yet the old soldier was deeply moved. "Tell my son how anxious

I am that . . . he may become the [worthy] possessor of those things that a grateful country has bestowed upon his papa—Tell him . . . [to] read & learn his Book . . . [because] his happiness thro life depends upon his procuring an education now; & . . . on all occasions to adhere to truth. . . . Never to make a promise unless on due consideration, and when made to be sure to comply with it. . . . Having experienced so much inconvenience from the want of a perfect education myself makes me so solicitious. . . . I would to god I could now leave the city. . . . Present me to all friends & neighbors & believe me to be your affectionate Husband."[61]

II

To gain votes, others might consume hours with fancy disquisitions on Jeffersonism, the tariff and internal improvements, or wear themselves thin contriving political combinations while, as John Quincy Adams observed, about all the Jackson people had to do was to shout "8th of January and battle of New Orleans."[62] The New Englander had foreseen something like this. At a time when no other rival pretended to consider the General seriously, Adams surprised a friend by saying that he regarded Jackson as a formidable candidate and a deserving one. If elected, he said the General would govern honestly and ably, which was more than could be expected of Crawford, Calhoun or Clay, though of the three he preferred Clay. Calhoun's "underhand course" was the object of especial resentment.[63]

Mr. Adams's distrust of Calhoun became more rankling when the Secretary of War hitched his vice-presidential ambitions to the Adams candidacy in New England. In the East Adams did not need the alert South Carolinian's help, and in the West, where he did need it, Calhoun was running under the Jackson colors. Presumably Adams knew that Jackson's high regard for Calhoun arose from the belief that he had supported the Florida invasion. The Secretary of State's idea of honor saved his colleague from exposure, but this was as far as he intended his aid and comfort should go. Adams told his lieutenants that another man must be found for the vice-presidency on his ticket.

But what man? Andrew Jackson, blandly replied the Secretary

of State. Old Hickory's character would lend a desirable lustre to the vice-presidential office and "afford an easy and dignified retirement for his old age."⁶⁴ No one seems to have raised the point that Jackson was the New Englander's senior by one hundred and eighteen days. Moreover, drolly continued the Secretary of State, "the Vice-Presidency . . . [is] a station in which the General could hang no one."⁶⁵

Under this proposed arrangement, a question of some moment was whether Jackson would accept the lesser honor; but the Secretary seemed at ease.⁶⁶ So a slogan was coined:

"John Quincy Adams
Who can write,
Andrew Jackson
Who can fight."⁶⁷

12

During all this while Congress was transacting business, though not a great deal of it. No senator, however, was more dutiful in his attendance than Andrew Jackson, and none stood less in the way of his fellow statesmen seeking to distinguish themselves in debate. In six months General Jackson took the floor only four times and altogether spoke less than twenty minutes: once to recommend a New Orleans veteran for a pension; twice to urge the construction of roads of military value; once to support a bill for the purchase of armament for fortifications. He voted, however, on every important division, consistently supporting internal-improvement legislation. Though unpopular with his supporters in the deep South, the only explanation Senator Jackson vouchsafed concerned the necessity of the projects for national defense.

The great issue was the tariff. Since January the lawmakers had been considering a bill which on March 31, 1824, Henry Clay espoused in the greatest protectionist speech in American history. The bill sought to erect a high-duty system in imitation of that of Great Britain, but this did not prevent Clay from christening it "the American System" and branding almost anything to the contrary a "foreign policy." Much that was native to Mr. Clay's character adorned that address: a warm and brilliant imagination, fervid felicity of phrase, shallow but showy research, half-knowledge dexterously disguised. Yet the effort constitutes a model for protectionist orators to this day.[68]

Daniel Webster answered the speaker. Here, too, was an indolent man, given to late hours and gay tavern company. But methodically he disclosed the historical and economic unsoundness of Mr. Clay's contentions.

Yet the American System carried the day in the House by five votes and came up to the Senate.

At this moment the Jacksonians were striving to complete their conquest of Calhoun's following in North Carolina. The situation prompted Dr. Littleton H. Coleman of Warrenton to suggest that a dig at the tariff from Jackson would assist his cause. The same post conveyed a similar expression from Colonel Arthur P. Hayne, now a planter in Alabama. "Manufacturing establishments I look upon as a *curse* to the country."[69]

To Coleman, Jackson replied:

"So far as the Tariff before us embraces the design of fostering, protecting, and preserving within ourselves the means of national defense . . . I support it. . . . Providence has filled our mountains and our plains with . . . lead, iron, and copper, and given us a climate and soil for growing hemp and wood. These being the grand materials of our national defense, they ought to have extended to them . . . protection, that our manufacturers and laborers may . . . produce within our own borders a supply . . . essential to war. . . .

"This . . . judicious . . . Tariff . . . possesses more fanciful than real dangers. . . . Where has the American farmer a market for his surplus products? Except for cotton he has neither a foreign nor a home market. Does this not clearly prove . . . that there is too much labor employed in agriculture? common sense points . . . the remedy. Draw from agriculture the superabundant labor, employ it in . . . manufacturers, thereby creating a home market for your breadstuffs. . . .

"Believing . . . my opinions . . . correct . . . I would not barter them for any office that could be given me."[70]

The publication of this challenging declaration caused a stir. Friends of the legislation seized so ardently upon the words "judicious tariff" that Henry Clay felt a twinge of jealousy. "Well, by ——, I am in favor of an *in*judicious tariff!"[71]

Jackson having declared himself on the tariff in the Grass Hat Letters eighteen months before, the really significant passage in the Coleman letter occurred in an aside which seemed to escape notice. "I am one of those who do not believe a national debt is a national blessing . . . as it is calculated to raise around the administration a moneyed aristocracy dangerous to the liberties of the country." This was a break from the past. The man of property, ever identified with the moneyed aristocracy in the West, had been raised on the shoulders of a resentful and impoverished populace to an eminence which overlooked exhilarating vistas. Something within Andrew Jackson responded to this allegiance—something not assignable to opportunism or to egocentric ambition. By degrees he was drifting into an acceptance of the protestations of these lowly supporters who claimed Old Hickory for their own. A member of the Tennessee Legislature had explained Jackson's election as senator in these words: "The commonality . . . thought him the only man . . . [to] revise what they thought a corrupt system of government, Meaning the caucus—the treasury and Bank influences."[72]

This appears to be the earliest mention of the Bank of the United States as one of the dragons Andrew Jackson was expected to slay.

13

The interminable tariff discussion wearied the junior Senator from Tennessee.

"My Dear wife, . . my heart bleeds when I read of the pain that our separation has cost you.[73] . . . I always believed I never was designed for a Legislator— I am sure I was not in the days like these whilst others are endeavoring by Log rolling . . . to defeat the Tariff Bill. . . . I shall leave here as soon as this Bill is acted on; before I cannot."[74]

"I have recd many letters on this subject . . . but I cannot be intimidated from doing that which my . . . conscience tells me is right . . . I will vote for the Bill."[75]

It passed the Senate and a wave of angry protest welled up from the South infusing new life into the languishing campaign of the Secretary of the Treasury. "The best judges believe," a visitor from Nashville warned John Overton, "that the stand taken by the Genl ... will give S. C. to Crawford."[76] The Georgian risked his life to take advantage of the first favorable turn of his political fortunes in more than a year. Summoning a carriage he quit his darkened room and, propped against pillows, showed himself in the streets of the capital. He attended cabinet meetings and visited the corridors of the all-important House of Representatives, led like a blind man.[77]

Another circumstance gave Mr. Crawford an unexpected lift at Jackson's expense. The Tennessean had endeavored to obtain the ministry to Mexico for the friend and protector of his boyhood, Colonel John Stokes of Salisbury, but the post went to a Calhoun worker, Ninian Edwards of Illinois. En route to assume his diplomatic duties, Edwards published charges accusing Crawford of official corruption, and forthwith was shuttled back to Washington to prove them. Edwards later declared that friends of Jackson had promised to support him. The glee with which certain Jacksonians received the new thrust at Crawford lends color to the assumption. But Jackson himself had nothing to do with this. "If an impeachment should be preferred against Mr. Crawford I would not sit upon his trial and will object to it."[78] A committee of the House dominated by anti-Crawford men delved into Edwards's accusations and submitted a report vindicating the Secretary.

Crawford scored again with the publication of the Jackson-Monroe correspondence of 1816. It will be remembered that William B. Lewis had won over the ex-Federalist Polk of North Carolina, with one of those letters, in which Jackson had urged Monroe to place a Federalist in his Cabinet. Polk, or someone, talked too much about the General's advice to Monroe, and all winter long the Crawford press had printed innuendoes assailing Jackson's record as a Republican. With the recrudescence of Crawford's drooping hopes in the spring, the editors grew bolder, and to clear the record Eaton was forced to publish the correspondence. This caused quite a commotion. Many good Republicans were dumbfounded that the Hero could have soiled paper with a considerate word for a Federalist. Nor were Federalists pleased to read that had the Hartford Convention been held within

General Jackson's military jurisdiction he would have hanged the leaders.[79]

In May, 1824, a Cumberland planter visiting in Washington sent John Overton a disturbing account of Jackson's prospects. "I think his strength is [giving] out. . . . Crd is undoubtedly the strongest man."[80] Daniel Webster surveyed the field with satisfaction. "Jackson's interest is evidently on the *wane*."[81]

With storms from every quarter swirling about his head, Old Hickory retracted nothing. To a criticism of his tariff vote, he flung back that he would not change it to place himself "in the Presidential chair."[82] The old warrior seemed content for the first time since he had become a senator. Another battle was behind him, and General Jackson did not tarry to witness the polysyllabic demise of Congress. The last week in May, 1824, saw him off through the young Virginia summer toward home and Rachel in too great haste for wayside hospitality. "I hope in god we will never be separated again until death parts us. . . . May Jehovah Take you in his holy keeping is the prayer of your affectionate Husband."[83]

CHAPTER XXIV

THE ELECTION

I

SENATOR JOHN HENRY EATON, who had scarcely permitted Jackson out of his sight since leaving Tennessee six months before, made his preparations to bear the General company on his return to Nashville. Eaton hoped to dissuade the candidate from his impractical resolution to decline invitations enroute. A little electioneering in Ohio, where a well-articulated Clay campaign was being pressed with vigor,[1] would be especially useful. It seemed that the thing could be arranged with a degree of naïveté sufficient to overcome the General's scruples. Merely for Old Hickory to show himself at a militia muster or a veterans' barbecue might spell the difference between winning the state or losing it. And Ohio would cast sixteen electoral votes.

These were the concerns uppermost in the mind of the senior Senator from Tennessee when, during one of the concluding sessions in the Upper Chamber, a pink envelope addressed in the flowing script of Margaret Timberlake was laid on Major Eaton's desk. The Senator scanned its contents and left the hall. At O'Neale's that evening Jackson found Peggy's eyes red from weeping and Eaton also visibly disturbed. As to the cause Eaton offered no explanation but later told his friend that he would be detained in Washington until after the adjournment.[2] So Jackson departed for the West attended by Congressman Richard K. Call. There were few stop-overs on the way for, like his patron, Captain Call felt a powerful attraction drawing him toward the graceful curves of the Cumberland.

Nashville first had known Dick Call at the close of the New Orleans campaign as a presentable aide-de-camp to General Jackson. He fell in love with Mary Kirkman. Though conceding her daughter's admirer to be "a splendid man, morally and physically," Mrs. Kirkman forbade the suit through a sense of loyalty to the memory of her late husband, Call being a protégé of Jackson and Thomas

Kirkman having quarreled with Jackson over a speculation in Indian lands.³ Old Hickory advised the young couple to elope or forget each other at once, adding that in case they wished to elope the Hermitage was at their disposal.⁴ They did not elope and four years of separation failed to bring forgetfulness—if the episode with Mrs. Timberlake can be classified as a momentary aberration.

In mid-June, 1824, the travelers reached Nashville. When General Jackson failed to obtain Mrs. Kirkman's blessing upon the proposed match, his own sufficed and the marriage was performed by Dr. A. D. Campbell of Hermitage Church.⁵ This little brick edifice, dedicated to the Presbyterian faith, had been completed during Jackson's absence. Mrs. Kirkman vowed to cut off her daughter without a penny and, bundling up copies of the letters that had passed between her and General Jackson when he was trying to win her consent to the marriage, she placed a ten dollar note on top of the pile and dispatched the whole to the editor of the *National Gazette*, Mr. Crawford's organ in Washington.⁶

The threat of disinheritance moved Jackson to another effort to soften the old lady's heart. Ellen Kirkman was perhaps the wealthiest woman in Tennessee. Her business interests extended from Philadelphia to New Orleans. Yet she lived upstairs over the hardware store at the corner of Cedar Street and the Square which her husband had founded upon their arrival in the West from Ireland.

Old Hickory climbed the steps to this abode.

"General Jackson, what are you doing in my house?" Mrs. Kirkman asked.

"I came to see you about Mrs. Call's property," replied the visitor in a pleasant tone.

"General Jackson, get out of my house," said Mrs. Kirkman. She spoke with a clipped Old Country accent.

"Not until I have had my say," parried Jackson.

From a drawer Mrs. Kirkman produced a large pistol, which she cocked and leveled at her caller.

"General Jackson, get out of my house."

For a moment Pakenham's conqueror looked her in the eyes. They were as blue and as steady as his.

"As you are a woman I will go," he said. "But if you were a man I would not."⁷

2

The *National Gazette* failed to publish Mrs. Kirkman's contribution in support of the hypothesis that a successful matchmaker might not necessarily embody the qualities required of a successful Chief Magistrate. The editor of this Crawford journal viewed with more favor, however, a literary production of Jesse Benton, and admitted it to his columns. Jesse Benton still resided in Tennessee. When his brother, the Senator from Missouri, took the hand of Andrew Jackson in friendship, a sense of humiliation moved Jesse to write thirty-four pages describing the General as bloodthirsty, dishonest and incompetent; a "mediocre politician," a cock-fighter, horse-racer, gambler, brawler and participant in shady land deals; a military chieftain whose renown rested on the deeds of subordinates.[8]

The appearance of this feuilleton sent the quills of John Henry Eaton and Andrew Jackson Donelson driving to establish that, detail for detail, the exact antithesis of Mr. Benton's portrait should be accepted as the true likeness.

This conscious effort to bring the campaign to an ideological plane, accessible to citizens who might fail to grasp the subtleties of opposed schools of thought on the tariff, worked no injury to General Jackson. Every slur on the name of the Hero seemed to raise up new defenders. An item of political sharp practice on the part of the General's adversaries was a sin against public morality and a poisoned spear pointed at popular rights. Similar practice on the part of the General's friends was a blow struck in the interest of virtue imperiled, or at worst an example of the end excusing the means.

The enforced consolidation of the Calhoun and Jackson interests had Crawford definitely on the defensive in North Carolina. In vain did the Secretary of the Treasury's supporters cry out that the "People's Ticket," the Jacksonian vehicle in that state, was a misnomer made up in an irregular way by a secret committee whose attachment to the shouting populace was of recent origin and questionable sincerity. "It is very difficult," one confessed, "to electioneer successfully against Genl Jackson— his character and his services are of the kind which *alone* the people can appreciate and feel— one cup of *generous whiskey* produces more military ardor than can be allayed in a month of reflection and sober reason."⁹

No vagary of a hurried pen should be blamed for the fact that this tribute from an adversary included Andrew Jackson's "character" among the rocks against which the opposition blunted its lances.

Whatever the flaws in the character of Jackson, vacillation, untrustworthiness and disloyalty were not among them. He deserved the reputation he bore for standing by those who stood by him. Only the public welfare, as he saw it, took precedence over the needs of a friend, and Jackson's normal impulse was to consider the two as coextensive. In matters upon which much depended, a sense of differentiation usually came to the rescue, however—the recent tariff controversy in Congress being a conspicuous example.

Less conspicuous, but not less notable, was the conduct of Senator Jackson on the subject of pensions. "Old soldiers in arms, hearing I have turned politician," he wrote during the late session, flooded his mail with "their long standing & almost obsolete claims."¹⁰ Jackson answered each letter and examined each claim, only one of which did he present to the Senate. It is difficult to see how his attitude toward this tempting subject could have exhibited a higher degree of integrity.

Yet, where many another man would have been ruined, Jackson's prestige suffered little. A phenomenon was arising with which American politicians were to wrestle for fifteen years to come, exclaiming in an apostrophe of impotent despair:

"General Jackson's popularity can stand anything!"¹¹

Already a legend was in the making as the masses displayed their unruly determination to accept the infallibility of the Hero. Primitive courage and a gift of leadership which animated followers to deeds beyond their strength, in truth, made it, in the words of the vexed North Carolinian, "difficult to electioneer successfully against Genl Jackson."

3

The recrudescence of Crawford hopes stimulated by early reactions to Jackson's tariff and internal improvement votes was transitory. The strain of personal leadership proved too much for the vitiated strength of the convalescent standard-bearer and, seven weeks after his resolute sally from the sick-room, Mr. Crawford collapsed again.

Hidden away in Virginia[12] where the most important of his political lieutenants failed to obtain dependable information of his condition, the afflicted candidate once more was the vortex of a hundred rumors. Those emanating from opposing political camps were ominous. "Mr. Crawford is *sick—very sick*," Webster wrote his brother. "In event of Mr. C's death (which I anticipate), Mr. Adams will be chosen by the *People* & by a great vote."[13] One Jackson supporter cheered another with these tidings: "A proposition to withdraw his name . . . would, I understand, have been made to Mr C———d by his friends before this—but for the *peculiar* and *unfortunate situation of his mind*!!"[14]

Martin Van Buren, bearing now the heaviest burden of the Crawford campaign, did not, could not, yield to the counsels of despair. His personal prestige and the complicated political organism in New York by which he maintained himself in public life were at stake. Needing a presidential candidate who would be an asset in his struggle to overcome the revolt against his dictatorship at home, the eminently practical sachem from the banks of the Hudson found himself saddled with a liability. But there was no turning back now. Anxiously he wrote to his confidential friends Messrs. Gales and Seaton, publishers of the *National Intelligencer,* for an account of the "real state of Mr Crawfords health." The reply was not reassuring. "Every function of his body was impaired unless perhaps his hearing."[15]

Van Buren was able to circumvent the popular demand to deprive the Legislature of its antiquated right to choose presidential electors only to behold unmistakable signs among the personnel of that body, soon up for re-election, of a drift from Crawford, who in a general plebiscite probably would have stood last among the presidential aspirants. Turning their eyes upon this scene of Mr. Van Buren's discomfiture, Mr. Clay and especially Mr. Adams felt a renewal of their hopes. In other quarters, however, these gentlemen perceived little for which to congratulate themselves.

Mr. Adam's extraordinary formula for effacing Jackson as Jackson had effaced Calhoun with an offer of the vice-presidency came to naught. The cases were dissimilar. In the West and the South Mr.

Calhoun had accepted second place on the Jackson ticket because his defeat in Pennsylvania made higher aspirations hopeless. Not even the wave of criticism following his refusal to compromise on the issues before the Senate reduced Jackson's campaign to that extremity, and the General's clever managers turned the Adams proposal into an endorsement of their chief in New England. Certainly, they told Mr. Adams, General Jackson would accept with pleasure the vice-presidential designation at the hands of Adams's eastern friends. But a withdrawal from the presidential lists elsewhere was a manifest impossibility. Jackson himself dropped his reserve to assure an eastern supporter that "the friends of Mr. Adams when they assert that I have 'abandoned the field in his favour' . . . are guilty of the grossest misrepresentation."[16]

Adams was politician enough to know who would reap the advantage of having Jackson a vice-presidential candidate in New England and a presidential candidate in the rest of the country. Consequently nothing more was done to disturb John C. Calhoun in the enjoyment of his reward as a virtually unopposed nominee for the second office.

In the mind of the ambitious South Carolinian this was a paltry prize, and the enjoyment thereof correspondingly meager. A friend described him as encompassed by gloom.[17] Indeed, the only speculation left to a driving intellect never to know the restorative powers of relaxation was whether the Calhoun star would fare better hitched to the wagon of Andrew Jackson or to that of John Quincy Adams. A Crawford journal in Washington surmised that he preferred Adams because a South Carolinian would stand a better chance of succeeding a northern man.[18] Another potential source of embarrassment in event of Jackson's election lay in the danger of disclosure of Calhoun's equivocal conduct in the Florida "war." When Mr. Calhoun's political situation rendered superfluous the expense of a personal organ in the national capital, his Washington *Republican* merged with Adams's *National Journal* which thereafter spoke in the interest of both candidates. With a foot in each camp the unhappy suitor for the vice presidency appeared circumspectly neutral, though a letter to his mother-in-law, a strong minded personage who spent much time under the Calhoun roof, referred to General Jackson without enthusiasm as "your candidate."[19]

4

Thus the campaign thundered into its final phase with every principal, excepting Jackson, beset by fresh anxieties. The flurry of disapproval over Jackson's tariff and internal improvement votes had amounted to nothing. In parts of the country where his stand ministered to local popularity, it was served up as campaign fodder. Elsewhere pyrotechnics in honor of a military conqueror diverted the spirit of objective inquiry. "[He] has slain the Indians & flogged the British & . . . therefore is the . . . wisest & greatest man in the nation."[20] How could a tariff orator expect to hold an audience against a rival who simply started the bung in a barrel of whisky and invited his auditors to step up and toast "Old Hickory, last of the Revolutionary patriots" whose "history is . . . the record of his country's glory?"[21] The cordiality of some of the responses indicates the effect of this mode of appeal to the judgment of the electorate: "May the SKINS of the enemies of Jackson be converted into a CARPETING for his friends to dance on."[22]

What other aspirant could display his qualifications as succinctly as this:

"Under Washington our independence was achieved; under Jackson our independence has been preserved . . .
"WASHINGTON, LAFAYETTE, and JACKSON,
"Brandywine, Yorktown and New Orleans."[23]

An epidemic of "straw" voting spread among mass meetings, militia musters and even grand juries. "He is a favorite of the people; he belongs to them; he has been raised with them; he has served them both in peace and war; they feel grateful."[24] This from a resolution by a North Carolina grand jury is notable only for the chaste tone of its language.

A sentiment often heard in the United States found its way across the ocean to the dinner table of an English baronet where someone remarked that Jackson's imperious temper would imperil Anglo-American relations. After Washington Irving had undertaken a defense of his countryman, Colonel William Thornton, late of His Majesty's Eighty-Fifth Regiment, asked permission to say a word.

"Had . . . Jackson not used the power confided to him in the high handed way alluded to, New Orleans would infallibly have been captured. As to the charge of implacable hostility, . . Genl. Jackson . . . [was] peculiarly courteous and humane."[25]

Alarm at the momentum of the sweep for Andrew Jackson betrayed opposing politicians into other incautious expressions. Said a Louisville newspaper reporting a militia muster in Ohio at which Jackson bested Clay in a test vote: "The Rowdies, . . . the very dregs of the community" won the day. "Can anything be more vexingly provoking?"[26] A commentary from North Carolina, across the mountains: "In almost every Captain's company the drums were beating and fifes whistling for the hero of New Orleans. The officers would treat the men, . . . and then raise the war whoop for General Jackson. Then the poor, staggering . . . creatures would sally forth to vote. The result was always in favor of Jackson."[27]

While the amount of liquor they could stow away at a muster should have made American militiamen heroes by Lord Nelson's definition, this was not in itself conclusive evidence that they sprang from the dregs of society. To assert as much fell short of an approach sufficiently tactful to woo their allegiance from Old Hickory.

5

Autumn saw Jackson leading the field and gaining. Flushed with confidence his supporters claimed that no other candidate had a chance for a victory at the polls, thus obviating a "run-off" election by the House of Representatives. Publicly the rival managers disputed this heartily, exhibiting columns of figures to support their contentions; privately most of them seemed reconciled to a House election as the best they could hope for. The vital concern of every politician was that his man should stand among the first three candidates and so be eligible to go on the ballot. This had been Clay's strategy almost from the first.

The Crawford-Van Buren cause was desperate. In mid-September the Secretary of the Treasury was carried back across the Potomac, his "recovery" proclaimed and the candidate himself placed on public exhibition to establish that he could, indeed, walk across a room, converse understandably and laboriously write his name on official papers. A less shrewd man than Martin Van Buren would have known that without an alliance the game was lost.

But to whom to turn? Before adversity waylaid his fortunes, William H. Crawford had carried on with hand so high as to excommunicate himself politically. Obviously no rapprochement with the exultant Jackson following was possible. Adams's sprouting hope of taking New York from Crawford barred the road to compromise with the New Englander. Clay, then, it must be; and Clay it was. Senator Van Buren threw all the persuasiveness of his subtle nature into a communication which, taken first and last, may be unique in the body of literature concerning contests for the presidency.

When revised and recopied, this letter filled seven pages and was dispatched to Benjamin Ruggles, a Clay lieutenant of St. Clairsville, Ohio.

Mr. Van Buren proposed a coalition of "men who ought never to have been separated & whose union is natural." With the Jackson victory in Pennsylvania, all chance of Mr. Clay's getting his name before the House was gone. But with Ohio and Kentucky Crawford could be elected "by the people." So argued Mr. Van Buren. If Clay were ever to support Mr. Crawford let him do it now. In exchange for this service would not the vice presidency appeal to the Speaker as a convenient stepping stone? The Kentuckian's friends should consider his future. The triumph of either Adams or Jackson would be injurious. But the union of Crawford and Clay "would constitute" a great new national party, "like . . . the old Republican Party, . . & such an one as I would be willing to stand or fall with." Let the minds of Mr. Clay's friends dwell on the choice of prospects that confronted them: their man eclipsed by the victory of Adams or Jackson, or their man serene in the vice presidency, leading "a powerful party" capable of crushing opposition to his advancement. And in conclusion the broadest hint of all: would not Henry Clay in the second office "relieve them [the Speaker's friends] from much of their apprehension on the score of Mr Crawfords health?"[28]

Not the least important facet of the situation which this letter ignored was the circumstance that Mr. Crawford already had a vice-presidential running mate, duly nominated by the caucus. But Albert Gallatin's distinguished services to his country belonged to a genera-

THE ELECTION

tion swiftly being shouldered into the shadows. His name had not brought the strength to the Crawford ticket that had been anticipated. Mr. Gallatin simplified matters by withdrawing, at the same time privately advising Van Buren against "negotiation with Mr Clay for the office of V. President. . . . It would only increase that gentleman's hope of success for the first office."[29]

Crawford himself failed to warm to the suggested bargain, and feebly expressed the hope that Clay would decline.[30] Yet Van Buren held to his course and was momentarily cheered by the significant support of Thomas Hart Benton. What poor, prostrated Crawford might hope counted for little now. The question was, Will Clay take the bait? Benton dangled this before him in its most enticing light: a certain door to the presidency. But the sick man had his wish. For Clay declined.[31]

After this, all that remained to Van Buren was the tenuous hope that should Crawford's name go to the House at all, he might slip in through a deadlock of the forces of Jackson and Adams.

To the end of the canvass, however, the shattered Crawford following continued its courtship of Clay, while its shrill attacks on the other candidates approached hysteria. An example of Mr. Adams's unfitness was construed from the allegation that he had endorsed the note of Mrs. Moulton, a milliner of Washington, and upon her default sought to avoid payment.[32] The Raleigh *Register's* concluding summary of General Jackson's career had the merit of brevity. "A disgusting detail of squabbling and quarreling—of pistolings dirkings & brickbattings and other actions reconciliable neither to regulations nor morals."[33]

Seven days before North Carolina voted, the same spirited journal lashed out again, and on this occasion established a dark and fruitful precedent. Clandestine whispers there had been, but, as far as can be discovered, this was the first time the innuendo that laid Charles Dickinson in his grave found its tortuous way to the printed page.

"I make a solemn appeal to the reflecting part of the community, and beg of them to think and ponder well before they place their tickets in the box, how they can justify it to themselves and posterity to place such a woman as Mrs. Jackson! at the head of the female society of the U. States."[34]

6

During the last weeks before the balloting began, General Jackson visited Melton's Bluff to make arrangements for the marketing of his Alabama cotton—an important detail, as the winter in Washington had been costly and the absentee planter was pressed for funds. Yet he found time to bestow on the trying task of managing the property of his ward, Andrew Jackson Hutchings, and to supervise the boy's schooling, along with that of Andrew junior, and Lincoyer, the young Indian. He also found some time for politics, though remaining to the end the least active of the candidates, not excepting the crippled Crawford.

He seemed to believe, however, that he would win, this being a fixed attribute of the Jacksonian character. Men (or horses) might fail *him*. The failure of means to an end on which he had set his heart was likewise possible. But a concept of failure as something indigenous to himself did not belong to the psychology of Old Hickory. *He* could do what he willed to do.

Yet, this fierce will had not wholly claimed the presidency as its perquisite. Moments of frank elation over a local victory were succeeded by moments of regret that he had allowed himself to be drawn into the contest at all. In Alabama, Jackson smoked his pipe on the porch with John Coffee to whom he could open his heart as to few men. Of the peace of that domestic scene the troubled traveler carried away a touching remembrance. "How much your situation are to be envied and how prudent you have been to keep yourself free of political life, surrounded as you are by your lovely children, and amiable wife, you ought not to abandon it for anything on earth— The man in office greeted with smiles and apparent friendship, his confidence often sought to be betrayed; surrounded thus, where a man must be always guarded, happiness cannot exist."[35]

7

By an act of Congress the twenty-four states had from October 27 until December 1 to select presidential electors. Ohio and Pennsylvania, where the choice was made by general election, acted first on October 29. Leisurely Louisiana and South Carolina, whose legislatures performed this duty, concluded the procession on November 22. As ballots were counted post riders, river steamers, coastwise vessels, indeed every traveler, bore the news piecemeal, to and fro. Not until mid-December, however, was the final result known in Washington.

Yet, from the moment of the receipt of the first fragmentary returns from Ohio and Pennsylvania, Jackson led the race and dominated every speculation concerning it. In Ohio Clay had waged a strenuous campaign, for victory there was indispensable to his hopes. The early news of the result placed Jackson so far ahead that many neutral and some opposition newspapers conceded the State to him. From Pennsylvania came word that Old Hickory was smothering his rivals under a majority of three to one.

Tennessee voted early in November and, with the slow count showing Old Hickory ahead by thirty to one, Senator Jackson, Rachel, Jack Donelson and his young wife Emily took their places in the morocco-lined carriage of Florida remembrance and, drawn by four horses, were on the long red road to Washington. The sight of this costly equipage moved a few unfriendly editors to comment on the insincerity of the candidate's democratic pretensions.[36] The fact is that the carriage was taken for the comfort of Mrs. Jackson whom the General, twelve months before, had determined to bring to Washington for companionship should he be obliged to make the pilgrimage again.[37]

Kentucky received the travelers warmly, staunch supporters of Henry Clay crowding around to shake Jackson's hand and to assure him of their allegiance in event the Speaker should be eliminated from the expected contest in the House. "Stick to Old Hickory—Give us a Western President."[38] Mr. Clay's elimination seemed more than likely. Kentucky's ballot boxes being opened as Jackson passed through, the result in Louisville (Clay, three hundred and eighty-seven; Jackson, seven hundred and forty-three) provided a surprise which sent expresses drumming the autumn highways in every direction. In the country at large the Louisville vote gave rise to an assumption that the Speaker might lose his own state.[39]

Then came tidings that Missouri, which Benton had counted in advance for Clay, was safe for Jackson.[40] With Missouri and Ohio in the Jackson column, the Speaker would be out of it, regardless of Kentucky.

His bags packed for Washington, Mr. Clay rode from his beautiful country seat to nearby Lexington and, unruffled by disappointment, begged his friends not to distress themselves whatever the issue of the election might be. He spoke well of General Jackson and was understood to say that he had written to solicit his company on the journey to Washington, but, having received no reply, had "given him out."[41] Yet, when state Senator Thomas Carneal announced that should Mr. Clay be excluded from consideration by the House he would introduce in the Legislature a resolution instructing the Kentucky delegation to vote for Jackson, Mr. Clay asked him not to do so. He said it would be best if the members remained uncommitted. Mr. Carneal promised not to put forward such a resolution, but, if introduced by another, he said he would vote for it because next to Clay Jackson was clearly Kentucky's choice.[42]

A few days after the Speaker had set out for the national capital, General Jackson arrived in Lexington and a respectable company of Mr. Clay's neighbors organized a ball in his honor.

John Quincy Adams's election news, though more encouraging than Mr. Clay's, also left much to be desired. The Secretary of State had New England's fifty-two votes as a matter of course, and he stood a good chance of getting the lion's share of the thirty-six from New York where Van Buren fought with his back to the wall. But Jackson won New Jersey and was leading in Maryland. On top of this the reports of his alarming pluralities in the West led at least two New England newspapers to admit the possibility of the Tennessean's election by the people.[43] Other eastern journals, such as the New York *Evening Post*, began to recall agreeable sides of the General's character which they had overlooked during the distractions of the campaign.

Next came the upheaval in New York, burying Van Buren's state ticket and electing Jackson's friend, DeWitt Clinton, governor. Before the echo of this overturn died away the Legislature met to consider the presidential question. One of Van Buren's advisers, Jacob Barker, hastened to Albany. A banker and lawyer not given to panic in a crisis, Mr. Barker surveyed the scene of chaos and contrived a formula calculated to salvage something from the wreck. "I pray you at once throw your whole influence into the scale for Jackson & do it promptly & openly & boldly—do not stop to count consequences. . . . No matter how hopeless the game may appear it will succeed . . . altho the probability is that it will make Jackson President without allowing the Question to go to the House."[44]

Mr. Van Buren failed to act on this suggestion and the Legislature he had so long exploited deserted the beaten politician, giving Adams twenty-six of New York's thirty-six votes.

This intelligence met Jackson in Virginia, and, coming on the heels of fresh tidings from the West, established that, after all, the finish of the race would be in the vaulted chamber of the House. For the reports of a Jackson victory in Ohio had proved to be premature, Clay carrying the state by seven hundred and ninety-eight votes out of fifty-nine thousand, nine hundred and ninety-two cast. Moreover the Speaker had carried Kentucky and Missouri, events which, combined with the collapse of Van Buren in New York, revived the Kentuckian's hope of nosing out Crawford and entering the House contest as the third man. But the first man would be Jackson with about one hundred electoral votes, and the second Adams with eighty votes or a little better.

This was the posture of affairs on December 7, 1824, when, on the twenty-eighth day of its journey, the carriage from Tennessee rumbled across the bridge into Washington. A strong current of opinion, by no means confined to the protagonists of General Jackson, favored the conclusion that the next President of the United States had attained the scene of his labors.

8

It went without saying that in the contest ensuing many who had opposed Andrew Jackson would stand their ground to the end. But when the editor of the Alexandria *Herald*, not a Jackson organ, forecast "a high game against gen. Jackson," involving "intrigue, . . . formidable opposition, . . . gross dissimulation,"[45] he was chided,[46] and properly it seemed, for seeing things under the bed.

Certainly this newspaper's surmise that Old Hickory would strike out against fancied machinations was wanting in confirmation; for lest one should mistake that, with the prize so nearly in his grasp, the Tennessean was prepared to liberalize his code of campaigning, Jackson promptly reiterated it.

"In no one instance have I sought either by promise or management to draw to myself the good opinion of a single individual in society. . . . That so many should have preferred me to take charge and to administer the affairs of our great and growing country, is to me a matter of the highest consolation, let the result now be what it may. . . . If any favourable result could be secured, through any intrigue, management or promises . . . I would at once unhesitatingly and without reserve spurn [it]. . . . The choice of a President is a matter for the people; to be installed against their wishes . . . I would feel myself [a] degraded man."[47]

This was a political letter written for dissemination, and apparently hurried off without benefit of the attentions that Eaton or Lewis sometimes bestowed upon their chief's correspondence. Otherwise, perhaps it would not have been directed to Samuel Swartwout, a colleague of Aaron Burr in his unfortunate western adventure of more than twenty years before. Some of the General's friends felt that a disclaimer of intrigue could have been more suitably addressed than to this protégé of a man still remembered for his equivocal part in a previous House election.[48]

Yet a charge of insincerity would be difficult to sustain against Jackson who wrote in the same vein to John Coffee, adding: "I am wearied with a public life, and if I could with propriety would retire, but my lott is cast, and fall as it may I must be content. should it be that I can retire next March to my home I will be happy. If confined here I must exercise my best exertions for the public weal until the four years runs around. . . . We are at Mr. Gadsbys tavern, well lodged, but *I pay for it*. How my funds may hold out I cannot say."[49]

They did not hold out very well and the General was obliged to ask his old friend for five hundred dollars.

THE ELECTION 413

"[This] will clear me of the city if I am permitted to leave it the 4th of March next. . . . How often does my thoughts lead me back to the Hermitage. there surrounded by a few friends would be a paradise . . . and . . . it would take a writ of habeas corpus to remove me into public life again."[50]

CHAPTER XXV

The Bargain

I

On December 16, 1824, the result of the vote in Louisiana reached Washington, calming somewhat the mounting fever of the politicians as Henry Clay's last hope of placing his name before the House of Representatives went glimmering. Louisiana had chosen three electors for Jackson and two for Adams, giving the General ninety-nine votes in the electoral college and Adams eighty-four. Mr. Crawford retained third place with forty-one. Clay was fourth with thirty-seven.

Weary of politics citizens turned to the eye-filling spectacle of Lafayette's triumphal pilgrimage, most of them apparently satisfied to dismiss the election with a perfunctory concession of Old Hickory's victory, and no hard feelings.[1] The New York *Statesman,* a journal not unfriendly to Mr. Adams, pointed out that Jackson, having carried eleven states to the New Englander's seven, needed only two more to prevail in the House. It predicted that he would get three on the first ballot—Ohio, Kentucky and Missouri.[2] In these states the Jackson vote had been more than double that of Adams.

Indeed, the histrionics of the long campaign seem to have bored the public even before the autumn elections. The rising of the masses, alternately courted and feared by political leaders, had not taken place. Though larger than in any previous presidential contest, the vote fell measurably below that in recent local elections. With a population of one million Pennsylvania had sent only forty-seven thousand men to the polls; Virginia, with a white population of six hundred and twenty-five thousand, sent fifteen thousand. Massachusetts cast thirty-seven thousand votes in contrast with sixty-six thousand for governor a year before; Ohio fifty-nine thousand, in contrast with seventy-six thousand for governor a month before.

THE BARGAIN

The weakness of opposition to Adams in New England and to Jackson in Tennessee and Pennsylvania was said to explain the light vote in those quarters; but this did not account for the apathy of closely-contested North Carolina, New Jersey and Ohio. Aside from the general overdoing of the campaign and the swing toward better times, the probable reason was a feeling that the plethora of candidates would throw the decision into the hands of the politicians anyhow.

When it transpired that this had come to pass, an occasional squib on current developments sufficed even partisan presses, which yielded entire pages to the phenomena of the marquis with the indestructible smile, bouncing over six thousand miles of half-made roads to be fêted from morning until night for eleven solid months, and gaining twelve pounds and a fortune meantime.

2

Nevertheless, the people had left an expression of their preference which congressmen, taking over the tavern houses of Washington, seemed inclined to respect. On the surface the removal of resourceful Mr. Clay as a contender seemed to facilitate this, for poor Crawford's cause was hopeless. Mr. Van Buren had slipped into town looking "like a wilted cabbage."[3]

Clay's most distinguished supporter in the West, Thomas Hart Benton, who had private reasons to oppose Jackson if any man had, promptly announced that as Missouri preferred Jackson to Adams he was for Jackson.[4] Senator Benton would not have the casting of Missouri's vote, however. That would be the duty of the state's sole representative, John Scott, whose one ballot would have as much bearing on the result as Pennsylvania's twenty-six or New York's thirty-four. When Scott declared that nothing could induce him to vote for Adams,[5] hasty observers, of whom there were many, counted the twelfth state for Jackson.

Under this view of things only one more would be required. It seemed within easy reach.

All the word from Kentucky indicated that its delegation would receive formal direction from the Legislature to support Old Hickory. Richard K. Call gleefully exhibited a letter from former

United States Senator John J. Crittenden, intimate of Clay and a power in the Blue Glass: "I hope you will be able to make the General beat the Yankee."[6] On the streets of Frankfort, a Kentuckian quoted Crittenden as saying, "Mr. Clay & the rest of the delegation" would support Jackson.[7] Representative Francis Johnson, a colleague of Mr. Clay, told a caller from home he had a sheaf of letters from constituents urging him to vote for Old Hickory.[8] "Kentucky," said he, "will come out strong for Jackson."[9] Clay, too, received such letters. "Sentiment in favour of Gen^1. Jackson grows . . . too powerful to be resisted," counselled William T. Barry, Secretary of State of Kentucky.[10]

Ohio was expected to follow Kentucky.

Georgia's Legislature instructed its delegation to regard Jackson as the choice after Crawford. This was taken to mean a complimentary vote for the doomed man and then a switch to Old Hickory should there be more than one ballot.

Even New York was not beyond hoping for. Henry Randolph Storrs, a Clay man from Utica, exclaimed that the only way Adams could get New York was through the support of the Crawford people. "And let them do it if they dare."[11]

These quick and uncritical calculations rested on the assumption that Jackson would hold the eleven states he had won in the electoral college. From the outset it was apparent that four of these states would bear watching: (1) Maryland, where Adams had received a small plurality of the popular vote, despite Jackson's capture of a majority of the electors; (2) North Carolina, a majority of whose representatives favored Crawford and seemed determined to give him a complimentary first-ballot vote, at least; (3) Illinois and (4) Louisiana, which had given Adams good second-place positions. Illinois's lone representative, Daniel P. Cook, was personally an Adams man. However, on his arrival in Washington, Mr. Cook said he would vote for Jackson in obedience to the will of the majority of his constituents.[12] When sounded out by the active R. K. Call, Brent of Louisiana sententiously observed, "Vox populi, vox Dei."[13] Call interpreted this to mean that Brent would vote for Jackson, rendering Louisiana secure as the state had only two other members, one of whom was Jackson's war-time friend, Edward Livingston.

A PORTRAIT BY THOMAS SULLY
From the original, owned by Mrs. Breckenridge Long of Laurel, Maryland. A conventionalization of this likeness of Jackson survives on the current twenty-dollar bill.

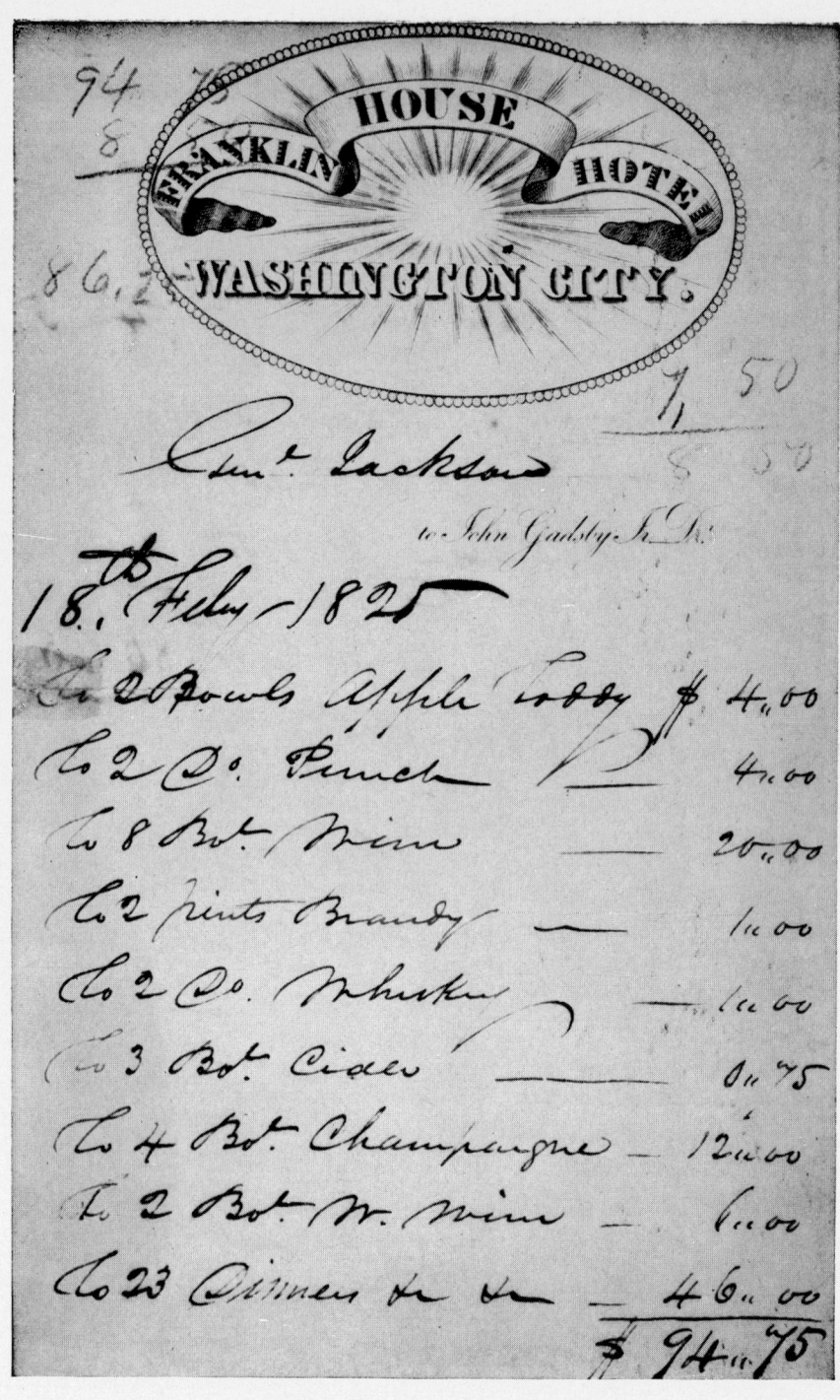

OLD HICKORY TOASTS HIS FRIENDS

Bill for a dinner to twenty-two supporters given by General Jackson after his defeat in the House election for President in 1825. The host received a refund of eight dollars and fifty cents for a pint of whisky, one of brandy and three bottles of wine which were not consumed

From the Jackson Papers, Library of Congress.

THE BARGAIN

These four potential sources of trouble notwithstanding, a judge of such matters so competent as Martin Van Buren considered Jackson's chances best by a considerable margin.[14] Able Willie P. Mangum of North Carolina picked the Tennessean to win, though he did not intend to vote for him.[15] After putting the best possible face on Mr. Adams's prospects, A. H. Everett of Massachusetts wrote, "I am not very sanguine."[16]

3

Not in two decades had an opening of Congress filled up Washington so promptly. Amid throngs that peopled inns, taprooms, Capitol corridors, theatres and made for a self-perpetuating series of balls and banquets, Jackson men were distinguishable by the buoyancy of their bearing. To place their chieftain's triumph beyond the pale of speculation, only one more voice was needed in his behalf—that of the Speaker of the House. "It is in fact very much in Mr. Clay's power to make the President," nervously declared an Adams adherent on the day the Louisiana vote came in.[17]

The thought did not alarm the Jacksonians. Benton's declaration, Crittenden's stand, the active sentiment of the Kentucky electorate, the friendly attitude of some of the Kentucky representatives, even the demeanor of the Speaker himself, were remarked as encouraging signs.[18]

Circumstances excused the Speaker from making an immediate public announcement of his choice. Not until mid-December did Mr. Clay know, beyond doubt, whether he, himself, was still a candidate. After that a decent interval seemed meet for the obsequies of his own aspirations. Meantime, the gayeties incident to Lafayette's arrival in town were not to be overlooked. During the thirty years of his residence in Washington, few men were more successful as hosts, or more sought for as guests, than the pleasure-loving statesman from Kentucky who seldom carried politics into a drawing-room. This attribute also served to explain his reticence on the topic that preoccupied every other tongue.

On December 8 General Jackson, Senator Eaton and Congressman

Call were traversing the rotunda of the Capitol when Clay hailed them.

"General, I have a *quarrel* with you: why did you not let me know you were coming through Lexington? I certainly should have waited for your arrival. We should have travelled together."[19]

This cordial meeting and an exchange of ceremonial calls concluded the intercourse between the two men, however. As the social affairs of the town partook more and more of the flavor of political forums, the General withdrew from them and rarely appeared in public except at church with his wife.

Mr. Clay's relation to the presidential issue served to make him the center of engaging attentions. "I am enjoying while alive," he wrote to a friend, "the posthumous honors which are usually accorded the venerated dead. . . .[20] I am sometimes touched gently on the shoulder by a friend (for example) of Genl Jackson, . . . 'My dear Sir, all our dependence is on you. . . . We want a western President—['] Immediately afterward a friend of Mr Crawford will accost me 'The hopes of the Republican party are concentrated on you'. . . . Next a friend of Mr. Adams, . . . 'Sir Mr Adams has always had the greatest . . . admiration of your talents'. . . . I sometimes wish it was in my power to accommodate each of them."[21]

Mr. Clay seems to have done something of this sort. John Floyd of Virginia quoted him as follows: "When I take up the pretentions of Mr. Adams and weigh them, . . . then take up the pretentions of General Jackson . . . I never was so puzzled in all my life as I am to decide between them."[22] Representative Thomas P. Moore of Kentucky was ill in his lodgings at Brown's Indian Queen Hotel when the Speaker called, and in the course of a conversation remarked: "We could vote for either of the three candidates and justify ourselves to our constituents."[23]

In this manner observers were favored with a picture, contrived from Mr. Clay's own words and those of men who knew him well, representing the Speaker in a nicely balanced attitude of indecision, hesitating among the three candidates.

Then came Congressman William Plumer, junior, of New Hampshire to add another shade to the portrait. Lafayette paid a visit of ceremony to the House of Representatives. When the affair was over Plumer congratulated Mr. Clay on the felicity of his address of wel-

THE BARGAIN

come in which, it seemed to the New Englander, the Speaker had especially emphasized the *civil* virtues" of the distinguished visitor.

"You will not find me, Mr. Plumer," said Clay, in acknowledgment of the complimentary remarks, "disposed by *any act of mine*, unnecessarily to increase the *military fever* which has already produced some *strange effects* upon us."

Thus on December 10, Mr. Clay appeared to be leaning from Jackson and Mr. Plumer went away happy.[24]

In view of other evidence which time was to bring to light, the wonder is that Clay said so little to Plumer. For it appears that prior to his departure from Kentucky, where the Speaker's friendly references to General Jackson created much comment, he had, at the same time, told a few friends he would never vote for the Tennessean for President;[25] that en route to the capital he had told a travelling companion that in a contest between Jackson and Adams he would support the latter;[26] and that, after his arrival in Washington, at a conference with Thomas Hart Benton, Mr. Clay had declined to follow his lieutenant into the Jackson camp and affirmed to him his intention to vote for Adams.[27]

In the light of these facts, later offered to show that Clay's determination to support Adams was of long standing and definitely settled by the time he reached the capital, why, then, did the Speaker send away Plumer, a member of Adams's inner circle, with no more than a shadowy hint of his supposed intentions? Nor is this the only feature of Mr. Clay's behavior, or of the general situation, that confounds ready explanation. Political secrets are so notoriously difficult to keep that one may almost set down the expression as a contradiction in terms. With all Washington clamoring for the least indication of Henry Clay's intentions, the gentlemen to whom he had confided this priceless information kept their tongues so well as almost to impose a strain upon credulity. Not only was a prying public left in the dark, but the whole Adams crew as well as many of Clay's most trusted friends both at home and in the capital; and also other politicians not often so badly misled.

4

So little did one Clay follower, Representative Thomas Moore of Kentucky, suspect that his chief could have committed himself to

Adams that, when the Speaker merely expressed a doubt as to how the Kentucky delegation should vote, Moore was surprised. Or so he said in a later account of the interview which took place in his bedroom at Brown's Hotel, the implication being that until then he had expected the Speaker to support Andrew Jackson. At any rate, when Mr. Clay had departed, Moore lost no time sending for Representative Robert P. Henry and United States Senator "Tecumseh" Johnson of Kentucky, to whom he repeated Clay's words. Henry said that Clay had made the same statement to him. Whereupon Moore and Henry, concluding that something was in the wind they did not fully understand, agreed forthwith to announce for Jackson.[28]

The public inferences, drawn from the avowal of two members from Kentucky, could not have been very comforting to those Jackson people who were counting on a majority of Kentucky's delegation of twelve. The question that intruded was, "What of the other ten?" Already afloat were vague stories that Clay was maneuvering in the direction of Adams. Assuredly something was happening to disturb the optimism of the Jacksonians. Van Buren reported them not in such high feather as before, but offered no speculation as to the cause.[29] Others did not hesitate to lay the Jacksonians' discomfiture at the door of Mr. Clay. "Late events," Mangum of North Carolina wrote on Christmas day, "leave Jackson's prospects more doubtful.... All depends on Kentucky.... Ohio and Missouri will go with her."[30] Still, neither he nor Van Buren saw reason to change their prediction that Jackson would win.

A feeling that more was going on than met the eye began to communicate itself to the country. "We *cannot* get a [dependable] whisper from Washington," complained a member of the Virginia State government at Richmond. "Now and then a faint rumour reaches us that *Adams* will be President." The Virginian was unprepared to accept such a contradiction of the portents, however. "Jacksons want of information [education] and his temperament are the only obstacles in his way. I think he will probably be the *man*. It is not however so certain now ... as *it appeared* to be."[31]

From an unexpected source came a ray of light on the Virginian's reference to Jackson's "temperament." Of a sudden Daniel Webster had shaken off the lethargy he had exhibited throughout the presidential contest, and, returning from an excursion beyond the Potomac, he repeated the substance of an interview with Thomas Jefferson. "I feel much alarmed," the philosopher of Monticello had said, "at the prospect of seeing General Jackson President. He is one of the most unfit men I know of for such a place. . . . His passions are terrible."[32] No sooner was this story in circulation than Thomas Hart Benton muddied the water a little more with a correction. Senator Benton had been to the Blue Ridge where he, too, climbed the bad road to the ill-kept mansion on the mountain which the sage inhabited by the indulgence of creditors, receiving callers in a stained dressing-gown and shabby slippers. "I told it [the report that Clay would support Adams] as my *belief*, . . . that Mr. Adams would, from the necessity of the case, . . . make up a mixed cabinet, . . . and asked Mr. Jefferson . . . how it would do? He answered: 'Not at all— would never succeed— would ruin all engaged in it.' "[33]

Mr. Benton's inexplicit allusion to the possibility of a "mixed" Cabinet was putting it delicately, for by this time a tale was abroad specifying the Secretaryship of State as the price of the Kentuckian's support of Adams. R. K. Call had this brought home to him in direct fashion, according to his own version. A man approached the member from Florida to ask Jackson's intention about filling the State Department. The visitor mentioned the superior qualifications of Mr. Clay. Call replied that he did not know the answer to the gentleman's question, which concerned a subject he could not mention to General Jackson.

"Then I venture to say," crisply observed Call's visitor, "that General Jackson will not be elected."[34]

5

It remained, however, for James Buchanan to carry to Andrew Jackson a statement of the alleged aspirations of Mr. Clay. This tall young man of good appearance and address, just elected to his third term from Pennsylvania, had been a good deal in the company of Clay's intimate set that winter. He was not anxious to undertake the rôle of courier between the headquarters of Clay and of Jackson, and had gone first to Major Eaton, then to Representative George Kremer from his own state, asking each of them to convey the substance of a message to Jackson. Learning what the message was they declined.³⁵

So Buchanan presented himself at Gadsby's Hotel, outstayed the rest of the company, and accepted the General's invitation to take a walk. The Pennsylvanian's opening speech gave him some trouble. He said he had come as a friend, and, whatever the General's reply to the communication he was about to make, he hoped that it would not alter their personal relationship. Jackson helped his caller over the difficulty by saying that his reputation was assurance of the purity of his motives. Whereupon Mr. Buchanan continued:

Friends of Mr. Clay had informed him that friends of Mr. Adams had approached them with the information that, if Mr. Clay would aid in Mr. Adams's election, he should be Secretary of State; that to induce the friends of Mr. Clay to accede to their proposal, Mr. Adams's friends said that, if Jackson were elected, he would continue Adams as head of the State Department. The friends of Mr. Clay were distressed to hear this. They had assured Mr. Buchanan that "the West did not wish to separate from the West"; if Jackson would permit a confidential associate to say that if he were elected Mr. Adams should not be Secretary of State, "a complete union of Mr. Clay and his friends would put an end to the presidential contest in one hour."

The General had his answer ready.

"Say to Mr. Clay and his friends that before I would reach the presidential chair by such means . . . I would see the earth open and swallow both Mr. Clay and his friends and myself with them. If they had not the confidence . . . that I would call to . . . the cabinet men of the first virtue, talent and integrity, [tell them] not to vote for me."³⁶

A disappointed young politician took his leave of General Jackson. To Kremer he argued the old soldier's ignorance of the seriousness of the situation and the necessity of meeting the opposition "with their own wepons."³⁷ Mr. Buchanan's motive seems not to have been more reprehensible than an effort to help Jackson despite himself, and to spare Clay the possible consequences of a dangerous game.³⁸ Concerning the nature of the Speaker's activities others had the same thought. Jefferson's opinion had been expressed to Benton. By this time Van Buren also had discovered the basis of the anxiety pervading the Jackson camp. When light-hearted Francis Johnson of Kentucky appealed to him to concert his influence with Clay's the New Yorker, who had reduced the science of politics to a settled system of diagnosis and pathology, declared that to elect Mr. Adams by the means proposed would be "Mr. Clay's political death warrant."[39]

In this situation James Buchanan himself determined to run a few risks. The message he set out to convey to Mr. Clay was not the message entrusted to him by General Jackson. Finding the Speaker in the lodgings of a messmate, Robert P. Letcher of Kentucky, Buchanan guided the conversation to the subject of cabinets, venturing that Jackson would bring forth the most notable ministry in the country's history. Letcher asked where he would find the equal of Jefferson's Cabinet in which were Madison and Gallatin.

Buchanan looked at Henry Clay. "He would not go outside of this room for a Secretary of State."

The Kentuckian laughed. The only Cabinet timber he saw in the room was the gentleman from Pennsylvania.[40]

How to construe the jest of this attractive, enigmatical man who seemed to take nothing over-seriously? Would he accept as a bona fide assurance from Jackson the daring bid of James Buchanan? Or had he more dependable information of Old Hickory's attitude? Or, again, was it now too late to turn him from Adams? Nearly a week of January had slipped by. Time was getting short.

6

Adams men, too, eyed the calendar. The time was as short for them as for the Jacksonians and much remained to do. But whereas the apprehensions of Hickoryites tended to increase, those of the Adams following subsided in almost direct proportion. In a little better than a month they had gained much.

In the beginning loyal Adams retainers had had enough to depress them as they pondered the possibility of drawing Henry Clay to their side. But ponder it they must, for the bristling antipathy of the Crawford group left no alternative. Moreover, none but Clay had the slightest chance of diverting from Jackson the western states Adams must have to succeed. These calculations could not have overlooked a consideration of the *raison d'être* Mr. Clay must advance for the desertion of the western candidate. Under this head were three distinct possibilities, one excellent and one plausible enough to serve.

Mr. Clay could support Mr. Adams on the high and well-nigh unassailable ground of his superior fitness.

He could support him on the ground that his tariff and internal-improvement views were more to Clay's liking than the views of Jackson on those issues.

He could support him on the negative ground of personal and political estrangement from Old Hickory, the core of which was the "military chieftain" charge.

This on one hand. On the other stood the unmistakable preference of the West, to which Clay owed his career, for General Jackson; the fact that in times past Adams and Clay had fought each other as bitterly as ever Jackson and Clay had fought, Adams branding the Kentuckian as a "half-educated" man of "loose public and private morals";[41] and the disconcerting indications of a happy adjustment of the differences that once had separated Jackson, Clay and their respective friends.

Such had been the unpromising outlook from the Adams watchtowers at the opening of December. Then, the slow but sure change. Presently the Adams people detected in the air signs that Clay was inclining toward their man. In this Mr. Clay's actual, not his ostensible, motive seemed to concern none of the reasons enumerated above. What the Speaker wished to know was how an alliance with Adams would affect the immediate political future of Henry Clay.

In any event so reasoned one of Mr. Adams's alert friends who lost no time in apprising his chief of the lay of the land. On the fifteenth day of December Edward Wyer called on Adams to say that the Speaker's support was available if, by that means, Clay "could be useful to himself."[42] Wyer was a political journalist close to Adams. He knew and Adams knew, if they knew anything, that without Clay's help Adams was lost. Benevolent neutrality would not do; it must be active help. Adams's reply to Wyer's feeler is not on record, but there was no rebuff such as Jackson was to give Buchanan. Next day the arrival of the Louisiana returns sent Wyer back to repeat his story.

From then on things moved apace. The day after Wyer's second trip Clay's friend Robert P. Letcher called on a pretext of State Department business. After an expansive exposition of the intricacies of Kentucky politics he asked Mr. Adams point-blank what he thought of Mr. Clay. The Secretary responded that he "harbored no animosity." Letcher said the Speaker's sentiments were similar. Before his visitor had departed Mr. Adams concluded that Wyer had given a true picture. "Clay would willingly support me if he could serve thereby himself. . . . [He wishes] a prominent share in the administration."[43]

Should he care for Mr. Clay's support on those terms, it was for Adams to convey such assurances as the Kentuckian would understand and would accept.

This was a difficult thing for one of John Quincy Adams's political training to do. For five days Clay waited, and heard nothing. On December 23, Letcher returned with definite and thinly veiled proposals, holding up to Adams the importance of carrying Kentucky, Ohio, Indiana, Illinois, Missouri and Louisiana on the first ballot, states which everyone believed without Clay's intervention, would go to Jackson. To this lucid demonstration of the obvious, the Secretary of State appears to have said little. John Quincy Adams was a master of euphemism. As a diplomat he could intrigue with the best, clothing a doubtful cause in language that made it shine forth as a thing above reproach. These talents he had used to the advantage of his country, but never to that of himself. With his political ideals undergoing the test of a lifetime Adams hesitated, sending Letcher away with an answer apparently not wholly satisfactory. That night a restless conscience relieved itself with a closing line in the Adams diary. "I consider Letcher as moving for Clay. . . . Incedo super ignes. [I walk over fires.]"[44]

On the next day William Plumer, jr., fully cognizant of the Kentucky game—"Clay's friends would have the merit of making Adams President, & have it to themselves"—found the Secretary in "better spirits" over his prospects than at any time before.[45]

Back went Letcher to say that Mr. Adams should meet the Speaker for a conference. To this the Secretary agreed "very readily." That evening—January 1—the two men found themselves seated together at a dinner to Lafayette. Clay requested "a confidential conversation" and Adams said to fix the time.[46]

Now it was Mr. Adams's turn to wait. In the meantime, Buchanan made his spirited sally, after which he, too, waited, and in vain, for a response from Henry Clay. The Speaker went his unruffled way. Privately he told Senator Bouligny of Louisiana,[47] and in reply to an audacious question he told Lafayette, that his intention was to vote for Adams.[48] Yet, in view of all the available evidence, it is difficult to confirm the claim later made that these and earlier conversations constituted commitments, and furnished proof that the Speaker had come to Washington imbued with a determination to support Mr. Adams from which he had never receded. With equal plausibility they could be placed in the category of tentative expressions which politicians less adroit than Henry Clay repudiate with impunity. Up to mid-January, or later, the accepted view was that Mr. Clay had not made up his mind. "It is not known," observed Nathaniel Macon, "for whom the friends of Mr. Clay will vote."[49] On January 10 Markley of Pennsylvania conversed with the Speaker without ascertaining whom he would support.[50] Cobb of Georgia saw the Clay crowd conscious of their possession of the balance of power, but apparently undetermined on a candidate. "Their conduct is extremely mysterious and doubtful."[51]

The anxiety in the Adams camp was plain to see.[52] In fact on January 8, when Mr. Adams had been a week without word from the Speaker, Clay was sure enough of his man to burn his bridges and take the decisive step. His first act was to notify a confidential lieutenant, Francis P. Blair of Kentucky, in a letter which does not appear to be the reflection of a man for weeks confirmed in his resolution to support John Quincy Adams.

"We are beginning to think seriously of the choice that must be made [between Adams and Jackson]. To both of these Gentlemen there are strong personal objections. . . . In the election of Mr Adams [however] we shall not . . . inflict any wound upon the character of our institutions. . . . I should much fear hereafter if not during the present generation that the election of General Jackson would give to the Military spirit a stimulus . . . that might lead to most pernicious results." This from a War Hawk of 1811. "[As] a choice of evils . . . I shall, with great regret, . . . support M^r

Adams. . . . My friends entertain the belief that their kind wishes toward me will . . . be more likely to be accomplished" by following suit. Therefore, would Mr. Blair write to his representative (the wavering David White) to vote for Adams? "Be pleased to shew this letter to Crittenden alone."[53]

With this missive, calculated to put in motion an important part of the machinery of the coalition, on its way, Mr. Clay asked permission to call at the Adams residence. The following evening, January 9, 1825, the "Kentucky gamester" and the Puritan met, talked long and parted allies to stand or fall together.[54]

7

Two days later the first shadow crossed the path of the new coalition: resolutions of the Kentucky Legislature directing Henry Clay and colleagues to vote for Andrew Jackson. This brought two other members of the delegation to the sides of Thomas Moore and R. P. Henry who had previously come out for the General. With Adams's cohorts in a state of "excessive alarm,"[55] Clay stemmed the revolt, holding the remaining Kentuckians in line for the New Englander.

Something now depended on how well Blair and Crittenden should do their work of setting backfires against the pronouncement of the Legislature.[56] They did as well as could be expected, considering that neither had his heart in it.

The letter of the ordinarily masterful Crittenden to the least distinguished of Kentucky congressmen was a shame-faced thing throughout, summarizing the business under review as "trashy politics." Jackson for President and Clay for Secretary of State would be the ideal slate, he said. This unattainable, "the common good is more concerned with Clay's being Secretary than it is . . . [with] whether Jackson or Adams shall be president."[57] Blair performed better, setting forth that, had it been known Adams intended Clay for the Cabinet, the Legislature "scarcely" would have hesitated to ask the Kentucky delegation to vote for him.[58] Then Mr. Blair sped to the Assembly chambers to importune members for letters in support of that interesting hypothesis.[59]

This and similarly inspired activity worked a temporary alteration in the complexion of congressional mail from Kentucky. Mr. Clay chanced to be present when the recalcitrant Moore broke the seal of a letter urging him, as he said, "to vote for whoever would make Mr. Clay Secretary of State, and intimating that Mr. Adams would do it." Clay genially asked the news from Kentucky. Moore observed that the missive was from a close friend of the Speaker.

"And what does he say?" pursued Mr. Clay.

"You know very well," replied Moore.

Mr. Clay smiled and moved away.[60]

8

Thus was the presidential question reopened, precipitating an unconcealed scramble for votes. The drama set Washington by the ears. "Society is now divided into separate battalions. . . . Mrs. Adams collected a large party [for the theatre], . . . Mrs. Calhoun another, so it was thought that Mrs. Crawford, . . . too [should] . . . show our strength."[61] Nerves were so jumpy that Lafayette imagined himself in danger of becoming involved. Living at the same hotel, he and General Jackson had been seen exchanging reminiscences of the Revolution. To repel suspicion of a deflection from his course of meticulous neutrality, the marquis abandoned his uniform, even when inspecting troops.

Deftly Mr. Clay moved against the Jackson lines, West and East. The switch of Cook of Illinois added the first new state to Mr. Adams's list. Storrs of New York promptly followed his Kentucky leader in the new alliance, and Brent of Louisiana seemed ill at ease in the presence of his old comrade, R. K. Call. Scott of Missouri was approached with less success. "[Though] one of Clay's best friends," Kremer of Pennsylvania related of the Missourian, "he [said he] would be damned if he would be sold like sheep."[62]

The ethical factor in the Adams-Clay understanding began to receive more attention. So open a confederation of men and forces, previously uncongenial, marked still another departure from the standards hitherto prevailing with reference to the presidency. It flew in the face of the swelling demand for a recognition of the will of the populace, noted on all sides as one of the distinguishing features of the campaign of 1824.

Out in the country, people were manifesting a revival of interest

THE BARGAIN

in the presidential question, and beginning to coin their own names for the phenomena narrated by the Washington dispatches. The names coined by John Campbell, an intelligent young Virginian, not at this time a partizan of Jackson, were uncomplimentary. From his family correspondence, composed with no eye to public effect: "Letters from Washington inform us that Adams is certainly to be the President. Clay & him have compromised. . . . *Bargain & sales* are going on . . . as infamous *as you* can imagine. This office & that are held out provided you *vote this way and that &c &c* What is this but bribery and corruption."[63] Regarding the effect on the fortunes of Henry Clay, Mr. Campbell voiced sentiments already expressed by Jefferson, Van Buren and Buchanan. "His conduct is beyond my comprehension. . . . What will the western people say?"[64]

If a more or less disinterested spectator could feel so strongly, the effect on the Jacksonian politicians may be imagined. "The monstrous union between Clay & Adams," exclaimed Senator Robert Y. Hayne of South Carolina, "[renders] the results doubtful. . . . We are in great danger."[65]

Old Hickory's followers did more than wring their hands, however. They took practical counter-measures. The strides of the coalition gave them something akin to a common cause with the friends of Crawford, however personally distasteful to all the gentlemen concerned that circumstance might be. One heard strange rumors. Aaron Burr's friend, Samuel Swartwout, was no head-in-the-clouds idealist, and his free access to the distinguished lodger at Gadsby's vexed some of the Jackson men who were jealous of their chief's reputation. Burr was close to Crawford leaders in New York. "Jackson's friends," wrote a New Yorker who was for Adams, "are pushing their intrigues to as desperate an extreme as Burr's did in 1801."[66] In proof whereof, the Representative made the astounding assertion that the General had called in person on William H. Crawford.

The news spread like quick-silver. Someone flew with it to Adams, now meeting his lieutenants daily to review the progress of their efforts. The reaction was a mixture of alarm, lest the Jackson and Crawford forces actually unite, and of relief over the fact that the pot could no longer call the kettle black. "Jackson last winter made up with all his other enemies—Clay, Benton, Cocke, Scott &c [but] kept aloof from Crawford," Plumer of New Hampshire, fresh from the Adams presence, reminded his father. "Now it is said that he has been to see Mr. Crawford & made very humble submissions and proffered him any terms which he might ask as the price of his cooperation."[67]

"Intrigue," "terms," "price": with something of relish Adams men rolled on their tongues syllables that were becoming too common for comfort in the threatening speech of the hard-pressed Jacksonians. The hubbub over the Crawford interview story was short-lived, though. Even before the letter to his parent was finished, Plumer learned that no such meeting had occurred.[68] Nevertheless, he insisted that friends of General Jackson and friends of Mr. Crawford were getting together.

Though no specific instance has been disclosed to the present writer, the general evidence supports this contention. Andrew Stevenson of Virginia, an influential man in the House, heard from his sister that Crawford partizans in Richmond were "universally denouncing Clay and Adams. . . . They would like Jackson now. . . . Quite a fashionable subject of conversation [is] 'who is to be bought and sold.' "[69]

Nor had the Jacksonians entirely abandoned their efforts to divert Clay men from the standard of the New Englander. The Ohio members seem to have been the object of a frontal attack by Jacksonians who "often repeated in a menacing manner that . . . [we] *durst not* vote for any other than General Jackson."[70] The approach of Sam Houston, however, gave less offense and suggests collaboration with James Buchanan. "Aid in electing General Jackson," John Sloane of Ohio, years later quoted Houston as having said, "and your man can have anything he pleases. What a splendid administration, . . . with Old Hickory as President and Mr. Clay as Secretary of State."[71] One flaw in these overtures was that Buchanan and Houston acted without the consent of their principal.

Adams-Clay men prosecuted their missions armed with that consent. This was verified by continuous contact with the Adams residence. Useful Robert Letcher brought in Scott with two things on his mind: first, the West's desire that Clay be in the administration; second, the plight of Scott's brother, a Federal judge who, having slain a dissenting member of the bench in a duel, imagined his robe in danger. Mr. Adams left Scott with the idea that Clay would be taken care of and the powder-stained jurist undisturbed. But, under the watchful care of Benton, Scott announced no change of allegiance.[72] Clay himself helped to pave the way for the visit of Daniel Webster who also had his boon to crave. Webster wished to be minister to England. Clay needed Webster's influence with the Federalist members from Maryland and Delaware. Webster left Mr. Adams's large brick house in F Street feeling the London appointment was to be his and straightway went to work on the Federalist congressmen.[73] In contrast to these gentlemen stood Cook of Illinois. Always an Adams man by personal preference, he had been one of the first accessions to the New Englander's camp. At this the Jacksonites had risen in their wrath and were making it uncomfortable for Cook when Mr. Adams asked him to dinner. Promises being unnecessary, for Cook had sought nothing in exchange for his vote, the object of the invitation seems to have been merely to bolster the Congressman's resistance. When the evening was over, Mr. Adams doubted whether he had done an effective job.[74]

Thus did the campaign etiquette of J. Q. Adams yield to the importunities of the times, giving way under the attrition of the stream of politicians, from Wyer to Webster, crowding across the New Englander's threshold, until the partnership with Clay manifested itself in a candid quest for votes by the time-honored means of promises, patronage and protection.

9

Exposed to identical importunities, Andrew Jackson yielded nothing. Though his rooms were usually filled, politics was a forbidden topic. His personal correspondence indicates that he closed his ears even privately to tales with which Eaton, Call, Houston, *et al.* were only too familiar.

While gossip of the Adams-Clay rapprochement filled Washington, he wrote to John Coffee: "There are various rumours . . . but whether any of them is founded in fact I do not know, as I do not . . . join in any conversation on the subject of the presidential election. . . . Altho Mrs J and myself goes to no parties . . . [tonight] the young [members of the Jackson entourage] are at parties and

Mrs J and myself at home smoking our pipe and send love to you Polly and the children."[75]

After sending Congressman Buchanan about his business the General confided to the same trusted friend: "Information of today gives some reasons to believe that a coalition is about to be formed . . . [of] the interest of Crawford, Clay and Adams combined for the purpose of defeating my election. be this as it may, I shall continue my course, . . . and I assure you I shall not envy the man who places himself in the chair of state by intrigue of his friends."[76]

When at length Mr. Clay admitted what nearly everyone already knew, and formally announced his alignment with Adams, Jackson referred to it in a letter to W. B. Lewis as "such an unexpected course."[77]

Once only did Old Hickory unbridle a flash of the spirit for which he was famous. Rumors that were thirty years old had preceded the arrival in Washington of Mrs. Jackson. "A dilemma was presented, and a grand debate ensued as to whether the ladies would visit her."[78]

They came, though Aunt Rachel would not have minded had they stayed away. "Oh, my dear friend," she wrote home to a neighbor, "how shall I get through this bustle, . . . from fifty to one hundred persons calling in a day." Lafayette delighted her. "He wears a wig and is a little inclined to corpulency. He is very healthy, eats hearty, goes to every party, and that is every night. . . . The General and myself . . . [go only to] church. Mr. Baker the pastor . . . is a fine, plain preacher. . . . The play actors . . . [requested] my countenance to them. No. A ticket to balls and parties. No, not one. Two dinings; several times to drink tea. Indeed, Mr. Jackson encourages me in my course."[79]

One gentleman was on the *qui vive* for a sight of the lady concerning whom he had heard "industriously circulated . . . a thousand slanders . . . of her awkwardness, ignorance and indecorum." Upon acquaintance he added: "I . . . find her striking characteristics to be an unaffected simplicity of manners, with great goodness of heart."[80]

It was a friend in Virginia who informed the General of "papers" imputing to Rachel shortcomings apparently more racy than unfamiliarity with the forms of polished society would evoke. These documents had been mysteriously left in the hands of "an individual

THE BARGAIN

in Alex.ª," who appeared so disturbed over their nature that "he is afraid to communicate or even speak about them." Yet Jackson was warned to be on his guard.[81]

To which Rachel's husband replied with a pen that fairly stabbed the paper:

"I can assure you that whenever my enemies think it worth while to investigate . . . the character of Mʳˢ. J I fear not . . . as I know how to defend . . . her."[82]

The pistol that killed Dickinson was behind in Tennessee; but still in order.

10

Mr. Clay's formal declaration for Adams came a fortnight before the question was to go before the House.[83] The Speaker had been too long in public life not to have expected a measure of recoil; but seasoned politician and man of courage though he was, Henry Clay was taken aback by the fury of the tempest that smote him. "The friends of —— [Jackson] have turned upon me. . . . I am a deserter from democracy; a giant at intrigue; have sold the West— have sold myself."[84]

"For God's sake be on your guard," warned Crittenden from Kentucky. "A thousand desperadoes . . . would think it a most honorable service . . . to shoot you."[85]

The *Columbian Observer* of Philadelphia, whose editor was a friend of John Henry Eaton, printed a statement purporting to be from a Pennsylvania representative:

"For some time past the friends of Clay have hinted that they, like the Swiss, would fight for those who pay best. Overtures were said to have been made by the friends of Adams . . . offering . . . [Clay] the appointment of Secretary of State. . . . The friends of Clay gave the information to the friends of Jackson and hinted that if the friends of Jackson would offer the same price they would close with them. . . . The friends of Jackson . . . [refused]."[86]

After which a Richmond editor asked whether Clay had "gone over to . . . Mr. Adams with a view to constitute a pair of his cabinet?"

Boldly Clay met the assault. "Do you believe it?" he countered in reply to the query of the Virginia journalist. "Then you ought not to respect me. Do you wish me to deny it? Then you cannot respect me. What do you desire?—That I should vote for Mr. Crawford? I cannot. For General Jackson? I will not."[87]

Yet, on the same day in another communication, Mr. Clay did deny it. "My dear Sir, I want no office."[88] And the implications of this letter differed from those of a missive penned twenty-four hours before the storm broke, in which the Speaker wrote with evident satisfaction: "I believe I can enter [Mr. Adams's Cabinet] in *any* situation I choose."[89] If Mr. Clay meant his statement that he wished no office, many of the Speaker's followers were supporting Adams under a misapprehension of the facts. Simple-minded Congressman White of Kentucky had put the case too bluntly for comfort, when he said he was not going "to vote for Mr. Adams but for Mr. Clay."[90]

The *Observer's* correspondent had sought to indict Mr. Adams jointly with Mr. Clay, yet only Clay felt that he must defend his name. In a published "card" the excited Kentuckian called upon the author to "unveil himself" and accept a challenge to the field of honor. Adams people were aghast at this display of western manners so long urged as a valid reason for rejecting the pretensions of Andrew Jackson.

However, the brave scene dissolved in quiet laughter when Mr. Clay's accuser briskly unveiled. He was George Kremer, a quaint little rustic from a "Pennsylvania Dutch" district, in private life a cross-roads storekeeper and in his official capacity hitherto conspicuous only because of the leopard-skin coat he wore on the floor of the House. "Mr. Kremer is a man," Webster informed his brother, "with whom one would think of having a shot about as soon as with your neighbor, Mr. Simeon Atkinson, whom he somewhat resembles."[91]

The dueling threat out of the way, Mr. Clay demanded an investigation by the House. Mr. Kremer rose in his place to say that he would appear before any properly constituted body and prove his charge. Thus Kremer in public, the flaming champion of political virtue, a rôle which, alas, Kremer in private seemed unable to sustain for, when taken off guard by irate friends of the Speaker, he bewilderingly denied any intention "to charge Mr. Clay with corruption."[92] After some delay a committee was chosen before which Mr. Kremer refused, on constitutional grounds, to appear. Although ultimately a good deal was made of Kremer's unseemly back-down, the Clay faction remained curiously silent at the time, it being tacitly understood by Clay, Adams and Jackson people alike that no good would come from pressing this inquiry too hard in face of the fact that every side had its secrets to guard. Mr. Clay believed the *Columbian Observer* letter to have been written by Eaton, and that may have been the way of it.[93]

The investigating committee receded from view, eventually to compose a milk-and-water report and lay it unnoticed before the House on February 9, 1825, a day which found that body engrossed in other concerns. Lafayette had returned to town to wedge his way into the gallery, for once a spectator, and not a spectacle. On the floor before him the representatives had come together to elect a President of the United States.

II

The domed, ill-ventilated chamber, outlined by a semi-circle of pillars of Potomac marble, breathed forth a sweet odor of wet wool and leather as the used-up air melted the snow which people tracked in. Before the canopied dais of the Speaker, the desks of members stood in concentric curves. On each desk was a snuff box, provided at public expense, and beside each desk a spittoon environed by a dark aura of stains—evidence that the astonished accounts of European observers concerning one particular of American marksmanship erred on the side of flattery. The interstices between pillars were filled by sofas and behind these were the galleries, raised only a foot or so above the common level. The sofas were grimly held down by excessively privileged characters while the less fortunate trod on their toes. A few representatives lounged in their seats. Others conversed in small groups or worked off their nervous vitality by visiting, from floor to foyer to gallery, as the hands of the marble-faced clock on the wall, chaperoned by a comely representation of History, measured the minutes. The special nature of the occasion was indicated by the fact that the members were not wearing their hats.

Galleries and politicians expected a long fight in which time would be the ally of General Jackson. Washington throbbed at the prospect, for the Clay-Adams coalition had reanimated the interest of the country. The Speaker's belated acknowledgment of that alliance was lashing the West into a lather beside which the local storm seemed as nothing. Missouri and Kentucky sent up cries of rage and Pennsylvania militiamen talked of laying siege to Washington if Jackson were not chosen.[94] With this wrathful wave of protest rolling eastward, Mr. Clay was in no position to prolong the contest. To win for Adams he must win quickly.

The snowy morning when the Speaker left his lodgings for the Capitol he did not have the thirteen states necessary to give Mr. Adams a majority on the first ballot. Lot Clark of New York, a Van Buren lieutenant and a clear-sighted observer, placed Adams's strength at ten states[95]—an estimate which must have been shared by many others. Actually Mr. Clay had been able to do better than that. In the face of a blistering denunciation from Benton, Scott of Missouri had announced for Adams[96] at the last moment, and Webster's drive on Maryland had won that state, for the first ballot only, by the margin of a single vote. Louisiana also was Adams's by one vote in the hands of a timid, unsteady man.

Nevertheless, the New Englander had the pledges of twelve states for the first ballot, or only one short of a majority. But on the second ballot it was said that he would lose Maryland where one member had promised to switch to Jackson.[97] In that event Adams would be two votes shy, and in no good position to regain the ground lost. On the other hand Jackson would be only beginning to show his second-line strength.

One effect of the Clay-Adams coalition had been to drive Crawford people into Jackson's arms where they found a hospitable welcome. On the eve of the balloting, such conspicuous Crawford adherents as John Randolph of Virginia, Cobb and Cuthbert of Georgia, and McLane of Delaware, equaled the Jacksonians in their hostility to Adams. Van Buren was more cautious in his expressions of preference, though it is significant that Cuthbert and McLane, supposed to look to the New York Senator for political guidance, shared with him a house in the capital.[98] The fourth resident of this congenial bachelor's hall was General Stephen Van Rensselaer, the Albany patroon and largest landowner in the eastern states.

On the first ballot Jackson was expected to poll the votes of seven states. After that Georgia, North Carolina and perhaps Virginia, having observed the amenities toward Crawford, seemed to be his. This assumption would give Jackson at least nine states to Adams's ten with the Jackson bloc probably in the better position to stand the hammering of a long contest.

Such were the prognostications on the morning of February 9. The hands on the marble clock-face moved toward the hour of noon. The tension in the crowded chamber increased. In the galleries were men who remembered the threats of armed intervention to bring an end to the seven-day battle between Jefferson and Burr. The son-in-law of Lafayette recalled the temper of the Pennsylvania militiamen he had seen. At ten minutes before twelve, a North Carolina member, "with countenance discovering deep concern," besought a colleague from Maryland. "I hope to God you may be able to terminate the election on the first ballot."[99]

But where was Mr. Clay? He had not appeared, as he often did, to mingle and jest with the members before taking up the gavel. The fact is that in the brief time that remained the Speaker was engaged elsewhere, in the effort of his life to win the one state needed to terminate the election on the first ballot. And unerringly he had picked the weakest link in the encircling chain of his adversaries.

12

The New York delegation was tied, seventeen votes for Adams and seventeen[100] in the hands of Van Buren which meant that, until the deadlock should be broken, the vote of the State would be counted for none of the candidates. Such was the utmost the Adams managers had been able to accomplish after weeks of effort, effort in which a promise of the ministership to England was said to have been whispered to DeWitt Clinton.[101] This story would have interested Daniel Webster whose zeal for Adams dated from the interview in which he had understood Mr. Adams to say that the London post should be his.

One of Van Buren's embattled band was General Van Rensselaer whose family exercised a sort of proprietary right to the congressional seat for the Albany district, the present incumbent being the fourth of his name to hold it. The old gentleman was immensely rich and sincerely pious; but in his veins the imperious blood of the line had run thin, so that the General often found himself in agreement with the views of the last person to speak to him, and especially his strong-minded wife. A dinner-party story had it that someone asked the General if he had read the Baron von Humboldt's latest work. He pondered and glanced at his wife. "Have I read Humboldt's work, my dear?" Margaret Schuyler frowned. "Certainly you have read it."[102]

In this situation Mr. Van Buren had made a personal concern of the political welfare of his aged protégé. Clay had been after him, had convoyed him to the Adams fireside along with the rest of the benighted he was struggling to show the light, but watchful Van Buren was able to counteract these ministrations. The old land baron clung to his determination to vote either for Jackson or for Crawford. The last preference he had expressed was for Jackson.

At breakfast on the ninth, Stephen Van Rensselaer had reassured his messmates. The four rode to the Capitol where Mr. Clay guided the patroon into the Speaker's private room. There they found Webster. These vigorous masters of persuasion plied Van Rensselaer with every word, every argument, every artifice at their command. They said the question of whether the House would or would not be able to select a President depended upon him. The two advocates agonized the old man with a dark picture of national chaos "that would in all probability result from the disorganization of the Government," the stake the Van Rensselaers with their vast estates had in the preservation of order, and so on.[103]

Though weak and shaken Van Rensselaer would not retract his promise to Van Buren. Leaving Clay and Webster he encountered McLane who was shocked by his colleague's distraught appearance.

"The election turns on my vote," stammered the old man. "*One vote will give Adams the majority*— This is a responsibility I cannot bear. What shall I do?"

"Do!" exclaimed McLane. "Do what honor, what principles direct. General, you are an old man. . . . You want nothing, you have no motive but duty to sway you. Look at me. . . . *My vote,* like yours, would turn the scale. [McLane was the sole representative from Delaware.] But, General, the greater the responsibility the greater the honor. . . . Let us march boldly in and do our duty."

This speech seemed what the old waverer needed. "I am resolved," he said. "Here is my hand on it."[104]

Feeling that the emergency called for a word from Van Buren, McLane sent for him. By the time Van Buren arrived Van Rensselaer had shuffled down the aisle toward his seat. Cuthbert of Georgia told the Senator that it would be unnecessary to trouble the old man with further questions as Van Rensselaer had just assured him that he would not vote for Adams. After reaching his desk the patroon made the same statement to J. J. Morgan, a Jackson member of the New York delegation.[105]

On the stroke of noon the forty-eight senators filed into the hall, two and two, led by their president *pro tempore*, the aged and wrinkled Gaillard of South Carolina. The senators took seats on the right of the dais. Mr. Gaillard occupied the Speaker's chair and Henry Clay that of the Clerk.

The first order of business was the formality of counting the electoral votes. This done, Gaillard announced the election of John C. Calhoun as Vice President, but that no candidate had received a majority of the votes for President.

The elder statesmen's participation in the tableau at an end, they solemnly filed out. Poised and pleasant-looking, Mr. Clay stepped behind his accustomed desk and, with the informal dignity that helped to make him the most popular moderator the House ever had, assumed the gavel.

State delegations were directed to poll their members. As the New Yorkers' box was passed General Van Rensselaer dropped his head on the edge of his desk in a silent appeal to his Maker. Removing his hand from his eyes he saw at his feet a discarded Adams ballot. Accepting this as an answer to his prayer, the old man picked up the ticket and dropped it in the box.[106] This act gave Mr. Adams a majority of one in the New York delegation, and the vote of that state.

Each delegation having balloted, the name of the candidate of its choice was written on two pieces of paper which were placed in separate boxes to be counted by the tellers, Webster and Randolph. The votes in the two boxes tallied. First Webster, then Randolph announced the result.

Adams had received the votes of thirteen states, Jackson of seven, Crawford four.

The Speaker arose. "John Quincy Adams, having a majority of the votes of these United States is duly elected President of the same."[107] Surely none had a better right than Henry Clay to give that message to the world.

A spattering of handclapping came from the astonished galleries; then a few hisses.

A Jackson firebrand from South Carolina leaped to his feet and demanded that the galleries be cleared. The applause, apparently, had angered him. Mr. Clay so ordered and the embarrassed sergeant-at-arms gestured toward the exits. In a few moments the benches were bare.

A motion to adjourn was carried and the members trooped out on the heels of their expelled guests.

Randolph of Roanoke's sallow face was hard. "It was impossible to win the game, gentlemen. The cards were packed." Cobb of Georgia stumped about the foyer muttering imprecations. "Treachery, treachery! Damnable falsehood!" Van Rensselaer was the target of his wrath. "The poor, miserable wretch!"[108]

13

Silently the crowd dispersed into snow-filled thoroughfares swept by a stinging wind. Only the alleys inhabited by free negroes resounded with rejoicing. No bonfires blazed for the victor, and the state of the weather discouraged a proposal by partizans of the vanquished to burn an effigy of Mr. Adams.[109]

A committee of the House repaired to the residence in F Street to perform the rite of notifying Mr. Adams. The President-elect presented an unforgettable spectacle. "Sweat rolled down his face. He shook from head to foot and was so agitated he could hardly stand to speak." One member of the committee thought he was going to decline the honor. With effort Mr. Adams begged leave to avail himself of the precedent set by Mr. Jefferson and reply in writing.[110]

Asbury Dickins, faithful chief clerk of the Treasury, bore the tidings to Crawford. "Is it possible!" exclaimed the invalid. "I thought it would . . . [be] Jackson."[111]

That night the President held his regular Wednesday levee. The crowd was immense and a pickpocket took General Scott's wallet.

Old Nathaniel Macon, the Nestor of Congress who had seen Andrew Jackson, a stripling from the wilderness, sworn in at Philadelphia in 1796, surveyed the scene. "Mr. Adams was there, but less an object of attention than General Jackson."[112] A lady of fashion observed "*Clay* walking about with . . . a smiling face . . . [and] a fashionable *belle* on each arm. . . . And Van Rensselaer, too, tho' . . . he looked more in want of support himself. . . . Poor man his messmates wouldn't speak to him. . . . More than one, pointing to A. said, there is our *Clay President*."[113] The rivals in the day's balloting found themselves face to face. "Mr. Adams was by himself; Gen. Jackson had a large, handsome lady on his arm. . . . Gen. Jackson reaching out his long arm said—'How do you do, Mr. Adams? I give you my left hand, for my right as you see is devoted to the fair; I hope you are very well, sir.' All this was gallantly and heartily done. Mr. Adams took the General's hand and said, . . . 'Very well, sir; I hope Gen. Jackson is well.'"[114]

14

Jackson accepted defeat in better part than many of his followers.

While members of the House were assembling to cast their votes he had remained in his hotel suite conversing with friends. Editor Hezekiah Niles of the *Register*, who had seen the General often during the winter, heard him mention the election for the first time. "He had no doubt but that a great portion of the citizens would be satisfied with the choice, . . . and he seemed to think it most probable that it would devolve upon Mr. Adams. . . . He observed that many . . . were unpleasantly situated, seeing that they were compelled to act either against Mr. Adams or himself. . . . And he further remarked that it was a matter of small moment to the people who was their president, provided he administered the government rightfully."[115] The day after the election the General quashed an impulsive move for a testimonial dinner because it "might be viewed as conveying . . . a feeling of complaint which I sincerely hope belong not to any of my friends."[116] The week following Jackson treated twenty-two men who had stood by him to a supper with champagne.[117]

This sportsmanlike attitude of a man beaten fairly, and the refusal to countenance tales to the contrary, had a practical side as well. Jackson could afford to wait; for, if the price of Mr. Clay's support were the Secretaryship of State, the fact could not be long concealed.

The disclosure came in five days when "Tecumseh" Johnson burst upon Jackson in hot blood with the story that Clay had been offered the first place in the Cabinet and probably would accept. The Jovian ire blazed forth, mayhap the fiercer for its long repression, though if Jackson had entertained prior suspicions of Clay his most intimate correspondence was not allowed to betray them. Nevertheless, the tone of the first brief explosion does not appear to be one of surprise. "So you see the *Judas* of the West has closed the contract and will receive the thirty pieces of silver. his end will be the same. Was there ever witnessed such bare faced corruption?"[118]

Though they made good use of it, neither Andrew Jackson nor his Washington entourage invented the "corrupt bargain" cry, a wealth of political folk-lore to the contrary notwithstanding. When Jackson wrote the foregoing, the sound and the fury of that cry already was sweeping upon the capital. It came from the country—West, South and to a slight extent East.

This had been an evolutionary process. The first faint accents of disapproval coincided with the obscure beginnings of the Adams-Clay understanding, and the stubborn impression that it embodied something that would not bear the light of day. As the objects of the alliance grew more distinct hostile murmurs increased. Mr. Clay's formal announcement, by chance or design timed so that western reactions could not reach Washington until after the eventful February 9, swelled these murmurs to a strident chorus. With the achievement of Mr. Adams's election and the punctual proffer of reward to Mr. Clay, the savage cry burst from savage throats.

An item from General Jackson's mail-bag:

"Pittsburgh March 4th a black fourth for the American nation—a black **1825**

"Your conduct and your behavior upon the late trying occasion both surpassed even the utmost stretch of thought. . . . Thy Throan shall be in Heaven"—the writer was Edward Patchell, the General's preacher friend—"at the right hand of Jehovah linked in the arm of the Immortal Washing [ton]," whereas "the corrupt Adams & Clay" would sizzle in hell "unless they be born again." As a starter Clay

THE BARGAIN

had been burned in effigy. "I . . . proposed sending a Barrel of whiskey to Grants hill to treat the fellows."[119]

Another:

"I have not the language to express the sorrow and Mortification that I feel. . . . The *West* surely will not protect those men . . . nor let them go unpunished. . . .

"Louisianians!—Degraded!—Ungrateful men!! to vote against you! you!! who under God they are indebted to for the . . . Chastity of their wives and daughters ! ! . .

"The Pride of Kentucky like Lucifer has fallen! . . .

"Your dignified conduct during the late Contest . . . and your subsequent Magnanimity has exacted praise even from those who . . . sacrificed you."[120]

Gems from the western press:

"HENRY CLAY, . . . morally and politically a gambler, a blackleg and a traitor."[121]

"We for one, should not be sorry to see [Henry Clay] *tarred and feathered*, nor shall we shrink from the responsibility of the expression."[122]

To such music did John Quincy Adams, after two sleepless nights, ride down the Avenue to take the oath.

"He will stand worse in four years than his father did," predicted a Crawford man from New York who witnessed the pageant. "Clay is ruined."[123] A Kentucky colleague shared these misgivings. "I fear we have done too much for our friend."[124]

A number of western congressmen made the dust fly in their rush for cover. Admitting that nineteen-twentieths of the people of Missouri were opposed to Adams, unhappy John Scott again and again justified himself on the ground that he had voted for Clay, not Adams. Virtuously he announced that he would accept no appointment under the administration.[125] Metcalfe of Kentucky was quoted as explaining his vote as an effort to prevent a deadlock which, if extended until March 4, would have made Calhoun President by default.[126] Another Kentuckian, David Trimble, hurried home to defend himself from the stump. The orator's success was not all that could be wished for. "If I had [carried] a gun," remarked one of his auditors, "I would have shot him."[127]

Representative Henry of Kentucky who had voted for Jackson asserted that Old Hickory could have had the vote of his state had he "authorized or permitted his friends to give . . . an assurance that Mr. Clay should . . . be made Secretary of State."[128]

Clay knew what he had done. On his desk lay a letter from Amos Kendall of Frankfort. This gifted man had been a member of the household at Ashland, a tutor to the Clay children. He had participated in the letter-writing calculated to stiffen the resolution of Kentucky congressmen to follow their chief for Adams. He edited the *Argus of Western America*, which had long fought the battles of Henry Clay. It could not fight them now. "Passion is taking the place of reason and you have little conception of the ferocious feelings." Kendall advised his patron to attempt no explanations, to emulate the *Argus* and keep still. "Even your voice would have little influence . . . [and] you might do yourself . . . much harm."[129]

Thus the spontaneous and national origin of the accusative cry roaring in from the land to claim its place in the argot of politics.

15

Seven days elapsed between the proffer of the State Department and its acceptance by Mr. Clay. They were days of doubt, divided counsels and indecision; days that have changed the face of much history. Though making light of it to Adams, Clay was troubled by the violence and volume of criticism. Adams men, once willing to offer almost anything for Clay's support, recoiled. They appealed to the warm-hearted Kentuckian to make a free gift of his great service to their cause, and, by declining the stipulated reward, bid the new Administration bon voyage on a tranquil sea. Clay's personal followers thought this hardly sporting. They pressed the Speaker to accept. Any other course would be an admission of wrong-doing, leaving them without an excuse for their votes. Had not Mr. Clay the right to support, and Mr. Adams to appoint, whom he chose?

They had that right. Mr. Clay could have supported Adams on lofty grounds, but he did not. His reason for his vote had alleged not the fitness of Mr. Adams, but the unfitness of General Jackson on the theatrical premise that he was a "military chieftain."[130] At best this was an oversimplification of the issue between Henry Clay and Andrew Jackson, thin and unconvincing. The man-on-horseback bogey derived from the Florida campaign which Adams had supported to the hilt. So people looked elsewhere for the real motive of Mr. Clay. They fancied they found it in what Mr. Adams had discerned after his first interview with Robert Letcher: Clay's ambition to advance himself. Adams had small talent for party leadership. Clay, then, could control the political machinery of the Administration, and apply it to prepare himself for the succession, not blinking the fact that it would be easier to succeed a New Englander than a fellow Westerner. Men who had followed Mr. Clay into his present interesting position accepted this line of reasoning.

Thus the Kentuckian's glove fell at the feet of Andrew Jackson, the last man to ignore so direct a challenge. He thought himself cheated, and Old Hickory bore affronts badly. His arresting countenance like a thundercloud, the General marched into the Senate chamber and, when Mr. Clay's name was presented for confirmation, he voted No. Thirteen other senators, an unprecedented number to oppose a Cabinet nomination, voted with him. He placed his seal of adoption on the bargain and corruption cry which impassioned liegemen were to make their *Marseillaise*, to damn Henry Clay with bell, book and candle, and harry him through the rest of his days.

Was the cry true? Jackson believed that it was. "What is this barter of votes for office but bribery?"[131] Thomas Hart Benton believed it. "No man, in his right senses, at the public scene of action as I was, could believe otherwise."[132] This is notable testimony. Benton and Clay were related by marriage. The Missourian viewed the course of his friend with regret rather than reproach, and strove to avoid too personal an application of the bargain charge. The private association of the two men long remained undisturbed. Their political separation constitutes a significant event in the march of American democracy as Benton turned to follow his constituents, Clay his star.

CHAPTER XXVI

A Preoccupied Cincinnatus

I

Bunland's Tavern at Washington, Pennsylvania, was thronged with Westerners homeward bound from Mr. Adams's inaugural. Word that General Jackson was passing through had brought out a good share of the townfolk as well. Andrew Wylie, president of Washington College and destined to be a man of mark among the educators of his day, introduced himself to the distinguished wayfarer.

"You return, General, from a boisterous campaign."

"Yes, sir," Old Hickory replied.

"A campaign in which you were not quite so successful as in some former ones," pursued Mr. Wylie.

"My success in those to which you allude was owing to the firmness of the brave men whom I had the honor to command."

Wylie was a Jackson man. "It is more honorable," said he, "to lose than to win if, indeed, things were managed as has been reported."

"Who can doubt it?" agreed Jackson.

The educator replied that many found it impossible to believe "that such men as Adams and Clay would, in the face of the nation, engage in such a transaction."

"Let any man in his senses," cut in Old Hickory, "take a view of the circumstances. Let him compare the prediction of honest George Kremer with its accomplishment."

Mr. Wylie repeated the argument that the "talents and local situation" of Mr. Clay sufficed to justify the appointment. "There is, however," he added, "another circumstance which, if true, will settle that point."

Jackson asked what it was.

"The proposition that is said to have been made to *you*? Is that a *fact*?"

The General's tone had been inaudible to those not standing very near him. At Wylie's last question he raised his voice. "Yes, sir, such a proposition *was* made. I said to the bearer, 'Go tell Mr. Clay, tell Mr. Adams, that if I go to that chair I go with clean hands.' "[1]

The words were welcome to the ears of western Jacksonians. They corroborated the continued accusations of their partizan editors. "Expired at Washington," one had written, "on the ninth day of February, of poison administered by the assassin hand of Henry Clay, the virtue, liberty and independence of the United States." "Five Western States," exclaimed another, "bought and transferred to the usurper like so many live cattle or a drove of negroes."[2] Yet, during the long journey over the National Road toward Wheeling, Jackson had sent ahead canceling acceptance of invitations made before his departure from the capital, and requesting that other demonstrations in his favor be omitted. Mrs. Jackson's health was the excuse. Nevertheless, crowds assembled. The General could not have been altogether displeased. His dander was up and the remarks to Mr. Wylie were characteristic rather than exceptional.

The further west Jackson went, the greater the enthusiasm of the people. Two newly-made fathers—Richard K. Call and Editor Stephen Simpson, whose *Columbian Observer* had been first to disclose the prediction of "honest George Kremer"—deplored the fact that their wives had presented them with daughters. A Kentuckian in like situation was more resourceful. "We shall call her Rachel Andrew Jackson Hitt."[3] Leaving the steamboat at Louisville, Old Hickory broke his resolution and attended a banquet.

2

As usual the General had brought some things for the Hermitage —on this occasion a lemon tree and a box of plants for Rachel's garden. Yet, the homecoming of April, 1825, differed from any other. Many times this far-faring man had turned his steps toward the comely Cumberland, sincerely determined to be done with offices and titles and to end his days on his own placid acres by the side of an adoring wife who, above all things, feared and distrusted renown's searching light. Always some emergency of war or peace or politics had drawn him forth again. In the ceaseless conflict Andrew Jackson had passed from a young man to an old man, Rachel from a radiant beauty to a dumpy little woman of fifty-eight, ill in body and in spirit. Now, for the first time, Jackson approached the Hermitage not as a permanent refuge from the cares of the world, but as winter quarters, wherein to rest, recruit and then sally forth to smash Henry Clay. Alas, for Rachel's peace of mind, this would mean another campaign for the presidency in 1828.

Before leaving the capital Old Hickory had served notice in an ostensibly private letter, already trickling through the press. "I became a soldier for the good of my country: difficulties met me at every step; I thank god it was my duty to surmount them. . . . If this makes me so, I am a 'Military Chieftain.' . . . To him [Henry Clay] I am no wise responsible. There is a purer tribunal to which in preference I would refer myself—to the Judgment of an enlightened patriotic and uncorrupted electorate."[4]

The document elicited from Mr. Clay a reply in which, contrary to advice, the Secretary not only defended his course in electing John Quincy Adams, but altered the provocative position he had assumed with reference to General Jackson. Greatly modifying the military chieftain charge, Clay praised Old Hickory's soldierly qualities, asserting that only Adams's superior statesmanship had drawn him to the side of the New Englander. To Kentucky constituents Mr. Clay offered ingenuous reasons for disregarding the instructions of the Legislature and the wishes of a majority of the voters.[5]

A copy of this production reached Jackson a few days after his arrival at the Hermitage. "How little common sense this man displays," the General wrote to John Coffee, "'O that my enemy would write a book.' . . . Silence would have been to him wisdom.[6] . . . Mr. Clay left himself so open to a severe scourging that it has been with difficulty I could withhold my pen." But, profiting by his rival's example, "for the present I have determined to be silent."[7]

3

There was scarcely more than time for a quick survey of his three plantations, including the one the General operated for his ward, Andrew Jackson Hutchings, when the Marquis de Lafayette arrived in Nashville. After five hundred receptions, a thousand speeches and

RACHEL JACKSON

This portrait, by Earl, hung in General Jackson's bed chamber at the Hermitage and at the White House. It was made about 1825. From the original, owned by the Ladies' Hermitage Association, Nashville.

DRAWN FROM LIFE, SEPTEMBER 23, 1829

The artist was James Barton Longacre. Reproduced from an old wet plate photograph of the original by Mathew B. Brady, owned by the L. C. Handy Studios, Washington.

the cheers of five million Americans, this remarkable traveler was still as fresh as the day he stepped from the ship. Formalities out of way, the party adjourned to the Hermitage. "The first thing that struck me," noted the visitor's son-in-law, "was the simplicity of his house. Still somewhat influenced by my European habits, I asked myself if this could really be the dwelling of the most popular man in the United States." Jackson's crops were flourishing. "We might have believed ourselves on the property of one of the richest and most skillful German farmers if, at every step, our eyes were not afflicted by the sad spectacle of slavery."

Someone begged Jackson to display his arsenal of ceremonial weapons. Lafayette recognized a pair of pistols he had given George Washington and expressed his delight at finding them still in worthy hands. The compliment was well turned and Old Hickory's eyes sparkled. The Marquis sought his host's counsel upon what he described as the "delicate But Very interesting Subject"[8] engrossing the energies of a young woman the Frenchman called his "daughter." She was Frances Wright, a tall, titian-haired Scottish lass of large means and larger ideals.

Having emancipated herself from the conventions that customarily surround unmarried females, Fanny Wright had conceived the idea of emancipating American negroes from slavery. Dropping in at the Lafayette country seat near Paris to discuss the matter she had remained there, off and on, for three years. When the Marquis came to the United States, Fanny would have been a member of the party except for an adverse ruling by the family, which held that Fanny's demonstrations of filial affection for her "venerable father" might be misunderstood in America. So the friend of freedom sailed under the chaperonage of his son, George Washington Lafayette, and his daughter's husband, Lavasseur. Fanny followed on another ship. On the day of the election in the chamber of the House, she sat beside the General, whose lusty appearance and gallant attentions did not allay gossip touching the "venerable" tourist and his beautiful protégée.

A few weeks after the Marquis's departure, Miss Wright appeared at the Hermitage in the company of George Fowler, one of her pupils in the manumission scheme. Jackson suggested the acquisition of a tract below Memphis. At Nashville the Scottish heiress purchased a coffle of negroes and marched them off toward the promised land[9] to establish what became rather too sweepingly known as "Fanny Wright's free love colony."

4

Expenses in Washington had been heavy beyond calculation, and the General had been obliged to borrow money to settle his hotel account and to defray the cost of the journey home where a fresh crop of bills awaited. The three boys—Andrew, junior, his cousin, Andrew Jackson Hutchings, and Lincoyer, the Indian—were in school where Andy II lived like a young lord. He had his own horse and a body servant to care for a wardrobe which included such newly purchased items as a suit, seventy-six dollars and eighty-seven cents; a hat, ten dollars; silk hose, a dollar fifty a pair, and imported kerchiefs. In six and one half months, the young man incurred indebtedness of three hundred and nine dollars to the establishment of Josiah Nichol who could outfit Nashville's *beau monde* from saddle blankets to hair oil.[10] The sum would have kept the average Tennessee family for a year.

And there were other claims on the time and purse of the planter. The overseer on the Hutchings boy's Alabama place died during cotton picking throwing the work into confusion. Jackson's first thought was for the care of the man's widow and children.[11] Colonel Robert Butler, husband of Rachel's favorite niece, Jane Hays, sent their son, Samuel, from Florida for Jackson to educate.[12] Thus were befriended by the master and mistress of the Hermitage three generations of Butlers, beginning with young Samuel's Revolutionary grandfather.

Fortunately, the long spell of hard times seemed at an end, with southern planters coming into their own again. Cotton prices were soaring. The first of the General's 1824 crop had brought thirteen and a half cents at New Orleans, the last thirty cents. "My [1825] crop is more promising than any I have ever seen." Jackson attributed the turn of the tide in large measure to a boom in domestic manufacturing which he hailed as vindication of his tariff vote, so roundly condemned by the planting class a year before.[13]

Politics also were booming. Four thousand vociferous Kentuckians got up a barbecue for their four congressmen who had voted for Jackson. Old Hickory resisted strong and subtle pressure calculated to inveigle him into attending. When Mr. Clay came home for the summer, invitations were sent forth to a dinner designed along more dignified and exclusive lines, which the Governor of the State and other notables, by their refusal to accept, rendered more exclusive than had been contemplated by the friends of the Secretary. Thus the breach in Kentucky widened as old Clay followers deserted and the organization of a permanent Jackson party got into its stride. Before Old Hickory's trunks were unpacked, invitations from a variety of states began to descend upon the Hermitage. A favorite approach was to bid the General to include this or that town in his itinerary to Washington next autumn.

This raised the first question Jackson must decide: whether to resign or to retain his seat in the Senate. Never happy as a legislator, the General's impulse was to resign. This was fortified by excellent reasons of policy. Congress would be a cock-pit of the Administration and anti-Administration forces. Would not the Hero present a fairer spectacle in pursuit of the occupation of a planter while others toiled amid the slippery gore of party conflict? A candid correspondent pointed out to the General that "opposition to the administration, and to the mode of the late election are very distinct and should be kept so." For General Jackson to express disapprobation of the "bargain" was proper, but as a disinterested patriot he should "support Mr Adams . . . so far as . . . the good of the country requires." At the end of four years the people "will select you whether at the *Hermitage* or in the *Senate* and I am not certain your remaining in the latter station will . . . give strength to the great cause."[14]

So the Hermitage it was. A graceful exit from the Senate was not difficult to contrive. Punctually the Tennessee Legislature renominated Andrew Jackson for the presidency. And how different the reception from that of the nomination of 1822. Without losing a day the General posted to Murfreesborough. In perhaps the longest political speech of his career, lasting fifteen minutes, Old Hickory told the assemblymen their step made it improper for him to continue in the Senate where events might place him under the imputation of shaping his official behavior to further his fortunes as a candidate.[15]

The General continued to comport himself with greater seemliness than the run of his followers. When Henry Lee, an unsteady son of Light Horse Harry, accepted the assistant postmaster-generalship under Adams, the Nashville *Republican*, owned by a personal friend of Old Hickory, attempted to drum Lee out of the Jackson camp. "I must regret the attack," Jackson assured the Virginian. "Sir, I am too charitable to believe that the acceptance of an Office under Mr Adams is either evidence of a change of principle or of corruption."

The Adams-Clay transaction stood on different legs, however.

"I had esteemed [Mr. Adams] as a virtuous, able and honest man; and when rumour was stamping the sudden union of his and the friends of Mr Clay with intrigue, barter and bargain I did not, nay, I could not believe that Mr. Adams participated. . . . When the election was terminated, I manifested publicly . . . my disbelief of his having had knowledge of the pledges which many men of high standing boldly asserted to be the price of his election. But when . . . Mr Clay was made Secretary of State . . . I could not doubt the facts. . . . I do not think the human mind can resist the conviction that . . . Mr. Adams by the redemption of the pledge stood before the American people as a participant in the disgraceful traffic of Congressional votes for executive office.

"From that moment I withdrew all intercourse with him, not however to oppose his administration when I think it useful to the Country. . . . Mr. Adams is the Constitutional President and as such I would be the last man . . . to oppose him on any other ground than principle."[16]

5

The appearance before the Tennessee Legislature was a little masterpiece. Jackson's resignation from the Senate, his few words and those so restrained, answered every purpose. The opposition had its leader: Andrew Jackson; its cry: the "bargain"; its cause: popular sovereignty.

In December, 1825, the nation's glance turned again to Washington for the convocation of the first Congress of the régime of Mr. Adams. There the opening guns of the new campaign would be touched off. Surely Mr. Clay must move in force to recapture the initiative, so boldly seized and so dexterously held during the House battle, but swept from his hands immediately thereafter by the sur-

A PREOCCUPIED CINCINNATUS

prising fury of the bargain charge. His first move as political impresario of the Administration had been defensive, a retreat from the defiant stand heretofore taken against Jackson. It had not been very successful.

The next skirmish entered about the President's message. This document was eagerly awaited. From a man of J. Q. Adams's training in the practical affairs of government, it proved to be an interesting production. Vainly had Mr. Clay contended for its modification. Since the decline of war-time nationalism, the trend had been toward Jefferson's dictum that the best government governed least. Against this the new President set his face with splendid idealism. Not only would he have the Federal authority construct roads, canals, harbors and light-houses, concerning which there was an active division of opinion in Congress; he would have it embark upon a great academic program embracing a national university, an astronomical observatory and geographical and exploring expeditions. The firmest believer in these projects could not have offered them at this time as an ideal foundation for a political party. The closing sentence was calamitous. "Are we to slumber in indolence . . . and proclaim to the world that we are palsied by the hands of our constituents?"

General Jackson privately observed that the President "gave evidence of a want of discretion,"[17] which was putting it more temperately than some of Mr. Adams's own people. Retaining the initiative Mr. Clay had sought to seize, Jacksonians deluged Congress with bills, resolutions and constitutional amendments aimed at the Administration. Ritchie's Richmond *Enquirer*, the most influential newspaper in the slave-holding states, the Albany *Argus*, whose editorial pen was guided by Van Buren, and Isaac Hill's blatant but effective *New Hampshire Patriot* joined the critics. Their swift metabolism into Jackson organs had begun.

Then Mr. Clay played a good card. Americans had watched with approval the collapse of Spanish power in the New World as colony after colony established itself as an independent state. No foreigner, except Lafayette, exceeded Bolivar in our esteem, and no other American statesman had championed the Latin-Americans with the eloquence and the fire of Henry Clay. Now he plumped before Congress a proposal that we join a council of the Latin nations called to meet, like that of the Greek republics, at the isthmus. This was the Panama Congress.

Here was something the "Friends of Jackson," as the opposition styled itself, could not so readily render ridiculous. But they did their best, pecking away, misrepresenting, and overlooking no opening to drag all discussions back to the bitter refrain of "bargain." A Tennessee member gleefully depicted for Jackson a scene in the House.

"Vance said he was peculiarly situated; that he had come from the lowest order of society; that at the Age of 22 years he could not connect the letters of the Alphabet; that promoted as he was by the People of Ohio when an Imputation of Corruption was cast on them he would sustain their character at the hazard of his life. Mr. Trimble of Kentucky made a Talk somewhat in the same way. . . .

"McDuffie [of South Carolina] in reply said Genl Vance . . . had not changed his . . . grade of society . . . [when he chose to follow] the great political Juggler, Poltroon and Puppy, the Secretary of State Clay. If Mr. Vance or Trimble thought themselves aggrieved he would for once forget they were not Gentlemen and would attend to their Calls. The House was a perfect scene of confusion for half an hour, . . . the Chairman crying out Order, Order, Order, hurly burly, helter skelter, negro states and Yankies."[18]

It remained for John Randolph, a senator now, to bring the debate to its climax. Never has our national legislature seen the counterpart of that imperious cynic, half mad, half genius. After twenty years in Congress, he would saunter down an aisle followed by a young negro and, flicking his riding boots with a whip, observe, "I have not the honor to know, even by name, a large portion of the members of this House."[19] Usually Randolph spoke without notes or other aid to memory than a flagon of porter which the colored boy periodically replenished from a jug. His speeches were long. Often they had nothing to do with the subject at hand. However, one interested in sprightly diction, salted impartially with classical allusions and the argot of the racing stable, was sometimes repaid for listening.

Senator Randolph's random remarks on the Panama Congress wore around to the bargain issue which he characterized as "the coalition of Blifil and Black George, . . . the Puritan and the Blackleg."[20]

This was more than Clay could stand. In what Thomas Hart Benton described as the last "high-toned duel" he was privileged to witness, Randolph, one of the best shots in Virginia, threw away his fire and took Mr. Clay's bullet through the coat-tail. Not to be outdone in magnanimity, the Secretary of State sent his adversary a new coat. But this did not save the Panama Congress or impede John Randolph's epigram which rang through the country.

6

Every few days Jackson received from John Henry Eaton an account of the progress of affairs at Washington.

"All that is necessary for you is to be still and quiet," he read after the duel. The General's friends promised to do the rest. "This administration, wretched & rotten, is already crumbling. . . . Hal [Clay] walks alone, crest fallen, dejected and almost without associates." He likened the sweep for Jackson to the current of the Mississippi.[21]

The figure was not amiss. Van Buren had thrown in with the Friends of Jackson. From New Hampshire to Georgia other leaders of the defunct Crawford organization were following suit. Deprived of a populace-rousing issue by the return of prosperity, the hard times party in Kentucky and Alabama, champion of paper money and state banks, overlooked the fact that Andrew Jackson had been largely responsible for the exclusion of similar economic experiments from Tennessee and clutched at the tail of Old Hickory's rising kite. Nor was this the only quarter in which General Jackson reaped where he had not sown. The "outs" of varying complexions began to drift to him. The task of accelerating the movement and regimenting disparate elements into an effective party was assumed by a group in Washington including Calhoun, Van Buren, Benton, Randolph, Sam Houston, McDuffie of South Carolina, Livingston of Louisiana and Duff Green of the *United States' Telegraph*. Intimacy with Jackson made Eaton their chief in name if not in fact.

This body formed central committees of correspondence in each state, and under them local committees which were furnished with materials for dissemination. It won over old newspapers and started new ones. Mass meetings, militia musters, barbecues and fish frys were provided with orators primed on the imperfections of the Administration, the iniquities of the bargain, and the virtues of General Jackson. In Congress the hostile drum-fire was unceasing. Nothing escaped. When an inventory of the belongings in the Executive Residence included a billiard table and chess men, a Georgia patriot let loose about squandering public money for "gaming tables and gambling furniture." In vain did Mr. Adams disclose that the articles had been purchased with his private funds: the original account was too good to be marred by a correction.

Well for Major Eaton and colleagues that General Jackson was not in Washington that winter. Never had any man or set of men acted with such authority in the concerns of the Old Chief. They told him what they thought he should hear and kept him satisfied. When John Overton's nephew protested that Randolph and some of the others were hurting his cause, Jackson did not answer the letter.[22] When Duff Green, a political adventurer from St. Louis, was selected to establish the *Telegraph*, Eaton went through the form of taking him to the Hermitage to discuss the policy of the periodical with Jackson. The General bade his caller godspeed with the admonition: "Truth is mighty and shall prevail."[23] On money raised by Eaton the paper appeared in March, 1826. Green proved an able partizan editor and organizer. Within a few months his aspersive columns were the pattern for fifty Jackson journals.

Eaton's reiterated injunctions to "say nothing and plant cotton" enabled the Friends of Jackson to point to a somewhat ink-stained Cincinnatus, tilling his farm, plying the quill over a mountainous if often trivial correspondence and, on the whole, discharging very well the campaign's lighter amenities.

"I beg you sir to accept my sincere thanks for this repeated assurance of your desire to see me in Massachusetts, and particularly on so interesting occasion as that of our national jubilee [July 4]." The invitation was declined, but with a reciprocal "proffer of such accomodations as the Hermitage affords to yourself and any of your friends should you ever be inclined to visit this section of the Union."[24]

He begged off from addressing a Bible society on the ground that "having lost many of my teeth it is with difficulty I can articulate. . . . [Moreover] I might be charged . . . with . . . [electioneering] hypocritically under the sacred garb of religion."[25]

A set of teeth made by a Nashville dentist removed Old Hickory's difficulty in speaking, but not his aversion to public appearances.

When the restoration of Mrs. Jackson's health canceled a proposed excursion to a healing spring in Kentucky, a friend of the General protested: "We hope that she may experience a slight relapse . . . and . . . wou^d beg to recommend . . . the Greenville, Blue-Lick & Bath Waters. . . . The people of Kentucky want to see Genl. Jackson. . . . The Public Interest requires that they shou^d see him. . . . He will be taken to some three or four barbecues. . . . Solicit Mrs Jacksons pardon for the freedom with which I have us^d her Name."[26]

The approach of the local elections of 1826, providing the first practical test of the new Jackson machine, found the Friends in jubilant spirits. "Don't forget my bets," reminded Van Buren. "This election . . . should make up for past losses." The Senator was willing to risk ten thousand dollars and, if that sum could not be placed, any smaller amount, "or even a suit of clothes."[27] Whatever the extent of the wagers, Mr. Van Buren could hardly have lost. Jackson candidates held all ground gained in 1824 with flattering accessions in New York, Ohio, Virginia and the old Crawford territory southward. Scott of Missouri and Cook of Illinois were beaten on the bargain issue. Of the eight Kentuckians who had supported Adams four were not candidates. One was defeated and three re-elected.

Sam Houston pictured to his patron the "consternation" of the Administration. "Desperation is their only hope!!"[28]

7

The Cumberland cotton grower was prepared to believe it. Before him lay a report of a dinner-table colloquy imputing to Secretary of Navy Southard the opinion that James Monroe deserved the laurels for New Orleans, Jackson having abandoned his army and taken the road home when Monroe's peremptory order sent him back to the threatened city.

Off to Sam Houston went a letter with instructions to deliver it to Mr. Southard.[29]

Houston was an energetic lieutenant. Only a month before he had left for dead on the field of honor a supporter of Mr. Clay who had offered to arbitrate with firearms an issue growing out of the campaign. In the present instance the Congressman acted with equal boldness. Instead of delivering the letter to Southard, he showed it to Eaton and other party managers. In their judgment, too, the tone was too severe for a Tennessee planter whose pacific temperament was a recurring theme of the Washington junto. So Houston prepared in his own name a courteous request that Mr. Southard state whether he had been correctly quoted and asked Jackson's permission to deliver it. If this would not do, Houston begged the General to recast his note in softer terms. "I trust that you will not for one moment suppose that my course has been dictated by an eye to your political advancement."[30]

Jackson answered that any communication to Southard must come from him. The Secretary might put Houston off. *"He must reply."*[31] Another note to Mr. Southard, much milder than the first, however, was enclosed.[32] By this time the story was in the newspapers. Monroe put in his oar, smugly taking credit to himself in a manner that made Jackson boil. In a letter to a United States Senator, Old Hickory declared the War Department's support of the Louisiana army had been so tardy and ineffective that, had New Orleans fallen, either Monroe or his ordnance officer should have been shot for "criminal neglect."[33]

Here was the making of a Jacksonian imbroglio of the first magnitude. Before things got any worse, Houston delivered the letter to Southard as the quickest way of ending the matter. The Secretary responded with a long and argumentative communication in which, however, he said, "My object was to vindicate Mr. Monroe and not . . . to depreciate your military exploits. They form a part of our national glory." Jackson's acknowledgment contained the crisp recommendation that at his "wine drinkings hereafter" Mr. Southard should be more careful with his tongue.[34]

There the matter rested, but the peace of mind of the gentlemen who hoped to keep General Jackson tending cotton was never the same again.

8

The next alarm came from North Carolina where the Fayetteville *Observer* printed an unsigned communication, reporting a social conversation at the Hermitage in which the General was quoted as saying that, in 1825, Clay would have dealt with Jackson had he said the word. Party managers were distressed not only because they preferred a candidate eloquently mum on the subject of his wrongs, but also because of a disturbing letter Duff Green had received from James Buchanan. "I had no authority from Mr. Clay or his friends. . . . I am clearly of the opinion that whoever shall attempt to prove by direct evidence any corrupt bargain between Mr. C—— and Mr. A—— will fail."[35] This was giving the celebrated visit a different face from what had been plain enough to Jackson, Eaton and Kremer at the time.

When the *Observer* item began to go the rounds of the papers, Henry Clay came out with a denial in which he expressed doubt that Jackson had made the remarks attributed to him. Coming on the heels of Buchanan's strange letter, the Secretary's assurance gave the General's campaign strategists a new cause for concern. Were the two events connected? Green speculated with the thought that the Pennsylvanian had been subtly reached by Mr. Clay. He advised Jackson to "leave the subject where it now is" and trust in his friends.[36] As soon as Congress adjourned Eaton deprived himself of the companionship of Margaret Timberlake and headed for Tennessee.

Jackson chose to act for himself. In response to questioning, Eaton gave his chief a memorandum stating that Buchanan had approached him with an offer of negotiation from the friends of Clay, and only after Eaton had refused to convey this to Jackson had Buchanan done so. George Kremer sent a statement along the same line.[37] Sure of his ground concerning Buchanan, Jackson then took up a letter signed Carter Beverley in which that gentleman, a recent house-guest at the Hermitage, admitted the authorship of the *Observer* letter and asked the General to confirm the quotations imputed to him. Jackson complied in detail with an account of the Buchanan interview in which he identified his caller as "a member of Congress of high respectability."[38] Beverley sent the letter to the *Telegraph* and Green, falling in with the master's plan, published it.

This pleased Clay, who fancied himself in possession of the initiative.[39] In a "direct, unqualified and indignant denial," he called upon General Jackson for proof. The American public, he said, should be the jury.[40]

Jackson came back with a lengthy broadside going over the whole story again. "This disclosure was made to me by Mr. James Buchanan."[41]

The challenge and the reply thundered through the press, partizans of each champion claiming the advantage. "Your letter . . . is a Death Stroke," boomed Captain Maunsel White, late of the Battalion of Uniformed Companies, now General Jackson's cotton broker in New Orleans. "But, they say, suppose Mr Buchanan denies it. That is impossible. Mr Eaton is a living witness."[42]

Surrounded by advisers who were in Nashville during the summer recess of Congress, General Jackson himself had pondered the possibility of Buchanan's failure to sustain him, and had taken steps to forestall it. Ahead of the newspapers which carried the General's statement eastward went a carefully composed, friendly but explicit letter to the Pennsylvania member. "I have no doubt . . . you will come forth and affirm the statement [you] made to Major Eaton, then to Mr. Kremer and then to me, and give the names of the friends of Mr. Clay who made it to you."[43]

It had been permitted to few men to refuse, with impunity, such a request from Old Hickory. The *Telegraph* exulted. "When Mr. Buchanan replies . . . we shall have more light to guide our way."[44] Fearing the worst, the Administration's *Journal* sought to impeach Buchanan's testimony in advance.[45]

Mr. Buchanan's reply came within a few days. This effort, also, showed scrupulous attention to composition; and it was tediously long. Up to the critical point the writer corroborated Jackson. Then, instead of giving the names the General called for, Mr. Buchanan declared that he had acted "solely on my individual responsibility and not at the agent of Mr. Clay or any other person."[46] In the light of this statement, Buchanan might have had some difficulty in explaining why he should have gone to Mr. Clay with a message impossible to justify, either on the basis of his or of General Jackson's version of their conversation. The Pennsylvanian avoided this embarrassment by omitting to mention the visit to Clay. When Clay himself offered to supply this detail, Buchanan begged him to be silent and Clay consented.[47]

Clay people threw their hats in the air and the *National Journal* repented its pre-judgment of Buchanan. A recent convert to the Jackson cause made a wry face. "This novel triangular controversy between Jackson, Clay & Buckhaun . . . has afforded a most singular triumph indeed to Henry Clay. Why does Genl. Jackson make such a *dam'd old fool* as Carter Beverley one of his confidential friends. . . . Who are the Generals advisers? Eaton, Sam Houston, Wm. B. Lewis & Tom Claiborne. I am apprehensive."[48]

Among the letters which poured upon the Hermitage was one from Frankfort, Kentucky, inscribed in an unfamiliar, delicate hand, fair enough for a lady's album.

"Although I have never had the pleasure of a personal acquaintance with you there are some circumstances of a peculiar nature which now induce me to address you. I am one of those who were told by one of his [Clay's] friends, as I think about the 20th day of January, 1825, that if Mr. Adams should be elected he would make Mr. Clay his Secretary of State and I was three times solicited to write to Mr. White, our representative, to vote for Mr. Adams on that account. Thus urged I did write."[49]

Below stood the legible signature of Amos Kendall, editor of the *Argus of Western America*. A second communication in the same small script:

"Buchanan's statement has been received here by the Adams men with much exultation but their joy has very much abated. 'Sweet in the mouth,' they find this document, 'but bitter in the belly.'"[50]

General Jackson replied at once to his new correspondent. "We live in days of wonder. It would be now only necessary for me to publish Major Eatons statement and Mr. Kreamers, contrast them with his [Buchanan's] and it would show that his recollection had materially failed him. . . . However, I shall deliberate fully before I act."[51] The deliberation was assisted by some direct advice, of which Martin Van Buren's is representative. "Our people do not like to see publications from candidates. . . . Although our friend Buchanan was evidently frightened and therefore softened and obscured the matter still the fact of your entire aversion to any and all intrigue or arrangement is clearly established, and nothing could be of more value."[52]

The General lapsed into silence. Kendall and Van Buren were more than a little right about the effect of the Buchanan letter, once the impact of unexpected disappointment passed. Cursing under his breath, Duff Green grimly set to work to make the most of the material at hand and the Jackson press throughout the land performed to perfection. Never did the bargain issue seem more alive and damning than during the afterclap of Mr. Buchanan's refusal to sustain it. The tides of fortune that had seemed in the eventful weeks of December '24 and January '25 persistently to favor the coalition which elevated J. Q. Adams to the presidency had run contrary for thirty months. Introspective and heartsick, Mr. Adams began to prepare his mind to accept defeat.

Not so the Secretary of State. "Clay is a man of hazards," remarked an observer whose vision remained comparatively unclouded by prejudice.[53] In the spring the Kentuckian had rushed west with the expectation of turning the tables on his rival. He failed, and midsummer brought no truce to the defensive battle. In the August election loss of the Kentucky Legislature was averted by a narrow squeak. With Adams useless as an ally, with hope abandoned for the strength-giving repose he had expected to find at Ashland, the man of hazards fought on—wan, ill, and, according to unfriendly report, lashing up with whisky his reserves of energy. Neither weapons nor tactics were scrutinized as closely as they might have been, until Mr. Clay's name was involved in a blow at General Jackson beside which the worst implications of the bargain charge seem an innocent party stratagem.

9

This touched the Sacred Name.

"There was at Frankfort," a correspondent in Kentucky, too circumspect to identify himself, wrote to John Overton, "an old ill looking Englishman named Day. His apparel was threadbare rusty and dirty, his professed employment was a collector of debts for the Baltimore and Philadelphia merchants. . . . He rendered himself conspicuous with the partisans of the coalition and . . . travelled at leisure to get such testimony as he might picked up [concerning General Jackson's marriage]. In this vindictive and diabolical occupation Day . . . passed through that part [of Kentucky] where Mrs. Jackson formerly resided; he then went to Nashville in Tennessee and then to Natchez."

Kentucky to Nashville to Natchez: the trail of romance blazed nearly forty years before by a headlong wilderness Lochinvar and the mismated wife of Lewis Robards.

"After an absence of some time he returned to Frankfort having obtained as he said what [enabled? Manuscript illegible.] him to demonstrate that General Jackson and his lady had never been married. he brought with him copys of some records from Mercer County Stating that Mr. and Mrs. Robards had been devorced . . . on the testimony of one Hugh McGary; this record and some other papers he showed in Frankfort to the partisans of the coallition; . . . after a while they were . . . left at Lexington, it has been said, with Mr. Henry Clay, who delivered them to Charles Hammond."[54]

When the shadow of Andrew Jackson's courtship threatened the campaign of 1824 Jackson had said, "I know how to defend *her*." He used that tone now. "I have lately got an intimation of some of his [Clay's] secrete movements which if I can reach with possitive and responsible proof I will wield to his political and perhaps his actual destruction. he is certainly the bases[t], meanest scoundrel that ever disgraced the image of his god. . . . Even the aged and virtuous female is not free from his . . . slander—but *anough, you know me*."[55]

Sam Houston, to whom this communication was addressed, did, indeed, know his patron, having trained for his recent duel on the Hermitage grounds under Jackson's experienced eye. He felt, however, that in the present canvass pistols had done all that could reasonably be expected of them. Yet, this might be serious: the Mercer County court records, Hugh McGary's testimony, in the hands of a man like Charles Hammond, editor of the Cincinnati *Gazette*. John Henry Eaton went straight to the Secretary of State. Mr. Clay admitted having seen Hammond during his recent stay in the West, but so emphatically did he deny knowledge of or agency in a contemplated attack on the character of Mrs. Jackson that Eaton wrote Jackson he believed the Secretary to be telling the truth.[56]

However, the General's friends did not place their sole reliance in Mr. Clay's veracity or in any endeavors that he might make to curb Hammond. Eaton in Washington and Lewis and Overton in Tennessee began collecting statements from old Cumberland residents giving their versions of Rachel's troubles with her first husband, her marriage to Jackson, her irreproachable character, and so on. A fortnight after the interview with Clay, Eaton felt this activity prudently undertaken. By that time he had begun to doubt the sincerity of the Secretary's protestations, and so told Jackson. Before him was an uninvited disclaimer from Hammond insisting that Clay had nothing to do with the affair. Eaton felt this inspired by the Secretary. Hammond confirmed the report that he had profited by the researches of Day. "What use I shall make of these documents depends upon future events."[57]

As he wrote, Hammond was already making use of Day's gleanings, steathily by word of mouth. From the Mississippi to the Atlantic spread underground tales of the annihilating revelations in Hammond's power to make. Jackson got wind of this and[58] the veteran's friends trembled lest he be goaded to some rash act. His threats grew bolder. "A day of retribution . . . [for] Mr Clay and his tool Col° Hammond must arrive should I be spared."[59] Eaton begged his chief to understand that this would be playing into the hands of the whisperers. "I know them all, & well, & everything I have to say is, be cautious— be still— be quiet. . . . Weigh & bale your cotton & sell it; and if you see any thing about yourself just throw the paper into the fire . . . & go on to *weigh the cotton.*"[60]

By the time, or shortly after, Eaton's letter was in Jackson's hands, the slander had attained the tangibility of print—and this from an unexpected source. Thomas D. Arnold, an East Tennessee candidate for Congress, published a hand-bill proclaiming that Andrew Jackson had "spent the prime of his life in gambling, in cock-fighting, in horse-racing . . . and to cap all tore from a husband the wife of his bosom." A vote for him would be a vote to sanction the code whereby if a man should fancy his neighbor's "pretty wife . . . he has nothing to do but to take a pistol in one hand and a horse whip in another and . . . possess . . . her."[61]

After this Hammond opened his *Gazette* to the story in more detail. "Gen. Jackson prevailed upon the wife of Lewis Roberts [*sic*] to desert her husband and live with himself." Then followed an account of the divorce on McGary's testimony of adultery, ignoring the three years the Jacksons had supposed themselves to be legally married.[62]

Arnold was an obscure country politician, Hammond an editorial

THE COFFIN HANDBILL

A campaign poster of 1828, published by John Binns of Philadelphia.

Reproduced from an original in the museum of the North Carolina State Historical Commission, Raleigh.

Some Account of some of the Bloody Deeds OF GENERAL JACKSON.

Jacob Webb   *David Morrow*   *John Harris*   *Henry Lewis*   *David Hunt*   *Edward Lindsay*

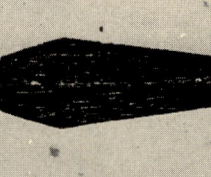
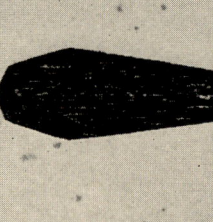

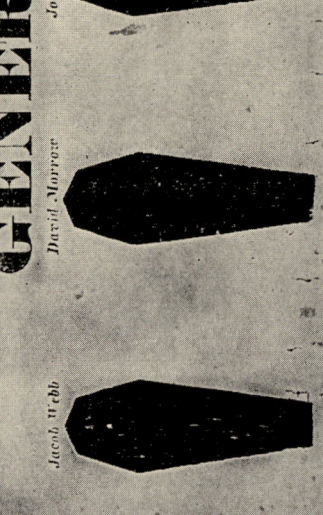

A brief account of the Execution of the Six Militia Men.

As we may soon expect to have the official documents in relation to the Six Militia Men, arrested, tried, and put to death, under the orders of General Andrew Jackson, this may not be an improper time to give to the publicsome of the particulars of their execution, as we have them from "AN EYE WITNESS," who appeals to Col. Russell, for the truth of every word he relates.

Harris was a Baptist preacher, with a large family. He had hired as a substitute for three months. This was the case with most of them. They were ignorant men, but obstinate in what they believed right, and what they had been told by their officers was right.— They were all sure they could not be kept beyond three months, and they gave up their musquets, and had provisions dealt out to them, from the public stores, before they left the camp. This confirmed their convictions that they were right and doing what was lawful.

Col. Russel commanded at the execution. The Militia men were brought to the place in a large wagon. The military dispositions being made, Col. Russell rode up to the wagon and ordered the men so descend. Harris was the only one who betrayed feminine weakness. The awfulness of the occasion; his wife and nine children; his paring with his son ; and the fear of a quickly approaching ignominious death! quite overcome him, and he sunk in unmanly grief. No feeling of military pride could brace him up.

Col. Russel, doubtless, felt as a man, but he felt also for the pride of the army, and desired to animate the men with fortitude. "You are about to die," said he, "by the sentence of a Court Martial—die like men—like soldiers. "You have been brave in the field—you have fought well—do no dishonor it to your country, or dishonour to the army, or yourselves, by any unmanly fears. Meet your fate with courage." Harris attempted to make some apology for his conduct, but while he spoke, he wept bitterly. "The fear of death, the idea that he should never again behold his wife and little ones, and his son weeping near him, had taken such entire possession of his mind that it was impossible he should rally.

Lewis, the gallant Lewis, said in a clear and manly tone, "Colonel, I have served my country well. I love it dearly, and would, if I could, serve "it longer and better. I have fought bravely—you know I have, and HERE "I have a right to say so MYSELF. I minutes he said—I give his very words: "Colonel"—the Colonel was close to him—"Colonel, I am not killed but am sadly cut and mangled." His body was now examined and it was found that but four balls had wounded him. "Colonel," said he, "did I behave well." "Yes, Lewis," said the Colonel in the kindest tone of voice—"like a man." "Well sir," said he, "have I notation ed for this offence? Shall I still live?" The Colonel was much agitated, and gave orders that the Surgeon should, if possible, preserve his life. They did all that skill and humanity could do—it was all of no avail. Poor Lewis expressed a great desire to live—"not," said he at one time, "that I fear death, "but I would repent me of some sins, "and I desire to live yet a little longer in the world." He suffered inconceivable agony, from his wounds, and died on the fourth day.

Many a soldier has wept over his grave. He was a brave man and much beloved. He suffered twenty deaths. Harris evidently trembled, and I could almost persuade myself that the heart of Lewis was enlarged, and that his bosom rose with manly courage to meet death. The fatal word was given and they all fell.

As we approached the scene of blood and carnage, Lewis gave signs of life; the rest were all dead—he crawled upon his coffin. After the lapse of a few minutes he said—I give his very words: from strong feelings of sympathy, or mistaken humanity failed to shoot him but four balls had entered his body.

"An Eye Witness" appeals to Col. Russell, who he thinks now lives in A. labama, for the perfect truth of this sketch. He does not fear but the Colonel will keenly recollect and faithfully depict the horrors of the day on which six Americans were shot to death under his command—but not by his orders.

The order bears date the very day after General Jackson returned in triumph to New Orleans, and the day before he joyfully went, under triumphal arches, to the Temple of the living God; where, says the historian, "they crowned their adored General with laurels," "The order for the execution of these six unhappy men bears date January 22, 1815. The tears of Laurels had not yet withered, when blood, the life's blood of his countrymen, of his fellow soldiers, flowed plentifully by his order. May that order and its consequences, sink deep into the hearts of the American people and steel them against him who had no flesh in his obdurate heart; who did not feel for Man, in the midst of Joy and Revelry, almost in the more immediate presence of his Creator, who issued the fatal order to put his fellow creatures to death, and to make their wives & children, widows and orphans.

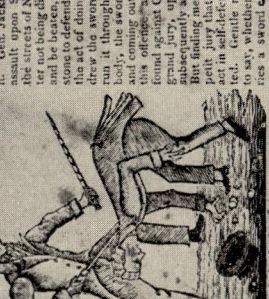

"O! DID you hear that plaintive cry
Borne on the solemn breeze;
Say Jars it was, that great pray
For mercy, on his knees?

"We thought our time of service out—
"Thought it our right to go—
"We meant to violate no law,
"Nor wish'd to shun the foe.

"At home an aged mother waits
"To clasp her only son:
"A wife, and little children—this are
"Alone depend upon.

"Twas all in vain, John Harris' pray'r,
"Tis past the soul's belief!
"Harris the flint was Jackson's heart,
"He would not grant relief.

See six black coffins rang'd along—
Six graves before them made;
Webb, Lindsey, Harris, Lewis, Hunt,
And Morrow kneeled and prayed.

All six militia men were shot.
And O! it seems to me
A dreadful deed—a bloody set
Of needless cruelty.

A short time before the execution of the militia-men, seven regular soldiers were shot near Nashville, by a kind of regulars scarcely sufficient to guard the prisoners.— They were confined in a house, and taken out and executed one at a time, there being scarcely enough men for the purpose of watching and guarding at the same time. An eighth soldier was to have been executed at the same time. He was a young man, who had deserted one month before his time had expired. General Jackson doomed him to die with the others. He was saved by a writ of habeas corpus from Judge M'Nairy, who fell under Jackson's displeasure for snatching this one victim from his blood-stained hand. If Jackson's army had been blind, no doubt M'Nairy would have shared the fate of Judge Hall and Judge Froment. Capital punishments in an army is not uncommon. It is necessary; but in this case it was a transaction of horror to peaceful citizens; no guilty was there to witness the bloody tragedy. He has never been a man of "blood and carnage."

Do not be startled, gentle reader at the picture before you. It is all true and every body ought to know it. A member of Congress, in an assault upon Samuel Jackson, in the streets of Nashville, & the latter not being disposed to stand still and be beaten, stooped down for a stone to defend himself. While in the act of doing so, Gen. Jackson drew the sword from his cane and run it through Samuel Jackson's body, the sword entering his back and coming out of his breast. For this offence an indictment was found against Gen. Jackson, by a grand jury, upon trial and evidence, the jury, under the oath, acquitted. Gentle reader, it is for you to say, whether this man, who carries a sword cane, and is willing to run it through the body of any one who may presume to stand in his way, is a fit person to be our President.

On the 27th day of March, 1814, General was to DESTROY many of them who had taken themselves under the banks of the river, concealed,—and the man who acts and speaks thus, who has half as much bold upon his conscience, as he has upon his hands,—he, forsooth, is to be called the peer and like of Washington, the happy warrior.—

POOR JOHN WOODS, he was generous hearted, noble fellow as ever lived, who had volunteered to come to his country. He was on guard one day at Fort Strother—the officer of the guard had permitted him to his tent, at which time a small meal was disposing of his scanty breakfast, waiting an order to eat it, an officer, who was not his equal at home, orders him to pick up and carry off some bones that lay scattered about the place. Woods refused, and the little officer attempted to compel him. At this instant, Gen. Jackson, having heard the dispute, came out of his tent, and without knowing any thing of the merits of the case, repeatedly vociferated— "Shoot the damn'd rascal!"— For this offence, the unfortunate Woods was shot. Before his trial, Gen. Jackson used this language to the continental.— "By the Eternal God! If you find him guilty, I will have him shot!"—Thus menaced a noble fellow in his promise, though he did offer pardon provide he would enlist in the regular service—This tendered a noble fellow to work as an his recompense. We continue— are the general's words;—these— "would make our little calaboose," which he once called our Court House, "a temple of liberty," in comparison with a military despotism under the control of our commander, the "hero" Jackson. Little fastidious, according to the customary appellation of our native rise into indigenous so strong is the feeling of our native rise into indigenous resentment, when we reflect upon the deep and bloody deeds! of such a man, in the face of the Law and the Constitution.

Gen. Jackson, detailing his progress among the Indians, in the course of which men, WOMEN and CHILDREN, were indiscriminately "exterminated," their town burnt and their country laid waste, with the utmost complacency and sang froid, says, in his letter, "Camp before St. Marks, April 9, 1818," "Capt. W Ever having hoisted the colours on board of his boats, Francis the Prophet, Homocomitchko and two Indians, were decoyed on board. There have been hung to-day." Reader, mark the perfect indifference with which Gen. Jackson shoots, hangs or stabs his fellow beings; what, no doubt, but, that the more than callous, aye, even exulting composure, with which he put to death his last victim, the tall bloody deeds of wielding bay onet aught, his fellow-citizens, and some of them his fellow soldiers, for no rag out, put to death by his thoughtful orders, together with the last bloody tragedy on our plains, our a number of prisoners, by an old man, in the face of the law and the constitution, might serve but to increase his popular glory.

FRANKLIN, Tenn. September 10, 1813.

A difference which had been for some months brewing between Gen. Jackson and myself, produced on Saturday, the 4th inst. in the town of Nashville, the most outrageous affray I ever witnessed in civilized country. In communicating the affair to my friends and fellow-citizens, I limit myself to the statement of a few facts, the truth of which I am ready to establish by judicial proof.

1. That myself and my brother Jesse Benton, arriving in Nashville on the morning of the affray, and knowing of General Jackson threats, but with no design to attack, though willing to work him the opportunity to execute his threat, went and put up at a tavern other in the one in which he staid.

2. That the General and some of his friends came to the tavern at which we had put up, and commenced the attack by leveling a pistol at me, when I had no weapon drawn, and advancing upon me a quick pace, without giving me time to draw one.

3. That seeing this, my brother fired upon General Jackson, when he had got within eight or ten feet of me.

4. That four other pistols were fired in quick succession, one by General Jackson at me, two by me at the General, and one by Col. Coffee at me. In the course of this firing General Jackson was brought to the ground, but I received no hurt.

5. That daggers were then drawn. Col. Coffee and Mr. Alexander Donaldson made at me, and gave me five slight wounds. Capt. Hammond and Mr. Stockly Hays engaged my brother, who being still weak from the effect of a wound he received at the battle of...

[Last paragraphs largely obscured]

THOMAS HART BENTON, Lieut. Col. 39th Infantry,
Judge, a member of the Senate of the United States.

A PREOCCUPIED CINCINNATUS   465

light of shifty character. The collaboration of the *National Journal*, Adams's mouthpiece and mentor of the Administration press, made them personages of note overnight. When this newspaper reprinted Arnold's screed, the assault on Rachel Jackson was before the country in a guise that could not fail of attention.

The General left off weighing cotton long enough to consent to a forthright counter-move. William B. Lewis signed a call for a mass meeting at the Davidson County court house at which, after "animated and eloquent" oratory, a committee was named to "detect and arrest falsehood and calumny." A preponderance of the wealth and prestige of the Nashville district was embodied in the eighteen men—not all unwavering admirers of Old Hickory—who served thereon.[63]

The committee produced a document notable for its judicial calm and accuracy. By the statements of the surviving witnesses in Virginia, Kentucky and Tennessee was traced the thorny path of Rachel Donelson's married life with Robards; her meeting with Jackson; the flight to Natchez; the supposed divorce; the marriage ceremony on Spanish soil; the actual divorce by ex-parte proceedings. Though the skillful work of advocates, little of importance in this recital can be overthrown by evidence we know today.[64] It shines by contrast with the reckless productions of the opposition. Plus flourishes by Duff Green, this was published in the *Telegraph,* filling ten columns, and in the Jackson press nationally.[65]

Arnold returned to the attack.

"Gen. Jackson has admitted that he boarded at the house of old Mrs. Donelson, and that Roberts became jealous of him, but he omits the cause of that jealousy . . . [namely] that one day Roberts surprised General Jackson and his wife exchanging most delicious kisses. . . . In this case Roberts acted a cowardly part" in that he failed to shoot "Jackson dead in his tracks." Concerning Mrs. Robards's voyage to Natchez in the company of Jackson and Colonel Stark, "the Gen. omitted to tell that . . . they slept under the same blanket."[66]

Hammond followed with a pamphlet said to have been distributed under the franks of Administration congressmen: "Ought a convicted adulteress and her paramour husband to be placed in the highest offices of this free and christian land?"[67]

Old Hickory fought for self-command. "How hard it is to keep the cowhide from these villains. I have made many sacrifices for my country—but being . . . unable to punish those slanders of Mrs. J. is a sacrifice too great to be well endured." Firm John Coffee counseled patience a little longer. "Controul your feelings. Let nothing draw you out."[68]

But the harried man could endure no more. He seized a pen.

"I could not [at first] believe that even you, sir, . . . could descend so low. . . . It did not seem possible to me that the Secretary of State, the second officer in the government of our Republic, . . . would travel through the country for the cowardly purpose of slandering a virtuous female—one who has passed from infancy to old age in the confidence and friendship of the good and pious citizens of every society in which she has lived and who [has] received the mark[ed] and I may say honored attentions of Mrs. Clay and yourself. . . . Were all these professions base hypocrisy? . . . Sir, assassination of character in all its horrid forms and colorings is not as bad as such conduct as this. . . ."

The object of this letter? Certainly not to split the hairs of social usage. That was never Jackson's way. He had started to draw up what looked like a summons to an interview at twenty paces, the form and language of which he knew by heart. Old Hickory took a fresh grip on the quill.

"Sir, One would have looked for something less degrading from a champion of the Pistol Gag Law. . . ."

Again the pen faltered sliding off into irrelevancies. Evil day, evil day when Andrew Jackson permitted himself to be caught up in the fatal web which had rendered him impotent to strike a blow for the woman he loved as he loved no other creature of earth. But the thing was done and Coffee was right: an aspirant to the presidency could not fight a duel.

Yet the pen ran on, tracing out sentences as futile as anything Andrew Jackson had uttered in twenty years.

". . . I have only to add that Mrs. J. and myself hurl at you our defiance. A virtuous and well spent life has assured her a skirt which such men as you and your worthy associate Charles Hammond cannot sully."

A PREOCCUPIED CINCINNATUS

There the baffled writer stopped. It is not known whether this letter ever was actually sent to Henry Clay.[69]

The free style of campaigning put Duff Green at no disadvantage. After an unheeded warning to Peter Force, publisher of the *Journal*, that further affronts would bring retaliation, Green smote his lyre and forth came a fabrication attributing to Mr. and Mrs. Adams premarital relations similar to those alleged against the Jacksons.[70] "Let Mrs. Jackson rejoice," the editor of the *Telegraph* reported to the Hermitage, "her vindication is complete."[71]

Old Hickory's rebuke was swift and final. "Female character should never be introduced or touched unless a continuation of attack should be made against Mrs. Jackson, and then only by way of *just retaliation* on the known GUILTY. . . . I *never war against females* and it is only the base and cowardly that do."[72]

This terminated the retaliation though, to Jackson's mind, the known guilty were John Quincy Adams and Henry Clay. The General believed that a word from Adams to Peter Force, such as Jackson gave to Green, would have halted the *Journal's* encouragement of Hammond's and of Arnold's filthy pens. The case of the Secretary of State is less negative. Disregarding questionable tales that reached Jackson's ears, such as that of a midnight meeting between Clay and Hammond,[73] it seems clear that Clay, an experienced politician and practiced manager of editors, was close enough to Hammond to have suppressed him had he wished to do so. More than that, Eaton's intuition had served him well when it attributed Hammond's effort to absolve Clay to the inspiration of Clay himself. The fact is that immediately after Eaton's visit the Secretary informed Hammond of the Senator's call. "I have now no recollection that the case of Mrs. Jackson formed any topic of conversation between us when you were at Lexington."[74] This was not the language Henry Clay had used to Major Eaton; nor was the effect of it the same. "Suppose you had furnished me the documents," brazenly replied Hammond, "what right had Gen. Jackson to complain? He keeps no terms with you."[75] Despite his virtuous disclaimer, Mr. Clay knew what his man Hammond was about, and gave silent consent to his depredations.

So much touching briefly on the question of responsibility for the episode which, above all others of his political life, Jackson never forgot or forgave. It appears to have gained the Administration no advantage with the voters; such assaults seldom do. The salient achievement was to lay waste to the joy of a life, desolating an aged and pious woman whose fortune had been in youth to be beautiful, to marry a bounder and, existence with him becoming intolerable, to win the heart of Andrew Jackson.

10

Jackson people, too, are accountable for the depths to which the campaign declined. The trend dates from the contest of 1824 in which the General was an unwilling candidate, his personal conduct the most proper of all the aspirants. Yet lieutenants were allowed to introduce militia muster and fish fry methods, long sanctioned in frontier elections but hitherto absent from presidential campaigns. The other candidates protested, perhaps the more passionately after each had attempted, without success, the western technique.[76] Jackson's border upbringing condoned the conduct of his aides who succeeded where rivals failed, Old Hickory being the only true borderer in the race.

The campaign of 1824, however, seems respectable by contrast with its successor in which the art of character assassination attained a perfection as yet unsurpassed. In this the Adams people were by a good margin the busiest practitioners. The ghosts of Dickinson, of poor John Woods, of six Tennessee militiamen executed in Alabama,[77] of Arbuthnot and Ambrister were caused to walk. Years later the tale was related of a New England Sunday school teacher who asked the name of the slayer of Abel. "General Jackson," a pupil replied.[78]

The case of the six militiamen was presented in the Coffin Handbill, perhaps the most easily remembered political broadside in our history, and in a pamphlet entitled *Official Record from the War Department* which deserves to be better known. This assumed the style of a government document and bore the legend, "Ordered to be Printed by the Congress." Distributed under the franks of Adams congressmen, it could be mistaken for an authentic transcript of the proceedings of the court-martial which sentenced the men. Actually it was a part of that record, so garbled as to constitute a forgery.

The Burr conspiracy was revived with éclat until the discovery that Henry Clay had appeared as an attorney for the accused. The *National Journal* published a *Sketch of the Life &c of General Jackson* convicting Old Hickory of the Florida "crimes" of which Mr. Adams had acquitted him at the time. Charles Hammond's *Gazette* had the last word, calling Jackson's mother a prostitute and his father a mulatto who had sold an older offspring of that union into slavery.[79]

In the light of this record, the comparatively minor allegations that Andrew Jackson drank, gambled and occasionally shot or sword-caned an acquaintance might have served to endow him with a few plausible failings. But the Hero's friends would not allow it. "Gen. Jackson *does not at any time play cards*," adjured Duff Green. "Neither does General Jackson swear."[80]

John Henry Eaton contributed to his reputation as an observer when he wrote his patron: "Nothing now to be said of you can . . . [work] the least injury. The Press has overthrown its own power through repeated falsehoods."[81]

Although the Hermitage was overrun with visitors, Jackson continued almost as removed from the purely political aspects of the campaign as he had been four years before. Then the attitude was genuine for, except when smarting under some hostile thrust, he had no deep-seated wish to be elected. Now he intended to triumph, and to that end permitted a dash of the conscious Cincinnatus to tincture the picture of masterly inaction. The General's cotton seemed to have suffered from inattention, however, the 1827 crop being no better than average in quality. A plague decimated the stables leaving Jackson without a team to take him to Alabama to straighten out an overseer tangle. Convinced that one plantation was enough for a man about to be called to other responsibilities, the General sold Melton's Bluff. Lincoyer, the Indian boy, died of tuberculosis and was buried as a member of the family. Andrew Jackson Hutchings was expelled from Cumberland College. "Tell him," his guardian wrote, "how much I have regretted the want of education and how much I wish him to possess one."[82] Henry Lee, having resigned his appointment under Adams, found himself homeless because of a sentimental affair with his wife's sister. Jackson took him in. "Black Horse Harry" fell to, helping Donelson write letters and even began a biography of his protector.

Old Hickory was persuaded to accept an invitation to go to New Orleans for the thirteenth anniversary of his greatest feat of arms. Attended by a mixed company of politicians and war veterans, the General and Mrs. Jackson boarded the steamer *Pocahontas* for the only electioneering tour he was ever to make in his own interest. One of the last persons to be included in the party was James Alexander Hamilton of New York, who had reached Nashville somewhat breathlessly on the eve of the sailing.

Colonel Hamilton, a son of the first Secretary of the Treasury, was of the cosmopolitan group engaged in promoting the advancement of Martin Van Buren. The New York statesman had come so far since his leadership of Crawford's doomed cause that only John C. Calhoun seemed to stand between him and the ultimate goal of a public man's ambition. Jackson's declaration not to seek re-election rendered the early settlement on an heir apparent a matter of first importance. Drifting down the Mississippi, Hamilton, W. B. Lewis, Sam Houston and other anti-Calhoun spirits were soon in congenial conversation. Several months previously Houston had endeavored to get in a lick at the South Carolinian by showing his chief an old letter, written by Monroe to Calhoun, throwing light on the subject which above everything Mr. Calhoun wished to conceal from Andrew Jackson: the truth of the Cabinet's secret deliberations concerning the Florida campaign. "My hair stood on end for an hour," exclaimed Jackson after reading the missive.[83] Conciliators had got busy, however. Old Hickory's gray locks came to rest and Sam's industry seemed wasted—until the apparently providential appearance of James Alexander Hamilton.

At New Orleans the celebration lasted longer than the battle and made almost as much noise. One relatively small act tended to make General Jackson's path in Louisiana smoother than it had been in 1814: he slept at the home of Bernard de Marigny de Mandeville.

Colonel Hamilton was not a member of the returning Jackson party. He was on his way to Georgia to try to get from William H. Crawford a statement on those old Cabinet confidences which Houston and Lewis fondly hoped would blow Calhoun sky high. Back in Nashville, Houston sought to prepare the way by stirring up things on the basis of the Monroe letter which had aroused Jackson momentarily the year before. This time Mr. Calhoun himself bore

A PREOCCUPIED CINCINNATUS

into the breach with wordy explanations. Then it transpired that Hamilton had performed his mission badly, failing to see Crawford and obtaining only a letter from Governor Forsyth giving a second-hand version of Calhoun's criticism of Jackson in 1818. Lewis felt the production too weak to present to the General. Calhoun's explanations succeeded. The campaign moved on with the ambitious South Carolinian still ascendant over his ambitious rival from New York.[84]

II

The sulphurous clouds of personal abuse all but obscured the only issues of policy before the country—the tariff and internal improvements—as well as the fact that on these heads there was not a great deal to choose between the candidates. Early in the campaign Jackson's advisers had pressed him to be discreet so as not to make difficulties for sectional leaders of the party. The object was to insinuate the General on the East as a friend of protection, on the West as a Federal road and canal advocate, on the South as a very mild tariff and improvements man. Old Hickory bristled. "I have nothing in my political creed to keep secrete."[85] He said he had voted for certain internal improvements and for Clay's American System, and still held the views those votes expressed. The managers persisted. "A laconic, very laconic note referring to your [tariff] votes would be ample."[86] Jackson did not retreat from the tariff position which had brought so much southern criticism in 1824. Though clear, his statements were brief enough to satisfy the strategists, however.[87] The "bargain" and slander farragoes made livelier reading, and what the General said about duties was not widely circulated. Consequently the practical idea of running him as a chameleon on the issues succeeded to some extent.

Yet, all these things gave way before the ruling consideration of personality: Old Hickory or John of Braintree? From the first a majority of people had seemed to prefer Jackson, which simplified the problems of his lieutenants. The campaign was almost an uninterrupted extension of that of 1824 which had opened with a populace in arms against hard times, determined to achieve a more equal distribution of wealth and of burdens. The defeat of their champion by the enterprise of Henry Clay afforded the most effective cry for 1828. Hard times passed. The place of the spur of want to drive the people on was supplied by a whipped-up frenzy of politicians mindful of their own needs and greeds—with the reticent figure of the outraged Hero etched upon their banners. Against this concatenation of circumstances, Adams began the race with less than an even chance. Soon the situation was desperate, which desperate measures failed to repair.

By midsummer, 1828, Jacksonites ceased to worry over the outcome. A party worker sent Lewis predictions on the vote in Kentucky, Indiana and Ohio merely to "enable our friends to make betts somewhat advisedly."[88] On election day a traveler in Illinois described a typical western polling place. "Platform some thirty feet high in front of the court house. . . . Thirty gallon barrel of whisky with the name of 'ANDREW JACKSON' written on it; and in a short time another barrel with the name of 'JOHN QUINCY ADAMS.'" The story was told of a stranger in a Tennessee town who saw no men on the streets. A hotel proprietor explained that they were looking for a couple of rascals. Asked what the rascals had done, the tavern-keeper said they had voted for Adams.[89]

In some New England precincts the situation was almost reversed. Heavy eastern majorities gave Mr. Adams a total popular vote within twelve per cent of that of his rival—508,064 to 647,276; but so much more widely diffused was Jackson's support that the triumph in the electoral college was overwhelming—one hundred and seventy-eight to eighty-three.

"I am filled with gratitude," he wrote simply to John Coffee. "Still, my mind is depressed."[90]

His heart ached for Rachel.

CHAPTER XXVII

End of Flight

I

AFTER handsome Charles Dickinson had futilely emptied a pistol into Andrew Jackson's breast and then folded his arms to receive the consequences of a hasty use of Rachel Jackson's name—in fact during all the early episodes that enliven Jackson's defense of his wife's reputation—precautions were taken to veil from Rachel the true nature of events. This was to small purpose. She always seems to have known more than she was supposed to know. Within her the conviction deepened that the only hope for peace lay in obscurity; and this proved a vain hope. When partizans of Mr. Adams branded Rachel Jackson an adulteress so publicly that pretense of concealment from her was useless, she faced the issue with the determined composure of one confronting an ordeal long expected.

Her own remonstrances were mildly put. "the enemys of the Genls have dipt their arrows in wormwood and gall and sped them at me. . . . they have Disquieted one that thaey had no rite to do." The afflicted woman prayed for her tormentors. "my judg will know how many prayers have I oferd up."[1]

There was also a reward for one of her champions, Moses Dawson, editor of *The* [Cincinnati] *Friend of Reform or Corruption's Adversary*—a suit of clothes woven and made up at the Hermitage, in part by Rachel's own hands. Such recognition all but deprived Mr. Dawson of the power of coherent speech.

"Madam

"With feelings which no language can discribe no eloquence express I received your very flattering letter and highly worthy estimable present by the hands of your respected Worthy friend Judge Isaacs. . . .

"To Advocate the cause of truth and to defend exemplary virtue and exalted worth against the pointless shafts of falsehood and malvolence is a task not only easy of performance, but, to a generous mind, is full and sufficient reward." Mr. Dawson promised that Rachel's gift "for the residue of my life [shall] be my only Holliday dress, and then left as an Heir loom in my family.

"Permit me at this time Madam to congratulate you on the event which. . . ." Then followed three lines of untrammeled prose, fortunately attended by a translation: "I mean the election that has called your illustrious Consort to the chief Magistracy of this great nation."[2]

William B. Lewis delivered this letter to the mistress of the Hermitage. It may be assumed that she made a proper—and properly spelled, thanks to Nephew Donelson—acknowledgment as she did to other messages in similar strain when the news of victory roused the Cumberland. But to Lewis she did not dissemble.

"For Mr. Jackson's sake I am glad. For my own part I never wished it."[3]

2

Friends noted a relinquishment of courage, a lapse into melancholy. "She supported herself under it [the slander] until the excitement produced by the late contest was over. From that moment her energy subsided, her spirits drooped, and her health declined—She has been heard to speak but seldom since."[4] Youthful Henry R. Wise, who had come to Nashville to practice law and had married the daughter of a clergyman dear to Rachel, called at the Hermitage with his bride and some members of the wedding party. Never was he to forget the marks of time and sorrow on the countenance of his hostess. "Mrs. Jackson was once a form of rotund and rubiscund beauty, but [is] now very plethoric and obese. . . . [She] talked low but quick, with a short and wheezing breath." Yet he found her "the very personification of affable kindness and of a welcome as sincere and truthful as it was simple and tender."[5]

The bridal couple accepted an invitation to pass their honeymoon under the roof that had sheltered so many newlyweds. "The house was full of guests, . . . visitors from all parts of the United States, numbering from twenty to fifty per day, constantly coming and going, all made welcome and all well attended to. The cost . . . [of this hospitality] was very great and burdensome; but the general showed no sign of impatience, and was alive and active in his attentions to all comers and goers. He affected no style, and put on no airs, but was plainly and simply . . . polite to all." Andrew Jackson Donelson, Stockley Donelson and Henry Lee assisted with the honors.

"General Jackson bade us feel at home but gave us distinctly to understand that he took no trouble to look after any but his lady guests; as for the gentlemen, there was the parlor, the dining-room, the library, the side-board and its refreshments; there were the servants, and all that was necessary was to ring. He was as good as his word. He did not sit at the head of the table, but mingled with his guests, and always preferred a seat between two ladies, seeking a chair between different ones at various times. He was quick to perceive every point of word or manner, was gracious in approval, but did not hesitate to dissent with courtesy when he differed. He obviously had a hidden vein of humor, loved aphorism, and could politely convey a sense of smart travesty. If put upon his mettle he was very positive, but gravely respectful. He conversed freely, and seemed absorbed in what the ladies were saying; but if a word of note was uttered at any distance from him audibly, he caught it by quick and pertinent comment, without leaving the subject about which he was talking to another person."[6]

On a soft October evening while facile Henry Lee entertained the company in the drawing room, young Wise was bidden to join a smaller and less fashionable group, though more difficult of access. He found Rachel in her first floor bedroom, seated beside an open window overlooking the garden. Her circle consisted of the General; old Judge Overton, bald, beak-nosed and toothless; the Reverend Obadiah Jennings, father-in-law of Mr. Wise; Mary Eastin, a pretty niece whom Rachel intended to take to Washington; and Henry Baldwin, son of a Jackson leader in Pennsylvania and a groomsman at the recent wedding. On hearing that Henry Wise was from Accomac County in Virginia, the home of her maternal ancestors, Mrs. Jackson had sent for him. As it turned out, the visitor was familiar with the hip-roofed mansion in which Rachel's mother was born, with Assawaman Church which she attended as a girl—in fact, the whole countryside of which Rachel had heard at her mother's knee. She asked the young man many questions.

There were other such evenings, as more and more the wife of the President-elect avoided the kaleidoscope of company, keeping to her chamber to sit with her Bible, or a few old friends, partaking of the additional consolation of a pipe of tobacco. Once she spoke of having "lived with Mr. Jackson for nearly forty years . . . [without] an unkind word passing between them, and the only subject on which they had ever differed . . . was his acceptance of appointments, . . . she being always unwilling for him to enter public life."[7]

On the eighth day of November, 1828, young Dr. Henry Lee Heiskell who made one or two trips a week to the Hermitage attending the negroes, examined Mrs. Jackson. He bled her, after which Rachel apparently felt better for a while. Yet the cause for concern was not removed. Forty years of selfless generosity had won Rachel Jackson an army of friends, but the thing went deeper than that as speculation arose as to the effect her brooding might have on the General.

Martin Van Buren was alert for news. John C. Calhoun still stood athwart the path of the New Yorker. With the South Carolinian already Vice President-elect, this was no time to permit Old Hickory's health to fail. Therefore, the news Mr. Van Buren received from Tennessee was not good news. "J^n appears to be well but (enter nous) he is wearing away rapidly. . . . Already J$^{n's}$ successor is as much spoken of as J$^{n's}$ late success."[8]

3

Something had been said of permitting Rachel to remain in Tennessee until the inaugural should be over and the General's administration under way. Eaton had agreed to this.

"That opinion is now changed since I have arrived here and heard the reasoning of your friends," wrote the Senator, again at the helm in Washington. "The storm was abated—the angry tempest has ceased to howl. . . . You cannot but look back on the past as an idle fading vision . . . that should produce to you [not] one moments feeling, one moments pain. . . . The attentions to be meted out to the general, and to you, are such as . . . [befits his triumph.] The

Ladies from . . . remote parts of the Union will be here . . . to manifest to you their feelings and high regard. . . . If you shall be absent how great will be the disappointment. Your persecutors may then chuckle and say that they have driven you from the field. . . . Such is my confidence that you will be along with the general that I shall no longer speak of it as doubtful."[9]

No respite. Arrangements for departure added to the scene of bustle at the Hermitage. The place was like a camp. A journey that would be so slow and tedious required an early start. State legislatures, municipal bodies, military organizations, political clubs feverishly planned what would amount to a continuous ovation along the route. A North Carolinian volunteered to drive the General and his lady all the way in a coach with six white horses. In Columbus, Ohio, sympathetic females chewed their quills over "an *Address* of Congratulation to Mrs. Jackson . . . as evidence of their contempt for those unprincipled slanderers."[10]

Nashville would take its leave on December 23, the anniversary of the Night Battle. A week beforehand old soldiers and politicos, new friends and hungry hangers-on began to put in an appearance from as far away as the Gulf until the little city, surprised from its accustomed leisure, was crowded to bursting. The General was expected down from the Hermitage in the morning "to receive the congratulations of his friends & partake with them a parting glass,"[11] the fête day closing with a banquet and ball at the Nashville Inn.

The overwhelming preparations engulfed Rachel, who desired no coach and six white horses, no address of congratulation, no ball and banquet at the Nashville Inn. The storm Major Eaton spoke of had not abated in her breast. "I assure you I had rather be a doorkeeper in the house of God than to live in that palace at Washington."[12] But as her immediate destination was taken to be the palace, a party of women friends assumed the task of making her ready for the journey. As usual Mrs. Jackson's wardrobe was in a state of neglect. The poor woman submitted to be borne off to Nashville to begin the process of measuring and fitting her unstylish form to attire deemed suitable for the first lady of the land.

Concerning one such expedition a story has been told in the Cumberland country so long that it is traditional. According to one version Aunt Rachel, who had retired to the parlor of the Nashville

Inn to rest off the fatigue of a session with the seamstresses, overheard a feminine conversation lamenting the impossibility of rendering presentable to official society this illiterate country-woman. Another account has it that in the office of a newspaper editor she chanced to pick up a pamphlet issued by the friends of the General, revealing that the foulest part of the slander had been kept from her after all. When her companions returned they found her "crouching in a corner," terror-stricken and hysterical. Rachel demanded her carriage. On the way home she stopped at a creek to bathe her tear-swollen eyes so that her husband might not know the depth of her grief.[13]

A few days later, on December 17, a horseman riding recklessly into Nashville's Square summoned young Doctor Heiskell and Dr. Samuel Hogg, the regular physician to the Hermitage household. Heiskell reached the plantation first, finding Mrs. Jackson's face contorted with pain from a "spasmodic affection of the muscles of the chest and left shoulder, attended with an irregular action of the heart." A physician Jackson had called in from the countryside bent over the patient. He had bled her without abatement of the distress. Heiskell bled her again. Toward evening Doctor Hogg repeated the operation. This "produced great relief," noted Heiskell, "and an entire subsidence of all alarming symptoms." In her high French bed Rachel was soon asleep. The physicians, but not Jackson, retired to a room adjoining. The vigil was rewarded. In the morning when he saw his wife open her eyes, the cruel marks of pain were gone from her countenance and she had gained strength.

For three days Rachel mended. She sat in a chair before the fire, received a few friends and seemed to be cheerful. Andrew was ever at her side. Perhaps not in a year had she enjoyed so much of her husband's company in so short a time. On Sunday evening, December 22, she sat too long and was put to bed with a cold and slight symptoms of pleurisy. The physicians brewed drinks, brought on a profuse sweat and, announcing that the incident was not serious, reminded General Jackson that he would be on the way to Nashville early in the morning. In the interest of his own health, they begged that he take himself to bed in another room. When Rachel seconded the suggestion he consented to go. It was one of the few times he had left her since the beginning of the illness. Presently the attending physicians retired.

They could bring repose to the body but not to the mind of their patient. Twice she had her maid Hannah help her to the chair by the fire and fill a pipe with tobacco. Sitting there in her night-dress shortly before ten o'clock, Aunt Rachel made a remark she had been heard to make before. "I had rather be a door-keeper in the house of God than to live in that palace."

Twenty minutes later she cried out, "I am fainting!" and collapsed in Hannah's arms.

The servant's screams roused the house. Jackson burst into the room in time to help lift Rachel to her bed. In her form he felt a convulsive muscular movement. Life? Andrew Jackson saw the doctors bend down and listen for the heart-beat. He saw them straighten and he read in their glance that life had gone.

Rachel Jackson's long flight from fame was over.[14]

4

"How shall I describe the agony," wrote Doctor Heiskell, "the heart-rending agony of the venerable partner of her bosom!"

The old chieftain's breast seemed to swell as if the heart within were about to burst.

"Bleed her!" he cried.

No blood flowed from her arm.

"Try the temple, Doctor."

Two drops, but no more, stained her cap.

Servants filled the house with piercing supplications to Heaven. They could not believe their mistress dead. "She's only fainting." Something of this blind negation entered the numbed mind of Jackson. He refused to leave his wife's side. When a table was brought in to lay her out he said:

"Spread four blankets upon it. If she does come to she will lay hard on that table."

By midnight relatives and neighbors and friends began to fill the house and fill the yard. Lewis came at dawn. In Hannah's simple language, he found Jackson "grieving"—alone with his loved one and with the paralyzing realization that a world can end. His head in his hands, his eyes dry, his long fingers thrust through his gray hair, the stricken husband was almost speechless. Thought seemed to have left him. A shaking hand stroked the cold brow as a child would to assure itself of the reality of an object by the sense of touch.

"John, can you realize that she is dead. I certainly can't."[15] This to John Coffee.

Throughout the day, except when she was being dressed in white for burial, Andrew Jackson remained by the side of the woman he had made his own thirty-seven years before and from that hour to this had defended against all things and all men. Physicians hovered watchfully, fearing even Andrew Jackson's resources unequal to the commands he placed upon them. Toward evening the General was induced to swallow a little coffee.[16]

At one o'clock in the afternoon of the next day—December 24—Rachel was buried in her garden one hundred and fifty paces from the east door of the house. Tennessee has never seen such a funeral. Ten thousand persons, or twice as many as lived in Nashville, filled the garden, the great lawn, and overflowed into the level pasture. The news of death had reached town after midnight. By daybreak on the twenty-third, handbills were spreading it through the streets and the countryside. Before posting to subscribers his issue of that date, the editor of the *Republican* had only time to scrawl on the margins, "*Mrs. Jackson has just Expired!*" The message surprised early-rising residents attiring themselves for a gala day. It intercepted conveyances on the roads from farms and plantations.

On the morning of the twenty-fourth the conveyances were on the roads again. Every buggy and carriage and coach in Davidson County was on the roads, and places in them could not be bought for money. Every manner of farm wagon and rig, every saddle horse and hundreds of work horses were on the road. Two or three thousand persons trudged on foot, taking short-cuts across fields, for every thoroughfare converging upon the Hermitage was choked as rich and poor, high and low, white and black, made their way as if impelled by instinct to the grave prepared for Rachel Jackson. Some there may have been who made the journey as a mark of respect to the memory of the wife of the President-elect, but they would have been strangers to the Cumberland country. Davidson County mourned Aunt Rachel for reasons with which her husband's fame and station had little to do.

Under a bleak sky, Sam Houston led the pallbearers along the

Emily Donelson

Niece of Rachel Jackson, wife (and cousin) of Andrew Jackson Donelson. She was mistress of the White House during General Jackson's administrations saving for a year of exile during the ascendency of Margaret Eaton whose calls Mrs. Donelson would not return. From a portrait by Earl, owned by Mrs. Donelson's great-granddaughter, Mrs. Pauline Wilcox Burke of Washington.

ANDREW JACKSON ("JACK") DONELSON

Nephew of Rachel Jackson and husband of Emily Donelson, reared at the Hermitage from the age of four, educated at West Point and at Transylvania University. Private secretary to General Jackson and later chargé d'affaires to the Texas Republic. He was the most disinterested and one of the ablest of Old Hickory's intimate counselors. From a portrait by Earl, owned by Mrs. Betty Donelson of Nashville.

curved garden walk to where the earth had been opened. Behind the casket walked Jackson as a man would walk in a trance, his arms linked with those of ever-dependable John Coffee and of Henry M. Rutledge; then a great train of Donelson relations; then the household servants, moaning and chanting. When Hannah flung herself beside the grave someone asked her to control her grief. Jackson shook his head, and Hannah lay there sobbing.

The Reverend William Hume spoke for twenty minutes. Seldom it is that words uttered on such an occasion are so free from exaggeration.

" 'The righteous shall be in everlasting remembrance.' These words might be applied to that venerable matron, with much propriety, as she gave every reasonable evidence that she was among the righteous. . . . Her character was so well known . . . that the following remarks will readily be acknowledged as true: . . .

"Her seat was seldom empty in the house of God. The tears of genuine penitence were often shed by her in the temple of the Lord. She had a tender and a feeling heart, and sometimes I have seen the tears bedewing her cheeks while she was speaking of . . . those around her, who seemed to be entirely careless about a future state.

"While she rejoiced in the honor of a nation, yet no unbecoming elation of mind, no haughtiness, no overbearing conduct, could ever be seen, even by an inimical eye, in this amiable lady. She was adorned with the ornament of a meek and quiet spirit. . . . By her kindness and affability, her husband was [rendered] more happy in his own family than in the midst of his triumphs.

"The tears and lamentations of the servants are proofs of her excellence as mistress of her household. . . . The widow and the orphan will long lament the death of Mrs. Jackson. . . . Blest with affluence, she had a heart to feel and a hand to relieve the poor and the needy. She viewed the bounties of Providence . . . as designed by her Benefactor to flow in channels leading to the doors of those who were perishing of thirst, that they, also, might quaff and be satisfied.

"Some, indeed, during the presidential struggle, with unfeeling hearts and unjustifiable motives, exerted all their powers to throw her numerous virtues into the shade. . . . Under this cruel treatment, Mrs. Jackson displayed the temper of a disciple of Him who was meek and lowly of heart. . . . She felt the injustice of the warfare. Her compassionate heart was wrung with sorrow. Her tears flowed, but there was no malevolence in her bosom. She could have received no pleasure in giving pain to her detractors. . . .

"While we cordially sympathize with the President of the United States in the irreparable loss he has sustained in the death of his amiable lady, whom he deemed so worthy, as he said, of our tears; we cannot doubt but that she now dwells in the mansions of glory in company with the ransomed of the Lord."[17]

For the first time since the tragedy tears coursed the white and taut cheeks of Jackson. "But one wish pervaded the assembly," wrote one who stood near. "That the individuals who had hastened this scene by their relentless attacks on an unoffending woman could be brought to witness the saddest spectacle that any present has ever beheld." When Doctor Hume ceased speaking Jackson, "by a muscular and almost superhuman effort, endeavored to check the current of his grief. 'I know 'tis unmanly,' said he, 'but these tears are due her virtues. She has shed many for me.' "[18]

The old soldier raised his voice a little, speaking slowly, in a tone that seemed to come from another world.

"In the presence of this dear saint I can and do forgive all my enemies. But those vile wretches who have slandered her must look to God for mercy."[19]

5

Pale was glory's coronet. With all that bound him to life returned to earth, the unconquered spirit of Andrew Jackson seemed on the brink of surrender. Some feared he might decline to make the effort to journey to Washington and take the oath. At best, it was felt that he could not long survive.

Old Captain Will Alexander, Cumberland pioneer and Revolutionary veteran, addressed Jackson by a title used, at this late day, perhaps by no other man.

"My dear Son,

"I have heard it remarked by your Sincere but I thought weak friends That the loss of your wife would impede the march of your Administration— your Bosome companion and my dear friend . . . is gone on a grand party of pleasure I hope—and I think I am not deceived— Religion in my opinion is a comprehensive term—it takes in every duty we owe to our God or our fellow creatures, even to our animals— Our departed friend . . . possessed that very kind of religion. . . . For my part I . . . [believe] you certainly have philosophy enough to Submit to a dispensation from the Great first cause of things. . . . Be temperate my Son in every thing you do."[20]

The sorrowing husband permitted no affair of state to intrude until all was done that he could do for his beloved. The grave was covered with a wooden shelter to shield it from the rain until a permanent tomb in the form of a Greek cupola could be erected. Corners of the burial plot were marked with cuttings from a willow tree planted by James Robertson, founder of Nashville and associate of Rachel's adventurous father. With all the directness of his feudal soul, Andrew Jackson had defended his wife in life. His breath on a stone would defend her memory. The legend for a long and moving epitaph contained these words: "A being so gentle, so virtuous, slander might wound but could not dishonor."

Impotent grief began to yield to a mood of sinewy hatred. "May God Almighty forgive her murderers as I know she forgave them. I never can."[21] To Washington, then, to ride down Adams and Clay, and to hunt their hirelings from the temple. It was easier to say than to do. On the eighteenth day of January, at the little landing where he loaded his cotton, the President-elect stepped on board a steamboat. "My heart is nearly broke. I try to summon up my usual fortitude but in vain."[22]

BOOK FIVE

THE "REIGN"

"Though we live under the form of a republic we are in fact under the absolute rule of a single man."
JUSTICE JOSEPH STORY,
United States Supreme Court,
in a letter to a friend.

BOOK FIVE

The Nixon

CHAPTER XXVIII

The Haggard Hero

I

"Mr Clay's furniture is to be sold this week," noted Margaret Bayard Smith, distinguished for her knack of discerning the pertinent minutiae of Washington's fashionable world. Notwithstanding prospects for an advantageous disposal of his household things —the sprawling city being crowded already with Jacksonians reckoning on a four-year stay—the spirits of the Secretary of State were overborne by gloom. Mrs. Smith was "shocked at the alteration of his looks. . . . His eyes [are] sunk in his head." At that, she found Mr. Clay in better case than his colleagues—the Secretary of the Treasury being "alarmingly ill," the Secretary of the Navy not out of his room for three weeks, the head of the War Office "almost blind from inflammation of the eyes," the Attorney General afflicted with vertigo and "loss of the sense of motion." Though least understanding the debâcle that had struck down his régime, Mr. Adams bore it the best of all. But even the President's legs had given out, obliging him to abandon his daily walks.

"Never before," continued Mrs. Smith who had seen every Executive except the first one come and go, "did the city seem to me to be so gloomy— so many changes in society— so many families broken up, and those of the first distinction. . . . Drawing rooms in which I have so often mixed with gay crowds, distinguished by rank, fashion, beauty, talent, . . . now empty, silent, dark, dismantled. Oh! 'tis melancholy!"[1]

A dirge for the days that were done. As for the days to come, Daniel Webster's guess seemed as good as any:

"General Jackson will be here abt. 15. of Feb.——
"Nobody knows what he will do.
"Many letters are sent to him; he answers none of them.
"His friends here pretend to be very knowing; but. . . .

"Great efforts are being made to put him up to a general sweep as to all offices; springing from great doubts whether he is disposed to do it.

"Nobody is authorized to say whether he intends to retire after one term. . . .

"Who will form the cabinet is as well known at Boston as at Washington. . . .

"My opinion is

"That when he comes he will bring a breeze with him.

"Which way it will blow I cannot tell."[2]

General Jackson's health was a universal topic. A rumor of his death gripped the nervous city for a day. "I hope it is not true," said a friend of Clay, "for I would rather trust him than Calhoun."[3] No better informed than Webster, the Vice President-elect was nevertheless a busy man. A grand plan was formulated to meet the General's party with a cavalcade at Pittsburgh and escort him to the city under the Calhoun aegis. Though this was abandoned the journey from Tennessee was ordeal enough. Frances Trollope saw Jackson disembark at Cincinnati and walk, uncovered, through exulting throngs to a hotel. "He was in deep mourning. . . . He wore his gray hair carelessly but not ungracefully arranged, and in spite of his harsh, gaunt features looked like a gentleman and a soldier." This English woman had not found occasion to describe many Americans as gentlemen. On the Pittsburgh-bound packet sensitive travelers were "disgusted by the brutal familiarity to which they saw him exposed at every place they stopped. . . . There was not a hulking boy from a keel-boat who was not introduced. . . . A greasy fellow accosted him thus:—

" 'General Jackson, I guess.'

"The General bowed assent.

" 'Why they told me you was dead.'

" 'No. Providence has hitherto preserved my life.'

" 'And is your wife alive too?' "

"Jackson shook his head sadly.

" 'Aye, I thought it was one or the t'other of ye.' "[4]

On February 12, 1829, while jabbering partizans planned a "formal" entry into the city, John Henry Eaton quietly sent his carriage into Maryland, and had the General safely in an apartment at Gadsby's four hours before the cannon supposed to signal his approach let loose.

2

The throng that was taking possession of Washington in the assured manner of an army of occupation laid siege to the hotel. Donelson, Lewis and Lee performed sentry duty, but the General's assumption that he had been elected by "the people" rather than by a party set much of their effort at naught. Democratic episodes of the journey from Tennessee were re-enacted at "the Wigwam," as scandalized representatives of the old order dubbed the Jackson ménage at Gadsby's. Night and day applicants for an audience filled lobby, stairways, corridors, pressing and jostling until nervous persons feared for the safety of the building.

During a change of administrations Washington was accustomed to a few days of stimulating confusion, but to no such horde as descended upon the embryonic city to see Jackson reap and allot the rewards of six years of championship of the common man. "It was like the inundation of northern barbarians into Rome. . . . Strange faces filled every public place, and every face seemed to bear defiance on its brow."[5] Tennessee backwoodsmen and pioneers from the Northwest mingled with Irish immigrants from the seaboard cities, old soldiers, politicians of high and low degree, editors, adventurers, schemers. "I never saw anything like it before," said Webster. "They really seem to think the country is [to be] rescued from some dreadful danger."[6] They roamed the streets, surging in and out of taprooms until the spectre of a whisky famine contributed to an outlook already unsettled. They overflowed Washington into Georgetown and Alexandria, sleeping five in a bed or on billiard tables, or on floors, or apparently not at all. They patronized barbers who advertised "haircutting in the Jackson style," and a haberdasher sold "Jackson stocks" copied from the old-fashioned neckwear the General had worn since the day when frankly one of the Cumberland uppercrust. Other defects in the proletarian composition of the scene met the eye. The sight of an Archer, a Hayne, a Van Ness, a Livingston, a Hamilton quitting his carriage at Gadsby's was evidence that not every scion of the Virginia tradition, the Cotton Kingdom, or the commercial East regarded himself an outcast on the morn of the people's triumph.

Against this encroachment it would be an error to assume that the lower orders stood as a band of brothers. The victory was won but the spoil undivided—some eleven thousand offices directly or indirectly within the gift of the President. Certain editors and politicians called for a "clean sweep," and the hosts liked the full-throated cry. Because it was mathematically obvious that even the cleanest sweep must fail to provide for every aspirant, or even those who had already come or sent in their petitions to Washington, rivalries began to cleave the democratic ranks. Little of this seems to have been lost on the sombre-faced old man in the Wigwam who listened to so many words and uttered so few. "It appeared," he wrote two years later, "that instead of love of principle it was love of office that had induced [many of] them to support the good cause as they pleased to term it, . . . that self-exertion was about to be abandoned and dependence for a livelihood placed upon the government."[7]

Such was the atmosphere in which General Jackson toiled over the first problem of appointments to confront a President: the selection of his Cabinet.

Long before, he had determined in event of election to bring into his official family one man who, in addition to the weight his counsel might contribute to the scale of public affairs, could be trusted as a steadfast and confidential friend. In this connection Tennessee's senators, John Henry Eaton and Hugh Lawson White, occurred to him. Judge White was the abler of the two, Eaton the closer friend. The choice fell upon White, to whom Jackson wrote before leaving Tennessee. Knowing White to be low in mind because of illness and death in his family, Jackson requested that, if for any reason the Senator could not accept, would he pass the letter on to Eaton who should construe it as an invitation to the Cabinet.

On Jackson's first night in the city White called to say that domestic afflictions unfitted him to participate in the Government. Jackson usually meant what he said, and there is every reason to believe that White was actually the first, and Eaton the second, choice for a Cabinet portfolio. Nevertheless, it appears that the undiplomatic effort to kill two birds with one stone, which made acceptance by White a virtual act of exclusion against Eaton, had some bearing on White's answer. On the next day Eaton also refused the office. Although he did not say so, domestic considerations were probably a factor in his declination, for the *haut monde* was still gasping over the Senator's recent marriage to Margaret Timberlake. "Public opinion," noted Mrs. Smith, "will not allow Genl. Eaton . . . [to] bring *his wife* into society."[8]

This was not the kind of talk to turn Andrew Jackson from a friend. The more Eaton demurred, the stronger grew Old Hickory's insistence that he join the Cabinet. "Surely . . . [you] and Judge White both would not desert me." After ten days of this sort of thing Eaton "very reluctantly," as Jackson said, consented to accept the War Office.[9] The whole episode suggests something of a game on Eaton's part, for it seems that he had desired the post all along.[10] And certainly his wife desired it for him.

By this time the other selections had been virtually decided. The State Department was for Van Buren, the Treasury for Samuel D. Ingham, Pennsylvania paper manufacturer and dull though successful business man with fourteen inconspicuous years in the House. Brilliant, caustic, vain John MacPherson Berrien of Georgia, an excellent lawyer and showy orator, was the choice for Attorney General. John Branch, Navy, represented the best social traditions of the slave-holding aristocracy. He had been an enlightened governor of North Carolina and a senator. John McLean of Ohio was to remain in charge of the mails, Jackson announcing his intention to raise the postmaster generalship to Cabinet rank. Though McLean had favored Jackson during the campaign, Adams had declined to replace for political considerations the ablest director of the postal service since Benjamin Franklin.

Publication of the list gave Jackson's adversaries their first cause for congratulation in many a day. It dismayed many of his friends. "The Millennium of the Minnows!"[11] exclaimed one who evidently thought himself a pretty big fish. "A miserable cabinet," intoned another. "Gen. Jackson came down to the city full of grief and out of health. . . . The eleventh-hour men flocked around and they forced upon the President men like themselves by every artifice."[12] The success of these eleventh-hour men was a fruitful cause of resentment, one old follower who now repented his politeness having written on the day after the General's arrival: "In consequence of the crowd of *new Converts* it behooves his old Troops to stand back."[13] Recalling Jackson's commitment against the appointment of congressman, Louis McLane of Delaware pointed out that three of his selections were from Congress and "of the least capacity in the country!"[14] James A. Hamilton, looking after Van Buren's interests, wrote his chief uneasy letters. The New Yorker had but one friend in the Cabinet—Eaton—while Calhoun had three. And so cleverly was the business managed that Eaton had been persuaded to go to Jackson with puffs for the eleventh-hour men, Berrien and Branch.[15]

Critics fairly pounced upon the War Office nomination. Various reasons for a change were urged, but what everyone had in mind was the Senator's matrimonial adventure. The Tennessee delegation in Congress screwed up enough courage to ask the General to drop their colleague. Another idea was to give him the Post Office and refrain from raising it to Cabinet rank. A foreign berth was also suggested—France, for example, or, in a less helpful spirit, Haiti, "that being the most proper Court for *her*." A spark of the old-time fire lighted the blue eyes of Old Hickory as he penned a stern answer to the respectfully worded protest of the Tennessee congressmen. Jackson forsake a friend! That kind of opposition almost made him forget his troubles, he said. John Henry Eaton would be the Secretary of War.[16]

Considered on the basis of its individual members, the Cabinet was not below average, every man on the list being competent to administer with credit the department assigned to him. Except in the case of Eaton, the dissatisfaction sprang from the fact that the selections represented the unequal results of a contest between the partizans of two candidates for the succession to the presidency.

3

Our diplomatic relations with Portugal reveal nothing calculated to attain so long or so honorable a survival as the *mot* of an emissary of Mr. Monroe's time who called Washington the "city of magnificent distances." In 1829 the most presentable thoroughfare was unpaved Pennsylvania Avenue, connecting the Capitol and the White House, at the four corners of whose newly-planted grounds stood the brick buildings, simple but in good taste, of the State, Treasury,

War, and Navy Departments. To the north and south of this street houses were scattered over a prodigious area as if sown by a careless farmer. To reach a neighbor one picked his way through swamps, across ditches and over hillocks clad in scraggly pine, extemporized roads and paths mocking the geometrical exactitude of L'Enfant's theoretical avenues. On a fair day a carriage was more than a convenience, in wet weather the only thing to save a wayfarer's clothing from ruin. In this paradise for hackney coachmen, the fastidious paid more for transportation than for bed and board.

Only a small proportion of the admirers of General Jackson who flocked to Washington could afford to be fastidious, and as the day of days—March 4—drew nigh, their weather-beaten exteriors lent verisimilitude to the dark forebodings of revolution. John Quincy Adams had signified his intention not to be present at the east front of the Capitol to see his authority pass to his successor. This suited Jackson, who gave promise of making good his word to show no mercy to those whom he regarded as slanderers of his wife. On his arrival he had vowed not to "go near" Mr. Adams, and consequently omitted the traditional courtesy call.[17] Deeply hurt, Adams sought to re-establish the amenities by sending a messenger to say that the Executive Residence would be ready for occupancy on March 4. Orally General Jackson replied that he hoped Mr. Adams would not subject his household to the inconvenience of a hasty removal. On the afternoon of the third, the Adams family departed for the suburban residence of a friend. The President of the United States followed on foot, alone, unrecognized, tortured by bitter reflections.

Next morning the cannons boomed. Pennsylvania Avenue and the sloping west lawn of the Capitol were dense with humanity. The ground was spotted by thin patches of snow, fortunately firm. The sun shone. As the erect, gray-haired figure emerged from Gadsby's a mighty cheer rolled up the Avenue toward Capitol Hill. Having vetoed a plan for a military pageant, the General and a small party made their way along the sidewalk. Tories who had come to scoff felt the exhilaration of the scene. "It is *true* greatness which needs not the aid of ornament and pomp," exclaimed Mrs. Smith. "I think I shall like him vastly when I know him." Francis Scott Key said, "Sublime!"[18]

Skirting the multitude on the east terrace, the President-elect scaled a wall and entered the Capitol by the basement. Reappearing on the roped-off portico, he stood for a moment bowing acknowledgment to the ovation "with a grace and composed dignity" which a doubting free trader from South Carolina confessed, "I never saw surpassed."[19] The crowd fell silent. Though it did not catch a word of the inaugural address, those who were nearest saw the pages tremble as the Hero turned them. To miss the speech was no great deprivation, most of it being too conservative to thrill a populace. But office-seekers would have applauded this line: "The task of *reform* . . . inscribes itself on the list of executive duties"—"reform" being a brief way of saying, "Turn the rascals out."

One of the least distinguished-looking persons on the portico, Chief Justice Marshall, administered the oath, thereby endangering, as he imagined, the work of a lifetime on the bench. Jackson raised a Bible to his lips; Marshall held out his hand; an active little man scrambled over the barricade and up the steps. The second person to congratulate the President was "honest" George Kremer, the People's Friend. That touch repaid the crowd for having missed the inaugural address.[20]

Down the Avenue the President rode on horseback with a mob at his heels which brought to one onlooker's mind descriptions of the march on Versailles. The destination was the White House where a reception had been announced. In the stately East Room long tables were spread with cakes and ice-cream and orange punch for the officially and socially eligible as defined by precedent. Precedent? The mob in the horseman's wake swept through the Mansion gates and through the portals, leaving the "eligible" to shift for themselves. Representative and Mrs. George Gilmer of Georgia got in by clutching the coattails of Representative and Mrs. John Floyd whose "two stout sons" cleaved a path. They remained long enough to see clothing torn, women faint, glasses and china broken. "One hundred-and-fifty-dollar official chairs [were] profaned by the feet of clod-hoppers" anxious for a glimpse of their President. "A regular Saturnalia," a South Carolinian informed Mr. Van Buren, happily detained at Albany. "It would have done Mr. Wilberforce's heart good to have seen a stout black wench eating a jelley with a gold spoon on the President's House."[21] Mr. Wilberforce was an English abolitionist.

But the rarest sight was Andrew Jackson, helpless, "sinking into a listless state of exhaustion." The Georgians left through a window, "in doing which," Mr. Gilmer related, "I had to sustain with a weak leg from a fracture scarcely healed the weight of Mrs. Floyd equalling three hundred pounds." Locking arms, men threw a cordon about the President enabling him to escape by the back way. As Old Hickory retreated to Gadsby's and to bed, the departure of the White House guests was facilitated by placing tubs of punch on the lawn.[22]

The eventful day closed with a ball at which Mrs. Andrew Jackson Donelson, Mrs. Calhoun, Mrs. Ingham and Mrs. Edward Livingston seemed unaware of the presence of Margaret Timberlake Eaton.

4

A solitary lamp shed its feeble beams in the vestibule of the White House. A single candle illuminated the study where the President sat with Major Lewis. In office three weeks, General Jackson looked grief-stricken and weary.

Emily Donelson had not taken wholly in good part the fatherly talk he had felt duty bound to administer after the neglect of the wife of the Secretary of War at the inaugural ball; and in this Emily's husband seemed to sustain her. True, she and Jack had returned a call of Major and Mrs. Eaton, but it was done as an act of obedience to their uncle, the President, and with no cordiality. This hurt the old man for he loved these young people. Emily, born a Donelson, was Rachel's niece by blood as well as marriage, and before her death Rachel had expressed the wish that Emily should go with her to Washington to manage the official entertaining. In making her the feminine head of his household, Jackson felt that he carried out the desire of the saint who slept in the Hermitage garden. Yet Emily must understand that John Henry Eaton was her uncle's friend, and that his wife must be accorded the courtesies due the wife of a friend as well as a Cabinet minister.

Old Hickory attributed the Eaton gossip to "Clay and his minions."[23] But no such convenient explanation would suffice for the criticism of the Cabinet and of other appointments, much of which came from the General's own followers. Jackson realized that his régime had not caught the airs of success. Deliberately he sought to stir his ebbing forces to greater effort. "You know when I am excited all my energies come forth. . . . If my constitution will bear me up for one year, . . have no fear."[24]

So the President sat chatting with Lewis when the Secretary of State was announced. Ah, Mr. Van Buren was punctual.

The smallish figure that paused in the doorway presented "a rather exquisite appearance. His complexion was a bright blond, and he dressed accordingly"—favoring for day-time wear snuff-colored coats, white trousers, lace-tipped cravats, yellow gloves and morocco shoes.[25] As the visitor's quick and perceptive glance rested on the haggard old man in the shadowy room, Martin Van Buren better understood some of the things he had heard on his journey to Washington, finished a little more than an hour ago.

Strong effort had been made to prevent Mr. Van Buren from undertaking that journey. He had been urged to sidestep the proffered Cabinet appointment on the ground that General Jackson's Administration was foredoomed to failure. Having accepted, he had been urged to withdraw his name because failure was at hand. On the way to Washington, this advice had been reiterated by a particular friend, Louis McLane, on the ground that failure was too far along for one man to arrest. Mr. McLane mentioned the mediocrity of the Cabinet and the widespread belief that, taking his appointments as a whole, Jackson seemed under the domination of "evil counsellors." Mr. Van Buren could understand his friend's poor opinion of the Cabinet since he, McLane, was not in it as he had expected to be. This factor, however, did not operate on the judgment of Edward Livingston whom the New Yorker had encountered in Philadelphia. Livingston had obtained a tender of the office he wanted— the ministry to France. Yet the Livingstons were doleful, very doleful. The egalitarian spirit of the first White House "reception," the Eaton situation—in short, the social aspect of matters, by which they saw our country's prestige degraded in foreign capitals, troubled the aspiring diplomat and his beautiful lady.

Descending at his hotel in Washington, Mr. Van Buren had confronted another aspect of the problem to which he had given much sober thought. A pack of patronage-seekers trailed the New Yorker to his room. Stretched on a sofa, Van Buren listened to them for an hour. Then he closed the interview saying, in his invariably pleasant way, that he disapproved of applicants appearing at the seat of government and suggested that they return to their homes. A few minutes later Martin Van Buren presented himself at the Executive Residence for his first meeting, as a political friend, with Andrew Jackson.

The native courtliness of the President's greeting struck the caller at once. Old Hickory seemed to lay aside his weariness as one would shed a dingy cloak. When business was mentioned it was Mr. Van Buren who must guard against over-taxing his strength. General Jackson could not think of burdening a man fatigued by travel, and appointed an hour of the next day. Van Buren took his leave in better heart than he had come. Something in "that noble old man" had moved him.[26]

5

If the rebuked patronage-hunters followed the advice of Mr. Van Buren their departure did not noticeably diminish the army that remained in town, parading their Jackson stocks, their Jackson haircuts, and their insistent claims. Forces that were stronger than the admonition of the tardily-arriving Secretary of State operated to keep them there.

After an unsuccessful campaign effort to commit Jackson to "rotation in office,"[27] editorial leaders of the spoilsmen had bided their time until after the election when they laid down a bombardment that seemed to take much for granted. "*Punish the* DECEIVERS, *but reclaim* the DECEIVED!" was the title of a masterful effort by Isaac Hill. "Shall we . . . appoint to office and continue in office the men who have . . . libel[ed] the purest patriots in the country? . . . Forbid it, Heaven!"[28] Old Hickory's failure to acknowledge himself a celestial agent did not arrest the pen of Duff Green. "*Jackson and Reform*. . . . Cleanse the Augean Stable."[29] Even Ritchie's respectable Richmond *Enquirer* chimed in. On Jackson's arrival in Washington the "reform" journalists increased their din. The *National Journal* denounced the coming Administration in advance while placeholders shook in their shoes. Duff Green was on the spot. Isaac Hill, Amos Kendall of the *Western Argus*, Mordecai Noah of the New York *Courier and Enquirer*, and half a dozen others lost no time getting there. In Lewis, in Henry Lee, and in Eaton, they found friendly spirits. Such was the coterie—the "evil counsellors," and the "eleventh-hour men," of whom critics spoke—that encircled Jackson at the time of his induction into office.

The first voice raised against their schemes came from the Cabinet in the person of Postmaster General McLean, who had at his disposal more patronage than the rest of officialdom combined. This able and abrupt Westerner told the President that, if he must remove postmasters who had taken part in the election, he would dismiss those who had worked for Jackson as well as those who had worked for Adams. Old Hickory took a turn of the room, puffing his pipe. "Mr. McLean, will you accept a seat on the bench of the Supreme Court?"[30] McLean was willing, and after four days as a Jackson minister he gave way to William T. Barry of Kentucky.

As nothing in Mr. Barry's brief catalog of distinctions suggested the McLean type of backbone, the reformers lifted high their hickory brooms—for the doctrinaires of the "clean sweep" had their visible symbol. Yet, bold as had been the propaganda and terrific the pressure, Jackson moved slowly. The first seventy-six names, including Cabinet nominations, sent to the Senate for confirmation were to supply existing vacancies. On March 17, however, the Senate adjourned, not to reconvene until December. Immediately the President announced a batch of "recess" appointments. All the "counsellors" received handsome rewards—and so the Kitchen Cabinet was born. The impatient champions of rotation had their taste of blood and, though only a taste, they made the most of it. *"The Barnacles Shall Be Scraped Clean from the Ship of State,"* shouted Isaac Hill's newspaper. Every "traitor" (*i. e.,* Adams man) must go.

Fear smote the hearts of thousands of placemen as the tranquil world in which they had their being was threatened with a Judgment Day. Though the heat of the late campaign had moved many of his kind to political activity, the average Federal appointee was not a party worker. Accepting changes of Administration as matters of course, he served each with equal fidelity, to which sometimes was added a touch of condescension. Removed from competitive employments, he was apt to be soft and leisurely. Mingling with the distinguished, he was apt to feel himself above the mass. Assured of an easy income, he was apt to be improvident. The civil servant's Elysium was not a difficult place in which to sow panic. Sensational journalism on both sides fanned the flames. Day after day Administration organs encouraged their followers with exaggerated accounts of the extent of the "purge." Crying "proscription," opposition sheets accepted their adversaries' fancy figures and presented exceptional cases—a lighthouse keeper's family penniless, a War Department clerk driven to suicide—as typical of "the terror."

David Campbell, one day to become an anti-Jackson Governor of Virginia, viewed things more sanely. Though his brother had obtained the important post of Treasurer of the United States, Mr. Campbell was no spoilsman.

"On Monday last," he wrote his wife, "John entered upon the duties of his office. The opposition prints . . . stated that Gen'l Clarks first notice of his removal was Johns walking into the Treasury office with his commission in his pocket. So far from this being the case Gen'l Clark some days before he went out of office called on John & myself and invited John to the office & sat nearly all day shewing John how the business was done. On Tuesday when he was about to leave the City he called . . . [and] wished . . . [John] good success. . . . I mention these circumstances to shew you how little credit ought to be given to the statements in the *National Intelligencer*. . . .

"The President has removed several . . . who have held their places for a long period and have been considered, perhaps more from that circumstance than any other, very faithful officers. But as it respects most of them it is not so. Old Mr. Nourse the Register of the Treasury had been in the employ of the government from the revolution. . . . Yet this old man is now a defaulter for about ten thousand dollars. . . . The conversation between him and the President was very interesting. . . . [Admitting] he was a defaulter . . . [Nourse] urged that he be retained. . . . The President endeavored to induce him to resign but he would not." Whereupon Jackson dismissed him saying, "'I would turn out my own father under the same circumstances.' The truth is that a considerable number of the officers who have been long in office are old men and drunkards. Harrison the first auditor . . . I have not yet seen sober."[31]

To regulate the business of reform, General Jackson wrote with his own hand an "Outline of Principles." "Every Head of Depar^t

[will conduct] a strict examination into the state of his Dep^t and report to the President . . . what . . . retrenchments can be made, . . . what offices dispensed with, and what improvements made in the economy and dispatch of public business." Moreover, chiefs would consider the "moral habits" of their subordinates, dismissing those found lax in "private or public relations." These clauses—no honest interpretation of which would impair the public service— were not the whole of the President's decree, however. "It becomes his duty to dismiss all officers who were appointed against the manifest will of the people or whose official station, by a subserviency to selfish electioneering purposes, was made to operate against the freedom of elections."[32] How the eyes of the hickory broom-bearers must have sparkled over that.

To the moral aspects of the situation the President gave his first attention. The dusty recesses of Government bureaus were aired as they had not been since Jefferson's day, bringing to light some curious circumstances. Amos Kendall, the Kentucky editor, taking the post of Fourth Auditor of the Treasury, found himself blessed with subscriptions to twenty-odd newspapers for which his predecessor had paid from the public funds. He discontinued them, as well as the favor of forwarding the letters of friends under his frank—a form of politeness long sanctioned by usage and almost universal in official circles, though against the law. But when Kendall declined to frank his wife's letters, fellow Jacksonians felt that to be holding the torch of reform too high. Then there was a matter of strange-looking charges for cord-wood for Marine officers, and for subsistence on shore for midshipmen, as well as disbursements for the hire of extra clerks who seemed to have had no corporeal existence. Digging deeper, Kendall and colleagues brought forth other interesting particulars. A large number of civil servants were habitually delinquent in their private obligations, some having taken the bankrupt's oath twelve times within a few months. Eighty-seven had jail records. In one Department, the Treasury, at least ten employees besides Mr. Nourse were short in their accounts with the Government.[33]

A defaulter in the amount of seven thousand dollars was found to be Tobias Watkins, Kendall's predecessor as Fourth Auditor. Watkins was a personal friend of Adams and Clay. During the campaign his political activity had given the Jackson managers considerable trouble. This ideal victim behaved admirably for the purposes of the stable cleansers. He fled, was caught, convicted, and sentenced, while the Jackson press and privately, Jackson himself, glowed with a consciousness of worthy accomplishment.[34]

While this *cause célèbre* did something to disarm criticism of the reform policy, the reform leaders were far from pleased. For all their talk and spilling of printer's ink, few heads had fallen. Even Barry, the mild-mannered, courteous new Postmaster General, in whom the clean sweepers had reposed implicit confidence, was writing "No cause for removal" opposite name after name on the lists the proscriptionists laid before him. Blunt, red-faced Duff Green, who even in repose wore the look of a man sitting for a portrait, called to see what was the matter. Failing to obtain the dismissal of the postmaster of Washington, Green stormed from Mr. Barry's office. *"I will pursue my course & leave you to yours,"* a trembling subordinate heard the editor roar as he strode from the building and directed his steps toward the White House.[35]

6

Martin Van Buren deplored this state of affairs. Schooled from young manhood in the ways of New York where politicians maintained an interesting form of communal life, the object of which was survival by rewarding the faithful, the Secretary of State regarded all this clatter attending Federal removals as the clumsy work of amateurs. In New York thrice as many public servants as Jackson had sent on their way might vanish into the void without awakening so much as an echo. Moreover, small as the number of Federal replacements had been, too many offices had fallen to friends of John C. Calhoun. That was Duff Green's doing. Mr. Van Buren addressed himself to the task of reforming the reformation.

A few days after their first conversation, the President received from his Secretary of State a communication on the subject of patronage. It was brief, merely asking "liberal and respectful consideration" of a letter from Thomas Ritchie, the Richmond editor, who saw the "bright prospect" of Jackson's Administration "somewhat clouded over within the short space of thirty days." "The Cabinet," continued Ritchie, "has disappointed many of the sincerest of the

President's friends." But the greatest danger arose from the nature of removals and of appointments. In the latter category were too many "personal friends," too many editors and congressmen—precisely the type of appointments for which Jackson had denounced Adams. "The enemies of the Administration are . . . availing themselves of all our errors."[36]

In a spirited rejoinder Old Hickory assured Mr. Van Buren that Ritchie was altogether wrong and the Administration altogether right. "The people expect reform—they shall not be disappointed; but it must be *Judiciously* done, and upon *principle*."[37] Noting the qualifying clause, the Secretary failed to press his point. Having declined a Supreme bench seat from Monroe, Mr. Van Buren did not wish one now.

Yet it well may be that Ritchie's letter, and others in similar vein, were not without effect on Jackson. In any event, the President's attitude continued to disappoint the spoilsmen. Anxious underofficials began to look hopefully to the Secretary of State to produce a split in the Administration ranks. "Parties have avowed [themselves]," one wrote. "Van B. refuses to assent to proscription. . . . Green greatly dissatisfied. . . . Messrs Eaton, Ingham, Hill [checked in their designs]."[38] Amos Kendall, ablest and, after Andrew Jackson Donelson, the least predatory of the Kitchen Cabinet, came to perceive a difference between the theory and the practice of rotation. "I turned out six clerks on Saturday, . . . the most painful thing I ever did."[39] To one the Fourth Auditor gave fifty dollars and started a fund to move his family back to Ohio. Dismay began to penetrate the ranks of job-seekers, watching their tavern bills climb.

Jackson himself showed growing impatience over their incessant importunities for "a tit . . . to suck the Treasury pap."[40] In all likelihood, more instances of distress could have been found among applicants who had blown themselves to bootless trips to the capital than among displaced appointees. "would you believe it," the President wrote a Tennessee neighbor, "that a lady who had once rolled in wealth, . . . and is an applicant for office, and well recommended, . . . with tears in her eyes . . . [assured] me that her children were starving, and to buy a morsel of bread she had to sell her thimble the day before. an office I had not to give, and my cash was nearly out, but I could not withhold from her half the pittance I had with me." These episodes were wearing. "Late in the night I retire to my chamber . . . deprived of all hope of happiness this side of the grave and often wish myself at the Hermitage there to spend the remnant of my days & drop a daily tear on the tomb of my beloved wife."[41]

After a White House reception an elderly man asked for a personal word with the Executive. He was the postmaster at Albany, New York. "The politicians want to take my office from me and I have nothing else to live on."

When Old Hickory did not reply, the caller began to peel off his coat. "I am going to show you my wounds." The postmaster had fought under George Washington.

"Put on your coat at once, sir!" exclaimed Jackson.

The next day Congressman Silas Wright presented a list of officials recommended for dismissal. The venerable postmaster was on it. Wright began to argue that he had supported John Quincy Adams. Old Hickory leaped to his feet and, in his excitement, threw his pipe in the fire. "By the Eternal! I will not remove the old man. Do you know that he carries a pound of British lead in his body?"[42]

A young man named David Buell bore an introduction from Van Buren's old New York associate, William L. Marcy, who illuminated contemporary history with the phrase, "To the victors belong the spoils." Considering this sponsorship, Buell's was a curious mission.

"Mr. President——"

Jackson interrupted to inquire if Marcy were correct in introducing his friend as an ex-soldier.

"Yes, sir."

"Then call me 'General.'"

The visitor spoke in behalf of another veteran, who had left a leg on a battlefield and needed to retain a small postmastership to support his large family. "But I must tell you that he voted against you."

"If he lost a leg fighting for his country," said Jackson, "that is vote enough for me."[43]

A Clergyman was an insistent applicant for a place.

"Are you not a Christian minister?" inquired the President.

"I am."

"Well, if you discharge the duties of that office, which is better than any I can confer, you will have no time for any other."[44]

After things had simmered for awhile Martin Van Buren himself brought up the office of collector of customs at New York. Samuel Swartwout was in town pulling wires. So unfavorably did the claims of this candidate impress the Secretary of State, that he refused to treat with him even by correspondence. But the letter he wrote to the President recommending another was a model of good temper. Nevertheless, Swartwout became collector, taking the most remunerative office in the gift of the Administration—that is to say, the office Mr. Swartwout was able to make the most remunerative. So agreeably did Van Buren accept the reverse that Jackson gave him the unexpected privilege of naming the district attorney for Nashville—an unequal exchange, but a significant gesture.[45] After weeks of close quarters with Eatons and Lewises and Greens, the President had begun to sense the contrasting mental stature of his Secretary of State.

Smoothly Van Buren moved on to another topic, which he prefaced with a series of confidential and intelligent talks on American problems before the foreign courts. These discourses included some incidental allusion to the qualifications desirable in the ministers who must act as the Secretary's agents in the business under review. Impulsively Jackson apologized for having named the envoys to England and France without consulting Van Buren. This was all the Secretary needed to know. Off went letters to Littleton W. Tazewell and to Edward Livingston, directing attention to the formidable state of affairs at their respective stations, and politely asking them to depart with the least delay. The effect was so discouraging to the diplomatic ambitions of these gentlemen that each relinquished his appointment. Whereupon, at Mr. Van Buren's suggestion, the President sent William C. Rives to Paris and Louis McLane to London,[46] thus obtaining two able foreign representatives and binding to the Administration a corps of valuable friends who were on the verge of estrangement. Thereafter, the quiet word of Martin Van Buren was supreme in his own department.

As the season advanced, the President sought occasional relaxation on horseback. Yielding to an urge dormant for years, Mr. Van Buren abandoned his carriage for a saddle. Sometimes the two rode together. Perhaps rather than advert to his companion's horsemanship, the courteous old gentleman jockey drifted into the habit of discussing with the New Yorker things that pertained to the domains of the other Cabinet officers.

7

The glories of the springtime on the Potomac brought scant satisfaction to the army of occupation. Less blatant, less convincing, was the rodomontade about a clean sweep. To be sure, the turnover in offices continued, but quietly—perhaps one might say *"Judiciously"* and "upon *principle*." In any case, machinations of the unblushing pack that swarms about thrones to live by bending great men to small uses were less easily discernible than before. A man at home seemed to stand as much chance of finding himself the happy possessor of a warrant as postmaster or deputy marshal or Indian agent, as a competitor resting his uneasy head on an expensive Capitol Hill boarding-house pillow. Private exchequers ran low, and the word was out that Jackson required strict explanations of those behind in their bills. Washington heard of the boarding-house mistress who had gone to the President with an unpaid account. Jackson bade her return with the delinquent's note for the amount due. Old Hickory wrote his name on the back as endorser. "I think he will pay it now."[47]

The host which had dominated the inaugural was disintegrating, its remnants inspiring sly ridicule where once they had inspired awe. To a bartender at Gadsby's was attributed an anecdote which genially grew with the years. It seems that an important-looking party worker, honoring the President with a call of congratulation, expanded on the warm nature of the contest in his district. "What I did, I did for my country—and I thought, sir, that I might be of further use to you in some official capacity." The Cabinet being filled, perhaps a post abroad would suit his particular gifts. Jackson replied that no diplomatic vacancies existed. A chief clerkship, then? Those places were filled by the respective heads of departments, the President said. Postmastership of Washington? Filled. A clerk's berth in that post office? It would be necessary to speak to the postmaster about that. "Well, then, General, haven't you an old black coat?"[48]

Mr. Van Buren had been right again. The cost of the siege was disproportionate to the gains. The army dwindled, dissolved. As crestfallen crusaders for preferment picked their ways homeward, richer only in experience, General Jackson, for the one time in his life, looked with complacency on the retreat of a force that had advanced under his banners. "Not one in five hundred," he remarked with some exaggeration, "had obtained office."[49] Angry subalterns among the spoilsmen sought to check the rout with subterranean threats of rebellion. "If the president pursues this course the party is Ruined and the sooner We begin to build up a new one the better."[50] The threats achieved nothing, the murmurs which arose with the dust of the retiring platoons moving not at all the man who had dealt with disaffection under sterner circumstances than this. "If I had a *tit* for every one of these *pigs* to suck at they would still be my friends."[51]

This observation was to John C. McLemore of Tennessee, who had brightened an hour in the busy life of the Executive with proof of exalted friendship. McLemore was married to one of Aunt Rachel's innumerable nieces. Plunged into debt by the failure of a man whose notes he had endorsed, he was striving desperately to save his plantation from seizure when Jack Donelson prevailed on Secretary of the Navy Branch to offer him the lucrative post of naval agent at Gibraltar. Though acceptance might mean the difference between solvency and ruin, McLemore had replied: "I cannot place myself in any situation likely to do Genl Jackson an injury. . . . It would at once be said that the Genl was bringing into Office his relations when others could be found better qualified."[52]

With the patronage situation leveling off, General Jackson heard his premier speak again of overseas affairs. Mr. Van Buren was considering a problem which had been on his mind since that talk with Livingston in Philadelphia. Few persons in the capital had been more apprehensive of the coming of the frontier President than the corps of foreign representatives. His actual arrival had not tended to subdue their alarms. In Europe and in Latin-America the appearance at a seat of government of a victorious soldier and his hardy partizans entailed consequences too often predictable.

THE HAGGARD HERO

Would it not be an excellent thing (Mr. Van Buren was saying) for the President to establish a personal acquaintance with the foreign representatives residing in Washington? Jackson, who liked nothing better than to form his opinions of men face to face, fell in with the idea. The Secretary suggested a private reception to the diplomatic corps at which the President, while "avoiding anything like a set speech," might diffuse certain sentiments useful to our concerns abroad. These sentiments Mr. Van Buren experimentally tabulated, with credit to Jackson's inaugural address. From this circumstance a careless observer might be led to doubt the diligence of the Secretary's scrutiny of that paper. The suggestions went farther than the address.

Many persons, some of them skeptical, have left their impressions of a first meeting with Andrew Jackson as President of the United States. In no instance which this writer recalls was the effect unfavorable to him. Instinctively one felt the presence of a superior being—a chieftain and a gentleman. Such was the impression of the ministers. The remarks suggested by the Secretary of State were spoken in a "happy and expressive manner." Guests began to request manuscript copies to forward to their governments. A dinner was served at which the "old-school manners of the host," and the "exceptional quality" of meat and drink completed the conquest[53] —justifying the "judicious" removal policy in one particular: General Jackson had retained Vivart, Mr. Adams's French cook.

The clouds at which Editor Ritchie had shaken his head seemed to be clearing from the skies over Washington.

CHAPTER XXIX

EMERGENCE OF A QUIET STATESMAN

I

ORIGINATING with the "light airs" which, on April 2, 1828, had coursed the remote Mediterranean, another spell of squally weather was on its way to the Potomac. On that day and on that sea John B. Timberlake departed this life aboard the frigate *Constitution,* thus relinquishing the employment Senator Eaton had obtained for him by posting a bond in the sum of ten thousand dollars to insure an improvement in the purser's accounting. The ship's record gave the cause of death as "pulmonary disease," the ship's gossip as drink. Presently the tale was abroad in Washington that the naval officer had cut his throat because he believed his wife to be living in sin with John Henry Eaton.[1] Timberlake dead proved even more of a problem than Timberlake living. On the rising of Congress the Senator returned to Tennessee, by his own admission, "anxious and distressed" in mind.

The election over, he laid the case before Jackson. "The hand of Providence . . . [has put it] in my power to snatch . . . [Mrs. Timberlake] from the injustice done . . . by a gossiping world. . . . All considerations of honor and of justice point to the course for me to pursue. . . . Under such circumstances it is not possible to hesitate [over] what is right and proper." Yet, if not hesitating, the Senator was able to refrain from unseemly precipitation. "At a *proper time*"—the words appeared to come with effort—"I will tender her the offer to share my life and prospects."[2]

"Major," Jackson replied, "if you love Margaret Timberlake go and marry her at once and shut their mouths."[3]

The Major had spoken of honor and justice, not love.

On his return to Washington the "proper time" was vaguely allocated to the future, "after the adjournment." Then Andrew Jackson would be President, and Eaton too, so he hoped, in a higher sphere of public usefulness. But before this cautious arrangement could be reported to Jackson, the Senator received, by private messenger, a pointed communication from the Hermitage. There should be no delay, Old Hickory said. Eaton should marry Peg "forthwith" or leave the O'Neale boarding house.[4]

In a long and labored letter Senator Eaton returned "sincere thanks ... for the kind suggestions made in reference to ... [this] delicate subject. Your admonition shall be regarded.... In the first week of January (the 6th) an honorable discharge of duty to myself and to her will be met and ... I rendered a happy and contented man. Judge! General, you who have known me long and well, if I could do such an act as this apart from the belief that she has a soul above everything of crime and design.... If I could entertain any wish more ardent than another it would be that you might honor us with your presence at the time, but the considerations you suggest are of a character so important as to induce us to forego this pleasure and close the business earlier than you can be here."[5]

Congressman Cambreleng apprized Martin Van Buren of the spirit in which Washington received the news of the betrothal. "Poor Eaton is to be married tonight to Mrs. T——! There is a vulgar saying of some vulgar man, I believe Swift, on such unions—about using a certain household —[sic] and then putting it on one's head."[6]

Five days sooner than Eaton had promised, that is to say on January 1, 1829, the vows were exchanged in the presence of the chaplain of the Senate. This could not have displeased the old chieftain, who laid so much store on the virtue of punctuality in the performance of his "admonitions." Yet the wedding failed to realize either the hopeful prediction of the troubled bridegroom or the emphatic one of its distinguished sponsor. "The General's friends are much disturbed. His enemies laugh and divert themselves." Ignorant of Jackson's compelling rôle, Margaret Bayard Smith overcredited the hand of the bride in the matter. "She is irresistible and carries whatever point she sets her mind on."[7]

2

Washington society said, "We shall see about that." The *haut monde,* from which Margaret Timberlake had been dropped by Mrs. Monroe, raised its barriers against Margaret Eaton. The ladies declined to call on her. Very well, Margaret would call on them—and, perhaps, as the fourth of March drew nigh, women with the welfare of their husbands at heart might read in the political skies portents that would suggest a reciprocation of those civilities. A card was left at the residence of Mrs. Daniel T. Patterson, wife of the Master Commandant of the Navy and as precise in her social relations as her spouse had been in the aim of his cannon at New Orleans. Mrs. Patterson did not return the call. One day, when Senator and Mrs. Eaton casually encountered the Commandant, Margaret remarked that she had called on Mrs. Patterson. Had Mrs. Patterson noticed the card? The surprised sea hero bowed. He presumed that the card had been received. "I had supposed," said Margaret, "that as she has not returned my visit, the card had not been received. Will you please tell her that I left it for her?" The Commandant bowed again and resumed his promenade.

"This anecdote," related David Campbell, "is perfectly characteristic of the lady."

Mr. Campbell's letters to his wife form an almost continuous narrative of the passing show in Washington. The Virginian had come to town prepared to judge Mrs. Eaton sympathetically. "I am under the impression that the stories I hear are not true." Campbell made his call. The bride of General Jackson's friend was twenty-nine years old. Her small, active form, well-rounded and voluptuous, trailed an odor of toilet water, which men were more apt to admire than women. Her apple complexion was still perfect; her large dark eyes, never still, could communicate much. Full lips were ready to part in a smile and, then with a tom-boyish toss of her head, the generous mouth would yield to immoderate laughter exhibiting the prettiest teeth in Washington. Deportment brought out the imperfections in the portrait. "She rose and saluted me very handsomely," Mr. Campbell continued, "and seemed to be very much at her ease." Eaton, on the contrary, appeared uncomfortable, although his wife went "out of the road to make us believe she was extremely fond of her husband. . . . Entering into conversation she talked *away* about anything and every thing—jumbling great and small subjects together. . . . She loves admiration and bedaubs every one almost with flattery who notices her. The gentlemen who call on Eaton

EMERGENCE OF A QUIET STATESMAN 511

[for political purposes], knowing this, pay her considerable attentions."

The polite Virginian's visit brought an invitation to dinner, after which Mr. Campbell made a prophecy. "Eaton can never get along [in public life] with such a woman."⁸

The fourth of March drew nigh with Old Hickory at the Wigwam and the town aswarm. The Eatons had taken a large house across the street from the British Legation. Their wines and food were good. They were blessed with numerous visitors from out of town. Cabinet-making time came on and the reluctance which Jackson saw in Eaton's attitude toward a portfolio was discernible to few others who were in the know. Margaret watched every move. When old and tried friends of the General suggested that the Senator be shifted to a foreign capital, Peggy put her foot down. She told her husband she would remain in Washington "in the presence of my enemies," and conquer there.⁹ More cards fluttered into her basket. The patrician Branch, his eye on the Navy Department, the fastidious Berrien, candidate of the Calhoun wing for Attorney General, were all smiles. When Jackson put it to him cold turkey "M^r. B[ranch] . . . disavowed any knowledge of any thing disreputable to M^{rs}. Eaton, or any belief of the rumors about her." Delighted with the behavior of his newly-found friends, Eaton went to Jackson with encomiums which Old Hickory later called the deciding factor in the appointments of Branch and of Berrien to the Cabinet.¹⁰

After these successes the snubbing that Margaret received at the inaugural ceremonies came as a shock. And this was not the end. The Cabinet sworn in, neither Mrs. Branch nor Mrs. Ingham nor the daughters of Mr. Berrien, who was a widower, visited the home of the recently popular Eaton. Mr. Calhoun left his own card but not that of his wife. Emily Donelson wrote to her sister, Mrs. John Coffee: "[Mrs. Eaton] is held in too much abhorrence ever to be noticed. The ladies here have determined not to visit her. To please Uncle we returned her first call. She talked of her intimacy with our family . . . [which] so disgusted . . . [me] that I shall not visit her again. I fear this is to be a source of great mortification to our dear old Uncle, . . . [but] if Major Eaton had felt any disinterested friendship he would have never accepted the [Cabinet] appointment."[11]

Emily had been listening to Mesdames Branch and Ingham, and one or two other ladies who were prepared to dispute Peg's claim to irresistibility. On the evening of April 9 two messages for Mrs. Donelson were delivered at the Executive Residence. Though signed by Eaton they could hardly have been written without the help of Margaret. "You are young and uninformed of the ways . . . of the world and therefore I speak to you. . . . I have understood that a certain family have gratuitously stepped forward to become councellors, to tell you what to do and what not to do; and in secret to whisper slanders respecting . . . me and my wife. . . . You yourself may become a victim of those meddling gossips. Your excellent aunt. . . ."[12]

Visitors meeting for the first time the person to whom Major Eaton's communications were addressed, were wont to describe her as "amiable," though something in the set of a well-shaped mouth and the candid glance of her hazel eyes suggested a mind of her own. Emily Donelson was good-looking and, in the opinion of Martin Van Buren, "unaffected and graceful" in demeanor. Her figure was slight and youthful, her countenance alert and of aristocratic cast, her most arresting feature a wealth of fine auburn hair. As Eaton said, Emily was young. Married at seventeen, she was now under twenty-one. Absent from her native West for the second time in her life, she had, indeed, much to learn, and the situation in which she found herself would have tried a more experienced woman. Yet, accustomed to the responsibilities of a large plantation homestead, she had energetically laid hold of the management of the Executive Residence with its eighteen servants, finding time to continue the lessons of her three-year-old son, Andrew Jackson, as well. A second baby was expected at the end of the summer.

The other feminine member of the President's household was Mary Eastin, a young cousin of Mrs. Donelson and a great pet of the General. This Cumberland Cinderella liked her new life. "I have a room fit for a Princess, with silk curtains, mahogany furniture, a carpet such as you Tennesseans have in your parlour, and a piano." She had a beau for every day in the week and Emily predicted a White House wedding before long. The attentions of Abra-

> Nov.
> *The* PRESIDENT,
> Requests the honor of
> Mr. Kendall's
> Company at dinner
> Monday the 18th inst at 4 o'clock
>
> The favor of an Answer is desired

SOUVENIR OF AN UNPLEASANT EVENING FOR MRS. EATON

Amos Kendall's card of invitation to the President's dinner to the Cabinet, at which the wife of the Secretary of War was snubbed by the ladies of the President's household. From the original, owned by Mrs. Arthur Chester of Rye, New York, a granddaughter of Mr. Kendall.

ANDREW JACKSON, JUNIOR

Nephew of Rachel Jackson, born December 22, 1809, and four days later legally adopted by General and Mrs. Jackson. From a portrait by Earl, owned by the Ladies' Hermitage Association, Nashville.

EMERGENCE OF A QUIET STATESMAN 513

ham Van Buren, a son of the Secretary of State, were such as to further this speculation. And the Secretary himself had been in town scarcely a week when this perspicacious young thing confided, "He has fine manners, . . . and bids fair to be our President one of these days."[13]

If Emily Donelson seemed qualified to discharge her duties with a fair amount of credit, General Jackson was even better served in the important matter of a private secretary. Jack Donelson had grown with the responsibilities of recent years. It is probable that no more intelligent or more useful man, excepting Van Buren, now stood closer to the President; and surely none was so selfless or so inconspicuous in his devotion. The once-modest Lewis, who also lived at the White House, had responded differently to developments. He seemed to swell rather than to grow. His jealousy of his prerogatives as the General's man Friday became noticeable to others.[14] This began to annoy Donelson. The fact that Lewis was a constant visitor at the Eatons, and an advocate of Margaret's cause with the President, failed to diminish the breach. Lewis and Eaton were brothers-in-law by Eaton's first marriage, but, this notwithstanding, Donelson remembered the time when the Major had induced Branch to remove his daughter from the O'Neale boarding house on the ground that her associates should be above suspicion.[15]

Eaton's unusual letters did not set well with Donelson and his wife. Particularly were they unable to appreciate the propriety of the Secretary of War's intimation that the mistress of the White House had placed herself under the guardianship of slanderers, or that an analogy existed between the history of Margaret Eaton and of the departed Aunt Rachel.[16] The missive, bearing Mrs. Donelson's name, which Secretary Eaton received in return for his pains was one that Talleyrand need not have disclaimed. Emily's husband was doubtless the actual co-author, however.

"It was with some surprise that I recd. your letters . . . and was not much relieved by a perusal of their contents. With regard to those who are understood to have 'stepped forward to be my councellors and advisors and to direct me what to do and what not to do' I must say I am totally unacquainted with such. . . .

"Having drawn my attention to slanders got up for political purposes to tarnish the reputation of my lamented Aunt you will suffer me to say that the most conclusive proof of her innocence was the respect in which she was universally held by her neighbours. . . . As to the probability of my becoming a victim to the slanders of this or any other place I feel it due to myself to say that altho I am conscious of possessing many faults . . . I hope I shall maintain my reputation as it has heretofore been, . . not only pure but unsuspected. . . .

"As you say I am young and unacquainted with the world, and therefore I will trouble myself as little as possible with things that do not concern me. . . . I do not wish to decide upon any persons character nor controul in any way the etiquette of this place; and that so far from arrogating to myself any honour or privilege from the circumstance of my being in the Gen[ls] family I shall act as if I was not a member of it nor expect to be considered in any light than the proper one as a private person. . . .

"very Respect.

"EMILY DONELSON."[17]

For the General's sake Donelson himself made a show of seeking to soften his wife's letter a little, writing one over his own signature in which, with more tact than truth, he assured Eaton that Emily placed no credence in the gossip she had heard.[18]

Then the President and his nephew, but not Emily, honored Mrs. Eaton with a call.

"The cloud is blowing over," the General wrote to one of Emily's connections in Tennessee. "Satelites of Clay are falling in the pitts [they] dug for Eaton."[19]

These amicable gestures fell short of what Margaret desired, however, and boldly she prepared to play for higher stakes. If Emily Donelson would not meet her, was it beyond the pale of possibility that a more amenable First Lady might find herself in the White House? William B. Lewis was Margaret's ally—and Lewis had a daughter, conveniently near, in Philadelphia. The Major had come to Washington with the expectation of remaining only long enough to see the General comfortably settled. Margaret, for one, and Jackson for another, begged him to prolong his stay—a suggestion that could not have been repugnant to the Major's own ideas of his enlarging importance. Mrs. Eaton was credited with helping to pull the strings whereby the Second Auditor of the Treasury was sacked and Lewis given the post.[20] Margaret also sought to bring Amos

Kendall within the sphere of her influence, and succeeded to the point of establishing social relations with his family. The account of a politically influential stage-coach firm, which had a contract for carrying mail, came to the desk of Mr. Kendall. He thought the account padded. According to a tale later related by Kendall's son-in-law, Mrs. Eaton informed Mrs. Kendall that a new carriage should be hers in event her husband passed the account. But this proved too much to ask of the officer who had declined to frank his wife's correspondence.[21]

Meanwhile Mrs. Eaton and Mrs. Donelson had met face to face for the first time since the notable exchange of letters. The occasion was a presidential excursion by water to Norfolk. Margaret offered Emily the use of her cologne bottle, which Mrs. Donelson refused in such a manner as to "shew a disposition not to be intimate with her." A little later Donelson noticed Mrs. Eaton's emotional confusion. Unaware of the cause, he proffered his arm. Whereupon Margaret poured forth an indignant account of the cologne bottle incident, adding that if Mrs. Donelson chose to persist in such behavior she might as well prepare to return to Tennessee. The President, she said, had given his word to pack Emily off unless she made amends.[22]

Thus the declaration of war. David Campbell gave his wife a candid impression of the contenders. Mrs. Donelson was "a very amiable little woman," though untrained "for court life." "Her ladyship [Mrs. Eaton] is *decidedly* the greatest fool I ever saw in a genteel situation."[23]

3

Emily neither made amends nor departed for Tennessee. The approaching accouchement excused her from formal society in which the Cabinet women avoided Mrs. Eaton more pointedly than ever. Yet, in the face of this formidable array, Margaret scored a series of triumphs. Martin Van Buren called on her. And so for the first time a Cabinet officer's card fell in Mrs. Eaton's basket and for the first time a Cabinet officer graced her dinner table, though alack, no Cabinet officer's lady, the Secretary of State being—and how fortunately, the envious said—a widower without daughters.

The want was soon supplied. Postmaster General Barry and his wife arrived from Kentucky. The Eaton carriage bore them off to the Eaton house, and Peggy had her Cabinet lady.

To this add the open protagonism of the President of the United States, which was assuming the dimensions of an Administration policy. The Reverend Ezra Stiles Ely of Philadelphia, an old friend of Jackson who had previously spoken well of Eaton, wrote Old Hickory a letter saying, among many other things, that Mrs. Eaton had borne a bad reputation from girlhood; that before their marriage she and Eaton had traveled together; that a gentleman breakfasting at Gadsby's had remarked that "Mrs. Eaton brushed by him last night . . . having apparently forgotten the time when she slept with him."[24]

General Jackson responded in a communication longer than his inaugural address. "The high standing of Mr. Eaton as a man of moral worth and a Mason [Timberlake also was a Mason] gives the lie direct" to the charges involving his name. As to the accusations involving other men, Jackson said he would entertain no "rumors or suspicions." But if Ely had "facts and proofs sustained by reputable witnesses in the light of day" let him bring them forth —a large order for Doctor Ely, or for anyone, to fill.[25]

The clergyman retreated before the slashing counter-attack, merely expressing the hope that Margaret's repentance would justify the President's faith in her. *"Repentance,"* Jackson shot back, "presupposes the existence of *crime.* . . . Where is the witness who has thus far come forth in substantiation of these slanderous charges?"[26] Doctor Ely could produce no witness. However, a gray-haired gallant in the person of Colonel Nathan Towson, the Paymaster General of the Army, came forward unasked. Jackson blasted him off his feet. "How fallen the military character whose boast is that they are the protectors of Female character."[27] Young R. K. Call came forward. Jackson taunted the former Congressman upon the admitted ill-success of his own effort at seduction. "My Dear Call *you* have a right to believe that Mrs. T. was *not* a woman of easy virtue."[28] The Reverend Mr. Ely returned to the lists, repeating to Jackson a story to the effect that Mrs. Timberlake had had a miscarriage at a time when her husband's absence at sea precluded him from responsibility in the matter.[29]

EMERGENCE OF A QUIET STATESMAN 517

Major Lewis was collecting contrary evidence in the form of testimonials as to the spotless nature of Margaret's reputation. In a city filled with politicians aspiring to office and office-holders aspiring to keep their places, the inescapable inference that to be on Mrs. Eaton's side was to be on Jackson's side did not obstruct the performance of the task. Statements to the effect that her character was as white as snow poured upon the President. This scramble for evidence, pro and con, made boudoir tales a topic of the day. True to prediction, no woman's reputation seemed safe. Duff Green heard a young buck holding forth at Gadsby's bar on the feasibility of carrying his campaign of conquest across the threshold of the White House where, he declared, "the female part of the family . . . were of easy virtue."[30] There is no proof that Green passed this particular morsel on to the male contingent in the Executive Mansion, and a world of presumption that he did not.

Mr. Van Buren increased the emphasis on his friendly attention to the Eatons. He intervened in their behalf with Mrs. Donelson and with Mary Eastin, but to no avail. On the other hand, John C. Calhoun and his followers remained conspicuously un-cooperative with Old Hickory's effort to induce society to accept the marriage he had pushed his friend into. Some of Van Buren's admirers thought this the wiser course. "God knows," insisted one, "we did not make him [Jackson] president to work the miracle of Making M^{rs} E—— an honest woman."[31] The Secretary of State declined to be diverted, however. Mr. Calhoun and his friends rejoiced. In their belief the position of Eaton and his empress of confusion was untenable. Were they to carry Martin Van Buren with them into obscurity that would be the simplest imaginable solution of the problem of the presidential succession.

In August, 1829, the President sailed down the Potomac for a short vacation on the Rip Raps, a breeze-swept islet in Hampton Roads, off Norfolk, returning September 1 somewhat invigorated by the rest and the sea bathing. That evening the Reverend John N. Campbell, pastor of the Presbyterian Church which Jackson attended in Washington, asked to speak to the President privately. They mounted to the study where Mr. Campbell revealed himself as the source of Doctor Ely's account of the alleged miscarriage. Campbell said he had the story from a physician named Craven, then dead, who had had professional knowledge of the case. He fixed the date as in 1821.

Thirty-six hours later, in the presence of Jack Donelson and Colonel Towson, General Jackson confronted the clergyman with documentary proof that Timberlake had been in Washington in 1821. Whereupon Mr. Campbell changed the date to 1822 when, it appears, Timberlake was at sea. Jackson read his pastor an explosive lecture on Christian charity. There was more to the interview, however. Campbell told of a call that he and Colonel Towson had made only a few hours before on Mrs. Craven, the physician's widow. This lady had described a previous visit to her residence by Major Eaton and his wife who, she said, had endeavored to frighten her with allusions to duels and law-suits into denying any knowledge of the miscarriage story. The widow, in truth, knew nothing of the reported miscarriage, but she said she had unhesitatingly told the Eatons that Timberlake had made a sort of father confessor of the old doctor and had left him with "impressions not favourable to the character of Mrs. T."[32]

Each of Mr. Campbell's three auditors drew from the recital what it pleased him to hear. Without presuming to pass on the truth or falsity of specific charges, Towson recalled a prophecy of his that the appointment of Eaton to the Cabinet would prove "most unfortunate." Donelson stressed the visit to the doctor's widow. To these things Jackson refused to listen. Like a shaft of lightning he fixed on the clergyman's change of dates, and declared that Campbell had told a wholly incredible tale.[33] Applied strictly to the miscarriage story this was hardly an exaggeration.

Swiftly Jackson moved to expand this victory into an acquittal of Mrs. Eaton of all the charges and rumors that overhung her name. Members of the Cabinet were summoned to a meeting unique in the history of that body, the explicit purpose being to examine evidence bearing on the private lives of the Secretary of War and his wife. Campbell and Ely accepted invitations to attend. Every Cabinet officer was present excepting Eaton, in whose place Lewis sat. Calhoun and Donelson were also there.

Before these statesmen Jackson laid the voluminous testimony Lewis had gathered as to Mrs. Eaton's impeccable character. Then he called on Ely, who admitted he had nothing of a tangible nature to convict Major Eaton of misconduct.

"Nor Mrs. Eaton either," broke in the President.

"On that point," said the pastor, "I would rather not give an opinion."

"She is chaste as a virgin!" exclaimed the President.

The Reverend Mr. Campbell started to offer his testimony. When he digressed to explain a point, Jackson interrupted to say that the clergyman had been summoned to "*give* evidence, not discuss it." Campbell declined to accept the ruling. Gathering up his papers, he bowed and withdrew declaring himself prepared to prove his case in a court of law. Whereupon the President adjourned the meeting with the air of one who had given Margaret Eaton's vindication the finished aspect of a *fait accompli*.[34]

4

The day florid-faced Duff Green ended a patronage dispute with Postmaster General Barry by stamping out of his Office and making tracks toward the White House, he had carried his point. The postmaster of Washington was removed in favor of a partizan of John C. Calhoun. Such a thing was not to happen often again, however. The editor's great influence with the program of "reform" was on the wane. Not without result had Martin Van Buren purchased a saddle horse and adopted the President's form of recreation. Not without consequences had been the fact that the Postmaster General was the only fellow-Cabinet officer the Secretary of State found in Margaret Eaton's drawing room. Years before the New Yorker had urged that, "instead of spending our time on small matters," steps should be taken to utilize the vast Postoffice Department as material for a political machine.[35] Monroe had interfered that time. Now the situation was different.

When Mr. Van Buren arrived in Washington, he was understood to be a foe of removals. Office-holders had rejoiced and looked to him to halt the proscription. In helping to rid the city of the army of job-hunters, that silent statesman had performed a service much appreciated by the President; and he had eliminated from the political landscape the most open and inconvenient advertizement of the work that was going on. But this was accomplished without checking the progress of "reform," for "slowly but surely," as one apprehensive postal official pointed out, the removals continued.[36] Before long a light began to dawn upon Government employees who had welcomed the Secretary of State as their protector. "Van Buren not Calhoun I believe is the head of the proscription party."[37] It was true. "The Post offices are swept clean in Newyork and eastward." Barry had resisted the brusque demands of Duff Green, representing the ambitions of Mr. Calhoun, to succumb to the suave suggestions of the Secretary of State, representing the ambitions of himself. Though the remark about a clean sweep of eastern post-offices was much exaggerated, the ascendency which Martin Van Buren had attained by almost imperceptible degrees was presently so well established that Duff Green confessed the defeat of his pro-Calhoun candidates in distant Illinois.[38]

The actual number of removals was the subject of much speculation and wide differences of opinion, however. After Congress convened in December, 1829, precise figures became available on the appointments which the President was obliged to submit to the Senate for confirmation. These included the famous recess appointments. The lists contained three hundred and nineteen names, of which one hundred and twenty-one were to supply the places of officials who had been removed by Jackson. In sixty-two instances incumbents were reappointed.[39] Considering the hullabaloo of both the Jackson press and the opposition press, as well as the prevailing opinion of more than a century, the noteworthy thing is not that actual removals had been so numerous, but so few.

Some of the appointments were subjected to severe criticism in the Senate, ten being rejected. Henry Lee, who had received the consulship at Algiers, was turned down by unanimous vote—Benton, Livingston and Hugh Lawson White joining the opposition. The senators also rejected Isaac Hill, and lived to regret it. Born in squalor, kicked and cuffed as a printer's ragged and oft-hungry apprentice, this frail, embittered cripple early in life had launched upon a career of revenge, opposing nearly everything the New England Brahmins held sacred. He refused to accept defeat now. Jackson stood by him and within a year the little lame Marat with a zealot's gleaming eyes returned to Washington, a senator from New Hampshire and a peer

ANDREW JACKSON HUTCHINGS
Great-nephew of Rachel Jackson and ward of General Jackson, reared at the Hermitage. From a portrait by Earl, owned by Edward Asbury O'Neal III, of Florence, Alabama.

A Portrait by Thomas Sully

Owned by the United States, it hangs in the Capitol at Washington. Sully painted several portraits of Jackson, one of which is reproduced in the first volume of this biography with comment by the writer which a few artists have taken as a disparagement of Mr. Sully's talent. Aware that nothing I can say will, or should, diminish Sully's reputation as a painter, I remain of the opinion that his delicately relaxed lines do not shadow forth Andrew Jackson as he seems to me to be.

of those who had pronounced him unfit for a subordinate office in the Treasury. The vote on Amos Kendall was a tie, which the Vice President broke in favor of the Kentuckian. Of the ten men rejected, four were later confirmed on renomination so that finally Old Hickory's will was overridden only in six of three hundred and nineteen instances. These figures indicate the need for revision of a good deal that has been written about the extent of the Senate's disciplinary action against the spoils proclivities of General Jackson.[40]

Over the bulk of Federal offices, numbering in the neighborhood of eleven thousand lesser posts, the Senate had no authority. Through this vast domain the "terror" was supposed to stalk unrestrained. In April, 1830, Holmes of Maine attacked proscription on the Senate floor, declaring that one thousand nine hundred and eighty-one persons had been thrown out of office in twelve months. The percentage of removals in Washington during the first year seemed to confirm these figures. In the Navy Department two out of nine clerks had been dropped; in the War Department eight out of forty; in the Treasury twenty-six out of one hundred and forty-five; in the Post-office Department fifteen out of forty-three, and in the Department of State, where Van Buren controlled in person, eighteen out of twenty-six.[41] The total was sixty-nine removals out of two hundred and sixty-three opportunities, or a little better than one in four.

Something like definite measures to halt the President seemed in the making. It was said that Justice McLean spoke privately of the feasibility of impeaching the man who had lately elevated him to the Supreme bench.[42] Daniel Webster, revolving similar thoughts in his mind, went so far as to consult unofficially McLean's colleague, the learned Justice Kent, on the constitutionality of certain removals. To this remarkable inquiry Kent regretfully replied that Jackson had acted within his rights. "That the President grossly abuses the power of removal is manifest," the gloomy jurist continued, "but it is the Genius of Democracy to be the sport of faction. . . . All theories of Government that suppose the mass of people virtuous and able to act virtuously are purely Utopian."[43] Practical rather than Utopian motives directed much of the opposition to removals, however. One of the things that irked McLean was the disruption, attempted by Calhoun and achieved by Van Buren, of the nucleus of an organization the former Postmaster General had created in that department to feather his own political nest.⁴⁴ Webster also revealed something of the spirit that actuated the senators in the discharge of their duties. "Were it not for the outdoor popularity of the President . . . [we] would have negatived more than half of his nominations."⁴⁵ And in view of what was said then and has since been widely repeated touching Mr. Adams's freedom from partizanship, it is interesting to note that in the closing days of his Administration he sent seventy-eight nominations to the Senate.⁴⁶

Duff Green answered Senator Holmes and other critics, claiming only nine hundred and nineteen removals in eighteen months, or about one in eleven, taking the civil list all in all. These figures seem to be nearly correct.⁴⁷ Moreover, by the time Green's figures appeared Jackson had greatly tempered the execution of his "reform" policy. Thenceforth comparatively few removals were made and one heard no more about a clean sweep—a term so offensive to the ears of soft-footed Mr. Van Buren. According to the best estimate available, Jackson replaced, during the eight years of his presidency, about one government employee in six, leaving more than nine thousand out of eleven thousand undisturbed.⁴⁸ The proportion of Jefferson's removals was almost as large.⁴⁹

Some good flowed from all this shaking-up. Smuggling along the southern coasts was cut down and the customs revenues rose. A notorious ring of grafters in the Indian service was smashed. The internal administration of departments and bureaus was simplified and, in the main, improved, an exception being the Post Office until Kendall succeeded the incapable Barry. Many unworthy and unfit and some dishonest officials were replaced by better ones. But to enumerate these things—and the list could be extended—is to make out a better case for rotation than General Jackson deserves. The aggregate of the defalcations so showily exposed by him comprises less than a fourth part of the million and a quarter dollars Old Hickory's friend Samuel Swartwout stole as Collector of the Port of New York. Though the President exercised commendable restraint in acting upon applications from his late wife's almost countless western connections, no objection came from him when the father and a brother-in-law of Mrs. Eaton appeared on the War Department payroll. The grand object of curtailing political activity among employees and rendering the public service free of partizan obligation failed utterly. In this respect Jackson was to leave the service a great deal worse than he found it, about the only political activity in which it was unsafe for an officer of the Government to engage being activity against the interests of General Jackson. Though succeeding presidents were to go further and to do much more than Andrew Jackson toward turning the civil service into a political tool, the fact remains that he had opened the door.

5

Up to December, 1829, when his first message to Congress was due, the most conspicuous issues to engross the energies of General Jackson had been the private life of Margaret Eaton and rotation in office. Friends of the Administration were under the impression that the country would appreciate a sight of Old Hickory in action in other fields. The message, an able and vigorous document, presented several possibilities.

Item, Foreign Affairs: For twenty years France had dodged and delayed negotiations for a settlement of our claims for damages arising from the Napoleonic wars; British West Indian ports had been closed to our commerce since the foundation of the Republic; the Maine boundary was in dispute; the South and the West desired to annex Texas. In these matters Jackson adopted a firm tone proposing "to ask for nothing that is not clearly right and to submit to nothing that is wrong."

Item, the Tariff: South Carolina, in revolt against the Act of 1828, threatened openly to "nullify" the law and refuse to pay the duties. This Act, a piece of political jugglery designed to promote the Jackson campaign alike in pro- and anti-tariff territory, had been framed with the expectation that New England votes would defeat it. But it became a law and now Jackson faced the consequences. He proposed conciliation and compromise.

Item, Indian Removal: True to the spirit of the West, Jackson would push the red people further back, exchanging new promises for promises broken. Reversing the policy of Adams, he sided with Georgia in its violent measures to expel the peaceable Creeks and Cherokees from lands guaranteed to them by Federal treaty.

Item, the National Debt: It should be paid and Jackson meant to pay it, thereafter distributing surplus revenue among the states.

Item, Internal Improvements: Small consolation for western appropriation-grabbers here. Jackson was for "constitutional" improvements, but his remarks on the debt and the surplus indicated his real intentions as to the disposition of Federal funds.

Item, the Bank of the United States: Its charter would expire in 1836, when the stockholders would apply for a renewal. The President suggested that Congress "and the people"—mark the phrase—begin to consider whether another agency might not be devised to replace the bank since it had "failed in the great end of establishing a uniform and sound currency."[50]

So much for the message. Before its delivery the tariff had been by long odds the pressing thing. Nor did the President's balanced treatment of that topic placate South Carolina where influential men spoke more openly than ever in favor of declaring the Act of 1828 to be null and void and Charleston to be a free port. One as capable as Jackson of smelling a fight from afar could not have been unaware of the significance of this. With the issue of nullification and the shadow of disunion at his gate what, then, was the object of that surprising paragraph on the Bank of the United States, whose charter had six years and more to run? If he held to his announced determination of refusing a second term, Jackson would be out of office by that time. Nicholas Biddle, president of the bank, stared with amazement at his newspaper. In November Biddle had had a long, cordial conversation with Lewis and a pleasant chat with the President. Moreover, there was Jackson's record in the West as a sound money man when it required courage to be one. At this moment the President's personal account was with the bank's Washington branch. And even if these things were not true what, in the name of veracity, did Andrew Jackson mean when he said the bank had failed to provide the country with a stable currency?

Mr. Biddle received no satisfactory answer to the enigma which, for the time being, slid into eclipse behind a façade of more timely concerns. Jackson seemed content that this should be. He seemed content to let the tariff pot boil a little longer. He had, however, selected an issue and determined upon the tactics by which he intended to see it boldly through. By a surprise move he meant to strike down the growing demands upon the Treasury for funds to build roads, canals and other internal improvements purely local in their benefits.

The plan originated in a series of talks casually begun by Martin Van Buren some months before. Throughout his public career, the Secretary of State had been an undeviating opponent of internal improvements as a Federal policy. This had set him apart from Clay, from Adams and—what was at this time of more importance—from John C. Calhoun. It had also set him apart from Jackson during the winter of 1823-24 when the General was in the Senate. Fresh from his frontier campaigns, Jackson had been dragged back into public life impressed with the military virtues of roads. On that ground he had voted for a comprehensive survey bill and for some minor roads. These votes he had continued to defend. From the mounting enthusiasm for public spending stemmed an evil difficult for the average congressman to resist. Having obtained appropriations for measures of national significance, members courted favor by proposing all sorts of local schemes to be paid for with public funds. Log-rolling alliances were beginning to be the talk of Capitol Hill. Would Representative A support Representative B's measure for a canal in return for B's promise to support A's bill for a highway connecting the county seats in his district? Van Buren believed that nothing short of prompt and drastic action would avert "a torrent of reckless legislation." Otherwise, he foresaw the improvement mania knit in with the reviving spirit of speculation in western lands, involving calls and renewed calls upon the Treasury. Another thing he could not have overlooked was the prospect of Mr. Calhoun riding the crest of the improvements wave.

Jackson agreed that the tendency should be stopped short, telling Van Buren to watch Congress and bring to the White House the first vulnerable bill to meet his eye. Few leaders, reflected the Secretary, would have behaved with equal resolution, for the "improvement" virus was at work in the veins of Jackson's western supporters. At the end of April, 1830, in the course of a horseback ride, Mr. Van Buren said he thought he had his bill—a measure to build a turnpike from Maysville to Lexington, Kentucky, through the heart of the strongest Jackson district in the State. It had passed the House and would pass the Senate. Returning to his study the President roughed out a veto message.[51]

Though the whole matter was supposed to be a secret between Jackson and the Secretary of State, a disturbing rumor brought Representative "Tecumseh" Johnson of Kentucky to the White House so agitated that he could hardly sit in a chair.

Nor was the Congressman's devotion to the cause of improvements the only thing to mark him as a faithful exemplar of border ideals. He wore no cravat. His nickname came from the War of 1812 in which he had reputedly slain Tecumseh in personal combat. To prove it some of his men came home with razor strops which they said had been cut from the Indian's hide.

Advancing toward the President with his left hand extended and his right fist clenched above his head, Johnson exclaimed: "General, if this hand were an anvil on which the sledge hammer of a smith were descending and a fly were to light upon it that fly would not be more surely crushed than you will crush your friends in Kentucky if you veto that bill."

Jackson sprang to his feet. "Sir, have you looked at the condition of the Treasury—at the amount of money it contains—at the appropriations already made by Congress—at the amount of other claims upon it?"

"Tecumseh" confessed that he had not.

"Well," said Old Hickory, "I have. There is no money to be expended as my friends desire. I stand committed before the Country to pay off the National Debt. This pledge I am determined to redeem."

The blustery Kentuckian returned to the Capitol a much-troubled man. "Nothing less than a voice from Heaven," he told fellow-Westerners who crowded around, "will prevent the old man from vetoing the Bill." And on second thought Johnson doubted the efficacy of a voice. Pennsylvania, linked to the West by strong ties of commerce, joined in the protest. On the morning the veto was due, Mr. Van Buren called at the White House. Eaton, Barry, Lewis, and Felix Grundy, who had succeeded to Eaton's Senate seat, were at breakfast with the President. Their "desponding" countenances told Van Buren what he had come to make sure of. Eaton was the president of a western canal company. The veteran at the head of the table tapped a bulging breast pocket. "The thing is here and shall go up as soon as Congress convenes."

This veto message was a work of art, to which Van Buren had given a final form that exhibited little more than a nodding acquaintance with Jackson's original outline. The document relied on Old Hickory's power over the imagination of the masses, and his uncanny ability to make his measures their measures—a phenomenon of statesmanship the country was to see much more of in the seven tumultuous years to come. Speaking over the heads of politicians and of politically-intrenched contractors, the President addressed the people, predicating his case on the welfare of the common man. Jeffersonian precedents were dexterously handled to the point, in one instance, of doubtful interpretation. An appeal to patriotism was supplemented by an appeal to self-interest. The payment of the national debt would diminish taxes, the pursuit of an unrestrained improvement policy increase them.

The performance was successful, one Pennsylvania member confessing astonishment at the way his constituents accepted the dictum of the Hero.[52] Out west Henry Clay let off steam in a speech against the veto, but, to their dismay, Clay men perceived the victory Jackson had wrought in holding "the allegiance of the south & Virginia with as little offense as possible to the North & West."[53] More than this, he had done the nation a service that was to endure for many years.

6

The most fortunate individual beneficiary was Van Buren, who had achieved much more than merely sealing up another source-spring of Mr. Calhoun's declining prestige. In the summer of 1829, when Jackson and his Secretary of State had first begun to discuss the subject, the President was so ill and vexed that he wrote a brother of Aunt Rachel:

"My time cannot be long upon earth. . . . My earthly house [is] in order and [I am] prepare[d] for another & I hope a better world." But if die he must it would be on the field of duty, however acute the longing to "withdraw from the scenes that surround me to the private walks of the Hermitage, . . . there to spend my [last] days . . . at the tomb of my Dr wife, . . . in peace from the toils & strife of this world with which I have long been surfeited. But this is denied me—I cannot retire with propriety."[54]

After the delivery of the message to Congress Jackson fell ill again. His legs swelled and Lewis, in alarm, feared a fatal attack of dropsy. Old Hickory frankly discussed his condition with the household. Lewis suggested that his old friend's political as well as his spiritual house should be in order and urged the claims of Van Buren against those of Calhoun as heir to the Jackson mantle. In the six months past, Old Hickory had leaned upon the New Yorker as never upon another man. Their collaboration on the message to Congress was just finished, the scheme to check internal improvements rounded into shape. Lewis suggested that Jackson leave, in effect, a political will to be used in case of his death. He did so in a letter to John Overton, of which Lewis retained a duplicate.

"Permit me to say here of Mr. Van Buren that I have found him everything that I could desire him to be, and believe him not only deserving of *my* confidence but the *confidence* of the *Nation*. Instead of his being selfish and intriguing, as has been represented by some of his opponents, I have found him frank, open, candid, and manly. As a Counsellor he is *able* and *prudent*, . . . and one of the most pleasant men to do business with I ever saw. He, my dear friend, is well qualified . . . to fill the highest office in the gift of the people. . . . I wish I could say as much for Mr. Calhoun. You know the confidence I once had in that gentleman. However, of him I desire not now to speak."[55]

Jackson usually knew when he had said enough.

CHAPTER XXX

Throb of a Distant Drum

I

IN DEFERENCE to orators who, with an eye on posterity, wished to revise their efforts after delivery the Washington newspapers sometimes lagged a fortnight behind in printing important speeches made before Congress. Jackson circumvented this delay by stationing Donelson or Lewis in the galleries to apprize him immediately on adjournment of a session's doings. On one of the coldest days of the winter, January 27, 1830, Major Lewis returned from such a tour of duty.

"Well, and how is Webster getting on?" inquired the President.

"Delivering a most powerful speech," replied Lewis. "I am afraid he's demolishing our friend Hayne."

"I expected it," said Old Hickory.[1]

Reluctant as Andrew Jackson was to say a good word for Daniel Webster, there was no blinking the fact that the New Englander had unmasked Hayne as too sympathetic with the South Carolina "nullifiers" to please the hero of New Orleans. And not only Hayne, but John C. Calhoun as well.

In the beginning, the President had been prepared to take a different view of the debate which Thomas Hart Benton had precipitated with an orthodox Jacksonian arraignment of eastern capitalists whom he charged with hindering western emigration to safeguard New England's cheap labor supply. There Robert Y. Hayne took up the thread. The Cotton Kingdom could not have wished for a more presentable advocate. Schooled in the best southern traditions of public service, the blond, mercurial Hayne at thirty-eight was one of the able men of the Senate, and in his social relationships one of the most popular. Branching out from Benton's rugged and rather sententious presentation, he gracefully invited the West to unite with the South against encroachments inimical to both sections. It was a skillful bid for an alliance in dealing with the frowning tariff and state rights questions.

As the South Carolinian began to speak, a thick-set, swarthy man in a blue coat with brass buttons tucked a bundle of papers under his arm and lounged against a pillar on the edge of the chamber. The lazy, card-playing Webster had been more than usually derelict that session in his attendance upon the deliberations of the Senate. He had just ascended the marble stairs from the quarters of the Supreme Court, where a rich practice occupied the greater part of the time he was willing to surrender to laborious concerns. Wholly ignorant of the nature of the issue before the Senate, he imagined himself too engrossed to pause for more than a moment. But as Hayne progressed, he took a seat and honored his southern colleague with strict attention.

On the next day Webster answered him. After an eloquent defense of the loyalty of New England, not altogether in agreement with the facts, the Senator from Massachusetts touched provocatively the weak spots in the Charlestonian's armor. Seizing on Hayne's declaration that "no evil was more to be deprecated than the consolidation of this government," Webster demanded proof. What was consolidation but the strengthening of the Union? He regretted a disposition—which he trusted Hayne did not share—of some in the South to "speak of the Union in terms of indifference, or even disparagement."

Hayne took the bait. In a bitter and brilliant reply, the South Carolinian attacked not only New England's long record of doubtful devotion to the Union, but Webster personally. With an array of historical precedent, he defended his State's contention for the right to set aside oppressive Federal legislation. This was nullification.

The speech, which many thought unanswerable and which Mr. Calhoun from his place on the dais had punctuated with smiles of approval, gave Webster the opportunity he had sought. He assailed Hayne's proposals as impossible of practical application, as ruinous to the welfare of all, and as unconstitutional. "The Constitution is not the creature of the State government. The very chief end, the main design, for which the whole Constitution was framed and adopted was to establish a government that should not . . . depend on State opinion and State discretion."

Webster was not a superficially dramatic type of orator. Using few gestures, he would speak for half an hour at a time in a tone only a little more formal than ordinary conversation. Yet the rich and deep voice, the sonorous rhythm of his sentences, and the glance of the great luminous dark eyes exercised something akin to an hypnotic sway. At the same time, listeners were left under the flattering impression that the appeal was to the intellect rather than to the emotions; for Webster dealt chiefly with arguments, not exhortations. The calmness, the good nature, the pervading sense of mastery and of subdued power clothed exaggeration in the confident garments of understatement. With Senate and galleries in his grip for two days, he delivered the most telling plea for the perpetuation of the Union that one man has ever made. In sentences that were to invite comparison with Demosthenes's *Oration on the Crown,* Mr. Webster concluded by urging the "folly" of the doctrine of "liberty first and Union afterwards." "Liberty *and* Union, now and forever, one and inseparable."

When John C. Calhoun's gavel and petulant cry of "Order, order!" broke the spell, others than Major Lewis were of the opinion that the man from Massachusetts had demolished Hayne.

A few hours later the contending giants met again at a White House levee.

"How are you this evening, Colonel Hayne?" asked Webster.

"None the better for you, sir," said the Southerner with a smile.[2]

As to the truth of that polite answer much, very much, would depend on the venerable host of the evening. After the last orator had spoken, Andrew Jackson must *act* on the issue which already had sensitive ears straining to catch the throb of a distant drum.

2

As somber shadows deepened, the incongruous note of travesty supplied by Mrs. Eaton continued its work of attrition on the inner harmony and the outward dignity of the Administration. General Jackson's extraordinary Cabinet meeting had failed of its purpose to open the portals of society for the lady of the Secretary of War, Branch making a particular display of his audacity. When Jackson withdrew from the church of the Reverend J. N. Campbell, an accuser of Mrs. Eaton, the Secretary of the Navy invited the clergyman to one of his dinners.³ Whereupon the President discontinued Cabinet meetings, assuming without complaint the added burden of work this threw on his shoulders. Andrew Jackson bore a heavy personal responsibility for the unpleasant situation in which his Secretary of War found himself. Weak in body but strong in loyalty, he did not shirk it. *"Eaton is the last man on earth I ought or would abandon.... I would sooner abandon life."*⁴ The strain of this lashing defiance was great. The veteran's hair turned from gray to white. "[The Eaton trouble]," said Jack Donelson, "has done more to paralize his energies than 4 years of the regular and simple operations of the Gov^t."⁵

The President's private secretary, well-balanced in his outlook on most things, felt that General Jackson's course did more credit to his heart than to his head. Donelson saw nothing added to his revered uncle's renown by a struggle that drained the energy needed for important public affairs. This view took for granted that the President's championship of Mrs. Eaton represented a purely personal determination to force upon society one whom a considerable proportion of that body did not think eligible to its privileges. In the affair's early stages, this narrow conception was widely accepted. Any political significance that might attach to the slighting of Mrs. Eaton was hastily shovelled onto the doorstep of Henry Clay. As time went on, however, the Clay theory ceased to hold water. The nature of the alignment for and against the Secretary of War's consort was becoming too plain for disguise. Against her were the friends and political followers of John C. Calhoun; for her, the friends and followers of Martin Van Buren. At the beginning of the Administration, Calhoun had had by far the larger and more distinguished retinue of the two. In eight months Van Buren had made important gains, no considerable part of which was attributable to the dapper little man's politeness to the wife of the President's friend.

So through the thick haze of his partizanship Andrew Jackson came to see Van Buren as the gallant champion of an innocent and injured female; Calhoun as the confidant of her traducers.

Thus, in the President's mind, the whole thing began to take on a new and larger growth, with the good name of Mrs. Eaton the ostensible stake in a game involving the prosperity of the Jackson Administration. Loyalty to Eaton and nothing more, probably would have induced Old Hickory to persist in this fierce strife, especially when one considers the secret which even Donelson (judging by his actions) appears not to have known: the fact that Jackson had prodded Eaton into a marriage he would have gladly postponed. But, all this aside, by autumn of 1829 the President had begun to feel that, in his fight for Margaret Eaton, he was defending a position upon which the ultimate prestige of his presidency might well depend.[6]

The events of the forthcoming social season were to throw this aspect of the situation into sharper relief.

Cabinet dinners formed the axis about which a Washington "season" revolved. The procedure was for the President first to entertain his official family, after which the Cabinet members, beginning with the Secretary of State, dined their colleagues in turn. Early in November, 1829, the President and Mr. Van Buren were taking a horseback ride—by this time an almost daily occurrence—when Jackson mentioned that thus far he had postponed his dinner to the Cabinet because of the situation prevailing. He doubted, however, whether he should delay much longer and thought "the sooner it was entered upon the better." So the invitations went out.

Not even the wit and spirit of the Secretary of State could raise the dinner that followed above the level of "a formal and hollow ceremony." When Mrs. Donelson rose to lead the ladies from the table, the President and the other gentlemen also filed out. After a halting attempt at drawing-room conversation the guests departed, leaving Old Hickory mortified and resentful.

Mr. Van Buren's dinner came next. Mr. Branch, Mr. Berrien and Mr. Ingham accepted for themselves but not for their wives or daughters, Branch offering the gratuitous excuse of "circumstances unnecessary to detail." Eaton and Barry, too, came without their wives. Mr. Van Buren, a notable judge of wine, later implied that the men made quite a night of it. No other Cabinet dinner was attempted, leaving society in a state of fluttering disorganization. When Mr. Van Buren distributed cards for a large but unofficial party, the *National Journal* proclaimed it an effort of the Secretary of State and his friend, the British Minister, to force into society an unwelcome figure. In a sprightlier contribution to the *belles-lettres* of the day, Mrs. Eaton became "Bellona, the Goddess of War," a name quickly taken up by the town. Nevertheless, Mr. Van Buren's affair was well-attended and it surpassed expectations when Bellona collided with the wife of a general while dancing, precipitating a scene which sent one nervous guest in quest of his host to act as peacemaker.

The Russian Minister, Baron Krudener, was also a friend of Mr. Van Buren's and, like his British colleague, unmarried. He goodnaturedly gave a ball at which he took Mrs. Eaton to supper, assigning the Secretary of War to Madame Huygens, the wife of the Minister from Holland. The Dutch diplomat's spouse failed to conceal her displeasure at the arrangement. A published report, doubtless exaggerated, said she left the table. In any event the story was soon abroad that Madame Huygens, Mrs. Ingham, Mrs. Branch and the daughters of Attorney General Berrien would give a series of dinners at which the danger of such contretemps would be obviated by the expedient of not inviting the Eatons.[7]

The Cabinet ladies gave their dinners. Eaton's friends retaliated with parties of their own, which the energies of Mr. Van Buren and of the bachelor diplomats rendered smarter in appearance than otherwise would have been the case. The political complexion of this division became more discernible every day. "Calhoun leads the moral party," noted an exceptionally detached spectator, John Quincy Adams of Massachusetts, "Van Buren that of the frail sisterhood."[8] Hostilities spread beyond the glass walls of the drawing rooms. "Branch and Eaton don't speak," recounted John Campbell of the Treasury. "How Old Hickory (who always becomes greater by difficulties) is to get out of the Scrape I cannot say." A Cabinet rupture was openly spoken of. In that case who should go? "The President . . . BELIEVES Eaton & his wife are innocent & would no longer be Andrew Jackson if any earthly consideration of popularity could induce him to give way and surrender them up." On the other hand "Branch & Ingham have many friends & to dismiss them . . . would shake the *old fellows* popularity confoundedly. So it is an *uggly affair* . . . [upon which] hangs a great deal more than you would suppose." Yet the blind faith of followers in his prowess remained, as ever, one of the General's greatest sources of strength. "Old Jackson," concluded Campbell, "will get thro' somehow."[9]

One morning before breakfast, Mr. Van Buren received a summons to come at once to the White House. Old Hickory's eyes were bloodshot, his face drawn from lack of sleep, his manner ominously calm. He had, he said, decided upon a course of action. If the reputed pact between Madame Huygens and the Cabinet ladies were true, he said he would dismiss Ingham, Berrien and Branch and hand Chevalier Huygens his passports. Jackson had sent for the Cabinet officers. Would Mr. Van Buren interview Madame Huygens?[10]

Though other items of our foreign policy were in delicate balance at the moment, the Secretary of State departed on his errand.

3

With the three distinguished gentlemen seated before him General Jackson held on his knee a single sheet of paper and began to read:

"I do not claim the right to interfere in the domestic relations or personal intercourse of any member of my Cabinet. . . . But from information and from my own observation I am fully impressed with the belief that you and your families have, in addition to the exercise of your and their undoubted rights, taken measures to induce others to avoid mrs Eaton and thereby to exclude her from society and degrade him. . . . If her character is such as to justify measures on the part of my cabinet, . . . it is I who am responsible for this alleged indignity to public morales. . . . I will not part with major Eaton and those of my cabinet who cannot harmonize with him had better withdraw, for harmony I must and will have."

Old Hickory removed his spectacles. What had the gentlemen to say?

The gentlemen had considerable to say. They were the last persons in the world to do an injustice to Major Eaton or his family.

Their wives' parties had had no such purpose in view. Naturally, they could not undertake to regulate each small detail of the social activities of their families, but— To these magnificent liars General Jackson responded with sentiments that did him credit. He was bound to accept, he said, the word of his Cabinet officers. But let them mark this, and mark it well: "An indignity to Major Eaton is an indignity to me." Let the gentlemen reflect. If they were not prepared to work in harmony with Eaton they should resign.[11]

The renewed invitation was not accepted and presently Martin Van Buren returned with Madame Huygens's assurance that she had been outrageously misquoted.

"The petticoat war has ended, no lives lost," chronicled Jack Donelson. "The General in the goodness of his heart thinks M^{rs}. E has attained a triumph."[12] And so thought a dazzled citizen of Ohio, attending his first White House levee, when he beheld Margaret sweep in, gloriously gowned in calico as an encouragement to American manufactures. "The Secretary's lady, whose form is symmetry itself, needed no ruffle or single ornament on her person. No sooner had she taken her place near the President's family than all the beauty and fashion in the room gathered around to do her honor."[13] Our western visitor barely mentioned that Emily Donelson and Miss Mary Eastin also wore calico. Had his preoccupation with the wife of the Secretary of War been less intent, he might have observed in the averted countenances of those ladies something to cause him to question the permanence of Bellona's ascendency.

4

Its interest whetted by fragmentary reports and alarms, the country fell hungrily upon the speeches which, after painstaking rectifications of phrase, Webster and Hayne at length gave to an impatient press.[14] By the tens of thousands the copies were snatched up; nullification was the topic of the hour at every cross-roads. After the speeches had been read the question was, "Does Jackson stand with Webster or with Hayne?" A word, a nod from him would decide the course of a host of people. Mayhap it would decide the issue.

Report had it that after Hayne had made his first speech the

The Third Hermitage

Completed 1831, destroyed by fire 1834. This structure represents an extensive remodeling of the second Hermitage which was built in 1818. On the right is Rachel Jackson's tomb. This likeness, reproduced from an engraving in the gallery of the Tennessee Historical Society, Nashville, appeared in early editions of the first volume of this work as the second Hermitage, erected in 1818. The Society and the writer have discovered their error and a proper likeness of the 1818 house has been substituted in Volume One.

SARAH YORKE JACKSON

Wife of Andrew Jackson, junior. Married in Philadelphia, November 24, 1831. "She has been more than a daughter to me," General Jackson wrote of her in his will. From a portrait by Earl, owned by the Ladies' Hermitage Association. Nashville.

President sent him a note of congratulation.¹⁵ This, however, was before the South Carolinian had been led into an open advocacy of the right of a state to sit in judgment upon an act of Congress. Certainly, since Webster's famous Second Reply, Old Hickory had kept his counsel, and neither principal to the great debate knew to what extent he had succeeded or failed to influence the views of an Executive who gave annoying evidence of a disposition to direct, rather than to obey, the masses that had elevated him to the chief magistracy. Webster, of course, had little chance to feel out the sentiment pervading the White House, which he visited only on formal occasions. On the other hand Hayne was a frequent social caller, familiar with the intimate atmosphere of the pipe-scented study on the second floor. In fact the President was contemplating the offer of a choice appointment to the Senator's brother who had fought at New Orleans. Mrs. Donelson and Miss Eastin were planning a trip to New York in company with the Senator's family.¹⁶ More than this, Benton, Felix Grundy and other Administration senators, not of the distinctly southern branch of the party, felt that for the benefit of his pro-tariff constituents Mr. Webster had overstressed the perils of the situation. On the floor Benton came to Hayne's defense, accusing the New Englander of going too far in his characterization of the South Carolina movement as a step toward disunion and civil war.¹⁷

Nevertheless, the continued silence of the President filled the Calhoun camp with vague misgivings. Writing under the eye of the Vice President, Duff Green began an increasingly warm series of editorial attacks on Webster's speech. "The doctrine contended for by General HAYNE is too well understood and too firmly established . . . to be shaken."¹⁸ Webster had joined Clay "in an unholy crusade against the administration."¹⁹ A praiseful column on Benton's rejoinder was made occasion for contrasting New England's attitude during the War of 1812 with that of the West in which Jackson's exploits were given significant attention.²⁰ As the *Telegraph* was supposed to reflect the views of the White House, Mr. Webster was moved publicly to dispute Green's interpretation of a passage from his speech.²¹ Whereupon Green dug up and reprinted a scurrilous campaign attack upon Jackson, which he said had appeared in a New England newspaper with "Mr. WEBSTER'S public sanction."²²

After a month of this, and no sign from the White House, a subtler plan was formed to draw Old Hickory closer to the side of the South Carolina group. A grand subscription dinner in ostensible tribute to the memory of Thomas Jefferson was announced for April 13, 1830, the anniversary of his birth. The affair was to be at once distinguished and democratic. A subscription list left on the bar of Brown's Indian Queen Hotel enabled the humblest disciple of the great promulgator of liberal political thought, now four years under Monticello's sod, to sign his name, pay his fee and get a ticket entitling him to sit and to sup with the famous. Less openly was the evening's program of speeches and toasts contrived, beginning on a broad note of appreciation of the Jeffersonian ideals, then narrowing to the Virginia Resolutions of 1798 adopted in opposition to the Alien and Sedition Laws, and then, as an analogous case, moving on to implied approval of South Carolina's resistance of the tariff. The President accepted an invitation to attend. This meant that, the prearranged speaking over, Andrew Jackson would offer the first volunteer toast of the evening.

As the date drew near, Old Hickory began to give thought to what he should say on that occasion. From the moment Webster had revealed the extent to which the nullification doctrine possessed the minds of the South Carolinians, Jackson had leaned toward the views of the Northerner, though this secret was so closely guarded that apparently only Lewis, Donelson and Van Buren knew it. Studiously these three observed the preparations for the banquet and reported to their chief. Van Buren's confidential man, C. C. Cambreleng of New York, and Benton and H. L. White, were on committees in charge of the dinner. The result was information leading Jackson to the conclusion that, if carried off as its promoters hoped, the affair "might menace the stability of the Union."²³ His direct mind swept aside the fulminations of Duff Green, the fine-spun arguments of Hayne, the criticisms of Benton. He saw, as Webster had seen, one central fact: the Union endangered. Jackson's political creed and social culture had been molded by the South. But his ideas of state sovereignty stopped short of any intention of allowing South Carolina to say what Federal statutes it would obey. Any tariff that was the law of the land Andrew Jackson would enforce. This line of reasoning placed him squarely beside Webster.

Taking up a pen Old Hickory fell to drafting a toast. Several sheets of paper went into the fire before a sentiment evolved that he regarded sufficiently compact and expressive. On the evening of the dinner he set out with Van Buren, as animated, the Secretary later said, as if he were preparing to defend the Union on a field of battle.[24]

At the Indian Queen they encountered a scene of excitement and suspense. A printed list of the regular toasts lay beside each plate. Members of the Pennsylvania delegation had read them and marched from the room. A few others also left. The banquet under way, Hayne started the oratory with a flowery address. Then came the regular toasts, twenty-four in number, building, bit by bit, support for the South Carolina point of view. Jackson sat impassive. The volunteer toasts were next in order. Toastmaster Roane introduced the President of the United States. Old Hickory stood, waiting for the cheers to subside. So many diners were on their feet that the diminutive Van Buren, whose place was at the foot of the second table, climbed on his chair in order to see the President.

Old Hickory fixed his glance upon John C. Calhoun.

"Our Union: It must be preserved."

Utter silence. "A proclamation of martial law in South Carolina," remarked Isaac Hill, "and an order to arrest Calhoun where he sat could not have come with more blinding, staggering force." The white-haired soldier raised his glass, a signal that the toast was to be drunk standing. Calhoun rose with the rest, his hand trembling so that a little of the yellow wine trickled down the side of the tumbler.[25] A moment more the chieftain stood there, as much the master as on the day he faced down a mutinous army at Fort Strother. Then, crossing to the far side of the room, he spoke to Benton. By this time the Senator from Missouri had altered his ideas concerning the impropriety of Webster's "Liberty *and* Union, now and forever," destined, with Jackson's strikingly similar phrase, to become a rallying cry in the long fight begun that night to strangle secession.

Hayne rushed up. Would the President consent to the insertion of one word in his toast before the text was given to the newspapers? What was the word? asked Jackson. It was "Federal," making the toast read, "Our Federal Union—" Mistakenly the Southerner imagined this might give the sentiment a state rights flavor, diluting a little the pungency of the rebuke. Jackson agreed and, like many another historic epigram, the toast went forth amended to the world. Curiously Hayne's suggestion gave the President's utterance the exact form he had intended it should have. In speaking he had left the written slip in his pocket, and so omitted one word unintentionally.[26]

When the gentlemen had resumed their places and the buzz of conversation ceased, the chairman called upon Mr. Calhoun for the second volunteer toast. The Vice-President arose slowly.

"The Union," he said, "next to our liberty, most dear."

After a moment's hesitation, and in a way that left hearers in doubt as to whether he was continuing the toast or beginning a speech, he added: "May we all remember that it can only be preserved by respecting the rights of the States and by distributing equally the benefits and burdens of the Union."[27]

Never to learn the art of brevity, the Vice-President had left the honors with Jackson. A little later when the President withdrew, two-thirds of the company followed within five minutes, leaving not more than thirty diners to bring Mr. Calhoun's banquet to a formal close.

Though Duff Green's eleven-column report covered the President's participation with only two lines of type,[28] the cat was out of the bag. A wave of nationalistic ardor swept the country, heartening the small Union Party in South Carolina which opposed the extremists' program.

The "reign" of Andrew Jackson had begun.[29]

5

John C. Calhoun sagged under the strain. Once more Martin Van Buren had scored over his rival in the contest to ride Old Hickory's popularity into the presidency. A visitor to the Senate gallery found the South Carolinian "more wrinkled and care-worn than I had expected from his reputed age." The Vice-President was forty-eight. "His voice is shrill and to my ear disagreeable. . . . His manners have in them an uneasiness, a hurried, incoherent air."[30] Mr. Calhoun was, in truth, uneasy. "The times are perilous beyond any that I have ever witnessed," he wrote following the banquet at Brown's Indian Queen.[31] The day after this sentiment was committed to the mails the Vice-President opened a communication which did nothing to allay his apprehensions.

"Sir . . . The Enclosed copy of a letter from William H. Crawford, Esq. . . . was placed in my hands on yesterday. . . . The statements and facts it presents being so different from what I had heretofore understood to be correct requires that it should be brought to your consideration. . . . My object in making this communication is to announce to you the great surprise which is felt, and to learn whether it is possible that the information given is correct. . . .

"I am, sir, very respectfully
            "Your humble servant
                "ANDREW JACKSON."[32]

The Florida campaign secrets again. Twice had Calhoun repelled the charge that he had stood for sacrificing Jackson on the altar of international comity when the conquest, undertaken with James Monroe's unwritten assent, brought a growl from the British lion. Could he do so again? The intervention of William H. Crawford, a party to the Cabinet meetings in question, was a new and difficult obstacle.

The Vice President acknowledged at once the receipt of his superior's letter, saying he would reply at length as soon as he had the leisure. Though usually impatient of delays, Jackson did not complain. "Time to explain . . . is due him. . . . *He shall have it,* but I am afraid he is in a dilemma."[33] In this state of mind, Jackson could afford to wait—1832 being a long way off as yet.

More than the Florida business stood against Calhoun on the black books this time. Clearly the part of the Vice President's followers in the Eaton affair encompassed something that struck deeper than a fastidious objection to a female of spicy background. Jackson's inclination to regard it as an effort to render his Administration ridiculous agreed with recent reports showing Ingham's hand at work to promote Calhoun's interests in Pennsylvania at Jackson's expense.[34] Added to this was the Webster-Hayne debate and the nullification banquet. Nor should one forget that nearly three months before throwing his oral hand grenade into the Vice President's dinner party, Old Hickory had privately placed with John Overton the codicil of political disinheritance. Now he sought only an excuse for a definite break, which an opportune and deliberate revival of the Florida issue seemed about to provide.

This was the clever work of Lewis, taking up where Sam Houston had left off two years before. In November, 1829, when feeling between the Eaton and the Calhoun cliques was acute, Jackson had entertained ex-President Monroe. After the company, with the exception of Eaton and Lewis, had retired, Jackson was having a meditative smoke while the others talked. A remark about the Florida campaign brought the General from his reverie. He asked Lewis to repeat it. Lewis said a guest had claimed that Mr. Monroe's entire Cabinet had opposed Jackson's course. The President said the man must be mistaken. Lewis said he was not sure of that.

"Why are you not?" demanded Jackson.

"Because I have seen a letter in which Mr. Crawford is represented as saying that it was not he but Mr. Calhoun who was in favor of your being arrested." Thus Lewis described the letter James Alexander Hamilton had obtained from Governor Forsyth of Georgia in 1828, which Lewis at that time had deemed too weak to show to Jackson.

"You saw such a letter as *that*?"

"Yes," repeated Lewis, adding that the letter was now in New York.

"I want to see it, and you must go to New York tomorrow."

Lewis returned with the story that Hamilton objected to turning over the letter without the consent of Forsyth, who was on his way to Washington to take a seat in the Senate. Forsyth also balked, saying he would have to consult Crawford[35]—as well he might, considering the supposed inviolability of Cabinet secrets. Not until after the nullification dinner did Forsyth write the former Secretary of Treasury, now partly recovered in health and charitably provided with a judgeship in Georgia. Back came a vindictive and astonishing epistle in which Crawford sought to cover up his former notorious hatred of Jackson and to throw the blame on Calhoun.[36]

"A poor tale this," reported wise old John Overton to whom the

President had passed the letter for comment, "scarcely fit to deceive a sensible school boy." He placed Crawford beneath the level of Calhoun who, though evading responsibility for an act, had not sought to fasten it on another. Yet Overton said he believed the part about Calhoun's participation in the criticism of Jackson.[37]

Such was the letter the President had sent to Mr. Calhoun. Overton thought his friend had blundered.

If so, Calhoun blundered more seriously. Pascal once apologized for the length of a letter, saying he had no time to write a short one. The Vice President took two weeks to cover fifty-two pages with his nervous scrawl. To an impartial judge he refuted Crawford's thin claim to Jackson's regard, and showed the whole to be a political intrigue.[38] What he did not show was the grace to admit his original position in 1818. Nor was any explanation offered as to why he had allowed Jackson to be deceived in that particular for all these years.

Eagerly Old Hickory made the most of this weakness. "In all your [previous] letters to me [you have] professed to approve... *entirely* my conduct in relation to the Seminole campaign.... Your letter now before me is the first intimation that *you* ever entertained any other opinion.... Understanding you now, no further communication with you on this subject is necessary."[39]

John C. Calhoun pondered the melancholy fact that when two ride the same horse one must ride behind.

6

Small was the personal satisfaction these events afforded the President. "My hope of hapiness had fled.... The only consolation this side of the grave is when I look forward to the time when I can again retire to the Hermitage, ... there to spend my latter days beside the tomb of the only solace of my life, ... and lay my bones beside her." Being President was only "dignified slavery,"[40] and times came when all the sense of duty that Jackson possessed was required to stimulate more than a serf's interest in his tasks.

During fifteen months of ceaseless toil, made the more burdensome by grief, by illness, and by disappointment in men he had given the hand of friendship, the hope of seeing the Hermitage once more remained before him like a mirage of cool springs beckoning a desert wanderer. From the brief reports of Graves Steele, the overseer, and of neighbors, he sought to give reality to the image of this nirvana. How fared the flowering shrubs and the willow slips by Rachel's grave? How fared the negroes, the stock of blooded horses, the work horses and mules, the work steers, the beef steers, the milch cows, the sheep? What of births and deaths—negro babies, colts, and calves? What the amount and the quality of cotton baled, of corn cribbed, of fodder stacked, of oats, of rye? The quantity and quality of meat in the smoke house? How went the work of clearing the "new ground," sending the large timber to the sawmill, making charcoal of the rest? How the work at the brick kiln?[41]

In the answers to these questions, rather than in councils of state, the old planter sought his personal solution of the riddle of life. No public career for his adopted son, Andrew, junior, now in his twentieth year. Let him stick to the Hermitage and learn the run of its affairs. "I have just . . . recd a letter advising me of the death of my negroman Jim," he wrote the boy. "I pray you examine minutely into this matter and advise with Col Love. . . . My negroes shall be treated humanely. . . . Since I left home I have lost three of my family. Old Ned I expected to die, but I am fearful of the cause of the death of Jack and Jim. . . . Your Uncle John Donelson writes that *Steel has ruled with a rod of iron*. . . . Unless he changes his conduct dismiss him."[42] Fortunately for Steele, Uncle John was mistaken.

Some understanding of the instincts of a horseman is necessary to comprehend the fact that General Jackson should have chosen this preoccupied time to re-establish his racing stable, with the hope of producing a champion from the Truxton strain. His principal partner was the Reverend Hardy M. Cryer of Gallatin, whose interests were evenly balanced between the Methodist pulpit and the turf. As Jackson's agent Cryer sold, on credit, the gray colt Tariff to two aspiring Kentucky sportsmen named Moore and Shaw. After winning several races, they staked their accumulated capital on a single contest. Parson Cryer admitted that it looked like a good stroke of business, Colonel George Elliott, one of Nashville's shrewdest connoisseurs of fast horseflesh, laying bets at two to one on the gray. Just before the race there was a rain and a freeze. Tariff lost, and a permanent injury to his wind was feared.

A WHITE HOUSE BRIDE

Mary Eastin, a grand-niece of Rachel Jackson, whom the General brought to Washington in 1829. She kept the hearts of various young men aflutter until 1832 when she married Lucius Polk, a relative of James K. Polk. This likeness, which shows Mrs. Polk with her son William, is from a portrait owned by Mrs. Sarah Polk Burch of Nashville.

"KING ANDREW I"
A cartoon of the campaign of 1832. From the Library of Congress collection.

The plight of the young Kentuckians also excited Cryer's compassion. Although Moore was "a strong Clay and Adams *Politician*," the sportsmanlike preacher consented to take Tariff off their hands and asked Jackson to approve the arrangement. He did so, requesting that the horse be rechristened Bolivar and turned over to Colonel Elliott. If fit for the track, Elliott was to enter him in the spring meets "for the benefit of my son." If windbroken, Bolivar was to be put to thoroughbred mares and several colts acquired. The tired pulse of the one-time proprietor of the Clover Bottom race course revived a little at the thought of the Hermitage colors carried to victory by a horse of the Truxton blood.[43]

Another restorative was the companionship of young folk, a hundred of whom the General could call by name. "Present me to Betsey and the children, to my good old friend Mrs Hays, [to] Narcissa, to Saml J. Hays and his sweet little wife and kiss my namesake, and [convey my remembrances] to the Doctor and Patsy and son, to Stockley and Lydia Jane and little Hickory and believe me your friend. . . ."[44] When correspondents neglected to include word of their broods Jackson would remind them of it. Childish shouts rang through the White House halls; little feet clattered on the stairs. The President did not complain. A conference was delayed when Mr. Van Buren entered the Executive study to find Emily Donelson's baby, Mary Rachel, asleep in the General's arms. The Secretary of State's prerogative of riding horseback with the President was usurped by ten-year-olds. "They are the only friends I have who never pester me with their advice."[45]

Andrew, junior, arrived for a visit bringing his cousins, Andrew Jackson Hutchings and Samuel Jackson Hays. Daniel Donelson, a brother of the President's secretary, came a little later. Young Hutchings had been expelled from another college. The President placed him in a Catholic institution at Georgetown, hoping the strict discipline would be a good thing. Young Hays ran up a haberdasher's bill of two hundred and eighty-three dollars, which the President paid. Andrew, junior, was recovering from the effects of unrequited love. The General had watched the progress of this romance. "You are very young, but having placed your affections upon Miss Flora I have no desire to interfere. . . . Early attachments are the most durable, and having been raised together in the same neighborhood I have only to recommend to you to say to her at once the object of your visit and receive her answer. . . . Should Miss Flora not favour your wishes, then my son I have one request to make of you. That is that you will give up all idea of Marriage for the present."[46]

Flora did not favor his wishes.

"I expected the result you name. . . . Flora is a fine little girl, . . . but as I told you she has give[n] herself up to coquetry. . . . I assure you I am happy at the result, as I seldom saw a coquett make a good wife, and I wish you to marry a lady who will make you a good wife and I a good daughter, as my happiness depends much upon the prudence of your choice. . . . I have councilled you through life to make no promises, or engagements, but what you punctually perform. . . . You are now free from all engagements and I trust you will keep so untill you advise with your father on this interesting subject."[47]

The four Tennessee blades, newly garnished by a Pennsylvania Avenue tailor, found the White House gay with girls—Cora Livingston, Margaret and Rebecca Branch, Rebecca McLane, and a Mary Smith of Abingdon, Virginia—who flocked about Mary Eastin and flirted becomingly. Donelson and Hays were soon in their toils. Mary Smith was able to expel from Andy II's mind the poignant memories of Flora. The young man brightened. "His countenance," observed a lady of experience (Mrs. Anne Royall, Washington's only newspaperwoman), "is sweetness and innocence itself, his eyes as soft as the dew-drop."[48] Pursuing Mary Smith to Virginia the innocent swain lost sight not only of his father's advice, but also of an important item in the etiquette of courtship. Reminding the President's son of this omission, the self-possessed young lady sent him jogging back to Washington.

General Jackson was deeply embarrassed. "Maj. Francis Smith, Dear Sir, This will be handed to you by my son. . . . He has erred in attempting to address your daughter without first making known to you and your lady his honorable intentions and obtaining your approbation. Admonished of this impropriety, he now awaits upon you to confess it. I find his affections are fixed upon her, and if they are reciprocated, with your approbation, he looks upon the step which would follow as the greatest assurance of his happiness. Mine, since the loss of my dear wife, has almost vanished except that which flows from his prosperity. He is the only hope for the continuation of my name; and has a fortune ample enough with prudence and economy. . . . With these prospects he presents himself again to your daughter." The suit was reinforced by the efforts of a friend of the President who wrote his brother in Abingdon. "Go with him to Smith's. He is after Mary & you must throw all facilities in his way." It was of no use. Having left Tennessee to forget one girl, Andy started back with the job to do over.[49] Mrs. Royall asked how he would like to be President. "Not at all, Madam," said Old Hickory's heir.[50]

The President missed this gullible though good-natured boy, for the agitating silhouette of Margaret Eaton again lay across the threshold of the Mansion. The Cabinet officers' glib pledges had amounted to nothing. In a black mood Old Hickory muttered renewed threats of dismissal and of public exposure of their infidelity to a promise. "The people shall judge."[51]

Choosing this auspicious moment to pour oil on the flames of her champion's ire, Mrs. Eaton declined, in writing, to dine at the Executive Residence. "It would only be another feast . . . [for a] part of your family . . . to make me the object of their censures and reproaches."[52]

General Jackson gave his niece and nephew the choice of receiving Mrs. Eaton or of banishment to Tennessee. Rather than "bow to her commands" they chose Tennessee. "[I shall part]," wrote Donelson, "[from one] to whom I have stood from my infancy in the relation of son to Father. . . . The wretched expedients . . . [of those who would] gratify the vain desire of being understood to possess the controul of his confidence . . . have served their turn."[53] With Mary Ann Lewis, daughter of Bellona's ally, "snugly recoiled in the White House,"—the irritated phrase is Donelson's—the Secretary of War and wife soared away to New York where Administration satraps burst their buttons to honor the lady whose ensign floated over Old Hickory's own tent.[54]

7

It would have been inconsistent with a record of forty years' indulgence toward members of the Donelson clan had General Jackson not abated a little his severity toward Emily and her husband. The concession took the unexpected form of an announcement that the President would accompany the transgressors to their seat of exile in Tennessee. A hundred ties and longings contributed to this decision, for which a petition of the Choctaw chiefs to meet the White Father in council furnished an official excuse. On June 17, 1830, they began the journey,[55] leaving Mary Ann Lewis mistress *ad interim* of the White House and her important-looking father in a situation that any man in the country might have envied. "I pray you," the President wrote en route, "to keep your eyes wide awake, and advise me of every occurrence"—with especial reference to John C. Calhoun, Duff Green, the Nullifiers and congressional partizans of the Bank of the United States. "Advise me whether Mary Ann got her pairsol we happened to bring on and sent back from Clarksburgh. Say to Mr. Van Buren I will be glad to hear from him often. . . . Affectionate regards to you and your amiable daughter and believe me yr. friend ANDREW JACKSON."[56]

This was, perhaps, the only time that a President of the United States has journeyed to an Indian council ground for the purpose of making a treaty. Although public attention was not directed to the exceptional nature of the General's hasty decision, circumstances justified his action. With his mind made up to oppose South Carolina in any effort to nullify Federal authority in the matter of the tariff, the President wished to get rid of another form of nullification which he had no intention of opposing. For forty years Indian treaties had been made only to be broken whenever frontiersmen should become sufficiently numerous or intrepid to do so. To this fast and loose policy of nullification of Federal instruments Andrew Jackson, in the successive rôles of border lawyer, land-speculator, frontier soldier and member of Congress, had frequently been a party.

His campaign of 1813 and '14 had broken forever the military power of the southern Indians. On the lands left to them after that disaster, the Cherokees and the Creeks in Georgia, the Choctaws and Chickasaws in Mississippi and Alabama, had kept their word to bury the tomahawk. They trod the white path, cultivating the civilized arts of peace in which the progress of the Cherokees was astonishing. Discarding tribal forms for those of a republic functioning under a written constitution modeled after our own, the Cherokees lived in houses, planted fields and orchards and established beef herds. They manufactured cloth, built roads, operated fair taverns and dependable ferries. A code of simple and apparently sensible laws was administered by native courts and peace officers. The duties of these functionaries were not burdensome, crimes of violence being rare in the Cherokee republic and disputes of the nature that usually clutter courts less numerous than among Caucasians.

This development, noteworthy in the whole history of primitive races, had begun to attract national notice and much encouragement in parts of the country sufficiently long-settled for the whites to cease to regard Indian problems from a frontier perspective. The other tribes were behind the Cherokees but making headway; and they gave their white neighbors no trouble.

The same cannot be said for the whites who, alarmed at the success of the Indians' cultural experiments, saw the red men on the road to permanent possession of their soil. To be sure, permanent possession had been guaranteed by the United States, in one case in a treaty to which Andrew Jackson, as commissioner, had affixed his signature;[57] but on a frontier the violation of an Indian treaty was regarded as a prerogative of the superior race. Georgia began a truculent course calculated to induce Cherokees and Creeks "voluntarily" to remove to wild lands in what is now Oklahoma. The dignified courtesy of the Indian refusal made strange reading beside the chaotic utterances of white statesmen ranting about "savages." Whereupon, shortly before General Jackson took office, Georgia tore up Federal treaties and annexed the territory of the Cherokee and Creek nations. Mississippi and Alabama did likewise in the cases of the Choctaws and Chickasaws. In his message to Congress, Jackson upheld the states though he spoke solicitously of the welfare of the Indians which, he said, would be promoted by their "voluntary" removal to the western wilderness to live free of white interference. Similar promises the Indians had heard made and had seen broken since George Washington's day. The answer of the intelligent Cherokees was to engage William Wirt of Baltimore, former Attorney General and an eminent constitutional lawyer, to take their case into court on the issue denying a state's right to annul a Federal contract. As no state possessed this right, the outcome of any such suit, once it should reach the Supreme Court, seemed a foregone conclusion.

General Jackson traveled westward to cut the ground from under the courts by persuading as many Indians as possible to agree to emigrate before any suit should come up for adjudication. Of the Choctaws and Chickasaws he had strong hope; and his emissaries were among the Creeks and Cherokees, reinforcing their arguments with those time-honored aids to Indian diplomacy, silver and whisky. Success would mean not only the accomplishment of a great stroke of western policy, but relief from the ticklish possibility of having to support nullification in three states while opposing it in another.[58]

The first reports General Jackson received at the Hermitage were dismaying. The Cherokees stood firm, and with them the Creeks. The behavior of the latter particularly incensed the old Indian fighter. "We have answered," he wrote Lewis, "that we leave them . . . to the protection of their friend Mr. Wirt. . . . The course of *Wirt* had been truly wicked. It will lead to the destruction of the Indians. I have used all the persuasive means in my power, . . . and now leave the poor deluded Creeks and Cherokees to their . . . wicked advisers." Jackson expressed the more enlightened frontier point of view in that his remarks included some concern for the fate of the Indians. His characterization of Wirt was more normally western, this lawyer's villainy arising merely from an assurance to the Indians that, in his opinion, the United States must protect their treaty rights or flout the authority of its own Supreme Court—a dilemma which General Jackson wished to avoid. "I am sure," continued Jackson, "the stand taken by the Executive was not anticipated. . . . It was expected that the more the Indians would hold out, . . . the greater would be the offers [of indemnity]. . . . The offer sent has blasted these hopes and if I mistake not the Indians will now think for themselves and send to the City [of Washington] a delegation prepared to cede their country and move X the M [across the Mississippi.]"[59]

Even the Choctaws, who had invited the President to their council, delayed assembling, and when he reached the meeting place only the Chickasaws had appeared. The President moved among chiefs and sub-chiefs, mingoes and headmen, greeting each one with grave respect. Old Indians were there who had long known General Jackson, and called him Sharp Knife. Indians were there who had fought at New Orleans. After the ceremonial pipe was passed, Sharp Knife addressed them, an interpreter translating.

"Friends and Brothers: . . You have long dwelt on the soil you occupy, and in early times before the white man kindled his fires too near to yours . . . you were a happy people. Now your white brothers are around you. . . . Your great father . . . asks if you are prepared and ready to submit to the laws of Mississippi, and make a surrender of your ancient laws. . . .

"Brothers, listen— To these laws, where you are, you must submit —there is no alternative. Your great father cannot, nor can Congress, prevent it. . . . Old men! Lead your children to a land of promise and of peace before the Great Spirit shall call you to die. Young chiefs! Preserve your people and nation. . . .

"Brothers, listen— Reject the opportunity which is now offered to obtain comfortable homes, and it may not [come] again. . . . If you are disposed to remove, say so, and state the terms you may consider just."[60]

The Indian dignitaries retired for consultation. General Jackson stepped into his carriage and drove away, leaving John Henry Eaton and General John Coffee to complete the negotiation. At the Hermitage he received word of the Chickasaws' capitulation. They would cross the Mississippi in 1832. Meantime the Choctaws had agreed to treat. Directing Eaton and Coffee to meet them, the President set out for Washington the first week in September.

8

Andrew Jackson Donelson accompanied his uncle, a circumstance representing the fruit of negotiations almost as complicated as those surrounding our Indian relations.

General Jackson had found his numerous family connections, and for that matter a large part of Tennessee, divided over the propriety of his defense of Mrs. Eaton. Bellona was an issue of the congressional campaign in the blue-blooded Gallatin district northeast of Nashville. Congressman Robert Desha, declining to run again, took the stump for ex-Governor William Hall and denounced the Secretary's lady as an "abandoned" woman. A supporter of Hall's opponent, running on a pro-Margaret platform, invited Desha to a fist fight. Desha won the fight and Hall the election.[61] This was somewhat offset by a gala dinner at the Hermitage for the Secretary and Mrs. Eaton. The combined pressure of the President, and of John Coffee, next in rank among the Donelson kith, brought a respectable family representation to the table.[62]

The banishment of Jack and Emily Donelson had failed, however, to strengthen Eaton's position in Tennessee, and Old Hickory sought a compromise. Consulting with Coffee and John Overton, he asked Donelson to return to Washington, leaving Emily in Tennessee, with the understanding that Eaton also should leave his wife behind. To this arrangement both the Donelsons and the Eatons consented. Margaret's consent, to be sure, was not heartily given. What woman could easily yield up the dream of a winter in Washington with the boon of White House favors hers to dispense? But Jackson was in earnest and went ahead with his plan to keep bachelor's hall. "A. J. Donelson, my son and Mr. Earle [the artist] will constitute my family." This word to Lewis tactfully foretold the end of Mary Ann's brief regency.[63]

The four men were hardly settled in the Mansion when General Jackson heard of the success of the Choctaw negotiation. Together with the Chickasaw treaty this provided for the cession of sixteen million acres in Mississippi, doubling the tillable area of that state, and of a million acres in Alabama. On the heels of this came an Executive proclamation of equal interest to the maritime and commercial people of the Atlantic littoral: a decree opening the British West Indian ports to American trade. Since our independence this rich market had been virtually closed. With the effective support of the President, Martin Van Buren had broken the deadlock in nineteen months. This conspicuous stroke in the field of foreign policy increased, in one year, the value of our commerce with those islands from one hundred and one thousand to more than two and a quarter million dollars annually.[64]

With these laurels to his credit, General Jackson turned to the knotty questions surrounding the Bank of the United States—a disturbing decision for those Administration statesmen who preferred to let sleeping dogs lie.

CHAPTER XXXI

A Greek Temple in Chestnut Street

I

A TALL and still room in a replica of a Greek temple facing Chestnut Street, Philadelphia, sheltered another man who pondered the affairs of the Bank of the United States—tireless, elegant Nicholas Biddle, his imaginative mind emboldened by success. After eight years as the presiding officer of that institution, Nicholas Biddle could contemplate a record of singular achievement. Through its twenty-seven branches and agencies, the Bank of the United States ruled the commerce, the industry, the husbandry of a nation; and Biddle ruled the bank. His control of the circulating medium was nearly absolute. By expanding or contracting credits he could make money plentiful or scarce, business brisk or dull in any locality in the land saving, to a certain extent, New England whose independent banks were strong and well-managed. Nothing short of a declaration of war could affect the everyday concerns of Americans as profoundly as this man, who looked more like a poet than a financier, could affect them by a stroke of the pen—with which he had, indeed, struck off some passable pentameters.

Though the son of a Philadelphia banker, Biddle had broken his own path to power in the realm of money. Completing at thirteen the prescribed studies at the University of Pennsylvania, Nicholas was refused a diploma because of his youth. At fifteen he was valedictorian of the class of 1801 at the College of New Jersey at Princeton. At eighteen, as secretary to the American Minister to France, a family friend, he handled important financial details of the Louisiana Purchase. Wandering the face of Europe, he discoursed with savants on the distinctions between classical and modern Greek. Art, architecture, history and languages also engrossed the handsome boy. Home again, upon finishing a law course, he turned to the editorship of a literary magazine of such elevated taste that few could appreciate its virtues. A more substantial work was a history of the Lewis and Clark expedition, a more delightful one the *Ode to Bogle*, immortalizing a versatile Philadelphia negro who had attained distinction as a fancy cook and as an undertaker. Biddle dedicated the book "with a mint stick" to his little daughter.

From these occupations Secretary of War James Monroe, who had known him in London, drew the rich young man into his country's service during the dire and splendid hours that followed the sacking of Washington by Admiral Cockburn. The Treasury empty and the Government paralyzed, hope of national survival seemed to rest on the issue of a collision impending somewhere near New Orleans between the mightiest military expedition Europe had ever sent to the New World, and a picked-up army led by a gaunt Indian fighter who had hardly seen the face of a civilized foe. With inspired energy Biddle fell upon Tangled Treasury records, obtaining loans to turn the wheels of government. Although his father, foreseeing the profits of his own bank trenched upon, opposed it, Biddle, junior, fought to re-establish the Bank of the United States as a means of lifting the country from financial chaos. The war over and the bank re-established, Biddle declined an invitation to become a director for the majority stockholders and prepared to return to the reposeful life of a literary dilletante. But when Mr. Monroe asked him to accept one of the five Government directorships he did so from a sense of duty.

Biddle became the best-informed man on the board. In 1823, at thirty-seven, he was elected president. A period of brilliant expansion followed, carrying the bank to the zenith of its power and usefulness.

The terms of this institution's charter favored a revival of the Hamiltonian ideal of concentrating control of the financial affairs of the people of the United States in the hands of a few men. The capital was thirty-five million dollars of which the Government subscribed seven million. Control resided in a board of twenty-five directors, five of whom were appointed by the President of the United States, the remainder by the outside stockholders. The bank was designated the depository for all Government funds, though the Secretary of the Treasury might deposit such funds elsewhere provided he informed Congress of the reason. On these deposits the bank paid no interest, but it was required to pay a bonus of a million and a half dollars, to transfer public money without charge, and to perform other services.

A GREEK TEMPLE IN CHESTNUT STREET

The bank might issue currency, providing each note was signed by the president of the institution and redeemed in specie on demand. Such currency was receivable for Government dues, a privilege extended to the notes of only such state-chartered banks as redeemed in specie.

Biddle made the most of these monopolistic concessions. By refusing to recognize the notes of state institutions which did not redeem in specie, the great bank did much to end the fantastic era of American banking born of the post-war boom and subsequent depression. Government patronage kept the great bank's notes at par. The great bank made state banks toe the mark by calling on them, at the first sign of undue expansion, to redeem in coin. The result, in a few years, was the most satisfactory currency the country had yet known.

Broad as was its charter, Biddle enlarged the domination of his bank beyond anything intended by the compact. While the charter specified no limit to the currency of the bank, the provision that each note must be signed by the bank's president was calculated to keep down this circulation. Biddle got around the restriction by devising "branch drafts." In appearance these drafts looked so much like notes of the parent bank in Philadelphia that Mr. Biddle said not one person in a thousand knew the difference. Actually they were checks on the parent bank drawn by the cashiers of branches and endorsed "to bearer." The Government received branch drafts in payment for public obligations and they circulated as money. In theory the drafts were redeemable in specie, though in practice the bank made this difficult, thus stretching its charter again. Redemption at par was possible only at the branch of origin. The bank would place these drafts in circulation remote from their places of origin, western drafts being released in the East and *vice versa*, so that a holder wishing coin was put to the expense of transporting across the country both the actual notes and the specie received in return. As a result he usually cashed them locally, at a discount. Thus the great bank was able to expand its paper issues beyond anything permitted to a state bank.[1]

Among men of business these were usually accounted small defects, however, and the advantages derived from the bank's operations proclaimed to outweigh the drawbacks. Conservative and very able management tended to minimize fear of an inflation of its own issues, as the branch draft adventure easily made possible. The bank had rehabilitated the currency and reformed banking practices. Its system of swift and cheap exchanges moved crops and facilitated commerce. It simplified the operations of the Treasury. The bank's stock was a good investment for the public and for the Government. The bank avoided politics, setting another good example for state banks. During the presidential campaign of 1828, which saw many things lugged in that had no business there, the Bank of the United States was not mentioned.

2

Yet, it would seem, Nicholas Biddle had been quietly preparing for Jackson's election. In 1827 he had sent his confidential man, Thomas Cadwalader, to Nashville to supervise the establishment of a branch of the bank. This skillful agent went out of the way to make himself agreeable at the Hermitage. He appointed W. B. Lewis and George Washington Campbell as directors of the branch. The presidency was conferred on Josiah Nichol, the wealthy merchant whom General Jackson customarily left in charge of his financial affairs when absent from Tennessee. After Cadwalader's departure friendly letters from him reached the Hermitage, congratulating Jackson on the triumph of his party in a Philadelphia city election. The bank's agent solicited Old Hickory's opinion of the officers of the Nashville tributary, intimating that changes were contemplated. Jackson sidestepped the diaphanous invitation. "Never having been connected with Banks, and having very little to do with this one here, I feel unable to give you any satisfaction."[2]

The deliberate immersion of the Nashville branch in influences friendly to the political aspirations of General Jackson represented a departure from Biddle's usual political code.[3] It wore the aspect of a conscious design to propitiate Old Hickory who, for some time past, had been falling away from his old position of cordiality, if not to the bank, at least to the friends of the bank. Mr. Biddle's task was rendered the more delicate by the fact that, taken as a whole, the General's attitude toward the Bank of the United States had followed a rather mixed pattern.

So early as 1815, or perhaps earlier, Jackson had bought a few shares of stock in the Nashville Bank, the pioneer institution of its kind in

Tennessee. The ownership of these securities gave Jackson "banking connections," but only in the sense that every wealthy man had such connections. In 1817 Jackson had opposed, though not conspicuously, the admission of branches of the Bank of the United States to Tennessee, approving of a state law which imposed a prohibitive tax of fifty thousand dollars a year on such subsidiaries. In this he showed independence, as most of the wealthy class were in favor of a branch at Nashville.[4] In 1821, however, while Governor of Florida, he had forwarded a petition for a branch at Pensacola—not because, as he was later to explain, he then favored the bank, but because the commercial sentiment of the town favored it.[5] Considering the extent to which personal opinions flavored Jackson's official acts in Florida, the suspicion arises that, had the General's antipathy to the bank been very strong at the time, he would have mentioned it when he dispatched the petition.

Reviewing the situation after his retirement from the presidency, Jackson said his early opposition rested on "grounds of expediency as well as of constitutionality."[6] The constitutional objection is not hard to understand, for Jackson was bred in the Jeffersonian state-rights school. The objection as to the expediency of the bank, however, seems difficult to reconcile with the General's known views on banking matters at the time. From 1818 until about 1824, the bank issue had been bound up with the Relief Party strife throughout the West. Jackson also was bound up in that strife, inveighing against popular but economically unsound hard-times legislation, and against equally popular and equally unsound printing-press banks[7] whose efforts to relieve the depression in reality had prolonged it. This attitude definitely placed the General on the side of the Bank of the United States, which was the particular obsession of the masses.

Such was Jackson's position when his name went before the country in 1822. Almost immediately he had found support among the very people whose economic legislation and banking philosophy he opposed—a fact explicable only on the ground of Jackson's military popularity. By 1826 when his second campaign for the presidency was getting under way, the depression was wearing out, and the Relief politicians needed a new cause. In Kentucky and in Alabama, they went over to Jackson almost in a body, taking with them their hatred of the bank. That same year the friends of the bank in Tennessee, who had been Jackson's political consorts during the hard-times upheavals, had moved to repeal the prohibitory tax. But Jackson opposed this, and only over his protest was the tax repealed.[8]

This brought the diplomatic Cadwalader to town to superintend the opening of the Nashville branch. Although the Philadelphian was courteously received at the Hermitage, other pilgrims returning from the General's home during the winter of 1827-28 quoted Old Hickory as speaking out against the bank.[9] So it came about that he had returned to his position in 1817. Jackson's inconsistency amounted to this: in normal times he had decried the bank's monopoly of our financial concerns but, in the abnormal depression period, he had deemed it a lesser evil than proletarian finance.

3

After the election had passed off, however, friends of the bank among the General's intimates were able to assert themselves strongly enough to exclude from the inaugural address a contemplated criticism of the institution.[10]

But the subject refused to stay down. During Jackson's first summer in the White House, John Catron, a Nashville lawyer close to Jackson and anxious to rise in the political scale, published in the Nashville *Banner & Whig* a series of attacks on the bank in which he declared the question of recharter to be the most important public issue of the day. Addressing himself to "the cultivators of the soil and the laboring people in Tennessee," Catron suggested a democratic substitute for Mr. Biddle's monopoly: all directors to be appointed by the President and Congress; branches to be set up only on petition of state legislatures; branch directors to be appointed by the legislatures. Catron disclaimed acting on impulse. "Some of us, gentlemen, have for years been pledged to stand together boldly and firmly, when the day should arrive for the execution of a policy new in these States."[11]

The articles kindled a local debate, one anonymous dissenter from Mr. Catron's views asking the *Banner's* readers to "call to mind that General Jackson is very hostile to the Bank of the United States, and has expressed sentiments very similar to those" embodied in Catron's substitute plan.[12] This dissenter turned out to be better informed than most people suspected at the time.

In the autumn of 1829 the President reviewed with Felix Grundy, Amos Kendall and James Alexander Hamilton his objections to the bank, which he called unconstitutional[13] and "dangerous to liberty." The latter criticism, inspired by the great power of the privately-chosen majority of the directorate, dealt with what the bank might do rather than with what it had done. No charge was made that Mr. Biddle and colleagues had misused their authority, the President restricting himself to the contention that such imperial power in the hands of a few persons, not responsible to the electorate, was inadvisable.[14] After this review the President asked Grundy, Kendall and Hamilton to transmit their observations on his remarks for consideration in connection with the Executive's first message to Congress.

The memoranda tendered by the President's confidants reveal the unmistakable affinity between Jackson's notion of an alternative to the Bank of the United States and the crude skeleton of Catron. Jackson wanted an institution in which the Federal and state governments should own all the capital stock and appoint all the officials. With a simple bank of deposit, or a bank of deposit and exchange, this might conceivably work. At that point perplexities began to embarrass the President's friends. The limited services such a bank could offer the commercial body of society would by no means compensate for the advantages withdrawn by the suppression of Mr. Biddle's helpful system. Yet to expand a "people's institution" into a bank of issue and discount, empowered to loan out depositors' money and do a general commercial banking business brought one face to face with complications inseparable from public ownership. Would people entrust their private funds to a bank run by office-holders in preference to one run by financiers disciplined by the profit motive? If the public would not entrust its funds to such a bank should the Government do so? Destroy confidence in a bank and what is left of it? To indicate potential, yea actual, evils of Mr. Biddle's bank was one thing. To devise, even on paper, a better bank was something else—particularly for four persons no better equipped by training for the task than Old Hickory and his present coadjutors.[15]

Even the loosest thinker among them, Felix Grundy, drew back. "A great difficulty [is] how are the Directors of Branches to be appointed?" he said. "To authorize the Directors of the principal bank to appoint them would give them an alarming power. To say that the Congress should do it would destroy anything like accountability. . . . To say that the State Legislatures should do it would be a very unstatesmanlike Idea."¹⁶ Amos Kendall, an old Relief Party man, had, from the security of his editorial chair in Kentucky, slashed at the bank like Mamaluke cavalry. In the privacy of the President's council chamber, he displayed greater discretion. "I am not prepared to say that . . . [your plan] is the best that can be devised. . . . I could wish that . . . [it] might not *as yet* be thrown before the public."¹⁷

Last of the triumvirate to report was Hamilton, a successful New York attorney whose career is a discouragement to enterprise in the field of political augury. On that July morning twenty-five years before when they rowed Alexander Hamilton home from Weehawken, who would have been willing to foretell a day when the dying man's son should be leagued with Aaron Burr in politics? Yet, such was another manifestation of Martin Van Buren's conciliatory magic. Again, who would have had the temerity to predict such a son at work to overturn the monetary system which the first Secretary of the Treasury regarded as his most enduring monument?

Hamilton's effort to knit Jackson's views into a workable scheme showed a firmer grasp of the realities and more constructive thought than the attempts of Grundy and of Kendall. An appreciation of the difficulties of successfully supplanting individual initiative with Government regulation troubled the New Yorker. A Government-owned bank denied the privilege of making loans must inevitably prove unsatisfactory, he informed the President. But for such a bank to make loans would be to run "the risk of far greater evils."¹⁸

So much, briefly, for the travail of three staunch critics of the bank unexpectedly summoned to scrutinize both sides of the question.

4

Nicholas Biddle's first counter-move uncovered a friend at court in the person of Major Lewis. In response to a reference to the appointment of new directors at Nashville, Lewis, himself no longer a member of the subsidiary board, warmly commended the selections. "If your Directory is composed of men . . . in whom the people have *confidence*, it will have a tendency to prevent opposition."[19] Placation was too menial an artifice for the proud Biddle to sustain for long, however. When Secretary of the Treasury Ingham, Senator Woodbury of New Hampshire and Isaac Hill framed a provocative protest alleging discrimination by the Portsmouth branch against Jackson men the financier saw red. "[Are we] to suffer ourselves to be tramped down by the merest rabble?"[20] he snorted in private, while striking back at the complainants as he had been accustomed to strike in his early battles to create and to preserve the great prestige of his bank. The branch, said he, had enforced the rules of prudent banking upon borrowers without regard to person or political affiliation. The bank would continue to operate on those lines regarding it "better to encounter hostility than appease it by unworthy sacrifices of duty." This was followed by a communication in which Mr. Biddle's racing pen got away from him entirely. Distorting the remarks of the Secretary into an assertion of the Treasury's right to interfere with the election of bank officials and to plunge them in politics, the banker read Mr. Ingham a lecture on the evils involved.

Actually the shoe was on the other foot, Biddle having been the one to introduce questions of political expediency into the hallowed rite of selecting the bank's personnel. Mr. Ingham replied with dry assurance. "In the arena of party conflict which you almost tempt me to believe unavoidable, the hostility to the bank, as a political engine, would be preferable to its amity." Washington friends of the bank were alarmed and Biddle saw that he had gone too far. In a good-tempered rejoinder to the Secretary, the banker retraced his steps without ruffling a feather and began to lay himself out to captivate the Administration.[21] But for all that, a new and subtly disquieting atmosphere pervaded the classic corridors of the Greek temple in Chestnut Street. Nicholas Biddle felt insecure. His change of front was too abrupt, his technique a trifle obvious.

Postmaster General Barry received an extension of a long-due loan.[22] To Asbury Dickins, the chief clerk of the Treasury, whose confidential asides on Ingham's firm state of mind had had something to do with Mr. Biddle's altered attitude, the bank expressed its gratitude in even more substantial terms, permitting Dickins to settle a loan for fifty cents on the dollar.[23] The friendly correspondence with Lewis was resumed. The testimony of a Jackson partizan was adduced to contradict a story circulated by Amos Kendall that bank money had been used against Jackson in Kentucky. The cashier of the New Orleans branch journeyed to the White House to refute a like report from his jurisdiction, and the President professed himself satisfied.[24] A batch of Jackson politicians were named branch directors from one end of the country to the other[25] and, when Lewis signaled that the time was ripe,[26] Biddle displayed his ace.

This was a request for a recharter of the bank four years ahead of time, coupled with a proposal for achieving the darling ambition of Andrew Jackson to extinguish the national debt, the final payment to be made January 8, 1833, the anniversary of another feat of his. We owed forty-eight million five hundred and twenty-two thousand dollars. Biddle's brilliant scheme was sound, simple in its essentials, and advantageous to the Government—though, on a second reading, as one became more inured to the fascination of millions marching into the limbo, the advantages to the Treasury appeared to be rather less and those to the bank rather more than the face of the figures revealed. Still, it was a fair offer.[27]

Mr. Biddle, himself, called on the President. The meeting of these strong men was pleasant, the conversation apparently casual, though Biddle strove to store away in memory every word spoken. General Jackson said he was grateful for the plan for paying the debt, which he would unhesitatingly recommend to Congress except for the recharter feature. "I think it right to be frank with you. I do not think that the power of Congress extends to charter a Bank out of the ten-mile square." The President went on to express appreciation of previous services of the bank in the liquidation of the debt, and said he would refer to them in his message. Ingham's name came into the interview. "He and you got into a difficulty thro' foolishness," the President observed good-naturedly. "Oh, that has all passed now," said the banker, and the awkward subject was dropped. Immensely pleased with the tenor of the interview the financier coupled to his adieux a happy little speech anticipating the pride with which he would read the promised allusion to the bank's help with the debt. "Sir," said Old Hickory, "it would only be an act of justice to mention it."[28]

5

But, despite Amos Kendall's tactful remonstrance the President persisted in the determination to illuminate his message with another mention of the bank as well.

Obstacles intruded at every step. Called upon for an opinion as to the constitutionality of the bank, Attorney General Berrien suggested that the question be deferred. "In the meantime I am bound to state respectfully to the President my opinion that it is not expedient . . . to make the proposed communication to Congress."[29] The Secretary of the Treasury, though still smarting from his brush with Biddle, dealt even less gently with his superior's proposal to present a tangible substitute for Biddle's bank. With deep concern Mr. Ingham cited "serious objections" to the idea. Before embarking on "a new and untried system," he suggested "mature reflection" as to whether the existing bank could not "be so modified as to evils it is liable to and secure the benefits desired." Nine days remained in which to complete the message. "I do apprehend Sir that we have not time to enter safely upon this complicated question."[30]

Jackson met his advisers half way. Following congratulatory remarks on its services in the matter of the debt, he declared that, in view of the doubtful constitutional status of the bank and in view of its failure "in the great end of establishing a sound and uniform currency," it might be wise to study the practicability of a substitute "founded upon the credit of the Government and its revenue."[31]

As soon as he could recover from his surprise, Biddle began to provide fodder for the efforts of editors and of the more articulate body of the public who disagreed with the President. Though impressive, the showing did not disturb Jackson. "I was aware the bank question would be disapproved by all the sordid and interested. . . . Although I disliked to act contrary to the opinion of so great a majority of my cabinet, I could not shrink from a duty so imperious. . . . I have brought it before the people, and I have confidence that they will do their duty."[32] Old Hickory's conception of the people's doing their duty was that they should sustain him in the issue he had raised in their behalf. This he did not doubt would be the case for Andrew Jackson understood the mind of the inarticulate mass well enough to know that he had spoken for a vast multitude seldom heard in the columns of the press or in the forums of statesmen. As one correspondent assured him: "The open mouthed million already Scorn and revile the institution. . . . It is our business to wrench from its gripe . . . a monopoly of the circulating medium, . . . calculated to make the few richer, the many and the poor still poorer."[33]

Standing committees of the Senate and of the House took notice of the references in the message. Both reported in favor of the bank and recommended its recharter. Commenting on the President's charge that the bank had failed to establish a uniform currency, the House report, with some exaggeration, declared that it had *"furnished a circulating medium more uniform than specie."* The constitutional objection was dismissed with reference to Supreme Court decisions, and Jackson's idea of a bank founded on Government revenues condemned as a dangerous experiment in patronage.[34] Duff Green published the committees' findings without rising to the defense of the Executive's program.[35]

To dispute Jackson was seldom to convince him. A reading of the congressional reports merely entrenched him in the opinion that the bank was a "hydra of corruption, dangerous to our liberties everywhere."[36] Had the General known the secret history of those documents he might have employed less temperate language. Nicholas Biddle had supplied the House committee with much of the data upon which its conclusions were based; and he had written the Senate report nearly word for word.[37]

Fresh objections to the hydra occurred to the President. Was not Government patronage the mainspring of its great wealth and power? The average monthly balance of public funds in the bank's keeping was seven million dollars and it drew no interest. The profits from this and from all other operations of the bank enriched a comparatively small number of stockholders. Jackson thought the profits of such an institution should "onure to the whole people, instead of a *few monied capitalists* who are trading on our revenue."[38] But the problem of attaining this goal still defied solution. Lewis cheered Biddle with the assurance that in the end the President would be satisfied with a few modifications of the existing institution.[39] Since Biddle had Lewis's word for it, Jackson must have seriously considered this possibility. But it was not what he wanted. He wanted a new bank, owned by the people and answerable to them. To serve the needs of trade, however, this must be a bank of discount as well as of deposit. Hamilton was sent back to his desk to devise a satisfactory pattern. At the end of five months he reported no success. A bank of discount in the exclusive hands of Government functionaries would fail of public confidence, said Hamilton. Depositors would be afraid of political loans. "The untiring watchfulness of individual interest is always a better manager of pecuniary concerns than Governments."[40]

While General Jackson was in Tennessee in the summer of 1830 his friend and counselor of forty years, John Overton, accepted a place on the board of the Nashville branch. Josiah Nichol, president of the branch and steward of the Hermitage finances, entertained Old Hickory at his home. Primed by Biddle, the host regaled his guest with the excellences of the bank, forthwith reporting to his chief: "I am well convinced that he will not interfere with Congress on the subject of renewing the Charter. Altho on this subject he keeps his opinion to himself he speaks of You in the most exalted terms and says No Gentleman would manage the Bank better."[41]

Encircled by pressure and persuasion Jackson did not give up. Guarding his tongue, he clung to the conviction that there must be a way of reshaping the financial structure so as to diminish the unwholesome power wielded over the masses by an isolated coterie of almost unreachable and almost unteachable men. In the familiar Cumberland Valley the impress of that power met the eye of the President. After years of close management of its money in the West, the bank had launched an era of free credit, the Nashville branch loaning out two million dollars. Family connections of Old Hickory were borrowing. This rush to mortgage the accumulations of thriftier seasons artificially accelerated business. "Those who borrow are encouraged in their extravagant modes of dressing and living which are greater than their means will justify," Alfred Balch, a prosperous planter of the Hermitage neighborhood, informed the President. "Many are building little palaces, furnishing them in very expensive style, and . . . [dress their] children as though they were the sons and daughters of Princes."[42] Andrew Jackson knew well the old, old story of such economic cycles, ever enticing in their beginnings. He himself had one time succumbed to the blandishments of easy credit, emerging within jail bounds for debt. From that day forth an abhorrence of debt, public as well as private, had been a guiding principle of Jackson's life.

Undeterred by the barren nature of Hamilton's researches, by the misgivings of Ingham, and the elbow-plucking of Lewis, the old pioneer pressed on impelled by an untranslatable instinct which Andrew Jackson would follow when he would not follow reason. Throwing off all importunities that his second message to Congress should restrict mention of the bank to a commendation of its continued usefulness in the matter of the debt, the President wrote into that document that his views on the bank "as at present organized" were unchanged.

Thus until the opening of 1831 the Executive's fight for the reformation of the monetary system was waged without the visible support of another figure of national calibre. Actively arrayed on the opposite side were all the organized wealth and a good share of the choice statesmanship of the United States. Though sympathetic, the masses who had carried Jackson on their shoulders into the White House were not stirred to the fighting pitch; the sting of necessity, as in 1820, was wanting to stir them. Surveying these circumstances, Thomas Hart Benton felt that a turning point was at hand. "The current was all setting one way," he later said. "I foresaw that if this course . . . [should continue] the Bank would triumph." After many attempts to dissuade him, the Senator from Missouri obtained the floor in February, 1831. In a long speech he arraigned the bank as a kingly autocracy with perilous power over the welfare of the people and the servants of their republic. Designed for popular consumption, the speech was somewhat demagogic, which quality was rather out of character for Benton. For the grand problem perplexing the President, he proposed a simple solution. "I am willing to see the charter expire without providing any substitute for the present bank. I am willing to see the currency of the federal government left to the hard money mentioned and intended in the constitution."[43]

"The President aims at the destruction of the Bank," cried Biddle.[44] With the masses poring over Benton's production, the financier prepared to set presses whirring in his own endeavor to carry the fight to the people. A friendly senator, better grounded in the subject of proletarian prejudices and impulses, advised him to hold off.

At this juncture the dissimilar careers of Margaret Eaton and of John C. Calhoun, their fates curiously joined, imparted a fresh aspect to the seemingly unrelated affairs of Nicholas Biddle.

CHAPTER XXXII

MARTIN VAN BUREN'S MASTERPIECE

I

BEFORE his departure for Tennessee in the summer of 1830, the President reminded Duff Green of the growing lack of warmth for Administration measures displayed by the *Telegraph*. To this the editor stiffly replied that, before he could advocate the measures of the Administration, he must know what they were.[1] The implications of the remark were true only in part. Although much less of a fixture in the presidential study than during the hectic pin-feather period of the Jackson régime, Green knew where Old Hickory stood on all the issues. Yet the platonic nature of his ardor had been a source of increasing irritation at the White House. Plainly Green and his influential newspaper preferred the orbit of Mr. Calhoun. The situation caused less positive men to hesitate, but not Jackson. "We must get another organ," he instructed Lewis.[2]

Upon the President's return at the end of September, the Kitchen Cabinet had agreed upon a candidate for the editorship of a new paper. Passing over all the established journalists who had won their spurs in Jackson's service, the choice had fallen upon a comparative unknown, Francis P. Blair of Kentucky. This was the work of Amos Kendall. Blair had begun his public career as a leader of the Relief Party whose ideas of public finance had virtually bankrupted Kentucky, and had quite bankrupted Blair. In 1825 Blair had supported Clay, to the point of some useful connivance in the "bargain" arrangements, though that issue later separated them. As a contributor to Kendall's *Argus*, he had done good work for Jackson since 1827. His style was terse, trenchant, direct. He opposed the Bank of the United States, internal improvements and nullification. Mr. Blair's position on the bank could be described either as a brave adherence to principle or an example of ingratitude. Owing that institution twenty thousand two hundred and forty-four dollars, the Kentuckian had been allowed to settle for ten cents on the dollar.[3]

Jackson confirming the nomination, Blair's arrival was eagerly awaited, only Kendall and Barry of the White House coterie having so much as seen the paragon from the Blue Grass picked to overthrow Duff Green and his mighty *Telegraph*. Interest was not diminished by the fact that some of the President's friends thought he had acted hastily, arguing that a safer policy would be to bring Green into line and to heal, if possible, the breach with Calhoun. With Henry Clay rallying the forces of opposition in the West it was felt that this was a time to avoid rather than to invite family discord.

On a November afternoon W. B. Lewis, prepared by Kendall's testimonials to confront a personage somewhat larger than life, descended the White House stairs to greet the recruit. The towering Major beheld an underfed-looking individual with one side of his bony head done up in court plaster, the result of a stage upset en route. From the travel-stained appearance of his frock coat, Lewis surmised that the visitor had no other coat. Mr. Blair was thirty-nine years old, five feet ten inches tall and weighed a little over a hundred pounds. He shook hands shyly and spoke in a low, modest voice. But his blue eyes returned a glance unwaveringly[4]—a thing Jackson liked. The President put the newcomer at his ease and within a few minutes they were deep in talk. Though usually more apparent than real, Old Hickory's lack of reserve often shocked Mr. Van Buren. This time Lewis seems to have been uneasy as Jackson unburdened himself on nullification, the bank, Henry Clay and the Eatons. "And there's my nephew, Donelson. I raised him. Let him do what he will, I love him. Treat him kindly but if he wants to write for your paper you must look out for him." The visit concluded with an invitation to dinner.

In formal black the President stepped into the East Room to greet the guests of the evening. A group of ambassadors and other personages, superbly costumed, made their bows. Beside a wall stood an abashed figure in a seedy frock coat and bandages. Mr. Blair had accepted the President's offer of hospitality thinking the dinner would be as casual as the invitation. General Jackson drew him into the center of the company, and at the table placed him on his right hand.[5] Frank Blair knew the formulas of polite society. He was well-born, well-educated and had been married in the governor's mansion in Kentucky. In the fluency and range of his social conversation was little to suggest the slashing manner of a partizan editor.

Nor was this manner apparent in the first issues of *The Washington Globe* which began their appearance on December 7, 1830, the day after Congress convened. Jackson himself solicited subscriptions. "I expect you all to patronize the Globe."[6] Names rolled in and a modest amount of Government printing was shifted from the columns of the *Telegraph*. Yet the care with which the new journal avoided offense to the Calhoun wing escaped no one. The latch-string on the door of reconciliation was out. Studiously did the Vice President, too, consider his every act, feeling the crisis of a political epoch at hand. Without importuning he, too, left unobstructed the way to harmony in case Jackson should make the first move. Unctuous Felix Grundy and forthright "Tecumseh" Johnson of Kentucky actively spread the sentiment in Jackson circles that by dragging in Crawford, Lewis had gone too far with his conspiracy to advance Van Buren at Calhoun's expense. Bluff, ingratiating Sam Swartwout came down from New York to lounge in the White House study and descant oracularly on the virtue of peace in the camps of friends. With pardonable satisfaction the Vice President wrote: "Those who commenced this affair are heartily sick of it."[7]

One day Martin Van Buren was conversing with his chief while Ralph E. W. Earl plied the brushes on one of his countless portraits of General Jackson. A servant announced Colonel Swartwout. Excusing himself, the President returned after a while to say that "the whole affair was settled." The unfriendly correspondence that had passed between the President and the Vice President was to be destroyed, Calhoun was to dine at the White House, and the estrangement to be ended signally. Perhaps no American in public life has equaled Martin Van Buren's control of tongue, pen and countenance in the face of adversity. The Secretary of State offered his congratulations on the restoration of amity in the executive councils.[8]

In the light of his traditional stubbornness, Andrew Jackson's announcement to Mr. Van Buren is extraordinary. Willingly had the President lent himself to Lewis's underhand machinations about Florida, virtually convicting Calhoun of Crawford's charges without a hearing. Now all that was to be sponged out for considerations of party harmony. Was it possible that the President also was looking to Mr. Calhoun for help with the nullification snarl in South Carolina?

With the reconciliation publicly spoken of as an accomplished fact, Mr. Calhoun was impatient to complete the demolition of his rival. The Florida lapse notwithstanding, the South Carolinian could exhibit a longer record of support of Andrew Jackson than Van Buren. In two years' time he had seen the prestige of that record dimmed almost to the vanishing point, while the clever New Yorker had installed himself at the President's right hand. Now Calhoun decided to strike back.

Why destroy the Jackson-Calhoun letters if they could be made to destroy Van Buren? With Duff Green the Vice President prepared the manuscript for a fat pamphlet embodying the correspondence and the statements of several other persons disputing the charges of Crawford. The object was to expose Van Buren as a plotter of party dissension. Grundy and Johnson asked Blair to publish this production in the *Globe*. What a stroke that would have been! It failed because the newcomer refused to fish in any such troubled waters. Then Grundy got Eaton in a hotel room and read him the manuscript, requesting that he indicate any changes necessary to make it acceptable to the President. Eaton offered several suggestions. The men parted with the understanding that Grundy was to submit the alterations to Calhoun and Eaton to lay the whole matter before the President. Nothing to which the General might object was to be published. The following day Grundy sent Eaton a note saying that Calhoun accepted the changes. To this Eaton made no reply and Grundy took the Secretary's silence as an indication of the President's approval. In the belief that he was acting with the knowledge and consent of Jackson, Calhoun ordered the publication of the pamphlet, which appeared on February 15, 1831, accompanied by a suitable review in the *Telegraph*.[9]

Whereupon the thunderbolt that flashed from the White House fairly stunned the unfortunate authors. "They have cut their own throats,"[10] flared Old Hickory.

Blair's moment had come. He reached for his broadax. "A firebrand [has been] wantonly thrown into the Republican party. . . .

Mr. Calhoun will be held responsible for all the mischief which may follow."[11] Fifty Administration presses echoed the *Globe's* cry. John C. Calhoun's long and precariously sustained attempt to ride the Jacksonian tide into the presidency was over.

So soon as they could assemble their wits, Calhoun and Green learned the simple cause of their downfall. John Henry Eaton had not so much as mentioned the existence of the manuscript to Andrew Jackson: a humiliated husband's revenge.[12]

2

The Secretary of War stood in need of the morale-lifting stimulus this achievement afforded, for his domestic difficulties had broken out anew.

The recurrence had its inception in the unexpected return from Tennessee of Bellona, bent on claiming the place in the sun she fancied the President's championship assured her. In this she was disappointed. "M^{rs}. Ingham gave a splendid party last night and left out M^{rs}. Eaton. Barry & wife did not go. Lewis was not there. Donelson & Earl were there."[13] Matters were further complicated when the Secretary of the Navy and Mrs. Branch announced the marriage of their daughter Margaret to Daniel Donelson, a brother of the President's secretary. After the honeymoon, the old General took the couple in for a visit, temporarily altering the bachelor aspect of the White House ménage in a manner distasteful in the last degree to Mrs. Eaton.

With the Secretary's lady in town Jack Donelson saw no reason why he, too, should not enjoy the society of his wife. In a moving letter, the President asked Mary Eastin to prevail upon Emily to return. "The House appears lonesome. . . . [I miss] you and Emily and the sweet little ones. . . . First and last [the separation] has almost destroyed me."[14] But if she came Emily must change her attitude toward Margaret Eaton. This controversy was no longer a personal affair involving only the fate of the Secretary of War and Mrs. Eaton. It was a political affair by which John C. Calhoun hoped to "weaken me . . . and open the way to his preferment on my ruin."[15] And aside from that Emily must remember Eaton as "the able defender of your dear aunt."[16] Mrs. Ingham and Miss

Rebecca Branch also were importuning Emily to return, but for less pacific reasons.[17]

Donelson suggested a middle course to his uncle. Within the four walls of the White House, but not elsewhere, Emily would accord Mrs. Eaton the civilities due her husband's station. Sadly Old Hickory said this would not do. The vein of iron in the amiable young man's composition refused to yield further. Though they continued to eat at the same table, virtually all but official intercourse ceased between the President and his private secretary. In a final endeavor to reach an agreement on the overshadowing issue, they resumed communication with each other by note. On one day five missives passed between them.[18] Useless. At the end of a week, they were further apart than ever.

Then followed a tense interview with his secretary in which the General announced that ministers whose families felt themselves the social superiors of Eaton would be dismissed.

Donelson said the step would be "fatal." "It is that which your enemies are looking for."

Let them do their worst, Old Hickory blazed back. "I will show the world that Jackson is still the head of the government."[19]

Donelson submitted his resignation to take effect at the President's pleasure.[20] With a breaking heart the old man wrote out his acceptance.

"My D'r Andrew, . . . if you should not think it too great a sacrifice, for which I ask of none, I will be glad that you remain until after the meeting of congress. . . . For upwards of a year you [have] appeared to be estranged from me, . . . which under my bereavements made my tears to flow often. . . . When you leave, whatever cause I have to regret or complain you will carry my friendship with you, and my prayers for your happiness and that of your amiable family I can never cease to love. . . . Very affectionately your uncle and sincere friend. . . ."[21]

So shaken did this rupture leave the old Spartan that friends took alarm. Fresh efforts were made to induce him to promote Eaton into the effacing mists of the diplomatic service. Of these maneuvers Donelson was informed and he was asked to be patient. "I implore you by all that is sacred *not to desert our dear old friend*."[22] Even Emily was unable to hold out against her uncle's desperate display of loyalty, tragically mistaken though she thought it to be. In a touching letter she told her husband that, despite everything, she loved the old man as she had loved him in her childhood. She said she would rather support her loneliness than have Andrew leave his side. More than that, if it would help matters, she offered to swallow her pride, return to Washington, and "to please our dear old Uncle . . . visit Mrs E. sometimes officially."[23]

On the scene in Washington was a nephew of John Overton reporting to that sound advisor of the Executive. "Public opinion does not sustain him in relation to Mrs. E. . . . This is a game too insignificant for a President."[24]

The renewed pressure to send Eaton abroad coincided with the effort to bring Jackson and Calhoun together again. Anxious days, these, for Martin Van Buren and for his handy man Lewis. Young Overton met a Tennessee friend, Samuel Bradford, on Pennsylvania Avenue.

"Bradford," said he, "there must be a change in the Cabinet."

"Change! What change, sir, do you mean?"

"Eaton must be removed," said Overton, adding that otherwise one hundred congressmen would go home dissatisfied.

Bradford relayed the conversation to Jackson. The fire of battle brightened Old Hickory's eyes. "Let them come— let the whole hundred come on—I would resign the Presidency sooner than desert my friend Eaton."[25]

What might have happened remains in the realm of conjecture, for the Calhoun pamphlet and attending earthquake gave the hundred congressmen something else to think about. By the time they were ready to reconsider the affairs of Margaret Eaton, the protection of that lady's social position had miraculously ceased to be a policy of the Jackson régime.

3

Mr. Calhoun's luckless pamphlet having removed all public doubt as to General Jackson's choice of a successor, Martin Van Buren found leisure to form the conclusion that he had done his full duty to the Eatons. The Secretary of State was able to see what hitherto he had professed not to see, namely, that Eaton was a liability to the party and a drag on the Administration. Should he resign, it would not only relieve Jackson of a vast burden but afford an excuse for a complete Cabinet house-cleaning, whereby the retirement of Messrs. Ingham, Branch and Berrien would remove the last trace of Calhoun influence from the President's official circle.

But how to face Andrew Jackson with a scheme, however artfully disguised, that included the unseating of John Henry Eaton as Secretary of War? The problem proved too much, on the spur of the moment, even for Martin Van Buren's ingenuity. At length, he decided to set the train of events in motion during a horseback ride. However, Van Buren returned from the canter to confess to his son, his only confidant, that he had lacked the heart for it. Twice, thrice, four times the same thing occurred, and Abraham Van Buren began to rally his illustrious sire.

Emily's generous offer of accommodation had availed nothing. Andrew Jackson Donelson joined his family in Tennessee, leaving the President much alone, indeed. Again the New Yorker and his chief rode out. The General spoke with feeling on the situation in his household, making a brave effort to look on the bright side.

"No, General," said the Secretary of State, "there is but one thing can give you peace."

"What is that, sir?" Jackson asked quickly.

"My resignation."

To the last year of his life, Martin Van Buren could recall the look on the General's face as he replied: "Never, sir! Even you know little of Andrew Jackson if you suppose him capable of consenting to such a humiliation of his friend by his enemies."

For four hours Van Buren argued that his withdrawal would smooth the way to a solution of many vexations, and the engrossed equestrians reached Washington very late for dinner. Jackson asked the Secretary to call in the morning.

The President's greeting was cool. "Mr. Van Buren, I have made it a rule thro' life never to throw obstacles in the way of any man who desires to leave me."

This was the turn the New Yorker had most feared the thing might take in Jackson's mind. Again the Secretary put forth his powers of persuasion, reassuring the President that the offer to resign proceeded wholly from a sense of loyalty to the Administration.

Old Hickory took his friend by the hand. "Forgive me. I have been too hasty." The President asked permission to consult with Postmaster General Barry. Van Buren consented—adding that the advice of Eaton and Lewis might also be useful.

The following night the resignation of the Secretary of State was agreed upon. As Eaton, Barry, Lewis and Van Buren emerged from the White House, the thoughtful New Yorker said that he had ordered a supper spread at his home. On the walk thither Eaton suddenly stopped. "Gentleman, this is all wrong! I am the one who ought to resign."

Had Martin Van Buren written the Secretary's lines, he could not have improved on that speech.

Eaton's companions said nothing. Silently the four men entered the house. At the table the Secretary of War seemed depressed. Again he said that he should resign, and this time Martin Van Buren spoke.

"What would Mrs. Eaton say to this?"

The Tennessean said that his wife would agree.

But Mr. Van Buren said he must be sure. He could not entertain the Secretary's suggestion until the views of his wife had been ascertained.

On the next evening the four again sat down at Mr. Van Buren's well-stocked board. The Secretary of War announced that his wife "highly approved" of his decision to retire.[26] The President, however, did not intend to part entirely from his favorites. Van Buren was to become minister to Great Britain, Eaton to carry on as a senator from Tennessee as soon as Jackson could bring about a vacancy.

On April 20, 1831, the two resignations and the President's notes of acceptance were published in the *Globe*. "Many a cigar [was] thrown aside ere half consumed," remarked a visitor to the city, "that the disinterested politician might give breath to his cogitations. . . . But not all the eloquence of the smokers, nor even the ultra-diplomatic expositions from the seceding secretaries themselves could throw any light on the mysterious business."[27]

Before Van Buren left Washington he and the President called on Mrs. Eaton. "Our reception," recorded the ex-Secretary, "was to the last degree formal and cold." Leaving the house Old Hickory shrugged his shoulders. "It is strange." As careful a student of human nature as Martin Van Buren could hardly have said as much.[28]

4

The President requested and received the resignations of Messrs. Ingham, Berrien and Branch, thus realizing the ultimate object of Martin Van Buren's masterpiece. Deprived of the public printing, Duff Green obtained a loan from Nicholas Biddle's bank. Thrust into the ranks of the opposition, he began to enliven the *Telegraph* with allusions to Mrs. Eaton. Other anti-Jackson prints joined the game. "Has the Administration been ruled by a *Madame Pompadour* or a *Duchess duBarry?*"[29] From the seclusion of the North Carolina hills, John Branch issued a communication to the press, upon which Eaton challenged him to a duel, using the columns of the *Globe* for that purpose. The former head of the Navy Department replied in the *Telegraph* loftily declining to accommodate.[30] Then Eaton challenged Ingham who couched his refusal in terms of insult. For a day or so the ex-Secretary of War ranged the town with a pistol seeking to interview his late Cabinet colleague. When Ingham's sudden departure for Baltimore seemed to render a meeting unlikely, Eaton challenged Berrien.[31] Again the result was disappointing.

The refusal of these gentlemen to submit their convictions to the test of powder and ball confirmed Old Hickory in his estimate of them. Tramping the floor, he sputtered about the "treachery" of Branch and "the *disgraceful flight of Ingham*. The Wicked Flee when no man pursueth." Berrien's behavior was the last straw. *"What a wretch!* This *southern hotspur* will not fight—My Creed is true— there never was a base man a brave one."[32] These philosophical lines were addressed to a philosophical man, Mr. Martin Van Buren. Alone of the retiring Cabinet functionaries, the ex-Secretary of State had taken his departure from Washington without a firearm by his side, to pack his trunks for London and the Court of St. James's.

With his enemies quiet or out of pistol shot Eaton lingered in the capital blustering, brooding and drinking. Disillusionment descended like a shroud upon the deserted pair sitting alone in the massive residence opposite the British Legation. The few who, like

"A Fine Old Well-Battered Soldier"

The characterization of Fanny Kemble, the English actress, who saw Jackson during the nullification crisis in 1833. The portrait, by Earl, is owned by the Ladies' Hermitage Association, Nashville.

Two White House Young Ladies

Mary Eastin (left), grand-niece of Rachel Jackson, and Mary Ann Lewis, daughter of William Berkeley Lewis. These girls were on opposite sides in the Margaret Eaton "war" and, when Mrs. Eaton's temporary triumph resulted in the banishment of Miss Eastin and Emily Donelson, it appeared as if Miss Lewis might become mistress of the White House. From a portrait owned by Mrs. Sarah Polk Burch, of Nashville, a descendent of Mary Eastin.

MARTIN VAN BUREN'S MASTERPIECE

Postmaster General Barry, remained loyal suffered agonies of embarrassment. The Major's recent demonstrations of his fitness to resume official life as a member of the Senate had only the spice of novelty to recommend them. The President was deluged with letters urging him to send the Eatons away. "But it is a subject," Lewis confessed to Van Buren, "upon which *I* cannot venture to speak to him."[33] At length, in September, 1831, while Margaret scornfully kept to her dismantled house, John Henry Eaton called at the Executive Mansion. With a warm handclasp, Andrew Jackson took leave of the man his hot friendship had done so much to ruin.

Harmony in his Cabinet, tranquillity in his home: the President seemed a new person. "Old Hickory is as full of energy as he was at New Orleans."[34] Although leaving Washington only for a brief sojourn at the Rip Raps, he approved and started work on a plan for remodeling the Hermitage. The changes projected were so sweeping as to alter the entire appearance of the house. The east and west wings were enlarged and extended, the east wing housing the library and a study, the west wing a dining room that would seat a hundred persons. Across the south front was flung a two-story portico supported by ten slender Doric columns, the line of which was broken by ornately figured balustrades, upstairs and down. The whole effect was one of elaborate ornamentation in contrast with the unostentatious lines of the original house.[35]

Jack Donelson, Emily and their children returned to the capital in September, bringing Mary Eastin and another Tennessee cousin, Mary McLemore, whom Justice Joseph Story, seldom inclined to flattery where the White House ménage was concerned, found a "pleasant and well-bred" dinner companion.[36] Andrew, junior, and his crony, Andrew Jackson Hutchings, also returned. Though Hutchings's college career had again been interrupted at the request of the faculty, the young man was on his good behavior just now, trying for the favor of Mary McLemore. The President encouraged the suit, reminding Hutchings that a bright girl such as Mary would have none but a "scholar." Mary Eastin's man of the moment was a Navy captain. Susceptible Andy, junior, wrote ardent letters to a little Quakeress in Philadelphia.

In this melting atmosphere came a traveler from the Waxhaws with news of the neighborhood where Andrew Jackson was born.

He spoke of Mary Crawford Dunlap, a widow with grown children. Memory swept the old cavalier back to the autumn forty-seven years before when he had courted Mary Crawford on the bank of the tumbling Catawba. After the caller had gone, the President wrote a short note to Mrs. Dunlap asking her to honor A. Jackson by accepting a snuff box in exchange "for the endearing recollection of the pleasure he enjoyed in his boyhood in the agreeable society of herself."[37]

5

Once Van Buren had opened the way, the statesmanlike manner in which Jackson had gone about the reconstruction of his Cabinet presented a refreshing contrast to the fumblings of the grief-ridden sexagenarian who had two years before suffered a Cabinet virtually to be imposed upon him through the zeal of second-rate wire-pullers.

The War Office was again tendered to Senator Hugh Lawson White, the President urging "the claims of private friendship" as well as those of public welfare. White was invited to bring his son and daughter and take quarters in the Executive Mansion. By this appointment, Jackson expected to draw into the Cabinet an excellent man whom he had always wanted there, and to provide a senatorial toga to cover the abrasions of John H. Eaton's dignity. Therefore, when White surprisingly refused the warmly proffered berth, Old Hickory's aspirations were doubly disappointed. So the war portfolio fell to Lewis Cass, a ponderous, solemn-faced man with a large bald head. But he had lived a life that Jackson could understand. Crossing the Alleghenies on foot, riding the rounds of backwoods courts as a border lawyer, this New England-born frontiersman had achieved the governorship of the wilderness called Michigan when the title was a risky distinction. For eighteen years General Cass held that office, leaving a record not surpassed in the annals of our territories.

Mr. Van Buren's place went to the awkward-looking but accomplished Senator Edward Livingston of Louisiana. The new Secretary of State wrote a letter to his charming wife. "Here I am in the very cell where the great magician, they say, brewed his spells."[38] Capable Louis McLane, who two years before had urged Van Buren to desert Jackson's standard, was called from London to be Secretary of the Treasury. Smug Levi Woodbury of New Hampshire, a former senator of above average ability, took the Navy Department. Isaac Hill said the only thing against him was his aristocratic background. The appointment that excited the most surprise was that of a Marylander named Roger B. Taney as Attorney General. Seemingly Nature had not modeled Mr. Taney—pronounced Tawney—for greatness. His form was spare, excessively stooped and carelessly clothed. Near-sighted eyes gave a perpetual squint to a narrow countenance, revealing uneven, tobacco-stained teeth. His flat voice was not designed for oratory. At fifty-one Taney was so little known outside of the state of his birth that apparently he preferred the uncomplicated life of a lawyer and a country squire. The insignificant, gentlemanly Barry remained as Postmaster General.

The selections were well-received, except by the dwindling party of Mr. Calhoun which was sure Van Buren controlled the Government.[39] It was true that all the new officials favored the former Secretary of State as Jackson's successor; but Jackson would have appointed none who did not. On the other hand, Van Buren's departure tended to quell the impression that the New Yorker had had more to do with shaping Jackson's policies than was healthy for the Administration. Some minor changes following in the wake of major ones were of consequence. With the return of the Donelsons, William B. Lewis found a residence of his own.[40] His importance diminished, that of Kendall and Blair grew.

"I was fortunate enough," wrote Harriet Martineau, "to catch a glimpse of the invincible Amos Kendall. . . . He is supposed to be the moving spring of the Administration; the thinker, the planner, the doer; but it is all in the dark. Documents are issued the excellence of which prevents them from being attributed to the persons that take the responsibility; a correspondence is kept up all over the country; work is done with goblin speed which makes men look about them with superstitious wonder. President Jackson's letters to his Cabinet are said to be Kendall's; the report on Sunday mails is attributed to Kendall; the letters sent from Washington to remote country newspapers, whence they are collected and published in the 'Globe' as demonstrations of public opinion, are pronounced to be written by Kendall. . . . The moment I went in [to the drawing room] intimations reached me from all quarters, 'Kendall is here.' 'There he is.' I saw at once that his plea for seclusion (bad health) is not a false one. The extreme sallowness of his complexion, the hair of such perfect whiteness is rarely seen in a man of middle age. . . . A member of congress told me he had watched through five sessions for a sight of Kendall and had never obtained one until now. . . . In a moment he was gone."[41]

An attractive rendering of an attractive legend which Kendall's recluse-like habits did much to sustain. It would be more than discourteous to censure an English woman for putting too much faith in it; most Americans did the same. But Francis P. Blair spoke from a point closer to the throne. "Old Hickory . . . is to his cabinet here what he was to his aids [in the army]."[42]

6

The Indian removal program, by which Jackson hoped to limit the issue of nullification to South Carolina, had struck a snag. Though the Chickasaw treaty was ratified by the United States Senate and declared operative, the Choctaws had rebelled against the removal agreement which some of their chiefs had made under the compelling spell of Old Hickory's presence. Jackson did not press them, but tactfully reopened negotiations looking toward a new arrangement acceptable to the rank and file of the tribe. This fortified the Cherokees and Creeks in their attitude of refusal to discuss removal on any terms, relying upon the Supreme Court to protect their land rights.

The matter came before that tribunal unexpectedly when a Cherokee named Corn Tassel killed another Indian within the limits of the Cherokee Nation. A court of the State of Georgia, which in violation of the Federal treaties had extended its jurisdiction to the Cherokee territory, sentenced Corn Tassel to be hanged. On behalf of the condemned Indian, application was made to the United States Supreme Court for a writ of error on the ground that Georgia's action was unconstitutional. The writ was granted and Georgia requested to show cause for its infringement on Cherokee sovereignty. The

Georgia Legislature instructed local officers to ignore the mandate of the Supreme Court. To give this defiance reality, the involuntary author of the crisis, Corn Tassel, was hastily restrained from further participation, by means of a rope.

Opposition presses which had applauded, albeit grudgingly, the President's "Federal Union" toast uttered grave warnings. "The Union is in danger. Gen. Jackson must sustain the Court." Friendly journals remained silent or offered lame excuses. South Carolina Nullifiers welcomed Georgia as an ally, jubilantly proclaiming the "usurpations" of Federal power "bravely met" by a sister state.[43] When anxious members of the Union Party in South Carolina planned a demonstration of strength in Charleston on July 4, the Nullifiers started to get up a counter demonstration. Jackson received an invitation from the Unionists. He sent a letter expressing the hope that the "declarations inconsistent with an attachment for the Union" reflected nothing more serious than "momentary excitement." But should the case prove otherwise, he promised to sustain the Union "at all hazards."[44]

Vexing their brains for an answering stroke, the Nullifiers turned to John C. Calhoun. The Vice President was summering in his native State, his mind a maelstrom of doubt and indecision. In a "feverish" conversation with a friend, "he spoke of the three great interests of the Nation, The North, the South and the West. . . . He thought the period was approaching that was to determine whether they could be reconciled or not so as to perpetuate the Union."[45] For three years the views of the South Carolinian had been in a state of transition. Covertly he had guided the Nullifiers without repudiating the support of his nationalist friends. The time was at hand when he must march under the one banner or the other.

South as well as north, nationalists implored the Vice President not to desert them. With no view to affording "pleasure to friends of Gen'l Jackson," a distinguished Georgian warned Mr. Calhoun that Georgia would oppose South Carolina's brand of nullification. "I could not desire my enemy a worse employment than to appear before the people on this subject." The Georgian followed exactly the reasoning of Jackson's Fourth of July letter. "Nullification . . . destroys not the [tariff] law but the government. And for what? For evils a thousand fold magnified, . . . Civil War."[46] Duff Green had rushed off to New York in an effort to beat up manifestations of friendly northern sentiment calculated to divert the Vice President from an open espousal of the state sovereignty cause. Green wrote to the Governor of South Carolina that at one swoop the Nullifiers were placing the strongest possible cards in Jackson's hands and snuffing out the career of their first citizen as a national statesman. "[He asks]," related the Governor, giving a digest of the letter, "if we were all crazy, . . . if we intended to start open rebellion and insure the empire of the whore of Washington (Mrs E. I suppose)." The Governor was unmoved. "to these civil things my Reply was . . . that whether we decreed perpetual empire to the W—— of Washington or not, or started into rebellion, we would abate not one jot our zeal . . . for Nullification."[47]

The fire-eaters prevailed. Three weeks after Jackson's message was read in Charleston, John C. Calhoun published a lengthy *Address*, taking the leadership of the nullification movement. In this way the challenging nationalist of 1824 at last stepped down from his pedestal to marshal the forces of sectionalism, though not without an eye to some combination of elements in the unpredictable panorama by which he might reascend to power. Emboldened by this adhesion, the nullificationist majority in the Legislature surpassed that of Georgia by singling out Jackson for attack. "Is this . . . [body] to legislate under the sword of the Commander-in-Chief?"[48] Secession was declared a right of any state, and it was defended as being neither treason nor insurrection.

But unlike Georgia, South Carolina did not suit action to the word. Andrew Jackson smoked his pipe and waited. Despite an almost irretrievable reputation for acting on impulse, Old Hickory could be very good at waiting. Strange it is how comparatively few persons observed that as he grew older much that passed for impulsiveness had been thought out ahead. Before the Legislature at Columbia had finished its brimstoning, the President privately assured a northern friend: "The *Union will be preserved*."[49]

CHAPTER XXXIII

Mr. Biddle's Dilemma

I

On a sparkling September day in 1831 the four dappled grays, which all Washington and the countryside had learned to recognize, whirled a carriage over Maryland roads to the princely estate of Charles Carroll of Carrollton. Deferentially the President of the United States stood before the only man living who had signed the Declaration of Independence. Memory carried the visitor back to the August day in 1776 when he had read the stirring words of that paper to the people gathered in his Uncle Robert Crawford's yard. Andy Jackson, "public reader" of the Waxhaws, was then nine years old. The present occasion was Charles Carroll's ninety-fourth birthday.

On the ride to this meeting the President had remarked to Secretary of the Treasury Louis McLane that he did not intend to pull down Mr. Biddle's bank merely to set up a similar one—an allusion, no doubt, to the ambitions of certain New York and Boston capitalists suddenly conspicuous for their affable interest in Jackson's monetary program. The Executive went further. He abandoned his objection to the bank based on the fact that much of its stock was owned abroad.[1] Foreign-owned shares had no voting power.

These sentiments were pleasing to Mr. McLane, who recently had confided to a senatorial friend of the bank: "If the old Chief would consent to recharter what a glorious operation I could make for him!"[2] At Carrollton the bank became the subject of a general conversation during which Old Hickory was reported to have declared himself willing to risk re-election "upon the principle of putting the bank down. . . . No bank and Jackson—or bank and no Jackson."[3] The outburst probably bothered the assembled Carrolls with their heavy investments in bank stock more than it did the Secretary of the Treasury who was beginning to understand the Executive's state of mind.

General Jackson was still at sea as to the best means of achieving his contemplated financial reforms—whether to hew out a new instrument to that end or to remodel the present one. Perhaps for the personal satisfaction it would give him because of some hastily-considered remarks made early in the contest, Jackson would have preferred to displace the bank; but, in the light of Hamilton's failures and advice from other quarters, caution deterred him. The flare-up at Carroll's indicated nothing conclusive, for Jackson leaned now this way, now that. It may well be that he was smarting under the effect of a recent election in Kentucky where friends of the bank had made the institution an issue, winning the contest by frightening the mercantile and debtor class with predictions of the bank's extinction under Jackson.[4] Such a challenge to Old Hickory could hardly be expected to pass without notice.

If vacillation and uncertainty were states difficult for Andrew Jackson to support with composure, they were doubly so for Nicholas Biddle. At least the initiative was Jackson's. He led, as he was accustomed to do, but Biddle must follow, must accommodate, must suit his mood and actions to conform to the shifting course of the President—a poor tonic for the nerves of a man used to ruling what he surveyed. Occasionally Biddle rebelled, only to draw back and truckle.

In the business under review, General Jackson had kept a tight rein on his headstrong streak. He listened to Amos Kendall, Blair, Benton and Isaac Hill, it is true. But in his new Cabinet he had placed three men friendly to the Bank of the United States, one who opposed it and one who turned out a straddler with the idea of backing the winning horse. Jackson listened to those who favored the bank, and they were men of weight—McLane, Livingston and Cass. Nicholas Biddle tried to see to it that his supporters in the Cabinet should be well informed. He primed his agent in the Treasury, Chief Clerk Asbury Dickins, with arguments to insinuate upon the attention of his chief. Particularly was Mr. Dickins to direct notice to the precedent that a secretary of the treasury could take the lead in a recommendation for recharter.[5]

Messrs. McLane and Livingston trod up and down the White House stairs. Usually Donelson was on hand, and sympathetic with their work. Smoking a long-stemmed pipe, Old Hickory would sit nodding, correcting, interpolating, as his lieutenants bent over an untidy desk developing modifications of the bank's structure and sweeping powers, which were calculated to remove the Executive's misgivings as to constitutionality. The Government's stock was to be sold to the public, although five Government directors would remain on the board; the bank was to carry out its part of the national debt payment program according to the Biddle plan of 1829; branch drafts were to be abolished in favor of currency of the mother bank which designated officers should sign; the bank was to be denied the privilege of loaning money on merchandise, branches limited to two in a state, the corporation made suable in and taxable by states, and its real estate holdings limited.[6]

These were steps, and long steps, toward the ideal Jackson had in mind. Mr. Biddle's assent was a guaranty of their practicability. Still, the modifications did not insure all that the President wished to accomplish. He withheld from the hovering secretaries the vital promise to sign a bill for recharter on the terms outlined. But McLane encouraged Biddle to be patient, that this would come in time.[7]

2

The President had cause for hesitation. In the beginning, his skepticism concerning the bank had included no reflection on the abilities or prudence of Mr. Biddle as a banker. On those scores Jackson had praised him. But in 1830 the President had noted in the liberalization of western credit a movement that more than once had desolated the West, its borrowers and bankers alike. Was history to repeat itself? Some were beginning to fear so. The 1831 crop was short. Instead of paying, borrowers were forced to increase their loans. From the consequences of his first serious banking error, Nicholas Biddle struggled to extricate himself. Balances with state banks were drawn upon, foreign balances likewise. They were not enough. The East felt the shock as its funds began to flow west to meet mounting demands. Biddle notified the Barings in London that he must draw to the limit of his standing credit of one million dollars. Then he asked for an additional million. The position of the Bank of the United States was fraught with peril.[8]

Although a banking error, the new western loan policy strengthened Biddle's hands politically. As in the case of Asbury Dickins, a debtor was more likely than not to do the bank's bidding. Thousands of Westerners who were at its mercy had no desire to see the bank legislated out of existence and their loans called. The Kentucky election had established that. Indeed, it seems probable that this was one of the things Nicholas Biddle had in mind when in 1830 he suddenly made credit easy in the section where the bank was politically weakest.

Mr. Dickins performed his work well.[9] McLane came to the President with a proposal to recommend in his annual report a renewal of the bank's charter with modifications. Jackson heard the Secretary out and offered no objection. "With a view to show the Pres^t the full extent to which his report might lead," McLane pointed out that the pro-bank House Committee on Ways and Means might use it as an excuse to report a bill for recharter. The Secretary said that he could not oppose such a course. "I should be sorry," observed the President, "if the question were forced upon me in that way." But Mr. McLane was in good form that day. Before taking his departure, he obtained the President's acquiescence not to mention the bank in his forthcoming message to Congress.

Off to Philadelphia posted the Secretary of the Treasury to lay the whole case before Biddle. He proposed so to link, in his annual report, the recommendation for recharter with the tariff and the public lands issues "that even Mr Benton would not attack it." However, he advised the banker not to petition for the charter's renewal until after the presidential election of 1832, lest Old Hickory take it as a campaign "dare" to veto the bill. In that event he would probably veto it, the Secretary said. After a triumphant re-election the situation would be different. "What I see of Genl Jackson I think he would be more disposed to yield when he is strong than when he is in danger."[10]

Nicholas Biddle accepted this sage advice, and Louis McLane returned to Washington believing the bank question solved.

3

A fortnight thereafter, in November, 1831, Henry Clay arrived to take a seat in the Senate. Social and political admirers flocked about the likable statesman. Margaret Bayard Smith, wife of the president of the Washington branch of the Bank of the United States, perceived little to remind her of their last meeting at the wake over Mr. Adams's régime. Two years and eight months at Ashland had restored the Kentuckian remarkably. His countenance was "animated," his spirit borne up by imperishable ambition[11] and a rare fund of good nature. The acknowledged leader of the opposition, whose nomination for the presidency on the anti-Jackson ticket was conceded, Mr. Clay seemed the picture of confidence. In this, appearances obscured reality, for the Kentuckian did not feel confident. "Something, however, may turn up," he wrote to a friend, "to give a brighter aspect to our affairs."[12]

Mr. Clay had canvassed the field: tariff and nullification, internal improvements, Indians, public lands, foreign relations. By skillful and effective handling of these questions General Jackson had, on the whole, strengthened his Administration in every part of the Union, save South Carolina; and Henry Clay was unprepared to champion nullification. The manipulation of patronage, plus a discipline reminiscent of Jackson's armies, had transformed into an energetic and obedient party the loose confederation of discrepant elements which had carried Old Hickory into power.

There remained, then, the bank. On this question alone, General Jackson's course had lacked the precision and clarity essential to the consolidation of political strength. His opposition to the bank "as organized" had been insufficiently defined or exploited to rouse up the anti-bank strength of the country. Mr. Clay was inclined to doubt its potentialities for popular exploitation. He had seen the bank issue used to defeat a Jackson slate in Louisville. He believed it afforded the most promising material available for a contest in the nation at large. A less nimble logician might have been embarrassed by the fact that Mr. Clay, at various times a member of the bank's corps of paid counsel, had hitherto advised Mr. Biddle to withhold an application for recharter until after the election. Brushing this aside, the Kentuckian came out for immediate action on the question. Adroitly he concerted pressure on Biddle to repudiate his tacit arrangement with Jackson and throw the bank into the campaign. This was what Henry Clay had in mind when he expressed the hope that something would turn up to brighten his prospects. And it was *his* prospects that concerned Candidate Clay foremost.

4

Early in December the Cabinet assembled to hear the first draft of the annual message. Donelson read it, pausing for discussion and to note suggested amendments. At length he reached the subject of the bank, which the President had finally decided to mention—in his own way. Actually, this had come about through the over-zealousness of Mr. Biddle. When McLane had reported the President's earlier promise to pass over the bank in silence, Biddle had suggested that judicious mention would be preferable to silence. Then the banker undertook to dictate that part of the message. The President, he said, should avoid a repetition of his previous criticisms and merely say that "having on former occasions brought the question before the Congress it was now left with the representatives of the people."[13] But McLane had been unable to bring this off. The President had written into the message that his opinion of the bank "as at present organized" was unchanged—after which he was willing to leave the matter to "an enlightened people and their representatives."

The silence that followed the reading of this passage seemed to denote unanimous approval until Attorney General Roger B. Taney remarked that the language proposed might suggest that the President had gone over to the side of the bank. McLane and Livingston disputed this. It was Taney's first Cabinet controversy, but after a mild beginning the countrified-looking Maryland lawyer warmed up. McLane warmly opposed him. Taney stood alone, not even Barry, the old Kentucky Relief Party man, uttering a word. After some indications of impatience, the President interrupted to say that he did not mean to imply that he would sign any bill that Congress might pass; nor did he mean that he would veto any bill. Donelson picked up the manuscript and read on, a sign that the bank paragraph was to remain intact. Taney left the meeting feeling that the Chestnut Street influence had been too much for him.[14]

The almost simultaneous appearance of the message and of McLane's report, recommending recharter, threw the anti-bank people into a spasm. Frank Blair leaped on the report with such vigor that McLane threatened to resign. The result was the softening of a further word of censure which the editor had ready for the typesetters.[15] "Mr. McLane and myself understand each other," the President reminded James Alexander Hamilton, another anxious member of the anti-bank group "and have not the slightest disagreement about the principles which will be a sine qua non to my assent to a bill rechartering the bank."[16] The nervous New Yorker thought of taking a fast vessel for England to consult Van Buren.

Mr. Clay also was disturbed, for he had committed himself and his party to a campaign predicated on Jackson's hostility to the bank. Six days after the President's message had gone to Congress the Clay party, under the new title of National Republican, had made its nominations, condemning Jackson as a foe of the bank. Mr. Clay's running mate was John Sergeant of Philadelphia, chief of the bank's legal staff. Should Jackson and Mr. Biddle come to terms, as it seemed that they were about to do, this fine work would be for nothing. Railing against Jackson's "deep game" to coast through the campaign without committing himself on the bank question, the Kentuckian intensified the effort to destroy the possibility of an accord between Mr. Biddle and the Administration, and to this Daniel Webster lent his practised hand. Friends of the bank with no ax to grind begged Biddle to stand fast.

Pulled this way and that, the banker sent Thomas Cadwalader to study the situation on the spot. For seven days and nights, without resting on Christmas, the indefatigable agent button-holed senators, congressmen, party managers and Washington nondescripts, covering page after page with cryptic tabulations indicating the expressed, probable or supposed sentiments of each of the two hundred and sixty-two members of Congress. At the outset McLane warned Cadwalader that Jackson would return a bill with his veto, which the Senate would sustain. The bank must wait until after the election. Then the Clay people began their work, which was finished to their satisfaction when Peter Livingston, a brother of the Secretary of State, but a supporter of Clay, whispered that Edward Livingston, McLane and Cass would prevent a veto. Cadwalader wound up the reports to his chief with a recommendation for the immediate submission of the question.[17]

One of Mr. Biddle's recurrent moods of boldness was setting in. Chafing under the necessity of bending his will to that of General Jackson, the banker grew captious. So small a thing as the President's insistence on his own rather than Biddle's formula for the message was made a subject for complaint.[18] No sooner did Cadwalader's last memorandum reach Philadelphia than, with a flaring gesture of independence, the financier plumped for recharter. "The bank cares not whether . . . [Jackson] is benefitted or injured," he proclaimed. "It takes its own time & its own way."[19]

Henry Clay's scheme had succeeded. Mr. Biddle had delivered the destiny of his bank into the keeping of a desperate candidate panting for an issue.

5

The eve of the battles, whose littered fields were to exhibit President Jackson's greatest contributions to the American saga, saw Old Hickory in the finest fighting trim since he had taken the oath three years before. His step was springier, his eye brighter. Something of the old banter reanimated his social conversation, making it, indeed, difficult to remember the heart-crushed old man of 1829, hauled about by second-rate politicians.

Yet the striking levels of success to which he had raised his Administration were not the sole causes of the new spirit which infused the veteran. For years the bullet which Thomas Hart Benton's brother had fired into Jackson's left arm in 1813, had periodically troubled him, at times rendering the arm almost useless. Physicians who concluded that the ball was poisoning Jackson's system hesitated to operate for fear of the shock to the heart against which lay another bullet which could never be disturbed—Charles Dickinson's. In January, 1832, when a visiting surgeon from Philadelphia expressed the opinion that the Benton bullet could be safely removed, Jackson asked him to take it out at once. The work was done in army field hospital style. Baring his arm to the shoulder, Old Hickory took a firm grip on his walking stick. In a few minutes the operation was over, and the President appeared at a small dinner party that evening.[20] His general health improved at once.

A story went around that Frank Blair had got hold of the bullet and offered it to Senator Benton. The Missourian declined the token, saying that Jackson had "acquired clear title to it in common law by twenty years' peaceable possession."

"Only nineteen years," corrected Blair.

"Oh, well," retorted Benton, "in consideration of the extra care he has taken of it—keeping it constantly about his person, and so on—I'll waive the odd year."[21]

Another measure to the General's cup of happiness was the continued felicity of his domestic circle, to which had been added a daughter-in-law.

Her arrival was a surprise. Early the preceding autumn, the fact that the vulnerable heart of Andrew, junior, had been touched by a girl in Philadelphia seems to have been occasion for little family comment. Nor was much attention paid to the matter when, late in October, the young man departed on a trip to the Pennsylvania city. Then came a letter to which General Jackson dispatched a reply that cost some effort.

"My son, . . . the sooner this engagement is consummated the better." Jackson was never a believer in long engagements. "You say that Sarah possesses every quality necessary to make you happy. . . . You will please communicate to her that you have my full and free consent that you be united in the holy bonds of matrimony; that I shall receive her as a daughter, and cherish her as my child. . . . Present me affectionately to Sarah for, although unknown to me, your attachment has created in my bosom a parental regard for her. That, I have no doubt, will increase on our acquaintance. I am
"Your affectionate father. . . ."[22]

It increased profoundly. An orphan of Quaker heritage, Sarah Yorke was small, of dark complexion, gentle voice and gentle manner. Except as the wife of the President's son, she would have been inconspicuous in the gay company that centered about Emily Donelson and Mary Eastin. She conquered the old General's heart as she had conquered young Andrew's. A large portrait of Mrs. Jackson by Earl hung in the General's bedroom. But the likeness he prized most was a miniature, painted by Anna C. Peale in 1815, which he wore about his neck suspended by a black cord under his garments.[23] At night after the General's mulatto body-servant, George, had assisted his master into a long white nightgown, Jackson would remove the picture and prop it up on a bedside table so that it might be the first thing to meet his eyes on awakening. In bed the General would open the worn Bible which had belonged to Rachel, and read a chapter before George snuffed the candle and stretched out to take his own sleep on a pallet on the floor beside the bed of his master. Sarah had not been in the house a month until she was permitted to hold the doubly sacred Book in her own hands and read the chapter to her "father," as she ever called him.[24]

The General's stories of Tennessee life thrilled Sarah. With a view to introducing to the ways of slavery this little Northerner who must one day be mistress of the Hermitage, Jackson gave her as a personal maid a bright young negress named Gracie. Within a few weeks, so great was his confidence in Sarah, Jackson acceded to the wish of the young couple to depart that spring to take formal charge of the plantation. "I mean to throw the care of the farm on . . . [Andrew], never more [to] pester myself with this worlds wealth— My only ambition is to get to the Hermitage so soon as the interest of my country . . . will permit me, and there to put my [spiritual] house in order and go to sleep along side my dear departed wife."[25]

The old soldier was ready to lay down his arms.

6

And he would lay them down in triumph—at the very hour when Henry Clay once would have had America believe that the "military chieftain," drunk with power, would only be ready to begin his real work of destruction in the field of popular liberty. Is it any wonder that, after three years of Jackson as President, the Kentuckian was obliged to bring forth a new issue for 1832?

Yet one may well ask: If General Jackson were sincere in his protestations about retirement why had he consented to stand as a candidate for re-election?

The answer to this question was known at the time to only two men—Andrew Jackson and Martin Van Buren.

Jackson had consented to run again to vindicate the record of his tenure of office. The New Yorker was to be the second man on the ticket. At the end of the first, or, at most, the second year of his new term, Jackson said that he intended to resign, by that means elevating Martin Van Buren to the chief magistracy. The magnanimous proposal, which stands alone in the history of American politics, was made in the fall of 1830 during a horseback ride over the Georgetown hills with the then Secretary of State. Almost overcome by the generosity of his superior, Mr. Van Buren, nevertheless, saw in the proposition "nothing but danger" to himself. Admitting the White House to be within the scope of his ambition, the Secretary said that he preferred to take his chances at the polls. Otherwise "enemies . . . would stigmatize the proceeding as a selfish intrigue designed to smuggle me into the Presidency and to gratify his [Jackson's] own resentment against" Calhoun. So tenaciously did the Secretary urge his point that, at length, the General admitted the possibility of having insufficiently considered the matter from Mr. Van Buren's point of view.[26]

Yet Jackson did not give up the idea. A year later he wrote about it to Van Buren in England. Three months thereafter, with delegates assembling at Baltimore to nominate Henry Clay, he wrote again, employing stronger terms.[27] In 1830 Jackson's proposal might have been susceptible of the interpretation of proceeding from weakness, for the current crisis of the Eaton affair had the old man in a wretched state of mind and health. But the end of 1831 saw the prestige of the Administration vastly improved, the President's family troubles solved, his health better. The bank issue seemed on the way to settlement. Of major matters pending only nullification remained, with which Old Hickory did not mistrust his ability to cope should South Carolina attempt to execute her threats. No possibility of misinterpreting the renewed proposal existed; it came from a consciousness of strength.

7

With these thoughts in his head, it was natural that General Jackson should have observed closely the performance of his Minister to the Court of St. James's. It was satisfactory, Martin Van Buren being in every way a credit to his country. Opposition eyes also ranged across the Atlantic. His opponents did not guess all that was in Jackson's mind with reference to the New Yorker, but this much they did know and it was enough to excite their ire: Van Buren would be the candidate for Vice President, and in 1836 he would be Jackson's choice for the succession. Clay, Calhoun and Webster joined in a plan to diminish the popularity of that too-fortunate politician.

Mr. Van Buren's had been a recess appointment. The three allies proposed that the Senate refuse to confirm the nomination, thus obliging the President to recall his minister with a stain on his political shield that would render him ineligible, as they imagined, to the second place on the Jackson ticket.

In January, 1832, a fastidious young idler from Philadelphia named Henry Wikoff visited the Senate gallery. He saw Mr. Clay "with his tall stately form, his urbane demeanor and courageous eye, indulging ever and anon in a pinch of snuff while listening to a member of the Opposition; Webster with his broad expanse of brow which looked like the very dome of thought, his tranquil mien and stolid figure; Calhoun, erect, slim, stern . . . and resolute; . . . the polished Hayne; . . . the stalwart Benton." He did not see so very much of them, however, because the galleries were cleared and the Senate went into executive session to consider, as all Washington knew, the nomination of Martin Van Buren.

On the evening of January 25, Mr. Wikoff called at the White House with a letter of introduction to the President. As General Jackson was presiding at a dinner party, his visitor was asked to wait in the Red Room—"a lofty, well-proportioned apartment," as Mr. Wikoff observed, "richly furnished in damask of the colour which designated it. . . . It was not long before the doors were thrown open and General Jackson entered at the head of his company, talking and laughing with much animation. . . . Seating himself near the fire, his friends formed a group about him. I was absorbed for some minutes scanning the face and mien of this remarkable man. In person he was tall, slim and straight. . . . His head was long, but narrow, and covered with thick grey hair that stood erect, as though impregnated with his defiant spirit; his brow was deeply furrowed, and his eye, even in his present mood, was one 'to threaten and command.' His nose was prominent and indicated force. His mouth displayed firmness. His whole being conveyed an impression of energy and daring." A touch on the elbow roused the young man from his contemplation. A friend offered to present him to the President. Before they could reach the Executive, however, another man entered the room hurriedly and gained his ear. Jackson sprang from his chair.

"By the Eternal! I'll smash them!"

The startled guests demanded to know what had happened. They learned that the Senate had rejected the nomination of Martin Van Buren.[28]

Benton brought intimate particulars of the secret sessions. A tie had been purposely contrived to give Mr. Calhoun the distinction of casting the deciding vote. Descending from his dais the Vice President had pronounced Martin Van Buren's obsequies. "It will kill him dead, sir, kill him dead. He will never kick, sir, never kick." All along Benton had been of a different opinion. When the vote was announced the Missourian turned to Gabriel Moore of Alabama. "You have broken a minister and elected a Vice President." "Good God!" exclaimed Moore, as the light began to dawn. "Why didn't you tell me that before I voted?"[29]

Billy Carroll of Tennessee furnished tidings from the West, where Van Buren had never been strong: "Two men know him now to one that knew him sixty days ago."[30]

8

"You wish to know, you say, precisely how the old Genl stands the wars," wrote John Campbell of the Treasury Department to his brother David in Virginia.

"The evening before last I spent with him. When I went in there were some 20 or 30 ladies & gentlemen seated and standing He was in the midst of the ladies in as fine a humour as I ever saw him He took me by the arm in his usual gallant style and introduced me to all the Ladies with whom I was not acquainted. . . . He then handed a young lady to the piano and stood by her while she play'd several airs. . . . He paid her some pretty compliments and then handed her back to her seat again. . . .

"At eight o'clock the whole party went off to a ball except [the President], Genl Gibson of the Army and My self. . . . We drew our chairs around the fire. . . . I asked [the President] if he was entirely relieved of pain since the ball was extracted [from his arm]. He reply'd that the strength of his arm had been completely restored so that he could manage a horse [with it]. . . . The old hero gave a very minute account of the manner in which his arm was broken *all to pieces* in his conflict with Benton [and] of its dreadful situation when he took command of the army to go into the Creek country— It remain'd in a sling for Six Months In a violent effort to draw his sword to cut [the retreating Colonel] Stump's head off in the battle of Enichopco [Enotachopco] . . . he tore the broken bones of the arm to pieces again."[31]

In April, 1832, the White House lost its bright-eyed ingénue when Mary Eastin, throwing over her navy captain after a wedding date had been set, was married to Lucius J. Polk, a boy from home, and set out for Tennessee to live.[32] Jackson missed her, but not so greatly as he missed Andrew, junior, and Sarah when they departed. The alterations at the Hermitage were finished and Jackson made a heavy purchase of furniture in Philadelphia to fit it out in style for Sarah. Andrew carried with him a compact manual on plantation administration, written in the General's own hand and concluding: "You will have to begin to learn the wants of a family & supply it— this will require oeconomy & care which you will have to attend to if you expect to get through life well by always knowing your means & living within them. . . . Write me fully as to the situation of all things— the health & condition of the negroes, the appearance of my stock, . . . the colts in particular, their form size and which promises best."[33]

And he wrote to Sarah: "I hope this night you are reposing under the peaceful roof of the Hermitage . . . and that you have found . . . [it] a pleasing home. . . . I wish I was there. I have spent a lonely time since you left me. . . . Do write me my Dr Sarah. . . . When alone in my room your letters will be company for me."[34]

The old man's thoughts were much on Tennessee. He said he envied Eaton his retirement.[35] The General might have spared himself. Margaret Eaton was not a social success in Tennessee, and many of the attentions she received bore the forced aspect of obedience to the wishes of husbands who desired to retain the good opinion of Andrew Jackson. Time hung heavily on the hands of the former Secretary of War whose distant view of the alignment of forces for the coming campaign filled him with wistful longing. Only four short years ago— Ah, but he could still do something.

The General had persevered in his ambition to build up a string of race horses from the Truxton strain. For the past year he had kept a number of colts in the White House stable. They were entered at the National City and other nearby tracks under the name of A. J. Donelson, but it was no secret to whom they actually belonged. Though none of them won an important race, the supervision of their care and training proved a wholesome relaxation for the President. In April, 1832, Major Eaton and his wife, stopping at the Hermitage, learned that on the day before, Steele, the overseer, had started on the road to Washington three horses and three colored jockeys. Behaving with the promptness that had once characterized his actions in larger concerns, the Major directed Steele to call back the horses. Then he wrote to Jackson. With a campaign coming on, further display of the President's sporting proclivities would be inadvisable; and to run the horses under Donelson's name would deceive no one.[36]

Old Hickory did not criticize the well-intentioned action of his friend. But he ordered the colts and jockeys sent on to Washington.[37]

Andrew Jackson Hutchings also put in an appearance at the Executive Residence, with his fourth notice of dismissal from a seat of learning—this time the University of Virginia. Old Hickory was discouraged in his effort to educate his ward. Giving the boy two hundred dollars, Jackson sent him to Tennessee to learn plantation management under the eye of John Coffee.[38] Other callers were W. H. Sparks and his bride of Natchez. Mrs. Sparks was the youngest daughter of Abner Green in whose home near Natchez Rachel Robards had found refuge at the end of the famous flight from Nashville. At the sight of her, memories more than forty years old engulfed Andrew Jackson.

"He did not speak, but held her hand . . . gazing intently into her face. His feelings overcame him and clasping her to his bosom he said, 'I must kiss you my child for your sainted mother's sake'; then holding her from him, . . . 'Oh! how like your mother you are— She was the friend of my poor Rachel when she so needed a friend.' "[39]

9

On January 9, 1832, three days before the Benton bullet was cut from Jackson's arm, Nicholas Biddle surprised the Administration and some of his own friends by memorializing Congress for the recharter of the Bank of the United States. The votes seemed at hand to pass a bill in both houses. The Clay forces felt that should Jackson veto the measure he would lose Pennsylvania in the coming election, and should he fail to veto it he would lose in the South and the West. The immediate effect, however, was to offend McLane and other pro-bank men in the Administration, and to restore to life all Jackson's personal antipathy to the "monster." "I will prove to them I will not flinch."[40]

It was Biddle who flinched, making overtures to McLane and Livingston. The bank, said Mr. Biddle, would go nine-tenths of the way to meet the President. "Let him write the whole charter with his own hands."[41] Bank men and Livingston put their heads together on the subject of modifications of the charter and, unaware that the President had begun to lose confidence in his Secretary of State,[42] Biddle's mercurial spirits rose. He had begun to perceive the difference between an alliance with Henry Clay and an alliance with Andrew Jackson.

But he was too late. Though the Livingston negotiations probably would have fizzled out in any event, Thomas Hart Benton made certain of this by proposing, through Representative Augustin S. Clayton, a new member from Georgia, an investigation of the bank by a committee of the House. Speaking from notes he endeavored to conceal because they were in Benton's handwriting, Clayton enumerated seven thumping violations of the bank's charter and fifteen "abuses" of the same.[43] The bank party was caught off guard. To accede to an investigation would be to surrender the initiative and go into the campaign fighting a defensive battle; to oppose an inquiry would be tantamount to an admission of guilt. There was nothing to do but yield. Whereupon anti-bank forces scored another victory, obtaining four places on the committee to the bank party's three.

This body was allowed the inadequate space of six weeks in which to conduct its researches. The result was three reports, one by the four majority members, one by two minority members and one by ex-President John Quincy Adams who had begun his long and singular career in the House. If the findings of the majority are to be believed fully—and they cannot be—virtually every charge when Benton had beguiled the inexperienced Clayton into laying before the House, was sustained. Yet these members, overwhelmed by a mass of abstract data thrown upon them by the bank in what appears to have been an attempt to confuse, did establish the dangerous, extra-legal nature of the branch draft system and other questionable points in the bank's conduct, such as leniency in the matter of loans to congressmen. Moreover, they reached behind the scenes and uncovered an interesting corollary to the abrupt switch of the New York *Courier and Enquirer*, the leading Jackson journal in the East, from an antibank to a pro-bank policy. A loan of fifteen thousand dollars, made in an irregular way for purposes of concealment, had immediately preceded this change of heart. And once in the bank ranks these useful journalists were quickly advanced thirty-five thousand dollars more.[44]

Where the majority report sought to prove everything, the minority reports sought to refute everything—another impossible task. In this the minority members enjoyed the warm co-operation of the bank officials, including Mr. Biddle, whom later events were to reveal as a too-accomplished explainer, if not a deliberately untruthful witness.[45]

With the bank issue in the campaign, Jackson placed his imprimatur on the report that favored his cause.

10

The investigation over, Biddle assumed personal command of the bank's Washington lobby and prepared to drive a bill for recharter through Congress. But unusual moderation tempered this act of defiance. Several amendments to the existing charter were incorporated —all in keeping with Jackson's ideas, though stopping short of the changes to which Biddle had consented the previous autumn. They included, however, a rectification of the important branch draft evil. This conciliatory policy won a few waverers to the bank's side, and even inspired some hope that Jackson might approve the bill. Without sharing this optimistic expectation, Mr. Biddle drew encouragement from the fact that McLane, Livingston and Cass had begun to urge upon the President that a veto should be mild, opening the way to further negotiation once the election were over and the issue out of politics.

An interested spectator of these negotiations was Attorney General Roger B. Taney who, since his reverse in December at the hands of the pro-bank members of the Cabinet, had not mentioned the subject to the President. The events of the seven months intervening had turned Mr. Taney more than ever against the bank. En route to court one morning, the Attorney General shared a hack with a member of the House who was supposed to be one of the President's personal friends. The member said he was going to make a speech against the bank bill, and asked Taney for pointers. When the bill came to a vote, Mr. Taney was surprised to see that the Representative in question had voted for it. Inquiry elicited the information that he had obtained a loan of twenty thousand dollars from the bank.

With the final passage of the bill only a matter of days, Mr. Taney visited the Executive Residence. He told the President that in his opinion the bill should be met with a positive veto which would close the door to any expectation that, at some future time, Jackson would agree to a continuation of the bank. Because he would be in court at Annapolis when the matter should come to the Executive for consideration, the Attorney General had put his reasons in writing. Jackson accepted the paper and said he would be glad to read it, but gave no indication as to his own attitude.

On July 3, 1832, the bill passed the House and Mr. Biddle's friends gave him a banquet. General Jackson summoned his Cabinet, with the exception of Taney who was in Annapolis. He had decided, he said, to return the bill with an uncompromising veto. Not a member of the official family sustained his chief. Importunities were renewed for a veto that would leave Jackson free to approve a modified bill in the future. Offers were made to help in framing such a message. Declining this assistance, the President dismissed the council and set Amos Kendall to work on a message of flat rejection. Kendall turned in a document which Jackson passed on to Donelson for revision. When this proved beyond his nephew's depth Old Hickory sent for Taney.

The Attorney General began his labors in seclusion at the White House, few being aware of his return to the city. On the second day Secretary of the Navy Woodbury, the fence-straddler, came to offer his services. On the third day the message was finished—the work of Taney, Jackson, Kendall and Donelson. On July 10, Jackson sent it to the Capitol.[46] At this juncture Martin Van Buren arrived from London. The President had overtaxed his strength and taken to bed. Holding the deposed diplomat's hand in one of his own and passing the other through his white locks Old Hickory said, "The bank, Mr. Van Buren, is trying to kill me, *but I will kill it.*"[47]

Such was the purpose of the message, destined to become the most widely read and discussed presidential veto in our annals. Since it was, in an important sense, a campaign document designed to cope with Henry Clay's stratagem in bringing the bank into the political vortex, the production contained unbalanced statements and weak though popular arguments. But it also contained sound and cohesive arguments—against the constitutionality of the bank and against the expediency of concentrating so much power in the hands of so few persons irresponsible to the electorate. Nor was this all. With deep and moving conviction, the message gave expression to a social philosophy calculated to achieve a better way of life for the common man.

"Distinctions in society will always exist under every just Government. Equality of talents, of education, or of wealth, can not be produced by human institutions. In the full enjoyment of the gifts of heaven and the fruits of superior industry, economy, and virtue, every man is equally entitled to protection by law. But when the laws undertake to add to these natural and just advantages, artificial distinctions, . . . to make the rich richer and the potent more powerful, the humble members of society, the farmers, mechanics, and laborers, who have neither the time nor the means of securing like favors to themselves, have a right to complain of the injustice of their government. Its evils exist only in its abuses. If it would confine itself to equal protection, and, as heaven does its rains, shower its favors alike on the high and the low, the rich and the poor, it would be an unqualified blessing. In the act before me, there seems to be a wide and unnecessary departure from these just principles."

Thus spoke not the frontier land lawyer and land baron, but the Andrew Jackson who in his canvasses for the presidency had accepted the support of the masses groping for leadership. And characteristically he meant to lead, not to follow, his flock.

That this philosophy and this form of leadership should fail to appeal to Nicholas Biddle is not surprising. "A manifesto of anarchy," he called the message.[48] So convinced of this was Mr. Biddle that he had printed, at the bank's expense, thirty thousand copies of the "manifesto," thinking its circulation would benefit Mr. Clay's campaign. This was not his major effort, however. Although it was at once obvious that Congress would uphold the veto, Mr. Biddle did not intend to let pass an opportunity to get something into the record. The brunt of this duty fell to Daniel Webster, of the bank's standing counsel. On July 11, the Senator from Massachusetts delivered his attack upon the message. Already in the bank's debt twenty-two thousand dollars, the following week he received an additional accommodation in the amount of ten thousand dollars, after which Mr. Biddle distributed one hundred and forty thousand five hundred copies of the address.[49] On July 13 the veto was sustained.

CHAPTER XXXIV

A Sword Against Disunion

I

WHILE Andrew Jackson was winning in Congress the fight into which Nicholas Biddle and Henry Clay had incautiously plunged the Bank of the United States, the twin-headed question of nullification thrust itself forward.

Elated by the triumph over the United States Supreme Court in the case of Corn Tassel, made possible by the benevolent neutrality of the Executive, Georgia had dealt the Indians another blow. White persons residing in the Cherokee country were ordered to take an oath of allegiance to the State. The New England missionaries, Samuel A. Worcester and Elizur Butler, refused and were imprisoned. The Supreme Court of the United States issued a writ of error which a Federal marshal served on the Governor of Georgia. The Governor denied the court's authority, and again the Georgia Legislature instructed local officers to decline to obey its orders.

In February, 1832, the missionaries' case was argued before a full bench in Washington. No counsel appeared for Georgia. The Chief Justice delivered the opinion of the court, holding that the Federal Government had exclusive jurisdiction over Indian lands and that Georgia was without authority to extend its laws over them. The judgment of the Georgia court was reversed, and a mandate issued calling for the release of Worcester and Butler. This mandate Georgia refused to obey, and again Jackson supported the State's defiance.

"John Marshall has made his decision, now let him enforce it." Years later a Whig congressman from Massachusetts attributed this remark to the President.[1] Jackson may have said it, for he wrote to John Coffee: "The decision of the supreme court has fell still born, and they find it cannot coerce Georgia to yield. . . . If a colision was to take place between them [the Indians] and the Georgians, the arm of the government is not sufficiently strong to preserve them from destruction."[2] This poor plea deceived no one. As much as any man living, Andrew Jackson could give strength to the arm of the government when he chose to do so. "The prerogatives of nullifying laws and political decisions by denying their conformity to the court," observed the *National Journal*, "makes . . . [the President] supreme—the final arbiter—the very Celestial Majesty."[3]

While yielding to the greed of the whites, Jackson endeavored to obtain a measure of practical justice for the Indians. Liberal terms were held out to them to remove peaceably beyond the Mississippi. The Creeks gave in and signed a treaty of evacuation. The Chickasaws signed a second treaty, so that by the end of 1832 only the Cherokees persisted in the struggle to retain the soil of their fathers.

These happenings bolstered the blustery confidence of the South Carolina Nullifiers, led now by the Vice President of the United States. In February a convention adopted menacing resolutions. "The State looks to her sons to defend her in whatever form she may proclaim her purpose to *Resist*."[4] South Carolina Unionists pinned their hope of averting a crisis to an effort to modify the tariff. Despite the preoccupation of Congress with the bank and presidential politics, an act was passed which Jackson signed the day after the bank veto was sustained. Though far short of what the radicals demanded, the new schedules certainly afforded a basis for amicable parley. But the Nullifiers rode boldly on. At the close of the eventful session in mid-July, 1832, Robert Y. Hayne and a majority of the South Carolina delegation issued an *Address*, calling upon their constituents as the "sovereign power" of the commonwealth to determine whether their liberties should be "tamely surrendered without a struggle or transmitted undiminished to posterity."

Jackson took notice of the declaration in his parting words to a South Carolina congressman who was setting out for home. "Tell . . . [the Nullifiers] from me that they can talk and write resolutions and print threats to their hearts' content. But if one drop of blood be shed there in defiance of the laws of the United States I will hang the first man of them I can get my hands on to the first tree I can find." In Benton's hearing, South Carolina's senior Senator expressed a doubt as to whether the President would go that far. "I tell you, Hayne," the Missourian replied, "when Jackson begins to talk about hanging, they can begin to look for the ropes."[5]

2

By this time the campaign was in its stride. A carefully timed entrance had returned Mr. Van Buren to his native shore, not in the rôle of repudiated public servant, but a party hero duly designated by a convention in Baltimore as Jackson's running mate. In 1824 Andrew Jackson had suffered the sort of defeat that solidifies a party. In 1828 he had won the kind of victory that tends to divide it, coalitions being impermanent by nature. But again the country was treated to the spectacle of common rules being without effect when Old Hickory was concerned. After some more or less deliberate pruning, such as the elimination of Mr. Calhoun, the President had knit the patchwork of 'Twenty-eight into a political machine of which he was the master. In the Eaton affair and in other matters, Mr. Van Buren had attained some distinction as a "magician." At the Baltimore convention, Jackson returned these favors in kind by making the New Yorker virtually the unanimous choice of the delegates for Vice President. A suggestion of the iron fist in the velvet glove was responsible for that appearance of unity, the Magician being far from the actual preference of Jackson men in many sections of the West and the South.

While uniting his own adherents, General Jackson divided those of the opposition. Henry Clay and his National Republican Party had won over Webster on the bank issue and most of the Calhoun group because they believed Clay the only man with a chance against Jackson. But the Kentuckian was unable to bring into his camp a curious political sect known as the Anti-Masons. This group had its beginning in western New York in 1826 when William Morgan, a wandering stone-setter, was kidnapped for attempted exposure of the secrets of Freemasonry and never seen again. By 1832 the Anti-Masons were fairly well organized in several states. Jackson's militant pride in his record as a Mason precluded union with Old Hickory's followers. The Anti-Masons, therefore, nominated for the presidency, William Wirt, Attorney General under Mr. Adams and more recently counsel for the Cherokee Indians in their actions against Georgia.

Frank Blair shortened the name National Republicans to "Nationals." Duff Green's *Telegraph*, wearing the livery of Mr. Clay, flung back "Democrats" at the Democratic Republicans, as the Jackson people called themselves.[6] The great issue was "Czar Nicholas" and his "hydra of corruption" which Blair accused of bribing statesmen and buying editors, charges the defenders of the institution were unable entirely to refute. Liberty-loving commoners were pictured at grips with the moneyed aristocrats. Senator Isaac Hill's *New Hampshire Patriot* struck a less impersonal note: "Twenty-one Reasons Why Henry Clay Should Not Be Elected President," reason number twenty being, "Because . . . he spends his days at the gaming table and his nights in a brothel."[7] Even scholarly William Cullen Bryant, editor of the decorous New York *Evening Post*, fell so far under the spell of the Hero as to cane a Clay supporter on Broadway.

The well-furnished purses of the opposition insured an equally spirited contest against "King Andrew I." The social status of Mrs. Eaton was engagingly discussed, point being lent to the case by her husband's effort to recapture, with General Jackson's blessing, the seat of Felix Grundy in the Senate. The spoils system and the incongruity of Martin Van Buren as a champion of the proletariat came in for lusty whacks. But mainly the Nationals stuck to the economic issue and a campaign of fear. The bank tried to frighten borrowers, with the exception of a few preferred editors and statesmen. Borrowers endeavored to pass on the shock. A Cincinnati wholesaler offered two dollars and fifty cents a hundred for pork in event Mr. Clay should win, a dollar fifty in event he lost. A Pennsylvania manufacturer laid off his hands until after election. A Clay newspaper in Pittsburgh announced a suspension of steamboat building along the Ohio.

In August Jackson went to Tennessee, making part of the journey on horseback. Wayside bills were paid in gold, which the bank in the effort to retrieve itself from the follies of over-expansion had almost driven from circulation. "No more paper money you see, fellow citizens, if I can only put down this Nicholas Biddle and his monster bank."[8] Long letters from the President to Jack Donelson reported Sarah's pregnancy and the state of roads, crops, stock and negroes. Politics was mentioned incidentally. "The veto works well. . . . Instead of crushing me it will crush the Bank."[9] To Hill he observed, "Isaac, it'll be a walk." The remark moved Benton to increase his election bets.[10]

Nor was the President especially aroused by the warning that "Nullification continues to rumble like distant thunder in the south."[11] "Calhoun is prostrate," Jackson replied. "I heard one of his best former friends say . . . he ought to be hung." Moreover, this "friend" had offered to march with ten thousand volunteers against the Nullifiers. "These," observed Old Hickory, "are and must be the sentiments of all honest men."[12]

3

That they were not the prevailing sentiments in Charleston General Jackson was soon to learn. He acted instantly. "To the Secretary of the Navy, *Confidential*. . . . *Efforts have been made, and perhaps not without succes*s . . . to disaffect the Officer of the Navy in command at charlston. . . . The idea is . . . to prevent a blockade. *This must be guarded against*." The squadron at Norfolk was ordered ready for sea.[13] In September the Nullifiers swept the State elections in South Carolina. On the heels of this, word reached the Hermitage that officers in command of the Regular troops at Charleston were prepared to surrender the harbor forts.

Ordering the garrisons replaced by detachments of unquestioned loyalty, Jackson left post haste for Washington. "My dear Sarah," he wrote en route, "yesterday and today [I] traveled 70 miles thro a broken country. . . . Until I hear of your confinement and safe delivery I shall have great anxiety."[14] And again: "My Dr. Sarah I regretted most of all being prevented from . . . visiting with you & Andrew alone [at] the tomb of my Dr departed wife. . . . When you visit me in the winter I trust we will be more to ourselves. I am happy to learn that all the necessary precautions have been taken to prepare you for your confinement. . . . Dr. Sarah your affectionate father ANDREW JACKSON."[15]

Ominous tidings awaited the President at the capital: South Carolina hopelessly in the hands of the extremists; the staffs of the customs houses corrupted; a call out for a convention to proclaim nullification of the revenue laws; demands for troops to "defend" the State against Federal "aggression." But the Navy was ready, the Charleston garrisons had been changed, and Major General Winfield Scott hurried south to command them. "The Secretary of War," further directed the President, "will cause secrete orders to be Issued to the officers commanding the Forts in the harbour of charleston So Carolina . . . to prevent a surprise in the night or by day. . . . *The attempt will be* made . . . by the militia, and must be . . . repelled with prompt and exemplary punishment."[16]

Frank Blair interrupted to present some campaign reports. "Thank you, sir," said the President, and putting down the papers he launched into a denunciation of the Nullifiers. The editor noted that the lines of the President's face "were hard drawn, his tones full of wrath and resentment."[17] Early in November, while the first returns from the polling places were coming in, Jackson received word of a plot to assassinate him,[18] and Jack Donelson heard from a neighbor that Sarah had been in labor for two or three days and was doing poorly. Ignoring the threatened assassination, Old Hickory rebuked Sarah's husband. "Why do you not write me— her fate must be sealed ere this."[19]

National Republicans and Anti-Masons had united on the same electoral slate in New York. National victories in a few state elections in August and September gave Mr. Clay's party further last-minute encouragement. But Andrew Jackson was not running on those state tickets. The earliest news from the presidential contest indicated a triumph for Old Hickory so overpowering that one opposition editor confessed he had "no heart to publish election returns."[20] But for this delicacy of feeling readers of the *Vermont Journal* might have learned sooner than they did that the popular vote for Jackson was six hundred and sixty-one thousand; for Clay, three hundred thousand; for the Clay-Wirt ticket in New York, one hundred and fifty-four thousand; for Wirt, one hundred thousand. The electoral vote was Jackson, two hundred seventeen; Clay, forty nine; Wirt, seven.[21]

Some of the more enthusiastic Jackson newspapers nominated the General for a third term. "My opinion," observed ex-Candidate Wirt, "is that he may be President for life if he chooses."[22]

The victor cherished other desires. "What would I not give to be free . . . and in retirement at the Hermitage.[23] . . . The best thing about this [huge plurality], gentlemen, is that it strengthens my hands in this [nullification] trouble."[24]

Strong hands were needed. On the Executive's desk lay a dispatch

A White House Belle

Mary Coffee, daughter of General John Coffee and grand-niece of Rachel Jackson. She spent the winter of 1833-34 at the White House and shortly after was married to General Jackson's ward, Andrew Jackson Hutchings. From a portrait by Earl, owned by Edward Asbury O'Neal III of Florence, Alabama, a descendant of General Coffee.

ONE OF THE WHITE HOUSE BABIES

Rachel Jackson Donelson, daughter of Andrew Jackson Donelson and Emily Donelson, born in the White House, April 19, 1834. From a portrait by Earl, owned by Mrs. Pauline Wilcox Burke of Washington.

from Joel R. Poinsett, the Unionist leader in South Carolina. "Grenades and small rockets are excellent weapons in a street fight." Mr. Poinsett had learned that in Mexico. "I would like to have some of them."[25]

The weapons sent,[26] the white-haired soldier bided the future more tranquil in mind than at any time since he had left Tennessee. For General Jackson was a grandfather; and Sarah was well; and they had named the baby Rachel. "I feel deeply indebted to you and my dear Sarah," he wrote to Andrew, junior. "Shall I be spared it will be a great pleasure to watch over and rear up the sweet little Rachel, and make her a fair emblem of her for whom she is called."[27]

4

Sergeant Sam Dale, a hero of the Creek and the Louisiana campaigns, had risen to become a general of Mississippi militia. After the election Dale appeared in Washington but was too modest to join the press of visitors that besieged his old commander. Whereupon Jackson sent Senator King of Alabama to bring in the veteran. The Mississippian found the President in the upstairs study discussing nullification with Benton and five or six others. Jackson put the visitor at ease by addressing his remarks to him. "General Dale, if this thing goes on our country will be like a bag of meal with both ends open. Pick it up and it will run out."

When the company took its leave, the President placed a decanter of whisky beside his friend. Jackson himself, never a heavy drinker, had abandoned the use of hard liquor almost entirely though he bought it by the barrel for his guests. At meal-time he would take a glass or two of wine and, though the White House table was famous, he dined sparingly, favoring the old army diet of rice.

They talked until late. "Sam, you have been true to your country, but you have made one mistake in life. You are now old and solitary, without a family to comfort you." Jackson started to speak of his wife but his eyes filled and he took a few turns of the room. "Dale," he said, at length, "they are trying me here; you will witness it; but, by the God in Heaven, I will uphold the laws."

General Dale expressed the hope that things would go right.

"They SHALL go right, sir!" exclaimed Old Hickory, bringing his hand down on a table so hard that he broke one of his pipes.

The President had a great collection of pipes. Admirers sent them from all parts of the world. "These will do to look at," he said, showing Dale the fancy specimens. "[But] I still smoke my corn cob, Sam. It is the sweetest and best pipe."[28]

South Carolina moved swiftly to precipitate a crisis before Congress should assemble. On November 24, 1832, the tariff acts were proclaimed void and not "binding upon this State or its citizens," after February 1, 1833. The truculent State declared that the use of force in an attempt to collect the duties after that date would be met by secession. Jackson jotted down a memorandum for his own eye. "South Carolina has passed her ordinance. . . . As soon as it can be had in authentic form, meet it with a proclamation. Nullification has taken deep root in Virginia, it must be arrested . . . by a full appeal . . . to the good sense of the people."[29]

In the case of South Carolina, the President continued his preparations to supplement this projected mode of persuasion. Seven revenue cutters and a ship of war were sent to Charleston. They anchored off the Battery, their guns commanding the fashionable waterfront lined with the homes and brick-walled gardens of the city's elect. General Scott strengthened harbor defenses against attack from the land side. With the Charleston post office in the hands of Nullifiers, a courier service was established to keep Jackson in constant touch with Joel Poinsett. "No state or states," the President wrote the leader of the Unionists, "has a right to secede. . . . Nullification therefore means insurrection and war; and other states have a right to put it down.[30] . . . [In this position] I am assured by all the members with whom I have conversed that I will be sustained by congress. If so, I will meet it at the threshold, and have the leaders arrested and arraigned for treason. . . . In forty days I can have within the limits of So. Carolina fifty thousand men, and in forty days more another fifty thousand."[31]

Elsewhere than in South Carolina anxious eyes turned toward Andrew Jackson. "Those who but yesterday," said Senator George M. Dallas of Pennsylvania, "opposed your re-election with ferocity now loudly profess their reliance on your saving the Union."[32]

Congress convened amid great excitement, which the President's message did little to allay. This document seemed poor company for the martial alarms and even more threatening private assertions of General Jackson. Its tone was conciliatory. Further tariff reductions were recommended and nothing said of resisting nullification by force. "The message," remarked John Quincy Adams, "goes to dissolve the Union . . . and is a complete surrender to the nullifiers."[33] Others asked if the intention were to permit South Carolina to emulate Georgia's successful defiance of the Federal Government. Nullifiers took heart. That scarred knight of the state sovereignty cause, Randolph of Roanoke, proffered the service of his lance to South Carolina and insinuatingly wrote the President: "You are now in a situation to recede with d[ignity]."[34]

There was no recession. On the day the message was read to Congress, Edward Livingston was engaged on Jackson's answer to the country's question, with Old Hickory peering over the Secretary's shoulder as he worked. "I submit the above as the conclusion of the proclamation," prompted the President. "Let it receive your best flight of eloquence. . . . The Union must be preserved, without blood if this be possible, but it must be preserved at all hazards and at any price."[35]

The Proclamation on Nullification was given to the world on December 10, 1832. The words are Livingston's, the initiative, the thought and the spirit Jackson's, comprising in all the greatest state paper of the spacious Jacksonian Epoch and one of the greatest to bear the name of an American president.

By skillful blending of argument, entreaty and warning the Executive addressed himself to the intelligence, the pride, the interests and the fears of the citizens of South Carolina; and he sought to unite the rest of the nation against the recalcitrant State.

Nullification was branded an "impractical absurdity." "If this doctrine had been established at an earlier day the Union would have been dissolved in its infancy. . . . Admit this doctrine and . . . every law . . . for raising revenue . . . may be annulled. . . . I consider, then, the power to annul a law of the United States, assumed by one State, incompatible with the existence of the Union, contradicted expressly by the letter of the Constitution, unauthorized by its spirit, inconsistent with every principle on which it was founded, and destructive of the great object for which it was formed."

The right of secession was categorically denied. "The Constitution ... forms a *government* not a league.... To say that any State may at pleasure secede from the Union is to say that the United States is not a nation." Relief from burdens of which South Carolina complained was foreshadowed by the "approaching payment of the public debt." But meanwhile the laws would be enforced.

"Fellow-citizens of my native State, let me admonish you. ... I have no discretionary power on the subject. ... Those who told you that you might peaceably prevent ... [the execution of the laws] deceived you. ... Their object is disunion. ... Disunion by armed force is treason. Are you really ready to incur its guilt? If you are, on the heads of the instigators of the act be dreadful consequences. ... [Your] first magistrate cannot, if he would, avoid the performance of his duty. ...

"ANDREW JACKSON

"By the President:
"EDW. LIVINGSTON, *Secretary of State*."[36]

Bonfires blazed, bells rang, men paraded. Military volunteers offered themselves, state legislatures denounced nullification. John Quincy Adams and Daniel Webster joined the President promptly and cordially. Embittered Henry Clay's tongue fell silent. In Illinois a village lawyer and captain of volunteers, lately returned from participation in a detail of Indian swindling which history obscures behind the respectable name of the Black Hawk War, pored over the proclamation. In 1861 Abraham Lincoln was to read it again before composing his inaugural address.

5

The story in South Carolina was different. "Gen Jackson's extraordinary proclamation has just reached me," wrote James H. Hammond, an editor of Columbia, to Robert Y. Hayne, who had resigned his Senate seat for the governorship of the embattled State. "Upon the timid and ignorant of our party I fear it will have great influence."[37] So did Hayne, who splashed his signature upon a counter-proclamation in which the Governor promised to maintain the sovereignty of South Carolina or perish "beneath its ruins." Proffers of military service poured upon the state Executive; calls for commissions, for pistols, sabers, powder and ball; for Hoyt's *Tactics* and an "'Abstract for the Manoeuvres of Infantry' adopted by the last Legislature." Hayne concentrated on the organization of *"Mounted Minute Men"* to enable him to throw "2,500 of the *elite* of the whole state upon a given point in three or four days. . . . The uniform of my staff will be the same as my Predecessors except *under boots* and a *short yellow crane* Plume. Palmetto Buttons of a beautiful pattern may be had at Roche's, Charleston."[38]

Union men refused to be overawed. "God and Old Hickory are with us."[39] Either would have sufficed Poinsett who continued to arm his men and to drill them at night.

John C. Calhoun quit these tense scenes to start north with the intention of resigning the vice presidency and taking the place in the Senate vacated by Hayne. The journey required courage. Friends of years' standing turned their backs. The curious gathered at every stage stop to stare at the man who, rumor said, would enter Washington a prisoner under charge of treason; and it seems more than probable that only the absence of an armed clash between the opposing forces in South Carolina averted this. Pale but determined, the South Carolinian walked into the Senate chamber on January 4, 1833, and swore to uphold and defend the Constitution of the United States.

Jackson charted a direct course. "I am now waiting," he apprized Van Buren, "for the [official] information from the assembly of So. Carolina of their having passed their laws for raising an army to resist the execution of the laws, which will be a levying of war, and I will make a communication to Congress . . . ask[ing] power to call upon volunteers to serve as a posse commitatus of the civil authority. . . . If the Assembly authorises twelve thousand men to resist the law, I will order thirty thousand to execute [it]".[40] Leaders of nullification would be seized wherever found "regardless of the force that surrounds them, [and] deliver[ed] into the hands of the judicial authority of the United States" to be tried for treason.[41] The President was already scrutinizing an inventory of infantry, cavalry and artillery weapons in the custody of the War Department. "Tenders of service is coming to me daily and from Newyork we can send to the bay of charleston with steamers such number of troops as we may be pleased to order, in four days."⁴²

On to this lively stage stepped comely Fanny Kemble, the English actress. She charmed Henry Clay and made John Marshall weep. Webster paid for his visit to the theatre with a cold. Aware that history was unfolding before her eyes, the visitor faithfully recorded impressions. Washington struck her as a "rambling red-brick image of futurity where nothing *is* but all things *are to be.* At night the scattered lights of the town looked like a capricious congregation of Jack-o'-lanterns, some high, some low, some here, some there, showing more distinctly by the dark spaces between them the enormous share that emptiness has in this congressional city." The envied Representative who escorted Miss Kemble through the Capitol said he had just left the President in a stern frame of mind. "They say the old General is longing for a fight," Fanny confided to her journal.

The Donelsons and Miss Mary Coffee, visiting from Alabama, attended the theatre, after which came the prized opportunity to call on the President. "Very tall and thin, but erect and dignified in his carriage," noted Miss Kemble, who used superlatives sparingly, "a good specimen of fine old well-battered soldier. . . . His manners are perfectly simple and quiet, therefore very good; so are those of his niece, Mrs. —— [Donelson], who is a very pretty person. . . . Of his measures I know nothing, but firmness, determination, decision, I respect above all things; and if the old General is, as they say, very obstinate, why obstinacy is so far more estimable than weakness, *especially* in a ruler, that I think he sins on the right side of the question."⁴³

6

Martin Van Buren would have preferred Fanny Kemble's acting to her opinion of General Jackson's attitude toward South Carolina. Remaining circumspectly aloof in Albany, the Vice President-elect moved subtly to modify the chieftain's Draconian impulses. "You will say I am on my old track—caution—caution—caution: but my Dr Sir I have always thought that considering our respective tem-

A SWORD AGAINST DISUNION

peraments there was no way perhaps in which I could better render you service."[44] The New Yorker politely disagreed with Jackson's contention that the mere raising of troops by South Carolina constituted actual treason.[45] Constructive treason it might be, but constructive treason was a vague accusation so abused in Europe that it was bound to be unpopular with Americans. The President's adviser went so far as to "regret" the inclusion in the famous proclamation of certain "doctrinal points," meaning, at bottom, Jackson's flat denial of the right of a state to secede. He said this was borrowing trouble. It had offended Virginia. Besides, "South Carolina has not and will not secede." Even if she did, would not the question of bringing her back by force be better decided by Congress than by the Executive? The letter closed with an intimation that a gesture toward tariff reduction might pave the way to a happy solution of everything.[46]

Mr. Van Buren's anxieties arose chiefly from the fact that, like many others, he regarded the crisis through the spectacles of partizan politics. This northern statesman had threaded his way to national eminence in candid alliance with southern state-rights leaders, notably those of Virginia. He feared the political aftermath of a break with them now. On the other hand Jackson had thrown such considerations to the winds, placing himself militantly at the head of the union sentiment of the nation, irrespective of person or party.[47]

Yet the man of caution had raised two points which the man of action could not ignore:

The first concerned the definition of actual treason and the constitutional right of the Executive to intervene in a state's affairs. Legally he could intervene only (1) at the request of the Governor to suppress insurrection, or (2) on his own initiative, to enforce the laws of Congress. In the latter case no clear procedure existed. In the past it had been contemplated that a Federal officer might summon a *posse comitatus* to aid in this duty. But, when Jackson notified Poinsett that in event of emergency his newly formed unionist military companies would be called to act as a *posse*, they objected. The word did not have the right ring. They preferred to be a part of the United States Army, which would give them the status of prisoners of war if captured.[48] The President promised to take the subject before Congress.

The second restraining consideration centered upon the necessity of keeping state-rightists in other commonwealths from making common cause with South Carolina. To South Carolina's surprise and discomfiture the high-hearted words of the proclamation had stunned most of that crowd into silence. Then came the parade of resolutions from state legislatures which, under pressure from Administration sources where necessary, soon were to isolate South Carolina from the declared support of a single state.

These circumstances constituted a salutary triumph for Jackson's leadership, a triumph which made things look better for him than they really were. The President was able to cheer Poinsett with the assurance that "the national voice from Main to Louisiana . . . declares . . . nullification and secession consigned to contempt and infamy."[49] But to a confidential friend he wrote: "There are more nullifiers here than dare avow it,"[50] and it was true. Virginia incurred Jackson's wrath by coupling to her resolution a proposal to mediate between South Carolina and the general government, and authorizing an agent to proceed to Columbia. New York legislators sat on their hands until a stiff letter from Jackson moved them to act. Then the resolution Mr. Van Buren wrote for them was so sleek and mild that the President filed it away without a word of comment.[51] Only the President's beneficent Indian policy averted difficulty in Georgia, Mississippi and Alabama. General John Coffee, wintering with his old comrade in the White House, wrote a relative in Memphis, "Nullification will be put down, but it has taken deeper root in the Southern States than any one could have supposed."[52]

While moving to cut off South Carolina from outside sympathy and succor, the President permitted an extension of the olive branch. In the last days of December Representative Verplanck of New York laid before the House a hastily drawn bill calling for heavy reductions of the tariff duties. This was no fresh or enforced concession. The principle was in keeping with a promise implied in the proclamation.

Such was the only offer of accommodation to the Nullifiers countenanced by Andrew Jackson.

7

The offer made, Old Hickory plowed grimly on rebuking the sly Van Buren, encouraging staunch Poinsett.

"No, my friend," reiterated the Executive to the Vice President-elect, . . . "[your policy] would destroy all confidence in our government both at home and abroad. . . . I expect soon to hear that a civil war has commenced. . . . [If] the leaders . . . are surrounded with 12,000 bayonets our marshall shall be aided by 24,000 and arrest them in the midst thereof."[53]

Silas Wright, whom Mr. Van Buren had just made a senator from New York, forwarded further disturbing details of the presidential state of mind. "He does not expect that . . . [any thing can] prevent an open rupture." Before a room filled with company, Wright had heard Jackson tell of a steamer sailing from Charleston with the stars and stripes upside down. " 'Sir,' said the old Gentleman, 'for this indignity to the flag she ought to have been instantly sunk, no matter who owned or commanded her.' "[54]

In the same crowded drawing room, the President spoke of the advisability of "disciplining" Calhoun and Hayne[55] as an object lesson to others. General Jackson could be something of an artist at dropping apparently unguarded expressions. Flying from tongue to tongue in the nervous capital, such threats grew with repetition. In the fullness of time, Congressman Letcher of Kentucky, so one story goes, called at the White House to learn the President's true intentions. Old Hickory said that "if one more step was taken he would try Calhoun for treason and, if convicted, hang him as high as Haman." In the middle of the night the South Carolina Senator is said to have been called from his bed to hear this not improbable tale. "There sat Calhoun," related a contemporary apt to improve a story in the telling, "drinking in eagerly every word, . . . pale as death and . . . [trembling] like an aspen leaf."[56]

Beyond doubt Jackson had them scared—Nullifiers and near-Nullifiers alike, along with political tight-rope performers of the Van Buren stamp. And not in Washington alone did knees shake behind façades of bravado. In December the President had said he would suspend positive action awaiting officially certified copies of the acts of the South Carolina Legislature giving effect to the ordinance of nullification. When these failed to arrive Jackson shot off a courier to fetch them. Ten days passed without word from the courier. It was January 16, 1833. Fifteen days remained until February 1 when the ordinance and supporting decrees were to go into force. Jackson waited no longer. Acting without the official copies, he asked Congress for authority to use military force to collect the customs. This would mitigate legalistic scruples about employing troops.

But what if Congress, in that short time, should fail to convey the power requested? Andrew Jackson was ready for the contingency. He would take unto himself the power, stretching the Constitution to suit the needs of the case. "The preservation of the Union is the supreme law."[57] On January 24 seven days remained in which to act before the first of February. The inability of Congress to agree on a bill seemed imminent. A hurried scrawl to Poinsett left Washington by night.

"Should congress fail to act, . . . [and should] So. Carolina oppose the execution of the revenue laws . . . [with] an armed force . . . I stand prepared to issue my proclamation warning them to disperse. should they fail to comply I will . . . in ten or fifteen days at farthest have in charleston ten to fifteen thousand well organized troops well equipped for the field, and twenty thousand, or thirty, more in their [sic] interior. I have a tender of volunteers from every state in the union. I can if need be, which god forbid, march two hundred thousand men in forty days to quell any and every insurrection that might arise." Should the Governor of Virginia attempt to prevent the passage of regiments bound for South Carolina, "I would arrest him at the head of his troops. . . .

"I repeat to the union men, fear not, *the union will be preserved*. . . . It is very late and my eyes grow dim. Keep me well advised, and constantly. . . . I keep no copy nor have I time to correct this letter. In haste. . . . ANDREW JACKSON."[58]

On the next day the President's proclamation was ready.[59] So were preparations to call on the governors of New York—Martin Van Buren, please note—Pennsylvania, Virginia—local Nullifiers ditto —North Carolina, Ohio, Tennessee, Alabama, Georgia and South

Carolina for thirty-five thousand men "ready to march at a moment's warning."[60]

Martin Van Buren later said that Andrew Jackson yearned to lead this force in person.[61] Who can doubt it for an instant?

But the proclamation was never issued; the requisitions on the governors never sent. The courier who bore the President's letter of January 24 to Poinsett passed a messenger hurrying northward with news that South Carolina had yielded. Jackson's awesome mobilization had been too much for the Nullifiers' nerves. On January 21 they had suspended their belligerent ordinance pending the outcome of the tariff debate.[62] Moving in an almost straight line, Old Hickory had outmaneuvered his foemen at every point and, sword in hand, faced them down.

8

The sword having had its vital hour, the time had come for the pen, and for many tongues. The major responsibility shifted to the halls of Congress, where the removal of the time limit encouraged loquacity. Although it was still known as an Administration measure, General Jackson had lost much of his early interest in Verplanck's tariff bill which, weighed down with amendments, made little headway. But the President insisted on the enactment, without one barb blunted, of the "Force Bill," or "Bloody Bill," as opponents variously called the measure authorizing the use of the military to collect the Government revenue. The demand unleashed an oratorical onslaught which John Tyler carried to a climax.

The Senator from Virginia called Charleston a "beleaguered city." Suppose, he said, this bill were to pass and "the proud spirit of South Carolina" should decline to submit. Would we then "make war upon her, hang her Governor, . . . and reduce her to the condition of a conquered province?" Mr. Tyler saw South Carolina's towns leveled, her daughters in mourning, her men driven "into the morasses where Marion found refuge." But he did not see them conquered. Rome had her Curtis, Sparta her Leonidas—and South Carolina had John C. Calhoun.

Mr. Calhoun did not repudiate the heroic part. "I proclaim it," said he, "that should this bill pass . . . it will be resisted at every hazard—even that of death."

Daniel Webster followed the South Carolinian. When he finished, the lamps in the Senate chamber had been lighted. Major Lewis hurried to the White House with an evaluation of the scene which the President passed on to Poinsett. "Mr. Webster replied to Mr. Calhoun yesterday . . . handled him like a child. . . . Keep me constantly advised of all movements in South Carolina."[63]

Oblivious to threat and to political entreaty, Jackson refused to give an inch. He insisted on the passage of the Force Bill. The last ten days of February were at hand, and on March 2 Congress must adjourn. Jackson could be angered by delay, but he could not be beaten. The votes to pass the Force Bill were pledged. Only something akin to a miracle could relieve John C. Calhoun of the unpleasant option of capitulating or of validating his menacing words.

The situation afforded Henry Clay, a practiced dispenser of parliamentary miracles, the opportunity that he sought. On the Force Bill the Kentucky Senator had been silent; he could not uphold nullification, and he would not uphold Jackson. The tariff, however, was Clay's specialty, and in this field he saw a number of serviceable possibilities: reconciliation between South Carolina and the general government; Calhoun rescued from his perilous position; something of the protective system saved from the devastations of the Verplanck Bill; Henry Clay in the rôle of pacifier instead of Martin Van Buren as would be the case should Verplanck's measure go through. The outcome was a bewildering maneuver which Clay counted on Calhoun's desperation to crown with success. As an independent "compromise," he introduced a bill which in ten years would lower tariffs by twenty per cent. The Verplanck Bill would cut them that much in two years or less. Yet Calhoun, sweating blood, was dragooned into supporting Clay's measure on the strange ground that it was promulgated as a compromise to which South Carolina could accede with dignity, notwithstanding the fact that the Administration bill embodied the more liberal terms.

This metaphysical proposition agreed to, the Force Bill was called up for a vote in the Senate. Mr. Calhoun and all his supporters except one left the chamber. Irate John Tyler of Virginia stayed and cast the only negative vote. Jackson ordered his congressional captains to drive the bill on through the House ahead of Clay's tariff.[64] Skillfully the Kentuckian spread the meshes of delay, and Jackson's captains failed. On the last day but one of the session, the two measures—Jackson's Force Bill and Clay's tariff—finished their legislative journeys together and at the same hour came to the President's desk. Old Hickory winced as he signed the tariff bill. South Carolina would make the most of the opportunity to accept peace from the hands of Mr. Clay rather than from those of General Jackson. But veto the bill he could not; that would be pushing Calhoun too far.

9

On Old Hickory's sixty-sixth birthday, March 15, 1833, South Carolina rescinded her ordinance of nullification. Snatched from the brink of civil war, the nation gave way to rejoicing that lifted Andrew Jackson's popularity to a pinnacle not before attained by a President of the United States. Daniel Webster extolled the Executive in a public address and Washington heard that, in event of the retirement of the aged John Marshall, the Senator from Massachusetts would be Chief Justice.

General Jackson regarded the demonstrations with sober mien. Twenty years as a popular idol had rendered him somewhat immune to the dangers of an excess of acclaim. His sensitive intuitions perceived too well the ever-tangling skein of our national life to accept the recent events as a cause for unqualified congratulation. With the plaudits of millions ringing in his ears, Jackson's private estimate of his accomplishment was modest. "Nullification and secession are for the present, I think, effectively, and I hope forever put down. But the coalition between Clay and Calhoun, combined . . . with a few nullifiers in Virginia and Poindexter [of Mississippi] and his coadjuters in the south and southwest portends no good, but much evil."[65] But the late crisis had ended more tamely than Jackson had reckoned on. "I thought I w^d. have to hang some of them & [I] wd. have done it."[66]

Charleston gave a "victory ball" for volunteers who had taken up arms against "the invader." It was easy to smile at the face-saving device; too easy. The President observed and reflected deeply. He knew the real issue to be slavery—as yet untouched and almost unavowed. From the shadow of the gallows John C. Calhoun emerged with a new and sinister prestige. In Virginia John Tyler responded to the toast, "Nullification the rightful and, as it proved, the efficient remedy." Andrew Jackson saw that the viper he had set out to kill was only scotched. "The nullifiers in the south intend to blow up a storm on the slave question. . . . This ought to be met, for be assured these men would do any act to destroy this union and form a southern confederacy bounded, north, by the Potomac river."[67]

As time furnished a clearer perspective of these scenes, many who had been in the thick of them came to believe that, had the resolute old man had his way with South Carolina in 1833, our national annals would have borne fewer blood stains in the end. Among these was Henry Clay who lived to regret the day he had stayed the upraised arm of Andrew Jackson.[68]

CHAPTER XXXV

"A Knightly Personage"

I

ON THE last official day of his first term of office, the President was about to sit down to dinner when word came that the House of Representatives had adopted the following:

"*Resolved,* that Government deposits may, in the opinion of the House, be safely continued in the Bank of the United States."

The parting slap was delivered with the combined strength of Henry Clay, John C. Calhoun and the pro-bank men of Jackson's own party. This performance took place twenty-four hours after the House, at Mr. Clay's bidding, had finished its equivocal part in the drama of nullification.

Old Hickory did not enjoy his dinner. With fire in his eyes, he drove to the Capitol, as precedent had established for these last hours, to sit in the little-used President's Room until Congress should adjourn *sine die*. John Coffee went with him—a fortunate choice of companion, for the nerves of Old Hickory were fraying. Few men have known the blessings of a deeper or more satisfactory friendship than John Coffee gave Andrew Jackson. The big, even-keeled, slow-spoken man who had commanded the left wing of the line of battle at New Orleans was a natural sedative to the other's temper. Though often invited, this was his first visit to Washington during his friend's presidency, and the last. He had kept Jackson company throughout the critical winter.

The presidential vigil did little to shorten the deliberations of the law-makers. As the night wore on bottles appeared on the desks. Half a dozen tipsy members of the House were on their feet at once. Rulings of the Chair were howled down. In shadowy ante-rooms, members of the bank's well-staffed lobby rubbed their hands with satisfaction. One such functionary, previously distinguished as the go-between in Mr. Biddle's purchase of the New York *Enquirer's* support, felt the historical impact of the scene. Snatching a moment he indited a message to his chief: "We have met the enemy and they are ours."[1] Two or three congressmen found time to use their pens. "I hope you will all feel satisfied with what has been done," reported the pliant tool, John Watmough of Pennsylvania, with the bland recommendation that Mr. Biddle open his purse to certain other members of the House.[2]

Hour after hour Jackson sat with John Coffee reading, writing, chatting of family things and bygone times. Although no other hostile resolutions received parliamentary recognition, Administration floor leaders, including the ordinarily efficacious James K. Polk, seemed powerless to stem the pointless talk—a situation upon which one student of causes and effects, Sam Houston, may have shed some light when he pronounced Polk a victim of the use of water as a beverage. Dawn of Sunday, March 3, 1833, was sketching in the profile of the low hills on the far side of the Anacostia when a delegation waited on the President to say that, if he had no further communications, their colleagues were prepared to adjourn. The Executive had no further communications. Whereupon the Twenty-second Congress of the United States reeled into history and its personnel into bed. President Jackson's first four years were behind him.

2

On the following day he began his second term with an inaugural as simple as Jefferson's. Snow covered the ground and thermometers stood at eleven degrees above zero. Outdoor arrangements were given up. Its floor cleared of broken glass, the House chamber served as the scene for administering the oath. No reception was held at the Executive Residence. Before dinner-time the President said goodnight and withdrew to his bedroom, leaving Jack and Emily Donelson, Andrew, junior, and Sarah, General Coffee and his daughter Mary, Lucius Polk and his wife Mary Eastin, Mary McLemore and R. E. W. Earl to represent the White House at the two inaugural balls.

As the General lay in bed turning the pages of Rachel's Bible, he hoped this quiet day might be prophetic. But would it? The incomplete nature of the victory over nullification, the prospect of the preservation of an harassing alliance between Clay and Calhoun, the stirring up of the bank issue even before the ghost of disunion was laid: these were vexing things. Though Andrew Jackson could look ahead from a height of personal popularity not scaled by another President, the burdens of the winter had sapped his strength. Now that a lull in the battle had come, suddenly he felt very old again and so tired and homesick that for almost the first time in his life Andrew Jackson admitted the need for rest and restoration. As ever, he looked longingly toward the Hermitage and the prospects of a visit there.

Yet the White House was a pleasanter abode and Washington a more sightly city than in 1829. A strip forty-five feet wide in the middle of expansive Pennsylvania Avenue had been paved. The grounds of the Executive Residence had been regraded, graveled walks laid and trees planted. The Mansion's pillared portico facing Pennsylvania Avenue was completed, giving the northern exterior the appearance it exhibits today. A show-place carriage house and stable, with stalls for ten horses, had supplanted the barn and sheds of wartime construction. Two friendly pumps were gone from the east and west yards, and the house was provided with running water, including hot and cold shower baths.

Life within doors retained the agreeable pattern re-established after the departure of Bellona. The young folk of courting age and the children remained the General's abiding joys. Emily's eldest, Andrew Jackson who was six, had his own pony and rode with his great uncle. Mary Rachel (Martin Van Buren her godfather) was three. Another baby was to arrive in May. When measles took them down in a row, the President fretted as much as their mother. He could hear a cry in the nursery as quickly as she. To encounter the General in the middle of the night making his way along the dim corridor to see that all was right with his "pets" was no rare occurrence. A new tooth, a first step, were attainments apt to take precedence in his family letters over the concerns of statecraft. When absent he worried constantly lest the little ones forget him. The crowning domestic event of the winter, of course, had been the arrival of Andrew, junior, and Sarah, with the pet of pets, the four-months-old granddaughter, Rachel.

No President before Jackson had so many house guests or spent so much on their entertainment. Young connections of the fabulous Donelson clan were especially favored. Sometimes their thoughtless antics vexed Uncle Andrew, but when the house was clear of them he would complain of loneliness. So on and on they came, to move through the enchantments of Washington like creatures in a fairy tale. The hour before dinner was a popular time. Wine and relishes waited on the tables of the Red Room. Youthful ornaments of the Army and the Navy clicked their heels; diplomatic underlings with well-turned compliments and continental bows and junior officials from the departments and from Capitol Hill came without specific invitation—three or four of them squiring each current White House belle. If he could possibly get away, the General would descend from his study to have a glass and a few jests with them.

In this way it was that Alphonse Pageot, of the French Legation, met Mary Lewis, the Major's daughter, whom he married, and Thomas P. Barton, a prospective light of our own foreign staff, began a swift conquest of the heart of alluring Cora Livingston, who had her mother's dark, communicative eyes. Wedding gifts became a standing item in the President's personal budget. However, Abraham Van Buren, an alumnus of West Point, and his brother, "Prince" John, spruced up in English clothes and evincing inherited talents for evasion, adroitly defended the bastions of bachelorhood against protracted sieges. Eliza Blair was a favorite of everyone, the General foremost. With her father, the editor, Jackson had developed the most enduring personal friendship of his presidential years. Frank Blair had more than one coat to his name now. He was preparing to buy a fine house and to provide it with running water. He kept cows and, learning that an increase of milk had been prescribed for the General's diet, at seven the next morning brought a foaming pailful to the White House door. Every morning thereafter a bucket from the Blair dairy was on hand, often carried by the journalist himself.

3

In April, 1833, Andrew Jackson Hutchings attained his majority. The President put the young man in possession of his estate, terminating a guardianship undertaken in 1818, in compliance with a death-bed request of Hutchings's father. "One word as to matrimony," was the General's parting advice.

"Seek a wife who will aid you in making a competency and will take care of it when made, for you will find it easier to spend two thousand dollars than to make five hundred. Look at the economy of the mother and you will find it in the daughter. recollect the industry of your dear aunt, and with what economy she watched over what I made, and how we waded thro the vast expence of the mass of company we had. nothing but her care and industry could have saved me from ruin. . . . Think of this before you attempt to select a wife. . . . I would bring to your view Genl Coffee and [his wife] Polly. take Coffee for your guide, receive his admonitions and pursue them. live within your means, never be in debt, and become no mans surety. If your friend is in distress aid him if you have the means to spare. if he fails to be able to return it, it is only so much lost. your property is not sold by the sheriff to raise it."[3]

The President's own money matters were on his mind at the time. For a year, or since paying for Mary Eastin's and Andrew, junior's weddings, Jackson had been short of funds. The ruin of a new carriage in a runaway had cost a thousand dollars, and two thousand had been spent to make the Hermitage more attractive for Sarah. During the visit to Tennessee in 1832, Jackson had changed plantation overseers. Though the new man, Burnard Holtzclaw, seemed energetic and capable, the Hermitage books showed an operating loss for the year. "So much for my absence," observed Jackson, with warm words of approval of young Hutchings's plan to keep the management of his place in his own hands.[4] "Settle all your debts the first of every year and you will know your means and can keep within it." To settle his own debts, Jackson had been forced to the distasteful expedient of asking friends to return personal loans. Yet not a tithe of what he had generously handed out came back.

Putting away adolescent foolishness, the young planter profited by this counsel, and seven months later he married Mary Coffee. Amid grave affairs the President paused to write a long letter. "To me it is joyfull. . . . I view her as a treasure."[5]

Treasure though Mary Coffee was in truth, when neither she nor her cousin Mary McLemore sent General Jackson a scratch of a pen during the homeward journey from the inaugural, he scolded both young ladies for "lasy toads."⁶ Tennessee news from other sources was cheering, however. Holtzclaw was taking hold of things at the Hermitage—a circumstance rendered the more desirable by the fact that, for all the General's coaching, Andrew, junior, seemed slow to get his bearings as a landed proprietor. Though the place still suffered from the slack stewardship of Steele, the new overseer had two hundred acres in cotton, three hundred in corn and a hundred and twenty in oats. Only the hay fields were in bad order. Stock was much improved, fences and gates repaired. The spinning jenny, the wheels and two looms were going. The negroes were well-clothed, including the children, whose numbers had increased to fifty-eight. On his latest visit General Jackson had gently expressed to Aunt Hannah, an aged negress who for nearly a generation had ruled the fowl yard, his "mortification" at finding no poultry fit for the table of the "big house." Through Major Lewis, Hannah reported that despite a visitation of "the gaps," carrying off many young turkeys and chickens, plenty of fowl would be on hand for the master's next homecoming.⁷

Though immensely gratified by these reports from home, General Jackson said that the excellent showing must not be permitted to prejudice the health of "the family." "Treat my negroes with kindness." Holtzclaw was further instructed to prevent Betty, the colored cook, from "abusing the little negroes that are under her about the kitchen. A small switch ought only to be used." The white folk's physician, Doctor Hogg, was directed to prescribe for the injured hip of a young victim of Betty's corrective measures. "I would be sorry [were] she [to] become a cripple."⁸

Then came news hard to bear. Dr. William Hume, Rachel's beloved pastor, wrote to say that John Overton was no more—John Overton, with whom the fiery young public prosecutor for the Mero District had shared a bed in the Widow Donelson's blockhouse in 1788. . . . His last words were of Andrew Jackson whom, like John Coffee, he had visited at the White House only once. "Altho," replied the President, "I could lament in the language and feelings of David for Absolom I am constrained to say, *peace to his manes,* let us weep for the living and not for the dead."⁹ A succeeding post brought the tidings that Parson Hume himself had passed to his reward. The world was emptying of familiar faces. The third blow in three months, taking off John Coffee, proved more than the old man's stoicism could parry. "[It was] so unexpected, . . . such a sudden shock upon us that . . . our philosophy fled & we were unmanned and I waited for composure of mind before I could acknowledge your letter."[10]

Andrew Jackson offered to stand in the place of a father to the children of his friend. At the request of one of them, he composed the epitaph which in an Alabama graveyard perpetuates "the memory of General John Coffee. . . . As a husband, parent and friend he was affectionate, tender and sincere. He was a brave, prompt and skillful general, a disinterested and sagacious patriot, an unpretending, just and honest man."[11]

4

Tranquillity seemed to elude the public as well as the private concerns of General Jackson. After the nullification crisis, he had indulged himself in the hope that the country "would be permitted to enjoy at least some repose." Before the second term was three weeks old, this aspiration seemed endangered by "a new combination between Clay and calhoun" actuated by "the corrupting influence of the Bank of the U. S. . . . These men are bound, I have no doubt, to have it rechartered." Were not "the late proceedings of Congress," declaring "the government deposits safe . . . evidence of the power of this institution over the government so strong as naturally to excite reflections on the subject?"[12]

Weary as the old man was, his meditations ranged a bold course. Jackson pondered a dramatic seizure of the initiative, striking the bank a disabling blow before it should strike him. The blow contemplated nothing less than the withdrawal of Government deposits, in defiance of the House resolution.[13]

This subject had been first mentioned officially at a Cabinet meeting in the November preceding—1832—when the conduct of the bank in the matter of the retirement of a series of three per cent Government bonds came under review.

The episode of the three per cents was something that not even the bank's warmest friends in Congress could defend. In the spring of 1832, the Treasury had told Biddle to be prepared to advance six million dollars of Government deposits on July 1, to take up these securities. Biddle obtained a postponement on the representation that the disbursement would derange commerce. The true reason was that Biddle's politically-minded liberality in the matter of loans had stripped the institution of the necessary funds. The bank's versatile journeyman, Cadwalader, hastening to London, arranged with the Barings to buy up several millions' worth of certificates and withhold them from the Government. This was a breach of faith and a violation of the charter. The Baring arrangement was to be secret, however, and might have succeeded but for a disclosure by the New York *Evening Post.*

Incensed, Jackson told the Cabinet he believed the bank unsafe and asked which would be the better course, to seek the revocation of its charter or to remove the Government deposits. The question reopened the squabble between Secretary of the Treasury McLane and Attorney General Taney, whereupon Jackson adjourned the meeting and turned to face nullification.[14]

Three months later, when the storm over South Carolina began to relent, the bank situation stood thus: in response to a suggestion in the President's annual message that Congress conduct a "serious investigation" to see whether the Government deposits were safe, two reports were submitted to the House by its Committee on Ways and Means. The majority report, offered by the committee chairman (Van Buren's friend Verplanck, author of the tariff measure which Mr. Clay put to sleep) in five printed pages, pronounced Mr. Biddle's bank sounder than the state banks taken as a whole. It recommended the retention of the deposits. The minority report, submitted by James K. Polk, comprised one hundred and eighty-four pages. Though partizan in tone, it bore evidence of an inquiry worthy of respect. This document indicated that the majority had waived aside much in order to give the bank a clean bill. In addition to other delinquencies, Polk exposed the critical, if not insolvent, condition of several western branches owing to Biddle's loan policy. It showed how "race horse bills" kept the weak branches afloat. That is to say Lexington would boost its assets by writing out a draft on Nashville, which Nashville would cover by drawing for like amount on Natchez, whose cashier would draw on his colleague in New Orleans, who would draw on Louisville, and so on again around the circle. The circulation of monetary fiction in this fugitive form ran into millions of dollars.[15]

Verplanck's report and the first forty-two pages of Polk's reached the House on March 1. The remainder of the Polk report was delivered on March 2, the last day of the session. Its forbidding length, the impending adjournment and the convivial state of many of the members, helped Mr. Clay's men to whoop through a resolution based on the conveniently brief findings of the majority.

5

General Jackson was correct in the assumption that this performance revealed a compact between Clay and Calhoun for the purpose of rechartering the bank. The Kentuckian was in a happy frame of mind. As soon as he had slept off the effects of that all-night tour of legislative duty, a letter went forward to Nicholas Biddle: "I do believe if we had two weeks more to go we could have renewed the charter in spite of all Vetoes."[16] Without waiting to go to bed, a North Carolina Congressman had assured the banker that, after the House vote, Jackson would not dare to remove the deposits.[17]

Nor was Old Hickory on the wrong scent when he spoke of "the corrupting influence of the Bank" in this regard.

Representative John Watmough had asked Biddle to show Congressman Verplanck "some attentions" during his passage through Philadelphia on his way home in New York; "to reinstate old Gilmore [a Representative from Pennsylvania] on his feet"; and to advance Representative Clayton of Georgia three thousand dollars "as the only means of preventing the terrible mischiefs which such men have it in their power to perpetuate."[18] Clayton, previously active against the bank, had grown cool toward the Administration during the nullification fight. After this Mr. Watmough spoke for himself. "I write you in the greatest possible state of distress." Mr. Biddle provided twelve hundred dollars to relieve it.[19] These and other generosities seem to have endowed the banker with an underground notoriety as a "soft touch." An editor wrote for two hundred dollars; a pamphleteer for five hundred; a wayfarer stranded in Philadelphia as a result of his own "imprudence" for twenty—each on the plea that he had been "useful" to the bank.[20] Duff Green rated his services higher; and General Jackson heard that the editor of the *Telegraph* had been allowed to overdraw his account ten thousand dollars.[21]

The turn of affairs fortified Jackson's conviction that the bank should go—and by the shortest practicable route. "I tell you, sir," the Executive was quoted as saying, "she's broke. Mr. Biddle is a proud man and he never would have . . . ask[ed] me for a postponement [of the three per cents] if the bank had had the money."

This, however, sounds more like something dressed up by Blair or Kendall for word-of-mouth dissemination than an accurate expression of the presidential mind.[22] True, the bank had not on hand the money for the three per cents, but, when the Baring trick failed, Biddle had been able to raise it; and in all his bank seems to have been as well off as the run of state institutions. On their own, some of the western branches[23] would have failed ere this, but as components of a national system few really doubted that eastern strength would pull them through. Jackson himself appreciated this, or he would not have continued to keep every dollar he owned in the Washington and Nashville branches.

On the other hand the events of the year past had, and with reason, tended to confirm Old Hickory's basic objections to the bank as a consolidation of power prejudicial to the purity of government and indifferent to the welfare of the plain people. Current embarrassments which Mr. Biddle sought to tide over by shady devices—race horse bills, the Baring deal—simply exposed a breach in the wall that could be attacked with advantage.

6

The President did not delay. Spurred by the offensive House resolution, he turned on the bank and turned furiously.

On March 19, the wheels were put in motion with a memorandum to the Cabinet asking: (1) Whether anything had occurred since December to lessen concern for the safety of deposits? (2) Has the bank been a faithful agent of the Government? (3) Should the charter be renewed with modifications? (4) Should there be a new bank, and if so with what privileges? (5) What should be done with the Government revenues? Commenting on his own questions,

Jackson said he was opposed to recharter and indicated that he favored removal of the deposits, but had not made up his mind whether they should be distributed among state banks or placed in a new national bank.[24]

Only two of the replies that reached the White House really mattered—those of the Attorney General and of the Secretary of the Treasury.

Taney's came first, leading off with a statement of "strong doubts whether the bank continued to be a safe depository for the public money." The Polk report, the Attorney General thought, "exhibits a true and faithful picture of the . . . Bank." Yet Taney did not commit himself to the proposition that the bank was insolvent. It "may be perfectly able to meet its engagements and yet be a very unsuitable agent to be trusted with the public money." "Gross and palpable violations of duty" were pointed out: the business of the three per cents and other items concealed from the Government directors "thus depriving the government of that knowledge of its affairs which the charter meant to secure"; the influence over the press and over the machinery of government.

Tellingly Taney demonstrated the significance of the twenty-million-dollar increase in loans since 1830 at a time, when by Biddle's own statement, the bank should have been contracting unless a renewal of the charter seemed probable. Why this policy? "Was it not to compel the people to continue . . . [the] monopoly not on account of the benefits incurred by it, but to escape from the sufferings which the corporation had the power to inflict?" Yes. "A fiscal agent which has thus endeavored to fasten itself upon the body politic, and to perpetuate its . . . exclusive privileges by the lash . . . is no longer worthy of the confidence or employment of the government." The Government could properly "dismiss it at once" from its service. In that event Mr. Taney preferred the distribution of revenue among "judiciously selected" state institutions to the formation of another national bank.

The Attorney General knew the sort of an ending to put to his effective letter. "I do not conceal from myself the fierce and desperate struggle which the Bank will make to . . . procure a restoration of the deposits"—already as good as removed! "Nor am I insensible of its power. But I . . . [rely] on prompt, firm and decisive measures on the part of the Executive, and for support on the intelligence and patriotism of the people. And I am Sir with highest respect yr. obt. st. R. B. TANEY."[25]

The fighting heart of Old Hickory responded. "I long for retirement & repose on the Hermitage. But until I can strangle this hydra of corruption, the Bank, I will not shrink from my duty or my part. I think a system can be arranged with the state banks."[26]

Frank Blair and Amos Kendall beamed with joy. All winter long they had been plugging with Jackson for the removal of deposits and the use of state banks. Taney's vigorous adherence to their cause was the greatest stroke yet. The smoke that curled from the Attorney General's long black cigars mingled more frequently with that of the corn-cob pipe in the second-floor study. A new vein showed itself in the White House correspondence and new faces appeared in the capital as state banks, scenting the atmosphere, by post and by agent began to insinuate their excellence on the Executive. One such agent, a Philadelphia financier currently without a connection, wrote that sporting men were willing to wager that the deposits would be removed.[27]

Another White House visitor, more tastefully attired than Mr. Taney, whose clothes appeared as if he had slept in them, regarded these events with distrust. Vice President Van Buren's restful office afforded opportunity for observation. Having laboriously ascended to the rank of heir apparent, all he need do was to hold what was already gained until 1836, granting that General Jackson should retire no sooner. But to encompass this with the fewest ripples, awkward episodes like that of nullification should be avoided. Already Mr. Van Buren had given an opinion—and for once precipitously it seemed—on the subject of deposits. He had opposed their removal.[28] Still, the Vice President could console himself with the reflection that the memorandum of his friend, the Secretary of the Treasury, was not as yet in the President's hands.

Jackson was growing impatient when on May 20, 1833, seven weeks after Taney had reported, Mr. McLane's opinion, a volume of ninety-one manuscript pages, reached the President's writing table. Under no circumstances, said the Secretary of the Treasury, should the Bank of the United States be rechartered. But there he and Mr. Taney parted company. McLane would form a new national bank, free of the evils that afflicted Mr. Biddle's, to receive and disburse the public revenue. The deposits should not be removed from the old institution before the new was ready, however. In the first place the President had no power to remove them. Only the Secretary of the Treasury had the power—to be exercised in accordance with his sense of duty. No adequate reason existed for the removal. The Bank of the United States was solvent—and that was the ruling consideration. Even the debts of the western branches were "safe and wholesome." To deposit in the state banks would be calamitous for a staggering variety of reasons. These banks were unsafe. They would not support each other as could branches of the great bank in time of stress. They could not transfer funds satisfactorily, and such transfers as they could make would be attended by annoyance and expense. Terms of the Government's dealings with the present bank were fixed by law and usage. With state banks terms would be "a matter of bargain." State banks could not maintain a uniform currency. Did the President wish to return to the chaotic conditions of wartime and after? Moreover, the Bank of the United States would set upon the state banks, ruin them and cause a panic.

"To restore harmony throughout the country seems now all that is left to complete the President's patriotic labors. . . . The winding up of . . . [the bank's] concerns without embarrassment is under the most favorable circumstances rather to be hoped for than expected. It is not for the government to add to the inherent difficulties of the task, but rather to aid in obviating them; *not for the sake of the bank but that of the community.* I have the honor, to be, Sir, with the highest respect. . . . LOUIS MCLANE."[29]

The President laid the last sheet on his table and penciled beneath the signature: "Some strong points in this view— all ably discussed."

Strong points there were indeed—points which had turned back foemen of the bank since 1829. But there were also points so weak that so imprecise a critic as Blair could expose them.[30] Mr. McLane did the cause of a national bank more than justice. He sought to prove too much. For better or for worse, Taney had made the more convincing presentation of his case for removal and for a trial of the state banks.

But before anything definite should be done, Jackson decided to refresh himself with a rest from official duties, and before he could do that he must make two Cabinet changes which had been agreed upon as far back as December. Accordingly on June 1, 1833, McLane stepped into Edward Livingston's shoes as Secretary of State and Livingston took the legation at Paris on which he had so long had an eye. William J. Duane, a Philadelphia lawyer and son of the celebrated editor of the Jeffersonian *Aurora*, became Secretary of the Treasury. Duane was McLane's nominee for the office, the arrangement having been made long before the emergence of the deposit question had elevated Taney to the actual post of premier.

7

The vacation opened with a junket to Fredericksburg, Virginia, to lay the cornerstone of a monument to Washington's mother. At Alexandria a well set-up young man boarded the steamer and approached the President as if to greet him. "Excuse my rising, sir," said General Jackson, whose chair was wedged between a berth and a table. The newcomer appeared to be taking off a glove. "Never mind your glove, sir," said the President extending his hand. The young man thrust his fist violently into Jackson's face as if to pull his nose.

"What, sir! What, sir!" Old Hickory's cry and the crash of the table as he kicked it away aroused the room.

McLane, Livingston and Washington Irving grappled the intruder who threw them off and darted through a door with Jackson after him, cane upraised. Friends blocked the President's path and closed the door. Pounding on the panel, Jackson commanded them to open up or he would break down the door.

Gaining the deck the President learned that his assailant had escaped down the landing stage surrounded by confederates posing as indignant passengers. He was recognized as Robert B. Randolph, a former lieutenant of the Navy dismissed for attempted theft of funds belonging to the late John B. Timberlake whom he had succeeded as purser of the frigate *Constitution*. A considerate Virginian offered to pursue and "kill Randolph in fifteen minutes." "No, sir," said the old soldier, "I want no man to stand between me and my assailants, and none to take revenge on my account."[30a]

The President later observed privately that, had he been on his feet and prepared for the attack, Randolph "never would have moved with life from the tracks he stood in."[31] That opportunity having been lost, Jackson declined to avail himself of the law to punish his assailant. Not until after Old Hickory had left the presidency was Randolph placed on trial. Jackson refused to give evidence for the prosecution, and asked that in event of conviction the sentence or fine be remitted. "I have to this old age complied with my mother's advice to indict no man for assault or sue him for slander."[32]

General Jackson returned from the outing "looking much better than when he left." "The [Randolph] affair seem'd to have put his blood in motion," said John Campbell of the Treasury.[33]

After this salutary beginning a large and important-looking presidential party set out on June 6 for the Chesapeake. "Met by a number of Citizens with the Steam Carrs [of the Baltimore & Ohio Railroad] 12 miles in advance of the City which took us into Baltimore in a few minutes," the General recorded.[34] The first ride of a President of the United States behind a locomotive was followed by three days of ear-splitting celebration which left the guest of honor with a headache.

Then he moved on to Philadelphia where the reception lasted four days and nights. Entering the city on a "white charger," the "savior of the Union" accepted the obeisances of the crowds for five hours and was badly sunburned. "How old, how very old he looks," seemed to be the common thought of those who filled streets, windows, roofs.[35] Though profoundly moved by the "feelings of the people, . . . I sincerely wish my trip was over," the President wrote his son. "Except to my Hermitage or to the watering places I think it is the last journey I shall undertake. Kiss my little Rachel."[36] Philip Syng Physick, America's most famous physician, examined the President. "Now, Doctor," he said, "I can do anything you think proper, except give up coffee and tobacco." So taken was he by the "gentleness, the peculiar and indescribable charm" of his patient that Doctor Physick could talk of little else for days.[37]

New York's welcome exceeded anything of the kind the metropolis had ever known. "I have bowed to upwards of two hundred thousand people today, . . . and I hope little Rachel will not forget me until I return."[38] As Jackson crossed the bridge from Castle Garden to the Battery, the overburdened structure gave way, precipitating Secretary Cass, Secretary Woodbury, Jack Donelson and a medley of attendant dignitaries into the water.

8

That night at the American House the President met Martin Van Buren for a long conversation on the bank question for which Amos Kendall had attempted to prepare the Vice President by letter.

"The President seems to have made up his mind that the public deposits must be withdrawn," Kendall informed Mr. Van Buren. "As to the manner and time he is not so well satisfied, and on those points, and perhaps upon the expediency of the whole measure, he will consult you."

There followed an outline for erecting a system of depositories comprised of state banks under definite regulation. To minimize the shock, fresh deposits only would go to the state banks. Existing deposits would remain in the Bank of the United States until withdrawn in the normal run of Government business. "As to the time of this movement, I am firmly of the opinion that it ought to be made soon enough to take the last dollar out of the U. S. Bank and present the new machine in complete operation before the next session of Congress [begins in December]. This cannot be done unless the deposits in the state banks commence as early as the first of August or at furthest the first of September." Kendall saw "the President's popularity" and the Government-supported state banks as the spearhead of a sudden assault to drive Biddle to the wall and end his power forever.

"I pray you to consider these points and . . . hope your great influence may be exerted to effect the desired object."[39]

The Vice President's great influence was not so exerted, thus affording no counterweight to the views of McLane, Cass and Woodbury, who were with the President constantly. On quitting the official party in New York, Mr. McLane left with his chief a lengthy memorandum urging that no action be taken until Congress should meet.[40]

Passing slowly through Connecticut amid continuous ovations, the General pondered this document whenever he could snatch a moment for himself. He had, indeed, determined to dispense with the

Bank of the United States as the Government depository. He meant to do this before Congress met. But the fresh objections of McLane, with which the President knew the new Secretary of the Treasury, Duane, to be in agreement,[41] moved Jackson to restate his reasons more fully than he had originally expected would be necessary. A detailed and explicit communication to Duane was begun—with only Donelson to help and apparently nothing except a memorandum by Kendall for a guide. When Hartford was reached, the President's young private secretary confessed himself worn out and anxious to shorten the tour.[42]

Across Rhode Island cannon boomed from town to town as if all New England were a battle line. Receptions overlapped each other. Though Jackson drove himself and his nephew unflaggingly, the letter to Duane was unfinished when, early in the morning of June 20, the travelers stood on the western end of a bridge across the Blackstone River beyond which lay Massachusetts. At their backs artillery roared a farewell salute, breaking so many windows in Pawtucket that the State provided new glass for nearly every householder who asked for it. General Jackson shook hands with his Rhode Island escorts and advanced toward the middle of the span. From the Massachusetts shore a man in the uniform of a member of the Governor's staff approached to welcome the President of the United States. He was Josiah Quincy, junior, a connection of General Jackson's predecessor in office, and he could have wished for a more congenial duty.

9

Reflecting that it is part of a lawyer's calling to be "equally fluent on all sides of a question," Barrister Quincy spoke the felicitations required of hospitality, for the President was in Massachusetts by express invitation of the State Legislature. This reverent body, which in 1815 had thanked the Almighty for the victory at New Orleans without mentioning General Jackson's name, appears to have felt it no longer necessary to ignore the existence of the man whose stand against nullification had won approval from "the God-like Daniel" Webster. After a ceremonial breakfast at Attleborough, the party inspected a factory. The manager produced a card of badges stamped with palmetto trees for the South Carolina "army." "You have been interfering with our business, Mr. President," he said with a smile, "and should feel honor bound to take these buttons off our hands."

As the afternoon wore on, Mr. Quincy began to thaw out, finding the President's conversation "interesting from its sincerity, decision and point." Before Boston was reached, the Governor's aide had caught the spirit of the occasion and sent ahead for a horse that the General might enter the city mounted. Pleased and grateful, Jackson left the barouche and swung his long legs into the saddle. At the city line, the Mayor awaited with a carriage in which a place was reserved for the guest of honor. Quincy argued that the President had been seated all day and preferred the saddle; but he argued in vain.

On the next day Old Hickory and the aide-de-camp were on excellent terms. A military review was scheduled to take place on the Common. Quincy had scoured Boston for handsome mounts for the President and his suite. As the visitors appeared in front of the troops, a salvo of artillery shook the earth. The borrowed horses reared and leaped. Controlling his mount perfectly, Jackson galloped along the line of troops, the Cabinet officers and miscellaneous notables following as best they could.

"Where is the Vice President?" exclaimed Old Hickory as he drew up his prancing horse to take the marching salute.

Riding alongside, Mr. Quincy answered him. "About as nearly on the fence as a gentleman of his positive political convictions can get."

Mr. Van Buren's bolting steed had brought up, tail first, against a fence and refused to budge.

General Jackson looked and laughed. "And you've matched him with a horse even more non-committal than his rider."[43]

Boston rubbed its eyes, scarcely able to believe the evidence of its own deportment. "Here is Pres. Jackson," apologetically wrote Edward Warren to his son, "for whom a short time ago no epithet was too bad, received with all the show of honor which we paid to Lafayette."[44] Quincy was unable to discern any particular injustice to Lafayette. Noting his tenderness to children and the wordless understanding the weatherbeaten warrior could at once establish with them, the aide-de-camp saw something incongruous in the old New

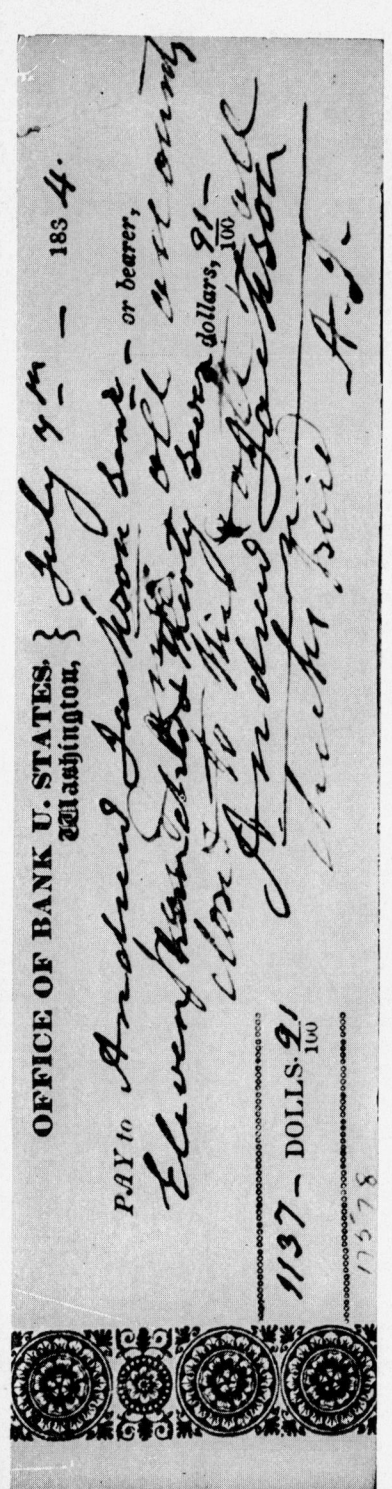
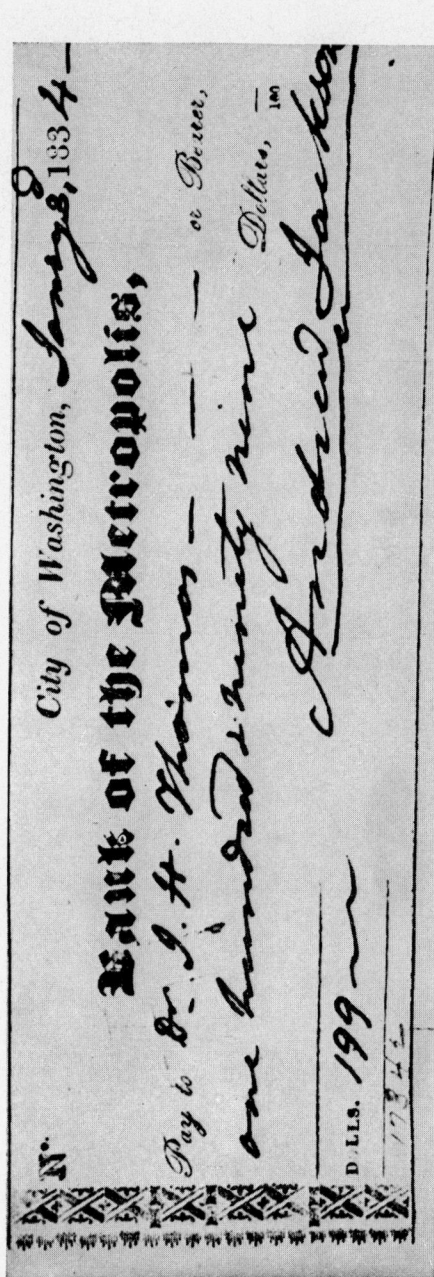

GENERAL JACKSON AND MR. BIDDLE SEVER BUSINESS RELATIONS

But not until they had been fighting each other officially for three years, and not until nine months after the President had transferred the Government deposits to other banks. Above is Jackson's last personal check on the Washington branch of the Bank of the United States, withdrawing his balance. Below is one of his first checks on an account he had started some months previously in Washington's "pet" bank. From the Jackson Papers, Library of Congress, Washington.

The White House

This popular name for the Executive Mansion received the accolade of polite usage during General Jackson's administrations. The portico was erected during his tenancy, and two pumps removed from the side yards. Unfortunately obscured by trees is the new stable, which Jackson filled with race horses and made as much a part of the presidential establishment as the East Room. From a print in the Library of Congress.

England custom of frightening young ones when they were naughty with the name of Andrew Jackson.

Only Beacon Street seems to have been able to make a decent show of curbing its emotions. When the presidential party passed through this residential holy of holies, Quincy confessed that the audience was "undemonstrative"—until a window flew up and an eager-faced child, a little girl, appeared waving a kerchief. Later Mr. Quincy learned the secret of the unexpected drama. Well back from his window, where he could see without being seen, Daniel P. Parker, merchant, was observing the procession. The carriage containing Jackson approached. A chill east wind tossed the Hero's white mane, but something less tangible bore the compelling magnetism of his presence into that parlor on Beacon Street. "Do someone come here," the merchant shouted, "and salute the old man!" Mr. Parker's little daughter did what her father could not bring himself to do.[45]

On his fourth day in Boston a severe cold and bleeding of the lungs[46] confined the President to his bed in the Tremont House. Physicians bled him. Quincy entertained the patient by reading from Seba Smith of the Portland (Maine) *Courier*, whose letters over the name of Major Jack Downing were the most widely reprinted and plagiarized newspaper humor of the day. The Major had long appeared in the rôle of an intimate counsellor of the President. In the present instance he assumed to be a member of the official touring party. His two most recent letters described incidents of the journey. At Philadelphia, when the President became exhausted by handshaking, the indispensable Major had stepped behind him and, thrusting his strong arm beneath Jackson's weary one, finished off the greetings as the President's understudy, with no one a whit the wiser. When the bridge broke in New York it was Major Downing who fished the dripping statesmen from the water.[47]

Old Hickory chuckled. "The Vice President must have written that. Depend upon it Jack Downing is only Van Buren in masquerade."[48]

On the fifth day also Jackson kept to his hotel while Quincy circulated among the brahmin set, singing the praises of Old Hickory with all the zeal of a new convert. He failed to convince his distinguished kinsman, the ex-President, that Jackson was even sick. John

Quincy Adams said he knew Andrew Jackson. The supposed illness was "four-fifths trickery," a mere bid for "sympathy."[49]

Young Mr. Quincy was more successful in communicating some of his enthusiasm to his father whom he assured that even General Jackson's ignorance of books had been exaggerated. This conversation had results that shook Boston to bed-rock. Though the president of Harvard College, Josiah Quincy, senior, was a lawyer and a man of action rather than a cloistered scholar who believed that all the knowledge in the world reposed between the covers of books. Calling the Harvard overseers together on that very day for a hurried and, as strict constructionists have said, "irregular" meeting, President Quincy obtained approval of a resolution to confer upon Andrew Jackson a degree of Doctor of Laws. John Quincy Adams was aghast. Was there no way, he asked the elder Quincy, to prevent this outrage? "None," replied the educator. "As the people have twice decided that this man knows law enough to be their ruler it is not for Harvard College to maintain that they are mistaken."[50]

The presentation ceremony was announced for the following morning.

10

During the two-day interim of illness, Jackson finished and Donelson began to copy two communications to Secretary of the Treasury William J. Duane, on the subject of discontinuing the use of the Bank of the United States as the depository for Government funds. The first, a letter of instructions, was fairly brief. The other, giving in deference to Duane's contrary views Jackson's reasons for the step, would fill twenty pages of this volume.

The letter of instructions suggested that on September 15, 1833, "at furthest," deposits in the Bank of the United States be discontinued and the balance remaining there drawn on until exhausted in the course of the ordinary needs of the Government. On that date, or before, deposits should go to a group of state banks whose composition would be determined as follows. An agent of the Treasury should proceed at once to Baltimore, Philadelphia, New York and Boston and in those four cities designate five banks (two in New York) as "primary banks." Later other primary banks might be chosen in western and in southern cities. The primary banks would select, with the Treasury's approval, "secondary banks" to assist them in receiving the deposits and performing all the functions for the Government hitherto performed by the Bank of the United States. This was to be done without cost to the Government.

Weekly reports on the state of deposits and monthly reports on the state of the banks would be submitted to the Treasury. At any time the Treasury could, on proper notice, drop a bank from the system "or break up the whole arrangement." Promptness was recommended in getting the preliminary survey under way and Amos Kendall was suggested as the agent for this work. Jackson said he wished "to present the new system to Congress, in complete and successful operation, at the commencement of the session."

The letter setting forth the President's reasons for dispensing with the services of Mr. Biddle's bank was largely a recast of Taney's indictment of that institution. Moreover, it took notice of McLane's contrary opinion which held that the power to remove the deposits from the Bank of the United States rested not with the Executive but with the Secretary of the Treasury. Jackson's whole communication was an implied denial of this, which the last line made more specific by adding that the President took "upon himself the responsibility."[51]

11

The seamed countenance of the old soldier was pale but "the spirit resolute to conquer infirmity," as Mr. Quincy wrote, when he set out for Harvard Yard. A full retinue attended, including the shade of Major Jack Downing. An address in Latin preceded the presentation of the degree. On receiving the scroll, the President expressed his thanks in a sentence or two. "[At this point]," recorded Major Jack, "the Gineral was going to stop but I says in his ear, 'You must give 'em a little Latin, *Doctor!*' . . . 'E pluribus unum,' says he, 'my friends, sine qua non.'"[52] This remark, destined to become the most widely quoted of all Major Downing's writings, was said to have been repeated in erudite circles as the President's veritable utterance. John Quincy Adams would have liked to believe it. Declining an invitation to honor the occasion with his presence, the ex-President wrote in his diary: "An affectionate child of my Alma Mater, I . . . [could not bear to] witness her disgrace in conferring her highest literary honor upon a barbarian who could . . . hardly spell his own name."[53]

After the degree had been conferred, a reception was held at the residence of President Quincy. The entire undergraduate body filed past. General Jackson began shaking hands with each one. "I am happy to see you, gentlemen." "I wish you all happiness." "Gentlemen, I wish you success in life." Perceiving the President's strength beginning to wane, friends discontinued the handshaking. When the faculty walked past, Doctor Palfrey led his two little girls by the hands. Jackson lifted the children up and kissed them.

So began an eventful day. Leaving Cambridge the President was driven in an open carriage to Charlestown, where he climbed the unfinished Bunker Hill Monument and listened to an oration by Edward Everett. Then followed a devastating series of receptions at which young Quincy, the aide-de-camp, rebelled. He begged Jackson to withdraw and conserve his strength. "These people have made their arrangements to welcome me," the old gentleman replied, "and so long as I am not on my back I will gratify them." In the middle of the afternoon, he was on his back—resting at Lynn while his suite struggled through a dinner in his honor, their fourth that day.

On to Marblehead, one of Massachusetts' rare Democratic towns. Quincy took matters in hand. After a brief pause a banquet was left untasted and a vast outpouring of genuine Jacksonians grievously disappointed while the carriage sped toward Salem. "An anxious drive," recorded Quincy, "the President was becoming weaker every moment." Dusk was falling as they entered Salem. The aide-de-camp ordered the carriage driven to a hotel by the quickest route. Before the citizenry was aware, he had Jackson in bed and under a doctor's care. Informing the local notables of the Executive's condition, Quincy suggested the cancellation of their program of arrangements. "Impossible," said the men of Salem. A barouche for the President was at the door and the procession actually in motion. Unconsciously or otherwise, Mr. Quincy borrowed an idea from Major Jack Downing. It had grown quite dark. He and Martin Van Buren entered the carriage of honor, which moved to its place in the parade. The applause was deafening. The hospitalities ended with dinner number five.

That night Jackson suffered a severe hemorrhage of the lungs. Quincy was sure the tour would have to be called off. In the morning Old Hickory walked in on his staff at breakfast. "An immaterial something flashed in his eye," wrote the aide-de-camp, "and it was evident that the faltering body was again held in subjection." On the next day, June 27, 1833, Mr. Quincy left the President at the New Hampshire boundary. "Come and see me at the White House, or better still at the Hermitage," said Jackson, taking his hand.

The two never met again. The letters to William J. Duane which Jackson had posted from Boston started a train of events that ended any chance of Josiah Quincy, junior's, allegiance to the Jackson cause, though nothing dimmed his admiration for the man. "A knightly personage," the Bostonian wrote in his old age, "prejudiced, narrow, mistaken upon many points, but vigorously a gentleman in his sense of honor and in his natural straightforward courtesies which are easily to be distinguished from the veneer of policy."[54]

12

The tour ended at Concord, New Hampshire, where the President collapsed. Borne back to Washington by steamer he suffered a relapse. For forty-eight hours his life seemed in danger.[55] Tiptoeing from the White House, Cabinet officers clustered anxiously about the spruce figure of Martin Van Buren. But the tough old gladiator rallied, thereby changing much history.

His first act was to direct Secretary of the Treasury Duane to start the machinery calculated to transfer the Government deposits from the Bank of the United States. That officer demurred and interposed subtle tactics of delay. McLane and Cass supported him. Mr. Van Buren sought the cooler temperature of Saratoga Springs, New York. Alone, and with noteworthy patience, Jackson contended against the refractory head of the Treasury, obtaining at the end of two weeks a promise that when the matter came up for final action Duane would co-operate or resign.[56] So racked by pain that to hold a pen was torture, General Jackson then indited a grave and kindly acknowledgment of another of his New England conquests, respectfully declining a proposal purporting to be from a Connecticut spinster whose object was matrimony.[57]

Not until the closing days of July, 1833, was Amos Kendall free to depart on his mission to select the key banks for the great experiment. Duane's quibbling had consumed precious time, and the President reconciled himself to a fortnight's delay in the execution of his plan. This deferred the beginning until October 1. As nothing could be done until Kendall reported, Jackson, still ill and very weary, embarked for his sea-island summer resort, the Rip Raps, taking the White House family including all the children and five servants.

CHAPTER XXXVI

Mr. Biddle's Biggest Gamble

I

ANDREW JACKSON paid his hotel bill at the Rip Raps with a personal check for three hundred and ninety-five dollars and seventy-five cents on Mr. Biddle's bank, and on August 23, 1833, he was at his desk in the White House after an absence of twenty-seven days. The relaxation of ocean bathing and games on the beach with the children had greatly improved though not restored his health. Yet, considering the distractions which marred this vacation, the change for the good was remarkable.

Kendall had immediately run into difficulties which every few days he reported to his chief. The enthusiasm of the state banks for Government deposits had suddenly begun to cool. In Baltimore one first-class bank refused to have anything to do with the proposal, another left the emissary's inquiry unanswered. Of three others which expressed a "desire" for a share of the deposits, only one seemed prepared to make the strict guaranties which Jackson demanded. Prospects in Philadelphia and New York seemed a little brighter; and in Boston brighter still, so far as the willingness of some of the banks was concerned. Yet, on the whole, the survey was very disappointing. The reasons for this were two: the safeguards demanded of the banks by the Government, and fear of the retaliatory power of Nicholas Biddle, who was making ready to strike back in earnest. As a sample of what he could do, the screws were put on Boston the week Kendall was there. In the face of a need by local merchants for a million dollars to pay duties on cargoes then at the wharves, the Bank of the United States discontinued discounts and demanded the return of its balances in the state banks. This so greatly crippled the state banks to which the importers applied that Kendall said unless relief were forthcoming some of the mercantile houses would have to suspend.[1]

Mr. Kendall's work was not made lighter by Secretary of State McLane, who had followed him to Philadelphia and to New York, talking up a proposal to postpone the transfer until January 1. Momentarily Kendall weakened. If McLane and Duane were not merely trying to throw up a screen behind which to defeat the whole project, Kendall told Jackson he would acquiesce. But after witnessing Mr. Biddle's demonstration against Boston, the President's agent said the state banks must be helped quickly: *"immediate removal or no removal"* at all.[2]

Duane continued recalcitrant and Jackson appealed to Van Buren for assistance. He received in return many mellifluous words attesting loyalty and admiration. The General's health being the prime consideration, the Vice President begged that he prolong his vacation. "The first weeks in September as you know are the worst in Washington." In the meantime the status of our public lands was suggested as a matter worthy of the Executive's especial attention. At last Mr. Van Buren mentioned the bank question, declaring himself in favor of preparing arrangements for the transfer, but deferring the execution thereof until the first of the year. All this was well and effectively said.[3]

If Martin Van Buren could write a seductive letter, Roger B. Taney could write one that was more so. The Attorney General said he did not close his eyes to developments which had "greatly strengthened the Bank and increased the difficulties to be surmounted by the Executive." Nor did he overlook the fact that if virtue were to prevail and vice be overthrown, it would be at the hands of Andrew Jackson because no other President would have the courage to carry to the death a fight with Nicholas Biddle. Still, the Attorney General would not press the issue upon his chief. "I should feel deeply mortified if after so many splendid victories, civil and military, you should in the last term of your public life meet defeat." The safe thing would be not to risk it. Mr. Taney would not presume to advise the President as to which course to take. But, in case Jackson wished to continue the fight, and to transfer the deposits now, he could count on Taney to stand by him.[4]

Instead of prolonging, Old Hickory curtailed his holiday. "is it possible," he asked Martin Van Buren, "that your friends are overawed by the power of the Bank. it cannot overawe me."[5]

Armed with stronger evidence than ever of the bank's moral unfitness—more secret loans to congressmen, more editors (including James Gordon Bennett) "bought up," sixty thousand dollars to printers for propaganda, light on the Asbury Dickins deal[6]—Jackson summoned his Cabinet on September 10. Presenting a report from Kendall claiming sufficient state banks available for immediate needs, the President said that the Government would change depositories on October 1. The meeting ended in an apparently irreconcilable disagreement—Taney and Woodbury supporting Jackson; McLane, Duane and Cass opposed; Barry absent.

On September 14, Jackson suggested that Duane retire in keeping with his promise. He refused. On September 19, Jackson read the Cabinet a statement of his reasons for removal which Taney, sustained by black cigars, had sat up most of the night revising.[7] Even Duane admitted it a strong document;[8] but he refused to sign an order discontinuing deposits in the Bank of the United States and he refused to resign. Had Mr. Duane been an officer of the bank, it is difficult to see how he could have served Mr. Biddle better. An interesting fact is that the banker knew six weeks in advance almost precisely the exasperating line the Secretary of the Treasury intended to take with his chief.[9]

Nicholas Biddle turned the screws of credit tighter, not in Boston alone but throughout the East, the West and the South. Every day of delay strengthened his hands and weakened those of the President. Not even in his bed chamber could Jackson find refuge from the incessant pressure, W. B. Lewis accosting him there to palliate the behavior of Duane and urge a postponement until Congress should meet. "No, sir," the General flashed back. "If the bank . . . [keeps the deposits until then] no power can prevent it from obtaining a charter— it will have it if it has to buy up all Congress."[10]

To add to these tribulations McLane and Cass threatened to abandon their posts, which would wreck, as many thought, popular confidence in the Administration.[11] Debilitating headaches and a pain in the chest constantly threatened to bring Old Hickory to bed. "Quite unwell today," he wrote. "Nothing but the excitement keeps me up."[12]

Through it all the Executive's forbearance was as remarkable as his inflexibility. Quarreling with no one, he met Duane's whimpering insolence with dignity. Not until September 23 did he dismiss this subordinate and name Roger B. Taney in his stead. The new Secretary of the Treasury lost no time giving official notice that Government deposits would not be made in the Bank of the United States after the last day of the month.

2

Nicholas Biddle thought Jackson would not dare to go that far, but, foresightedly enough, the banker had long and carefully prepared for any eventuality. He had placed his bank in tip-top shape and slyly drawn state banks into its debt. These astute measures were counted on to break up the removal campaign in its early stages. "When we begin," he told the head of his New York branch, "we shall crush the Kitchen Cabinet at once."[13] The beginning, which Amos Kendall had witnessed in Boston, brought on great consternation but failed to achieve its end. So, on October 1 Mr. Biddle turned the screws again, and hardest in the West and the South. Discounts were further reduced, more balances against state banks called in, the receipt of the notes of state banks restricted, bills of exchange limited to sixty days, exchange rates raised and rigged in favor of the East to draw capital in that direction. Sixteen days later western offices were required to squeeze their communities tighter still.[14]

The bank claimed these harsh measures necessary to its security, and this false statement contained a deceptive element of truth. Some contraction was necessary, the exact extent of which probably no two persons could have agreed on. Under the cover of this necessity Biddle went far and away beyond anything required by conservative banking.[15] At the outset his bank was in an exceptionally strong position. On October 1, Government money in its vaults amounted to nine million eight hundred and sixty-eight thousand dollars, to be drawn out gradually over a period of several months. The banker's deliberate purpose was to make people suffer, to bring upon the Administration a storm of protest by the threat of panic and, if that did not suffice, by panic in fact. The blame, he felt, would fall on Jackson and ruin him. Had not the then Secretary of the Treasury, Mr. McLane, solemnly warned the President of this identical calamity six months before? So Mr. Biddle sowed the wind, topping off that achievement with a manifesto in his jauntiest style, representing Jackson as an angry ignoramus intent upon the demolition of an institution whose aim was to scatter seeds of benevolence among a prosperous, a happy and a virtuous people.

Biddle's object was measurably assisted by the lame start the "pet banks," to use the opposition's term, made at taking over the work of the "monster." Amos Kendall, who did much of the actual work of erecting the new system, was a keen man and a capable organizer. Four years as Fourth Auditor of the Treasury, a post beneath his talents, had taught him something of the mysteries of banking and finance; and his constant thought had been to supplant the Bank of the United States. McLane and Duane so retarded his efforts, however, that in September he had brought Jackson an instrument admittedly imperfect. Confronted by the alternatives of giving battle with half an army or retiring from the field, Old Hickory chose to fight.

Roger B. Taney, taking over the subordinate command, sought to arm a few of the state banks with the means of defense should Biddle suddenly call on them to redeem large quantities of their notes in specie. Accordingly he issued to each of the New York depositories and to one depository in Philadelphia a draft for five hundred thousand dollars on the Bank of the United States. A Baltimore depository got three drafts for a hundred thousand each. These transactions were unnoted in the reports of the Treasury to the Bank of the United States, the strict understanding being that the drafts should be presented only in event of aggression by Mr. Biddle.

Temptation overcame some of the recipients of this ammunition. Finding itself adversely involved in speculation, the Union Bank of Baltimore cashed one of the one-hundred-thousand-dollar drafts. The situation was made worse by the fact that Thomas Ellicott, president of this institution, was a close friend of Taney, himself a small stockholder. Then, in defiance of renewed pledges, Ellicott cashed the other two. The Philadelphia bank followed with its five-hundred-thousand-dollar draft, as did one of the New York banks. Biddle met these demands on the spot but filled the air with entirely justified remonstrances because of the intentional omission of the drafts from the Treasury statements. For awhile it looked as if the Baltimore bank would fail and, all in all, Mr. Taney was in an ugly fix—as he deserved to be. But he pulled out, no more emergency drafts being presented. Gradually additions were made to the chain of depositories until the country was covered. By day-and-night industry, the Treasury chief began to co-ordinate their activities.

3

Nicholas Biddle was equally busy, and the results of his handiwork made the improvements in Mr. Taney's system difficult to appreciate. The repressive proceedings of the great bank were bearing fruit. Commerce slackened, industry drooped, prices of securities and of agricultural products slumped; hands were laid off; wages cut; gold and silver were hoarded, money rates climbed from eight to twenty-five per cent and business houses began to go to the wall. Nor could all the inconveniences be attributed directly to Mr. Biddle, though it was in his power to relieve them. As the Government's fiscal agent the great bank had provided a national currency that was fairly uniform. A bill on an Atlantic seaboard branch was honored on the Mississippi River for about ninety-eight cents on the dollar. Mr. Taney's thrown-together group was unable to duplicate this arrangement. Troops transferred from Virginia to Alabama found their money had depreciated twelve and a half per cent. Government employees and creditors in Missouri and Illinois, heretofore paid in notes of the great bank's St. Louis branch receivable locally at par, got the paper of the "pet" bank in Washington, D. C., which they found hard to dispose of at a five percent shaving. Such things discomfited a stratum of society where Jackson's supporters were most numerous.

Mr. Biddle beat the drums and let the people know. More manna for congressmen, editors and pamphleteers quickened the spread of his gospel. The waters of public discontent began to rise and some of Jackson's personal followers to fall away. Clayton of Georgia, House leader of the anti-bank forces in 'Thirty-one, accepted a loan and apologized for his error. The banker's hireling, Representative Watmough of Pennsylvania, in receipt of a fresh accommodation of sixteen hundred and fifty dollars, made overtures to Major Lewis.

Though fearful of the future, Lewis remained loyal,[16] as did McLane; and Cass's opposition changed to timid acquiescence. As for Martin Van Buren, he kept away from Washington until nearly Christmas time, carefully explaining that this was from motives of delicate consideration for the fame of his great leader. Once the die was cast, the Vice President assured Jackson that he was with him through thick and thin. "[But]," added the self-effacing statesman, "it would not do to expose the great measure to prejudice by doing anything that would tend in the slightest degree to withdraw it from the protection of your name."[17] No evidence to the contrary appearing, it would seem that General Jackson read this with a perfectly straight countenance; and to the end of his official life he deprecated the injustice of calling such a guileless soul "the Magician."

With at least the show of a friendly Cabinet behind him, Jackson struck back with all the vigor of a still well-disciplined Administration machine. Blair and Kendall prodded the partizan press to onslaughts as fierce as anything Mr. Biddle's rival troupe of performers could deliver. Results, however, were unsatisfactory in consequence of the fact that the campaign was predicated on a stupendous miscarriage of prophecy. From the first the Jackson press had taken the line that no public distress existed—only scare-talk put out by the bank to disguise its own distress. In Amos Kendall's vivid metaphor, the Secretary of the Treasury had his heel on the bank viper's head and could crush it at will. These statements were susceptible of the criticism of being untrue. The bank was strong and arrogant, and public distress was nearing the panic stage. Frightened hoarders virtually withdrew the stock of precious metals from circulation. Communities began to supply the shortage of small coins with scrip, derisively called "Jackson money."

For years opponents had nourished their self-esteem in defeat with the reflection that "General Jackson's popularity can stand anything." Now it seemed that Nicholas Biddle had found the heel of Achilles. From the apex of the nullification victory, the fabulous Jacksonian prestige was falling like a spent rocket. Along the route of the grand tour from Maryland to New Hampshire, banquet orators who had strewn the Hero's path with the flowers of rhetoric publicly proclaimed their apostasy. The people were invited to button their waist-bands tighter and survey the state of the nation.

Six months ago mills humming, farm prices high. Now—all a ruin. Why? Because Andrew Jackson, carried away by delusions of grandeur, had chosen to disregard the implicit warnings of two secretaries of the treasury in favor of the schemes of a reckless crew of politico-financial adventurers.

Though few had the courage to resist the pack in full cry, one rather surprising exception was Robert Vaux who in Philadelphia bore a name almost as well-known as that of Nicholas Biddle. A man of wide culture, Mr. Vaux's patronage of the arts, his philanthropies and his works of prison reform had been copied throughout the United States and in Europe. On the bank question, he remained silent until his views were solicited. Then he expressed apprehension that "a Government Bank was perhaps a dangerous institution, as it might in the hands of unscrupulous men be used as a lever against popular liberty." Philadelphia rang with denunciations. "From mouth to mouth," recorded an eye-witness, "flew the exclamation, 'Robert Vaux is a Jackson man.' An edict of social extermination was registered against him. To the right and left he was shunned. A crusade was organized to eject him from all societies he had for the most part founded, and it was done."[18]

With the breaking storm's sharp growl assailing every ear, statesmen made their ways to Washington for the Twenty-third Congress which was to convene on December 2, 1833. Clay, Calhoun and Webster stood forth as the giants of an opposition whose prospects never had seemed brighter. Jackson's shaken ranks realized the supreme crisis of their leader's public life to be at hand, with the odds against him the heaviest ever faced. As never before his lieutenants needed a ringing battle cry to electrify the spirits of their followers. They needed to regain the initiative and carry a fight to the enemy.

Through it all Old Hickory himself remained detached and tranquil, singularly so. Though seldom without headaches and chest pains, he seemed on the whole to gain strength. Minutely he followed the multifarious details of managing the Hermitage establishment. A colt he had given to Sarah won a four-mile purse at Baltimore. When Andrew, junior, and the little family left for Tennessee a stream of letters followed them. "My dear Sarah, I dreaded the long travel for our sweet little pet, fearful that it might get sick &

no doctor near. I have not rested well at night since you left me—every thing appeared silent & in gloom about the House, and when I walked into your room—found it without its occupants—everything changed, the cradle of my little pet without it, and its little waggon there—my feelings were overcome for the moment."[19] He would sit in his bedroom with Sarah's or Andrew's letters in his hand, gazing at a portrait of the grandchild as if to give reality to the parents' descriptions of her. "I wish I could see her walk, and hear her begin to prattle."[20] The long, unhurried missives contained no word of politics.

In his message, read to Congress on December 3, the Executive clung to the malapropos tactics of defense. "I am happy to know that through the good sense of our people the effort to get up a panic has hitherto failed. . . . No public distress has followed the exertions of the bank."[21] No battle cry to drown the clamors for bread welling up from a stricken land. Administration men shook their heads despairingly.

4

The bank struck first, respectfully memorializing Congress to direct the restoration of the deposits on the ground that their transfer represented a breach of contract. Two days later Henry Clay, wearing the air of a man with grave purposes afoot, moved to call on the President to lay before the Senate the "paper" he was "alleged" to have read to the Cabinet on September 18 last. As this paper, giving reasons for his contemplated action on the deposits, has been printed in every newspaper in the country, Senator Clay's request for an official copy seemed to foreshadow some direfully legalistic procedure. Courtly John Forsyth of Georgia, Administration floor leader in the Upper House, asked the object of the unprecedented request. Was it, by any chance, for the purpose of impeaching the President of the United States? This unruffled anticipation left the quick-witted Kentuckian for once without a ready reply.

His resolution was adopted, however; Jackson refused to comply. "As well I might be required to detail to the Senate the free and private conversations I have held with those cabinet officers relating to their duties."[22] Under the spur of Clay and of Calhoun, the Senate refused to receive the President's reply, though this bit of ill-humor failed to alter the fact that Jackson had acted clearly within his constitutional rights. Mr. Clay countered with an equally constitutional victory for the bank, the Senate rejecting four of the President's five renominations of Government directors. These men had been a thorn in the flesh of Mr. Biddle and useful to Jackson in exposing the banker's autocratic irregularities. The House, too, aimed a charge of bird-shot at the Executive. Ignoring the well-heeled agents of the bank who overran the ante-rooms, a resolution was introduced to exclude the President's none-too-happy observer, Major Lewis. It failed of passage.

Picayunish preliminaries seemed at an end, though, when, on December 26 Mr. Clay began a tremendous speech, his first of sixty that session. It took three days to deliver, and is one of that statesman's finest philippics. Jackson's whole record as President came under review. Finally Mr. Clay moved a resolution of censure proclaiming that "in relation to the public revenue" Andrew Jackson had violated the Constitution and the laws. The speaker was rewarded with such demonstrations of approval that Vice President Van Buren, who had tardily taken up his gavel only a few days before, suffered a lapse of his traditional urbanity. He cleared the galleries.

While Mr. Clay's motion did bear on the bank issue, Mr. Biddle would have greatly preferred a direct demand for the restitution of deposits. But neither he nor Henry Clay had been honest with the other. In 1832 Biddle had sought to use Clay for the purposes of the bank. Now Clay was using the bank to promote his own fortunes with an eye to 1836. The fate of the bank was only incidental to the harassment of Jackson and Van Buren. The Clay speech started a tide of oratory, pro and con, which veered further and further from the specific object that was vital to Nicholas Biddle.

The banker moved to get his forces in hand and throw them behind a resolution for the return of the deposits. He thought it could be shoved through quickly,[23] and to this end Mr. Biddle adopted grim and practical means.

In January the panic struck, and some of Biddle's allies winced at the carnage. "I should be very well pleased to see the scarcity of money increased," wrote one, describing the scenes in New York, "if it were not . . . [injuring] *your friends*."[24] It was perhaps natural for Editor James Watson Webb of the *Courier and Enquirer*, gambling on the fall of stocks, and for Congressman Watmough, who had not felt the pinch, to offer contrary advice:[25] "Do not alter your course the thousandth of a point."[26] Yet the plea of a woman who seems to have known Nicholas Biddle in happier days must have been difficult to resist. She asked for twenty dollars to buy a lottery ticket as a last cast to save her aged father from ruin.[27]

One may hope that Mr. Biddle lent her twenty dollars and that she held a lucky number, but, if the banker did that, it was about all he did to ameliorate distress except among congressmen susceptible of cultivation and other supposed molders of public opinion. On the contrary he turned the screws again, on January 23, 1834, directing his branch heads to squeeze three million three hundred thousand dollars more from a prostrate public in forty days. This would bring the contraction since August 1 to eighteen million three hundred thousand dollars, or more than one third of the total discounts of the bank. The contention that such excesses were necessary to protect the bank would be difficult to prove.[28] In private, Biddle's mask slipped. To the head of his Boston branch he wrote: "Nothing but the evidence of suffering abroad will produce any effect in Congress. . . . A steady course of firm restriction will ultimately lead to . . . the recharter of the bank."[29] Dropping all pretense that the retrenchment was anything but a lash applied to the backs of the voters, the realistic Webb told Biddle that his measures were not severe enough. "If you do not curtail, and largely too, you must & will lose . . . the approaching election in New York."[30]

To make out Jackson the culprit, Nicholas Biddle created an engine of propaganda the like of which no private person had set in motion before. Its fuel was cash. In his latest distribution of largess, Mr. Biddle had omitted Daniel Webster, possibly feeling that thirty-two thousand dollars in "loans" exclusive of outright fees should suffice the man from Massachusetts. If so he reckoned without a proper understanding of the facility with which the "God-like" one could run through money. The following reached the Greek temple in Chestnut Street: "I believe my retainer has not been renewed or *refreshed* as usual. If it be wished that my relation to the Bank should be continued it may be well to send me the usual retainers. yours with regard DAN^L WEBSTER."[31]

Mr. Clay, too, was advanced a paltry thousand dollars;[32] but, unlike Webster, he gave security for all his loans and paid them. The Kentuckian was not above recommending extraordinary favors for others, however. "Mr. Knower [a bankrupt] is, you know, the father in law of Gov Marcy and he belongs to that powerful interest in N. York. The desired accommodation would have the best effects."[33] While pressing honest merchants to the wall, Mr. Biddle could assure a North Carolina congressman of elastic convictions that "in paying off the whole or any part of the loan you will consult exclusively your own convenience."[34] In John Forsyth, the first man in the Senate to raise his voice for Andrew Jackson, the banker found a legislator of different stuff. Owing twenty thousand dollars he could not pay, the Georgian offered to deed over property in that amount.[35]

On the banker's roster of acquisitions from the profession of letters were such men of standing as Thomas Ritchie of the Richmond *Enquirer* and Thomas Cooper, president of South Carolina College,[36] as well as a personage entitled to standing of a different sort, Charles Hammond of the Cincinnati *Gazette*.[37] But, oddly enough, the most useful services in this field were performed by a talented amateur, Charles Augustus Davis, whose brilliant counterfeits of Major Jack Downing were to win the author a permanent place in the annals of American humor. Davis was a New York City-bred silk-stocking. Yet his imitations of the homely parable for which Major Downing was famous were often better than the originals of Downing's creator, Seba Smith, a Maine country editor. Many readers[38] confused Davis's Downing with Smith's, concluding that the true Major Jack, who might spoof General Jackson but was usually for him, had turned his coat. "Squire Biddle," the hero of the new Downing letters, was a democratic and kindly character whose droll and plausible philosophy of finance fascinated cross roads store audiences throughout the land: a vastly different individual from the terrible "Czar Nick" of the Jackson press. Davis's letters were more widely read than the speeches of Webster and of Clay combined. Appreciating their value and always the litterateur, Biddle flooded his author with guidance and rewarded him with a post on the board of directors on the New York branch.[39]

5

The banker was not always so fortunate in the matter of immediate dividends from his propaganda investments, however. When Henry Clay led the Senate astray with his self-seeking resolution of censure, Mr. Biddle asked Webster to bring it back to earth. "You *must make a speech,* one of your calm, firm, solid, stern works."[40] Despite a meticulous insistence on pay for his work Mr. Webster, like his Kentucky colleague, reserved to himself considerable latitude as to what that work should be. On the occasion in question he made no speech. Instead, this acute observer directed Mr. Biddle's attention to the results of a significant change in Administration tactics. For the Jackson press had abandoned its ostrich-like policy on the general distress. Distress was admitted and Biddle blamed for it. The effect was adverse to the bank, said Webster, who recommended that Biddle moderate his pressure.[41]

The banker refused, bluntly instructing one of his Washington lobbyists, the distinguished-looking Judge Joseph Hopkinson of the Federal bench: "The relief must come from Congress and Congress alone.... The bank feels no vocation to redress the wrongs inflicted by these miserable people. This worthy President thinks that because he has scalped Indians and imprisoned Judges he is to have his way with the Bank. He is mistaken."[42] And to a member of Congress: "All the other banks and all the merchants may break, but the Bank of the United States shall not break.... [Those who doubt this] must rely on Providence or Amos Kendall."[43]

The worthy President kept his counsel and let subordinates do the talking. The bank continued to attack, finding a spectacular weapon in the ancient right of petition. "Memorial from the city of Portsmouth, New Hampshire," noted the journal of the Senate, "complaining of great embarrassment and pecuniary distress ... [owing] to the removal of deposits from the Bank of the United States." Memorial from New Orleans, Louisiana, praying that deposits be restored. Same from Bridgeport, Connecticut, Plymouth, North Carolina, Madison County, Kentucky; same from Philadelphia, signed by seven hundred "cabinet-makers, chair-makers, upholsterers &c." A meeting in Bucks County, Pennsylvania, offered "the deliberate opinion . . . that if Andrew Jackson . . . is sustained in his reckless usurpations . . . this country . . . will cease to be a republic."

Singly and by twos and threes and tens such documents showered upon Congress, each an occasion for a speech, and sometimes five or six. Administration tacticians answered with counter-petitions. Memorial of seven thousand citizens of Boston "explicitly approving the course of the President"; resolutions of the Ohio State Legislature endorsing the removal of deposits;[44] resolutions of the "freemen" of Schuylkill County, Pennsylvania, declaring "the United States Bank . . . corrupt and corrupting, and now, in its desperation a vampyre that would draw the last drop of blood from the honest yeomen of the country." The whole number of memorials from both sides mounted from the hundreds to the thousands, the speeches keeping pace: Clay, Calhoun, Webster, bell-wethers for the bank; Benton, Forsyth, James K. Polk, for Jackson—a Niagara of oratory seeking to drench a Vesuvius.

The bank people seemed to have the better of it. By the wide margin of one hundred and fifty-one thousand names to seventeen thousand, they presented the more numerously signed memorials. The histrionics of their orators were professionally superior. Calhoun, by no means the most vehement of the President's critics, pronounced the looting of the Roman exchequer by Caesar less reprehensible than the conduct of Jackson and the Kitchen Cabinet. "They have entered the Treasury, not sword in hand, as public plunderers, but with the false keys of sophistry, as pilferers, under the silence of midnight."

In private the President occasionally bridled up. "Oh, if I live to get these robes of office off me, I will bring that rascal to a dear account," he exclaimed of Henry Clay. The editor of the *Globe* exhibited what he described as notes for a speech by a member of the House which characterized the President's revolutionary exploits as electioneering fiction. "The damned, infernal scoundrel," roared the old man, pointing to the deep scar on his forehead. "Put your finger there, Mr. Blair."[45]

On the whole, however, the President seems to have betrayed less anxiety than Martin Van Buren, on whom devolved the unenviable duty of listening to hostile speeches day after day. Early in the session the Vice President enclosed to General Jackson a letter received from a friend. Old Hickory replied at once:

"I have read Col H.⁴⁶ with attention. he is in a *panic*. . . . I am not in any panic. were all the worshippers of the golden Calf to memorialize me and request a restoration of Deposits I would cut my right arm from my body before I would do such an act. . . . I am mortified at the . . . [timidity of] our friends."⁴⁷

That spirit had won the Greek campaign. But Red Eagle had not at hand the resources of Nicholas Biddle.

6

In proof of this the technique of the hostile petition was immensely improved. Instead of sending their memorials by post, signers were instructed to choose delegations to bring them to the capital. These emissaries filled hotel lobbies with their bitter talk and lined the benches of House and Senate galleries. The bolder ones began to finish off their sojourns by calling on the President. The first were received with stately courtesy, the Executive saying little in reply to their remonstrances. At length the time came when the old fighter's battle-instinct told him the hour was at hand to turn to other uses the pit Nicholas Biddle had been digging for Andrew Jackson. Old Hickory took the offensive.⁴⁸

A delegation from Philadelphia brought the largest petition of all, bearing ten thousand signatures. Jackson received the representatives courteously, but before the spokesman had uttered a dozen words he interrupted.

"Go home, gentlemen, and tell the Bank of the United States to relieve the country by increasing its business." The old man's voice was shrill. "Sooner than restore the deposits or recharter the bank I would undergo the torture of ten Spanish inquisitions. Sooner than live in a country where such a power prevails I would seek an asylum in the wilds of Arabia."⁴⁹

At the allusion to Arabia, Nicholas Biddle smiled and said the General might "as well send at once and engage [his] lodgings."⁵⁰

A committee of mechanics and artisans of New York presented itself. "Well, what do you want?" demanded Old Hickory. "I tell you I will never restore the deposits. I will never recharter the United States Bank. Here I am receiving one or two anonymous letters every day threatening me with assassination. Is Andrew Jackson to bow the knee to the golden calf? I tell you if you want relief go to Nicholas Biddle."[51]

That was it. The very cry. "Go to Nicholas Biddle!" The old warrior drove it home.

Members of Congress, Jackson members, were not so sure of their leader's strategy. A parcel of them brought to the White House a rumor of a Baltimore "mob" which did not intend to be turned aside with words. It would lay siege to the Capitol until the deposits were restored. "Gentlemen," said the President, "I shall be glad to see this mob on Capitol Hill. The leaders I will hang as high as Haman to deter forever all attempts to control the congress by intimidation."[52]

No mob came from Baltimore to encamp on Capitol Hill, but a respectful deputation to present its memorial in the regular way, and to seek an audience with the President.

"General," said the chairman, "the committee has the honor to be delegated by the citizens of Baltimore, without regard to party, to come to you, sir, the fountain head, for relief . . ."

"Relief, sir!" the high-pitched tones cut like a knife. "Come not to me, sir! Go to the monster! It is folly, sir, to talk to Andrew Jackson."

"Sir, the currency of the country is in a dreadful situation."

"Sir, you keep one-sided company," retorted the President. "Andrew Jackson has fifty letters from persons of all parties daily on this subject. Sir, he has more and better information than you, sir, or any of you."

"The people, sir. . . ."

"The people! The people, sir, are with *me*."[53]

Lengthy accounts of these interviews in the Biddle press represented the President as a cantankerous old man about as amenable to reason as a bolt of lightning. More friendly reporters did not destroy this impression entirely;[54] and the Executive himself had the bad taste to let Blair publish some of the letters threatening assassination.[55]

The simulation of rage was an old Jackson trick, and effective. Young Henry A. Wise, who as a bridegroom had visited the Hermitage, was serving his first term with the Virginia delegation in Congress. He witnessed one of the President's harangues. When the petitioners had gone Jackson lighted his pipe. "They thought I was mad," he chuckled, and went on coolly to instruct his lieutenants "on the policy of never, never to compromise a vital issue."[56] One afternoon as Frank Blair reviewed the situation Jackson's eye lighted on the head-dress proffered by Black Hawk as a token of his surrender. Old Hickory put it on and shook his head until the quills rattled. "I don't think those fellows would like to meet me in this."[57] Thomas Hart Benton usually dropped in after the Senate had adjourned for the day. "We shall whip them yet," Old Hickory would tell the big Missourian. "The people will take it up after a while."[58]

When Andrew Jackson said, "Go to Nicholas Biddle!" it was not as if an ordinary man had said it.

CHAPTER XXXVII

Doom of the Bank

I

In February of 1834 the bank fight reached the zenith of its fury. Flying the flag of no quarter, Nicholas Biddle threw his reserves into the effort to bring the country to its knees, and with it Andrew Jackson. The white-haired President, ill and rarely free from pain for an hour, counter-attacked so savagely that it seemed to some as if the gods were about their business of making mad one whom they had marked for destruction. On the other side is the testimony of Congressman Wise that deliberate calculation prompted Old Hickory's flailing exhortations to "Go to Nicholas Biddle." The General's personal correspondence and the administration of his private affairs during this critical period appear to bear out Mr. Wise. Instead of a man beside himself with passion, they reflect an example of extreme self-possession.

For instance, not until January, 1834, did the President select another depository in the capital for his personal funds. This was three months after he had discontinued the public deposits in the Bank of the United States. An account was opened with the Bank of the Metropolis, the "pet" institution in Washington, though the President was in no haste to withdraw the balance remaining in Mr. Biddle's vaults. On July 7 when he closed out the account it amounted to eleven hundred and thirty-seven dollars.[1]

At the beginning of the year the General's private concerns seemed to be flourishing. Andrew, junior, reported one hundred and eighty to two hundred thousand pounds of cotton on the way through the gin. Though the young man was a little late with that operation, his father did not complain. The crop, as estimated, stood to net at least fifty thousand pounds baled, which at fifteen cents, a low estimate, would gross seventy-five hundred dollars,[2] an excellent showing for a beginner. Typically the old frontiersman thought of branching out and creating a greater estate for his son. Hunter's Hill, which Andrew Jackson had been obliged to relinquish at forced sale in 1804, was said to be on the market. The place embraced five hundred and sixty-three acres adjoining the Hermitage. The two properties could be thrown together nicely and operated as a unit. Telling the boy to open negotiations with an inquiry as to the price expected,[3] the President turned to a subject nearer his heart. "I am truly delighted to hear our dear little Rachel has cut her jaw teeth. we have now a right to hope that she has passed the dangerous stage of teething."[4]

His running horses, too, were coming on, with three promising fillies in the White House stables—Emily, Lady Nashville and Bolivia. At the Hermitage two fillies and three young stallions engaged the old turfman's particular interest. As three of them were all that could be trained without hiring professional help, Jackson wrote his son to breed the fillies and train the studs, forwarding opinions "of the action of each."[5]

The first thing to divert the President's attention from the breaking in of the Hermitage colts was a small matter but "mortifying," as he expressed it. A Mr. George Hibb of Cumberland, Maryland, had presented a demand note for two hundred dollars signed by Andrew, junior. The instrument had been given in part payment for a negro girl whom the young man, already traveling with five servants, bought on his way to Tennessee the autumn previous. This was a violation of the General's instructions on the subject of debt. He paid the note, gently voicing the hope that the transaction had not impaired his son's credit.[6] The boy begged his father's pardon and wrote pridefully that sixty-three bales of cotton had been shipped to New Orleans, and that when the ginning should be finished he hoped for one hundred bales. The corn was not all gathered, Andrew said—writing on January 25—"but we are at it." General Jackson replied that the information concerning the cotton was of little value as the weight of the bales had been omitted, also the handling charges. Moreover, had the cotton been sold or merely shipped? And finally, no statement of the plantation's obligations at the beginning of the year had been received. Jackson had repeatedly directed his son to reckon up his debts on the first of each year, arrange for their payment out of the proceeds of the crops, and order his scale of living accordingly.

Nor was this all. The young man placidly announced the purchase of Hunter's Hill: price ten thousand dollars, "in one and two years payments," with a possible extension to three years. Other details were as meager as they had been about the cotton: "I could get it for no less. . . . What think you of it. I think the place worth it." Though General Jackson thought the place far from worth it, he merely requested his son to ask for no extension of time and to forward at once the weight of the cotton, the charges against it, and other outstanding bills. But the old man was worried. When four days elapsed and no copy of the agreement with Harry R. W. Hill, the seller of Hunter's Hill, arrived he wrote again. "I am anxious to receive your contract with Mr. Hill. he is a very keen man, and do nothing with him but what is reduced to writing."[7]

Two months later Jackson was still writing his son for the contract with Hill, the weight of the cotton and the amount of the Hermitage debts. Then came word from Maunsel White, the General's broker and honest friend, announcing the arrival in New Orleans of the first shipment. The cotton was of inferior quality, the shipping charges excessive and the shipping agreement negligently drawn from the standpoint of the owner of the cotton. White did not mention the weight of the cotton, doubtless assuming that Jackson knew it, and he mentioned only casually that he would pay the proceeds of the sale over to N. and J. Dick & Company, assuming that Jackson must have known of that arrangement also. This was disconcerting information. The Dicks were the New Orleans agents of Harry R. W. Hill. "Is it possible," Old Hickory asked his son, "[that] you have given Mr. Dick a power to receive the proceeds of our crop? . . . I am fearful you have been dealing too loosely with Mr. Hill . . . [who is] a keen mony making man. . . . I have had much writing on this subject, and uneasiness."[8]

The apprehensions were justified. The Dicks were, indeed, empowered to collect at New Orleans the proceeds from the sale of the Hermitage cotton and to hand the money over to Harry R. W. Hill. This was a part of the agreement between Hill and Jackson, junior, a copy of which Jackson, senior, had been vainly trying to get hold of for ninety days. The reason the young man failed to send it seems to have been that he had no copy in his possession. Jackson, senior, directed him to obtain one at once "or you will have *trouble*." The arrangement with Dick also was most unfortunate, the father said. "He is unworthy of trust, my deadly enemy." Although under no delusions as to the advantage the sharp Hill had taken of his inexperienced son, Old Hickory meant to stand by and to liquidate as quickly as possible any bargain the boy had made. Quotations for cotton were up in Liverpool—fifteen to twenty cents. Maunsel White was a competent trader. At these prices fifty thousand pounds should easily bring five thousand dollars clear of all charges and plantation debts. By taking something out of his salary as President—twenty-five thousand dollars a year, payable monthly—Jackson hoped to be clear of Mr. Hill in short order.[9]

The next letter from the Hermitage brought tears of joy to the old man's eyes. Sarah was a mother again—this time of a "fine son" already named Andrew. "Present to my dear Sarah and the sweet little babe my blessings, and a kiss to each. Kiss my dear little Rachel and tell her [that] Granpa, if he is permitted to get to the Hermitage this summer, will bring her a pretty."[10]

Subsequent news was less pleasant. The whole of the cotton crop weighed thirty-seven thousand eight hundred pounds, not fifty thousand as anticipated. It had sold for eleven and a quarter cents, bringing a net sum of thirty-nine hundred and seventeen dollars, or about half the amount originally counted on. At the same time Jackson received the terms with Hill: five thousand dollars payable in May, 1834, and five thousand on January 1, 1835. By drawing on his own funds, Jackson placed in his son's hands enough to complete the first payment on time.

With this went tender letters patiently directing the young man's attention to several things. The price paid for Hunter's Hill was high out of reason; five thousand dollars would have been enough. No excuse existed for the overestimate of the weight of the cotton crop. An accurate "cotton book" kept day by day during the picking season would obviate that. Baling costs were too great. Jackson said he could bale fifty thousand pounds for what the boy had spent on thirty-seven. "My son these things are only brought to your view that you may profit by them hereafter." The young man must remember that he had another five thousand dollars to pay on the first of the year. Only by economy and prudent management could it be done. "And there is no certainty that I will live to aid you."[11]

Tardily the young man replied that seven late frosts—three in April and four in May—had killed much of the new cotton. A poor half-crop was about all they could hope to market in 1835. Still, he was cheerful and optimistic, qualities that never seemed to desert Andrew Jackson, junior.[12]

2

John R. Montgomery was a lawyer from the pleasant town of Lancaster, Pennsylvania, the home of James Buchanan. Coming to Washington on Supreme Court business, the attorney bore letters of introduction which brought an invitation to dine at the Executive Residence. After that experience, had he been permitted to read the admonitions of frugality which the President pressed on his son, Mr. Montgomery might have found the General's words inconsistent with his example. On February 20, 1834, the visitor wrote for his daughter Letitia a narrative of the evening's entertainment.

"About 5 o'clock I got to the White House, as the President's mansion is generally termed. The company had mostly assembled, for the party was small. There were three gentlemen from New York, a Tammany Committee, Judge Hopkinson [the bank lobbyist] of Philadelphia, Mr. Ham[m], our late charge to Chile, Mr. David of Baltimore, the Vice-President and his son, Major [Abraham] Van Buren, Mr. Rogers and myself. These constituted the party, with the President's own family and Mrs. Sherman from Baltimore and Miss [Elizabeth] Martin, a very pretty little girl from Tennessee." Miss Martin was a member of the Donelson clan, and a cousin, therefore, of Emily.

"About ½ after six o'clock we sat down to dinner. The table was very splendidly laid and illuminated. There was a large chandelier hanging over the middle of it with 32 candles besides those on the table, mantles and on the piers. The first course was soup in the french style; then beef bouille, next wild turkey boned and dressed with brains; after that fish; then chicken cold and dressed white, interlaided with slices of tongue and garnished with dressed salled; then canvass back ducks and celery; afterwards partridges with sweet breads and last pheasants and old Virginia ham. The dishes were placed in succession on the table, so as to give full effect to the appearance and then removed and carved on a side table by the servants. The first dessert was jelly and small tarts in the turkish style, then blanche mode and kisses with dryed fruits in them. Then preserves of various kinds, after them ice cream and lastly grapes and oranges.

"The wines on the table were Sherry and Port to drink with soups and the first course of meats. When the wild turkey and fish were served, Madeira was handed and while the wild fowl was eaten Champaigne was constantly poured out by the servants; after these were gone through with, Claret was substituted to be taken with the dessert and old Cherry was put on to drink with the fruits. As soon as all had taken what their appetites could possibly endure, we left the table and returned to the drawing room.

"I think I can hear Bud say, if father ate and drank all this he must have needed an 'Eoff pill.' But french servants know how to guard American appetites from the ill effects of too much indulgence and in helping to any one dish do it so sparingly as to leave room for another and yet another to follow. We were at table until nearly 9 o'clock and were eating and talking all the time. The President was very affable and his niece, Mrs. Donnelson, the lady of the house, near whom I sat, a very agreeable woman, so that the evening passed very pleasantly. Soon after our return to the drawing room, a cup of coffee was handed, then the ladies played the piano and sung and after this a glass of 'liquer' was sent around as the signal for adjournment and the party broke up about ½ past nine o'clock."[13]

This had been an informal affair, a degree removed from a family dinner. General Jackson's state entertainments were marked by a richness and a dignity devoid of stiffness unequaled since Washington's day. He brought to the Executive Mansion and all its concerns the tangy savor of the best that was in Tennessee. The stable, with its complement of colored jockeys, was as much a part of the White House establishment as the East Room, and as frequently honored by eminence and fashion.

On a spring day in 1834 the President rode out to the National Jockey Club to watch a trial of the White House horses. Jack Donelson, Congressman Balie Peyton of Tennessee and other devotees of the turf were in the party; also Martin Van Buren, who had bet more money on elections than on horse races. At the track were the fillies Emily and Lady Nashville, nominally owned by Donelson, Bolivia owned by Jackson, and a celebrated stallion, Busirus, owned by a friend of Jackson named Irvine.

The General admired Busirus and later acquired some of his progeny. He was an immense animal and two men were required to hold him so that Jesse, a jockey from the White House stable, could mount. When the holders let go, Jesse lost control of the horse which plunged against a fence. The crowd scattered. Jackson's high-pitched voice was heard above the commotion. "Get behind me, Mr. Van Buren! They will run over you, sir." The Vice President safe, Old Hickory turned his attention to the refractory stallion. "Hold him, Jesse! Don't let him break down that fence." He berated the horse's trainer. "Why don't you break him of those tricks? I could do it in an hour."

Behind his hand Balie Peyton observed that he would like to see any man break Busirus of those tricks in a week.

The remainder of the day's performances was satisfactory and Jackson left the course in fine humor. As he rode home, scenes from famous races of other days swam before the old sportsman: the Truxton-Greyhound match at the Hartsville course in 1805; the great contest between Newton Cannon's Expectation and Jackson's Doublehead in 1811 at Jackson's own Clover Bottom track. Doublehead had won and Jackson had collected a side bet of five thousand dollars from Colonel Cannon.

Expectation had been heavily backed by Cannon's friends. They took their losses to heart, which threatened serious consequences to Patton Anderson, a member of Jackson's racing set. "[After the race]," related the President, "I went to the stable to see the old horse cool off, and about dusk observed Patton Anderson approaching at a brisk walk, pursued by a crowd of excited men. . . . I was bound to take up common cause with Patton." Facing the mob across a stile, Jackson denounced their conduct as unmanly and promised that Anderson should meet any one of them at sunrise. And if Anderson did not Jackson would. The challenge gave Anderson an opportunity to escape into the tavern house that adjoined the stables.

The mob insisted on adjusting matters on the spot. "I saw there remained but one chance for us," Old Hickory continued. "Putting my hand behind me, into my coat pocket, I opened a tin tobacco box, my only weapon, and said, 'I will shoot dead the first man who attempts to cross that stile.' "

One man set his foot on the first step.

"I raised my arm and closed the box with a click very like the cocking of a pistol. It was so dark they could not distinguish what I had in my hand—and, sir, they scampered like a flock of deer!"

Jackson turned to the Vice President. "I knew there were men in that crowd who were not afraid to meet me or any other man. But, Mr. Van Buren, no man is willing to take a chance of being killed by an accidental shot in the dark."[14]

Fortunately the Vice President was never to find occasion to test the accuracy of General Jackson's conclusion. The phrase of the day destined to become most highly treasured in the fragrant memorabilia of the Jackson Era was Old Hickory's "Get behind me, Mr. Van Buren."

3

A saying that had a more immediate bearing on events, however, was "Go to Nicholas Biddle." The people were beginning to repeat it.

A politician wise in the ways of popular trends cautioned the banker as to the consequences. If the bank were to continue its policy of contraction without regard for public suffering the public would be persuaded that the institution was too powerful and deserved destruction. Mr. Biddle was advised to retreat. Hezekiah Niles of Baltimore, whose long-standing friendship for the bank was not dependent on subsidies, declared in his influential *Register* that the bank had shown too much ability to protect itself. Its power over the common welfare was too great; "which power," concluded the editor, *"I would not agree to continue."*[15] A New York adherent also sought to stay the hand of the banker. "Our friends complain, Our enemies exult." Sentiment was growing for "a new bank and a New Deal."[16]

Contemptuously Biddle scorned them all. He would yet force the nation to accept the old bank and the old deal and be thankful for them. "Rely upon it that the Bank has taken its final course and that it will not be frightened nor cajoled from its duty by any small drivelling about relief to the country."[17]

The bank's agents asked Governor George Wolf[18] of Pennsylvania, to address a strong pro-bank message to the Legislature.[19] So confident was Biddle of Wolf's continued friendship,[20] and so little did he do to retain it, that the State of Pennsylvania found it impossible to borrow three hundred thousand dollars. Incensed, Wolf denounced the bank for trying to bludgeon from Congress a charter and a return of deposits "by bringing indiscriminate ruin on an unoffending community."[21]

The effect was electrical. Unmindful of Mr. Biddle's hysterical threats, the Upper House of the Pennsylvania Legislature adopted resolutions declaring (1) "That the present bank of the United States *ought not to be rechartered by congress,*" and (2) "That the *government deposits . . . ought not to be restored.*" Forty-eight hours later the Governor of New York recommended the creation by the State of a stock issue of four or five million dollars to be loaned to state banks to ease the stringency. The Legislature authorized six million.[22]

While these momentous measures were in the making at Harrisburg and at Albany a committee of New York City merchants and bankers was formed under the chairmanship of James G. King. The object was to obtain relief. Previously Mr. King had piloted a similar group to Washington to present the usual memorial to Congress and to call at the White House. "What do you come to me for?" rasped the President. "Go to Nicholas Biddle."[23] Shortly after, the *Globe* had announced that the Executive would see no more memorialists. They had served their purpose—or more correctly, Andrew Jackson's.

Mr. King took the advice. In the name of the merchants' committee he asked the banker to relax the pressure in New York. Endorsing the plea, aged Albert Gallatin, whose prestige in American finance was second only to that of Mr. Biddle, reminded the banker that it was within his power to afford the relief requested. Hitherto Mr. Gallatin had heartily espoused the cause of the bank.

"Sprightly as a Little Fairy"

General Jackson's characterization of his idolized first grandchild, Rachel, daughter of Andrew, junior, and Sarah Yorke Jackson, born at the Hermitage, November 1, 1832. From a portrait by Earl, owned by the Ladies' Hermitage Association, Nashville.

"QUI PAYE SES DETTES S'ENRICHIT"

A French jibe at their government for bowing to Jackson's terms in the debt settlement. The caption, "Who Pays His Debts Enriches Himself," accuses the government of wringing money from the country not only to satisfy the United States but to line its own pocket as well. From a contemporary cartoon in the collection of Emil Edward Hurja of New York City.

So ended a black week, beginning with the message of Governor Wolf. The drum-fire of disaster left its mark on the architect of the Greek temple in Chestnut Street. Nervously fingering the demands of King and the warning of Gallatin, Mr. Biddle was no longer a jaunty autocrat conscious of his power, but a cornered man.

He hesitated, he blundered. He told King that he would have eased the plight of New York ere this except for the action of the Governor of Pennsylvania.[24] So New York must continue to suffer because Pennsylvania abused the bank.

Fatal admission. The mask was off, revealing Mr. Biddle and his panic in their true colors. The bank party had said much of the one-man rule of Andrew Jackson. What now of the one-man rule of Nicholas Biddle?

What other modern prototype of robber baron has had the power to be so ruthless and so callous on so large a scale?

Mr. King coolly replied that the banker's reason for withholding relief "would not be deemed sufficient by our community."[25] When Albert Gallatin threatened to say the same thing publicly, Biddle struck his flag. It was no voluntary capitulation. "The Bank had to do something for the evil of such an announcement [from Gallatin] would have been enormous."[26] True; but Mr. Biddle's private apology for succoring New York overlooked the more important fact that the evil of his own conduct was beyond repair entirely. New York accepted as a right too long denied the relief wrung from reluctant hands—and not as a favor for which it owed a debt of gratitude. The bank's goose was cooked.

General Jackson expressed his thanks to Governor Wolf of Pennsylvania. "It was to have been hoped that our past experience had sufficiently demonstrated the futility of all attempts, however formidable in their character or source, to controul the popular will: but there are unfortunately too many amongst us who are not only destitute of knowledge of the people, but who seem wholly incapable of acquiring it."[27]

This precise statement of the crowning weakness of Nicholas Biddle's temperament contained nothing to indicate the part Andrew Jackson's generalship had played in making that weakness serve the people's ends.

4

In the ensuing weeks of March, 1834, the retreat of the bank's forces in Congress became a rout. Mr. Biddle had met his Waterloo, a Pennsylvania senator exclaimed, with only himself to blame. The Pennsylvania delegation, led by the senators, deserted almost in a body. Everywhere the lines gave way. Too late Calhoun and Webster repudiated the self-centered leadership of Clay and introduced bills for recharter on a temporary basis. Perceiving the hopelessness of the cause, Webster tabled his own bill. Clay, too, knew the bank was gone, but enough life remained to serve the purposes of the Kentuckian's private feud with the Administration. This remarkable parliamentarian brought up his almost-forgotten resolution of censure of the President. Marshaling apostate bank senators who had been none too cordially received in the camp of the victorious Jacksonians, Mr. Clay obtained the passage of the resolution on March 28 by a vote of twenty-six to twenty. The President replied that the Senate's act was unconstitutional and asked that this protest be entered in the journal of that body. The Senate declining to receive the reprimand, the censure alone remained in the record.

This personal triumph for Clay, signifying nothing so far as the bank was concerned, precipitated a victory for Jackson in the House which impressed the seal of formality on the doom of Mr. Biddle's institution. Though not a spectacular legislator, James K. Polk, Chairman of the Committee on Ways and Means, was an exceedingly competent one. On April 4 he reported four sweeping resolutions.

1. "That . . . the bank of the United States ought not to be rechartered."

It was carried by a vote of one hundred and thirty-four to eighty-two.

2. "That the public deposites ought not to be restored."

Ayes, one hundred and eighteen; noes, one hundred and three.

3. "That the state banks ought to be continued as the places of deposites."

Carried by the close vote of one hundred and seventeen to one hundred and five.

4. That a committee of the House investigate the bank's affairs and the reasons for the commercial crisis.

Carried by the vote of all but the bank die-hards, one hundred and seventy-five to forty-two.

"The history of this day," wrote one of Mr. Biddle's directors who observed the scene, "should be blotted from the annals of the Republic. . . . The Chief Magistrate of the United States seized the public Treasure, in violation of the law of the land; and the Representatives of the People have confirmed the deed!!!"[28]

Jackson's comment was briefer. "I have obtained a glorious triumph," he said in a letter otherwise dealing with a proposal to bring out a biography of General John Coffee.[29]

Disobeying a subpoena to produce the bank's books and defying arrest, Biddle defeated the attempted investigation. The net result was to confirm in the popular belief all the Administration charges. In June Henry Clay did what Mr. Biddle had hoped he would do in December and laid before the Senate a resolution asking for a restoration of deposits. Moreover, the resolution was adopted and went to the House. A desperate gambler's hope glowed in the breast of Nicholas Biddle. Casting ordinary precautions aside, he made the frankest offer of all to exchange the bank's money for political support, promising Louisiana two million dollars in relief loans in return for eleven votes which he thought were needed to pass the resolution in the House.[30] The banker was wasting his time. The House had spoken on April 4. It laid the Clay resolution on the table.

The Kentuckian had one more arrow in his quiver. He launched it when Jackson, waiting until within a week of the close of the session, presented to the Senate the name of Roger B. Taney for confirmation as Secretary of the Treasury. The nomination was rejected, and this time Jackson's white anger was real. Lost to the Cabinet was the one man who had not faltered an instant in the fight. It availed Mr. Biddle nothing. Like Wolfe on the plains of Abraham, Taney fell victorious, "the fate of the Bank," as Jackson observed, "sealed forever."[31]

5

Louisiana received her two million, and more, without paying any price whatsoever in votes. Boston was relieved, Pennsylvania relieved—relief everywhere, credit rushing like a stream long dammed to the farthest reaches of the country as the beaten Biddle cut the dikes with a stroke of the pen on July 11, 1834. By the end of the month, money was plentiful and commerce reviving so rapidly that one was apt in the bustle to pass by the stark débris of ruined careers and impoverished families. Taney's system of state depositories was working better. Though not all that its creator had hoped, the performance was superior to anything that the anti-removal people in the Administration had imagined possible. Many reflective men, and a multitude of others who had thought differently a year before, or had not thought at all, accepted the new order as an expedient preferable to perpetuating the authority of such a man as Nicholas Biddle had shown himself to be.

Jackson's popularity soared again. But Old Hickory found a deeper satisfaction in penning an affectionate letter to his former ward, Andrew Jackson Hutchings, who had married Mary Coffee. The young fellow was proving a far better planter than he had been a college student, his place showing a larger profit than the Hermitage. "You have not hinted whether a cradle will be necessary to compleat the furniture of your house. do inform me."[32]

6

On the evening of August 5, 1834, four very tired horses pulled a dust-stained coach past the brick gate-posts of the Hermitage. An old man in black alighted wearily. In his arms was a doll—the "pretty" he had promised Rachel. "I found . . . [her] as sprightly as a little fairy and as wild as a little partridge. . . . [The doll] was the only thing that induced her to come to me." The young lady's diffidence did not endure. She and her grandfather were soon inseparable.[33] Another measure to the patriarch's cup of happiness was the news that Mary Coffee Hutchings was going to have a baby. She being unable to journey to the Hermitage, the President replied that he would take a stage to Alabama and visit her. Only the sudden illness of Sarah deterred him.

In all it was the quietest visit the President had enjoyed in Tennessee. Yet there was a good deal to do. Andrew, junior, had run into debt again. Holtzclaw was let go and Edward Hobbs engaged as overseer. The cotton yield would be no more than half of normal, and exacting Harry Hill would expect satisfaction for young Jackson's five thousand dollar note. Not in twenty years had the Hermitage stood so in need of close and watchful handling.

Moreover, there was the self-perpetuating problem of what to do with the Eatons. Once had Hugh Lawson White and twice had the Tennessee Legislature politely defeated General Jackson's design to return the former Secretary of War to public life by way of the Senate. Eaton, himself, no longer cared a great deal. His library and his lands might have occupied him agreeably enough but for the inclinations of his wife. Margaret was bored by the provinces, though existence there was not so dull as it might have been without her. Tennessee had witnessed a pistol affray over Bellona's private life and the undoing of one of her active detractors—the wife of a former congressman of the blue blood and from the blue grass of the fastidious Gallatin district. In Washington this mighty lady had declined an introduction to Mrs. Eaton. She was now an exile in the remoter province of Missouri, disowned by her husband as a result of the disclosure of a liaison with one of his nephews.[34] Jackson offered Eaton the governorship of Florida. After sulking a while, presumably in the expectation of something better, he and Peggy departed for Tallahassee.

In September the President reluctantly entered his coach and started eastward, writing ahead to Major Lewis to have the White House rid of bed bugs.[35]

7

Thoughts on the future of the Hermitage and the Hermitage family kept General Jackson uneasy company on that journey. No letters overtook him en route, and none awaited in Washington though Andrew had promised faithfully to write. Two weeks more and no letter. "My son, Thirty one days has elapsed since we left sarah on a sick bed and the babe [Andrew] not recovered from its attack. I am wearied with anxiety and disappointment." The cotton, too, concerned him. Were the gin and the press working well? Much depended on these things if Hill were to be paid in January. Economy, economy: the old farmer dinned it in. Plant more potatoes and garden truck. That was one way to stop the leaks and make a place sustaining.[36]

Bring the hay and grazing fields back to where they were when Jackson was in charge, and cease buying feed for the stock. "The blue grass I want sowed in the two small lotts near the stud stable—The Timothy with a small portion of clover say one quart to the acre in the old timothy Lott, or mares lot, adjoining the north western field of cotton— the herds grass in the colts lott south of the timothy, and such other lots as you judge best for grazing and cutting. . . . The timothy lott ought to be prepared in the winter and sowed in the month of March— It ought to be thrown over by the large patent plow and four horses— after lying exposed to the frost until February it ought to be plowed with a small plow and when ready for sowing ought to be harrowed with the iron harrow, the seed sowed & harrowed in, and then rolled with a heavy logg drawn by two horses." Explicit directions followed for rigging the log.[37]

Pages of such instruction flowed from Jackson's pen. He sent to Philadelphia for seed. Andrew, junior, was cautioned to be careful with the clover. "It has cost me $83.75 besides the freightage."[38]

Forty-eight hours after the last of these letters had left his hands, Jackson heard from his son. The Hermitage had been swept by fire. The beloved house was a ruin.

Letters from neighbors who had rallied about the young man further enabled the President to reconstruct the calamity. On the afternoon of October 13, 1834, the roof had caught from a spark from the dining room flue. The family was absent. Hands from the Hermitage and from neighboring fields tried to mount the roof with buckets but could find no ladder. When Andrew and Sarah arrived, Sarah turned her attention to saving the furniture. Nearly all the downstairs and most of the upstairs things were carried out, some much damaged. The General's papers were saved. Rescued also was Rachel Jackson's wardrobe which had remained in her closet as it was on the day of her death. Considerable of the thick walls resisted the flames and, if protected from the weather, they could be used in rebuilding. To this end Robert Armstrong, the heroic artilleryman of Enotachopco who had eloped to the Hermitage with Josiah Nichol's daughter and married her there, undertook to "assist" Andrew the younger. Three whipsaws were started in the timber lot, and carpenters called from their work of building a house for Jack Donelson on the property adjoining. By the time the tidings of the disaster reached Washington the scaffolding was going up.[39]

The news was received with one of the few recorded expressions of submission to pass the lips of Andrew Jackson. "The Lords will be done. it was he that gave me the means to build . . . my dwelling house and he has a right to destroy it. Tell Sarah [to] cease to mourn its loss. I will have it rebuilt."[40] On reflection the old man altered that brave declaration to say that the reconstruction would be in the hands of a "benevolent providence . . . [who] will spare me long enough to have it rebuilt." And as a final token of humility he took his pen and after the word "enough" traced "I hope."[41]

Gratefully he approved the prompt procedure of Armstrong.[42] "was it not on the site selected by my dear departed wife I would build it higher up on the Hill. . . . Have it covered in before the hard frost and rain injures the walls. Have a tin roof put on it. . . . I write to . . . [Philadelphia] to send on by the Ship *Chandler Price* via New Orleans as much tin as will cover a House 80 feet by 44. This will enable you to borrow tin in Nashville from any one who has it."[43]

Other matters equally important remained. "In all your bustle my son have your cotton picked and Housed, gin'd, baled and sent to markett.[44] . . . My son, I regret to see that we are without seed wheat and that the negroes are without shoes in these heavy frosts. . . . [This] shows careless management." Nor were the sweet potatoes gathered. "They must be all tainted [by frost] and will rot before spring."[45] More detailed reports on the fire indicated that the early estimates of the loss of furniture were far too low.[46] "My son economy now upon all hands must be used . . . [if we are] to pay Hill for the land, meet my other engagements and rebuild my house. . . . Have the useless stock sold, the blooded stock well attended."[47]

8

Nicholas Biddle, too, could look adversity in the face, though not with the composure of Andrew Jackson. He knew this. Instinctively and from the first this singular man—poet, glass of fashion, philanthropist, in whom the quiet tastes of an esthete joined the reckless courage of a marauder—had felt Jackson the superior being. His whole conduct betrays it, and betrays more: a nervous anxiety to preserve "face," to o'ermaster Jackson as he had o'ermastered every other man who had stood in his way. In December, 1831, Mr. Biddle, himself, had made the decision that destroyed the bank when deliberately he chose to unite with Clay, whom he regarded as his inferior in ability, rather than with Jackson.

By autumn of 1834, the financier had sufficiently recovered from the débâcle of the spring preceding to try quietly to turn the fall elections in favor of the bank. He backed the Whigs. (Mr. Clay's party had dropped the name, National Republicans, and the Jacksonians frankly called themselves Democrats.)[48] But the Administration forces kept the initiative. The coinage of gold had been resumed that summer. "Jackson's yellow boys," they called the glittering pieces. Democratic stump-speakers were provided with long green purses to jingle before the huzzaing crowds as they flayed the bank. Riots startled the cities. Sending his wife and children to the country on election night, Mr. Biddle filled his residence and the Chestnut Street temple with armed men. He himself stood guard until dawn when he learned that the Democrats everywhere had been victorious.

"We bet largely," a field captain wrote in, "all the money you sent us, hoping by that means we might influence the election. but we have *not* succeeded. Almost all the anti-Bank members of Congress elected. . . . All hope is now in bribery! I think some of the members of Congress might be sounded successfully! You understand.——"[49]

Yes, Mr. Biddle understood—that the time had passed for that. Confessing final defeat, he good-naturedly turned to the task of selling the branches of the Bank of the United States, preparatory to winding up its affairs on the date of the expiration of the charter, March 3, 1836.

CHAPTER XXXVIII

The Etiquette of Collecting Twenty-five Million Francs

I

ANDREW JACKSON PAGEOT, the capital's youngest subject of King Louis Philippe, had never seen the land of his paternal ancestors. He had never seen anything very far away from his birthplace, a large house in Washington which his proud maternal grandsire, Major William Berkeley Lewis, had strapped himself to provide. This infant's father, Alphonse Pageot, the attaché of the French Legation, had courted Mary Lewis in the White House. Their marriage had received the benediction of its venerated occupant and their son, his godchild, was christened in the Red Room.

These events were responsible for the cordial personal intercourse between the Executive Residence and the French Legation, a circumstance which added to the embarrassments of Louis Sérurier, the French minister and Monsieur Pageot's superior, when, on October 22, 1834, he donned his silk hat to pay the Secretary of State an official visit. Unfortunately the official relations between Monsieur Sérurier's government and that of the United States no longer could be defined as cordial.

When General Jackson took office, the United States for twenty years had been endeavoring to interest the government of France in sundry damage claims of our citizens arising from the depredations of Napoleon. Though they paid similar claims to other nations, the French refused to pay ours. Presidents came and went, so able a diplomat as John Quincy Adams getting nowhere against an almost intangible barrier of polite evasion and delay. With equal politeness Jackson adopted a firmer, stronger line than his predecessors, the result of which was rather surprising. In 1831 a treaty was signed and in 1832 ratified providing for the disbursement of twenty-five million francs in six annual installments, in consideration of which we should reduce the duty on French wines. Coming on the heels of the reopening of the British West Indian market to American trade, the French agreement was hailed as another triumph for the vigorous foreign policy of the soldier president.

We lowered the wine tariff. In 1833 the first installment of the French settlement was due and, though Louis Philippe's government had said nothing of any arrangement for meeting it, Jackson directed the Secretary of the Treasury to write out a draft for the amount. This was handed to the Bank of the United States for collection. The draft came back unpaid and the Treasury received a bill for one hundred and seventy-five thousand dollars in protest fees and the like. The French explanation was that the Chamber of Deputies had failed to make the necessary appropriation. The excuse did not rest well with Jackson who saw an effort to resume the old game of hide-and-seek. When the Chamber went further, defeating a bill to provide the funds, Old Hickory ordered the Navy ready for sea duty[1] and began to speak of laying the matter before the country in a "strong" message to Congress.[2]

This was the situation that brought Monsieur Sérurier to the State Department on October 22, 1834. The French diplomat had seen enough of Andrew Jackson's strong messages not to wish his country the subject of one. Our Secretary of State was courtly John Forsyth of Georgia, promoted for his part in the last battle against the bank. His greeting to the Frenchman was courteous but cool. When Sérurier expressed the hope that the United States would pursue a "discreet" course, Mr. Forsyth said that the President, "deeply mortified" by the behavior of France, was determined to inform Congress of the state of affairs. Sérurier continued his persuasions. Forsyth was unmoved. At length the French minister said:

"What do you wish, Monsieur, a collision between us or the execution of the treaty?"

Collision is one of diplomacy's less obscure synonyms for war.

The usual urbanity of the Secretary of State did not desert him. "The execution of the treaty," he replied adding, however, that the President deemed the people entitled to an explanation of the recent proceedings, and intended that they should have it.[3]

A month later the French minister repeated his request. Forsyth repeated his refusal and Sérurier wrote his government to expect "very painful" developments.[4]

2

To date General Jackson's conduct of our foreign affairs presented an almost unbroken pageant of successes: the West Indian agreement of 1830; claims against Denmark favorably settled the same year; claims against the Kingdom of Naples settled 1832; against Spain 1834; several commercial treaties conceding us most-favored-nation advantages. Only the effort to annex Texas presented a diplomatic spectacle about which the less said by Jackson partizans the better. And now this French question also approached a stage from which one party or the other would find it difficult to recede with dignity. The same, however, had been true of the situation with Naples when King Bomba found multiple excuses for not paying up. Whereupon Jackson sent a commissioner to receive the money, but he did not send him alone. Master Commandant Daniel T. Patterson and five men-of-war sailed into the Bay of Naples, with cannon firing—though merely the salutes required by international etiquette. They sailed out again—with the commissioner and the money. Would Jackson risk a similar line of tactics with France? Thinking he would, the captain of a Liverpool packet delayed the sailing of his vessel in order to be the first man to reach Europe with the President's message to Congress.[5]

One or two evenings later Frank Blair's partner in the printing business, John C. Rives, brought to the White House study a proof of the document, as revised by Forsyth. Donelson began to read it while Jackson patrolled the carpet with a pipe in his hand. Rives thought he heard the private secretary intentionally slur over a passage. Jackson paused in his walk. "Read that again, sir," he said. Donelson repeated the words more distinctly. "That, sir, is not my language," said the President taking up a pen. He scratched out the amended passage and wrote on the margin of the proof the robust words of the original draft.[6]

The packet-master's precautions were justified, the French minister's forebodings borne out. Without a trace of bluster, Jackson nevertheless had spoken of France as he had not spoken of another foreign power, going further than the energetic Edward Livingston, our minister at Paris, or most of the President's supporters at home, had expected to be asked to follow.

The time had come, he said, to "take redress into our own hands." "After the delay on the part of France of a quarter of a century in acknowledging the claims by treaty it is not to be tolerated that another quarter of a century be wasted in negotiation about the payments." Therefore, in view of France's continued "violation of pledges given through her minister here, . . . I recommend that a law be passed authorizing reprisals upon French property in case provisions shall not be made for the payment of the debt at the approaching session of the French Chambers." The next sentence disclaimed an intention to wound French honor. The law requested "ought not to be considered by France as a menace. Her pride and power are too well known to expect anything from her fears. . . . She ought to look upon it [only] as the evidence of an inflexible determination on the part of the United States to insist on their rights."[7]

Couriers spurred their horses, perspiring firemen piled wood beneath the boilers of locomotives and steamboats to speed the message to the country. The two hundred and twenty-five miles to New York were covered in thirteen hours and forty minutes. A flurry swept the seaboard's commercial marts. Marine insurance companies refused to assume risks resulting from a rupture with France. Pride swelled the breasts of common men: "Hurrah for Jackson!" Such a persistent heckler of the Administration as Philip Hone of New York privately characterized the message as "dignified, and its sentiment manly and patriotic."[8] A Massachusetts politician, grooming Webster for 1836, woefully admitted that in event of war the Whigs would have to support the President because he was right.[9] Despite a minor strain of criticism, Old Hickory had the country with him. His touch had changed an obscure question, with which other presidents had fumbled in the dark, into a popular national issue.

3

Having rallied the country, Jackson restrained himself. He pursued the substance and not the shadow.

The French section of the message went to the Senate Committee on Foreign Relations, three of whose five members, Clay among them, were of the opposition. No three men in the French Chambers, sputtered the *Globe*, would take greater delight in "thwarting the measures of General Jackson's administration."[10] This statement, however, was not to be borne out by events. Though neither Congress nor the country showed a disposition to recede from the high ground the President had taken, a sentiment existed that we should do nothing further until the French Chambers had had a chance to act.[11] In a lengthy report the Senate Committee presented an exposition of the French issue not materially different from that of the President. It was suggested that Congress await the action of the French Chambers. Clay introduced a resolution to this effect which, with Jackson's silent consent,[12] was adopted by a unanimous vote. Some of the opposition senators, however, could not resist the temptation to make a wholesale distribution of the resolution as political propaganda against the President.

The atmosphere was growing tense a fortnight later when, on January 30, 1835, General Jackson visited the House chamber to attend funeral services for the late Representative Warren R. Davis of South Carolina. The burden of the chaplain's sermon was that life is uncertain, particularly for the aged. "There sat the gray-haired president," wrote an English visitor, Harriet Martineau, "looking scarcely able to go through this ceremonial."[13] The discourse finished, he filed past the casket and with the Cabinet descended to the rotunda of the Capitol.

A stranger of good appearance, his face covered by a thick black beard, was standing six feet away. No one noticed him draw the small, bright pistol he aimed at the Executive, but, as he pressed the trigger, the report rang through the stone chamber "like a rifle shot." Calmly the man produced another pistol. Jackson was one of the first to realize what was happening. Clubbing his cane he started for the man. "*Crack!*" went the second weapon. Old Hickory lunged at his assailant, but a young army officer reached the man first.[14]

The President was unharmed. Only the caps of the pistols had exploded, the charges failing to go off, although the weapons had been properly loaded "with fine glazed duelling powder and ball." Jack Donelson recapped one and squeezed the trigger. It fired perfectly. An expert on small arms calculated that the chance of two successive misfires was one in one hundred and twenty-five thousand. Rushing to the White House to congratulate the President on his narrowest escape from death, Martin Van Buren found him with the Donelson children in his lap, talking of something else to Major General Winfield Scott.[15]

The assailant said he was Richard Lawrence and that Jackson had killed his father. When it developed that Lawrence was an Englishman whose parents had never been in America, the prisoner described himself as the heir to the British crown. He said that he wanted to put General Jackson out of the way in order to strengthen his claims to the throne. When the prisoner was committed to a lunatic asylum, partizans on both sides objected to that undramatic disposition of the case, Frank Blair hinting that Lawrence was a tool of Jackson's enemies and Duff Green that the affair had been devised to create popular sympathy for the President.[16]

It did create sympathy for him, John C. Calhoun detaining the Senate with a denial of complicity, and John Quincy Adams proclaiming his allegiance on the floor of the House. These protestations were succeeded by the report of another explosion, set off by the arrival of the President's message in France. Gallic honor was officially outraged and Louis Sérurier appeared at the State Department to demand his passports. He received them and left with the Secretary a defense of his country's conduct:

"Les plaintes que porte M. le Président contre le prétendu non-accomplissement des engagements pris par le Gouvernment du Roi . . . ne sont pas seulement étranges par l'entière inexactitude des allégations sur lesquelles elles reposent, mais aussi. . . ."[17]

The State Department's staff linguist rendered this as conveying the idea that General Jackson had made charges against the French government which he knew to be untrue. Edward Livingston was directed to inquire whether these were the sentiments of the French government, and if so to say that they would not be tolerated by the government of the United States.[18]

General Jackson asked Congress for heavy military expenditures, and the martial ardor of America matched that of the Parisian boulevards. As chargé d'affaires, Alphonse Pageot succeeded to the uncomfortable station of France's diplomatic agent in the United States. Beside himself with anxiety for his daughter and his grandson, poor Major Lewis trunneled to the White House letters which Mary Lewis

Pageot had translated in the French Legation to show that not all her husband's countrymen were spoiling to fight us.[19]

So, for the time being, the matter sank into a state of uneasy repose.

4

Breaking the seal on a letter from George C. Childress, a kinsman of Mrs. James K. Polk, the President read that New Orleans had started public subscriptions to rebuild the Hermitage. To accommodate as many contributors as possible, no offering of more than fifty cents would be accepted. Mr. Childress desired to father such a movement in Tennessee.

General Jackson scribbled a notation at the foot of the page directing Donelson to thank Mr. Childress and the citizens of New Orleans and to give the money already raised to charity. "I am able to rebuild [my home]."[20] At the same time the proud old man wrote his son: "Draw on me for fifteen (1500) hundred dollars. This is as much as I can spare." If more were needed to pay the carpenters, borrow on the cotton crop.[21]

A new Hermitage was rising from the ruins of the old. Jackson's first impulse had been to reconstruct it brick for brick and timber for timber except for a fireproof roof. But as the abode his cherished Rachel knew had been altered almost out of recognition in 1831, the President consented to further extensive changes. The house was to be taller. The elaborate and rather vain front portico gave way to a simpler, statelier one supported by six great white pillars. This is the Hermitage that we know today.[22]

Andrew, junior's, family had found shelter in the remnant of the ancient blockhouse—the original Hermitage—which still stood on the place. Jackson professed to count this no hardship, recalling that he had spent some of the happiest days of his life in that log fort.[23] Nevertheless he asked Lewis, who was in Tennessee, to bring Sarah and the two children to Washington. They arrived shortly before midnight on November 26, 1834. "Grandpa, the great fire burnt my bonnet," little Rachel said. Sarah complained of fatigue. "I gave her a dose of medicine and she is quite lively this morning," the President related.[24]

She was lively enough to brave the rigors of a shopping tour, for the great fire had burned mamma's bonnet also. On Pennsylvania Avenue, she found others that struck her fancy—a "Blue Lame Toque," for ten dollars, a "Pink Silk Hat & flower $12" and a "Pink Bérét & feathers $13." Then the expedition was fairly under way: "14 yds Bleu Fig^d. Satin [$] 21, 14 yds Bro[wn] Fig^d. Silk 17.50, 14 yds Plain Silk 12.25, 1 Blond scarf 25., 3 Pr Worked Silk Hose, 9., 2 Pr. Plain Silk Hose 4, 2 Pr Long Gloves 9. . . ." General Jackson paid the bill—three hundred and forty-five dollars and eighty cents.[25] Nor was that the last of Sarah's shopping.

If compensatory economies marked the management of the White House, they were invisible to a boy from Ohio who, reporting for his first cruise as a second lieutenant of Marines, viewed everything in the capital with fresh, astonished eyes. A note from Mr. Van Buren had procured an invitation to partake of a family dinner at the Mansion, served at the proper Tennessee hour of four o'clock. One could judge the degree of formality of a White House dinner by the time the guests sat down. An affair for the diplomatic corps might be as late as seven thirty.

Walking very erectly in his new, high-collared uniform, Lieutenant Caldwell met the other guests in what he described as an "anti-chamber." After a little the President entered, greeted every one and chatted for fifteen minutes. Then a "porter" announced that the meal was served. "Led by the porter we passed through a spacious Hall and entered another finely furnished room which was darkened by the window curtains and blinds and contained two tables richly laden with fine plate and dishes and tall splendid lamps— around one table were chairs, so we were seated— What attracted my attention first was the very nicely folded napkin on each plate with a slice of good light bread in the middle of it." Light bread, made of wheat flour, was so designated to distinguish it from ordinary or corn bread. "Well, all being seated the Gen. asked the blessing, then the servants about the table, I believe one to every man, commenced—'Will you have some roast beef?— some corn beef?— some boiled beef?— some beef stake?'

"Well, the beef being through with away goes your plate and a clean one comes. 'Will you have this kind or that kind or the other kind of fish?' Fish being through, a new plate & then comes some other dish. Then a new plate comes and some other dish— then a new plate and the pies— then the desert— then & in the mean time the wines— sherry, madaira & champagne. . . . [We] drink one another's health— then after so long a time, all of which made very agreeable by miscellaneous conversation, we retire again to the Chamber whence we had come, where being seated in comes a servant with a dish of coffee for each of us. . . . Directly aside looking at my watch [and] find[ing] it almost 7 o'clock I conclude to retire. So I takes the Prest. by the hand and says Gen, I bid you good-night and it will always be my pride to do you honor.' "[26]

The Chief of State thus honored concealed the private worries that plagued his mind. "My son, I have waited with great anxiety to receive a Statement of the precise amount of our cotton that I might make a probable calculation . . . of the debt to Mr. Hill which becomes due the first of next month. . . . Surely these long nights you might write a few lines to your D'r sarah if you cannot write to me. Your own interest is involved."[27] Sarah exhibited less tolerance toward her husband's inattention and wrote that flirting proved a sovereign antidote for the shades of melancholy. Andrew, junior, replied that this was a fact he, too, knew very well, naming as the objects of his gallant addresses "the Beautiful *Mrs. Haggatt* . . . and the all accomplished and gentle *Mrs. Baldwin*. . . . So you see I am going ahead of you. . . . I will say no more except that you must try to enjoy yourself."[28]

Anxious to be useful in any particular, Major Lewis escorted Sarah to Baltimore and to Philadelphia to choose wall paper and furniture for the new Hermitage. In their absence General Jackson heard that his son was carrying on a game that went beyond innocent flirtation.

"I now address you with the fondness of a father's heart. how careful then ought you to be to shun all bad company, or to engage in any dissapation whatever and particularly intoxication. When I reflect on the fate of your cousin Savern, reduced to the contempt of all by his brutal intemperance I shudder when I see any appearance of it in any other branch of our connection. . . . [The happiness of] your charming little wife and sweet little ones depends on your upright course. this my son ought always to be before your eyes. . . .

"You must, *to get thro' life well,* practice industry with economy. . . . Nothing can be more disgraceful than the charge truly made that he has promised to pay money at a certain day, and violating that promise. Our real wants are but few, our imaginary wants many, which never ought to be gratified by creating a debt to supply them. These subjects [are] so essential to your happiness here and hereafter and that of your charming little family."²⁹

Yet despite all young Jackson could do, or his father do for him, the five-thousand-dollar note held by Harry Hill which Andrew, junior, had promised to pay on January 1, 1835, was not met. It began to draw interest at six per cent.

5

More fortunate in the field of public finance, General Jackson was able seven days later, on January 8, to pay the final installment of the national debt. Owing no one and with a surplus in its Treasury, this Government enjoyed a fiscal standing unique in the history of the modern world. The favorable balance showed every indication of increasing, for in eight months the country had passed from a depression to a state of prosperity, with visions of overflowing abundance which French war clouds failed to dispel.

In the spring of 1835 the march of plenty crossed the line into the green pastures of speculation. The impetus came in part from a speculative wave in Europe, in part from the momentum of over rapid recovery from the Biddle panic, in part from the Treasury surplus creating an excess of loanable funds in the custody of the "pet" banks. The phenomena of inflation began to appear. New state banks were chartered by the score, most of them bidding for a share of the Government deposits, many of them getting it, and all printing their own money. Bad money drives out good. "Jackson's yellow boys," the gold pieces minted in 1834, vanished into the hiding places of the thrifty who knew that gold could be spent any day but were less certain of the current flood of paper. Bank notes flew from hand to hand in fantastic transactions of purchase and sale.

As prices rose the builders of the Hermitage were unable to keep within their estimates or to find carpenters or masons. "Hands cannot be got. I have written to Cincinnati, Louisville, Huntsville and Lexington."³⁰ Everywhere it was the same as artisans, shopkeepers, factory workers, farmers, judges, statesmen neglected their pursuits to take the easier road to fortune. City folk gambled in commodities, houses, rentals and stocks, making such terms as "bull" and "bear" and "corner" a part of the common speech. Everyone gambled in that illimitable American resource—land. A timber tract in Maine, bought for twenty-five cents an acre seven years before, was sold at an advance of thirty-six hundred per cent, profit two hundred and fifteen thousand dollars. The proprietor of an estate on the Hudson ten miles from New York subdivided it into a hundred parts, selling each for two thousand dollars. A farm near Louisville was turned over for two hundred and seventy-five thousand dollars. Secretary of War Cass exchanged a part of his farm adjoining the village of Detroit for one hundred thousand dollars. Lots in the swampy hamlet of Chicago sold for seven thousand dollars each. As a possible way out of his private involvements, the President sent his son to Mississippi to report on property the Chickasaw Indians were vacating for a site beyond the western line of Arkansas Territory.[31] Nothing came of the trip so far as Jackson was concerned, though Jack Donelson bought nine hundred and twenty acres.

The greatest stake in the speculative saturnalia was our almost incalculable public domain—an unpeopled stage of empire billowing from the westernmost settlements toward the sunset. This land was purchasable from the Government for a minimum of a dollar and twenty-five cents an acre. Speculating syndicates fell upon it and, elbowing aside genuine homesteaders, bought by the fifty-thousand-acre swoop, hoping for resale at ten and fifteen dollars an acre. In wilderness and prairie solitude, towns and cities were sketched in imagination and linked to the markets by imaginary railroads, canals and turnpikes. Public land sales rose in one year from four million to fourteen million dollars. The consideration therefor was the paper money of the deposit banks and of such other banks as the deposit banks would honor. As the banks could not hold this money idle in their vaults, they loaned it out to other speculators who purchased more land—a perpetual metamorphosis of paper dollars into paper towns and paper railroads emerging from a paper horn of plenty.

Another form of property, and the political ideas concerning the same, affected by this whirligig was the negro slave. As Jackson saw, slavery and not the tariff was the soil that nurtured the roots of disunion; eliminate the one and you eliminated the other. The early 'Thirties found Virginia, Kentucky, North Carolina and to some extent Tennessee debating proposals for gradual emancipation. The movement received a setback when Nat Turner's slave rebellion in Virginia took sixty white lives. Then the boom enhanced the prices of negroes. The Cotton Kingdom burst from the bud to a flower whose narcotic perfumes put to sleep emancipation schemes under the convenient delusion that, for better or for worse, the black race was a part of the South's heritage and could be controlled only in slavery. "The county court of Davidson," General Jackson was informed, "last week refused to emancipate the negroes of your [lately deceased] Uncle Alexander [Donelson] unless they would go to Liberia. They refuse to go. Their obstinacy will give you two or three negroes—a kind of property I suppose you but little care about."[32]

Fanatical William Lloyd Garrison launched his abolition crusade in Boston which, mistakenly it seems, was supposed to have been Nat Turner's inspiration. A storm swept the South, which southern members carried into Congress, for the exclusion of abolition literature from the mails. "On this great question," Jackson read in a letter from the New Orleans veteran, A. P. Hayne, "the South must stand or fall. *Man* loves *property* as he *does* his *life* and no government where the right of property is not secure can be looked upon as a good government."[33] So marched the South in these deceiving times, counter to the current of the world. With England liberating its blacks in the adjacent West Indies, our South sought to throw about itself a wall behind which to eternize a self-contained anachronism, Mr. Calhoun going so far as to proclaim slavery "a good—a positive good" for both races.

For the times it was not a bad life for the negro, as those of the late Alexander Donelson somehow realized when they preferred slavery in Tennessee to freedom in Africa. At the Hermitage was a black man named Sam whom Jackson had freed in 1816, but could not induce to leave the place. In retrospect it seems fairly clear that nowhere in the contemporary world did the negro find tutelage in the arts of civilization on the whole so beneficial to him as in the American slavery states. The overtone of Mr. Garrison's theme was the brutal treatment of the serfs. In the mill towns encircling Boston the average factory worker fared no better, if as well. A mill master could work his hands out of health without paying the doctor's bill. Deprived of civil status, property and family rights, the southern negro imperceptibly had acquired something greater—the power to mold the economic and social pattern of a people. Nearer the truth than Garrison, Hayne or Calhoun was General Jackson's Yankee friend, Washington Irving, when, taking a close-range view of slavery, he penciled in a pocket note-book: "In these establishments the world is turned upside down—the slave the master, the master the slave. The master has the idea of property, the latter the reality."[34]

And now began another phase as the enslaved race commenced to exercise its fatal influence on the political destinies of the free.

Andrew Jackson viewed the gilded panorama with apprehension. The perils of inflation were bad enough, as Old Hickory knew from dear experience. But the perils of slavery struck deeper, and would be the more difficult to meet.

6

Jackson did not direct his policy of rotation in office against political adversaries alone. Nowhere was it employed more freely than in the President's own official family.

In 1835 the General faced across his Cabinet table but one man who had held the same post a year before—Secretary of War Lewis Cass, and he was presently to go. The strong frontier face of the man from Michigan had lost its tan and grown a little soft under the blandishments of Washington living. With the French crisis on, Jackson complained of having to be his own Secretary of War. Old Hickory had no such fault to find with the man who sat at his right hand—the fourth occupant of the chair of the Secretary of State under Jackson. John Forsyth bore his responsibilities without troubling the President over details—and without neglecting the tailor who turned out the Georgian in splendid velvet-collared coats and black stocks reaching to the chin.

By trimming his sails to suit prevailing breezes, Levi Woodbury had ridden out the bank storm, making port as Jackson's fifth Secretary of the Treasury when the Senate refused to confirm Taney. Whereupon Mahlon Dickerson of New Jersey, a Jacksonian subaltern in the Senate, had received a handsome promotion as the third Secretary of the Navy. Martin Van Buren's law partner, Benjamin F. Butler,[35] with small black eyes and thin white fingers restlessly riffling the papers before him, was the third holder of the portfolio of Attorney General. At the foot of the table sat no stranger, but quiet, slender Amos Kendall, the only Kitchen Cabinet member to attain actual Cabinet rank. Jackson had lifted the unobtrusive Kentuckian from his insignificant closet in the Treasury to become his third Postmaster General barely in time to avert a scandal from Barry's amiable and innocent mismanagement.

Of all who had passed in and out of the Cabinet Jackson most sorely missed Roger B. Taney. Determined to reward the Marylander for his part in the bank war, the President nominated him for a place on the Supreme bench. But the opposition still controlled the Senate. On the last day of the session the clock in the Upper House was stopped at midnight, and Daniel Webster moved the indefinite postponement of action on the nomination. It was carried by three votes.

His Administration harried by a captious opposition, the country beset by fresh problems at home and abroad, Old Hickory was confronted by a revolt in his own party. It came about over the unbending insistence on Van Buren for Democratic standard-bearer in 1836. In 1832 Jackson had been able to quell but not extinguish opposition to the New Yorker. He was able to point to Van Buren's record of four years as the Executive's most useful lieutenant. He could point to no such record in 1835. In the nullification and the bank fights Benton, White, Taney, Forsyth and Polk, to name only those in the forefront, had served the cause of the embattled chieftain with greater fortitude and effectiveness. Yet Jackson clung to Van Buren, and would listen to no other word from anyone. The serious nature of the insurrection could no longer be disguised when the Tennessee delegation jumped the traces and, with only White, Grundy, Polk and one other absent, formally presented for the consideration of the forthcoming Democratic National Convention the name of Hugh Lawson White for president. Tacitly accepting the honor, Senator White's intercourse with the Executive Residence ceased.

Old Hickory refused to treat with the insurgents. Denouncing them as victims of a scheme of Henry Clay to "divide and conquer" the Administration, he toiled to tie up the convention for the Magician.[36] The revolt spread, gaining adherents in other states. Whereupon Jackson served notice that he would relieve the convention of the responsibility of selecting a vice-presidential candidate as well.

his designee being Colonel Richard M. ("Tecumseh") Johnson of Kentucky.

This was an astonishing choice. Admitting the expediency of a western running-mate for Van Buren, Jackson could have found half a dozen men who were Johnson's superior in the qualities desirable in a candidate. Chief Justice John Catron of the Tennessee Supreme Court wrote the President a long and earnest letter. Mentioning only in passing the Kentuckian's want of capacity, Judge Catron rested his case on Johnson's open acknowledgment of a mulatto mistress, and the liberal education bestowed on two octoroon daughters who "rode in carriages and claimed equality." He suggested that to force the party to accept such a man would meet with a success in the South similar to that of Johnson's own efforts to introduce his daughters to society.[37]

7

Following the recall of Louis Sérurier, France strengthened its naval stations in the West Indies, which England took as a preparation to blockade our coast in event of war. At the same time, however, Louis Philippe laid before the Deputies a bill for the payment of the indemnity which, in May, 1835, we learned, had become a law—with an amendment to the effect that nothing should be paid until France received "satisfactory explanations" of the language of Jackson's message to Congress.

This time our national pride was touched. Jackson immediately recalled Livingston from Paris, leaving his son-in-law, Thomas P. Barton, behind as chargé. "France will get no apology," spread-eagled the *Globe*, "nothing bearing even a remote resemblance to one."[38] The President's bitterest foe dared not intimate anything else. Once more the country stood firm and ready behind old Jackson.

The spectacle was not lost on the statesmen in the Quai d'Orsay. In September when Secretary of State Forsyth returned from his summer holiday, he found young Monsieur Pageot awaiting an audience. By some means—Major Lewis is an obvious suspect[39]—the President had received notice of the object of the visit. The chargé asked leave to acquaint the Secretary with the contents of a letter from the Duc Achille de Broglie, the French Minister for Foreign Affairs. The communication occupied the twilight zone between official and unofficial papers wherein a minister who has something too delicate for state utterance may assume to step, with one foot, out of his official character and speak as a private person. Considering the saber-rattling that had gone on in France and the powdery amendment to the indemnity-payment law, Broglie's letter was astonishingly pacific. His Majesty's government would accept as meeting the requirements of the amendment a statement from our Government explaining "the true meaning and real purport" of Jackson's message in terms that would banish the idea that any affront to the French *amour propre* was intended. As Jackson had made this explicit statement in the message itself, all France asked was a formal repetition of the disclaimer.[40]

At the end of his visit, Pageot asked permission to leave with the Secretary a copy of Broglie's interesting letter. Mr. Forsyth knew what to say, for Jackson had told him. He could not receive the communication. To do so would be to admit the right of a foreign nation to concern itself in a purely domestic affair of the United States such as a President's communication to a co-ordinate branch of the Government. Such an admission would be degrading to the United States.[41]

On this display of French weakness Jackson acted at once. With his own hand he drafted instructions to Barton in Paris to say that the United States stood ready to receive the indemnity. If this note were not answered in three days, Barton was to ask when payment might be expected. If in five days this did not bring the payment or definite arrangements for the same, Barton was to close the legation and come home.[42]

Before Barton could be heard from, the time came to prepare the annual message of 1835 to Congress. Again Pageot attempted to press upon Forsyth the Broglie letter and again he was rebuffed.

"The honor of my country," wrote General Jackson in that message, "shall never be stained by an apology from me for the statement of truth or the performance of duty." This, however, was preceded by a statement that his message of the year before was not intended "to menace or insult the Government of France."[43]

Amid the almost universal acclaim this utterance evoked, the country learned that Barton had asked for his passports. Pageot immediately did the same. The first week of January, 1836, Andrew Jackson

Pageot, attended by his anxious parents, began the long journey to the land of his paternal forbears, while his distinguished godfather plied the pen over a special message to Congress which Edward Livingston regarded as tantamount to a declaration of war.[44]

The united efforts of Livingston, Forsyth and Van Buren induced the old chieftain to tone down the document, but the version that went to Congress was no skimmed-milk affair. In view of the "peremptory refusal [of France] to execute the treaty except on [inadmissible] terms," the Executive requested "large and speedy appropriations for the increase of the Navy and the completion of our coast defenses." Nothing, said the President, would remain undone by him to "preserve the pecuniary interests of our citizens, the independence of our Government, and the honor of our country."[45]

At this juncture England stepped in to save the face of Louis Philippe with an offer of mediation. France immediately, and Jackson after just enough hesitation to avoid a look of precipitation, agreed to arbitrate. A sigh of relief was heard on two continents. "The war of etiquette," wrote Philip Hone, "is on a fair way now of being averted."[46]

8

France solemnly accepted General Jackson's message of 1835 as proof that nothing in the message of 1834 had been intended to wound her sensibilities. But before the British could congratulate themselves on the success of their pacific offices, the United States presented the note of ex-Minister Sérurier.

"*Les plaintes que porte M. le Président contre le prétendu non-accomplissements des engagements. . . .*"

Our translator had rendered this as follows:

"The complaints which the President brings against the pretended non-fulfillment of the engagements. . . ."

In fine, the issue of peace or of war between France and the United States ostensibly had been narrowed down to the meaning of one word. It was the word *"prétendu,"* which we translated as "pretended." In the text under review our linguist held that this conveyed the idea that Jackson had acted in bad faith. Against this rendering the British and the French foreign offices opposed their combined erudition. The whole trouble, the diplomats said in chorus, lay in our faulty translation. *"Prétendu"* meant "alleged," and nothing in the entire passage was susceptible of a construction implying that General Jackson was aught but the soul of truth and honor.[47]

This explanation was accepted as satisfactory to the government of the United States, and for the enlightenment of posterity and the advancement of the study of the French language in America a memorandum to that effect was filed in the archives of the State Department.

On May 10, 1836, the President made a gracious announcement of his complete victory. Four back installments of the twenty-five-million-franc indemnity had been paid with interest. Cordial relations were re-established with France.

To wipe the slate clean the two countries were to staff their respective legations with new personnel. Jackson arranged to send Lewis Cass to Paris and consented to receive as the French minister one Édouard Pontois. Imagine, then, his surprise when who should turn up to reopen the legation in Washington but Alphonse Pageot with his wife Mary Lewis and son Andrew Jackson. The tricky French again! Much as General Jackson loved Mary Lewis and his little godson, and much as he respected Pageot as a man, he was for packing the three of them back across the ocean.

So great was the presidential ire that a thoroughly alarmed Major Lewis came forward with explanations. The French were not villains in this affair, but the victims of a side-door intrigue between the good Major and the new minister to the court of Louis Philippe, Lewis Cass. Naturally, the Major wanted his daughter back. So he had connived with Cass to get from Jackson, in private conversation, an expression of his personal friendship for the chargé. This Cass had transmitted to Paris in such a way that the French monarch had consented to restore Pageot to his old post as a private compliment to his esteemed fellow-ruler, the brave General Jackson. Still, as a rebuke to Cass, Jackson was for making a clean breast of it to Louis Philippe, and asking for Pageot's recall. At this point the British Minister resumed his capacity as mediator and, with Major Lewis bringing to bear the weight of forty years of loyal friendship, Old Hickory relented and let the Pageot family stay.[48]

CHAPTER XXXIX

THE PRAIRIE ROSE

I

THE French question triumphantly disposed of, in the autumn of 1835 General Jackson turned to another problem in his foreign portfolio which, at the moment, seemed to be getting badly out of hand. For this the Executive himself was largely to blame.

Through the whole labyrinth of Jacksonian diplomacy, the topic of Texas had threaded a secretive and, as inhospitable critics were wont to imply, a sordid course. Two years before he became President, the General had received at the Hermitage a letter postmarked Jackson, Mississippi. "I have been into Texas," it read, "[and examined] the Soil, climate & local advantages of the country— It must belong to the United States and I hope that it may be one of the Acts of your administration to obtain it."[1] The writer was Colonel Anthony Butler,[2] a bumptious South Carolinian who had ranged the western border from the Lakes to the Gulf and fought at New Orleans. When this letter was written, in 1827, he was a member of the Mississippi Legislature and one of the increasingly numerous company of American speculators in Texas lands. They did much to keep alive the patriotic cry for a rectification of the international boundary which would bring their holdings under the stars and stripes.

In the summer of 1829 Colonel Butler joined another numerous company, that of General Jackson's super-serviceable friends gathered in Washington for the patriotic purpose of assisting the new Administration along the pathway of an illustrious destiny. Armed with maps and memoranda, he readily qualified as an expert on the Texas question with which John Quincy Adams had grappled for four years in vain. The grief-stricken Jackson listened to his oracular friend and instructed Secretary of State Van Buren to open negotiations for a boundary following the watershed between the Nueces

River and the Rio Grande, with a cash inducement of five million dollars to enable the Mexican officials the better to appreciate the justice of our claim.[3] Adams had offered one million for about the same thing. Instructions for our minister at Mexico City, the competent Joel R. Poinsett, were quickly prepared. Owing to their confidential nature, these documents were not entrusted to the ordinary channels of communication. They were handed to Anthony Butler to deliver in person. Moreover, in the business at hand, Mr. Van Buren advised Poinsett to avail himself of the collaboration of the special courier.[4] Jackson himself added a personal note. "Col Butler . . . is entitled to your entire confidence."[5]

Four years' residence in mercurial Mexico had rendered Joel R. Poinsett somewhat immune to surprise. He has not illuminated the record with a description of his emotions when, a few days after the arrival of the Administration's breezy bearer of confidential dispatches, the newspapers of Mexico City announced that Colonel Butler had come with an offer to purchase Texas for five million dollars. The Government organ, *El Sol,* assured its readers that consideration of so degrading a proposal was unthinkable. Three weeks later Poinsett left for home. He resigned and Butler was named in his stead. The rise from obscure political adventurer to minister plenipotentiary with millions to dangle before Mexican statesmen was phenomenal even for the era of the "clean sweep."

Nor was this Colonel Butler's only remarkable achievement. For five years he held that post by the basically simple formula of redeeming one promise with another. At length, when the President's patience began to wear thin, Butler proposed military occupation of "that part of Texas which is ours. . . . [Place] me at the head of the country that is to be occupied [and] I will pledge my head that we shall have all we desire in six months." Jackson handed the letter to Donelson with the following endorsement: "A. Butler: What a scamp. The Secretary of State will . . . recall him."[6] Not until a year later, however—June, 1835—did the minister reach Washington. He did not come empty-handed. The new proposal was to cross the palm of one Father Hernandez, confessor of the sister of Antonio López de Santa Anna, the current president of Mexico, with five hundred thousand dollars as a stimulus to further negotiation. This suggestion had the advantage of being cheaper than others of a similar nature which Butler had laid before the Government.

Jackson replied: "Nothing will be countenanced by the Executive to bring the Government under the remotest imputation of being engaged in corruption." Our virtue thus made a matter of record, the Executive indicated no further readiness to interfere to an impractical degree with what Butler represented as a prevailing custom of Mexican statecraft.[7] Once the five million—no more—was paid over it would be no concern of ours as to the pockets the money might eventually reach. The President expressed himself more delicately, however: "The public functionaries of Mexico may apply it as they deem proper to extinguish *private claims* and give us the cession free of all encumbrance."[8]

Pleading for another chance and promising to work wonders, this man Butler was permitted to return to Mexico. He accomplished nothing and in December Jackson yanked him home for good. The diplomat expostulated against the ingratitude of republics. "Just at the period when a favorable moment presented itself to renew the work I am discharged from office."[9]

2

General Jackson did not despair. The Texas question was in the throes of another experiment, rendered the more exhilarating because it revolved about a personage whose history had run a course more bizarre than that of Colonel Butler—Sam Houston of Tennessee.

On the tearful January morning in 1829 when Andrew Jackson turned from his wife's grave to the road to Washington, he had paused to bestow his personal and political benedictions on Governor Houston. The occasion for the personal blessing was the announcement of Houston's prospective marriage into the influential Allen family of Gallatin. The Governor was thirty-five years old, six feet six inches tall, handsome, captivating, able. Marriage and a less roistering mode of life, his friends felt, were all that were necessary to complete his conquest of the heights. The occasion for the political blessing was the forthcoming contest in which Houston would be opposed for re-election by the powerful William Carroll, three times occupant of the State's executive chair. The weight of Jackson's influence, it was believed, would insure victory for Sam Houston, after which predictions as to his future ranged from the Cabinet to the White House itself.[10]

Twelve weeks after his marriage to Eliza Allen the glamorous Governor of Tennessee left his yellow-haired girl bride, resigned his office and under an assumed name boarded a steamboat for the western wilderness beyond the pale of civilization. The only explanation vouchsafed a stunned populace was that "private afflictions, deep, incurable," for which he alone was to blame had wrecked his happiness. Actually, Houston had accused his bride of infidelity, only to follow her to her father's house and on his knees withdraw the hot words and ask forgiveness. But it was then too late. A moment of wild accusation was paid for with a lifetime of regret.[11]

Twenty years before, Sam Houston, carrying a copy of the *Iliad* and a rifle, had run off from school to live with the Indians. That sojourn had lasted four years, a minor chief named Oo-loo-te-ka taking Sam into his family and naming him The Raven. In 1829 ex-Governor Houston again sought the wigwam of Oo-loo-te-ka, then principal chief of the Western Cherokees in what is now Oklahoma. He became again The Raven.

The first story Andrew Jackson received of the spectacular ruin of his protégé's fortunes included a report that he intended to rehabilitate himself by conquering Texas. Ordering a surveillance of Houston's movements, the President exacted from him a "pledge of honor" to respect the sovereignty of Mexico.[12] With little to lose and forgetfulness to gain, the exile turned to the whirlpool of internal Indian politics, momentarily giving Washington almost as much of a start as if he had gone to Texas. Under his leadership, border tribes united to oppose a resistance to white rapacity which gained a new respect for the rights of southwestern Indians. But on the whole he maintained good terms with Jackson, countenancing his policy of removal of the southern Indians as the best thing the red men could hope for. So passed three confusing years, during which The Raven stood forth, now an inspired leader of his adopted people, now a tribal vagabond known by another Cherokee name which casually translated means "Big Drunk."

Twice The Raven visited Washington, attractively clad in beaded buckskins and a blanket, to insist on the performance of Indian treaties. Jackson shocked the conservative wing of society by inviting him to the White House. On the second visit, in 1832, the President suggested a trip to a tailor and paid the bill. Never to be outdone in the matter of gifts was a part of Indian etiquette. From about his neck Sam Houston removed a small buckskin sack which for years had passed as a Cherokee witch charm. Opening the little bag, The Raven presented to Sarah Yorke Jackson Eliza Allen's engagement ring. Attired as a white man Sam Houston listened to his patron speak of Texas. Butler was getting nowhere, and Jackson desired dependable information from the Mexican province. Sam Houston left the capital with a War Department commission to hold parleys with nomadic Indians who pitched their camps at will on the Mexican and the American sides of the Red River. The instrument has the appearance of a subterfuge to cover a reconnaissance of Texas for the confidential use of General Jackson.[13]

3

The first activity of the unofficial envoy pleased Jackson no more than the diplomacy of Anthony Butler. Openly playing the game of the American land-speculating clique, hot for revolution, Houston aroused the suspicions of Mexico City so promptly that Jackson disavowed him.[14]

Houston changed his tune and sided with the conservatives who wished Texas under the stars and stripes rightly enough, but preferred the Jacksonian scheme of purchase to war. As prospects for a settlement by this means grew dimmer and Santa Anna's repressive measures harsher, Texas began to arm. General Jackson closed his eyes to an extraordinary emigration of American "settlers," lugging guns rather than ploughshares. The guns began popping in 1835 and, with Sam Houston one of their generals, the Americans in Texas drove the weak Mexican garrisons across the Rio Grande. The South and the West were alive with sentiment for the revolutionists, but Jackson preserved a stern show of official neutrality, sharply rebuking the Texan commissioner Stephen F. Austin when he requested the United States "openly" to take up the cause of the rebellious province.[15] Sam Swartwout incurred his chief's displeasure by presiding at a meeting in New York to raise funds for the friends of freedom in Texas.[16] Colonel Swartwout and other conspicuous New York Jacksonians were large shareholders in the great Galveston Bay and Texas Land Company, of which General Houston, in addition to his military duties, was the resident attorney.

Yet, despite the formal rectitude of Jackson the President, in his private character Old Hickory was unable to suppress a certain sympathy for the ardor of his southern and western countrymen, or an almost paternal interest in the fortunes of his old subaltern Sam Houston, now commander-in-chief of the scattered bands of adventurers grandiosely known as the Armies of the Texas Republic.

Early in 1836 came startling news. Santa Anna was north of the Rio Grande with seven thousand men. Houston ordered a general retreat and concentration. The leaders of the bands, remembering the easy victories of the year before, refused to obey. Santa Anna surrounded the Alamo and slew its defenders to a man. Then he wiped out a larger band at Goliad. Then another and another. With the government of the republic and the civil population in flight toward the United States border, Sam Houston managed to reach what remained of the "army," numbering three hundred and seventy-four men, and to get them out of Santa Anna's reach.

In the littered White House study Andrew Jackson pored over a map, trying to give reality to each meager, hysterical report from Texas. The one clear military fact seemed to be that Houston was making a zig-zag retreat, adding to his force while Santa Anna divided his in pursuit. The best that most observers hoped for was Houston's escape to American soil. Jackson disagreed. Sam Houston would turn and fight. Old Hickory's long forefinger crinkled the map at the western shore of Galveston Bay. He would fight *there*, the President said, or *there*—indicating a stream called Buffalo Bayou.[17]

In May came tidings too fantastic for belief: the Mexican army annihilated, Santa Anna a prisoner of war.

A few days later a travel-worn lieutenant of United States dragoons presented himself at the White House with dispatches from General Edmund P. Gaines, commanding our frontier troops—and from Sam Houston. Jackson fairly grasped the papers from the young man's hand. The old soldier's eyes lighted up as he read, exclaiming

THE FOURTH HERMITAGE

Finished 1835 after its predecessor had been destroyed by fire, save for portions of the exterior walls which were used in rebuilding. In the background, right, is Tulip Grove, the residence of Andrew Jackson Donelson. From an engraving made in 1856 and owned by the Ladies' Hermitage Association.

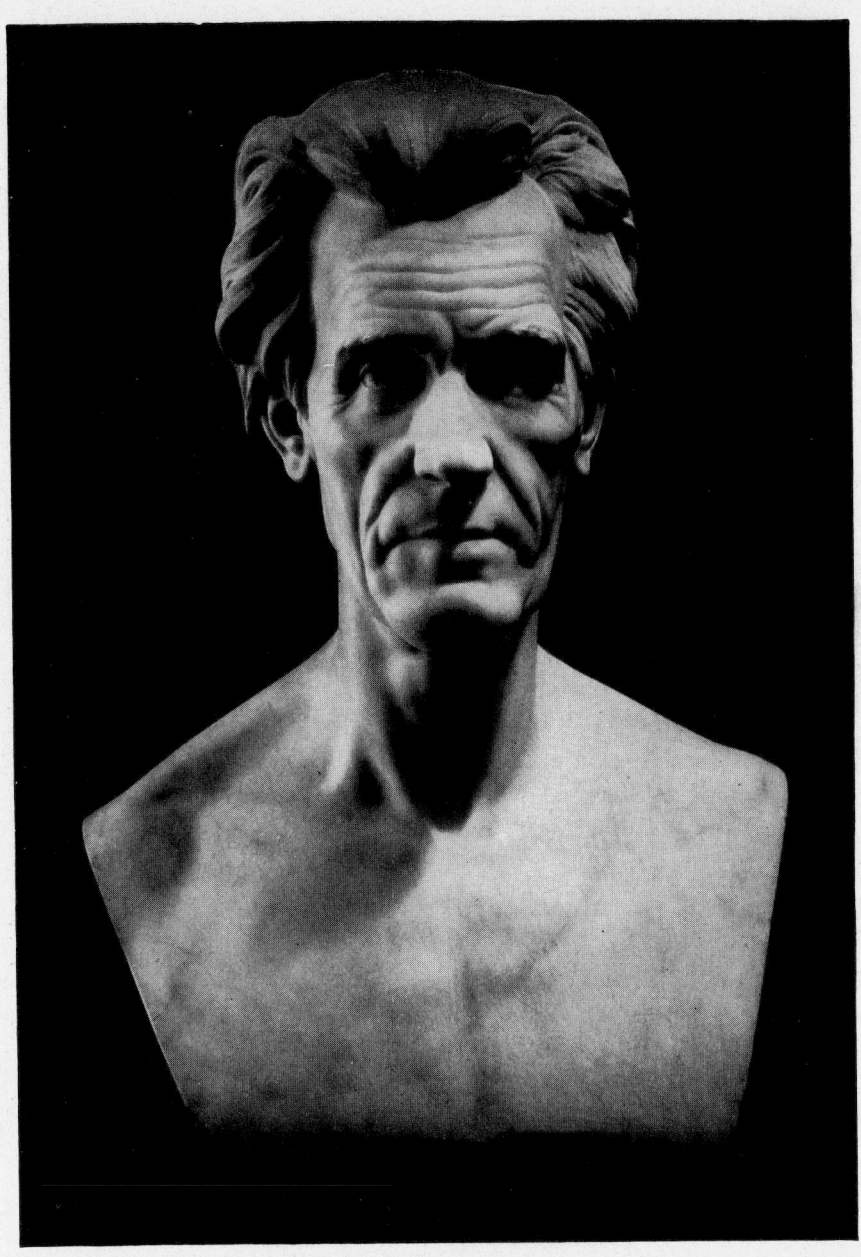

SCULPTOR AND DATE UNKNOWN
A bust of General Jackson, owned by Dr. Isaac M. Cline of New Orleans, and loaned by him to the Louisiana State Museum.

over and over, "Yes, that is his writing. I know it well. That is Sam Houston's writing. There can be no doubt about what he says."[18]

The fantastic tale was true. After a retreat of thirty-eight days, Houston had taken Santa Anna by surprise at the junction of Buffalo Bayou and San Jacinto River, obliterating the army under his immediate command and capturing the president of Mexico.

A note of congratulation went off to the conqueror. "I hope there may be no delay or discord in organizing a stable government to make the best use of the Independence you and your brave men have so bravely won. . . . Subscriptions are being made in Tennessee and elsewhere to aid you; to which I need not say I have contributed to the extent of my means."[19]

4

Before a week was out John C. Calhoun arose in his place in the Senate. He said there were "powerful reasons" not only for the recognition of the independence of Texas, but for her admission to the Union.

To add to the glory of Andrew Jackson was not among the ambitions of the statesman from South Carolina. He made this speech because Texas under the flag would open a vast field for the expansion of slavery and its peculiar political doctrines. So quickly did the dew begin to fall from the prairie rose and the thorns to appear. General Jackson could sympathize with many of the current complaints of the southern people. He had asked Congress for a law prohibiting the circulation of inflammatory abolition literature through the mails. Yet the Executive had no desire to risk the estrangement of conservative northern opinion by throwing Texas into the bubbling cauldron of slavery issues. Consequently a sharp line continued to divide the personal sentiments from the presidential behavior of Andrew Jackson as he strove to keep Texas from falling from the plane of national to that of sectional questions.

San Jacinto set the South and the West on fire. The Tennessee fund to which (in his personal capacity) General Jackson had contributed went to equip volunteers whose ambition was to conquer all Mexico. Troops swarmed into Texas until Houston had thrice as many as he could feed. Vainly he expostulated that the war was over and that

Texas needed people to plant corn and not to perform military exercises. Even the ordinarily level-headed Gaines took leave of his senses. At a critical juncture of Santa Anna's invasion, Jackson had ordered this officer to march a small force a short distance across the international line ostensibly to avert border incidents. With Santa Anna a prisoner and the "On to Mexico" cry sweeping the West, Gaines called on the governors of five adjacent states for re-enforcements of militia. Jackson countermanded this at once, lecturing the Governor of Tennessee on "the obligations of our treaty with Mexico . . . to maintain a strict neutrality."[20]

5

Those not stricken by the Texas fever found ample excitement at home as the craze for land speculation reached new heights in 1836. One of the springs from which this speculation fed was the ever-mounting Federal surplus on deposit in the "pet" banks. In 1829 Jackson had pronounced in favor of distributing such a surplus among the states. Now he was less certain of the wisdom of this. But the people wanted it, not as a means of curbing speculation but as a means apparently of getting something for nothing. So a bill was passed for the distribution of the surplus, beginning in 1837, which in June, 1836, Jackson signed with misgivings.

Alarmed by the multiplication of banks and of paper money, the President perceived flaws in the "pet" bank deposit system,[21] which had begun to present evils as patent as those he had fought to extinguish in his long battle against the Bank of the United States. Deposit banks were lending Government funds on security of doubtful value, and were adding to the flood of paper currency far in excess of their power conveniently to redeem.

The best thing that could be said of the distribution of the surplus revenue was that it would force deposit banks to curtail their loans to the extent of thirty-odd millions. This might check, but it would not stop, the course of currency inflation so long as the land boom lasted. And land gambling would continue so long as the products of the other paper money mills were receivable at the Government land offices. Benton introduced a resolution providing that only gold and silver should be taken in payment for public lands. The grip of the speculative mania was too powerful, and it failed of passage. Jackson then took the responsibility on himself, directing the Secretary of the Treasury to issue the famous Specie Circular which appeared on July 11, 1836. Before the earth-shaking protests of the speculative fraternity, the President remained unmoved, and the land boom received a death blow. The fall of fictitious real estate prices carried down other prices. The inevitable inconveniences of this readjustment brought complaints from those who believed a paper prosperity could endure forever.

6

In still other details Old Hickory showed himself the master.

He gave his party as candidates not only Martin Van Buren but "Tecumseh" Johnson as well. Going through with his threat to secede, Hugh Lawson White accepted an independent nomination from the Tennessee Legislature. But as the Jackson party divided, so did the opposition. Massachusetts put forth Webster as an independent nominee. South Carolina played a lone hand, declining to affiliate with anyone. Under these circumstances the only chance to defeat Van Buren seemed to lie in throwing the election into the House, and Henry Clay showed little enthusiasm for that. Standing graciously aside, the Kentuckian permitted the apparently hopeless Whig nomination to go to William Henry Harrison of Ohio.

In the face of party revolt the old leader also achieved in 1836 a victory which did much to alter the controlling social philosophy of the United States Supreme Court.

John Marshall had died the year before. Jackson called him one of "the greatest men of his age, . . . [although] perhaps it is proper that I should say . . . [that I] dissent from some of his expositions of our constitutional law."[22] In a word, Marshall set property rights above human rights and Jackson did not, though in their differences over the Cherokee Indian cases this distinction does not hold. On the whole John Marshall had carried on the social philosophy of Hamilton while Jackson was revitalizing that of Jefferson.

Strange this was, because the two Democrats, the greatest of their century, disliked and distrusted each other. For all his service to Jeffersonian ideals, Jackson inconsistently regarded their author as a feathery doctrinaire; Jefferson looked on Jackson as a border ruffian. Actually the men were not well acquainted, neither having had an opportunity to see beneath the top layer of the other's personality. Twice only did they meet after Jefferson's retirement in 1809, once in 1815 and again in 1823. Neither meeting got beyond the scrupulous exchange of amenities. Earlier encounters seem to have been even more superficial. Yet, from these brief contacts were derived those hasty first impressions which crystallized into lifetime convictions—with which, however, neither man seems to have been wholly satisfied.

For Marshall's successor Jackson nominated Roger B. Taney. Perhaps personal reasons swayed him as much as any other. Perhaps partizan considerations, as much as any other, moved the Senate to confirm this nomination after having twice rejected Mr. Taney for lesser offices. Nevertheless, the accession of Chief Justice Roger B. Taney marked the beginning of an era in the history of the Supreme Court which was to remold its thought and carry into its decisions (excepting on the negro question) the liberal social spirit having as its goal the greater well-being of common men.[23] In Jackson's last days in office, Congress helped along the trend by increasing the number of justices from seven to nine. Of these Jackson, in his eight years, named six, or more than any previous President except George Washington. He could have named seven, for the court was passed on to his successor with one vacancy.

7

"Kiss your dear Sarah for me and my two sweet little ones," Andrew Jackson wrote to his son. "Tell the children grandpa is coming. . . . If convenient have the two year old filly out of the virginia mare broke by the time I get out."[24]

On July 10, 1836, the White House coach rolled across the bridge into Virginia behind four mettlesome horses, fresh for the long journey. The last thing the President had done before leaving was to borrow money to settle household bills, though the arrival of an unexpected draft for eighteen hundred dollars for work on the Hermitage obliged him to leave with some of the local items unpaid.

Bad roads and bad weather met the travelers at the outset. Every few hours a horse would throw a shoe, and repairs to the coach cost as much as meals and lodging for its occupants. One day they were seven hours going ten miles, after which a single-tree and both fore-axles gave way. More drafts met the traveler en route. "My dear Andrew," he wrote ahead, "draw on me no more until I can get funds." On August 4 the coach creaked into the Hermitage drive. Notifying Frank Blair of his arrival, Jackson described the condition of the horses. Then he briefly accounted for himself. "The continued dampness gave me a bad cold and cough and I fear I will have to use the lancet soon."[25]

The handsome new Hermitage was finished. New curtains hung at the windows, new carpets covered the floors. Much new furniture appeared in the spacious rooms, with more to come replacing the eighteen crates from Philadelphia which had been lost when the steamboat *John Randolph* burned at Nashville. Moreover all was paid for, the bills footing up to more than ten thousand dollars, which was nearly four times the amount of the first estimates Jackson had received of the probable cost of repairing the damage wrought by the fire.[26] On top of this the five thousand dollar note in the hands of Harry Hill had been paid.

Drastic economies at the White House—fewer guests and less lavish fare—had made these things possible, for the 1835 cotton crop (for which Jackson normally would have been paid in April, 1836) represented the greatest failure in the history of the Hermitage.[27] This was the second failure in two years. Old Hickory anxiously looked forward to the time when he should be master of his own acres. "The eye of the owner maketh the ox fat."[28]

A source of trouble was the fact that Andrew, junior, shifted too many burdens to the shoulders of his overseer. The young man was frequently absent from the plantation. A letter from the harried superintendent reflects the diversity of the problems left behind.

"Your directions concerning the purchase of some mares shall be attended to. I shall also use my best exertions to sell your riding horses. I could have sold your grey horse long since had it not been for his eyes. As respects the tap for the screw [for the cotton press] I had the pattern made at home by Ned with the assistance of sharp

3 or 4 days to instruct him and it is now at the furnace . . . [for] casting. . . . I have the timbers all ready and so soon as I can get the Casting I will put up the press again. I have the shingles nearly ready for covering the gin house. . . . We have a great many other Jobs to do, such as fixing our Corn houses, repairing lot fences and one or two of the negro houses wants new shingles. We have all our winter cloth for the negroes done. Our shues I have not yet began. I have been trying my best to get the leather. I shall finish gathering of fodder this week.

"Our neighbors are becoming a little alarmed about our cotton crop on account of verry cold rainy weather. I was at Mr. Pools a few days since and saw the colts gallop, they appear to be doing finely. Pool makes some considerable calculations on the black colt and Majr. Donelson's horse Mombrino he feels verry confident of taking the mile. . . . Some sickness Amongst us but nothing very serious. Aron the Blacksmith and Tom Franklin was both taken . . . [with] verry hot fever all night. I gave them a large dose of Calomel and Jalap this morning. Littleton is laid up with Gonerea, he got it from his wife."[29]

Such was the nature of the things with which the planter grappled on his last visit home before retirement from his country's service. Both Andrew, junior, and Overseer Hobbs came in for a strict talking to. The White House salary could not be depended on much longer to cover the losses of the farm. "My son, you must assume energy, and command our concerns. . . . We must make better crops and preserve our stock better or we will soon be in a state of *want* and *poverty*."[30] With increasing dismay the old man surveyed stables, stock lots and fields: not enough blue grass or herd's grass or wheat; more land in oats, hemp and millet than needed, and this "slovenly sowed." "We must plow better and cultivate less [acreage] and we will produce more."[31]

After six weeks of study General Jackson concluded, years in advance of his time, that the underlying defect in the Cumberland Valley's scheme of agriculture was an overdependence on cotton as a money crop. "We must change our culture in part to stock, hemp and perhaps tobacco." Preliminary arrangements were made accordingly,[32] and in September the President started for Washington for the last time, leaving Jack Donelson behind. Emily was very ill.

8

The desk in the second-floor study was nearly buried beneath a pile of papers which the winnowing of Donelson could have reduced to half. The President bent to the task encouraged by the thought that, after all, the end was in sight.

Angrily Jackson conned the reports on the Seminole campaign in Florida, the second Indian "war" of his administrations. The Seminoles had declined to fulfill an agreement by which their pampered chiefs had consented to remove the tribe beyond the Mississippi. Jackson had sent Winfield Scott with an impressive body of Regulars and militia to teach the recalcitrants a thing or two about the sanctity of treaties—when broken by an Indian. Unfortunately the soldiers of General Scott's numerous army had simply got in each other's way, leaving the Indians in unenlightened possession of their swamps. Veterans of Jackson's celebrated Florida expedition filled the mails with derisive letters. The President recalled General Scott. Brigadier General Richard K. Call of the Florida militia, who in 1818 had followed Old Hickory as a captain, was given command. He promised to show the country an Indian campaign, Jackson style.

Another problem arose from an enthusiastic effort to quicken the work of destiny in Texas. That republic had elected Sam Houston president, voted overwhelmingly for annexation to the United States, and started a minister to Washington under the cordial assumption that everything would be as easy as falling off a log. Slavery extremists were in transports of joy, while Abolitionists uttered the most menacing threats yet. General Jackson thought the impulsive Texans, like the Seminoles, had something to learn.

In the midst of these difficulties it was a pleasure to consider the presidential campaign. Old Hickory could see nothing but a sweep for Van Buren.

9

Jack Donelson was on the way to Washington, making a journey which naught but a Jacksonian sense of duty could have impelled him to undertake. He had left his beautiful wife dying, as he believed, of "quick" consumption.

There being no appropriation for a private secretary to the President, Jackson had given his nephew a minor place in the Land Office. Ordinarily the duties were slight, but during the past summer forty thousand land patents had accumulated which only Donelson's signature could validate. It was imperative that they be signed. Fortunately, when Jack reached the capital, his wife was reported to be better. He fell to work night and day, and Jackson said he must start for home the instant the job was done.[33] By the time he had written his name forty thousand times, better news came of Emily. So strong was the hope for recovery that Donelson concluded to help with the annual message and return by way of Philadelphia to buy furniture for the new house he had built at Tulip Grove, his plantation which adjoined the Hermitage.

The message was begun—the last to bear the name of Andrew Jackson. As he worked the President was seized with coughing. Blood gushed from his mouth. Doctors cupped and blistered him. As if the hemorrhage had not taken enough, they drained his veins of sixty ounces of blood. For two days it was not known whether the President would live or die.[34]

Forty-eight hours later the incredible invalid was sitting up. They placed in his hands a letter which had come from Emily. It was a cheerful letter. Emily was able to leave her bed and to take a little exercise each day. A succeeding post, however, had brought tidings of a setback. Propped against pillows, Jackson began an answer to Emily. It does not appear that he was shown the letter bearing the bad news. He did not need to see it. Tuberculosis ran in the Donelson strain. Old Hickory had seen too many of the clan go to feel sanguine about Emily. At the time of their parting in Tennessee he had feared her doomed.

Yet the letter began in a hopeful vein. "I rejoice, my dear Emily, to find your spirits are good. This is necessary to your perfect recovery. . . . You are young——"

Yes, twenty-eight. In the eight years since General Jackson had brought her on to be the mistress of the White House, the bright, inexperienced country girl had matured into a notable hostess and lady of fashion. In the transformation nothing was lost of her youthful warmth and gaiety, her courage and integrity. She had matched that courage against the courage of her dear old uncle, preferring the public humiliation of exile to countenancing Margaret Eaton. Incidentally General Jackson's once-flaming championship of Bellona was a thing he no longer spoke of. Not that the old man had repudiated the obligations incurred in sponsoring that mésalliance. Florida proving too undistinguished a theatre, he had made Eaton the minister at Madrid. Tales that drifted back were not pleasant to hear: Margaret smoking cigars with her guests while her husband steeped himself in rum.[35]

The brave tone faded from General Jackson's missive. "We know not when we may be called home. Then let us live so that we can say with the sacred poet:

> " 'Deal gently, Lord, with those
> Whose faith and pious fear,
> Whose hope, and love, and every grace,
> Proclaim their hearts sincere. . . .'

"My blessing to you and the children. Emily farewell."[36]

Jackson begged Emily's husband to leave him. Concealing his almost unbearable anxiety Jack Donelson remained until the message was finished. December 3 he started for Tennessee. On the night of the sixteenth a dream of death alarmed the President. Three weeks later he learned that on the day before that dream Emily had suffered the relapse which took away hope. She asked that her bed be moved so that she could look from a window commanding the road by which her husband would return. Telling her children good-bye, she sought to save what remained of her strength for the effort to keep alive until Jack should come. At noon on December 20 Emily Donelson turned her head toward the window and closed her brown eyes forever. Jack was then a two days' ride away.[37]

10

In the course of these trials, General Jackson learned that Martin Van Buren had been elected his successor, though not by the margin Old Hickory had anticipated. Tennessee, including the Hermitage polling district, had gone for Hugh Lawson White. This was hard to bear. "We live in a day of personal and political changes," the old man said—accurately enough before his emotions got the upper hand, "and I must add, of depraved morals."[38] Another example of depravity, in General Jackson's estimation, occurred when the Electoral College, for once exercising the independence intended by the framers of the Constitution, failed to supply the majority required to make "Tecumseh" Johnson Vice President. The Senate elected him, however.

Strangely, the Senate which convened in December was a body more than usually amenable to the Jacksonian will, due to changes during the recess brought about by deaths and by resignations. Old Hickory had always had trouble with the Upper House, the lair of Clay, Webster and Calhoun. The great victory over the bank was won in the teeth of a hostile Senate, which had retaliated with a resolution of censure against the President. At the time and on the spot Thomas Hart Benton had served notice that one day he would see this slur wiped from the official journal of the Senate.

The vow was kept. For nearly three years the Missourian waited and watched. Compromises were offered. Would the Senator consent to the "abrogation" or "rescinding" of the resolution? No, he would not. The resolution must be "expunged"—physically expunged from the journal. The annoyingly logical Webster asked how the Senate could be said to "keep" a record if it were to vote to destroy a part of it. To no purpose: Benton had his majority for expunging. On Saturday night, January 14, 1837, about a table laden with cold meats and wine, the expungers planned their course.

A resolution was introduced at the opening of Monday's session. At midnight the opposition surrendered. The Clerk of the Senate produced the thick ledger for 1834 and turned to the resolution of censure. In the presence of a gallery packed to the last inch and of such senators as cared to bear witness, he drew heavy lines around the offending act and wrote across its face, "Expunged by order of the Senate, this 16th day of January, 1837."

This tinsel, twilight triumph pleased the old man as much as if it had contributed something material to his fame. His eyes would kindle as he displayed the pen the Clerk had used—a gift from Benton.

II

On the twentieth of December, 1836, William H. Wharton, Envoy Extraordinary and Minister Plenipotentiary of the Republic of Texas, spread his credentials before Secretary of State Forsyth. At the moment of their preparation, the republic being without an official seal, Sam Houston had stamped the documents with the impress of one of his cuff links instead. The treasury of the republic being innocent of funds to defray the traveling expenses of its diplomatic staff, Mr. Wharton had used his own. He had used them with taste and propriety. No minister from the Court of Saint James's has presented a more confident façade in the interest of his country. This was needful. En route Mr. Wharton had read the President's message. To Texans as well as to our own southern and western expansionists, the passage on Texas was little short of dumfounding. As to annexation—not one word. As to recognition, mere acknowledgment that Texas was independent of Mexico—these lines:

"Recognition at this time . . . would scarcely be regarded as consistent with that prudent reserve with which we have heretofore held ourselves bound to treat all similar questions."

Mr. Forsyth told Mr. Wharton that the clamor for annexation had "embarrassed" the United States. In view of the ruction stirred up by the Abolitionists would it not be best if the matter were taken care of "under the administration of a Northern President?"

Mr. Wharton could see no point to giving Martin Van Buren more honors than he had already received at the hands of Andrew Jackson. Post haste he set out for the White House, intent that Old Hickory should not be "robbed" of "glory" rightly his.[39]

Wharton was a native Tennesseean whom Jackson remembered well. He received the envoy kindly—in his study, for since his illness in November the President no longer came downstairs. But Wharton's mention of glory awakened no spark. Recognition, the President said, was a matter for Congress. Congress, countered Wharton, would not act without a special message removing the impression of the previous one. Jackson declined to write a special message. This was another way of saying, "Leave it to Mr. Van Buren."

Again and again Wharton returned to the Executive Residence, each time to be rebuffed. He did not give up. "Night and day," the envoy assured Sam Houston, "I shall . . . [persevere in] every argument that can operate on his pride and his sense of justice."[40]

From these incessant interviews a better acquaintance grew between Sam Houston's energetic agent and the feeble old President. General Jackson laid aside his reserve. He had not relinquished, he said, his desire to bring Texas under the flag. But a more ardent desire was for the security of the Union. To annex Texas now, or to recognize its independence, would be fuel to the flames of sectionalism—too dear a price for any man to pay for the gratification of ambition. But Jackson said he saw a way whereby the acquisition of Texas could be made to bind together the Union instead of rending it apart. "Texas," he said, and his voice was thin and high-pitched, "Texas must claim the Californias. The fishing interest of the North and East wish a harbour on the Pacific." Offer it to them and they would forget their cry against the spreading of slavery through the southern reaches of Texas.[41]

General Jackson was too tired to say more—if more needed to be said. "A day of changes," in sooth. Who knew better than the man who had made it that the era of Florida conquests was over?

And the spacious "reign" was nearly so. Three weeks remained. The sick old soldier took his meals in bed. When unable to don an ancient dressing gown and hobble to his study, he worked on a couch strewn with official papers.

Three weeks seemed a long time.

CHAPTER XL

THE SCEPTER PASSES

I

BENEATH the mask of pre-inaugural gaieties, a feeling of sadness pervaded Washington. People crowded into the capital not so much to greet the new President as to tell the old good-bye. They brought parting gifts—pipes, canes, a light wagon made of hickory with the bark on, a splendid phaeton of timbers from the frigate *Constitution*, a cheese four feet in diameter and weighing fourteen hundred pounds, a hat from a hatmaker who begged leave to honor the man who had "bestowed the Blessings of Government upon the Poor as well as the Rich."[1] The services of Frank Blair were commandeered to help acknowledge the letters, resolutions and addresses which streamed in from the world over from all grades and degrees of men. As the editor's chirography was notorious, Jackson cautioned him to write "not in cypher but so it can be read."[2]

On Washington's birthday the cheese formed the *pièce de résistance* of President Jackson's last public levee. The people made this affair their own in a manner faintly reminiscent of the President's first "reception" in 1829. Draymen and milliners' girls touched elbows with Cabinet ladies and diplomats. Each sliced himself a piece of cheese and decorously departed. Leaning on the arms of his son and of Jack Donelson, who had come on to witness the closing scenes, the President descended the stairs and bowed to his guests for a while.

Upstairs packing boxes and trunks stood in the hallways. Rooms were being shorn of the eight-year accumulation of Jacksoniana, which included five gift busts of the General and twenty-eight pictures. Outside, the banter and soft, easy laughter of negroes no longer quickened life in the once populous stable. Gone were Marse Gen'l's corps of jockeys and hostlers and horse-wise hangers-on who had slept wherever they could spread a blanket and foraged victuals from the presidential kitchen. Sporting congressmen and major generals had used to seek them out as authorities on the points and performances of horses. Carefree, anomalous company of slaves—whose like no White House establishment had seen before or would see again —whose sojourn there drives into the core of the American saga: now on the winding, red road to Tennessee, convoying the racing, saddle and carriage stock. Only the four gray coach horses and their driver, the gigantic Charles, remained.

At the Mansion a caller announced himself with a speech which apparent practice had rendered letter-perfect: "Patrick Cunningham, sir; corporal Seventh Regulars, sir, at Pensacola and New Orleans; now for many years in Snyder's livery stable." Though Jackson rarely saw visitors except on official business, the Irishman's self-introduction so amused John Rives that he repeated it to the General. The President said to admit ex-Corporal Cunningham. The veteran counted out twelve dollars and handed them to his old commander. He had borrowed the money three years before.[3] Jackson could use it. The bill for crating and getting all his plunder home was two thousand dollars.

Money was scarcer everywhere, as the pendulum began its downward arc from the speculative zenith of 1836. In that desperate try which is always made to shore up an artificial prosperity, the blame fell upon the Specie Circular. Placards appeared on the streets of New York:

"BREAD! MEAT! RENT! FUEL!
Their Prices Must Come Down!
The voice of the people shall be heard and will prevail . . ."[4]

An apprehensive Senate voted to rescind the Specie Circular. The President's impulse was to veto the rescinding bill. He began to draft a message of rejection. Friends said a veto would be overridden, bringing upon the country a fresh flood of paper currency which could only postpone the day and aggravate the degree of retribution. Though he preferred to win his legislative battles in open fighting, Jackson "pocketed" this bill, and let it die.

William R. Wharton continued to press the claims of Texas for recognition. He was at the White House nearly every day, and the rest of the time on Capitol Hill. He wiggled into the diplomatic appropriations bill a line providing for the expenses of a minister to the "Independent Republic" of Texas. The line was stricken out. Another line was inserted providing funds for such a minister "whenever the President may receive satisfactory evidence that Texas is an independent power." This seemed harmless and was allowed to stay. When the bill was passed four days of Jackson's term remained.

Wharton flew to the White House. He repeated all his old arguments and invented new ones. On the afternoon of March 3, 1837, his last day in office, Old Hickory yielded, sending to the Senate the nomination of Alcée La Branche, of Louisiana, "to be chargé d'Affairs to the Texas Republic." One of the last acts of that body was to confirm this appointment. The hands of the White House clocks were converging upon midnight when Andrew Jackson and William R. Wharton, standing in the dismantled study, raised their glasses to Sam Houston's republic,[5] which Old Hickory had said should open the way to American dominion over the shore of the Pacific Ocean.

In his bedchamber General Jackson read a chapter from Rachel's Bible. He closed the Book and the mulatto George pinched out the candle. The "reign" was over.

2

The next day was bright and balmy. Andrew Jackson left the top floor of the White House for the fifth time since his illness in November. Seated beside Martin Van Buren, he rode toward the Capitol in the *Constitution* carriage drawn by the famous Jackson grays. Cheers stopped in the throats of the thousands who lined Pennsylvania Avenue. In reverential silence they removed their hats. "For once," wrote Thomas Hart Benton, "the rising was eclipsed by the setting sun."[6]

The multitude that filled the east lawn of the Capitol fell silent when the two men appeared on the portico. After Taney had administered the oath and Mr. Van Buren had delivered his inaugural address, the ex-President started slowly to descend the broad steps. The *Constitution* carriage, Charles and the grays waited at the bottom to bear the hero away. As in obedience to a signal a mighty shout burst from the throng. "[It was a cry]," recalled Benton, "[such] as power never commanded, nor man in power received. It was affection, gratitude and admiration, . . . the acclaim of posterity breaking from the bosoms of contemporaries. . . . I felt an emotion which had never passed through me before."[7]

Midway down the stone stairs General Jackson uncovered and bowed. A gentle wind stirred his silvery locks. The tumult died.

3

Why was it that the people loved him so?

In thronged Washington, where men slept in barbers' chairs, the question was debated that night as it was destined to be debated a hundred years to come.[8]

Mr. Justice Story, who thought that he instead of Taney should have had John Marshall's place, did not know the answer. "Though we live under the form of a republic we are in fact under the absolute rule of a single man."[9]

Senator Daniel Webster's opinion, as usual, had the merit of particularity. "General Jackson is an honest and upright man. He does what he thinks is right, and does it with all his might."[10]

A German nobleman recorded the views of an unnamed senator who assumed to speak without partizanship. "He called himself the people's friend and gave proofs of his sincerity. The people believed in General Jackson as the Turks in their prophet. With this species of popularity it is vain to contend; and it betrays little knowledge of the world and the springs of human action to believe that those who possess it [are] men of ordinary capacity. General Jackson understood the people of the United States better, perhaps, than any President before him, and developed as much energy in his administration as any American statesman. . . . Whether all his measures were beneficial to the people [is beside the point]; they were . . . in unison with his political doctrines and carried through with an iron [disregard of personal] consequence, notwithstanding the enormous opposition that wealth and talent could put in the way of their execution."[11]

William Cullen Bryant, a theoretical rather than a practical democrat, spoke further of this opposition, which he knew so well. "Faults he had, undoubtedly; such faults as often belong to an ardent, generous, sincere nature—the weeds that grow in rich soil. Notwithstanding this, he was precisely the man for the period in which he well and nobly discharged the duties demanded of him by the times. If he was brought into collision with the mercantile classes, it was more their fault than his own. No man, even the most discreet and prudent, could under the same circumstances have done his duty without exasperating them. The immediate and apparent interests, though not the permanent and true interests, of trade were involved in the controversy with the national bank. Artfully party leaders exaggerated the cause of the offense until they were almost entirely alienated. Had Zeno himself been President the result would have been the same."[12]

The trouble with Mr. Story's observation lies in the jurist's ignorance of the mass. At heart the people do not wish to govern themselves, all the catchwords of proletarianism notwithstanding. They wish to be governed. Their striving raises up two demagogues to one honest liberal of capacity; and a Jackson comes along about once in a century. Jackson knew this peculiarity of the people, knew it instinctively without conscious process of thought. In that way he knew many things. His early applications of this knowledge were not designed for the benefit of the common man. Jackson was born and reared in a frontier aristocracy—unpretentious, it is true, but all that an aristocracy could attain to in the Waxhaws of that day and time. Hacking his way upward in the Tennessee wilderness, he rose to the height of spokesman for one frontier class against another—nabobs versus leathershirts. Climbing higher, Jackson became a spokesman for the whole almost-autonomous West in the contests arising from the opposed interests of the settled, commercial seaboard. The things the West, even the nabob West, advocated then seemed alluring to the landless and the propertyless of the tidewater cities. This fermentation, shaped into a political movement during the hard times of 1818-22, found the underprivileged and the lack-alls of the East one with the established currents of western thought.

Andrew Jackson brought to the presidency fewer personal ambitions than any man excepting Washington. The gradual alteration from border conservative to national liberal is noteworthy, but other eminent men have spanned a greater scale of change. John Adams and Patrick Henry storm into history not as liberals but as revolutionists shouting for bayonets and barricades. They rattle out not as conservatives merely, but as cantankerous reactionaries.

Emerging as a people's man, Jackson proffered no ordinary claims to that much-courted distinction. No mere arbiter between factions of followers, he strode forth to inspire, to lead, to govern. He not only reigned but ruled. He saw for the people what they could not see for themselves. The bank issue was as good as dead after the passing of the hard times of the Twenties. Jackson revived it, lashed up an apathetic public, lashed up apathetic lieutenants, silenced the unwilling; and drove on to victory. All this rested on the philosophy of majority rule. When a majority was at hand Jackson used it. When a majority was not at hand he endeavored to create it. When this could not be done in time, he went ahead anyhow. *He* was the majority *pro tem*. Unfailingly, at the next election, the people would return a vote of confidence, making his measures their own. This confidence was not misplaced. If not every day in the year providing a government *of* and *by* the people, Andrew Jackson did provide one *for* them.

He lived by valor. The people like that because it is exciting and because it clothes them in the mantle of Fortuna, with enormous power over the destiny of a public servant. Andrew Jackson carried his political life in the hollow of his hand, ready to risk it for the cause of the hour whether that cause were great or small, good or bad—the Bank of the United States, the Spoils System, the French indemnity, Margaret Eaton. Time and again, heedlessly and needlessly, he exposed himself to destruction by the popular will. That the people did not destroy him bewildered the opposition. "Jackson's luck" became a Whig byword. Jackson's luck was the kind that gains respect for the proverb that fortune favors the brave.

Fortune also favors the competent. The opposition to Andrew Jackson has been mentioned. It was not composed of straw men. No other President has confronted a coalition of adversaries so able or so well furnished with the ordinary resources of political welfare. Henry Clay, Daniel Webster, John C. Calhoun, Nicholas Biddle: Old Hickory met these great captains and their legions separately and in alliance. He beat them to their knees.

Nor were the peculiar gifts Jackson brought to the presidency successful alone in the management of the domestic concerns of a democracy. His foreign policy raised the prestige of the young American nation to a height not before attained among the powers of the world. Genuine respect abroad for American rights dates from Jackson.

Through it all he had walked humbly. Departing for home one summer he directed that mail be forwarded to him, readdressed as follows:

> "Hermitage
>   near the Fountain of Health
>   Davidson County
>   Tennessee"

The Fountain of Health was a healing spring of popular resort and, in the General's estimation, the most widely known place in the locality.

After eight years he laid down his burden, unsuspecting that on his times was an impress so characteristic and so deep that posterity would accord to Andrew Jackson an honor not as yet vouchsafed another American—that of marking out an Epoch in our national history and calling it by the name of one man.

4

The day after Mr. Van Buren's inauguration, and before the Jacksonian Epoch had been formally christened, the General conducted his own critique of the "reign." He had dropped in at Frank Blair's three-story house. The editor, Benton and young Senator-elect William Allen, a Jackson idolator from Ohio, were there. Old Hickory lighted his pipe and took his ease. The conversation ranged from the Carolina campaign of 1780 to the current moment.

His best piece of work as President, the General said, was getting rid of the Bank of the United States as the Government's fiscal servant. The problem was not solved, though. The state of the currency was alarming, and trying times doubtless were in store. But the people had been saved from the worse evil of placing themselves at the mercy of a monopoly for the enrichment of the few. If there must be paper money, let the issue be direct from the Treasury, based on the faith and the wealth in gold of the Government alone; no bank notes.

The tariff? A bad thing, a thing done only half right. Could the conflicting needs and wants and greeds ever be satisfactorily adjusted? Texas? That would work itself out.

Oregon? Firmness and courage needed there, lest England "cheat our frank and candid statesmen." "Our motto should be, gentlemen, the words of our young friend Allen—'Fifty-four-Forty or Fight!'" Then England would yield. She would not go to war for the Northwest.

Regrets? General Jackson admitted two regrets. He had been unable to shoot Henry Clay or to hang John C. Calhoun.[13]

5

On the following morning, March 6, 1837, the *Constitution* carriage rolled from the White House drive. Mr. Van Buren had protested that Jackson was too tired to travel. This unavailing, he had directed Surgeon General Thomas Lawson to accompany the party. When Old Hickory undertook to alter this arrangement, Mr. Van Buren smilingly observed that the Surgeon General of the Army was under the orders of the President of the United States. The journey had been arranged with every consideration for the comfort of the distinguished traveler. The party would proceed by the steam cars to the western terminus of the Baltimore & Ohio railroad at Ellicott's Mills, Maryland, thence by coach to Wheeling, and by steamer to Nashville.

Almost as many people lined the thoroughfares as on inauguration day. They enveloped the railroad depot at Second Street and Pennsylvania Avenue, Northwest. They flowed onto the switch-tracks and the right-of-way. They took over every point from which one could see the waiting train. General Jackson stood on the rear platform, his hat off, his white mane flowing. No sound came from the multitude.

The conductor rang his bell. With a hiss of steam the cars began to move. General Jackson bowed. The crowd stood still. The train swung around a curve, its course described by a trailing plume of smoke. When this dissolved in the air the crowd began to melt away feeling, one has said, "as if a bright star had gone out of the sky."[14]

BOOK SIX

TWILIGHT OF A CHIEFTAIN

> "I bequeath . . . my sword . . . with the injunction that . . . [it be] used when necessary in support and protection of our glorious Union."
>
> ANDREW JACKSON in his last will and testament.

BOOK SIX

Twilight of a Chieftain

CHAPTER XLI

Shadows on the Hermitage

I

Ah, the Hermitage: memory-haunted garden; dark earth curling from the plow; blue hills standing in a blue haze on the river's yonder bank. Forty-nine years ago a raw, unsuspected heir to chieftainship first had beheld the Clumberland. So like the river had the course of his own life run—ever seeking, never finding tranquillity; until now, perhaps, at seventy.

"I am very thankful to a kind providence for sparing me to reach my home. I hope rest in due time may restore my health so as to be enabled to amuse myself in riding over my farm and visiting my neighbors."[1] So many concerns to catch up with. "I learn from Mrs. Donelson that your dear Mary is not well, [and] that Mrs. John Coffee [junior] was so much indisposed that she was obliged to wean her little infant. I hope that all this is not real."[2] On the journey home, he was never so honored as when his old soldiers brought their children to receive the chieftain's blessing. "I congratulate you and your dear Mary on the birth of a son. kiss the babe for me. Please say to Mary that she must constantly keep the croup sirup by her on the mantle piece. Sarah could not have raised Andrew . . . [without it]."[3]

The burdens of a patriarch supplanted those of a president. Had the old man surrendered a lock of his abundant white hair to everyone who requested it he would have resembled a moulting rooster. Had he complied with every request for a line from his pen, there would have been little time for anything else. To gratify every appeal for a loan would have swallowed his property. "An unknown youth," he scrawled on the back of a letter, "wants money to aid his education. I wish I had the means to supply his wants."[4]

This question of means was a serious one. When he took the presidency, General Jackson had carried five thousand dollars to Washington. He returned with ninety in his wallet. This he divided with Jack Donelson on overhearing his ex-secretary say he needed money to buy corn. Jackson's corn also was out, and oats and fodder, too. The stock was lean; the store of bacon low; the new tin roof of the mansion leaking; his son in debt for negroes bought to work Hunter's Hill. Yet Old Hickory fended without borrowing, though he did add his name to Andrew, junior's, notes for negroes. Virtually his only asset aside from the Davidson County farms was eight hundred and forty acres in West Tennessee. If need be he would sell that land to keep in the clear until the home places were paying again. To the restoration of the Hermitage the planter directed his immediate efforts. A field was carefully turned over and sowed in wheat with seed from Egypt.[5]

2

To stay free of debt in the spring of 1837 was a measure of elementary prudence, though a measure few could adopt because of involvements in the speculative craze, now on the brink of the abyss. On his way to Tennessee General Jackson had seen and heard alarming things: paper money falling in value everywhere; a blue-sky bank in Mississippi, chartered for fifteen million dollars, gone to the wall; planters "deeply indebted and paying 30 per cent for money"; prime negroes down from eighteen hundred dollars to five hundred. "The speculators and borrowers in Mississippi and Alabama are broke," Jackson observed. "Their Bank paper at Neworleans and Nashvill, as I am informed, are at ten to 15 per cent below par and going down."[6]

The stories were true. Nashville was in a fever. During the two years past that keen real estate trader, Harry R. W. Hill, had bloomed forth as a capitalist of imposing stature with hundreds of trusting "investors" in his train. He was desperate. His fall would spread ruin like a holocaust. The banks of Nashville clubbed together to advance Hill three hundred and nineteen thousand dollars in one day when, as General Jackson dryly observed, an ordinarily solvent citizen could not discount a note for twenty-five hundred.[7]

Frenzied speculators, borrowers, bankers—all who found themselves in the path of the avalanche of tumbling paper—invoked the wrath of Heaven and of Martin Van Buren to strike down the iniquitous Specie Circular, or Treasury Order, as General Jackson always called it. Let the Government receive paper for public lands and confidence would return, and the American people regain their threatened Eden.

Old Hickory forgot his Egyptian wheat long enough to give the President a different view. "My dear sir, the Treasury order is popular with the people everywhere I have passed. But all the speculators, and those largely indebted, *want more paper*. the more it depreciates the easier they can pay their debts. . . . Check the paper mania *and the republic is safe and your administration must end in triumph*."[8] The storm grew fiercer. Nicholas Biddle joined the fray. Jackson expressed no surprise. "The gamblers and speculators, in and out of Congress, unite [against the Treasury Order]. . . . I thought it absolutely necessary at the time. . . . Its continuance [is] imperious now for the safety of the revenue. . . . I have done my duty to my country and my god, [and] have given [you] my opinion freely. . . . *I say, lay on, temporise not, it is always injurious.*"[9]

The time was when Andrew Jackson thought the state banks safe custodians of the public revenue. He thought otherwise now. Caught up in the coils of speculation, going to the rescue of such men as Harry Hill, some of the depositories were falsifying their books to hide their peril. The Nashville banking house of Yeatman, Woods & Company suspended. Dark tales flew concerning the Government's local depositories, the Union and the Planters' banks. Old Hickory warned Van Buren to examine all deposit banks and get the Treasury funds in places of safety. The local anti-Jackson newspaper reprinted from the *National Intelligencer* of Washington a piece to the effect that General Jackson would be called on to redeem three hundred thousand dollars in notes bearing his endorsement held by the Yeatman bank, and that Jackson's draft for six thousand dollars had been protested in New York.[10]

These false stories made a small sensation in the East. The Old Chief hoisted on his own petard! New York merchants drafted a memorial to Nicholas Biddle to save them from the consequences of Jacksonian finance.

After a long silence Jackson heard from Martin Van Buren. The letter was dated April 24. "You cannot form an adequate idea of the dreadful state of the money market in New York. . . . My situation has been one of peculiar delicacy and difficulty. . . ."[11] Not a word as to the fate of the Specie Circular.

The same mail brought a letter, dated April 23, in the hieroglyphics of Frank Blair, which Old Hickory never learned to read easily. "Biddle was here yesterday and paid a complimentary visit to the President."[12]

By the Eternal!

3

Mr. Biddle's visit availed nothing. Martin Van Buren preserved the Specie Circular. The banks of New York City suspended payments in coin. Others followed the country over. The United States Government could not get gold or silver for its funds. A panic was on which most articulate persons laid at the door of Andrew Jackson's financial policies, particularly the Specie Circular, the distribution of the Treasury surplus and the transfer of deposits from the Bank of the United States.

This incorrect view was destined for a long survival and is still widely held. Jackson's contribution to the boom had been a minor one. In view of efforts he made to arrest this inflation, his responsibility for the ensuing crash can be no greater than his participation in the original cause. Far from causing the crash, Jackson's measures rendered that inevitable catastrophe less severe than it would otherwise have been. The boom here was an extension of one originating in Europe. When the inflation of land values on these shores got under way, foreign funds poured across the ocean to participate in the quick and rich rewards. Early in 1836 things began to tighten abroad, and European investors to withdraw their capital. The Specie Circular counteracted this movement, tending to keep coin at home and definitely checking the lavish use of paper here. But for that Circular, the disastrous reckoning might have been deferred at the expense of greater losses when it came; it could not have been avoided. The distribution of the surplus, depriving the deposit banks of additional loanable capital, certainly did not promote and it may have acted as another check on inflation.[13] Otherwise this act was bad, as Jackson realized at the time. He signed it reluctantly. Had he vetoed it the veto would have been overridden. The later cry against it sprang from wisdom after the fact.

As to the third point—the transfer of deposits from the Bank of the United States: in the bank fight, Jackson's primary aim had been to free the country of the shackles of a monopoly whose power he deemed too great, and whose public morals he believed too loose for the country's good. Stripping Nicholas Biddle naked, he had proved those indictments. As an experiment which he had believed would be successful, deposits were shifted to the state banks. Long before he left office, Old Hickory had begun to doubt the sagacity of this, and was examining plans by which the Treasury should care for its own funds and issue its own money based on the metal in its vaults.[14]

Swollen with public revenues, the "pet" banks were a factor in promoting the boom. How much more wisely Mr. Biddle might have handled those revenues is a matter of conjecture. One can draw inferences, however, from the manner in which he handled the funds of private depositors, for Mr. Biddle was still in the banking business. As the Federal charter was about to expire, Mr. Biddle had sent his agents to mingle with the members of the State Legislature at Harrisburg. The agents spent four hundred thousand dollars and obtained, by means corrupt on their face,[15] a charter to continue operations under the deceptive title of the United States Bank of Pennsylvania. Mr. Biddle's revamped bank plunged gaily into the waters of speculation and in May, 1837, ceased specie payments with the rest. But not from weakness, the glib wizard of finance was quick to explain. His bank had the means to go on; only a duty to his depositors, who might be forced to pay their debts in coin while others paid in paper, had induced him to suspend. "A great disaster has befallen the country. I shall strive to repair it."[16]

A drought was killing the Egyptian wheat, but Old Hickory had larger matters on his hands. "Mind not the clamour of . . . Biddle and Co," he wrote Martin Van Buren. "[Mind not] the demagogues, the Bankmen and gamblers. . . . Recollect the former panic and pressure; the present will soon blow over. . . . Be ye therefore steady, firm and unwavouring in your course and all is safe."[17]

Van Buren was steady. Calling Congress into special session in September he yielded nothing to the panic-stricken. He asked for a law rendering the Government independent of all banks, the revenues to be retained in the Treasury which would issue its own money—gold and silver for units under fifty dollars, notes for units over that. The plan was essentially Jackson's, forwarded from the Hermitage.[18]

On a raw October day in 1837 Amos Kendall, visiting at the Hermitage, found his host a quarter of a mile from the house without a coat, awaiting the mail coach with news of the Independent Treasury Bill. Jackson followed the progress of that measure— "Divorce Bill" in the vernacular—as keenly as he had followed any legislation in his days of power. His days of power— They were not done. With hearing failing, right eye nearly useless, and memory uncertain,[19] the white-haired warrior was still a chieftain—guiding, inspiring, strengthening faint hearts from his inexhaustible store of courage. Illness did not deter him, nor adverse election returns. Jackson's personal and political protégé Robert Armstrong was defeated for Governor of Tennessee. In the Hermitage countryside friends and family connections deserted the hickory standard. The chieftain heeded them not. Hold fast! he told Van Buren twenty times. Fight on!

Winter came and waned. Spring of 1838 brought word of the Divorce Bill's victory in the Senate, summer word of its defeat in the House.

Old Hickory cheered his successor. Never mind. "The eyes of the people are fast opening." Fight on![20]

4

Better success attended General Jackson in another battle. Conforming to his custom he paid his bills on January 1, beginning the year 1838 free of debts though it cost him his land in West Tennessee.[21] "I have no opinion of holding property when I need the money, and I will not borrow. . . . Since last spring we have paid upwards of seven thousand dollars." Most of this was to save Andrew, junior, from legal complications as a result of endorsing the notes of others, often as his father had told him to be no man's surety. "Andrew was inexperienced, and he happened to fall into the hands of men who pretended to be his friends."[22] The Hermitage was showing the results of the master's hand. Notwithstanding the drought, seventy-four bales of cotton went to New Orleans that spring. Jackson said the receipts would put him "in funds," and the eventual passage of the Divorce Bill restore prosperity to all.

But until that time should come the General meant to keep expenses within current means. He pressed those who owed him, placing claims in the hands of attorneys. When the cash was not available, he gave up a trip to one of Tennessee's many healing springs, relying on Matchless Sanative, a cough medicine which he said was making "a new man" of him. Frank Blair wrote that he hoped not, because "the old man" was good enough. Jackson recommended Matchless Sanative to ailing friends, with the advice to "carefully attend to . . . [the] directions [which] accompany each bottle."[23]

In July he joined the church, standing among the congregation in the little Presbyterian edifice he had helped to build for Rachel, and making a formal profession of faith. He would have done this much sooner, he said, but for the fear that this act might have been given a political interpretation. The hardest thing for Old Hickory to say was that he had forgiven his enemies; and he made it clear that only *his* enemies were absolved. Those who had slandered *her* remained for God to deal with.[24]

Banks were resuming specie payments. The outlook for the Hermitage was so promising that General Jackson permitted his son to buy Halcyon Plantation, a property of more than eleven hundred acres on the Mississippi River in Coahoma County, Mississippi. The price was twenty-three thousand seven hundred dollars, payable in four installments, a year apart, beginning March 1, 1839.[25] This transaction completed without the use of a dollar of ready money, young Jackson stopped off at Nashville on his way home and bought a piano the same way.

In September Jackson suffered a great loss in the death of Ralph E. W. Earl. Seventeen years before a wandering portrait painter had turned up at the Hermitage—to find the only home he had ever known. Lovable, devoted, gently mocking at life—"Blair's the King's printer and I'm the King's painter"—[26] Earl had become almost as indispensable to the General's comfort as the mulatto George. "He was my constant companion when I travelled," the old man said. "Had I a wish to travel I have now no one to go with me."[27]

Autumn brought more adverse election news, and Samuel Swartwout, whom Jackson had made Collector of the Port of New York in the face of objections from Van Buren and from nearly everyone else, sailed for Europe. An examination of his accounts disclosed that Colonel Swartwout was entitled to the distinction of being the first American to steal a million dollars. This resounding blow to the prestige of the "reign" came at a moment when hard-pushed Mr. Van Buren was planning to sun himself in the Hero's renown. He had gone so far as to announce to friends a political fence-fixing junket in the South, to culminate in a reunion at the Hermitage. James K. Polk, who was running for Governor, suggested the omission of the reunion. The old man's feelings were hurt. "A visit to me surely could not be used to disadvantage the cause."[28]

Nevertheless, the tour was called off.

5

The year 1839 came in with cold weather. General Jackson put on a pair of woollen socks Mrs. Frank Blair had made, remarking that they would last him to the grave. This was intended as a compliment to Mrs. Blair's knitting, for the General was in a cheerful state of mind. He believed the end of hard times in sight. Though it took all he had, he paid his bills; and then turned his attention to an effort to solve the riddle of the death of Frank, the fiddler.

Frank was a colored man, lately the property of Stockley Donelson. The mulatto George and three other Hermitage negroes were in jail at Nashville charged with murder. General Jackson went to town and told his four "boys" to speak the truth. He heard the depositions of other negroes who had witnessed the killing, penciling notes on their testimony with his own hand. The trouble had taken place during a holiday spree and dance at which someone had asked Frank to stop his music until a fire could be built. This had started a fight in which about forty negroes joined. Frank was killed by a blow on the head with a rock.

Stockley Donelson had obtained the warrants for Jackson's four negroes. Stockley had gone over to the Whigs. He took his politics as seriously as did General Jackson, and for some time relations between them had been strained. Declaring his negroes innocent,

Jackson denounced their arrest as spite work and engaged a lawyer to defend them. They were acquitted at a trial which cost the General a thousand dollars. He borrowed the money.[29]

The expectation of relief from the depression proved illusory. It was a hard year. Business continued at a standstill and money scarce. Negroes were almost the only article of commerce that could command cash. With notes of hand circulating with a freedom that recalled Jackson's trading post days at the beginning of the century, one had to be careful whose note he accepted or endorsed. In this situation Old Hickory not only kept the Hermitage on a paying basis, but he raised funds sufficient to meet the first installment of five thousand one hundred and seventy-six dollars on Andrew, junior's, Halcyon Plantation.

Meanwhile, louder were growing the cries against the financial policies of the Jackson régime, bolder the bids of the reviving Biddle group for the restoration of their favorite to power, when suddenly the wheel of fortune turned. The hard year had been too much for Mr. Biddle. Financial wizardries were no longer equal to the task of sustaining the inverted pyramid of his speculations. His drafts were protested in Paris and the United States Bank of Pennsylvania closed its doors. So destructive to confidence was this failure that half of the specie-paying banks in the country again suspended. Nicholas Biddle buried himself on his country estate, his power seemingly gone forever. The greatest obstacle to the Independent Treasury Bill appeared to be removed.

Richard Rush whose last act as Secretary of the Treasury under John Quincy Adams had been to recommend the recharter of the Bank of the United States, wrote to Jackson: "[This] puts the seal to the foresight and wisdom of your course."[30]

At the next session of Congress, that of 1839-40, the Independent Treasury Bill became a law, taking the fiscal affairs of the nation out of the hands of the banks and completing the work commenced by Jackson in 1829. The mail coach waited beside the Hermitage gate while Old Hickory scribbled a note of congratulation to Mr. Van Buren.[31]

"Jackson's luck," said the Whigs of Mr. Biddle's misfortune. The old man's popularity revived so much that Martin Van Buren thought the sight of Old Hickory at a formal observance of the twenty-fifth anniversary of the Battle of New Orleans would be a good thing for the cause of Democracy. So an invitation reached the Hermitage. Amos Kendall felt it "cruel" to ask the old man to make the long mid-winter journey,[32] and the veteran himself perceived obstacles. "Again I am out of funds, and I cannot bear to borrow or travel as a pauper."[33]

As he wrote this, the General had before him a letter from Major Lewis asking for the satisfaction of a two-years-overdue note for five hundred and fifty dollars signed by Andrew Jackson, junior. The money had been used to purchase a carriage concerning which young Jackson had told his father a story contradicted by the evidence of the note. That must have pained the old man more than the debt. "I have exerted all my means," he informed the Major, "to clear . . . [my son] from his foolish as well as useless debts. . . . They are all exhausted, I can do no more." But on Andrew's return from Mississippi the father promised to "stimulate him to use every exertion to meet it."[34]

Never before had Andrew Jackson adopted such a tone toward a creditor of his adopted child.

6

General Jackson seems to have given up the idea of going to New Orleans in favor of a quiet Christmas season at his own fireside when the Nashville community was rocked by the financial collapse of Albert Ward, a son of the late Colonel Edward Ward, Jackson's long-time friend and one of the richest men in Middle Tennessee. Creditors pounced on Ward's properties, began to tear them to pieces and to pursue with judgments and with writs of attachment those who had gone security for the unfortunate man.

Chief on the list of these sureties was Andrew Jackson, junior.

The amount of his commitments no one seemed to be able to tell, both Ward and young Jackson being absent. But clearly this was no matter of the price of a carriage. Ward's liabilities would run high into the thousands of dollars. Moreover, the involvement brought to light other debts Andrew, junior, had contracted unknown to his father, as frightened creditors began to present their claims.[35]

At New Orleans Twenty-five Years After

So ill he could scarcely stand, General Jackson endured ten nights and days of festivity marking the twenty-fifth anniversary of the Battle of New Orleans, in 1840. The object of the journey was to raise money to pay his son's debts. This portrait, by Jacques J. Amans, was painted during the visit. The original hangs in the Brown University Library, Providence, Rhode Island.

JACKSON IN RETIREMENT
From a print of a drawing from life by William H. Brown, owned by Emil Edward Hurja of Washington.

Any resolution the humiliated father may have contemplated at the time of the discovery of the Lewis note was discarded.

First he made an arrangement with the Ward creditors to gain time.[36]

Next, he would go to New Orleans. If the trip should help the prospects of the Democrats well and good; the real object was to relieve his son.[37]

The time was short. On December 23 the General drove to Nashville and drew in advance on his cotton. After paying two notes for young Andrew and a few other bills only enough remained for traveling expenses to New Orleans. So he borrowed three thousand dollars which was placed to the credit of his son.

On the day before Christmas Andrew, junior, had not returned from Mississippi. Jackson could delay his departure no longer. Scratching directions to the boy to pay the Lewis note and other debts to the extent of three thousand dollars, Old Hickory was off for Louisiana to make his first public appearance in nearly three years.[38]

En route he wrote his son to sell Hunter's Hill, and to levy an execution on the negroes of a debtor named Cheatam. The negroes could be used to pay for the piano and other things. New Year's day of 1840 was spent aboard an Ohio River packet menaced by drifting ice. At Memphis Jackson obtained from Albert Ward pledges which he hoped would balance Andrew, junior's, obligations to the Ward creditors. Stopping briefly at Halcyon Plantation, Old Hickory was struck by its money-making possibilities. He obtained a modification of the terms under which his son had bought the place. In the most cheerful letter since his departure, he expressed the hope that two years hence would see all debts paid and Andrew, junior, assured of "ease and plenty."[39]

On January 4, the steamer *Vicksburg*, chartered by the State of Mississippi and loaded with notables, took the General aboard. What followed was a nightmare. Stricken with a hemorrhage which made every breath torture, the veteran drummed out the last reserves of his will-power "determined to go through [with the journey] or fall in the struggle." "I have long found that complaining never eased pain," he said.[40] The endless receptions, the speeches, the pageantry, the fireworks, the shouting, were somehow endured for ten days and nights. Leaning on his cane the chieftain slowly mounted the mouldering ridge that had been the rampart beside the Rodriquez Canal. Dim old eyes looked on a level field of cane stubble, . . . which memory may have peopled with pulsing platoons in red tunics latticed by white cross-belts, . . . hedges of bayonets receding into infinity. . . .

Alone in the cabin of a homeward bound steamer, the pain passed and a feeling of peace filled the heart of the soldier. He hoped he had done something to save Mr. Van Buren. In any event, he believed he had saved Andrew. "Recollect my son that I have taken this trip to endeavour to relieve you from present embarrassments, and if I live to realize it I will die contented in the hope that you will never again encumber yourself with debt that may result in the poverty of yourself and the little family I so much Love."[41]

7

The Whigs nominated William Henry Harrison for President and John Tyler, of Virginia, for the second place. Henry Clay swallowed a stiff drink of whisky. "I am," he said, "the most unfortunate man in the history of parties: always run by my friends when sure to be defeated, and now betrayed when I, or any one, would be sure of election."[42]

General Jackson, Mr. Van Buren and most other Democrats sympathized with Mr. Clay. They would have preferred him as an opponent. General Harrison exhibited too many possibilities reminiscent of the Jackson appeals of 1824 and 1828: a fine military record; a respectable if virtually forgotten civil record as a territorial governor and frontier congressman; and no record whatever on any current issue. Such a standard-bearer presented few points for attack.

Perceiving the necessity of a strong vice-presidential candidate, Old Hickory advised Van Buren to drop "Tecumseh" Johnson in favor of James K. Polk. The suggestion was wise. Stemming the Whig tide, Polk had reclaimed the governorship of Tennessee. Jackson declared that he would insure the victory of the national ticket in the West and the South.[43]

When Martin Van Buren took the oath in 1837, he had laid aside the magician's wand for the toga of a statesman. Courageously and high-mindedly he had fought for the right things, as he saw them, rather than for the politically expedient. Now for a moment he resumed his old trick to trying to please both sides. The Democratic Convention which renominated Mr. Van Buren for President left the choice of a vice-presidential candidate to the states. The idea was that Johnson should run in the North and the East where he was strong, and that Polk should run in the South and West. The scheme collapsed when Polk declined to co-operate, and Van Buren entered the campaign saddled with a running mate poorly equipped to woo votes in the slaveholding states.

Amos Kendall retired from the Cabinet to direct the Van Buren press, but surely he could not have been responsible for the squib by which the Baltimore *American* sought to belittle the pretensions of General Harrison:

"Give him a barrel of hard cider and settle a pension of two thousand a year on him and, my word for it, he will sit the remainder of his days in a log cabin."[44]

A genius among the Whigs agreed with the Democratic editor. Yes, the Hero of Tippecanoe could live comfortably on what Martin Van Buren spent on his wardrobe. A log cabin, a barrel of hard cider for his friends, plain folk like himself, and William Henry Harrison would be content.

Log cabins and barrels of cider began to blossom forth at Harrison rallies. In New York City a wealthy dabbler in politics enlivened a meeting with a song:

"What has caused this great commotion, motion,
    Our country through?
    It is the ball a-rolling on,
For Tippecanoe and Tyler too, Tippecanoe and Tyler too.
And with them we'll beat little Van, Van, Van;
    Van is a used-up man."

The song, the log cabins, the barrels of cider spread through the country. The West gave birth to another roundelay:

"Ole Tip he wears a homespun suit,
He has no ruffled shirt—*wirt—wirt*;
[*Wirt wirt* simulated by spitting through the teeth.]
But Mat he has the golden plate,
And he's a little squirt—*wirt—wirt*"

Nicholas Biddle's bank was reopened (with another man as president), while the wizard himself came from retirement to raise funds to provide more log cabins and more cider. He also supplied advice for the candidate's managers. "Let him say not a single word about his principles or his creed—let him say nothing, promise nothing. Let the use of pen and ink be wholly forbidden."[45]

This course was followed. By mid-summer a greatly enlarged and improved edition of the Jackson campaign of 'Twenty-four was before the public: log cabins on wheels, transparencies showing Old Tip in a 'coonskin cap trapping the Red Fox; rivers of cider to loosen the vocal cords. "Tippecanoe and Tyler too!" . . . "Van, Van, is a used-up man!"

The initiative was with the Whigs. The best rebuttal the Democrats could offer in kind was a thin

> "Rumpsey, Dumpsey,
> Colonel Johnson killed Tecumsey. . . ."

8

In April General Jackson received two hundred and forty dollars in cash for three town lots in Florence, the last of his possessions in Alabama. The money came barely in time to save Andrew, junior, "from the sheriffs grasp."[46] Old Hickory regarded the revival of activity by his son's creditors as a reflex of the political campaign. "Every Whigg that he is indebted to has either sued or warranted him."

The hounded young man took to bed with "chills, shakes and fever," ailments common to the Mississippi country whence he had lately returned, though his father attributed the attack to visits by the bailiff. Jackson, senior, also was ill, but did not take to bed. He tried to get from his son an understandable statement of the sum of his debts and suretyships. From what Andrew said, the General judged these to be in the neighborhood of six thousand dollars.[47] On his journey to New Orleans General Jackson had established a line of credit, the particulars of which accessible records do not fully disclose.[48] In July the old man went to Nashville to settle once and for all Andrew, junior's, accounts.

He found them to total not six but twelve thousand dollars. He paid eleven thousand in cash, and promised the balance in a week. "My mind being relieved . . . of the great pressure of Andrews debts . . . I believe I will maintain better health." Andrew's health improved at once.[49]

The campaign pressed on, with Nashville an especial object of Whig attention—carrying the war into Africa. An Ohio delegation made a pilgrimage to present a canoe and a live 'coon to the Tippecanoe Club of Nashville. General Jackson's facile friend J. G. Harris, editor of the *Union*, wrote some amusing rhymes in the meter of *'Possum up de Gum Tree*:

> "Mum is the word, boys,
> Brag is the game,
> Cooney is the emblem
> Of Old Tip's fame."

Brag was a favorite card game of Henry Clay, and a forerunner of poker.

The Whigs incorporated the verses in their repertoire and the 'coon gained new authority as a Harrison emblem.

In August a rally at Nashville attained national proportions, with delegations and marching clubs from half the states of the Union. In a pageant with log cabins and 'coons galore, one banner took formal and respectful notice of General Jackson. It showed a fox following a lion. Henry Clay was the orator of the day. His effort also contained respectful allusions to "the illustrious captain in this neighborhood. . . . He was a great chieftain."[50]

Old Hickory did not relish the compliment. "The great gathering at Nashville to worship the coon and sour cider and desecrate the sabath had injured the Federal [Harrison] cause. . . . It is saying to . . . the people . . . that they can be led by hard cider, coons, Log cabins and demagogues. I have a higher opinion of the intelligence of the american people than this. I think Tennessee will give Mr. Van Buren a good majority." On the other hand Democratic rallies were models of deportment. After attending three, Jackson said he had "never seen more order or decorum in a church." Worldly campaigners among the General's friends were not so sure that this was a good sign. Unceremoniously turned out of the diplomatic corps, John Henry Eaton had hit the hard cider trail. In Florida Richard K. Call had done the same. "What apostacy! . . . *O tempo, O Mores,*" exclaimed Andrew Jackson.[51] Less affected by ethical considerations, a prominent Democratic editor sighed, "We have taught them how to conquer us!"[52]

No one had taught them how to conquer Andrew Jackson. Indignantly Old Hickory announced that he would take the stump for Van Buren—something he had never done for himself. When he was ready to start, it developed that not all of Andrew's obligations had been settled. Nevertheless, the old man set out, writing back: "Sell all [the beef] you can spare. . . . Sell the fillies if you can get five hundred dollars for the two *in cash*. If you can get as much for my riding mare as two hundred dollars let her go and pay Mr. Crutcher and Capt Dodson what you owe."[53] In the slightly conflicting capacities of public hero and electioneer, he traveled westward with James K. Polk as far as Jackson, Tennessee, blessing babies, giving autographs, shaking hands, and haranguing enormous crowds at highly respectable barbecues—not a drop of hard stuff, apparently, in sight. He thumped the banks and the speculators and the paper money people. He made light of Harrison's military achievements, a subject on which Major General Jackson had expressed a different view in 1814.[54] Back at the Hermitage, he was sure that Tennessee and the country were safe.

The first returns reversed the opinion about Tennessee where, it was said, there was not a sober Whig in the State on election day. The victors serenaded Editor Harris and presented him with a jug of corn whisky—a delicate gesture, for no Democrat would soil his lips with cider. Next, the country seemed in doubt. News that Pennsylvania and New York had gone for Harrison took the heart out of most western Democrats, though not old Hickory. "I do not believe a word of it," he wrote the President. "Nor will I believe that you are not elected until I see *all* the official returns."[55] It was unnecessary to wait so long. Though the popular vote was close, Van Buren received the electoral votes of only seven states.

"Beaten by such a man as Harrison!" penned one western editor, slowly recovering the use of his senses. "Sung down, lied down, drunk down."[56] Hope seemed dead.

But not in the breast of the chieftain. *"Beaten but I trust not con-*

quered, . . . I do not yet despair of the Republick."[57] Reform the shattered battalions. Rally "round Mr. Van Buren and elect him by a triumphant Majority should he live to November 1844."[58]

"Should he live. . . ."

"Should I live" would have been a presumption on the good nature of Providence.

9

New Year's day, 1841.

In three months Andrew Jackson would be seventy-four. The exertions of the year closed had taken their toll. He was weaker and feebler. Only the inextinguishable spark of his spirit preserved him from all the marks of an old, old man; though the General himself gave the credit to the restorative powers of Matchless Sanative.

On this New Year's day the master of the Hermitage could scarcely reckon his debts, leave alone pay them, for every week seemed to add to the sum. The twelve thousand dollars laid out in August to clear his son of the Ward endorsements was not enough. In December the total had risen to fifteen thousand, ten thousand of which represented, in the General's view, "swindles" perpetrated on Andrew, junior.[59] The extra three thousand had no more than been found when word came that the negroes on Halcyon Plantation were shivering and starving—provisions out and no shoes; then notice of an action at law by the overseer for back wages.[60]

The Hermitage began to wear a look of neglect—the house out of repair and needing paint, the stable stripped of the master's saddle mare, the very beef from the smoke-house sold, the products of its soil indentured for years to come. Of all the children General Jackson and his wife had reared or cared for, the one he had adopted and given his name seemed the least equipped to make his own way through life. Not only had Andrew, junior, involved himself in this bottomless bog of debt, he had told his father untruths.[61] Andrew's falsehoods were not of the vicious kind; nor were they clever, for he was sure to be found out. They were the momentary refuge of the weak and immature. General Jackson was not legally liable for the debts of his son. He assumed them from a supersensitiveness to personal honor, and because of an affection for the boy which nothing had been able to destroy. Never, apparently, did it occur to Jackson to investigate the possibility of invoking the new bankruptcy law in behalf of his son. The General had opposed this statute as providing a means for dishonest debtors to bilk their creditors, and now he advocated its repeal.[62]

With characteristic faith in those he loved, old Jackson clung to the conviction that once Andrew was relieved, never would he be so gullible as to encumber himself again. He looked beyond Andrew to Andrew's children. These growing youngsters were ever by their grandfather's side. They invaded his disordered study, covering his papers with their scrawls. For their security he set himself to provide.

In all these private trials, the correspondent to whom Jackson most freely unburdened himself was his son's schoolmate, the once reckless Andrew Jackson Hutchings to whom Andy, junior, had been held up as a model. How differently young Hutchings had turned out, bravely and ably meeting life's adversities—hard times, the death of a baby boy, the death of his wife, lovely Mary Coffee. Now Hutchings himself battled against tuberculosis. A trip to Cuba having brought no relief, the young man had come home, as he knew, to die. Jackson set aside money to visit him in Alabama. Andrew, junior's, needs swept away the little nest-egg. Tied to the Hermitage, the old man could only write: "I urge your attention to the Matchless Sanative."[63]

10

It was a relief to turn from such things to the theatre of our public affairs, however unpromising from a Democratic standpoint it might appear to be. The General wrote to inquire, "Can Clay succeed in his attempt this session to have the independent treasury law repealed and a National Bank charter passed."[64] The answer came that the Whigs would try it. Their chances of success would depend on contingencies as yet difficult to foretell. But the General was told that he could take consolation from one thing: Nicholas Biddle's day was done. Even Clay was through with him.[65]

A month later General Jackson received confirmation of the opinion about Biddle. In a last gamble for power, the United States Bank of Pennsylvania had resumed specie payments. A run followed. The bank closed, its entire capital of thirty-five million dollars lost, thousands of stockholders and depositors ruined. Haggard and friendless, the man who had once disputed with Andrew Jackson for the control of the United States reached the end of his road at a prisoner's dock charged with fraud. A legal technicality saved Nicholas Biddle from the penitentiary.

With the ardor of an evangelist, the chieftain spent his failing strength to reanimate the drooping spirits of his party. To an admirer who wished a sentiment to preserve as a memento: "The Republic . . . may suffer under the present imbecile chief, but the sober second thought of the people will restore it at our next Presidential election."[66] To Amos Kendall: "The Mock Hero, the president elect, I see has reached Washington."[67]

General Harrison was, indeed, at Gadsby's Hotel, smothered by the most shameless swarm of fortune hunters the capital had seen since the coming of another Hero twelve years before. To afford the distressed man a sanctuary, Martin Van Buren offered to vacate the Executive Mansion in advance. Declining to avail himself of this distinguished courtesy, General Harrison was worn to distraction before inauguration day. A week thereafter a caller found the lower floor of the White House in the possession of patronage seekers. They filled every room and defied eviction. The President opened a door, expecting to meet his Cabinet. The spoilsmen crushed about him. Soon the Executive's pockets were filled with their petitions, then his hat, then his arms; and thus he staggered upstairs to revive himself with "stimulants."[68]

On his twentieth day as President, General Harrison took to bed. On the thirty-first day he died.

"A kind and overruling providence," said Andrew Jackson, "has interfered to prolong our glorious Union, . . . for surely Tyler . . . [will] stay the corruptions of this clique who has got into power by deluding the people by the grossest of slanders . . . and hard cider."[69]

CHAPTER XLII

A Taper Burning Low

I

On one of his trips down Chesapeake Bay to the Rip Raps, President Jackson was accompanied by George Washington Parke Custis, a rotund, fussy little gentleman with snuff on his lace who delighted in the appellation of "the child of Mount Vernon." He was a grandson of Martha Custis, and the adopted son of George Washington. The appearance of a storm arising, Mr. Custis had expressed a premonition of disaster. General Jackson smiled. "My good friend, you never traveled with me."

The President's companion was vexed. Next to his connection with the Father of His Country, Mr. Custis prided himself on an acquaintance with the classics. He confided to Blair that General Jackson had indifferently rendered the words of the Roman emperor to a pilot who hesitated to put out in a storm: "Why do you fear, you carry Caesar?"

The editor often recalled the incident with amusement.[1] Those who traveled with Old Hickory counted for security not on their chief's awareness of what another captain had said or done: they counted on that secret spring of certainty from which flowed Andrew Jackson's confidence in himself.

This still remained true.

Mr. Clay carried his bill for the re-creation of a national bank. Tyler vetoed it, as Jackson had predicted. For a second time in the same session Mr. Clay forced the bill through. For the second time the session it passed, Tyler vetoed it again, and was sustained.

Democratic spirits rose. The letter of a grateful citizen of Baltimore expressed a prevailing sentiment.

"To providence and to you we give thanks—and some to Tyler. It was you who gathered the Democrats together on this subject after they had been separated and scattered and deceived. . . . Every where, at every turn and every corner the expression may be heard —'It will do old Hickory's heart good when he hears of the Veto.' ... 'Egad, he has found one of old Jackson's pens.' "[2]

2

Other prospects also were fair. On the way down the Mississippi the winter before, one swift view of Halcyon Plantation had revealed to General Jackson its advantages as a fueling station for steamers. Accordingly, a woodyard was established at the water's edge under management of Andrew, junior. It was immediately profitable. The land needed clearing to extend the cotton acreage, and good Democratic packet-masters made a special point of stopping at the Jackson woodyard. Transactions were cash, a dollar fifty a cord, and one hand could turn out two cords in a day.

"My son has become the man of business," Old Hickory proudly related. "Our plantation on the Mississippi, hitherto unproductive, this year [1841] will yield us some profit, and in two years will produce in cotton and wood at least a neat income of eight thousand dollars." With this statement of the family's prospects, Jackson authorized Major Lewis to contract a loan of six thousand dollars for six years. He wished to consolidate the obligations incurred in freeing his son "of some of the greatest scamps, sharpers and swindlers that honest and unsuspecting youth was ever surrounded with."[3]

Lewis submitted two proposals. From New Orleans came a volunteer proposal from Major Jean B. Plauché who, though he himself would have to borrow the money, asked the honor of assisting his old commander. Jackson agreed to accept the gallant old Creole's proposal, and proffered security—presumably a mortgage on the Hermitage, which was the security he had tendered to others. Plauché would not take it. The matter was settled by Jackson remitting a note signed by himself and his son, which Plauché accepted under protest rather than lose "the only opportunity which has ever presented itself of being agreeable to you." Then he sent a letter of credit for seven thousand dollars instead of the six.[4] Jackson declined to use the extra thousand.

Whig newspapers reported the General's money troubles in a

way that would have impaired another man's credit. James C. Pickett, the United States chargé d'affaires to Peru, wrote Blair that a secret fund must be raised to discharge Jackson's debts. Picket asked to be put down for a share. Frank Blair knew such a proposal would meet a fate similar to that of the purse raised long ago to pay the thousand-dollar fine Judge Hall had imposed on General Jackson after the Battle of New Orleans, and of the attempt to rebuild the Hermitage by public subscription. Yet something should be done. Blair himself was closely run, the Whigs having given the public printing to another man. However, the Government owed him twenty thousand dollars due to be paid shortly. In the name of himself and his partner, John C. Rives, Blair wrote that half of this sum was at Jackson's disposal.[5]

In Congress Jackson's friends introduced a bill to refund, with interest, the New Orleans fine.

The veteran said he would accept a refund of the fine because of the bearing such an act of Congress might have on the future safety of the country. The time might come again when it would be the duty of an army commander, ringed about with foes, to take in his hands extraordinary powers. No threat of penalties a civil authority might impose should be allowed to deter him.[6]

Acceptance of Blair's generous offer rested on another plane. The cotton crop of 1841 at the Hermitage was a failure and seven blooded horses had died, cutting off revenues by which Jackson had expected to meet the installments due on Halcyon Plantation. The loan would meet this unpaid balance and future crops would meet the loan. Once more that vision of tranquillity which Andrew Jackson had pursued through a long life seemed an attainable reality. "This loan will place me at ease, and secure to him [my son] and his dear little ones and charming wife an ample fortune— therefore you see the obligation you lay me under."[7] For the ten thousand dollar advance General Jackson devised, over Blair's protest, the following security: a mortgage on Halcyon Plantation; a bill of sale for "thirty-odd negroes now on said plantation"; a note jointly signed by Andrew, junior, and himself; a codicil to his will directing that all bequests under it be suspended until the debt should be paid.[8]

A sense of release and of accomplishment comforted the old man. "My son A.J. junr. seeing his way now clear begins to look up like a freeman. When I discovered his embarrassments, found out how he had been swindled and imposed upon, that he had been adopted and raised by my dear wife and myself, was the only representative to perpetuate my name, and when I viewed the goodness and amiability of his dear wife and little children I could not withstand stepping forward to extricate him."[9]

3

The Democrats also were beginning to lift up their heads in the manner of freemen. Mr. Tyler's veto of the bank bills, and other examples of independent behavior, tended to estrange him from the Whig leaders who saw themselves despoiled of the fruits of their hard cider victory. Dissension wracked the lately triumphant party and, in the elections of 1841 and 1842, the Democrats made striking gains—circumstances agreeable, indeed, to the two ex-Presidents who ruled over the destinies of that party, consulting each other occasionally by correspondence.

Martin Van Buren had retired not to his law practice in New York City, but to the neighborhood of his birth at Kinderhook, a village on the Hudson about twenty-five miles below Albany. He addressed General Jackson as one country squire to another touching, not too exhaustively, on the state of agriculture. "My health has never been better, nor my spirits either." Improvements on the residence at Lindenwald, as Mr. Van Buren had named his seat, were going forward. "How greatly would be its value increased if I could promise myself to see you at it. To come as near as practicable I have our friend Col Earles likeness of you well framed . . . [for] my dining room."[10]

It was a stately dining room that Earl's portrait looked upon, with places for many guests. Van Buren had bought the property during his presidency, thus reidentifying himself with a community which he had been glad to forsake as a boy. The Van Buurmalsens had come over as articled servants of the Van Rensselaers. One of their number simplified the name to Van Buren, needlessly it seems, for he could not write. Rising out of the indentured class, in a land and a time abounding with opportunities, they rose little higher during the next hundred years. Seven families of Van Burens residing in Kinderhook during the Revolution seemed to have contributed to freedom's cause two militiamen of short-time service.

Into perhaps the most prosperous of these households was Martin Van Buren born in 1782, his father the neglectful proprietor of a small tavern. From this environment Martin escaped to perfect his knowledge of English (Dutch was the family tongue), to become a man of fashion, master politician, and, as he mentioned in his inaugural address, the first President of the United States not born a British subject. He returned a newly-made country gentleman, consciously treading the paths of his predecessors to the Executive Chair—saving the Adamses, townfolk whose careers, especially in their latter parts, Mr. Van Buren had no desire to emulate. The squire's son made light of the struggle to select a right-sounding name for Lindenwald which, except for antecedent use by James Fenimore Cooper, would have become The Locusts.[11]

Unlike the master of Lindenwald, General Jackson was not enjoying good health. "I have been scarcely able to write— with pain in my ears, head and eyes it is quite an effort."[12] Yet, as Frank Blair observed, he had something better than strength of flesh. He had strength of spirit. "Your life is of the soul, more than the body."[13]

His finances readjusted, the General took a more active interest in public affairs, with two ambitions before him, the realization of which Old Hickory regarded as his final contributions to his country. He wished to insure James K. Polk second place on the ticket which in 1844 would achieve a restoration of the Jacksonian dynasty; and he wished to bring Texas into the Union.

After the defeat of 1840, the next vice-presidential nomination seemed Polk's for the asking. Mr. Van Buren saw the error of his strategy in the late disastrous campaign: with Polk instead of Johnson the Democrats might have polled a majority of the popular vote. Then came the encouraging returns of 1841, marred only by what seemed at a distance to be the incomprehensible defeat of Polk for re-election as Governor of Tennessee. Viewed at close range the defeat was susceptible of explanation: the Tennessee Whigs had discovered a *deus ex machina* in the person of "Slim Jimmy" Jones.

James Chamberlain Jones was born on a small farm almost within sight of the Hermitage. When General Jackson made his triumphal return from the Battle of New Orleans, Jimmy was six years old,

A TAPER BURNING LOW

fatherless and beginning to feel the weight of life's responsibilities. But care rode lightly on his sloping shoulders. Jimmy grew up to attain renown as a rustic buffoon and mimic. He moved away, married a wife who had a baby every year, and made a good country living. In 1840 his broad humor was ideal for the hard cider campaign, and in 1841 the Whigs nominated him for Governor. James K. Polk was a hard-working public servant with no frivolities and little humor. On the stump he did not thrill crowds; he sought to win their respect by earnest discussions of the issues. Slim Jimmy dogged Polk's steps throughout the State. When his adversary had concluded an address, Jones would draw a 'coonskin from his pocket and stroke it. "Did you ever see such fine fur?" In a few moments the voters would be splitting their sides over Jimmy's clownish misrepresentations of Polk's record.

Polk's defeat made party satraps uneasy and General Jackson very indignant indeed. To lose one's own state was not a good recommendation for vice-presidential honors.

The Texas question also presented perplexities. The taint of sectionalism would not wash off, and for this the indiscreet ardor of the slavery expansionists was largely responsible. During Van Buren's administration the republic had again offered itself for annexation. The President, fighting for his political life and not anxious to add to his troubles, had declined to act. Tyler's efforts to place the issue on nationalistic grounds by linking it to the Oregon question were unfruitful. Meanwhile, harassed by border raids and threatened with a determined attempt at reconquest by Mexico, Sam Houston's situation was critical. Turning to Europe for help, he found sympathetic ears in the chancelleries of England and of France. It would be to the interests of those countries to build up on the vulnerable southwestern flank of the United States a strong nation under European patronage.

Jackson had envisaged the acquisition of the Californias by a Texas which one day would become a part of the Union. The statesmen in London and in Paris did not overlook the possibilities of an identical conquest—by a Texas united to Europe by friendly ties.

These maneuvers were quickly noticed in the United States. Tyler was worried, and the southern extremists raised a great hullabaloo. New England Abolitionists replied in kind, John Quincy Adams scenting a "plot" on the part of the President and the "slavocrats" to encompass annexation.[14] On the other hand, the fear of foreign intervention revealed the germs of an influential northern sentiment for annexation arising from the old national policy of Jackson and from the fear of a loss of commercial advantage to our manufacturing states.

Already the question was beginning to disturb the serenity of political managers looking to 1844.

4

The extra places at Martin Van Buren's dinner table were filled by hopeful Democrats from the country over who beat a path to Lindenwald. As to 1844, they found their host receptive. When other aspirants—J. C. Calhoun, James Buchanan, Lewis Cass—began to appear, the squire of Lindenwald adopted less passive measures to impress his receptivity on the public mind. A pilgrimage to the Hermitage was announced, and in February, 1842, the pilgrim set out. The latter part of March he had progressed as far as South Carolina, when a letter from Henry Clay came to his hand.

His immediate aspirations confounded by Tyler, the Kentuckian also was bound for the shades of retirement, there to await the call of his party in 1844. Mr. Clay had given notice of his resignation from the Senate and soon would be at Ashland, which he cordially asked Mr. Van Buren to include in his all-embracing itinerary. The invitation was accepted. Six weeks thereafter the traveler reached the Cumberland. By contrast with refurbished Lindenwald the debt-plagued Hermitage looked seedy.

Though suffering from a chill, General Jackson bestirred himself to sponsor his guest to the community. Of private conversations neither principal has left a line for the enlightenment of posterity. Yet it is impossible to believe that Texas was not mentioned, or that Mr. Van Buren expressed any view on that subject which aroused a suspicion in Jackson's mind that he would interpose obstacles to annexation. The exertions of the visit left Old Hickory so weary that several days elapsed before he gave his friend Blair an account of the impression the candidate had made. "Instead of a dwarf dutchman, a little dandy who you might lift out of a bandbox, the people found him a man of middle size, plain and affable. W[h]iggery is done in Tennessee."[15]

The plain, affable traveler passed on to Kentucky. Some time went by before General Jackson heard from him. "The hospitable roof of our friend Col. ["Tecumseh"] Johnson affords me the first opportunity to drop you a line. . . . At Lexington the crowd was large and everything well conducted." Admirably so, it would appear. "Mr. Clay presented himself and remained some time surrounded by a dense mass of Democrats. He inquired respectfully and kindly about your health." For forty-eight hours the candidate remained in Lexington at the disposal of the Democratic reception committee. "After that I spent two or three days with Mr. Clay, and returned to the City for a day longer."[16]

Well as Martin Van Buren knew his patron's love of frankness, not one syllable did he utter concerning his visit to the home of the man in all probability to be the Whig nominee for President in 1844, and regarded by Andrew Jackson as "a pure unadulterated demagouge."[17] Was not "two or three days" a curiously vague phrase to use at a time when Van Buren's schedule was so closely packed that hours and minutes must be taken into account? He had tarried at the Hermitage less than three days.

On the poplar-shaded, secluded lawn at Ashland the two statesmen, too clever by far for their own good, had sat, their thoughts tending toward ambition. Neither has left the least record of that interesting rendezvous. It has remained for friendly biographers to offer the suggestion that they struck a bargain to omit Texas from the list of campaign issues.[18] Certainly the developments support this view.

Though political expediency had been the lodestar of each, Mr. Van Buren had shown disinterested statesmanship in dealing with the financial troubles dating from 1837 and Henry Clay had shown it on the looming menace of slavery. Their understanding, if they had one, is susceptible of an interpretation by no means unworthy. For one candidate to come out for annexation would be to gain votes in the South and the West, lose them in the East, and probably fan the fires of sectionalism. For both to come out, no political advantage would accrue, and a sectional issue be raised needlessly.

If both remained aloof, the campaign might be waged around less combustible issues.

The detail this convenient formula left out of the reckoning was the peril arising from the possibility of European intervention in Texas. This complication had not been present in 1836 when Jackson retreated before the frowning visage of slavery. Believing the designs of England presented the greater danger, Old Hickory was determined to yield no more. Yet, should Andrew Jackson die before 1844, who would have the authority to revoke any gentleman's agreement Martin Van Buren and Henry Clay may have made?

5

The veteran's sands seemed to be running out. "I have been brought low with a severe attack of chills and fevers."[19] He could hardly see to write, and his discourse had an old man's way of rambling. Correspondence was neglected. Too poor to employ a secretary, he retained, however, the futile habit of jotting on the covers of unanswered letters the gist of replies which, in other days, Jack Donelson would have made. They were the responses of a man finished with worldly vanities. On the letter of a portrait painter: "The last sitting I fully determined I would sit no more. I am now too old and infirm." On a communication from Clinton College, in New York: "I am too old to accept honorary titles that I do not merit." On the letter of a society wishing to confer a membership: "I am too old to be of any use."[20]

Too old? The bill to refund the New Orleans fine was altered to make the proposed restitution a gratuity to General Jackson rather than the rectification of a miscarriage of justice. Instantly new vigor fortified the flagging pen at the Hermitage. Andrew Jackson would scorn the benefits of such an act. "I would starve," he stormed in private, "before I would touch one cent of the money under that odious & insulting amended bill."[21] In long letters he elucidated his claim "on the basis of justice alone."[22]

When opponents of the original bill cited Martin's *History of Louisiana* in support of their contentions, Old Hickory indicated his familiarity with that work. Statement after statement he challenged, some on evidence difficult to controvert, though the sum-mation—"a greater tissue of falsehoods never before eminated from a wicked head and corrupted heart"—hardly entitles General Jackson to recognition as a dispassionate critic of our historical literature.[23] The effort seemed to serve the more useful purpose of replenishing his energy. "I am like a taper. When nearly exhausted [it] will sometimes have the appearance of going out, but will blaze up again for a time."[24]

Now high, now low flared the taper, consuming its last inch. The continuance of gratifying election results proved a wonderful revitalizer. "[With] the overwhelming victory in Newyork, Pennsylvania, ohio and other states Clays fate is sealed. . . . I can scarcely hope to live to see the termination of the next Presidential election—should providence will it, and Van Buren [be] elected, and [I be] able to travel, I would cheerfully go on, take my constitution carriage and take him in it, to the capitol to be inaugurated, but my dear friend I have small hopes that I will be spared so long."[25]

To George Bancroft's request for reminiscences of the Revolution for inclusion in his history of the United States, the veteran replied: "From my weak and debilitated state I can only refer you to Major J. H. Eatons life of Jackson."[26] Amos Kendall applied for permission to write his patron's biography. The former Postmaster General was ill and in debt as a result of a judgment (subsequently reversed) obtained by avaricious mail contractors whose profits he had curtailed.

To help a friend old Jackson laboriously turned to his mountain of papers, the accumulation of half a century. Captivating fragments of the past drifted back: the titanic feud with John Sevier; the North Carolina land fraud; hoof beats at Clover Bottom. Alack, the task of assorting these documents proved quite beyond the old man. Kendall was under restriction of the court not to leave the District of Columbia. So a nephew of his, James A. McLaughlin, arrived at the Hermitage in December, 1842.

6

Intelligent, industrious, obliging, immediately this young man won the hearts of the General and of all his household. The quickening pulse of an alert and purposeful spirit infused with new life the shabby mansion and debt-burdened family, dependent in everything on the feeble chief of clan whose next step might be his last. Burrowing into the papers, McLaughlin soon had ready a boxful of material for his uncle. It went off with a note from the subject of the projected biography: "I hope . . . [the] Book may relieve you from pecuniary embarrassments. . . . I am pressed to earth. I have not had one dollar in three years that I could call my own."[27]

Distinguished counsel on research came from the harassed Kendall who perceived what was scarcely visible to another writer of his day: the distinction between history and biography. "Your Biographies thus far," he wrote the General, "are destitute of incidents connected with your private life."[28] The public man is half the man, and sometimes less than half. With pencil and pad on his knee McLaughlin held long conversations with the General, leading him back and forth over the years in an effort to recapture those informal things which are the most elusive of the biographical ingredients. After a session the young man would put his notes in connected form.

"Narrative of a trip made in the winter of 1811 from *Nashville Tenn to Natchez Miss. T.*

"The road lead through the Chickasaw and Choctaw country. . . . The station of the U. S. agent for the Choctaw nation was on this road. The Genl. was going to Natchez for the purpose of getting some negroes. . . . On reaching the Agency he found some 7 or 8 families detained there. . . . They told him they were removing to Natchez but had been stopped by the Agent until one of their number should go down to Natchez and obtain a passport. In the meantime they were splitting rails for the Agent at 25 cents per 100 and buying corn from him at from $1.00 to $1.50 per bushel. The Genl. went with them to the Agent and . . . inquired how this happened. . . . The Agent with much severity inquired of the Genl. if *he* had a passport. 'Yes Sir,' he replied, 'I always carry it with me. I am a free born American and . . . [that is] sufficient passport to take me wherever my business leads me.' He then told the emigrants to gear up their wagons and start and if anyone attempted to stop them to shoot him."[29]

Soon Jackson's pen, too, was busy:

"Lord Rawden advanced in the fall of 1780 or 81 & encamped on

Major Robt. Crawfords plantation at the crossing of the Waxhaw Creek— before Lord Rawdons advance Gen¹ Lasley or Col Lasly of the British army with Infantry & Tarleton with dragoons advanced, . . . passing our dwelling but we all *hid out*— Tarleton passed within a hundred yards of where I & a cousin crawford had concealed ourselves— I could have shot him."[30]

When Tarleton raided the Waxhaws Andy Jackson was thirteen years old. He wrote the above at seventy-six. That birthday anniversary—March 15, 1843—brought a flood of greetings, delaying work on the biography. "Wants my autograph," scribbled Jackson. "An entire stranger— having refused thousands I cannot from my debility & custom conform with this."[31] Some of the letters contained solicitations that were impossible to decline. "Dear General you will not I hope refuse even from a little girl eight years old the tribute of respect and affection on your birthday. Papa has taught us all to love you very much. . . . CAROLINE L. BUTLER."[32]

7

Another task of composition interrupted the labor of the memorialist.

"Hermitage, June 7, 1843.

"In the name of God Amen, I Andrew Jackson Senr. being of Sound mind memory and understanding, and impressed with the great uncertainty of life, and the certainty of death, and . . . whereas since executing my will of the 30th of September, 1833 my Estate has become greatly involved by my liabilities for the debts of my well beloved and adopted Son Andrew Jackson Jnr which makes it necessary to alter the same, Therefore I . . . do make, ordain publish and declare this my last Will and Testament, revoking all other wills by me heretofore made,

"I bequeath my body to the dust whence it comes . . . [to] be buried by the side of my dear departed wife in the garden of the Hermitage.

"To meet the debt [to] my good friends Genl. J B Plauché and Co of New Orleans for the sum of six thousand dollars with the interest accruing thereon . . . also a debt of ten thousand dollars borrowed of my friends Blair and Rives of the city of Washington

District of Columbia with the Interest accruing thereon . . . I hereby bequeath all my Real and Personal estate.

"After these debts are fully paid thereby, I give and bequeath to my adopted son Andrew Jackson Junr, the tract of Land whereon I now live known by [as] the Hermitage . . . with all my negroes that I may die possessed of with the exceptions hereafter named, . . . all the Household furniture farming tools, Stock of all kind . . . to him and his heirs forever."

Jackson's language was clear. Yet to avoid any possibility of misconstruction he repeated:

"The true intent and meaning of this my last Will and Testament is that all my Estate real personal and mixed, are hereby first pledged for the payment of the above recited debts and Interest, and when they are fully paid, the residue of all my Estate, are hereby bequeathed to my adopted Son A Jackson Junr. with the exception[s] hereafter named."

Then followed a number of specific bequests of negroes to Sarah, who "has been more than a daughter to me," and to the grandchildren.

"I bequeath to my well beloved Nephew Andrew J Donelson, Son of Samuel Donelson deceased, the elegant sword presented to me by the state of Tennessee, with this injunction that he fail not to use it when necessary in support and protection of our glorious Union. . . . This from the great change in my worldly affairs of late is with my blessing all I can bequeath him, doing justice to those creditors to whom I am responsible.

"To my Grand Nephew Andrew Jackson Coffee I bequeath the elegant sword presented to me by the rifle company of New Orleans . . . with this injunction, that he wield it . . . against all invaders whether foreign foes, or intestine traitors.

"I bequeath to my beloved Grand son Andrew Jackson, son of A Jackson Junr. and Sarah his wife, the sword presented to me by the Citizens of Philadelphia, with this Injunction, that he will always use it in defence of our glorious Union.

"The pistols of Genl Lafayette I bequeath to George Washington Lafayette.

"The Gold box presented to me by the Corporation of the City of New York, the large Silver vase presented by the Ladies of Charleston, South Carolina, my native State, . . . I leave in trust to my Son A Jackson Junr with directions that should our happy country not be blessed with peace, he will at the close of the war present each of said articles to that patriot residing in the city or state from which they were presented, who shall be adjudged to have been the most valient in defence of his country. . . .

"As a memento of my high regard for Genl. Robert Armstrong . . . I give and bequeath to him, my case of pistols and sword, worn by me throughout my military career, well satisfied that in his hands they will never be drawn without occasion, nor sheathed but with honor,

"Lastly, I leave to my Beloved Son all my walking canes and other relics, to be distributed among my young relatives (name sakes)."

Though no sword was to go to Andrew, junior, General Jackson named him "my whole and sole Executor, . . and [I] direct that no security be required of him."[33]

A month later Sarah's fourth child was born. "Thinking as I was of Emuckfau heights, Enotochopco and Talladega we named him Robert Armstrong—remembering [that] when he [Armstrong] fell desperately wounded, he cryed out, . . ['] save the cannon [']. . . . If the child live he may perchance aid in saving our glorious Union."[34] Had the child lived it is probable that he would have followed his two brothers into the army of the Confederacy; but he did not live. Jackson saw the little lifeless form taken from the sobbing mother's breast. "It was the most distressing scene I ever witnessed."[35]

8

The pleasant young McLaughlin gathered up his notebooks and departed, planning to return as soon as his uncle should exhaust the material in hand. The Hermitage never saw him again. After *Harper's Magazine* had published seven installments, Amos Kendall's life of Andrew Jackson was abandoned following an estrangement between the author and Frank Blair. The widespread Democratic triumphs of 1843 had assured a majority in Congress sufficient to elect a public printer of the Jacksonian faith. By right of party service the place belonged to the firm of Blair & Rives. Harried by debts, Kendall entered the lists against his old friends, losing the favor of Andrew Jackson as well as failing to win the printership.[36]

Old Hickory mingled with his congratulations to Blair & Rives a painful request for the postponement of principal and interest due on his debt of ten thousand dollars. In an effort to obtain a better price, Jackson had shipped his 1842 cotton to Liverpool. He obtained no more than he could have had at New Orleans, and carrying charges virtually devoured the proceeds. The 1843 crop at Halcyon Plantation was ruined by a flood. On the heels of these events it transpired that Andrew, junior, had been endorsing notes again—"swindled," as Jackson put it, by his cousin Stockley Donelson. In anguish the old man wrote: "I have grappled with every debt Andrew ows and I trust I will be able to meet [these new ones]."[37] Governor Pierce Butler of South Carolina, was in Nashville looking for horses. Old Hickory asked Jack Donelson to offer three thoroughbred colts from the depleted Hermitage stable for a thousand dollars, then for nine hundred, then "as your judgment may direct.... I want mony.... The bay filly [alone] is worth $1000."

Andrew Jackson wanted money badly to throw away his horses for such prices. Butler took them.[38]

On January 1, 1844, for the fourth consecutive New Year's Day, the General was obliged to forego payments of his debts and to pray the indulgence of his creditors. Yet there were rifts in the clouds. With éclat the new Congress voted to wipe out the New Orleans fine. President Tyler himself enclosed to the master of the Hermitage a draft on the Treasury for two thousand seven hundred and thirty-two dollars and ninety cents (which included interest from 1815), accompanied by a most cordial letter. The event was celebrated from one corner of the country to the other. In New York City a transparency stretching across Broadway proclaimed:

JUSTICE TO THE BRAVE
Judge Hall's
Sentence on
GENL JACKSON
Repudiated by the
Nation
Feb. 14th 1844[39]

When the Treasury order arrived Jackson did not have a dollar. Ignorant of the exact terms of the refunding act, the old man asked Blair if he could "with honor" cash the draft.[40]

Blair extended for one year what was due on the ten thousand dollar loan. The veteran's gratitude was touching. This generous act, he said, and one good crop would rehabilitate the finances of the Hermitage. "To your unsolicited liberality and that of my friend Genl Plauché I ascribe the happy prospects of my dear adopted son and his precious little wife and sweet children. . . . How long a kind providence may permit me to remain in the land of the living he only knows, . . . but when providence pleases to make the call I will go without any regrets . . . where the wicked cease to trouble and the weary are at rest."[41]

9

Eleven days after this was written a young man appeared at the Hermitage—William D. Miller, private secretary to the president of the Texas Republic. Beneath his careful courtesy was an air of settled resolution. Mr. Miller handed General Jackson a letter marked "Private" in the swelling script of Sam Houston.

It was a long letter. Feeble eyes strained over sheets held so close they almost touched the hero's nose. They contained alarming news. Could it be true what Jackson had heard about Sam Houston's intrigues with England?[42]

Old Hickory reconsidered his hasty preparations for Paradise. Texas must first be ours.

CHAPTER XLIII

LAST LEAVE

I

SAM HOUSTON had come a long way since the days of The Raven and of Big Drunk. When Andrew Jackson ordered Houston to a tailor for a suit of white man's clothes,[1] Old Hickory did not suspect that he was setting the stage for a drama in which one day Sam Houston should emerge as the dictator—and Jackson the one dictated to.

The constitution of the Texas Republic limited a president to two terms, and these not consecutive. Houston's first administration was a notable achievement in statecraft. Annexation unexpectedly refused by the United States, the executive confronted the task of molding into a nation, which could stand alone, a white population of thirty thousand distributed over an area as large as France. A high proportion of these prospective citizens were adventurers who preferred the rifle and the bowie knife as instruments of government. From these materials Sam Houston gave Texas the appearance of a sovereign state, its domestic concerns reasonably ordered and prosperous, its rights respected abroad.

His successor in the executive chair was Mirabeau Buonaparte Lamar, a gentleman afflicted with visions as soaring as his name. In three years the machinery of the republic virtually had ceased to function. Currency was worthless, Indians on the war path and Santa Anna gathering his forces for invasion. Another offer of annexation had been refused by the United States. Resuming the presidency in 1841, Sam Houston calmly looked into the face of chaos. Skillfully he inaugurated a foreign policy calculated to alarm the United States and to excite the cupidity of Europe.

Twice in the autumn of 1843, President Tyler offered to reopen negotiations for annexation. Unmindful of the desperate improvisations by which he kept his republic alive, Sam Houston replied with cold dignity. "[By] the interposition of foreign friendly governments . . . an armistice has been established between Texas and Mexico. . . . Were Texas to agree to annexation [to the United States] the good offices of the powers would, it is believed, be withdrawn, and were the [annexation] Treaty to Fail of ratification by the Senate of the United States Texas would be . . . without a friend."[2]

Tyler's reply was a mixture of persuasion, threat and entreaty. Immediate annexation was guaranteed. The Senate had been sounded and *a clear constitutional majority of two-thirds are in favor of the measure.* The United States would not consent to see a rival power built up on her border, and would go to war to prevent it. What had Texas to gain from precipitating such a conflict?[3]

But Mr. Tyler was not so confident of his ability to cope with Sam Houston as he pretended to be. He sought the help of Jackson, currying favor by an espousal of the bill to remit the New Orleans fine. This was followed by a letter to the Hermitage from the President's confidant, Senator Robert J. Walker of Mississippi: "I think the annexation of Texas depends *on you.* May I request you to write by the first mail to President Houston?"[4]

Jackson wrote.

"You know my dear General that I have been & still am your friend. . . . Some of your enemies have been & are circulating at the City of Washington that you are endeavoring to athwart the wishes of an overwhelming majority in Texas to become annexed to the United States—that you are desirous to become closely allied to great Britain. . . . I have denied . . . the slanders, . . . [saying] that you never could become the dupe of England. . . . My strength is exhausted and I must close."[5]

More disconcerting reports from Mr. Tyler's confidants, and five days later the old man wrote again—a long letter scrawled amid such bodily and mental anguish that the wonder is the pen did not fall from the enfeebled fingers before the task was done:

"My dear Genl I tell you in all sincerity and friendship, if you will achieve this annexation your name & fame will become enrolled amongst the greatest chieftains. . . . Now is the time to act & that with promptness & secrecy & have a treaty of annexation laid before the United States Senate where I am assured it will be ratified.... It will be an unfailing laurel in your ploom.... I am scarcely able to write— The Theme alone inspires me with the strength.... Let me hear from you if only three lines.... your friend,

"ANDREW JACKSON."6

2

Instead of three lines, in which Sam Houston could have told Andrew Jackson all he wished to know and put his fears at rest, the Texas Talleyrand wrote three hundred lines. This was the communication Old Hickory received from the hand of Houston's private secretary, William D. Miller, on March 11, 1844.

It had not been an easy piece of composition. With relish Sam Houston could play off England, France, Mexico and the United States against each other in the cockpit of diplomacy. To play on the heart-strings of the frank and brave old patriot whom he truly loved was another order of business—but necessary to the game Houston had started. Old Hickory's painful letters contained nothing the Texan did not fully know from his alert chargé d'affaires in Washington. Far from being chagrined by the "slanders" connecting him with European intrigue, Houston had deliberately conducted that affair in a manner calculated to insure those tales a wide circulation. By stirring to action old Jackson, they had served one of their definite objects. Though the hand of death might be on his shoulder, Andrew Jackson could still do more than any other American to call to arms a national sentiment for annexation.

"Venerated Friend," began Sam Houston's long letter, "so far as I am [personally] concerned, I am determined upon immediate annexation to the United States." Houston could not consider the matter from a personal point of view, however. He must act as a chief of state, putting thoughts of self aside. "Our situation has been peculiar.... Surrounded with internal difficulties as well as external dangers, it was my duty as Executive to have an eye to every emergency that might arise." It was his duty to safeguard the future of Texas. He had done so. A friendly interposition of the powers having given the republic peace, "she has nothing to apprehend for years to come." With confident strokes Houston sketched the rise of a great nation, untroubled by the ominous question so determinedly dividing the United States into hostile camps, Texas being all of one mind on slavery. Indeed, "Texas with peace could exist without the U. States; but the U. States cannot, without great hazard, exist without Texas." As if old Jackson were not aware!

Notwithstanding previous humiliations at her hands, Texas was not without affection for the motherland. Houston was willing to offer once more to unite the destinies of the two nations. A "Secret Legation," with power to negotiate a treaty of annexation, was being formed in Washington, of which young Miller, the bearer of this letter, would be the secretary. The offer could not be made without reservation, however. The United States must guarantee Texas security from invasion "during the progress of negotiations." Moreover, there must be no delay. "An effort to postpone . . . [discussions] may be tried in the U. States, to subserve party purposes and to make a President; Let them beware! . . . [Texas] has been sought by the United States, and this is the third time she has consented. Were she now to be spurned, it would forever terminate expectation on her part; and . . . she would seek some other friend [among the nations of the world]."[7]

Jackson pondered these stipulations. To protect the integrity of Texas during the progress of negotiations was beyond the constitutional authority of a president of the United States. Did Houston mean to insist on impossible conditions?

England was permitted to gather that such was the case.[8] Old Hickory was more discerning. He ignored the unsatisfactory parts of Houston's letter and made use only of the satisfactory parts. He assured Houston's emissary, Miller, that the speedy action his chief insisted on could be had, reading confidential letters from Washington in support of this. Then he enclosed to Senator Walker a copy of Houston's letter to be passed around as a spur to action. Then he wrote W. B. Lewis, who stood close to Tyler, to cultivate Miller's acquaintance and to press forward the negotiations. These letters were handed to Miller to deliver, and the young man departed after a sojourn of only a few hours. But he had tarried long enough to yield to the almost inescapable spell which the old leader could cast over men.[9]

Four days later, on his seventy-seventh birthday, Jackson replied to Sam Houston. Gone was the tone of entreaty which had marked (and how strangely) his earlier messages to the Texan. Old Hickory spoke as one who had gathered up the reins of authority once more. "My dear Sir, your much esteemed favor I [have] perused with much pleasure and satisfaction. . . . I sincerely congratulate you upon . . . [your statesmanship as president of the republic.] You have a mixed population, heterogeneous and difficult to govern. I rejoice to find that you have triumphed." The chieftain rejoiced also in the bright future of Texas. "I have no doubt but that the Treaty will be ratified by the Senate." Confidential polls indicated "that 39 senators will vote for it," or four more than the two-thirds required.

General Jackson briefly noted his own endeavors to stimulate the energies of the senators, holding out to them the dire prospect of a Texas driven into the arms of England and lost to us "forever." That had been very well to tell the senators. Jackson himself did not mean that Texas should be lost "forever." Houston had emphasized his and his country's desire for peace, the implication being that English protection would afford it. Jackson painted a different picture. Granted that Great Britain should get "an ascendency over Texas," and then move on into Oregon forming, with her West Indies, "an iron hoop about the United States." This would bring Texas not peace but war. For the United States would "burst asunder" that iron hoop though "it cost oceans of blood & millions of money. . . . yr. friend

ANDREW JACKSON."[10]

Nowhere in this meaty letter was the least allusion to the audacious stipulations Houston had mentioned as a *sine qua non* to negotiation.

3

Yet, by the time his commissioners began their secret meetings with the commissioners of the United States, it appeared that Sam Houston had done his work almost incredibly well. The "impossible" demand for the protection of Texan integrity had been made, and a compromise wrung from Tyler. Moreover, dust had been thrown in England's eyes, and her guaranties, too, remained in force. Houston had maneuvered his country, two years before a disregarded mendicant among nations, into a position where it could scarcely lose, however the cards might fall.[11]

The deliberations of the negotiators were not altogether a secret from General Jackson whose spirits, though not his health, improved daily as he scanned the Washington mails. That a treaty would be signed was a foregone conclusion. Disconcerting news came from the ranks of the senators, however. Thirty-nine votes for ratification could no longer be counted on. Clay men spoke of laying the matter over until the next Congress. Even Van Buren men, emulating the silence of their chief, seemed to grow cool. "Much, very much, my dear General," wrote young Miller, "depends upon your continued efforts."[12]

Others thought the same. Partizans of Texas polished up an old letter of Jackson's urging annexation and, changing the date from 1843 to 1844, published it in the Richmond *Enquirer*.[13] Quickly the rejuvenated communication spread through the press. News of the secret sittings of the negotiators began to leak, and the country to bubble with the Texas question. The continued silence of the candidates after everyone else had begun to talk was placing followers at a loss. But not Jackson. Clay's silence pleased the veteran; Van Buren's did not disturb him. At the proper moment the man from Kinderhook would come out and ride high on the Texas tide. Old Hickory was certain of it.

On April 22, 1844, the treaty of annexation, signed by plenipotentiaries of the respective nations, was laid before the United States Senate.

Sentiment for Texas swept Tennessee like a cyclone. In Nashville a great mass meeting was planned for May 4. On the night before, the eastern mail brought copies of the *National Intelligencer* for April 27 which threw the Democrats into ecstasy and the Whigs into gloom. The newspaper contained a letter from Henry Clay against annexation.

"Clay [is] a dead political Duck," succinctly observed Andrew Jackson.[14]

Who could doubt it? The meeting was a thunderous affair, at which more than one Whig solemnly repudiated his leader. James K. Polk drove out to make his obeisances at the Hermitage. He found the master looking "years" younger. Now for a swinging pro-Texas pronunciamento from Mr. Van Buren and Polk was sure the election was safe.[15]

Stirring days these, at the Hermitage. As in bygone times, a stream of callers flowed to and fro. Democrats came to pledge allegiance, Whigs to confess their sins and beg absolution; and all to cut hickory canes. A hickory cane was the badge of a Jackson man, a hickory cane cut at the Hermitage the badge of a Jackson man who had been to Mecca. Had all the saplings that went into walking sticks been allowed to grow, they would have furnished enough stake and rail to fence the Hermitage's nine hundred and sixty acres.

At daybreak on May 6, General Jackson awakened to find Robert Armstrong and Willoughby Williams awaiting an audience. So brimming with Texas was the veteran that he began to talk the moment he caught sight of his friends. "I knew Clay would not be President. . . . [I knew] he would commit some indiscretion. Gentlemen, mark what I tell you: no man can be President who opposes annexation."

"General," said Willoughby Williams, a forthright man, long the sheriff of Davidson County, "General, we came to submit other developments to you. The late mail brought a letter from Mr. Van Buren in which he takes the same ground that Mr. Clay has taken."

"It's a forgery," exclaimed Jackson. "Mr. Van Buren never wrote such a letter."

Williams placed in Old Hickory's hands a copy of the *Globe*. Then the two visitors strolled over toward the spring house, leaving the General to read and reflect alone. The *Globe* bore the date April 27, as did the *Intelligencer* which contained Mr. Clay's letter. Being a morning newspaper, the *Intelligencer* had reached Nashville one tri-weekly mail ahead of its evening contemporary.

Van Buren's statement filled eight columns. After an hour Armstrong and Williams returned. The chieftain had accepted the fact. If it was in Frank Blair's paper it was so.

"Mr. Van Buren must write a second letter explaining himself," General Jackson said quietly.

Armstrong ventured that a second letter would do no good. The Tennessee delegation to the Democratic National Convention would

IN AN INVALID'S CHAIR

Mathew B. Brady of New York, the most celebrated American photographer of his day, transported his cumbersome daguerreotype equipment to the Hermitage and made this picture on April 15, 1845, when Jackson had less than two months to live. Three likenesses of Jackson by this process are known, of which Brady's is the best. When photographic plates came into use Brady made one from the original tin-type. This reproduction is from that plate, owned by Brady's successor, the L. C. Handy Studios, Washington.

THE DYING CHIEFTAIN

Painted in May, 1845, by George P. A. Healy who visited the Hermitage under commission of Louis Philippe of France. A dropsical swelling having spread to Jackson's face, only the eyes, the right one blind, the forehead and the hair were painted from life. The remainder was adapted from a portrait by Earl. The majesty of the dying leader moved Healy to make two portraits, one of which now hangs in the Louvre, the other in the Hermitage. This is a reproduction of the latter, which is owned by the Ladies' Hermitage Association.

be leaving for Baltimore in a few days. Whom should it support? Cass? Silas Wright? Calhoun?

Old Hickory shook his head. His eyes were wet.

Jack Donelson rode up. Presently there was quite a crowd. Jack was a delegate to the convention. After more earnest talk Donelson, Armstrong and a few others withdrew to summon James K. Polk to the Hermitage.[16]

4

On May 11 Old Hickory wrote to Frank Blair:

"I am quite sick really, and have been ever since I read V. B. letter. . . . Political matters out of the question, Texas [is] the key to our future safety. . . . We cannot bear that Great Britain have a Canedy on our west as she has on the north. . . . Some good democrat must be selected, with Polk [as vice president]. . . . can Wright be brought out and will he pledge himself, will Woodbury, or Buchanan."[17]

The chieftain wrote merely to relieve his harrowed feelings. By the time Blair's reply should be at hand the fate of the party, aye of the Union as Jackson believed, would be in the hands of the delegates at Baltimore. If anything were to be accomplished, Jackson must act now. Hours were too precious to waste on regrets.

As of old, Jackson prepared to appeal the question from the politicians to the people. He composed a letter to his friend Harris of the Nashville *Union*. The General began by saying that he had been asked whether Mr. Van Buren's statement had caused him to change his opinions on Texas. He had not changed them. The acquisition of Texas was not a party question. It was a question of national security. The theme was effectively developed. In conclusion a tactful paragraph gave the New Yorker a chance to retrace his steps.[18]

On May 13 Jack Donelson started to Nashville with this production. On the way he met Polk and Armstrong en route to the Hermitage. Polk had been in Nashville for a day and a night closeted with General Jackson's friends in preparation for the Hermitage interview. Martin Van Buren had never been popular in Nashville. Jack Donelson had declined a place in his Cabinet. On every street corner, men were drawing unpleasant inferences from the simultaneous announcements of Clay and of Van Buren on Texas; and "bargain" was a memorable word in the lexicon of Jacksonians. When Polk looked at the letter Donelson was taking to the *Union*, he knew that many true blue Nashville Democrats would regard it as dealing too gently with the squire of Lindenwald. Donelson knew this, too.

At the Hermitage Polk and Armstrong were patient, respectful, lucid. They emerged victorious, and James K. Polk headed for Nashville with high thoughts throbbing in his cool, intent and always practical brain. The chieftain had yielded up Martin Van Buren—reluctantly and with a heart of lead, but had yielded him up.

Mr. Polk had previously selected a field marshal to handle his vice-presidential ambitions at Baltimore—a needful precaution, for those aspirations had received a setback by reason of a second unfortunate encounter with Slim Jimmy Jones.[19] Upon this marshal, Congressman Cave Johnson of Tennessee, larger burdens now devolved. Back from the Hermitage Polk wrote Johnson a long letter.

"The Genl . . . speaks most affectionately of *Mr. Van Buren* but is compelled to separate from him. . . . [He says] the Convention must select another man," and he "hoped" that in the interest of harmony Van Buren would withdraw.

Who should take his place?

"Genl. J. says the candidate for the first office should be an annexation man."

As everyone knew, several such men were available—Cass, Buchanan, Calhoun, possibly Wright.

But General Jackson directed that he should be "from the Southwest, and that he and other friends should insist on that point."

Cass was from Michigan, Buchanan, Pennsylvania, Wright, New York; Calhoun—impossible on any ground. But Polk left nothing to inference. "I tell them, and it is true, that I have never aspired so high. . . . I aspire only to the 2nd office. . . . I am however in the hands of my friends and they can use my name in any way they think proper."[20]

Thus the picture contrived for Cave Johnson: the chieftain's word being law, what could Polk do but make the race?

This representation failed—or did it?—to take account of one thing: General Jackson's public appeal, due to appear in the next day's *Union*, containing no mention of Polk, but urging Van Buren to reverse himself on Texas, lead his party to victory and his country to peace. Its publication might seem to contradict Mr. Polk at vital points.

The General's letter did not appear in the next day's *Union*, however—and for an extraordinary reason, if one is to place implicit confidence in the prompt explanation of J. K. Polk. Editor Harris's paper was overset, as printers say, making it necessary to leave out a few items. The custom in such cases, naturally, is to omit the items of least public interest. Harris omitted Andrew Jackson's letter. And, before the type could be placed in the form for the succeeding issue, Old Hickory recalled the communication for "further consideration."[21]

Thus a little coterie of politicians in Nashville, who for years under the compelling eye of the master had pounded the tocsin for Martin Van Buren, edged a step nearer the goal so dear to their hearts. But Polk warned Johnson against over-optimism. Old Hickory would probably "insist" on the publication of his letter after all. If so, it would be read in Baltimore before the opening of the convention, and would inspire the Van Buren people with hope.[22]

That same day, however, brought news from Washington that Van Buren appreciated the critical nature of his situation. Cave Johnson wrote that Senator Silas Wright had assured him that, in event of Van Buren's withdrawal, only James K. Polk could unite the northern Democrats.[23] Wright was Van Buren's friend and lieutenant.

Polk became a little bolder. Without revisiting the Hermitage for additional inspiration, he answered Johnson, quoting Jackson in stronger language than he had attributed to him the day before. Not only did Old Hickory agree with Senator Wright, he went further: Van Buren "has been misled and ruined" by his opposition to Texas; he "will and ought to withdraw," leaving Polk "the most available man." The convention must take Polk, with a running mate from the northern states. Thus the orders of the chieftain, as transmitted by James K. Polk with incidental expressions of surprise and modesty.

Though bold, Polk was not too bold. Let his friends speak at first not of Polk but of "saving the party" from the evils of internal strife.

"I suggest a practical plan," continued the candidate. "[Prior to the convention] get one Delegate from each State in a room at Brown's Hotel and" talk to them about harmony—the particular brand of harmony of which J. K. Polk would be the corporeal embodiment. This should be done with delicacy, avoiding offense to the Van Buren people whose votes would be needed. Finally, Polk's friends must bear in mind that he was still a candidate for vice president—in case the first prize should be another's.[24] After this, the candidate drove back to his home in Columbia. He had done all any man in his situation could do.

Jack Donelson departed for Baltimore, leaving his uncle on the brink of mental confusion. Never before had the chieftain been so nearly at a loss for a handhold on the things he saw passing before his eyes; never so close the feeling that he had lost his grip on the ropes of destiny; never had his commands been so ambiguous and conflicting. Pressed by his vigorous young friends, one day the old man had consented to drop Van Buren and make the gamble for Polk. Next day he had muttered a prayer for a revelation from on High to reconvert Mr. Van Buren and return him the nominee on a Texas platform. Indeed, Jack Donelson carried with him a letter in which Old Hickory implored the New Yorker to reverse himself.[25] Two days after Donelson's stage had rolled away, the *Union* published Jackson's letter, the pro-Van Buren part of which the editor somewhat nullified with an out-and-out anti-Van Buren editorial.[26]

Sinking into a chair the sick chieftain awaited the Baltimore post.

After two days of balloting Van Buren and Cass were neck and neck, the party apparently irrevocably divided and the convention on the verge of dissolution, when a few cool heads brought about an adjournment. Most of the delegates were up all night. At dawn an agreement was reached. At nine o'clock the sleepy politicians tumbled into their seats. By acclamation they nominated James Knox Polk of Tennessee—"Young Hickory."

5

"Polk and Dallas!" rang the battle cry. "Oregon and Texas!"

George M. Dallas, of Pennsylvania, was Young Hickory's running mate.

The chieftain revived.

"Every letter brings us Joyfull news. You will get twenty states at least."[27] And to Mrs. Polk: "Daughter, I will put you in the White House if it costs me my life!"[28]

Not every pleasant letter pertained to the campaign.

"Dear Uncle
 "I presented my husband with a fine Son which we have named Andrew Jackson. . . . Yr aff Niece
 "SARAH K. SEVIER."[29]

Andrew Jackson Sevier, great-grandson of John Sevier: here was something to tickle the ears of Nolichucky Jack should Old Hickory chance to meet him on the golden stairs.

Lines from one of the multitude of children Rachel had befriended:

"Derr Sir I have herd of your bad helth. . . . You have not now my good Freind Mrs Jackson [to nurse you]. I often Shed Teirs when I think of hur for I found her a kind Mother in a foren land. I have come through many troubles & trials since I left the Hermitage. I am now a widow living in the far west [Haw Creek, Missouri] with 8 children six sons & two dawters. It was my lot to get a triffling compannion but blessed be god the best of children. I have not been able to given them any schooling only what I could myself teach. I begin to look old and feels old I am now close on to fifty & not a gray hair in my head but remains respectfuly LATITIA CHAMBERS."[30]

Seldom a week without something like this:

"Honored Genl
 "I have long thought of Coming to See you but poverty forbids. I have not Seen you Since when the army was returning from st Marks—1817, but hope that you will write me a few Lines that I may have the handwriting of my Genl to Look upon. Respectfully Sir JOHN GREERE."[31]

Prospects for cotton and for feed crops were good, both at the Hermitage and "below," as the General spoke of Halcyon Plantation —until July when the Mississippi swept over Halcyon. The fences, most of the stock and sixty thousand pounds of cotton went with the yellow flood.[32] The loss was a small fortune. No debts could be paid that year or the next. Blair and Rives, who had bet twenty-two thousand dollars on Polk, would need their money in case the Whigs should win.

6

The campaign ran head-foremost into a serious complication.

Since April the United States Senate had been tossing the annexation treaty about as if it were a hot potato. The Democratic platform provided a welcome solution: "Polk and Texas!" "Very well, Mr. Polk, you shall have the honor." So saying, the senators stood aside, rejecting the treaty by a smashing vote.

Haughtily Sam Houston turned to England's door. The latchstring was out. Jackson could not find it in his heart to blame him. "Houston has been most cruelly treated."[33] The olympian scorn of the chieftain was reserved for "those craven hearted Senators, Traitors to our country and to our Glorious Union. . . . [Must we now] go to war with England and France to gain Texas, offered to us on honorable terms [and] rejected for political effect?"[34]

Polk's election seemed the only alternative, and to elect him the rank and file of the Democratic Party would have to display greater unity and spunk than its leaders had done in the Senate. To this task the Old Chief gave his strength unsparingly. By August he could no longer ride—he who had spent a lifetime on horseback. By September he was too short of breath to walk the hundred and fifty steps to Rachel's grave without an arm to lean on. Propped before his writing table he labored on, sowing letters broadcast in an effort to arouse the country to a realization of its peril. Tyler was running on an independent ticket. He should withdraw, he must withdraw, the white-haired warrior said, and throw those votes to Polk. Jackson played his hand with the skill of a politician in the prime of his powers. Tyler withdrew.[35] He did more. To counteract European influence, the President diffused the atmosphere of the Hermitage about Sam Houston, appointing Andrew Jackson Donelson chargé d'affaires to the Texas Republic.

America began to respond, the tide for Texas to rise. Clay men strove to beat it down. "Slavery is the paramount issue," shouted an alarmed editor in Cincinnati, making common cause with Garrison's *Liberator*. But the current was setting the other way—even in

New England where a young man had the effrontery to remind John Quincy Adams that Nature had given us Texas "and we must have it." The New Haven *Register* declared annexation a subject on which Democrats North and South should unite. Once more, and for the last time, the nation was taking its stride from Andrew Jackson.[36]

The warrior spurred his protégé to press the advantage, and never let up. "Lash Clay on Texas."[37] Young Hickory lashed him. The Whigs began to waver. Taking fright, Clay compromised, declaring that he would be glad to receive Texas into the Union if it could be done without war and with the people's consent.

When the voters went to the polls in November, in one sense Old Hickory's success had been too sweeping. Clay as well as Polk had profited by Jackson's exploitation of the Texas issue. The General no longer claimed twenty states; he knew the result would be close. So did Polk. Glancing up from a page of tabulations in his own precise hand, the cool, objective contestant said that only fourteen states with one hundred and thirty-four electoral votes were sure, and that victory might turn on the votes of the doubtful states of New York and Tennessee.[38]

Slowly recovering from a hemorrhage and panting for breath, Jackson marked down the returns. It was a long ordeal. From Maine to Louisiana the candidates seemed to have run a dead heat. As votes were counted, it was found that Polk had carried exactly the fourteen states he had said would go to him. These were not enough to elect. Clay won Tennessee and its thirteen electoral votes by a popular majority of one hundred and thirteen. Now Polk must have New York to win. He got it by five thousand votes, making the count in the electoral college one hundred and seventy to one hundred and five. Polk's popular plurality was thirty-eight thousand out of two million six hundred thousand votes cast.[39]

The star of Henry Clay's ambition set in the ashes of his hopes. Finished was the long sequel to the drama of February 9, 1825, which the Kentuckian already recognized as the greatest error of judgment of his life.[40] Yet this engaging statesman's farewell to presidential aspirations was not a farewell to greatness. The finest days of Henry Clay's career were to come when he left Ashland for the last time to lead a courageous band of Southerners, mostly old Jackson men, in the hopeless fight against the trend toward secession.

7

At the Hermitage the architect of victory grew weaker, the last reserves of his strength seemingly gone. "I await with resignation the call of my god."[41]

But first he would see the fruits of his victory secure. While messages of congratulation piled up unacknowledged, Andrew Jackson wrote to his nephew in Texas. "Col Polk spent two nights with me. We had a full and free conversation upon all matters and things. . . . Congress will at an early day of her *now* session . . . [pass] a bill for the reannexation of Texas. . . . The voice of the people has pronounced upon the subject. . . . England wants Texas, next Cuba, and then Oregon." America must defeat this and save Texans from the fate of "Hewers of wood and drawers of water for the . . . [British] aristocracy. . . . My kind regards to Genl Houston. Bring those things which I have expressed to his view. . . . [He has] too much patriotism . . . [to make Texas] a Colony of England."[42]

Sam Houston begged Major Donelson to thank the Old Chief for his counsel. The words of Andrew Jackson would be prized as treasures.[43]

A fortnight later Houston finished his second term of office. "The attitude of Texas now," he said in his farewell address, "is one of peculiar interest. The United States have spurned her. Let her, therefore, work out her own political salvation," pushing her boundary to the Pacific. "If Texas goes begging again for admission to the United States she will only degrade herself." Suppose the United States should open her door? Ah, in that event the course of Texas would be a matter for Houston's successor to consider. Houston himself would be occupied with the more congenial task of farming and finished forever with public affairs.[44]

The new president of Texas was Anson Jones, a sort of orderly-clerk for Sam Houston. The imperialistic tone of the valedictory did not disturb Donelson. After a private talk with the retired executive, Jack assured his uncle that Houston's true goal was annexation. "He is devoted to you, considering that he owes his success at the battle of San Jacinto to the recollection of your plans of battle in your campaigns against the Creek Indians. . . . He says that his greatest ambition is to make a pilgrimage to the Hermitage and obtain your blessing on his boy. You may expect him this spring."[45]

Jackson pressed the Administration to strike while the iron was hot. Half a dozen resolutions, differing in detail, were plumped before Congress. The annexationists began to bicker and divide, the opposition to unite. His strength ebbing daily, Jackson took to an invalid's chair fitted with an attachment to write on. To indite a page made him "gasp" for breath.[46] Yet many pages were written, appealing for harmony. Polk sped to Washington to co-operate with Tyler. After anxious days an opposition senator exclaimed, "The pressure of two presidents and an ex-President is too much for us."[47] A resolution offering Texas a place as a state of the Union was adopted. Mr. Tyler signed it on March 1, 1845, three days before leaving office.

"I congratulate you, Dear General,"[48] exclaimed Frank Blair.

The man in the invalid's chair replied: "I congratulate my beloved country."[49]

8

Informed of the flood's damage to Halcyon Plantation, Blair and Rives again deferred all payments on account of their ten thousand dollar loan. "My Dear General, your convenience alone must be consulted."[50]

No sooner had this been arranged than a fresh revelation of the business practices of Andrew, junior, almost broke the old gentleman down. A note to Jack Donelson breathed despair. "Poverty stares us in the face."[51] Young Jackson had never thought highly of his father's idea of running a woodyard, and had neglected it for cotton. When the cotton was washed out, it transpired that Andrew had been duped by his overseer into closing the woodyard, his only source of ready money until another crop could be grown. Whereupon the overseer had leased land adjoining Halcyon and established his own fuel station which he palmed off on packet captains as belonging to Jackson. This was not all. Andrew had contracted debts amounting to six thousand dollars. At any rate that was what the

General and Sarah computed them to be, confirmation being impossible due to Andrew's absence from home. Were creditors to learn of this state of affairs "the sheriff [would be] at our doors."[52]

The only thing, as Jackson saw it, was to sell Halcyon. "My son has not sufficient energy to conduct an establishment at a distance," the afflicted father wrote to W. B. Lewis in Washington. "You are in the thoroughfare of rich farmers." Here was "a certain fortune" for someone. "If there were ten thousand cords [of wood] on the Bank it would all be taken at a dollar and a half a cord by the middle of June." But all Jackson asked was enough money to pay his son's debts. He would let Halcyon, with all improvements, go for twelve dollars an acre. As virtually wild land it had cost twenty. "My dear Major aid me in getting a purchaser and I will die happy."[53]

Sarah was reading the General's mail to him when she crumpled something to her breast and burst into tears. It was a single sheet covered with Frank Blair's cabalistic scrawl. "Major Lewis has just shown me your letter about Andrew's affairs." General Jackson must not sacrifice his Mississippi property. The firm of Blair & Rives would advance the money needed. John Rives confirmed this. "Mr. Blair and myself are indebted to you for *all we are worth*."[54] Enclosed was the following:

"Washington, March 12, 1845

"General Andrew Jackson is authorized to draw upon us at one day's sight for any sum between one and one hundred thousand dollars and his draft shall be honored, . . . payable at Baltimore, Philadelphia or New York.

"BLAIR & RIVES."[55]

Before Sarah had finished, tears were trickling down the chieftain's cheeks. Again, the old man and his daughter-in-law pored over Andrew's muddled ledger. To be safe they decided to draw for seven thousand dollars. Andrew reached home in time to correct this estimate. So the General drew for eight thousand, raising to twenty-four thousand dollars the total of his indebtedness on his son's account. "Mr. A. Jackson junr will not create another debt of one dollar until he is clear of . . . [this]."[56] The hope that declined to die.

9

The thread of life can spin itself incredibly fine. Many who witnessed the unforgettable scene of General Jackson's departure from Washington in 1837 did not believe that he could survive to reach the Hermitage. Ever since that time Jackson men had journeyed thither with hastened steps, in the belief that the last chance to see the Old Chief alive was at hand. On March 4, 1845—Young Hickory's inaugural day—the cane of crippled Isaac Hill thumped the peeling planks of the Hermitage portico. He had come from New Hampshire to spend that day with Old Hickory.

"If he were another man I could scarcely suppose he would live a week. For the last four months he has not attempted to take his customary meals with the family. He sits through the day in a well constructed easy chair, with his writing materials, his miniature bible and hymn book before him. As soon as the mail arrives his first inquiry is for the daily Washington newspapers and the letters bearing the postmark of the capital. The absorbing topic with him is Texas. . . .

"His complaint is pulmonary: one lobe of the lungs he believes to be entirely consumed. His feet and ankles are swollen from continued sitting, and he finds a substitute for exercise in the bathing of his limbs every evening in those emolients calculated to produce a healthy reaction of the skin.—Weak as he is he shaves with his own hand and adjusts the ample gray hair which continues to add to the dignity of his appearance."[57]

On March 15 a group of old Jackson men gathered in Washington to celebrate the General's seventy-eighth birthday. It was a solemn company—until Auguste Davézac, of Louisiana campaign remembrance, raised his glass.

"There are craven hearts," the Creole said, "who would have refused the boon of an empire lest the accepting of it should lead to war: a war, they said, to be dreaded by a nation having no army, no leader to match the great commanders of European nations. No leader! They forget that Jackson still lives. Even if the hero were dead, go to the Hermitage, ye men of little faith; Go! ask for that old *cocked hat*; it is still there; take it; raise it on the top of a long hickory pole! One hundred thousand American horsemen, rallying around that standard, will tread down Europe's or Mexico's mercenaries like the grass of the Texan prairies."[58]

A naval officer brought from over the water the sarcophagus of a Roman emperor which he offered to General Jackson. "With the warmest sensations that can inspire a grateful heart I must decline the honor intended," Old Hickory replied. "I have prepared an humble repository for my mortal body beside that wherein lies my beloved wife."[59]

In April Justice John Catron reached the Hermitage. His appointment to the United States Supreme bench had been one of the last that Jackson made. The General said he knew that he would never leave his chair. "He then asked me to give him an account of the start our friend President Polk had made. This I did for an hour at which he laughed heartily, understanding to the letter the office-seeking horde." General Jackson had not lessened Mr. Polk's burden, his own recommendations for appointments ranging from Cabinet officers to copying clerks.

After the visit Justice Catron fell to meditating on the qualities that made Andrew Jackson great. He decided in favor of a natural gift of chieftainship, and the paralysing swiftness with which he translated thought into action. "If he had fallen from the clouds into a city on fire, he would have been at the head of the extinguishing hosts in an hour." Perhaps the Justice had heard of the Jonesborough fire in 1803. "He would have blown up a palace to stop the fire with as little misgiving as another would have torn down a board shed. In a moment he would have willed it proper and in ten minutes the thing would have been done. . . . He cared not a rush for anything behind: he looked ahead."[60]

He looked ahead now—with one eye on eternity, the other on Texas.

10

Disturbing reports came from Jack Donelson.

Anson Jones, Houston's successor as president, had declined to call the Texan congress to consider the ratification of the resolution of annexation. This was ominous, for Donelson knew Jones to be a pawn of Sam Houston. Old Hickory's nephew sought out the hero of San Jacinto. The interview was painful. The Texan dictator objected to the American terms on various far-fetched grounds.

A mighty struggle fevered the mind of Sam Houston. He had come to Texas an outcast. Now the first statesmen of two hemispheres addressed him in terms of equality. With his own hands and brain he had created a nation, which Sam Houston had no fear should become a British colony. Thrice had he offered this treasure to the United States. Thrice it had been rejected. Now that the United States, pricked in the tender flesh of self-interest, had deigned to change its mind, should Houston oblige: should he relinquish this personal possession of his, this republic which he had made strong; or should he keep it, snatch from Mexico the Pacific Coast and establish himself at the head of a nation which one day might rank with the powers of the world?

The acute Donelson had done more than communicate the American resolution of annexation to the Texan, however. He had placed in his hands a letter from Andrew Jackson, in which the Old Chief cordially chose to assume opposition to the American terms by Houston to be unthinkable. "I congratulate you, I congratulate Texas and the United States. Glorious result! in which you, General, have acted a noble part."[61]

Still, the Texan hesitated. Donelson warned his uncle: "Houston has disappointed me."[62]

The master of the Hermitage was sinking, the dropsical swelling taking possession of his whole body. Edward George Washington Butler, classmate of Jack Donelson at West Point and godson of General Jackson, arrived to take his last leave. With agony in his dying eyes, the right one blind, Old Hickory said:

"Edward, what will Houston do?"

In a vigorous letter Butler relayed the question to the Texan.[63] Donelson added to the pressure.

Surrendering his shimmering dream, Sam Houston signed to Jones to prepare to furl the flag of the lone star.

This decision was typical of the men who marched under the ensign of Andrew Jackson: a loyal breed. Long after the old leader was in the grave that power of his lived on. When the sections came to the parting of the ways, Frank Blair, junior, did much to save

Missouri for the Union, Sam Houston tried to save Texas, and Andrew Johnson helped to reclaim Tennessee.[64]

On May 26 news of Houston's decision reached the Hermitage from Donelson. Nor was that all. The Texas titan himself was on the way to Tennessee to account in person to his chief.

Glorious tidings! Old Hickory traced a note to James K. Polk. "I knew British gold could not buy Sam Houston."

Fighting for breath, Jackson signed his name.[65] "My lamp is nearly burned out, and the last glimmer has come."[66]

Sam Houston, make haste.

11

The dying man could no longer lie down. His nights were spent propped up in bed, his days on the pillowed chair. The swelling extended to his face. The train of pilgrims grew in volume. On May 29 more than thirty persons, from every walk of life, made their brief farewells. A king's painter came—from Louis Philippe—to take a likeness for the royal gallery. The artist was George P. A. Healy, a young American residing in Paris. Painting the eyes, forehead and hair from life, he adapted the rest from a portrait by Earl.[67]

When Mr. Healy had finished, the General asked him "as a personal favor" to remain long enough to make a portrait of his "dear child," Sarah. Having already painted two portraits, not one, of Jackson, Healy had overstayed his time. The King had given him other American commissions to execute, among them a likeness of Henry Clay. Mr. Clay was at the moment passing through Nashville and Healy told the General he wished to join him there. The artist never forgot the look in Jackson's eyes at the mention of Henry Clay's name.

"Young man," Old Hickory said, "always do your duty."

Healy remained to paint Sarah. On the belated arrival at Ashland Mr. Clay observed to him:

"I see that you, like all who approached that man, were fascinated by him."[68]

On Sunday, June 1, the General asked the members of the family to cease their vigil and go to church. "This is the holy Sabbath, and apparently the last one I will be with you."[69] That night he slept little. The next day was one of great pain. He prayed to God to help him bear it. Opiates were given more freely. On Thursday he rallied, and listened to an account of plantation affairs from his son. Asking for pen and paper, he began a letter to Plauché in New Orleans:

"We want a supply of Pork & bacon at our Mississippi plantation—one thousand pounds of bacon, midlings, if to be had bottom shoulders, and five barrels of Miss[issippi] pork in all 2000#."

Alas, Andrew had mentioned a subject other than pork: money.

. . . ["May we] draw upon you a bill to mature the first of March next for not more than $2,000 before which maturity we shall have ample assets [the cotton crop] in your hands to cover. . . . You may rest assured that A. Jackson Jnr will never again draw unless covered by assets My health is bad. . . . I remain y^r. friend
"Andrew Jackson."[70]

Late that night after George had lifted his master into bed, it was Sarah's turn on watch. The beam of a candle cast restless shadows on the sufferer's face. The lips moved. Sarah bent nearer. She caught snatches of a prayer and the words of a hymn:

"When through the deep waters I call thee to go
The rivers of woe shall not then overflow."

At midnight Sarah asked her father how he felt. "Pretty comfortable," he said, "but I cannot be long with you all. I wish to be buried without display or pomp." And he added: "Or any superfluous expense."[71]

On awakening the next morning, which was Friday, the patient said he still felt "comfortable." About eleven o'clock he told his son he wished to write his friend Polk, and that this might be his last letter. Andrew suggested that it be put off until tomorrow.

"Tomorrow," the father said, "I may not be here."

"*—confidential—*
"Hermitage
"June 6th, 1845

"James K. Polk
 "president of the
  "United States—
   "My dear Sir,
    "Your letter of the 12th ultimo, (*confidential*) has been received — Be assured my friend that it is truly gratefull to learn from you that you have a united & harmonious Cabit——"

The dying man's hand was steady, the letters, though slowly formed, distinct and strong. His mind was clear. Looking back he missed the word "gratefull," written for "gratifying," but "Cabit" for "Cabinet" caught his eye and was corrected.

". . . Sarah is truly grateful to learn from you that Mr. Taggart [a petitioner for office] will be provided for as you promised—We all salute you & M^{rs}. Polk with the kindest good wishes.

"My dear Sir, I wish you to recollect the caution I gave you about the Treasury Department—." For a page and a half Old Hickory proceeded with the topic that was his object in writing. Mr. Polk had named Senator Robert J. Walker as Secretary of the Treasury—an appointment dictated by expediency, not choice. Walker was the head of a pro-Texas group which demanded recognition. Jackson had heard that he was also backed by speculators in depreciated script in the hope that a Treasury order would restore it to par. "I say put your veto on . . . [this scheme] or you and your Secretary will be blown sky high. . . . I can write no more—friendship has aroused me to make this attempt— yr friend

"Andrew Jackson."[72]

The signature, free and fair, stretched two-thirds of the way across the sheet.

At two o'clock Andrew returned.

"There is my letter to my friend Polk. Fold and back [address] it for me, for I am too exhausted, my son, to do it."[73] A little strength returning, his mind dwelt on the sunset rainbow of Sam Houston's momentous decision. "All is safe at last!" His "old friend and comrade in arms" had been true to his trust. British gold could not buy Sam Houston. . . . That left Oregon. Polk would attend to Oregon. Polk would be firm. Polk would get Oregon—Jackson hoped without war. "If not," the soldier said, "let war come."[74]

Sunday, June 8, dawned still and hot. In the forenoon General Jackson swooned away. A cadenced cry from the servants spread through the rooms.

"Oh, Lord! Oh, Lord! Old Massa's dead. Old Massa's dead."

Those outside the house caught up the wail, carrying it to the outbuildings and the stables. Now close at hand it sounded, now far **away.**

~~Confidential~~

Hermitage
June 6th 1845

James. K. Polk
President of the
United States

My dear sir,

Your letter of the 12th ultimo, (Confidential) has been received. Be assured my friend that it is truly gratefull to learn from you, that you have a united & harmonious Cabinett — May it so continue to exist thro' your administration, is the prayer of your friend. Sarah is truly gratefull to learn from you, that her friend Mr Taggart is to be provided for as you promised — We all salute you & Mrs Polk with the kindest good wishes.

My dear sir; I wish you to recollect the caution I gave you about the Treasury Department — Here you are to be assailed, and without great vigilence & energy in yourself, your administration wounded deeply, and in the strictest confidence as your real friend, I read your attention again to it. I was well advised, and by Mr Walkers friends, that Mr Walker would be pressed for this office by all those who were interested in those cheated fraudulent claims, & by those deeply interested in them, and in their negotiation. There never was a greater fraud attempted & committed than in these claims, and a thorough probing investigation will throw shame & desgrace upon all concerned. The passed acts by congress on this subject you cannot repeal, but look well to the future. Scrip has been issued upon these fraudulent claims to the amount of

---

JACKSON'S LAST LETTER
Written two days before his death. This reproduction, four-fifths of actual size is from the original in the Jackson Papers, Library of Congress, Washington.

1,510,000 — this is now worth 58 cents in the dollar. for certain I am told — the great aim of those Speculators are to get Walker as Secretary of the Treasury, by a circular, to place this scrip upon the same footing as the =Stocks, and at once to raise 100 pct, putting $750,000 in the pockets of these fraudulent Speculators — Look to this my friends — let the scrip rest on its own basis on which Congress has placed it. do you not believe that such an act on the Secretary of your Treasury would blow you & your administration sky high.

But again, I am informed thro' a channel in which I have a right to confide, and is a man of much truth himself — that the late executive of the Treasury for the short time he was at the head of it, made ninety thousand dollars, by arrangements with the two brokers Banks of Newyork where large Sums of the public money was deposited & other deposit Banks in N. York. Enquire cautiously amongst the clerks in the city of Washington, by which you will find a key that may unlock the door — is a proper one — But on enquiry by the Whiggs are prepared for you, should Mr Walker have the folly to have any thing to do with either of these abominable projects — I say to you, putyou reto upon them both, if you do your Secretary will be blown sky high. And whatever these corrupt Speculators do for you, or hire characters of, if can get hold of the cash — I can write no more — friend=ship has caused me to make this attempt — if

Andrew Jackson

"Old Massa's dead. Oh, Lord! Old Massa's dead."[75]

A spoonful of brandy revived the General. He said farewell to the household servants, kissed and blessed each member of the family, his glance resting longest on the little granddaughter whose name was Rachel Jackson. "My dear children, and friends, and servants, I hope and trust to meet you all in Heaven, both white and black—both white and black."

The yard had begun to fill with people: a mixed and sorrowing company, some of them drawn, it would seem, by a force stronger than volition. John Henry Eaton and Margaret were there. Eaton had seen his Old Chief perhaps three times in five years, Margaret not for nearly ten. In life they were not to see him again. Negroes trooped from across the fields. Field hands at the Hermitage enjoyed unusual privileges. Not segregated in "quarters," they lived in individual cabins scattered all over the plantation. Forming a group a little distance from the house, they began to chant and pray. Two large south windows of the master's first-floor bedroom gave upon the spacious gallery. The household servants collected on the porch before them, chanting softly.

William Berkeley Lewis came at noon. "Major," said the dying man, "you had like to have been too late." He gave his friend messages for Sam Houston, for Thomas Hart Benton and for Frank Blair.

Someone asked Hannah, in whose arms the first Rachel Jackson had died, to leave the room. "I was born on this place," the old negress said, "and my place is here."

At half past five Andrew, junior, leaned over the bed. "Father, do you know me?"

The voice was very weak. "Yes, I know you. I would know you all if I could see. Bring my specs."

The moans of the servants peering through the windows reached his ears.

"Oh, do not cry. Be good children, and we shall all meet in Heaven."

The chant on the porch sank to a whisper. The chieftain closed his eyes. At six o'clock his head fell forward. His heart stood still.[76]

12

At dusk a coach drawn by galloping horses careened into the Hermitage drive. A travel-stained, arresting figure dismounted, leading a very small boy by the hand. The newcomer towered half a head above the next tallest man present. Not everyone at first recognized Sam Houston.

The greatest of Old Hickory's expeditionary captains stood motionless before the candle-lit couch of death. Then he dropped to his knees, and sobbing, buried his face on his chieftain's breast.

The proprietor of the Texas Republic drew the boy to his side.

"My son, try to remember that you have looked on the face of Andrew Jackson."[77]

THE END

NOTES

Part One

The Border Captain

CHAPTER I

[1] Previous biographies of Jackson, including that of Reid and Eaton, prepared under the General's eye, say that Jackson's parents landed at Charleston and reached the Waxhaws by the southern route. The same statement appears in a document, not in Jackson's hand, found in the Library of Congress collection of Jackson Manuscripts (CXVIII, 33). This gives an account of Jackson's father in Ireland and of his father's three brothers. After he became famous General Jackson from time to time was in receipt of genealogical information from persons claiming kinship. All such material examined by this writer seems warped to meet the aspirations of the authors. For example, *The Genealogy of the Jackson Family,* by Reverend Hugh Parks Jackson and others (1890), 6-11; also an engaging letter dated County of Down, Ireland, September 21, 1821, William M. McCully to "General Jackson near New Orleans, North America." (Library of Congress.)

Had the Jacksons landed at Charleston at any time between 1761 and 1775 their debarkation would have been noted in the records of His Majesty's Council for South Carolina, which are intact in the original manuscript in the office of the Historical Commission of South Carolina at Columbia. These list all immigrants passing through that port. The only member of the Waxhaw clan to which General Jackson was connected by blood or marriage thus shown is James Crow who disembarked a single man, was granted land in the Waxhaws in 1768, when Jackson was one year old, and married Grace Hutchinson, Jackson's aunt. Grace was the sixth Hutchinson sister to turn up in the Waxhaws. When she came is not known, though it is barely possible that she accompanied Jackson's parents in 1765.

This is negative evidence that the Jacksons came by the northern route, but it is practically conclusive and moreover reenforced by other circumstances. The Crawfords who, the widely copied Parton (I, 49) says, accompanied the Jacksons from Ireland, were born in␣Scotch-Irish dominated southeastern Pennsylvania, the sons of Colonel John Crawford, a native of Ayrshire, Scotland. (*Daughters of the American Revolution Magazine,* November, 1920, p. 640. The unnamed Crawford brother of this article is James who married General Jackson's aunt, Jennet Hutchinson in Pennsylvania.) Most of the Waxhaws was settled by Scotch-Irish who came the Pennsylvania route, many of them second generation Americans. After the Revolution when counties were organized in that part of South Carolina, the three in the Waxhaw region were named Lancaster, York and Chester after counties in Pennsylvania. See also: a letter, J. G. Wardlaw, York, South Carolina, to A. S. Salley, junior, May 20, 1922, private collection of Mr. Salley, Columbia, South Carolina; James D. Craig memoir, dated September 24, 1858, in Walter Clark Manuscripts, III, 332, North Carolina Historical Commission, Raleigh.

In view of the inaccuracies of the latter document, to which the writer adverts in Note No. 17 *post,* anything in it must be considered with caution. Yet it contains material worthy of belief as, for instance, the landing in Pennsylvania of the Jackson emigrants. Although the writer has refrained from using several details of the landing which are patently the result of poor memory on the part of old Mr. Craig or his informant, others which appear credible are incorporated as the best evidence on the subject extant.

The Craig Memoir states that the Jacksons "Landed at Caninigigo Pennsylvania & Jackson came Straight to the Carolinas." Mr. Craig's "Caninigigo" rather clearly refers to the Scotch-Irish settlements along Conowingo Creek, a tributary of the Susquehanna. The place of actual debarkation was probably Philadelphia, but possibly Port Deposit, Maryland, at the head of navigation of the shallow Susquehanna, a few miles below the mouth of Conowingo Creek. The place of embarkation—Larne, County Antrim—is "Learn" in the Craig manuscript.

[2] Craig Memoir, Walter Clark Manuscripts, III., 332, North Carolina Historical Commission, Raleigh.

[3] Reminiscence of William Allen, member of Congress from Ohio during the Jackson Administration, reporting a conversation with Jackson, from Augustus C. Buell, *A History of Andrew Jackson* (1904), I, 20.

[4] Craig Memoir, Walter Clark Manuscripts, III, 332, North Carolina Historical Commission, Raleigh.

[5] Thus she signed herself (June 1, 1774. See Deed Book H., p. 100, Lancaster County, South Carolina, records, Lancaster), but survives in the Waxhaw tradition and in print as Jane, although in several contemporary records the spelling is Jean. (S. H. Walkup, reprinted in *North Carolina University Magazine*, X, 225, and *Congressional Record*, June 18, 1926, p. 11582.)

[6] *The Daughters of the American Revolution Magazine*, November, 1920, p. 640, gives date of arrival of the three Crawford brothers in the Waxhaws as "about 1760." In 1763 Robert and Joseph Crawford bought the Crawford lands in the Waxhaws. (Deed Book 5, p. 215, Mecklenburg County records, Charlotte.) Joseph died shortly thereafter and James occupied the portion of the land on which General Jackson said he was born; at any rate, was reared, though James did not get a title to this land until September 12, 1768. Such delay in executing titles after possession was not unusual. The grant stated that he was then resident on the land and had "improved" it.

[7] Walkup, who correctly cites the land records.

[8] "Lessley" is their own spelling. John Lessley's land was ordered surveyed October 7, 1766, by the South Carolina authorities. (Manuscript, Journal of Council, Historical Commission of South Carolina, Columbia.) Settlers often occupied lands before they were surveyed. No record of land owned by Samuel Lessley has been found.

[9] The declaration of entry, by which Ewing initiated his claim to his land, is missing from the records, but he had made such declaration prior to April 20, 1766, when it was surveyed. (Land Grant Records, Office of Secretary of State, Raleigh.)

[10] *Ibid.*

[11] George Howe, D.D., *History of the Presbyterian Church in South Carolina* (1870), I, 289.

[12] Walter Clark Manuscripts, III, 331, North Carolina Historical Commission, Raleigh.

[13] Reminiscence of H. E. Coffey, Rock Hill (South Carolina) *Record*, August 19, 1920.

[14] The story of the temporary loss of the body of Andrew Jackson, senior, is unsupported by any contemporary documentary evidence that the writer has been able to discover, but it is supported by the uncontradicted and unanimous tradition of the locality. I have had it from collateral descendants of General Jackson, many of whom still reside in the Waxhaws. On October 8, 1931, the Fort Mill (South Carolina) *Times*, published a few miles from where the burial took place, reprinted an account of T. D. Faulkner, a third cousin of General Jackson, who died in 1916. Mr. Faulkner was born in 1825 and his grandparents may have attended the funeral. Mrs. Anne Hutchison Bigger, of Rock Hill, South Carolina, and others assure me of the existence of an account of the funeral written in the 1840's by Reece Massey from the recollections of persons who were present. Reece Massey was a distinguished local figure. His father, uncles and aunts went to school with General Jackson, and his grandparents, whose farm adjoined the Crawfords', attended the funeral. Though unable to find Mr. Massey's narrative, I feel that some day it will be publicly available.

[15] The location of the grave of Andrew Jackson, senior, is not known with assurance, but generations of old residents pointed to a brown stone, weather-worn to a knob about a foot high, as marking the burial place. In 1931 an inscribed boulder was ceremoniously dedicated to mark this spot definitely as Jackson's resting-place. According to published accounts of local origin (see Yorkville *Enquirer*, York, South Carolina, April 14, 1931), this ceremony originated with the visit in 1931 of an "unidentified stranger" carrying a broken piece of stone in a motor-car. He said he had brought it from Tennessee. Digging into the supposed grave another stone was found. The broken edge of the two fitted together. The conclusion is that some one, presumably General Jackson, had transported to Tennessee half of his father's gravestone. Some old residents of the Waxhaws with whom the writer has corresponded are skeptical of this form of "proof." Others whose veracity is unassailable have given me affidavits as to the visit of the stranger and the fitting of the stones together. In Tennessee the existence of such a stone is unknown to history.

[16] Andrew Jackson to James H. Witherspoon, August 11, 1824. *Correspondence of Andrew Jackson,* edited by John Spencer Bassett, III, 265. Circumstances surrounding this letter are mentioned in Note 17 following.

[17] Andrew Jackson has been accredited with eight birthplaces or one more than Homer. The controversy began in 1815, a few weeks after the Battle of New Orleans made him famous.

I shall dismiss without discussion the claims advanced in favor of Ireland, England, the high seas, York County, Pennsylvania; Augusta County, Virginia; Berkeley County, Virginia (now West Virginia); also the narratives, respectably sponsored, making, on one hand, his father a mulatto and his mother an army camp follower; and on the other hand his mother "the only child of John Vance (a corruption of de Valebus) who . . . claimed royal descent."

There remains the seasoned controversy as to whether Andrew Jackson was born in South Carolina or in North Carolina. He was born in South Carolina, a fact established by Crown authority fixing the limits of the North and South provinces which made the thirty-fifth parallel of latitude the boundary in the Waxhaws. To reach this parallel it was necessary first to run the boundary up in a northwesterly direction from the coast to it. This line was properly started in 1735. In 1737 a surveyor in the service of the provinces set out to complete it and thought he had done so. But he miscalculated and instead of driving his stake at the thirty-fifth parallel, where actually the boundary turned west, he drove his stake in a meadow about eleven miles south of the thirty-fifth parallel.

As the country filled up a guessed-at westward projection of a line from the stake was mistakenly thought to be the boundary. The brothers-in-law, James Crawford and George McKemey, got lands by North Carolina authority in the eleven-mile strip. In 1764 commissioners representing the two provinces came to the Waxhaws with surveyors to finish running the boundary. From a stake in the meadow they started the line westward. When they got to the Charleston-Salisbury post road, a mile south of James Crawford's house, they discovered the error and went no farther, but set a stake beside the road in the shade of a hickory tree and reported to the authorities. The matter was referred to London, and things became lively in the Waxhaws where the sovereignty of the eleven-mile strip was in contest between North Carolina and South Carolina. Law was on South Carolina's side. The land was legally hers. But possession was largely on North Carolina's side. Owing to the surveyor's blunder, North Carolina had made grants to settlers within the strip and taken other measures to establish her authority there.

In 1771 the King approved a compromise. South Carolina surrendered to North Carolina the eleven-mile strip in the Waxhaws, in exchange for which North Carolina surrendered to South Carolina about an equal amount of land west of the Catawba River. In 1772 this decision was carried into effect on the ground. The line of 1764, from the stake in the meadow to the stake under the hickory beside the road, was legalized, but not extended. At the stone the line turned north, following the windings of the highway north for about eight miles, to where this road cut across a corner of the Catawba Indian reservation.

As the McKemey house was on the east side of the road, this arrangement put it in North Carolina. The Crawford house, being on the west side of the road, landed in South Carolina. Thus both houses stood within shouting distance of the border for more than forty years when again the line was changed slightly. The shifting highway had proved an unsatisfactory boundary, and two states collaborated to fix the line without reference to the vagaries of the road. The conferences were long-drawn-out. Whether the Governor of South Carolina's quotable amenity to the Governor of North Carolina about its being a long time between refreshments hastened a conclusion is not known, but in 1813 the line, as it stands to-day, was determined. This left the McKemey house four hundred and seven yards over the border in North Carolina and the Crawford house a good half-mile in South Carolina. (For original documents on the boundary controversy see A. S. Salley, junior, *The Boundary Line between North Carolina and South Carolina* (1929), and William L. Saunders [Editor], *Colonial Records of North Carolina* (1887), V, xxxv *et seq*.)

North Carolina's claim to being the state of Andrew Jackson's nativity rests on the assumption that he was born in the McKemey house, although this house was not on North Carolina soil until Jackson was four years old. A North Carolina Chapter of the Daughters of the American Revolution has erected of the stones from a cabin that stood on McKemey's land a monument on that site which records that Jackson was born there. Two and a half miles away a South Carolina Chapter of the Daughters of the American Revolution has put up a conspicuous marker on the site of the James Crawford homestead. Between the merits of these opposed claims the historian must choose, though the choice does not affect the fact that both houses were in South Carolina at the time of Andrew

Jackson's birth. My choice is in favor of the Crawford place because Jackson said he was born there, and I think it more likely than not that he knew.

Nevertheless, the McKemey house claim is worthy of examination in some detail. As promulgated in 1858 by Samuel H. Walkup, a lawyer of Union County, North Carolina, in which the McKemey lands lie, it convinced James Parton when he visited the Waxhaws the year following in quest of material for his biography. If not the most accurate work of its kind, Parton's three volumes remain after seventy-five years the most readable and the most copiously copied of the many lives of General Jackson. The acceptance without investigation of Parton's conclusion has done much to give the McKemey claim the authority of fact.

Contrary to a wide-spread belief, which one finds even among some who have studied the subject, the McKemey claim did not originate with the labors of Mr. Walkup. He merely consolidated, in the form of a very respectable case, a body of hearsay that had been current in the Waxhaws for more than a generation. Two months after the Battle of New Orleans had made him famous there was a discussion in Charleston as to Jackson's birthplace. Colonel William Richardson Davie, who had known Jackson from childhood, being appealed to, affirmed a statement that "he is a native of Lancaster [District, now County] in this state." (Charleston *City Gazette and Commercial Daily Advertiser*, March 27, 1815.) This *may* mean that Davie believed him to have been born in the Crawford rather than the McKemey house which was then in North Carolina, and, in 1815, seems generally thought to have always been there.

In the autumn of 1815 the South Carolina Assembly formally acknowledged Jackson as a native son in a resolution of thanks for the victory at New Orleans. On February 9, 1816, Jackson expressed his appreciation in a letter to Governor Williams in which he said his pleasure was enhanced by the fact that the resolution came from "that state which gave me birth." (*Correspondence*, II, 229.) This is the earliest of a long series of statements in Jackson's own hand fixing his birthplace in South Carolina, though mindful that North Carolina had its claimants owing to the McKemey house tradition.

In 1817 Reid and Eaton's life of Jackson appeared. The writer has examined the opening chapters in the original manuscript. Jackson supervised the production of this pioneer biography and let stand the loose statement that he was born "about forty-five miles above Camden." This vagueness was one of the things that stimulated Mr. Walkup to his researches under the mistaken idea that Jackson was uncertain in his own mind as to his exact birthplace. In 1819 S. Putnam Waldo's *Memoirs of Andrew Jackson* came out, making the General a native of South Carolina. The statement prompted Thomas Watson of Baltimore to write Jackson asking if the statement were true, and Jackson replied under date of March 4, 1820, that it was. (For his letter see New York *Times*, November 4, 1922.)

In 1820 South Carolina began the compilation of a state map under the direction of Robert Mills, one of the eminent cartographers and engineers of the day. The contract for Lancaster District was sublet to J. Boykin, a native of the region. Present-day surveyors in the Waxhaws testify as to the fidelity of Mr. Boykin's lines, and tactical historians have found him fairly exact in locating Revolutionary battles and skirmishes. Boykin placed a star on his map to denote the James Crawford homestead as "Genl A. Jackson's Birth Place." The map was published in 1825 and Mills, who had fought under Jackson at New

Orleans, sent him a copy at the Hermitage. The reminiscent glow its perusal afforded is reflected in a warm letter of acknowledgment. "A view of the map pointing to the spot that gave me birth brings fresh to my memory many associations dear to my heart, many days pleasure with my juvenile companions; but alas most of them are gone to that bourne from which no one returns. . . . Most of the names of the places [plantations] are changed; all the old generation appears to have passed away. . . . The crossing of Waxhaw creek within one mile of which I was born, is still, however, I see, possessed by Mr. John Crawford, son of the owner (Robert) who lived there when I was growing up and at school. . . . From the accuracy with which this spot is marked on the map I conclude the whole must be correct." (Dated July 8, 1827. Private collection of Thompson D. Dimitry of New Orleans, a descendant of Mr. Mills.)

In 1824, in response to an inquiry from James H. Witherspoon, a prominent resident of Lancaster District, Jackson wrote: "I was born in So Carolina, as I have been told at the plantation whereon James Crawford lived about one mile from the Carolina road [crossing] of the Waxhaw Creek." (*Correspondence*, III, 265.)

None of these assertions by the General was published, however, and the Eaton biography, with the vague statement as to his place of birth, remained the account generally accepted and read. For this or some other reason the McKemey tradition quietly persisted. The first reference to it in print known to this writer appeared in 1824 in a brief note, signed "K," to the editor of the Columbia (South Carolina) *Telescope*, copied on November 24, 1824, by the Charleston *Courier*: "There has been much uncertainty in regard to General Jackson's birthplace; some asserting that he was born in North Carolina, others . . . that he was born in South Carolina, and others that he is a native of Ireland. I am glad that I have it in my power to settle this question. . . . After the death of his father, his mother . . . went to live with her brother-in-law, a Mr. McAmey. . . . General Jackson was born at the house of Mr. McAmey, and therefore in the State of North Carolina. When he was about six weeks old his mother removed with him to the house of Mr. James Crawford, another brother-in-law, on the South Carolina side of the road."

The death of General Jackson in 1845 revived interest in the question, and in a Fourth-of-July oration that year Mr. Walkup obtained the signed statements of two aged and respectable residents of the Waxhaws to support his position. Benjamin Massey declared that "about the year 1822" he had heard Mrs. Sarah Lathan say that Jackson was born at the McKemey house and that, as a child of seven, she was present at the birth. Sarah Lathan was a first cousin of General Jackson, her mother, Sarah Hutchinson Lessley, being Jackson's aunt. The other statement was by John Carnes who said he had often heard Mrs. Sarah Hutchinson Lessley say that Jackson was born at McKemey's.

Thirteen years later, in 1858, a Virginia claim to the nativity of Jackson, brought forth the now celebrated "Walkup evidence," to which, despite voluminous subsequent controversy and extravagant claims pro and con, nothing material has been added. It was published originally in a weekly newspaper, the *North Carolina Argus* (Wadesboro), September 23, 1858. Later it appeared as a pamphlet. The most available reprints appear in the *North Carolina University Magazine*, X, 225-44, and the *Congressional Record* for June 18, 1926, pp. 11535-40. From the ambiguities of Reid and Eaton's and other biographies Mr. Walkup concluded that "there was no settled opinion by General Jackson himself of the place of his birth. . . . He just supposed that he was born at Crawford's place . . . because his earliest associations were connected with it. . . . I think it can be as clearly demonstrated as any such thing can be at this distance of time that Gen. Jackson . . . was born at the house of George McKemey or McCamie." In the light of evidence then publicly known, this was a reasonable assumption, and not a reckless claim for the testimony Mr. Walkup had to offer.

This testimony consisted of written statements by six persons (including the Massey and Carnes statements of 1845) that they had heard Sarah Lessley, or her daughter Sarah Lathan, say that they knew Jackson was born at McKemey's because they were present. One of Mrs. Lathan's sons and two of her nephews, second cousins therefore of General Jackson, were among those so testifying. All had to remember rather a long way back for Mrs. Lathan had then been dead thirty years and Mrs. Lessley fifty years. The composite story of the six statements is this: After the death of Andrew Jackson, senior, the widow started from the Twelve Mile Creek place to James Crawford's to make her home, but at the McKemey house, two and a half miles short of her destination, was taken with pains of labor. In the nighttime Sarah Lessley, Mrs. Jackson's sister and a midwife, was sent for. She went, taking her seven-year-old daughter along, and assisted at the birth.

Additionally there were seven written statements of old persons who had heard it said on no named authority that Jackson was born at McKemey's, and one statement to the effect that the birthplace "has always been disputed" by partizans of the Crawford and McKemey sites.

I am unable to dismiss this evidence as cavalierly as some modern proponents of the Crawford claim are inclined to do, but this is true: it presents one side of the case, argued in professional fashion by a lawyer. If the McKemey claim had "always" been disputed, as one of Mr. Walkup's witnesses admits, there must have been some basis in local evidence for the Crawford pretensions. But unfortunately no one reduced this to writing, or rounded it out in the form of a case. Whereas the McKemey claim had the benefit of an energetic and skilled advocate who traveled about gathering depositions, prompting witnesses, and, in at least one instance amplifying and correcting testimony when it presented demonstrable errors in detail which, if given to the public, might have impaired belief in the whole.

I do not challenge the sincerity of Mr. Walkup's research, notwithstanding a perusal of his papers in the original manuscript (Walter Clark Manuscripts, III, North Carolina Historical Commission, Raleigh) suggests that at times his method was that of a barrister rather than a historian. The affidavit of James Faulkner, Jackson's cousin, was one of the most important offered. The published affidavit is one of three made by Mr. Faulkner that are preserved in the manuscripts. All appear in the hand of Mr. Walkup, though signed by Mr. Faulkner and sworn to. The first deposition, dated August 26, 1858, contains several small errors, due no doubt to slips of memory, and corrected with a different pen and ink by Mr. Walkup. The deposition published also bears the date of August 26, 1858, but as a matter of fact could not have been written earlier than September sixth, because it appears on the same four-page folio with two other depositions bearing date of September sixth, and was unmistakably written *after* these depositions were. The published Faulkner declaration is a recasting of the original with corrections. A third Faulkner declaration, dated

September fifteenth, is more positive on some points than the published statement.

Another thing one hears much about is the "Craig evidence" in favor of the McKemey contention. This was first mentioned by Parton (I, 55) who says Mr. Craig "remembers hearing old James Faulkner [father of James Faulkner of the preceding paragraph] say that, while sleeping with Andrew Jackson in the McKemey house Andrew told him that he was born in that house." What old Mr. Craig really said in the letter which Parton perused was that Faulkner "Slept with Andrew. . . . A Lad about 14 years old & understood"—not understood Jackson to say—"he was Born in that house." (Walter Clark Manuscripts, III, 332. North Carolina Historical Commission, Raleigh.)

The origin of the Craig evidence is this. When Mr. Walkup was gathering his data he wrote to James D. Craig who had moved to Mississippi twenty years before. Mr. Craig's reply came too late for inclusion in the publication in the *North Carolina Argus*, but Walkup showed it to Parton whose misquotation gave it an importance that has grown with the years until it has been represented as settling the question absolutely by supplying what the Walkup evidence lacks to make out a prima-facie case. "The weakness in the [Walkup] case," writes Dr. Archibald Henderson of the University of North Carolina (Raleigh *News and Observer*, October 3, 1926), "inhered in the fact that the affidavits set forth not the statements of eye-witnesses . . . of Jackson's birth but statements of neighbors who heard the narrations of alleged eye-witnesses." The Craig evidence, continues Doctor Henderson, supplies this deficiency in a manner "unimpeachable." During the campaign of 1828 when the born-in-Ireland, the negro-father and other stories were being circulated against the General, Mr. Craig, at the request of a Jackson manager in Ohio, gathered certain affidavits as to Jackson's parentage and place of birth, which was designated as the McKemey house. The affidavits were lost and no one has been found who ever saw any scrap of them. Thirty years later Mr. Craig undertook to repeat to Mr. Walkup the substance of the lost affidavits and succeeded, according to Doctor Henderson, in recalling "an exact summary" of the originals.

If this is true, the originals were almost worthless because the 1858 summary contains so many grotesque, if entirely unintentional, misstatements of known facts. James Faulkner, who is reported to have slept with Andrew, is made to say that Jackson's father arrived in the Waxhaws with "2 Daughters & Settld in No Caroling 12 Mile Creek Afterwards his 2 Daughters Married A Lassely & James Crawford." Another affidavit gives an account of the military service of Andrew Jackson and his two brothers in the Revolutionary War that is inaccurate in almost every particular. In a third affidavit "Mrs. Mary Cowsar An Aged Lady I believe Daughter of Magor [Robert] Crawford" [incorrect] says she called at the McKemey house the morning Andrew was born and "Before . . . [he] was Dressed." This is the eye-witness testimony that is supposed to clinch everything. Such is the Craig evidence, often alluded to but never published, except such excerpts as support the particular contention under review.

Between 1922 and 1928 the subject of Jackson's birthplace was periodically discussed in the House of Representatives in connection with the compilation of the *Biographical Dictionary of the American Congress*. Representative William F. Stevenson, of South Carolina, leaning heavily upon the researches of A. S. Salley, junior, for twenty-seven years secretary of the Historical Commission of South Carolina, and the late Representative William C. Hammer, of North

Carolina, were the opposing champions. While rather declamatory their speeches are repositories of valuable evidence on both sides. (*Congressional Record*, February 23, 1922, p. 3395; June 18, 1926, p. 11534; May 24, 1928, p. 10116; July 2, 1928, p. 11312.)

My opinion is that neither party has proved its case, but that the Crawford house has a little the better of it on Jackson's own testimony. Jackson became a conscious performer before the glass of history. After the Battle of New Orleans he began filing away papers endorsed "for the historian." He knew of this dispute. The boundary question agitating the Waxhaws during his childhood, I think, should have tended to fix in his mind his exact birthplace. When he wrote that he had been told that he was born at Crawford's, I think that statement clearly represented his own belief in the matter, attained after weighing the evidence. Mr. Walkup has a case—for which he claimed less than his modern followers—but I do not think that this case, resting as it does on the distant recollection of conversations with two aged women, one of them a child of seven when the event took place, is sufficient to refute Jackson himself.

[18] Deed Book XX, 21, Mecklenburg County records, Charlotte. Jackson owned this property until after his marriage in Tennessee, selling it in 1793. (Deeds, Book D, old, p. 227, Lancaster County records, Lancaster.)

[19] Some particulars of this boundary dispute, as it concerns the controversy over the state of Jackson's nativity given in Note No. 17 *ante*.

[20] Reminiscences of Susan Smart Alexander, *National Intelligencer*, August 1, 1845.

[21] Howe, I, 416.

[22] Buell, I, 37.

[23] John Reid Manuscript, p. 1, Tennessee Historical Society, Nashville. John Reid, Jackson's aide-de-camp in the War of 1812, began a life of his chief immediately thereafter. With about a third of the work completed, Reid died and John Henry Eaton finished the book which was published under their joint authorship in 1817. In 1823 Eaton brought the work to date and Reid's name was dropped. Two manuscript copies of Reid's effort exist. One is in the Tennessee Historical Society at Nashville and one in the Library of Congress. The Nashville copy seems to be the first draft. I presume that Jackson influenced several changes that appear in the printed text in the interest of accuracy and policy.

[24] Charles C. Royce and Cyrus Thomas, "Indian Land Cessions in the United States," *Eighteenth Annual Report*, Bureau of American Ethnology (1899), II, 632.

[25] Sydney George Fisher, *Men, Women & Manners in Colonial Times* (1898), II, 327.

[26] Revolutionary Accounts, Audited, No. 1592, South Carolina archives, Historical Commission of South Carolina, Columbia.

[27] Buell, I, 37, 38.

[28] No autograph of James Crawford can be found. The name is spelled Crawford in these pages to avoid confusion, inasmuch as his brother and nephews invariably, and his sons usually, used that form. In those days it was not a mark of illiteracy, as now understood, for one to vary the orthography of one's name. In this book the writer has endeavored to spell the name of persons as the individuals themselves usually wrote them which explains numerous departures from other printed texts. Concerning persons who, like George McKemey,

could not write, I have made arbitrary decisions, in his case taking the spelling that appears on his tombstone in the Waxhaw churchyard.

[29] Buell, I, 38. William Allen's reminiscence, quoted by Buell, is corroborated by local tradition.

CHAPTER II

[1] Walter Clark Manuscripts, III, 318, North Carolina Historical Commission, Raleigh.
[2] Parton, I, 64.
[3] *Ibid.*
[4] *Correspondence* I, 2. The original in the Library of Congress has been called the earliest known example of Jackson's handwriting. It is not in Jackson's hand.
[5] Reid and Eaton, *The Life of Andrew Jackson* (1817), 11.
[6] Unpublished researches among Revolutionary manuscripts by A. S. Salley, junior, secretary of the Historical Commission of South Carolina.
[7] Reid and Eaton, *The Life of Andrew Jackson* (1817), 11.
[8] David Ramsay, M. D., *The History of South Carolina* (1809), I, 367.
[9] Revolutionary Accounts, Audited, No. 1592, South Carolina archives, Historical Commission of South Carolina, Columbia.
[10] Buell, I, 52.
[11] Revolutionary Accounts, Audited, No. 1592, South Carolina archives, Historical Commission of South Carolina, Columbia.
[12] *Ibid.*, Nos. 1587, 1589 and 1594; and Jackson to James H. Witherspoon, August 11, 1824, *Correspondence,* III, 265.
[13] Parton, I, 73. See also reminiscences of Susan Smart Alexander in *National Intelligencer*, August 1 and 29, 1845. Parton is in error calling her Mrs. Smart. Smart was her maiden name. I am unable to reconcile Mrs. Alexander's statement in the *Intelligencer* that Mrs. Jackson and her two sons were at her home in August, when it is known that the boys were in the field with Davie most of that month, and Jackson's own statement is that the flight into North Carolina took place in September. I, therefore, accept Parton's version of her story which places her meeting with Jackson in September.
[14] Banastre Tarleton, *Campaigns of 1780-1781 in the Southern Provinces* (1787), 186.
[15] Amos Kendall, *Life of Andrew Jackson* (1843), 19.
[16] Every published reference to this action that the writer has seen calls it Wahab skirmish and similarly misspells the name of Captain Wauchope who, incidentally, was the paternal grandfather of S. H. Walkup of "Walkup evidence" renown (Note No. 17, Chapter I). See S. H. Walkup to David L. Swain, September 25, 1857, Swain Manuscripts, North Carolina Historical Commission, Raleigh, and Deed Book XI, 112-13, Mecklenburg County records, Charlotte.
[17] An old but undated clipping from the Charlotte (North Carolina) *Observer*, in the collection of Waxhaw memorabilia of Mrs. Anne Hutchinson Bigger of Rock Hill, South Carolina.
[18] Revolutionary Accounts, Audited, No. 1592, South Carolina archives, Historical Commission of South Carolina, Columbia.
[19] A manuscript account among the Jackson Papers, Library of Congress, apparently prepared by Amos Kendall for his biography from conversations with Jackson. See also: Kendall, 45; Buell, I, 52; Parton, I, 86.

[20] Reid Manuscript, 5, Tennessee Historical Society, Nashville; Parton, I, 87; Reid and Eaton, 12.

[21] Jackson to Amos Kendall, May 15, 1843, collection of Thomas F. Madigan, New York City; Parton, I, 89.

[22] *Correspondence,* I, 2. The original in Jackson's hand (Library of Congress) is dated "April 1781," but apparently was written in 1843, for Kendall's uncompleted biography.

[23] W. H. Sparks, *The Memories of Fifty Years* (1870), 147. I prefer this version of Elizabeth Jackson's last words to her son because they sound more natural than in the better known account of Jackson's godson, Thomas Butler (Buell, I, 56). Colonel Sparks knew Jackson well and had no ax to grind. His book is filled with the solecisms of sincerity and an unrefreshed memory, but is no less valuable on that account. He has Jackson parting from his mother after the war when he left to practise law. But the substance of her words is identical with that of Butler, who allocates them correctly and improves their literary quality.

[24] Jackson to James H. Witherspoon, August 11, 1824, *Correspondence,* III, 265. Governor's Gate was probably the gate to the avenue of Belvedere plantation, which one time had been the home of the governors of South Carolina. Forty-three years after his mother's death, Jackson made an unsuccessful attempt to locate her grave.

[25] Buell, I, 56.

CHAPTER III

[1] Revolutionary Accounts, Audited, No. 1594, South Carolina Historical Commission, Columbia. The official record of this appraisal represents the earliest known example of the handwriting of Andrew Jackson, then fifteen years old.

[2] *Ibid.*

[3] Unpublished researches from Revolutionary Manuscripts of A. S. Salley, junior, secretary of South Carolina Historical Commission.

[4] Revolutionary Accounts, Audited, South Carolina Historical Commission, Columbia.

[5] Buell, I, 63; Parton, I, 96. The report mentioned by Parton and disputed by Buell, that Jackson challenged Galbraith to a duel is supported by local tradition.

[6] Buell, I, 56.

[7] I fix the time of year by the fact that Jackson was there for the racing; the year itself by the fact that in the spring of 1782 and 1784 Jackson appears otherwise engaged at home.

[8] Kendall, 68, whose account of Jackson's early life is based on conversations with the subject of his memoir. A. S. Salley, junior, secretary of the Historical Commission of South Carolina, whose opinions I respect, says no Charleston refugees went to the Waxhaws.

[9] Johann David Schoepf, *Travels in the Confederation* (1785), English translation (1911), 167-68.

[10] John B. Irving, *The South Carolina Jockey Club* (1857), 11.

[11] *Ibid.,* 20, 42.

[12] *Ibid.,* 45.

[13] *Cabinet and Talisman* (1829), 4. Quoted from Parton, I, 98.

[14] Reminiscences of Susan Smart Alexander, *National Intelligencer,* August 1, 1845.

[15] Anne Hutchinson Bigger of Rock Hill, South Carolina, to the writer, communicating a local tradition. The Massey farm adjoined Major Crawford's.

[16] Revolutionary Accounts, Audited, No. 1594, South Carolina Historical Commission, Columbia. The date of the appraisal, December 4, 1784, fixes Jackson's departure at a date later than has been given hitherto.

[17] An old clipping in the scrap-book of Dr. William A. Pressly of Rock Hill, South Carolina, quotes a letter written by Stephen Decatur Miller, former United States Senator, Governor of South Carolina, and a friend of Jackson, as authority for the romance with Major Crawford's daughter who later married Dr. Samuel Dunlap.

[18] Parton, I, 104.

[19] Mrs. Anne (Nancy) Jarret Rutherford, from Augustus C. Buell, *A History of Andrew Jackson* (1904), I, 68.

[20] Rowan County Court Minute Book 1785-86.

[21] Parton, I, 107, whose authorities, withheld at their request, were Misses Christine and Maria Howard and their mother, the latter being present. For this and certain other information in this chapter, I am indebted to Mr. Walter Murphy, of Salisbury, a nephew, three generations removed, of Jackson's preceptor, Colonel John Stokes.

[22] Anson County (North Carolina) Records, Wadesborough, from S. G. Heiskell, *Andrew Jackson and Early Tennessee History,* I, 428.

[23] Buell, I, 68.

[24] Malter Murphy, of Salisbury, North Carolina, and Miss Katherine Hoskins, Summerfield, North Carolina, to the writer; Bassett, I, 13; Dr. Archibald Henderson in Raleigh *News and Observer,* October 17, 1926.

[25] Miss Katherine Hoskins, of Summerfield, North Carolina, a student of local history, to the writer, September 23, 1931.

[26] *Ibid.* Miss Hoskins's researches have made her familiar with the character of McNairy whom she admires. She believes Jackson to have been the inspiration of their decision to go West.

[27] *State Records of North Carolina,* XX, 270.

[28] The regular course would have been for the Legislature to have named the attorney-general, as Parton implies that it did by naming Jackson before he crossed the mountains. Jackson received his first legislative appointment to that office in 1789 (*State Records,* XXI, 403), which has led some to assume that he did not reach Nashville until then. But McNairy first appointed him to the office in November, 1788, a few days after their arrival in Nashville (*Ibid.,* XXI, 637).

CHAPTER IV

[1] Dr. Archibald Henderson, "Jackson's Loose Living Common Sin of the Period," Raleigh (North Carolina) *News and Observer,* October 17, 1926.

[2] *Correspondence,* I, 5.

[3] Henderson, *op. cit.*

[4] John Allison, *Dropped Stitches in Tennessee History* (1897), 8.

[5] Minute Book No. 1 in the Davidson County archives supports the generally accepted statement that Judge McNairy's first court was held there in January,

1789. *State Records of North Carolina,* XXI, 637, disclose that court was held in November, 1788, and that Jackson was paid for his services as prosecutor. *The American Historical Magazine* VIII, 294, reproduces the indictment in November, 1788, of George Gibson who, according to evidence presented by Jackson, "feloniously and Burglarously did Break and enter" William Barr's house and "steal take and carry away one Bever Skin."

[6] Parton, I, 135.

[7] Ancestry of John and Rachel Stockley Donelson derived mainly from unpublished studies of Miss Butler Chancellor, of Washington, D. C., a great-niece of Rachel Donelson Jackson. Her work is based on original documents in Maryland and Virginia county archives.

[8] Spelled Caffrey by some of his present-day descendants in Louisiana.

[9] The circumstances of Colonel Donelson's decision to go to the Cumberland, his short stay there and later removal to Kentucky, are derived from unpublished studies from original documents by Dr. William A. Provine, secretary of the Tennessee Historical Society. These researches, generously placed at the author's disposal, correct practically everything previously written on the subject, notably A. W. Putnam's widely copied *History of Middle Tennessee* (1859). Putnam's book is very valuable, but too eulogistic of the Robertson and Donelson families. The author disregarded fact to make Donelson a permanent settler in 1780.

[10] From a copy of Donelson's journal, contemporary or nearly so, Tennessee Historical Society, Nashville. This copy has generally been mistaken for the original, only four pages of which exist. These are in the private collection of John Donelson, of Nashville.

[11] Mary Donelson Wilcox in *Leslie's Weekly*, quoted from Heiskell, III, 279.

[12] See Note 9 *ante*.

[13] Jackson Manuscripts, Library of Congress. The entry was made April 6, 1784.

[14] Statement of John Overton *United States Telegraph,* June 22, 1827. The *Telegraph* article, referred to frequently in the documentation of this chapter and the next, was compiled by a committee of Jackson's friends in answer to attacks on Mrs. Jackson's character by partizans of John Quincy Adams in the presidential campaign of 1828. It was widely copied and later issued as a pamphlet. Although a campaign document, and susceptible of refutation in some of its details (for one thing the contributors wrote from memory after a lapse of thirty-seven years), it is much more worthy of belief on the whole than the literature to which it is a reply. Some of the contributors, such as Judge McNairy, were then opposed to Jackson, but had the grace to speak in defense of his wife.

[15] Statement of Elizabeth Craighead, *ibid*.

[16] Mary Donelson Wilcox, *op. cit.*

[17] Statement of John McGinnis, *United States Telegraph,* June 22, 1827.

[18] Statement of Elizabeth Craighead, *ibid*.

[19] Statement of George L. Davidson, Parton, I, 168.

[20] Dr. W. A. Provine, secretary of the Tennessee Historical Society, to the writer.

[21] Statement of John Overton, *op. cit.*

[22] *Ibid*. "*At length* I communicated to Mr. Jackson the unpleasant situation." Overton's words thus indicate that it was not done *at once*. His actual apprizal of Jackson of the lay of the land will be reached in the logical course of the narrative.

[23] John W. Monette, *History of the Discovery and Settlement of the Valley of the Mississippi* (1846), II, 16.

[24] Kendall, 90.

[25] February 13, 1789, *Correspondence*, I, 7.

[26] John Haywood, *Civil and Political History of the State of Tennessee* (1823), reprint of 1915, p. 251.

[27] Smith to Miró, March 11, 1789, Papeles de Cuba, Legajo 196. Photostatic copy in Lawson McGhee Library, Knoxville, Tennessee. Original in Spanish archives, Seville, Spain.

[28] Robertson to Miró, February 18, 1789, *ibid.*, 41.

[29] Dispatch dated April 23, 1789, quoted from Charles E. Gayarré, *History of Louisiana*, II, 262.

[30] Miró to Smith, April 20, 1789, Draper Manuscripts, State Historical Society of Wisconsin, Madison.

[31] Haywood, 256.

[32] *Ibid.*, 257.

[33] *Ibid.*, 258.

[34] Jackson apparently started for Natchez shortly after the close of the October, 1789, term of court, which Minute Book No. 1, pp. 318-32, shows he attended at Nashville. A marginal note on page 8 of the Reid Manuscript (Tennessee Historical Society copy) reading, "1789 went to Natz," suggests that the author may have intended to expand the theme. No mention of the journey, or for that matter any journey of Jackson to Natchez, prior to 1813, appears in Reid and Eaton's biography, however.

[35] Dated March 14, 1790, *Correspondence*, I, 8.

[36] W. H. Sparks, *Memories of Fifty Years* (1870), 151.

[37] *Ibid.*, 149.

[38] Dated November 8, 1790, *Correspondence*, I, 9.

[39] Dated February 26, 1791, private collection of Andrew Jackson IV.

[40] Robertson to Gayoso, May 17, 1790, Papeles de Cuba, Legajo 203. Photostatic copy in Lawson McGhee Library, Knoxville. Original in Spanish archives, Seville.

[41] In the Jackson Manuscripts, Library of Congress, is a bill from Melling Woolley, a Natchez merchant, to Jackson, chiefly for liquor, totaling two hundred and thirty-four dollars and one cent, dated "July 1790." These purchases may have been made during the earlier visit, or may have been ordered by letter. The rapidity of Jackson's movements constantly astonishes the researcher, but I do not believe he could have left Nashville as late as May 17, 1790, and returned in time to have "eloped" with Mrs. Robards from Mercer County, Kentucky, on July first. In 1793 this "elopement" was proved in court. It took place some time in July, though possibly not on July first. Jackson's presence in Nashville on July fourteenth, however, is established by Minute Book No. 1 of the Davidson County Court, p. 373.

[42] Statement of John Overton, *op. cit.*

[43] Mary Donelson Wilcox, *op. cit.*

[44] Statement of Thomas Crutcher, *United States Telegraph*, March 28, 1828.

[45] The whereabouts of the original of the court record of the Robards divorce is unknown. Some time since 1891 it has been abstracted from the court-house files at Harrodsburg (modern spelling), and C. E. Rankin, a local attorney, informs the writer that "I think some historical crank is responsible." In 1891 it

was there, however, and was copied by a correspondent of the St. Louis *Post-Dispatch*. From this transcription the excerpt quoted in the text is taken. The *Dispatch* article is reproduced in Thomas E. Watson's *Life of Andrew Jackson* (1912), a work of low values, so hostile to Jackson as to impair confidence in almost anything it contains. I have been able, however, to corroborate the essential particulars of the *Dispatch* copy by other testimony, practically all from sources friendly to Jackson, and entertain no doubt but that the *Dispatch* copy is a faithful reproduction of the originals, possibly the only one in existence. Suffice to note in this place that Mary Donelson Wilcox (*op. cit.*) mentions Jackson's presence in Kentucky at this time, and also Robards's formal allegation that his wife "had eloped and was cohabiting adulterously with one A. Jackson." Mrs. Wilcox is mistaken in her suggestion that Jackson's name appeared in the documentary record, however.

CHAPTER V

[1] Robertson to Miró, September 2, 1789, *Mississippi Valley Historical Review*, XII, 171.
[2] Jackson Manuscripts, Library of Congress.
[3] *Ibid.*, January 15, 1791.
[4] Jo C. Guild, *Old Times in Tennessee* (1878), 61.
[5] Haywood, 340.
[6] Statement of John Overton, *United States Telegraph*, June 22, 1827. Overton, who omits a great deal, does not mention the Kentucky trip, but he gives Rachel's residence during the summer of 1790 as at the Hays house.
[7] The universal assumption, that Rachel's journey under Jackson's protection to Natchez in 1791 constituted the grounds upon which Robards obtained his divorce, is untenable because this journey did not take place until after the passage by the Virginia Legislature of the enabling act under which the action for divorce was instituted.
[8] Parton, I, 168.
[9] James L. Armstrong, *General Jackson's Juvenile Indiscretions* (1832), 4.
[10] Statements of Thomas Crutcher and John Overton, *United States Telegraph*, June 22, 1827.
[11] Statement of Overton, *op. cit.*
[12] *Ibid.*
[13] *Ibid.*, Thomas Crutcher (*op. cit.*) fixes the start in December, 1790, or January, 1791. Mary Donelson Wilcox (*op. cit.*) says December. Overton is more nearly right. From a check of evidence of Jackson's known presence in Nashville, it appears that the journey could only have been made between January twentieth and April twelfth, or April eighteenth and July twelfth, 1791. (*Correspondence*, I, 9; Davidson County Court Minute Book No. 1, p. 415; *Correspondence*, I, 11; Minute Book No. 1, p. 432.) My opinion is that they departed in January.
[14] Virginia *House Journal* (1790), 123, 127, 147; *Senate Journal*, 53, 62, 72. In 1827 James Breckenridge, a member of the Legislature in 1790, declared he had voted for the bill under the impression that Mrs. Robards would establish her innocence in court. (*United States Telegraph*, June 22, 1827.)
[15] *Acts Passed at a General Assembly of the Commonwealth of Virginia* (1790), 155.

[16] Robards to Hays, January 10, 1791. Jackson Manuscripts, Library of Congress.

[17] Robards wrote from Mercer County, Kentucky, twenty-one days after the Virginia Assembly had passed the enabling act, but owing to the state of the roads in winter may not have received news of it. But as the Legislature was to adjourn on December thirty-first, he knew his petition had been acted on one way or another, and apparently was confident that action had been favorable.

[18] Mary Donelson Wilcox (*op. cit.*).

[19] *Ibid.*

[20] *Ibid.*

[21] In 1922 James Payne Green, eighty-six years old, a graduate of Yale in 1857 and a great-grandson of Thomas M. Green, junior, gave the late S. G. Heiskell, of Knoxville, Tennessee, a written statement of what had come down to him about Jackson's marriage. He said that T. M. Green, junior, performed the ceremony (Knoxville *Sentinel*, November 26, 1922). James Payne Green then lived at Gayoso, the house built by Gayoso de Lemos and owned by Abner Green during Rachel's stay in the Natchez district before her marriage. No documentary record of the marriage has ever been found though in 1827 when it became an issue in the presidential campaign Jackson's confidant, W. B. Lewis, went to Natchez presumably for that purpose.

Another tradition of the Green family is that before the marriage, Rachel obtained a divorce from the Spanish authorities. (Sparks, 151. Mr. Sparks married the youngest daughter of Abner Green.) This seems impossible for two reasons: the extreme difficulty of obtaining divorces under Spanish law and that, if true, there would have been no need two years later for a second ceremony. When Robards finally decided to complete his divorce transaction, Rachel could have exhibited her Spanish papers in proof of the fact that she had not been Robards's wife for two years.

In 1785 the Greens had espoused the cause of Georgia, which claimed the Natchez territory and attempted to exercise sovereignty there by forming the district into a county called Bourbon and appointing magistrates and a register of probates. Abner Green accepted the latter office and both T. M. Green, senior, and junior, were magistrates. The elder Green got in jail for his zeal and was obliged to transfer his property to his sons. In 1788 Georgia abandoned the conquest which terminated the official powers of the Greens. Therefore, when Jackson was married in 1791, Green was not a magistrate, but, as the frontier viewed such matters, that fact alone would not have placed the ceremony outside the pale. It sometimes happened that in frontier communities there was no one authorized by the letter of the law to perform marriages. In such cases a ceremony before any person of T. M. Green's standing would have been recognized by a court of review, in case no legal impediment to the union existed. Springfield, the house in which the marriage took place, is still standing.

[22] *Op. cit.* Mrs. Wilcox is in all probability mistaken, as I can not imagine that the fruitless quest made in 1827 for documentary evidence of the ceremony failed to include an examination of church records.

[23] George Cockran to Jackson, with an enclosure to Mrs. Jackson; undated, but filled with papers for 1796 in Jackson Papers, Library of Congress.

[24] Kendall, 94.

[25] Jackson Papers, January 1, 1792, Library of Congress.

[26] On February 23, 1792, the two hundred acres on Twelve Mile Creek in the

Waxhaws, where Andrew Jackson's father had established the family on his arrival from Ireland in 1765, were sold possibly to help meet the expenses of establishing Rachel at Poplar Grove.

[27] Now called Hadley's Bend.

[28] Parton, I, 136.

[29] *Ibid.*, I, 138.

[30] Dated November 6, 1893, private collection of Andrew Jackson IV.

[31] Jackson to Jesse Wilkinson, January 6, 1797, refers to the sale of land in Sumner County which he had never seen. Private collection of S. P. Hessel, Woodmere, Long Island, New York.

[32] January 30, 1793, *Correspondence,* I, 12.

[33] *American State Papers, Indian Affairs,* I, 44; Charles C. Royce, "The Cherokee Nation of Indians," in *Fifth Annual Report,* Bureau of American Ethnology (1887), 148-71.

[34] Haywood, 380.

[35] The Knoxville *Gazette,* September 14, 1793, contains an account of an attack on nearby Henry's Station in which an Andrew Jackson distinguished himself. Later writers have assumed that this was the Andrew Jackson who forms the subject of this book. Actually he was another man of the same name.

[36] Parton, I, 146; Watson, 74; Blount's draft, dated June 11, 1796, Jackson Papers, Library of Congress.

[37] Statement of John Overton, *United States Telegraph,* June 22, 1827.

[38] *Ibid.*

[39] Statements of John Overton, Sally Smith, Thomas Crutcher, Judge John McNairy, Elizabeth Craighead, the latter a sister of Senator Brown, Robards's attorney, *ibid.*

[40] *United States Telegraph,* June 27, 1827. This defense of Jackson, filling ten columns, consisted of the statements of a number of persons, several of which have been referred to in foregoing notes, with explanatory remarks by a committee of eighteen of the most prominent men in the Nashville district—not all of them blind followers of Jackson—who deplored the level to which some of Mr. Adams's protagonists had brought the campaign. The quotation referred to is from the committee's remarks.

[41] Court record, from Watson, 73. Why did Robards wait two years before taking action under the Legislature's enabling act? Why did he, by his silence if nothing more, countenance the false report of a divorce in 1791? No one knows, though the suppositions are not creditable to Robards. The accepted theory, however, that the consequences of the false report provided Robards with grounds to obtain his divorce—grounds he may have lacked when he appealed to the Legislature—is unsupportable. The acts established in court as cause for the divorce antedated, as was necessary under the law, the enabling act of December 20, 1790. The fact that Robards remarried shortly after the divorce may be the key to the riddle, supposing that he instituted the court action with that in view. His second marriage was happy and he had no part in the politically inspired attacks on Mrs. Jackson's name in 1827.

[42] Court record, *ibid.,* 73.

[43] Committee report, *United States Telegraph,* June 22, 1827.

[44] Tennessee State Library, Nashville. It is an interesting, though probably not significant, fact that during this trying period when Overton and Jackson were so closely associated, Robards was a client of Overton. Robards's appre-

hensions of a division of his Cumberland property in 1791 had been without basis. But on February 19, 1794, less than a month after Jackson's remarriage, Robards gave Overton power of attorney to dispose of his Cumberland holdings. Acting under this authority, Overton sold the farm to John Shannon on March seventeenth (Deed Book D, 42; Deed Book C, 277, Davidson County records). Two years later Jackson bought the place of Shannon. It adjoined the property later known as the Hermitage.

[45] Marriage Records, 1789-94, Davidson County records, Nashville. Thomas Crutcher (*United States Telegraph,* June 22, 1827) says the ceremony was performed January seventeenth. According to a local tradition Reverend Thomas B. Craighead officiated, but his widow does not mention this in her statement published in 1827 (*United States Telegraph,* June 22).

[46] March 8, 1795, *Correspondence,* I, 13.

[47] Jackson to Overton, June 19, 1795, *ibid.,* I, 14.

[48] Jackson-Allison "Indenture," June 11, 1796, *ibid.,* I, 21; Jackson to Overton June 9, 1795, *ibid.,* I, 14; Parton, I, 242.

[49] Jackson to James Jackson, August 25, 1819, *Correspondence,* II, 427.

[50] Jackson's "Account of Expences May and August 1795," *ibid.,* I, 15.

[51] Jackson to Overton, June 9, 1795, *ibid.,* I, 14.

[52] James Grant to Jackson, August 13, 1795, private collection of Andrew Jackson IV.

[53] Jackson to Nathaniel Macon, October 4, 1795, *Correspondence,* I, 17.

[54] Mark Mitchell to Jackson, November 21, 1795, Library of Congress.

[55] J. G. M. Ramsey, *Annals of Tennessee* (1853), 655.

[56] Jackson to James Jackson, August 25, 1819, *Correspondence,* II, 427.

CHAPTER VI

[1] Parton, I, 196.

[2] Andrew Jackson to Hays, December 6, 1796, collection of Thomas Madigan, New York City.

[3] Jackson to Hays, December 16, 1796, Library of Congress.

[4] Parton, I, 214.

[5] Jackson to John Sevier, January 18, 1797, *Correspondence,* I, 27.

[6] January 8, 1797, *ibid.,* I, 24.

[7] Jackson to his wife, May 9, 1796, private collection of Andrew Jackson IV.

[8] Jackson to Sevier, May 8, 1797; to McNairy, May 9, 1797; Sevier to Jackson, May 11, 1797; McNairy to Jackson, May 12, 1797, *Correspondence,* I, 31 *et seq.*

[9] November 2, 1797, *ibid.,* I, 38.

[10] Jackson to James Robertson, January 11, 1798, *ibid.,* I, 41.

[11] Jackson to Robert Hays, January 25, 1798, *ibid.,* I, 44.

[12] Jackson to Cocke, June 24 and 25, 1798; Cocke to Jackson, June 25, 1798, *ibid.,* I, 48-50.

[13] Private collection of Andrew Jackson IV.

[14] August 16, 1799, *Correspondence,* I, 56.

[15] An affidavit dated June 15, 1800, *ibid.,* I, 57.

[16] Memoir of Mary Donelson Wilcox, Heiskell, III, 280.

[17] Narrative of Isaac T. Avery, Parton, I, 167.

[18] A warrant for the arrest of Russell Bean, dated February 12, 1802, is preserved in the Washington County records, Jonesboro (modern spelling). This

discloses that Bean had been at large for more than a month when the fire lured him from hiding.

[19] James A. McLoughlin to Amos Kendall, January 3, 1843, *Correspondence*, I, 65.

[20] One purchase of books Jackson made in Philadelphia, January 7, 1797, as listed by the seller: "Vattel, Law of Nations, Powell on Contracts, Espinasse Nisiprius, Gilbert's Law of Evidence, Butler's Nisiprius, Comyn's Digest 6 Vols, Vessey's Reports, Brown Reports, Vernon's Chancery, William's Report 3 Vols, Hawkin's Pleas of the Crown, Laws of the United States, Impey's Practice 2 Vols, Equity Cases Abridged, Hinde's Practice, Gilbert on Equity, Atkyns' Reports, Coke upon Littleton 5 Vols, Wilson's Reports 3 Vols, Raymond Reports, Burns Law Dictionary, Sheridan's Dictionary, Barnes Notes." Jackson Manuscripts, Library of Congress.

[21] Thomas Perkins Abernethy, *From Frontier to Plantation in Tennessee* (1932), 171 *et seq.*

[22] Knoxville *Gazette*, July 27, 1803.

[23] Narrative of Isaac T. Avery, Parton, I, 164.

[24] W. W. Clayton, *History of Davidson County Tennessee* (1886), 142.

[25] October 3, 1803, *Correspondence*, I, 71.

[26] Clayton, 142.

[27] Petitions dated October 5 and 7, 1803, *Correspondence*, I, 72-73.

[28] Superior Court record book No. 3, Knoxville.

[29] October 9, 1803, *Correspondence*, I, 73.

[30] Superior Court record book No. 3, Knoxville.

[31] Sevier to Jackson, October 10, 1803, Clayton.

[32] Affidavit of Andrew Greer, October 23, 1803, *American Historical Magazine*, V, 208. See also Thomas J. Van Dyke to Jackson, November 5, 1803; William Dickson to Jackson, November 20, 1803, Library of Congress. The tree that Sevier interposed between himself and Jackson's pistol was long pointed out by Jackson's friends.

[33] John H. DeWitt, editor, "Journal of John Sevier," *Tennessee Historical Magazine*, VI, 36.

CHAPTER VII

[1] August 7, 1803, *Correspondence*, I, 67.

[2] Division Order, August 7, 1803, *ibid.*, I, 68.

[3] Concerning these transactions: Jackson to Coffee, January 7 and February 28, 1804, and one undated letter, *ibid.*, I, 80, 82, 83; to Hutchings, March 17, 1804, *ibid.*, I, 84.

[4] April 6, 1804, *ibid.*, I, 87.

[5] Jackson to George W. Campbell, April 28, 1804, *ibid.*, I, 90.

[6] "Account of Expence," dated "Spring 1804," *ibid.*, I, 94.

[7] July 24, 1804.

[8] Jackson to Edward Ward, May 7, 1805, private collection of Andrew Jackson IV.

[9] Parton, I, 253.

[10] The date of Jackson's removal to the Hermitage has been a subject of speculation. It was between August 25, and September 21, 1804. On the former date Jackson dated a letter to N. Davidson, "Hunter's Hill" (*Correspondence*,

I, 106), and on the latter date William Preston Anderson addressed a note to Jackson at the Hermitage (Library of Congress). In "August 1804" Deaderick & Littler of Nashville billed Jackson for a 125-gallon still (Library of Congress), it would seem, for the new farm.

[11] Jackson & Hutchings to Boggs, Davidson & Co., Philadelphia, July 31, 1804, *Correspondence,* I, 101.

[12] To Jackson, Library of Congress.

[13] "Patton" is his own spelling.

[14] Dr. Felix Robertson, son of James Robertson, founder of Nashville; from Parton, I, 249.

[15] Jackson to John Coffee, June 21, 1804, *Correspondence,* I, 95.

[16] Jackson & Hutchings to Boggs, Davidson & Co., July 31, 1804, *ibid.,* I, 101.

[17] August 25, 1804, *ibid.,* I, 106.

[18] To Theodosia Alston, May 29, 1805. From Matthew L. Davis, *Memoirs of Aaron Burr* (1837), II, 370.

[19] "If Burr has any treasonable intentions in view he is the bases[t] of all human beings. I will tell you why. he always held out the idea of settling the Washita unless a war with Spain [should take place]. in that event, he held out the idea that from his intimacy with the Secretary of War, he would obtain an appointment, and if he did he would revolutionize Mexico." Jackson to George W. Campbell, January 15, 1807 (*Correspondence,* I, 168). This was written when Jackson suspected Burr and was searching for him with twelve companies of militia.

[20] James B. Ranck, "Andrew Jackson and the Burr Conspiracy," *Tennessee Historical Magazine,* October, 1930.

[21] See Note No. 19 *ante.*

[22] Burr to Theodosia Alston, August 13, 1805. From Davis, II, 372.

[23] Jackson to Ward, June 10, 1805, private collection of Andrew Jackson IV.

[24] From John Morrell & Son, January 8, 1805, Library of Congress.

[25] From John Smith & Son, June 5, 1805, *ibid.*

[26] Memorandum of purchase, May 11, 1805, *Correspondence,* I, 113.

[27] Balie Peyton, "Sumner County Races 1804-05," *The Rural Sun,* 1873. From James Douglas Anderson, *Making the American Thoroughbred* (1916), 242.

[28] *Ibid.*

[29] Balie Peyton, "President Jackson's Orders and Reminiscences," *The Rural Sun,* 1873; from Anderson, 246.

[30] Balie Peyton, "Sumner County Races 1804-05," *The Rural Sun,* 1873; from Anderson, 242.

[31] Parton, I, 269; Guild, 219.

[32] Statements of Jackson and John Hutchings dated February 10 and 5, 1806, *Correspondence,* I, 127, 128.

[33] Jackson to Swann, January 7, 1806, *ibid.,* I, 124.

[34] Swann to Jackson, January 12, 1806, *ibid.,* I, 139.

[35] Statement of John Coffee, February 5, 1806, *ibid.,* I, 130.

[36] *Ibid.*

[37] *Ibid.,* I, 122. The original, in the Tennessee Historical Society, Nashville, was found where General Coffee had preserved it among his papers.

[38] *Ibid.,* I, 138.

[39] February 1, 1806, Library of Congress.

⁴⁰ March 15, 1806.
⁴¹ Jackson to Hutchings, April 7, 1806. Jackson misdated this letter "1805," under which date it appears in *Correspondence,* I, 111. The original is in the Library of Congress.
⁴² *Ibid.*
⁴³ March 24, 1806. From Parton, I, 313.
⁴⁴ Hutchings to Jackson, April 24, 1806, *Correspondence,* I, 141.
⁴⁵ Parton, I, 291.
⁴⁶ *Correspondence,* I, 142.
⁴⁷ May 23, 1806, *ibid.,* I, 144.

CHAPTER VIII

¹ This account of the duel is drawn from the documents concerning the same and from the files of the *Impartial Review* (Nashville) as reproduced in Bassett's *Correspondence,* I, 144-49; from a memorandum of Catlett and Thomas Overton dated May 25, 1806, and a letter, John Overton to Jackson, "June, 1806," private collection of Andrew Jackson IV; from Parton, I, 289-301, who consulted most of the foregoing and in 1857 interviewed residents of Nashville who had had their accounts from witnesses; from Buell, I, 167-82, whose partizanship of Jackson nowhere is more marked, but who discovered one useful source that escaped Parton—the gist of Jackson's conversation en route to the field, as related by Thomas Hart Benton; from Mary Donelson Wilcox's memoir, Heiskell, III 293; and from Major Ben Truman's *Field of Honor* (1884), 280-84. Additional material on the duel is extensive, but nothing of which I am aware adds to the facts.

² Joseph Erwin in the *Impartial Review* (Nashville), June 21, 1806, in which the writer admitted the agreement that a half-cock should not constitute a fire, but held that this article was not in force because it had not been committed to writing. This drew from Overton and Catlett, the second, the public rejoinder that the duel had been fought in accordance with stipulations agreed upon by all parties.

³ Overton to Jackson, dated "Nashville June, 1806," private collection of Andrew Jackson IV.

⁴ Parton, I, 302.

⁵ Jackson to an unnamed correspondent, September 25, 1806, *Correspondence,* I, 149.

⁶ Parton, I, 316.

⁷ Jackson to Daniel Smith, November 12, 1806, *Correspondence,* I, 154. Jackson fails to name Fort in this letter, but does so in his letter to Campbell. See Note No. 10 *post.*

⁸ Henry Lee Manuscript, p. 55, Library of Congress. This is my designation of this manuscript, and may be incorrect, but will be used in these pages for purposes of identification. The manuscript appears to be a fragment of an unpublished biography of Jackson, and was written during his lifetime. It consists of twenty-two pages, numbered from 53 to 75, and is preserved in Volume III of the Library of Congress collection of Jackson papers. Comparison has been made with the handwriting of Coffee, Benton, Kendall, Lee and others and it seems to resemble that of Lee who, while Jackson's secretary and a resi-

dent of the Hermitage, is known to have begun a life of his patron. Whoever the author was, he drew from sources close to Jackson.

[9] Jackson to Daniel Smith, November 12, 1806, *Correspondence*, I, 154.

[10] Jackson to George W. Campbell, January 15, 1807. The original of this letter, owned by Mrs. Susan P. Brown, of Franklin, Tennessee, is reproduced in *Correspondence*, I, 167. It gives the name of Jackson's caller concerning whom historians have been curious for more than a century. The Henry Lee Manuscript, p. 55, mentioned in Note No. 8 *ante*, describes Fort, without naming him, as "a natural son of Burr . . . on his way from N. York to join him." Burr had such a son, but his name was not Fort, nor is there any other testimony as to his connection with his father's Western schemes. A Fort family was prominent in New Jersey where Burr had numerous adherents, but there is no direct evidence to connect Jackson's caller with it. In 1828 when Jackson's political enemies were accusing him of collusion with Burr, Campbell published Jackson's letter, deleting the name of Fort and making other small changes. Parton (I, 330) had access to the original letter, but he also made textual changes and omitted the names of Fort and Swartwout.

[11] Jackson to Smith, November 12, 1806, *Correspondence*, I, 153.

[12] Jackson to Campbell, *ibid.*, I, 167.

[13] *Ibid.*

[14] November 12, 1806, *ibid.*, I, 152.

[15] Jackson to Jefferson, November 12, 1806, Parton, I, 319.

[16] November 12, 1806, *Correspondence*, I, 152.

[17] Jackson to Campbell, *ibid.*, I, 167.

[18] *Impartial Review* (Nashville), December 20, 1806.

[19] Henry Lee Manuscript, p. 54, Library of Congress. The author mistakenly ascribes the incident to Burr's summer visit, however.

[20] Albert J. Beveridge, *Life of John Marshall* (1916-19), III, 327; Henry Adams, *History of the United States* (1889-1911), III, 228, and Parton, I, 321, are among those who mistakenly cite Stockley Hays's journey as proof of Jackson's full confidence in Burr. The letters Stockley carried can not be found, but Jackson's letter to Claiborne of January 8, 1807 (*Correspondence*, I, 163), states what his suspicions were at the time.

[21] Statements of J. B. McMaster (*History of the People of the United States*, III, 72), of Beveridge (*Marshall*, III, 326), and of others that the President's proclamation for the apprehension of Aaron Burr arrived in Nashville on December nineteenth, before Burr's departure, are incorrect. Parton (I, 322) and Bassett (I, 46) say it arrived a few days after Burr's departure, and the effigy burning followed at once. This puts Jackson in little better light. Buell (I, 198) says the proclamation came late on December twenty-second, or early on the twenty-third, when it was published. None cites an authority.

I can not discover exactly when the proclamation arrived, but it was several days after Burr had gone—too long to overtake him, as General James Robertson makes clear in his letter to Senator Daniel Smith, dated February 2, 1807 (*Correspondence*, I, 164). The *Impartial Review* does not mention the proclamation until its issue of January third. The issue of December twenty-seventh contains a brief mention of Burr's departure. In 1828 a committee, friendly to Jackson (*Correspondence*, I, 167), held that the proclamation arrived on December twenty-seventh. All the evidence that I can find tends to support this. No evidence supports the implications of McMaster and Beveridge that Jackson conspired in the escape of Burr from Nashville. The extraordinary sluggishness with which the proclamation traveled in the West calls for explanation, but the explanation probably lies in what Jackson had already heard about the arrangements for delaying news inimical to Burr.

[22] Jackson to Patton Anderson, January 4, 1804, Parton, I, 328; to Claiborne, January 8, 1807, *Correspondence*, I, 183.

[23] From the private collection of Emil Edward Hurja, New York City.

[24] January 8, 1807, *Correspondence*, I, 163.

[25] George Smith to Daniel Smith, January 15, 1807, Jackson papers, Library of Congress.

[26] Undated draft, *Correspondence*, I, 177.

[27] March 17, 1807, *ibid.*, I, 172.

[28] Buell, I, 206.

[29] June 16, 1807, *Correspondence*, I, 181.

[30] Josiah Meigs to Return J. Meigs, August 29, 1807, Lawson McGhee Library, Knoxville.

[31] Excerpt from a version published in 1824 by Thomas Ritchie, the distinguished Richmond editor. Once asked concerning its accuracy, Jackson said it was not strong enough.

[32] Jackson to J. Stephenson, March 11, 1804, Library of Congress.

[33] Their mother was Polly Smith, daughter of General Daniel Smith. On March 24, 1807, William Ballard sent Jackson a timid reminder that seventeen dollars, due for the boys' schooling, would be very acceptable (*ibid.*).

[34] Ben Smith to Jackson, May 10, 1810, *ibid.*

[35] Statement of November, 1808, *Correspondence*, I, 190. An ininteresting analysis of the statement appears in Douglas Anderson's "Andrew Jackson, Frontier Merchant," Nashville *Tennessean*, April 13, 1928.

[36] Jackson to Daniel Smith, November 28, 1807, *Correspondence*, I, 183.

[37] Jackson to an unnamed correspondent, *ibid.*, I, 198.

[38] Jackson to James Jackson, August 25, 1819, *ibid.*, II, 427.

[39] Abernethy, *From Frontier to Plantation in Tennessee*, 263.

[40] Guild, 59.

[41] Parton, I, 349-60.

[42] *Ibid.*, I, 344. Parton probably had the story from W. B. Lewis or some one else close to Jackson. Jackson's great interest in this trial is attested by the fact that after his death between fifty and sixty pages of manuscript bearing on it were found among his papers. They are now in the Jackson Papers, Library of Congress, in a folder marked, "Doubtful and Undated." They are not in Jackson's handwriting. They give attorneys' arguments and the substance of the testimony of witnesses. On the point above one reads that "Genl Jackson deposed generally to A.^{s} character. A heart humane, honest and generous; the natural enemy of villains and scoundrels."

[43] Thomas Hart Benton, *Thirty Years' View* (1854), I, 737.

[44] Jackson to Whiteside, February 10, 1810, *Correspondence*, I, 199.

[45] Donelson Caffery to Jackson, December 5, 1810, *ibid.*, I, 201.

[46] Deaderick to Jackson, June 4, 1810, Library of Congress.

[47] Deaderick to Jackson, April 25, 1807, *ibid.*

[48] Deaderick to Jackson, March 5, 1809, *ibid.*

[49] Certificates of George Blakemore, Benjamin Rawlings, Robert Williamson

and Shadrach Nye, dated March 22, 1808; of Robert Purdy, February 15, and—Boyd, March 12, Jackson Papers, Library of Congress.

[50] Donelson Caffery to Jackson, July 10, 1810, *ibid.*
[51] Lem Hutchings to Jackson, May 31, 1811, *ibid.*
[52] Isabella Vinson to Jackson, September 10, 1810, *ibid.*
[53] Jackson to Whiteside, February 10, 1810, *Correspondence,* I, 199.
[54] *Ibid.*
[55] A letter to Jackson, June 4, 1811, from which the sheet containing the writer's signature is missing, Library of Congress.
[56] Hampton to Jackson, December 9, 1810, *Correspondence,* I, 205.
[57] February 10, 1810, *ibid,* I, 199.

CHAPTER IX

[1] To "Arbitrators" (in a business dispute), February 29, 1812, *Correspondence,* I, 217. An interesting letter, showing Jackson in a conciliatory frame of mind and also still interested with the Green family in the slave trade at Natchez which he began twenty-three years before. Jackson was now related to this family, two of Abner Green's sons having married nieces of Rachel.
[2] Division Orders, *ibid.,* I, 220.
[3] Pronounced Wylie Blunt. He was a half-brother of Territorial Governor and ex-Senator Blount.
[4] Donelson Caffery to Jackson, December 5, 1810, *Correspondence,* I, 201.
[5] Buell (I, 247-51) rescued from oblivion the ride of Billy Phillips. He quotes a receipt of Governor Blount for Phillips's dispatches, dated Nashville, June 21, 1821. This must be an error. Blount's letters in the Jackson Papers, Library of Congress, show that the Governor was in Knoxville on June twenty-third. Thus he would have had to travel almost as fast as Billy to have been in Nashville two days before.
[6] P. Perkins to Jackson, July 5, 1812, Library of Congress.
[7] Blount to Secretary of War, June 25, 1812, Library of Congress.
[8] Parton, I, 361.
[9] The Club's premises were the old Clover Bottom track purchased from Jackson and his associates.
[10] Secretary of War to Blount, October 21 and 23, 1812, Library of Congress.
[11] November 11, 1812, *Correspondence,* I, 238.
[12] To Coffee, September 15, 1812, Library of Congress.
[13] Parton, I, 368.
[14] Promissory note, dated December 30, 1812, Library of Congress.
[15] To George W. Campbell, November 29, 1812, *Correspondence,* I, 244.
[16] January 18, 1813, *ibid.,* I, 271.
[17] January, 1813, *ibid.,* 272.
[18] January 25, 1813, *ibid.,* I, 274.
[19] *Ibid.,* I, 273.
[20] To W. B. Lewis, March 4, 1813, private collection of Oliver R. Barrett, Chicago.
[21] April 5, 1813, Chamberlain Manuscripts, Boston Public Library.
[22] February 6, 1813, *Correspondence,* I, 275. The copy of the letter Jackson received from Secretary Armstrong was misdated January 5, 1813, giving rise to the confusion in the mind of Jackson and of historical commentators. In a

subsequent letter March 22, 1813 (*ibid.*, I, 300), the Secretary reveals when the order was written.

23 March 8 and 16, 1813, *Correspondence*, I, 290, 296.

24 To John P. Hickman, December 26, 1837, private collection of William M. Hall, Memphis.

25 March 15, 1813, *Correspondence*, I, 296.

26 T. W. B. Lewis, April 9, 1813, *ibid.*, I, 304.

27 Parton, I, 382.

28 "Carroll . . . is I think the best Brigade Major in the armies of the United States—he ought and must be at the head of a regiment." (Jackson to W. B. Lewis, March 4, 1813, private collection of Oliver R. Barrett, Chicago.) This is one of several examples of Jackson's ability to recognize a military leader in the embryo.

29 The Carroll-Benton duel: Carroll's statement, October 4, 1824, *Correspondence*, I, 311; a statement by the opposing parties' seconds, Andrew Jackson and John M. Armstrong, August 23, 1813, Jackson Papers, Library of Congress; Jackson to Armstrong with marginal notations by the latter, August 9, 1813, *ibid.*; statement of Felix Robertson, August 5, 1813, *ibid.*; Parton, I, 387; Bassett, I, 67.

30 The fight with the Benton brothers: Andrew Hynes to Jackson, July 16, 1813; T. H. Benton to Jackson, July 25; Benton's statement, September 10; Jackson to Benton, July 19 and July 28 (?); James W. Sitler's statement, September 5, *Correspondence*, I, 309-18; Parton, I, 390.

31 George S. Gaines's account, Pickett Manuscripts, Alabama State Library, Montgomery.

32 General Order, September 24, 1813, Library of Congress.

CHAPTER X

1 Jackson to Blount, October 13, 1813, *Correspondence*, I, 332.

2 John Strother to Jackson, October 9, 1813, *ibid.*, I, 329.

3 J. Lyon to Jackson, October 27, 1813, Library of Congress; Jackson to Leroy Pope, October 31, 1813, *Correspondence*, I, 339.

4 To Pope and others, October 23, 1813, *ibid.*, I, 335.

5 To W. B. Lewis, October 24, 1813, *ibid.*, I, 336.

6 Order dated Fort Deposit, October 24, 1813, *ibid.*, I, 337.

7 Reid to W. B. Lewis, October 24, 1814, Parton, I, 432.

8 Reid Manuscript, 38, Tennessee Historical Society, Nashville.

9 Reid to W. B. Lewis, October 24, 1813, Parton, I, 432.

10 October 27, 1813, Library of Congress. James Jackson, a Nashville merchant, held the note.

11 David Crockett, *Life of David Crockett* (1865), 75.

12 To Blount, November 4, 1813, *Correspondence*, I, 341.

13 Parton, I, 439.

14 Crockett, 78.

15 Reid and Eaton, 56-58.

16 John Henry Eaton, *Life of Andrew Jackson* (1824), 66.

17 Reid and Eaton, 60.

18 General Orders, November 13, 1814, *Correspondence*, I, 344.

19 Reid and Eaton, 70; Kendall, 217; Parton, I, 464.

[20] Library of Congress. James Jackson held the note.
[21] Jackson to Blount, November 19, 1813, *Correspondence*, I, 362.
[22] To Jackson, December 9, 1813, Library of Congress.
[23] December 9, 1813, *Correspondence*, I, 378.
[24] Reid and Eaton, 84.
[25] Jackson to his wife, December 14, 1813, *Correspondence*, I, 391.
[26] December 12, 1813, *ibid.*, I, 387.
[27] To Coffee, December 22, 1813, *ibid.*, I, 404.
[28] December 29, 1812, *ibid.*, 416. Original in Library of Congress. Reid and Eaton (110) contains a refined version of this letter that has been widely copied.
[29] Morning reports, or returns, showing the strength at Fort Strother are available only periodically, but on January fourteenth the last of the militia departed. The 800 new troops came up the same day and on the seventeenth the march began. In his report to Pinckney, dated January 29, 1814 (*Correspondence*, I, 447), Jackson gives the "remainder of my force," exclusive of the 800 recruits, on January seventeenth as 130.
[30] Jackson to Pinckney, *ibid.*; to his wife January 28, 1814, *ibid.*, I, 444; Reid and Eaton, 128.
[31] To Pinckney, *op. cit.*, 451.
[32] Reid and Eaton, 136.
[33] February 10, 1814, *Correspondence*, I, 459.
[34] To Lewis, February 21, 1814, Parton I, 502.
[35] To Lewis, February 25, 1814, New York Public Library.
[36] Parton, I, 508.
[37] *Ibid.*, 509-12.
[38] Reid Manuscript, 131, Tennessee Historical Society, Nashville.
[39] Jackson to Blount without date, Buell, I, 325. This letter contradicts the substance of the letter to Pinckney referred to in the note immediately following. Jackson wrote Blount that as the hour of execution drew near he mounted his horse and rode out of ear-shot.
[40] To Pinckney, March 14, 1814, *Correspondence*, I, 481.
[41] Two notes of $1,000 each, payable to James Jackson, dated February 9 and March 2, 1814, Library of Congress.
[42] General Orders, March 24 (?), 1814, *Correspondence*, I, 488.
[43] Charles Edwards Lester [and Sam Houston], *Life of Sam Houston* (1855), 33.
[44] Jackson to his wife, April 1, 1814, *Correspondence*, I, 493.
[45] *Ibid.*
[46] To Blount, March 31, 1814. A report entitled "Battle of Tehopisko or the Horse Shoe," Tennessee Historical Society, Nashville.
[47] W. G. Orr, in *Publications of Alabama Historical Society*, II, 57. Mr. Orr writes from memories of conversations with his father who saw the surrender.
[48] Albert James Pickett, *History of Alabama* (Reprint of 1896), 594. I favor Pickett's version which was derived from witnesses.
[49] The quotation thus far is taken from an undated fragment of a letter in the hand of John Reid (Tennessee Historical Society, Nashville). At this point Reid's letter ends. I have finished the quotation from Reid and Eaton, 166. Pickett calls Reid and Eaton's version of Weatherford's speech camp gossip. I do not think so. That part of their book was written by Eaton, but the Weatherford incident follows, almost literally, Reid's private letter.

CHAPTER XI

[1] May 8, 1814, *Correspondence*, II, 1.
[2] To Josiah Nichols, June 9, 1814, *ibid.*, II, 5.
[3] John Overton to Jackson, May 8, 1814, *ibid.*, II, 1.
[4] G. W. Campbell to Jackson, May 29, 1814, Library of Congress. Jackson's first appointment, on May twenty-second, was as a brigadier-general, vice Wade Hampton resigned, following his failure in Canada. Six days later the retirement of Harrison, virtually driven from the service, resulted in the proffer of the higher rank. Jackson accepted both appointments, the former, June 8, the latter, June 20, 1814.
[5] Armstrong to Jackson, June 25, 1814, *Correspondence*, II, 11.
[6] June 27, 1814, *ibid.*, II, 12.
[7] To Benjamin Hawkins, July 11, 1814, *ibid.*, II, 14.
[8] August 10, 1814, private collection of Oliver R. Barrett, Chicago.
[9] Kendall, 89.
[10] August, 1814, Library of Congress.
[11] Eaton, 205.
[12] *American State Papers, Indian Affairs*, I, 837; see also Hayne to Jackson, March 27, 1816, and statement of Benjamin Hawkins, April 16, 1816, *Correspondence*, II, 237.
[13] The Creek Nation has kept alive a claim against the United States for the compensation for the lands taken from the friendly tribes by Andrew Jackson. In 1853 the Commissioner of Indian Affairs was Luke Lea, of Tennessee, an old follower of Jackson. He informed a committee of the House of Representatives: "The . . . claim is eminently just. . . . The case is simply this, that a great Government, at the close of a war . . . forces . . . her allies, who fought bravely in every battle . . . to make a treaty. . . . In the history of our country it does not appear that any such [similar] case has ever occurred; nor has the Government ever desired to take lands from friendly Indians except . . . for a satisfactory compensation." The most recent opinion of the Indian Bureau, under the signature of Commissioner C. S. Rhoads, May 27, 1930, takes an opposite view of the justice of the Creek claim (Senate Report 1527, 71st Congress, 3rd session).
[14] August 10, 1814, private collection of Oliver R. Barrett, Chicago.
[15] Jackson to Manrique, July 12, 1814, *Correspondence*, II, 15.
[16] John Gordon to Jackson, July 30 (original misdated July 20), 1814, *ibid.*, II, 17.
[17] July 17, 1814, *ibid.*, II, 16.
[18] July 24, 1814, *ibid.*, II, 19.
[19] Eaton, 212; Bassett, I, 128.
[20] August 10, 1814, private collection of Oliver R. Barrett, Chicago.
[21] Jackson to Blount, August 5, 1814, *American State Papers, Military Affairs*, III, 792.
[22] Charles Warren, *Jacobin and Junto* (1931), 269.
[23] Parton, I, 567.
[24] Jackson to Monroe, January 6, 1817, *Correspondence*, II, 272.
[25] To Robert Butler, August 27, 1814, *ibid.*, II, 31.
[26] August 28, 1814, *ibid.*, II, 35.

²⁷ Major Howell Tatum, "Topographical Notes and Observations on the Alabama River, August 1814," *Publications of the Alabama Historical Society,* II, 173; Jackson to Manrique, September 9, 1814, *Correspondence,* II, 44.

²⁸ To the Secretary of War, August 25, 1814, Library of Congress.

²⁹ Major A. Lacarrière Latour, *Historical Memoir of the War in the West* (1816), xxiv.

³⁰ Bibliotheca Parsoniana, New Orleans.

³¹ Dated August 21, 1814, writer and addressee undisclosed, Jackson Papers, Library of Congress.

³² Fragment of a letter dated Havana, August 13, 1814, apparently addressed to Jackson or intended for him, Jackson Papers, Library of Congress.

³³ August 24, 1814, *Correspondence,* II, 29.

³⁴ Marquis James, "Napoleon, Junior," *The American Legion Monthly,* III, No. 4. An account of Jean Laffite's rôle in the New Orleans campaign. In this article the author spelled the name Laffitte, as the individual in question sometimes spelled it. A more extensive study of Laffite manuscripts in Bibliotheca Parsoniana, which is the notable private collection of Edward A. Parsons, of New Orleans, and in the Rosenberg Library, Galveston, prompts the use, in this volume, of the form, Laffite, because Laffite himself seems to have preferred it.

³⁵ *Ibid.*

³⁶ *Ibid.*

³⁷ *Ibid.*

³⁸ August 31, 1814, Bibliotheca Parsoniana, New Orleans.

³⁹ September 1, 1814, *ibid.*

⁴⁰ Jean Laffite to Lockyer, September 4, 1814 (". . . *Je serai tout à vous.*"), *ibid.*

⁴¹ Percy to Lockyer, August 30, 1814, *ibid.*

⁴² Tatum, 174.

CHAPTER XII

¹ Tatum, 175.

² September 14, 1814, *Correspondence,* II, 48.

³ Tatum, 176.

⁴ Jackson to Robert Butler, September 17, 1814, *Correspondence,* II, 49.

⁵ McKinley to Stewart, September 9, 1814, Jackson Papers, Library of Congress.

⁶ Tatum, 177.

⁷ To Robert Butler, September 17, 1814, *Correspondence,* II, 49.

⁸ Lawrence's loss was 4 killed, 5 wounded; the British, 32 killed, 40 wounded. The size of the British landing force and of Lawrence's force has been variously stated. Jackson's report to the Secretary of War, September 17, 1814 (*Correspondence,* II, 50) gives the latter as 158 "fit for duty," and the former as 110 marines, 20 artillerymen and 200 Indians. The British figures, 60 marines and 120 Indians, are probably more accurate. The crews of the ships numbered 600.

⁹ Jackson to John Rhea, October 11, 1814, private collection of Mrs. Charles R. Hyde, Chattanooga, Tennessee.

¹⁰ September 4, 1814, Bibliotheca Parsoniana, New Orleans. Blanque is generally supposed to have been a close friend of Laffite. This letter, however, is

couched in formal terms and in a note to Claiborne (*ibid.*), Blanque declared himself unacquainted with Laffite.

[11] Bibliotheca Parsoniana, New Orleans. The original is without date. Laffite's letters to Lockyer, Blanque and Claiborne appear in Latour whose versions of them have been accepted by all subsequent writers. Latour wrote in French. His manuscript was translated for publication by H. P. Nugent whose polished rendering of Laffite's language effaces much of the flavor and simplicity of the original. Laffite was a man of quiet force and personal charm, but no scholar. His orthography and grammar are Jacksonian and his penmanship worse than Monroe's. In an effort to approximate the true expression of the man, the translation is rather literal. In the French of Laffite the excerpts quoted read:

"*Dans la ferme persuasion que le choix qui éte fait devous pour . . . d'Emploi de premier Magistrait . . . a eté par L'Estime & accorde au Merite, Je M'addresse avous avec confiance pour un objet dont peut dependre la Salut de l'Etat. Je vous offre Rendres á cette Etat plusiers Citoyens, Qui peut-Etre 'ont perdu a vos yeux catitre sacré. Jevous offre . . . Leurs Efforts pour La Déffense delapatrie.*

"*Cepoint dela Louisienne que j'occupe est d'une Grand Importance dans la situation présente. Je m'offre ala déffendre. . . . Je suis la Brebie Égarrié qui désire rentrit au l'un dutroupeau . . . vous penitre de mes fauts tille quelles sonts. . . .*

"*Au cas, Monsieur Le Gouverneur, que votre Response, Ne soit favorable a mes desires ardents, je vous déclare que je part desuite pour N'étre pas tenu, d'avoir Co-opéré à une invasion. . . . Ce qui ne peut Manquer d'avoir lieu, et me son mettre entièrment au jugement de ma consience.*

"*Jai L'honneur d'étre, M. Le gouverneur*

"Laffite"

[12] To Jackson, September, 1814, Library of Congress.

[13] October 3, 1814, *Correspondence*, II, 66. After the war Colonel Ross and Commandant Patterson went to court with a dispute over their personal shares of the booty.

[14] Jackson to Livingston, October 23, 1814, *ibid.*, II, 81.

[15] September 30, 1814, *ibid.*, II, 63.

[16] *Ibid.*, II, 57.

[17] Claiborne to Jackson, October 24, 1814, *ibid.*, II, 81.

[18] Gayarré, IV, 354.

[19] Claiborne to Jackson, September 19 and 20, 1814, *Correspondence*, II, 54 and 55.

[20] Committee on Defense to Jackson, September 18, 1814, *ibid.*, II, 51. Although sent in the name of the committee, the document is Livingston's work.

[21] Jackson to Livingston, April, 1804, Buell, I, 148.

[22] September 30, 1814, *Correspondence,* II, 63.

[23] September 30, 1814, *ibid.*, II, 65.

[24] To Monroe, February 18, 1815, *ibid.*, II, 174.

[25] On September 25, 1814, Monroe wrote Governor Blount of British intentions to attack "thro' the mobile" (*ibid.*, II, 62). A copy of this letter was forwarded to Jackson who received it probably late in October. Not until after

Jackson had departed for New Orleans in November did Monroe begin his oft-cited requests for the General to hasten to the defense of the city.

[26] Thomas L. Butler to Holmes, September 30, 1814, *ibid.*, II, 64.
[27] October 21, 1814, *ibid.*, II, 78.
[28] *Columbian Centinel* (Boston), September 10, 1814.
[29] Monroe to Jackson, September 27 and October 10, 1814, *ibid.*, II, 60 and 71.
[30] From Charles Cassidy, October 15, 1814, Library of Congress.
[31] To John Rhea, October 10, 1814, private collection of Mrs. Charles R. Hyde, Chattanooga, Tennessee.
[32] Robert Butler to Robert Hays, October 21, 1814, Jackson Papers, Library of Congress.
[33] To his wife, October 21, 1814, *Correspondence,* II, 78.
[34] John Coffee to his wife, without date, Buell, I, 358.
[35] To Monroe, October 26, 1814, *Correspondence,* II, 82.
[36] Charles Cassidy to Jackson, September 23, 1814, Library of Congress.
[37] Reid and Eaton, 226.
[38] Jackson left Pensacola November 9, 1814, the day after the flight of the British, arriving on the Tensas, November thirteenth. Casualties at Pensacola: American, 7 killed, 11 wounded; Spanish, 4 killed, 6 wounded. (Richard L. Campbell, *Historical Sketches of Colonial Florida* [1892], 233.)
[39] Reid and Eaton, 235.
[40] November 22, 1814, Library of Congress.
[41] Jackson to Blount, November 14, 1814, *ibid.*
[42] November 5, 1814, *Correspondence,* II, 90.
[43] Claiborne to Jackson, November 16, 1814, *ibid.*, II, 100.
[44] To Winchester, November 22, 1814, *ibid.*, II, 106.
[45] October 10, 1814, *ibid.*, II, 70.
[46] General Order, November 16, 1814, *ibid.*, II, 100.
[47] To Winchester, November 22, 1815, *ibid.*, II, 106.
[48] *Ibid.*
[49] November 20, 1814, *ibid.*, II, 101.
[50] James Jackson to Jackson, December 14, 1814, Library of Congress.

CHAPTER XIII

[1] Louisiana usage of the term Creole ofttimes is imperfectly understood in other parts of the United States. In 1814, as now, it had a meaning different from that in the French and Spanish West Indies where it designates a native of part negro blood. Louisiana Creoles are white persons of French or Spanish extraction. "Creole negroes" in Louisiana are negroes reared among the French-speaking inhabitants.
[2] Alexander Walker, *Jackson and New Orleans* (1856), 14.
[3] Jackson to Coffee, December 11, 1814, *Correspondence,* II, 112; Claiborne to Monroe, December 9, 1814, Gayarré, IV, 379.
[4] Jackson to Winchester, November 22, 1814, *Correspondence,* II, 106; to Monroe, December 10, 1814, *ibid.*, II, 111.
[5] Walker, 13.
[6] *Ibid.*, 16.
[7] *Ibid.*, 15.
[8] *Louisiana Historical Quarterly,* VI, 82. This article is a translation by Grace

King of Marigny's pamphlet, *Reflexions sur la Campagne du Général André Jackson en Louisiane* (1848).

9 Walker, 17.
10 Grace King, *Creole Families of New Orleans* (1922), 33.
11 Walker, 17.
12 *Ibid.*, 18.
13 Marginal note in Jackson's hand on Monroe's letter to Jackson, December 10, 1814, *Correspondence*, II, 110.
14 Vincent Nolte, *Fifty Years in Two Hemispheres* (1854), 207.
15 Livingston's statement, Buell, I, 366.
16 *Louisiana Historical Quarterly*, VI, 82.
17 To James Brown, February 4, 1815, Library of Congress.
18 Jackson's address to the New Orleans volunteers, December 18, 1814, *Correspondence*, II, 118.
19 Jackson to James Brown, February 4, 1815, Library of Congress.
20 Captain Alexander White to Jackson, December 14, 1814; Lieutenant B. M. Stokes to Brigadier-General Morgan, December 21, 1814, Jackson Papers, Library of Congress.
21 December 10, 1814, *Correspondence*, II, 111.
22 December 11, 1814, *ibid.*, II, 112.
23 January 21, 1815, Louisiana State Museum, New Orleans.
24 *Correspondence*, II, 114.
25 Parton, II, 57.
26 *Ibid.*, 55.
27 Latour, 72.
28 Report of Lieutenant Colonel McRea to Jackson, December 12, 1814, *Correspondence*, II, 120.
29 Latour, 64.
30 Parton, II, 56.
31 *Ibid.*
32 December 16, 1814, *Correspondence*, II, 116.
33 Parton, II, 56.
34 December 16, 1814, *Correspondence*, II, 116.
35 Proclamation of marital law, December 16, 1814, Parton, II, 60.
36 Latour, 72.
37 Sister Superior Marie Olivier to Jackson, December 20, 1814, Library of Congress.
38 *Friend of the Laws*, January 16, 1815.
39 Nolte, 208.
40 *Louisiana Historical Quarterly*, VI, 65.
41 *Ibid.*
42 *Ibid.*
43 Latour, 71. Latour's assertion that it was Jackson who interceded with Judge Hall to obtain the safe conduct is at variance with Marigny's account, which is undoubtedly correct. Marigny wrote in 1848 after differences with Jackson during the campaign were long forgotten and he had become a belligerent supporter of Jackson's policies in national affairs.
44 December 22, 1814, Bibliotheca Parsoniana, New Orleans.
45 Walker, 143.
46 *Ibid.*, 154.

⁴⁷ Nolte, 203.

⁴⁸ An incomplete manuscript narrative, in Carroll's hand, describing incidents of the river journey and the subsequent engagements near New Orleans, including that of January eighth, gives December twentieth as the date of his arrival (private collection of Albert Lieutaud, New Orleans). Other authorities give the dates of December twenty-first and twenty-second. Jackson was mistaken in his assertion (*Correspondence,* II, 110) that Carroll arrived without arms.

⁴⁹ Carroll's Manuscript Narrative, *op. cit.*

⁵⁰ *Ibid.*

⁵¹ *Correspondence,* II, 123.

⁵² His own spelling. The name is usually written Delaronde.

⁵³ Latour, 87.

⁵⁴ Walker, 151.

⁵⁵ I follow tradition in preserving for Gabriel Villeré the conspicuous rôle in bringing word of the British landing because research seems to justify it. Walker (151), who gives a detailed account of Villeré's arrival, is trustworthy. Although he did not record the incident until thirty-three years later, he was in New Orleans at the time and knew all the persons concerned. Moreover he is supported by contemporary evidence. The next morning—December 24, 1814—the Eastern mail left the city at daybreak when the results of Jackson's night battle were still in doubt. This mail carried a private letter written by a soldier who mentions Villeré, and no one else, as the bearer of the news of the British coup. "Without this providential warning," says the writer, "we should probably have been taken by entire surprise" (*Columbian Centinel* [Boston], January 28, 1815).

The prior visit of Rousseau, however, is apparently authenticated by Walker (151). Reid and Eaton (284) give the credit solely to Tatum whom Jackson had known for thirty years. Eaton may have relied on an undated memorandum of Colonel Arthur P. Hayne, now among the Jackson Papers at the Library of Congress, which merely says that Jackson was informed at two P.M. of the British landing by Howell Tatum. In view of Tatum's own statement, it is impossible to believe that this officer reached headquarters in advance of Villeré ("Major Howell Tatum's Journal," *Smith College Studies in History,* VII, 107). The modest Tatum does not even mention his own name, merely saying that "this day the Commanding General received information, by Maj. Latour, that the enemy had effected a landing."

CHAPTER XIV

¹ Losses: American, 45 killed and wounded; British, 95 killed and wounded, Bassett, I, 169.

² [George Robert Gleig] *A Narrative of the British Campaigns against Washington, Baltimore and New Orleans* (1821), 264. He calls it Pine Island. Jackson's men would have lived on ducks which Gleig found "so timorous that it was impossible to approach within musket shot."

³ Gleig, 266. The British writer calls his informants "American deserters." Latour (93) gives the names of three Louisianians in the Spanish service who, he says, had joined the British at Pensacola. Walker (118) identifies them as "ex-officials of the Spanish government in Louisiana" who had never acquiesced to the transfer of the country to the United States.

⁴ Called by British writers Bayou Catalin or Cataline. On old maps of Louisiana it appears as River St. Francis.

⁵ To Holmes, December 25, 1814, *Correspondence,* II, 124; to Blount, February 6, 1815, Library of Congress.

⁶ Lest my remarks in the main text should be taken as innuendo reflecting on the patriotism of General Villeré, which is unimpeachable, I shall say exactly what is in my mind. The route of Bayou Mazant and Bayou Bienvenue was the commonly used way from the Villeré plantation to the lake. Had it been blocked as Jackson ordered, it would only have had to be cleared again after the campaign at the cost of much labor. As did most Louisianians, and Jackson himself, Villeré thought the British would attempt the Bayou Chef Menteur. Under these circumstances did the General seek to avoid what he deemed a useless inconvenience to his property by casually overlooking this one bayou during his obstructing operations? The question may be very unjust to General Villeré, but history shows many examples wherein small personal interests have swayed the official conduct of perfectly upright persons.

Major Villeré's negligence, however brilliantly atoned for, is clear. Jackson's "astonishment" at the discovery that Bayou Bienvenue had not been obstructed, bordered on suspicion. (Jackson to Holmes, December 25, 1814, *Correspondence,* II, 124.) Young Villeré participated in the battle of December twenty-third (Jackson to Monroe, December 27, 1814, *Correspondence,* II, 127), but later Jackson deprived him of his sword and placed him under arrest. After the news of peace he was tried for "harboring and protecting the enemy" and "neglect of duty." Major Hinds of the Mississippi Dragoons was president of the court. It was alleged that on the night of December twenty-second one of the Spanish fishermen informed Villeré of the British landing, and Villeré denounced him as a spreader of false alarms. Villeré entered no defense and was acquitted. Of the first charge he was innocent. Of the second, the war being over, the court took a lenient view. (General Orders, Headquarters Seventh Military District, March 3, 1815. Louisiana State Museum, New Orleans; Latour, cxxxi.)

⁷ Latour, 104. Bassett (I, 172) says 1,688 "rank and file" which is practically the same thing.

⁸ Gleig, 278.

⁹ I am unable to account for this coincidence. Walker (124) states that Ducros and his comrades deceived the British by prearrangement. I think Latour (86), who probably had the story from Ducros himself, more plausible in his suggestion that the men had honestly fallen into one of the most common of errors among untrained soldiers, that of overestimating the magnitude of any force.

¹⁰ Nolte, 209.

¹¹ Walker, 157.

¹² *Ibid.;* Parton, II, 73.

¹³ Reid and Eaton, 503; from a statement of Colonel Robert Butler, Jackson's adjutant-general. Latour (105) enumerated 2,131, not counting staff: the *Louisiana Gazette,* June 10, 1815, 2,325. In a letter to Monroe, December 27, 1814 (*Correspondence,* II, 127), Jackson gave his force as "not exceeding in all fifteen hundred." The Commander's preoccupation with more important matters may account for this underestimate.

¹⁴ These trees which to-day conduct one to the ruins of Versailles form the

most magnificent double row of oaks in Louisiana. They are now erroneously known as the Pakenham Oaks. See Note No. 39, Chapter XV.

[15] Hayne Manuscript, Jackson Papers, Library of Congress.

[16] A manuscript account in the handwriting of Jackson, hereinafter referred to as Jackson's Manuscript Narrative, Library of Congress. This account, which Jackson wrote sometime in 1815, gives a succinct running story of events from December 23, 1814, to January 19, 1815, with the exception of happenings between December twenty-eighth and about ten A.M. on January eighth. These sheets are missing.

[17] Jackson to Laffite, undated, Bibliotheca Parsoniana, New Orleans.

[18] Hayne Manuscript, Jackson Papers, Library of Congress.

[19] Jackson's Manuscript Narrative, *ibid*.

[20] Latour, 112.

[21] Walker, 171.

[22] Jackson to Monroe, December 27, 1814 (*Correspondence*, II, 128), does not mention his participation in this affair, but gives the credit to Colonels Butler and Piatt and Major Chotard, who rushed into the scene of confusion beside the General.

[23] Latour, 97.

[24] *Ibid.*, 240.

[25] The brigade had dismounted before going into action and the horses let run loose. Latour's map of the battle is in error where it indicates two companies detached to hold the horses. Eventually most of the mounts were retaken by the Tennesseans, but the British caught a good many of them. Colonel Henry R. Richmond, U. S. A., who has made a careful study of the campaign from British sources, believes that six months later some of these captured Tennessee horses were ridden on the field of Waterloo.

[26] Gleig, 294.

[27] To his father, undated, Parton, II, 101.

[28] Jackson's Manuscript Narrative, Library of Congress.

[29] Latour, 102, clx.

[30] Jackson's Manuscript Narrative, Library of Congress.

[31] To Jackson, December 25, 1814, *Correspondence*, II, 125.

[32] December 27, 1814, *ibid.*, II, 128.

[33] December 24, 1814, *ibid.*, II, 124.

[34] Anderson, 97.

[35] Walker, 212.

[36] Livingston to Jackson, December 25, 1814, *Correspondence*, II, 125.

[37] Parton, II, 102.

[38] François-Xavier Martin, *The History of Louisiana* (1882), 376.

[39] Nolte, 214.

[40] Latour, 114.

[41] Martin, 376.

[42] Jackson to John McLean, March 22, 1824, *Correspondence*, III, 239; affidavit of T. L. Butler, May 23, 1815, *ibid.*, II, 210; Gayarré, IV, 562.

[43] This is the most innocuous construction that can be placed on Declouet's understanding of Guichard's remarks, and the one admitted by Marigny (*Louisiana Historical Quarterly*, VI, 68). Abner Duncan and Auguste Davézac said under oath that Declouet told them Guichard tried to obtain his adhesion to a scheme of capitulation in event the Rodriquez Canal line was taken. This

is a grave charge. The whole subject of "treasonable" intentions on the part of Guichard and other members of the Legislature was investigated by a committee of that body after the battle of January eighth. The result was exoneration. Gayarré (IV, 534-77) analyzes the testimony with his usual conservatism and care. That of Guichard is remarkable and, as Gayarré broadly hints, difficult of belief. The body of evidence leaves this writer with the impression that an influential coterie in the Legislature did hope to contravene the plans of Jackson and save the city should matters come to that extremity.

44 Gleig, 309.
45 Walker, 226.
46 To a committee of the Legislature, December 31, 1814, Gayarré, IV, 540; Plauché to Phillips, January 17, 1843, Jackson Papers, Library of Congress; Parton, II, 145; *Louisiana Historical Quarterly,* VI, 68; Reid and Eaton, 320.

CHAPTER XV

1 Patterson to Secretary of Navy, December 29, 1814, Latour, xlix.
2 *Louisiana Historical Quarterly,* VI, 68.
3 To John McLean, March 22, 1824, *Correspondence,* III, 240. Marigny's version (*Louisiana Historical Quarterly,* VI, 68) is that Jackson accepted his assurances of the patriotic intentions of the Legislature and merely said to "Return to the City. Reassure your colleagues." After the campaign Jackson defined his meaning of a warm session. "I should have . . . fired . . . the city . . . and fought the enemy amidst the surrounding flames. . . . Nothing for the comfortable maintenance of the enemy would have been left. . . . I would have . . . occupied a position above the river, cut off all supplies, and in this way compelled them to depart from the country" (Parton, II, 143).
4 *Ibid.*, II, 140. During this engagement Jackson had 3,282 men on his line, though only the artillerymen and a small body of infantry under Carroll were engaged. The British strength was about 5,500. American losses were 9 killed, and 9 wounded, including one seaman wounded on board the *Louisiana.* The British made no separate return of casualties for December twenty-eighth, but for the period of December 25-31 reported 16 killed, 42 wounded, 2 missing (Latour, clxxi).
5 Contemporaries barely mention the use of cotton bales of which so much subsequently has been made (Latour, 134; Nolte, 216 and 232). The latter, who owned two hundred and fifty bales seized by Jackson, says no others were used in the works. Isaac Edward Morse, a member of Congress from Louisiana whose father served under Jackson, wrote to his sons in 1853: "The story of the cotton bales was greatly exaggerated, only a few hundred were used . . . mostly as platforms to place cannon on (private collection of Miss Ethel Morse, Tampa, Florida)."
6 Latour, preface, xvii.
7 Walker, 257-58.
8 Nolte, 218.
9 Losses: American, 11 killed, 23 wounded. The British reported 32 killed, 42 wounded and 2 missing between January first and fifth (Latour, clxxii).
10 John F—— (illegible) to Jackson, January 2, 1815, Library of Congress.
11 Library of Congress.
12 January 3, 1815, *Correspondence,* II, 130.

13 Jackson's Manuscript Narrative, Library of Congress.
14 January 3, 1815, *Correspondence*, II, 132.
15 Buell, I, 423.
16 January 7, 1815, *Correspondence*, II, 132.
17 Walker, 319.
18 *Ibid.*
19 Jackson Manuscript Narrative, Library of Congress.
20 Buell, II, 8.
21 *Ibid.*, II, 10.
22 Statements of Jackson's strength vary considerably. Bassett (I, 192) places it at 3,989, adding that the estimate is based on Latour and is not far from the figures Jackson cited in his controversy with Adair in 1817. The *Louisiana Gazette*, June 15, 1815, listed 4,698. My figure is based on the consolidated morning reports for January eighth of the commands stationed behind the Rodriquez line (Jackson Papers, Military, Library of Congress). It includes only officers and men marked present for duty. It is perhaps doubtful if all these actually were on the line during the fighting and certainly the figure includes some troops who had no arms.
23 Buell, II, 12.
24 *Ibid.*
25 *Ibid.*
26 Jackson to Monroe, January 9 and 13, 1815, *Correspondence*, II, 136 and 142.
27 Buell, II, 20.
28 To Monroe, January 13, 1814, *Correspondence*, II, 143.
29 Parton, II, 208.
30 The action on the west bank brought the total of American casualties to 13 killed, 39 wounded, and 19 missing. The British losses as reported to the home government on January tenth were 291 killed, 1,262 wounded and 484 missing in the actions on both sides of the river (William James, *Military Occurrences of the Late War between Great Britain and the United States* [1818], II, 554). Of the wounded many did not live to reach the fleet. Combat casualties since December twenty-third had been 2,694 or about half of the number actually engaged.
31 To Robert Hays, January 26, 1815, *Correspondence*, II, 156.
32 Parton, II, 212.
33 Bassett, I, 203.
34 January 9, 1815, *Correspondence*, II, 137.
35 Morgan to Claiborne, January 25, 1815, Louisiana State Museum, New Orleans.
36 General Orders, February 25, 1815, *ibid.*
37 Nolte, 224.
38 Jackson's Manuscript Narrative, Library of Congress.
39 Pierre Favrot to his wife, January 21, 1815, Louisiana State Museum, New Orleans. The avenue of oaks leading from the ruins of Versailles, the de La Ronde plantation château, are known as the Pakenham Oaks from a tradition that the British commander died under their branches. Stanley Clisby Arthur of New Orleans has rediscovered the fact that Pakenham died under a group of four oaks on the Colomb plantation. These trees are still standing.
40 G. M. Ogden to Jackson, February 3, 1815, *Correspondence*, II, 156.

[41] Jackson to Hays, February 4, 1815, *ibid.*, II, 157.
[42] February 4, 1815, Library of Congress.

CHAPTER XVI

[1] McMaster, IV, 249.
[2] National *Intelligencer,* Washington, January 20, 1815.
[3] To his wife, February 9, 1815, from Samuel Eliot Morison, *Life and Letters of Harrison Gray Otis* (1913), II, 163.
[4] *Ibid.,* February 12, 1815.
[5] *Ibid.*
[6] *Correspondence,* II, 150.
[7] January 21, 1815, Louisiana State Museum, New Orleans.
[8] Latour, 199.
[9] To Robert Hays, February 9, 1815, Library of Congress.
[10] Jackson to Winchester, January 19, 1815, *Correspondence,* II, 150.
[11] January 21, 1815, Louisiana State Museum, New Orleans.
[12] Parton, II, 288.
[13] To Hays, February 17, 1815, Collection of Thomas F. Madigan, New York City.
[14] February 14, 1815, Library of Congress.
[15] February, 13, 1815, *ibid.*
[16] February 19, 1815, Latour, xc.
[17] Jackson to Holmes, February 21, 1815, *Correspondence,* II, 178.
[18] February 13, 1815, *Correspondence,* II, 177.
[19] Nolte, 227.
[20] Nolte, 227; Jackson to Godwin B. Cotten, editor of the *Gazette,* February 21, 1815, *Correspondence,* II, 179. The latter is a rough draft differing slightly from the version of Nolte which evidently was taken from the newspaper.
[21] Rachel Jackson to Robert Hays, March 5, 1815, Library of Congress.
[22] James Jackson to Jackson, January 26, 1815, *ibid.*
[23] Nolte, 238.
[24] Parton, 323.
[25] Rachel Jackson to Robert Hays, *op. cit.*
[26] *Ibid.*
[27] Nolte, 238.
[28] To Robert Hays, *op. cit.*
[29] Order dated February 28, 1815, *Correspondence,* II, 181.
[30] Jackson to Arbuckle, March 5, 1815, *ibid.,* II, 183.
[31] Jackson to Monroe, March 6, 1815, *ibid.,* II, 184.
[32] March 6, 1815, *ibid.,* II, 184.
[33] Gayarré, IV, 611.
[34] Latour, cxiv.
[35] *Ibid.,* cxiv.
[36] Buell, I, 56.
[37] General Order, January 21, 1815, Latour, clxxv; Jackson to [Pierre] Laffite, without date, Bibliotheca Parsoniana, New Orleans. On Jackson's representations Madison pardoned the Laffites and their followers, thus ending the proceedings against them suspended by Judge Hall in order that they might bear arms in the defense of the city.

[38] Jackson Papers, XXXIV, Library of Congress.
[39] *Ibid.*
[40] Gayarré, IV, 625.

CHAPTER XVII

[1] Dated April 15, 1815, Library of Congress.
[2] Jackson to Coffee, April 24, 1815, Library of Congress.
[3] Jackson to Dallas, July 11, 1815, *Correspondence,* II, 213.
[4] James Kearns to Jackson, February 22, 1815, Library of Congress.
[5] Stephen Kingston to John Rhea, February 24, 1815, private collection of Mrs. Charles R. Hyde, Chattanooga, Tennessee.
[6] Balie Peyton, "Haynie's Maria Against the World," the *Rural Sun* (1873), Anderson, 259.
[7] *Ibid.,* 260.
[8] Guild, 249.
[9] Abernethy, *From Frontier to Plantation in Tennessee,* 263 *et seq.* It will be remembered that in 1811, Jackson had averted possible ruin by a bold and astonishingly successful bargain which put him in a position to demand a settlement from the sellers of eighty thousand acres, in order to clear their warranted titles. All met his terms except Andrew Erwin who precipitated a long court and legislative contest. Finally, in 1823, Jackson let Erwin off on a plea of his wife that an enforcement of the claim would impoverish the family.
[10] Library of Congress. Jackson's deposit book for this period is filed with papers for June, 1815.
[11] September 20, 1815, *Correspondence,* II, 215.
[12] October 4, 1815, *ibid.,* II, 217.
[13] Andrew Hynes to Jackson, October 24, 1815, *ibid.,* II, 218.
[14] November 7, 1815, *ibid.,* II, 220.
[15] November 15, 1815, Chamberlain Manuscripts, Boston Public Library.
[16] Parton, II, 334.
[17] Reid to an unidentified correspondent, November 21, 1815, Tennessee Historical Society, Nashville.
[18] Monroe to Jackson, July 3, 1816, Library of Congress; Bassett, I, 224.
[19] Coffee to Jackson, January 21 and February 8, 1816, *Correspondence,* II, 225 and 228; Jackson to Coffee, February 13, 1816 (two letters), *ibid.,* II, 230 and 231; Jackson to Colbert, a Cherokee chieftain, February 13, 1816, *ibid.,* II, 233.
[20] January 2, 1816, collection of Thomas F. Madigan, New York City.
[21] Jackson to James Brown, September 6, 1816, *Correspondence,* II, 259.
[22] April 8, 1816, *ibid.,* II, 238.
[23] April 22, 1816, *ibid.,* II, 241.
[24] Jackson to Monroe, October 23, 1816, *ibid.,* II, 261.
[25] July 27, 1816. The actual operation was conducted by Colonel Clinch of the Army and Sailing Master Loomis of the Navy.
[26] March 1, 1817, *Correspondence,* II, 276.
[27] Jackson to Monroe, March 18, 1817, collection of Thomas F. Madigan, New York City.
[28] Abernethy, *op. cit.,* 271.

[29] March 17, 1817, *American Historical Magazine,* V, 235.
[30] Parton, I, 105.
[31] February 24, 1817, *Correspondence,* II, 275.
[32] Division Order, April 22, 1817, *ibid.,* II, 291.
[33] Parton, II, 376.
[34] September 8, 1817, *Correspondence,* II, 325.
[35] October 4, 1817, *ibid.,* II, 327. Parton's estimate of Scott's letter (II, 377) as "every thing that . . . it should have been" has found general acceptance among historians, but Parton apparently saw only such excerpts of the letter as appears in Mansfield's *Life of Scott,* 171.
[36] December 3, 1817, *Correspondence,* II, 338.
[37] January 2, 1818, *ibid.,* II, 344.
[38] Carroll to Jackson, September 11, 1817, Library of Congress. Parton (II, 383-91) covers this controversy rather thoroughly, drawing from the pamphlet, *Letters of General Adair and General Jackson,* published at Lexington, Kentucky, in 1817.
[39] August 4, 1817, *Correspondence,* II, 320.
[40] Monroe to Jackson, July 3, 1816, Library of Congress.
[41] December 14, 1816, *Correspondence,* II, 266.
[42] Bassett, I, 242.
[43] Captain Ferdinand Amelung to Jackson, June 4, 1816, *Correspondence,* II, 243.
[44] Livingston to Jackson, February 2, 1816, Library of Congress.
[45] October 4, 1817, *Correspondence,* II, 329.
[46] Rhea to Jackson, November 27 and December 24, 1817, *Correspondence,* II, 335 and 341.
[47] Jackson to Monroe, October 22, 1817, *ibid.,* II, 332; Monroe to Jackson, December 29, 1817, collection of Thomas F. Madigan, New York City; Calhoun to Jackson, December 29, 1817, *Correspondence,* III, 343.
[48] *Ibid.,* 342.
[49] January 6, 1818, *ibid.,* II, 345.
[50] Monroe to Jackson, December 28, 1817, collection of Thomas F. Madigan, New York City.

CHAPTER XVIII

[1] Jackson to his wife, January 27, 1818, Heiskell, III, 289.
[2] The Rhea letter controversy broke in 1830 during the political warfare between Jackson and Calhoun, breeding a question which nonpartizan historians have been unable to settle to their satisfaction. The contentions of Monroe and Jackson are diametrically opposed, and, on the face of existing evidence, Monroe has the better of the case. Dr. Bassett (I, 247) calls it an issue of veracity and of memory between the two men, equally truthful. But, being obliged to choose, Bassett thinks Monroe, possessing the more trained and orderly mind, would be the more reliable as to memory. On the point of memory I follow with some misgivings my distinguished predecessor, but as to comparative veracity, or "honesty" to use Bassett's broader term, I submit that the record of Mr. Monroe's dealings with Andrew Jackson leaves room for a dissenting opinion.

At an early date Mr. Monroe sought to disassociate himself from the "say

Mr. J. Rhea" suggestion. On December 18, 1818, when the Administration was arduously striving to throw responsibility for the Florida campaign on Jackson—Monroe going so far as to propose a "correction" of Jackson's dispatches—the President wrote the General: "Your letter of January 6th was received while I was seriously indisposed. Observing it was from you, I handed it to Mr. Calhoun to read. . . . He remarked after perusing the letter that it was a confidential one relating to Florida, which I must answer" (Benton, I, 170).

Later Crawford happened in and read it but made no comment.

The original of the letter in question is now in the Monroe Papers in the New York Public Library. It bears this endorsement in Monroe's hand: "I was sick when I recd. it, and did not read it, till after . . . [the campaign]. Hearing afterwards that an understanding was imputed to me. I asked Mr. Rhea, if anything had ever pass'd between him and me. He declard that he had never heard of the subject before. I knew the suggestion to be false, but . . . it being possible that Mr. Rhea might have spoken to me by distant allusion, . . . to which I might have innocently given, from a desire to acquire Florida, a reply, from which he might have inferred a sanction not contemplated, I was glad to find that nothing of the kind had occurred."

Two weeks before his death, Mr. Monroe repeated the substance of the above. The striking feature about the whole thing seems to me to be this. Florida was the dominating issue before the Administration at that moment. Jackson was the dominating personality of that issue. He writes the President a confidential letter on this topic which had been the subject of many confidences. The Secretary of War says it is something the President must attend to personally. Yet, the President lays the letter aside and forgets about it until after the war when the prickly question of responsibility arises. The incident does not speak well for Mr. Monroe's memory, or for his judgment.

With Mr. Monroe's version, Jackson's story is irreconcilable. His account of the delivery of Rhea's reply at Big Creek is contained in an "Exposition," written or dictated by him at the White House in 1831 during the quarrel with Calhoun. It was not given to the newspapers, as intended, and was first published by Benton (I, 169-80) in 1854. Though he does not say so, Jackson received Monroe's disclaimer of December 18, 1818, either while in Washington or on his way there in January, 1819. This was during the Congressional investigation of the Florida campaign. While in Washington, Jackson apparently took up the Rhea matter with the President, and, if his Exposition sets forth the facts correctly, he did it in such a way as to refresh Monroe's memory. In any event, Jackson says that Monroe asked him to burn Rhea's letter when he got home, which Jackson says he did, making an entry in his letter-book opposite the copy of his confidential letter of January sixth: "Mr. Rhea's letter in answer is burnt this 12th April, 1819" (*ibid.*, 179; Jackson to Rhea, June 2, 1831, *Correspondence*, IV, 288).

Jackson's official letter book for this period is missing, but the General's private copy of his letter of January 6, 1818, is available in the Jackson Papers in the Library of Congress. It bears the notation: "Mr. J. Rhea's letter in answer is burnt this 12th April 1818," which was obviously a slip of the pen for 1819.

Thus far we have a good deal of corroboration of Jackson's account, unless one would assume him guilty of faking the endorsement just quoted. Such an assumption is not in character with Jackson. Mr. Monroe is the only party to this controversy who has proposed the amendment of public documents in an effort to prove something by them which they did not prove when written.

Other facts and circumstances, however, tend to weaken Jackson's case. With the exception of John Overton, no one has been found who claims to have seen the Rhea letter in question, and Overton's statement is indefinite (Overton to Jackson, June 2, 1831, *Correspondence,* IV, 287). It might have referred to some other Rhea letter.

Moreover during the passage of confidential letters between Jackson and Monroe in 1818 over the question of responsibility, Jackson makes no allusion to the indirect permission to seize Florida that he claims was given (Jackson to Monroe, August 19, 1818, *Correspondence,* III, 389; to Monroe, November 15, 1818, Parton, II, 525). And most significant, Rhea himself appears to have had no recollection of having sent any such letter as Jackson says he received. This is shown by his letter of December 18, 1818, to Jackson (*Correspondence,* II, 403), and by his behavior in 1831 when Jackson appealed to him for support. Rhea was then seventy-nine years old and his faculties were weak; but surely, if he had been the secret link between Monroe and Jackson in a matter such as the Florida campaign, he would not have forgotten it.

He was willing to help his old friend, however, and wrote three times to find out exactly what Jackson wanted him to say (Rhea to Jackson, January 4, 1831, *ibid.,* III, 221; March 30 and April 2, 1831, *ibid.,* III, 254). When he finally got the matter straight in his mind, he wrote Monroe (Rhea to Monroe, June 3, 1831, *ibid.,* IV, 288) repeating Jackson's whole story and asking the ex-President's corroboration. Monroe was dying when he received the letter, but in the presence of witnesses he dictated a denial, and signed it two weeks before the end came. Rhea died less than a year later and relatives questioned his competence to make a will (Margaret B. Hamer, "John Rhea of Tennessee," *East Tennessee Historical Society's Publications,* January, 1932).

Only one of Jackson's letters to Rhea has been found. Judging from Rhea's answers the others seem to have been filled with promptings. Mrs. Charles R. Hyde, of Chattanooga, a niece of John Rhea, has several of her uncle's papers, among which is a fragment which resembles the handwriting of Andrew Jackson. It is undated and reads:

"I wish to See the Letters That Gen'l Jackson addressed to John Rhea respecting a Letter that Should have been written by John Rhea to him to authorise him to go to pensacola and also secure a Coppy of the Letter in my hand write to John Rhea directed to me dated———"

This may explain the absence of Jackson's other letters to Rhea.

Certainly Jackson would not have gone to all the trouble he did had he not honestly believed that he received some kind of letter from Rhea at Big Creek which he interpreted as containing Monroe's assent to the Florida adventure. Rhea was writing Jackson often during those days, and had acted as mediator in the dispute arising from Jackson's General Order of April 22, 1817. On January 12, 1818, Rhea wrote Jackson a letter (*Correspondence,* II, 348) which quite possibly was delivered at Big Creek, and which, by a wide stretch of the imagination, Jackson may have misconstrued. Another guess is that Rhea may have written Jackson on his own responsibility and dared not confess it.

[3] To Isaac McKeever, March, 1818, Parton, II, 447. See also Colonel George Gibson to Jackson, February 12, 1818, *Correspondence*, II, 354.
[4] *Ibid.*, II, 357.
[5] To John Arbuthnot, April 2, 1818, *American State Papers, Military Affairs*, I, 722.
[6] *Ibid.*, I, 721-28.
[7] *Ibid.*, I, 731.
[8] *Ibid.*, I, 734.
[9] *Ibid.*, I, 734.
[10] Memoir of Lieutenant J. B. Rodgers, who was present, Parton, II, 477.
[11] Jackson to Monroe, June 2, 1818, *Correspondence*, II, 378.
[12] Proclamation, May 29, 1818, *ibid.*, II, 374.
[13] *American State Papers, Foreign Relations*, IV, 496.
[14] Charles Francis Adams (editor), *Memoirs of John Quincy Adams* (1875), IV, 107 *et seq.*
[15] July 19, 1818, Library of Congress.
[16] August 19, 1818, *Correspondence*, II, 389.
[17] To Thomas Cooper, August 24, 1818, Library of Congress.
[18] James Gadsden to Jackson, September 18, 1818, Library of Congress. For other light on the Secretary's change of heart see Calhoun to Charles Tait, July 20, 1818, *Gulf States Historical Magazine*, I, 92, and Calhoun to a friend, September 5, 1818, *ibid.*, I, 94.
[19] Monroe to Jackson, October 20, 1818, and Jackson to Monroe, November 15, 1818, *Correspondence*, II, 398.
[20] *American State Papers, Foreign Relations*, IV, 539 *et seq.*
[21] October 5, 1818, *Correspondence*, II, 398.
[22] Heiskell, II, 443.
[23] January 2, 1819, Library of Congress.
[24] Jackson to Andrew Jackson Donelson, January 31, 1819, *Correspondence*, II, 408.
[25] Jackson to James Gadsden, August 1, 1819, *Correspondence*, II, 241; Gadsden to Jackson, February 6, 1820, Library of Congress.
[26] Bassett, I, 283; Parton, II, 536.
[27] Parton, II, 569.
[28] This story was published by Mr. Lacock in 1828. Decatur was killed in a duel the following year and apparently left no record of the incident. In a campaign letter in 1827 Jackson made a guarded allusion to his conduct in Washington on this occasion, which is not, however, sufficiently explicit to form a basis for contradicting the Lacock story (Parton, II, 569-71).
[29] Adams, IV, 243.

CHAPTER XIX

[1] Jackson to Robert Butler, December 31, 1815, *Correspondence*, II, 223.
[2] Jackson to Andrew Jackson, junior, October 23, 1834, *ibid.*, V, 302.
[3] Parton, II, 644.
[4] The house here described is not to be confused with the Hermitage of to-day, which was built in 1834 and '35. The first house was begun in 1818 and occupied in that year or early in 1819. In 1831 it was extensively remod-

eled, along the lines of the present structure, erected three years later when a fire had left little except the walls of the original standing.

[5] John Jackson to Andrew Jackson, April 30, 1819, Library of Congress.

[6] John H. DeWitt, "Andrew Jackson and his Ward Andrew Jackson Hutchings," *Tennessee Historical Magazine,* series II, Vol. I, No. 2.

[7] February 27, 1821, Library of Congress.

[8] March 4, 1821, *ibid.*

[9] March 23, 1821, *ibid.*

[10] Rachel Jackson to R. E. W. Earle, February 23, 1819, *ibid.*

[11] *Ibid.*

[12] July 3, 1819, Library of Congress.

[13] Jackson vs. Kerzee, *et al.* Section A, Bin 9, State Supreme Court Records, 1819, Nashville.

[14] It appears from one paper bearing Jackson's money accounts that in the twelve months ending March 31, 1819, his Alabama investments absorbed more than six thousand dollars (*Correspondence,* II, 412).

[15] Thomas Perkins Abernethy, "Andrew Jackson and Southwestern Democracy," *American Historical Review,* XXXIII, p. 67.

[16] Jackson to James Gadsden, August 1, 1819, *Correspondence,* II, 421.

[17] November 6, 1819, *ibid.,* II, 439.

[18] James Houston to Jackson, September 24 and November 17, 1819, *ibid.,* II, 430 and 440.

[19] November 21, 1819, *ibid.,* II, 440.

[20] December 10, 1819, *ibid.,* II, 447.

[21] To Calhoun, January 10, 1820, *ibid.,* III, 2.

[22] To Jackson, January 23, 1820, *ibid.,* III, 12. Jackson's letter to Calhoun is not available, but the Secretary's reply reveals its substance.

[23] Jackson to James C. Bronaugh, February 12, 1820, *ibid.,* III, 14.

[24] Adams, IV, 76.

[25] Eaton to Jackson, March 9, 1821, Library of Congress.

[26] Jackson to Coffee, March 1, 1821, *Correspondence,* III, 39.

[27] Jackson to James C. Bronaugh, February 11, 1821, *ibid.,* III, 39.

[28] To Monroe, February 11, 1821, *ibid.,* III, 38.

[29] Jackson to Coffee, *op. cit.*

[30] Andrew Jackson in account with S. W. Stout & Company of Nashville, April 14, 1821, *Correspondence,* III, 48.

[31] Rachel Jackson to Eliza Kingsley, April 27, 1821, Parton, II, 595. I have not encountered the original of this letter, the orthography and grammar of which is here reproduced as rectified by Mr. Parton or some other copyist. The same applies to the other letters of Mrs. Jackson to Mrs. Kingsley quoted in this chapter.

[32] To Eliza Kingsley, June 21, 1821, *ibid.,* II, 597.

[33] Jackson to Andrew Jackson Donelson, March 31, 1821, *Correspondence,* III, 46.

[34] To Coffee, May 11, 1821, *ibid.,* III, 55.

[35] *Ibid.*

[36] *Ibid.*

[37] To Calhoun, May 22, 1821, *ibid.,* III, 59.

[38] Order and postscript as they appear in Jackson's Letter Book are in *Correspondence,* III, 62. The copy in Parton, II, 590, has been extensively altered.

[39] To Eliza Kingsley, July 23, 1821, Parton, II, 603.
[40] *Ibid.*
[41] *Ibid.*
[42] To Andrew Jackson Donelson, July 3, 1821, *Correspondence*, III, 87.
[43] To Calhoun, May 22, 1821, *ibid.*, III, 58.
[44] June 9, 1821, *ibid.*, III, 65.
[45] June 19, 1821, *ibid.*, III, 71.
[46] July 15, 1821, *ibid.*, III, 104.
[47] June 20, 1821, *ibid.*, III, 72.
[48] July 14, 1821, *ibid.*, III, 89.
[49] To Eliza Kingsley, July 21, 1821, Parton, II, 603.
[50] July 16, 1821, *Correspondence*, III, 104.
[51] Rachel Jackson to Eliza Kingsley, *op. cit.*

CHAPTER XX

[1] *American State Papers, Foreign Relations*, IV, 751.
[2] To Eliza Kingsley, July 23, 1821, Parton, II, 606.
[3] *Ibid.*
[4] Narrative of H. M. Breckenridge, Alcalde of Pensacola, Parton, II, 614.
[5] August 3, 1821, *Correspondence*, III, 111.
[6] The firm name was then Panton, Leslie & Company. McGillivray was buried on Panton's estate.
[7] H. M. Brackenridge to Jackson, August 24, 1821, *American State Papers, Miscellaneous*, II, 811; affidavit of Brackenridge, October 21, 1821, *ibid.*, 829.
[8] James C. Bronaugh to Jackson, August 23, 1821, *Correspondence*, III, 112; affidavit of Brackenridge, October 21, 1821, *American State Papers, Miscellaneous*, II, 829.
[9] *Ibid.*
[10] Dated August 22, 1821, *ibid.*, 805.
[11] Affidavit of Brackenridge, *op. cit.*
[12] Minutes of Callava's examination, *Correspondence*, III, 113.
[13] *Ibid.*
[14] Affidavit of J. C. Connor, September 22, 1821, *American State Papers, Miscellaneous*, II, 825; affidavit of Brackenridge, October 21, 1821, *ibid.*, 830.
[15] The Vidal case was thrown into the courts where it had a long career. What, if anything, the heirs ultimately received from Innerarity does not appear in such records as are included in the *State Papers*. Court records at Mobile or Pensacola should show this, however. Parton's assertion (II, 639) that the estate was found to owe Forbes & Company one hundred and fifty-seven dollars seems incorrect. This was the decision of a court at Mobile which did not, however, mark the end of the litigation. See Bassett, I, 309.
[16] August 26, 1821, *Correspondence*, III, 115. Apparently in an effort to improve the appearance of the record, Fromentin on October third wrote Jackson two letters in which he gave his own version of the interview. Jackson flung back challenging answers (*American State Papers, Miscellaneous*, II, 820). A question of veracity between these men should not be difficult to decide.
[17] *American State Papers, Foreign Relations*, IV, 768. My characterization of Callava's account is based on a comparison with the reports of Jackson and his

subordinates covering the same incidents. Parton pays considerable attention to Callava's story, and through him it has colored several subsequent accounts.

[18] To an unidentified correspondent, September 24, 1821, Chamberlain Manuscripts, Boston Public Library.
[19] *Correspondence*, III, 122.
[20] From John C. Mitchell, October 24, 1821, Library of Congress.
[21] To Richard K. Call, November 15, 1821, *Correspondence*, III, 131.
[22] Bill of S. Seignouret, May 16, 1821, Jackson Papers, Library of Congress.
[23] Bill of A. H. Inskeep & Company, New Orleans, May 16, 1821, *ibid*.
[24] February 9, 1821, *ibid*.
[25] To James Gadsden, May 2, 1822, *Correspondence*, III, 161.
[26] To Andrew Jackson Donelson, April 16, 1820, *ibid.*, III, 21.
[27] March 21, 1822, *ibid.*, III, 156.
[28] Parton, II, 354.
[29] November 15, 1821, *Correspondence*, III, 130.
[30] Jackson to James Gadsden, May 2, 1822, *ibid.*, III, 160.
[31] To Jackson, October 29, 1821, Library of Congress.
[32] December 11, 1821, *ibid*.
[33] To James Gadsden, December 6, 1821, *Correspondence*, III, 140.

NOTES

PART TWO

Portrait of a President

CHAPTER XXI

[1] Planters in the Tennessee River Valley of Alabama sent their cotton over the Muscle Shoals with the rise of the waters in February, and thence to New Orleans via the Tennessee, Ohio and Mississippi Rivers. This long journey was easier of accomplishment than to haul the cotton overland to the head of navigation of the Alabama for shipment to Mobile.
[2] Nashville *Whig*, January 2, 1822.
[3] *Ibid.*, January 16, 1822.
[4] Bill of Thomas Barron & Company, dated April 23, 1822. Jackson Papers, Library of Congress, Washington.
[5] Philadelphia *Aurora*, January 23, 1822.
[6] Knoxville *Register*, February 26, 1822.
[7] Nashville *Whig*, March 20, 1822.
[8] Rachel Jackson to Mary Donelson, February, 1822, Augustus C. Buell, *A History of Andrew Jackson* (1904), II, 157.
[9] *Ibid.*, 155. Buell was acquainted with Campbell and doubtless had this anecdote from his lips. I have taken the liberty to correct Buell's text where he gives Jackson's age as fifty-four. See also Campbell to W. Jones, Philadelphia, April 1, 1822, private collection of Emil Edward Hurja, New York City.
[10] Nashville *Whig*, January 2, 1822.

[11] Jackson to Andrew Jackson Donelson, July 5, 1822, *Correspondence of Andrew Jackson,* edited by John Spencer Bassett (1926-1935), III, 167.
[12] Nashville *Whig,* May 15, 1822.
[13] *Ibid.*
[14] Jackson to J. C. Bronaugh, June 2, 1822, Jackson Papers.
[15] Jackson to R. K. Call, May 2, 1822, *Correspondence,* III, 162.
[16] Jackson to R. K. Call, May 20, 1822, Jackson Papers.
[17] Jackson to A. J. Donelson, April 22, 1822, Donelson Papers, Library of Congress.
[18] Jackson to Gadsden, May 2, 1822, *Correspondence,* III, 161. It is not known what became of Gadsden's ambition to write a book about Jackson, and if Jackson forwarded him the papers requested they were returned long before Jackson's death. In 1825 a *Civil and Military History of Andrew Jackson* was published under the authorship of "An American Officer." In *The Raven, a Biography of Sam Houston,* I intimate that Houston may have written this book. I am now inclined to believe that he did not write it. Possibly the author was Gadsden, but this is merely a guess.
[19] Jackson to A. J. Donelson, May 2, 1822, Donelson Papers.
[20] Jackson to A. J. Donelson, April 12, 1822, *ibid.*
[21] Jackson to A. J. Donelson, May 20, 1822, *Correspondence,* III, 162.
[22] John M. Lea was the son-in-law who burned the papers. The incident was related to the writer in 1933 by Lemuel R. Campbell of Nashville who had it from Mr. Lea. This evidence being destroyed, the reader may properly inquire as to the source of the author's statement that Judge Overton played a "masterful" part in the campaign. A few political papers escaped Mr. Lea and are in the Overton Papers, Tennessee Historical Society, Nashville. Others are in the Coffee Papers (Tennessee Historical Society), Jackson Papers (Library of Congress) and elsewhere. The correspondence of other members of the junto shows Overton's constant activity and a general deference to his views. In the matter of answering the slanders against Mrs. Jackson in 1827 Overton emerged for once. There his work was patently masterful. So greatly did he surpass in ability the other members of the junto that, to a person who has studied the whole situation, there can be no doubt as to the extent of his contribution to the eventual result.
[23] Jackson to James Gadsden, December 6, 1821, *Correspondence,* III, 140.
[24] Narrative of W. B. Lewis, written in 1858, James Parton, *Life of Andrew Jackson* (1859-60), III, 19-20.
[25] Jackson to James Gadsden, December 6, 1821, *Correspondence,* III, 140.
[26] Parton, III, 20.
[27] Nashville *Whig,* May 1, 1822.
[28] *Ibid.,* April 24, 1822.
[29] *Ibid.,* August 28, 1822.
[30] Jackson had acquired Melton's Bluff from John Melton who had grown wealthy by robbing the boats which passed along the Tennessee River. Melton had built a mansion for his Cherokee wife, but when the Creeks, displeased by his encroachments, began to make threats against his life, he disposed of his extensive property, which he had made famous by lavish expenditures and cruelties to his hands, and moved to the other side of the river. Anne Royall visited the plantation in 1818, and found Jackson's overseer living on the first floor of the Melton house and the second story bulging with stores of cotton.

"No language can convey an idea of the beauties of Melton's Bluff," Mrs. Royall wrote. "I can sit in my room and see the whole plantation; the boats gliding down the river, . . . the ducks, geese, and swans, playing . . . on the bosom of the stream, with a full view of the many islands. . . . I took a walk with some ladies over the plantation. . . . We approached the mansion, by a broad street, running up the river bank east of the town. The street seems suspended between heaven and earth, as the whole premises for two miles, all in sight, appears to be elevated above the horizon. . . . We entered the courtyard, fronting the house, by a stile; and the first thing we met was a large scaffold overspread with cotton. Being damp from dew and often rain, it must be dried in this manner. The mansion was large, built with logs, shingled roof. . . . All the trade of East Tennessee passes by the Bluff, and halt here to take in their pilots." (Anne Royall, *Letters from Alabama* [1830], 59-62.)

[31] Jackson to Egbert Harris, April 13, 1822, *Correspondence*, III, 158.
[32] Jackson to A. J. Donelson, June 28, 1822, *ibid.*, 166.
[33] Jackson to A. J. Donelson, June 28, 1822, *ibid.*, 167.
[34] Felix Grundy to Jackson, June 27, 1822, *ibid.*, 163.
[35] Jackson to A. J. Donelson, August 6, 1822, *ibid.*, 173: "I have recd many letters from every quarter of the united states on this subject the presidency; I have answered none." This was written after the Grundy letter had been received.

Bassett (I, 328) states that Jackson did answer Grundy's letter, under date of July 18, and gives the summary of the answer, the original of which the author says is in the Library of Congress. Bassett apparently has mistaken a letter Jackson wrote to James Bronaugh on July 18 for an answer to Grundy. The summary he gives exactly fits the Bronaugh letter. In the Library of Congress collection of Jackson manuscripts or in no other collection to which Bassett had access, or in no collection to which I have had access, have I been able to discover a reply to the Grundy letter. The letter to Bronaugh is in the Library of Congress collection, as is also Grundy's letter to Jackson, bearing this endorsement in Jackson's hand "Mr. Grundy's confidential letter of the 27th of June 1822," but nothing to indicate that it was answered. Bassett included the Grundy letter and the Jackson letter to Bronaugh in the *Correspondence*, III, 163-170, but no answer to the former appears.

[36] The contemporary spelling of Murfreesborough, and of all other proper names, is used in this volume. The town is now Murfreesboro.
[37] Jackson to A. J. Donelson, July 16, 1822, Donelson Papers.
[38] Nashville *Clarion*, July 18, 1822.
[39] Jackson to J. C. Bronaugh, July 18, 1822, *Correspondence*, III, 170.
[40] Jackson to A. J. Donelson, August 6, 1822, *ibid.*, 173.
[41] John Spencer Bassett, *The Life of Andrew Jackson* (1911), I, 328.
[42] Jackson to Bronaugh, August 1, 1822, S. G. Heiskell, *Andrew Jackson and Early Tennessee History* (1921), III, 158.
[43] Sam Houston to Jackson, August 3, 1822, Jackson Papers.
[44] *Ibid.*

CHAPTER XXII

[1] New York *Evening Post*, August 22, 1822.
[2] Knoxville *Register*, January 29, 1822. The statement was also true of August of the same year.

[3] *Columbian Observer,* Philadelphia, June 23, 1822.
[4] *Western Carolinian,* Salisbury, August 20, 1822.
[5] Jackson to A. J. Donelson, August 6, 1822, *Correspondence,* III, 174.
[6] Jackson to A. J. Donelson, August 6, 1822, *ibid.,* 174.
[7] Jackson to A. J. Donelson, August 28, 1822, *ibid.,* 178.
[8] Jackson to A. J. Donelson, October 11, 1822, *ibid.,* 179.
[9] Parton, II, 585.
[10] J. H. Eaton to Jackson, January 11, 1823, Jackson Papers.
[11] *Ibid.*
[12] James Monroe to Jackson, January 30, 1823, private collection of Henry M. Flynt, New York City.
[13] Jackson to A. J. Donelson, January 8, 1823, Donelson Papers, Library of Congress.
[14] William Carroll to Henry Clay, February 1, 1823, Clay Papers, Library of Congress.
[15] Henry Shaw to Henry Clay, February 11, 1823, *ibid.*
[16] Benton, Jesse, *An Address to the People of the United States on the Presidential Election,* 1824, 8; "Curtius," *Torch Light, . . . an Examination of the . . . Opposition to the Administration . . .* 1826, 7.
[17] J. C. Calhoun to Virgil Maxcy, December 31, 1821, Maxcy Papers, Library of Congress.
[18] J. C. Calhoun to Jackson, January 20, 1823, *ibid.*
[19] J. H. Eaton to Jackson, January 11, 1823, Jackson Papers.
[20] Jackson to James Monroe, February 19, 1823, Monroe Papers, New York Public Library.
[21] Eaton to Jackson, March 23, 1823, Jackson Papers.
[22] J. H. Eaton to Jackson, January 11, 1823, *ibid.*
[23] Jackson to John Coffee, March 10, 1823, *Correspondence,* III, 192.
[24] *Ibid.*
[25] John M. Farland to Jackson, August 14, 1824, Jackson Papers.
[26] Edward Patchell to Jackson, August 7, 1824, *Correspondence,* III, 263.
[27] H. W. Peterson to Jackson, February 3, 1823, Jackson Papers.
[28] Jackson to H. W. Peterson, February 23, 1823, *Correspondence,* III, 189.
[29] J. M. Farland to Jackson, August 14, 1824, Jackson Papers.
[30] The only attempt at a biography of Crawford is J. E. D. Shipp's *Giant Days or the Life and Times of William H. Crawford* (1909), a brief and unsatisfactory work. *The Dictionary of American Biography,* IV, 529, contains a good sketch of Crawford's career by Ulrich B. Phillips. In a bibliographical note Professor Phillips adds: "His rivals for the presidency lived on to great prominence, attracting biographers each of whom wanted a foil for his hero. Crawford was made to serve, until the time of Carl Schurz (*Henry Clay,* I, 223) he was reduced to a reputation of a reputation." The biographer who can tell us in detail how it was that a figure now so obscure as Crawford rose among the men who then peopled the American stage to stand not once but twice on the threshold of the presidency will have made a distinct contribution to our political history.
[31] Worthington C. Ford, *Writings of John Quincy Adams,* VII, 272.
[32] C. Vandewater to Virgil Maxcy, July 10, 1823, Maxcy Papers.
[33] George McDuffie to an unnamed correspondent, January 18, 1823, Fisher Papers, State Historical Commission of North Carolina. This document is from

"The Presidential Election of 1824 in North Carolina" (p. 237), an unpublished thesis by A. R. Newsome, head of the History Department of the University of North Carolina. Dr. Newsome kindly placed a copy at the disposal of the writer. Other copies are in the library of the University of Michigan.

[34] F. J. Wharton to Henry Clay, August 13, 1823, Clay Papers.
[35] John McKinley to Henry Clay, June 3, 1823, *ibid*.
[36] T. H. Benton to Henry Clay, July 7, 1823, *ibid*.
[37] A writer, whose signature is illegible, to Virgil Maxcy, July 24, 1823, Maxcy Papers.
[38] J. C. Calhoun to Virgil Maxcy, August 6, 1823, *ibid*.
[39] Dallas to Maxcy, March 8, 1823; Calhoun to Maxcy, March 12 and 13; Kent to Maxcy, March 2, 1823, Maxcy Papers; George McDuffie to Montfort Stokes, April 7, 1823, Fisher Papers, University of North Carolina, Chapel Hill.
[40] Jane Hays to Rachel Jackson, May 10, 1823, private collection of Andrew Jackson IV, Los Angeles.
[41] Robert Patterson to Rachel Jackson, March 20, 1823, New York *Evening Post*, July 31, 1823, reprinted from the *Franklin Gazette*, Philadelphia.
[42] Rachel Jackson to Robert Patterson, May 17, 1823, *ibid*.
[43] Robert Patterson to Jackson, March 20, 1823, *ibid*.
[44] Jackson to Robert Patterson, May 17, 1823, *ibid*.
[45] Was Jackson sincere in his first abrupt rejections of any suggestion that he stand for the presidency?

I think that he was. Whatever his shortcomings the General was truthful. Had he desired the presidency and assumed indifference to promote his cause, I do not think that he would have found it necessary to lie to Andrew Jackson Donelson whom he regarded with the affection of a father and before whom he desired to appear as a worthy criterion. Moreover Jackson loved his wife as he loved no other creature of earth. He appreciated his responsibility in the private considerations that had made her a fugitive from the white light of renown, and made an honest effort to order his life accordingly. There was little personal vanity of the meaner sort in Jackson's composition. His sense of self-esteem was considerable, but he knew that his place in history was secure. Leadership of men, however, was a birthright which Jackson was as powerless to alter as the color of his eyes.

The ardor of his spirit and an inherent love of combat, first directed against Crawford and Clay against whom he had valid grievances and later involved with the allurements of fame and switched to his own interests, I think, are the factors that swept him into the contest rather than any settled plan or disguised *a priori* ambition.

CHAPTER XXIII

[1] The letter appears in *Correspondence*, II, 263. In later years, Lewis, an old man, liked to regard himself as the person responsible for Jackson's career in the White House, and talked a great deal on the subject. The series of letters to Monroe, of which this is one, attained a position of great importance in his mind. He imagined them almost wholly the product of his own intellect, and written with a view to future political use. These statements are not susceptible of proof. Parton accepted Lewis's story without critical analysis, and his exaggerated account of Lewis's importance as Jackson's political monitor has col-

ored most subsequent biographies and historical accounts. Bassett (*Jackson*, I, 339 *et. seq.*) gives the correct history of the correspondence.

[2] W. B. Lewis to Lewis Cass, a very lengthy letter which, though undated, is shown by internal evidence to have been written in 1844 or 1845. It appears in John Spencer Bassett, "Major Lewis on the Nomination of Andrew Jackson," *Proceedings* of the American Antiquarian Society, New Series, XXXIII, 20; also, with some textual changes in Parton, III, *et seq.* Manuscript copies are in the New York Public Library and the Henry E. Huntington Library, San Marino, California, in the later place under the date of 1850.

[3] George McDuffie to Charles Fisher, December 14, 1823, Polk Papers, University of North Carolina, Chapel Hill, Newsome thesis, 247.

[4] George McDuffie to an unnamed correspondent, probably Charles Fisher, December 12, 1823, Fisher Papers, University of North Carolina, Newsome thesis, 245.

[5] George McDuffie to an unnamed correspondent, probably Charles Fisher, November 21, 1823, *ibid.*, 244.

[6] J. C. Calhoun to Virgil Maxcy, August 27, 1823; L. Williams, Jr., to Maxcy, September, 1823, Maxcy Papers.

[7] George McDuffie to Charles Fisher, December 14, 1823, Polk Papers, University of North Carolina, Newsome thesis, 248.

[8] J. P. Kennedy to Virgil Maxcy, October 11, 1823, Maxcy Papers.

[9] B. B. Smith to Charles Fisher, January 24, 1824, Fisher Papers, University of North Carolina, Newsome thesis, 109.

[10] Shipp, 174.

[11] W. B. Lewis to Lewis Cass, *op. cit.*, 28.

[12] *Ibid.*, 29.

[13] Jackson to John Coffee, October 5, 1823, *Correspondence* III, 210.

[14] Nashville *Whig*, October 6, 1823.

[15] W. B. Lewis to Lewis Cass, *op. cit.*, 29.

[16] Jackson to John Coffee, October 5, 1823, *Correspondence* III, 210.

[17] Jackson to John Coffee, October 24, 1823, *ibid.*, 213.

[18] Jackson to his wife, November 28, 1823, Henry E. Huntington Library *Bulletin*, No. 3, 118.

[19] Jackson to his wife, November, 1823, *ibid.*, 119.

[20] Jackson to his wife, December 3, 1823, *ibid.*, 121.

[21] Jackson to his wife, December 7, 1823, *Correspondence* III, 216.

[22] J. H. Eaton to Rachel Jackson, December 18, 1823, *ibid.*, 217.

[23] Jackson to A. J. Donelson, December 5, 1823, Jackson Papers.

[24] J. R. Bedford to John Overton, December 11, 1824, Overton Papers, Tennessee Historical Society, Nashville.

[25] Hull & Townsend to Jackson, December 15, 1823; Jackson to Hull & Townsend, December 20, 1823, Jackson Papers.

[26] Notice of protest of draft, January 9, 1824; A. J. Donelson to Bedford & Macy, January 23, 1824, *ibid.*

[27] Wyoming, (pseud.) *Letters . . . to the People of the United States*, (1824), 5. The contents of this pamphlet first appeared in the *Columbian Observer* of Philadelphia.

[28] Winfield Scott to Jackson, December 11, 1823; Jackson to Scott, same date, *Correspondence* III, 216-17.

[29] James L. Armstrong, *General Jackson's Juvenile Indiscretions* (1832), 8.

³⁰ Henry Clay, *Address to the Public,* (1827).
³¹ J. H. Eaton to Rachel Jackson, December 18, 1823, *Correspondence* III, 217.
³² Jackson to G. W. Martin, January 2, 1824, *ibid.,* 222.
³³ Daniel Webster to Ezekiel Webster, February 2, 1824, Fletcher Webster, editor, *Private Correspondence of Daniel Webster,* (1856), I, 346.
³⁴ Elijah H. Mills to his wife, January 22, 1824, [Elijah Hunt Mills] *Selections from Letters of the Hon. E. H. Mills* (1881), 21.
³⁵ Jackson to his wife, December 21, 1823, *Correspondence* III, 218.
³⁶ Jackson to John Coffee, December 31, 1823, *ibid.,* 220.
³⁷ Jackson to Francis Preston, January 27, 1824, Huntington Library *Bulletin,* No. 3, 124. See also Jackson to Samuel Swartwout, December 16, 1823, *Proceedings* of the American Antiquarian Society, New Series, XXXI, 74.
³⁸ Sam Houston to G. Mowry, December 13, 1823, Jackson Papers; see also D. W. White to J. J. Crittenden, February, 1824, Crittenden Papers, Library of Congress.
³⁹ Jackson to G. W. Martin, January 2, 1824, *Correspondence* III, 221.
⁴⁰ Jackson to A. J. Donelson, January 21, 1824, *ibid.,* 224.
⁴¹ Jackson to A. J. Donelson, January 18, 1824, *ibid.,* 224.
⁴² James Buchanan to Hugh Hamilton, December 14, 1823, private collection of Emil Edward Hurja, New York City.
⁴³ T. J. Green to William Polk, February 2, 1824, Newsome thesis, 120.
⁴⁴ Raleigh (North Carolina) *Register,* March 5, 1824.
⁴⁵ Phoebe Morris to Mrs. James Madison, January 19, 1825 (misdated 1824), Allen C. Clark, *Life and Letters of Dolly Madison* (1914), 217.
⁴⁶ Jackson to his wife, December 21, 1824, *Correspondence* III, 218.
⁴⁷ The statements concerning Miss O'Neale's early life and loves are derived from her memoirs, written in 1873 and published in 1932 under the title of *The Autobiography of Peggy Eaton.* This document, almost as remarkable for its admissions as for its omissions, was composed while the author was reflecting upon the consequences of the last amours of her eventful history. At the age of sixty she had captivated her granddaughter's dancing master, a youth of nineteen, named Buchignani, and married him. Whereupon Buchignani possessed himself of his wife's large fortune and eloped to Italy with the granddaughter. These events appear in a somewhat clearer perspective in Queena Pollack's *Peggy Eaton, Democracy's Mistress* (1931). A minor example of the literary license of which Mrs. Buchignani availed herself in her memoirs was to spell her maiden name O'Neil.
⁴⁸ Pollack, 59.
⁴⁹ Jackson to W. B. Lewis, September 10, 1829, *Correspondence* IV, 72.
⁵⁰ George McDuffie to Charles Fisher, December 14, 1823, *North Carolina Historical Review,* VII, 490; Henry Clay to James Erwin, December 29, 1823, private collection of Mrs. H. L. Bateman, Nashville, Tennessee.
⁵¹ J. H. Eaton to John Overton, February 8, 1824, Overton Papers.
⁵² Jackson to A. J. Donelson, January 21, 1823, *Correspondence* III, 225.
⁵³ *Niles Register,* XXV, 405.
⁵⁴ Daniel Webster to Ezekiel Webster, February 22, 1824, *Private Correspondence of Daniel Webster,* I, 346.
⁵⁵ "Pennsylvania is as firm as a rock," Calhoun wrote to J. G. Swift on Jan-

uary 25, 1824. See Thomas Robson Hay, "John C. Calhoun and the Presidential Campaign of 1824," *North Carolina Historical Review*, XII, 39.

[56] William C. Meigs, *Life of John C. Calhoun* (1917), 305-06; *Franklin Gazette* (Philadelphia) February 19, 1824.

[57] J. C. Calhoun to Virgil Maxcy, February 27, 1824, Maxcy Papers.

[58] Jackson to W. B. Lewis, March 31, 1824, Lewis Papers, New York Public Library.

[59] Jackson to his wife, January 21, 1824, Huntington Library *Bulletin* No. 3, 123.

[60] Jackson to A. J. Donelson, March 6 and 7, 1824, Donelson Papers.

[61] Jackson to his wife, March 16, 1824, Huntington Library *Bulletin* No. 3, 127.

[62] Charles Francis Adams (editor) *Memoirs of John Quincy Adams, Comprising Portions of His Diary* (1876), VI, 340.

[63] William Plumer Jr., to his father, December 3, 1823, Everett Somerville Brown (editor), *The Missouri Compromises and Presidential Politics, 1820-1825, from the Letters of William Plumer Jr.* (1926), 85; Adams, VI, 273.

[64] Adams, VI, 633.

[65] *Ibid.*, 333.

[66] *Ibid.*, 269, 274, 279, 285, 293.

[67] Harrisburg *Pennsylvanian*, May 4, 1824, from Herman Hailpern, "Pro-Jackson Sentiment in Pennsylvania," *Pennsylvania Magazine of History and Biography*, L, 203.

[68] Mr. Clay's speech appears in *Annals of Congress*, 18th Congress, 1st Session, 1862 *et seq*. Characterizations of it to which the present writer is indebted appear in Carl Schurz, *Henry Clay* (1899) I, 216.

[69] A. P. Hayne to Jackson, April 16, 1824, Jackson Papers.

[70] Jackson to L. H. Coleman April 26, 1824. The first publication of this letter was by the Raleigh (North Carolina) *Star*, May 28, 1824, after Coleman had obtained Jackson's leave to print. Parton (III, 35) was the first biographer to reproduce it, and in doing so he began the circulation of a curious error repeated in many other books. He printed what purports to be the letter from "L. H. Colman" that elicited Jackson's response. This is dated Warrenton, Virginia, and in it the writer is made to describe himself as a member of the Virginia Legislature. No Colman or Coleman was in the Virginia Assembly at the time. The author was a physician of Warrenton, North Carolina, and not a member of the Legislature of his state. The importance of this letter has been overstated, and the missive itself strangely misinterpreted. For example Sumner (*Andrew Jackson* (1899), 95) called it an "ambiguous" bit of "electioneering, muddled . . . by contradictory suggestions." For the letter in full see Parton, III, 35, Bassett, I, 345 or Correspondence, III, 249.

[71] [Martin Van Buren] *Autobiography of Martin Van Buren* (1920), 240.

[72] P. M. Miller to Charles Fisher, January 3, 1824, Fisher Papers, University of North Carolina, Chapel Hill, Newsome thesis, 263.

[73] Jackson to his wife, April 23, 1824, *Correspondence* III, 249.

[74] Jackson to his wife, May 5, 1824, private collection of Andrew Jackson IV, Los Angeles, California.

[75] Jackson to A. J. Donelson, April 27, 1824, *Correspondence* III, 251.

[76] Alfred Balch to John Overton, May 4, 1824, Overton Papers. Tennessee Historical Society, Nashville.

[77] William Plumer Jr. to his father April 1, 1824, Brown, 108.
[78] Jackson to A. J. Donelson, April 23, 1824, Donelson Papers.
[79] Bassett, I, 339 *et seq.* gives a lengthy history of the Jackson-Monroe correspondence episode interesting to those whose ideas of the details of this affair have been derived from Parton.
[80] Alfred Balch to John Overton, May 4, 1824, Overton Papers.
[81] Daniel Webster to Ezekiel Webster, June 5, 1824, Claude H. Van Tine (editor), *Letters of Daniel Webster* (1902), 106.
[82] Jackson to John Coffee, July 1, 1824, *Correspondence* III, 258.
[83] Jackson to his wife, April 23, 1824, *ibid.*, 249.

CHAPTER XXIV

[1] A sidelight on the Clay campaign in Ohio concerns the grandfather of Woodrow Wilson, James Wilson, editor of the *Western Herald and Steubensville Gazette*. A violent free-soiler, Mr. Wilson originally opposed Clay as a friend of slavery and sponsor of the Missouri Compromise, but in the spring of 1824 he joined the Clay ranks and rendered useful service to the future standard-bearer of the Whig Party. Had Mr. Wilson worked as hard for Jackson it is not recklessness to assume that the Tennessean might have carried Ohio, without which it is almost impossible to see how Adams could have been elected.
[2] Pollack, 65.
[3] Farrell-Kirkman family papers, from the private collection of Mrs. Louis Farrell, Nashville, Tennessee. Mrs. Farrell is a great-great-granddaughter of Ellen Kirkman, mother of Mary Kirkman.
[4] Jackson to R. K. Call, November 15, 1821, *Correspondence* III, 130.
[5] Davidson County, Tennessee, records, Nashville. The ceremony was performed July 14, 1824.
[6] J. M. Glassell to Jackson, August 1, 1824, Jackson Papers.
[7] Farrell-Kirkman family papers, *op. cit.*
[8] Benton, Jesse, *An Address to the People* (1824).
[9] John Owen to Bartlett Yancy, July 21, 1824. Miscellaneous Papers, Series One, II, 105, North Carolina Historical Society, Newsome thesis, 173.
[10] Jackson to Samuel Swartwout, March 4, 1824, *Proceedings* of the American Antiquarian Society, New Series, XXXI, 75.
[11] Parton, III.
[12] Joseph Gales, Jr., to Martin Van Buren, October 25, 1824, Van Buren Papers, Library of Congress.
[13] Daniel Webster to Ezekiel Webster, June 5, 1834, *Private Correspondence of Daniel Webster,* I, 346.
[14] A. S. H. Burges to William Polk, Polk Papers, Library of Congress, Newsome thesis, 127.
[15] Gales and Seaton to Martin Van Buren, September 15, 1824, Van Buren Papers. The letter is in the hand of Joseph Gales, junior.
[16] Jackson to Samuel Swartwout, September 27, 1824. *Proceedings* of the American Antiquarian Society, XXXI, 77.
[17] [Smith, Margaret Bayard] *First Forty Years in American Society* (edited by Gaillard Hunt) (1906), 164.
[18] Washington *Gazette*, July 26, 1824. This item is from a manuscript thesis.

"The Washington Press in the Jackson Period" (p. 31) by Culver H. Smith of the University of Chattanooga, a copy of which Dr. Smith kindly placed at the disposal of the writer. Additional copies are in the library of Duke University.

[19] Calhoun to Floride Colhoun, November 12, 1824, J. Franklin Jameson (editor), "Correspondence of John C. Calhoun," *Annual Report American Historical Association* for 1899, II, 227. Though Calhoun and his mother-in-law were blood kin, she spelled her name Colhoun.

[20] P. H. Mangum, Orange County, North Carolina, April 15, 1824, Mangum Papers, Library of Congress, Newsome thesis, 165.

[21] A Jackson broadside in North Carolina, *ibid.*, 65.

[22] Alexandria (D. C.) *Herald*, June 30, 1824. This item is from a manuscript thesis, "The National Election of 1824" (p. 72) by Curtis W. Garrison, librarian of the Pennsylvania State Library, Harrisburg, a copy of which Dr. Garrison kindly placed at the writer's disposal. Additional copies are in the library of Johns Hopkins University.

[23] A Jackson broadside, *ibid.*, 74.

[24] Davidson County, North Carolina, May, 1824, Newsome thesis, 165.

[25] Washington Irving to W. M. Blackford, October 27, 1833, collection of the late Thomas F. Madigan, New York City.

[26] Louisville *Public Advertiser*, October 9, 1824, Garrison thesis, 73.

[27] Robert Williamson to Bartlett Yancy, July 26, 1824, Newsome thesis, 176.

[28] Martin Van Buren to Benjamin Ruggles, August 26, 1824, Van Buren Papers.

[29] Gallatin to Van Buren, October 2, 1824, *ibid.*

[30] Joseph Gales, Jr., to Van Buren, October 17, 1824, *ibid.*

[31] Van Buren, 665.

[32] *National Gazette*, September 7, 1824.

[33] Raleigh *Register*, October 12, 1824, Newsome thesis, 170.

[34] *Ibid.*, November 5, 1824.

[35] Jackson to John Coffee, December 27, 1824, *Correspondence*, III, 270.

[36] Parton, III, 51.

[37] Jackson to John Coffee, October 24, 1823, *Correspondence*, III, 213.

[38] Testimony of John S. Hitt at an investigation conducted by the Kentucky Legislature, 1828, of the conduct of Henry Clay during the House election of 1825. Apparently the only surviving record of this proceeding appears in the *Argus of Western America* (Frankfort), February 25, 1828, from which it was copied by the *United States' Telegraph*, Extra No. 1, March 1, and Extra No. 12, May 10, 1828.

[39] New York *Evening Post*, November 24, 1824.

[40] *Ibid.*

[41] Testimony of Oliver Keene and Francis McAlear, Kentucky legislative investigation, *op. cit.* Clay later denied having sent and Jackson having received such an invitation.

[42] Testimony of Thomas D. Carneal, Kentucky legislative investigation, *op. cit.*

[43] Salem *Gazette* and Boston *Courier*, quoted by New York *Evening Post*, November 18, 1824.

[44] Jacob Barker to Martin Van Buren, November 7, 1824, Van Buren Papers, Library of Congress.

[45] Alexandria (D. C.) *Herald*, December 1, 1824.

⁴⁶ Richmond *Enquirer*, December 4, 1824.
⁴⁷ Jackson to Samuel Swartwout, December 14, 1824, *Correspondence*, III, 268.
⁴⁸ Charles Tutt to Jackson, *ibid.*
⁴⁹ Jackson to John Coffee, December 27, 1824, *ibid.*, 270. "Mr. Gadsbys tavern" was the Franklin House which had become renowned under the proprietorship of William O'Neale, father of the even more renowned Margaret Timberlake.
⁵⁰ Jackson to John Coffee, January 23, 1824, *ibid.*, 274.

CHAPTER XXV

¹ The *New-England Galaxy* (Boston), December 24, 1824, predicted that Jackson's administration would be satisfactory. See also Jabez Hammond, *History of the Political Parties in the State of New York* (1845), II, 188. Hammond was an Adams man.
² New York *Statesman*, December 17, 1824.
³ Hay, 42.
⁴ Benton, I, 48-49 does not state at what time he went over to the Jackson side but there could not have been much delay, despite John Scott's assertion (*An Address of Henry Clay to the Public Containing Certain Testimony in Refutation of the Charges Made By Gen. Andrew Jackson*, 1827, p. 49), which is probably correct, that the Missouri Senator's first impulse was to support Crawford. Several Clay men, including, it seems, the Speaker himself, appear to have flirted with this possibility.
⁵ George Kremer of Pennsylvania to his constituents, Washington *Gazette*, February 28, 1825.
⁶ Statement of T. P. Moore, Kentucky Representative in 1824, *United States' Telegraph* Extra No. 1, March 1, and Extra No. 12, May 10, 1828. Moore says Call exhibited as from Crittenden the letter in question and read the sentence quoted. No such letter to Call appears in the Library of Congress collection of Crittenden Papers. It was generally known, however, that Crittenden was at this time in favor of Jackson's election. (See Crittenden to Clay, September 3, 1827, *An Address of Henry Clay to the Public,* 50.) The quotation in the text, therefore, would have been a correct representation of Crittenden's views.
⁷ A. L. Burnley to J. J. Crittenden, March 2, 1828, Crittenden Papers.
⁸ Testimony of John S. Hitt, Kentucky legislative investigation, *op. cit.*
⁹ George Kremer of Pennsylvania, quoting Johnson, in a letter to his constituents, Washington *Gazette*, February 28, 1825.
¹⁰ W. T. Barry to Henry Clay, January 10, 1825, Clay Papers.
¹¹ George Kremer to his constituents, *op. cit.*
¹² Duff Green to Ninian Edwards, July 14, 1828, Green Papers, Library of Congress.
¹³ Statement of R. K. Call, *United States' Telegraph* Extra No. 12, May 10, 1828.
¹⁴ Martin Van Buren to B. F. Butler, December 27, 1824, Van Buren Papers. In this letter Van Buren still puts Jackson first but remarks that the confidence of his supporters is waning. One gathers that before evidence of an Adams-Clay coalition began to accumulate the New Yorker considered Jackson's advantage very impressive.

[15] W. P. Mangum to Bartlett Yancey, December 25, 1824, *James Sprunt Historical Publications*, X, No. 2, 51.

[16] A. H. Everett to J. Blunt, November 28, 1824, private collection of Stanley Horn, Nashville.

[17] William Plumer, junior, to his father, December 16, 1824, Everett S. Brown (editor), *Missouri Compromises and Presidential Politics*, 123.

[18] Statements of R. K. Call and T. P. Moore, *United States' Telegraph* Extra No. 12, May 10, 1828; Kremer to his constituents, Washington *Gazette*, February 28, 1825. Call says that he arrived in Washington confident that Clay would vote for Jackson. I think that is putting it too strongly. Clay's *Address*, p. 57, contains a statement by John Braddock, a tavern-keeper of Rockville, Maryland, which relates that General Jackson's party, of which Call was a member, stopped at his house of entertainment en route from Tennessee to the capital. Discussing the presidential question, Braddock says Call "declared that the friends of Gen. Jackson did not expect Mr. Clay to vote for him, and if he did so, it would be an act of duplicity on his part." This seems the more reasonable statement of Call's attitude immediately upon his arrival in Washington. Very shortly, however, receipt of the Crittenden letter and other favorable straws in the wind doubtless changed Call's views until he entertained, if not the expectation, at least a strong hope that Clay would find himself in a position where he could hardly avoid supporting Jackson.

[19] Statement of R. K. Call, *United States' Telegraph* Extra No. 12, May 10, 1828. In his own account of this meeting Mr. Clay says: "I was very desirous that he [Jackson] should arrive [in Lexington] prior to my departure, . . . that I might offer him the hospitality of my house." However, Clay avers that he did not contemplate traveling with the General, having already made other arrangements. (*Address*, 28). Jackson's account of the meeting is similar to Call's. (Jackson to Thomas Hickey, September 25, 1827, Jackson Papers.)

[20] Henry Clay to an unnamed constituent, quoted in his "Address to Constituents" of March 26, 1825, Calvin Colton, *Works of Henry Clay* (1897), V, 302.

[21] Henry Clay to F. P. Blair, January 8, 1825, Clay Papers. In the original, misdated 1824.

[22] Statement of John Floyd, *United States' Telegraph* Extra No. 12, May 10, 1828.

[23] Statement of Thomas P. Moore, *ibid*.

[24] Statement of William Plumer, junior, *Supplement to an Address of Henry Clay*, 17. In this recital of the incident, written more than three years after its occurrence, Plumer shows that time had dimmed his memory of the actual event. In 1828 Plumer went so far as to say of Mr. Clay's reply to his felicitations, "I drew from it the obvious allusion that Mr. Clay intended to vote for Mr. Adams." Mr. Plumer's own letters, and his conversations with Adams as recorded by the latter in his diary, are proof that he drew no such inference at the time. The Plumer-Clay conversation took place December 10. Not until December 17 did the rapprochement between Clay and Adams begin. Plumer assumed from the outset that Clay was sounding out Adams to see what he would get in return for his support. Anxiously Plumer watched the development of this matter, and not until January, 1825, was he satisfied that Clay would vote for Adams. Plumer's letters are in Brown, *Missouri Compromises*.

[25] Statements of David Trimble, J. J. Crittenden and James Davidson, *An Address of Henry Clay*, 41, 50, 51.

[26] Statement of Alexander Robertson, *Supplement to an Address of Henry Clay*, 19.

[27] Benton, I, 48, who fixes the time of the conversation as prior to December 15.

[28] Statement of Thomas P. Moore, *United States' Telegraph* Extra No. 12, May 10, 1828.

[29] Martin Van Buren to B. F. Butler, December 27, 1824, Van Buren Papers.

[30] W. P. Mangum to Bartlett Yancey, December 25, 1824, *James Sprunt Historical Publications*, X, No. 2, 51.

[31] John Campbell to David Campbell, January 12, 1825, Campbell Papers, private collection of Lemuel R. Campbell, Nashville.

[32] For accounts of Webster's interview with Jefferson see George Tichnor Curtis, *Life of Daniel Webster* (1870), I, 222 and *The Writings and Speeches of Daniel Webster* (1903), XVII, 371; for proof that Webster repeated Jefferson's remarks on his return to Washington, William Plumer, junior, to his father, December 24, 1824. In Brown, *Missouri Compromises*, 125.

[33] Benton, I, 48. Though the Benton interview places Jefferson in a better light as a prophet, it is impossible to say whether the Missourian or Webster gave the more accurate representation of the sentiments of the former President. A grandson of Jefferson later questioned the fidelity of Webster's quotation; see Henry S. Randall, *Life of Thomas Jefferson* (1858), III, 507.

[34] Statement of R. K. Call, *United States' Telegraph* Extra No. 12, May 10, 1828.

[35] Jackson to Samuel Swartwout, May 16, 1825, *Proceedings* of the American Antiquarian Society, New Series, XXXI, 87; George Kremer to Jackson, March 8, 1825, *Correspondence*, III, 281.

[36] According to Jackson's recollection, the Buchanan interview took place "early in January" 1825; according to Buchanan, December 30, 1824. This particular discrepancy is of no importance, and is noted here only that the reader may fix in his mind the approximate time. Two accounts of the meeting exist: Jackson's in a clear and vigorous letter to Carter Beverley, June 5, 1827, *Correspondence*, III, 355; and Buchanan's, in a letter to his constituents, August 18, 1827, which appears in John Bassett Moore (editor), *Works of James Buchanan* (1908), I, 263. Something of the history of these letters will appear in the next chapter. Suffice to say here that Buchanan's account is labored, incomplete and somewhat obscure, though on the whole a corroboration of Jackson's story of the interview. The most important point of difference is Buchanan's denial that in the matter he acted as an emissary of Clay. On March 8, 1825, (*Correspondence*, III, 281) shortly after the event George Kremer wrote Jackson an account of his conversations with Buchanan which strengthens Jackson's contention. Moreover the deletion by Buchanan from his own account of any mention of his meeting with Clay and Letcher, as subsequently will be related in the text on Clay's authority, is such a serious omission as to impair confidence in the Buchanan version. The direct quotations in the text are from Jackson's account. See also Note No. 40 *post*.

[37] George Kremer to Jackson, *op. cit.*

[38] James Buchanan to Thomas Elder, January 2, 1825, Moore, I, 120.

[39] Van Buren, 150.

⁴⁰ Calvin Colton, *Works of Henry Clay*, I, 441. This is Clay's own account of the interview, made public in 1844. Clay says he meant to include it in his *Address* of 1827, but refrained to do so on that and several subsequent occasions at the urgent request of Buchanan. It is no wonder that in 1827 Buchanan was disturbed by the thought of a public revelation of his visit to Clay, which he, Buchanan, had tactfully omitted from his own restrained version of the Jackson interview incident documented in Note No. 36 *ante*.

⁴¹ Bennett Champ Clark, *John Quincy Adams, Old Man Eloquent* (1932), 186.

⁴² Adams, VI, 444.

⁴³ *Ibid.*, VI, 447.

⁴⁴ *Ibid.*, VI., 452-53.

⁴⁵ William Plumer, junior, to his father, December 24, 1824, Brown, 124.

⁴⁶ Adams, VI, 457.

⁴⁷ Statement of Bouligny, *Address of Henry Clay*, 54. Bouligny fixed the date of his conversation with Clay as December 20.

⁴⁸ Statement of Lafayette who fixed the date "in the latter end of December," *ibid.*, 56.

⁴⁹ Nathaniel Macon to Charles Tait, January 7, 1825, Shipp, 179.

⁵⁰ Colton, *Works of Henry Clay*, I, 378.

⁵¹ T. W. Cobb to a constituent, January 15 (?), 1825, Joseph B. Cobb, *Leisure Labors* (1858), 214. The contemporary evidence of alert politicians should be given at least equal weight with the statements of Clay's friends (see Notes No. 25, 26 and 47 *ante*). The former statements were written on the spot. They were designed neither to accuse nor defend Mr. Clay, but merely to indicate the prevailing impression of uncertainty as to his position as late as mid-January. The latter statements were made from memory two or three years after the event by friends of Clay anxious to deliver him from the difficulties in which his alliance with Adams had enmeshed him. I do not think it unfair to caution the reader that after this interim others besides Mr. Plumer may have been suffering from an impairment of memory as to precisely what happened in the autumn and winter of 1824.

⁵² William Plumer, junior, to his father, January 4, 1825, Brown, 126.

⁵³ Henry Clay to F. P. Blair, January 8, 1825, Clay Papers.

⁵⁴ When Mr. Clay departed John Quincy Adams penned in his diary the entry which furnishes the only contemporary narrative of this meeting. Having attended church twice that day, Mr. Adams first gave the text of the sermons, and told how he had spent the time between services. Clay arrived at six. His opening speeches are given rather fully—how a Crawford man had approached him, and how friends of Mr. Adams, "always claiming to act on their own responsibility," had also come "urging considerations personal to himself." No mention is made of the Buchanan or any other visit in Jackson's interest. Next, Mr. Clay asked Adams "to satisfy him with regard to some principles of great public importance" which the diarist does not identify. Then the entry ends abruptly: "He had no hesitation in saying that his preference would be for me." The unsatisfactory feature of the account is that at no time does Adams report his part of the conversation. From Letcher and others Adams knew that the purpose of Clay's visit was to formulate a political working agreement. Clay's opening statement, as quoted by Adams, confirms this. Whatever Mr. Adams replied to this and other speeches of Clay, it was agreeable to the Speaker

because from that day forth the two acted in concert. Clark, in his sympathetic biography (*John Quincy Adams*, 224), says this meeting marked the perfection of the Adams-Clay "alliance." In a conversation with the writer in 1933 Senator Clark said that from his knowledge of politics and of the circumstances of the Adams and Clay meeting he was sure that the terms of the alliance, as later carried out by each party, were understood beforehand by both Adams and Clay; and that a political adversary was within his rights in calling this understanding a "bargain."

[55] Cobb, 214; Adams, VI, 467-69.

[56] Mr. Clay's defiance of the instructions of the Legislature involved a repudiation of his prior views on that subject. Notably in 1816 Clay had expressed a strong reverence for such instructions and denounced Congressmen who violated them. He did the same in 1839.

[57] J. J. Crittenden to David White, January 21, 1825, *United States' Telegraph* Extra No. 12, May 10, 1828. Crittenden also wrote to Francis Johnson (*ibid.*) and probably other Congressmen. None of these letters appears in the Library of Congress collection of his papers. In White's case this may be explained by the fact that Crittenden admitted, in the letter mentioned in the text, that he had so little stomach for his task that he was sending off the communication without reading it; apparently, therefore, he retained no copy. As time passed Crittenden overcame a measure of his distaste for Adams and supported Clay in his course more stoutly. This is established by the Crittenden Papers.

[58] F. P. Blair to David White, January 21, 1825, *ibid.*

[59] Testimony of J. Dudley, a member of the Legislature, Kentucky legislative investigation, *op. cit.*

[60] Statement of T. P. Moore, *United States' Telegraph* Extra No. 12, May 10, 1828.

[61] [Margaret Bayard Smith], *The First Forty Years in Washington Society*, edited by Gaillard Hunt (1906), 172.

[62] Kremer to his constituents, February 25, 1825, Washington *Gazette*, February 28, 1825.

[63] John Campbell to his brother, probably David, January 25, 1825, Campbell Papers.

[64] John Campbell to James Campbell, February 1, 1825, *ibid.*

[65] R. Y. Hayne to S. V. Grimke, January 28, 1825, New York Historical Society.

[66] A. H. Tracy to Thurlow Weed, January 23, 1825, Thurlow Weed, *Autobiography* (1883), I, 175.

[67] William Plumer, junior, to his father, January 24, 1825, Brown, 136.

[68] Two or three days *after* the House election Jackson paid Crawford a brief call, externally a mere visit of courtesy. (Shipp, 191) This was their first meeting in several years and in view of the attitude of the Crawford following toward the election of Adams it is difficult to regard it as without political significance.

[69] Betty Coles to Andrew Stevenson, February 3, 1825, Stevenson Papers, Library of Congress.

[70] Statement of Representative Duncan McArthur of Ohio, *An Address of Henry Clay*, 32.

[71] Calvin Colton (editor), *Private Correspondence of Henry Clay* (1856), 489; Curtis, I, 574. Mr. Sloane delayed making this disclosure until 1844, a cir-

cumstance difficult to understand in view of Mr. Clay's need for and his efforts to obtain just such testimony to include in his *Address* of 1827. The statement Sloane contributed to the *Address* contains only an indistinct allusion to the "importunity of some of his [Jackson's] Congressional friends." Why he should have waited until the General's public career was over to expand this vague phrase into a specific accusation against one of Jackson's intimates is a question no weigher of testimony can ignore.

[72] Adams, VI, 473; Senator Thomas W. Cobb of Georgia to a constituent, January 15 (?), 1825, Cobb, 214. This letter shows that the Crawford people also had been after Scott. Cobb, a Crawford leader, sums up a long analysis of the situation with the assertion that Jackson would probably be elected on the first ballot.

[73] Claude Moore Fuess, *Daniel Webster* (1930), I, 320-22.

[74] Adams, VI, 476.

[75] Jackson to John Coffee, December 27, 1824, *Correspondence*, III, 270.

[76] Jackson to John Coffee, January 5, 1825, *ibid.*, III, 273. So far as his known correspondence discloses, Jackson mentioned his suspicions only to Coffee, and to him he minimized the situation. Buchanan's visit was not specifically mentioned. As Coffee lived in Alabama, a three-weeks' journey distant, the letters could not have been designed to promote a backfire against Clay.

[77] Jackson to W. B. Lewis, January 29, 1825, Lewis Papers.

[78] Mrs. William Seaton, in Anne Hollingsworth Wharton, *Social Life in the Early Republic* (1902), 199.

[79] Mrs. Jackson to Eliza Kingsley, December 23, 1824, Parton, III, 52.

[80] Bassett, I, 355.

[81] Charles P. Tutt to Jackson, January 9, 1825, Jackson Papers. On the same subject Tutt wrote on January 4 and 6. These letters have not been found.

[82] Jackson to C. P. Tutt, January 6, 1825, *ibid.*

[83] This was accomplished rather obliquely on January 24 by the announcement that a majority of the Kentucky and Ohio delegations would vote for Adams. A few days later a letter from the Speaker to Francis Brooke (see note 88 *post.*), dated January 28, was published. In this the Speaker declared his personal intention to vote for Adams.

[84] Henry Clay to F. P. Blair, January 29, 1825, *Private Correspondence of Henry Clay*, 112.

[85] J. J. Crittenden to Henry Clay, February 15, 1825, Crittenden Papers.

[86] *Columbian Observer*, January 28, 1825.

[87] Henry Clay to a member of the Virginia Legislature, February 4, 1825, *Supplement to the Address of Henry Clay*, 22.

[88] Henry Clay to Francis Brooke, February 4, 1825, *ibid.*, 21.

[89] Henry Clay to James Brown, January 23, 1825, Clay Papers.

[90] Statement of T. P. Moore, *United States' Telegraph* Extra No. 12, May 10, 1828. In a weak and involved statement in *A Supplement to the Address of Henry Clay* (p. 20), White defended his course. "So far as I have been implicated, in connection with my late colleagues, in the alleged management, bargain, sale &c . . . I plead conscious innocence." Moreover he stated that as far as he knew the other Kentucky members who supported Adams had done nothing "criminal." In 1828, when this was written, White, like several other congressmen, had lost his seat on account of his vote for Adams and was knocking for admission to the Jackson party.

⁹¹ Quoted from William O. Lynch, *Fifty Years of Party Warfare* (1931), 310.
⁹² Statement of Representative William Brent of Louisiana, *Address of Henry Clay*, 59.
⁹³ Mr. Clay also expressed the "probability" that this was done with the knowledge and approval of Jackson (*ibid.*, 23-24), a supposition supported by no other evidence and opposed by much evidence. Kremer declared (*United States' Telegraph* Extra No. 12, May 10, 1828) that neither Jackson nor Eaton had knowledge of the letter until it was published. He said it was written on his own desk and, by implication, with his own hand. The letter itself, however, is good evidence that Kremer, a man of little schooling, did not write it.
⁹⁴ A. Levasseur, *Lafayette in America* (1829), II, 24.
⁹⁵ Lot Clark to Roger Skinner, February 28, 1825, Van Buren Papers. On January 24, Plumer of New Hampshire sent his father an optimistic prediction, indicating an Adams victory on the first ballot (Brown, 136). A day earlier, however, Clay had privately expressed himself as uncertain of the result (Clay to James Brown, Clay Papers).
⁹⁶ T. H. Benton to John Scott, February 8, 1825, Parton, III, 62.
⁹⁷ Van Buren, 152.
⁹⁸ Contemporary evidence that most of the broken Crawford following in Congress preferred Jackson to Adams is plentiful. On February 15, before he knew the result of the House balloting, Crittenden wrote Clay (Crittenden Papers) specifically mentioning New York and Virginia as reported to have gone over to Jackson. Georgia and North Carolina were certain to prefer him to Adams in a long contest. According to McLane's statement on January 24 (Brown, 136), Delaware intended to stand by Crawford to the end. After the election McLane went over to the Jackson camp speedily enough, however.

In his *History of the Political Parties in the State of New York* (II, 190), published 1845, Jabez Hammond reports that Van Buren contrived the tie with the expectation of throwing his support to Adams on a later ballot and appropriating some of the credit which otherwise would redound to Clay as a president maker. Nathan Sargent in his *Public Men and Events* (1875), 77-78, tells the same story, though the premise on which he bases his conclusions is faulty in one particular at least. (See Note 106 *post.*) Although such competent students of the period as Bassett (I, 364), and Lynch (313), are inclined to accept the Hammond-Sargent view, my reading of the evidence causes me to question it. [Since the foregoing was written I have discovered that Mr. Hammond experienced similar doubts, for in the fourth printing of his work in 1852 he inserted at the end of the volume (II, 540) a note correcting his text in that particular, and stating that Van Buren intended to support Crawford throughout the balloting.]

Mr. Van Buren's motives were seldom transparent and, with his fortunes at the low ebb that they were in 1825, there can be no doubt but that he had his own welfare in mind when charting his course in the House election.

If Van Buren really meant that Jackson should be beaten (and by his own statement after the first ballot the votes of two additional states would be required to elect Adams, owing to the defection of Maryland), he was very lenient toward his messmates, McLane and Cuthbert, both avowed anti-Adams men. Moreover the post-election wrath of Van Buren's intimates is significant. To say that it sprang not from the fact that Jackson was beaten but merely that Adams had been elected without Van Buren's having had time to get on the bandwagon, would be to say something I find hard to believe.

When the House balloting began time fought on the side of Jackson and in a long contest every vote the Crawford men kept from Adams would be half a vote for Jackson, a fact a politician of Van Buren's acumen could not have overlooked.

[99] Statement of Representative Kent of Maryland quoting Saunders of North Carolina, *Address of Henry Clay*, 60.

[100] Actually Van Buren's personal following numbered only fifteen men who were for Crawford, but the delegation contained two Jackson men who by their determination to vote against Adams were counted, for practical purposes, as part of the Van Buren strength. Indeed, without them the leader could not produce the tie that he hoped to produce on early ballots. One of the fifteen, Van Rensselaer, vacillated between Crawford and Jackson. It is significant that Van Buren should regard this with complacency, his only request being that the old man should *not* vote for Adams.

[101] Lot Clark to Roger Skinner, February 28, 1825, Van Buren Papers. Clark was apparently correct in his surmise, for after the election Clinton, not Webster, received the offer of the English mission. He declined it.

[102] Mrs. Smith, 185.

[103] Van Rensselaer's account of the interview as reported by Van Buren, 152. No other direct account exists, though Mrs. Margaret Bayard Smith's relation of McLane's meeting with Van Rensselaer directly afterward establishes that such an interview had taken place and gives McLane's version of its dire effect on the old man.

[104] Mrs. Smith, 191.

[105] Van Buren, 150; Mrs. Smith, 192.

[106] Van Buren, 152. Sargent (77) gives an entirely different story of how Rensselaer came to vote for Adams. He says the patroon was informed that Van Buren had purposely contrived the tie vote so as to throw his strength to Crawford on the second ballot, and thus snatch from Clay the credit for making a President. Therefore Van Rensselaer voted for Adams to defeat the scheme of Van Buren to whom he was "antagonistic." One trouble with this account is that Van Rensselaer and Van Buren were not antagonistic. Moreover, uncandid as Mr. Van Buren often was, it is difficult to believe that in his old age he deliberately invented a falsehood to explain Van Rensselaer's vote. The weight of probability, therefore, seems on the side of his story and not Sargent's.

[107] *Niles' Register,* February 12, 1825.

[108] Mrs. Smith, 181; Shipp, 185.

[109] Mrs. Smith, 186.

[110] *Ibid.,* 186.

[111] *Ibid.,* 173; Shipp, 183.

[112] *Ibid.,* 186.

[113] Mrs. Smith, 181, 183.

[114] Samuel G. Goodrich, *Recollections of a Lifetime* (1866), II, 403.

[115] Parton, III, 65.

[116] Jackson to Samuel Swartwout and others, February 10, 1825, *Proceedings* of the American Antiquarian Society, New Series, XXXI, 80.

[117] Bill for food and drink, dated February 18, 1825, Jackson Papers.

[118] Jackson to W. B. Lewis, February 14, 1825, *Correspondence,* III, 276.

[119] Edward Patchell to Jackson, March 4, 1825, Jackson Papers.
[120] John Pemberton to Jackson, Philadelphia, February 15, 1825, *ibid*.
[121] Allegheny *Democrat*, quoted by *Columbian Observer* (Philadelphia), March 2, 1825.
[122] Pittsburg *Observer*, quoted by Columbian *Observer*, March 10, 1825.
[123] Lot Clark to Roger Skinner, February 28, 1825, Van Buren Papers.
[124] Testimony of John T. Johnson, brother of the Kentucky Senator, quoting Representative Metcalfe before Kentucky legislative investigation, *Argus of Western America,* February 25, 1825, and *United States' Telegraph* Extras Nos. 1 and 12, March 1 and May 10, 1828.
[125] Statements of John T. Johnson and O. B. Brown, *ibid.,* No. 12, May 10, 1828.
[126] Testimony of John Desha reporting a conversation with Metcalfe, Kentucky legislative investigation, *op. cit.* All during the winter this had been regarded as one of the remote possibilities. On December 12 James Hamilton, junior, of South Carolina wrote Van Buren: "Keep a sharp look out as to the Calhouns movement If I know the man and his friends he will endeavour to prevent a choice. look to it with all your eyes." (Van Buren Papers.) On February 18, the day Clay accepted Adam's offer of the secretaryship of state Calhoun wrote his political lieutenant in Maryland, Virgil Maxcy, somewhat enigmatically as follows: "Things have taken a strange turn. It would require a little volume to detail all of the occurrences of the last two months. . . . I wish to see you much so that you may clearly understand the present extraordinary . . . crisis. Form no opinion from what you see on the surface. Be here at least on the 4th of March." (Maxcy Papers) Mr. Desha's testimony was given under oath. Mr. Metcalfe's own account of his vote, which appears in Mr. Clay's *Address*, p. 45, does not mention Calhoun, and says that he voted for Adams because of "the *army,* the *anti-tariff* and *anti-internal improvements*" views of Jackson.
[127] Affidavit of John Griffith and others, *United States' Telegraph* Extra No. 12, May 10, 1828.
[128] Statement of A. Greer, *ibid*.
[129] Amos Kendall to Henry Clay, March 23, 1825, Clay Papers.
[130] I speak here of the reasons Mr. Clay advanced for his vote prior to the election, not after it, when, to his surprise, the storm of criticism grew in volume instead of dying away as he had expected. In an effort to pour oil on the troubled waters the Secretary, disregarding the advice of Kendall, issued a circular to his constituents, dated March 26, 1825. The immediate occurrence which seems to have called it forth was the publication of a letter from Jackson to Samuel Swartwout (February 22, 1825, *Correspondence,* III, 278), in which Old Hickory recapitulated his army services and said if that record made him a "military chieftain" he would not disown the title. Clearly, this letter was written for dissemination. In his reply Clay greatly toned down his military chieftain charge. Praising the General's career as a soldier, he said that only Jackson's lack of statesmanship had caused him to vote for Adams whose proved statesmanship made him the more intelligent choice. (Colton, *Works of Henry Clay,* V, 299.)

All very true, but these reasons, put forth in a defensive argument after the event, form no part of the picture with which we are here concerned: Clay, the political partner of Adams, toiling among the congressmen to encompass the defeat of his western rival. Note Clay's private letter to Blair dated January 8, 1825 (see Note No. 53 *ante*) which contained the barest indirect allusion to Mr. Adam's fitness and rested the weight of the case on the military chieftain charge. Note the letter to Francis Brooke, dated January 28, in which Clay publicly set forth his position: "I have interrogated my conscience as to what I ought to do, and that faithful guide tells me I ought to vote for Mr. Adams." This letter contained no reference to Adam's statesmanship or to Jackson's lack of it, and continued, "As a friend of liberty and to the permanence of our institutions I cannot consent by contributing to the election of a military chieftain to give the strongest guaranty that this Republic will march in the fatal road which has conducted every other Republic to ruin." (Colton, *Works of Henry Clay*, IV, 111.)

Taking the evidence as a whole, of which the foregoing are fair samples, it seems conclusive that by design Clay set out to defeat Jackson on the old militarism issue of 1819. Only when the repercussions became too great did the Secretary seek to shift his ground to Mr. Adam's superior qualifications as a civil servant. Nor is this the only particular in which Mr. Clay sought to alter the aspect of the past to support later contingencies. His *Address* of 1827 and the *Supplement* of 1828 seek to establish that, from October, 1824, he had not faltered in his resolution to support Adams. The object of this was to create the inference that if Mr. Clay had decided in October to vote for Adams, a bargain over that vote in December would have been impossible. What Mr. Clay omitted to make clear was that, so closely did he guard his secret, not only were Adams men in doubt as to his preference but also many of his own confidants, for example Crittenden and Blair who heard the news with surprise and dismay in January.

Kremer's letter to his constituents, probably written by Eaton, was published February 28, 1825, and may be taken as the earliest statement in detail of the Jacksonian point of view. This accepted the premise that before leaving Kentucky Clay laid the groundwork for his vote for Adams, but veiled his intentions until, step by step, he had worked into a position where he could carry with him a sufficient number of western congressmen to elect the New Englander. No evidence Mr. Clay and his partizans has brought to light seriously impairs this contention. Evidence from impartial sources tends to confirm it. Though, as Mr. Clay declared, the person cannot be found who ever heard him say he would vote for Jackson, it nevertheless remains that his cordial behavior toward the General led many Jackson people to hope and many Adams people to fear that he would do so. It is impossible to believe that a man of Clay's intuitions was unaware of this. By his cautious and indirect approach to Adams, Clay, at the outset, gave the impression of a man seeking a bargain. By the time Adams and his intimates learned that the support of Clay was a probability the bargain aspect of the arrangement was taken for granted by them.

To epitomize, this is my view: before coming to Washington, Clay hoped to be able to bring about a situation whereby he could benefit himself by supporting Adams; upon his arrival there he assumed an attitude of aloofness designed to put the Adams people on the anxious seat and bring them to his terms; after which Mr. Adams met the terms. The alternative is an assumption that Clay's support of Adams and Adams's appointment of Clay were merely a coincidence.

[131] Jackson to George Wilson, February 20, 1825, Tennessee Historical Society, Nashville.

¹³² Colton, *Life of Henry Clay*, 319, quoting Benton's words to a constituent in 1827. Benton was not entirely consistent in his attitude toward the bargain charge, however. In 1854 in his final word on the subject (Benton, I, 48), the Missouri Senator said that the charge had been used "unjustly in prejudicing the public mind against Mr. Adams and Mr. Clay."

CHAPTER XXVI

¹ Statement of A. Wylie, *Supplement to the Address of Henry Clay*, 6.
² John Bach McMaster, *History of the People of the United States* (1883-1924), V, 489.
³ J. T. Hitt to Jackson, April 22, 1825, Jackson Papers.
⁴ Jackson to Samuel Swartwout, February 22, 1825, *Correspondence*, III, 278.
⁵ See Note 130, Chapter V.
⁶ Jackson to John Coffee, April 24, 1825, *Correspondence*, III, 283.
⁷ Jackson to Samuel Swartwout, May 16, 1825, *ibid.*, 285.
⁸ Marquis de Lafayette to Jackson, August 21, 1825, *ibid.*, 290.
⁹ Una Pope-Hennessey, *Three English Women in America* (1929), 41.
¹⁰ Bill of Josiah Nichols to Jackson, December 26, 1825, Jackson Papers.
¹¹ Jackson to John Coffee, October 20, 1825, *Correspondence*, III, 296.
¹² Robert Butler to Jackson, September 15, 1826, Jackson Papers.
¹³ Jackson to John Coffee, May 19, July 23, 1825, *Correspondence*, III, 285 and 288.
¹⁴ James Gadsden to Jackson, September 15, 1825, Jackson Papers.
¹⁵ Jackson to the Tennessee Legislature, October 12, 1825, *Correspondence*, III, 293.
¹⁶ Jackson to Henry Lee, October 7, 1825, *ibid.*, III, 291.
¹⁷ Jackson to R. K. Call, March 9, 1829, Jackson Papers.
¹⁸ John H. Marable to Jackson, April 3, 1826, *ibid.*
¹⁹ Charles H. Peck, *The Jacksonian Epoch* (1899), 107.
²⁰ Blifil, a hypocritical rogue, and Black George, a candid rogue with some redeeming virtues, are characters in Henry Fielding's novel *Tom Jones*.
²¹ Eaton to Jackson, May 5, 1826, Jackson Papers.
²² Samuel R. Overton to Jackson, July 5, 1826, *ibid.*; Samuel R. Overton to John Overton, August 28, 1826, Overton Papers.
²³ Duff Green, *Facts and Suggestions, Biographical and Historical* (1866), 29.
²⁴ Jackson to James Loyd, July 14, 1826, Jackson Papers.
²⁵ Jackson to a Committee of the Davidson County Bible Society, September 30, 1826, *Correspondence*, III, 315.
²⁶ John Rowan to Jackson, August 20, 1826, Jackson Papers.
²⁷ Van Buren to C. C. Cambreleng, November 8, 1826, Van Buren Papers.
²⁸ Sam Houston to Jackson, January, 1827, *Correspondence*, III, 329.
²⁹ Jackson to Sam Houston, October 23, 1826, *ibid.*, VI, 485.
³⁰ Sam Houston to Jackson, December 13, 1826, *ibid.*, 486.
³¹ Jackson to Sam Houston, January 5, 1827, *ibid.*, 488.
³² Jackson to Secretary of Navy, January 5, 1827, *ibid.*, III, 329.
³³ Jackson to H. L. White, February 7, 1827, *ibid.*, 334.
³⁴ S. L. Southard to Jackson, February 9, 1827; Jackson to Southard, March 6, *ibid.*, 342 and 345.
³⁵ James Buchanan to Duff Green, October 16, 1826, Jackson Papers.

[36] Duff Green to Jackson, June 9, 1827, *Correspondence,* III, 361.
[37] Jackson to W. B. Lewis, May 5, 1827, *ibid.,* 355; to Amos Kendall, September 4, 1827, *ibid.,* 381.
[38] Jackson to Carter Beverley, June 5, 1827, *ibid.,* 356.
[39] Solomon Penn, junior, to Jackson, July 5, 1827, *ibid.,* 370.
[40] Parton, III, 125.
[41] Dated July 18, 1827. *United States' Telegraph,* August 9, 1827.
[42] Maunsel White to Jackson, August 4, 1827, Jackson Papers.
[43] Jackson to James Buchanan, July 15, 1827, *Correspondence,* III, 374.
[44] *United States' Telegraph,* August 9, 1827.
[45] *National Journal* (Washington), August 9, 1827.
[46] *United States' Telegraph,* August 13, 1827.
[47] See Note 40, Chapter V.
[48] John Campbell to his brother, probably James, August 23, 1827, Campbell Papers.
[49] Amos Kendall to Jackson, August 22, 1827, Tennessee State Library, Nashville.
[50] Amos Kendall to Jackson, August 27, 1827, *ibid.*
[51] Jackson to Kendall, September 4, 1827, *Correspondence,* III, 381.
[52] Martin Van Buren to Jackson, September 14, 1827, *ibid.,* 384.
[53] David Campbell to his brother, probably James, March 29, 1827, Campbell Papers.
[54] A communication signed "An Enquirer," which internal evidence shows to have been written in 1827, to John Overton. Private collection of J. M. Dickinson of Nashville, a great-great-grandson of Overton. Having been written in 1827 this could not have been the first evidence the Jackson people had of Day's activities or Clay's supposed knowledge of them, but the record indicates that the information they did have late in 1826 was almost precisely what this communication sets forth.
[55] Jackson to Sam Houston, December 15, 1826, *Correspondence,* III, 325.
[56] J. H. Eaton to Jackson, December 27, 1826, Jackson Papers.
[57] Charles Hammond to J. H. Eaton, January 3, 1827, *Truth's Advocate,* January, 1828; Eaton to Jackson, February 4, 1827, Jackson Papers.
[58] E. G. W. Butler to Jackson, Cincinnati, January 11, 1827, *ibid.;* Sam Houston to Jackson, January 5, 1828, *Correspondence,* III, 331; *United States' Telegraph,* March 8, 1827.
[59] Jackson to W. B. Lewis, December 12, 1826, private library of J. P. Morgan, New York City.
[60] J. H. Eaton to Jackson, January 27, 1827, Jackson Papers.
[61] This appeared in February, according to Arnold's second hand-bill, dated May 24, 1828, a copy of which is in the Tennessee State Library, Nashville. The writer has not seen a copy of the original. The quotation in the text is from the *National Journal's* reprint, March 26, 1827.
[62] *Liberty Hall & Cincinnati Gazette,* March 23, 1828. In this article Hammond does not mention Arnold but assumes to publish the story in reply to a "challenge" from the Cincinnati *Advertiser* which, taking notice of Hammond's whispering campaign, had called upon him to unmask himself in print.
[63] Nashville *Banner & Whig,* March 21, 1827.
[64] Surviving fragments of the private correspondence of John Overton indicate that the committee adopted a critical attitude toward evidence unusual

under the circumstances. On May 27, 1827, Overton wrote to Jackson: "In the *defence* now in progress . . . it may be necessary to state explicitly that Hugh McGary . . . *never saw you and* Mrs Jackson together either *before or since he came in company with you both Sept 1791* . . . with nearly 100 . . . [others] in the trip from *Natchez* to *Nashville*. Such I believe to be the fact and if so please communicate it. This letter nor your answer intended for publication but . . . your answer necessary to satisfy some of the Committee." (Jackson Papers.)

Jackson's reply cannot be found but apparently it deviated slightly from Overton's idea of the facts. In any event a slight deviation is found in the committee report, which seems to indicate the careful work of that body. On McGary's testimony the divorce was granted on ground of adultery in 1793. (See first volume of this work, pp. 74-78.) After mentioning the ex parte nature of that hearing the committee reflects on McGary's competence as a witness: "Hugh McGary . . . never saw Gen. and Mrs. Jackson together until the month of Sept. 1791, after their marriage at Natchez, when they were living together as married persons; in the most fair, honest and innocent belief that they were lawfully joined in wedlock. Hugh M'Gary came through the Indian country from Natchez to Nashville . . . in the same company in which General and Mrs. Jackson came, in Sept. 1791, and circumstances then occurred calculated to excite in M'Gary a strong feeling of dislike toward Gen. Jackson, which it is unnecessary to detail as they related solely to a meditated attack by the Indians."

While sparing no pains to blacken the characters of Jackson and his wife, the Adams papers portrayed Robards as a good husband, grievously wronged. Though evidence abounds that Robards was not a good husband, the Nashville committee was considerate of him. This testimony was not used: "I resided with the [Robards] family whilst they lived together [in Kentucky] & his conduct towards her was cruel, unmanly & unkind; . . . her deportment exhibited the exemplary & affectionate wife. . . . Lewis Robards was in the habit of leaving his wife's bed & spending the night with the negro women." The deponent said that Mrs. George Robards, a sister-in-law, would corroborate this. "She states that . . . the breach arose from Roberts's own improper conduct." (John Downing to J. H. Eaton, December 20, 1826, private collection of J. M. Dickinson, Nashville.)

Mr. Dickinson also has two letters to Overton from Henry Banks, a well-known figure of Frankfort, Kentucky, touching on Rachel's attachment to Peyton Short, which illuminate Robard's character and the length Rachel was prepared to go to escape from him. Had this material been available at the time, it would have been included in Chapter V of the preceding volume of this work. It is useful in the reconstruction of the background of experience which undoubtedly had its effect on Rachel's peace of mind in later life.

Under date of June 4, 1827, Banks wrote that not long before his death Short, whom Banks had known from youth, vowed "that so far as he knew or believed Mrs. Jackson was as pure and virtuous as an Angel. . . . That in consequence of the politeness of his deportment to Mrs. Robards Captain Robards became jealous of his wife, and therefore treated her in a rude and cruel manner. That the discontent appeared to be mutual. That they had agreed to part, and that she was about to go to Tennessee where her mother resided. That he (Short) was so much excited, both by his sympathy for Mrs. Robards and his respect and affection for her, as induced him to form a determination to marry her after the intended separation should take place. That he was then about to go to Virginia with an intention of converting his patrimony into money or slaves—and if Mrs. Robard would accept him as a husband to go with her to the Spanish Dominions on the Mississippi; and there to settle himself for life.

"With such views, and under such excitements, when on his way to Virginia he sent a letter to The Crab Orchard to Mrs. Robards which was enclosed to a friend authorizing Mrs. Robards to obtain what goods, etc. she might want, on his account. That Captain Robards obtained possession of this letter, and followed him to Virginia, uttering threats & vengeance against him. That being informed of what Robards had said he caused an enquiry to be made of him to know whether he sought blood or pecuniary atonement. That he was informed that Robard would be appeased by money. In consideration of which . . . Robards was paid and satisfied.

"Before Short returned to Kentucky Mrs Robards had gone to Natchez, and there married General Jackson."

In another letter, dated May 10, 1827, Banks gave his own testimony regarding the settlement between Short and Robards in Richmond. "Short . . . let him know that if blood was his object he should be ready to meet him, . . . but if a compromise could be made with money, it would be given." The two met at Gault's Tavern, and in Banks's presence "Short paid over about $1,000.00."

[65] *United States' Telegraph,* June 22, 1827. Later the material was issued as a pamphlet. Members of the committee who produced the document included John Overton, W. B. Lewis, John McNairy, G. W. Campbell, Alfred Balch, Edward Ward, Felix Robertson and John Catron. The restrained, judicial tone sounds like the work of Overton. The text refers to the final report of the committee, completed in June, 1827. A preliminary report was published in April to which Arnold's second production quoted in the text was a reply. In the interest of terseness the preliminary report is not mentioned in the text.

[66] Broadside by Arnold, May 24, 1824, Tennessee State Library, Nashville.

[67] [Charles Hammond], *A View of Gen. Jackson's Domestic Relations* (1828). The material appeared originally in *Truth's Advocate* (Cincinnati), a campaign sheet edited by Hammond.

[68] Jackson to Coffee, June 2, 1828, *Correspondence,* III, 409; Coffee to Jackson, July 2, 1828, Jackson Papers.

[69] Rough draft of an undated letter, Jackson to Henry Clay, private collection of Andrew Jackson IV, Los Angeles. My opinion is that the letter was not sent. Otherwise some sort of sequel would hardly have been avoidable.

[70] *United States' Telegraph,* June 16, 1827.

[71] Duff Green to Jackson, July 8, 1827, *Correspondence,* III, 372.

[72] Jackson to Duff Green, August 13, 1827, Jackson Papers.

[73] Thomas Henderson to Jackson, July 28, 1827, *ibid.*

[74] Henry Clay to Charles Hammond, December 23, 1826, *Truth's Advocate,* January, 1828.

[75] Charles Hammond to Henry Clay, January 3, 1827, Clay Papers.

[76] The writer has consulted newspapers published in practically every state from 1822 to 1824. He believes that nearly any Adams, Crawford, Clay or

Calhoun journal west or south of the Potomac that he examined will bear out the statement in the text.

77 See page 275, Volume I of this work.
78 Harriet Martineau, *Society in America* (1837), III, 166.
79 Jackson to R. K. Call, August 16, 1828, *Correspondence,* III, 426; Holmes Alexander, *The American Talleyrand* (1935), 237.
80 *United States' Telegraph,* April 10, 1828.
81 Eaton to Jackson, August 21, 1828, *Correspondence,* III, 429.
82 Jackson to Andrew Jackson, junior, November 27, 1827, Jackson Papers.
83 Jackson to H. L. White, March 30, 1828, *Correspondence,* III, 396.
84 Parton, III, 315 *et seq.*; J. C. Calhoun to Jackson, April 30, May 25, July 10, 1828, *Correspondence,* III, 400, 404, 413.
85 Jackson to James K. Polk, December 27, 1826, Bassett, II, 396.
86 J. H. Eaton to Jackson, March 28, 1828, Jackson Papers.
87 Jackson to J. B. Ray, Governor of Indiana, February 23, 1828, private collection of Stanley Horn, Nashville; to G. W. Campbell, February 14, *Correspondence,* III, 390. On June 5, 1828 (Jackson Papers), R. Y. Hayne of South Carolina wrote Jackson a polite but strong warning that the South would expect him to meet its wishes on the tariff and improvements.
88 L. Campbell to W. B. Lewis, October 30, 1828, Jackson Papers.
89 Harvey Lee Ross, *Early Pioneers of Illinois* (1899), 153-54.
90 Jackson to John Coffee, November 24, 1828, *Correspondence,* III, 447.

CHAPTER XXVII

1 Rachel Jackson to Elizabeth Watson, July 18, 1828, *Correspondence,* III, 416.
2 Moses Dawson to Mrs. Jackson, October 24, 1828, Jackson Papers.
3 Parton, III, 153.
4 A communication signed "L" in the Cincinnati *National Republican,* January 23, 1829.
5 Henry A. Wise, *Seven Decades of the Union* (1872), 101.
6 *Ibid.,* 98-99.
7 Cincinnati *National Republican,* January 23, 1829.
8 Alfred Balch to Van Buren, November 27, 1828, Van Buren Papers.
9 John H. Eaton to Mrs. Jackson, December 7, 1828, *Correspondence,* III, 449.
10 Columbus (Ohio) *Monitor,* reprinted in Lebanon (Tennessee) *Democrat,* January 17, 1829.
11 Nashville *Banner,* December 26, 1828.
12 Wise, 113.
13 *Ibid.;* Bassett, II, 406, who had the newspaper-office detail from a daughter of Francis P. Blair.
14 Dr. Henry Lee Heiskell in a letter to the Winchester *Virginian,* January, 1829; a bill for professional services, Doctor Heiskell to Jackson, October 22 to December 22, 1828, private collection of C. Norton Owen, Glencoe, Illinois; letter dated Nashville, December 23, 1828, Philadelphia *Mercury,* January 17, 1829; Parton, III, 156.
15 Buell, II, 210.
16 Heiskell, *op. cit.;* Parton, III, 156.
17 Scrapbook of Jacksoniana, Tennessee State Library, Nashville.

[18] A letter signed "L" in the Cincinnati *National Republican*, January 23, 1829.
[19] Louisville *Courier-Journal*, quoted in Ben Truman, *The Field of Honor* (1884), 283.
[20] Will Alexander to Jackson, December 26, 1828, Jackson Papers.
[21] Buell, II, 204.
[22] Jackson to John Coffee, January 17, 1829, *Correspondence*, IV, 2.

CHAPTER XXVIII

[1] Mrs. Smith, 257.
[2] Quoted from Lynch, 357.
[3] John Chambers to J. J. Crittenden, January 29, 1829, Crittenden Papers.
[4] Frances M. Trollope, *Domestic Manners of the Americans* (Reprint of 1904), 125.
[5] Parton, III, 169.
[6] *Private Correspondence of Daniel Webster*, I, 473.
[7] Undated manuscript in Jackson's hand probably written in 1831, Jackson Papers, Item 242, Volume V, Second Series; see also Jackson to J. C. McLemore, December 25, 1830, Jackson Papers, New York Historical Society. This letter is catalogued as from Jackson to Calhoun. By a slip of the pen Jackson wrote "Mr. Jno. C. Calhoun" on the last page, but the content shows it to be one of a series of letters he wrote John C. McLemore on later developments in the imbroglio arising from Eaton's appointment.
[8] Mrs. Smith, 282.
[9] Undated manuscript in Jackson's hand, Item 242, Volume V, Second Series, Jackson Papers; Jackson to H. L. White, April 9, 1831, *Correspondence*, IV, 258. James A. Hamilton in his *Reminiscences* (1869), 91, speaks of the War Office being offered to L. W. Tazewell of Virginia, an assertion several biographers and historians repeat. Hamilton is sometimes unreliable in such details, and no other evidence of this offer appears to exist.
[10] On February 23, when Jackson understood Eaton to be firm in his refusal to accept an office, Eaton wrote to White plainly indicating his desire for a cabinet post, if it could be had without offending White. (Bassett, II, 414.)
[11] William Wirt to William Pope, March 22, 1829, John P. Kennedy, *Life of William Wirt* (1849), II, 228. Mr. Wirt was quoting, without malice, a Jackson man.
[12] Caleb Atwater, *Remarks on a Tour to Prairie du Chien* (1831), 277.
[13] James Hamilton, junior, to Martin Van Buren, February 13, 1829, Van Buren Papers.
[14] Louis McLane to Martin Van Buren, February 19, 1829, Van Buren Papers.
[15] Jackson to J. W. Campbell, November 8, 1831, Jackson Papers.
[16] Mrs. Smith, 282; J. A. Hamilton to Van Buren, February 23, 1829, Van Buren Papers.
[17] W. B. Lewis to Lewis Cass, undated but written in 1844 or 1845, Bixby Collection, Henry E. Huntington Library, San Marino, California.
[18] Mrs. Smith, 284; Bassett, II, 422.
[19] James Hamilton, junior, to Martin Van Buren, March 5, 1829, Van Buren Papers.

[20] George R. Gilmer, *Sketches of Some of the Settlers of Upper Georgia* (Reprint of 1926), 244.
[21] James Hamilton, junior, to Martin Van Buren, March 5, 1829, Van Buren Papers.
[22] The quotations are from Gilmer, 245. See also Parton, III, 170; McMaster, V, 525; Bassett, II, 423; Claude G. Bowers, *Party Battles of the Jackson Period* (1922), 47.
[23] Jackson to John Coffee, March 22, 1829, *Correspondence*, IV, 15.
[24] *Ibid.*
[25] Henry B. Stanton, *Random Recollections* (1886), 32.
[26] Van Buren, 229-32.
[27] M. D. L. Sharp to Jackson, June 28, 1828; Jackson's reply, July 5, Jackson Papers.
[28] *New Hampshire Patriot & State Gazette,* November 24, 1828.
[29] *United States' Telegraph,* November 24, 1828.
[30] Ben: Perley Poore, *Perley's Reminiscences* (1866), I, 98.
[31] David Campbell to his wife, June 3, 1829, Campbell Papers.
[32] Dated February 23, 1829. Letter Book for 1829, Jackson Papers, Second Series.
[33] William Stickney (editor), *Autobiography of Amos Kendall* (1872), 308-16; Bassett, II, 488; Bowers, 75.
[34] James Schouler, *History of the United States* (1913 edition), III, 458; Jackson to J. C. McLemore, April, 1829, *Correspondence,* IV, 20.
[35] W. T. Simpson to John McLean, April 14 and 17, 1829, McLean Papers, Library of Congress.
[36] Martin Van Buren to Jackson, March 31; Thomas Ritchie to Van Buren, March 27, 1829, *Correspondence,* IV, 17.
[37] Jackson to Van Buren, March 31, 1829, *ibid.,* 19.
[38] W. T. Simpson to John McLean, April 14 and 17, 1829, McLean Papers.
[39] Amos Kendall to his wife, June 1, 1829, Stickney, 292.
[40] Jackson to John Coffee, March 22, 1829, *Correspondence,* IV, 14.
[41] Jackson to H. M. Cryer, May 16, 1829, *ibid.,* 33.
[42] John W. Forney, *Anecdotes of Public Men* (1873), 283.
[43] Buell, II, 213.
[44] *Harper's Magazine,* January, 1855.
[45] Martin Van Buren to Jackson, April 23, 1829, *Correspondence,* IV, 25; Bowers, 69.
[46] Van Buren, 251-60.
[47] Bassett, II, 448.
[48] Francis J. Grund (editor), *Aristocracy in America* (1839), II, 224.
[49] Jackson to John Coffee, March 22, 1829, *Correspondence,* IV, 14.
[50] J. J. Coddrington to Jesse Hoyt, March 29, 1829, Green Papers.
[51] Jackson to J. C. McLemore, April, 1829, *Correspondence,* IV, 21.
[52] J. C. McLemore to A. J. Donelson, April 3, 1829, Donelson Papers.
[53] Van Buren, 261.

CHAPTER XXIX

[1] Pollack, 74, 75. Though Timberlake's death was apparently due to tuberculosis, a few months before, he had attempted to end his life by cutting his

throat. See Thomas Norman, a shipmate, to Margaret Eaton, April, 1829, New York Historical Society.

[2] J. H. Eaton to Jackson, Washington, December 7, 1828, private collection of Andrew Jackson IV, Los Angeles. In this letter Eaton, by way of recapitulation, repeats a conversation with Jackson that had taken place at the Hermitage some time before. For the sake of smoothness I have substituted the present for the past tense which Eaton used.

[3] This is Mrs. Eaton's version of the reply, given in her *Autobiography,* 80. Parton's version (III, 185), which he probably had from Lewis, is much like it. Eaton (*op. cit.*) covered Jackson's answer in these words: "It was a matter of infinite satisfaction to me to find that your advice and opinions accorded with my own; from that moment I was inspired with a new and fresh decision as to the course to be pursued."

[4] Eaton to Jackson, *op. cit.*

[5] *Ibid.*

[6] C. C. Cambreleng to Martin Van Buren, January 1, 1829, Van Buren Papers. The Congressman was attempting to quote Montaigne.

[7] Mrs. Smith, 252.

[8] David Campbell to his wife, May 24, 27 and June 3, 1829, Campbell Papers. The description of Mrs. Eaton is not Campbell's. It comes from many sources included in probably five hundred manuscripts the writer has read on the Eaton affair. Of numerous portraits of Mrs. Eaton that have been reproduced none made before her forty-fifth birthday is an authentic likeness.

[9] Pollack, 86; Mrs. Eaton, 80.

[10] Undated Memorandum in Jackson's hand, written after reorganization of the Cabinet in 1831. Posted in Jackson Papers, LXXIII, under date of September, 1829.

[11] Emily Donelson to Mary Coffee, March 27, 1829, private collection of Mrs. Andrew Jackson Martin, Memphis, Tennessee, a great-granddaughter of Mrs. Coffee.

[12] J. H. Eaton to Emily Donelson, April 8, 1829, *Correspondence,* IV, 29.

[13] Mary Eastin to Mrs. Stockley Donelson, April 9, 1829, private collection of Mrs. Mary Wharton Yeatman, Columbia, Tennessee; Emily Donelson to Mary Coffee, March 27, 1829, private collection of Mrs. Andrew Jackson Martin, Memphis; the attentions of Abraham Van Buren are a family tradition, communicated to the writer by Mrs. Lucius E. Burch, Nashville.

[14] David Campbell to his wife, May 28, 1829, Campbell Papers; R. G. Dunlap to Jackson, August 10, 1831, *Correspondence,* IV, 331.

[15] A. J. Donelson to J. C. McLemore, April 30, 1830, Donelson Papers.

[16] Fragment in Donelson's hand to Jackson, *ibid.,* for October, 1830.

[17] Emily Donelson to J. H. Eaton, April 10, 1829, private collection of Mrs. Pauline Wilcox Burke, Washington, D. C. Mrs. Burke is a great-great-granddaughter of Emily Donelson. Her copy of this letter is in the hand of A. J. Donelson.

[18] A. J. Donelson to J. H. Eaton, April 10, 1829, *Correspondence,* IV, 30.

[19] Jackson to J. C. McLemore, May 3, 1829, Jackson Papers, New York Historical Society.

[20] J. M. L. to Jackson, October 3, 1831, Jackson Papers.

[21] Stickney, 351. Though Stickney is not the most reliable of sources, the incident does no violence to Mrs. Eaton's established character.

22 A. J. Donelson to Jackson, October 25, 1830, *Correspondence,* IV, 190.
23 David Campbell to his wife, May 28 and June 3, 1829, Campbell Papers.
24 E. S. Ely to Jackson, March 18, 1829, Parton, III, 186; Pollack, 90.
25 Jackson to E. S. Ely, March 23, 1829, Parton, III, 187-92.
26 Jackson to E. S. Ely, April 10, 1929, *ibid.,* 192-95.
27 Undated memorandum in Jackson's hand, posted in Jackson Papers as Item 242, Volume V, Second Series.
28 Jackson to R. K. Call, May 18, 1829, *Correspondence,* IV, 35.
29 I have been unable to locate the letter in which Ely communicated the story of the miscarriage. That such a communication was made prior to the Reverend J. N. Campbell's visit to Jackson on September 1, 1829, appears from Jackson's letter of September 3 to Ely (*Correspondence,* IV, 67), and from Jackson's memorandum of Campbell's visit, also dated September 3. (Parton, III, 197.)
30 Duff Green to David Henshaw, April 15, 1829, Green Papers.
31 James Hamilton, junior, to Van Buren, July 16, 1829, Van Buren Papers.
32 For Jackson's account of the two interviews see Parton, III, 197-202; for Donelson's account of the second interview, at which he was present, see *Correspondence,* IV, 68-72. Both are dated September 3, 1829. The direct quotation is from Donelson.
33 The reactions of Jackson are taken from his account of the second interview, that of Towson and of Donelson from Donelson's account. (See note preceding.) The account which Towson himself left of the interview cannot be found.
34 Lewis's account of the Cabinet meeting, Parton, III, 202-05; Van Buren's account, Van Buren to J. A. Hamilton, September 24, 1829, Hamilton, 146.
35 Denis Tilden Lynch, *An Epoch and a Man: Martin Van Buren and His Times* (1929), 356.
36 C. K. Gardner to John McLean, May 12, 1829, McLean Papers.
37 P. Bradley to John McLean, May 6, 1829, *ibid.*
38 Duff Green to Ninian Edwards, October 8, 1830, E. B. Washburne (editor), *The Edwards Papers* (1884), 548.
39 Erik M. Eriksson, "The Federal Civil Service Under President Jackson," *Mississippi Valley Historical Review,* XIII, 524.
40 *Ibid.,* 525.
41 *Ibid.,* 529, quoting special reports of the heads of the departments named. These are to be found in *House Executive Documents,* Twenty-first Congress, First Session, Nos. 20, 27, 28, 97 and 105.
42 T. L. Homer to John McLean, February 16, 1830, McLean Papers.
43 James Kent to Daniel Webster, January 21, 1830, Kent Papers, Library of Congress.
44 Various letters, 1829-32, McLean Papers.
45 Parton, III, 276.
46 Eriksson, 527. Thirty-eight of these nominations were not acted upon, a fact that has been held up as additional evidence of Jackson's spoils proclivities. Except in Professor Eriksson's undeservedly obscure study, I have never seen an allusion to the fact that forty of Adams' eleventh-hour nominations were confirmed after Jackson's inauguration.
47 *Ibid.,* 527-28. Green's figures on removals from March, 1829, to September, 1830, given in the *Telegraph* for September 27, 1830, follow:

	Officers Removed	Total Number Office-holders
State Department	6	24
Treasury Department	22	174
War Department	3	20
Navy Department	5	23
General Post Office	5	61
Postmasters	543	8,356
Marshalls and attorneys	30	60
Territorial governments	4	12
Surveyors of public lands	7	21
Registrars of land offices	16	42
Receivers of public moneys	16	42
Indian agents and subagents	11	55
Collectors of customs	49	98
Appraisers	8	15
Naval Officers	6	14
Surveyors	14	68
Light house keepers	16	186
Subordinate customs officers	151	801
Consular and diplomatic service	7	21
Totals	919	10,093

I do not guarantee these figures, though on the whole they have not been overthrown by dependable evidence. In one respect Green did the cause of "reform" an injustice, for actually the total number of office holders was nearly 11,000. Therefore if his number of removals is correct the proportion is lower than he stated. On the other hand his figures for removals in the Washington offices are lower than those given by the various heads of departments whose evidence is certainly preferable to Green's. See note 41 *ante*.

[48] Eriksson, 529-30.
[49] Carl Russell Fish, *The Civil Service and Patronage* (1905), 51.
[50] James D. Richardson (editor), *Messages and Papers of the Presidents* (1899), II, 462; Jackson's uncompleted rough draft, *Correspondence*, IV, 97.
[51] Jackson's notes for the Maysville Road Veto appear in *Correspondence*, IV, 137. Van Buren (319-38) takes credit for suggesting and intimates that he wrote the veto message. Jackson's rough notes support the latter claim. The message as delivered differs in form and substance from Jackson's notes.
[52] The narrative of the Maysville veto is derived from Van Buren (312-38), and from Bassett (II, 374-96) who believed Van Buren reliable, but in his usual careful manner amplified the New Yorker's account with a study of other contemporary sources. In no communication that I can find did Jackson so much as mention the subject in his correspondence—one indication of the correctness of Van Buren's assertion that the matter was a secret between the President and himself.
[53] A. T. Burnley to J. J. Crittenden, June 13, 1830, Crittenden Papers.
[54] Jackson to John Donelson, June 7, 1829, *American Historical Magazine* (Nashville), IV, 232.

⁵⁵ Jackson to John Overton, December 31, 1829, with an explanatory note appended by W. B. Lewis, *Correspondence,* IV, 108.

CHAPTER XXX

¹ Parton, III, 282.
² Charles W. March, *Reminiscences of Congress* (1850), 151.
³ Undated memorandum in Jackson's hand. Posted with papers for September, 1829, Volume LXXIII, Jackson Papers.
⁴ Jackson to Samuel Swartwout, September 27, 1829, *Correspondence,* IV, 77.
⁵ A. J. Donelson to John Coffee, August 27, 1829, Donelson Papers.
⁶ Though another nine or ten months was to elapse before, in the summer of 1830, Jackson was in his private correspondence openly to accuse Calhoun of being the fomenter of the Eaton troubles, his course of action and his correspondence from autumn 1829 onward indicates that he suspected it and acted accordingly. (See Jackson to J. C. McLemore, November 24, 1829, Jackson Papers, New York Historical Society.) On October 24, 1830, he wrote Emily Donelson (*Correspondence,* IV, 187) that he had "long known" Calhoun to be "at the bottom of this" effort to strike him through Mrs. Eaton. The truth of the thing seems to be that it was all a struggle over the succession between Van Buren and Calhoun, in which Van Buren was ultimately successful as a result of excessive cleverness on his own part and some shady practices on the part of Lewis and of Eaton, his friends. At this stage Calhoun had done nothing in the Eaton affair calculated to discredit the Administration.
⁷ Van Buren, 347-52; Parton, III, 290.
⁸ Adams, VIII, 185.
⁹ John Campbell to his brother David, December 27, 1829, Campbell Papers.
¹⁰ Van Buren, 353.
¹¹ Memorandum by Jackson, *Correspondence,* IV, 123; Jackson to J. H. Eaton, July 19, 1830, *ibid.,* 163; to Martin Van Buren, August 8, 1831, *ibid.,* 328. After the dissolution of the Cabinet in 1831 Ingham, Branch and Berrien published statements which included their own versions of this interview (see Parton, III, 303-09). In the main I have followed Jackson's accounts, believing them the more reliable.
¹² A. J. Donelson to J. C. McLemore, April 30, 1830, Donelson Papers.
¹³ Atwater, 269.
¹⁴ Hayne's opening speech, delivered January 19, 1830, and Webster's reply, delivered January 20, appeared in the *United States' Telegraph* on February 3. Hayne's second speech, delivered January 21 and 25, appeared in the *Telegraph* on February 15 and 16. Webster's reply to this, delivered January 26 and 27, appeared in the *National Intelligencer,* February 23, 25 and 27. The *Telegraph* published it March 4 to 8.
¹⁵ Fuess, I, 386.
¹⁶ Jackson to R. Y. Hayne, April 26; to A. P. Hayne, April 27, 1830, *Correspondence,* IV, 135.
¹⁷ Benton, I, 148.
¹⁸ *United States' Telegraph,* January 28, 1830.
¹⁹ *Ibid.,* January 30, 1830.
²⁰ *Ibid.,* February 2, 1830.

[21] *Ibid.*, January 29, 1830.
[22] *Ibid.*, February 3, 1830.
[23] Van Buren, 413.
[24] *Ibid.*, 414; Parton, III, 284.
[25] Quoted from Frederic Austin Ogg, *The Reign of Andrew Jackson* (1919), 165.
[26] Van Buren, 415.
[27] Ogg, 165.
[28] *United States' Telegraph*, April 17, 1830.
[29] Jackson's "reign" was a contemporary expression which in the early 'Thirties became common among the opposition.
[30] Atwater, 289.
[31] J. C. Calhoun to Christopher Van Deventer, May 12, 1830, *Calhoun Letters*, 272.
[32] Jackson to J. C. Calhoun, May 13, 1830, *Correspondence*, IV, 136.
[33] Jackson to J. A. Hamilton, May 29, 1830, *Correspondence*, IV, 140.
[34] H. Petrikin to Jackson, April 2; Jackson to Coffee, April 10, 1830, *ibid.*, 131 and 134.
[35] Lewis's narrative, Parton, III, 322-25.
[36] W. H. Crawford to John Forsyth, April 30, 1830, Richard K. Crallé (editor), *Works of John C. Calhoun* (1850-56), VI, 360.
[37] John Overton to Jackson, June 16, 1830, *Correspondence*, IV, 151.
[38] J. C. Calhoun to Jackson, May 29, 1830, Jackson Papers. The letter is also in Calhoun, *Works*, VI, 362.
[39] Jackson to J. C. Calhoun, May 30, 1830, *Correspondence*, IV, 141.
[40] Jackson to R. J. Chester, November 30, 1829, *ibid.*, 96.
[41] Charles J. Love to Jackson, enclosing "Memorandum of Stock Crops etc etc at the Hermitage," January 15, 1830, *ibid.*, 119.
[42] Jackson to his son, July 4, 1829, *ibid.*, 49.
[43] H. M. Cryer to Jackson, December 26, 1829; Jackson to Cryer, January 10 and February 28; Jackson to C. J. Love, February 28, 1830, *ibid.*, 106, 117, 126, 125.
[44] Jackson to R. J. Chester, November 7, 1830, Tennessee Historical Society, Nashville.
[45] Buell, I, 34.
[46] Jackson to his son, July 26, 1829, *Correspondence*, IV, 57.
[47] Jackson to his son, September 21, 1830, *ibid.*, 76. The only further clue to the identity of Flora given by this correspondence is that she was the orphaned daughter of a friend of Jackson's and the ward of Colonel Edward Ward, at whose home she lived near Nashville.
[48] Royall, 213.
[49] Jackson to Francis Smith, May 19, 1830, private collection of Andrew Jackson IV, Los Angeles; John Campbell to David Campbell, June 16, David Campbell to John Campbell, November 2, 1830, Campbell Papers.
[50] Royall, 213.
[51] Jackson to J. H. Eaton, July 20, 1830, *Correspondence*, IV, 164.
[52] Margaret Eaton to Jackson, June 9, 1830, *ibid.*, 145.
[53] Donelson's endorsement, dated June 10, 1830, on Mrs. Eaton's letter, *ante, ibid.*, 146; A. J. Donelson to Jackson, October 30, 1830, *ibid.*, 195.

⁵⁴ A. J. Donelson to J. C. McLemore, April 30, 1830, Donelson Papers; Jackson to John Coffee, July 9, 1830, *Correspondence,* IV, 160.

⁵⁵ On May 19, 1830, in his letter to Major Francis Smith, (See note No. 49 *ante*) Jackson mentioned that he would remain in Washington during the summer, though Mr. and Mrs. Donelson were going to Tennessee. On June 9 occurred the dinner which Mrs. Eaton would not attend, and apparently immediately thereafter (See Donelson's memorandum on her letter and his letter to Jackson, October 30, 1830, *Correspondence,* IV, 146, 195) the sentence of banishment was pronounced. On June 14, Jackson wrote John Overton (*ibid.,* 146) that he was leaving for home.

⁵⁶ The quotation is from Jackson to W. B. Lewis, June 21 and July [blank], 1830, *ibid.,* 156 and 159. See also Jackson to Lewis, June 26 and August 25, 1830, *ibid.,* 156 and 177.

⁵⁷ The Choctaw treaty of October 8, 1820.

⁵⁸ Seymour Dunbar, *A History of Travel in America* (1915), II, 484-587.

⁵⁹ Jackson to W. B. Lewis, August 25, 1830, *Correspondence,* IV, 176.

⁶⁰ Dunbar, II, 575.

⁶¹ James Given to Jackson, October 16, 1830, Jackson Papers.

⁶² Jackson to John Coffee, July 20, 1830, *Correspondence,* IV, 165; to W. B. Lewis, July 21 and 28, August 17, 1830, *ibid.,* 165, 167, 173; to J. H. Eaton, August 3, 1830, *ibid.,* 168.

⁶³ Jackson to W. B. Lewis, August 7, 15, 17 and 25, 1830, *ibid.,* 170, 173, 174, 178.

⁶⁴ For detailed expositions of the West Indian trade settlement see William MacDonald, *Jacksonian Democracy* (1906), 200-204; Bassett, II, 657-63; Van Buren, 521-27.

CHAPTER XXXI

¹ The account in the text of the abuse and danger of the branch draft system is taken from a manuscript account of Jackson's fight against the Bank of the United States, written by Roger B. Taney, and now in the Library of Congress. This manuscript is quoted extensively—and for the first time—in Carl Brent Swisher's *Roger B. Taney*, (1935), which the present writer will hereafter use in citing Taney's account. The criticism of the branch drafts appears on pp. 167-68. The difficulty in obtaining coin for drafts is also cited by Alfred Balch to Jackson, January 7, 1830, *Correspondence,* IV, 115.

² Thomas Cadwalader to Jackson, October 15; Jackson's answer, November 21, 1828, *Correspondence,* III, 438 and 445.

³ This statement is true despite the fact that in Kentucky, for example, the bank's officers and supporters were almost solidly with Clay. This was a condition due to the vagaries of politics in Kentucky, where the banking question had long been an issue, rather than to any deliberate act of Biddle to pack the Louisville and Lexington branches with anti-Jackson men. In Nashville, of course, Biddle would have found it difficult to have erected a branch organization without including supporters of Jackson, as in New England it would have been difficult to have erected such a directorate politically favorable to Jackson. At the same time it seems plain that Cadwalader meant to demonstrate to Jackson that the bank had picked men favorable to his

cause, and Cadwalader's ingratiating letter cited in the note foregoing is a clear bid to turn the Nashville branch over to Jackson organization. This was something new in the bank's affairs. For Biddle's customary position on mixing banking and political matters see Ralph C. H. Catterall, *The Second Bank of the United States,* (1903), 171, 243-51; also Biddle's letters in Reginald C. McGrane, *The Correspondence of Nicholas Biddle* (1919), 63, 68, 70, 72.

[4] Jackson to T. H. Benton, November 29, 1837, Jackson Papers. In this review of the situation Jackson says "the Aristocratic few at Nashville" wanted a branch of the bank in 1817, but omits to indicate that he was a member of that aristocratic group at the time. Indeed his failure to go along with the nabobs on the bank question is one of the few instances when Jackson, at that period of his life, opposed the majority of the frontier aristocrats.

[5] Bassett, II, 590.

[6] Jackson to T. H. Benton, *op. cit.*

[7] Jackson to A. J. Donelson, October 11, 1822, *Correspondence,* III, 179.

[8] Jackson to T. H. Benton, *op. cit.;* Catterall, 183; St. George L. Sioussat, "Tennessee Politics in the Jackson Period," *American Historical Review,* XIV, 62.

[9] Hamilton, 69; Bassett, II, 592.

[10] In 1833 Jackson's recollection was that two paragraphs on the bank included in an early draft of the address were stricken out after the President-elect's arrival in Washington. In none of the four drafts now among the Jackson Papers, Library of Congress, showing the address in process of evolution, do these paragraphs appear, however. See Bassett, II, 425-30.

[11] Sioussat, *op. cit.,* 64, 65.

[12] *Ibid.,* 65.

[13] In view of the Supreme Court's ruling in the case of McCulloch *versus* Maryland, upholding the bank, it is simple enough for modern commentators to dismiss Jackson's constitutional objections to the Bank of the United States as evidence of unenlightened thinking. The present day reader should bear in mind that the authority of Supreme Court decisions was not at that time generally established, except among lawyers. John Marshall's bold assumption of the court's right to be the final judge of the constitutionality of acts of Congress had in itself slender constitutional basis. To this day competent constitutional students challenge that right. In 1829 there was much doubt about it in the minds of the masses of the people, particularly in the West. Jackson's constitutional suggestions to the bank were a reflection of a widely spread western opinion. In the phrasing of J. A. Hamilton (*Correspondence,* IV, 113) they follow: "The present bank is unconstitutional: 1. Because it is a corporation which Congress had no constitutional power to establish. 2. Because it withdraws the business of Bank discounts and the property of private citizens from the operation of State laws and particularly from the taxing power of the states. . . . 3. Because it purchases . . . real estate within the States without their consent, under an authority purporting to be derived from Congress, when the General Government itself possesses no such constitutional power."

[14] The substance of Jackson's objections is derived from the memoranda Kendall and Hamilton submitted in response to the President's requests. The former, with a covering letter dated November 20, 1829, is in Jackson Papers,

Ladies' Hermitage Association, Nashville; the latter, with covering letter dated January 4, 1830, in *Correspondence,* IV, 112. Grundy's reply, dated October 22, (*ibid.,* IV, 83), throws little light on the objections, confining itself to a rough and rather poorly stated plan for a substitute bank.

[15] Memoranda of Grundy, Kendall and Hamilton, *op. cit.*
[16] Grundy's letter, *op. cit.*
[17] Kendall's letter, *op. cit.*
[18] Hamilton's letter, *op cit.*
[19] W. B. Lewis to Nicholas Biddle, June 28, 1829, Catterall, 186.
[20] Nicholas Biddle to Thomas Cadwalader, August 28, 1829, *Biddle Correspondence,* 75.
[21] The Biddle-Ingham correspondence is in *Reports of Committees,* First Session, Twenty-second Congress, IV, 437 *et seq.*
[22] Catterall, 182.
[23] *Ibid.,* 178, 254; Samuel Smith to Nicholas Biddle, September 22; Biddle to Asbury Dickins, September 16 and 30, 1829, *Biddle Correspondence,* 53, 75 and 77.
[24] Catterall, 187-88.
[25] *Ibid.,* 189, 246.
[26] W. B. Lewis to H. Toland, November 11, 1829, *ibid.*
[27] Bassett, II, 598-99; Catterall, 189-91; S. D. Ingham to Jackson (three letters), November 24, 1829, *Correspondence,* IV, 86-91.
[28] Biddle's memorandum of the conversation, *Biddle Correspondence,* 93. See also Nicholas Biddle to Alexander Hamilton, a brother of James A., November 28 and to Robert Lenox, December 4, 1829, Biddle Papers, Library of Congress.
[29] J. M. Berrien to Jackson, November 27, 1829, *Correspondence,* IV, 94.
[30] S. D. Ingham to Jackson, November 26 and 27, *ibid.,* IV, 92, 93.
[31] The passage appearing in the message apparently evolved from a draft by J. A. Hamilton, now preserved in the Jackson Papers, Library of Congress. In his *Reminiscences* (pp. 149-51) Hamilton implies that he wrote the entire message. An incomplete draft in Jackson's hand (*Correspondence,* IV, 97-104) and a later draft in Van Buren's (Jackson Papers), tallying closely with the message as submitted, casts doubt on the assertion of Hamilton.
[32] Jackson to J. A. Hamilton, December 19, 1829, Hamilton, 151.
[33] W. Catron to A. J. Donelson, December 31, 1829, Donelson Papers.
[34] Catterall, 198.
[35] Later Jackson got J. A. Hamilton to write a criticism of the report which the *Telegraph* was obliged to publish.
[36] Jackson to J. A. Hamilton, June 3, 1829, Hamilton, 167.
[37] Catterall, 198.
[38] Jackson to an unnamed correspondent, July 17, 1830, Bassett, II, 603.
[39] W. B. Lewis to Nicholas Biddle, May 25, 1830, Catterall, 200.
[40] J. A. Hamilton to Jackson, June 7, 1830, Hamilton, 168.
[41] Josiah Nichol to Nicholas Biddle, July 20, 1830, *Biddle Correspondence,* 106.
[42] Alfred Balch to Jackson, January 7, 1830, *Correspondence,* IV, 115.
[43] Benton, I, 187.
[44] Nicholas Biddle to Joseph Hemphill, January 15, 1831, Catterall, 207.

CHAPTER XXXII

[1] Parton, III, 277.
[2] Jackson to W. B. Lewis, June 26, 1830, *Correspondence*, 156.
[3] Catterall, 171.
[4] The description of Blair is by John C. Rives, quoted from Smith thesis, 252.
[5] Lewis's narrative, Parton, III, 336. See also William Ernest Smith, *The Francis Preston Blair Family in Politics* (1933), I, 62.
[6] Jackson to Samuel Hays, December 7, 1830, private collection of Samuel Jackson Hays, Memphis.
[7] J. C. Calhoun to J. H. Hammond, January 15, 1831, *Calhoun Letters*, 283.
[8] Van Buren, 377, 379.
[9] This is Van Buren's version (pp. 377-79), extraordinary for its frankness. Bassett (II, 517) bases his account on Duff Green's story, which is that he, Green, handed Eaton the manuscript to show to Jackson. Green says Eaton returned the production unchanged, from which Green concluded that Jackson had approved it. Eaton denied this, though admitting his interview with Grundy and his subsequent equivocal behavior in withholding the manuscript from Jackson. (Van Buren, *op. cit.*) As early as January 13, 1831, Lewis knew of the project to publish the correspondence (Lewis to John Overton, Overton Papers), and intimated that Jackson knew of it. On February 3, J. A. Hamilton, writing to Jackson, mentioned Calhoun's "plan to publish." (Hamilton, 195.) In view of this evidence one is surprised to find Jackson writing Donelson on March 24 that "I was thunderstruck when I saw the publication." (*Correspondence*, IV, 253.) The best that can be said for the General is that, although he had previously heard gossip about the intended publication, the actuality came to him as a surprise. By curious reasoning, in his letter to Donelson, he exculpates Eaton of questionable conduct, attributing everything to the "wickedness" of Green which is not evident to an impartial observer. Not even Van Buren, writing twenty-three years later, questions that Eaton's conduct deceived Calhoun into the belief that he was acting with Jackson's approval.
[10] Jackson to C. J. Love, March 7, 1831, *Correspondence*, IV, 245.
[11] Washington *Globe*, February 21, 1831.
[12] See Note No. 9 *ante*.
[13] John Campbell to his brother David, November 6, 1830, Campbell Papers.
[14] Jackson to Mary Eastin, October 24, 1830, *Correspondence*, IV, 186.
[15] Jackson to Emily Donelson, November 28, 1830, *ibid.*, 208.
[16] Jackson to Mary Eastin, October 24, 1830, *ibid.*, 187.
[17] Mrs. S. D. Ingham to Emily Donelson, November 28, 1830; Rebecca Branch to Emily Donelson, October [blank], 1830, private collection of Mrs. Pauline Wilcox Burke, Washington, D. C.
[18] Various notes between Jackson and A. J. Donelson dated from October 25 to October 30, 1830, *Correspondence*, IV, 189-97.
[19] A. J. Donelson's memorandum of a conversation with Jackson, dated November 10, 1830, *ibid.*, 202. I give the General's words in the present tense. Donelson used the past.
[20] A. J. Donelson to Jackson, October 25 and 27, 1830, *ibid.*, 189 and 192.
[21] Jackson to A. J. Donelson, October 30, 1830, *ibid.*, 194.
[22] John C. McLemore to A. J. Donelson, November 10, 1830, *ibid.*, 197.

²³ Emily Donelson to her husband, November 30, 1830, private collection of Mrs. Pauline Wilcox Burke, Washington, D. C.
²⁴ W. H. Overton to John Overton, December 21, 1830, Overton Papers.
²⁵ Samuel Bradford to W. B. Lewis, February 28, 1832, Jackson Papers.
²⁶ Van Buren, 402-07.
²⁷ Trollope, 286.
²⁸ Van Buren, 407.
²⁹ Pollack, 146.
³⁰ *Ibid.*, 152.
³¹ *Ibid.*, 159; Jackson to A. J. Donelson, June 24; to J. C. McLemore, June 27, 1831, *Correspondence*, IV, 302, 304.
³² Jackson to Coffee, May 26, *ibid.*, 285; to R. G. Dunlap, July 18, *American Historical Magazine*, IX, 85; to Van Buren, August 8, 1831, *Correspondence*, IV, 330.
³³ W. B. Lewis to Martin Van Buren, June 27, 1831, Bixby Collection, Henry E. Huntington Library, San Marino, California; W. T. Barry to John Overton, July 1, 1831, Overton Papers.
³⁴ F. P. Blair to J. J. Crittenden, June 10, 1831, Crittenden Papers.
³⁵ D. Morrison (the builder) to Jackson, December 6, 1831, Mary French Caldwell, *Andrew Jackson's Hermitage* (1933), 78-80.
³⁶ William W. Story, *Life and Letters of Joseph Story* (1851), II, 118.
³⁷ Jackson to Mrs. Mary Dunlap, October 13, 1831, *Correspondence*, IV, 359.
³⁸ Charles H. Hunt, *Life of Edward Livingston* (1864), 361.
³⁹ J. C. Calhoun to Virgil Maxcy, May 16, 1831, Maxcy Papers.
⁴⁰ Jackson was strongly urged to get rid of Lewis altogether. R. G. Dunlap, a plain-speaking friend of army days wrote: "It raises a suspicion of your fitness to rule, . . . when it is said Billy Lewis is your councillor." (June 30, 1831, Jackson Papers.)
⁴¹ Harriet Martineau, *A Retrospect of Western Travel* (1838), I, 155.
⁴² F. B. Blair to J. J. Crittenden, June 10, 1831, Crittenden Papers.
⁴³ Contemporary press quotations from Charles Warren, *The Supreme Court in United States History* (1922), II, 194-95.
⁴⁴ Jackson to a committee of citizens of Charleston, June 14, 1831, Parton, III, 370.
⁴⁵ Memorandum of J. H. Hammond, March 18, 1831, *American Historical Review*, VI, 742-45.
⁴⁶ Tomlinson Fort to J. C. Calhoun, July 15, 1831, private collection of George Fort Milton, Chattanooga, Tennessee. Mr. Milton is a great-grandson of Mr. Fort.
⁴⁷ James Hamilton, junior, to J. H. Hammond, June 11, 1831, *American Historical Review*, VI, 747.
⁴⁸ Excerpt from a legislative report, Frederick Bancroft, *Calhoun and the South Carolina Nullification Movement* (1928), 101.
⁴⁹ Jackson to J. A. Hamilton, November 12, 1831, Hamilton, 231.

CHAPTER XXXIII

¹ Biddle's memorandum of a conversation with McLane, October 19, 1831, *Biddle Correspondence*, 132.
² Louis McLane to Samuel Smith, August 24, 1831, Swisher, 174.

[3] Roswell L. Colt to Nicholas Biddle, October 3, 1831, Biddle Papers, Library of Congress. Colt was a gossip, and was not present at Carroll's. He said he had the story from a "Mr. Caton,"—presumably Carroll's son-in-law. The tale sounds likely enough, however.

[4] Worden Pope to Jackson, August 6, 1831, *Correspondence*, IV, 327. The cashier of the Lexington, Kentucky, branch had urged that loans be made to help pro-bank candidates there, saying that Clay thought it advisable. Biddle vetoed the idea. (Catterall, 251.)

[5] Biddle's memorandum of a conversation with Louis McLane, October 19, 1831, *Biddle Correspondence*, 131.

[6] *Ibid.*, 129; Catterall, 211, 212; Edward Shippen to Nicholas Biddle, December 6, 1831, *Biddle Correspondence*, 136.

[7] Biddle memorandum, *op. cit.*; for Livingston's view of the matter, Parton, III, 395.

[8] Catterall, 145.

[9] Biddle gave Dickins credit for inducing McLane to move for recharter. See Biddle's memorandum of a conversation with McLane, October 19, 1831, *Biddle Correspondence*, 128.

[10] *Ibid.*, 128-31. I have changed the remark—"I should be sorry," etc.—attributed to General Jackson from the third person, which Biddle used, to the first person.

[11] Mrs. Smith, 325.

[12] Henry Clay to Francis Brooke, December 9, 1831, Clay's *Works*, IV, 321.

[13] Biddle's memorandum of a conversation with McLane, October 19, 1831, *Biddle Correspondence*, 129, 130.

[14] Taney's manuscript account, Swisher, 175-78.

[15] Robert Gibbes to Nicholas Biddle, December 11, 1831, *Biddle Correspondence*, 179.

[16] Jackson to J. A. Hamilton, December 12, 1831, Hamilton, 234. Doctor Bassett (II, 616) thinks that up to this time and, indeed, until the collapse of the final efforts at compromise in February, 1832, Jackson "played a game, concealing his real purpose from the bank democrats and working for party harmony." This is possible, though I think Bassett overstresses the case. Clay was clearly the leading gamester in the picture. Jackson watched the progress of his effort to throw the bank issue into the campaign. If Jackson were playing a game I think it more of a countergame to Clay's than anything else. Doctor Bassett supports his statement with the following evidence:

On December 19, John Randolph, a bitter anti-bank man, wrote that if Jackson made peace with the "Chestnut Street Monster," his, Randolph's vote for the Jackson ticket would "be delivered with forceps." On December 22, Jackson replied that he was still opposed to the bank and that the McLane report committed him to nothing. On January 3, Randolph wrote again, and in reply Jackson said, "Never fear the triumph of the U. S. Bank while I am here." (Bassett, 612-13; *Correspondence*, IV, 386, 387, 395.)

In his rendering of the substance of Jackson's letter of December 22, Bassett merely says Jackson declared himself still opposed to the bank, whereas the President's exact language was "the bank as at present organized." True, Jackson's letters to Randolph were mollifying in tone and to that extent aimed at the preservation of party harmony. But his use of the qualifying phrase quoted reduces the depth of the "game," if any, which the President was playing. Moreover, this phrase has the effect of qualifying Jackson's assurance of January third in this sense: "Never fear the triumph of the U. S. Bank as at present organized," etc. The recharter of the bank on modified terms such as Jackson would agree to could not have been regarded as a victory for that institution. I think that is what Jackson had in mind when he wrote Randolph, and I point to his letter of December 12 to Hamilton, another anti-bank man, as confirmation of this.

Of course, when Clay succeeded in his effort to induce Biddle to throw the question into the campaign, all Jackson's latent hostility to the bank sprang to life again. Compromise was no longer politically possible—but this had been Clay's doing, not Jackson's. As the fight reached its heated climax Jackson forgot his early efforts at compromise and made a number of strong and hasty statements which, detached from their antecedents, might seem to support the contention that he could never have seriously considered the idea of compromise. Yet he had entertained such an idea, as a wealth of evidence shows.

[17] For Cadwalader's and Biddle's exchanges of letters during the former's stay in Washington, December 20 to 26, 1831, see *Biddle Correspondence*, 146-61.

[18] Nicholas Biddle to Asbury Dickins, December 12, 1831, Catterall, 213.

[19] Nicholas Biddle to Samuel Smith, January 4, 1832, *Biddle Correspondence*, 163.

[20] Boston *Gazette,* January 21, 1832; Parton, III, 415.

[21] Buell, II, 268.

[22] Jackson to Andrew Jackson, junior, October 27, 1831, *Correspondence*, IV, 365.

[23] Reproduced facing page 144, first volume of this work.

[24] Amos Kendall, "Anecdotes of General Jackson," *Harpers Magazine,* September, 1842.

[25] Jackson to H. M. Cryer, June 17, 1832, *Correspondence,* IV, 448.

[26] Van Buren, 506.

[27] Jackson to Martin Van Buren, September 5 and December 6, 1831, *Correspondence*, IV, 348 and 379.

[28] Henry Wikoff, *Reminiscences of an Idler* (1880), 29-31.

[29] Benton, I, 215, 219.

[30] William Carroll to Jackson, February 20, 1832, Jackson Papers.

[31] John Campbell to his brother David, March 8, 1832, Campbell Papers.

[32] The Eastin-Polk nuptials took place April 10, 1832. On January 21, Jackson had written to Coffee that on February 4 next she would marry Captain W. B. Finch, *Correspondence,* IV, 401.

[33] Undated memorandum in Jackson's hand, filed with papers for 1832, Jackson Papers.

[34] Jackson to Sarah Yorke Jackson, April 30, 1832, *ibid.*

[35] Jackson to John Coffee, November 21, 1831, *Correspondence,* IV, 377.

[36] J. H. Eaton to Jackson, April 10, 1832, Jackson Papers.

[37] Jackson to Andrew Jackson, junior, April 30, 1832, private collection of Andrew Jackson IV, Los Angeles.

[38] Jackson to John Coffee, March 26, 1832, Coffee Papers.

[39] W. H. Sparks, *Memories of Fifty Years* (1870), 151.

[40] J. A. Hamilton quoting Jackson, March 14, 1832, Hamilton, 243.

[41] Nicholas Biddle to C. J. Ingersoll, February 13, 1832, *Biddle Correspondence*, 182.

[42] Jackson to Martin Van Buren, December 17, 1831, *Correspondence*, IV, 385.

[43] Benton, I, 238.

[44] Bassett, II, 625; Catterall, 258-64. James Watson Webb was the editor of the *Courier and Enquirer*.

[45] Sumner, 311-316.

[46] Taney's account, Swisher, 187-95; for the message see Richardson, II, 576-91.

[47] Van Buren, 625.

[48] Nicholas Biddle to Henry Clay, August 1, 1832, *Clay Correspondence*, 341.

[49] Swisher, 200; D. T. Lynch, 357.

CHAPTER XXXIV

[1] Horace Greeley, *The American Conflict* (1864), I, 106.

[2] Jackson to John Coffee, April 7, 1832, *Correspondence*, IV, 430.

[3] *National Journal*, April 7, 1832.

[4] David F. Houston, *A Critical Study of Nullification in South Carolina* (1896), 105.

[5] Buell, II, 245.

[6] Privately Green suggested the name Whigs in 1832, but not until the spring of 1833 did the Jackson opposition take up that name. See Duff Green to R. K. Crallé, March 12 and 28, 1832, Green Papers.

[7] Washington *Globe*, September 25, 1832, a reprint from the *New Hampshire Patriot*.

[8] Parton, III, 420.

[9] Jackson to A. J. Donelson, August 9, 1832, Donelson Papers; August 16, *Correspondence*, IV, 467.

[10] Bowers, 251.

[11] Louis McLane to Jackson, August 3, 1832, Jackson Papers.

[12] Jackson to Martin Van Buren, August 30, 1832, *Correspondence*, IV, 470.

[13] Jackson to Secretary of the Navy, September 11, 1832, *ibid.*, 474.

[14] Jackson to Sarah Yorke Jackson, October 5, 1832, Jackson Papers, Ladies' Hermitage Association, Nashville.

[15] Jackson to Sarah Yorke Jackson, October 21, 1832, Private collection of Andrew Jackson IV, Los Angeles.

[16] Jackson to Lewis Cass, October 29, 1832, *Correspondence*, IV, 483.

[17] Buell, II, 277.

[18] Henry S. Crabb to Jackson, November 6, 1832, Jackson Papers.

[19] Jackson to Andrew Jackson, junior, November 8, 1832, *ibid*.

[20] Washington *Globe*, November 24, 1832, quoting *Vermont Journal*.

[21] Statements of the popular vote cast in 1832 vary considerably, most historians giving Jackson in the neighborhood of 700,000 and Clay in the neighborhood of 350,000, excluding the votes he received on the fusion ticket in New York. I have used the figures of Samuel R. Gammon, junior, in his *The Presidential Campaign of 1832* (1922), 153, 170. Professor Gammon has, I believe, made the most careful study of the question from contemporary

sources that we have to date. South Carolina cast its electoral vote for John Floyd of Virginia.

[22] Parton, III, 432; William Wirt to J. T. Lomax, November 15, 1832, Kennedy, II, 331.

[23] Jackson to Mary Eastin Polk, November 26, 1832, private collection of Lucius Polk Brown, Columbia, Tennessee.

[24] A remark to Blair and Kendall, Bowers, 253.

[25] J. R. Poinsett to Jackson, November 16, 1832, *Correspondence,* IV, 488.

[26] Jackson to J. R. Poinsett, December 2, 1832, *ibid.,* 493; Poinsett to Jackson, March 21, 1833, *ibid.,* V, 45.

[27] Jackson to Andrew Jackson, junior, November 12, 1832, private collection of Andrew Jackson IV, Los Angeles.

[28] J. F. H. Claiborne, *Life and Times of Gen. Sam Dale* (1860), 178.

[29] Bassett, II, 564.

[30] Jackson to J. R. Poinsett, December 2, 1832, *Correspondence,* IV, 494.

[31] Jackson to J. R. Poinsett, December 9, 1832, *ibid.,* 498.

[32] G. M. Dallas to Jackson, December 6, 1832, *ibid.,* 496.

[33] Adams, VIII, 503.

[34] John Randolph to Jackson, December 6, 1832, *Correspondence,* IV, 497.

[35] Jackson to Edward Livingston, December 4, 1832, *Correspondence,* IV, 495.

[36] Richardson, II, 640-656.

[37] J. H. Hammond to R. Y. Hayne, December 20, 1832, *American Historical Review,* VI, 751.

[38] R. Y. Hayne to F. W. Pickens, December 26, 1832, *ibid.,* 755.

[39] James O'Hanlon to Jackson, December 20, 1832, *Correspondence,* IV, 504.

[40] Jackson to Martin Van Buren, December 16, 1832, *ibid.,* 500.

[41] Jackson to Martin Van Buren, December 25, 1832, *ibid.,* 506.

[42] Jackson to Lewis Cass, December 17, 1832, *ibid.,* 502.

[43] Frances A. Kemble, *Journal* (1835), II, 120, 131, 132, 138.

[44] Martin Van Buren to Jackson, December 27, 1832, *Correspondence,* IV, 507.

[45] Jackson to Martin Van Buren, December 25, 1832, *ibid.,* 506.

[46] Martin Van Buren to Jackson, December 27, 1832, *ibid.,* 506. See also Van Buren, 445.

[47] Bassett, II, 573, 578, 580; D. T. Lynch, 366; Alexander, 301.

[48] J. R. Poinsett to Jackson, January 16, 1833, *Correspondence,* V, 6.

[49] Jackson to J. R. Poinsett, February 7, 1833, *ibid.,* 15.

[50] Jackson to H. M. Cryer, February 20, 1833, *ibid.,* 19.

[51] Jackson to Martin Van Buren, January 25, 1833, *ibid.,* 12; Van Buren, 553.

[52] John Coffee to G. W. Martin, February 25, 1833, private collection of Miss Estelle Lake, Memphis, Tennessee.

[53] Jackson to Martin Van Buren, January 13, 1833, *Correspondence,* V, 3.

[54] Silas Wright to Martin Van Buren, January 13, 1833, *ibid.,* 4.

[55] *Ibid.*

[56] Poore, 138; Benton, I, 143.

[57] Jackson to Van Buren, December 25, 1832, *Correspondence,* IV, 506.

[58] Jackson to J. R. Poinsett, January 24, 1833, *ibid.,* V, 11.

[59] Jackson to Martin Van Buren, January 25, 1833, *ibid.,* 13.

⁶⁰ A fragment in Jackson's hand, posted as Item 376, Jackson Papers, Second Series, Volume V.
⁶¹ Van Buren, 544.
⁶² This action was not taken by the nullifying convention, which had adjourned, but by a mass meeting at Charleston dominated by men who had been members of that convention. The action of this body was fully respected by the South Carolina authorities. It had all the effect of an action by the convention, with certain face-saving graces added.
⁶³ Jackson to J. R. Poinsett, February 17, 1833, *Correspondence*, V. 18.
⁶⁴ Jackson to Felix Grundy, February 13, 1833, *American Historical Magazine*, V, 17.
⁶⁵ Jackson to H. M. Cryer, April 7, 1833, *Correspondence*, V, 53.
⁶⁶ P. P. F. Degrand to Nicholas Biddle, July 4, 1833, Biddle Papers, reporting a remark by Jackson to the Mayor of Boston in June of that year. In transcribing the quotation I have substituted the first person for the third which Degrand used.
⁶⁷ Jackson to John Coffee, April 9, 1833, *Correspondence*, 56.
⁶⁸ Schurz, II, 21.

CHAPTER XXXV

¹ S. E. Burrows to Nicholas Biddle, March 2, 1833, Biddle Papers.
² J. G. Watmough to Nicholas Biddle, March 2 and 12, 1833, *ibid*.
³ Jackson to A. J. Hutchings, April 18, 1833, *Correspondence*, V, 60.
⁴ *Ibid*.
⁵ Jackson to A. J. Hutchings, November 3, 1833, *ibid*., 223.
⁶ Jackson to John Coffee, April 9, 1833, *ibid*., 56; Mary Coffee to Jackson, April 29, private collection of Andrew Jackson IV, Los Angeles.
⁷ W. B. Lewis to Jackson, April 21, 1833, *Correspondence*, V, 61-65.
⁸ Jackson to W. B. Lewis, May 4, 1833, *ibid*., 73.
⁹ Jackson to W. B. Lewis, April 29, 1833, *ibid*., 66.
¹⁰ Jackson to A. J. Hutchings, September 6, 1833, Jackson Papers, Tennessee Historical Society, Nashville.
¹¹ Jackson to Mary Coffee, September 15, 1833, *Correspondence*, V, 188; to J. D. Coffee, December 24, 1834, Coffee Papers.
¹² Jackson to H. L. White, March 24, 1833, *Correspondence*, V, 46.
¹³ *Ibid*.
¹⁴ Swisher, 208-13.
¹⁵ For both reports see *House Reports* No. 121, Twenty-second Congress, Second Session.
¹⁶ Henry Clay to Nicholas Biddle, March 4, 1833, Biddle Papers.
¹⁷ Lewis Williams to Nicholas Biddle, March 2, 1833, *ibid*. Williams was a brother of Jackson's implacable enemy, Ex-Senator John Williams of Tennessee.
¹⁸ J. G. Watmough to Nicholas Biddle, March 2 and 12, 1833, *ibid*.
¹⁹ J. G. Watmough to Nicholas Biddle, April 25, 1833; Watmough's notes dated April 25 and May 1, *ibid*.
²⁰ S. Simpson to Nicholas Biddle, February 20, 1833; anonymous letters to Biddle, March 7, March 31, April 1 and 2, *ibid*.
²¹ Jackson to H. L. White, March 24, 1833, *Correspondence*, V, 46.

22 Parton, III, 498. Parton does not give his source or the quotation, though it appears to have been Blair who, in 1859 (October 10, Van Buren Papers), wrote Van Buren an account of a conversation with Jackson. Virtually the same words as Parton uses are attributed to the General. I am still disposed to question the accuracy of Blair's memory for nothing in Jackson's letters, official or private, which this writer has seen, expresses doubt as to the solvency of the bank. The fact that Jackson kept his money in Biddle's bank seems to be the best evidence that he believed it safe.

23 The Nashville branch owed other offices $1,653,326 and had due it from other offices only $205,998, and adverse balance of $1,369,187. The specie in the branch was only $244,893. Some of the other western branches were in little better state. (Amos Kendall to Louis McLane, March 16, 1833, Jackson Papers.)

24 Jackson to his Cabinet, March 19, 1833, *Correspondence*, V, 32.
25 R. B. Taney to Jackson, April 3, 1833, *ibid.*, 33-41.
26 Jackson to H. M. Cryer, *American Historical Magazine*, IV, 238.
27 R. M. Whitney to Jackson, April 3, 1833, Jackson Papers.
28 Parton, III, 504.
29 Louis McLane to Jackson, May 20, 1833, *Correspondence*, V, 75-101.
30 F. P. Blair to Jackson, a memorandum without date, *ibid.*, 102-104.
30a A. J. Donelson to John Coffee, May 19, Donelson Papers; Jackson to A. J. Hutchings, June 2, Jackson Papers, Tennessee Historical Society, Nashville; Parton, III, 487.
31 Jackson to Martin Van Buren, May 12, *Correspondence*, V, 74.
32 Jackson to Martin Van Buren, December 4, 1838, *ibid.*, 573.
33 John Campbell to David Campbell, May 12, 1833, Campbell Papers.
34 Jackson to Andrew Jackson, junior, June 6, 1833, *Correspondence*, V, 107.
35 *United States Gazette* (Philadelphia), June 10, 1833.
36 Jackson to Andrew Jackson, junior, June 10, 1833, *Correspondence*, V, 109.
37 Parton, III, 489.
38 Jackson to Andrew Jackson, junior, June 14, 1833, *Correspondence*, V, 109.
39 Amos Kendall to Martin Van Buren, June 6, 1833, *ibid.*, 107.
40 Van Buren, 602. The McLane memorandum which Van Buren gives the date June 4, 1833, was handed to the President on June 14, the day McLane left New York. I can find no account of the President's New York conference with Van Buren except the brief and vague mention the New Yorker makes in his autobiography. My statement that Van Buren did not oblige Kendall by exerting his influence in support of the removal plan is based on a study of Van Buren's behavior throughout the deposit transfer episode, some glimpses of which may be had in succeeding pages of the text.
41 Duane had given Jackson his views before the President left Washington. See [William J. Duane], *Narrative and Correspondence Concerning the Removal of the Deposites* (1838), 9.
42 Jackson to Andrew Jackson, junior, June 17, 1833, *Correspondence*, V, 110.
43 Josiah Quincy, *Figures of the Past* (1883), 353-58.
44 Edward Warren to J. M. Warren, July 4, 1833, J. S. Bassett, "Notes on

Jackson's Visit to New England," *Proceedings* of the Massachusetts Historical Society, LVI, 245.

⁴⁵ Quincy, 361-63.

⁴⁶ Quincy does not mention the bleeding of the lungs which is established from other sources. Amos Kendall in "Anecdotes of General Jackson," *Democratic Review,* September 1842, mentions it.

⁴⁷ [Seba Smith] *Life and Writings of Major Jack Downing* (1834), 214, 217.

⁴⁸ Quincy, 359.

⁴⁹ Adams, IX, 5.

⁵⁰ Quincy, 361.

⁵¹ Jackson to W. J. Duane, two communications, June 26, 1833, *Correspondence,* V, 111-28.

⁵² New York *Advertiser*, June 29, 1833. Inasmuch as Mr. Davis will appear in the main text of the succeeding chapter I have not interrupted the narrative at this point to mention the fact that this well-known quotation from Jack Downing was written not by Seba Smith, the creator of the character, but by Charles Augustus Davis, the most brilliant of Smith's many imitators. The comments of Smith's Downing on the Harvard degree are amusing, but not quite so good as those of Davis's Downing.

Smith, a Maine farmer boy who became editor of the Portland *Courier*, began the Downing letters in January, 1830. By 1833 they were being copied in newspapers throughout the Union. When the President appeared in New York in June of that year Davis, a city-bred silk-stocking and, like his friend Nicholas Biddle, a literary dilletante, began a second series of Downing letters in the New York *Advertiser*. These quickly attained a wide-spread popularity, so much so that most general historians and biographers seem to think Davis the originator and Smith the imitator. Davis, as we shall see, was in reality one of Mr. Biddle's controlled propagandists. Smith was a ruggedly independent commentator. The bank fight over, Davis ceased to write while Smith continued at intervals until after the commencement of the Civil War.

⁵³ Adams, VIII, 346.

⁵⁴ Quincy, 353, 367-74.

⁵⁵ Van Buren, 602.

⁵⁶ Jackson to Van Buren, *Correspondence,* V, 128-43.

⁵⁷ On July 2, 1833, Martin Van Buren received a letter signed Louisa C. Tuthill soliciting an introduction to the President in order to offer to marry him. Van Buren forwarded the letter to Jackson who replied through Van Buren under date of July 24. On receipt of the President's kindly refusal, Miss Tuthill wrote Van Buren (August 8) that the original letter to him signed by her name was a forgery, despite the remarkable similarity of the handwriting. The foregoing correspondence is in the Van Buren Papers.

CHAPTER XXXVI

¹ Amos Kendall to Jackson, August 2, 11, 14 and 25, 1833, *Correspondence,* V, 145, 150, 156, 169; see also Catterall, 293; Sumner, 351.

² Amos Kendall to Jackson, August 14 and 25, 1833, *Correspondence,* V, 156 and 170.

³ Martin Van Buren to Jackson, August 19 and September 4, 1833, *ibid.,* 159, 179.

pp. 648-658]   NOTES—*Portrait of a President*   877

⁴ R. B. Taney to Jackson, August 5, 1833, *ibid.*, 147.

⁵ Jackson to Martin Van Buren, September 8, 1833, *ibid.*, 183.

⁶ H. D. Gilpin and two other directors of the Bank of the United States to Jackson, August 19, 1833, *ibid.*, 160-665; manuscript in Jackson's and entitled "Charges against the Bank," *ibid.*, 174-76; Jackson to Martin Van Buren, August 18 and September 8, *ibid.*, 168, 183.

⁷ For the finished document commonly known as "The Paper Read to the Cabinet" see Richardson, III, 5-19; for Jackson's early draft, *Correspondence*, V, 192-203.

⁸ Jackson to Martin Van Buren, September 19, 1833, *ibid.*, 203.

⁹ Nicholas Biddle to John Potter, August 1, 1833, Biddle Papers.

¹⁰ Parton, III, 506.

¹¹ F. P. Blair to Martin Van Buren, November 13, 1859, Van Buren, 608.

¹² Jackson to Martin Van Buren, September 29, 1833, *Correspondence*, V, 212.

¹³ Nicholas Biddle to Robert Lenox, July 30, 1833, Biddle Papers.

¹⁴ Catterall, 316-20.

¹⁵ Catterall, 329, who makes the assertion without qualification and supports it with figures. I select this citation because Professor Catterall's book, once regarded as the standard work on the bank and still the most useful, has lost caste within recent years because it does that institution more than justice.

¹⁶ John Watmough to Nicholas Biddle, November 6 and 28, December 18, 1833, Biddle Papers.

¹⁷ Martin Van Buren to Jackson, October 2, 1833, *Correspondence*, V, 214.

¹⁸ Wikoff, 65-66.

¹⁹ Jackson to Sarah Yorke Jackson, October 6, 1833, Henry E. Huntington Library *Bulletin*, No. 3, p. 133.

²⁰ Jackson to Andrew Jackson, junior, November 13, 1833, January 5, 1834, *Correspondence*, V, 224 and 239.

²¹ Richardson, III, 31.

²² *Ibid.*, III, 36.

²³ Nicholas Biddle to Horace Binney, January 8, 1834, Biddle Papers.

²⁴ James Dunlap to Nicholas Biddle, December 14, 1833, *ibid.*

²⁵ J. W. Webb to Nicholas Biddle, February 4, 1834, *ibid.*

²⁶ John Watmough to Nicholas Biddle, December 18, 1833, *ibid.*

²⁷ L. Henry to Nicholas Biddle, January 15, 1834, *ibid.*

²⁸ Catterall, 319-21.

²⁹ Nicholas Biddle to William Appleton, January 27, 1834, *Biddle Correspondence*, 219.

³⁰ J. W. Webb to Nicholas Biddle, March 11, 1834, *ibid.*, 227.

³¹ Daniel Webster to Nicholas Biddle, December 21, 1833, Biddle Papers.

³² Henry Clay to Nicholas Biddle, January 17, 1834, *ibid.*

³³ Henry Clay to Nicholas Biddle, February 2, 1834, *ibid.*

³⁴ Nicholas Biddle to W. B. Shepherd, February 28, 1834, *ibid.*

³⁵ John Forsyth to Nicholas Biddle, December 25, 1833, *ibid.*

³⁶ Catterall, 256.

³⁷ Nicholas Biddle to Charles Hammond, March 11, 1834, *Biddle Correspondence*, 225.

³⁸ Many latter-day historians have followed their example.

³⁹ In the Biddle Papers from September, 1833, to October, 1834, are about

twenty letters which passed between the banker and C. A. Davis. They have never been consulted by a writer on American humor of the period. Davis's writings are collected in [Charles Augustus Davis] *The Letters of J. Downing, Major* which ran through several editions between 1834 and 1836. See also Mary A. Wyman, *Two American Pioneers* (1924), 70-82 and Jeanette Tandy, *Crackerbox Philosophers* (1925), 32-38.

[40] Nicholas Biddle to Daniel Webster, January 8, 1834, Biddle Papers.

[41] Horace Binney to Nicholas Biddle, February 4, 1834, *Biddle Correspondence*, 220. Binney wrote at Webster's direction.

[42] Nicholas Biddle to Joseph Hopkinson, February 21, 1834, *ibid.*, 222.

[43] Nicholas Biddle to J. G. Watmough, February 8, 1834, *ibid.*, 221.

[44] Examples of these petitions may be found on almost any page of the *Congressional Globe* for the First Session of the Twenty-third Congress, from mid-January forward. Niles' *Register* is also filled with them.

[45] Parton, III, 542 and 554.

[46] James Alexander Hamilton of New York.

[47] Jackson to Martin Van Buren, January 3, 1834, *Correspondence*, V, 238.

[48] As early as January 3, 1834 (Jackson to Martin Van Buren, *ibid.*) Jackson had complained of the inaction of his followers in Congress and urged offensive measures, but it was not until more than a month later that he personally took the initiative and struck back at the delegations that flocked to the White House.

[49] *United States Gazette* (Philadelphia), February 24, 1834, McMaster, VI, 202.

[50] Nicholas Biddle to Joseph Hopkinson, February 21, 1834, *Biddle Correspondence*, 222.

[51] McMaster, VI, 202.

[52] F. P. Blair to George Bancroft, June 24, 1845, Bancroft Papers, New York Public Library.

[53] *United States Gazette* (Philadelphia), February 13, 1834; McMaster, VI, 203.

[54] Stickney, 412.

[55] Washington *Globe*, February 14, 1834.

[56] Wise, 107.

[57] F. P. Blair to Martin Van Buren, October 10, 1859, Van Buren Papers.

[58] Parton, III, 548; see also Van Buren, 353.

CHAPTER XXXVII

[1] Material regarding Jackson's personal bank accounts derived from canceled checks in the Jackson papers. These indicate that the Bank of Metropolis account was started early in January, 1834, and that the Bank of United States account was closed July 7 of that year. The amount of the balance remaining on July 7 raises a question whether actual deposits in the Bank of the United States ceased when the other account was opened. It appears that Jackson's Nashville funds were transferred to the Union Bank there in the fall of 1833.

[2] Jackson to Andrew Jackson, junior, November 25, 1833, May 4, 1834, *Correspondence*, V, 227 and 264.

[3] Jackson to Andrew Jackson, junior, November 25, 1833, *ibid.*, 227.

[4] Jackson to Sarah Yorke Jackson, January 5, 1834, *ibid.*, 239.

⁵ Jackson to Andrew Jackson, junior, January 26, 1834, *ibid.*, 242.
⁶ Jackson to Andrew Jackson, junior, February 16, 1834, *ibid.*, 248.
⁷ Andrew Jackson, junior, to Jackson, January 25, 1834, *ibid.*, 240-41; Jackson to Andrew, junior, February 12 and 16, *ibid.*, 247 and 248.
⁸ Jackson to Andrew Jackson, junior, March 16 and 26, *ibid.*, 255 and 256.
⁹ Jackson to Andrew Jackson, junior, February 12, 1834, *ibid.*, 247; March 16, *ibid.*, 255; April 6, *ibid.*, 259.
¹⁰ Jackson to Andrew Jackson, junior, April 15, 1834, *ibid.*, 261.
¹¹ Jackson to Andrew Jackson, junior, April 27, May 4 and May 5, 1834, *ibid.*, 263 and 264.
¹² Andrew Jackson, junior, to Jackson, May 25, 1834, private collection of Andrew Jackson IV, Los Angeles.
¹³ J. R. Montgomery to his daughter Letitia, February 20, 1834, private collection of Emil E. Hurja, New York City.
¹⁴ James Douglas Anderson, *Making of the American Thoroughbred* (1916), 241-47. This is Balie Peyton's account, written after he had read in Parton (I, 341) who relates the details of the tobacco-box incident somewhat differently.
¹⁵ Catterall, 339.
¹⁶ John Rathbone to Nicholas Biddle, January 18, 1834, Biddle Papers.
¹⁷ Nicholas Biddle to Joseph Hopkinson, February 21, 1834, *Biddle Correspondence*, 222.
¹⁸ This was his name though Catterall, usually accurate in such details, calls him Simon Wolf and others repeat the error.
¹⁹ Senator William Wilkins of Pennsylvania to the Senate, April 29, 1834, Catterall, 340.
²⁰ Niles' *Register* (Baltimore), March 15, 1834.
²¹ *Ibid.*, March 8, 1834.
²² Catterall, 340-41.
²³ Parton, III, 549.
²⁴ Nicholas Biddle to J. G. King, February 28, 1834, Catterall, 343.
²⁵ J. G. King to Nicholas Biddle, March 11, 1834, *ibid.*, 343.
²⁶ Nicholas Biddle to J. G. Watmough, March 17, 1834, *ibid.*, 343.
²⁷ Jackson to George Wolf, February, 1834, *Correspondence*, V, 243.
²⁸ John Connell to Nicholas Biddle, April 4, 1834, Catterall, 342.
²⁹ Jackson to J. D. Coffee, April 6, 1834, *Correspondence*, V, 260.
³⁰ Nicholas Biddle to Senator Alexander Porter of Louisiana, June 14, 1834, Biddle Papers: "If such a vote were secured the Bank would feel no reluctance in giving one, or if necessary two, millions of loans to Louisiana as requested for her relief. This could be done because such a vote is peace and harmony & confidence between the Bank & the Congress. In truth I know of no way in which all the interests on the Western waters could be more immediately & substantially advanced than by such a vote. . . . I should think there were men enough in the House to do that good service even if it did cost them a frown from the palace."
³¹ Jackson to Amos Kendall, July 8, 1834, private collection of Mrs. Arthur Chester of Rye, New York. Mrs. Chester is a great-granddaughter of Amos Kendall.
³² Jackson to A. J. Hutchings, June 7, 1834, *Correspondence*, V, 269.
³³ Jackson to F P. Blair, August 7 and 30, 1834, *ibid.*, 281 and 287.

[34] R. M. Barton to Jackson, February 13, 1833, Jackson Papers.
[35] Jackson to W. B. Lewis, September 14, 1834, *Correspondence*, V, 292.
[36] Jackson to Andrew Jackson, junior, October 11, 1834, *ibid.*, 293-94.
[37] Jackson to Andrew Jackson, junior, October 15, 1834, Jackson Papers.
[38] Jackson to Andrew Jackson, junior, October 21, 1834, *Correspondence*, V, 301.
[39] Robert Armstrong to Jackson, October 14, 1834; S. D. Donelson to Jackson, same date, *ibid.*, 295-97.
[40] Jackson to Andrew Jackson, junior, October 23, 1834, *ibid.*, 302.
[41] Jackson to Andrew Jackson, junior, October 25, 1834, Jackson Papers.
[42] Jackson's endorsement dated October 24, 1834, on Robert Armstrong's letter of October 14, *Correspondence*, V, 296.
[43] Jackson to Andrew Jackson, junior, October 23, 1834, *ibid.*, 302.
[44] *Ibid.*
[45] Jackson to Andrew Jackson, junior, October 30, 1834, *ibid.*, 303-04.
[46] Bills for new furniture for the Hermitage, *ibid.*, 382-83, 357-58. Some of Jackson's military papers also were lost.
[47] Jackson to Andrew, junior, October, 1834, *ibid.*, 304.
[48] These changes of name had come about gradually. The Whig party represented more than a rechristening of the National Republicans. It took a large number of state rightists and some lesser elements. The Jackson party did not officially adopt the name of Democrats until the national campaign of 1844, though it was in almost universal popular use ten years earlier.
[49] David Gulliver to Nicholas Biddle, October 16, 1834, Biddle Papers.

CHAPTER XXXVIII

[1] Jackson to Secretary of the Navy, June 6, 1834, Jackson Papers.
[2] Jackson to Martin Van Buren, October 5, 1834, Van Buren Papers.
[3] Louis Sérurier to Count Henri de Rigny, French minister of Foreign Affairs, October 22, 1834, *British and Foreign State Papers, 1812-1922*, from Richard Aubrey McLemore, a manuscript thesis, "The French Spoliation Claims, 1816-1836" (1932), 162. This is the most thorough study that has been made of the diplomatic masterpiece of the Jackson administrations. It establishes that Jackson personally deserves a larger share of the credit than historians generally have been disposed to give him. A twenty-one-page condensation of Dr. McLemore's study appears in the *Tennessee Historical Magazine*, Series II, Volume II, Number 4, and has been published as a pamphlet. Unfortunately, the complete manuscript of three hundred-odd pages is as yet unpublished. Dr. McLemore who is professor of history at Judson College, Marion, Alabama, kindly provided the author with a copy for which he is deeply indebted as subsequent documentation will show in part.
[4] Louis Sérurier to Count Henri de Rigny, November 29, 1834, *ibid.*, 164. Parton (III, 568) makes a statement concerning the President's determination, subsequently carried out, to write a "strong" message on the French question, which a few later writers repeat. He says that Louis Philippe assured Livingston, our minister at Paris, of his embarrassment over the dilatory behavior of the French Chamber and suggested that a more "earnest" statement of the American case might remedy this. This information Livingston is said

to have passed on to Jackson who acted on it. Parton apparently had the story from Thomas P. Barton, Livingston's son-in-law and a member of the Legation staff during the French crisis. Though nothing has been found in Livingston's or in Jackson's official or private correspondence to corroborate it, McLemore (*op. cit.*, 188) brings to light that the same report was afloat in Paris at the time. So there may be something to it. The matter is of little importance, however. Jackson needed no suggestion from Louis Philippe to take a firm course with France. He had started that in June, 1834, when he ordered the Navy in readiness. As early as October 5, he had told Van Buren he meant to make strong representations in his annual message.

[5] [Hone, Philip] *The Diary of Philip Hone* (1889), I, 121, McLemore thesis, 164-65.

[6] Wise, 145-46.

[7] Richardson, III, 106-07.

[8] Hone, I, 122, McLemore thesis, 174.

[9] Taggard to Webster, December 17, 1834, Webster Papers, Library of Congress, McLemore thesis, 174.

[10] Washington *Globe*, December 17, 1834.

[11] Sir Charles Vaughn, British minister at Washington to Lord Palmerston, minister of foreign affairs, December 20, 1834, British Foreign Office Papers (copies), Volume 293, Library of Congress, McLemore thesis, 175.

[12] Obvious from the unanimous vote and from the changed tone of the *Globe* (January 15, 1835) which passed over the Senate's action without objection.

[13] Martineau, *Western Travel*, I, 161.

[14] Alexandria *Gazette*, February 2, 1835; John Tyler to Robert Tyler, January 31, 1835, Bixby Collection, Huntington Library, San Marino, California.

[15] *United States' Telegraph*, February 2, 1835; Van Buren, 353.

[16] Washington *Globe*, February 3; *United States' Telegraph*, February 2, 1835.

[17] Louis Sérurier to John Forsyth, February 23, 1835, State Department Manuscripts, McLemore thesis, 197.

[18] John Forsyth to Edward Livingston, March 5, 1835, State Department Manuscripts, *ibid.*, 198.

[19] W. B. Lewis to J. A. Hamilton, March 14, 1835, Hamilton, 284.

[20] G. C. Childress to Jackson, November 16, 1834, *Correspondence*, V, 310.

[21] Jackson to Andrew Jackson, junior, November 19, 1834, *ibid.*, 311.

[22] Jackson's agreement with the builders for reconstructing the Hermitage, dated January 1, 1835, is in *Correspondence*, V, 315. The stipulated expenditure of thirty-nine hundred and sixty dollars was exceeded, however, the final bill being five thousand one hundred and twenty-five.

[23] *Continental Monthly*, September, 1862.

[24] Jackson to Andrew Jackson, junior, November 27, 1834, *Correspondence*, V, 313.

[25] Items 18,136, 18,137, and 19,145, Jackson Papers for December, 1834.

[26] Robert Caldwell to his father, December 29, 1834, *American Historical Review*, XXVII, 273.

[27] Jackson to Andrew Jackson, junior, December 9, 1834, *Correspondence*, V, 313.

[28] Andrew Jackson, junior, to Sarah Yorke Jackson, December 14, 1834, private collection of Andrew Jackson, IV, Los Angeles.
[29] Jackson to Andrew Jackson, junior, April 14, 1835, *Correspondence,* V, 335.
[30] Robert Armstrong to Jackson, August 13, 1835, *ibid.,* 362.
[31] Jackson to Andrew Jackson, junior, March 1, 1836, *ibid.,* 388.
[32] R. M. Burton to Jackson, February 1, 1835, Jackson Papers.
[33] A. P. Hayne to Jackson, November 11, 1835, *ibid.*
[34] Note-book No. 6, Washington Irving Papers, New York Public Library.
[35] Not the General Benjamin F. Butler of Civil War and Reconstruction notoriety.
[36] Jackson to Alfred Balch, February 16, 1835, *Correspondence,* V, 327.
[37] John Catron to Jackson, March 21, 1835, *ibid.,* 330-32.
[38] Washington *Globe,* May 29, 1835.
[39] Jackson to John Forsyth, September 6, 1835, *Correspondence,* V, 363, speaks of having received information on the French situation from the letter of one Harris. Levitt Harris, an American in Paris, was corresponding at the time with Major Lewis and Lewis was quoting him in a effort to show the pacific nature of French sentiment. See Lewis to J. A. Hamilton, March 14, 1835, Hamilton, 284.
[40] Duc Achille de Broglie to Alphonse Pageot, June 17, 1835, *National Intelligencer,* January 22, 1836, McLemore thesis, 211-14.
[41] Jackson to John Forsyth, September 6, 1835, *Correspondence,* V, 363. In this letter the Secretary of State was instructed to receive the document officially or not at all. Unofficially he was neither to "hear" nor to receive the document. It is apparent from what followed that while Forsyth may not have "heard" the document in a literal sense he received, orally from Pageot, a correct idea of its contents.
[42] "Instructions for Thomas P. Barton," September 14, 1835, *ibid.,* 364. Forsyth's formal letter to Barton conformed to this draft. See McLemore thesis, 215.
[43] Richardson, III, 158, 160.
[44] Edward Livingston to Jackson, January 11, 1836, Hunt, 428.
[45] Richardson, III, 192.
[46] Hone, I, 196.
[47] Lord Palmerston to H. S. Fox, British minister to the United States, April 22, 1836, British Foreign Office Papers (copies), Volume 307, Library of Congress, McLemore thesis, 262-63.
[48] Two memorandums in Jackson's hand, dated November 15, 1836, *Correspondence,* V, 436-38; McLemore thesis, 267-68.

CHAPTER XXXIX

[1] Anthony Butler to Jackson, January 4, 1827, Jackson Papers.
[2] Anthony Butler, of Mexican problem distinction, and Jackson's one-time ward, Anthony Wayne Butler, were different persons.
[3] Jackson to Martin Van Buren, August 12, 1829; "Notes on Poinsett's Instructions," August 13; Jackson to Van Buren, August 14, *Correspondence,* IV, 57-61.

⁴ Martin Van Buren to Joel R. Poinsett, October 16, 1829, George Lockhart Rives, *The United States and Mexico* (1913), II, 243.
⁵ Jackson to J. R. Poinsett, August 17, 1829, *Correspondence*, IV, 66.
⁶ Anthony Butler to Jackson, March 7, 1834, *ibid.*, 251-52.
⁷ Anthony Butler to Jackson, February 6, 1834, *ibid.*, 245.
⁸ Memorandum by Jackson dated June 22, 1835, Rives, II, 258.
⁹ Anthony Butler to John Forsyth, January 15, 1836, *ibid.*, 260.
¹⁰ Marquis James, *The Raven, a Biography of Sam Houston* (1929), 71-73, 76.
¹¹ *Ibid.*, 78, 82, 139.
¹² Jackson's fragmentary journal, May 21, 1829, Jackson Papers; Jackson to Sam Houston, June 21, 1829, Henderson Yoakum, *History of Texas* (1856), I, 307.
¹³ Buell, II, 351, states that Jackson loaned Houston five hundred dollars to help finance the trip to Texas. This may be corroborated by a statement of Jackson's in a letter written from the Hermitage on August 16, 1832, to A. J. Donelson in which he speaks of having lost a note "on Houston for money advanced to him whilst in the city." (Jackson Papers.) As to the real object of the journey see James, 192.
¹⁴ Jackson to Anthony Butler, October 30, 1833, *Correspondence*, V, 221; James, 190-94.
¹⁵ Jackson's endorsement on a letter of Austin dated at New York, April 15, 1836, *ibid.*, V, 398.
¹⁶ Samuel Swartwout to A. J. Donelson, May 6, 1836, Donelson Papers.
¹⁷ Buell, II, 352; see also reminiscences of N. P. Trist, New York *Evening Post*, July, 1853, Parton, III, 605.
¹⁸ Journal of Lieutenant Hitchcock, Clarence R. Wharton, *The Texas Republic* (1922), 165.
¹⁹ Buell, II, 352.
²⁰ Jackson to Newton Cannon, August 6, 1836, *Correspondence*, V, 417.
²¹ Frederick Jackson Turner, *The United States 1830-1850* (1935), 257.
²² Jackson to J. R. Chandler, September 18, 1835, *Correspondence*, V, 366.
²³ James Truslow Adams, *The Living Jefferson* (1936), 298-301; Ernest Sutherland Bates, *The Story of the Supreme Court* (1936), 136-155; William Bennett Munro, *The Makers of the Unwritten Constitution* (1930), 53-113; Warren, II, 273-312; Swisher, 380-392.
²⁴ Jackson to Andrew Jackson, junior, July 4, 1836, Jackson Papers.
²⁵ Jackson to Andrew Jackson, junior, July 10 and 23, *ibid.*; to F. P. Blair, August 12, 1836, *Correspondence*, V, 418.
²⁶ Though conservative, this figure is in part an estimate, as the cost of the furniture lost on the *John Randolph* has not been ascertained exactly. The work on the house totaled five thousand one hundred and twenty-five dollars (itemized statement, *ibid.*, 414-15), against a first estimate of twenty-five hundred to three thousand dollars (Robert Armstrong to Jackson, November 4, 1834, *ibid.*, 305) and a formal contract for thirty-nine hundred dollars (*ibid.*, 315-16.). New furnishings exclusive of those burned on the *Randolph* cost thirty-seven hundred dollars (*ibid.*, 382-83, 457) exclusive of transportation costs.
²⁷ Robert Armstrong to Jackson, August 13, 1835, *ibid.*, 361; Jackson to

Andrew Jackson, junior, October 25, 1835 and March 29, 1836, *ibid.,* 372 and 396.

[28] Jackson to E. Breathitt, March 30, 1835, Jackson Papers.

[29] Edward Hobbs to Andrew Jackson, junior, August 26, 1835, *Correspondence,* V, 361.

[30] Jackson to Andrew Jackson, junior, March 25, 1836, *ibid.,* 394.

[31] Jackson to Andrew Jackson, junior, August 23, 1836, *ibid.,* 423.

[32] Jackson to Andrew Jackson, junior, August 23 and September 22, 1836, *ibid.,* 423 and 426.

[33] Jackson to Emily Donelson, October 31, 1836, *ibid.,* 433.

[34] A. J. Donelson to Emily Donelson, November 20 and 21, 1836, Donelson Papers; Jackson to Emily Donelson, November 27, 1836, *Correspondence,* V, 439.

[35] C. P. Van Ness to Martin Van Buren, Madrid, February 10, 1837, Van Buren Papers.

[36] Jackson to Emily Donelson, November 27, 1836, *Correspondence,* V, 440.

[37] A. J. Donelson to Emily Donelson, November 20 and 21, 1836, Donelson Papers; A. J. Donelson to Jackson, December 23, *ibid.;* Jackson to Mary Eastin Polk, December 22, private collection of Mrs. Mary Wharton Yeatman, Columbia, Tennessee; Jackson to A. J. Donelson, December 17, *Correspondence,* V, 442.

[38] Jackson to H. M. Cryer, November 13, 1836, Cryer Papers, Tennessee Historical Society, Nashville.

[39] W. H. Wharton to Stephen F. Austin, Secretary of State, Texas Republic, December 22, 1836, and January 6, 1837, George P. Garrison (editor), *Diplomatic Correspondence of the Republic of Texas* (1908), I, 158, 169.

[40] W. H. Wharton to Sam Houston, February 2, 1837, *ibid.,* 179-80.

[41] W. H. Wharton to T. J. Rusk, Secretary of State, Texas Republic, undated, but about February 15, 1837, *ibid.,* 194-95.

CHAPTER XL

[1] W. Peck to Jackson, February 27, 1837, Jackson Papers.

[2] Jackson to F. P. Blair, February 25, 1837, *ibid.*

[3] Buell, II, 357.

[4] D. T. Lynch, 397.

[5] W. H. Wharton to J. P. Henderson, March 5, 1837, *Texas Diplomatic Correspondence,* I, 201.

[6] Benton, I, 735.

[7] *Ibid.*

[8] It is a coincidence that these lines were written on March 4, 1937.

[9] Story, II, 154.

[10] Buell, II, 297.

[11] Grund, II, 241-43.

[12] New York *Evening Post,* December 3, 1836.

[13] Buell, II, 364-66, from conversations, long afterward, with Blair and Allen.

[14] An unsigned article in *Harper's Magazine,* January, 1855.

CHAPTER XLI

[1] Jackson to Martin Van Buren, March 30, 1837, *Correspondence,* V, 466.
[2] Jackson to A. J. Hutchings, April 4, 1837, *ibid.,* 473.
[3] Jackson to A. J. Hutchings, April 4, 1838, *ibid.,* 547-48.
[4] An undated fragment, representative of many such, Jackson Papers.
[5] Jackson to A. D. Campbell, March 15, 1837, *Correspondence,* V, 465; to A. J. Donelson, April 22, *ibid.,* 477; to A. J. Hutchings, April 4, *ibid.,* 473; to F. P. Blair, May 11, *ibid.,* 481; to Martin Van Buren, August 7, *ibid.,* 504.
[6] Jackson to Martin Van Buren, March 22, March 30, 1837, *ibid.,* 465 and 467; to F. P. Blair, April 2, April 18, *ibid.,* 473 and 476.
[7] Jackson to F. P. Blair, April 18, 1837, *ibid.,* 476.
[8] Jackson to Martin Van Buren, March 30, 1837, *ibid.,* 467.
[9] Jackson to F. P. Blair, April 18, 1837, *ibid.,* 476.
[10] *National Intelligencer,* April 28, 1837; Nashville *Banner & Whig,* May 10, 1837; Jackson to F. P. Blair, May 11, 1837, *Correspondence,* V, 481.
[11] Martin Van Buren to Jackson, April 24, 1837, *ibid.,* 479.
[12] F. P. Blair to Jackson, April 23, 1837, *ibid.,* 477.
[13] The late Professor Edward Channing of Harvard cannot be regarded as a historian over-friendly to the political and economic ideals of General Jackson. From him, therefore, I quote: "The causes of the Panic of 1837 are by no means so simple of ascertainment as our historians have usually held. Jackson's financial misdeeds could not have had much effect in bringing on the crisis, because it was worldwide." These sentences summarize a treatment of the subject conforming to my own in the preceding paragraphs of the text. (See his *History of the United States* (1923-1926), V, 453-56.
[14] Turner, 459.
[15] Sumner, 395-96.
[16] Nicholas Biddle to J. Q. Adams, May 13, 1837, Niles' *Register,* LI, 182.
[17] Jackson to Martin Van Buren, May 12, 1837, *Correspondence,* V, 483.
[18] Jackson to Martin Van Buren, June 6, 1837, *ibid.,* 489; to Amos Kendall, June 23, *ibid.,* 489-90; to F. P. Blair, July 23, *ibid.,* 500.
[19] Amos Kendall to Martin Van Buren, October 20 and November 6, 1838, Van Buren Papers.
[20] Jackson to Martin Van Buren, July 6, 1838, *Correspondence,* V, 555.
[21] Jackson to N. P. Trist, February 6, 1838, *ibid.,* 536.
[22] Jackson to A. J. Hutchings, April 9, 1838, *ibid.,* 549.
[23] Jackson to A. J. Hutchings, March 15, 1838, *ibid.,* 542; to same, December 3, 1839, *ibid.,* VI, 41; F. P. Blair to Jackson, May 20, 1839, *ibid.,* 15; S. C. McWhorter to Jackson, August 14, 1838, Jackson Papers.
[24] Nashville *Republican,* July 20, 1838; Jackson to W. P. Lawrence, August 24, *Correspondence,* V, 565, Parton, III, 644-49.
[25] Memorandum of agreement dated November 20, 1838, *Correspondence,* V, 571.
[26] F. P. Blair to Jackson, October 19, 1838, *ibid.,* 567.
[27] Jackson to A. J. Hutchings, September 20, 1838, *ibid.,* 566.
[28] J. K. Polk to Jackson, February 7, 1839, Jackson Papers, Tennessee Historical Society, Nashville; Jackson to Martin Van Buren, March 4, 1839, *Correspondence,* VI, 6.

²⁹ Jackson to J. A. Shute, January 3, 1839, *ibid.*, 1; to J. K. Polk, February 11, *ibid.*, 4; to A. J. Hutchings, May 20, *ibid.*, 14.
³⁰ Richard Rush to Jackson, October 22, 1839, Jackson Papers.
³¹ Jackson to Martin Van Buren, July 13, 1840, Van Buren Papers.
³² Amos Kendall to Jackson, March 4, 1840, Jackson Papers.
³³ Jackson to H. M. Cryer, December 10, 1839, *Correspondence*, VI, 41.
³⁴ Jackson to W. B. Lewis, November 11, 1839, *ibid.*, 40.
³⁵ Jackson to A. J. Hutchings, December 19, 1839, *ibid.*, 43.
³⁶ Jackson to Andrew Jackson, junior, December 31, 1839, *ibid.*, 46.
³⁷ *Ibid.*
³⁸ Jackson to Andrew Jackson, junior, December 24, 1839, *ibid.*, 44.
³⁹ Jackson to Andrew Jackson, junior, December 27 and 31, 1839, *ibid.*, 45-46; to Sarah Yorke Jackson, January 4, 1840, *ibid.*, 47.
⁴⁰ Jackson to Amos Kendall, April 16, 1840, *ibid.*, 58.
⁴¹ Jackson to Andrew Jackson, junior, December 31, 1839, *ibid.*, 46. Though written on the journey to New Orleans the quotation expresses exactly Jackson's sentiments on his way home.
⁴² Wise, 170.
⁴³ Jackson to F. P. Blair, February 15, 1840, *Correspondence*, VI, 49-51; to Martin Van Buren, April 3, Van Buren Papers; to Amos Kendall, April 16, *Correspondence*, VI, 58.
⁴⁴ Alexander, 370.
⁴⁵ *Ibid.*, 366.
⁴⁶ Jackson to A. J. Hutchings, May 1, 1840, *Correspondence*, VI, 60.
⁴⁷ On his return from New Orleans Jackson had borrowed on two notes of hand dated January 20, 1840, four thousand nine hundred and sixty-four dollars (Jackson Papers). The amount is hardly large enough to explain the source of the fifteen thousand dollars he raised during the year to apply on Andrew's debts, for the earnings of the Hermitage, including sales of stock, hardly could have made up the balance. On December 10, 1842, Hunter's Hill, which Jackson had had on the market since 1840, was sold to Mrs. Elizabeth E. Donelson for twelve thousand dollars (Transcribed Deed Book No. 9, Davidson County Records, Nashville). This money appears to have gone at once to satisfy old obligations, leaving Jackson still hard pressed.
⁴⁸ Jackson to A. J. Hutchings, August 3, September 7 and 11, 1840, *ibid.*, 69, 74, 77.
⁴⁹ Jackson to A. J. Hutchings, August 3 and 12, 1840, *ibid.*, 70.
⁵⁰ James Phelan, *History of Tennessee* (1888), 386-90; Parton, III, 637.
⁵¹ Jackson to F. P. Blair, September 26, 1840, *Correspondence*, VI, 78.
⁵² *Democratic Review*, June, 1840, p. 486.
⁵³ Jackson to Andrew Jackson, junior, September 28, 1840, *Correspondence*, VI, 79.
⁵⁴ Buell, II, 373-74.
⁵⁵ Jackson to Martin Van Buren, November 12, 1840, *Correspondence*, VI, 82.
⁵⁶ Wheeling (Virginia) *Times*, McMaster, VI, 590.
⁵⁷ Jackson to Martin Van Buren, November 24, 1840, *Correspondence*, VI, 83.
⁵⁸ Jackson to F. P. Blair, December 18, 1840, *ibid.*, 85.

⁵⁹ Jackson to W. B. Lewis, December 26, 1839, *ibid.*, 87.
⁶⁰ James Howerton to Andrew Jackson, junior, October 21, 1840, Jackson Papers; J. M. Parker to Jackson, February 21, 1841, *Correspondence,* VI, 91; James Howerton to Jackson, April 5, *ibid.,* 99-102.
⁶¹ Jackson to W. B. Lewis, November 11, 1839, *ibid.,* 40; to A. J. Hutchings, September 11, 1840, *ibid.,* 77.
⁶² Endorsement in Jackson hand on letter of L. Thompson to Jackson, June 26, 1842, Jackson Papers.
⁶³ Jackson to A. J. Hutchings, January 14, 1841, *Correspondence,* VI, 91.
⁶⁴ Jackson to Amos Kendall, January 2, 1841, *ibid.,* 89.
⁶⁵ John Catron to Jackson, January 3, 1841, *ibid.,* 89-90.
⁶⁶ Jackson to E. F. Purdy, March 16, 1841, private collection of Arthur G. Mitten, Goodland, Indiana.
⁶⁷ Jackson to Amos Kendall, February 17, 1841, Jackson Papers.
⁶⁸ F. P. Blair to Jackson, April 4, 1840, quoting General Alexander Hunter, *Correspondence,* VI, 97-98.
⁶⁹ Jackson to F. P. Blair, April 19, 1841, *ibid.,* 105.

CHAPTER XLII

¹ F. P. Blair to Jackson, November 13, 1842, *Correspondence,* VI, 175.
² D. S. Carr to Jackson, August 18, 1841, *ibid.,* 119.
³ Jackson to W. B. Lewis, August 18, 1841, *ibid.,* 120.
⁴ J. B. Plauché to Jackson, December 21, 1841, *ibid.,* 129.
⁵ F. P. Blair to Jackson, January 18, 1842, *ibid.,* 136; Jackson to Blair March 29, 1842, *ibid.,* 148, referring to a letter from Blair dated February 16 in which the offer of ten thousand dollars is made.
⁶ Jackson to L. F. Linn, March 12, 1842, *ibid.,* 143-46.
⁷ Jackson to F. P. Blair, February 24, 1842, *ibid.,* 140.
⁸ Jackson to W. B. Lewis, February 28, 1842, *ibid.,* 141.
⁹ Jackson to W. B. Lewis, March 26, 1842, *ibid.,* 147.
¹⁰ Martin Van Buren to Jackson, May 15, 1841, *ibid.,* 112.
¹¹ Alexander, 14-16, 361.
¹² Jackson to F. P. Blair, April 23, 1842, *Correspondence,* VI, 150.
¹³ F. P. Blair to Jackson, May 24, 1842, *ibid.,* 154.
¹⁴ The southern "conspiracy" idea with reference to the annexation of Texas has been plentifully exploited by historians and biographers. Turner (p. 512) concludes that there is nothing in it, and cites good evidence.
¹⁵ Jackson to F. P. Blair, May 23, 1842, *Correspondence,* VI, 152.
¹⁶ Martin Van Buren to Jackson, May 27, 1842, *ibid.,* 155.
¹⁷ Jackson to F. P. Blair, April 23, 1842, *ibid.,* 150.
¹⁸ D. T. Lynch, 478; Edward M. Shepard, *Martin Van Buren* (1888), 343; Schurz, II, 244.
¹⁹ Jackson to F. P. Blair, July 18, 1842, *Correspondence,* VI, 159.
²⁰ Miscellaneous endorsements without dates, *ibid.,* 416.
²¹ Jackson to F. P. Blair, June 4, 1842, Jackson Papers.
²² Jackson to L. F. Linn, June 2, 1842; to Amos Kendall, June 18; to F. P. Blair, July 14; to J. W. Breedlove, August 1, *Correspondence,* VI 156-62.
²³ Jackson to J. W. Breedlove, October 3, 1842, *ibid.,* 172. See also Jackson to F. P. Blair, September 9, and October 3, *ibid.,* 165, 171.

24 Jackson to Amos Kendall, *op. cit.*
25 Jackson to F. P. Blair, November 25, 1842, *ibid.,* 178.
26 Jackson to George Bancroft, December 9, 1841, *ibid.,* 128.
27 Jackson to Amos Kendall, January 10, 1843, Tennessee State Library, Nashville.
28 Amos Kendall to Jackson, November 29, 1842, Jackson Papers.
29 J. A. McLaughlin to Amos Kendall, January 30, 1843, *Correspondence,* VI, 186.
30 Fragment posted as item 23,655, Volume CVII, Jackson Papers.
31 Fragment posted as item 23,783, Volume CIX, Jackson Papers.
32 C. L. Butler to Jackson, March 15, 1843, Jackson Papers.
33 Jackson's Will, *Correspondence,* VI, 220-23.
34 Jackson to F. P. Blair, July 14, 1843, *ibid.,* 224.
35 Jackson to Amos Kendall, November 13, 1843, *ibid.,* 242.
36 F. P. Blair to Jackson, November 26, 1843; Jackson's reply, December 5; Blair to Jackson December 6, *ibid.,* 244-45, 247, 248. Before Jackson's death Kendall and Blair were reconciled and in the last weeks of his life Jackson solicited a federal appointment for Kendall from James K. Polk.
37 Jackson to F. P. Blair, November 22, 1843, *ibid.,* 243.
38 Jackson to A. J. Donelson, October 15, 1843, *ibid.,* 234; to Blair, *op. cit.* Accessible records do not give the prices Butler paid for the horses.
39 Henry Lieberman to Jackson, February 19, 1844, Jackson Papers.
40 Jackson to F. P. Blair, February 24 and 29, 1844, *Correspondence,* VI, 266, 267. Blair's reply to Jackson's specific request is not available, but the tenor of subsequent letters, and Jackson's disposition of the money, indicates its nature.
41 Jackson to F. P. Blair, February 29, 1844, *ibid.,* 267-68.
42 The letter delivered by Miller, Sam Houston to Jackson, February 16, 1844, and Jackson's reply under date of March 15, appear in more detail in the next chapter. See notes 7 and 9 *post.*

CHAPTER XLIII

1 James, 167.
2 Anson Jones, Secretary of State of Texas, to Isaac Van Zandt, Texan chargé d'affaires to the United States, December 13, 1843, *Texan Diplomatic Correspondence,* II, 232-33.
3 A. P. Upshur, Secretary of State, to W. S. Murphy, American chargé to Texas, January 16, 1844, Justin H. Smith, *The Annexation of Texas* (1911), 158-59.
4 R. J. Walker to Jackson, January 10, 1844, *Correspondence,* VI, 255.
5 Jackson to Sam Houston, January 18, 1844, private collection of the late Houston Williams, Houston, Texas. Mr. Williams was a grandson of Sam Houston.
6 Jackson to Sam Houston, January 23, 1844, *ibid.*
7 Sam Houston to Jackson, February 16, 1844, *Correspondence,* VI, 260-64.
8 J. H. Smith, 164.
9 Jackson to Sam Houston, March 15, 1844, Houston (Texas) Public Library; to W. B. Lewis, March 11, *Correspondence,* VI, 272; W. D. Miller to Jackson, April 7, *ibid.,* 276.

[10] Jackson to Sam' Houston, March 15, 1844, Houston (Texas) Public Library.
[11] J. H. Smith, 166-76.
[12] W. D. Miller to Jackson, April 7, 1844, *Correspondence,* VI, 276; W. B. Lewis to Jackson, March 28, *ibid.*
[13] Jackson to A. V. Brown, February 12, 1844, Richmond *Enquirer,* March 22, 1844. In subsequent contemporary publications the date was changed to 1843, which was correct. A copy of the original letter, under date of February 9, 1843, appears in *Correspondence,* VI, 201-02, which shows that the language of the published copy was dressed up quite a bit.
[14] Jackson to F. P. Blair, May 7, 1844, *Correspondence,* VI, 283.
[15] James K. Polk to Cave Johnson, May 4, 1844, St. George L. Sioussat, "Letters of James K. Polk to Cave Johnson 1833-1848," *Tennessee Historical Magazine,* I, 238-39.
[16] Willoughby Williams to John Trimble, December 1, 1877, Jo. C. Guild, *Old Times in Tennessee* (1878), 163-64; J. K. Polk to Cave Johnson, May 13, 1844, Sioussat, *Polk Letters,* I, 242; Jackson to F. P. Blair, May 11, *Correspondence,* VI, 286: "I have shed tears of regret over [Van Buren's letter]."
[17] *Ibid.*
[18] Nashville *Union,* May 16, 1844. Jackson also sent to Van Buren a manuscript copy of the letter which is reproduced, from the Van Buren Papers, in *Correspondence,* VI, 289-91.
[19] In 1843 Jones had defeated Polk for Governor of Tennessee a second time.
[20] J. K. Polk to Cave Johnson, May 13, 1844, Sioussat, *Polk Letters,* I, 239-40.
[21] J. K. Polk to Cave Johnson, May 14, *ibid.,* 242.
[22] *Ibid.*
[23] Cave Johnson to J. K. Polk, May 8, 1844, Polk Papers, Library of Congress.
[24] J. K. Polk to Cave Johnson, May 14, 1844, Sioussat, *Polk Letters,* I, 242-43.
[25] Jackson to B. F. Butler, May 14, 1844, Jesse S. Reeves, "Letters of Gideon J. Pillow to James K. Polk, 1844," *American Historical Review,* XI, 833-34. Butler, the former Attorney General, was Van Buren's campaign manager. The letter was intended for Van Buren's eye. It is quite possible that it was designed to cover the further contingency of averting a break with Van Buren with a view to bringing more pressure to bear, should Van Buren be nominated on a platform silent on Texas.
[26] The letter appeared in the *Union* for May 16, 1844, the editorial in the succeeding issue, May 18.
[27] Jackson to J. K. Polk, June 29, 1844, *Correspondence,* VI, 299.
[28] Buell, II, 384.
[29] Sarah Knox Sevier to Jackson, February 3, 1844, Jackson Papers. The writer was one of the regiment of Rachel Jackson's grand-nieces. She was also related to James Knox Polk.
[30] Latetia Chambers to Jackson, January 15, 1844, *ibid.*
[31] John Greere to Jackson, November 20, 1844, *ibid.*
[32] J. M. Parker to Jackson, August 2, 1844; Jackson to W. B. Lewis, September 17, *Correspondence,* VI, 309 and 319.
[33] Jackson to F. P. Blair, August 15, 1844, *ibid.,* 313.
[34] Jackson to W. B. Lewis, July 12, 1844, *ibid.,* 302.
[35] Jackson to J. K. Polk, July 26, 1844; to J. Y. Mason, August 1; to W. B. Lewis, August 1, *ibid.,* 303-08; John Tyler to Jackson, August 18, *ibid.,* 315.

[36] J. H. Smith, 297-307.
[37] Jackson to J. K. Polk, July 23, 1844, Polk Papers.
[38] Jackson to F. P. Blair, September 19, 1844, *Correspondence,* VI, 322; J. K. Polk to Cave Johnson, October 30, Sioussat, *Polk Letters,* I, 253.
[39] The following tabulation (from Turner, 528) shows, in some measure, the extent to which Jackson had been able to popularize the cause of Texas in New England, where at the start of the campaign it was very weak, and the extent to which Clay was able to pick up pro-Texas votes in the West and South, where the Texas cause was overwhelmingly strong:

	Polk	Clay	Birney [Abolitionist]
New England	178,474	186,586	25,861
Middle Atlantic	442,618	432,003	19,081
South Atlantic	171,706	171,271	....
South Central	198,099	185,162	....
North Central	346,346	324,040	17,358
	1,337,243	1,299,062	62,300

It would not do, of course, to accept these figures as a reflection on Texas alone. The tariff, the currency question and other issues entered in. A high-tariff letter was credited as responsible for Polk's victory in Pennsylvania, for example. But Texas was the greatest single issue, and the foregoing figures can be considered with that in mind.

[40] A speech by Clay at Lexington, Kentucky, in 1842, in a collection of Clay's speeches in the library of the University of Chicago; see also Henry S. Foote, *Casket of Reminiscences* (1874), 27.
[41] Jackson to A. J. Donelson, November 18, 1844, *Correspondence,* VI, 330.
[42] Jackson to A. J. Donelson, December 2, 1844, *ibid.,* 334-36.
[43] A. J. Donelson to the Secretary of State, November 24, 1844, J. H. Smith, 370-71.
[44] *Ibid.,* 373.
[45] A. J. Donelson to Jackson, December 28, 1844, *Correspondence,* VI, 349-50.
[46] Jackson to F. P. Blair, January 21, 1844, *ibid.,* 367.
[47] James, 353.
[48] F. P. Blair to Jackson, February 28, 1844, *Correspondence,* VI, 375.
[49] Jackson to F. P. Blair, March 10, 1844, *ibid.,* 378.
[50] F. P. Blair to Jackson, December 22, 1844, *ibid.,* 348.
[51] Jackson to A. J. Donelson, without date but containing internal evidence of having been written in February, 1845, *ibid.,* 367.
[52] Jackson to W. B. Lewis, February 12, 1844; to F. P. Blair, March 3, *ibid.,* 368 and 376.
[53] Jackson to W. B. Lewis, February 12, 1844, *ibid.,* 368-69.
[54] F. P. Blair to Jackson, February 21, 1845, *ibid.,* 370; J. C. Rives to Jackson, March 12, *ibid.,* 380; W. B. Lewis to Jackson, March 13, Jackson Papers.
[55] Heiskell, II, 408.
[56] Jackson to F. P. Blair, March 3, 1844; to W. B. Lewis, March 22, *Correspondence,* VI, 376 and 386.
[57] Isaac Hill in an unsigned letter to the *New Hampshire Patriot* reprinted in *The Madisonian* (Washington), March 29, 1845.

⁵⁸ From a scrapbook of old newspaper clippings, Tennessee State Library, Nashville.
⁵⁹ Jackson to J. D. Elliott, March 27, 1845, *Correspondence,* VI, 391.
⁶⁰ John Catron to James Buchanan, June 11, 1845, The New York *Sun,* January 8, 1882. This item kindly furnished by Lindsey House, Tulsa, Oklahoma.
⁶¹ Jackson to Sam Houston, March 12, 1845, Yoakum, II, 441.
⁶² A. J. Donelson to Elizabeth Donelson, for Jackson's eye, April 16, 1845, Donelson Papers.
⁶³ E. G. W. Butler to W. C. Crane, April 9, 1881, William Carey Crane, *Life and Select Literary Remains of Sam Houston* (1885), 251.
⁶⁴ An example of the respect of humble citizens for the authority of Jackson's name occurred in Alabama in 1866 in a case involving a cloud on a land title. It appears that a patent originating during Jackson's administration exhibited some small irregularity. The holder was asked to surrender the same to have the technicality rectified. He responded as follows: "You think you are gon to git my paytent. I reckon not. I am not afeard of you. My paytent is signed A-N-D-R-E-W J-A-C-K-S-O-N. Now tech that if you dar." (Washington correspondence of the New York *Evening Post,* dated August 8, 1866.) This item kindly communicated by David Rankin Barbee, Washington, D. C.
⁶⁵ Jackson to J. K. Polk, May 26, 1845, *Correspondence,* VI, 412.
⁶⁶ Diary of William Tyack, May 29, 1845, Niles' *Register,* June 21, 1845; also in Parton, III, 673.
⁶⁷ John Catron to Sarah Yorke Jackson, May 19, 1845, *ibid.,* 409; Niles' *Register,* June 21, 1845.
⁶⁸ George P. A. Healy, *Reminiscences of a Portrait Painter* (1894), 144, 149.
⁶⁹ William Tyack's diary, *op. cit.*
⁷⁰ Jackson to J. B. Plauché, June 5, 1845, from an old clipping, apparently from a New Orleans newspaper. For an account of the writing of this letter see Andrew Jackson, junior, to J. K. Polk, October 10, 1845, Jackson Papers.

This draft for two thousand dollars raised the total of General Jackson's indebtedness, exclusive of household bills, to twenty-six thousand dollars at the time of his death. The principal creditors, Blair, Rives and Plauché, were specifically protected by the terms of Jackson's will. Blair and Rives did not avail themselves of this protection, making no claim against the estate. What Plauché did I do not know. In 1856 Andrew Jackson, junior's, debts had mounted to forty-eight thousand dollars. The State of Tennessee came to his relief, purchasing the Hermitage, and enabling Jackson to make a fresh start. In 1860 the State invited him to return to the Hermitage as a tenant at will. He died there in 1865. His widow, Sarah, died there in 1888.

The last of the Hermitage "family"—to use the term as General Jackson used it, meaning persons both white and black—to leave the old place was Alfred, an ex-slave. He died in 1901 at the age of 98, and was buried beside his master and mistress in the garden.

Long before his death Alfred became a personage of distinction, constantly pressed for reminiscences of General Jackson. The old darky did his best to accommodate, and in this way his name has become considerably involved with the local Jacksonian tradition. Alfred is usually referred to as the General's body servant. The remark attributed to him which I like best was one the late Judge John H. DeWitt, president of the Tennessee Historical Society, used to repeat. Someone asked the old negro if he thought General Jackson would get to Heaven on Judgment Day. Alfred replied: "If Gen'l Jackson takes it into his head to git to Heaven who's gwine to keep him out?"

Though a household negro, Alfred was not General Jackson's body servant. He was one of the four negroes tried in 1840 for the murder of Frank, the fiddler, and acquitted. Another of the defendants—George, the mulatto—was the General's body servant and constant attendant during the last twenty years of his life. During Jackson's last illness George's understudy and assistant appears to have been a negro named Dick. George married Manthis, the property of Albert Ward. In 1840 Ward offered to sell her to Jackson for one thousand dollars so that the couple might be together. At that time Jackson did not have the money to make the purchase, but later he made it for the two were at the Hermitage in 1845.

In 1858 they were separated again. Andrew Jackson, junior, sold George to Dr. John Donelson Martin. He sold Manthis to a Presbyterian minister named Carr who handed her over to Nathan Bedford Forrest, a slave dealer in Memphis, soon to achieve renown in another field. There Martin bought her in order to unite the couple at his place in Alabama where both died during the last year of the War Between the States. (For the history of George and Manthis after leaving the Hermitage I am indebted to Mrs. Mary Martin Frost of Florence, Alabama. The deeds of sale are in her family.)

[71] Andrew Jackson, junior, to A. O. P. Nicholson, June 17, 1845, Jackson Papers, New York Historical Society.

[72] Jackson to J. K. Polk, June 6, 1845, Jackson Papers, Library of Congress. Jackson signed his name once more after writing this letter when, on the following day, June 7, he franked a letter for Andrew, junior, to former Congressman Thomas F. Marshall of Kentucky. (Andrew Jackson, junior, to A. O. P. Nicholson, *op. cit.*) Emil Edward Hurja, who has studied the life of Walker from the sources, and who owns manuscript material concerning him, informs me that Jackson's misgivings concerning the influence of the Mississippi speculators were unfounded. Walker made a good Secretary of the Treasury, and financed the Mexican War without a bond issue.

[73] Andrew Jackson, junior, to J. K. Polk, October 10, 1845, *ibid.*

[74] Andrew Jackson, junior, to A. O. P. Nicholson, *op. cit.;* Parton, III, 676.

[75] Healy, 145.

[76] Statements of Dr. Esselman and W. B. Lewis, *ibid.,* 677-78; Andrew Jackson, junior, to A. O. P. Nicholson, *op. cit.;* statement of Hannah, the slave, *Correspondence,* VI, 415.

[77] Related to the writer in 1927 by the late Nettie Houston Bringhurst, of San Antonio, Texas, a daughter of Sam Houston; see also Sam Houston to J. K. Polk, midnight, June 8, 1845, *Correspondence,* VI, 415.

BIBLIOGRAPHY

Part One

The Border Captain

BIBLIOGRAPHY

[In the following lists appear the full title of sources and authorities referred to in the text and notes of this volume. It is not a complete roster of sources read or consulted, and omits a few works which, though not directly cited or quoted, were extremely helpful. These, with other light on sources, appear in the remarks entitled "Personal Acknowledgments."]

MANUSCRIPT SOURCES

Public Collections

Alabama State Library, Montgomery, Pickett Manuscripts.
Boston Public Library, Chamberlain Manuscripts.
Davidson County (Tennessee) court, marriage and land records.
Harvard University, Museum of Comparative Zoology, Journal of J. J. Audubon.
Knox County (Tennessee) court records.
Lancaster County (South Carolina) land records and wills.
Lawson-McGhee Library, Knoxville, miscellaneous manuscripts.
Library of Congress, Washington, Jackson Papers. This is the largest and most notable collection of Jackson manuscripts in existence, numbering approximately forty thousand items of which about twenty thousand pertain to the period covered by this volume.
Louisiana State Museum, New Orleans, miscellaneous manuscripts.
Mecklenburg County (North Carolina) land records and wills.
Mercer County (Kentucky) court and marriage records.
New York Public Library, Lewis Manuscripts, a collection of more than two hundred items, only a few of which, however, bear on the period treated by this book.
North Carolina Historical Commission, Raleigh, Walter Clark and Swain Manuscripts.
North Carolina, office of Secretary of State, colonial land grant records.
Rosenberg Library, Galveston, Texas, Laffite Manuscript.
Rowan County (North Carolina) court records.
South Carolina, Historical Commission of, Columbia, Revolutionary Accounts and the Journal of His Majesty's Council for South Carolina and miscellaneous manuscripts. These papers are indispensable to an understanding of the environment of Jackson's youth.
Tennessee Historical Society, Nashville. This society's collection of Jackson papers and those of his contemporaries contains perhaps six hundred manuscripts and is second in importance to that in the Library of Congress.
Tennessee State Library, Nashville, miscellaneous manuscripts.
Tennessee State Supreme Court records, Nashville.
United States District Court records, New Orleans.

Washington County (Tennessee) records, Jonesboro.
Wisconsin, State Historical Society of, Madison, Draper Manuscripts.

PRIVATE COLLECTIONS

Oliver R. Barrett, Chicago.
Bibliotheca Parsoniana (collection of Edward A. Parsons), New Orleans.
Thompson D. Dimitry, New Orleans.
William M. Hall, Memphis.
S. P. Hessel, Woodmere, New York.
Emil Edward Hurja, New York City.
Mrs. Charles R. Hyde, Chattanooga.
Andrew Jackson IV, Los Angeles.
Albert Lieutaud, New Orleans.
Thomas F. Madigan, New York City.
Miss Ethel Morse, Tampa, Florida.
Alexander S. Salley, junior, Columbia, South Carolina.

PRINTED SOURCES

Thomas Perkins Abernethy, "Andrew Jackson and Southwestern Democracy," *American Historical Review*, XXXIII.
———, *From Frontier to Plantation in Tennessee* (1932).
Acts Passed at a General Assembly of Virginia (1790). Re Robards divorce.
Henry Adams, *History of the United States* (1889-1911).
Susan Smart Alexander, reminiscences of Andrew Jackson, *National Intelligencer*, August 1 and August 29, 1845.
John Allison, *Dropped Stitches in Tennessee History* (1897).
American Historical Magazine, V, contains affidavit of Andrew Greer, re Jackson-Sevier encounter; VIII, indictment in case with which Jackson was connected in November, 1788.
American State Papers, Foreign Relations.
American State Papers, Indian Affairs.
American State Papers, Military Affairs.
American State Papers, Miscellaneous.
Douglas Anderson, "Andrew Jackson, Frontier Merchant," Nashville *Tennessean*, April 13, 1929.
James Douglas Anderson, *Making of the American Thoroughbred* (1916).
James L. Armstrong, *General Jackson's Juvenile Indiscretions* (1832).
John Spencer Bassett, editor, *Correspondence of Andrew Jackson* (1926-33).
———, *Life of Andrew Jackson* (1911).
Thomas Hart Benton, *Thirty Years' View* (1854).
Albert J. Beveridge, *Life of John Marshall* (1916-19).
Biographical Dictionary of the American Congress.
Augustus C. Buell, *A History of Andrew Jackson* (1904).
Mary French Caldwell, "Massacres in this Section," Nashville *Tennessean*, August 30, 1931.
Richard L. Campbell, *Historical Sketches of Colonial Florida* (1892).
Charleston (South Carolina) *City Gazette and Commercial Daily Advertiser*, March 27, 1815. Colonel William Richardson Davie's statement about Jackson's birthplace.

BIBLIOGRAPHY—*The Border Captain*

Charleston (South Carolina) *Courier*, November 24, 1814. Letter signed "K" about Jackson's birthplace.

W. W. Clayton, *History of Davidson County, Tennessee* (1886).

H. E. Coffey, reminiscences of the Waxhaws, Rock Hill (South Carolina) *Record*, August 19, 1920.

Columbian Centinel (Boston), September 10, 1814. Attitude of the East toward the war with England; January 28, 1815, news of the December 24 attack on New Orleans reaches New England.

Congressional Record, discussions about Jackson's birthplace, February 23, 1922; June 18, 1926; May 24, 1928; July 2, 1928.

David Crockett, *Life of David Crockett* (reprint of 1865).

Daughters of the American Revolution Magazine, November, 1920. Arrival of the Crawford brothers in the Waxhaws.

Matthew L. Davis, *Memoirs of Aaron Burr* (1837).

John H. DeWitt, "Andrew Jackson and His Ward Andrew Jackson Hutchings," *Tennessee Historical Magazine*, Series II, Vol. I, No. 2.

———, editor, "Journal of John Sevier," *Tennessee Historical Magazine*, VI. *East Tennessee Historical Society's Publications*.

John Henry Eaton, *Life of Andrew Jackson* (1824).

———and John Reid, *Life of Andrew Jackson* (1817).

T. D. Faulkner, reminiscence of Jackson's father, reprinted in the Fort Mill (South Carolina) *Times*, October 8, 1931.

Sidney George Fisher, *Men, Women & Manners in Colonial Times* (1898).

Friend of the Laws (New Orleans).

Charles E. Gayarré, *History of Louisiana* (1866).

[George Robert Gleig] *A Narrative of the British Campaigns against Washington, Baltimore and New Orleans* (1821).

Jo C. Guild, *Old Times in Tennessee* (1878).

Gulf States Historical Magazine.

Margaret B. Hamer, "John Rhea of Tennessee," *East Tennessee Historical Society's Publications*, January 3, 1932.

John Haywood, *Civil and Political History of the State of Tennessee* [1823] (reprint of 1915).

S. G. Heiskell, *Andrew Jackson and Early Tennessee History* (1920-21).

Archibald Henderson, article about Jackson's birthplace, Raleigh (North Carolina) *News and Observer*, October 3, 1926; "Jackson's Loose Living Common Sin of the Period," *News and Observer*, October 17, 1926.

George Howe, D.D., *History of the Presbyterian Church in South Carolina* (1870).

Impartial Review and Cumberland Repository (Nashville), files for 1806 and 1807 consulted re Burr conspiracy, Dickinson duel and other matters.

John B. Irving, *The South Carolina Jockey Club* (1857).

Reverend Hugh Parks Jackson, *Genealogy of the Jackson Family* (1890).

Marquis James, "Napoleon, Junior," *The American Legion Monthly*, III, No. 4. Account of Laffite's rôle in New Orleans campaign.

William James, *Military Occurrences of the Late War between Great Britain and the United States* (1818).

Amos Kendall, *Life of Andrew Jackson* (1843).

Kentucky *Gazette* (Lexington), 1790 to 1793, re Robards divorce.

Grace King, *Creole Families of New Orleans* (1922).

Knoxville *Gazette*, September 14, 1793. An article on Indian warfare in vicinity of Knoxville; July 27, 1803, Jackson's exposé of Sevier's North Carolina land fraud.

Knoxville *Sentinel*, November 26, 1922. Statement of James Payne Green on Jackson's marriage in Natchez.

Major A. Lacarrière Latour, *Historical Memoir of the War in the West* (1816).

La Courrière de la Louisiane (New Orleans).

Charles Edward Lester [and Sam Houston], *Life of Sam Houston* (1855).

Letters of General Adair and General Jackson, published at Lexington, Kentucky, in 1817.

Louisiana *Gazette*, various dates in 1814 and 1815.

Louisiana Historical Quarterly, VI. Grace King's translation of Bernard Marigny's pamphlet on the New Orleans campaign.

Edward Deering Mansfield, *Life of General Winfield Scott* (1848).

François-Xavier Martin, *History of Louisiana* (reprint of 1882).

John Bach McMaster, *History of the People of the United States* (1883-1906).

Mississippi Valley Historical Review.

John W. Monette, *History of the Discovery and Settlement of the Valley of the Mississippi* (1846).

Samuel Eliot Morison, *Life and Letters of Harrison Gray Otis* (1913).

Niles's *Weekly Register.*

Vincent Nolte, *Fifty Years in Two Hemispheres* (1854).

North Carolina Argus (Wadesboro), September 23, 1858. First publication of the famous "Walkup evidence," relating to Jackson's birthplace. Reprints appear in the *North Carolina University Magazine,* X, and the *Congressional Record,* June 18, 1926, pp. 11535-40.

W. G. Orr, memoir of Wetherford's surrender, *Publication of Alabama Historical Society,* II, 57.

James Parton, *A Life of Andrew Jackson* (1859-60).

Albert James Pickett, *History of Alabama* (reprint of 1896).

Publications of Alabama Historical Society.

A. W. Putnam, *History of Middle Tennessee* (1859).

David Ramsey, M.D., *History of South Carolina* (1809).

J. G. M. Ramsay, *Annals of Tennessee* (1853).

James B. Ranck, "Andrew Jackson and the Burr Conspiracy," *Tennessee Historical Society Magazine,* October, 1930.

John Reid and John Henry Eaton, *Life of Andrew Jackson* (1817).

Charles C. Royce, "The Cherokee Nation of Indians," *Fifth Annual Report,* Bureau of American Ethnology (1887).

Charles C. Royce and Cyrus Thomas, "Indian Land Cessions," *Eighteenth Annual Report,* Bureau of American Ethnology.

A. S. Salley, junior, *The Boundary Line between North Carolina and South Carolina* (1929).

William L. Saunders, editor, *Colonial Records of North Carolina* (1887).

Johann David Schoepf, *Travels in the Confederation* (1785, English translation 1911).

Senate Report 1527, 71st Congress, 3rd Session.

W. H. Sparks, *The Memories of Fifty Years* (1870).

State Records of North Carolina.

Lieutenant-Colonel [Banastre] Tarleton, *Campaign of 1780-1781 in the Southern Provinces* (1787).

Major Howell Tatum, "Topographical Notes and Observations on the Alabama River, August, 1814," *Publications of the Alabama Historical Society,* II.

——"Major Howell Tatum's Journal," *Smith College Studies in History,* VII.

Cyrus Thomas and Charles C. Royce, "Indian Land Cessions," *Eighteenth Annual Report,* Bureau of American Ethnology.

Major Ben Truman, *Field of Honor* (1884).

United States Telegraph (Washington, D. C.), June 22, 1827, article answering attack on character of Mrs. Jackson; March 28, 1828, statement of Thomas Crutcher.

Virginia House Journal (1790). *Re* Robards divorce.

Virginia Senate Journal (1790). *Re* Robards divorce.

S. Putnam Waldo, *Memoirs of Andrew Jackson* (1819).

Alexander Walker, *Jackson and New Orleans* (1856).

S. H. Walkup, *North Carolina University Magazine,* X, 225. An article on Jackson's birthplace. Reprinted in *Congressional Record,* June 18, 1926. Originally appeared in *North Carolina Argus* (Wadesboro), September 23, 1858.

Charles Warren, *Jacobin and Junto* (1931).

Thomas E. Watson, *Life of Andrew Jackson* (1912).

Yorkville Enquirer (York, South Carolina), April 14, 1931. An article about grave of Jackson's father.

BIBLIOGRAPHY

PART TWO

Portrait of a President

[No attempt is made here to give a full list of the sources, manuscript or printed, which have been read or examined. Only such manuscript collections are named as yielded something which is quoted in the text or cited in the Notes. The list of printed sources is confined to a recapitulation by full title of authorities referred to in the Notes, where short titles are used after the initial mention. Further remarks on sources appear under "Personal Acknowledgments."]

MANUSCRIPT SOURCES

PUBLIC COLLECTIONS

George Bancroft Papers, New York Public Library.

Nicholas Biddle Papers, Library of Congress, Washington.

Bixby Collection, miscellaneous manuscripts, Henry E. Huntington Library, San Marino, California.

ANDREW JACKSON

Henry Clay Papers, Library of Congress.
John Coffee Papers, Tennessee Historical Society, Nashville.
John J. Crittenden Papers, Library of Congress.
Hardy M. Cryer Papers, Tennessee Historical Society.
Davidson County (Tennessee) Records, Nashville.
Andrew Jackson Donelson Papers, Library of Congress.
Charles Fisher Papers, University of North Carolina, Chapel Hill.
Duff Green Papers, Library of Congress.
Washington Irving Note Books, New York Public Library.
Andrew Jackson Papers, Ladies' Hermitage Association, Nashville.
Andrew Jackson Papers, Library of Congress. Manuscripts from this collection usually are designated in the Notes simply as "Jackson Papers." Manuscripts from other public collections of Jackson papers are identified by giving the location of the collection each time it is mentioned, for example, "Jackson Papers, Ladies' Hermitage Association, Nashville."
Andrew Jackson Papers, New York Historical Society, New York City.
Andrew Jackson Papers, Tennessee Historical Society.
James Kent Papers, Library of Congress.
William B. Lewis Papers, New York Public Library.
Virgil Maxcy Papers, Library of Congress.
John McLean Papers, Library of Congress.
Miscellaneous manuscripts, Houston (Texas) Public Library.
Miscellaneous manuscripts, New York Historical Society.
Miscellaneous manuscripts, Tennessee Historical Society.
Miscellaneous manuscripts, Tennessee State Library, Nashville.
James Monroe Papers, New York Public Library.
John Overton Papers, Tennessee Historical Society.
James K. Polk Papers, Library of Congress.
Andrew Stevenson Papers, Library of Congress.
Martin Van Buren Papers, Library of Congress.

Private Collections

Oliver R. Barrett, Chicago.
Mrs. H. L. Bateman, Nashville.
Lucius Polk Brown, Columbia, Tennessee.
Mrs. Pauline Wilcox Burke, Washington.
Campbell Papers, Lemuel R. Campbell, Nashville.
Mrs. Arthur Chester, Rye, New York.
J. M. Dickinson, Nashville.
Mrs. Louis Farrell, Nashville.
Henry M. Flynt, New York City.
Mrs. Mary Martin Frost, Florence, Alabama.
Samuel Jackson Hays, Memphis.
S. P. Hessel, Woodmere, Long Island, New York.
Stanley Horn, Nashville.
Emil Edward Hurja, Washington.
Andrew Jackson IV, Los Angeles.
Miss Estelle Lake, Memphis, Tennessee.
The late Thomas F. Madigan, New York City.
Mrs. Andrew Jackson Martin, Memphis.

George Fort Milton, Chattanooga, Tennessee.
Arthur G. Mitten, Goodland, Indiana.
J. P. Morgan, New York City.
C. Norton Owen, Glencoe, Illinois.
The late Houston Williams, Houston, Texas.
Mrs. Mary Wharton Yeatman, Columbia, Tennessee.

UNPUBLISHED THESES

Curtis W. Garrison, "The National Election of 1824," manuscript copy in the library of Johns Hopkins University, Baltimore.
Richard A. McLemore, "The French Spoliation Claims, 1816-1836," manuscript copy in the library of Vanderbilt University, Nashville.
Arthur R. Newsome, "The Presidential Election of 1824 in North Carolina," manuscript copy in the library of the University of Michigan, Ann Arbor.
Culver H. Smith, "The Washington Press of the Jackson Period," manuscript copy in the library of Duke University, Durham, North Carolina.

PRINTED SOURCES

Charles Francis Adams (editor), *Memoirs of John Quincy Adams, Comprising Portions of His Diary* (1876).
James Truslow Adams, *The Living Jefferson* (1936).
Holmes Alexander, *The American Talleyrand, the Career and Contemporaries of Martin Van Buren* (1935).
Alexandria (D. C.) *Gazette.*
Alexandria (D. C.) *Herald.*
American Antiquarian Society *Proceedings*, New Series, XXXI.
American Historical Magazine.
James Douglas Anderson, *Making of the American Thoroughbred* (1916).
"An American Army Officer," *Civil and Military History of Andrew Jackson* (1825).
Annals of Congress.
Argus of Western America (Frankfort, Kentucky).
James L. Armstrong, *General Jackson's Juvenile Indiscretions* (1832).
Caleb Atwater, *Remarks on a Tour to Prairie du Chien* (1831).
Frederick Bancroft, *Calhoun and the South Carolina Nullification Movement* (1928).
John Spencer Bassett (editor), *Correspondence of Andrew Jackson* (1926-35).
——, "Major Lewis on the Nomination of Andrew Jackson," *Proceedings* of the American Antiquarian Society, New Series, XXXIII.
——, "Notes on Jackson's Visit to New England," *Proceedings* of the Massachusetts Historical Society, LVI.
——, *The Life of Andrew Jackson* (1911).
Ernest Sutherland Bates, *The Story of the Supreme Court* (1936).
Jesse Benton, *An Address to the People of the United States on the Presidential Election* (1824).
Thomas Hart Benton, *Thirty Years' View* (1854-56).
[Nicholas] *Biddle Correspondence.* See R. C. McGrane.
Boston *Gazette.*
Claude G. Bowers, *Party Battles of the Jackson Period* (1922).

Everett Somerville Brown (editor), *The Missouri Compromises and Presidential Politics 1820-1825, from the Letters of William Plumer, Jr.* (1926).
Margaret Eaton Puchignani. See Margaret Eaton.
Augustus C. Buell, *A History of Andrew Jackson* (1904).
Mary French Caldwell, *Andrew Jackson's Hermitage* (1933).
[John C.] *Calhoun Letters.* See J. F. Jameson.
[John C.] *Calhoun's Works.* See R. K. Crallé.
Ralph C. H. Catterall, *The Second Bank of the United States* (1903).
Edward Channing, *History of the United States* (1923-26).
J. F. H. Claiborne, *Life and Times of Sam Dale* (1860).
Allen C. Clark, *Life and Letters of Dolly Madison* (1914).
Bennett Champ Clark, *John Quincy Adams, Old Man Eloquent* (1932).
[Henry Clay], *Address of Henry Clay to the Public, Containing Certain Testimony in Refutation of the Charges Made by Gen. Andrew Jackson* (1827).
[——], *Supplement to an Address by Henry Clay* (1828).
[Henry] *Clay Correspondence.* See Calvin Colton.
[Henry] *Clay's Works.* See Calvin Colton.
Cincinnati *Advertiser.*
Cincinnati *Gazette.* Full title *Liberty Hall & Cincinnati Gazette.*
Cincinnati *National Republican.*
Joseph B. Cobb, *Leisure Labors* (1858).
Calvin Colton (editor), *Private Correspondence of Henry Clay* (1856).
—— and others (editors), *Works of Henry Clay* (1897).
Columbian Observer (Philadelphia).
Congressional Globe.
Continental Monthly.
Correspondence of Andrew Jackson. See J. S. Bassett.
Richard K. Crallé (editor), *Works of John C. Calhoun* (1850-56).
William Carey Crane, *Life and Select Literary Remains of Sam Houston* (1885).
George Tichnor Curtis, *Life of Daniel Webster* (1870).
"Curtius," *Torch Light, . . . an Examination of the Opposition to the Administration* (1826).
[Charles Augustus Davis], *The Letters of J. Downing, Major* (1834).
Democratic Review.
[William J. Duane], *Narrative of Correspondence Concerning the Removal of Deposites* (1838).
Seymour Dunbar, *A History of Travel in America* (1915).
[Margaret Eaton], *The Autobiography of Peggy Eaton* (1932).
Erik M. Eriksson, "The Civil Service Under President Jackson," *Mississippi Valley Historical Review*, XIII.
Carl Russel Fish, *The Civil Service and Patronage* (1905).
Worthington C. Ford, *Writings of John Quincy Adams* (1913-17).
John W. Forney, *Anecdotes of Public Men* (1873).
Franklin Gazette (Philadelphia).
Claude Moore Fuess, *Daniel Webster* (1930).
Samuel R. Gammon, junior, *The Presidential Campaign of 1832* (1922).
George P. Garrison (editor), *Diplomatic Correspondence of the Republic of Texas* (1908).

George R. Gilmer, *Sketches of Some of the Settlers of Upper Georgia* (Reprint of 1926).
Samuel G. Goodrich, *Recollections of a Lifetime* (1866).
Horace Greeley, *The American Conflict* (1864).
Duff Green, *Facts and Suggestions, Biographical and Historical* (1866).
Francis J. Grund (editor), *Aristocracy in America* (1839).
Jo. C. Guild, *Old Times in Tennessee* (1878).
Herman Hailpern, "Pro-Jackson Sentiment in Pennsylvania," *Pennsylvania Magazine of History and Biography*, L.
James A. Hamilton, *Reminiscences* (1869).
[Charles Hammond], *A View of Gen. Jackson's Domestic Relations* (1828).
Jabez Hammond, *History of the Political Parties in the State of New York* (1845).
Harper's Magazine.
Thomas Robson Hay, "John C. Calhoun and the Presidential Campaign of 1824," *North Carolina Historical Review*, XII.
George P. A. Healy, *Reminiscences of a Portrait Painter* (1894).
House Reports No. 121, Twenty-second Congress.
David F. Houston, *A Critical Study of Nullification in South Carolina* (1896).
Charles H. Hunt, *Life of Edward Livingston* (1864).
Henry E. Huntington Library *Bulletin* No. 3.
Marquis James, *The Raven, a Biography of Sam Houston* (1929).
J. Franklin Jameson (editor), "Correspondence of John C. Calhoun," *Annual Report of the American Historical Association* (1899).
Frances A. Kemble, *Journal* (1835).
Amos Kendall, "Anecdotes of General Jackson," *Harper's Magazine*, September, 1842.
John P. Kennedy, *Life of William Wirt* (1849).
Kentucky Legislature, investigation of Henry Clay's part in House Election of 1825, *United States' Telegraph* Extras No. 1 and No. 12.
Knoxville (Tennessee) *Register.*
Lebanon (Tennessee) *Democrat.*
A. Levasseur, *Lafayette in America* (1829).
Liberty Hall & Cincinnati Gazette.
Louisville (Kentucky) *Public Advertiser.*
Denis Tilden Lynch, *An Epoch and a Man: Martin Van Buren and His Times* (1929).
William O. Lynch, *Fifty Years of Party Warfare* (1931).
The Madisonian (Washington).
Charles W. March, *Reminiscences of Congress* (1850).
Harriet Martineau, *Society in America* (1837).
———, *A Retrospect of Western Travel* (1838).
William MacDonald, *Jacksonian Democracy* (1906).
Reginald C. McGrane, *The Correspondence of Nicholas Biddle* (1919).
John Bach McMaster, *A History of the People of the United States* (1883-1924).
William C. Meigs, *Life of John C. Calhoun* (1917).
[Elijah Hunt Mills], *Selections from the Letters of the Hon. E. H. Mills* (1881).

John Bassett Moore (editor), *Works of James Buchanan* (1908).
William Bennett Munro, *The Makers of the Unwritten Constitution* (1930).
Nashville *Banner*.
—— *Banner & Whig*.
—— *Clarion*.
—— *Republican*.
—— *Union*.
—— *Whig*.
National Gazette (Washington).
National Intelligencer (Washington).
New-England Galaxy (Boston).
New Hampshire Patriot & State Gazette.
New York *Advertiser*.
—— *Evening Post*.
—— *Statesman*.
Niles' *Register*.
North Carolina Historical Review.
Frederic Austin Ogg, *The Reign of Andrew Jackson* (1919).
James Parton, *Life of Andrew Jackson* (1859-60).
Charles H. Peck, *The Jacksonian Epoch* (1899).
James Phelan, *History of Tennessee* (1888).
Philadelphia *Aurora*.
—— *Mercury*.
Ulrich B. Phillips, "William H. Crawford," a sketch in the *Dictionary of American Biography*, IV.
Queena Pollack, *Peggy Eaton, Democracy's Mistress* (1831).
Una Pope-Hennessey, *Three English Women in America* (1929).
Ben: Perley Poore, *Perley's Reminiscences* (1866).
Josiah Quincy, *Figures of the Past* (1883).
Raleigh (North Carolina) *Register*.
—— *Star*.
Henry S. Randall, *Life of Thomas Jefferson* (1858).
Jesse S. Reeves, "Letters of Gideon J. Pillow to James K. Polk, 1844," *American Historical Review*, XI.
Reports of Committees, First Session, Twenty-third Congress, IV.
James D. Richardson (editor), *Messages and Papers of the Presidents* (1899).
Richmond (Virginia) *Enquirer*.
George Lockhart Rives, *The United States and Mexico 1821-1848* (1913).
Anne Royall, *Letters from Alabama* (1830).
Harvey Lee Ross, *Early Pioneers of Illinois* (1899).
Nathan Sargent, *Public Men and Events* (1875).
James Schouler, *History of the United States of America* (Edition of 1913).
Carl Schurz, *Henry Clay* (1899).
Edward M. Shepard, *Martin Van Buren* (1888).
J. E. D. Shipp, *Giant Days, or the Life and Times of William H. Crawford* (1909).
St. George L. Sioussat, "Letters of James K. Polk to Cave Johnson 1833-1848," *Tennessee Historical Magazine*, I and II.
——, "Tennessee Politics in the Jackson Period," *American Historical Review*, XIV.

Justin H. Smith, *The Annexation of Texas* (1911).
[Mrs. Margaret Bayard Smith], *The First Forty Years of Washington Society* (Gaillard Hunt, editor) (1906).
[Seba Smith], *Life and Writings of Major Jack Downing* (1834).
William Ernest Smith, *The Francis Preston Blair Family in Politics* (1933).
W. H. Sparks, *Memories of Fifty Years* (1870).
James Sprunt Historical Publications, X.
Henry B. Stanton, *Random Recollections* (1886).
William Stickney (editor), *Autobiography of Amos Kendall* (1872).
William W. Story, *Life and Letters of Joseph Story* (1851).
William G. Sumner, *Andrew Jackson* (Edition of 1899).
Carl Brent Swisher, *Roger B. Taney* (1935).
Jeanette Tandy, *Crackerbox Philosophers* (1925).
Texas [Republic] *Diplomatic Correspondence*. See G. P. Garrison.
Frances M. Trollope, *Domestic Manners of the Americans* (Reprint of 1904).
Ben Truman, *The Field of Honor* (1884).
Truth's Advocate (Cincinnati).
Frederick Jackson Turner, *The United States 1830-1850* (1935).
United States Gazette (Philadelphia).
United States' Telegraph (Washington).
[Martin Van Buren], *Autobiography of Martin Van Buren* (John C. Fitzpatrick, editor) (1920).
Claude H. Van Tine (editor), *Letters of Daniel Webster* (1902).
Charles Warren, *The Supreme Court in United States History* (1922).
E. B. Washburne (editor), *The* [Ninian] *Edwards Papers* (1884).
Washington *Globe*.
[Daniel Webster], *The Writings and Speeches of Daniel Webster* (1903).
[———], *Letters of Daniel Webster*. See C. H. Van Tine.
Fletcher Webster (editor), *Private Correspondence of Daniel Webster* (1856).
Thurlow Weed, *Autobiography* (1883).
Western Herald and Steubensville (Ohio) *Gazette*.
Western North Carolinian (Salisbury).
Anne Hollingsworth Wharton, *Social Life in the Early Republic* (1902).
Clarence R. Wharton, *The Texas Republic* (1922).
Mary Emily Donelson Wilcox, *Christmas Under Three Flags* (1900).
Winchester *Virginian*.
Henry A. Wise, *Seven Decades of the Union* (1872).
Henry Wycoff, *Reminiscences of an Idler* (1880).
Mary A. Wyman, *Two American Pioneers* (1924).
"Wyoming," *Letters . . . to the People of the United States* (1824).
Henderson Yoakum, *History of Texas* (1856).

BIBLIOGRAPHY—Portrait of a President

Justin H. Smith, *The Annexation of Texas* (1911).
Mrs. Margaret Bayard Smith, *The First Forty Years of Washington Society* (edited Hunt, 1906).
Sol. Smith, *Late and Younger of Major Jack Downing* (1834).
William Ernest Smith, *The Francis Preston Blair Family in Politics* (1933).
W. H. Sparks, *Memories of Fifty Years* (1870).
Jones Sprawl Historical Publications, X.
Henry R. Stanton, *Random Recollections* (1886).
William Stickney (editor), *Autobiography of Amos Kendall* (1872).
William W. Story, *Life and Letters of Joseph Story* (1851).
William C. Sumner, *Andrew Jackson* (Edition of 1899).
Carl Brent Swisher, *Roger B. Taney* (1935).
Bayard Tuckey, *Cruise to Reminiscences* (1942).
Texas (Republic) Diplomatic Correspondence. See C. P. Garrison.
Frances M. Trollope, *Domestic Manners of the Americans* (Reprint of 1901).
Ben Truman, *The Field of Honor* (1884).
Tuttle's Almanac & Cincinnati.
Frederick Jackson Turner, *The United States 1830-1850* (1935).
United States Gazette (Philadelphia).
United States Telegraph (Washington).
[Martin Van Buren]. *Autobiography of Martin Van Buren* (John C. Fitzpatrick, editor) (1920).
Claude H. Van Tyne (editor), *Letters of Daniel Webster* (1902).
Charles Warren, *The Supreme Court in United States History* (1922).
E. B. Washburne (editor), *The [Zzziqui] Edwards Papers* (1884).
Washington Globe.
[Daniel Webster], *The Writings and Speeches of Daniel Webster* (1903).
—— *Letters of Daniel Webster*. See C. H. Van Tyne.
Fletcher Webster (editor), *Private Correspondence of Daniel Webster* (1869).
Thurlow Weed, *Autobiography* (1883).
Western Herald and Steubenville (Ohio) Gazette.
Western Carolinian (Salisbury).
Aime Hollingsworth Wharton, *Social Life in the Early Republic* (1902).
Clarence R. Wharton, *The Texas Republic* (1922).
Mary Emily Donelson Wilcox, *Christmas Under Three Flags* (1900).
Winchester Virginian.
[Henry], *Wise*. *Seven Decades of the Union* (1872).
Henry Wynoff, *Reminiscences of an Idler* (1880).
Mary Austin Wynoff, *The Jackson Wreath* (1951).
Wyoming, *Letters . . . to the People of the United States* (1824).
Hendersen Yoakum, *History of Texas* (1856).

PERSONAL ACKNOWLEDGMENTS

Part One

The Border Captain

PERSONAL ACKNOWLEDGMENTS

CARLYLE observed of biography that a well written life is almost as rare as a well spent one. If this narrative shall be received as a partial exception to the first case the circumstance is due in considerable measure to the good companions, casual and constant, who have attended the biographer during his years of labor.

This book would not be finished now, possibly would not have been finished at all, and in any event would have been more deficient in merit than it is, had it not been for the unfailing collaboration of my wife, Bessie Rowland James. To assist me she laid aside important and engaging researches of her own, for a life of Anne Royall. In connection with this book of mine much of her work has integrated itself with the whole so as to leave no distinctive impress, though if it were absent the finished product would be measurably poorer. But much of her work is of the positive kind that bears its own banner.

David Laurance Chambers of Indianapolis is another who has traveled the long road which had its beginning when a few stray discoveries in the course of research for *The Raven* determined the undertaking of this study. Though Laurance Chambers is the head of the Trade Department of the publishing house whose mark this volume bears I have fallen into the habit of regarding him more particularly as a keen, critical and useful student of Americana, who, very fortunately for me, appreciates the material problems arising from a task of historical inquiry of this stamp.

The present volume is derived from contemporary sources almost entirely and benefits by the scrutiny of a large body of manuscript not previously consulted by a biographer of General Jackson, or, indeed, for any historical purpose. Some of these papers have turned up in strange places, as one cache aggregating more than twelve hundred letters and documents, especially culled for their biographical value, that was found in Massachusetts, not more than a three hours' journey from Northampton where the late John Spencer Bassett labored the greater part of a lifetime to perfect his knowledge of Andrew Jackson.

While occupied chiefly with manuscripts the author has paid careful attention to published sources and has profited by the learning of those who have been over the ground before him. They comprise a numerous company, for of the presidents only the names of Washington and Lincoln appear more often on the printed page. From the bulk of this material the task of weeding the important from the unimportant is not, however, as serious as one might suppose. As those who have read the preceding pages may remember, the first biography of Jackson was begun by John Reid, completed by John Henry Eaton and published in 1817. As a contemporary account it is valuable and no subsequent biographer of Jackson has been able to ignore it. The present writer has obtained a little deeper insight into the historical method of Reid than appears on the printed page from a perusal of two copies of his manuscript, one at the Tennessee Historical Society in Nashville and the other, which is a later draft, among the "find" of twelve hundred Jackson papers above referred to, which within the past year have been acquired by the Library of Congress.

The next biography of significance is the unfinished one by Amos Kendall, a Kentucky editor who became an auditor in the Treasury Department and a member of the "Kitchen Cabinet" during the Jackson Administrations. In 1842 Jackson turned over to Kendall a great many of his papers. The following year seven parts of a projected fifteen-part life were published. The financial returns were not what the author had expected, Kendall became associated with Morse in the sale of stock in his telegraph company and the biography was neglected.

Jackson was not very well satisfied with what Kendall had written, and before his death in 1845 Old Hickory directed Kendall to turn over the papers to Francis Preston Blair, who had been editor of the *Globe*, the Jackson organ at Washington. Blair wished George Bancroft to write a life of Jackson. Kendall relinquished a few of the Jackson papers, but kept the more vital ones, and relations between him and Blair became strained. In 1857 James Parton appeared on the scene and began his energetic researches. Blair gave him some assistance and Kendall gave him some, but without disclosing the contents of the most important part of the General's papers which he still retained. Parton was a man of too independent mind to gain the complete confidence of either of these uncritical Jackson partizans. Parton's first volume appeared in 1859, his other two in 1860. Their success with the public was instantaneous, and despite the flood of Jacksoniana that has appeared since, this popular attachment continues. At the time many of the General's old friends and admirers, including Blair, were not so well pleased, however.

The mantle of this displeasure has descended to several authoritative and precise historians of the present day who are at pains to point out that Mr. Parton was an indifferent and superficial historian with a faulty comprehension of the underlying historical forces of the period. Therefore the background before which he causes Jackson to move is defective, sometimes to an extreme degree, and the likeness of the central character thus contrived, however entertaining, is not always an accurate or properly proportioned portrait.

These criticisms are true and they are important, but not all-important. The fact remains that *a man* walks through the numerous pages of Mr. Parton, and that man, in the main, is Andrew Jackson, whom the reader comes to know as he knows a friend or neighbor. Such is James Parton's contribution to our knowledge of Jackson and to the art of American biography; and it is the secret of his enduring popularity. Biography is not history in the general sense. It is a more personal and individual thing, and more difficult to do well. Yet in this country biography has been regarded as a sort of bi-product of history, rather than the cellular life of the same. The spotlight must ever be on the central character. Background must remain background and by selection and emphasis be kept from swamping the man we are trying to tell about. This is the salient contribution that "moderns," for all their general lack of scholarship and disinclination toward serious or laborious research, have brought to this branch of letters—and I am unable to except some of the "debunking" brethren, their keyhole views of creation and original ideas of taste notwithstanding.

Parton ever dogged the man, Jackson. He is the only biographer of the General (excepting the one who now bores you) to visit practically every place that Jackson visited, absorb something of its local flavor and dig for his materials on the spot. Parton began these travels only twelve years after his

PERSONAL ACKNOWLEDGMENTS

subject had been laid to rest in the Hermitage garden. Persons who had known Andrew Jackson as a boy were still living. Everywhere he talked to those who had been Jackson's friends, foes and acquaintances and thus preserved a body of reminiscence and anecdote which but for him must have perished. Parton was superficial, he was hasty, undiscriminating, needlessly voluminous and often carried away merely by the picturesque—but he did preserve. It is easy to understand why written documents were a secondary consideration to this agile gatherer who had so many priceless living sources at his command. Instead of wishing too ardently that some one might have done this better than Parton we should be grateful that it was done at all.

The success of Parton's lively books was the death of Blair's ambition to induce Bancroft to immortalize his patron. Kendall's half-hearted determination to finish his work also faded, and when the ex-auditor died the Jackson papers in his possession passed to a daughter who stored them in a warehouse in Washington. Shortly thereafter this building burned and the papers were assumed to have been lost.

In 1882 Professor William G. Sumner of Yale published his *Andrew Jackson*, thus marking the singularly belated entry of scholarship into the populous field of Jacksonian biography. As a study of administrations of the seventh president this book is valuable. As a proportioned biography it lacks distinction. The first chapter carries Jackson to the age of forty-five, when the forces that formed his character had completed their work. It is impossible to understand the man and difficult to understand some of his official conduct without a more intimate view of the origin and play of those forces.

Dr. John Spencer Bassett of Smith College understood the shortcomings of his predecessors and, as the preface to his first edition indicates, sought to correct them by associating a human and personable Jackson, such as Parton recreated, with the proper historical environment. For the latter task he seemed eminently qualified. A scholar who derived his materials from original sources, he had an all-round knowledge of the Jackson period which no one to date has surpassed, though amplifications and corrections are possible. His two volumes appeared in 1911. Although the most valuable work on Jackson in existence, Dr. Bassett's books are rarely seen in the hands of the general reader, because, alas, as reading they are saltless fare. The author failed to impart the savor of life to his man. If Parton, in his researches, emphasized field work to the neglect of library work, Bassett reversed the order.

But in the cloister he was supreme and when the Carnegie Institution decided to publish six volumes of Jackson's correspondence there was no question but that the most competent hand for the task was John Spencer Bassett. The first of these volumes appeared in 1926. Dr. Bassett died in 1928 but the text, annotation and arrangement of the fourth, fifth and sixth volumes had been completed by him. The remaining work of preparing them for publication fell to Dr. J. Franklin Jameson, chief of the Division of Manuscripts of the Library of Congress. A seventh volume will be issued of selections from the twelve hundred manuscripts whose acquisition the Library announced in December, 1932. These comprise the bulk of the so-called "Kendall Papers" which, after all, had survived the Washington warehouse fire. By a fortunate turn of events the writer had been able to begin his study of them before their existence was known to the Library. After the purchase, and before they were made publicly available, Dr. Herbert Putnam, Librarian of Congress, and Dr.

Jameson generously permitted me to complete my examination of them in Washington, so as not to delay the appearance of this volume.

Throughout my researches the valuable volumes of Bassett's *Correspondence of Andrew Jackson* have never been far from my side, but in justice to my own endeavors I will say that, within and somewhat beyond the scope of the present work, I have examined in the original manuscript nearly every document reproduced therein. In my "Notes" credit is given to the *Correspondence*, not only because it is owing to the labors of Dr. Bassett, but for the convenience of those who may wish to consult the full text of a given document. Space limitations prevented Dr. Bassett from publishing more than a selected part of the Jackson manuscripts available to him. He used his judgment in eliminating what seemed to him unessential. A desire to make decisions on this head for myself induced me to go over collections in the wake of the editor. It has not been altogether unprofitable work. Nothing I can say would liquidate my debt to this scholar, yet I have found many documents omitted or condensed by him that seem to me to be useful in an interpretation of Andrew Jackson.

And I suppose that I might as well confess a certain predilection for work among manuscripts. They convey something, some essence, that is lost in the transition to type. For the same reason I like to visit places that one time or another have been the environment of my man. The opportunities that were Parton's of course are not mine. But it is possible by the study of old maps, deeds, wills, court records and general accumulated memorabilia fairly to reconstruct the past. Concerning the military operations about New Orleans, for example, I first wrote or sketched out, largely from contemporary sources, a full story of the campaign, and then pared it down to the requirements of biography, which I repeat are not synonymous with those of history. Incidentally, a general is often one of the hardest men in an army to follow through a battle, and I think this was especially true of Jackson.

After more than a year of library work a sense of duty took Mrs. James and myself to the Carolinas. Really I did not expect to find much that would be new or of value, and was prepared to remain only a few days. I remained six weeks, and had not so many kindly and competent assistants sprung up in my path my stay would have been longer. The result is a rather fresh picture of the youthful Andrew. I am especially indebted to Alexander S. Salley, junior, of Columbia, for twenty-seven years secretary of the Historical Commission of South Carolina, and to A. R. Newsome, of Raleigh, secretary of the North Carolina Historical Commission. In my opinion these gentlemen know the source materials and the histories of their native commonwealths as well as any one knows them. After pointing the way to invaluable data they were good enough to read the manuscript of the first three chapters of this book. Inasmuch as that is still a controversial subject in those parts, and some others, I may say that neither expressed dissatisfaction with the accuracy of my conclusions as to the birthplace of the subject of this memoir. For other assistance in these early stages of the work I am indebted to A. E. Hutchison, Mrs. Anne Hutchison Bigger and Dr. William A. Pressly of Rock Hill, and to William R. Bradford of Fort Mill, South Carolina; to Miss Katherine Hoskins of Summerfield, Walter Murphy of Salisbury and Mrs. Lindsay Patterson of Winston-Salem, North Carolina; to G. Walter Barr of Keokuk, Iowa, and to Miss Queena Pollack, of Philadelphia.

Moving across the Blue Ridge the canvas enlarges. The young solicitor

PERSONAL ACKNOWLEDGMENTS

becomes a chip on the eddy of big events, and I find in the recapitulation which I have passed off as a "Bibliography" of this volume no mention of Frederick J. Turner's *Rise of the New West* and *Frontier in American History*. These books formed the framework of my understanding of the frontier, though devotees will perceive the extent of some of my departures from the doctrine of the essential democracy of the border. I discover that Edward Channing's *History of the United States* is not acknowledged. On this work I relied for the general pattern of national affairs for the period covered by this narrative, irrespective of certain departures, especially with respect to the attitude of New England during the War of 1812. I also profited by my readings of Schouler and Von Holst, likewise unmentioned elsewhere.

Judge John H. DeWitt, of Nashville, president of the Tennessee Historical Society and himself a fine critical historian was an unfailing friend and counselor during the long and pleasant course of my work in Tennessee, and in the end he read in manuscript Chapters IV to VIII of this book. I am also particularly obligated to Miss Mary U. Rothrock and her amiable colleagues of the Lawson-McGhee Library at Knoxville, which was my headquarters for two months. When I think back on places like this and like Dr. Paul DeWitt's lodge on the Cumberland and the Pflanze's hotel at Montvale Springs in the Big Smokies I do not regret that I still have a volume on Jackson to write.

I am indebted to Mrs. Samuel G. Heiskell of Knoxville, widow of the author of *Andrew Jackson and Early Tennessee History*, which is a veritable mine of material not to be found elsewhere. Mrs. Heiskell gave me the freedom of her husband's papers. I am indebted to Mrs. John Trotwood Moore of Nashville, State Librarian and Archivist of Tennessee, and to my friend George Fort Milton of Chattanooga, who interrupted his labors on a life of Stephen A. Douglas to lend a helping hand. I also express my gratitude to P. E. Cox, Mrs. Elsie W. Stokes, Miss Alice Stockell, Reau E. Folk, Mrs. Mary French Caldwell and William Henry Morgan of Nashville; to James Douglas Anderson of Madison, Tennessee; to John Jennings, junior, Knoxville, and Professor P. M. Hamer of the University of Tennessee, Knoxville; to Mrs. L. W. McCown of Johnson City, to Hugh L. Taylor of Elizabethton, and to the owners of privately owned manuscripts, in Tennessee and elsewhere, whose names are recorded under "Bibliography." Later it will be a pleasure to acknowledge the donors of material which does not fall within the compass of this book.

Andrew Jackson IV of Los Angeles is the grandson of Andrew Jackson, junior, nephew and adopted son of General Jackson. Several years ago he placed in my hands copies of a hundred or more manuscripts for use in this book. My account of the ancestry of Rachel Jackson is based on researches among Maryland and Virginia archives by a grand-niece, Miss Butler Chancellor of Washington. My narrative of the early years of the Donelson family in Kentucky and Tennessee is derived largely from the unpublished researches of Dr. William A. Provine, of Nashville, secretary of the Tennessee Historical Society. Miss Elizabeth Pickett of Montgomery, a granddaughter of Albert James Pickett, the Alabama historian, examined for me the Pickett Papers in the Alabama State Library. I have also profited by the assistance of Captain Samuel A. Greenwell of the office of the Chief of Staff of the Army, Judge E. J. Van Court of Eufaula, Oklahoma, Edward Caffery of San José, Costa Rica, Mrs. Julia Welder of Liberty, Texas, William MacLean of Larchmont, New York, and Emil Edward Hurja, Frank L. Jones and David Kirchenbaum of

New York City. I call myself fortunate for having been able to induce Lowell L. Balcom of Norwalk, Connecticut, to execute the maps that appear in these pages.

New Orleans has been a pleasant place as long as I have known it, that is to say since 1913 when James Evans Crown tried to teach me something about the profession of letters as practiced by his reporters on the *Item*. There were few journeymen journalists in my day who had not learned something from Jim Crown. To contemporaries of that spacious era I would report that Mr. Crown liked New Orleans too well to leave for long. In the same case is Stanley Clisby Arthur who, in the fulness of time, has become an authority on such matters as may be found in his book *Old Families of Louisiana*. Colonel Henry R. Richmond of the Regular service has been stationed in New Orleans for four years. Jackson's Louisiana campaign is his hobby. I am in the debt of Colonel Richmond for giving me the benefit of his tactical studies, to Mr. Arthur for leads on sources and to both for reading Chapters XII to XV. I wish to thank Miss Josie Cerf of the Louisiana State Museum for her courtesies and Edward A. Parsons for the use of his notable private library.

At the Library of Congress I have been much helped by the scholarship, counsel and general interest in my method and subject manifest by Dr. Thomas P. Martin, assistant chief of the Division of Manuscripts. I have also to thank Martin Arnold Roberts of the circulating division and his assistant David C. Mearns for the investigations in my behalf they caused to be made at the Public Record Office in London. I am grateful to the memory of the late William A. Taylor of the American History Room of the New York Public Library, to the New York State Library at Albany and to my neighbor Mrs. Evelyn H. Allen and her assistants of the Free Library of Pleasantville, New York, who by their contacts with other institutions have demonstrated how greatly a small library can shorten the hours of labor involved in an undertaking of this nature.

Every student of American history owes a debt to William O. Lynch of Indiana University for his *Fifty Years of Party Warfare*. My obligations are somewhat greater. Professor Lynch read the whole of this book before publication, and his suggestions have added materially to its soundness.

M. J.

Pleasantville, New York,
January 12, 1933.

PERSONAL ACKNOWLEDGMENTS

Part Two

Portrait of a President

Frederick Jackson Turner's *The United States 1830-1850* fills a volume about as thick as this one. The fruit of twenty years of work, it was published in 1935, posthumously and unfinished. In his preface Professor Avery Craven writes that the author "disliked to find his researches halted and his ideas crystallized by publication. There were new facts to be unearthed; new findings might alter old conclusions. Until all the evidence was in, the time had not come for the last word."

The evidence is never all in and the time for the last word remains a figure of speech. Only seven years have gone by, and how swiftly, since the present writer began his formal research for the undertaking which this book completes. One pleasant summer in the early days of that work, the base for my operations was a cabin in the Big Smoky Mountains of East Tennessee. One week-end two or three history professors turned up. One asked how many volumes my biography would be. With some emphasis I said, "One volume." Perhaps had I done my work as well as I then hoped it might be done one volume would have sufficed, though I am not sure. The one thing I am sure of is that I had trouble telling in two volumes the story of Andrew Jackson as he seems to me to be; and I may add, for the comfort it gives me, that I had professional encouragement to string it out beyond that length.

In the course of my preparation for this second volume I have examined in manuscript about forty thousand documents, exclusive of sources consulted more conveniently in print. Week by week and year by year the notes pile up, and there is born an insidious urge to justify or parade this labor by giving a place in the sun to too much of the resultant memoranda. Thus research may partake of the nature of vanity, and a book reflect a picture of the author's progressive grubbings in such strong light as to cast a shadow on the concerns of the other individual whose name appears on the title page. A biographer (I speak for myself only) must resist a temptation to compete with his subject for the reader's favorable notice. Oscar Wilde's observation that any fool can make history but that it takes a genius to write it should not be taken as a final judgment.

Usually worse than too much or too obvious research is too little. I am sorry that I feel bound to say "usually" and not "invariably": otherwise the task of those who would like to do something toward ameliorating the lowly estate biography occupies as a department of letters would not be so trying. The confusing truth is that biographies are available which, despite an average of one error of fact per page, attain a sort of truth beyond the facts, giving a fairly faithful representation of the subject as a human being. There are biographies that approach factual perfection but leave the reader with a less adequate idea of the kind of *human being* the writer was trying to tell about than the average person could pick up in a fifteen-minute face-to-face conversation; and subjects of biography were human beings before they were soldiers or presidents or what not. Further disconcerting circumstances are that so many good writers who now and again dash showily into the biographical lists are careless, lazy and shallow about their research, whereas most of the honest and competent researchists can't write for sour apples. Though in the minority, the good writers, being easier to read, spread the greater number of submarginal ideas about the personnel of history. Yet one should not condemn them too roundly. Submarginal ideas may be better than none.

I have heard biographers imply that the public's preference for novels is a reflection on its taste. I am inclined to think it a reflection on the biographers. A sizable class of readers turn to novels for dependable representations of life and character, finding them in greater profusion than in the pages of biography. Though an inconsiderable reader of novels, in no biography that comes to mind offhand is there a character so real to me as Huckleberry Finn, Becky Sharp, Tom Jones or George Babbitt.

A biographer may argue that his task is technically the more difficult; and he is on solid ground there. He may point out that a novelist merely has to invent and create whereas a biographer is confined to a work of re-creation, and the re-creation of a particular person and not just any person. A palæontologist's is also a work of re-creation, but in a different way. He can take the shin bone of an extinct animal and reconstruct the complete skeleton, but this will not be the skeleton of the particular animal whose shin bone was found but of an average representative of the species. From the shin bone of an extinct person a biographer cannot reconstruct that particular person except by guesswork. The other bones must be found or accounted for.

Another thing a novelist can do more easily than a biographer is to give his story architectural symmetry. His supply of materials is limited only by his capacity for creation. A biographer's materials are limited, first by the question of their physical survival in the form of reliable record, and second, by the biographer's success, through the exercise of patience, intelligence, imagination and industry, in bringing that record to light. A biographer may be perfectly aware that he is not proportioning his narrative with proper regard for the art of story-telling, or even the balanced re-creation of personality, and be able to do nothing about it because he cannot find the materials to fill certain gaps. A good novelist is never in such a dilemma.

The second and some of the other early chapters of this book are badly balanced, being top-heavy with politics at a time when General Jackson's actual life was far from so. Politics was a great and threatening force playing about him but not touching him to the extent that my treatment would indicate, despite explicit disclaimers in the text which the reader may fail to notice because they are so weakly supported by corroborative evidence that actually Jackson had very much of anything else on his mind. I am sure that he had much else on his mind in the way of private and personal affairs, and in a general way I know what those things were. But specifically I could learn little.

To a novelist this would present no problem at all. On the other hand I had to choose between pruning the politics to balance my meager store of personal information and presenting an unbalanced picture. I pruned until to prune any more would have been to default an obligation to history. I had discovered a number of undisclosed facts concerning Jackson's emergence and progress as a candidate for the presidency, making, indeed, something of a new story of it. So I present this story; I present it ostensibly as biography of Andrew Jackson for that period of his life, and as such it lacks much. Dull and imperfect chapters in the fore part of a book are a bad thing. I feel pretty sure that some readers will chuck this book before they get to the more supportable parts of it.

There are professional historians who will not be impressed by the reverential mention of my obligation to history. In their opinion I give history short shrift nearly all through this book, compressing and generalizing too much. On the other hand many things which do not touch the main stream of history at all have been treated extensively. Though these things have little to do with history they had much to do with Jackson. History has concerned me only as it touched Jackson or as Jackson touched it. An excellent historian, to whose painstaking counsel I am truly indebted, notes on the margin of a page of the

PERSONAL ACKNOWLEDGMENTS

last chapter of the manuscript: "I am sorry that you have not mentioned Calhoun's period as Sec'y of State [under Tyler], and that he also did much to bring about the annexation of Texas. Every reviewer of your book will sharply criticize you for the writing of the history of annexation without mention of Calhoun."

If reviewers assume that I have attempted to write a history of the annexation of Texas their criticism will be justified. I have not attempted to do this, however. I have attempted to write a life of Andrew Jackson, giving such parts of the history of the annexation of Texas as seemed to me to bear thereon.

Before these maundering remarks become more involved I shall conclude with an attempt to justify their title, for without the good scholarship, the good companionship and the sound and serviceable help of many persons this book would be a poorer thing than it is. Of perhaps twenty authors of books about Jackson, I owe a basic debt to the biographers Parton, Sumner and Bassett. Though careless of the facts of history, and with little sense of its larger forces, Parton was one of the best of American biographers and *Jackson* is his best work. His treatment of the subject's early life, which is not covered in this volume, is, however, far superior to his treatment of the presidential years; yet he keeps by the side of his man as no other Jackson student does. Writing less than fifteen years after Old Hickory's death his work has almost a contemporary flavor.

Professor Sumner of Yale came along in the 'Eighties. Of Jackson the human being he tells us little but, considering the limited documentary evidence then readily available, Jackson the public figure is well-placed on the stage of history. Doctor Bassett's *Life* appeared in 1911. Here was the most indefatigable Jackson student of his generation. He greatly improved on the work of Sumner, though to the casual reader the result is apt to appear a little cloudy; for Doctor Bassett had small insight into human values and next to no idea of what constitutes a literary pattern. Bassett's services to those who would study Jackson do not end with his biography. He tackled the mountain of manuscripts in the Library of Congress and in several other public depositories, in 1926 beginning the publication of selections therefrom under the title of *Correspondence of Andrew Jackson*. After Doctor Bassett's death Dr. J. Franklin Jameson, chief of the Manuscript Division of the Library of Congress, brought the work to a notable conclusion with the publication of the sixth volume in 1935.

To me research is the buoyant part of an adventure of this kind, filled with exhilarations of discovery that efface the memory of weeks of unexciting and sometimes poorly rewarded toil. In a moment I shall mention some of the persons met along the paths of research. Their names lie before me now as I jotted them down at different times, here, there and everywhere that part of the work called me. They bring back a flood of recollections, all pleasant and many light-hearted. Then there is a smaller list I have just made up of people who have been close to me during the last year and more which has been devoted exclusively to composition. Like most old hands from the city room I like to diffuse the impression that I write easily. I fancy I could bring evidence to support that premise, though this book would form no part of it. For in the main the going has been tough; and no one has borne the brunt of this to the extent that my wife has. Bessie has shared too much of the drudgery involved in this book and too little of the fun—a circumstance rendered inescapable by the fact that she is the best critic of composition I know.

Professor William O. Lynch of Indiana University generously read this book in primitive manuscript form. His advice and comments have been of great value. Further, I am indebted to Professor William MacDonald, late of Brown University and author of *Jacksonian Democracy*, and to Professor Thomas C. Cochran of New York University for reading it before publication and for their comments; likewise to Professor Allan Nevins of Columbia for reading a part of it. I am indebted for enlightenment on the campaigns of 1824 and 1828 to assistance from Professor Arthur R. Newsome of the University of North Carolina, Dr. Culver H. Smith of the University of Chattanooga and Curtis W. Garrison, librarian of the Pennsylvania State Library, Harrisburg; also to Dr. Richard A. McLemore of Judson College, Marion, Alabama, on the subject of the French claims.

This acknowledgment, however, is not intended to imply that these gentlemen approve of everything I have written. David Laurance Chambers, a careful student of Americana and the president of the publishing house whose imprint this volume bears, should be mentioned for knightly conduct. He read the chapters as they were pulled from a typewriter and declined to be discouraged.

I am under especial obligation to Doctor Jameson of the Library of Congress and to his genial assistant, Dr. Thomas P. Martin; to Sylvester Vigilanti and to Miss Dorothy P. Miller of the American History Room of the New York Public Library; to Mrs. E. A. Lindsey, former regent, and to Mrs. Mary French Caldwell, of the Ladies' Hermitage Association, Nashville; to Clarence S. Brigham of the American Antiquarian Society, Worcester, Massachusetts; to Mrs. John Trotwood Moore, Nashville, librarian and archivist of the State of Tennessee; to the late Judge John H. DeWitt, president, Tennessee Historical Society; to Mrs. Evelyn H. Allen and staff of the Pleasantville (New York) Free Library; to the New York Historical Society, New York City; and to the New York State Library, Albany; and to the Troy (New York) Public Library.

The owners of private manuscript collections which I have kindly been permitted to examine are named under "Bibliography," but here I cannot forbear mentioning that Lemuel R. Campbell of Nashville shortened my labors by providing the services of his secretary to help go through the papers of his Campbell ancestors, fifteen hundred of which papers bear on the Jackson administrations.

For permission to reproduce pictures that appear in this volume I am, in addition to persons and institutions mentioned elsewhere, indebted to the Brown University Library, Providence; Mrs. Sarah Polk Burch, Nashville; Mrs. Pauline Wilcox Burke, Washington; Mrs. Arthur Chester, Rye, New York; Dr. Isaac Cline, New Orleans; Mrs. Betty Donelson, Nashville; Emil Edward Hurja, Washington; Mrs. Breckenridge Long, Laurel, Maryland; the North Carolina Historical Commission, Raleigh; Edward Asbury O'Neal III, Florence, Alabama.

For contributions to research, in addition to those mentioned elsewhere, I am indebted to David Rankin Barbee, Washington; Allen Churchill, New York City; Burton Craige, Winston-Salem, North Carolina; Dr. J. B. Cranfill, Dallas, Texas; Charles P. Everitt, New York City; Miss A. L. Frantz, Lancaster, Pennsylvania; Mrs. Mary Martin Frost, Florence, Alabama; Miss Estelle Lake, Memphis, Tennessee; Andrew Jackson Martin, Memphis; George Fort

Milton, Chattanooga; J. F. Spainhaur, High Point, North Carolina; Mrs. Elsie Warren Stokes, Nashville; Miss Claude Wier, Dallas, Texas; Mrs. Mary Wharton Yeatman, Columbia, Tennessee; Mrs. Marshall Elise Janney, Montgomery, Alabama.

M. J.

Pleasantville, New York,
June 13, 1937.

INDEX

Parts One and Two

The Border Captain

Portrait of a President

INDEX*

Aaron, slave, 710.
Abingdon, Va., 546, 547.
Abolition, 692, 705, 711, 715, 751.
Abridgement of the Law, 45.
Accomac County, Virginia, 49, 475.
Adair, Brigadier-General John, 46, 242, 243, 244, 245, 248, 270, 280.
Adams, John, 77, 81, 721.
Adams, John Quincy, appointed Secretary of War, 276; champions Jackson's seizures in Florida, 291; note to Spanish Minister defending Jackson, 292; withering dispatch to Spain in support of Jackson, 295; presidential aspirations, 297; 298; signs treaty with Spain for Florida purchase, 301; 308, 313, 321, 326, 332; Cabinet officer, 337, 350; presidential candidate in 1824, 347, 352, 355, 357-359, 363, 366-368, 373-376, 382, 384, 388, 389, 391-393, 402-403, 406-407, 410-411, 414-440; diplomacy of, 356, 681, 699, 700; President-elect, 440-442; inaugural of, 443, 446; as President, 448, 451-453, 456, 457, 462, 468, 487, 491-493, 502, 507, 522, 525, 587, 605, 735, 841; presidential candidate in 1828, 461, 471-473, 498; connected with slanders, 467, 483; 534; supporters of, 498, 500, 503, 545; in House of Representatives, 599, 611, 612, 686; 641, 643, 721, 751, 775, 855.
Adams, Mrs. J. Q., 384, 428, 467.
Adventure, flatboat, 49, 50, 64, 100.
Africa, 692.
Alabama, 154, 157, 177; Jackson's acquisitions in, 277, 285, 303, 306, 329, 394, 552, 595, 609, 614, 652, 677, 740, 744, 892; Legislature of, 358; plantations, 335, 336, 348, 349, 350, 378, 450, 469; political senti-

Alabama—*Continued*
ments in, 361, 370, 384, 388, 455, 557; military executions in, 468; Indians, 548, 616; Governor of, 618; speculators in, 728.
Alamo, the, 704.
Albany *Argus,* 453.
Albany, N. Y., 410, 436, 437, 494, 503, 614, 672, 749.
Alexander family of South Carolina, 7.
Alexander, Susan Smart, 21, 34.
Alexander, Captain Will, 482.
Alexandria, D. C., 433, 489, 636.
Alexandria *Herald,* 411.
Alexandria, Virginia, 181.
Alfred, household negro, 892.
Algiers, 520.
Alien and Sedition Laws, 538.
Allegheny Mountains, 578.
Allen, Eliza, 701-702, 703.
Allen, Thomas, 72.
Allen, William, 723.
Allison, David, 75, 76, 77, 81, 84, 133.
Alston, Joseph, 271, 272.
Alston, Theodosia Burr, 102, 103, 271.
Ambrister, Lieutenant Robert C., 288; trial and execution of, 289; 296, 297; Congressional investigation of execution of, 298; 301, 468.
Amelia Island, Florida, storehouse of pirates, 281; 282, 296.
America, 449, 592, 686.
see also United States.
American House, New York, 638.
American System, 471.
see Tariff.
Ames, Fisher, 180.
Anacostia River, 624.
Anderson, Joseph, 84.
Anderson, Patton, 100, 106, 107, 108, 111, 121, 125, 134, 136, 150, 670.

* Index compiled in part by Pauline Peirce.

Anderson, William Preston, 100, 107, 108, 130.
Andrew Jackson, steamboat, 278.
Andrews, Miss, of Philadelphia, 372.
Annapolis, Md., 375, 600.
Anti-Masons, 605, 608.
Appraisals. See prices.
Arabia, 661.
Arbuthnot, Alexander, 286, 287; Jackson arrest, 287; trial and execution of, 289; 296, 297; Congressional investigation of execution of, 298; 301, 321; 468.
Arbitration of French claims, 697.
Argus of Western America, 444, 461, 497, 567.
Arkansas Territory, 691.
Armstrong, Captain John, 174.
Armstrong, John, Secretary of War, 148, 149, 175, 179, 195.
Armstrong, Robert, 679, 732, 759, 768-769.
Arnaud, Major, of Louisiana, 248.
Arnold, Thomas D., 464, 467.
Ashe, Judge Samuel, 37, 90.
Ashland, home of Henry Clay, 462, 587, 752, 753, 775, 782.
Ashland, Tennessee, 54.
Assawaman Church, Virginia, 475.
Attleborough, Mass., 639.
Augusta, Georgia, 331.
Aury, "Commodore" Louis, 282, 283.
Austin, Stephen F., 703.
Avery, Colonel Waightstill, duel with Jackson, 45.

Baker, the Reverend Mr., of Washington, 432.
Balch, Alfred, 565.
Baldwin, Henry, 475.
Baldwin, Mrs., of Nashville, 689.
Ballard, William, 811.
Baltimore, 370, 375, 386, 462, 549, 576, 593, 605, 637, 642, 647, 654, 662, 668, 671, 689, 746, 769, 770, 771, 772, 778.
Baltimore *American,* 739.
Baltimore, Maryland, shelled by British in 1814, 181; 218, 252, 270, 281, 287; ovation for Jackson, 300, 301.

Baltimore & Ohio Railroad, 637, 724.
Baltimore, Union Bank of, 651-652.
Bancroft, George, 755.
Bank of England, 80.
Bank of the United States, 305.
Banks, 335, 340, 351, 362, 369, 380, 395, 455, 733, 735, 740; Bank of the Metropolis, 664; Bank of the United States, 369, 395, 524, 552, 553-568, 576, 583-586, 598-602, 603, 605, 623-625, 629-636, 638-639, 642, 645-664, 671-676, 680, 682, 693, 694, 706, 714, 722, 723, 730-731, 735; Nashville branch of, 556-558, 560, 565, 630, 632; *see also* Andrew Jackson, Presidential Administrations, Bank controversy; deposit banks, *see* "Pet" banks; failures of, 728-730; national bank bills, 744, 746, 749; "Pet" banks, 651, 652, 664, 690, 706, 731, *see also* state banks; Planters' Bank, Nashville, 729; printing-press banks, 557; state banks, 555, 585, 630, 632, 633, 634, 635, 638, 642, 645-653, 672, 674, 676, 690, 691, 729, 731; Union Bank of Baltimore, 651-652; United States Bank of Pennsylvania, 731, 735, 744.
Banks, Henry, 855-856.
Bargain, the "Corrupt," election of 1824 thrown into House, 414; Jackson's election on first ballot predicted, 414; popular vote light but congressmen impressed by people's preference for Jackson, 414-415; line-up of state delegations indicates Jackson's strength in electoral college, 415-416-417; Adams's strength, 415-416-417; Crawford weak third, 416; Jackson men sanguine at opening of Congress, 417; Clay's support uncertain, although Kentucky expressed preference for Jackson, 418-419; two Kentucky congressmen declare for Jackson, 420; Clay's maneuvers injure Jackson's prospects, 420; Webster quotes Jefferson as opposed to Jackson, 420-

INDEX 925

Bargain—*Continued*
421; Clay rumored to have traded support for place in Adams Cabinet, 421; Buchanan tenders Jackson offer of Clay's support in exchange for Cabinet appointment, 421-422; Jackson declines to make a bargain, 422; Buchanan tries to win Clay for Jackson, 423; apprehension in Adams camp, 423; Clay annoys Adams by his indecision, 426; Clay and Adams meet as allies, 427; Kentucky Legislature instructs delegation for Jackson, 427; "Corrupt Bargain" talk, 429; Jacksonians take steps to regain lost ground, 429; Adams holds votes with more concessions, 430-431; Jackson aloof, 431-432; Clay formally declares for Adams, 433; adverse comment from country, 433-434; Kremer incident, 434-435; scene in House on election day, 435; Clay lacks one vote to give Adams majority on first ballot, 436; Van Rensselaer breaks tie in New York to win, 437-439; Adams notified, 440; Jackson complacently accepts defeat, 441; Adams names Clay Secretary of State, 442; Jackson aroused by evidence of "bargain," 442; Clay's "bargain" denounced through country, 443; Jackson votes against Clay's confirmation, 445; *see also* J. Q. Adams *and* Henry Clay.
Barings, the, English bankers, 585, 630, 632.
Barker, Jacob, 410.
Barr, William, 801.
Barron, Thos. & Co., New Orleans, 336.
Barry, Dr. Redmond Dillon, 228.
Barry, William T., Secretary of State of Kentucky, 416; Postmaster-General, 498, 501, 519, 575, 579; in Eaton affair, 516, 533, 571; his retirement from office; 522, 694; and the Bank, 588, 649, 694.
Barry, Mrs. William T., 516, 571.
Barton, Thomas P., 626, 695-696.

Baton Rouge, Louisiana, 184, 199, 206, 209, 211, 259.
Bay of Naples, 603.
Bayou Pierre, Mississippi, 59; Jackson spends honeymoon at, 67; 137.
Beale, Captain, of Louisiana, 223, 241.
Bean, Russell, arrested by Jackson, 87, 91; marshal of Memphis, 306; 806.
Beasley, Major Daniel, 157.
Bell, Caroline S., 304.
Bell, Hugh F., 58.
"Bellona."
  see Margaret Eaton.
Belluché, Captain, 213.
Bennett, James Gordon, 649.
Benton, Jesse, 151, 152; pistol fight with Jackson, 153; 351, 400, 591, 596, 598.
Benton, Thomas Hart, 150, 151, 152; pistol fight with Jackson, 153; 306; supports Clay, 370, 407, 409, 415, 419, reconciliation with Jackson, 382, 400, 429; in Senate, 382, 520, 529, 537-539, 566, 594, 595, 604, 706; supports Jackson, 415, 417, 419, 431, 455, 609, 663, 714, 719, 723; talks with Jefferson, 421, 422; denounces Scott, 436; separates from Clay, 445; witnesses duel, 454; and the bank, 566, 584, 586, 598, 599, 660, 694; bullet story, 590-591; election bets, 608; Jackson's last message for, 785.
Berrien, John MacPherson, 491, 492, 511, 533, 535, 563, 574, 576.
Betty, cook at the Hermitage, 628.
Betty, mulatto maid, 314.
Beverley, Carter, 459, 461.
Bibbs, Governor, of Alabama, 285.
Biddle, Nicholas, president, Bank of the United States, 524; early history, 554-555; *Ode to Bogle,* 554; policy as head of Bank, 555-556; establishes branch at Nashville, 556-557; growing controversy over recharter of Bank, 558-565; accuses Jackson of aiming at Bank's destruction, 566; loan to Duff Green, 576; friends in Cabinet and Treasury, 584; liberalization of

926   ANDREW JACKSON

Biddle—*Continued*
  western credit endangers Bank,
  585-586; agrees to postpone renewal
  petition until after election, 586-
  588; attempt to dictate Bank paragraph of Jackson's annual message,
  588; recharter issue falls into Clay's
  hands, 590; petitions Congress for
  recharter, 598; Congressional investigation of Bank, 598; bill for
  recharter, with amendments, passes
  House, 600; bill is vetoed by Jackson, 600; Biddle reprints veto message, 602; Blair styles "Czar Nicholas," 605-606; House votes to
  continue government deposits in
  Bank, 623-624; "race horse bills,"
  630; loans to friends of Bank, 631;
  Jackson sends memorandum to
  Cabinet regarding Bank, 632;
  Taney recommends state banks,
  and McLane, new national bank,
  633-635; Jackson proposes state
  banks, 638; crippling of state banks,
  647-652; beginning of panic, 652-
  655; Bank petitions restoration of
  deposits, 655; renomination of directors rejected by Senate, 656;
  policy during panic, 656-663; Pennsylvania's support lost, 672; New
  York's support lost, 672-673; Bank
  refused recharter by Congress, 674;
  end of panic, 676; Biddle and Jackson contrasted, 680; speculation results from panic recovery, 690;
  Biddle is great adversary of Jackson, 722; against Specie Circular,
  729, 730, 731; private bank, 731,
  735; political advice, 739-740;
  charged with fraud, 745; *see also*
  Andrew Jackson, Presidential Administrations, Bank controversy.
"Big Drunk"
  see Sam Houston
Big Warrior, Creek chief, 178.
Bissell, Captain, 126, 127.
Blackburn, John, 58.
Black Hawk, 663.
Black Hawk War, 612.
Blackstone River, 639.

Blair, Eliza, 626.
Blair, Mrs. F. P., 734.
Blair, Francis P. (Frank), Clay supporter, 426, 427; editor of Washington *Globe*, 567-571, 589, 605, 608,
  626, 653, 660, 662, 686, 746, 769;
  adviser of Jackson, 579, 580, 584,
  632, 634, 635; house, 626, 723; in
  printing business, 683, 759, 778;
  correspondence, 709, 733; handwriting, 717; creditor of Jackson, 748-
  749, 757, 760-761, 773, 777-778, 891;
  on Jackson, 750; message for, 785.
Blair, Francis P., jr., 781.
Blair & Rives, 759, 778; *see also* Francis P. Blair *and* John C. Rives.
Blakemore, George, 135.
Blanque, Jean, 190.
Bledsoe, Anthony, 63.
Blennerhasset, Harman, 124.
Blount, William, Governor of Territory south of River Ohio, 62; 69;
  Senator from Tennessee, 77; 80; 82;
  expelled from Senate, 88; 90.
Blount, Willie, Governor of Tennes-
  see, 143; recommends Jackson to
  War Department, 144; 145; com-
  missions Jackson a major general,
  146; 148; recommends retreat to
  Jackson in Creek campaign, 165;
  169, 175, 180, 215.
Blue Grass, 568.
  see Kentucky.
Blue Ridge, the, 420.
Boggs, Davidson, & Company, of Phil-
  adelphia, 101.
Boleck, Creek chief, 288, 290.
Bolivar, race horse.
  see Tariff, race horse.
Bolivar, Simon, 453.
Bolivia, race horse, 670.
Bomba, King of Naples, 683.
Bonaparte, Napoleon, 84, 96, 142, 180,
  181, 186, 218, 229, 242, 289, 294.
Bordeaux, France, 186.
Bosley, Captain John, 57.
Boston, 390, 488, 640-641, 642, 645,
  647-650, 657, 660, 676, 692; Com-
  mon, 640; Beacon Street, 641.

INDEX

Boston, Massachusetts, 15, 181, 251.
Bouligny, Senator, 426.
Boundary dispute between North and South Carolina, 10, 11, 791.
Boyd, Mrs., friend of Elizabeth Jackson, 28.
Boyd, "King," Nashville tavern keeper, 48.
Boyd, William, 12.
Boykin, J., 793.
Brackenridge, Henry M., 321, 322, 324, 325.
Bradford, Samuel, 573.
Bradley, Ed, 145.
Braintree, Mass., 367, 471.
Branch, John, Secretary of the Navy, 491, 492, 506, 571; Eaton affair, 511, 513, 531-532, 533, 534; 576, 577; retirement of, 574.
Branch, Mrs. John, 511, 512, 534, 571.
Branch, Margaret, 546, 571.
Branch, Rebecca, 546, 572.
Brandywine, battle of, 404.
Breckenridge, James, 803.
British, in Waxhaws and South during Revolutionary War, 15, 17, 18, 19, 20, 21, 22, 23, 24, 27, 40; contemplate reconquest, 56; 70, 83, 102, 130; in Florida, 156, 175, 176, 178, 179, 180; at Mobile, 182, 184; seek Laffite for ally, 185, 190; fail to take Fort Bowyer, 190; fleet advances on New Orleans, 194; defeated by Jackson at Pensacola, 197; advance on New Orleans, 199, 200, 203, 208, 209, 210, 211, 216, 217; land below New Orleans, 218; first battle for New Orleans, 223, 224; second battle, 231; battle of January 8, 1815, 240; 250, 252, 255, 265, 267, 273, 275, 289, 321. See England.
Brent, Representative, 416, 428.
Bribery, 429, 445, 680; *see also* Corruption.
Bridgeport, Conn., 659.
British, 404, 697, 698, 756.
British Legation, 511, 576.
British West Indies, 523, 552, 682, 692, 766.

Broglie, Duc Achille de, French Minister of Foreign Affairs, 695.
Bronaugh, Dr. James C., 303, 315, 316, 320, 322, 323, 327, 332, 351, 352.
Brooke, Colonel, 322, 323, 327.
Brown, General, 380.
Brown, Major General Jacob, 310, 313, 332.
Brown, John, Senator from Kentucky, 63, 72, 102.
Brown, William, 58.
Brown's Indian Queen Hotel, Washington, 418, 420, 538, 541, 772.
Brown's Station, Tennessee, 63.
Bryant, William Cullen, 606, 720.
Buchanan, James, 384, 421-423, 426, 429, 430, 432, 459-462, 668, 752, 769, 770.
Buchanon's Station, Tennessee, 58.
Bucks County, Pa., 659.
Buell, David, 503.
Buffalo Bayou, Texas, 704.
Buford, Colonel Abraham, 19, 30, 37.
Bunker Hill Monument, 644.
Bunland's Tavern, Washington, Pa., 446.
Burr, Aaron, 77, 83, elected Vice-President, 95; duel with Hamilton, 102; conspiracy, 102; wins Jackson's support, 103; 110, 112, 116, 117, 119, 120; collapse of conspiracy, 121; trial, 129; 132, 136, 144, 204, 271, 273; 412, 429, 437, 469, 560.
Busirus, racehorse, 670.
Butler, Anthony Wayne, ward of Jackson, 130, 270, 380.
Butler, Colonel Anthony, 699-701, 703.
Butler, Benjamin F., 693.
Butler, Caroline L., 757.
Butler, Edward, 130.
Butler, Edward George Washington, ward of Jackson, 130, 280, 781.
Butler, Elizur, 603.
Butler, Pierce, 760.
Butler, Rachel Hays, niece of Rachel Jackson, 106, 135, 180, 199.

Butler, Col. Robert, 380, 450.
Butler, Robert, ward of Jackson, 135, 180, 182, 201, 238, 240, 297, 322, 323, 330.
Butler, Samuel, 450.
Butler, Colonel Thomas, 95, 96, 118, 121, 131, 135.
Butler, Captain Thomas L., ward of Jackson, 230.
Butler, Dr. William E., 380.

Cabildo, at New Orleans, 96, 214.
Cabinet, Monroe's, 337, 359, 374, 396, 470, 541, 542; predictions, 420-421; Adams's, 434, 442, 487; 702, Van Buren's, 739, 769; Harrison's, 745; Polk's, 780, 783; *see also* Andrew Jackson, *passim*.
Cabot, George, 251.
Cadwalader, Thomas, 556, 558, 589, 630.
Caffery, John, 49, 51.
Caffery, Mary Donelson, sister of Rachel Jackson, 49, 180.
Caldwell, Lieutenant, 688.
Calhoun, John C., 142; appointed Secretary of War, 283; orders Jackson to Florida against hostile Indians, 283; 285, 291; favors disavowal of Jackson's acts in Florida, 292; conceals earlier attitude toward Jackson, 295; asks Jackson for military program in second movement against Florida, 309; 313, 332, 827; in Monroe's Cabinet, 337; as presidential candidate in 1824, 347, 354-355, 358-359, 362-363, 365-368, 370-371, 373, 375-376, 382, 384, 388, 389-390, 392, 396; vice-presidential candidate, 390-392, 400, 402; as Vice President, 439, 518, 527, 530-531, 548, 604-605; resigns vice-presidency, 613; 443, 455, 488, 566, 686, 714; versus Van Buren group, 470, 471, 476, 492, 511, 517, 519-520, 521, 525, 528, 532, 534, 540, 573, 579, 594; supporters of, 492, 501, 517, 519, 532, 537, 538, 567, 605; nullification, 529, 539-540, 581, 582, 604, 613, 617, 619-622; breach with Jack-

Calhoun—*Continued*
son, 541-543, 548, 568-574, 593, 607, 722, 724; *Address*, 582; combination with Clay, 621, 623, 625, 629, 654, 655, 660; slavery, 674, 692; presidential possibility in 1844, 752, 769, 770.
Calhoun, Mrs. John C., 428, 495.
Californias, the, 716, 751.
Call, Captain Richard, 315, 331.
Call, Richard K., 342, 379, 387, 398-399, 415-418, 421, 428, 431, 447, 516, 711, 742.
Call, Mrs. Richard K. *see* Mary Kirkman.
Callava, Colonel José, Spanish Governor of West Florida, 315; differs with Jackson about terms of Florida transfer, 315, 316; formally turns over Florida, 317, 318; 319; defies Jackson over Vidal records, 322; arrested and questioned, 323, 326, 332.
Cambreling, C. C., 509, 538.
Cambridge, Mass., 644.
Camden, South Carolina, 7, 21, 26.
Cameron, Governor, of New Providence (Bahamas), 289.
Campaigns, presidential
1824: 364, 366, 370-371, 373-376, 381, 383, 387-396, 398-408, 414, 415, 416, 463, 468, 471, 738, 740, 834, 841;
1828: 448, 452, 455-469, 497, 556, 738;
1832: 586-590, 597, 598, 602, 605-608;
1836: 694, 706-707, 711;
1840: 738-742, 750;
1844: 750, 752-755, 772, 774.
Campbell, Dr. A. D., 399.
Campbell, David, 499, 510-511, 515, 595.
Campbell, George Washington, 118, 132, 338-340, 345, 556.
Campbell, John, 429, 534, 595-596, 637.
Campbell, Rev. John N., 517-519, 532.
Canada, 144, 148, 149, 151, 175, 199, 769.
Cannon, Newton, 670.

Capitol, the, 381, 417, 418, 436, 438, 492, 493, 526, 601, 614, 662, 685, 719; President's room, 623.
Capitol Hill.
see under Washington, D. C.
Carneal, Thomas, 410.
Carolina campaign of 1780, 723.
Carolina, schooner, 210; at defense of New Orleans, 223, 224; 228; blown up by British, 231; 232, 241.
Carr, Reverend Mr., 892.
Carrickfergus, Ireland, 4, 14, 31.
Carroll, Chas., of Carrollton, 583, 584.
Carroll, Major General William, 147; duel with Jesse Benton, 151; at battle of Enotachopco Creek, 168; 199; at defense of New Orleans, 211, 215, 216, 220, 222, 229, 233, 234, 235, 242, 243, 244, 245, 248; urges Jackson to stand for presidency in 1816, 270; 278, 280, 338, 341, 345, 358, 361, 595, 701.
Carrollton, 583.
Carron, British man-of-war, 182, 188.
Cartwright, Peter, Methodist circuit rider, 296.
Cass, Lewis, in Jackson's Cabinet, 578, 584, 590, 600, 638, 645, 649, 653, 691, 693; Minister to France, 698; presidential possibility, 752, 769, 770, 772.
Catawba, River, 578.
Catawba Indians, 4.
Catawba Traders' Path, 3, 4.
Catlett, Dr. Hanson, 115, 117.
Catron, Justice John, 558, 559, 695, 780.
Caucus system, 345-346, 354, 355, 365, 366, 388-389, 406.
Chalmette plantation, 236, 243.
Chamber of Deputies, 682, 695; see also French Chambers.
Chambers, Latitia, 773.
Charles, negro coachman, 718, 719.
Charles, runaway slave, 348.
Charleston, S. C., 524, 530, 581, 582, 607, 608, 610, 613, 617, 619, 621, 758.

Charleston, South Carolina, 5, 11, 13, 14, 15, 17, 18, 19, 28, 30; visited by Jackson in 1783, 31; 32, 35, 69, 74, 105, 137, 153, 163, 262, 281, 309.
Charles Town. See Charleston.
Charlestown, Mass., 644.
Charlotte, North Carolina, 7, 14, 21, 23, 34.
Charlottesville, Virginia, 272.
Chase, Supreme Court Justice, 101.
Cheatam, debtor of Jackson, 737.
Cherokee Indians, 4, 24, 47, 49; whites violate treaty with, 69; 74, 81, 83, 84, 94; allies of Jackson in Creek campaign, 158; 166, 275, 276, 523, 548-550, 580, 603-604, 702-703, 707, 834.
Chesapeake, United States man-of-war, 130.
Chesapeake Bay, 370, 637, 746.
Chesterfield County, Virginia, 105.
Cheves, Langdon, 142.
Chicago, 691.
Chickasaw Indians, 548-552, 580, 604, 691, 756.
Chickasaw Road, 64, 66.
Childers, British man-of-war, 188.
Childress, George C., 687.
Childress, John, 93.
Chile, 668.
Choctaw Indians, 134; allies of Jackson in Creek campaign, 158; 166, 223, 275, 276, 548-552, 580, 756.
Chotard, Major, of Louisiana, 201.
Chotard, Mlle. Eliza, 204.
Cincinnati, Ohio, 102, 488, 606, 690, 774.
Cincinnati *Friend of Reform or Corruption's Adversary,* 473.
Cincinnati *Gazette,* 463, 464, 469, 658.
City Hotel, Nashville, 152, 153.
Civil war, threat of, 581, 617, 621.
Claiborne, Tom, 461.
Claiborne, William Charles Cole, 82; appointed governor of Louisiana, 97; 123, 125, 184, 185, 186, 190; informed by Laffite of British plans, 191; 192, 193, 198, 200; welcomes Jackson to New Orleans, 202; 202,

Claiborne—*Continued*
204, 209, 227, 233; closes Louisiana Legislature, 236; 255, 259.
Clark, Daniel, 202.
Clark, General, 499.
Clark, Lot, 436.
Clarksburgh, 548.
Claxton's, Mrs., boarding house, Washington, 382.
Clay, Henry, attorney for Aaron Burr, 123; speaker of House of Representatives, 143; member Ghent peace commission, 276; presidential aspirations in 1824, 297; attacks Jackson's record in Florida, 298; 308, 341, 469, 525, 532, 537, 612, 614, 684, 694, 714, 722, 741, 782; presidential candidate in 1824, 343, 355-364, 368, 370, 371, 373, 382, 384, 388, 390, 392, 398, 402, 405-407, 409-411, 414-416; American System, 393-394; political bargain, 417-448, 452, 460-462, 472, 567; in Kentucky, 451, 462, 527; Secretary of State, 452-455, 457, 458-459, 462, 466, 467, 487; supporters of, 451, 457, 460, 488, 500, 514, 527, 545, 567, 589, 598, 605, 767, 774, 841; connected with slander of Mrs. Jackson, 462-464, 466-467, 483, 568, 724; presidential candidate in 1832, 587-589, 592-594, 598, 601-603, 605, 606, 608; pacifier, 620-622; alliance with Calhoun, 621, 623, 625, 629, 654, 655, 660, 674; uses Bank issue, 656-659, 674-675, 680, 744, 746; passed over in 1840, 738; agreement with Van Buren, 752-755, 767-770; defeated in 1844.
Clay, Mrs. Henry, 466.
Clayton, Augustin S., 598-599, 631, 652.
Clinton, Governor DeWitt, 300, 332, 337, 366, 410, 437.
Clinton College, 754.
Clover Bottom, Tennessee, 51; Jackson & Hutchings's store at, 99; 101; Jackson's racing stable and track at, 106; 108; Truxton-Ploughboy race at, 111; 113, 121, 124, 134, 303.

Clover Bottom race course, near Nashville, 545, 670, 755.
Clover Bottom Tavern, 124.
Coahoma County, Mississippi, 733.
Cobb, Representative Thomas W., 298, 426, 436, 440.
Cochrane, Sir Alexander, sacks coast towns of United States, 180; 218; captures Jackson's gunboats on Lake Borgne, 219; 221; low opinion of American soldiers, 228; 237, 239, 244, 256.
Cockburn, Admiral, 554.
Cocke, General John, 342, 429.
Cocke, Major General John, 160, 161, 164, 169.
Cocke, William, Senator from Tennessee, 77, 84.
Cock-fighting, 18, 34, 98.
Cockran, George, 67.
Coffee, Andrew Jackson, 758.
Coffee, Brigadier-General, 96, 99, 109; duel with Nathaniel McNairy, 110; 116, 121, 124, 131; with Jackson's Natchez expedition, 146; in Benton fight, 153; in Creek campaign, 154, 157, 159, 162, 164, 165, 166, 167, 168; 179, 182; Mobile campaign, 196, 197, 199; at defense of New Orleans, 209, 211, 214, 215, 216, 220, 223, 224, 225, 228, 233, 234, 235, 242, 243, 245, 246, 248; 267, 274, 277, 306, 312, 316.
Coffee, General John, planter, 348, 350, 597, 627; Jackson's adviser and traveling companion, 350-351, 466, 551; Jackson's letters to, 361, 378, 408, 412, 431, 448, 472, 603; political influence, 370; at Rachel Jackson's funeral; in Washington, 616, 623-624; death of, 629; biography proposed, 675.
Coffee, Mrs. John, 432, 511, 627.
Coffee, Mrs. John, jr., 727.
Coffee, Mary, 614, 624, 627, 744. *see also* Mary Coffee Hutchings.
Coffin Handbill, 468.
Coleman, Dr. Littleton H., 394, 395.

INDEX

College of New Jersey (Princeton), 338, 553.
Columbia, S. C., 582, 612, 616.
Columbia, Tenn., 772.
Columbus, Ohio, 477.
Concord, Massachusetts, 15.
Concord, N. H., 645.
Congress of the United States, 62, 77, 101, 118, 132, 142, 143, 193, 215, 266, 270, 293, 297, 301, 309, 310, 312, 320. See House of Representatives and Senate.
Congress, members of, 338, 381, 386, 440, 454, 492, 548, 572, 580, 589, 659, 662, 680, 692, 748; 343, 388, 389, 393, 401, 451, 453, 455, 464, 468, 529, 551, 554, 729; close of sessions, 397, 459, 460, 508, 623-624; acts of, 408, 523-525, 536, 538, 588, 604, 615, 619-620, 705, 708, 731-732, 735, 760; convening of, 417, 452, 520, 527, 610, 638, 639, 649, 654; messages to, 523-524, 528, 549, 559, 566, 586, 588, 611, 630, 655, 683, 695-697; Bank controversy, 560, 562, 565, 566, 588, 589, 598, 599, 602-604, 629, 630, 643, 649, 657, 659, 672-674, 731-732, 735; nullification, 610, 613, 618-620; French debt affair, 682, 683, 685, 686, 695-697; Texas, 716, 767, 776-777.
Connecticut, 143, 638, 646, 659.
Conowingo Creek, Pennsylvania, 3.
Conrad's boarding house, Washington, D.C., 97.
Conscription Bill, 215.
Constitution, Jackson's carriage, 717, 719, 724, 755.
Constitution, U. S. S., 386, 508, 636, 717.
Constitution of the United States, 16, 56, 62, 95, 530, 611, 613, 618, 656.
Cook, Daniel P., 416, 428, 431.
Cook, Peter B., 288.
Cooper, James Fenimore, 750.
Cooper, Thomas, 658.
Corn Tassel, Cherokee Indian, 580-581, 603.

Cornwallis, Earl of, 19, 21, 22, 23, 28, 33.
Corruption, charge of, against Clay denied by Kremer, 434; "corrupt bargain" first disclosed to Jackson, 442; cry sweeps country, 442-445; Jackson's letter to Henry Lee concerning, 452; issue in campaign, 452-454, 459, 462, 471; introduction of spoils system corrupts civil service under Jackson, 519-523; nullifiers corrupt South Carolinian customs officers, 607; in Bank of United States, 631-634, 649, 660; in diplomatic dealings with Mexico, 700-701; Jackson accuses Whigs of, 745.
see also Bargain, the "Corrupt."
Cotton, 335-337, 340, 394, 456-458, 464, 465, 483; Hermitage crops of, 357, 378-380, 408, 469, 677, 678, 679, 689, 733, 737, 834; Andrew Jackson, junior's, report, 664-668; crop failure, 709-710, 748; shipment to Liverpool, 760; encouraging prospects, 773; flood damage, 777.
Cotton, John, 50.
Cotton Kingdom, 489, 529, 692.
Cotton, Lazarus, 105.
County Antrim, Ireland, 3, 227.
Courts, 362, 368, 463, 549, 550, 580-581, 600, 659, 692, 755; U. S. Supreme Court, 368, 498, 502, 521, 530, 549, 550, 564, 580-581, 603, 668, 694, 707-708, 780; Supreme Court of Kentucky, 340; Supreme Court of Tennessee, 695.
Courts and records, 36, 37; Jackson's first trip with traveling court, 37; 40; in Nashville, 47; 60; Jackson preserves dignity of, 62; Robards hales Jackson to, 64; divorce case of Robards, 65, 71; 101; Aaron Burr in court, 123, 128; Judge Hall releases Laffite and his pirates, 212, 213; trial of Jackson before Judge Hall, 263; 322, 326; record of Robards's divorce action, 802; record of Jackson's remarriage, 806.

Cowan, John, 72.
Cowsar, Mrs. Mary, 796.
Crab Orchard, Tennessee, 856.
Craig, James D., 796.
Craighead, Alexander, 119.
Craighead, Reverend Alexander, 7, 8.
Craighead, Reverend Thomas B., 68, 806.
Craven, Dr., figure in Eaton affair, 517.
Craven, Mrs., 518.
Crawford, James, uncle of Jackson by marriage, 5, 7, 9; Jackson born at house of, 10, 793, 794; property involved in boundary dispute between North and South Carolina, 11, 792; 14, 15, 18; services in Revolutionary War, 18, 24, 28; 34, 789, 797.
Crawford, James, junior, cousin of Jackson, 20, 21.
Crawford, Jennet (called Jane) Hutchinson, aunt of Jackson, 5, 10, 14, 789, 790.
Crawford, Colonel John, 789.
Crawford, John, cousin of Jackson, 794.
Crawford, Joseph, 790.
Crawford, Joseph, cousin of Jackson, 19, 21, 28.
Crawford, Major Robert, 583, 757.
Crawford, Robert, 14, 15, 16, 18, 19, 20, 21, 22, 24, 25, 30, 31, 34, 80, 790.
Crawford, Thomas, cousin of Jackson, 14, 25.
Crawford, William, cousin of Jackson, 19, 21, 28, 30, 31.
Crawford, William H., Secretary of War with presidential aspirations in 1816, 270; 273; modifies Jackson's Creek treaty and gains his enmity, 275; 282, 292; aspires to presidency in 1824, 297; fosters investigation of Jackson's Florida campaign, 298; 300, 308, 309, 310, 332; Rhea letter controversy, 828.
Crawford, Mrs. William H., 428.
Crawford, William Harris, in Monroe's Cabinet, 337, 354, 365; pres-

Crawford—*Continued*
idential candidate, 346, 352, 358, 359, 361-368, 370-371, 373, 376-377, 383, 387-389, 392, 396-397, 400-402, 405-408, 411, 414-416, 418, 429-430, 432, 436, 438; supporters of, 360, 370, 416, 418, 423, 429, 436, 443, 455; press, 367, 377, 399, 400, 403; illness, 376-377, 387, 401-402, 406; territory, 379, 457; 440; anti-Calhoun intrigue, 470-471, 541-543, 569-570.
Crawley, Lieutenant, United States Navy, 242.
Creek, Jackson's campaign against, 339, 609, 661, 777.
Creek Indians, 56, 58, 83; war with, 1813-14, 154; 161; Jackson makes treaty with, 176; 195, 198, 266, 267, 268, 273, 275, 286; Clay disclaims against Jackson's treaty with, 298, 344, 523, 548-550, 580, 596, 604, 834.
Creoles, 96, 102, 200, 204, 209, 210, 212, 230, 241, 258, 259, 261; *see also* Auguste Davézac and J. B. Planché.
Crews, Micajah, 47.
Crittenden, John J., 416, 417, 427, 433.
Crockett, Davy, 159, 378.
Crow, Grace Hutchinson, aunt of Jackson, 787.
Crow, James, uncle of Jackson by marriage, 789.
Cruzat, Secretary to Callava, 324, 325.
Cryer, Rev. Hardy M., 544-545.
Cuba, 184, 309, 322, 776.
Cumberland College, Nashville, 344, 469.
Cumberland country, the, 397, 463, 477, 480, 482, 512.
Cumberland County, Pennsylvania, 5.
Cumberland, Md., 665.
Cumberland River, 336, 340, 371, 398, 447, 457, 474, 489, 752.
Cumberland Road, 47, 54, 68, 305.
Cumberland Valley, 335, 565, 710.
Cummins, Francis, 18.
Cunningham, Patrick, 718.

INDEX

Currency, Jackson's stand on, 369; policy of hard times party regarding, 455; soundness and uniformity of, under Bank of United States, questioned by Jackson, 524, 563-564; Bank of United States allowed to issue, 555; Benton's demagogic statement regarding, 566; branch drafts to be abolished in form of, 585; uniformity impossible for state banks to maintain, 635, 652; Baltimore delegation's statement to Jackson regarding, 662; speculative, 690-691, 706, 718, 728-729, 742; Jackson's appraisal of condition of, 723; Texan, under Lamar, 762.
Cusack, Adam, 20.
Custis, George Washington Parke, 746.
Custis, Martha, 746.
Cuthbert, Representative, 436, 439.
Cypress Land Company, 277.

Dale, Colonel, British Army, 246.
Dale, General Sam, 609-610.
Dallas, Acting Secretary of War, 273.
Dallas, George Mifflin, 371, 390, 610, 772.
Daquin, Major, of Louisiana, 224, 225, 242.
Darden, Mr., in Tennessee duel, 342.
Dart family, South Carolina, 32.
Dauphin County (Pennsylvania) Committee, 364, 374.
Davézac, Auguste, 212, 241, 779-780, 822.
Davézac, Gaston, 303.
David, Mr., of Baltimore, at White House, 668.
Davidson Academy (later Cumberland College), 68, 329.
Davidson County, Tennessee, 76, 86, 306, 345, 465, 480, 723, 728, 768.
Davidson, George, 53.
Davidson, N., 101, 808.
Davie, Archibald, 13.
Davie, Colonel William Richardson, 12, 18, 20, 22, 23, 30, 207; opinion on place of Jackson's birth, 793.

Daviess, Joseph Hamilton, 123, 124.
Davis, Charles Augustus, 658.
Davis, Warren R., 685.
Dawson, Moses, 473-474.
Day, Mr., figures in slander of Mrs. Jackson, 462-464.
Deaderick, Captain, 182.
Deaderick, George M., 85, 135.
Deaderick, Mrs. George M., 135, 136.
Dearborn, Henry, Secretary of War, 104; letter to Jackson about Burr conspiracy, 125; 127, 144, 151, 165.
Decatur, race-horse, 132, 145.
Decatur, Captain Stephen, 301.
Decker, J., 340, 342.
Declaration of Independence, 583.
Declouet, Colonel, hears Louisiana legislators are prepared to make peace with British, 230; 233, 236, 822.
Dedham, Massachusetts, 180.
De la Croix, Dussau, 217.
Delahoussaye, Pelletier, 205.
De La Ronde, Colonel Pierre, 216, 217, 223, 226.
Delaware, 143, 376, 431, 436, 438, 492.
De Lemos, Manuel Gayoso, 59, 60, 66.
Democratic National Conventions:
  1832: 605;
  1936: 694;
  1840: 739;
  1844: 768-772.
Democratic Party, 774.
  see also Democrats.
Democratic Republicans, 606.
  see Democrats and Republicans.
Democrats, 390, 606, 680, 694, 707-737, 741, 742, 745, 746-747, 749, 752, 753, 759, 767, 771, 775.
De Monbreun's tap-room, Nashville, 98.
Denmark, 683.
De Oñis, Don Luis, 291, 292, 301.
Depressions, financial, 335, 340, 374, 650-651, 652, 735.
Deschert rifles, 24.
Desha, Robert, 551.
Detroit, Mich., 691.
DeWett mare, a race horse, 336.

DeWett, sportsman, 267, 268.
Dick, a negro jockey, 268.
Dick, N. and J., & Co., New Orleans, 666-667.
Dickinson, Charles, quarrels with Jackson, 107, 108, 109, 110; Jackson challenges and the duel, 113-118; 125, 136, 152, 227.
Dickerson, Mahlon, 693.
Dickins, Asbury, 440, 561, 584, 649.
Dickinson, Charles, 407, 433, 468, 473, 590.
Dinsmore, Silas, 134, 136.
Diomed, race horse, 337.
District of Columbia, 755, 758.
see also Washington, D. C.
Disunion, 612, 625.
see also Nullification and Secession.
Ditto's Landing, Alabama, 157.
Divorce Bill.
see Independent Treasury Bill.
Donelson, Alexander, 692.
Donelson, Major Alexander, 167.
Donelson, Andrew Jackson, ward of Jackson, 131, 278, 307, 317, 320, 330, 811; letters from Andrew Jackson, quoted, 341, 343-344, 350-352, 355, 380, 391, 513, 606, 776, 777; in Tennessee, 374, 475, 574, 679, 710, 713, 728, 760; messenger for Jackson, 378, 409, 552, 638, 711, 772; private secretary of Jackson, 400, 469, 474, 538, 585, 588, 600, 639, 642, 683, 687, 700, 754; in Washington, 489, 529, 552, 568, 577, 579, 608, 624, 711-712, 717; Eaton affair, 495, 513-515, 518, 532, 533, 536, 547, 571, 574; in Kitchen Cabinet, 502; 506, 685, 691; horse-racing, 597, 669-670, 710; sword bequeathed to, 758; Democratic Convention delegate, 769, 770, 772; in Texas, 774, 776, 780-782.
Donelson, Andrew Jackson, jr., 512, 624, 686.
Donelson, Captain, nephew of Rachel Jackson, 229, 277, 287.
Donelson, Daniel, 344, 545, 571.

Donelson, Emily, wife of A. J. Donelson, trips, 409, 537; Eaton affair, 495, 511-517, 533, 536, 547, 552, 571-573; children of, 545, 577, 625, 686, 713; see also Andrew Donelson, junior, and Mary Rachel Donelson; in Washington, 577, 579, 591, 624; descriptions of, 614, 669; illness of, 710-712; death of, 713.
Donelson, Colonel John, father of Rachel Jackson, 48, 49, 51, 52, 86, 277.
Donelson, John, 544.
Donelson, John, junior, brother of Rachel Jackson, 49, 50, 51, 68, 131, 225.
Donelson, John III, ward of Jackson, 131, 278, 811.
Donelson, Mrs. John, mother of Rachel Jackson, 465, 628.
Donelson, Mary, 337.
Donelson, Mary Rachel, 545, 625.
Donelson, Polly Smith, mother of John and Andrew Jackson Donelson, Jackson's wards, 811.
Donelson, Rachel.
see Rachel Jackson.
Donelson, Mrs. Rachel Stockley, mother of Rachel Jackson, 48, 53, 66.
Donelson, Samuel, brother of Rachel Jackson, 53, 68, 131, 266, 758.
Donelson, Severn, brother of Rachel Jackson, 131.
Donelson, Severn (Savern), 689.
Donelson, Stockley, brother of Rachel Jackson, 59, 90.
Donelson, Stockley, 475, 734, 760.
Donelson, Colonel William, 337.
Donelson, Mrs. William, 337, 727.
Doublehead, race-horse, 209, 267, 670.
"Downing, Major Jack," 641, 643, 644, 658.
Drayton, Colonel William, 374-375.
Drayton, William H., 276.
Duane, William J., 636, 639, 642-643, 645, 646, 648-651.
DuBourg, Abbé, 252, 254.
Ducros, Joseph Rodolphe, 221, 222.

INDEX 935

Duels, Jackson-Avery, 46; 83, 84, 90, 92, 93, 94, 102, 109, 110; Jackson-Dickinson, 113; 151, 152, 279, 320.
Duels, 342, 370, 375, 381, 385, 430, 434, 454, 455, 457, 463, 466, 473, 518, 576, 590, 596, 670, 677.
Duncan, Abner, 233, 234, 235, 822.
Duncan, Joseph, 93.
Duncan, Stephen, 93.
Dungannon, race-horse, 145.
Dunham, killed by Indians, 58.
Dunham's Station, Tennessee, 58.
Dunlap family of South Carolina, 13.
Dunlap, George, 13.
Dunlap, Mary Crawford, cousin of Jackson, 34, 578.
Dunlap, Nancy Craighead (Richardson), 8, 12, 13, 28.

Eagle Tavern, Richmond, Virginia, 129.
Earle, Jane Caffery, niece of Rachel Jackson, 304.
Earl, Ralph E. W., 304, 340, 342, 552, 569, 571, 591, 624, 733, 749.
East, the, 392, 442, 471, 555, 585, 599, 649, 650, 716, 721, 729, 739, 753.
Eastin, editor *Impartial Review* (Nashville), 113, 119.
Eastin, Mary, 475, 512, 517, 536, 537, 546, 571, 577, 591, 596, 624, 627.
Eaton, John Henry, 275, 277, 287; elected senator from Tennessee, 297, 301, 303, 310; promotes Jackson for President, 338, 345, 356-357, 360-361, 363, 377-378, 381; companion and friend of Jackson, 379, 382, 384, 398, 417, 488, 516, 526, 573, 576-577, 785; and Margaret O'Neale Eaton, 385-387, 459, 491, 495, 508, 509, 510-511, 513-514, 517, 534, 535, 568, 593, 605; quoted, 388; supporter and adviser of Jackson, 400, 412, 421, 431, 433, 435, 456, 458-461, 467, 477, 498, 502, 504, 541-542, 551-552; correspondence, 455, 464, 469, 476, 512-514; proffered Cabinet position, 490; as Secretary of War, 491-492,

Eaton, John Henry—*Continued*
518, 531-532, 536, 547; revenge, 570-571; retirement from Cabinet, 574-575, 596; attempted duels, 576; return to politics, 606, 677; Governor of Florida, 677, 713; Minister at Madrid, 713; in Whig camp, 742; *Life of Jackson*, 755; *see also* Andrew Jackson, Presidential Administrations, Eaton affair.
Eaton, Margaret, marriage to Eaton, 491, 509, 517; reputation and criticism of, 492, 495-496, 512-514, 516-519, 523, 531-533, 534, 536, 541, 547, 566, 568, 571-574, 575-576, 582, 593, 713; descriptions of, 510, 516, 535; ambitions, 511, 515, 552, 571, 575, 596, 677; patronage, 522; nicknamed, 534; honored, 547; 605, 606, 625, 722, 785; *see also* Margaret O'Neale *and* Margaret Timberlake, *and* Andrew Jackson, Presidential Administrations, Eaton affair.
Edwards, Ninian, 396.
Egypt, 728.
El Sol, Mexico City, 700.
Elections:
  1824: 408-412, 414-415, 435, 440, 441, 452, 605.
  1826: 457.
  1828: 472, 474, 497, 605.
  1832: 586, 608.
  1834: 680.
  1836: 713-714.
  1840: 742-743, 750.
  1841 and 1842: 749, 750.
  1844: 745, 755, 775.
Ellicott, Thomas, 651.
Ellicott's Mills, Md., 724.
Elliott, Colonel George, 268, 544, 545.
Ely, Reverend Ezra Stiles, 516-519.
Emancipation, 691-692.
  see Slavery.
Emigration, over Catawba Traders' Path in 1765, 5; 88. See immigration.
Emily, race horse, 670.
Emuckfaw, battle of, 166, 759

England, 26, 39, 76, 80, 84, 100, 102, 104, 116, 132, 142, 157, 218, 262, 276, 286, 301, 431, 437, 504, 589, 593, 692, 695, 697, 724, 754, 761, 763-767, 774, 776; Court of St. James's, 576, 593, 715. See British.
Enotachopco, Battle of, 167, 174, 596, 679, 759.
Eppes, Senator, of Virginia, 301.
Erwin, Andrew, 826.
Erwin, Captain Joseph, 106, 107, 108, 111, 152.
Europe, 506, 553, 554, 615, 654, 683, 690, 730, 751, 762, 780.
Evans & Co., John B., of Philadelphia, 75, 76.
Everett, A. H., 417.
Everett, Edward, 644.
Everett, John, 63.
Ewing, Thomas, 6, 10, 790.
Exchange Coffee House, New Orleans, 260, 264.
Executive Residence.
  see White House.
Expansionists, 356.
  see Texas.
Expectation, race horse, 670.

Fagot, Captain André, 54, 55, 56, 57.
Fairfield, plantation, 374.
Farland, John M., 364.
Faulkner, James, cousin of Jackson, 795.
Faulkner, James, senior, 796.
Faulkner, T. D., cousin of Jackson, 791.
Favrot, Pierre, 209, 252.
Fayetteville (N. C.) *Observer*, 458-459.
Fayetteville, Tennessee, 157.
Federalist Party, 346.
Federalists, 77, 78, 79, 199, 216, 269, 270, 367, 374, 375, 396, 431.
Fernandina, Florida, pirate village, 281.
Findley, James, 9.
Fishing Creek, South Carolina, 21.
Flaugeac, General Garriques, 242, 245.
Flora, Miss, and Andrew Jackson, junior, 546.

Florence, Alabama, 277, 329, 349, 740.
Floriant, Mme., of New Orleans, 253.
Florida, 83, 102, 112, 144, 149; Creek Indians of, 158; 172, 178; Jackson's eyes on, 177, 178; British gather forces in, 180; alarm in United States over conditions in, 274; 275, 277, 280; United States negotiates for purchase of, 282; Jackson has plan to seize, 283; 285, 287, 291, 294, 295; Secretary Adams's note to Spain regarding, 295; 299; purchase offer by United States, 301; Spain hesitates to sell, 306; Jackson's program for new invasion of, 309; 310; Monroe names Jackson governor of, 311; 315; formally transferred to United States, 318; 319, 321; Jackson departs from, 327; 328, 343, 359, 383, 409, 421, 450, 469; Jackson's governorship of, 336, 339, 345, 356, 557; Jackson's campaign in, 338, 339, 356, 392, 403, 445, 470, 541-543, 548, 569-570, 711; Scott's campaign in, 711; 677, 716, 742.
Floyd, John, of Georgia, 494.
Floyd, Mrs. John, of Georgia, 494.
Floyd, John, of Virginia, 418.
Forbes, Colonel, 315.
Forbes & Co., Pensacola, 287, 289, 321; influence in Florida, 321.
Force Bill, 619-621.
Force, Peter, 467.
Forrest, Nathan Bedford, 892.
Forsyth, John, Governor of Georgia, 471, 542; Senator, 655, 658, 660; Secretary of State, 682-683, 693-697; 715.
Fort Barrancas, Florida, 183, 185, 197, 291, 308, 309, 325.
Fort Bowyer, Alabama, 182, 183, 188; besieged by British, 189; 194, 197, 198, 208, 211, 219; captured by British, 255; 260.
Fort, Captain, 121, 122, 126.
Fort Deposit, Mississippi Territory, 157.
Fort Gadsden, Florida, 291.
Fort Jackson, Mississippi Territory, 172, 176.

Fort Massac, Ohio, 126.
Fort Mims, Mississippi Territory, 154, 155, 159, 171, 172.
Fort Patrick Henry, North Carolina, 49.
Fort Scott, Georgia, 286.
Fort St. Jean, Louisiana, 200, 202, 223.
Fort St. Michael, Florida, 196, 197.
Fort St. Philip, Louisiana, 208, 211.
Fort St. Rose, Florida, 196.
Fort Strother, Alabama, 539.
Fort Strother, Mississippi Territory, 159, 160, 161, 163, 166, 169.
Fort Toulouse, 155, 172. See Fort Jackson.
Foster, J., 58.
Fountain of Health, near Hermitage, 723.
Fowler, George, 449.
Fowltown, Georgia, 282.
Fraize, John, 36.
France, 56, 58, 80, 84, 155, 156, 186, 270, 380, 492, 496, 504, 523, 553; spoliation claims, 681-684, 686-687, 690, 693-699; 762, 764, 774; *see also* Andrew Jackson, Presidential Administrations, Foreign policy.
Francis, Creek leader, 286, 288.
Frank, a slave, 734, 892.
Frankfort, Ky., 102, 123, 416, 444, 462, 463, 855.
Franklin, Benjamin, 491.
Franklin County, Ala., 348.
Franklin House, Washington, 385, 386.
Franklin, Tennessee, 134, 150, 152, 275.
Franklin, Tom, slave, 710.
Fredericksburg, Va., 379, 380, 636.
Freemasonry, 605.
French Chambers, 684, 685.
  see also Chamber of Deputies.
French Legation, 626, 681, 687, 698.
Friend of the Laws, 212.
"Friends of Jackson," 456-457; *see also* Jacksonians.
Fromentin, Judge Eligius, 321, 323; trouble with Jackson, 326, 832, 332.

Frontier, in Pennsylvania, 3; in North and South Carolina, 6, 7; passing of Waxhaws, 14; 88, 89, 137, 277, 330.
Frost, William, 303.
Fugitive slaves.
  see Slavery.
Fullarat, Antoine, 324, 325.
Fulton, Robert, 193.

Gadsby, John, 386.
Gadsby's Hotel, Baltimore, 252.
Gadsby's Hotel, Washington, 412, 422, 429, 488-489, 493, 505, 516, 517, 745.
Gadsden, Captain James, 295.
Gadsden, Colonel James, 343.
Gaillard, Senator, 439.
Gaines, Brigadier-General Edmund P., president of Louaillier court martial, 261; 266, 275, 276, 282, 283; presides at court martial of Arbuthnot and Ambrister, 289; 293, 294.
Gaines, General Edmund P., 704, 706.
Galbraith, Captain, 31.
Gales and Seaton, Messrs., 402.
Gallatin, Albert, 79, 389, 406, 423, 672.
Gallatin, Tenn., 54, 544, 551, 677, 701.
Galveston Bay, 704.
Galveston Bay and Texas Land Co., 704.
Garçon, slave leader, 275.
Garrison, William Lloyd, 692, 774.
Gates, General Horatio, 21, 27.
Gault's Tavern, Richmond, 856.
George, body-servant of Jackson, 592, 719, 733, 734, 783, 892.
George III, 33.
Georgetown, D. C., 252, 385, 386, 489, 545.
Georgia, 18, 38, 92, 101, 133, 143, 158, 177, 195, 267, 270, 275, 281, 283, 285, 286, 292, 298, 304, 331, 365, 426, 436, 437, 439, 440, 455, 470, 491, 494, 542, 598, 631, 652, 655, 682; political sentiments in, 376, 388; Legislature of, 416, 581, 582, 603; Indian trouble, 523, 548-549,

Georgia—*Continued*
580, 603-604, 605, 611, 616; Governor of, 618.
Georgians, 376, 396, 495, 581, 603, 693.
Ghent, Belgium, 195, 199, 216, 254, 256, 265, 275, 276, 298.
Gibbs, General, British Army, 243, 244, 245, 246.
Gibraltar, 506.
Gibson, General, 595.
Gilbert, runaway slave, 348, 349.
Giles, William Branch, 129.
Gilmer, George, 494.
Gilmer, Mrs. George, 494.
Gilmore, Representative, 631.
Girod, Mayor, of New Orleans, 202, 227.
Gleave, Michel, 85.
Glen, John, 63.
Gold coinage, 680, 690.
Goliad, Texas, 704.
Goode, Thomas, 105.
Goose, Dorotha, 36.
Gordon, Captain John, 179, 182.
Gorham, Nathaniel, 39.
Graham, George, 278.
Grass Hat Letters, 372-373, 395.
see Tariff.
Great Britain, 84, 141, 187, 373, 393, 575, 763, 766, 769.
see also British and England.
Green, Abner, 59, 66, 597, 804.
Green, Duff, editor of *United States' Telegraph*, 455, 456, 462, 465-467, 469, 537, 538, 540; Jackson adviser, 459, 497, 504; and the patronage, 501, 519-520, 522, 861-862; 517; joins opposition, 548, 564, 567, 570, 576, 581-582, 686; and the Bank, 576, 631.
Green, James Payne, 804.
Green, Thomas Marston, junior, 59, 67.
Green, Thomas Marston, senior, 804.
Greene, Nathanael, 24, 27.
Greer, Andrew, 94.
Greere, John, 773.
Greyhound, race-horse, 105, 106, 107.

Grundy, Felix, 134, 174, 297, 335, 345, 350-352, 358; in Senate, 526, 537, 606; on Bank, 559-560; anti-Calhoun efforts, 569-570, 694.
Guibert, Captain, of New Orleans, 203, 214.
Guichard, Magloire, 230, 236, 822.
Guilford County, North Carolina, 23.
Guilford Court House, North Carolina, 24, 38.
Guillemard, Lieutenant, Spanish Army, 190.
Gulf of Mexico, 477, 699.

Haggatt, Mrs., of Nashville, 689.
Haiti, 492.
see also Santo Domingo.
Halcyon Plantation, 733, 735, 737, 743, 747, 748, 760, 773, 777, 778.
Hall, Judge Dominick, 212, 260, 261, 262, 263, 265, 275; of New Orleans, 748, 760.
Hall, William, 551.
Hall of Representatives, 383, 389, 435-436.
Hamilton, Alexander, 102, 117, 554, 560, 707.
Hamilton, James Alexander, member of electioneering party, 470; looks after Van Buren's interests, 492; letter from Georgia Governor, 542; and the Bank, 559-560, 565, 566, 584, 589.
Hamm, Mr., Chargé to Chile, 668.
Hammond, Charles, 463-465, 466, 467, 658.
Hammond, James H., 612.
Hampton Roads, Va., 517.
Hampton, Wade, 137.
Hanging Rock, battle of, 21, 30.
Hannah, Aunt; slave, 628.
Hannah, negro maid of Rachel Jackson, 479-481, 785.
Harding, Private James, 255, 261.
Hard times, 80; in Tennessee in 1819, 305.
Harper's Magazine, 759.
Harris, Egbert, 349.
Harris, J. G., 741, 742, 769, 771.

INDEX

Harrisburg *Commonwealth*, 364.
Harrisburg, Pa., 363, 364, 369, 371, 375, 391, 672, 731.
Harrison, Reuben, 50.
Harrison, Treasury employee, 499.
Harrison, William Henry, 175, 707, 738-742, 745.
Harrison's Mill, Kentucky, 115.
Harrodsburgh, Kentucky, 52, 61, 71, 136.
Harrodsburgh Spring, Ky., 350, 351.
Hartford, Conn., 250, 639.
Hartford Convention, 181, 215, 250, 251, 270, 396.
Hartford, Georgia, 285.
Hartman, Susannah, 36.
Hartsville, Tennessee, 105, 228.
Hartsville, Tenn., race course, 670.
Harvard College, 642, 643.
Harvy, George W., 349.
Havana, Cuba, 184, 194, 289, 315.
Haw Creek, Mo., 773.
Hawkins, Benjamin, 156, 176, 178.
Hay, District Attorney, 129.
Hayne, Colonel Arthur P., 198, 269, 394, 692.
Hayne, Senator Robert Y., 489, 594, 604; statement concerning Clay and Adams, 429; Cotton Kingdom advocate, 529; debate with Daniel Webster, 529-531, 541; the President's attitude toward policies, 536-540; nullification banquet, 537-540; reaction to Proclamation on Nullification, 612.
Haynie, Jesse, 132, 145, 209, 267, 269, 336.
Hays, Jane Donelson, sister of Rachel Jackson, 63, 371-372, 450.
Hays, Mrs., connection of General Jackson, 545.
Hays, Narcissa, 320.
Hays, Colonel Robert, 63, 66, 67, 70, 73, 79, 80, 81, 169, 216.
Hays, Samuel, 371, 545.
Hays, Stockley, 124, 153.
Haywood, John, 326.
Healy, George P. A., 782.

Heiskell, Dr. Henry Lee, 476, 478-481.
Henry, Patrick, 721.
Henry, Robert P., 420, 427, 444.
Henry's Station, 70.
Hermes, British man-of-war, 182, 188, 190.
Hermitage Church, 372, 399.
Hermitage, Jackson moves to, 99, 807; 103, 116, 121, 124, 125, 130, 131, 135, 137, 141, 150, 152, 154, 158, 169, 174, 199, 257, 267, 269, 296; Jackson builds new, 302; 306, 307, 309, 311, 327, 329, 794.
Hermitage, the, 335, 336, 340, 343, 344, 350, 355, 357, 361, 373, 374, 378, 413, 448, 450, 451, 461, 463, 467, 473, 474, 477, 478, 495, 509, 527, 543, 545, 550, 551, 565, 592, 607, 608, 625, 634, 637, 645, 654, 676, 699, 712-713, 723, 727, 735, 742, 750, 754, 760, 763, 771, 774, 776, 779, 781, 783; crops, 335, 544, 665-667, 677-678, 679, 728, 732-733, 748, 761, 773; visitors to, 342, 345, 350, 449, 456, 459, 469, 480, 556, 558, 597, 662, 732, 733, 752-753, 755, 759, 767-770, 777, 779, 785-786; slaves, 349, 476; 544, 692, 734, 758, 784-785; remodeling and purchases for, 447, 577, 596, 627, 679, 687, 689, 690, 708-709; debts, 627, 679, 708-709, 728, 733, 735, 743, 747, 748, 756, 761, 773; fire, 678-679; purchased by the state, 890-892; *see also* Andrew Jackson, Master of the Hermitage.
Hernandez, Father, 700.
Hibb, George, 665.
Hickman, William, 100.
Hickory Guards, 372.
Hill, Harry R. W., 666-667, 677, 678, 679, 689, 690, 709, 728-729.
Hill, Isaac, 453, 497, 498, 502, 520, 539, 561, 579, 584, 606, 779.
Hill, Lord, 209.
Hillsboro, North Carolina, 5.
Hinds, Colonel, at defense of New Orleans, 211, 216, 222, 223, 227, 229, 232, 247, 248.

Hitt, Rachel Andrew Jackson, 447.
Hobbs, Edward, 677, 709-710.
Hobkirk's Hill, battle of, 27, 51.
Hodge, Mr., Tennessee clergyman, 372.
Hogg, Dr. Samuel, 478, 628.
Holland, 534.
Holmes, Senator, 521, 522.
Holtzclaw, Burnard, 627, 628, 677.
Homollimicke, Creek chief, 288.
Hone, Philip, 684, 697.
Hopkinson, Judge Joseph, 659, 668.
Hornet, United States sloop-of-war, 315.
Horses, racing.
  see Andrew Jackson, Master of the Hermitage, horses and horse-racing.
Horse-racing, 33, 34, 100, 105; Truxton vs. Greyhound, 106; Truxton vs. Ploughboy, 111; 131, 134, 145, 209, 267.
Hôtel du Trémoulet, New Orleans, 185, 193.
Hotels. See Taverns.
House of Representatives, Jackson elected to, 78, 79, 81; 95, 129, 143, 193, 283; resolution disapproving execution of Arbuthnot and Ambrister, 297; various resolutions aimed against Jackson, but he is vindicated, 307.
House of Representatives, Speaker of, 368, 417; battles in, 370, 452-455; election of President in, 383, 405-407, 408-412, 435-440, 449, 707; votes on bills, 393, 525, 600, 621, 631, 732; committees, 396, 435, 440, 586, 598-599, 630, 674; Lafayette visits, 418; members of, 430, 441, 491, 599, 600, 623, 686; reports, 564; bills, 616; chamber, 624, 685; resolutions, 629, 632, 655, 675; leader, 652; gallery, 661.
Houston, Sam, 171, 303; Nashville lawyer, 340, 345; visits to the Hermitage, 342, 786; urges Jackson for President, 351, 352-353, 355; member of Congress, 381, 383, 430, 431, 455, 457, 458, 461, 463; duels, 457,

Houston, Sam—*Continued*
  463; anti-Calhoun efforts, 470, 541; at Rachel Jackson's funeral, 480; 624; and Texas, 701-706, 711, 715, 716, 719, 751, 761-766, 774, 776, 780-782, 784.
Hudson River, 402, 691, 749.
Hughes, James, 36.
Hughes, Major, at Natchez, 201.
Hull, Lieutenant, duel at Pensacola, 320.
Humbert, General Jean, 247.
Humboldt, Baron, 438.
Hume, Dr. William, 481-482; 628.
Humphrey, Captain, at New Orleans, 238, 241.
Humphries, William, 13, 17.
Hunter, American Revolutionary soldier, 33.
Hunter, Captain, 58.
Hunter's Hill, Jackson's plantation, 76, 79, 82, 84, 86, 96, 98, 99, 104, 302.
Hunter's Hill Plantation, 362, 665-667, 728, 737.
Huntsville, Alabama, 157, 159, 174, 329, 690.
Hutchings, Andrew Jackson, ward of Jackson, 303, 306, 329, 330; schooling of, 344, 408, 450; 379; plantation of, 448, 450, 626, 676; expelled from schools, 469, 545, 577, 597; marriage of, 627, 676; burdens of, 744.
Hutchings, John, 96, 99, 100, 101, 104, 113, 180, 275, 306.
Hutchings, Lem, 136.
Hutchings, Mary Coffee, 627, 676; *see also* Mary Coffee.
Hutchings, S. D., 303.
Hutchinson sisters, marital fortunes in United States, 4, 5; 13, 16, 789.
Huygens, Chevalier, Dutch minister, 535.
Huygens, Madame, 534-536.

Illinois, 358, 390, 396, 416, 425, 428, 431, 457, 472, 520, 612, 652.

INDEX 941

Impartial Review and Cumberland Repository (Nashville), 110, 111, 113, 119, 120, 124, 125.
Independent Treasury Bill, 732, 733, 735, 744.
Indian lands, 399, 552, 587, 603.
Indian policy.
 see Andrew Jackson Presidential Administrations, Indian policy.
Indian Queen Hotel.
 see Brown's Indian Queen.
Indian Queen, race-horse, 105.
Indian removal, 523, 550-551, 604, 691; see also Cherokee, Chickasaw, Choctaw, Creek and Seminole Indians.
Indian treaties, 548-549, 552, 580, 604.
Indiana, 277, 358, 425, 472.
Indians, 4, 14, 24, 47, 49, 50, 51, 52, 53, 54, 55, 58, 63, 69, 70, 74, 81, 89, 95, 159, 175, 176, 179, 183, 190, 198, 274, 275, 286, 287, 288, 289, 290, 296, 383, 404, 548, 603, 702-703, 762; see also Black Hawk War, Catawbas, Cherokee, Chickasaw, Choctaw, Creek, Seminole Indians and Andrew Jackson, Military Activities and Memoirs, and Andrew Jackson, Presidential Administrations, Indian policy.
Inflation, 555, 690, 693, 706, 730.
 see also Currency.
Ingham, Samuel D., 491, 502, 533, 534, 561-563, 566, 574, 576.
Ingham, Mrs. Samuel D., 495, 511, 512, 534, 571.
Innerarity, John, 321, 323, 325, 326.
Innes, Judge Harry, 123.
Internal improvements, 369, 392, 424, 453, 471, 524-528; favored by Pennsylvania, 362; advocated by Calhoun and Clay, 362; Crawford opposes, 365; Adams's friendly attitude toward, 366; Van Buren's policies, 367; Jackson votes for, 393, 404; item in Jackson's first message to Congress, 524; Van Buren's opposition to, 525-527; Blair's disapproval of, 567-568.
Ireland, 3, 4, 12, 14, 31, 266, 399.

Irving, Washington, 404, 636, 693.
Isaacs, Judge, of Tennessee, 473.
Isbel, Mr. who fooled the Tories, 25.
Iturbide, Emperor of Mexico, 360.

Jack, slave, 544.
Jackson, Andrew—
 Ancestors in Ireland, 3; arrival of parents in Pennsylvania in 1765, 3, 789; their journey to the Waxhaws, 4, 5; Mrs. Jackson's kinfolk in Waxhaws, 5; the Jacksons affiliate with Waxhaw Church, 8; father's death and funeral, 9, 791.
Birth and Early Years in South Carolina—
 Birth, 10, 791; landed proprietor at age of three, 10; debate about place of birth, 11, 791 et seq.; schooling, 13, 14; his mother's ambition he enter ministry, 17; nurses wounded soldiers, 19; joins army at age of thirteen, 20; night encounter with Tories, 24; prisoner of war, 25; witnesses battle of Hobkirk's Hill, 27; near death with smallpox, 28; death of mother, 28, 29; apprenticed to saddler, 31; trip to Charleston to claim grandfather's legacy, 31; loses inheritance at horse-races, 33.
Lawyer and Judge—
 A care-free law student, 34 et seq.; admitted to bar, 37; first case of record, 38; promised appointment as attorney-general of Western District, 38; quarrel and duel with Colonel Waightstill Avery, 45; arrives in Nashville, October 26, 1788, 47; boarder at Donelson blockhouse, 48; deals with a bully, 54; interested in Western intrigues with Spain, 55, 57; fights Indian marauders, 58; buys property near Natchez and enters slave trade, 59, 802; takes oath of allegiance to United States, December 15, 1790, 62; reappointed attorney-general, 62; appointed to Superior Court Bench, 1798, 85; captures Russell Bean, 87, 88; in-

Jackson, Andrew—*Continued*
Lawyer and Judge—*Continued*
terpretation of law, 89; a purchase of law books, 807; seeks governorship of Louisiana, 98; resigns from bench, 98; seeks judgeship in Mississippi Territory, 137.
Courtship and Marriage—
Captain Lewis Robards's jealousy, 53; quarrels with Robards, 60; arrested on Robards's complaint, 64; escorts Rachel Donelson Robards from her home in Kentucky, 63; accompanies her to Natchez, 64; accused of adultery by Robards, 65, 803; marries Rachel, 67, 804; learns marriage is irregular, 71; second wedding ceremony, 73, 74, 806; defense of wife against slanderers, 136.
Lawmaker, Business Man and Land Speculator—
Large land holdings, 69; trouble with Indians, 70; trade trip to Philadelphia, 74; elected delegate to Territorial Convention, 76; financial difficulties, 76, 81, 133; elected to House of Representatives, 78; criticizes statesmanship of George Washington, 80; record as representative, 82; elected to Senate, 83; love for children, 86; genesis of quarrel with John Sevier, 90; challenges Sevier, 92; expands mercantile business, 96, 97; buys the Hermitage, 99, 807; mercantile firm of Jackson & Hutchings, 99, 100; cotton planter, 101; meeting with Aaron Burr, 103; buys race-horse Truxton, 105; trouble with Charles Dickinson, 108; canes Thomas Swann, 109; race between Truxton and Ploughboy, 111; challenges Dickinson, 140; kills him, 118; host to Burr and collapse of the conspiracy, 119, 120; at trial of Burr, 128, 129; wards and adopted son, 130, 131; killing of Patton Anderson, 134.

Jackson, Andrew—*Continued*
Early Military Activities—
Judge advocate of Davidson County militia, 68; major general of Tennessee militia, 91; a military gesture against Spain, 96; prepares troops to aid Aaron Burr, 113; puts troops under arms to capture Burr, 126; studies French military regulations, 132; calls for volunteers, 1812, 141; offers militia to President Madison, 143; War Department fails to accept, 144; appointed major general of United States Volunteers by Governor Blount, 146; starts south to war, 146; dismissed from service at Natchez, 149; refuses to demobilize volunteers, 149; nicknamed "Old Hickory," 150; quarrel and pistol fight with Benton brothers, 152.
Creek Campaign—
Prepares expedition against Creeks, 154; battle of Talladega, 160; ill with dysentery, 161; quells mutiny in hungry militia, 162; second mutiny for lack of food, 164; Jackson declines to retreat, 165; battle of Emuckfaw, 166; battle of Enotachopco, 167, 168; court martial of Private John Woods, 169, 170; battle of Tohopeka (Horseshoe Bend), 170; William Weatherford surrenders, 172; Jackson returns to Tennessee a hero, 174; appointed major general in command of Seventh Military District, 175; Creek treaty, 177; instructs Rachel in conduct becoming a major general's lady, 180.
Mobile and New Orleans Campaigns—
Learns British plan of attack on Southern coast, 180; arrives at Mobile, 182; military preparations to meet British, 182; defense of Fort Bowyer, 189; denounces pirate Jean Laffite, 192; fortifies Mobile, 194; prepares to go to New Orleans, 198; reception at New Orleans, 200;

Jackson, Andrew—*Continued*
Mobile and New Orleans Campaigns
—*Continued*
misunderstanding with Bernard de Marigny, 205; fortifies territory around New Orleans, 206; difficulties of organizing city's defense, 209, 210; proclaims martial law, 211; accepts services of Laffite and the Baratarians, 212, 213; mobilization and review of troops, 214; learns of British landing below city and decides to attack immediately, 217; preparations for night attack, 222; surprises British, 224; entrenches in Rodriquez Canal, 227; preparations against next British attack, 231; second battle for New Orleans, 234; third battle for New Orleans, 239; victory of January 8, 1815, 244; hailed in New Orleans, 252; city objects to martial law, 254, 255; troops mutiny, 259; arrest of Louis Louaillier and Judge Dominick Hall, 262; Jackson fined by Hall, 264; court martial and acquittal of Gabriel Villeré, 821.

After War of 1812—
Returns to Hermitage, 265; horse-racing again, 267; great popularity in United States, 269; dispels presidential illusions of friends, 271; reception in Washington, 272; Southern tour of military inspection, 275; declines War Office, 277; land speculations in Alabama, 277; a difference with War Department and challenge to Major General Winfield Scott, 278, 279.

Florida Expeditions—
Florida Jackson's true goal since beginning of military career, 175; investigates hostile British proceedings in Florida, 179; capture of Pensacola, 1814, 197; fires Monroe with vision of conquering Florida and extending frontiers, 273; alarm over activities at Negro Fort, 275; Secretary of War Crawford readjusts Creek treaty, 275; Jackson ordered

Jackson, Andrew—*Continued*
Florida Expeditions—*Continued*
to Florida by Secretary of War Calhoun to bring Seminole Indians to terms, 283; Jackson writes Monroe his plan to seize Florida, 283; captures St. Marks, 287; trial and execution of Arbuthnot and Ambrister, 289; Pensacola surrenders, 291; Administration has difficulty justifying seizure of Florida, 291; Monroe suggests "correction" of Jackson's dispatches, 293; near break with Administration, 294; Secretary of State Adams's dispatch to Spain in support of Jackson, 295; Jackson goes to Washington to defend military actions, 297; investigation in House of Representatives and vindication, 298; ovations in Philadelphia, New York, Baltimore, 300; Senate investigation, 301.

After Florida Campaign (1818-21)—
Builds new Hermitage for Rachel, 302; welcomes President Monroe to Tennessee, 304; hard pressed for money in depression of 1819, 306; wishes to resign from Army, 307; a critic of style in writing, 307; retires from Army, 313.

Governor of Florida—
Receives confidential instructions to prepare for military movement against Florida, 308; sends Calhoun program for Florida invasion with private letter suggesting seizure of Cuba, 309; accepts governorship of Florida, 311; formal negotiations with Governor Callava for transfer strike a snag, 315; enters Pensacola, 317; difficulties as governor, 319; arrests Callava, 323; interference of Judge Fromentin, 326; 832; resigns and leaves for Tennessee, 327.

Retirement—
Family circle at Hermitage, 330; "I am not fit to be President," 330; an anonymous letter-writer reveals political intrigue of President Monroe and other public men, 331; opin-

ANDREW JACKSON

Jackson, Andrew—*Continued*
Retirement—*Continued*
ions of candidates in presidential campaign of 1824, 332.

Characteristics and Descriptions—14, 17, 21, 33, 34, 35, 37, 79, 83, 88, 101, 201, 204, 330, 382-383, 392, 400, 401, 457, 469, 507, 568-569, 594, 595, 614, 645, 717, 720-721, 754, 779, 780, 782.

And His Wards—
See Anthony Wayne Butler, Andrew Jackson Hutchings, Andrew Jackson, junior, Lincoyer.

And His Wife—
Kindnesses to her relatives, 343-344, 450, 495; church attendance with her, 372, 418, 432; his letters to her, 379, 384-385, 391, 392, 395, 399; his concern for her, 379, 391, 395, 397, 409; travel with her, 409, 470; slander concerning, 407, 432-434, 462-468, 473, 474, 477, 478, 482-483, 493, 513-514, 571, 733, 834, 855-856; home life with, 431-432, 475-476; her death and funeral, 479-482, 701; thoughts after her death, 482-483, 488, 528, 543, 547, 591-592, 597, 607, 609, 627, 679, 687, 733, 757, 774, 780.

Military Activities and Memories—
Florida campaigns, 338, 339, 356, 359, 392, 403, 445, 469, 470, 541-543, 548, 569-570, 711; Creek campaign, 339, 596, 661; Louisiana campaign, 623, 750, 759; Gadsden desires to write his military history, 343; presentation of ceremonial sword, 350; newspapers laud military career, 354; attends anniversary celebration of Battle of New Orleans, 357; received medal voted by Congress in 1815, 391; British Colonel defends his conduct at New Orleans, 404; credit for New Orleans disputed, 457-458; execution of the six militiamen, 468; attends anniversary celebrations at New

Jackson, Andrew—*Continued*
Military Activities and Memories—*Continued*
Orleans, 470, 736-737; battle of Enotachopco, 596, 759; visit of former corporal, 718; Carolina campaign of 1780, 723; New Orleans fine refunded, 748, 754, 760; writes of Tarleton's raid, 757.

Master of the Hermitage—
A good "hard times" manager, 335; bank shareholder, 335, 556-557; charities, 336; purchases for the Hermitage, 336, 447, 596, 709; dysentery, 336, 339, 343; horses and horse-racing, 336, 337, 469, 544-545, 596, 597, 654, 665, 669-670, 708-709, 710, 717-718, 742, 743, 748, 760; subscriber to twenty newspapers, 336-337; G. W. Campbell visits the Hermitage, 338-340; inflammation of the lungs, 339; his favorite Nashville resort, 340; Houston's duel story, 342; friendship with Overton, 344; inspects Melton's Bluff Plantation, 348, 408; runaway slaves, 348-349; slave-owner, 349; cautions overseer, 349; Coffee accompanies him home, 350; guests at the Hermitage, 342, 459; bullet wound and cough give trouble, 351; markets cotton crop, 357, 408; contribution to church building, 372; leaves for Washington during cotton-ginning time, 378; borrows from Overton, 378; cotton brings good prices, 380; pays Butler notes, 380; an aid to Cupid, 399; visits John Coffee, 408; survey of his plantations, 448; visit of Lafayette, 448-449; aids Frances Wright's manumission scheme, 449; debts increase, 450; cares for overseer's family, 450; cotton prices soar, 450; gets new set of teeth, 456; sells Melton's Bluff, 469; gives refuge to Henry Lee, 469; host to large numbers, 474-475; arrangements for departure, 477-478; leaves the Hermitage, 483; reports from

Jackson, Andrew—*Continued*
  Master of the Hermitage—*Continued*
  overseer, 544; looks to welfare of negroes, 544, 596, 628; visits Hermitage, 550, 551; Josiah Nichol, steward of Hermitage finances, 565; abhors debt, 565-566; remodels Hermitage, 577, 596, 627; puts son in charge of plantation, 592, 596; writes manual on plantation administration, 596; short of funds, 627; new overseer, 627; plantation operates at a loss, 627; cotton crop a disappointment, 664-667; son's bad bargain with H. R. W. Hill, 665-667; son's debts increase, 665-666; son's poor management of plantation, 666-668, 709-710; visits Hermitage, 676; engages new overseer, 677; plantation in poor condition, 677; gives advice on crops, 678, 679; Hermitage burns, 678-679, 687; plans to rebuild, 679, 687, 690, 708; worries about debts, 688, 689-690; borrows anew, 708; new Hermitage completed, 709; worst cotton crop failure, 709; sees overdependence on cotton, 710; home to the Hermitage, 727; burdens of a patriarch, 727; sows Egyptian wheat, 728, 731; financial state, 728; false rumors about, 729; health failing, 732, 750; free of debt, 732; improves the plantation, 733; relies on "Matchless Sanative," 733, 743, 744; joins church, 733; death of R. E. W. Earl, 733; wool socks from Mrs. Blair, 734; defends his slaves, 734; arranges to pay son's debts, 737-738, 740-742; establishes woodyard at Halcyon Plantation, 737-747, 777-778; stricken with a hemorrhage, 737; sells town lots in Alabama, 740; son's debts grow, 743, 760, 777-778; conditions bad at Halcyon, 743; borrows from Plauché, 747, 761, 783, 891; cotton crop fails, 748; Blair offers loan, 748, 761, 777, 778, 891; visit of

Jackson, Andrew—*Continued*
  Master of the Hermitage—*Continued*
  Van Buren, 752; neglects correspondence, 754; Bancroft requests reminiscences, 755; Kendall asks to write biography, 755-756, 759; writes last will and testament, 757-759; ships cotton to Liverpool, 760; has bad year, 760; gets refund of New Orleans fine, 760; cotton flooded at Halcyon, 773; last illness, 781, 782-785; visit of Isaac Hill, 779; offered Roman sarcophagus, 780; Catron visits Hermitage, 780; last visitors, 785; servants gather, 785; death, 785.
  Political Activities to 1829—
  Governorship of Florida, 336, 342, 343, 345; rejects suggestion that he run for President, 337, 339; opposed to rising of the masses, 341; for sound money, 341; suspicious of William Carroll, 341; thinks Houston should be in Congress, 342; advice to Captain Call, 343; creed of public service, 343, 363; predicts Clay can't be elected, 343; friends map out his destiny, 344-347; feeling against Crawford, 346; inveighs against stay law and loan bureau bill, 346; Lewis bids for Stokes's support, 347; Grundy asks if he will be a presidential candidate, 350; disapproves of Kentucky's banking policy, 351; agrees to go to Murfreesborough, 351; newspapers boom his candidacy, 351; "I have never been a candidate for any office," 351; Tennessee Legislature nominates him for presidency, 352; wishes to stay in retirement, 355; says Legislature is not the people, 355; Monroe attempts to sidetrack candidacy with Mexican offer, 356-357, 358; Jackson silent as to his candidacy, 358; question of Jackson's withdrawal, 358-359, 370; "a stalking horse for Henry Clay," 359, 368-369; refuses

Jackson, Andrew—*Continued*
Political Activities to 1829—*Continued*
appointment to Mexico, 360, 363; aversion to presidential politics is changing, 360-362; Pittsburgh enthusiastic for him, 363; agrees formally to his candidacy, 363-364, 369; his availability, 369; popular opinion for, 370, 375, 384, 390-391; comes out for protective tariff, 373; Donelson becomes his secretary, 374; advocates non-partizan Cabinet selections, 375, 396; William Polk declares for him, 375, 376; elected Senator, 378; goes to Washington with Eaton, 378; at O'Neale's boarding house, 379, 385, 387, 391; orders new clothes, 380; reconciliations with former enemies, 382; social conquests, 380, 382, 384; chairman of Committee on Military Affairs, 382; defends Margaret Timberlake, 387; against caucus system, 388-389; Pennsylvania for him, 390; Adams considers him formidable rival, 392; suggests him for Vice President on Adams ticket, 393, 402; slogan, 393; on floor of Senate, 393, 401; supports protective tariff, 394, 395, 401; responding to allegiance of the masses, 394-395; criticism of tariff stand strengthens his resolves, 397; hastens home, 397; campaign personalities, 400-401, 404-405; Calhoun's attitude toward him, 403; favorite in "straw" votes, 405; slander Mrs. Jackson as political weapon, *see* Andrew Jackson and His Wife; election returns, 408-411, 414-415; travels to Washington, 409-411; against intrigue, 411, 422, 431, 433; at Gadsby's Tavern, 412, 422; borrows from Coffee, 411; Clay makes a bargain with Adams, 429-430, 433, 436-440; *see also* Bargain, the "Corrupt"; Adams is elected on first ballot, 439; greets Adams, 441; stops testimonial din-

Jackson, Andrew—*Continued*
Political Activities to 1829—*Continued*
ner plan, 441; "corrupt bargain" cry, 442-445, 472; homeward bound, 446; remarks to Mr. Wylie on the bargain, 446-447; announces candidacy for 1828, 448; politics booming, 450; invitations to appear, 451; renominated for presidency, 451, 452; resigns from Senate, 451, 452; makes his longest political speech, 451; campaigning free style, 453-469, 472; desperate elements drift to him, 455; the *Telegraph* established, 456; "say nothing and plant cotton," 456, 458, 464; test of new party machine, 457; successful in 1826 elections, 457; imbroglio with Southard, 457-458; Clay involved in Jackson slander, 462-468; electioneering tour, 470; anti-Calhoun intrigue, 470-471; chameleon on issues, 471; election stories, 472; triumphant at the polls, 472.
Presidential Administrations—
Bank Controversy—
History of Jackson's feeling toward Bank of the United States, 556-559; suggests establishment of some agency to take place of Bank, 524; Biddle tries to bluff Administration, 560-561; he fails and seeks its friendship, 561-562; Jackson plans for an alternative to the Bank, 558-560, 584-585; testimony on use of Bank money in elections, 562; Biddle calls on Jackson, 562; Jackson insists on mentioning the Bank in his message, 563-564, 566; calls Bank a "hydra of corruption," 564; still working on Bank substitute, 564-566; Biddle willing to compromise, 585; Jackson apparently willing, 586; Bank question seems on way to settlement, 586; Clay works to disrupt Jackson-Biddle rapprochement, 588; he succeeds,

INDEX 947

Jackson, Andrew—*Continued*
Presidential Administrations—*Continued*
Bank Controversy—*Continued*
590; Jackson men counter with House investigation of Bank, 598-599; Biddle forces pass bill for recharter, 599-600; Jackson's vetoes sustained, 602; House retorts that government deposits are safe, 623; Jackson resentful, contemplates their withdrawal, 629-630, 632-634; Cabinet divided, 630-649; Biddle's suspicious loans to congressmen, 631; Taney favors withdrawal, 633-634; McLane opposed, 634-635; Jackson plans to withdraw deposits, 634-636; Secretary of Treasury, 638-639, 642-643; 645-648; Duane declines to issue withdrawal order, 645, 648-649; Jackson makes Taney Secretary of Treasury and he discontinues deposits, 650; Biddle strikes back, calling loans of state banks, 650-651; country feels stringency, 652; outcry against Jackson, 654; battle begins in Congress, 655 *et seq.*, panic strikes country, 656; Biddle's loans to congressmen and propagandists, 657-659; Jackson resumes offensive; "Go to Nicholas Biddle," 661-663; trend turns against Bank, 671-673; Biddle weakens, 673; Biddle unmasked, 673; Jackson victorious in House, 675; Bank doomed, 680; *see also* Bank of the United States *and* Nicholas Biddle.

Eaton Affair—
Advises Eaton not to delay marriage, 508-509; insists that Eaton accept Cabinet position, 491; foreign berth suggested for Eaton, 492; President is adamant, 492; chides Emily Donelson for her treatment of Mrs. Eaton, 495; blames Clay for Eaton gossip, 495; deciding factor in Branch and Ber-

Jackson, Andrew—*Continued*
Eaton Affair—*Continued*
rien appointments, 511; feminine members of White House family, 512; Lewis advocates Margaret's cause, 513, 514, 518; President and his nephew call, 514; Emily threatened with exile, 515; correspondence on reputation of Mrs. Eaton, 516; taunts R. K. Call, 516; Calhoun party unco-operative, 517-532; refutes testimony against Mrs. Eaton, 518-519, 523; unique Cabinet meeting, 518, 531; feels responsible for Eaton's unfortunate position, 532, 533; Cabinet dinner a "hollow ceremony," 533; threatens Cabinet members with dismissal, 535, 547; banishes niece and nephew, 547-548, 552; Eaton issue in Tennessee, 552; considers it now a political affair, 571; Emily offers to compromise, 572-573, 574; Donelson resigns, 572, 574; resists pressure to send Eaton away, 573; Eaton resigns, 575; parts from Eaton, 577; in the campaign of 1832, 606; offers Eaton governorship of Florida, 677; sends Eaton to Madrid, 713; *see also* John H. Eaton, Margaret Eaton, *and* Margaret Timberlake.

Foreign Policy—
Mentioned in first message to Congress, 523; British West Indian ports opened, 552; claims against Naples settled, 683; against Spain, 683; against Denmark, 683; French asked to pay, 681; treaty signed, 681-682; French refuse to keep it, 682; Jackson's strong message, 683, 684; martial ardor in France and America, 684-686; France offers to pay if we apologize, 695; Jackson refuses, 696; diplomatic relations severed, 697; France backs down, 697-698; Texas annexation long desired, 356, 699; failure of Jackson's early efforts, 699-701; Hous-

Jackson, Andrew—*Continued*
  Foreign Policy—*Continued*
    ton's early career in, 702-705; Jackson hears of victory at San Jacinto, 705; his equivocal policy toward Mexico, 705; Texas issue involved with slavery, 705; Jackson refuses to press for annexation, 715; urges Texas to claim Californias, 716, 751; recognizes Texas Republic, 719; *see also* Texas *and* Andrew Jackson, Political Influence after Retirement.
  Indian Policy—
    Mentioned in final message to Congress, 523; supports Georgia, Alabama and Mississippi in their violation of Federal treaties, 549; relation to nullification in South Carolina, 548; attempts to keep question out of courts, 550; addresses Chickasaws, urging them to move West, 550-551; Chickasaws sign removal treaty, 551; Choctaws sign, 552; Chickasaws repudiate removal treaty, 580; Cherokees and Creeks refuse to remove, 580; Georgia overrides United States Supreme Court, 580; Jackson declines to interfere, 581; South Carolina nullifiers elated, 581; Georgia again defies Court, 603; "John Marshall has made his decision. Let him enforce it," 603-604; Chickasaws sign new removal treaty, 604; Creeks sign, 604; Policy helps Jackson against South Carolina, 616; Houston supports policy as best Indians can hope for, 702; Black Hawk War, 612; Seminole War, 711; southwestern frontier tribes, 702.
  Nullification in South Carolina—
    Proposes conciliation and compromise on tariff, 523-524; thinks Hayne too sympathetic with nullifiers, 529; must act on the issue, 531; for Webster or Hayne, 536-537; Jefferson dinner, 538-540, 542; toast to the Union, 540, 581;

Jackson, Andrew—*Continued*
  Nullification in South Carolina—*Continued*
    to oppose South Carolina's efforts, 548, 580; warns nullifiers, 581, 582, 604; waits for South Carolina to start trouble, 607-608, 610-611, 615; denounces nullifiers, 608, 610, 617; Nullification Proclamation, 610-612, 617-619; Van Buren disagrees, 615-616; tariff compromise proposed, 616, 619-620; supports Unionists, 618; South Carolina yields, 619, 621; Jackson insists upon Force Bill, 619-621; realizes nullification question not settled, 622, 624.
  Spoils System—
    Job seekers overflow Washington, 489-490, 491; 496, 497; McLean objects to removals, 498; Jackson's "principles" on, 499, 500; patronage seekers disappointed, 496-506; Jackson opposes "clean sweep" of offices, 498; exaggerated accounts of removals, 499; Van Buren's part in, 501-502, 504, 506; he obtains ascendency over Calhoun, 520; talk of Jackson's impeachment, 521; approximate total of removals, 520-522, 861-862; good and bad effects, 522.
  Texas—*see* Andrew Jackson, Presidential Administrations, Foreign policy.
  Minor Incidents—
    Arrival in Washington awaited, 488; death rumored, 488; at Gadsby's, 488, 493; Cabinet selection, 490-492, 495, 496, 511; inauguration, 493-495; disorderly reception at the White House, 494; Kitchen Cabinet, 498, 650, 660, 694; changes made in diplomatic appointments, 504; reception for diplomatic corps, 507; private secretary, 513; vacation at Rip Raps, 517, 746; first message to Congress, 523, 528, 549; means to pay national debt, 524, 526, 527, 562;

INDEX

Jackson, Andrew—*Continued*
Minor Incidents—*Continued*
cool toward internal improvements, 524, 524, 525; Maysville Road veto, 525-527; "Tecumseh" Johnson objects, 526; appeal to the people, 527; ill health, 527-528; leaves a political will, 528; 542; observers in Congress, 529; anti-Calhoun feeling, 540-543; feels Presidency is only "dignified slavery," 543; visits Indians, 548-551; dissatisfied with Green's *Telegraph*, 567-568; visits Tennessee, 567; meets Frank Blair, 567-569; starts the Washington *Globe*, 569; moves for reconciliation with Calhoun, 569; Calhoun "cuts his own throat," 570, 573; Van Buren offers to resign, 574-575; makes Van Buren Minister to Great Britain, 576; sojourn at Rip Raps, 577; reconstructs Cabinet, 578-579; visits Charles Carroll of Carrollton, 583; recalls reading the Declaration when 9 years old, 583; has old Benton bullet removed, 590-591; health improves, 590, 596; consents to run for re-election, 592; plans to elevate Van Buren by resigning, 593; his choice for the succession in 1836, 594; Senate rejects Van Buren for Minister to Great Britain, 595; unites his adherents into strong party machine, 605; re-elected President, 608; pipe collection, 610; end of first term, 624; simple inaugural, 624; milk from Blair's diary, 626; changes in Cabinet, 636; attempted attack on, 636; first ride on railroad, 637; reception in Philadelphia, 637; New York welcome, 637-638; triumphal procession through Connecticut and Rhode Island, 638-639; honored in Boston, 640-642; confined to bed, 641, 645, 645; Harvard confers honorary degree, 643; tour ends at Concord, N. H., 645; declines a proposal of

Jackson, Andrew—*Continued*
Minor Incidents—*Continued*
marriage, 646; vacation at Rip Raps, 646-647, 648; threatened with assassination, 662; typical dinner party described, 668-669, 688-689; Senate censures, 674; Senate rejects Taney's nomination, 675; attempted assassination, 685-686; pays last of national debt, 690; inflation appears, 690, 706, 730; land speculation rife, 691, 706; national slavery trouble, 692-693; further Cabinet changes, 693-694; revolt in party, 694, 707; insists on succession of Van Buren, 694-695, 707; distributes surplus to states, 706, 730; Specie Circular, 707, 718, 729, 730; opinion of Marshall, 707; opinion of Jefferson, 707-708; appoints Taney to Supreme Court, 708; prepares last message for Congress, 712, 713; seriously ill, 712; Van Buren elected as successor, 713; Senate expunges resolution of censure, 714; last reception, 717; pockets rescinding bill, 718; crowds bid farewell, 719-720; appraisals of, 720-722; his two regrets, 724; journeys homeward, 724.
Political Influence after Retirement—
Urges keeping Specie Circular in force, 729; suggests examination of deposit banks, 729; plans for independent treasury, 731-732, 735; encourages Van Buren, 731; Van Buren's visit to Hermitage is called off, 734; tour helps Democratic prospects, 737-738; would prefer Clay to Harrison as opponent, 738; suggests Polk for Vice President, 738; condemns Whig campaign methods, 741-742; takes stump for Van Buren, 742; favors Tyler, 745-747; indignant at Polk's defeat for Governor, 751; strives for Texas annexation, 754, 761, 763-767, 769-772, 774-777, 780-782; surprised at

Jackson, Andrew—*Continued*
Political Influence after Retirement—*Continued*
Van Buren-Clay agreement, 768; backs Polk's candidacy, 769-772, 774-775; gets Tyler to withdraw, 774; writes to Polk, 783-784.

Jackson, Andrew, junior, adopted son of General Jackson, 131, 134, 147, 149, 171, 174, 182, 194, 257, 265, 266, 288, 330; schooling, 343, 392; 379; debts, 450, 666-668, 677, 687, 689, 709-710, 728, 732-738, 740-744, 748-749, 757, 760, 777-778, 783; Jackson's letters to, 544, 591, 609, 637, 667, 677-679, 687, 689-690, 708, 737-738, 742; love affairs of, 545-547, 577; in Washington, 545-547, 577, 624, 625, 717; in care of the Hermitage, 592, 596, 608, 627, 628, 654, 664-668, 676-679, 687, 708-711, 743-744, 891-892; manager of woodyard, 747, 777-778; 748, 761, 784, 785; inheritance, 758-759.

Jackson, Andrew, senior, father of Jackson, arrives in Pennsylvania in 1765, 3; family of, 4; journey to Waxhaws, 5; homesteader, 6; death and funeral, 9; 791, 796.

Jackson, Andrew III; grandson of General Jackson, 667, 678, 727, 744, 758.

Jackson, Elizabeth Hutchinson, mother of Jackson, 4; sisters and kinfolk in Waxhaws, 5; 9; widowed, 9; birth of Jackson, 10; 12, 13, 14, 17, 18, 20, 23, 28; death, 29; 37, 798, 799.

Jackson, Hugh, brother of Jackson, 4, 9, 10, 18.

Jackson, Hugh, grandfather of Jackson, 31.

Jackson, Hugh, uncle of Jackson, 4.

Jackson, Rachel Donelson (Robards), 48, 50, 51; marries Lewis Robards in 1785, 52; husband's jealousy, 53; 59; final quarrel with husband, 61; returns with Jackson to Tennessee, 63; refuses Robards's plea for rec-

Jackson, Rachel Donelson—*Continued*
onciliation, 63; flees from husband with Jackson to Natchez, 64; Robards sues for divorce, 65, 803, 804; marries Andrew Jackson, August, 1791, 67, 804; learns marriage to Jackson is irregular, 71; remarried to Jackson, 73, 74, 806; 78, 79, 80, 81, 82, 83; her lonely life, 85, 86; 92, 97, 99, 100, 106, 107, 110, 115, 116, 118, 124, 130, 131, 135; aged forty-three, description of, 136; 143, 147, 148, 149, 152, 169, 174, 175, 176, 178, 179, 182, 194, 199, 209, 228, 257, 258, 259, 260, 265, 266, 269, 273, 274, 285; Jackson's letter telling of capture of St. Marks and arrest of Arbuthnot, 288; opposes Jackson's becoming governor of Florida, 311; 312; letter describing Florida, 314; 316, 317, 319, 320; back to Hermitage and happy, 327; wife of General Jackson, 336, 340, 344, 488, 547, 597, 607, 609, 627, 678, 679, 687, 773; "a fugitive from fame," 338, 342, 360, 372, 378, 391, 395, 448, 472, 474, 475, 476; correspondence, 337, 371-373, 379, 382, 384, 391, 392, 395, 397, 432, 473-474, 476-477; relatives of, 344, 351, 450, 475, 481, 483; 495, 506, 522, 527, 743; health, 382, 391, 447, 457, 474-479; slander concerning, 407, 432-433, 463-468, 473, 474, 477, 478, 482-483, 493, 513, 571, 733; new light on her first marriage, 834, 854-856; travel, 409, 470; religion, 418, 432, 473, 475, 733; life in Washington, 431, 432; descriptions, 432, 448, 474, 477, 481; Bible, 476, 591-592, 624, 719; death and funeral, 479-482, 785; grave, 480, 483, 543, 607, 701, 757, 774, 780; *see also* Andrew Jackson and His Wife.

Jackson, Rachel II, granddaughter of General Jackson, 609, 625, 637, 655, 665, 667, 687, 744, 785.

Jackson, Robert, brother of Jackson, 4, 9, 10, 19, 20, 23, 24, 26, 28.

INDEX

Jackson, Sam, uncle of Jackson, 4.

Jackson, Sarah Yorke, wife of Andrew Jackson, junior, Jackson's regard for, 591-592, 596, 627, 678, 689, 708, 748, 749, 758, 761, 782-784; Jackson's letters to, 596, 606-608, 654-655; pregnancy, 606-608; children of, 609, 625, 667, 727, 748, 749, 758, 759; *see also* Andrew Jackson III *and* Rachel Jackson II; in Washington, 624, 625, 687-689; illness of, 677-678; gift ring, 703; 778.

Jackson, Miss., 699.

"Jackson money," 653.

Jackson, Tenn., 742.

"Jackson's Well," 68.

Jacksonian Epoch, 723.

Jacksonians, 363, 394, 396, 417, 420, 430, 431, 436, 487, 500, 644, 655, 680, 770, 779; *see also* Democrats.

Jamaica, B. W. I., 179, 180, 181, 194, 195, 219, 314.

James, Captain, "surest scout of Marion," 33.

Jarret, Nancy, 35, 37, 41, 79.

Jay, John, 76.

Jefferson, Thomas, 77, 81; elected President, 95; 97, 116, 117, 118, 123; orders arrest of Aaron Burr, 123; 129; denounced by Jackson at Burr trial, 130; 132; reconciliation with Jackson, 272; 274, 301, 307, 310, 339, 365, 421, 422, 429, 437, 440, 453, 500, 522, 538, 624, 707-708; ideals of, 367, 392, 527, 538, 557, 707.

Jennings, Johnathan, 50.

Jennings, Reverend Obadiah, 475.

Jesse, colored jockey, 670.

Jesuits, 58, 326.

Jim, slave, 544.

John Randolph, steamboat, 709.

Johnson, a South Carolina Tory, 25.

Johnson, Andrew, 782.

Johnson, Cave, 770-771.

Johnson, Francis, 416, 423.

Johnson, Lieutenant Littleton, 151.

Johnson, Richard M., 142.

Johnson, Col. Richard M. ("Tecumseh"), 420, 442, 526, 569, 570, 707, 714, 738, 740, 753.

Johnson, Colonel William R., 267.

Johnson's landing, Nashville, 98.

Johnsonville, North Carolina, 37.

Jones, Anson, 776, 780, 781.

Jones, Chamberlayne, 348.

Jones, James Chamberlain ("Slim Jimmy"), 750, 770.

Jones, Lieutenant Thomas Ap. Catesby, 208, 209, 210, 218, 219.

Jonesborough fire, 780.

Jonesborough, Tennessee, 39, 40, 41, 45, 68, 85, 87, 306.

Jones's Bend, Tennessee, 68.

Jouitt, John, 65.

Judges, 430.

see Courts.

Jugeat, Pierre, 223.

Junto, the Nashville, Jackson's earliest presidential supporters, 345-346, 350, 352-353, 354, 359, 361, 363, 381, 834.

Keane, Major General, 199; at attack on New Orleans, 218, 219, 220, 221, 222, 223, 225, 226, 243, 246; Jackson returns sword to, 249.

Kemble, Fanny, 614.

Kendall, Amos, editor of *Argus of Western America,* 444, 461, 497, 567; Fourth Auditor of Treasury, 500, 521; "Kitchen Cabinet," 502, 694; Eaton affair, 515; Postmaster General, 522, 694, 739; Bank controversy, 559-563, 639, 643, 646-651, 653, 659; adviser and friend of Jackson, 567, 568, 579-580, 584, 600-601, 632, 634, 638, 732, 736, 745; biography of Jackson, 755-759.

Kennedy, John Pendleton, 375-376.

Kent, Justice, 521.

Kentuckians, 411, 424, 425, 447, 450, 521, 526, 567, 587, 588, 589, 592, 605, 621, 631, 655, 658, 674, 675, 694, 695, 707, 752, 775.

Kentucky, 49, 51, 52, 56, 60, 63, 64, 65, 71, 75, 102, 103, 115, 116, 117, 121, 123, 142, 194, 195, 199, 240, 242, 246, 248, 259, 261, 266, 267, 270, 278, 279, 298, 329; Legislature of, 340, 358, 415, 427, 448, 462; Supreme Court of 340; 350, 368, 417, 418, 419, 420, 423, 426, 428, 433, 434, 443, 444, 454, 457, 462, 463, 465, 498, 500, 516, 525, 526, 544, 560, 562, 567, 617, 620, 659, 691, 695, 753, 855, 856; political sentiments in, 384, 390, 406, 409, 410, 414, 417, 425, 436, 451, 455, 457, 472, 557, 569, 584, 586, 588; see also Bargain.

Kentucky Reporter, 280.

Kentucky Road, 48, 116, 305.

Kerr, Doctor, 205.

Key, Francis Scott, 493.

Kidd, Captain William, 193.

Kinderhook, 749-750, 767.

King, James G., 672-673.

King's Mountain, South Carolina, 24, 40, 87.

King, Senator, 609.

Kingsley, Captain Alpha, 340.

Kingston, Tennessee, 94.

Kirkman, Mrs. Ellen, 399.

Kirkman, Mary, 398.

Kirkman, Thomas, 398-399.

Kirkpatrick, Major, 58.

"Kitchen Cabinet," 498, 502, 567, 650, 660, 694.

Knower, Mr., of New York, 658.

Knoxville *Gazette*, 91, 93, 94.

Knoxville *Register*, 354.

Knoxville, Tennessee, 70, 75, 77, 82, 90, 91, 94, 305, 337, 352.

Kremer, George, 421, 422, 428, 434-435, 446, 447, 459, 461, 494.

Krudener, Baron, 534.

La Branche, Alice, 719.

Lacock, Abner, 301, 307.

Lacoste, Captain, 242.

La Courrière de la Louisiane, 259, 260.

Lady Nashville, race horse, 670.

Lafayette, George Washington, 449, 758.

Lafayette, Marquis de, 404, 453, 640; American tour, 414, 415, 417, 426, 428; visits House of Representatives, 418, 435, 449; Mrs. Jackson's description of, 432; son-in-law of, 437, 449; and Francis Wright, 449-450; pistols, 449, 758; visits Jackson, 449.

Laffite, Jean, sought as ally by British, 185; 188; offers services to Governor Claiborne of Louisiana, 191; 202, 206, 210, 212; services accepted by Jackson, 213; at defense of New Orleans, 219, 229; 263, 280, 282.

Laffite, Marc, 186.

Laffite, Pierre, 186, 187, 192, 224.

Lamar, Marabeau Buonaparte, 762.

Lambert, General, 243, 246, 247, 248, 260.

Lancaster County, Pennsylvania, 3.

Lancaster, Pa., 668.

Land, Captain, of South Carolina, 24.

Land Companies, 89, 277.

Land Office, 712.

Lands, 358, 399, 523, 552, 586, 587, 603, 648; speculation in, 690-691, 699, 703, 706-707, 712; 728-730, 755; in the Waxhaws, 5; "tomahawk rights," and early colonial forms of land acquisition, 6; of Jackson in Waxhaws, 10; exchange of, between North and South Carolina in boundary dispute, 11; of James Crawford in Waxhaws, 14; 48; of Jackson near Nashville, 68; 70, 74, 75, 77, 81, 89, 90, 96, 99; Hermitage, 99, 807, 808; 106, 133, 134, 157, 269, 276; Cypress Land Company, 277; 286; founding of Memphis, 306; 307; 804, 805; of Lewis Robards sold, 806.

Larne, Ireland, 3.

Lasley, General, 757.

Lathan, Mrs. Sarah, cousin of Jackson, 794.

Latin-American affairs, 360, 454, 506; see also Mexico.

INDEX

953

Latour, Major A. Lacarrière, 213, 216, 217, 229, 243.
Laval, Captain, 189, 197.
Lavasseur, 449; *see* Lafayette, son-in-law of.
Lawrence, Captain, 251.
Lawrence, Major, at Fort Bowyer, 182, 183, 188, 189, 190.
Lawrence, Richard, 686.
Laws, replevin, 340.
Lawson, Surgeon General Thomas, 724.
Lea, John M., 834.
Lebanon Pike, 338, 374.
Lebanon Road, 99, 121.
Lebanon, Tennessee, 99.
Lee, Henry, 452, 469, 475, 489, 498, 520.
Lee, "Light Horse Harry," 452.
Leopard, man-of-war, 130.
Lessley, John, uncle of Jackson by marriage, 6, 790.
Lessley, Mary Hutchinson, aunt of Jackson, 6.
Lessley, Sarah Hutchinson, aunt of Jackson, 6, 794, 795.
Lessley, Samuel, uncle of Jackson by marriage, 6, 790.
Letcher, Robert P., 423, 425, 430, 445, 617.
Lewellen, Abednego, 58.
Lewis and Clark Expedition, 554.
Lewis, Mary Ann, 547, 548, 552, 626; *see also* Mary Lewis Pageot.
Lewis, Seth, 328.
Lewis, Major William B., 146, 302, 804; promotes Jackson for President, 345-347, 363, 374-375, 377-378, 390, 412, 461, 472; Jackson correspondence, 391, 412, 432, 550, 552, 567, 677, 736, 765, 778; adviser of Jackson, 461, 498, 504, 526, 528, 538, 548, 575; 579, 628, 689; and Rachel Jackson slanders, 463, 465, 474; anti-Calhoun efforts, 470, 471, 542, 569, 573; in Jackson's household, 489, 495, 568; Eaton affair, 513, 514, 516, 518, 571, 577; Bank, 524, 556, 560-562, 564, 566, 649, 652-653; observer for Jackson, 529, 656; connected with French Legation, 626, 681, 686, 695, 698; and Jackson's debts, 736, 747; Jackson's last message to, 785.
Lewis, Major William Terrell, 111.
Lewis, Mrs. William B., 346.
Lexington, Ky., 266, 305, 329, 366, 410, 418, 463, 525, 630, 690, 753.
Lexington, Massachusetts, 15.
Lexington, North Carolina, 143.
Liberator, the, 774.
Liberia, 692.
Lile, David, 76, 86.
Lincoln, Abraham, 612.
Lincoln, General Benjamin, 19.
Lincoyer, Indian ward of Jackson, 159, 266, 288, 329, 344, 408, 450, 469.
Lindenwald, Van Buren's home, 749-750, 752, 770.
Littleton, slave, 710.
Liverpool, England, 667, 683, 760.
Livingston, Cora, 257, 546, 626.
Livingston, Edward, 186, 191, 193, 198, 202, 203; host at New Orleans to Jackson, 204; 206, 210, 212, 214, 217, 229, 240, 248, 255, 256, 262, 281, 416, 455, 489, 506; offered ministry to France, 496; relinquishes appointment, 504; in Senate, 520; Secretary of State, 578, 584, 585, 588, 590, 598, 600, 611-612; Minister to France, 636, 686, 695, 697.
Livingston, Mrs. Edward, 204, 212, 257, 495, 496.
Livingston, Peter, 589.
Lockyer, Captain Charles, 185, 187, 188, 191, 219.
London, England, 431, 437, 504, 554, 579, 585, 601, 630, 751.
Lottery, 657.
Louaillier, Louis, 212; arrest of, 260; court martial and release, 261, 262; 289.
Louis Phillippe, 681, 682, 695, 697-698, 782.

Louisiana, 41, 49, 51, 55, 57; purchase of, 96; 97, 100, 102, 121, 122, 124, 131, 137, 157, 158, 175, 180, 183, 184, 187; British prepare for attack on, 191; 193, 194, 199; defense of New Orleans, 200, 202, 204, 205, 206, 208, 209, 210, 212, 214, 219, 228, 230, 231, 236, 240, 241, 247; 250, 254, 256, 259, 261, 263, 267, 280, 281, 322.

Louisiana Gazette, 186, 192, 256.

Louisiana Legislature, 205, 210, 212, 213, 230; closed by Jackson, 235; 236, 238, 254.

Louisiana, man-of-war, 210, 228, 231, 234.

Louisiana, political sentiments of, 358, 361, 384, 390, 414, 416, 424, 425, 436, 616; 428, 455, 578, 659, 675, 719; Legislature, 409; army, 458; Jackson visits, 470, 737; campaigns, 609, 779.

Louisiana Purchase, 553.

Louisianians, 443.

Louisville, Kentucky, 102, 405, 409, 447, 587, 630, 690.

L'Ouverture, Toussaint, 203.

Love, Colonel, of Nashville, 544.

Lucy, race-horse, 33.

Lynch, Colonel, 268.

Lynch, David, 362.

Lynchburgh, Virginia, 272.

Lynn, 644.

Macarté, Augustin, 227; house Jackson's headquarters below New Orleans, 231, 232, 238.

Macay, Spruce, 34, 36.

MacGregor, Gregor, 281.

Macon, Nathaniel, 426, 441.

Madison County, Ky., 659.

Madison, Dolly, 273, 384.

Madison, James, 81; elected President in 1808, 132; 179, 195; Jackson administers nerve tonic to, 196; 215; bleak outlook of Administration, 250; Jackson's victory at New Orleans restores political fortunes of, 252; 272, 276, 278, 305, 308, 365, 423.

Madrid, 713.

"Magician," the.
see Martin Van Buren.

Magness, David, 134.

Maham, Colonel, 33.

Maine, 388, 390, 521, 523, 616, 641, 658, 691.

Mandeville, Bernard de Marigny de, 470.

Mangum, Willie P., 417.

Manrique, Don Matteo González, 179, 183, 190, 197, 198.

Mansker, Casper, 51, 60.

Mansker's Station, Tennessee, 64.

Manthis, slave, 892.

Marblehead, Mass., 644.

Marchand, Captain, 155.

Marchand, Sehoy, 155.

Marcy, William L., 503, 658.

Maria, race-horse, 132, 145, 209, 267, 268, 269, 336.

Marietta, Ohio, 124.

Marigny de Mandeville, Bernard de, 202; Jackson declines hospitality of, 205; 208, 210, 212, 230, 235, 236, 254.

Marion, General, 33.

Markley, Representative, 426.

Marriages, Margaret O'Neale and John B. Timberlake, 385; Mary Kirkman and Richard Call, 398; Henry R. Wise, 474-475; Margaret Timberlake and John H. Eaton, 491, 509, 518; Margaret Branch and Daniel Donelson, 571; Andrew Jackson, junior, and Sarah Yorke, 591, 627; Mary Eastin and Lucius J. Polk, 596, 627; Mary Lewis and Alphonse Pageot, 626, 681; Mary Coffee and Andrew Jackson Hutchings, 627, 676; Robert Armstrong and Josiah Nichol's daughter, 679; Eliza Allen and Sam Houston, 701-702; of Hugh Jackson, 4; of Hutchinson sisters, 4, 5; Dr. William Richardson and Nancy Craighead, 8; George Dunlap and Nancy Richardson, 13; of Crawford heirs, 14; Dr. Samuel Dunlap and Mary

INDEX

Marriages—*Continued*
 Crawford, 800; John Donelson, senior, and Rachel Stockley, 49; John Donelson, junior, 50; Lewis Robards and Rachel Donelson, 52; Andrew Jackson and Rachel Donelson Robards, 67, 73, 804; Samuel Donelson and Polly Smith, 811; Robert Butler and Rachel Hays, 135; of Sehoy Marchand, 155; Captain Armstrong and Miss Nicholls, 174; Ralph E. W. Earle and Jane Caffery, 304.
Marshall, Chief Justice John, 494, 603, 614, 621, 707, 720.
Marshall, John, 107, 124, 129.
Martin, Elizabeth, 668.
Martin, Governor, of North Carolina, 38.
Martin, Dr. John Donelson, 892.
Martin's *History of Louisiana*, 754.
Martineau, Harriet, 579-580, 685.
Martinsville, North Carolina, 37.
Maryland, 113, 326, 371, 375, 384, 388, 390, 410, 417, 431, 436, 488, 583, 588, 653, 665, 724.
Marylanders, 579, 694.
Masons, the, 156, 516, 605.
Massachusetts, 39; opposes war of 1812, 181; 199, 251; ignores Jackson in public thanks for New Orleans victory, 252; 358, 383, 414, 417, 456, 530, 531, 534, 602, 603, 621, 639, 644, 657, 684, 707; Legislature, 639.
Massacres, Indian, 58, 63, 69, 154.
Massey, Benjamin, 794.
Massey, Mary, 34.
"Matchless Sanative," Jackson's cough medicine, 733, 743, 744.
Maxey, Colonel Virgil, 375.
Mayfield's Station, Tennessee, 63.
Maysville, Ky., 525.
McColloch family of North Carolina, 23.
McCrady's Tavern, Charleston, 33.
McCulloh, Henry Eustace, 7.
McDonough, Commodore John, 181.
McDougall, Captain, aide-de-camp of Pakenham, 245.

McDuffie, George, 375, 388, 454, 455.
McGary, Betty Crawford, cousin of Jackson, 25.
McGary, Hugh, 72, 73, 463-464, 855.
McGary, Martin, 25, 31, 47, 72.
McGillivray, Alexander, 155, 156, 321.
McGillivray, Lachlan, 155.
McKee, Colonel John, 69.
McKeever, Lieutenant Isaac, U. S. Navy, 287.
McKemey, George, uncle of Jackson by marriage, 4, 5, 9; house said to be Jackson's birthplace, 10, 795; house in North and South Carolina boundary dispute, 11, 792, 793, 797.
McKemey, Margaret Hutchinson, aunt of Jackson, 4, 5.
McKinley, John, 303.
McLane, Louis, opposes Adams in balloting, 436-437; criticizes Jackson's appointments, 392; friend of Van Buren, 496; Minister to France, 504; becomes Secretary of the Treasury, 579; favors rechartering of Bank of United States, 583-590; is offended by Biddle petition, 598; urges mild veto of recharter bill, 600; opposes Taney on Bank question, 630; recommendation to Jackson, 634-635; becomes secretary of State, 636; influence on Jackson, 638-639; reference to views in Jackson's letter to Duane, 643; supports Duane against Jackson, 645; recommends postponement of government deposits' transfer, 648-649; threatens to resign, 649; warning recalled by Biddle, 650; remains loyal to Jackson, 653.
McLane, Rebecca, 546.
McLaughlin, James A., 755-756, 759.
McLean, John, 491, 498, 521.
McLemore, John C., 506.
McLemore, Mary, 577, 624, 627.
McMinn, Governor, of Tennessee, 303.
McNairy, John, 36, 37; elected judge of Superior Court, 38; 39, 41, 45, 54, 83.

McNairy, Nathaniel A., 109, 110, 111, 116.
McQueen, Peter, Creek chief, 286.
McRae, Lieutenant Colonel, at New Orleans, 198.
McRory, 63.
McWhorter, George, 17.
McWilliams, Captain, British Colonial Marines, 185.
Mecklenburg County, North Carolina, 7.
Meeker, Cochran & Company, of Philadelphia, 75, 76.
Melton, John, 834.
Melton's Bluff Plantation, 335, 348, 349, 408, 469, 834.
Memphis, Tennessee, founding of, 306; 449, 616, 737.
Mercer County, Kentucky, 51, 52, 61, 463.
Mero District, 39, 40, 41, 45, 54, 55, 56, 57, 62, 113, 258, 628.
Metcalfe, Representative, 443.
Methodists, 544.
Mexico, 102, 121, 123, 124, 356-357, 358, 359, 396, 609, 700-706, 715, 751, 763, 764, 780, 781.
Mexico City, 356, 700, 703.
Mexico Libre, a stolen ship, 282.
Michigan, 578, 693, 770.
Milfort, General Leclerc, 156.
Milledgeville, Ga., 366.
Miller, Pleasant M., 352.
Miller, Robert, 8.
Miller's Tavern, Kentucky, 117.
Miller, William D., 761, 764, 765, 767.
Mills, killed by Indians in Tennessee, 58.
Mills, Mrs. E. H., 383.
Mills, Elijah Hunt, 383.
Mills, Robert, 793.
Mims, Samuel, 157.
Miranda, General, 112.
Miró, Don Estéban, Spanish Governor of Louisiana, 55; fosters Spanish alliance with Cumberland settlers, 56, 62; 83, 96, 156, 202.
Mississippi, 137, 211, 220, 222, 261, 299, 336, 359, 361, 384, 548, 550, 552, 609, 616, 621, 691, 699, 728,

Mississippi—*Continued*
733, 736, 740, 756, 763, 778, 783; Legislature, 699.
Mississippi River, 455, 464, 470, 550, 604, 652, 711, 733, 747, 773, 856.
Mississippi Territory, 154, 158, 175.
Missouri, 358, 370, 390, 400, 409, 411, 414, 415, 420, 425, 428, 436, 443, 457, 539, 566, 652, 677, 773.
Missouri Compromise, 329, 366, 841.
Missourians, 591, 595, 604, 663, 714.
Mitchell, Major, British Army, 225.
Mitchell, Mark, 76.
Mobile, Alabama, 102, 148, 158, 166, 178; Jackson defends, 182, 188; 194, 195, 196, 197, 198, 199, 200, 205, 211, 254, 267.
Mombrino, race horse, 710.
Money.
see Currency *and* Banks.
Monkey Simon, a jockey, 268.
Monroe, James, 132; 337, 338, 356-358, 360, 374, 391, 396, 440, 458, 470, 492, 502, 541-542, 554; Secretary of State, 143; Secretary of War, September, 1814, 195; supports Jackson's expedition against Florida, 196; 197, 198, 199, 208; difficulty in financing War of 1812, 216; 227, 239, 248, 270; Aaron Burr's opinion of, 271; 273, 274; elected President 1816, 276; 278, 280, 282; Jackson's plan for seizure of Florida sent to, 283; "approval" of seizure, 285; 286; ready to disavow Jackson's acts in Florida, 292; suggests Jackson "correct" his Florida dispatches, 294; rebuffed, 295; 298, 301; welcomed to Tennessee by Jackson, 304, 305; 307; his insincerity toward Jackson, 310, 315, 327, 331; 310, 313, 319, 321, 326, 327; version of Rhea letter controversy, 827, 828.
Monroe, Mrs. James, 386, 509.
Montgomery, John R., 668-669.
Montgomery, Letitia, 668.
Monticello, home of Jefferson, 365, 421, 538.
Montpelier, Alabama, 312, 313.

INDEX

957

Moore, Gabriel, 595.
Moore, Thomas, P., 418, 419, 427-428, 544-545.
Moore, Colonel William, 37.
Morales, Don Juan Ventura, 202.
Morgan, Brigadier-General David, 240, 243; Jackson's anger over defeat at New Orleans, 247.
Morgan, J. J., 439.
Morgan, William, 605.
Morganton, North Carolina, 40, 41, 45.
Morrell, Jack, 126, 127.
Moulton, Mrs., Washington dressmaker, 407.
Mount Vernon, Washington's home, 746.
Mountz, Lieutenant, at Pensacola, 323.
Murfreesborough, Tenn., 176, 351, 352-355, 359, 361, 377-378, 451.

Naples, Bay of, 683.
Naples, Kingdom of, 683.
Napoleon, 681.
Napoleonic wars, 523.
Nashville, 45; description of, in 1788 when Jackson arrived, 47; 54, 55, 56, 58, 63, 66, 68, 70, 74, 75, 89; described in 1804, 98; 103, 106, 107, 109, 110, 113, 115, 116, 119, 124, 125, 136, 143, 146, 148; Benton brothers fight with Jackson in, 152, 153; after Creek campaign, Jackson's reception, at, 174; 180, 215, 258; description of, in 1815, 265; 266, 269, 274, 283, 296, 303, 304, 305, 310, 311, 329; improvements in 1821, 329.
Nashville Bank, 135, 269, 277, 305, 335, 380.
Nashville *Banner & Whig*, 558.
Nashville *Clarion*, 351.
Nashville Female Academy, 330.
Nashville *Gazette*, 209, 345.
Nashville Inn, 98, 152, 329, 335, 340, 477.
Nashville Jockey Club, 132, 145, 266.
Nashville junto.
  see Junto.
Nashville *Republican*, 452, 480.

Nashville, Tenn., 336, 342-344, 347, 354, 359, 361, 362, 373, 387, 391, 396, 398, 448, 449, 456, 463, 465, 470, 474, 477, 478, 480, 485, 504, 544, 551, 556, 557, 558, 597, 630, 679, 709, 724, 728, 729, 733, 734, 736, 740, 741, 756, 760, 767, 768, 769, 771, 782, 854, 855; Cedar Street, 399; Court House Square, 340, 399, 478; Tippecanoe Club of, 741.
Nashville *Union*, 741; 769-771, 772.
Nashville *Whig*, 337, 340, 351.
Nassau, Bahamas, 287, 289.
Natchez, Mississippi, 59, 60, 64, 66; Jackson escorts Rachel to, 66; 71, 73, 97, 143; encamps at, in 1813, 147, 148, 149; 150, 151, 163, 267, 329, 462, 463, 465, 597, 630, 855.
Natchez Trace, 64, 146.
Natchitoches, Louisiana, 124, 137.
National City race course, Washington, 597.
National Gazette, 399, 400.
National Intelligencer, 315, 327, 357, 402, 499, 729, 767-768.
National Jockey Club, Washington, 669.
National Journal, Washington, 367, 403, 460, 465, 467-469, 497, 534, 604.
National Republican Party, 605.
National Republicans, 589, 608, 680.
National Road, 447.
Nationals.
  see National Republicans.
Ned, slave, 544, 709.
Neely, Alexander, 63.
Negroes, 340, 440, 447, 454, 476, 544, 554, 592, 596, 606, 628, 665, 691-693, 695, 708-710, 717-718, 728, 734, 735, 737, 743, 748, 756, 758, 784-785, 855; *see also* Slaves and Slavery.
Negro Fort, Florida, 275; blown up by General Gaines, 276, 291. See Fort Gadsden.
Nelson, Lord, 405.
Nesbit, Captain, Revolutionary soldier, 25.

958 ANDREW JACKSON

Newburn, Va., 379.
"New Deal," 671.
New England, 142, 168, 181; for ending War of 1812 on any terms, 195; 199, 216; opposition to war, 250; 251, 252, 255; friendly to Jackson in 1816, 269, 366, 367, 371, 375, 390, 392, 393, 403, 406, 410, 414, 415, 419, 427, 430, 431, 436, 445, 448, 468, 472, 520, 523, 529, 530, 537, 538, 553, 578, 603, 639, 640-641, 646, 751.
New Englanders, 529, 537.
New Hampshire, 38, 418, 429, 455, 520, 561, 579, 645, 653, 659, 779.
New Hampshire Patriot, 453, 606.
New Haven, Connecticut, 251, 380.
New Haven *Register*, 775.
New Jersey, 371, 375, 390, 410, 415, 693; College of, 338, 553.
Newman, Captain, 211.
New Orleans, 41, 55, 56; seat of Spanish Governor Miró conspiring to separate Cumberland country from Union, 57; 69; United States takes possession of in 1804, 96; 98, 101, 102, 104, 109, 112, 119, 121, 124, 144, 145, 148, 155, 181; British prepare to cut off, 184; 186, 187, 190, 191, 192, 194, 197, 198, 199; Jackson arrives and prepares to defend, 200; battle of December 23, 1814, 223; second battle, 234; battle and victory of January 8, 241; 249, 250, 251, 252; hails Jackson, 252; 253, 254, 255; Rachel arrives in, 257; 260; Jackson's trial before Judge Hall, 262; 265, 266, 269, 270, 273, 275, 279, 281, 285, 286, 300, 303, 309; described as "great Babylon" by Rachel Jackson, 311; 319, 326, 328, 335, 336, 341, 374, 380, 384, 393, 398, 399, 450, 457, 458, 460, 470, 554, 577, 630, 659, 665, 666, 679, 687, 692, 718, 728, 733, 736, 740, 747, 754, 757, 758, 760, 763, 783.
New Orleans, Battle of, 357, 392, 405, 470, 510, 529, 537, 550, 623, 639, 699, 736, 748, 750.

New Port, Tennessee, 85.
Newspapers, 336-337, 367, 377, 389, 399, 400, 403, 405, 409, 415, 443, 448, 462, 465, 501, 529, 536, 540, 563-564, 581, 652, 747; Alexandria *Herald*, 411; Albany *Argus*, 453; *Argus of Western America*, 444, 461, 497, 567; Baltimore *American*, 739; Cincinnati *Friend of Reform or Corruption's Adversary*, 473; Cincinnati *Gazette*, 463, 464, 469, 658; *El Sol*, 700; Fayetteville *Observer*, 458-459; Harrisburg *Commonwealth*, 364; Jeffersonian *Aurora*, 636; Knoxville *Register*, 354; Nashville *Banner & Whig*, 558; Nashville *Clarion*, 351; Nashville *Gazette*, 345; Nashville *Republican*, 452, 480; Nashville *Union*, 741, 769-771, 772; Nashville *Whig*, 337, 340, 351; *National Gazette*, 399, 400; *National Intelligencer*, 357, 402, 499, 729, 767-768; *National Journal*, 367, 403, 460, 465, 467-469, 534, 604; *New Hampshire Patriot*, 453, 606; New Haven *Register*, 775; New York *Courier and Enquirer*, 498, 599, 624, 657; New York *Evening Post*, 354, 410, 606, 630; New York *Statesman*, 414; Niles's *Register*, 441, 671; of Mexico City, 700; Philadelphia *Aurora*, 336; Philadelphia *Columbian Observer*, 354, 433, 434, 447; Portland *Courier*, 641; Raleigh *Register*, 407; Richmond *Enquirer*, 453, 497, 658, 767; Salisbury *Western Carolinian*, 354; *United States' Telegraph*, 455, 456, 459, 460, 465, 467, 537, 567-569, 570, 576, 605, 632, 861; *Vermont Journal*, 608; Washington *Globe*, 569-571, 575-576, 580, 660, 685, 695, 768; Washington *Republican*, 403.
New York, Van Buren's influence in, 365, 366, 383, 390, 402, 436, 437, 501, 616; Legislature of, 365, 390, 411; political sentiments in, 371,

INDEX

959

New York—*Continued*
375, 376, 388, 402, 406, 410, 411, 415, 416, 437, 457, 605, 608, 657, 742, 775; 428, 429, 436, 439, 443, 470, 503, 520, 538, 560, 617, 631, 645, 661, 668, 671, 672, 673, 704, 754; Governor of, 618.

New York *Advocate*, 332.

New York City, 82, 112, 121, 143, 144, 193, 271, 278, 279; ovation and banquet for Jackson in 1819, 300; 367, 385, 504, 537, 542, 569, 582, 583, 613, 637, 641, 656, 671, 684, 691, 718, 729, 739, 749, 758; Port of, 522, 734; Broadway, 606, 760; Battery, 637; Castle Garden, 637; banks, 642, 647-652, 658, 778.

New York *Columbian*, 279.

New York *Courier and Enquirer*, 498, 599, 624, 657.

New Yorkers, 423, 439, 476, 492, 496, 505, 519, 528, 560, 570, 574, 575, 579, 589, 593, 605, 615, 694, 769, 772.

New York *Evening Post*, 354, 410, 606, 630.

New York *Statesman*, 414.

Nichol, Josiah, 450, 556, 565; daughter of, 679.

Nicholas, Wilson Carey, 129.

Nicholls, Lieutenant Colonel Edward, British Army, proclamation inviting Louisiana to become ally of Great Britain, 183; 187; invites Laffite to join British, 187; 190, 192, 194, 286, 296

Nichols, Josiah, 174

Niles, Hezekiah, 441, 671.

Niles's *Register*, 287, 441, 671.

Noah, Mordecai, 497.

Nolte, Vincent, 230.

Norfolk, Va., 515, 517, 607.

Norrington, Joseph, 58.

Norris, Lieutenant, United States Navy, at New Orleans, 241.

North Carolina, 5, 7; controversy with South Carolina over boundary, 10, 11, 18; in Revolutionary War, 21,

North Carolina—*Continued*
23, 34, 38; difficulties with State of Franklin, 39; 45, 49, 56, 57, 58, 59, 62, 79, 80, 90, 92, 143, 266, 346, 347, 354, 367, 371, 374-376, 383, 384, 388, 390, 394, 400, 405, 407, 415-417, 420, 437, 458, 477, 576, 618, 631, 658, 659, 691, 755; birthplace of Jackson, 791, 792.

Nourse, Mr., defaulting Treasury official, 499, 500.

Nueces River, 699-700.

Nullification, threatened by South Carolina, 523-524; Webster-Hayne debate, 529-531; Jackson's uncertain attitude toward, 536-538; Jackson's toast at Jefferson dinner, 539-540; nullification of Indian treaties, general, 548, by Georgia, 549; Cherokees fight treaty nullification, 549-550; Jackson averts issue by visit to Indian council, 548-551; Blair opposes nullifiers, 567; proposed reconciliation between Jackson and Calhoun fails, 570-571; issue of Indian treaties reopened in Georgia, 580-581; South Carolinians seek support of Georgians, 581; Calhoun and nullification, 581-582; Clay unwilling to champion, 587; Jackson confident of victory against, 593; Worcester-Butler case and aftermath, 603-604; activities of Hayne, Calhoun, *et al,* 604; Jackson's threat, 604; crisis in South Carolina, 607-619; South Carolina passes ordinance of nullification, 610; Proclamation on Nullification, 611-612, 615-616; bill to lower tariff introduced in House, 616; Jackson asks Congress to authorize military force to collect customs, 618-619; South Carolina yields, 619; the "Force Bill" and Clay's tariff bill passed, 619-621; South Carolina rescinds ordinance of nullification, 621; Jackson predicts civil war, 622; Jackson's stand on nullification

Nullification—*Continued*
meets approval in Massachusetts, 639-640; Van Buren lukewarm opponent of 634, 694; *see also* Andrew Jackson, Presidential Administrations, Nullification in South Carolina.
Nullifiers, 581, 604, 607-608, 610, 616-619.

Ode to Bogle, 554.
Ohio, 124, 270, 277; Legislature, 358, 660; political sentiments of, 384, 388, 390, 398, 406, 408, 409-411, 414-415, 420, 425, 430, 454, 457, 472, 755, 841; women of, 477; 491, 502, 536, 688, 707, 723; Governor of, 618; delegation, 741.
Ohio River, 606, 737.
Ohio River Valley, 340.
Oklahoma, 549, 702.
"Old Hickory."
  see Andrew Jackson.
O'Neale boarding house, 379, 384-387, 391, 398, 509, 513.
O'Neale, Peggy.
  see Mrs. Margaret Timberlake *and* Mrs. Margaret Eaton.
O'Neale, Major William, 379, 384-387, 391, 398.
Oo-loo-te-ka, 702.
Oregon, 724, 751, 766, 772, 776, 784.
Orpheus, British man-of-war, 182.
Otis, Harrison Gray, 251, 252.
Otis, Mrs. Harrison Gray, 252.
Overton, Judge John, 52, 53, 60, 64, 65, 66; discovers Jackson's marriage is illegal, 71; signs Jackson's marriage bond, 73; 74; inaugurates written court decisions, 89; 113, 115, 119, 133, 174, 175, 303, 306, 805; and Rachel Jackson slanders, 344, 462, 463-464, 834, 854, 855; Jackson creditor, 378; political aide, 396, 397; 475; letter, 528, 542; adviser of Jackson, 542, 552; Bank director, 565; his nephew, 573; death of, 628.

Overton, General Thomas, Jackson's second in Dickinson duel, 114; 120, 180.

Pacific Coast, 776.
Pacific Ocean, 716, 719, 776.
Pacolet, race-horse, 209, 267.
Pageot, Alphonse, 626, 681, 686, 695-698.
Pageot, Andrew Jackson, 681, 696-697, 698.
Pageot, Mary Lewis, 686-687, 698; *see also* Mary Lewis.
Pakenham, Major General Sir Edward, 225; takes command of British below New Orleans, 227; 228, 233, 234, 235; battle of December 28, 1814, 236, 237, 238, 240; plan of attack on January 8, 1815, and its failure, 243; death, 246, 249.
Palfrey, Dr., of Harvard, 644.
Palmetto State.
  see South Carolina.
Panama Congress, 454, 455.
Panics, 650, 653-655, 656, 690, 730-731; *see also* Depressions.
Paper money.
  see Currency.
Paris, France, 449, 504, 636, 695, 698, 735, 751.
Parish, Captain, 182.
Parker, Daniel P., 641.
Parties, political.
  see Anti-Masons, Democrats, National Republicans, Relief, Republicans, Union Party, Whigs.
Patchell, Edward, 363, 442.
Pathkiller, Chief, 159.
Patronage, Adams and, 431; Jackson and, 489-492, 494, 722; Van Buren trailed by seekers of, 496-497; Jackson faces many controversial and divergent problems arising from, 497-506; dispute ended by Duff Green, 519-520; Van Buren and, 519-520, 606; number of Jackson appointments and removals, 520-521, 861-862; disappointed seekers of, 520-521; reform policy tempered, 522; and the Bank, 555, 564;

INDEX

Patronage—*Continued*
successful manipulation of, by Jackson, 587; General Harrison and, 745; Jackson sends many recommendations for, to Polk, 780; *see also* Andrew Jackson, Presidential Administrations, Spoils system.
Patterson, Commandant Daniel T., 510, 683; 187, 202, 210, 224; wrecks British artillery at December 28 attack on New Orleans, 234, 236; 241, 243, 247.
Patterson, Mrs. Daniel T., 510.
Patterson, Colonel Robert, 372-373.
Pawtucket, R. I., 639.
Payne, Mr., killed by an Indian, 50.
Peacock, British man-of-war, 251.
Peale, Anna C., 592.
Peddie, Captain, British Army, 220.
Peire, Major, at Pensacola, 196.
Pennsylvania, arrival from Ireland of Jackson's parents in, 3; 5, 270; 459, 460.
Pennsylvania, political sentiment in, 358, 362, 364, 367, 370, 371, 375, 376, 384, 388, 390, 391, 403, 406, 408-409, 414, 415, 526, 541, 606, 742, 755; protectionists, 373; congressmen of, 421, 426, 428, 433, 491, 527, 539, 610, 624, 631, 652; 446, 475, 659, 668, 676, 770, 772; militiamen, 436, 437; Governor of, 618; banks, 671-674, 731; Legislature of, 672, 731.
Pennsylvania, University of, 553.
Pensacola, 339, 557, 718.
Pensacola, Florida, 148, 156, 158; Jackson's true goal, 175; 179; British occupy, 182; 190, 194, 196; Jackson drives British from, 197; 198, 202, 280, 283; occupied by Jackson, 291; 293, 295, 296, 298; House of Representatives approves seizure of, 300; 308, 309, 313, 315, 316, 317; Jackson enters, for transfer of Florida, 317; 320, 321, 322, 331; 339, 557, 718.
Pensions, 393, 401.

Percy, Sir William H., 187, 188, 189.
Perry, Colonel, at New Orleans, 242.
Peru, 748.
"Pet banks."
    see Banks.
Peter, a slave of Jackson, 307.
Peterson, H. W., 363-364.
Petit, Mr., of New Orleans, 59.
Peyton, Balie, 106, 669.
Peyton, Ephraim, 50.
Phifer family of South Carolina, 7.
Philadelphia, 5, 58, 69; Jackson's first trip to, 74; 76, 77; Jackson in Congress at, 79; 80, 82, 83; Jackson in Senate at, 83; 88, 90, 96, 97, 99, 101, 103, 105, 133, 204, 251, 255, 294; reception to Jackson in 1819, 300; 371, 372, 399, 441, 462, 496, 506, 514, 516, 554-556, 577, 586, 589, 590, 591, 594, 596, 631, 634, 636, 637, 641, 642, 647, 648, 651, 654, 659, 661, 668, 678, 679, 689, 709, 712, 758, 778; Chestnut Street, 553, 561, 589, 657, 673, 680.
Philadelphia *Aurora*, 336.
Philadelphia *Columbian Observer*, 354, 433-435, 447.
Phillips, Lieutenant Billy, 143, 241, 243.
Phoenix, John Lewis, 289.
Physick, Dr. Philip Syng, 637.
Pickett, James C., 748.
Pierce's Stockade, Mississippi Territory, 196.
Pike, Miss, of Philadelphia, 372.
Pinckney family of South Carolina, 32.
Pinckney, Major General, 158, 164, 176, 177.
Pistol Gag Law, 466.
Pittsburgh, Pa., 75, 125, 126, 151, 362, 363, 366, 442, 448, 606.
Pittsylvania County, Virginia, 49.
Planters' Bank, Nashville, 729.
Plauché, Captain, at New Orleans, 203, 214, 216, 224, 225, 241.
Plauché, Jean B., 747, 757, 761, 783, 891.
Ploughboy, race-horse, 107, 110; race against Truxton, 111, 268.

Plumer, William, junior, 418, 425, 429.
Plymouth, N. C., 659.
Pocahontas, steamboat, 470.
Poindexter, Representative, of Mississippi, 299.
Poindexter, Senator, 621.
Poinsett, Joel R., 360, 609, 613, 615, 616, 618-619, 700.
Polk family of North and South Carolina, 7.
Polk, James K., in Congress, 624, 630, 633, 660, 674; 694, 734; vice-presidential possibility, 738, 750, 751; and Jackson, 742, 767-768, 769, 776, 782, 783, 784; presidential candidate, 769-774; elected, 775; as President, 777, 779, 780.
Polk, Lucius J., 596, 624.
Polk, Mrs. James K., 687, 773, 784.
Polk, Mary Eastin.
  see Mary Eastin.
Polk, Thomas, 11.
Polk, William, 374-375, 376, 384, 396.
Polly, fugitive slave, 349.
Pontois, Édouard, French minister, 698.
Pools, Mr., 710.
Poplar Grove plantation, Jackson takes bride to, 63, 69, 70, 75.
Popular sovereignty, 452.
Portland, Me., 366.
Portland *Courier,* 641.
Portsmouth, N. H., 659.
Portsmouth Branch, Bank of U. S., 561.
Portugal, 492.
'Possum up de Gum Tree, 741.
Potomac River, 405, 505, 508, 517, 622.
Presbyterian Church, 351, 399, 517, 733.
Press.
  see Newspapers.
Prices, Money, Appraisals, etc., 10, 15, 30, 31, 32, 33, 34, 35, 40, 47, 48, 59, 68; Jackson's mercantile purchases in Philadelphia, 75; 76, 77, 80, 81, 96, 97, 98, 99, 104, 105, 107, 108, 121, 124; condition of firm of

Prices—*Continued*
  Jackson & Hutchings, 131; 133, 146, 159, 163, 181, 196, 199, 216, 250, 266, 267, 277, 301, 305, 311; Hermitage furniture, 328; 329; Jackson's liquor bills, 802.
Princeton, New Jersey, 12, 49.
Princeton, N. J., College of New Jersey, at, 338, 553.
Prior, Norton, 133.
Propaganda, 657-659, 685.
Pryor, Captain Samuel, 107, 108, 111.
Public domain.
  see Land.

Quai d'Orsay, 695.
Quarter House Tavern, Charleston, 32.
Quebec, 98, 144, 145, 180, 181.
Queen's Museum, Charlotte, Jackson attends, 34.
Quincy, Josiah, 642, 643-644.
Quincy, Josiah, junior, 639-642, 644-645.

Rafignac, Monsieur, of Louisiana Legislature, 212.
Raleigh, N. C., 374, 376.
Raleigh *Register,* 407.
Randal, Lieutenant, 320.
Randolph, John, 129, 436, 439, 440, 454, 455, 611.
Randolph, Robert B., 636-637.
"Raven, The."
  see Sam Houston.
Ravenel, Mr., of Charleston, 33.
Rawdon, Lord, 28, 756.
Rawlings, Mr., innkeeper of Jonesborough, Tennessee, 85.
Read, Captain, at Pittsburgh, Pennsylvania, 125.
Red Eagle. See William Weatherford.
Red Heifer Tavern, 48.
Red River, 703.
Regular Army of United States, 70, 93, 95, 96, 121, 126, 132, 146, 149, 151, 156, 158, 169, 170, 175, 182, 187, 196, 197, 198, 211, 224, 225,

INDEX

Regular Army of United States—Continued
238, 242, 261, 266, 286, 289, 295, 309, 310, 312.
Reid, Major John, 159, 163, 172, 201, 239, 240, 256, 259, 265, 266, 269, 273, 274.
Reid, Maria, 274.
Relief Party, 557, 560, 567, 588.
Remenhill, Joseph, 93.
Removals from office.
see Andrew Jackson, Presidential Administrations, Spoils system.
Rennie, Colonel, British Army, at New Orleans, 246.
Republican Party, 338, 346, 364, 389, 396, 406, 418.
Republicanism, 367.
see Republican Party.
Republicans, 103, 116, 270, 276.
Revolutionary War, in the Carolinas, 15, 16, 17, 18, 19, 20, 21, 22, 23, 25, 26, 27; disillusionment after, 38, 39; 70, 156.
Reynolds, Major, 213.
Rhea, John, 377; Representative, 282; Jackson declares he receives famous letter from, 285; 295; controversy between Jackson and others over letter, 827.
Rhode Island, 143, 388, 639.
Rice, Joel, 74.
Richardson, Nancy Craighead. See Dunlap.
Richardson, William, D.D., 8, 10, 12.
Richmond *Enquirer*, 125, 453, 497, 658, 767.
Richmond, North Carolina, 37.
Richmond, Virginia, 72, 82, 128, 130, 271, 272, 383, 433, 856.
Riddle, James, 362.
Rio Grande, 356, 700, 703.
Rip Raps, Virginia, 517, 577, 646, 647, 746.
Ritchie, Thomas, 453, 497, 501, 507, 658.
Rives, John C., 683, 718, 748, 757, 759, 773, 777-778, 891; *see also* Blair & Rives.

Rives, William C., 504.
Roan Knob, North Carolina, 24.
Roane, Archibald, 90.
Roane, Representative, 539.
Roanoke, Va., 440.
Robards, Captain Lewis, 38; marries Rachel Donelson in 1785, 52; jealousy of Jackson, 53; refuses Jackson's invitation to duel, 60; divorces Rachel, 63, 65, 71, 72, 803; 99, 303, 805; death mentioned, 344; Rachel Jackson as "unhappy wife" of, 371; divorce scandal renewed, 463-468; character of, 855; in Peyton Short affair, 855-856.
Robards, Mrs. George, 855.
Robards, Mrs., mother of Lewis, 52.
Robards, Rachel Donelson. See Rachel Jackson.
Roberts, Brigadier-General Isaac, 169.
Roberts, Lewis. See Robards.
Robertson, Elijah, 77.
Robertson, Dr. Felix, 119.
Robertson, James, 49, 51, 57, 60, 62, 110, 120, 126, 483.
Robertson, Private Joe, 242.
Robertson's Station, Tennessee, 58.
Roche, Captain, at New Orleans, 214.
Roche's, at Charleston, 613.
Rodriquez Canal, 738.
Rodsmith, Paul, 36.
Roebuck, race-horse, 33.
Rogers, Mr., guest of White House, 668.
Rome, 489, 619.
Ross, Colonel, at New Orleans, 187, 192.
Rotation in office.
see Andrew Jackson, Presidential Administrations, Spoils system.
Rousseau, Augustin, 216.
Rowan House, Salisbury, North Carolina, 34, 36.
Roy, Lieutenant, at Fort Bowyer, 188, 189.
Royall, Mrs. Anne, 546, 547, 834.
Ruggles, Benjamin, 406.
Rush, Richard, 735.

Russell, Captain, in Creek campaign, 160.
Russia, 339.
Russian Minister, 534.
Rutledge, Henry M., 481.

Sabine River, 356.
St. Augustine, Florida, 283, 308, 309, 320.
St. Clairsville, Ohio, 406.
St. Gême, Captain, at New Orleans, 203, 212, 214.
St. Genevieve, Louisiana, 100.
St. Louis, Mo., 370.
St. Louis Branch Bank of U. S., 652.
St. Marks, Florida, 285; Jackson captures, 287; 288, 291, 293, 295, 308, 309, 773.
St. Petersburg, Russia, 339.
Salem, Mass., 644.
Salisbury, North Carolina, 5, 7, 35, 36, 37, 41, 55, 79, 396.
Salisbury *Western Carolinian*, 354.
Sam, freed slave, 692.
San Jacinto, Battle of, 705, 776-777, 781.
San Jacinto River, 705.
Santa Anna, Antonio López de, 703-705, 762; sister of, 700.
Santo Domingo (Haiti), 203, 275.
Saratoga Springs, N. Y., 645.
Savannah, Georgia, 18, 281.
Schools, 12, 13, 17, 18, 31, 34, 49, 68, 107, 150, 283, 300, 304, 307, 329, 330, 811.
Schuyler, Margaret, 438.
Schuylkill County, Pa., 660.
Scotch-Irish settlers in Pennsylvania, 3, 7.
Scotland, 338.
Scott, John, Representative, of Missouri, 415, 428, 429, 430, 436, 443.
Scott, John, Tennessee planter, 349.
Scott, General Winfield, 381, 383, 440, 607, 610, 686, 711; 279, 310, 332.
Scott, Major Thomas B., 349.
Secession, 582, 610-612, 615, 616, 621, 776.

Sectionalism, 367, 582, 716, 751, 753.
Seminole campaign, 543.
Seminole Indians, 198, 282, 283, 286, 293, 314, 711.
Senate, United States, 79, 82, 90, 102, 103, 122, 297, 301, 310, 320; members of, 370, 388, 529, 577, 587, 606, 658; chamber, 382, 445; 382, 398, 439, 451, 509, 526, 530, 531, 542, 594, 612, 613, 655, 661, 677, 686, 694, 705, 714, 752; committees of, 382, 564, 684; bills and resolutions presented and considered, 393, 401, 403, 525, 590, 659, 675; bills and resolutions passed, 396, 620-621, 674, 718, 732; adjournment, 498, 663; on presidential appointments, 520-521, 595, 675, 693, 708, 719; on treaties, 580, 763, 766, 767, 774.
Sergeant, John, 589.
Sérurier, Louis, French minister, 681, 682-684, 686, 695, 697.
Sevier, Andrew Jackson, 773.
Sevier, Catherine Sherrill (Bonny Kate), 40.
Sevier, Charles, 164.
Sevier, George Washington, 94.
Sevier, John, 24; governor of State of Franklin, 40; 41, 49, 62, 70, 71; governor of Tennessee, 1796, 77; 81, 83, 88; Jackson exposes fraudulent land deals of, 90; insults Mrs. Jackson and refuses duel with Jackson, 92; 108, 143.
Sevier, John, 338, 755, 773.
Sevier, Sarah K., 773.
Shannon, John, 806.
Shaw, Henry, 358, 359.
Shaw, Kentucky sportsman, 544.
Shelby, Evan, 58.
Shelokta, Creek chief, 178.
Sherman, Mrs., guest of White House, 668.
Short, Peyton, 52, 65, 855-856.
Sign of the Indian King Tavern, 93.
Simpson, Stephen, 447.
Sitler, James, 153.
Skipwith, Fulwar, 230.

INDEX

Slaves and Slavery, Jackson's personal ownership of slaves, 340, 348-350, 592, 692; Calhoun supported by slave-holding states, 362; J. Q. Adams's views regarding, 366; "Fanny Wright's free love colony," 449-450; Richmond *Enquirer's* influence in slave-holding states, 453; Branch represents best traditions of slave-holding aristocracy, 491; Jackson sees slavery as chief nullification issue, 621-622, 691; early proposals for emancipation, 691; Nat Turner's rebellion, 692; abolition crusade launched under Garrison, 774; emancipation in West Indies, 692; Calhoun proclaims slavery a good thing for both races, 692; condition of negroes, 692; Washington Irving on slavery, 693; Calhoun advocates admission of Texas to Union with view to slavery expansion, 705; Texas' application for admission delights slave-holders, 711; Jackson attempts to balance northern and eastern interests in Texas against slave-holders', 716; W. H. Harrison unpopular in slaveholding states, 739; slavery question delays annexation of Texas, 751-752; statesmanship of Henry Clay in dealing with problem, 753; Texans take united stand on, 765; slavery declared paramount issue in question of Texas annexation, 774; James Wilson as free-soiler, 841; Peyton Short intends to buy slaves, 856; illicit relations of Robards with slaves, 855.

Slave trade, 14, 59, 74, 104, 134, 275, 315.

Sloane, John, 430.

Smart family, North Carolina, 21.

Smart, Susan. See Alexander.

Smiley, Major, of Kentucky at New Orleans, 246.

Smith, Brigadier-General Daniel, 54, 56, 57, 62, 122, 278, 810.

Smith, Major Francis, 546-547.

Smith, J. Kilty, 200, 201, 208.

Smith, Margaret Bayard, 487, 491, 493, 509, 587.

Smith, Mary, 546-547.

Smith, Seba, 641, 658.

Smith, William, 131.

Smuggling, 522.

Social philosophy, in Jackson's Bank veto message, 601-602; Jackson's and Marshall's compared, 707-708.

Somerset County, Maryland, 48.

Songs and rhymes, campaign, 739, 740, 741.

Sophie, British brig, 182, 185, 187, 188.

Sousa, Lieutenant Domingo, 322, 324, 325.

Southard, Secretary of Navy, 457-458.

South Carolina, controversy with North Carolina over boundary, 10, 791; birthplace of Jackson, 11, 791; in Revolutionary War, 15, 18, 19, 24; 30, 142, 163, 266, 271, 276, 283; political sentiments, 358, 367, 384, 388, 390, 396, 409, 707; 375, 429, 439, 454, 455, 494, 685, 705, 752, 758, 760; nullification controversy, 523-524, 537-540, 548, 570, 580-582, 587, 593, 604, 607-622, 630, 640; Legislature, 582, 618.

South Carolinians, 347, 368, 370, 371, 403, 470, 471, 476, 494, 538.

South, the, 335, 348, 366, 391, 396, 402, 442, 471, 523, 527, 529, 538, 581, 598, 605, 621, 649, 650, 692, 695, 703, 705, 734, 738, 753.

Southwest Point, Tennessee, 94.

Southwest, the, 340, 770.

Spain, 41; conspiracy to separate Cumberland country from Union, 55; 77, 83, 96, 102, 103, 104, 112, 120, 121, 122, 123, 127; silent ally of Britain and supporter of Creeks, 158; 175; extends hospitality in Florida to hostile Indians, 179; 182, 183, 190, 191; displays bad faith in Mobile campaign, 197; 202, 210, 218, 245, 274, 280, 281; surrenders St. Marks to Jackson, 287; demands

Spain—*Continued*
restitution of captured forts of Florida and punishment of Jackson, 291; 293, 295, 296; signs treaty transferring Florida to United States, 301; 306, 308; ratifies Florida purchase treaty, 309; formally transfers Florida to United States, 317; 324, 339, 356, 453, 683.
Spanish. See Spain.
Spanish territories, 349, 465, 856.
Sparks, Captain, 92.
Sparks, W. H., 597.
Sparks, Mrs. W. H., 597.
Specie Circular, 707, 718, 729-731.
Speculation, 399, 548, 690, 699, 703, 706-707, 728-729, 731, 735, 742, 784.
Spencer, Captain, 220.
Spoils system.
see Andrew Jackson, Presidential Administrations, Spoils system.
Spotts, Lieutenant, 242.
Stamp Tax, resented by colonists, 6, 7.
Stark, John, 64, 65.
State of Franklin, 39, 40, 47, 62, 88.
State-rights, 365, 530, 537, 539, 540, 557, 610, 615.
Staunton, Va., 379.
Steele, Graves, 544, 597, 628.
Steele, Robert, 363.
Stevenson, Andrew, 430.
Stokes, Colonel John, 36, 346, 396.
Stokes, Montfort, 346-347.
Stono Ferry, battle of, 18.
Storrs, Henry Randolph, 416, 428.
Story, Justice Joseph, 577, 720, 721.
Strater's Hotel, Washington, D. C., 297.
Stuart, James, 77.
Stuart, John, 93.
Stump, Colonel, in Creek campaign, 596.
Stump-the-Dealer, race-horse, 267.
Sugar Creek Church, Mecklenburg County, North Carolina, 7.
Sumner County, Tennessee, 62, 132, 228.
Sumter, Colonel Thomas, 19, 20, 21.
Sumter's Surprise, 30.

Superior Court of Tennessee, 85, 87, 91, 93. See Superior Court of Western District.
Superior Court of Western District, 38, 45, 54, 59, 61.
Swann, Thomas, 107, 108, 109, 110, 125, 152.
Swartwout, Samuel, 122 124, 130, 412, 429, 504, 522, 569, 703, 734.
Sycamore Shoals, North Carolina, 24.

Taggart, Mr., applicant for office, 784.
Tait, Captain, of British Army, 155.
Talbot's Hotel, Nashville, 98, 120.
Talladega, battle of, 160, 166, 759.
Tallahassee, Fla., 677.
Tallushatchee, battle of, 159, 266.
Tammany Committee, 668.
Tammany Hall, 300.
Tam O'Shanter, race-horse, 267.
Taney, Roger B., 643; appointed Attorney General, 579; first Cabinet controversy, 588; opposed to the Bank, 600-601; squabble with McLane, 630; views on the Bank, and fight against, 633-636, 643, 648-652; Senate rejects nomination for Treasury post, 675, 693; rejected for Associate Justice, 694; appointed and confirmed as Chief Justice, 708; Administers oath to Van Buren, 719.
Tanner, race-horse, 106, 107.
Tariff, Calhoun and Clay high-tariff, 362; Crawford anti-tariff, 365; Adams high-tariff, 366; Calhoun's stand on, wins him support in Pennsylvania, 367; Jackson's stand unknown, 369; Grass Hat letters force Jackson's declaration, 372-373; issue of anti-Jackson forces, 392; great protectionist speech of Clay, 393; "American system" wins, 394; Jackson declares for "judicious tariff," 394; protests against tariff measure encourage Crawford, 396; Jackson refuses to recant, 397, 401, 471; opponents of Jackson's views on tariff weaken, 401, 404; Clay finds Adams's tariff new basis for

Tariff—*Continued*
support, 424; tariff issue obscured by personal abuse, 471; mentioned in first message to Congress, 523; growing protests against, in South Carolina, 524; Webster-Hayne debate, 530, *et seq.*, 536-537; Jackson determines to enforce, 539, 548; nullification of tariff deplored by Southern Nationalists, 581-582; McLane proposes to link recharter with tariff and public lands issues, 586; South Carolina proclaims tariff void, 610; Verplanck bill presented, 616; Jackson asks Congress to authorize military force to collect customs, 618; Verplanck measure, Clay compromise and "Force Bill", 619-621; Jackson signs "Force Bill" and Clay tariff bill, 621; duty on French wines lowered, 682; tariff less contributory to disunion than slavery, 691; *see also* Andrew Jackson, Political Activities to 1829, *and* Andrew Jackson, Presidential Administrations, Nullification in South Carolina.

Tariff, race horse, 544-545.

Tarleton, Lieutenant Colonel Banastre, 19, 21, 22, 23.

Tarleton's raid of the Waxhaws, 757.

Tatum, Major Howell, 217.

Taverns, Hotels, etc., see Quarter House Tavern, Charleston; McCrady's Tavern, Charleston; Rowan House, Salisbury, North Carolina; Red Heifer, Nashville; Sign of the Indian King, Knoxville; Conrad's boarding house, Washington, D. C.; De Monbreun's tap-room, Nashville; Talbot's, Nashville; Winn's Tavern, Nashville; Nashville Inn, Nashville; Miller's Tavern, Kentucky; Clover Bottom Tavern, Tennessee; Eagle Tavern, Richmond; City Hotel, Nashville; Hôtel du Trémoulet, New Orleans; Gabsby's Hotel, Baltimore; Exchange Coffee House, New Orleans; Strater's Hotel, Washington, D. C.

Taverns—*Continued*
Taverns, hotels, boarding houses, etc., 670, 750; *see also* American House, Brown's Indian Queen, Claxton's, Franklin House, Gadsby's, Gault's Tavern, Nashville Inn, O'Neale's, Tremont House.

Taxes, 336, 346.

Tazewell, Littleton W., 504.

Tecumseh, 156, 157, 178, 526, 740.

Telford, Lieutenant, 70.

Tennessee Legislature, 165, 306.

Tennessee named, 77; 78, 79, 80, 81, 82, 84, 85; growth of, 88; 90, 91, 92, 95, 97, 99; support of Burr's conspiracy, 102; 106, 113, 115, 119, 125, 133, 134, 135, 137, 142, 143, 144; mobilizes for war with England in 1812, 146; 149, 150, 151, 157; supports Creek campaign, 159; 175, 178, 180, 182, 194, 196; supports New Orleans campaign, 199, 207, 211, 215, 228, 254, 259; 268, 273, 275, 283, 285, 287, 298; President Monroe visits, 304; excludes branches of Bank of the United States, 305; 306, 326.

Tennesseans, 381, 396, 412, 419, 512, 575, 715, 841.

Tennessee, plantations and planters, 336, 458; 338, 374, 411, 433, 450, 468, 476, 480, 488, 489, 490, 515, 547, 548, 551, 556, 565, 567, 571, 573, 574, 592, 596, 597, 606, 609, 627, 628, 654, 665, 687, 688, 691, 692, 701, 712, 713, 718, 721, 723, 736, 742, 756, 758, 782, 855, 891; Legislature of, 341, 346, 347, 351-355, 358, 361, 363, 377-378, 388, 395, 451, 452, 677, 707; residents of, 344, 399, 506, 514, 546, 558, 577, 595, 668, 772; congressmen of, 356, 381, 382, 386, 398, 454, 490, 492, 508, 575, 669, 770; Governor of, 358, 618, 702, 732, 738, 750; political sentiments in, 358, 361, 362, 370, 384, 409, 415, 694, 705, 706, 741, 753, 767, 768-769, 775; West, 371, 728, 732; East, 464, 835;

Tennessee—*Continued*
   banks, 556, 557; Supreme Court of, 695.
Tennessee River, 349, 834.
Territory South of the River Ohio, 62, 73, 76.
Texas, 102, 103, 281, 356, 523, 683, 699-706, 711, 715-716, 718, 724, 750-754, 761-770, 771-772, 774-777, 779-782, 784, 786; *see also* Andrew Jackson, Presidential Administrations, Foreign policy.
"The Great Waggon Road," Pennsylvania, 3.
Thomas, Major General, of Kentucky militia, 199, 211, 240, 242.
Thompson, Lieutenant, 231.
Thompson, noted Whig of South Carolina, 26.
Thompson, Smith, 354.
Thornton, Colonel William, British Army, 221, 225, 243, 244, 247, 248, 404.
Timberlake, John B., 386-387, 508, 516, 518, 636.
Timberlake, Margaret, 384-387, 398, 459, 508-510, 517; *see also* Margaret Eaton, *and* Andrew Jackson, Presidential Administrations, Eaton affair.
Tippecanoe, 739.
   see also William Henry Harrison.
Tippecanoe Club, of Nashville, 741.
Tipton, John, 40.
Titsworth family of Tennessee, 58.
Tobacco-growing, 340, 710.
Tohopeka, Mississippi Territory, 166; battle of, 170; 251.
"Tomahawk rights" to lands, 6.
Tonnant, British man-of-war, 218.
Tories, of South Carolina, 19, 20, 24, 25, 26, 31, 47.
Tousard, Louis de, 259.
Towson, Colonel Nathan, 516-518.
Trade, in the Waxhaws, 14; in Mero District, 55, 56; 74, 96, 99, 100, 142.
Trails and Roads. See "The Great Waggon Road"; Catawba Traders' Path, Charles Town-Salisbury Road; Cumberland Road; Chickasaw

Trails and Roads—*Continued*
   Road; Natchez Trace; Kentucky Road; Lebanon Road; War Path.
Translyvania University, 330, 340, 344, 355.
Treason, 610, 615, 617.
Treasury.
   see United States Treasury Department.
Treasury Order.
   see Specie Circular.
Treaties.
   see United States, treaties of.
Tremont House, Boston, 641.
Trimble, David, 443, 454.
Trollope, Frances, 488.
Truxton, race-horse, 105, 106, 107, 110, 336, 337, 544, 545, 597; race against Ploughboy, 111; 113, 132, 143, 268.
Tulip Grove, home of A. J. Donelson, 712.
Tulip Hill Plantation, home of Virgil Maxcy, 375.
Turner, Nat, slave rebellion of, 692.
Tyler, John, 619, 620, 622, 738-740, 745, 746, 749, 751, 752, 760, 762-763, 765, 766, 774, 777.

Union Bank of Baltimore, 651-652, 729.
Union Party, in South Carolina nullification episode, 540, 581, 604, 609, 610.
United States, 62, 69, 70, 77, 80, 96, 101, 120, 121, 123, 127, 129, 134, 141, 144, 146, 149, 156, 158, 187, 191, 202, 216, 250, 262, 263, 275, 287, 289, 296; 356, 360, 389, 390, 404, 407, 411, 420, 440, 447, 449, 474, 482, 507, 539, 549, 550, 554, 566, 583, 604, 611, 613, 615, 637, 639, 654, 674, 681, 682, 684, 686, 696-698, 699, 703, 715, 720, 724, 730, 744, 751, 762-767, 776, 781; signs treaty for purchase of Florida, 301; 321; Bank of, *see under* Banks; boundaries of, 699-700, 724, 751; governmental de-

INDEX 969

United States—*Continued*
partments of: navy, 386, 491, 493, 511, 521, 576, 579, 862; post office, 491, 492, 521; state, 491, 493, 504, 682, 686, 698, 862; treasury, 195, 362, 395, 491, 492, 499, 500, 521, 525, 526, 534, 554-556, 560-562, 579, 584, 595, 629, 637, 642-643, 645, 650-651, 660, 682, 690, 693-694, 723, 731, 760, 784; war, 458, 491-495, 499, 521, 522, 578, 613, 703, 862; national debt, 524, 526, 527, 562, 585, 690; treaties of, 51, 69, 70, 74, 76, 80, 356, 523, 548-552, 580, 604, 681-684, 697, 702-703, 706, 711, 763-767, 774.

United States Bank of Pennsylvania, 731, 735, 744.

United States Navy, 208.

United States' Telegraph, 455, 456, 459, 460, 465, 467, 537, 567-569, 570, 605, 632, 861.

University of Pennsylvania, 553.

University of Virginia, 597.

Ursuline Sisters, 104, 212, 261.

Utica, N. Y., 416.

Van Buren, Abraham, 512-513, 574, 626, 668, 750.

Van Buren, John, 626, 750.

Van Buren, Martin, 144; political influence in New York, 365-366, 383, 390, 402, 411, 436, 437, 501, 616; allied with Crawford, 365, 367, 389, 402, 405-407, 410; description of, 415, 496; predicts Jackson victory, 417, 420, 423, 429, 436, 438, 453, 455, 461, 509, 512, 526, 527, 539, 548, 560, 568, 569, 570, 578, 605, 606, 613, 618, 619, 625, 645, 686, 688, 715; supporters of, 436, 470, 492, 503, 630, 693; election bets, 457, 669-670; anti-Calhoun efforts, 471, 476, 492, 501, 527, 528, 534, 540, 569-570, 573, 579; Secretary of State, 491, 496-497, 504-505, 506, 521, 525, 535, 545, 552, 569, 575; on patronage, 496, 501-502, 504, 506, 519, 521, 522; sons of, 512-513, 574, 750; Eaton affair, 515-518,

Van Buren, Martin—*Continued*
519, 532-536, 574-577; horseback rides, 519, 533, 545, 574, 593, 640; Minister to Great Britain, 575, 589, 593-595, 601, 605; for Vice President, 594-595, 605; on nullification, 614-617, 620, 699-700; as Vice President, 617, 634, 638, 641, 644, 648, 653, 656, 660, 668, 671, 697; presidential candidate, 694, 695, 707, 711; as President, 713, 719, 723-724, 729-731, 734, 735, 738, 745; candidate for re-election, 738-742; defeated, 742; aspires to 1844, 749-752, 755; agreement with Clay on Texas, 753-754, 767-772.

Van Buren family, 749-750.

Van Dyke, Dr. Thomas J., 94.

Van Rensselaer family, 749.

Van Rensselaer, Stephen, 436, 437-439, 440-441.

Vance, Representative, 454.

Vaux, Robert, 654.

Verell, Major John, 105, 106, 107, 108, 109, 111.

Vermont Journal, 608.

Verplanck, Representative, 616, 619, 620, 630, 631.

Versailles, 494.

Vicksburg, steamboat, 737.

Vidal, Mercedes, 322.

Vidal, Nicolas Maria, 322, 326.

Villeré, Célestin, 222.

Villeré, Major General Jacques Phillippe de, 212, 220, 221, 230, 236.

Villeré, Major René Phillippe Gabriel, warns Jackson British have landed below New Orleans, 220; captured by British, 222; acquitted at court martial, 821.

Virginia, 4, 5, 14, 19, 24, 49, 52, 59, 71, 92, 105, 128, 180, 267, 268, 272, 274, 292, 301; political sentiments in, 343, 376, 388, 414, 457, 527, 610, 615, 616, 622; 365, 368, 376, 379, 380, 383, 386, 387, 397, 402, 411, 418, 430, 432, 434, 436, 465, 475, 489, 499, 546, 595, 619, 621, 652, 662, 708, 738, 856; Governor of, 618; slave rebellion, 692.

Virginia Dynasty, 365.
Virginia, General Assembly of, 65, 66, 71, 72, 128.
Virginia Resolutions of 1798, 538.
Virginia, University of, 597.
Virginians, 429, 452, 510, 511, 636.
Vivart, White House chef, 507.
Vives, Francisco Dionisio, 309.

Wadesborough, North Carolina, 37.
Walker, Robert J., 362, 763, 765, 784.
Ward, Albert, 736-737, 743, 892.
Ward, Colonel Edward, 341, 348, 736.
Ward, Edward, 99, 104, 267, 303, 304, 306.
War Department, 96, 125, 144, 145, 146, 148, 151, 166, 175, 176, 194, 198, 203, 215, 254, 266, 279, 282, 294.
War Hawks, 142, 283, 368, 426.
War of 1812, 345, 526, 537.
War Path, 305.
Warren, Edward, 640.
Warrenton, Va., 394.
Washington Branch Bank of U. S., 587, 632.
Washington College, 446.
Washington County, Mississippi Territory, 137.
Washington, D. C., 97, 102, 150, 151, 152, 181, 194, 215, 218, 220, 225, 252, 255, 260, 270, 271, 280, 289, 297, 299, 300, 301, 306, 310, 327, 332, 344, 360, 367, 370, 371, 375, 376, 377, 378, 379, 381, 385, 387, 390, 391, 396, 398, 399, 407, 408, 409, 410, 411, 415, 416, 417, 419, 426, 428, 429, 431, 435, 442, 447, 450, 451, 452, 455, 456, 463, 475, 476, 482, 483, 487, 488, 489, 492, 495, 496, 497, 501, 505, 507, 508, 509, 510, 511, 517, 519, 520, 521, 524, 529, 533, 542, 546, 550, 551, 552, 554, 561, 573, 574, 575, 576, 579, 582, 583, 586, 589, 597, 599, 603, 607, 609, 613, 614, 617, 621, 623, 625, 626, 632, 648, 652, 654, 659, 664, 668, 672, 677, 681, 693, 698, 699, 700, 701, 702, 711, 717,

Washington, D. C.—*Continued*
720, 727, 728, 729, 745, 757, 763, 764, 765, 767, 771, 777-779, 862; Capitol Hill, 382, 387, 493, 505, 525, 626, 662, 718; F Street, 431, 440; Pennsylvania Avenue, 492, 493, 494, 546, 573, 625, 719, 724; Second Street, 724.
Washington, George, 18, 49, 56, 62, 70; Jackson suggests impeachment of, 76; 79, 80, 81, 95, 117, 176, 193, 258, 304; 344, 358, 366, 404, 442, 449, 503, 549, 669, 708, 721, 746; mother of, 636.
Washington *Globe*, the, 569-571, 575-576, 580, 660, 672, 685, 695, 768.
Washington junto. *See* Junto.
Washington, Pa., 446.
Washington *Republican*, 403.
Watauga Fort, North Carolina, 40.
Watkins, Tobias, 500.
Watmough, John, 624, 631, 652, 657.
Watson, Thomas, 85, 99, 793.
Wauchope, James, 23.
Waxhaw Church, South Carolina, 8, 9, 10, 12, 13, 19, 25, 37.
Waxhaw Creek, South Carolina, 757.
Waxhaws, 3, 4, 5; description of settlement and growth, 5, 6; 13, 14; sends food to Boston after Tea Party, 15; in Revolutionary War, 15, 18, 19, 20, 21, 22, 32, 33, 35, 47; 68, 72, 84; boundary dispute, 791; 374, 577, 583, 721, 757.
Weakley, Robert, 64.
Weatherford, Charles, 156, 175.
Weatherford, John, 156.
Weatherford, William, 661; ancestry of, 155; destroys Fort Mims, 157; 158, 159, 161, 163, 166, 167, 171; surrenders to Jackson, 172; 275.
Webb, James Watson, 657.
Webster, Daniel, quoted, 358, 383, 389, 397, 402, 420-421, 487-489, 720; 375, 439, 614, 714, 722; opinion of Jackson, 383, 397, 487-488, 521, 720; personal qualities, 394, 530, 531; speeches in Congress, 394, 530-531, 537, 541, 621; political

INDEX

Webster, Daniel—*Continued*
ambitions, 431, 437, 621, 684, 707; political activity, 436, 438, 594, 694; nullification, 529, 531, 536-539, 541-542, 612, 620, 639; Bank controversy, 589, 602, 605, 654, 657-660, 674.
Weehawken, N. J., 560.
Wellington, Duke of, 180, 181, 182, 183, 218, 227, 254.
West, the, 335, 356, 359, 366, 368, 370, 375, 391, 392, 395, 398, 399, 403, 410, 411, 415, 422, 424, 430, 433, 436, 442, 443, 463, 471, 512, 523, 524, 525, 527, 529, 537, 557, 565, 568, 581, 585, 595, 598, 605, 649, 650, 703, 705, 721, 738, 739, 753.
Western District. See Mero District.
Western Light, race-horse, 267, 336.
West Indies, 683, 695; *see also* British West Indies.
West Point (United States Military Academy), 278, 280, 300, 307, 344, 385, 626, 781.
Weymss, Major, British Army, 20.
Wharton, William H., 715-716, 718-719.
Wheeling, Va., 447, 724.
Whig Party, 841.
Whigs, 603, 680, 684, 707, 722, 734, 735, 738-742, 744, 748, 749, 750, 753, 767, 774, 775.
White, Captain, Andrew, 92.
White, David, 427, 434.
White House, 492, 493, 495, 496, 501, 512, 513, 517, 519, 525, 526, 535, 537, 552, 558, 562, 566, 567, 568, 570, 571, 577, 578, 593, 596, 600, 617, 624, 626, 645, 646, 647, 662, 672, 677, 683, 686, 688, 702, 704, 708, 709, 710, 715, 716, 718, 719, 724, 745, 773; receptions, 494, 503, 507, 531, 536; guests, 494, 568-569, 591-592, 594, 597, 601, 609, 625-626, 628, 634, 668, 703; East Room, 494, 568, 669; mistresses, 512-513, 514, 548, 712; young people, 545, 546, 577, 625-626; Red

White House—*Continued*
Room, 594, 626, 681; stable, 597, 669; described, 625.
White, Hugh Lawson, 490-491, 520, 538, 578, 677, 694, 707, 713.
White, Brigadier General James, 160.
White, Dr. James, 58, 62.
White, Captain Maunsel, 203, 214, 460, 461, 666, 667.
Whiteside, Senator Jenkin, 133, 134, 137.
Wikoff, Henry, 594.
Wilberforce, Mr., English Abolitionist, 494.
Wilcox, Mary Donelson, 67.
Wildcat banks.
see Banks.
Wilkinson, Major, 246.
William and Mary, College of, 107, 150.
Wilkesboro, N. C., 346.
Wilkinson, General James, 96, 102, 120, 121; betrays Burr, 124; 125, 127, 128, 129, 130, 132, 144, 145, 147, 148, 151, 175, 214.
Williams, Berry, 268.
Williams, Colonel John, 377-378.
Williams, Judge John F., 37.
Williams, Willoughby, 768.
Wilson, George, 345.
Wilson, James, grandfather of Woodrow Wilson, 841.
Wilson, John, 23.
Winchester, Brigadier General James, 144, 148, 198, 205, 211, 254; founds Memphis, 306.
Winn's Tavern, Nashville, 98, 109.
Wirt, William, 549, 550, 605, 608.
Wise, Henry A., 662, 664.
Wise, Henry R., 474-476.
Witherspoon, James H., 794.
Wolf, Governor George, of Pennsylvania, 672, 673.
Wood, Molly, 36.
Wood, Rachel, 36.
Woodbine, Captain George, 286, 287, 289, 296.
Woodbury, Levi, 561, 579, 601, 638, 649, 693, 769.

Woods, Private John, 169, 468.
Wooley, Melling, 802.
Worcester, Samuel A., 603.
Wrenn, William, 24.
Wright, Frances, 449-450.
Wright, Silas, 503, 617, 769, 770, 771.
Wyer, Edward, 424-425, 431.
Wylie, Andrew, 446-447.

Yale College, 380.
Yale University, 283, 304.

Yeatman, Thomas, 340.
Yeatman, Woods & Co., Nashville bankers, 729.
York, Pennsylvania, 3.
Yorke, Sarah.
 see Sarah Yorke Jackson.
Yorktown, Virginia, 28.
You, Dominique, pirate, 186, 212, 213; at defense of New Orleans, 232, 238, 241.
"Young Hickory."
 see James K. Polk.